KEYS TO ECONOMIC PROSPERITY

 These keys to the economic prosperity of a nation are highlighted throughout the text. When they appear, they are indicated with this special icon.

1. **Human Ingenuity.** Economic goods are the result of human ingenuity and action; thus, the size of the economic pie is variable, not fixed. [*Economics* Chapter 2; *Macroeconomics* Chapter 2; *Microeconomics* Chapter 2]

2. **Private Ownership.** Private ownership provides people with a strong incentive to take care of things and develop resources in ways that are highly valued by others. [*Economics* Chapter 2; *Macroeconomics* Chapter 2; *Microeconomics* Chapter 2]

3. **Gains from Trade.** Trade makes it possible for individuals to generate a larger output through specialization and division of labor, large-scale production processes, and dissemination of improved products and production methods. [*Economics* Chapter 2; *Macroeconomics* Chapter 2; *Microeconomics* Chapter 2]

4. **Invisible Hand Principle.** Market prices coordinate the actions of self-interested individuals and direct them toward activities that promote the general welfare. [*Economics* Chapter 3; *Macroeconomics* Chapter 3; *Microeconomics* Chapter 3]

5. **Profits and Losses.** Profits direct producers toward activities that increase the value of resources; losses impose a penalty on those who reduce the value of resources. [*Economics* Chapter 3; *Macroeconomics* Chapter 3; *Microeconomics* Chapter 3]

6. **Competition.** Competition provides businesses with a strong incentive to produce efficiently, cater to the views of consumers, and search for innovative improvements. [*Economics* Chapter 21; *Microeconomics* Chapter 9]

7. **Entrepreneurship.** The entrepreneurial discovery and development of improved products and production processes is a central element of economic progress. [*Economics* Chapter 22; *Microeconomics* Chapter 10]

8. **Link between Productivity and Earnings.** In a market economy, productivity and earnings are closely linked. In order to earn a large income, one must provide large benefits to others.[*Economics* Chapter 25; *Microeconomics* Chapter 13]

9. **Innovation and the Capital Market.** If the potential gains from innovative ideas and human ingenuity are going to be fully realized, it must be relatively easy for individuals to try their innovative and potentially ingenious ideas, but difficult to continue if the idea is a bad one. [*Economics* Chapter 26; *Microeconomics* Chapter 14]

10. **Price Stability.** When monetary policy makers consistently achieve price stability, they are providing the foundation for both economic stability and the efficient operation of markets. [*Economics* Chapter 15; *Macroeconomics* Chapter 15]

11. **International Trade.** When people are permitted to engage freely in international trade, they are able to achieve higher income levels and living standards than would otherwise be possible. [*Economics* Chapter 17; *Macroeconomics* Chapter 17; *Microeconomics* Chapter 16]

12. **Government and the Environment for Prosperity.** Governments can promote economic progress by establishing an environment that encourages entrepreneurship, investment, skill development, and technological improvements. Key elements of this are the protection of individuals and their property, enforcement of contracts, open competition, price stability, free trade, low taxes, and provision of a limited set of "public goods." [*Economics* Chapter 16; *Macroeconomics* Chapter 16]

Economics: Private and Public Choice
Tenth Edition

THOMSON

SOUTH-WESTERN

Australia · Canada · Mexico · Singapore · Spain · United Kingdom · United States

Economics: Private and Public Choice
Tenth Edition

James D. Gwartney

Florida State University

Richard L. Stroup

Montana State University

Russell S. Sobel

West Virginia University

David A. Macpherson

Florida State University

Australia · Canada · Mexico · Singapore · Spain · United Kingdom · United States

Economics: Private and Public Choice, 10th Edition

James D. Gwartney, Richard L. Stroup, Russell S. Sobel, David A. Macpherson

VP/Editor-in-Chief:
Jack Calhoun

Team Leader:
Michael Roche

Acquisitions Editor:
Peter Adams

Developmental Editor:
Andrew McGuire

Senior Marketing Manager:
Janet Hennies

Production Editor:
Robert Dreas

Manufacturing Coordinator:
Sandee Milewski

Compositor:
Pre-Press Company, Inc.

Production House:
Elm Street Publishing Services, Inc.

Printer:
Von Hoffmann Press
St. Louis, Missouri

Design Project Manager:
Michael Stratton

Internal Designer:
Bill Brammer, fusion 29 visual communication

Cover Designer:
Bill Brammer, fusion 29 visual communication

Photography Manager:
Deanna Ettinger

Photo Researcher:
Annette Coolidge

Library of Congress Cataloging-in-Publication Data
Economics: private and public choice / James D. Gwartney ... [et al.] -- 10th ed.
        p.cm.
Rev. ed of Economics: private and public choice / James D. Gwartney, Richard L. Stroup, Russell S. Sobel, 9th ed. Fort Worth, Tex.: Dryden Press, 2000.
Includes bibliographical references and index.
        ISBN 0-03-034398-4
1. Economics I. Gwartney, James D. II. Gwartney, James D. Economics.

HB171.5. E3377 2002
330--dc21
                2002006775

As in the past, our goal in this edition is to provide students with a user-friendly text that challenges the reader to develop the economic way of thinking. Put simply, this text is about: (a) making economics understandable, (b) illustrating the power and relevance of economics to our daily lives, and (c) explaining why both individuals and nations prosper. Throughout, we seek to communicate basic, and in some cases fairly complicated, ideas in a manner that is understandable for college freshmen and sophomores. We believe that this edition does that better than ever. The accompanying exercises, test questions, and even the PowerPoint package are designed to make the concepts of economics come alive.

The study of economics does not have to be either difficult or "watered down." *Economics: Private and Public Choice, 10th Edition* is a comprehensive text, rich in detail. But it is written with the student in mind. We have avoided abstractions and mechanical exercises that stress obscure details rather than basic concepts. The primary objective of our writing style is clarity. We have worked hard to make the material as clear as possible. Examples, illustrations, and visual aides are used to reinforce basic concepts. Simplicity, however, is not substituted for depth. Rather, our aim is to highlight the power, accessibility, and relevance of economic concepts.

More than ever before, the world is characterized by dynamic change, instant communication, and interaction between people in different nations. New products and technologies are constantly replacing the old ways of doing things. In fact, sometimes new products become obsolete just a few years after they are introduced. How will these developments affect your life? What will the U.S. economy be like ten or twenty years from now? Why do some countries prosper while others regress? As we proceed, we will use the tools of economics to address these and many other important issues that affect our lives.

DIVISION INTO CORE CHAPTERS AND SPECIAL TOPICS

Beginning with the 9th edition, the text was divided into core chapters and a concluding special topics section. The 27 core chapters cover all of the material taught in most principles courses and they are presented in the usual manner. Examples and data from the real world are used to reinforce the analysis. In addition, the Beyond the Basics section provides 14 relatively short features (about one-third the length of a regular chapter) that focus on high profile special topics. These features, designed for coverage during a single class period, provide a solid foundation for discussing important topics such as the stock market, the future of social security, the organization of health care and education, and the impact of unions. See the front endpapers for a complete listing of the special topics of the Beyond the Basics section. This core/special-topic structure has been quite popular, largely because it makes it easier for instructors to tailor their course to fit their own preferences.

CHANGES IN THE 10TH EDITION

David Macpherson has now officially joined the author team. He has been involved with this project for several years and was responsible for both the *Instructor's Manual* and *Test Bank* of the last edition. Professor Macpherson is both an outstanding researcher and an excellent teacher. On several occasions, Florida State University has recognized his outstanding teaching abilities, particularly in large lecture principles classes. His writing skills and in-depth knowledge of labor markets and monetary economics have both strengthened the author team and contributed significantly to the quality of this edition.

The authors enjoy working together and we have an excellent balance regarding our areas of expertise, alternative perspectives, and even youth and experience. We look forward to a cooperative effort on this project for many years to come.

Keys to Prosperity Series

Our own teaching experience indicates that students often fail to appreciate organizational and institutional factors that provide the foundation for economic progress. In order to help remedy this situation, this edition incorporates a new "Keys to Economic Prosperity" series that highlights the importance of factors like gains from trade, secure property rights, competition, and free trade as sources of economic prosperity. In all, twelve of the most important factors that underlie modern economic prosperity are highlighted at appropriate places throughout the text. These "keys to prosperity" are also listed in the front cover endpapers.

Beyond the Basics Section

The Beyond the Basics section of this edition contains new features on the impact of the Internet, the economics of health care, school choice, and government spending and taxation. In addition, the features from the last edition have been updated and, in several instances, substantially revised. This section provides background material on current issues that students will find both interesting and challenging.

Core Macroeconomics

The modifications to the core macro material include the following:

✗ Several modifications designed to enliven the mechanics of national income accounting and adjustments of price changes were incorporated into Chapter 7. Using gasoline prices as an example, this edition contains a new feature explaining how to convert income and price data for earlier years into current dollars. The material on cross-country and cross-time period GDP comparisons was expanded. An exercise on the real revenues derived from highly successful movies was also added.

✗ A new section "Price Level, Inflation, and the AD/AS Model" was incorporated into Chapter 10. This feature focuses on the relationship between (a) a change in the price level and (b) an inflation rate that differs from the rate that was expected.

✗ New material on both fiscal and stabilization policy has been incorporated. Chapter 12 includes a new section, "Fiscal Policy of the United States." The material on "Stabilization Policy and the U.S. Economy" in Chapter 15 is also new.

✗ Chapter 16 on economic growth has been substantially revised. This chapter also contains an extensive analysis of the Irish Miracle and the policies underlying it.

Core Microeconomics

The following changes were made to the core micro material:

✗ The importance of the entrepreneur has been elevated throughout the core micro material. Fred Smith (FedEx) and Pleasant Rowland (American Girl dolls) are now included along with Ted Turner and Bill Gates in the Chapter 22 feature on real world entrepreneurs.

✗ Chapter 23 incorporates new material on both the Microsoft case and the California electricity crisis.

✘ The material on productivity in Chapter 25 was updated and current debate about whether the 1996–2000 increase in productivity is temporary or permanent is highlighted.

✘ A new feature on millionaires in America and how to become one is now included in Chapter 25.

✘ The debate about the pattern of outcomes versus the fairness of the process has been incorporated into the chapter on income distribution and poverty.

ORGANIZATIONAL FEATURES

We have employed several organizational features designed to make the presentation more interesting and more understandable.

1. Applications and Measures in Economics. The Applications in Economics boxed features apply economic theory to real-world issues and controversies. The Measures of Economic Activity boxes explain how important economic indicators such as the unemployment rate and the index of leading indicators are assembled.

2. Chapter Focus Questions and Closing Key Point Summaries. Each chapter begins with several questions that summarize the focus of the chapter. Following the end of each chapter is a Key Points section that provides the student with a concise statement of the material (chapter learning objectives). Reviewing the focus questions and these concise key points will help the student better understand the material and integrate it into the broader economic picture.

3. Key Terms. The terminology of economics is often confusing to introductory students. Key terms are introduced in the text in bold type; simultaneously, each term is defined in the margin opposite the first reference to the term. A glossary containing the key terms also appears at the end of the book.

4. Critical Analysis Questions. Each chapter concludes with a set of discussion questions and problems designed to test the student's ability to analyze economic issues and to apply economic theory to real-world events. Appendix B at the end of the text contains suggested answers for approximately half of the critical analysis questions. We think these answers, illustrating the power of economics, will interest students and will help them develop the economic way of thinking.

SUPPLEMENTARY MATERIALS
For the Student

The Wall Street Journal Edition

Instructors can enhance the real-life applications in the text by ordering *The Wall Street Journal Edition* of the textbook instead of the regular textbook. This special edition of the textbook is the same as the standard edition but includes a discounted 20-week subscription of *The Wall Street Journal* for students. Professors get a free subscription when ten or more of their students order the *Journal. The Wall Street Journal* provides a nice tie-in with the text, since new examples of economic principles can be found in each day's paper. Students can activate their subscriptions by simply completing and mailing the business reply card found in the back of the book. Instructors interested in finding out more about this program can contact their sales representative or simply call 1-800-782-4479. This option is available for both the hardcover version of the book and the paperback splits.

Coursebooks

The *Coursebooks* for this edition were prepared by coauthor Professor Russell Sobel and are now available not in two, but three versions, covering all three courses: economics, microeconomics, and macroeconomics. The *Coursebooks* are more than study guides. Each includes numerous multiple-choice, true/false, and discussion questions permitting students to self-test their knowledge of each chapter. Answers and short explanations for most questions are provided in the back of each *Coursebook*. Each chapter also contains problem and project exercises designed to improve the student's knowledge of the mechanics. A set of short readings chosen to supplement the classroom teaching of important topics is also included. Like the textbook, the *Coursebook* is designed to help students develop the economic way of thinking.

Favorite Ways to Learn Economics Student Manual

Authors David Anderson (Centre College) and Jim Chasey (Homewood Flossmoor High School) use experiments to bring economic education to life. This is a growing trend and for good reason. It works! Students are far more likely to retain new knowledge when it is reinforced with hands-on experiments. *Favorite Ways to Learn Economics* is a lab manual for the classroom and for individual study. This manual of experiments and problem sets reinforces the key principles of microeconomics and macroeconomics covered in most college and AP courses. Students will enjoy this active approach to learning. Instructors will see improvement in their students' comprehension. Like a finely tuned lecture, these experiments and problem sets bring economics to life.

PowerPoint Note-taking

For years, we have encouraged students to think rather than focus on note-taking in our classes. It was a hard sell—many feel uncomfortable if they are not developing a set of notes. This note-taking version of the PowerPoint slides contains all slides (both the notes and graphics), along with space for additional note-taking next to each slide. This supplement permits students to focus on the classroom activities while providing them with confidence that they have an excellent set of notes for future reference.

Gwartney Xtra! CD-ROM

Gwartney Xtra! CD-ROM, packaged with every new text, provides students with complimentary access to the robust set of additional on-line learning tools found at the site. If students don't have the CD, they can purchase access to the on-line version at http://gwartneyXtra.swcollege.com. Here is a tour through some of the study support features you will find there:

✗ **The Graphing Workshop.** For most students, graphing is one of the most difficult aspects of the Principles course. The Graphing Workshop is your one-stop learning resource for help in mastering the language of graphs. You'll explore important economic concepts through a unique learning system made up of tutorials, interactive tools, and exercises that teach you how to interpret, reproduce, and explain graphs.

✗ **SEE IT!** Animated graphing tutorials provide step-by-step graphic presentations and audio explanations.

✗ **TRY IT!** Interactive graphing exercises have you practice manipulating and interpreting graphs with GraphIt—a hands-on Java graphing tool. You can check your work on-line.

✗ **APPLY IT!** Interactive graphing assignments challenge you to apply what you have learned by creating your own graph from scratch to analyze a specific scenario. You can print out and/or e-mail answers to your instructor for grading.

✗ **Video Lecture and Applications.** Via streaming video, difficult concepts from each chapter are explained and illustrated by an economics instructor. These "Ask the Instructor" video clips can be extremely helpful review and clarification tools if you had trouble understanding an in-class lecture or if you are more of a visual learner who sometimes has difficulty grasping concepts as they are presented in the text. In addition, CNN video segments bring the "real world" right to your desktop. The accompanying CNN video exercises help to illustrate how economics is an important part of your daily life.

✗ **Additional Self-Testing Opportunities.** In addition to the open-access, chapter-by-chapter quizzes found at the Gwartney Product Support Web site (http://gwartney. swcollege.com), Gwartney Xtra! offers you an opportunity to practice for midterms and finals by taking on-line quizzes that span multiple chapters.

✗ **econ@pps: (Economic Applications).** These economic applications are also available through the Gwartney Xtra! CD. EconDebate Online, EconNews Online, EconData Online, and EconLinks Online, all deepen your understanding of theoretical concepts through hands-on exploration and analysis of the latest economic news stories, policy debates, data, and Web sites. These applications are updated on a regular basis.

Web Site

Valuable resources for students can be found on the Internet at the Gwartney textbook support site: http://gwartney.swcollege.com. Students will find links to economics-related Internet sites, automatically graded practice quizzes, PowerPoint slides for their review, a sample chapter from the study guide, access to Gwartney Xtra! and other resources.

South-Western Economics Resource Center

A unique, rich, and robust on-line resource for economics instructors and students (http://economics.swcollege.com) provides customer service and product information, teaching and learning tips and tools, information about careers in economics, access to all of our text-supporting Web sites, and other cutting-edge educational resources.

InfoTrac College Edition

If you bought a new copy of the *InfoTrac College Edition* of this text, don't forget to take advantage of your subscription. With *InfoTrac College Edition*, you can receive anytime, anywhere, on-line access to a database of full-text articles from hundreds of scholarly and popular periodicals. You can use its fast and easy search tools to find what you're looking for among the tens of thousands of articles—updated daily and dating back as far as four years—all in this single Web site. It's a great way to locate resources for papers and projects without having to travel to the library. To log on and get started, visit http://www.infotrac-college.com

Economics Alive! CD-ROMs

These interactive multimedia study aids for economics are the high-tech, high-fun way to study economics. Through a combination of animated presentations, interactive graphing exercises, and simulations, the core principles of economics come to life and are driven home in an upbeat and entertaining way.

Macroeconomics Alive! CD-ROM
ISBN: 0-538-86850-3
Microeconomics Alive! CD-ROM
ISBN: 0-538-84650-X

For more details, visit the Economics Alive! Web site http://econalive.swcollege.com.

Economics: Hits on the Web

This resource booklet supports your students' research efforts on the World Wide Web. The booklet covers materials such as: introduction to the World Wide Web, browsing the Web, finding information on the World Wide Web, e-mail, e-mail discussion groups, and newsgroups, documenting Internet Sources for research, and it provides a listing of the hottest Economic sites on the Web.

The New York Times Guide to Economics
by Bernard F. Sigler, Cheryl Jennings, and Jamie Murphy

More than just a printed collection of articles, this *Guide* provides access, via password, to an on-line collection of the most current and relevant *New York Times* articles that are continually posted as news breaks. Also included are articles from *CyberTimes*, the online technology section of *The New York Times* on the Web. Correlation guides for many South-Western economics texts are available on the South-Western/*New York Times* Web site at http://nytimes.swcollege.com.
ISBN: 0-324-04159-4

The Tobacco Wars

The Tobacco Wars, by Walter Adams (Michigan State University) and James W. Brock (Miami University of Ohio) presents the economic theory surrounding the tobacco litigation as a creative dialogue between many key players in the debate—including tobacco industry executives, consumers, attorneys, economists, health care professionals, historians, and political activists. Their fictional conversations illustrate the real-life issues, controversies, and points of view currently at play, giving readers a balanced and provocative framework to reach their own conclusions. The text provides a unique way to illustrate microeconomic principles, such as:

✗ Consumer behavior

✗ Industrial organization and public policy

✗ Antitrust policy

✗ Externalities, social costs, and market imperfections

ISBN: 0-324-01296-9

For the Instructor
Test Banks

The *Test Banks* for the 10th Edition were prepared by the author team. The two *Test Banks* contain approximately 7,000 questions—multiple-choice and short answer—most of which have been class tested. Within each chapter, the questions correspond to the major subheadings of the text. The first ten questions of each chapter are suitable for use as a comprehensive quiz covering the material of the chapter. The multiple-choice questions from the *Coursebook* are also included in a special section of the *Test Bank*. Thus, instructors who would like to provide their students with a strong incentive to study the *Coursebook* can easily access these questions and incorporate them into their quizzes and exams.

Computerized Test Banks

The computerized Test Banks for this edition have been enhanced significantly. *Examview—*Computerized Testing Software contains all of the questions in the printed *Test Bank*. ExamView is an easy-to-use test creation software compatible with both Microsoft Windows and Macintosh. Instructors can add or edit questions, instructions, and answers and select questions by previewing them on the screen, selecting them randomly, or selecting them by number. Instructors can also create and administer quizzes on-line, whether over the Internet, a local-area network (LAN), or a wide-area network (WAN).

PowerPoint

Prepared by Chuck Skipton, we believe our PowerPoint presentation is the best you will find in the principles market. The new package comes in three formats to suit the various needs of instructors.

✗ The first format provides chapter-by-chapter lecture notes with fully animated, hyperlinked slides of the textbook's exhibits. The dynamic slides and accompanying captions make it easy for instructors to present (and students to follow) sequential changes. The dynamic graphics are also used to highlight various relationships among economic variables. In order to facilitate discussion and interaction, questions are strategically interspersed throughout the chapters to help students develop the economic way of thinking. We have used the material in our own classes and can assure you that students find this method of presentation both enjoyable and helpful. Economic principles are developed rather than merely portrayed. This makes it so much easier to visualize relationships.

✗ The second version contains all of the slides mentioned in the first version, but they are not fully animated and hyperlinked. This is to suit those instructors with slower modems or less classroom capabilities.

✗ The third version contains exact replica slides of all of the exhibits in the book so that an instructor can present these graphs and figures without going through the entire set of lecture note PowerPoint slides.

Instructions explaining how professors can easily add, delete, and modify slides in order to tailor the presentation to their liking are included with the *Instructor's Resource* CD-ROM. If instructors want to make the PowerPoint presentation available to students, they can place it on their Web site (or the site for their course). It is also available on the Web site for this text at http://gwartney.swcollege.com.

South-Western Economics Resource Center

A unique, rich, and robust on-line resource for economics instructors and students (http://economics.swcollege.com) provides customer service and product information, teaching and learning tips and tools, information about careers in economics, access to all of our text-supporting Web sites, and other cutting-edge educational resources.

Instructor's Manual with Classroom Games

The *Instructor's Manual* was prepared by David Macpherson. Instructions and information on how to use and modify the PowerPoint material is contained in the front of the manual. Also included at the front of the manual is information on the enhancements to the new *Examview*—Computerized Testing Software. The remainder of the manual is divided up by corresponding text chapter, with each manual chapter divided into three parts. The first part is a detailed outline of each chapter in lecture-note form. It is designed to help instructors organize and structure their current lecture notes according to the format of the 10th Edition. Instructors can easily prepare a detailed, personalized set of notes by revising the computerized version of the notes. The second part of each chapter contains teaching tips, sources of supplementary materials, and other helpful information. Part 3 of each chapter provides instructors with in-class games designed to illustrate and enliven important economic concepts. Contributed in part by Professor Charles Stull of Kalamazoo College, the games are an enormously popular feature with instructors. We hope you will try them. We believe you will find them extremely useful for classroom learning.

Instructor's Resource CD-ROM

For the first time, the instructor's supplements accompanying this textbook are now conveniently available on one CD-ROM. Included on the CD-ROM are the PowerPoint slides, *Instructor's Manual,* and *Test Banks.* The CD-ROM also displays a navigation bar, allowing professors to easily search among the microeconomics and macroeconomics versions of the supplements.

Color Transparencies

Color transparencies of the major exhibits of the 10th Edition have been prepared for use with overhead projectors. They are available to adopters upon request in sets for micro-economics and macroeconomics.

South-Western Publishing will provide complimentary supplements or supplement packages to those adopters qualified under our adoption policy. Please contact your sales representative to learn how you may qualify. If as an adopter or potential user you receive supplements you do not need, please return them to your sales representative.

Principles of Economics Videotape

Principles of Economics is a 40-minute videotape that offers students an insightful overview of ten common economic principles: Tradeoffs, Opportunity Cost, Marginal Thinking, Incentives, Trade, Markets, Government's Role, Productivity, Inflation, and The Phillips Curve.

Principles of Economics shows viewers how to apply economic principles to their daily lives. This video is filled with interviews from some of the country's leading econo-mists, and includes profiles of real students facing economic choices, as well as showing the economy's impact on U.S. and foreign companies.

This video can be used at the beginning of a term to give students a general overview of economics, or used one section at a time prior to teaching one of these principles in your course.

CNN Economics Videos

Professors can bring the real world into the classroom by using the CNN Principle of Eco-nomics Video Updates. This video provides current stories of economic interest. The video is produced by Turner Learning Inc.

WebTutor/WebTutor Advantage

On-line learning is growing at a rapid pace. Whether instructors are planning to offer courses at a distance, or to offer a Web-enhanced classroom, South-Western/Thomson Learning offers them a solution with WebTutor. WebTutor provides instructors with text-specific content that interacts in the two leading Course Management Systems available in Higher Education—WebCT and Blackboard. WebTutor is a turnkey solution for instruc-tors who want to begin using technology like Blackboard or WebCT, but do not have Web-ready content available or do not want to be burdened with developing their own content. South-Western offers two levels of WebTutor—WebTutor and WebTutor Advantage.

WebTutor—An interactive Study Guide, WebTutor uses the Internet to turn everyone in your class into a front-row student. WebTutor offers quizzing, concept review, flash cards, discussion forums, and more. Instructor tools are also provided to assist communication between students and faculty.

WebTutor Advantage—More than just an interactive study guide, WebTutor Advantage delivers innovative learning aids that actively engage students. Benefits include automatic and immediate feedback from quizzes; interactive, multimedia-rich explanation of concepts, such as flash-animated graphing tutorials and graphing exercises that utilize an on-line graph-drawing tool; streaming video applications; on-line exercises; flashcards; and greater interaction and involvement through on-line discussion forums. Powerful instructor tools are also provided to assist communication and collaboration between students and faculty. Contact your sales representative for more information on WebTutor products.

Favorite Ways to Learn Economics Instructor's Manual

Authors David Anderson (Centre College) and Jim Chasey (Homewood Flossmoor High School) use experiments to bring economic education to life. This is a growing trend and for good reason. It works! Students are far more likely to retain new knowledge when it is reinforced with hands-on experiments. *Favorite Ways to Learn Economics* is a lab manual for the classroom and for individual study. This manual of experiments and problem sets reinforces the key principles of microeconomics and macroeconomics covered in most college and AP courses. Students will enjoy this active approach to learning. Instructors will see improvement in their students' comprehension. Like a finely tuned lecture, these experiments and problem sets bring economics to life.

NOTE TO THE INSTRUCTOR

In trying to improve the book from one edition to the next, we rely heavily on our experiences as teachers. But our experience using the book is minuscule compared with that of the hundreds of instructors who use it nationwide. If you encounter problems or have suggestions for improving the book, we urge you to let us know by writing to us in care of South-Western / Thomson Learning, 5191 Natorp Blvd., Mason, OH 45040. Such letters are invaluable, and we are glad to receive both praise and suggestions for improvement. Many such suggestions that were accumulated since publication of the 9th Edition have found their way into this new book.

Acknowledgments

A project of this type is a team effort. We would like to express our appreciation to Chuck Skipton, who assisted us in numerous ways. Most significantly, he developed what we believe is the very best set of PowerPoint slides accompanying an introductory economics text. In the past, Woody Studenmund of Occidental College prepared the Coursebook and Gary Galles of Pepperdine University coauthored the *Instructor's Manual*. Both of these supplements still bear the imprint of their contribution.

Through the years, numerous people have supplied us with quality questions for the Test Banks. We would like to acknowledge specifically the contributions of J. J. Bethune, University of Tennessee–Martin; Edward Bierhanzl, Florida A&M University; Tim Sass, Florida State University; and Woody Studenmund. Amy Gwartney helped with the proofing and provided assistance in several other areas.

We have often revised material in light of suggestions made by reviewers, users, friends, and even a few competitors. In this regard, we would like to express our appreciation to the following people for their contributions to recent editions: Douglas Agbetsiafa, Indiana University, South Bend; James C.W. Ahiakpor, California State University, Hayward; Ali T. Akarca, University of Illinois at Chicago; Stephen A. Baker, Capital University; Alana Bhatia, University of Colorado at Boulder; Edward J. Bierhanzl, Florida A&M University; Charles A. Booth, University of Alabama at Birmingham; Ford J. Brown, University of Minnesota–Morris; Dennis Brennen, Harper College; James Bryan, Manhattanville College; Darcy R. Carr, Coastal Carolina University; Mike Cohick, Collin County Community College; David S. Collins, Virginia Highlands Community College; Jim F. Couch, University of North Alabama; Steven R. Cunningham, University of Connecticut; George W. Dollar, Clearwater Christian College; Jeff Edwards, Collin County Community College; Robert C. Eyler, Sonoma State University; James R. Fain, Oklahoma State University; Kathryn Finn, Western Washington University; Marsha Goldfarb, University of Maryland Baltimore County; David Harris, Northwood University; Ronald Helgens, Golden Gate University; Robert E. Herman, Nassau Community College/SUNY; William D. Hermann, Golden Gate University, San Francisco; Brad Hobbs, Florida Gulf Coast University; Woodrow W. Hughes, Jr., Converse College; Rob H. Kamery, Christian Brothers University; Frederic R. Kolb, University of Wisconsin, Eau Claire; Barbara Kouskoulas, Lawrence Technological University; David W. Kreutzer, James Madison University; George Kuljurgis, Oakland University; Randy W. LaHote, Washtenaw Community College; Tsung-Hui Lai, Liberty University; Bob Lawson, Capital University; Don R. Leet, California State University, Fresno; George P. Lephardt, Milwaukee School of Engineering; Joe LeVesque, Northwood University; G. Dirk Mateer, Grove City College; John McArthur, Wofford College; Ed Mills, Kendell College; David M. Mitchell, Oklahoma State University; Hadley T. Mitchell, Taylor University; Glen A. Moots, Northwood University; John R. Neal, Lake-Sumter Community College; Lloyd Orr, Indiana University, Bloomington; Judd W. Patton, Bellevue College; Robert Reinke, University of South Dakota; Robert C. Rencher, Jr., Liberty University; Dan Rickman, Oklahoma State University; Karin L. Russell, Keiser College; Lewis F. Schlossinger, Community College of Aurora; Thomas W. Secrest, USC Coastal Carolina; Ben S. Shippen, Jr., Mercer University; Charles D. Skipton, Florida State University; Ken Somppi, Southern Union State Community College; William A. Steiden, Jefferson Community College; Richard D.C. Trainer, Warsaw School of Economics; Scott Ward, East Texas Baptist University; Tom Lee Waterston, Northwood University; Jim Wharton, Northwood University; Janice Yee, Wartburg College; and Anthony Zambelli, Cuyamaca College.

Many people made important contributions to the 10th Edition by providing us with insightful feedback and astute reviews. The following reviewers helped us make substantial improvements:

Ljubisa Adamovich, Florida State University; Gayla Ashford, Calhoun State Community College; Laurie Bates, Bryant College; Joseph P. Cairo, LaSalle University; Shawn Carter, Jacksonville State University; Christopher Clark, University of South Alabama; Richard

Ebeling, Hillsdale College; Pat Euzent, University of Central Florida; Andrew W. Foshee, McNeese State University; Stephen Gohmann, University of Louisville; Darren Grant, Georgia Southern University; Ashley Lyman, University of Idaho; Thomas McCaleb, Florida State University; Rex Santerre, Bentley College; Eric Schansberg, Indiana University Southeast; Kevin Stokes, Jefferson Community College; Thomas Tacker, Embry-Riddle Aeronautical University; David Theissen, Lewis-Clark State College; Chris Westley, Jacksonville State University.

We are also indebted to the excellent team of professionals at South-Western Publishing: Peter Adams, acquisitions editor, for his help and support of our efforts; Andy McGuire, developmental editor, who managed the project; Bob Dreas, production editor, for orchestrating the copyediting, proofreading, and countless other production tasks; Bill Brammer, who designed the book; Carrie Hochstrasser, who designed the preface and preview guide. We'd also like to thank all those at Elm Street Publishing Services and Pre-Press Company for their help in production and composition, and Janet Hennies for her work in marketing this text.

Finally, we would like to acknowledge the assistance of Amy Gwartney, Jane Shaw Stroup, Terri Sobel, and Karen Macpherson for their encouragement throughout the project. Without their contributions, we would have been unable to meet the demands and deadlines of this project.

A Note to Students

This text contains several features that we think will help you maximize (a good economic term) the returns derived from your study effort. Our past experience indicates that awareness of the following points will help you use the book more effectively.

✘ Each chapter begins with a series of focus questions that communicates the central issues of the chapter. Before you read the chapter, briefly think about the focus questions, why they are important, and how they relate to the material of prior chapters.

✘ The textbook is organized in the form of an outline. The major headings within the text are the major points of the outline. Minor headings are subpoints under the major headings. In addition, important subpoints within sections are often set off and numbered. Bold, italicized type is used to highlight material that is particularly important. Sometimes thumbnail sketches are included to help the reader better organize important points. Careful use of the headings, highlighted material, and thumbnail sketches will help you master the material.

✘ A Key Points summary appears at the end of each chapter. Use the summary as a checklist to determine whether you understand the major points of the chapter.

✘ The key terms introduced in each chapter are defined in the margins. As you study the chapter, go over the marginal definition of each key term as it is introduced. Later, you may also find it useful to review the marginal definitions. If you have forgotten the meaning of a term introduced earlier, consult the glossary at the end of the book.

✘ The boxed features provide additional depth on various topics. In general, the topics of the boxed features have been chosen because of their relevance as an application of the theory or because of past student interest in the topic.

✘ The critical analysis questions at the end of each chapter are intended to test your understanding of the economic way of thinking. Solving these questions and problems will greatly enhance your knowledge of the material. Answers to approximately half of these questions are provided in Appendix B.

✘ Economics is about obtaining the most value from the available resources. At appropriate places throughout the text, the Keys to Prosperity Series (indicated with a key-shaped icon) stresses the importance of 12 elements that are central to the achievement of this objective. Students should make sure that they understand these factors because they will enhance their knowledge of the conditions underlying economic prosperity. The front endpapers contain a list of the 12 elements.

✘ If you need more practice, be sure to obtain a *Coursebook* and solve the questions and problems for each chapter. The Coursebook also contains the answers to the multiple-choice questions and a brief explanation of why an answer is correct (and other choices incorrect). In most cases, if you master the concepts of the test items in the Coursebook, you will do well on the quizzes and examinations in your course.

✘ For extra help utilizing multimedia tools, use the Gwartney X-tra CD-Rom or go to http://gwartneyXtra.swcollege.com, where you will find practice quizzes, PowerPoint reviews of each chapter, video clips that answer frequently asked questions, tutorials on graphing, and other helpful learning tools.

About the Authors

James D. Gwartney

James Gwartney is Professor of Economics in the DeVoe Moore Center for the Study of Critical Issues in Economic Policy at Florida State University. Professor Gwartney, who received his doctoral degree from the University of Washington, served as Chief Economist of the Joint Economic Committee of the U.S. Congress from 1999 to 2000. He is the author of numerous books and articles, including *Economic Freedom of the World* and *What Everyone Should Know about Economics and Prosperity*—a book that has been translated into 14 languages. His writing has appeared in the *Wall Street Journal, New York Times,* and *Investor's Business Daily,* among many others.

Richard L. Stroup

Richard Stroup is Professor of Economics at Montana State University, and Senior Associate at the Political Economy Research Center. With a Ph.D. in economics from the University of Washington, Professor Stroup has served as Director of the Office of Policy Analysis at the Department of the Interior and has been published widely in professional journals. He is a contributing editor of numerous books on the economics of resources and the environment, and has lectured throughout the United States and abroad to professional and general audiences.

Russell S. Sobel

Russell Sobel is an Associate Professor of Economics at West Virginia University. Receiving his Ph.D. in economics from Florida State University in 1994, Professor Sobel regularly teaches courses in both principles of economics and public economics. His enthusiastic teaching style has earned him many university teaching awards, and he regularly gives lectures at economic education outreach programs on basic economic principles. Professor Sobel's research focuses on the economic effects of state and local tax policy specifically, and on political behavior in general.

David A. Macpherson

David Macpherson is a new addition to the authorship team. The Abba Lerner Professor of Economics at Florida State University, he has received two university-wide awards for teaching excellence. Professor Macpherson is also the author of many articles in leading labor economics and industrial relations journals—including the *Journal of Labor Economics, Journal of Human Resources,* and *Industrial and Labor Relations Review*. His current research interests include pensions, discrimination, labor unions, and the minimum wage. Professor Macpherson received his undergraduate degree and Ph.D. from Pennsylvania State University.

Brief Contents

Table of Contents

RELATIONSHIP BETWEEN MAIN EDITION AND THE MACRO/MICRO EDITIONS

PART 1

"Life is a se

THE ECONOMIC WAY OF THINKING

Economics is about how people choose. The choices we make influence our lives and those of others. Your future will be influenced by the choices you make with regard to education, job opportunities, savings, and investment. Furthermore, changes in technology, demographics, communications, and transportation are constantly altering the attractiveness of various options and the opportunities available to us. The economic way of thinking is all about how incentives alter the choices people make. It can help you make better choices and enhance your understanding of our dynamic world.

CHAPTER **1**

The Economic Approach

[Economics] is

not a body of

concrete truth,

but an engine for

the discovery of

concrete truth.

—*Alfred Marshall*[1]

Chapter Focus

- Why is scarcity a key economic concept, even in a relatively wealthy economy?

- How does scarcity differ from poverty? Why does scarcity necessitate rationing and cause competition?

- What are the basic principles underlying the economic way of thinking? What is different about the way economists look at choices and human decision making?

- What is the difference between positive and normative economics?

[1]Alfred Marshall, *The Present Position of Economics* (1885), p. 25.

Now is an exciting time to study economics. Recent political campaigns in the United States have centered on economic issues such as health care, the budget deficits and surpluses, the structure and level of taxes, and social security reform. The market economies of Western Europe are struggling to develop a single, integrated economy with a common currency and legal structure. Several countries of Eastern Europe and the former Soviet Union are continuing their struggle to move from socialist central planning toward market-directed economies. Several Asian nations are trying to recover from recent financial difficulties and regain the prosperity they achieved throughout most of the 1980s and 1990s. Latin American and African leaders are searching for economic prescriptions that will generate prosperity and upgrade living standards.

Economies around the world are becoming more and more interrelated. Many of the goods at your favorite shopping mall are produced, at least in part, by people who speak a different language and live in a country far from your own. Similarly, many Americans work for companies that market their products in Europe, Japan, Latin America, or Africa. The pension funds of American workers commonly own stocks from around the world. Ownership shares of American companies are traded not only in New York City but also on stock exchanges in London, Tokyo, and throughout the world.

How will our current economic policies and rapidly changing world affect the economic status of Americans? What impact will the globalization of our economy have on our living standards, lifestyles, and future opportunities? This book will help you better understand these issues, and the world in which you live. This is not to imply that economics provides easy answers for problems. As Alfred Marshall stated more than a century ago, economics is a discovery process—a way of thinking—rather than a "body of concrete truth" (see the chapter opening quote). Our goals are to present the tools of economics and illustrate how the economic way of thinking can enhance your understanding of our rapidly changing world.

OUTSTANDING ECONOMIST

The Importance of Adam Smith, the Father of Economic Science

Economics is a relatively young science. The foundation of economics was laid in 1776, when Adam Smith (1723–1790) published *An Inquiry Into the Nature and Causes of the Wealth of Nations*. Smith presented what at that time was a revolutionary view. He argued that the wealth of a nation did not lie in gold and silver, but rather in the goods and services produced and consumed by people. According to Smith, coordination, order, and efficiency would result without the planning and direction of a central authority.

Adam Smith was a lecturer at the University of Glasgow, in his native Scotland. Morals and ethics actually were his concern before economics. His first book was *The Theory of Moral Sentiments*. For Smith, self-interest and sympathy for others were complementary. However, he did not believe that charity alone could provide the essentials for a good life. He stressed that free exchange and competitive markets would harness self-interest as a creative force. Smith believed that individuals *pursuing their own interests* would be directed by the "invisible hand" of market prices toward the production of those goods that were most advantageous to the society.

Ideas have consequences. Smith's ideas greatly influenced not only Europeans but also those who mapped out the structure of the U.S. government. Since then, the effectiveness of the "invisible hand" of the market has become accepted as critical to the prosperity of nations.*

---

*For an excellent biographical sketch of Adam Smith, see David Henderson, ed., *The Fortune Encyclopedia of Economics* (New York: Warner Books, 1993), pp. 836–838.

The origins of economics date to Adam Smith's classic book *An Inquiry Into the Nature and Causes of the Wealth of Nations* (for more information see the Outstanding Economist box on Adam Smith). As the title suggests, Smith sought to explain the forces underlying the creation of wealth and the sources of income differences across regions and nations. Just as during the time of Smith, understanding the process of wealth creation continues to be the central issue of economics. Reflecting this importance, the following icon 🔑 will be used throughout the text to highlight "Keys to Economic Prosperity." A full listing of these keys to economic prosperity is presented inside the front cover of this book. These keys and accompanying discussions will help identify the central factors underlying growth and prosperity. ■

[Economics is] the science which studies human behavior as a relationship between ends and scarce means which have alternative uses.

—Lionel Robbins[2]

WHAT IS ECONOMICS ABOUT?

Economics is about people and the choices they make. The unit of analysis in economics is the individual. Of course, individuals group together to form collective organizations, such as corporations, labor unions, and governments. Individual choices, however, still underlie and direct these organizations. Thus, even when we study collective organizations, we will focus on the ways in which their operation is affected by the choices of *individuals*.

Scarcity and Choice

Would you like some new clothes, a nicer car, and a larger apartment? How about better grades and more time to watch television, go skiing, and travel? Do you dream of driving your brand new Porsche into the driveway of your ocean-front house? As individuals, our desire for goods is virtually unlimited. We may want *all* of these things. Unfortunately, both as individuals and as a society we face a constraint called **scarcity** that prevents us from being able to completely fulfill our desires. Scarcity is a condition that indicates that there is less of a good or resource freely available from nature than people would like. Some things, such as air or seawater are not scarce—there is as much available freely from nature as we all would like. Almost everything else you can think of—even your time—is scarce. The unlimited nature of our desires coupled with the limited nature of the goods and resources that are available to satisfy them require that we make choices. Should I spend the next hour studying or watching TV? Should I spend my last $20 on a new CD or on a shirt? Should this factory be used to produce clothing or furniture? **Choice**, the act of selecting among alternatives, is the logical consequence of scarcity. In our choices we are constantly faced with making important trade-offs between meeting one desire or meeting another. To meet one need we must let another go unmet. The basic ideas of *scarcity* and *choice*, along with the *trade-offs* we must face as decision makers are the basic ingredients of economic analysis.

Resources are the inputs used to produce goods and services. In essence, they are tools that we can use to battle scarcity. There are three general categories of resources. First, there are human resources—the productive knowledge, skill, and strength of human beings. Second, there are physical resources—things like tools, machines, and buildings that enhance our ability to produce goods. Economists often use the term **capital** when referring to these human-made resources. Third, there are natural resources—things like land, mineral deposits, oceans, and rivers. The ingenuity of humans is often required in order to make these natural resources useful in production. For example, until recently the yew tree was considered a "trash tree," having no value. Then, scientists discovered that the tree produces taxol, a substance that could be used to fight cancer. Human knowledge and ingenuity made yew trees a valuable resource. Natural resources are important, but recognizing the best ways to produce goods, and which goods to produce under changing circumstances, is as important as the existence of the resources themselves.

Scarcity
Fundamental concept of economics that indicates that there is less of a good freely available from nature than people would like.

Choice
The act of selecting among alternatives.

Resource
An input used to produce economic goods. Land, labor, skills, natural resources, and capital are examples. Throughout history, people have struggled to transform available, but limited, resources into things they would like to have—economic goods.

Capital
Man-made resources (such as tools, equipment, and structures) that are used to produce other goods and services. They enhance our ability to produce in the future.

---

[2]Lionel Robbins, *An Essay on the Nature and Significance of Economic Science* (1932).

SCARCE GOODS	LIMITED RESOURCES
Food (bread, milk, meat, eggs, vegetables, coffee, etc.)	Land (various degrees of fertility)
Clothing (shirts, pants, blouses, shoes, socks, coats, sweaters, etc.)	Natural resources (rivers, trees, minerals, oceans, etc.)
Household goods (tables, chairs, rugs, beds, dressers, television sets, etc.)	Machines and other human-made physical resources
Education	Nonhuman animal resources
National defense	Technology (physical and scientific "recipes" of history)
Leisure time	Human resources (the knowledge, skill, and talent of individual human beings)
Entertainment	
Clean air	
Pleasant environment (trees, lakes, rivers, open spaces, etc.)	
Pleasant working conditions	

EXHIBIT 1
A General Listing of Scarce Goods and Limited Resources

History is a record of our struggle to transform available, but limited, resources into goods that we would like to have.

Exhibit 1 provides a listing of the various categories of both scarce goods and the limited resources that might be utilized to produce them. Because of scarcity we will never be able to produce enough goods to fulfill human desires completely. With the passage of time, however, better technology, improved knowledge, human ingenuity, and discovery, allow us to produce more goods with the same amount of limited resources. Primitive cavemen had the same physical natural resources available as are present today, but their ability to produce desired goods from these resources was not as great. While these advances help to ease the grip of scarcity through time, it can never be eliminated. Some desires will always have to remain unsatisfied. Making matters worse, if we devote more of today's resources toward investment in new technology, education and skill enhancement, more tools and machines, or more factories, then fewer resources will be available to produce goods for consumption right now.

Put simply, the basic economic problem concerns how we as individuals decide to allocate our limited resources among the many competing uses. Which desires should we attempt to satisfy and which should we leave unsatisfied? Economics is about trade-offs.

Scarcity and Poverty

During the past 250 years, we have loosened the grip of scarcity a little. Think for a moment what life was like in 1750. People all over the world struggled 50, 60, and 70 hours a week to obtain the basic necessities of life—food, clothing, and shelter. Manual labor was the major source of energy. Animals provided the means of transportation. Tools and machines were primitive by today's standards. As the English philosopher Thomas Hobbes stated in the seventeenth century, life was "solitary, poor, nasty, brutish, and short."[3]

Throughout much of South America, Africa, and Asia, economic conditions today continue to make life difficult. In North America, Western Europe, Oceania, and some parts of Asia, however, substantial economic progress has been made. Of course, scarcity is still a fact of life in these areas, too; the desire for goods and services still far outstrips the ability of people to produce them. But from a material standpoint, life is more comfortable. As diet and health care have improved, so has life expectancy. Modern energy sources, means of transportation, appliances, and recreational opportunities have reduced physical hardship and the drudgery of life in North America and other wealthy parts of the world. In these areas, a typical family might worry about financing a summer vacation, obtaining a better

---

[3]Thomas Hobbes, *Leviathan* (1651) Part I, Chapter 13.

home computer or an additional car, and providing for the children's college education. Subsistence levels of food, shelter, and clothing are taken for granted. As anyone who watched the CBS reality TV show "Survivor" knows, we take for granted many of the basic needs that modern technological advances have allowed us to fulfill. Participants on the show struggled with even basic things like making fire, shelter, and catching fish. Not only were they more than thrilled at winning basic items such as shampoo, rice, and toilet paper at the reward challenges, but during the second "Survivor" series, survivor Elisabeth Filarski eagerly outbid everyone at an auction to get a small chocolate bar and a spoonful of peanut butter for $260 Australian (equivalent to about $132 U.S.).

It is important to note that scarcity and poverty are not the same thing. Poverty implies some basic level of need, either in absolute or relative terms. Absence of poverty means that the basic level has been attained. In contrast, the absence of scarcity would imply that we have as much of *all* goods as we would like. Both individuals and countries may win the battle against poverty—people may achieve income levels that allow them to satisfy a basic level of need. But it is painfully obvious that we will not triumph over scarcity. Even in the wealthiest of countries, productive capabilities cannot keep pace with material desires. People always want more goods for themselves and others they care about; societies always want more and better medical care, schooling, and national defense than can be produced with available resources.

Scarcity Necessitates Rationing

Rationing
An allocation of a limited supply of a good or resource to users who would like to have more of it. Various criteria, including charging a price, can be utilized to allocate the limited supply. When price performs the rationing function, the good or resource is allocated to those willing to give up the most "other things" in order to obtain ownership rights.

When a good (or resource) is scarce, some criterion must be set up for deciding who will receive the good (or resource) and who will go without it. Scarcity makes **rationing** a necessity.

Several possible criteria could be used in rationing a limited amount of a good among citizens who would like to have more of it. The rationing criterion chosen will influence human behavior. If the criterion were first-come, first-served, goods would be allocated to those who were fastest at getting in line or to those who were most willing to wait in line. This is often how space in college classes is rationed. If beauty were used, goods would be allocated to those who were thought to be most beautiful. The political process might determine allocations, and goods would be distributed on the basis of political status and ability to manipulate the political process to personal advantage. In a market setting, price

The degree to which modern technology and knowledge allow us to fulfill our desires and ease the grip of scarcity is often taken for granted—as the cast of the CBS reality show "Survivor" soon found out when they had to struggle to meet even basic needs such as cleaning their bodies and clothes, eating, and cooking.

is used to ration things; goods and resources are allocated only to those who are willing to pay the prevailing market price. One thing is certain: Scarcity means that methods must be established to decide who gets the limited amount of available goods and resources.

Competition Results From Scarcity

Competition is a natural outgrowth of scarcity and the desire of human beings to improve their conditions. Competition exists in every economy and every society. It exists both when goods are allocated by price in markets and when they are allocated by other means—political decision making, for example.

Moreover, the rationing criterion will influence which competitive techniques will be used. When the rationing criterion is price, individuals will engage in income-generating activities that enhance their ability to pay the price. The market system encourages individuals to provide goods and services to others in exchange for income. In turn, the income will permit them to procure more scarce goods.

A different rationing criterion will encourage other types of behavior. When the appearance of sincerity, broad knowledge, fairness, good judgment, and a positive television image are important, as they are in the rationing of elected political positions, people will use resources to project these qualities. They will hire makeup artists, public relations experts, and advertising agencies to help them compete. We can change the form of competition, but no society has been able to eliminate it, because no society has been able to eliminate scarcity and the resulting need for rationing. When people who want more scarce goods seek to meet the criteria established to ration those goods, competition occurs.

THE ECONOMIC WAY OF THINKING

One does not have to spend much time around economists to recognize that there is an "economic way of thinking." Admittedly, economists, like others, differ widely in their ideological views. A news commentator once remarked that "any half-dozen economists will normally come up with about six different policy prescriptions." Yet, in spite of their philosophical differences, the approach of economists covers a common ground.

That common ground is **economic theory**, developed from basic postulates of human behavior. Economic theory, like a road map or a guidebook, establishes reference points indicating what to look for, and how economic issues are interrelated. To a large degree, the basic economic principles are merely common sense. When applied consistently, however, these commonsense concepts can provide interesting and powerful insights.

> *It [economics] is a method rather than a doctrine, an apparatus of the mind, a technique of thinking which helps its possessor to draw correct conclusions.*
>
> —John Maynard Keynes[4]

Economic theory
A set of definitions, postulates, and principles assembled in a manner that makes clear the "cause-and-effect" relationships of economic data.

Eight Guideposts to Economic Thinking

The economic way of thinking requires the incorporation of certain guidelines—some would say the building blocks of basic economic theory—into one's thought process. Once these guidelines are incorporated, we believe that economics can be a relatively easy subject to master. Students who have difficulty with economics have almost always failed to assimilate these principles. We will outline and discuss eight principles that characterize the economic way of thinking and that are essential to understanding the economic approach.

1. The use of scarce resources is costly; trade-offs must always be made.
Economists sometimes refer to this as the "there is no such thing as a free lunch" principle. Because resources are scarce, the use of resources to produce one good diverts those resources from the production of other goods that are also desired. At any time a parcel of

---

[4]John Maynard Keynes (1883–1946) was an English economist whose writings during the 1920s and 1930s exerted an enormous impact on both economic theory and policy. Keynes established the terminology and the economic framework that are still widely used when economists study problems of unemployment and inflation.

Reprinted with special
permission of King Features
Syndicate.

undeveloped land could either be used for a new hospital, a parking lot, or simply left un-developed. No option is free of cost—there is always a trade-off. The choice to pursue any one of these options means the others must be sacrificed. Economists refer to the highest valued alternative that must be sacrificed as the result of a choice as the **opportunity cost** of that option. For example, if you use one hour of your scarce time to study economics, you will have one hour less time to watch television, read magazines, sleep, work at a job, or study other subjects. Time spent working at a job, or even time spent sleeping, might be viewed as your highest valued option forgone. In economics, the cost of an action is the highest valued option given up when a choice is made.

It is important to recognize that the use of scarce resources to produce a good is always costly regardless of who pays for the good or service produced. In many countries, various kinds of schooling are provided free of charge *to students*. However, provision of the schooling is not free *to the community*. The scarce resources (for example, buildings, equipment, and skills of teachers) used to produce the schooling could have been used in-stead to produce more recreation, entertainment, housing, or other goods. The cost of the schooling is the highest valued option that must now be given up because the resources required for its production were instead used to produce the schooling.

By now the central point should be obvious. As we make choices, we are continu-ously faced with trade-offs. The use of more resources to do one thing implies fewer resources with which to achieve other objectives. For example, while mandating air bags in automobiles may save lives, economic thinking forces us to ask if that money and those resources could have been used in an alternative way to save even more lives. In the next chapter we will look more closely at this key concept and some of its implications.

2. Individuals choose purposefully—they try to get the most from their limited resources.

Recognizing the restrictions imposed by the limited resources available to them (income, time, talent, and so on), individuals will try to select those options that best advance their personal objectives. They will not deliberately waste their valuable resources. In turn, the objectives or preferences of individuals are revealed by the choices they make. **Economizing behavior** results directly from purposeful (rational) decision making. Econ-omizing individuals will seek to accomplish an objective at the least possible cost to them-selves. When choosing among things that yield equal benefit, an economizer will select the cheapest option. For example, if a pizza, a lobster dinner, and a sirloin steak are expected to yield identical benefits for Mary (including the enjoyment of eating them), economizing behavior implies that Mary will select the cheapest of the three alternatives, probably the pizza. In the same way, when choosing among alternatives of equal cost, economizing decision makers will select the option that yields the greatest benefit. If the prices of several dinner specials are equal, for example, economizers will choose the one they like the best—the one that provides them the most benefit.

Purposeful choosing implies that decision makers have some basis for their evalua-tion of alternatives. Economists refer to this evaluation as **utility**—the benefit or satisfac-tion that an individual expects from the choice of a specific alternative. Utility is highly subjective, often differing widely from person to person. The steak dinner that delights one person may be repulsive to another (a vegetarian, for example).

Opportunity cost
The highest valued alternative that must be sacrificed as a result of choosing among alternatives.

Economizing behavior
Choosing with the objective of gaining a specific benefit at the least possible cost. A corollary of economizing behavior implies that, when choosing among items of equal cost, individuals will choose the option that yields the greatest benefit.

Utility
The subjective benefit or satis-faction a person expects from a choice or course of action.

THE FAMILY CIRCUS®   **By Bil Keane**

"Everybody wants to be sick.
I'm using M&M's for pills."

Reprinted with special permission
of King Features Syndicate.

3. Incentives matter—choice is influenced in a predictable way by changes in incentives.

This guidepost to clear economic thinking might be called the basic postulate of all economics. *As the personal benefits from choosing an option increase, other things constant, a person will be more likely to choose that option. In contrast, as the personal costs associated with the choice of an item increase, the individual will be less likely to choose that option.* For a group, this basic economic postulate suggests that making an option more attractive will cause more people to choose it. In contrast, as the cost of a selection to the members of a group increases, fewer of them will make this selection.

This basic postulate of economics is a powerful tool because its application is so widespread. Incentives affect behavior in virtually all aspects of our lives, ranging from market decisions about what to buy to political choices concerning for whom to vote. If beef prices rise, making beef consumption more expensive relative to other goods, the basic postulate indicates that consumers will be less likely to choose it. As a result, less beef will be consumed at the higher price. Similarly, the "incentives matter" postulate indicates that a voter will be less likely to support candidates favoring higher taxes to provide goods the voter finds unattractive.

Why do store owners reduce
their prices on various items?
Do they believe that consumers
respond to incentives?

To show its broad scope, we can apply this basic postulate of economics to the examination process. If a classroom instructor makes it more costly to cheat, students will be less likely to do so. There will be little cheating on a closely monitored, individualized essay examination. Why? Because it is difficult (that is, costly) to cheat on such an exam. Suppose, however, that an instructor gives an objective "take-home" exam, basing students' course grades entirely on the results. Among the same group of students, more will be likely to cheat because the benefits of doing so will be great and the risk (cost) minimal.

Most errors in economic reasoning occur because of a failure to remember and consistently apply the simple postulate that incentives matter. Probably because economics focuses on efforts of individuals to satisfy material desires, casual observers often argue that the relevance of the incentives matter postulate hinges on selfishness. This view is false. People are motivated by a variety of goals, some humanitarian and some selfish. The basic postulate of economics applies to both. For example, even an unselfish altruist would be more likely to attempt the rescue of a small child from a three-foot swimming pool than from the rapid currents approaching Niagara Falls. Similarly, people are more likely to give a needy person their hand-me-downs rather than their best clothes.

It is clear that incentives, whether they be monetary or nonmonetary, matter in human decision making. People will be less likely to walk down a dark alleyway than a well-lit one, they will be more likely to take a job if it has good benefits and working conditions than if it doesn't, and they will be more likely to bend down and pick up a quarter lying on the sidewalk than they will a penny.

4. Individuals make decisions at the margin.

When making a choice between two alternatives, individuals generally focus on the *difference* in the costs and benefits between the alternatives. Economists describe such decisions as **marginal**. The last time you went to eat fast food you probably were faced with a decision that highlights this type of thinking. Should you get the cheeseburger for $1.50 and the medium drink for $1.00, or should you get the value meal that has a cheeseburger, a medium drink, and a medium order of fries for $3.00? Naturally, individual decision making focuses on the difference between the alternatives—the value meal costs 50 cents more (this would be the marginal cost of going with the value meal) while it contains one extra food item, the fries (this would be the marginal benefit of going with the value meal).

Marginal
Term used to describe the effects of a change in the current situation. For example, the marginal cost is the cost of producing an additional unit of a product, given the producer's current facility and production rate.

Marginal choices always involve the effects of net additions to or subtractions from the current conditions. In fact, the word *additional* is often used as a substitute for *marginal*. For example, we might ask, "What is the marginal (or additional) cost of producing one more unit?" Marginal decisions may involve large or small changes. The "one more unit" could be a new factory or a new stapler. It is marginal because it involves additional costs and additional benefits. Given the current situation, what marginal benefits (additional sales revenues, for example) can be expected from the new factory, and what will be the marginal cost of constructing it? The answers to these questions will determine whether building the new factory is a good decision.

It is important to distinguish between *average* and *marginal*. A manufacturer's current average cost of producing automobiles (which would be the total cost of production divided by total number of cars produced) may be $20,000, but the marginal cost of producing an additional automobile (or an additional 1,000 automobiles) might be much lower, say, $5,000 per car. Costs associated with research, testing, design, molds, heavy equipment, and similar factors of production must be incurred whether the manufacturer is going to produce 1,000 units, 10,000 units, or 100,000 units. Such costs will clearly contribute to the average cost of an automobile, but they will change very little as additional units are produced. Thus, the marginal cost of additional units may be substantially less than the average cost. Should production be expanded or reduced? That choice should be based on marginal costs, which indicate the *change* in total cost due to the decision, rather than the current average cost.

We often confront decisions involving a possible change from the current situation. The *marginal benefits* and *marginal costs* associated with the choice will determine the wisdom of our decisions. What happens at the margin is therefore an important element of the economic way of thinking.

5. Although information can help us make better choices, its acquisition is costly.

Because we must devote time and resources to gather information, we will almost always make choices based on limited knowledge. Information that will help us make better choices is valuable. Like other resources, however, it is also scarce and therefore costly to acquire. As a result, individuals will economize on their search for information just as they economize on the use of other scarce resources. For example, when purchasing a pair of jeans, you may check price and evaluate quality at several different stores. At some point, though, you will decide that additional shopping—that is, acquisition of additional information—is simply not worth the trouble. You will make a choice based on the limited knowledge that you already possess.

The process is similar when individuals search for a restaurant, a new car, or a roommate. They will seek to acquire some information, but at some point, they will decide that the expected benefit derived from gathering still more information is simply not worth the cost. When differences among the alternatives are important to the decision maker, more time and effort will be spent to make a better individual decision. People are much more likely to read a consumer ratings magazine before purchasing a new automobile than they are before purchasing a new can opener. Because information is costly to acquire, limited knowledge and resulting uncertainty about the outcome generally characterize the decision-making process.

6. Economic actions often generate secondary effects in addition to their immediate effects.

Failure to consider secondary effects is the most common source of economic error. Frederic Bastiat, a nineteenth-century French economist, stated that the difference between a good and a bad economist is that the bad economist considers only the immediate, visible effects, whereas the good economist is also aware of the **secondary effects**, effects that result from the initial policy, but that may be seen or felt only with the passage of time.

> **Secondary effects**
> Consequences of an economic change that are not immediately identifiable but are felt only with the passage of time.

Perhaps a simple example involving both immediate and secondary effects will help us grasp this point. The immediate effect of an aspirin is a bitter taste in one's mouth. The secondary effect, which is not immediately observable, is relief from a headache. The immediate effect of drinking six quarts of beer might be a warm, jolly feeling. The secondary effect is likely to be a sluggish feeling the next morning, and perhaps a pounding headache.

In economics, the immediate, short-term effects that are highly visible are often quite different from the long-term effects. Changes in economic policy often alter the structure of incentives, which indirectly affects how much people work, earn, invest, and conserve for the future. But the impact of the secondary effects is often observable only after the passage of time—and even then only to those who know what to look for in evaluating them.

Consider tariffs, quotas, and other restrictions that limit imports. Proponents of such restrictions argue that they will increase employment. Indeed, for a short period of time, this may be the case. If, for example, the supply of foreign-produced automobiles to the U.S. market were restricted, Americans would buy more American-made automobiles, increasing output and employment in the domestic auto industry. These would be the immediate, easily identifiable effects. But consider the secondary effects. The restrictions would also reduce supply to the domestic market and increase the price of both foreign- and American-made automobiles. As a result of the higher prices, many auto consumers would pay more for automobiles and thus be forced to curtail their purchases of food, clothing, recreation, and literally thousands of other items. These reductions in spending would mean less output and employment in those areas. There would also be a secondary effect on sales to foreigners. Since foreigners would be selling fewer automobiles to Americans, they would acquire fewer dollars with which to buy American-made goods. U.S. exports, therefore, would fall as a result of the restrictions on automobile imports.

Once the secondary effects are considered, the net impact on employment of the import restrictions is no longer obvious. Although restrictions may increase employment in the auto industry, they will reduce employment in other industries, particularly export industries. Primarily, they will reshuffle employment rather than increase it. As this example illustrates, consideration of secondary effects is an important ingredient of the economic way of thinking.

7. The value of a good or service is subjective.

Preferences differ, sometimes dramatically, between individuals. How much is a ticket to see tonight's performance of the Bolshoi Ballet worth? Some would be willing to pay a very high price, while others might prefer to stay home and avoid the ballet performance, even if tickets were free! Circumstances can change from day to day, even for a given individual. Alice, a ballet fan who usually would value the ticket at more than its price of $100, is invited to a party, and suddenly becomes uninterested in the ballet tonight. Now what is the ticket worth? If she knows a friend who would give her $40 for the ticket, it is worth at least that much. If she advertises on a bulletin board and gets $60 for it, a higher value is created. But if someone who doesn't know of the ticket would have been willing to pay even more, then a potential trade creating even more value is missed. If tonight's performance is sold out, perhaps someone in town would be willing to pay $120. One thing is certain: The value of the ticket depends on several things, including who uses it and under what circumstances.

Economics recognizes that people can and do have legitimately different subjective values for similar goods. Mike may prefer to have a grass field rather than a parking lot next to his workplace, and is willing to bear the cost of walking farther from his car each day. Ken, on the other hand, may prefer the parking lot and the shorter walk. As a science, economics does not place any inherent moral judgment or value on one person's preferences over the other—in economics all individuals' preferences are counted equally.

Seldom will one individual know how others would value an item. Consider how difficult it often is to know what would make a good gift, even for a close friend or family member. So, arranging trades, or otherwise moving items to higher-valued users and uses, is not a simple task. The entrepreneurial individual, who knows how to locate the right buyers and arranges for the goods to flow to higher-valued uses, can create huge increases in value from existing resources. In fact, encouragement of individuals to (a) move goods toward those who value them most and (b) combine resources into goods that individuals value more highly than the resources required for their production is a vitally important source of economic progress. As we proceed, we will investigate this issue in more detail. The fact that value is subjective helps to make trade between individuals possible—and to make trade mutually beneficial to both parties involved.

8. The test of a theory is its ability to predict.

Scientific thinking
Development of a theory from basic postulates and the testing of the implications of that theory as to their consistency with events in the real world. Good theories are consistent with and help explain real-world events. Theories that are inconsistent with the real world are invalid and must be rejected.

Economic thinking is **scientific thinking**. The proof of the pudding is in the eating. The usefulness of an economic theory is proved by its ability to predict the future consequences of economic action. Economists develop economic theory from scientific thinking, using basic postulates to analyze how incentives will affect decision makers, and comparing the analysis against events in the real world. If the events in the real world are consistent with a theory, we say that the theory has *predictive value* and is therefore valid.

If it is impossible to test the theoretical relationships of a discipline, the discipline does not qualify as a science. Because economics deals with human beings who can think and respond in a variety of ways, can economic theories really be tested? The answer to this question is yes, if, on average, human beings respond in predictable and consistent ways to certain changes in economic conditions. The economist believes that this is the case even though not all individuals will respond in a specified manner. Economists usually do not try to predict the behavior of a specific individual; instead, they focus on the general behavior of a large number of individuals.

In the 1950s, economists began to do laboratory experiments to test economic theories. Individuals were brought into laboratories to see how they would act in buying and selling situations, under differing rules. For example, small but concrete cash rewards were given to individuals who, when an auction was conducted among them, were able to sell at high prices and to buy at low prices, thus approximating real-world market incentives. These experiments have verified many of the important propositions of economic theory.

Laboratory experiments, however, cannot duplicate all real economic interactions. How can we test economic theory when controlled experiments are not feasible? This is a problem, but economics is no different from astronomy in this respect. Astronomers can use theories tested in physics laboratories, but they must also deal with the world as it is. They cannot change the course of the stars or planets to see what impact the change would have on the gravitational pull of the earth. Similarly, economists cannot arbitrarily change the prices of cars or unskilled labor services in real markets, just to observe the effects on quantities purchased or levels of employment in the real world outside the laboratory. However, economic conditions (for example, prices, production costs, technology, and transportation costs), like the location of the planets, do change from time to time. As actual conditions change, an economic theory can be tested by comparing its predictions with real-world outcomes. Just as the universe is the main laboratory of the astronomer, the real economic world is often the laboratory of the economist.

POSITIVE AND NORMATIVE ECONOMICS

Economics as a social science is concerned with predicting or determining the impact of changes in economic variables on the actions of human beings. Scientific economics, commonly referred to as **positive economics**, attempts to determine "what is." Positive economic statements postulate a relationship that is potentially verifiable or refutable. For example: "If the price of gasoline were higher, people would buy less." Or, "As the money supply increases, the price level will go up." We can statistically investigate (and estimate) the relationship between gasoline prices and gallons sold, or between the supply of money and the general price level. We can analyze the facts to determine the correctness of a statement about positive economics. Remember, a positive economic statement need not be correct, it simply must be testable.

Normative economics involves the advocacy of specific policy alternatives, because it uses ethical or value judgments as well as knowledge of positive economics. Normative economic statements concern "what ought to be," given the preferences and philosophical views of the advocate. Value judgments may be the source of disagreement about normative economic matters. Two persons may differ on a policy matter because one is a socialist and the other a libertarian, because one wants cheaper food while the other favors organic farming, or even because one values wilderness highly while the other wants more improved campsites that can be easily reached by roads. They may agree as to the expected outcome of altering an economic variable (that is, the positive economics of an issue), but disagree as to whether that outcome is desirable.

Positive economics
The scientific study of "what is" among economic relationships.

Normative economics
Judgments about "what ought to be" in economic matters. Normative economic views cannot be proved false, because they are based on value judgments.

A positive science may be defined as a body of systematized knowledge concerning what is; a normative or regulative science is a body of systematized knowledge relating to criteria of what ought to be, and concerned therefore with the ideal as distinguished from the actual.

—John Neville Keynes[5]

[5]John Neville Keynes, *The Scope and Method of Political Economy,* 4th ed. (1917), pp. 34–35.

In contrast with positive economic statements, normative economic statements can neither be confirmed nor proven false through scientific testing. "Business firms should not maximize profits." "The use of pesticides on food to be sold in stores should not be allowed." "More of our national forests should be set aside for wilderness." These normative statements cannot be scientifically tested because their validity rests on value judgments.

Normative economic views can sometimes influence our attitude toward positive economic analysis. When we agree with the objectives of a policy, it is easy to overlook warnings of potential problems implied by positive economics. Although positive economics does not tell us which policy is best, it can provide knowledge that also serves to reduce a potential source of disappointment with policy. Those who do not understand how the economy operates may advocate policies that are actually inconsistent with objectives they would like to see achieved. The actual effects of policy alternatives often differ dramatically from the objectives of their proponents. A new law forcing employers to pay all employees at least $12 per hour might be intended to help low-skill workers, but the resulting decline in the number of workers employed (and increase in the number unemployed) would be disastrous despite the good intentions. Proponents of such a law, of course, would not want to believe the economic analysis that predicted the unfortunate outcome.

The task of the professional economist is to expand our knowledge of how the real world operates, both in the private and the public sectors. If we do not fully understand the implications, including the secondary effects, of alternative actions, we will not be able to choose intelligently. Yet, it is not always easy to use economic thinking to isolate the impact of a change in an economic variable or a change in policy. Let us consider some of the potential pitfalls to avoid in economic thinking.

PITFALLS TO AVOID IN ECONOMIC THINKING

Violation of the Ceteris Paribus Condition

Ceteris paribus
A Latin term meaning "other things constant," used when the effect of one change is being described, recognizing that if other things changed, they also could affect the result. Economists often describe the effects of one change, knowing that in the real world, other things might change and also exert an effect.

Economists often preface their statements with the words **ceteris paribus**, a term from Latin meaning "other things constant." "Other things constant, an increase in the price of housing will cause buyers to reduce their purchases." Unfortunately for the economic researcher, we live in a dynamic world. Other things seldom remain constant. For example, as the price of housing rises, the income of consumers may also be increasing. Each of these factors—higher housing prices and an expansion in consumer income—will have an impact on housing purchases. In fact, we would generally expect them to have opposite effects: higher prices reducing housing purchases but the rise in consumer income increasing the demand for housing. The task of sorting out the specific effects of two or more variables when all are changing at the same time is difficult, though with a strong grip on economic theory, some ingenuity, and enough data, it can often be done. In fact, the major portion of the day-to-day work of many professional economists consists of statistical research.

Association is Not Causation

In economics, causation is very important, and statistical association alone cannot establish causation. Perhaps an extreme example will illustrate the point. Suppose that each November a witch doctor performs a voodoo dance designed to arouse the cold weather gods of winter, and that soon after the dance is performed, the weather in fact begins to turn cold. The witch doctor's dance is associated with the arrival of winter, but does it cause the arrival of winter? Most of us would answer in the negative, even though the two are linked statistically.

Unfortunately, cause-and-effect relationships in economics are not always self-evident. For example, it is sometimes difficult to know whether a rise in income has caused people to buy more or, conversely, whether an increase in people's willingness to buy more has created more business and caused incomes to rise. Similarly, economists sometimes argue whether rising money wages are a cause or an effect of inflation. Economic theory, if rooted to the basic postulates, can often help to determine the source of causation, even though competing theories may sometimes suggest differing directions of causation.

Fallacy of Composition

What is true for the individual (or subcomponent) may not be true for the group (or the whole). If you stand up for an exciting play during a football game, you will be better able to see. But what happens if everyone stands up at the same time? What benefits the individual does not necessarily benefit the group as a whole. When everyone stands up, the view for individual spectators fails to improve; it may even become worse.

People who mistakenly argue that what is true for the part is also true for the whole are said to be committing the **fallacy of composition**. What is true for the individual can be misleading and is often fallacious when applied to the entire economy. Potential error associated with the fallacy of composition highlights the importance of considering both a micro view and a macro view in the study of economics. Because individual decision makers are the moving force behind all economic action, the foundations of economics are clearly rooted in a micro view. **Microeconomics** focuses on the decision making of consumers, producers, and resource suppliers operating in a narrowly defined market, such as that for a specific good or resource.

As we have seen, however, what is true for a small unit may not be true in the aggregate. **Macroeconomics** focuses on how the aggregation of individual micro-units affects our analysis. Like microeconomics, it is concerned with incentives, prices, and output. Macroeconomics, however, aggregates markets, lumping all 100 million households in this country together to study such topics as consumption spending, saving, and employment. Similarly, the nation's 7 million business firms are lumped together in "the business sector."

What factors determine the level of aggregate output, the rate of inflation, the amount of unemployment, and interest rates? These are macroeconomic questions. In short, macroeconomics examines the forest rather than the individual trees. As we move from the micro components to a macro view of the whole, it is important that we beware of the fallacy of composition.

Fallacy of composition
Erroneous view that what is true for the individual (or the part) will also be true for the group (or the whole).

Microeconomics
The branch of economics that focuses on how human behavior affects the conduct of affairs within narrowly defined units, such as individual households or business firms.

Macroeconomics
The branch of economics that focuses on how human behavior affects outcomes in highly aggregated markets, such as the markets for labor or consumer products.

ECONOMICS AS A CAREER

If you find yourself doing well in this course, and find economics an interesting field of study, you may want to think about majoring in economics. Graduating with a major in economics provides a variety of choices. Many students go on to graduate school in economics, business, public administration, or law. Graduate M.B.A. and law programs find economics majors particularly attractive because of their strong analytical skills.

A graduate degree (a master's or doctorate) in economics is typically required to pursue a career as a professional economist. About one-half of all professional economists are employed by colleges and universities as teachers and researchers. Professional economists also work for the government or private businesses. Most major corporations have a staff of economists to advise them in business decisions, while governments employ economists to analyze the impact of policy alternatives. The federal government has a Council of Economic Advisers whose purpose is to provide the president with analyses of how the activities of the government influence the economy.

Students who major in economics, but who do not pursue graduate school, have many job opportunities. Because economics is a way of thinking, knowledge of economics is a valuable decision-making tool on almost any job. Undergraduate majors in economics typically work in business, government service, banking, or insurance. There are even increasing opportunities for persons with only undergraduate economics majors to teach economics at the high school level. This is not to say that a major in economics limits your job prospects to the narrow field of economics—Arnold Schwarzenegger (movie star), Mick Jagger (singer for the Rolling Stones), John Elway (former NFL quarterback), and Ronald Reagan (former U.S. president) are among the long list of famous undergraduate economics majors!

The average salary offer for a beginning economics graduate is comparable to those with finance and accounting majors, and is generally higher than for management or marketing. Professional economists with graduate degrees in economics who work for private business average approximately $90,000 per year, and those who choose to work as teachers and researchers at colleges and universities earn approximately $75,000 annually. Although salaries vary substantially, the point is that a career in economics can be rewarding both personally and financially. If you are interested in learning more about a major in economics, and the job opportunities available, you might visit your school's career center or speak with your school's undergraduate advisor in economics.

Even if you choose not to major in economics, you will find that your economics courses will broaden your horizons and increase your ability to understand and analyze what is going on around you in the world of politics, business, and human relations. Economics is a social science, often overlapping with the fields of political science, sociology, and psychology. Because the economic way of thinking is so useful in making sense of the abundance of available economic observations and data, and because there is ample opportunity for productive research using economic science in the real world, economics has sometimes been called the "queen of the social sciences." Reflecting this lofty position, economics is the only social science for which the Nobel Prize of the Swedish Academy of Science is awarded.

LOOKING AHEAD

The primary purpose of this book is to encourage you to develop the economic way of thinking so that you can separate sound reasoning from economic nonsense. Once you have developed the economic way of thinking, economics will be relatively easy. Using the economic way of thinking can also be fun. Moreover, it will help you become a better citizen. It will give you a different and fascinating perspective on what motivates people, why they act the way they do, and why their actions sometimes go against the best interest of the community or nation. It will also give you some valuable insight into how people's actions can be rechanneled for the benefit of the community at large.

KEY POINTS

▼ Scarcity and choice are the two essential ingredients of an economic topic. Goods are scarce because desire for them far outstrips their availability from nature. Scarcity forces us to choose among available alternatives. Every choice entails a trade-off.

▼ Every society will have to devise some method of rationing the scarce resources among competing uses. Markets generally use price as the rationing

device. Competition is a natural outgrowth of the need to ration scarce goods.

▼ Scarcity and poverty are not the same thing. Absence of poverty implies that some basic level of need has been met. An absence of scarcity would imply that all our desires for goods were fully satisfied. We may someday eliminate poverty, but scarcity will always be with us.

▼ Economics is a way of thinking that emphasizes eight points:

1. The use of scarce resources to produce a good always has an opportunity cost.
2. Individuals make decisions purposefully, always seeking to choose the option they expect to be most consistent with their personal goals.
3. Incentives matter. The likelihood of people choosing an option increases as personal benefits rise and personal costs decline.
4. Economic reasoning focuses on the impact of marginal changes; decisions will be based on marginal costs and marginal benefits (utility).
5. Since information is scarce, uncertainty is a fact of life.
6. In addition to their initial impact, economic events often generate secondary effects that may be felt only with the passage of time.
7. The value of a good or service is subjective and varies with individual preferences and circumstances.

8. The test of an economic theory is its ability to predict and to explain events in the real world.

▼ Economic science is positive; it attempts to explain the actual consequences of economic actions. Normative economics goes further, applying value judgments to make suggestions about what "ought to be."

▼ Microeconomics focuses on narrowly defined units, while macroeconomics is concerned with highly aggregated units. When shifting focus from micro- to macro-units, one must beware of the fallacy of composition.

▼ The origin of economics as a systematic method of analysis dates to the publication of *The Wealth of Nations* by Adam Smith in 1776. Smith believed a market economy would bring individual self-interest and the public interest into harmony.

CRITICAL ANALYSIS QUESTIONS

1. Indicate how each of the following changes would influence the incentive of a decision maker to undertake the action described.
   a. A reduction in the temperature from 80° to 50° on one's decision to go swimming.
   b. A change in the meeting time of the introductory economics course from 11:00 A.M. to 7:30 A.M. on one's decision to attend the lectures.
   c. A reduction in the number of exam questions that relate directly to the text on the student's decision to read the text.
   d. An increase in the price of beef on one's decision to have steak.
   e. An increase in the rental price of apartments on one's decision to build additional housing units.

*2. "The government should provide such goods as health care, education, and highways because it can provide them free." Is this statement true or false? Explain your answer.

3. a. What method is used to ration goods in a market economy? How does this rationing method influence the incentive of individuals to supply goods, services, and resources to others?
   b. How are grades rationed in your economics class? How does this rationing method influence student behavior? Suppose the highest grades

were rationed to those whom the teacher liked best. How would this method of rationing influence student behavior?

*4. In recent years, both the personal exemption and child tax credit have been increased in the United States. According to the basic postulate of economics, how will the birthrate be affected by policies that reduce the tax liability of those with children?

*5. "The economic way of thinking stresses that good intentions lead to sound policy." Is this statement true or false? Explain your answer.

6. Economic theory postulates that self-interest is a powerful motivation for action. Does this imply that people are selfish and greedy? Do self-interest and selfishness mean the same thing?

*7. Congress and government agencies often make laws to help protect the safety of consumers. New cars, for example, are required to have many safety features before they can be sold in the United States. These rules do indeed provide added safety for buyers, although they also add to the cost and price of the new vehicles. What secondary effects can you see happening as the result of mandating air bags in automobiles? What incentives do you see changing for drivers as the result of making cars safer? Do you think the millions of dollars spent by consumers on air bags each year could be better spent elsewhere to save even more lives?

*8. "Individuals who economize are missing the point of life. Money is not so important that it should rule the way we live." Evaluate this statement.

*9. "Positive economics cannot tell us which agricultural policy is better, so it is useless to policymakers." Evaluate this statement.

*10. "I examined the statistics for our basketball team's wins last year and found that, when the third team played more, the winning margin increased. If the coach played the third team more, we would win by a bigger margin." Evaluate this statement.

11. Which of the following are positive economic statements and which are normative?
   a. The speed limit should be lowered to 55 miles per hour on interstate highways to reduce the number of deaths and accidents.

   b. Higher gasoline prices cause the quantity of gasoline that consumers buy to increase.
   c. A comparison of costs and benefits should not be used to assess environmental regulations.
   d. Higher taxes on alcohol result in less drinking and driving.

12. "Economics is about trade-offs. If more scarce resources are used to produce one thing, fewer will be available to produce others." Evaluate this statement.

13. Do individuals "economize"? If so, what are they trying to do? Do you economize when you shop at the mall? Why or why not?

*Asterisk denotes questions for which answers are given in Appendix B.

ADDENDUM

Understanding Graphs

Economists often use graphs to illustrate economic relations. Graphs are like pictures. They are visual aids that can communicate valuable information in a small amount of space. A picture may be worth a thousand words, but only to a person who understands the picture (and the graph).

This addendum illustrates the use of simple graphs as a way to communicate. Many students, particularly those with some mathematics background, are already familiar with this material, and can safely ignore it. This addendum is for those who need to be assured that they can understand graphic illustrations of economic concepts.

The Simple Bar Graph

A simple bar graph helps us to visualize comparative relationships and to understand them better. It is particularly useful for illustrating how an economic indicator varies among countries, across time periods, or under alternative economic conditions.

Exhibit A-1 is a bar graph illustrating economic data. The table in part (a) presents data on the income per person in 1999 for several countries. Part (b) uses a bar graph to illustrate the same data. The horizontal scale of the graph indicates the total income per person in 1999. A bar is made indicating the income level (see the dollar scale on the *x*-axis) of each country. The length of each bar is in proportion to the per person income of the country. Thus, the length of the bars provides a visual illustration of how per capita income varies across the countries. For

example, the extremely short bar for Nigeria shows immediately that income per person there is only a small fraction of the comparable income figure for the United States, Japan, Switzerland, and several other countries.

Linear Graphic Presentation

Economists often want to illustrate variations in economic variables with the passage of time. A linear graph with time on the horizontal axis and an economic variable on the vertical axis is a useful tool to indicate variations over time. **Exhibit A-2** illustrates a simple linear graph of changes in consumer prices (the inflation rate) in the United States between 1960 and 2000. The table of the exhibit presents data on the percentage change in consumer prices for each year. Beginning with 1960, the horizontal axis indicates the time period (year). The inflation rate is plotted vertically above each year. Of course, the height of the plot (line) indicates the inflation rate during that year. For example, in 1975 the inflation rate was 6.9 percent. This point is plotted at the 6.9 percent vertical distance directly above the year 1975. In 1976 the inflation rate fell to 4.9 percent. Thus, the vertical plot of the 1976 inflation rate is lower than that for 1975. The inflation rate for each year shown in part (a) is plotted at the corresponding height directly above the year in part (b). The linear graph is simply a line connecting the points plotted for each of the years 1960 through 2000.

The linear graph is a visual aid to understanding what happens to the inflation rate during the period. As the graph

COUNTRY	TOTAL INCOME PER PERSON, 1999
Switzerland	$38,350
Japan	32,230
United States	30,600
Germany	25,350
Sweden	25,040
United Kingdom	22,640
Canada	19,320
Mexico	4,400
China	780
India	450
Nigeria	310

(a)

EXHIBIT A-1
International Comparison of Income Per Person

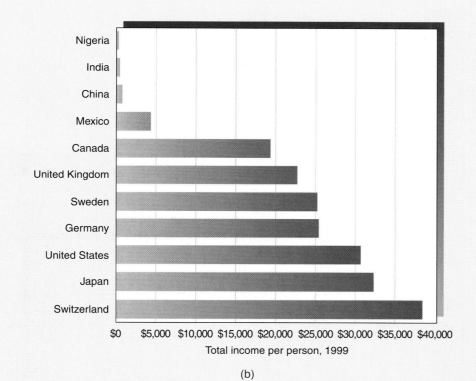

(b)

Source: The World Bank, *World Development Report,* 2000/2001, Table 1. Income per person shown is GNP per capita derived by the purchasing power parity method.

shows, the inflation rate rose sharply between 1967 and 1969, in 1973–1974, and again in 1977–1979. It was substantially higher during the 1970s than in the early 1960s or the mid-1980s and 1990s. Although the linear graph does not communicate any information not in the table, it does make it easier to see the pattern of the data. Thus, economists often use simple graphics rather than tables to communicate information.

Direct and Inverse Relationships

Economic logic often suggests that two variables are linked in a specific way. Suppose an investigation reveals that,

other things constant, farmers supply more wheat as the price of wheat increases. **Exhibit A-3** presents hypothetical data on the relationship between the price of wheat and the quantity supplied by farmers, first in tabular form in part (a) and then as a simple two-dimensional graph in part (b). Suppose we measure the quantity of wheat supplied by farmers on the *x*-axis (the horizontal axis) and the price of wheat on the *y*-axis (the vertical axis). Points indicating the value of *x* (quantity supplied) at alternative values of *y* (price of wheat) can then be plotted. The line (or curve) linking the points illustrates the relationship between the price of wheat and the amount supplied by farmers.

EXHIBIT A-2
Changes in Level of Prices in United States, 1960–2000

The tabular data (a) of the inflation rate are presented in graphic form in (b).

Year	Percent Change in Consumer Prices	Year	Percent Change in Consumer Prices
1960	1.4	1981	8.9
1961	0.7	1982	3.8
1962	1.3	1983	3.8
1963	1.6	1984	3.9
1964	1.0	1985	3.8
1965	1.9	1986	1.1
1966	3.5	1987	4.4
1967	3.0	1988	4.4
1968	4.7	1989	4.6
1969	6.2	1990	6.1
1970	5.6	1991	3.1
1971	3.3	1992	2.9
1972	3.4	1993	2.7
1973	8.7	1994	2.7
1974	12.3	1995	2.5
1975	6.9	1996	3.3
1976	4.9	1997	1.7
1977	6.7	1998	1.6
1978	9.0	1999	2.7
1979	13.3	2000	3.4
1980	12.5		

(a)

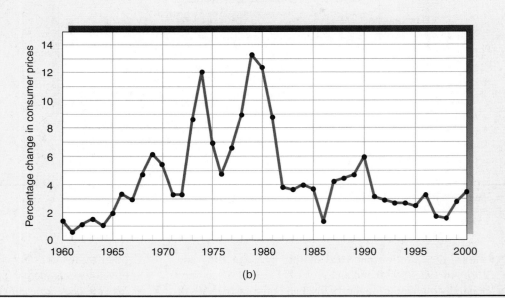

(b)

Source: Bureau of Labor Statistics (http://www.bls.gov/cpi/).

In the case of price and quantity supplied of wheat, the two variables are directly related. When the *y*-variable increases, so does the *x*-variable. When two variables are directly related, the graph illustrating the linkage between the two will slope upward to the right, as in the case of SS in part (b).

Sometimes the *x*-variable and the *y*-variable are inversely related. A decline in the *y*-variable is associated with an increase in the *x*-variable. Therefore, a curve picturing the inverse relationship between *x* and *y* slopes downward to the right. **Exhibit A-4** illustrates this case. As the data of the table indicate, consumers purchase less as

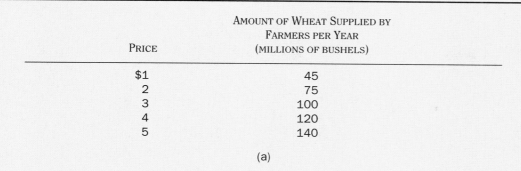

PRICE	AMOUNT OF WHEAT SUPPLIED BY FARMERS PER YEAR (MILLIONS OF BUSHELS)
$1	45
2	75
3	100
4	120
5	140

(a)

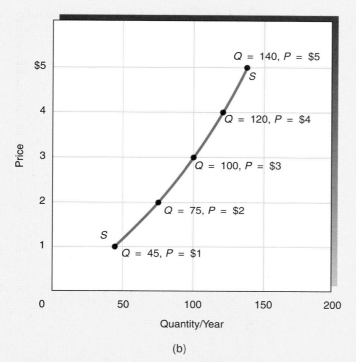

(b)

EXHIBIT A-3
Direct Relationship Between Variables

As the table (a) indicates, farmers are willing to supply more wheat at a higher price. Thus, there is a direct relation between the price of wheat and the quantity supplied. When the *x*- and *y*-variables are directly related, a curve mapping the relationship between the two will slope upward to the right like *SS*.

the price of wheat increases. Measuring the price of wheat on the *y*-axis (by convention, economists always place price on the *y*-axis) and the quantity of wheat purchased on the *x*-axis, the relationship between these two variables can also be illustrated graphically. If the price of wheat were $5 per bushel, only 60 million bushels would be purchased by consumers. As the price declines to $4 per bushel, annual consumption increases to 75 million bushels. At still lower prices, the quantity purchased by consumers will expand to larger and larger amounts. As part (b) illustrates, the inverse relationship between price and quantity of wheat purchased generates a curve that slopes downward to the right.

Complex Relationships

Sometimes the initial relationship between the *x*- and *y*-variables will change. **Exhibit A-5** illustrates more complex relations of this type. Part (a) shows the typical

relationship between annual earnings and age. As a young person gets work experience and develops skills, earnings usually expand. Thus, initially, age and annual earnings are directly related; annual earnings increase with age. However, beyond a certain age (approximately age 55), annual earnings generally decline as workers approach retirement. As a result, the initial direct relationship between age and earnings changes to an inverse relation. When this is the case, annual income expands to a maximum (at age 55) and then begins to decline with years of age.

Part (b) illustrates an initial inverse relation that later changes to a direct relationship. Consider the impact of travel speed on gasoline consumption per mile. At low speeds, the automobile engine will not be used efficiently. As speed increases from 5 mph to 10 mph and on to a speed of 40 mph, gasoline consumption per mile declines. In this range, there is an inverse relationship between speed of travel (*x*) and gasoline consumption per mile (*y*). However,

EXHIBIT A-4
Inverse Relationship
Between Variables

As the table (a) shows, consumers will demand (pur-
chase) more wheat as the
price declines. Thus, there
is an inverse relationship between the price of wheat and
the quantity demanded. When
the *x*- and *y*-variables are inversely related, a curve showing the relationship between
the two will slope downward
to the right like *DD*.

PRICE	AMOUNT OF WHEAT DEMANDED BY CONSUMERS PER YEAR (MILLIONS OF BUSHELS)
$1	170
2	130
3	100
4	75
5	60

(a)

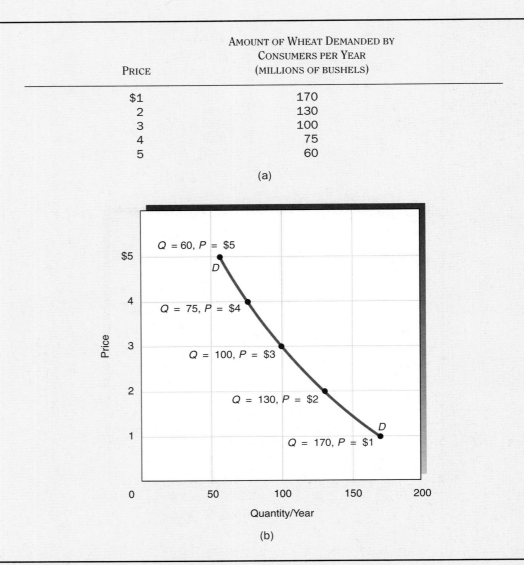

(b)

as speed increases beyond 40 mph, air resistance increases
and more gasoline per mile is required to maintain the additional speed. At very high speeds, gasoline consumption per
mile increases substantially with speed of travel. Thus,
gasoline consumption per mile reaches a minimum, and a
direct relationship between the *x*- and *y*-variables describes
the relationship beyond that point (40 mph).

Slope of a Straight Line

In economics, we are often interested in how much the
y-variable changes in response to a change in the *x*-vari-
able. The slope of the line or curve reveals this information. Mathematically, the slope of a line or curve is equal
to the change in the *y*-variable divided by the change in the
x-variable.

Exhibit A-6 illustrates the calculation of the slope for
a straight line. The exhibit shows how the daily earnings
(*y*-variable) of a worker change with hours worked (the

x-variable). The wage rate of the worker is $10 per hour,
so when 1 hour is worked, earnings are equal to $10. For
2 hours of work, earnings jump to $20, and so on. A
1-hour change in hours worked leads to a $10 change in
earnings. Thus, the slope of the line ($\Delta y/\Delta x$) is equal to 10.
(The symbol Δ means "change in.") In the case of a
straight line, the change in *y*, per unit change in *x*, is equal
for all points on the line. Thus, the slope of a straight line
is constant for all points along the line.

Exhibit A-6 illustrates a case in which a direct relation
exists between the *x*- and *y*-variables. For an inverse relation, the *y*-variable decreases as the *x*-variable increases.
So, when *x* and *y* are inversely related, the slope of the line
will be negative.

Slope of a Curve

In contrast with a straight line, the slope of a curve is different at each point along the curve. The slope of a curve

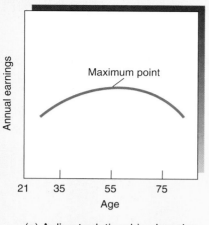

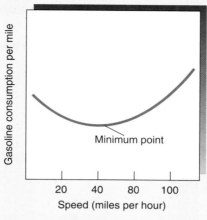

(a) A direct relationship changing to inverse

(b) An inverse relationship changing to direct

EXHIBIT A-5
Complex Relationships Between Variables

At first, an increase in age (and work experience) leads to a higher income, but later earnings decline as the worker approaches retirement (a). Thus, age and annual income are initially directly related but at approximately age 55 an inverse relationship emerges. Part (b) illustrates the relationship between travel speed and gasoline consumption per mile. Initially, gasoline consumption per mile declines as speed increases (an inverse relationship), but as speed increases above 40 mph, gasoline consumption per mile increases with the speed of travel (direct relationship).

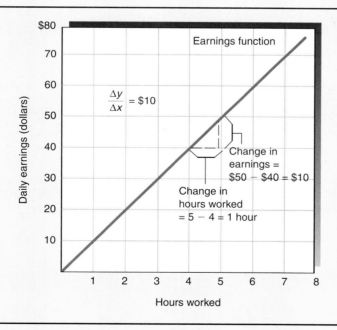

EXHIBIT A-6
Slope of a Straight Line

The slope of a line is equal to the change in y divided by the change in x. The line opposite illustrates the case in which daily earnings increase by $10 per hour worked. Thus, the slope of the earnings function is 10 ($10 ÷ 1 hr). For a straight line, the slope is constant at each point on the line.

at a specific point is equal to the slope of a line tangent to the curve at the point, meaning a line that just touches the curve.

Exhibit A-7 illustrates how the slope of a curve at a specific point is determined. First, consider the slope of the curve at point A. A line tangent to the curve at point A indicates that y changes by one unit when x changes by

two units at point A. Thus, the slope ($\Delta y/\Delta x$) of the curve at A is equal to 0.5.

Now consider the slope of the curve at point B. The line tangent to the curve at B indicates that y changes by two units for each one unit change in x at point B. Thus, at B the slope ($\Delta y/\Delta x$) is equal to 2. At point B, a change in the x-variable leads to a much larger change in y than was

EXHIBIT A-7
Slope of a Nonlinear Curve

The slope of a curve at any point is equal to the slope of the straight line tangent to the curve at the point. As the lines tangent to the curve at points *A* and *B* illustrate, the slope of a curve will change from point to point along the curve.

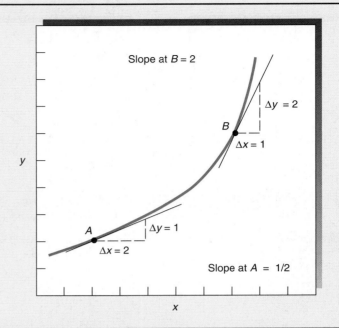

true at point *A*. The greater slope of the curve at *B* reflects this greater change in *y* per unit change in *x* at *B* relative to *A*.

Graphs Are Not a Substitute for Economic Thinking

By now you should have a fairly good understanding of how to read a graph. If you still feel uncomfortable with graphs, try drawing (graphing) the relationship between several things with which you are familiar. If you work, try graphing the relationship between your hours worked (*x*-axis) and your weekly earnings (*y*-axis). Exhibit A-3 could guide you with this exercise. Can you graph the relationship between the price of gasoline and your expenditures on gasoline? Graphing these simple relationships will give you greater confidence in your ability to grasp more complex economic relationships presented in graphs.

This text uses only simple graphs. Thus, there is no reason for you to be intimidated. Graphs look much more complex than they really are. In fact, they are nothing more than a simple device to communicate information quickly and concisely. Nothing can be communicated with a graph that cannot be communicated verbally.

Most important, graphs are not a substitute for economic thinking. Although a graph may illustrate that two variables are related, it tells us nothing about the cause-and-effect relationship between the variables. To determine probable cause and effect, we must rely on economic theory. Thus, the economic way of thinking, not graphs, is the power station of economic analysis.

CHAPTER **2**

Some Tools of the Economist

Chapter Focus

- What is opportunity cost? Why do economists place so much emphasis on it?

- Why do people engage in exchange?

- How does private ownership affect the use of resources? Will private owners pay any attention to the desires of others?

- What does a production-possibilities curve demonstrate?

- What are the sources of gains from trade? How does trade influence our modern living standards?

- What are the two major methods of economic organization? How do they differ?

The key insight of Adam Smith's **Wealth of Nations** *is misleadingly simple: if an exchange between two parties is voluntary, it will not take place unless both believe they will benefit from it. Most economic fallacies derive from the neglect of this simple insight, from the tendency to assume that there is a fixed pie, that one party can gain only at the expense of another.*

—Milton and Rose Friedman[1]

[1]Milton and Rose Friedman, *Free to Choose* (Harcourt Brace, 1990), p.13.

n the preceding chapter, you were introduced to the economic way of thinking. We will now begin to apply that approach. This chapter focuses on four topics: opportunity cost, trade, property rights, and the potential output level of an economy. These seemingly diverse topics are in fact highly interrelated. The opportunity cost of goods determines which ones it makes sense for an individual or a nation to produce and which should be acquired through trade. In turn, the structure of both trade and property rights will influence the level of output. These tools of the economist are important in understanding how each economy can answer the basic economic questions: what to produce, how to produce it, and for whom will they be produced. We will begin by taking a closer look at the concept of opportunity cost. ∎

WHAT SHALL WE GIVE UP?

Because of scarcity, we cannot have as much of everything as we would like. We constantly face choices that involve trade-offs between competing desires. Most of us would like to have more time for leisure, recreation, vacations, hobbies, education, and skill development. We would also like to have more wealth, a larger savings account, and more consumable goods. However, all these things are scarce, in the sense that they are limited. Our efforts to get more of one will conflict with our efforts to get more of the others.

Opportunity Cost

An unpleasant fact of economics is that the choice to do one thing is, at the same time, a choice *not* to do something else. Your choice to spend time reading this book is a choice not to spend this time playing tennis, listening to a math lecture, or going to a party. These things must be given up because of your decision to read. As we indicated in Chapter 1, the highest valued alternative sacrificed in order to choose an option is called the *opportunity cost* of that choice. In economics when we refer to the "cost" of an action, we are referring to opportunity cost.

Opportunity costs are subjective. (So are benefits. After all, an opportunity cost is a sacrificed benefit!) A cost exists in the mind of the decision maker. It is based on expectation—the expected value of the forgone alternative. Opportunity cost can never be directly measured by someone other than the decision maker because only the decision maker can place a value on what is given up.[2] Others, including experts and elected officials, who try to choose for the individual (or group of individuals), face an exceedingly difficult information problem. Individuals differ in the trade-offs they prefer to make, and those preferences change with time and circumstances. Only individuals are in a position to properly evaluate options for themselves, and to decide whether a specific trade-off is a good thing for them, in their specific circumstances of time and place.

Cost, however, often has a monetary component that enables us to approximate its value. For example, the cost of attending a movie (or a football game) is the highest valued opportunity lost as a result of (1) the time necessary to attend and (2) the use of purchasing power—the money—necessary to obtain a ticket. The monetary component is, of course, objective and can be measured. So long as individuals are paying the money price in voluntary exchange, it represents opportunity costs for them. When *nonmonetary* considerations are relatively unimportant, the monetary component will approximate the total cost of an option. We should notice, though, that to a buyer (or to one who refuses to sell), the item is probably worth more than the market price. However, to a seller (or one who does not buy), the item is worth less than the market price.

Opportunity Cost and the Real World

Is real-world decision making influenced by opportunity cost? Remember, the basic economic postulate that incentives matter states that an option is more likely to be chosen

---

[2]See James M. Buchanan, *Cost and Choice* (Chicago: Markham, 1969), for an analysis of the relationship between cost and choice.

Gabrielle Reece understands opportunity cost. A star volleyball player at Florida State University, she forfeited her $4,500 scholarship (the NCAA prohibits outside employment by scholarship athletes) in order to embark on a six month modeling tour following her freshman year. After an appearance on the cover of *Vogue*, her modeling opportunities soared. Even though she was both a good student and super volleyball player, she left school prior to graduation. Given her potential earnings as a model, the opportunity cost of school was simply too great.

when its cost to the decision maker is less. So economic theory does tell us that differences (or changes) in opportunity cost will influence decisions. Recognizing opportunity costs can help us to understand decisions—those made by college students, for example.

Consider your own decision to attend college. Your opportunity cost of going to college is the value of the next best alternative, which could be measured as the salary you would earn if you had chosen to work rather than go to college. Every year you stay in college, you give up what you could have earned by working that year. The typical student incurs an opportunity cost of probably more than $80,000 in forgone income during their stay in college. Changes in this opportunity cost of going to college will affect the choices of potential students. Suppose, for example, that you received a job offer today for $250,000 per year as an athlete or an entertainer, but the job would require so much travel that school would be impossible. Would this change in the opportunity cost of going to college affect your choice as to whether to continue in school? For many students it would; such a large increase in the cost of remaining in school would cause many students to leave. (See the feature on Gabrielle Reece above.) It is clear that one of the most important costs of attending college is the value of the next best alternative: the opportunity cost.

Even when their parents pay all the monetary expenses of their college education, some students are surprised to learn that they are actually incurring more of the total cost of going to college than their parents. For example, the average monetary cost (tuition, room and board, books, and so forth) for a resident student attending a public four-year college is about $10,000 per year. Even if the student's next best alternative was working at a job that paid only $15,000 per year, then over a four-year college career, he or she will incur $60,000 of the cost of college in the form of forgone earnings, while the parents will incur only about $40,000 of the cost.[3]

Now consider another decision made by college students—whether to attend a particular meeting of class. The monetary cost of attending a class (bus fare or parking and gasoline, and so on) remains fairly constant from day to day. Why then do students choose to attend class on some days and not on others? Even though the monetary cost is fairly constant, the opportunity cost—the highest valued alternative given up—can change dramatically from day to day. Some days the next best alternative to attending class may be sleeping in or watching TV. Other days, the opportunity cost may be substantially larger, perhaps the value of attending a big football game, getting an early start on a holiday break,

[3]From the standpoint of the family's total economic cost of sending a child to college, some of the monetary costs, such as room and board, are not costs of choosing to go to college. The cost of living does have to be covered, but it would be incurred whether or not the student went to college.

or having additional study time for a crucial exam in another class. As options like this increase the cost of attending class, more students will decide not to attend.

Failure to consider opportunity cost often leads to unwise decision making. Suppose that your community builds a beautiful new civic center. The mayor, speaking at the dedication ceremony, tells the world that the center will improve the quality of life in your community. People who understand the concept of opportunity cost may question this view. If the center had not been built, the resources might have funded construction of a new hospital, improvements to the educational system, or housing for low-income families. Will the civic center contribute more to the well-being of the people in your community than these other facilities? If so, it was a wise investment. If not, however, your community will be worse off than it might have been if decision makers had chosen a higher-valued project (that must now be forgone).

TRADE CREATES VALUE

Why do individuals trade with each other, and what is the significance of this exchange? In the preceding chapter we learned that value is subjective. It is wrong to assume that a particular good or service has a fixed value just because it exists.[4] The value of goods and services generally depends on who uses them, and on circumstances, such as when and where they are used, as well as on the physical characteristics. Some people may love onions while others dislike them horribly. Thus, when we speak of the "value of an onion," this makes sense only within the context of its value to a specific individual. We must ask, "Its value to whom?" In the hands of some the onion may have great value, while it is worthless to others. It is this difference in subjective values that makes trade between individuals possible, and mutually beneficial.

Consider the case of Mary, who loves tomatoes but hates onions, and John, who loves onions but hates tomatoes. They go out to dinner together and the waiter brings their salads. John turns to Mary and says, "I'll trade you the tomatoes on my salad for the onions on yours." Mary gladly agrees to the exchange. This simple example will help us to illustrate two important aspects of voluntary exchange.

1. When individuals engage in a voluntary exchange, both parties are made better off.

In the above example, Mary had the option of accepting John's offer of a trade or declining it. Mary would only agree to this exchange if she expected to be better off as a result. Because she likes tomatoes better than onions, Mary's enjoyment of her salad will be greater with this trade than without it. On the other side, John has voluntarily made this offer of an exchange to Mary because John believes he will also be better off as the result.

OUTSTANDING ECONOMIST

Thomas Sowell (1930–)

Thomas Sowell, a senior fellow at the Hoover Institution, recognizes the critical importance of the institutions—the "rules of the game"—that shape human interactions. His book, *Knowledge and Decisions*, stresses the difficulty of obtaining knowledge and explores the way different institutional arrangements provide different kinds and amounts of scarce information.

---

[4]An illuminating discussion of this subject, termed the "physical fallacy," is found in Thomas Sowell, *Knowledge and Decisions* (New York: Basic Books, 1980), pp. 67–72.

People tend to think of making, building, and creating things as productive activities. Agriculture and manufacturing are like this. They create something genuinely new, something that was not there before. On the other hand, trade—the mere exchanging of one thing for another—does not create new material items. Therefore, some conclude that the situation is one in which one person's gain is necessarily an equal loss to another. A closer look at the motivation for trade helps us see through this popular fallacy. Exchange is based on the mutual expectation of gain. If both parties did not expect the trade to improve their well-being, they would not agree to the trade. Because trade is mutually advantageous, it must be a positive-sum productive activity.

As the chapter opening quote by Milton and Rose Friedman illustrates, most errors in economic reasoning stem from the failure to remember that voluntary trade makes both parties better off. While Henry Ford earned a fortune making and selling automobiles, it would be wrong to conclude that this fortune came at the expense of others. Henry Ford made millions, but at the same time enriched consumers by providing them with cars that they were better off for having purchased.

2. By channeling goods and resources to those who value them most, trade creates value and increases the wealth created by a society's resources.

Preferences are subjective and differ among individuals. As a result, the value of an item can vary greatly from one person to another. Therefore, movement of goods to those who value them more can create value. The simple exchange between John and Mary illustrates this point. Imagine for a moment that John and Mary had never met and instead were both eating their salads alone. Without the ability to engage in this exchange, both would have eaten their salads but not had as much enjoyment from them. When goods are moved to the individuals who value them more, the total value created by a society's limited resources is increased. The exact same two salads create more when the trade ocurs than when it doesn't.

It is easy to think of material things as wealth, but material things are not wealth until they are in the hands of someone who values them. A highly technical book on electronics that is of no value to an art collector may be worth several hundred dollars to an engineer. Similarly, a painting that is unappreciated by an engineer may be of great value to an art collector. Therefore, a voluntary exchange that moves the electronics book to the engineer and the painting to the art collector will increase the value of both goods. By channeling goods and resources toward those who value them most, trade creates wealth for both the trading partners, and for the nation.

Transaction Costs—A Barrier to Trade

How many times have you been sitting home late at night, hungry, wishing you had a meal from your favorite fast-food restaurant? You would gladly pay the $4 price for the value meal you have in mind, but you feel it is just not worth the time and effort to get dressed and make that drive. The costs of the time, effort, and other resources necessary to search out, negotiate, and conclude an exchange are called **transaction costs**. *High transactions costs can be a barrier to potentially productive exchange.*

Transaction costs
The time, effort, and other resources needed to search out, negotiate, and consummate an exchange.

Because of transaction costs, we should not expect all potentially valuable trades to take place, any more than we expect all useful knowledge to be learned, all safety measures to be taken, or all potential "A" grades to be earned. Frequent fliers know that if they never miss a flight, they are probably spending too much time waiting in airports. Similarly, the seller of a car, a house, or a ballet ticket knows that to find that one person in the world who would be willing to pay the most money is not worth the enormous effort required to locate that buyer. Information is costly. That is one reason that perfection in exchange, as in most things we do, is seldom reached.

The rapid expansion of the use of the Internet has significantly lowered transaction costs in a variety of ways. For example, the auction web site eBay permits sellers to offer their products for sale to millions of people with little effort and low monetary cost. Buyers can easily search the vast web site for items they desire. Also reducing search costs for buyers are the web sites MySimon and Pricescan, which continually scour numerous on-line shopping sites to find the lowest price for many products. In addition, the Internet enables consumers to readily find detailed information about products. The prominent Web site Amazon.com provides user reviews as well as manufacturer information about the goods it sells. By reducing transaction costs, the Internet creates value and wealth, by expanding the number of productive exchanges.

The Middleman As a Cost Reducer

Middleman
A person who buys and sells or who arranges trades. A middleman reduces transaction costs.

Because gains from exchange are facilitated by information, some people, called **middlemen**, specialize in providing information at a lower cost, and in arranging trades. Middlemen are generally not very popular; many think that they just add to the buyer's expense without performing a useful function. Once we recognize that transaction costs deter gains from trade, the real contribution of middlemen is obvious: They provide services that reduce the cost of transactions and thereby promote the realization of additional gains from trade. The auto dealer, for example, can help both the manufacturer and the buyer. By keeping an inventory of autos, and by hiring knowledgeable salespeople, the dealer lowers the cost for the car shopper to learn about the many cars offered, and how each car looks, performs, and "feels." (Since preferences are subjective and not objectively known to others, the reports of other users may not fully inform the potential buyer.) Car buyers also like to know that the local dealer will honor the warranty and provide parts and service for the car. The car maker, by using the dealer as a middleman, is able to concentrate on designing and making cars, leaving to middlemen—that is, dealers—the tasks of marketing and servicing.

Grocers also provide middleman services. Each of us could avoid the grocer by dealing with farmers and other food producers directly. If we did, though, transaction costs would be high and it would be more difficult to squeeze the tomatoes! Alternatively, we could form consumer cooperatives, banding together to eliminate the middleman, using our own warehouses and our own volunteer labor to order, receive, display, redistribute, and collect payment for the food. In fact, some cooperatives like this do exist, but most people prefer instead to pay the grocer to provide all these middleman services.

Stockbrokers, publishers of the Yellow Pages, and merchants of all sorts are middlemen—specialists in selling, guaranteeing, and servicing the items traded. For a fee, they reduce transaction costs both for the shopper and for the seller. By making exchange cheaper and more convenient, middlemen cause more efficient trades to happen. In so doing, they themselves create value.

THE IMPORTANCE OF PROPERTY RIGHTS

Private Ownership

Private ownership provides people with a strong incentive to take care of things and develop resources in ways that are highly valued by others.

Property rights
The right to use, control, and obtain the benefits from a good or service.

Private property rights
Property rights that are exclusively held by an owner, or group of owners, and that can be transferred to others at the owner's discretion.

The buyer of an apple, a CD, a television set, or an automobile generally takes the item home. The buyer of a steamship or an office building, though, may never touch it. When exchange occurs, it is really the rights—the **property rights**—to the item that change hands.

Private property rights involve three things: (1) the right to exclusive use, (2) legal protection against invaders—those who would seek to use or abuse the property without the owner's permission, and (3) the right to transfer to (exchange with) another. Private owners cannot do anything they want with their property. Most significantly, they cannot use their property in a manner that invades or infringes on the property of another. For example, I cannot throw the hammer that I own through the television set that you own. If

I did, I would be violating your property right to your television. The same is true if I operate a factory that harms you or your land by spewing air pollution.[5] Because an owner has the right to control the use of property, the owner also must accept responsibility for the outcomes of that control.

Clearly defined and enforced private property rights are a key to economic progress because of the powerful incentive effects that follow from private ownership of goods and resources. The following four factors are particularly important.

1. Private owners can gain by employing their resources in ways that are beneficial to others and they bear the opportunity cost of ignoring the wishes of others.

Realtors often advise home owners to use neutral colors for countertops and walls in their house because they will improve the resale value of the home. As a private owner you could install bright green fixtures and use deep purple paint around your house, but you will bear the cost (in terms of a lower selling price) of ignoring the wishes of others who might want to buy your house. On the other hand, by fixing up a house and doing things to it which others find beneficial you can reap the benefit of a higher selling price. Similarly, you could spray paint orange designs all over the outside of your brand-new car, but private ownership gives you an incentive not to do so because the resale value of the car depends on the value that *others* place on it.

Let's now consider an example of a parcel of undeveloped land near a university. The private owner of that land could do many possible things with the land, for example, she could leave it undeveloped, make a metered parking lot, erect a restaurant, or build rental housing. Will the wishes and desires of the nearby students be reflected in her choice even though they are not the owners of the property? The answer is yes. Whichever use is more highly valued by potential customers will earn her the highest reward from investment. If housing is relatively hard to find but there are plenty of other restaurants, the profitability of using her land for housing will be higher than the profitability of using it for a restaurant. Private ownership gives her a strong incentive to cater to the wishes of others as to the use of her property. And if she decides to leave the property undeveloped, withholding it from these potential uses that would benefit the nearby students, she will bear the opportunity cost of forgone income from the property.

"Their house looks so nice. They must be getting ready to sell it."

From the *Wall Street Journal*—permission, Cartoon Features Syndicate.

As a second example, suppose Ed owns a house and will be out of town all summer. Will his house stay vacant, or will Ed let someone else use it during those months? We don't know, but we do know that Ed can rent the house to someone else if he chooses, and that if he does not, he will incur the opportunity cost—the rental payments he could earn, minus any damages, added upkeep, and transaction costs. Ed will pay a price (the net income forgone) if he chooses not to rent the house. Thus, private ownership provides him with a strong incentive to consider the wishes of others—the value that someone else places on the use of the house during the summer.

Finally, consider the owner of an apartment complex near your campus. The owner may not care much for swimming pools, workout facilities, study desks, or green areas, for example. Nonetheless, private ownership provides the owner with a strong incentive to provide these items if students and other potential customers value them enough to cover the cost of their provision. Why? The owner will be able to lease the apartment units for more if they include amenities that are highly valued by others. Investment property owners have a strong incentive to consider the desires of others.

[5]For a detailed explanation of how property rights protect the environment, with several real-world examples, see Roger E. Meiners and Bruce Yandle, *The Common Law: How It Protects the Environment* (Bozeman, Mont.: PERC, 1998), available online at <www.perc.org>.

When apartments and other investment properties are owned privately, the owner has a strong incentive to provide amenities that others value highly relative to their cost.

2. The private owner has a strong incentive to care for and properly manage what he or she owns.

Will Ed change the oil in his car? Will he take care to see that the seats do not get torn? Probably so, since being careless about these things would reduce the car's value, both to him and to any future owner. The car and its value—the sale price if he sells it—belong just to Ed, so he would bear the burden of a decline in the car's value if the oil ran low and ruined the engine, or if the seats were torn. Similarly, he would capture the value of an expenditure that improves the car, such as providing a new paint job. As the owner, Ed has both the authority and the incentive to protect the car against harm or neglect, and even to enhance its value. Private property rights concentrate the owner's interest and attention, providing a strong incentive for good stewardship.

Do you take equally good care not to damage an apartment you rent as you would if it were your own house? If you share an apartment with several roommates, is it generally the case that common areas of the apartment or house (such as the kitchen and living room) are as neatly kept up as the bedrooms? Our guess is that the answer to both of these questions is probably "no." Property that is owned in common—that is, jointly by many people—is generally not as well maintained as property that is owned privately by a single individual. In 1998, the student government association at Berry College in Georgia purchased 20 bicycles to be placed around campus for everyone's use.[6] These $200 Schwinn Cruiser bicycles were painted red and were marked with a plate reading "Berry Bike." The bikes were available on a first-come, first-serve basis, and students were encouraged to take them whenever they needed them and leave them anywhere on campus wherever they were finished. What do you think happened to these bikes? Within two months, most of these top-quality bikes were severely damaged or lost. This is despite the fact that there had been no prior problems on campus with privately owned bikes being lost or abused. The campus newspaper reported of "mangled corpses of twisted red metal that lie about campus." All the bikes were replaced or fixed over the summer break, and despite pleas by the student government to "treat the bikes as if they were your own prop-

---

[6]Daniel L. Alban and E. Frank Stephenson, "The 'Berry Bikes': A Lesson in Private Property," *Ideas on Liberty* 49, no. 10 (October 1999), pp. 8–9.

Without clearly defined private property rights there is less of an incentive to take proper care of things—as the student government administration at Berry College found out when they provided common property bikes to be used around campus.

erty," the program resumed in the fall with similar results. After only one more month, the student government association abandoned the program and began leasing the remaining bicycles on a semester-by-semester basis to individual students. As this example illustrates, there is no denying the strong incentive that private ownership creates for owners to care for their property (or more precisely, the lack of this incentive when private ownership is not clearly defined and enforced).

The incentive for good care and management by the individual extends also to private investments that yield income. The owner of a hotel does not want to neglect electrical or plumbing problems, if taking care of them now avoids large repair costs due to electrical fires or water leaks. The wealth of the owner, in the form of the value of hotel ownership, is a hostage to the owner's good management. Poor management will reduce the hotel's value, and thus the owner's personal wealth. Again, ownership concentrates the owner's interest and attention on good management of the asset owned.

3. The private owner has an incentive to conserve for the future if the property's value is expected to rise.

Suppose our man Ed owns a case of very good red wine, which is only two years old. Age will improve it substantially if he puts it in his cellar for another five years. Will he do so? Well, if he does not, he will personally bear the consequences. He (and presumably his friends) will drink wine sooner, but they will sacrifice quality. Also, Ed will forgo the chance to sell the wine later for much more than its current worth. The opportunity cost of drinking the wine now is its unavailability later, for drinking or for sale. Ed bears that cost. Private property rights assure that Ed has the authority to preserve the wine, and that he gains the benefits if he does so. If the greater quality is expected to be worth the wait, then Ed can capture the benefits of not drinking the wine "before its time."

In a similar way, if Ed owns land, or a house, or a factory, he has a strong incentive to bear costs now, if necessary, to preserve the asset's value. His wealth is tied up in its value, which reflects nothing more than the net benefits that will be available to the owner in the future. So Ed's wealth depends on his willingness and ability to look ahead, maintain, and conserve those things that will be highly valued in the future.

4. With private property rights, the property owner is accountable for damage to others through misuse of the property. Private ownership links responsibility with the right of control.

Ed, the car owner, has a right to drive his car, but he has no right to drive in a drunken or reckless way that injures Alice. A chemical company has control over its products, but, exactly for that reason, it is legally liable for damages if it mishandles the chemicals. Courts of law recognize and enforce the authority granted by ownership, but they also enforce the responsibility that goes with that authority. Because private property owners can be held accountable for any damage they cause, they have a powerful incentive to use their property responsibly and to take steps to reduce the likelihood that their property will harm others.

Private Ownership and Markets

The incentives provided by the private ownership of property are very useful. As we will discuss in more detail later, private ownership and competitive markets provide the foundation for cooperative behavior among individuals. They provide each individual, however selfish or narrow-minded, with both the information and the incentive to engage in productive activities and cooperate with others. *When private property rights are protected and enforced, permission of the owner is required for the use of a resource. Put another way, if you want to use a good or resource, you must either buy or lease it from the owner. This means that each of us faces the cost of using scarce resources.* Furthermore, when their actions are directed by market price signals, private owners have a strong incentive to consider the desires of others and to use and develop their resources in ways that are valued highly by others. The resulting market exchanges generate what F. A. Hayek, the 1974 Nobel laureate in economics, called the "extended order." Hayek used this expression to describe the tendency of markets to direct individuals from throughout the world to cooperate with each other in mutually beneficial ways despite the fact that they do not know each other, and that they often have vastly different backgrounds, lifestyles, and cultural values.

In contrast, in a community that does not recognize private ownership rights, whoever has the power or the political authority can simply take command of an item, ignoring the wishes of both the person in possession and other potential users. Without private property rights, other methods must be found to provide the incentives for good stewardship of property, and for proper concern for others by the users of property. For example, if the owners of a factory are not held responsible for damages their pollutants impose on the person and property of others, then other measures may be needed to control polluting behavior. The accompanying Applications in Economics feature, "Protecting Endangered Species and the Environment with Private Property Rights," explores some of these issues. We will return to this issue in Chapter 5 and in other sections of the book as well.

Production possibilities curve
A curve that outlines all possible combinations of total output that could be produced, assuming (1) the utilization of a fixed amount of productive resources, (2) full and efficient use of those resources, and (3) a specific state of technical knowledge. The slope of the curve indicates the rate at which one product can be traded off to produce more of the other.

PRODUCTION POSSIBILITIES CURVE

Purposeful decision making and economizing behavior imply that individuals seek to get the most from their limited resources. The nature of the economizing problem can be made more clear with the use of a conceptual tool, the production possibilities diagram. A **production possibilities curve** reveals the maximum amount of any two products that can be produced from a fixed set of resources, and the possible trade-offs in production between them.

APPLICATIONS IN ECONOMICS

Protecting Endangered Species and the Environment with Private Property Rights

Column 1	Column 2
Cows	African Rhinos
Pigs	Bald Eagles
Chickens	Spotted Owl
Dogs	American Bison
Cats	African Elephants

Compare the two columns of animals above. The animals listed in column 2 are endangered species while those in column 1 are not. Why the difference? The answer may surprise you—all of the animals listed in column 1 can be privately owned, while those in column 2 generally cannot. In this chapter you have learned about the powerful incentives for careful management and conservation created by private property rights. This application considers how the power of these incentives is being harnessed to protect endangered species and the environment.

What do you think would happen to the total population of cows if people wanted less beef? Beef prices would fall, and the incentive for individuals to dedicate land and other resources to the raising of cattle would decline. It is precisely the market demand for beef which *creates* the incentive for suppliers to maintain herds of cattle, and to protect them from any harm.

The rhinoceros is similar in some ways to a cow. It is a large and rather unpredictable animal. A rhino, like a large bull in a cattle herd, may charge if disturbed. And at 3000 pounds, a charging rhino can be very dangerous. Also like cattle, rhinos can be valuable, and they are more scarce. A single horn from a black rhino can sell for as much as $30,000. But that makes it a favorite target of poachers— people who hunt illegally for such animals. Rhinos are very different from cattle in one important respect: In most of Africa where they naturally range, the rhinoceros cannot be privately owned, or sold by anyone who might protect them. In those areas, poachers may be helped by local people more interested in personal safety. We should not be surprised that in these circumstances, the rhino is in danger of becoming extinct.

One reaction to this problem is to outlaw the hunting of rhinoceros and to forbid the sale of any rhino parts. That happened, as an international treaty signed by many nations outlawed such sales of black rhino in 1977. Nearly 20 years later, however, in 1994, the black rhino was closer to extinction than ever before. According to South African economist Michael 't Sas Rolfes, the trade ban "has not had a discernible effect on rhino numbers and does not seem to have stopped the trade in rhino horn. If anything, the . . . listings led to a sharp increase in the black market price of rhino horn, which simply fueled further poaching and encouraged speculative stockpiling of horn." Incentives for poachers and local people had not changed, and between 1970 and 1994, black rhinos suffered a 95 percent decline in Africa.[1]

Then a very different strategy for the black rhino was developed in the southern African nation of Zimbabwe. While rhinos cannot be privately owned there, landowners can fence and manage the game animals on their property. Many of the remaining black rhinos were relocated to private land in the early 1990s. Able to profit from protecting the big animals, some ranchers shifted their operations from cattle to wildlife protection, eco-tourism, and hunting. They often combined several ranches into one conservancy in the process, since some wild animals, including rhinos, can range over a large area and are difficult to fence. Revenues from the conservancies come from both hunting the many big game animals and from non-consumptive uses of wildlife. A stay at the Barberton Lodge in the Bubiana conservancy in Zimbabwe costs about $160 per night for a photo safari. Other Bubiana properties charge between $500 and $1,000 per day for a hunting safari, on top of whatever trophy fees are incurred. For an animal like a leopard, the trophy fee can be over $3,000. No elephants are hunted in the conservancies, but elsewhere in Zimbabwe, hunters pay up to $36,000 for a three-week chance at tracking and killing an elephant. And while no black rhino may be hunted in Zimbabwe, it has been estimated that the fee for a permit to hunt one could be as high as $250,000. Because of the low overhead and high return, hunting is the reason why, even without the hunting of elephant and rhino, all of the ranchers in the Bubiana partnership are turning a profit from their wildlife operations.

Rhinos are the biggest attraction, and at least one local person is commonly hired and armed to follow each rhino, in order to protect them. Not a single animal had been poached by the turn of the century on these private conservancies. Rhino populations have climbed there. Cattle had been introduced to the area in the 1950s and 1960s. When they were removed from some of the conservancies to make way for rhinos, native grasses and shrubs came back in strength, and so did other big game and other forms of wildlife. A similar success story is unfolding in South Africa for the African white rhino.[2] Property rights that allow owners of land to

(continued)

(continued)

capture some of the benefits of conserving wildlife and protecting them can often make conservation pay. Doing good for the wildlife becomes a way for landowners and local people to do well for themselves.

In Africa, elephant numbers also show the value of property rights and market tools for conservation. Zimbabwe and Botswana have for years allowed landowners and local tribes to benefit financially from the presence of elephants. They have also made trade in ivory legal. Other countries, such as Kenya, have banned the ivory trade and they have forbidden such gains to landowners from the elephants, instead making their government responsible for protecting them. From 1979 to 1989, property rights and market conservation pushed elephant numbers from 50,000 up to 94,000 in Zimbabwe and Botswana, while Kenya's elephant population fell from 65,000 to 19,000. The trend did not stop there. From 1989 to 1995, elephant populations in Zimbabwe and Botswana rose by about 15 percent, while the rest of Africa *lost* about 20 percent of their elephants.

So long as property rights exist, or landowners can manage wildlife and gain from doing so, market conservation can work. Yet many environmentalists fail to see the benefits of markets for conservation, especially when hunting is involved. But as Dave Foreman, a founder of EarthFirst! and now head of the Wildlands project, has said, "I find shooting elephants . . . repulsive. I'd never do it. But if hunting will save elephants . . . then I support it."[3] With private ownership, entrepreneurs can often find ways to do good work for conservation, while doing well for themselves. In fact an entire book has been written on the topic. Terry Anderson and Don Leal, in *Free Market Environmentalism: Revised Edition* (New York: Palgrave, 2001), provide an overview and dozens of case studies on market conservation of water, wildlife and wilderness, scenic views, and pollution-free environments for the interested reader or researcher.

[1]See Michael De Alessi, *Private Conservation and Black Rhinos in Zimbabwe: The Savé Valley and Bubiana Conservancies*, San Francisco: Center for Private Conservation, 2000, available online at: http://www.cei.org/CPCCaseReader.asp?ID=883. Our information on the rhino comes mainly from that case study, one of many available from the CPC and its Web site.

[2]See "The Rhinos Are Baaack!" in *Smithsonian Magazine,* March 2001 (pp. 76–86).

[3]Quoted in Michael DeAlessi, noted above.

Exhibit 1 illustrates the production possibilities curve for Susan, an intelligent economics major. This curve indicates the combinations of English and economics grades that she thinks she can earn if she spends a total of 10 hours per week studying for the two subjects. Currently she is choosing the material to study in each course that she expects will help her grade the most, for the time spent, and she is allocating 5 hours of study time to each course. She expects that this amount of time, carefully spent on each course, will allow her to earn a B grade in both, indicated at point *T*. But if she took some time away from studying one of the two subjects and spent it studying the other, she could raise her grade in the course receiving more time. If she spent more hours on economics and fewer on English, for example, her expected economics grade would rise as a result, while her English grade would fall.

Susan's production possibilities curve indicates that the additional study time required to raise her economics grade by one letter, to an A (point *S*), would require giving up two grades in her English class, not just one grade, reducing her English grade to a D. As she shifts more time away from English, she gives up some time that would have been spent studying the most important (grade-increasing) material. In contrast, as she reallocates more and more study time to economics, much of that time is spent studying additional material that is likely to be a little less helpful in producing grade points than the material chosen at point *T*. The curve is flatter to the left of point *T*, and steeper to the right, showing that, as Susan takes more and more of her resources (time, in this case) from one course and puts it into the other, she must give up greater and greater amounts of productivity in the course getting fewer resources.

Of course, Susan could study more economics *without* giving up her English study time, if she gave up some leisure, or study time for other courses, or her part-time job in the campus bookstore. If she gave up leisure or her job to add to the 10 hours of study time for economics and English, the entire *STU* portion of the curve in Exhibit 1 would shift

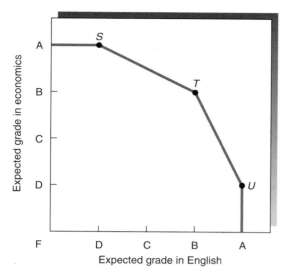

The production possibilities for Susan, in terms of grades, are illustrated for 10 hours of total study time. If Susan studied 10 hours per week in these two classes, she could attain (1) a D in English and an A in economics (point *S*), (2) a B in English and a B in economics (point *T*), or (3) a D in economics and an A in English. [Note: Spending even more of her 10 hours on economics than at point *S*, moving along the curve to the left, would decrease her English grade toward an F, but could not improve her A in economics. Similarly, spending more time on English than at point *U*, moving her downward on the curve from there, would decrease her economics grade toward an F, but could not increase her A in English, so we assume that Susan will not choose to spend time on these parts of her production possibilities curve.]

Could Susan move the entire curve outward, making higher grades in both? Yes, if she were willing to apply more resources, perhaps by giving up some leisure or her job.

outward. She could get better grades in both classes by devoting more of her scarce time to studying for both of them.

Can the production possibilities concept be applied to the entire economy? The answer is yes. We can grow more soybeans if we grow less corn, since both can be grown on the same land. Beefing up the military requires the use of resources that otherwise could be used to produce nonmilitary goods. When scarce resources are being used efficiently, more of one thing requires the sacrifice of others.

Exhibit 2 shows a production possibilities curve for an economy producing only two goods: food and clothing. The curve is convex, or bowed out from the origin, just as Susan's was in the previous exhibit. Why? Resources are not equally well suited to produce food and clothing. Consider an economy that is using all its resources to produce clothing. At that point (*S*), food production can be expanded by transferring those resources that are best suited for production of food (and least suitable for clothing production) from clothing to food production. Since the resources transferred are those that are highly productive in food and not very productive in clothing, in this range the opportunity cost (clothing forgone) of producing additional food is low. However, as more and more resources are devoted to food production, and successively larger amounts of food are produced (moving from *S* to *A* to *B* and so on), the opportunity cost of food will rise. This results because, as more and more food is produced, additional food output can be achieved only by using resources that are less and less suitable for the production of food relative to clothing. Thus, as food output is expanded, successively larger amounts of clothing must be forgone per unit of additional food.

What restricts the ability of an economy, once resources are fully utilized, from producing more of everything? The same constraint that kept Susan from making a higher grade in both English and economics—lack of resources. There will be various maximum combinations of goods that an economy will be able to produce when:

EXHIBIT 2
Concept of Production Possibilities Curve for an Economy

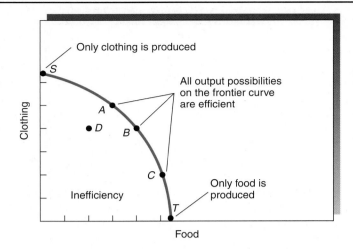

When an economy is using its limited resources efficiently, production of more clothing requires the economy to give up some other goods—food in this simple example. With time, a technological discovery, expansion of the economy's resource base, or improvement in its economic organization could make it possible to produce more of both, shifting the production possibilities curve outward.

Or the citizens of the economy might decide to give up some leisure for more of both goods. These factors aside, limited resources will constrain the production possibilities of an economy.

1. It uses some fixed quantity of resources.

2. The resources are used efficiently.

3. The level of technology is constant.

When these three conditions are met, the economy will be at the edge of its production possibilities frontier (points such as *A*, *B*, and *C* in Exhibit 2). Producing more of one good, such as clothing, will necessitate less production of other goods (for example, food).

When the resources of an economy are used inefficiently, output will be at a point inside the production possibilities curve—point *D*, for example. Why might this happen? It happens if the economy is not properly solving the economizing problem. A major function of economic decision making is to help us get the most out of available resources, to move us out to the production possibilities frontier. We will return to this problem again and again.

Shifting the Production Possibilities Curve Outward

Could an economy ever have more of all goods? In other words, could the production possibilities curve be shifted outward? The answer is yes, under certain circumstances. There are four major possibilities.

1. An increase in the economy's resource base would expand our ability to produce goods and services.

If we had more and better resources, we could produce a greater amount of all goods. Many resources are human-made. If we were willing to give up some current consumption, we could invest more of today's resources into the production of long-lasting physical structures, machines, education, and the development of human skills. This **investment** would provide us with better tools and skills in the future and thereby increase our

Investment
The purchase, construction, or development of capital resources, including both nonhuman capital and human capital (such as better education). Investment expands the availability of capital resources in an economy. The process of investment is sometimes referred to as capital formation.

ability to produce goods and services. **Exhibit 3** illustrates the link between investment and the future production possibilities of an economy. The two economies illustrated begin with the same production possibilities curve (*RS*). However, since Economy A (part a) allocates more of its resources to investment than does Economy B, A's production possibilities curve shifts outward with the passage of time by a greater amount. The growth rate of A—the expansion rate of the economy's ability to produce goods—is enhanced because the economy allocates a larger share of its output to investment. Of course, more investment in machines and human skills requires a reduction in current consumption.

2. Advancements in technology can expand the economy's production possibilities.

Technology determines the maximum physical output obtainable from any particular set of resource inputs. New technology can make it possible to get more from our given base of resources. An important form of technological change is **invention**—the use of science and engineering to create new products or processes. In recent years, for example, inventions have allowed us to develop photographs faster and cheaper, get more oil from existing fields, and send information instantly and cheaply by satellite. Such technological advances increase our production possibilities, shifting the entire curve outward.

An economy can also benefit from technological change through **innovation**—the practical and effective adoption of new techniques. Such innovation is commonly carried out by an **entrepreneur**—one who seeks profit by introducing new products or improved techniques to satisfy consumers at a lower cost. To prosper, an entrepreneur must undertake projects that convert and rearrange resources in a manner that will increase their value, thus expanding the size of our economic pie.

It is interesting to reflect on how some very famous entrepreneurs have impacted our lives, for example, Henry Ford, an entrepreneur who changed car-making technology by pioneering the assembly line. With the same amount of labor and materials, Ford made

Invention
The creation of a new product or process, often facilitated by the knowledge of engineering and scientific relationships.

Innovation
The successful introduction and adoption of a new product or process; the economic application of inventions and marketing techniques.

Entrepreneur
A profit-seeking decision maker who decides which projects to undertake and how they should be undertaken. A successful entrepreneur's actions will increase the value of resources and expand the size of the economic pie.

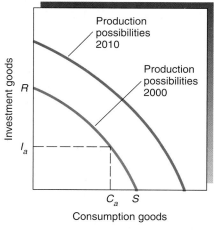

(a) Economy A, high investment

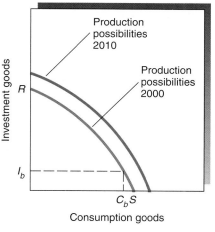

(b) Economy B, low investment

EXHIBIT 3
Investment and Production Possibilities in Future

Here we illustrate two economies that initially confront identical production possibilities curves (*RS*). The economy illustrated on the left allocates a larger share of its output to investment (I_a compared to I_b for the economy on the right). As a result, the production possibilities of the high-investment economy will tend to shift outward by a larger amount than will be true for the low-investment economy.

more cars, more cheaply. Another entrepreneur, the late Ray Kroc, purchased a hamburger restaurant from Richard McDonald and built it into the world's largest fast-food chain. Kroc revolutionized fast food by offering an attractive menu at economical prices and developing a system of franchising and inspection that resulted in uniform quality across a worldwide chain of establishments. More recently, entrepreneurs like Steven Jobs (Apple Computer) and Bill Gates (Microsoft) helped develop the personal computer and accompanying software programs and thereby dramatically increased their usefulness to both businesses and households. The activities of entrepreneurs like these and many others shift the production possibilities curve outward with the passage of time.

3. An improvement in the rules under which the economy functions can also increase output.

The legal system of a country influences the ability of people to cooperate with one another and produce desired goods. Changes in legal institutions that promote social cooperation and enhance the incentive of people to produce will increase production possibilities.

Historically, legal innovations have been an important source of economic progress. During the eighteenth century, a system of patents provided inventors with a private property right to their ideas. At about the same time, the recognition of the corporation as a legal entity reduced the cost of forming large firms that were often required for the mass production of manufactured goods. Both of these legal changes improved economic organization and thereby accelerated the growth of output (that is, shifted the production possibilities curve outward more rapidly) in Europe and North America.

Sometimes governments, perhaps as the result of ignorance or prejudice, adopt legal institutions that reduce production possibilities. Laws that restrict or prohibit trade among various groups provide an illustration. For example, the laws of several southern states prohibited the employment of African Americans in certain occupations, and restricted other economic exchanges between blacks and whites for almost 100 years following the Civil War. This legislation was not only harmful to African Americans, it retarded progress and reduced the production possibilities of these states.

The recent experience of Russia also illustrates the importance of economic institutions. Following the collapse of communism, Russia was unable to develop legal institutions capable of protecting property rights and enforcing contracts. The absence of these institutions not only retarded investment and gains from trade, but also led to inefficient use of resources and movement of capital to other places where property rights were more secure. Therefore, even though Russia has a well-educated labor force and abundant natural resources, its economic performance has been abysmal. The weak legal structure and insecurity of ownership rights are important elements underlying the economic struggles of Russia.

4. By working harder and giving up current leisure, we could increase our production of goods and services.

Strictly speaking, this is not an expansion in the production frontier because leisure is also a good. We are giving up some of that good to have more of other things.

The work effort of individuals depends not only on their personal preferences but also on public policy. For example, high tax rates may induce individuals to reduce their work time. The basic economic postulate implies that, as high tax rates reduce the personal payoff from working (and earning taxable income), individuals will shift more of their time to other, untaxed activities, including the consumption of leisure, moving the production possibilities curve for market goods inward. (Recall, from Exhibit 1, how Susan's production possibilities for grades would shift *outward* if she changed from 10 hours of study per week to more than 10 hours. The reverse would occur if she were to reduce study time below 10 hours.) Any reduction in market work time due to higher taxes not only reduces output directly, but is likely also to reduce the gains from the division of labor, as more people do more work for themselves because doing so is untaxed. We turn now to a consideration of how trade influences production possibilities and economic prosperity.

TRADE, OUTPUT, AND LIVING STANDARDS

 Trade makes it possible for individuals to generate a larger output through specialization and division of labor, large-scale production processes and dissemination of improved products and production methods.

Gains from Trade

As we previously discussed, trade creates value by moving goods from people who value them less to people who value them more. However, this is only part of the story. Trade also makes it possible for individuals to expand output through specialization and division of labor, large-scale production, and dissemination of better products and production methods.

Gains From Specialization and Division of Labor

Business firms can achieve higher output levels and greater productivity per worker through specialization and division of labor. More than 200 years ago, Adam Smith noted the importance of this factor. Observing the operation of a pin manufacturer, Smith noted that when each worker specialized in a productive function, ten workers were able to produce 48,000 pins per day, or 4,800 pins per worker. Without specialization and division of labor, Smith doubted an individual worker could produce even 20 pins per day.[7]

The division of labor separates production tasks into a series of related operations. Each worker performs one or a few out of perhaps hundreds of tasks necessary to produce a commodity. This process makes it possible to assign different tasks to those individuals who are able to accomplish them most efficiently (at the lowest cost). Furthermore, a worker who specializes in just one narrow area becomes more experienced and more skilled in that task with the passage of time.

Trading partners can also benefit from specialization and division of labor. The **law of comparative advantage** explains why. *Initially developed in the early 1800s by the great English economist David Ricardo, the law of comparative advantage states that the total output of a group of individuals, an entire economy, or a group of nations will be greatest when the output of each good is produced by the person (or firm) with the lowest opportunity cost.*

Law of comparative advantage
A principle that states that individuals, firms, regions, or nations can gain by specializing in the production of goods that they produce cheaply (that is, at a low opportunity cost) and exchanging those goods for other desired goods for which they are high-opportunity-cost producers.

The principle of comparative advantage is applicable to trade among individuals, business firms, regions, and even nations. When trading partners are able to use more of their time and resources producing those things they do best (while trading for those things for which they are a high-cost producer) they will be able to produce a larger joint output than would otherwise have been possible. In turn, the larger output will lead to mutual gain and higher levels of income

If a good or service can be obtained more economically through trade, it makes sense to acquire it in this manner. For example, even though most doctors might be good at record keeping and arranging appointments, it is nonetheless generally in their interest to hire someone to perform these services. Time they spend keeping records is time they could have spent seeing patients. Given the value of their time with patients, their earnings will be reduced as more of their time is spent keeping records, and less seeing patients. The relevant issue is not whether doctors are better record keepers than the assistants they could hire, but rather how doctors use their time most efficiently.

Once one thinks about it, the law of comparative advantage is almost common sense. If someone else is willing to supply you with a good at a lower cost than you can produce it yourself, doesn't it make sense to trade for it and use your time and resources to produce more of the things for which you are a low-cost producer? Consider the situation of Andrea, an attorney who earns $100 per hour providing legal services. She has several

---

[7]See Adam Smith, *An Inquiry into the Nature and Causes of the Wealth of Nations* (1776; Cannan's ed., Chicago: University of Chicago Press, 1976), pp. 7–16, for additional detail on the importance of the division of labor.

documents that need to be typed and she is thinking about hiring a word processor who earns $15 per hour. Andrea is an excellent typist, much faster than the prospective employee. Thus, she could do the job in 20 hours, while it will take the word processor 40 hours to complete the task.

Because of her greater typing speed, some might think Andrea should handle the job herself. This is not the case. Even though Andrea is a fast typist, she is still a high-opportunity-cost producer of typing service. If she types the documents, the job will cost $2,000, the opportunity cost of 20 hours of her lost time as a lawyer earning $100 per hour. Alternatively, the cost of having the documents typed by the word processor is only $600 (40 hours at $15 per hour). Andrea's comparative advantage thus lies in practicing law. She will increase her own productivity, and gain income accordingly, by hiring the word processor to do the job.

The implications of the law of comparative advantage are universal. Any group will be able to produce a larger output from the available resources when each function is undertaken by the low-opportunity-cost producer. This insight is particularly important when considering the role of markets. Purposeful decision-making indicates that both businesses purchasing resources and consumers purchasing goods will seek to get the most from their expenditures. They will not knowingly choose a high-cost option when a lower-cost alternative is available. This places low-cost suppliers at a competitive advantage. Thus, they will generally survive and prosper in a market economy. As a result, there will be a tendency for markets to allocate goods and resources in accordance with the law of comparative advantage.

Most recognize that Americans benefit from trade among the 50 states. For example, the residents of Nebraska and Florida are able to produce a larger joint output and achieve higher income levels when Nebraskans specialize in the production of wheat and other grain products and Floridians specialize in the production of oranges and other citrus products. The same is true for trade among nations. Like the Nebraskans and Floridians, people in different nations will be better off if they specialize in the production of those

Trade channels goods to those who value them most. It also makes it possible for us to produce a larger output as the result of specialization, division of labor, use of large-scale production methods, and innovative improvements. These factors underlie our modern living standards.

goods and services that they are able to produce at a low cost, while trading for those items for which they are high-cost producers. See the addendum to this chapter for evidence on this point.

Gains From Mass Production Methods

Trade also promotes economic progress by making it possible for firms to achieve lower per unit costs through the adoption of mass production methods. In the absence of exchange, self-provision and small-scale production would be the rule. Exchange permits business firms to sell their output over a broad market area, so they can plan for large outputs and adopt complex large-scale production processes. Using such mass production procedures often leads to a more efficient utilization of both labor and machinery and enormous increases in output per worker. Without trade, these gains could not be achieved.

Gains From Innovation

Trade also makes it possible to realize gains from the discovery and dissemination of innovative products and production processes. In the modern world, economic growth increasingly involves brain power, innovation, and the application of technology. Observation of and interaction with individuals employing different technologies often induces others to emulate successful approaches. Trade across geographic areas and national boundaries is also likely to encourage modifications that improve the original technology and/or make it more suitable for the local area. Thus, the development and dissemination of innovative ideas and new technologies is enhanced by trade.

It is difficult to exaggerate the gains derived from division of labor, specialization, large-scale production, and innovation. Trade makes these gains possible. Can you imagine the difficulty involved in producing your own housing, clothing, and food, to say nothing of radios, television sets, dishwashers, automobiles, and telephone services? Yet, most families in North America, Western Europe, Japan, and Australia enjoy all these conveniences. They are able to do so largely because their economies are organized in such a way that individuals can cooperate, specialize, and trade, thereby reaping the benefits of the enormous increases in output—both in quantity and diversity—that can be generated. On the other hand, countries that impose obstacles that retard exchange—either domestic or international—reduce the ability of their citizens to realize gains from trade and achieve more prosperous lives.

IS THE SIZE OF THE ECONOMIC PIE FIXED OR VARIABLE?

 Economic goods are the result of human ingenuity and action; thus, the size of the economic pie is variable not fixed.

Human Ingenuity

We do not live in the Garden of Eden. Resource scarcity limits our ability to generate goods and services. Through time we have expanded the supply of tools, machines, and other human-made resources and figured out how to get more from the available natural resources. While this has enhanced our productive capacity, our ability to produce goods and services today is both constrained and dependent upon human effort. This is the message of the production possibilities curve.

With the passage of time, however, the bonds of scarcity can be loosened. Human ingenuity is particularly important in this regard. As better ways of doing things and improvements in knowledge about how to transform potential resources into desired goods and services are discovered, output can be expanded. Thus, when viewed over time, knowledge even more than resources is the constraining factor limiting economic progress.

Without the advancements of knowledge achieved during recent decades and certainly those of the last 250 years, production of the vast array of goods and services that underlie our modern living standards would be impossible. Thomas Sowell highlights this point when he notes: "The cavemen had the same natural resources at their disposal as we have today, and the difference between their standard of living and ours is a difference between the knowledge they could bring to bear on those resources and the knowledge used today."[8]

The size of the economic pie reflects the physical effort and ingenuity of human beings. It is not an endowment from nature. With time, output can be expanded through human creativity and the discovery of better ways of doing things. This also highlights another important point: if one individual—Bill Gates for example—creates more goods, this does not mean that there are fewer goods available for others. As individuals use their skills to produce more, they are also enlarging the total size of the economic pie.

ECONOMIC ORGANIZATION

Every economy must answer three basic questions: (1) What will be produced? (2) How will goods be produced? and (3) For whom will they be produced? These questions are highly interrelated. Throughout, we will consider how alternative forms of economic organization address these three questions.

As we have stressed in this chapter, the availability of most goods we enjoy—our food, clothing, housing, medical services, and so on—reflects cooperative efforts by numerous people, most of whom we have never met. This cooperation does not occur automatically. Economic organization and institutions influence both the type and degree of cooperation.

Two Methods of Economic Organization: Markets and Political Planning

There are two broad ways that an economy can be organized: markets and government (or political) planning. Let us briefly consider each.

Market Organization

Capitalism
An economic system based on private ownership of productive resources and allocation of goods according to the signals provided by market prices.

Private ownership, voluntary contracts (often these contracts are verbal), and reliance upon market prices are the distinguishing features of market organization, or **capitalism,** as it is sometime called.[9] In market economies, people have private ownership rights to productive assets, as well as to consumption goods and their own labor services. Private parties are permitted to buy and sell ownership rights at mutually acceptable prices in unregulated markets. Government plays the limited role of a rule maker and neutral referee. The rule maker role involves the development of a legal structure that recognizes, defines, and protects private ownership rights, enforces contracts, and protects people from violence and fraud. But the government is not an active player in the economy; ideally, the political process avoids modifying market outcomes or favoring some participants at the expense of others. For example, the government does not prevent sellers from undertaking price reductions and quality improvements to compete with other sellers. Nor does it prevent buyers from offering higher prices to bid products or productive resources away from others. No legal restraints (for example, government licensing) limit potential buyers or sellers from producing, selling, or buying in the marketplace. Under market organization, there is no central planning authority. The three basic economic questions are answered through market coordination of the decentralized choices of buyers and sellers.

---

[8]See Thomas Sowell, *Knowledge and Decisions* (New York: Basic Books, 1980), p. 47.
[9]*Capitalism* is a term coined by Karl Marx.

In a market setting, individuals communicate both directly and indirectly. They directly give voice to their desires to buy or to sell by advertising, whether in print or broadcast, or informally by word of mouth, on bulletin boards, and by letters of request and complaint, and other means. They send messages also by exiting or entering exchange relationships, as when they stop purchasing Coke and switch to Pepsi. The indirect, or "exit" option gives special power to their "voice," or direct statements. Indeed sellers, when markets are competitive, often hire experts to seek out the statements and desires of potential buyers. Buyers, too, are eager to know what sellers want—special terms of payment or delivery, for example—hoping that sellers might be willing to reward cooperation with a better deal.

Political Planning

The major alternative to market organization is **collective decision making**, the use of political organization and government planning to allocate resources. An economic system in which the government owns the income-producing assets (machines, buildings, and land) and directly determines what goods they will produce is called **socialism**. Alternatively, the government may maintain private ownership in name, but use taxes, subsidies, and regulations to resolve the basic economic questions. In either instance, political rather than market forces direct the economy. In both cases, government officials and planning boards hand down decisions to expand or contract the output of education, medical services, automobiles, electricity, steel, consumer durables, and thousands of other commodities. This is not to say that the preferences of individuals have no importance. If the government officials and central planners are influenced by the democratic process, they have to consider how their actions will influence their election prospects. That means they will listen to the voices of the voters, as they seek to win over a majority. Otherwise, like the firm in a market economy that produces a product that consumers do not want, their tenure of service is likely to be a short one. However, the exit option is seldom available, except to citizens who can "vote with their feet" and leave the nation. One's voice may disagree with the planners' decisions, but unlike a market setting, one cannot refuse to pay the taxes and buy instead from a competing supplier, or buy a competing product. Nor can one fail to do what the planners have ordered.

In summary, both the market and the government planning forms of economic organization must solve the same basic problems. To succeed, each must give voice to citizens, must motivate decision makers and other workers to listen, and in the modern world must coordinate a highly complex system of economic production and exchanges. A basic difference between these two broad kinds of economic organization is that the market system, with its exit option, allows diversity, constant competition, and marketing to diverse groups, while the central planning system, in a democracy, responds primarily to the votes of the majority.

Collective decision making
The method of organization that relies on public-sector decision making (voting, political bargaining, lobbying, and so on) to resolve basic issues.

Socialism
A system of economic organization in which (1) the ownership and control of the basic means of production rest with the state, and (2) resource allocation is determined by centralized planning rather than by market forces.

The next two chapters present an overview of the market sector, with real-world applications of the supply and demand model of market behavior. Chapters 5 and 6 focus on how the public sector—the democratic collective decision-making process—functions. The tools of economics can be used to analyze the operation of and allocation of resources in both the market and political sectors.

We think this approach is important, fruitful, and exciting. How does the market sector really work? What does economics say about which activities should be handled by government? What types of economic policies are politically attractive to democratically elected officials? Why is sound economic policy sometimes in conflict with good politics? All these questions will be tackled in the next four chapters.

LOOKING AHEAD

KEY POINTS

▼ The highest valued activity sacrificed in making a choice is the opportunity cost of the choice; differences (or changes) in opportunity costs help explain human behavior.

▼ Mutual gain is the foundation of trade. When two parties engage in voluntary exchange, they are both made better off. Trade creates value because it channels goods and resources to those who value them the most.

▼ Transaction costs—the time, effort, and other resources necessary to search out, negotiate, and conclude an exchange—are an obstacle to the realization of gains from trade. Middlemen perform a productive function by reducing the costs of transactions.

▼ Private property rights provide strong incentives for owners to use their resources in ways that benefit others. Private property rights also provide strong incentives for owners to take proper care of their resources, and to conserve them for the future.

▼ The production possibilities curve reveals the maximum combination of any two products that can be produced with a fixed quantity of resources and constant level of technology.

▼ With the passage of time, the production possibilities curve of an economy can be shifted outward through (1) investment, (2) technological advances, (3) improved institutions, and (4) greater work effort (the forgoing of leisure). Thus, the size of the economic pie is variable, not fixed, across time periods.

▼ The law of comparative advantage indicates that the joint output of individuals, regions, and nations will be maximized when each productive activity is undertaken by the low-opportunity-cost supplier. When a good can be acquired through trade more economically than it can be produced directly, it makes sense to trade for it.

▼ In addition to the gains derived from the movement of goods toward those who value them most, trade also makes it possible to expand output through specialization, division of labor, mass production processes, and innovation. These elements underlie our modern living standards.

▼ The two basic methods of making economic decisions are the market mechanism and public-sector decision making; in each, the decisions of individuals using voice and exit strategies will influence the result.

CRITICAL ANALYSIS QUESTIONS

1. "If Jones trades a used car to Smith for $5,000, nothing new is created. Thus, there is no way the transaction can improve the welfare of people." Is this statement true? Why or why not?

*2. Economists often argue that wage rates reflect productivity. Yet, the wages of house painters have increased nearly as rapidly as the national average, even though these workers use approximately the same methods that were applied 50 years ago. Can you explain why the wages of painters have risen substantially even though their productivity has changed so little?

3. It takes one hour to travel from New York City to Washington, D.C., by air, but it takes five hours by bus. If the air fare is $110 and the bus fare is $70, which would be cheaper for someone whose opportunity cost of travel time is $6 per hour? For someone whose opportunity cost is $10 per hour? $14 per hour?

*4. "People in business get ahead by exploiting the needs of their consumers. The gains of business are at the expense of suffering imposed on their customers." Evaluate this statement from the producer of a prime-time television program.

5. With regard to the use of resources, what is the objective of the entrepreneur? What is the major function of the middleman? Is the middleman an entrepreneur?

6. If you have a private ownership right to something, what does this mean? Does private ownership give you the right to do anything you want with the things that you own? Explain. How does private ownership influence the incentive of individuals to (a) take care of things, (b) conserve resources for the future, and (c) develop and modify things in ways that are objectionable to others? Explain.

7. What is the law of comparative advantage? According to the law of comparative advantage, what should be the distinguishing characteristics of the goods that a nation produces? What should be the distinguishing characteristics of the goods that the nation imports? How will international trade of this type influence the level of production and living standard of the populace? Explain.

*8. Does a 60-year-old tree farmer have an incentive to plant and care for Douglas fir trees that will not reach optimal cutting size for another 50 years?

*9. What forms of competition does a private-property, market-directed economy authorize? What forms does it prohibit?

10. What are the major sources of gains from trade? Why is exchange important to the prosperity of a nation? How do physical obstacles (such as rivers, mountains, and bad roads) that increase transaction costs influence gains from trade and the prosperity of a nation? How do human-made obstacles (for example, tariffs, quotas, and legal restrictions limiting trade) that increase transaction costs influence gains from trade and prosperity?

*11. "Really good agricultural land should not be developed for housing. Food is far more important." Evaluate this statement.

*12. In many states, the resale of tickets to sporting events at prices above the original purchase price ("ticket scalping") is prohibited. Who is helped and who is hurt by such prohibitions? Can you think of ways ticket owners who want to sell might get around the prohibition? Do you think it would be a good idea to extend the resale prohibition to other things—automobiles, books, works of art, or stock shares, for example? Why or why not?

13. Consider the choices of women age 30 to 50 years with (a) a college education and (b) less than a high school education. Which of the two will have the larger percent in the work force? Which will have the larger average number of children? Explain your answers.

14. Consider the questions below:
   a. Do you think that your work effort is influenced by whether there is a close link between personal output and personal compensation (reward)? Explain.
   b. Suppose the grades in your class were going to be determined by a random draw at the end of the course. How would this influence your study habits?
   c. How would your study habits be influenced if everyone in the class were going to be given an A grade? How about if grades were based

entirely on examinations composed of the multiple-choice questions in the course book for this textbook?
   d. Do you think the total output of a nation will be influenced by whether or not there is a close link between the productive contribution of individuals and their personal reward? Why or why not?

15. In the chapter it was stated that a private property right also involves having the right to transfer or exchange what you own with others. However, selling your organs is a violation of federal law, a felony punishable by up to five years in prison or a $50,000 fine. Because of this, in September 1999 eBay intervened when a person put one of his kidneys up for sale on eBay (the bidding reached $5.7 million before it was pulled). Does this lack of legal ability to exchange mean that individuals do not own their own organs? Explain.

16. During the last three decades entrepreneurs like Bill Gates, Sam Walton, and Ted Turner earned billions of dollars. Do you think the average American is better off or worse off as the result of the economic activities of these individuals? Explain your response.

*17. As the skill level (and therefore earnings rate) of an architect, computer specialist, or chemist for example increases, what happens to their opportunity cost of doing other things? How is their time and expenditures on leisure likely to change?

18. What are the sources of gains from trade? How does trade influence the quantity of output that trading partners are able to produce? In a market economy, will there be a tendency for both resources and products to be supplied by low-cost producers? Why or why not? Does this matter? Explain.

19. [*This question relates to the material from the addendum to this chapter.*] The tables below show the production possibilities for two hypothetical countries, Italia and Nire. Which country has the comparative advantage in producing butter? Which country has the comparative advantage in producing guns? What would be a mutually agreeable rate of exchange between the countries?

Italia		Nire	
Guns	Butter	Guns	Butter
12	0	16	0
8	2	12	1
4	4	8	2
0	6	4	3
		0	4

*Asterisk denotes questions for which answers are given in Appendix B.

Comparative Advantage, Specialization, and Gains from Trade

This addendum is for instructors who want to assign a more detailed numerical example demonstrating comparative advantage, specialization, and mutual gains from trade. Students who are uncertain about their understanding of these topics may also find this material enlightening. The international trade chapter later in the text provides still more information on trade and how it affects our lives.

We begin with hypothetical production possibilities curves for two countries, Slavia and Lebos, shown in **Exhibit A-1**. The numerical tables represent selected points from each country's production possibilities curve. To make calculations easier, we have assumed away increasing opportunity costs in production so that the production possibilities curves are linear.

Without trade, each country would only be able to consume what it can produce for itself. Let's arbitrarily assume that for survival Slavia requires 3 units of food and Lebos requires 6 units of food. As can be seen by point A in the exhibit, if Slavia were to produce the 3 units of food it requires, it would have enough resources remaining to produce 2 units of clothing. Similarly, if Lebos were to produce the 6 units of food it requires, it would have enough resources left to produce 6 units of clothing, again shown by point A in the exhibit. As we proceed we will use this outcome in the absence of specialization and trade between the countries as our benchmark.

Economic analysis suggests that both countries could gain if each were to specialize in the production of the good for which they have the comparative advantage and then trade for the other. First, let's figure out which country has a comparative advantage in the production of clothing. To do so requires calculating the opportunity cost of producing clothing for each country. Because, in this example, the opportunity costs are constant at all points along the production possibilities curve, rather than increasing, this can be found by first selecting any two points on the production possibilities curve (or equivalently by comparing any two rows of numbers in the numerical tables given in the exhibit). For Slavia, moving from the point of producing 6 food and 1 clothing to the alternative point of producing 3 food and 2 clothing we see that Slavia gains 1 clothing but must give up 3 units of food. For simplicity, the opportunity cost for Slavia can be written as $1C=3F$ where C stands for clothing and F for food. You might note that this same numerical tradeoff is true for Slavia anywhere along its production possibilities curve (for example beginning from 9 food and 0 clothing, it would also have to give up 3 food to gain 1 unit of clothing in this example).

Using a similar approach (taking any 2 points or 2 rows in the table) for Lebos shows that for every 3 units of clothing they wish to produce, they must give up 3 units of food ($3C=3F$). This can be treated as any other mathematical equation, and can be simplified by dividing both sides by 3, resulting in an opportunity cost of 1 clothing equals 1 food ($1C=1F$). Now, compare this to the opportunity cost for Slavia ($1C=3F$). Slavia must give up the production of 3 units of food for every 1 unit of clothing it produces, while Lebos only has to give up 1 unit of food for every 1 unit of clothing it produces. Thus, Lebos gives up the production of *less* food for every unit of clothing. Lebos is the low opportunity cost producer of clothing, and thus it has a comparative advantage in the production of clothing.

Because comparative advantage is a relative comparison, if one country has the comparative advantage in the production of one of the products, the other country must have the comparative advantage for the other good. Thus, because Lebos has the comparative advantage in clothing, it will be true that Slavia has the comparative advantage in food. However, it is worthwhile to show this here as well. To produce 1 unit of food, Lebos must give up 1 unit of clothing (recalling the $1C=1F$ opportunity cost). To produce 1 unit of food, Slavia must give up the production of only one-third of a unit of clothing (recalling the $1C=3F$ opportunity cost and noting that mathematically it can be rewritten as $1/3\,C=1F$ by dividing both sides of the equation by three). Thus, Slavia gives up the production of *less* clothing for every unit of food produced. Slavia is the low opportunity cost producer of food, and thus has a comparative advantage in the production of food.

Suppose that according to their comparative advantages, Lebos specializes in producing clothing and Slavia in food. From the last row of the table for Lebos, it would be able to produce 12 units of clothing (and 0 food) if it specialized in producing all clothing. From the top row of the table for Slavia, it would be able to produce 9 units of food (and 0 clothing) if it specialized in producing all food. Note, this joint output (9 food and 12 clothing) is greater than the benchmark joint output (9 food and 8 clothing) produced and consumed without trade.

The countries now must find a mutually agreeable rate of exchange if they are to trade. Any rate of exchange *between* the two opportunity costs of $1C=3F$ and $3C=3F$ would be mutually agreeable. Here we will use $2C=3F$.

Recall that Slavia requires 3 units of food for survival. Now, however, they are specializing and producing 9 units of food. Using the rate of exchange above, Slavia would send its extra 6 units of food to Lebos in exchange for 4 units of clothing. After trade Slavia would then have 3 units of food and 4 units of clothing. Compare this to the situation without specialization and trade, in which Slavia had only 3 units of food and 2 units of clothing to consume. Specialization and trade has created 2 additional units of clothing for Slavia relative to the situation without trade.

With specialization, Lebos is producing 12 units of clothing. In the trade with Slavia, Lebos gave up 4 units of

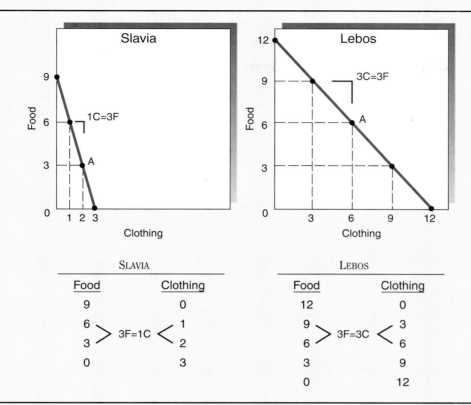

EXHIBIT A-1
Production Possibilities for Slavia and Lebos

For Slavia, the opportunity cost of producing 1 unit of clothing is equal to 3 units of food (1C=3F). For Lebos the opportunity cost of producing 3 units of clothing is equal to 3 units of food (3C=3F or thus 1C=1F). The difference in the opportunity costs of production will make mutually beneficial trade between the countries possible, with each specializing in their area of comparative advantage.

SLAVIA		
Food		Clothing
9		0
6	3F=1C	1
3		2
0		3

LEBOS		
Food		Clothing
12		0
9	3F=3C	3
6		6
3		9
0		12

clothing to obtain 6 units of food. After trade, Lebos has 8 units of clothing remaining and 6 units of food imported from Slavia. Compare this to the situation without specialization and trade, in which Lebos had only 6 units of food and 6 units of clothing to consume. For Lebos, specialization and trade have also created 2 additional units of clothing relative to the situation without trade.

As this simple example shows, total output is greater and *both* countries are better off when they specialize in the area where they have a comparative advantage. By doing so each is able to consume a bundle of goods and services that exceeds what could have been achieved in the absence of trade. This concept applies equally to individuals, states, or nations. The typical worker could not begin to produce by themselves all of the things they can afford to buy with the money they earn in a year by specializing and working in a single occupation. As our world has become more integrated over the past several hundred years, the gains from specialization and trade that have occurred are at the root of the significant improvements in well-being that we have experienced.

PART 2

"There are two primary

methods of allocating

scarce resources: markets

and governments"

MARKETS AND GOVERNMENTS

Economics has a great deal to say about how both markets and governments allocate scarce resources. It provides insights concerning the conditions under which each will likely work well (and when each will likely work poorly). The next four chapters will focus on this topic.

VISUALIZING MARKET ALLOCATION

Business firms purchase resources, such as materials, labor services, tools, and machines, from households in exchange for income. Firms incur costs as the resources are bid away from their alternative uses. Businesses transform the resources into products, such as shoes, automobiles, food products, and medical services, and supply them to households in exchange for revenues. In a market economy, businesses will continue to supply a good or service only if the revenues from the sale of the product are sufficient to cover the cost of the resources required for its production.

VISUALIZING ALLOCATION THROUGH GOVERNMENT

Allocation through government involves a more complex three-sided exchange. In a democratic political setting, a legislative body levies taxes on voter-citizens and these revenues are subdivided into budgets, which are allocated to government bureaus and agencies. In turn, the bureaus and agencies use the funds from their budgets to supply goods, services, and income transfers to voter-citizens. The legislative body is like a board of directors elected by the citizens. The competitive pressure to be elected provides legislators with a strong incentive to cater to the views of voters. In turn, a voter will be more likely to support a legislator if the value of the goods, services, and transfers received by the citizen (link between bureau and citizen) is large relative to the citizen's tax liability (link between voter and legislator). Goods, services, and income transfers will tend to be supplied through government if, and only if, a majority of the legislators perceive that the provision will enhance their electoral prospects, in other words, the likelihood they will win the next election.

CHAPTER **3**

Supply, Demand, and the Market Process

I am convinced that if it [the market system] were the result of deliberate human design, and if the people guided by the price changes understood that their decisions have significance far beyond their immediate aim, this mechanism would have been acclaimed as one of the greatest triumphs of the human mind.

—Friedrich Hayek,
Nobel Laureate[1]

From the point of view of physics, it is a miracle that [seven million New Yorkers are fed each day] without any control mechanism other than sheer capitalism.

—John H. Holland, scientist,
Santa Fe Institute

Chapter Focus

- What are the laws of demand and supply?

- How do consumers decide whether to purchase a good? How do producers decide whether to supply it?

- How do buyers and sellers respond to changes in the price of a good?

- What role do profits and losses play in an economy? What must a firm do in order to make a profit?

- How is the market price of a good determined?

- How do markets adjust to changes in demand? How do they adjust to changes in supply?

- What is the "invisible hand" principle?

[1]Friedrich Hayek, "The Use of Knowledge in Society," *American Economic Review* 35 (September 1945), pp. 519–530.

To those who study art, the *Mona Lisa* is much more than a famous painting of a woman. Looking beyond the overall picture, they see and appreciate the brush strokes, colors, and techniques embodied in the painting. Similarly, studying economics can help you to gain an appreciation for the details behind many things from your everyday life. On your last visit to the grocery store, you probably noticed the fruit and vegetable section. Next time, take a moment to ponder how potatoes from Idaho, oranges from Florida, apples from Washington, bananas from Honduras, kiwi fruit from New Zealand, and other items from around the world got to your local grocery store. Literally thousands of different individuals, *working independently*, were involved in the process. Their actions were coordinated such that the quantity of each good was just about right for your local community. Furthermore, the goods, including those transported great distances, were both fresh and reasonably priced.

How does all this happen? The short answer is, "It is the result of market prices, and the incentives and coordination that flow from them." To the economist, the operation of markets—including the local grocery market—is analogous to the brush strokes and techniques underlying a beautiful painting. Reflecting on this point, Professor Hayek speculates that if the market system had been deliberately designed, it would be "acclaimed as one of the greatest triumphs of the human mind." Similarly, computer scientist John H. Holland argues that, from the viewpoint of physics, the feeding of millions of New Yorkers "day after day with very few shortages or surpluses" is a miraculous feat.

Amazingly, markets coordinate the actions of millions of individuals *without* central planning. There is no individual, political authority, or central planning committee in charge. Considering that there are nearly 300 million Americans with widely varying skills and desires, and roughly 7 million businesses producing a vast array of products ranging from diamond rings to toilet paper, the coordination derived from markets is indeed an awesome achievement.

This chapter focuses on supply, demand, and the determination of market prices. For now, we will analyze the operation of competitive markets—that is, markets with rival sellers (and buyers) without restrictions limiting potential rivals from entering and competing in the market. We will also assume that the property rights to both resources and goods are well defined. Later, we will consider what happens when these conditions are absent.

When you sell a car through a classified newspaper ad, as the seller you have in mind a minimum price you will accept for your car. A potential buyer, on the other hand, has in mind a maximum price he or she will pay for the car. If the potential buyer's

The produce section of your local grocery store is a great place to see economics in action. Literally millions of individuals from around the world have been involved in the process of getting these goods to the shelves in just the right quantities. Market prices underlie this feat.

maximum price is greater than your minimum price, mutual gains from trade are possible. As this simple example shows, the desires and incentives of both buyers and sellers underlie the operation of markets and the determination of prices. We will begin with the demand (buyer's) side, then turn to the supply (seller's) side of the market. ■

CONSUMER CHOICE AND LAW OF DEMAND

Our desire for goods is far greater than our income. Even high-income consumers are unable to purchase everything they would like. We all must make choices as consumers. Seeking as much satisfaction (value) as possible from our limited income, we choose those alternatives that are expected to enhance our welfare the most, relative to their cost. Clearly, prices influence our decisions. As the price of a good increases, we are required to give up more of *other* goods if we buy at the more expensive price. Thus, we might say that as the price of a good rises, its opportunity cost increases (in terms of other goods forgone).

Law of demand
A principle that states there is an inverse relationship between the price of a good and the amount of it buyers are willing to purchase. As the price of a product increases, other things constant, consumers will purchase less of the product.

The basic postulate of economics indicates that if an option becomes more costly people will be less likely to choose it. ***The law of demand** reflects this postulate. The law states that there is an inverse relationship between the price of a good and the quantity of it that consumers are willing to purchase. As higher prices make the good more costly to consumers, they will purchase less of it. At lower prices, a larger quantity will be purchased.*

Substitutes
Products that serve similar purposes. They are related such that an increase in the price of one will cause an increase in demand for the other (for example, hamburgers and tacos, butter and margarine, Chevrolets and Fords).

The availability of substitutes—goods that perform similar functions—underlies the negative relationship between price and quantity purchased. No single good is absolutely essential; each good can be replaced by other goods. A chicken sandwich can be substituted for a cheeseburger. Wood, aluminum, bricks, and glass can take the place of steel. Going to the movies, playing tennis, watching television, and going to a football game are substitute forms of entertainment. When the price of a good increases, people turn to substitute products and economize on their use of the more expensive good. Prices really do matter.

Market Demand Schedule

Exhibit 1 shows a hypothetical demand schedule for cellular telephone service with differing prices and the quantities that consumers would demand at each price.[2] Here, price is measured as the average monthly cost, and quantity demanded is the number of subscribers to cellular phone service. In the table, when the price of cellular phone service is $143 per month, just over 2 million consumers subscribe. As the price falls to $85, the quantity rises to 11 million; when the price falls to $41 per month, the quantity of subscribers increases to just over 69 million.

Exhibit 1 also provides a graphic presentation of the law of demand called the *demand curve*. When representing the demand schedule graphically, economists measure price on the vertical or *y*-axis, and the amount demanded on the horizontal or *x*-axis. Because of the inverse relationship between price and amount purchased, the demand curve will slope downward to the right.

Read horizontally, the demand curve shows how much of a particular good consumers will buy at a given price. Read vertically, the demand curve also reveals important information about consumer preferences—their valuation of goods. *The height of the demand curve at any quantity shows the maximum price that consumers are willing to pay for that additional unit.* If consumers value an additional unit of a product highly, they will be willing to pay a large amount (a high price) for it. Conversely, if their valuation of an additional unit of the good is low, they will be willing to pay only a small amount for it.

---

[2]These data are actual prices (adjusted to 2000 dollars) and quantities annually for 1988 to 1998 taken from *Statistical Abstract of the United States* (Washington, D.C.: U.S. Bureau of the Census, various years). *If we could assume that other demand determinants (income, prices of related goods, etc.) had remained constant,* then this hypothetical demand schedule would be accurate for that time period. Because it is possible that some of these other factors changed, we treat the numbers as hypothetical, depicting alternative prices and quantities *at a given time.*

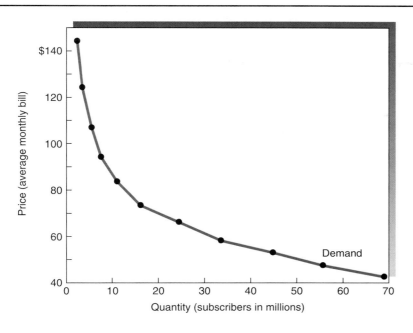

EXHIBIT 1
Law of Demand

As the table indicates, the number of people subscribing to cellular phone service (just like the consumption of other products) is inversely related to price. The data from the table are plotted as a demand schedule in the graph. The inverse relation between price and amount demanded reflects the fact that consumers will substitute away from a good as it becomes more expensive.

CELLULAR PHONE PRICE (AVERAGE MONTHLY BILL)	QUANTITY OF CELLULAR PHONE SUBSCRIBERS (IN MILLIONS)
$143	2.1
124	3.5
107	5.3
92	7.6
85	11.0
73	16.0
65	24.1
58	33.7
53	44.0
46	55.3
41	69.2

Because the amount a consumer is willing to pay for a good is directly related to the good's value to the consumer, the demand curve indicates the marginal benefit consumers receive from additional units. When viewed in this manner, the demand curve reveals that as consumers have more and more of a product, they will value additional units less and less.

Consumer Surplus

Previously, we indicated that voluntary exchange makes both the buyer and seller better off. The demand curve can be used to illustrate the gains of the consumers. Suppose that you value a particular good at $50, but you are able to purchase it for only $30. Your net gain from buying the good is $20. Economists call this net gain of buyers **consumer surplus**. In effect, consumer surplus is the difference between the amount that consumers would be willing to pay and the amount they actually pay for each unit of a good. **Exhibit 2** illustrates the measurement of consumer surplus for an entire market. The height of the demand curve measures how much the various buyers value each unit of the good, while the price indicates the amount they actually pay. The difference between these two—the area under the demand curve but above the price paid—is a measure of the total consumer surplus generated in the market. The size of the consumer surplus is affected by the market price. A reduction in the market price will lead to an expansion in quantity purchased and a larger

Consumer surplus
The difference between the maximum price consumers are willing to pay and the price they actually pay. It is the net gain derived by the buyers of the good.

EXHIBIT 2
Consumer Surplus

Consumer surplus is the area below the demand curve but above the actual price paid (P_1). This area represents the net gains to buyers from market exchange.

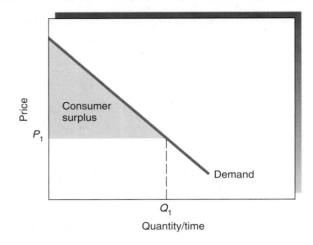

consumer surplus. Conversely, a higher market price will reduce the amount purchased and shrink the surplus (net gain) of consumers.

In aggregate, the total value (the entire area under the demand curve) to consumers of the units purchased may be far greater than the amount they pay. When additional units are available at a low price, the marginal value of a good may be quite low, even though its total value to consumers is exceedingly high. For example, this is generally the case with water. Of course, water is essential for life and the value derived from the first few units consumed per day will be exceedingly high. The consumer surplus derived from these units will also be large when water is plentifully available at a low price. As more and more units are consumed, however, the *marginal value* of even something as important as water will fall to a low level. Thus, when water is cheap, people will use it not only for drinking, cleaning, and cooking, but also for washing cars, watering lawns, flushing toilets, and keeping fish aquariums. While consumers will tend to expand consumption until price and *marginal value* are equal, price reveals little about the *total value* derived from the consumption of a good.

Responsiveness of Quantity Demanded to Price: Elastic and Inelastic Demand Curves

As we previously noted, the availability of substitutes is the main reason why the demand curve for a good slopes downward. Some goods, however, are much easier to substitute away from than others. As the price of tacos rises, most consumers find hamburgers a reasonable substitute. Because of the ease of substitutability, the quantity demanded of tacos is quite sensitive to a change in their price. Economists would say that the demand for tacos is relatively *elastic* because a small price change will cause a rather large change in the amount purchased. Alternatively, such goods as gasoline and electricity have fewer good substitutes. When their prices rise, it is harder for consumers to easily substitute away from these products. When good substitutes are unavailable, even a large price change may not cause much of a change in the quantity demanded. Economists would say that the demand for such goods is relatively *inelastic*.

Graphically, this different degree of responsiveness is reflected in the steepness of the demand curve, as is shown in **Exhibit 3**. The flatter demand curve (D_1, left frame) is for a product—tacos—for which the quantity demanded is highly responsive to a change in price. As the price increases from $1.25 to $2.00, the quantity demanded falls sharply from 10 to 4 units. The steeper demand curve (D_2, right frame) is for a product—gasoline—where the quantity purchased is much less responsive to a change in price. For gasoline, an increase in

EXHIBIT 3
Elastic and Inelastic Demand Curves

The responsiveness of consumer purchases to a change in price is reflected in the steepness of the demand curve. The flatter demand curve (D_1) for tacos shows a higher degree of responsiveness and is called relatively elastic, while the steeper demand curve (D_2) for gasoline shows a lower degree of responsiveness and is called relatively inelastic.

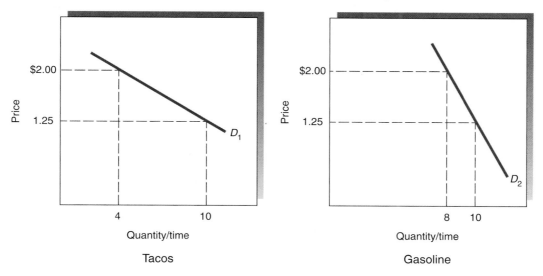

Tacos   Gasoline

price from $1.25 to $2.00 results in only a small reduction in the quantity purchased (from 10 to 8). An economist would say that the flatter demand curve D_1 was relatively elastic, while the steeper demand curve D_2 was relatively inelastic. The availability of substitutes is the main determinant of whether the demand curve is relatively elastic or inelastic.

What would a demand curve that was perfectly vertical represent? Economists refer to this as a perfectly inelastic demand curve, and it would represent a situation in which the quantity demanded was the same regardless of the price of the good. While it is tempting to think that the demand curves are vertical for goods considered to be essential to human life (or goods that are addictive), this is inaccurate for two reasons. First, we live in a world of substitutes. In varying degrees, there are substitutes for everything, and as the price of a good rises the incentive for suppliers to invent even more new substitutes increases. Thus, even for goods that currently have few substitutes, if the price were to rise high enough alternatives would be invented and marketed causing a reduction in the quantity demanded of the original good. The second reason why demand curves are unlikely to be vertical is that scarcity and limited income restrict our ability to afford goods as they become very expensive. As the price of a good rises to high levels we begin to forgo many things that we "need"—or at least think we need. In affluent countries, families are thought to need at least one bathroom with hot and cold running water, a sink, a toilet, and a bathtub or shower. Yet the typical family in many poorer countries would perceive such a bathroom to be a luxury.

CHANGES IN DEMAND VERSUS CHANGES IN QUANTITY DEMANDED

The demand curve isolates the impact of price on the amount of a product purchased. Economists refer to a change in the quantity of a good purchased that occurs in response to a price change as a "change in *quantity demanded*." A change in quantity demanded is a movement along a demand curve from one point to another. Changes in factors like income and the prices of closely related goods will also influence the decision of consumers.

If one of these other factors changes, the entire demand curve will shift inwards or outwards. Economists refer to such shifts in the demand curve as a "change in *demand*."

Failure to distinguish between a change in demand and a change in quantity demanded is one of the most common mistakes made by beginning economics students.[3] *A change in demand is a shift in the entire demand curve. A change in quantity demanded is a movement along the same demand curve in response to a price change.* In essence, if the change in the amount purchased is due to a change in the price of the good, it is a change in quantity demanded. Alternatively, when the change in the amount purchased is due to *anything other than price* (a change in consumer income, for example), it is a change in demand. When we put supply and demand together later in this chapter, the distinction between a change in demand and a change in quantity demanded will become more clear visually. Let us now take a closer look at some of the factors that cause a change in demand—an inward or outward shift in the entire demand curve.

1. Changes in consumer income.

An increase in consumer income makes it possible for consumers to purchase more goods. If you were to win the lottery, or if your boss were to give you a raise, you would respond by increasing your spending on many products. Alternatively, if the economy were to go into a recession, falling incomes and rising unemployment would cause consumers to reduce their purchases of many items. A change in consumer income will result in consumers buying more or less of a product *at all possible prices for the product.* When consumer income increases, individuals will generally purchase more of a good. This is shown by a shift to the right (or an outward shift) in the demand curve. Such a shift is called an increase in demand. A reduction in consumer income generally causes a shift to the left (or an inward shift) in the demand curve, which would be called a decrease in demand.

Exhibit 4 highlights the difference between a change in demand and a change in quantity demanded. The demand curve D_1 indicates the initial demand curve for compact discs. At a price of $30, consumers would purchase Q_1 units. If the price declined to $10, there would be an increase in *quantity demanded* from Q_1 to Q_3. Arrow A indicates the change in *quantity demanded*—a movement along the original demand curve D_1. Now, alternatively suppose that there is an increase in consumer income. The *demand* for compact discs would increase from D_1 to D_2. As indicated by the B arrows, the entire demand curve would shift. At the higher income level, consumers would be willing to purchase more compact discs

---

EXHIBIT 4
Change in Demand Versus Change in Quantity Demanded

Arrow *A* indicates a change in *quantity demanded*, a movement along the demand curve D_1, in response to a change in the price of compact discs. The *B* arrows illustrate a change in *demand*, a shift of the entire curve, in this case due to an increase in consumer income.

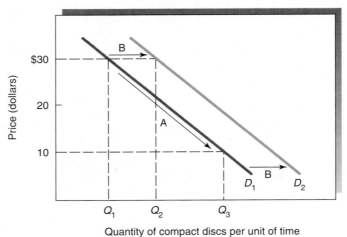

Quantity of compact discs per unit of time

---

[3]Questions designed to test the ability of students to make this distinction are favorites of many economics instructors. A word to the wise should be sufficient.

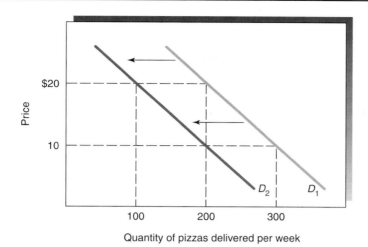

than before. This is true at a price of $30, at $20, at $10, and at every other price. The increase in income leads to an increase in *demand*—a shift in the entire curve. Alternatively, a decrease in consumer income would have led to a decrease in demand—the demand curve would have shifted in the opposite direction (for example, from D_2 inward to D_1).

2. Changes in the number of consumers in the market.

Businesses that sell products in college towns are greatly saddened when summer arrives. As you might expect, the demand for many items—from pizza delivery to beer—falls during the summer. **Exhibit 5** shows how the falling number of consumers in the market caused by students going home for the summer affects the demand for pizza delivery. With fewer customers, the demand curve shifts inward from D_1 to D_2. There is a decrease in demand; pizza stores will sell fewer pizzas than before regardless of what price they were originally charging. Had their original price been $20, then demand would have fallen from 200 pizzas per week to only 100. Alternatively, had their original price been $10, then demand would have fallen from 300 pizzas to 200. When fall arrives and the students come back to town, there will be an increase in demand, restoring the curve to near its original position. As cities grow and shrink, and as international markets open for domestic firms, changes in the number of consumers have an effect on the demand curves for many products.

3. Changes in the price of a related good.

Changes in prices of closely related products also influence the choices of consumers. Related goods may be either substitutes or complements. When two products perform similar functions or fulfill similar needs, they are generally *substitutes*. Economists define goods as substitutes when there is a direct relationship between the price of one and the demand for the other (an increase in the price of one increases demand for the other). For example, margarine is a substitute for butter. If the price of butter rises, it will increase the demand for margarine as consumers substitute margarine for the more expensive butter. Similarly, lower butter prices would reduce the demand for margarine, shifting the entire curve to the left. A substitute relationship exists between beef and chicken, pencils and pens, apples and oranges, coffee and tea, and so forth.

Other closely related products are consumed jointly, so the demands for them are linked together in a positive way. Examples of goods that "go together," so to speak, could be jelly and peanut butter, CDs and CD players, or tents and other camping equipment. For these combinations of goods, called **complements**, a decrease in the price of one will not only increase its quantity demanded, it will also increase the demand for the other. With complements, there is an inverse relationship between the price of one and the demand for the other. For example, lower prices for DVD players during the 1990s increased the demand for DVD movie discs. Similarly, if hamburger is on sale this week at

Complements
Products that are usually consumed jointly (for example, peanut butter and jelly). They are related such that a decrease in the price of one will cause an increase in demand for the other.

the grocery store, the store can also expect to sell more hamburger buns, even if the price of buns is unchanged.

4. Changes in expectations.

Consumers' expectations about the future also can affect the current demand for a product. If consumers begin to expect that a major hurricane will strike their area, the current demand for such goods as batteries and canned food will rise. Expectations about the future direction of the economy can also affect current demand. If consumers become pessimistic about the economy, they might start spending less, causing the current demand for goods to fall. Of perhaps most importance is how a change in the expected future price of a good affects the current demand. When consumers expect the future price of a product to rise, their current demand for it will increase. "Buy now, before the price goes up." On the other hand, consumers will delay a purchase if they expect the item to decrease in price. No doubt you have heard someone say, "I'll wait until it goes on sale." When consumers expect the price to be lower in the near future, they will reduce their current demand for the product.

5. Demographic changes.

The demand for many products is strongly influenced by the demographic composition of the market. An increase in the size of the elderly population during the past decade increased the demand for medical care, retirement housing, and vacation travel, shifting the demand for these goods to the right. During the 1980s, population in the 15–24 age grouping fell by more than 5 million. Because young people are a major part of the U.S. market for jeans, the demand for jeans declined. Sales, which had topped 500 million pairs in 1980, fell to less than 400 million pairs in 1989.[4] Luckily for jeans producers, this trend leveled off in the 1990s.

6. Changes in consumer tastes and preferences.

Why do preferences change? Preferences change because people learn and change. Consider how consumers responded to new medical information linking certain fats and oils to heart disease. They purchased less of such products as whole milk, butter, and beef, which were thought to be dangerous, and increased their demand for such goods as olive oil and canola oil, thought to be much more "heart-healthy." As consumers became more aware of the health implications of their diet, their preferences changed, shifting the demand for various foods. Trends in clothing, toys, collectibles, and in the types of leisure activities that are popular cause continuous changes in the demand for products. Firms may even try to increase the demand for their own products through advertising and information brochures targeted at changing consumer tastes.

THUMBNAIL SKETCH

Factors That Cause Changes in Demand and Quantity Demanded

This factor increases (decreases) the quantity demanded of a good:

1. A decrease (increase) in the price of the good

These factors increase (decrease) the demand for a good:

1. A rise (fall) in consumer income
2. An increase (decline) in the number of consumers in the market

3a. A rise (fall) in the price of a substitute good
3b. A fall (rise) in the price of a complementary good
4. A rise (fall) in the expected future price of the good
5. Demographic changes: Population increases (decreases) in age groups with strong demand for a good
6. Preferences: Increased (reduced) consumer desires for the good

---

[4]These figures are from Suzanne Tregarthen, "Market for Jeans Shrinks," *The Margin* 6, no. 3 (January–February 1991), p. 28.

The **Thumbnail Sketch** summarizes the major factors that cause a change in *demand*—a shift of the entire demand curve—and points out that *quantity demanded* (but not demand) will change in response to a change in the price of a good.

PRODUCER CHOICE AND LAW OF SUPPLY

We have now completed the examination of demand and will shift our focus to the supply side of the market. How does the market process determine the amount of each good that will be produced and supplied? We cannot answer this question properly unless we understand the factors that influence the choices of those who supply goods, the producers of goods and services. Often using the business firm, producers:

1. organize productive inputs and resources, such as land, labor, capital, natural resources, and intermediate goods;

2. transform and combine these factors of production into goods and services; and

3. sell the final products to consumers for a price.

Production involves the conversion of resources into commodities and services. Producers will have to purchase the necessary resources at prices that are determined by market forces. Predictably, owners will only supply resources at prices that are at least equal to what they could earn elsewhere. Stated another way, each resource employed has to be bid away from all other uses; its owner will have to be paid its opportunity cost. *The sum of the producer's cost of employing each resource required to produce the good will equal the product's* opportunity cost of production.

There is an important difference between the opportunity cost of production and standard accounting measures of a firm's cost. Accountants generally do not count the cost of such assets as buildings, equipment, and financial resources *owned by the firm*. These assets have alternative uses and, therefore, costs are incurred when they are used to produce a good. Unless these costs are covered, the resources will eventually be employed in other ways. For now, it is sufficient to think of this cost of employing assets owned by the firm as a normal return (or "normal profit rate") that these assets could earn if employed in another way. For example, the millions of dollars worth of capital, buildings, and equipment held by a shirt manufacturer could also be used in other ways. For one thing, the firm's operating funds could be drawing interest at a bank. If the interest rate was 10 percent, a firm with $100,000 worth of operating capital could place these funds in a bank (or mutual fund) and earn $10,000 in interest income per year. This income forgone because the funds are tied up running the business is an opportunity cost.

Firms will not remain in business for long unless they are able to cover the cost of all resources employed, including the opportunity cost of resources owned by the firm. Typically, economists will use some measure of an average or normal rate of return as an indicator of the employment cost of assets owned by the firm.

Opportunity cost of production
The total economic cost of producing a good or service. The cost component includes the opportunity cost of all resources, including those owned by the firm. The opportunity cost is equal to the value of the production of other goods sacrificed as the result of producing the good.

Role of Profits and Losses

 Profits direct producers toward activities that increase the value of resources; losses impose a penalty on those who reduce the value of resources.

Profits and Losses

Business decision makers have a strong incentive to undertake activities that generate revenues greater than cost. If an activity is to be profitable, the revenue derived from the sale of the product must exceed the cost of employing the resources required for its production. The opportunity cost of producing a good indicates the value of other goods that might have been produced with the same resources. For example, if the opportunity cost of producing a pair of jeans is $30, this means that the resources used to produce the jeans could have been used to produce other items worth $30 to consumers (perhaps a denim backpack). If consumers are willing to pay more than $30 for the jeans, producing them increases the value of the resources.

Profit

An excess of sales revenue relative to the opportunity cost of production. The cost component includes the opportunity cost of all resources, including those owned by the firm. Therefore, profit accrues only when the value of the good produced is greater than the value of other goods that could have been produced with those same resources.

Loss

Deficit of sales revenue relative to the opportunity cost of production. Losses are a penalty imposed on those who misuse resources in lower-valued uses as judged by buyers in the market.

Firms that use resources to supply goods and services for which consumers are willing to pay more than the opportunity cost of the resources will make a profit. The willingness of consumers to pay a price greater than a good's opportunity cost indicates that they value the good more than other things that could have been produced with the same resources. Viewed from this perspective, profit is a residual "income reward" earned by entrepreneurs who use resources to produce goods consumers value more highly than other goods those resources might have been used to produce. In essence this profit is a signal that an entrepreneur has increased the value of the resources under his or her control.

Sometimes decision makers use resources unwisely. When resources are employed to produce a good or service that has less value to consumers than other things that might have been produced, losses are incurred. Loss results because the sales revenue derived from the project is insufficient to cover the opportunity cost of the resources. Losses indicate that the firm has reduced the value of the resources. It would have been better if the resources had been used to produce other things. In a market economy, losses will eventually cause firms to go out of business and the resources will be directed toward other things that are valued more highly.

Profits and losses play a very important role in a market economy. They determine which firms and products will expand and survive, and which will contract and be driven from the market. In 1998, more than 155,000 new businesses started in the United States. During the same year, more than 71,000 businesses failed. Although the business failure rate was only 76 out of every 10,000 firms, many more firms incurred losses. Some were taken over by new owners. Marketing studies indicate that only about 55 to 65 percent of the new products introduced are still on the market five years later. Firms come and go at a rapid rate. In the wave of dot-com failures in 2000, at least 210 Internet companies shut their doors.[5] Business failures are not necessarily bad. To the contrary—as our preceding discussion highlights, losses and business failures free up resources that are being used unwisely so they may flow toward productive activities that are more highly valued.

Losses are capable of disciplining even the largest of firms. After 129 years in business, including many years as the second largest retailer in America, Montgomery Ward department stores went out of business in 2001 because it failed to adapt to changing market conditions. There are also famous examples of major, established firms suffering losses when they attempted to introduce new products that did not match consumer desires. Some of these include the introduction of "New Coke" by Coca-Cola in 1985, the Cadillac Allanté by General Motors in 1987, the McArch Deluxe by McDonald's in 1996, and the XFL professional football league started by the WWF and NBC in 2001. In each of these cases, the firms suffered losses on these products and eventually withdrew them from the market.

Supply and the Entrepreneur

Entrepreneurs undertake production organization, deciding what to produce and how to produce it. The business of the entrepreneur is to figure out which projects will be profitable, and then to convince a corporation, a banker, or individual investors to invest the resources needed to give the new idea a chance. Since the profitability of a project is affected by the price consumers are willing to pay for a product, the price of resources required to produce it, and the cost of alternative production processes, successful entrepreneurs must either be knowledgeable in each of these areas or be able to obtain the advice of others who have such knowledge. Being an entrepreneur means taking on the risk of failure.

---

[5]See Robert E. Litan and Alice M. Rivlin, *Beyond the Dot.Coms: The Economic Promise of the Internet* (Washington, D.C.: Brookings Institute and Internet Policy Institute, 2001) for a discussion of the dot-com failures and the overall economic impact of the Internet.

To prosper, business entrepreneurs must convert and rearrange resources in a manner that will increase their value. An individual who purchases 100 acres of raw land, puts in a street and a sewage-disposal system, divides the plot into one-acre lots, and sells them for 50 percent more than the opportunity cost of all resources used is clearly an entrepreneur. This entrepreneur "profits" because the value of the resources has been increased. Sometimes entrepreneurial activity is less complex. For example, a 15-year-old who purchases a power mower and sells lawn service to the neighbors is also an entrepreneur seeking to profit by increasing the value of resources—his time and equipment. In a market economy, profit is the reward to the entrepreneur who discovers and acts upon an opportunity to produce a good or service that is valued more highly than the resources required for its production. Profit also creates an incentive for rival entrepreneurs to enter the market and further expand the production of the good for consumers.

Market Supply Schedule

How will producer-entrepreneurs respond to a change in product price? Other things constant, a higher price will increase the producer's incentive to supply the good. New entrepreneurs, seeking personal gain, will enter the market and begin supplying the product. Established producers will expand the scale of their operations, leading to an additional expansion in output. Higher prices will induce producers to supply a greater amount. *The law of supply states that there is a direct relationship between the price of a product and the amount of it that will be supplied. As the price of a product increases, producers will be willing to supply more. Correspondingly they will supply less, if the price declines.*

Like the law of demand, the law of supply reflects the basic economic postulate that incentives matter. Higher prices increase the reward entrepreneurs receive from selling their product. When it becomes more profitable, they will be willing to supply more. Conversely, as the price of the good falls, so does the profitability, and thus the incentive to supply the good. Just think about how many hours of tutoring services you would supply for different prices. Would you be willing to supply more hours of work at a wage of $50 per hour than at $5 per hour? The law of supply suggests that you would, and producers of other goods and services are no different.

Exhibit 6 provides a graphic presentation of the law of supply called the *supply curve*. Because of the direct relationship between price and the amount offered for sale by suppliers, the supply curve will slope upward to the right. Read horizontally, the supply curve shows how much of a particular good producers are willing to produce and sell at a given price. Read vertically, the supply curve reveals important information about the cost of production. *The height of the supply curve indicates both (1) the minimum price necessary to induce producers to supply that additional unit and (2) the opportunity cost of*

Law of supply
A principle that states there is a direct relationship between the price of a good and the amount of it offered for sale. As the price of a product increases, other things constant, producers will increase the amount of the product supplied to the market.

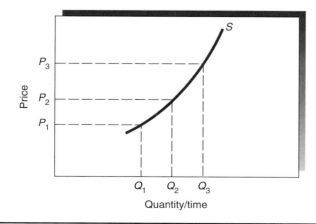

EXHIBIT 6
Supply Curve

As the price of a product increases, other things constant, producers will increase the amount of the product supplied to the market.

producing the additional unit of the good. These are both measured by the height because the minimum price required to induce a supplier to sell a unit is precisely the marginal cost of producing it. Just as the demand curve can also be used as a marginal benefit curve, the supply curve can also be used as a marginal cost curve.

Producer Surplus

Producer surplus
The difference between the minimum supply price and the actual sales price. It measures the net gains to producers and resource suppliers from market trade. It is not the same as profit.

We previously used the demand curve to illustrate consumer surplus, the net gains of buyers from market exchange. The supply curve can be used in a similar manner to derive the net gains of producers and resource suppliers. Suppose that you are an aspiring musician and that you would be willing to perform a two-hour concert for $100. If a promoter offers to pay you $150 to perform the concert, you will accept, and receive $50 more than your minimum price. This $50 net gain represents your **producer surplus**. In effect, producer surplus is the difference between the amount a supplier actually receives (based on the market price) and the minimum price required to induce the supplier to produce the given units (their marginal cost). The measurement of producer surplus for an entire market is illustrated by the shaded area of **Exhibit 7**.

It is important to note that producer surplus represents the gains that accrue to all parties that contribute resources used to produce the good. Producer surplus is fundamentally different from profit. Remember, profit is a return that accrues to the owners of the firm when sales revenues exceed the *total* cost of production. The supply curve reflects *marginal* costs (not total or average) of producing various quantities. As production of a good is expanded, the prices of the resources required to produce the good may rise. If so, the rising resource prices generate gains for resource suppliers and these gains are an integral part of producer surplus. In contrast, the higher resource prices increase the costs of firms producing the good, and thereby reduce their profit. Profit accrues to the owners of the firm, while producer surplus encompasses the net gains derived by all resource owners that help to produce the good, including those employed by or selling resources to the firm.

Responsiveness of Quantity Supplied to Price: Elastic and Inelastic Supply Curves

As in the case of demand, the responsiveness of quantity supplied to a change in price will differ among goods. The supply curve is said to be elastic when a modest change in price leads to a large change in quantity supplied. This is generally true when the additional resources needed to expand output can be obtained with only a small increase in their price. Consider the supply of soft drinks. The contents of soft drinks—primarily carbonated water, sugar, and flavoring—are abundantly available and a sharp increase in the use of

EXHIBIT 7
Producer Surplus

Producer surplus is the area above the supply curve but below the actual sales price (P_1). This area represents the net gains to producers and resource suppliers from production and exchange.

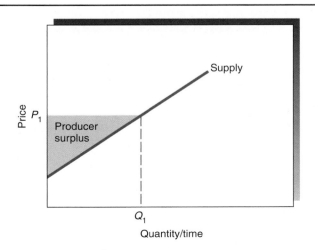

these ingredients by soft drink producers is unlikely to push their price up much. Therefore, as **Exhibit 8** illustrates, if the price of soft drinks rose from $1 to $1.50, producers would be willing to expand output sharply from 100 million to 200 million cans per month. A 50 percent increase in price leads to a 100 percent expansion in quantity supplied. The larger the increase in quantity in response to a higher price, the more elastic the supply curve. The flatness of the supply curve for soft drinks reflects the fact that it is highly elastic.

In contrast, when quantity supplied is not very responsive to a change in price, supply is said to be inelastic. Physician services provide an example. If the earnings of doctors increase from $100 to $150 per hour, there will be some increase in quantity of the services provided. Some physicians will work longer hours; others may delay retirement. These adjustments, however, are likely to result in only a small increase in quantity supplied. It takes a long time to train a physician and the number of qualified doctors who are doing other things or who are outside of the labor force is small. Therefore, as Exhibit 8 (right frame) shows, a 50 percent increase in the price of physician services leads to only a 20 percent expansion in quantity supplied. Unlike soft drinks, higher prices for physician services do not generate much increase in quantity supplied. Economists would say that the demand for physician services is inelastic.

The responsiveness of supply to a change in price is affected by time. The great English economist Alfred Marshall introduced the concepts of *short run* and *long run* in order

EXHIBIT 8
Elastic and Inelastic Supply Curves

Frame (a) illustrates a supply curve that is relatively elastic and therefore the quantity supplied is highly responsive to a change in price. Soft drinks provide an example. Frame (b) illustrates a relatively inelastic supply curve, one where the quantity supplied increases by only a small amount in response to a change in price. This is the case for physician services.

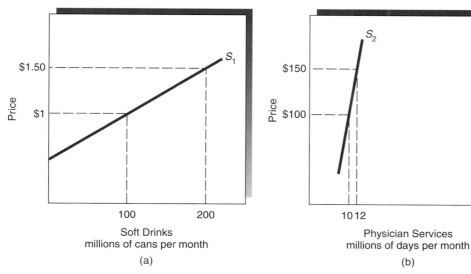

Short run
A time period of insufficient length to permit decision makers to adjust fully to a change in market conditions. For example, in the short run, producers will have time to increase output by using more labor and raw materials, but they will not have time to expand the size of their plants or to install additional heavy equipment.

Long run
A time period of sufficient length to enable decision makers to adjust fully to a market change.

to highlight this point. In the **short run**, firms do not have enough time to build a new plant or expand the size of their current one. Producers are stuck with their existing facility in the short run; they can increase output only by using that facility more intensely. As a result, the immediate supply response to a price change will be limited. Thus, the supply curve for many goods will be relatively inelastic (like the right frame of Exhibit 8) in the short run.

The **long run** is a time period lengthy enough for existing firms to alter the size of their plant and for new firms to enter (or exit) the market. Predictably, the change in quantity supplied in response to a change in the price of a good will be greater in the long run than in the short run. Compared to the short run, the supply curve in the long run will be much more elastic (like the left frame of Exhibit 8).

CHANGES IN SUPPLY VERSUS CHANGES IN QUANTITY SUPPLIED

As with demand, it is important to distinguish between a change in *quantity supplied* and a change in *supply*. When sellers alter the number of units supplied in response to a change in price, this movement along the same supply curve is referred to as a "change in *quantity supplied.* "

As we previously discussed, profit-seeking entrepreneurs will produce a good only if the sales price of the good is expected to exceed its opportunity cost. Therefore, changes that affect the opportunity cost of supplying a good will also influence the amount of it that producers are willing to supply. These "other factors," such as the price of resources and level of technology, are held constant when drawing a supply curve. Changes in these other factors that influence the opportunity cost of providing the product will shift the entire supply curve for the good. This shift in the entire supply curve is referred to as a "change in *supply.*" Factors that increase the opportunity cost of providing a good will discourage production and decrease supply (shift the entire curve inward to the left). Similarly, changes that decrease the opportunity cost of producers will increase supply (shift the entire curve outward to the right).

Let us now take a closer look at the primary factors that will cause a change in supply, a shift in the entire curve to either the right or the left.

1. Changes in resource prices.
How will an increase in the price of a resource, such as the wages of workers or the materials used to produce a product, affect the supply of the good? There are two ways to view the effects of changing resource prices. First, higher resource prices will increase the cost of production, reducing the profitability of firms buying the resources to supply the good. The higher cost will induce firms to cut back their output. With time, some may

EXHIBIT 9
A Decrease in Supply

Crude oil is a resource used to produce gasoline. When the price of crude oil rises, it increases the cost of producing gasoline and results in a decrease in the supply of gasoline.

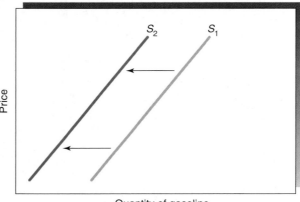

even be driven out of business. As **Exhibit 9** illustrates, the higher resource prices and increased opportunity cost will reduce the supply of the good, causing a shift to the left in the supply curve from S_1 to S_2. A second way to view the effect of a change in resource prices is to remember that the height of the supply curve measures the marginal cost of production. Thus higher production costs can be thought of as shifting the supply curve upward, showing that the cost of producing each and every unit has now gone up. We would encourage you, however, to think of an increase in supply as a shift to the right and a decrease as a shift to the left. When remembered this way, decreases in both supply and demand are shown by a shift to the left, while increases in both are shifts to the right.

Suppose that the price of a resource used to produce a good falls. How will this affect the supply of the good? Lower resource prices will reduce the cost of producing the good. Suppliers will respond with a larger output, causing the supply curve to shift outward to the right.

2. Changes in technology.

Like lower resource prices, technological improvements—the discovery of new, lower-cost production techniques—reduce production costs, and thereby increase supply (shift the curve to the right). Technological advances have in fact affected the cost of almost everything. Before the invention of the printing press, books had to be handwritten. Just imagine the massive reduction in cost and increase in the supply of books caused by this single invention. Technologically improved farm machinery has reduced cost and vastly expanded the supply of agricultural products through the years. Technological improvements in the production of computer chips have drastically reduced the cost of producing such electronic products as calculators, DVD players, cell phones, and compact disc players. Robotics have reduced the cost of airplanes, automobiles, and several other types of machinery.

3. Elements of nature and political disruptions.

Natural disasters and changing political conditions may also alter supply, sometimes dramatically. During some years, highly favorable weather can lead to higher yields and "bumper crops," increasing the supply of various agricultural products. At other times, droughts may reduce yields, reducing supply. War and political unrest in the Middle East region have exerted a major impact on the supply of oil several times during the past few decades. Such factors as these will reduce supply.

4. Changes in taxes.

If the government increases the taxes on the sellers of a product, the result will be the same as any other increase in the cost of doing business. The added tax to be paid by sellers will reduce their willingness to sell at any given price. At each price, only those units for which the price covers all opportunity costs, including the tax, will be offered for sale. For example, the Superfund law placed a special tax on petroleum producers based on petroleum output (not on the producer's past or present pollution level). That raised the cost of producing petroleum products, decreasing the supply of those products.

5. Changes in the number of firms in the market.

With the passage of time, it is possible for new firms to enter an industry and for existing firms to leave the industry. Predictably, entry will tend to occur in industries that have higher than average profit rates, while exit will tend to occur in industries suffering below average profit rates (or losses). Other things constant, an expansion in the number of firms in the market will cause an increase in supply, while a reduction in the number of firms in the market will cause a decrease in supply.

The accompanying **Thumbnail Sketch** summarizes the major factors that cause a change in *supply*—a shift of the entire supply curve—and points out that *quantity supplied* (but not supply) will change in response to a change in the price of a good.

THUMBNAIL SKETCH

Factors That Cause Changes in Supply and Quantity Supplied

This factor increases (decreases) the quantity supplied of a good:

1. An increase (decrease) in the price of the good

These factors increase (decrease) the supply of a good:

1. A fall (rise) in the price of a resource used in producing the good

2. A technological change allowing cheaper production of the good

3. Favorable weather (bad weather or a disruption in supply due to political factors or war)

4. A reduction (increase) in the taxes imposed on the producers of the good

5. An increase (decline) in the number of firms in the market

HOW MARKET PRICES ARE DETERMINED: SUPPLY AND DEMAND INTERACT

Market
An abstract concept that encompasses the trading arrangements of buyers and sellers that underlie the forces of supply and demand.

Consumer-buyers and producer-sellers make decisions independent of each other, but markets coordinate their choices and influence their actions. To the economist, a **market** is not a physical location, but an abstract concept that encompasses the forces generated by the buying and selling decisions of economic participants. A market may be quite narrow (for example, the market for grade A jumbo eggs), or it may be quite broad when it is useful to aggregate diverse goods into a single market, such as the market for all "consumer goods." There is also a wide range of sophistication among markets. The New York Stock Exchange is a highly computerized market in which, each weekday, buyers and sellers, who seldom formally meet, exchange shares of corporate ownership worth billions of dollars. In contrast, the neighborhood market for lawn-mowing services, or tutoring in economics, may be highly informal, since it brings together buyers and sellers primarily by word of mouth.

Equilibrium
A state of balance between conflicting forces, such as supply and demand.

*Equilibrium **is a state in which conflicting forces are in balance. When a market is in equilibrium, the decisions of consumers and producers are brought into harmony with one another. In equilibrium, it will be possible for both buyers and sellers to realize their choices simultaneously.*** What could bring these diverse interests into harmony? We will see the answer is market prices.

Market Equilibrium

As Exhibit 1 illustrates, a higher price will reduce the amount of a good demanded by consumers. On the other hand, Exhibit 6 shows that a higher price will increase the amount of a good supplied by producers. The market price of a commodity will tend to change in a direction that will bring into balance the quantity of a good desired by consumers with the quantity supplied by producers. That is, price will tend to move toward equilibrium. If the price is too high, the quantity supplied will exceed the quantity demanded. Producers will be unable to sell as much as they would like unless they reduce their price. Alternatively, if the price is too low, the quantity demanded will exceed the quantity supplied. Some consumers will be unable to get as much as they would like, unless they are willing to pay a higher price. Thus, there will be a tendency for the price in a market to move toward the price that brings the quantity demanded by consumers into balance with the quantity supplied by producers.

Exhibit 10 illustrates supply and demand curves in the market for a basic calculator. At a high price—$12, for example—producers will plan to supply 600 calculators per day, whereas consumers will choose to purchase only 450. An excess supply of 150 calculators (distance *ab* in the graph) will result. Production exceeds sales, pushing the inventories of

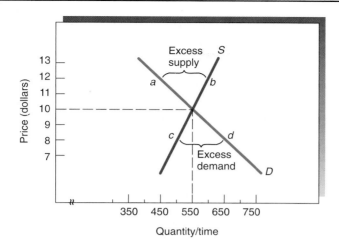

EXHIBIT 10
Supply and Demand

The table indicates the supply and demand conditions for calculators. These conditions are also illustrated by the graph. When the price exceeds $10, an excess supply is present, which places downward pressure on price. In contrast, when the price is less than $10, an excess demand results, which causes the price to rise. Thus, the market price will tend toward $10, at which point supply and demand will be in balance.

PRICE OF CALCULATORS (DOLLARS)	QUANTITY SUPPLIED (PER DAY)	QUANTITY DEMANDED (PER DAY)	CONDITION IN THE MARKET	DIRECTION OF PRESSURE ON PRICE
13	625	400	Excess supply	Downward
12	600	450	Excess supply	Downward
11	575	500	Excess supply	Downward
10	550	550	Balance	Equilibrium
9	525	600	Excess demand	Upward
8	500	650	Excess demand	Upward
7	475	700	Excess demand	Upward

producers upward. To reduce undesired inventories, some producers will cut their price in order to increase their sales. Other firms will have to lower their price also, or sell even fewer calculators. The lower price will make production less attractive to producers. Some producers may go out of business, while others will reduce their output. How low will the price go? When it has declined to $10, the quantity supplied by producers and the quantity demanded by consumers will be in balance at 550 calculators per day. At this price ($10), the choices of buyers and sellers are brought into harmony. The amount that producers are willing to supply just equals the amount that consumers want to purchase.

What will happen if the price per calculator is lower—$8, for example? The amount demanded by consumers (650 units) will exceed the amount supplied by producers (500 units). An excess demand of 150 units (*cd* in the graph) will be present. Some consumers who are unable to purchase the calculators at $8 per unit because of the inadequate supply would be willing to pay a higher price. Recognizing this fact, producers will raise their price. As the price increases to $10, producers will expand their output and consumers will cut down on their consumption. At the $10 price, equilibrium will be restored.

People have a tendency to think of consumers wanting lower prices and producers wanting higher prices. Although true, price changes frequently work in exactly the opposite direction. When a local store has an excess supply of a particular item, how does it get rid of it? By having a sale or somehow otherwise lowering its price (a "blue-light special"). Firms often lower their prices in order to get rid of excess supply. On the other hand, excess demand is solved by consumers bidding up prices. Children's toys around Christmas provide a perfect example. When first introduced, Sony Play Station 2, Furby, the Tickle-Me-Elmo stuffed Muppet, and Teletubbie dolls were immediate successes. The firms producing these products had not anticipated the overwhelming demand. Soon every child wanted one for Christmas. Some stores raised their prices, but the demand was so strong that lines of parents were forming outside stores before they even opened. Often, only the first few in line were able to get the toys (a sure sign that the store had set the price below equilibrium). Out in the parking lots, in the classified ads, and on eBay, parents were offering up to $100 or more for these items. If stores were not going to set the prices right, parents in these informal markets would. These examples show that rising prices are often the result of consumers bidding up prices when excess demand is present. A similar phenomenon can be seen in the market for Ty Beanie Babies as their immediate value on the resale market can be much higher than the original retail price if, at that price, the original quantity supplied is not adequate to meet the quantity demanded.

Efficiency and Market Equilibrium

Economic efficiency
A market meets the criterion of economic efficiency if all the gains from trade have been realized. An action is consistent with efficiency only if it creates more benefits than costs. With well-defined property rights and competition, market equilibrium is efficient.

When a market reaches equilibrium all the gains from trade have been fully realized; **economic efficiency** is present. This criterion is important because economists often use it as a standard with which to judge outcomes under alternative circumstances. The central idea of efficiency is a cost versus benefit comparison. Undertaking an economic action will be efficient only if it generates more total benefits than the total costs. On the other hand, undertaking an action that generates more costs than benefits is inefficient. For a market to satisfy the criterion of economic efficiency, all trades that generate more benefits than costs need to be undertaken. In addition, economic efficiency requires that no trades creating more costs than benefits be undertaken.

A closer look at the way in which markets work can help us to understand the concept of efficiency. The supply curve reflects producers' opportunity costs. Each point along the supply curve indicates the minimum price for which the units of a good could be produced without a loss to the seller. Assuming no other third parties are affected by the production of this good, then the height of the supply curve represents the opportunity cost to society of producing and selling the good. On the other side of the market, each point along the demand curve indicates the consumer's valuation of an extra unit of the good—the maximum amount the consumer is willing to pay for the extra unit. Again assuming that no other third parties are affected, the height of the demand curve represents the benefit to society of producing and selling the good. Any time the consumer's valuation of a unit (the benefit side) exceeds the producer's minimum supply price (the cost side), producing and selling the unit is consistent with economic efficiency. The trade will result in mutual gain to both parties. When property rights are well defined, and only the buyers and sellers are affected by production and exchange, competitive market forces will automatically guide a market toward an equilibrium level of output that satisfies economic efficiency.

Exhibit 11 illustrates why this is true. Suppliers of a good, bicycles in this example, will produce additional units as long as the market price exceeds the production cost. Sim-

EXHIBIT 11
Economic Efficiency

When markets are competitive and property rights are well defined, the equilibrium reached by a market satisfies economic efficiency. All units that create more benefit (the buyer's valuation shown by the height of the demand curve) than cost (opportunity cost of production shown by the height of the supply curve) are produced. This maximizes the total gains from trade, the combined area represented by consumer and producer surplus.

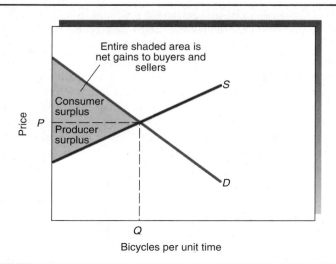

ilarly, consumers will gain from the purchase of additional units as long as their benefits, revealed by the height of the demand curve, exceed the market price. Market forces will result in an equilibrium output level of Q: All units providing benefits to consumers that exceed the costs to suppliers will be produced. Economic efficiency is met because all potential gains from exchange (the shaded area) between consumers and producers are fully realized. Market equilibrium is consistent with maximizing the combined area reflecting both consumer and producer surplus.

When less than Q bicycles are produced, some units that are valued more than their opportunity cost of production are not being produced. This is inconsistent with economic efficiency. On the other hand, if output is expanded beyond Q, inefficiency would also result because, in this range, some of the bicycles would cost more to produce than their value to consumers. With competitive markets, consumers and producers alike will be guided by the pricing system to output level Q, just the right amount from the standpoint of economic efficiency.

HOW MARKETS RESPOND TO CHANGES IN DEMAND AND SUPPLY

How will a market adjust to a change in demand? **Exhibit 12** illustrates the market adjustment to an increase in demand. For most of the year, the demand for eggs is primarily for breakfast or the making of other food products. The demand D_1 and supply S indicate the typical conditions throughout most of the year. Typically, the equilibrium price of eggs is P_1. Around Easter time, however, many people purchase extra eggs to decorate or dye with coloring. During the two weeks before Easter, U.S. farmers sell about 600 million more eggs than the average throughout the rest of the year. Thus, at Easter time, there is a sharp increase in demand for eggs (shift from D_1 to D_2 in Exhibit 12). This increase in demand for eggs will push their price upward. During the holiday, egg prices are typically about 20 cents higher per dozen. Note that if the price of eggs did not rise, excess demand would be present. At the P_1 price present throughout most of the year, consumers at Easter time would want to purchase more than producers were willing to supply. At the higher P_2 price, consumers will moderate their additional purchases and producers will supply a larger quantity (Q_2 rather than Q_1). Because hens lay fewer eggs when they are molting, farmers take costly steps to avoid having the hens molt around Easter. This can be done by changing the quantity and types of feed used, and by changing the brightness of lighting in the birds' sheds. In addition, farmers attempt to build up larger than normal inventories of eggs before Easter. Eggs are typically about two days old when consumers buy them, but can be up to seven days old during Easter.

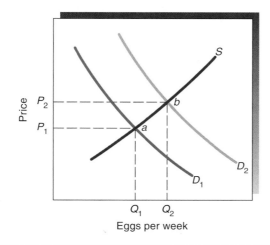

EXHIBIT 12
Market Adjustment to Increase in Demand

Here we illustrate how the market for eggs adjusts to an increase in demand such as generally occurs around Easter time. Initially (before the Easter season), the market for eggs reflects demand D_1 and supply S. The increase in demand (shift from D_1 to D_2) pushes price up and leads to a new equilibrium at a higher price (P_2 rather than P_1) and larger quantity traded (Q_2).

The tradition of coloring and hunting for eggs causes an increase in demand for eggs around Easter. As Exhibit 12 illustrates, this leads to higher egg prices and costly actions by producers to supply a larger quantity during this period.

In a market economy, when the demand for a good increases, its price will rise, which will provide (1) consumers with more incentive to search for substitutes and to moderate their additional purchases and (2) producers with a stronger incentive to supply more of the product. These two forces will keep the quantity demanded and quantity supplied in balance.

When the demand for a product declines, the adjustment process will provide buyers and sellers with just the opposite signals. Take a piece of paper and see if you can diagram a decrease in demand and how it will affect price and quantity in a market. If you've done it correctly, a decline in demand (a shift to the left in the demand curve) will lead to a lower price and a lower quantity traded. What's going on in the diagram is that the lower price (caused by lower consumer demand) is reducing the incentive of producers to supply the good. Thus, when consumers no longer want as much of a good, market prices send the signal to producers to cut back on their production. The reduced output allows these resources to be freed up to go into the production of other goods.

How will markets respond to changes in supply? **Exhibit 13** uses the example of romaine lettuce to illustrate the market's adjustment to a reduction in supply. Severe rains and flooding in California during the spring and early summer of 1998 destroyed a large portion of the romaine lettuce crop. This reduction in supply (shift from S_1 to S_2) caused the price of romaine to increase sharply (to P_2). Consumers cut back on their consumption of the now more expensive good. Some switched to substitutes—in this case, probably other varieties of lettuce and leafy vegetables. Producers took extraordinary steps to expand output and replenish the supply. Vegetable farmers shifted from other crops to romaine lettuce. Some greenhouses were even converted to produce romaine lettuce. The higher prices kept the quantity demanded and quantity supplied in balance and provided suppliers with an incentive to expand supply. Eventually, weather patterns returned to normal and the price fell from its temporary high level.

As the lettuce example illustrates, a decrease in supply will lead to higher prices and a reduction in the equilibrium quantity. How would the market adjust to an increase in supply, such as would result from a technological breakthrough or lower resource prices that reduce production cost of a good? Again, try to draw the appropriate supply and demand curves to illustrate this case. If you do it correctly, the graphic will illustrate that an

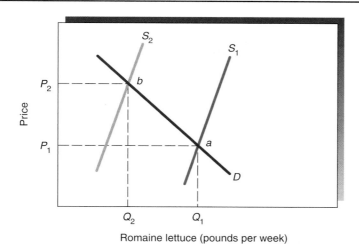

Romaine lettuce (pounds per week)

EXHIBIT 13
Market Adjustment to a Decrease in Supply

Here, using romaine lettuce as an example, we illustrate how a market adjusts to a decrease in supply. Adverse weather conditions substantially reduced the supply (shift from S_1 to S_2) of romaine during the spring and summer of 1998. The reduction in supply led to an increase in the equilibrium price (from P_1 to P_2) and a reduction in the equilibrium quantity traded (from Q_1 to Q_2).

increase in supply (a shift to the right in the supply curve) leads to a lower market price and a larger quantity.

The following Thumbnail Sketch summarizes the impact of changes—both increases and decreases—in demand and supply on the equilibrium price and quantity. The cases listed in the thumbnail sketch, however, are for when only a single curves shifts. Sometimes market conditions can be affected by a simultaneous shift in both demand and supply. For example, consumer income might increase at the same time that a technological advance was reducing the cost of producing a good. These two changes will cause both demand and supply to increase at the same time—both curves will shift to the right. The new equilibrium will definitely be at a larger quantity, but the direction of the change in price is indeterminate. Price may either increase or decrease, depending on whether the increase in demand or increase in supply is larger. When both supply and demand shift, either the resulting price or quantity will be indeterminate. Which would be indeterminate if an increase in supply and a reduction in demand occurred at the same time? The correct answer is: Price will definitely fall, but the new equilibrium quantity may either increase or decrease. Draw the supply and demand curves for this case and make sure that you understand why.

THUMBNAIL SKETCH

How Changes in Demand and Supply Affect Market Price and Quantity

Changes in Demand

1. An increase in demand (a shift to the right of the demand curve) will cause an increase in both the equilibrium price and quantity.
2. A decrease in demand (a shift to the left of the demand curve) will cause a decrease in both the equilibrium price and quantity.

Changes in Supply

1. An increase in supply (a shift to the right of the supply curve) will cause a decrease in the equilibrium price and an increase in the equilibrium quantity.
2. A decrease in supply (a shift to the left of the supply curve) will cause an increase in the equilibrium price and a decrease in the equilibrium quantity.

TIME AND THE ADJUSTMENT PROCESS

When market prices change, both consumers and producers adjust their behavior to the new structure of incentives. The adjustment process will not be instantaneous, though. Sometimes various signals are sent out by changing market prices and are acted upon only gradually, with the passage of time.

In the 1950s and 1960s, Americans were in love with large high acceleration automobiles. Why did those vehicles lose their appeal? The adjustment to higher gas prices provides the answer and it also illustrates the importance of time in the market process. Gas prices rose sharply following the 1973 Arab-Israeli war and again in the late 1970s as a result of political turmoil in Iran, an important oil producer. As **Exhibit 14** illustrates, a reduction in supply (shift from S_1 to S_2) pushed gas prices sharply higher. Adjusted for inflation, gasoline prices rose from $0.70 in 1978 to $1.20 in 1980. *Initially*, consumers responded to rising prices by cutting out some unnecessary trips and leisure driving, by carpooling, and using gasoline additives to get better gasoline mileage. Adjustments like these allowed consumers to reduce their consumption of gasoline, but only by a small amount (from 7.4 million to 7.0 million barrels per day), moving them up D_{sr} from point a to point b. The demand for gasoline in the short run was relatively inelastic, being not very responsive to the change in price.

Given additional time, however, consumers were able to make other adjustments that influenced their consumption of gasoline. For example, as those big gas-guzzling autos that were so popular a few years earlier wore out, they were replaced with smaller vehicles that got better gas mileage. Given sufficient time, consumers were able to reduce their gasoline consumption by a larger amount, causing the demand to become more elastic. By late 1981, consumption of gasoline had declined to 6.6 million barrels per day, and there was downward pressure on prices.

As gas prices trended downward throughout most of the 1980s and 1990s, Sport Utility Vehicles (SUVs) and other heavier, less gas-efficient vehicles once again increased in

EXHIBIT 14
Time, and Adjustment to a
Reduction in Supply

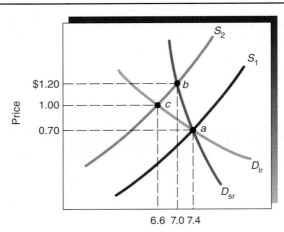

Here we illustrate the adjustment of a market to an unanticipated reduction in supply, such as occurred in the market for gasoline during 1978–1982. Initially, the price of gasoline was 70 cents (equilibrium *a*). Supply declined (shifted from S_1 to S_2) as the result of military conflict and political unrest in the Middle East. In the short run, prices rose sharply to $1.20, and consumption declined by only a small amount (equilibrium moved from *a* to *b*). In the long run, however, the demand for gasoline was more responsive to the price change. As a result, in the long run the price increase was more moderate (equilibrium moved from *b* to *c*).

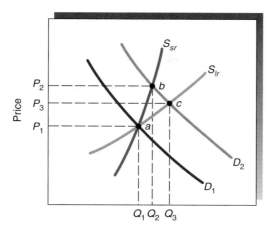

EXHIBIT 15
Time, Supply, and
Adjustment to an
Increase in Demand

The quantity supplied is generally more responsive to a price change in the long run than in the short run. If the market for notebook computers was initially in equilibrium at P_1 and Q_1, an unexpected increase in demand would push the price of the notebooks up sharply to price P_2 (moved from *a* to *b*). Given more time, however, producers will expand output by a larger amount. Therefore, the long-run supply curve will be more responsive to a price change than the short-run curve (S_{lr} is flatter than S_{sr}). The more responsive supply will place downward pressure on price (moved from *b* to *c*) with the passage of time.

popularity. When gas prices shot up again in 2000, it was difficult to reduce gasoline consumption quickly. Similarly, when gasoline prices fell in 2001, only small adjustments were made quickly. Long-run adjustments, such as a shift to or from smaller, more fuel efficient automobiles, occur slowly.

This adjustment process for gasoline is typical. The consumption response to a price change will usually be smaller in the short run than over a longer period of time. As a result, an unexpected reduction in the supply of a product will generally push the price up more in the short run than in the long run.

Similarly, the adjustments of producers to changing market conditions take time. Suppose that specialized new computer software is developed that causes an increase in demand for notebook computers. How will this change be reflected in the market? **Exhibit 15** provides an overview. The increase in demand is shown by the shift from D_1 to D_2. Initially, suppliers of notebook computers see a decline in their inventories as the computers move off their shelves more rapidly. Discounts will be more difficult to find, deliveries to buyers will be slower, and prices will begin to rise as sellers ration their limited supplies among the increased number of buyers. The market price rises from P_1 to P_2.

A few aggressive entrepreneurs in the computer-producing business may quickly expand their production of notebook computers. They increase the quantity supplied quickly, by rush orders of new materials, having employees work overtime, and so on. But since it is costly to expand output quickly, the higher market price (P_2) will lead to only a modest increase in output from Q_1 to Q_2 in the short run. The higher prices and improved profitability, however, will encourage other, more deliberate efforts to supply more notebooks. *With the passage of time*, more resources will be brought into notebook computer production. Some resource prices will have to be bid higher in order to obtain larger quantities. This raises costs, but over time relatively low cost expansion will take place. In the long run the quantity supplied will be more responsive (S_{lr} rather than S_{sr}) and the price increase will be more moderate (P_3 rather than P_2). All these responses will take time, however, even though economists sometimes talk as if the process were instantaneous.

INVISIBLE HAND PRINCIPLE

**Invisible Hand
Principle**

 Market prices coordinate the actions of self-interested individuals and direct them toward activities that promote the general welfare.

More than 200 years ago, Adam Smith, the father of economics, stressed that personal self-interest *when directed by market prices* is a powerful force promoting economic progress. In a famous passage in his *Wealth of Nations*, Smith put it this way:

> Every individual is continually exerting himself to find out the most advantageous employment for whatever capital [income] he can command. It is his own advantage, indeed, and not that of the society which he has in view. But the study of his own advantage naturally, or rather necessarily, leads him to prefer that employment which is most advantageous to society. . . . He intends only his own gain, and he is in this, as in many other cases, led by an invisible hand to promote an end which was not part of his intention. By pursuing his own interest he frequently promotes that of the society more effectually than when he really intends to promote it.[6]

Invisible hand principle
The tendency of market prices to direct individuals pursuing their own interests into productive activities that also promote the economic well-being of the society.

Using the terminology employed by Smith, economists refer to the tendency of competitive markets to direct the actions of self-interested individuals and bring them into harmony with the general welfare (economic progress) as the **invisible hand principle**. Smith's major point was that market prices are able to harness self-interest and put it to work for the benefit of society. Is this really true? Next time you sit down to have a nice dinner, think about all the people who help make it possible. It is unlikely that any of them, from the farmer to the truck driver to the grocer, was motivated by a concern that you have an enjoyable meal. Market prices, however, bring their interest into harmony with yours. Farmers who raise the best beef or turkeys receive higher prices; truck drivers and grocers earn more money if their products are delivered fresh and in good condition; and so on. Let us now take a closer look at how the invisible hand of market prices brings the interests of individuals into harmony with economic progress.

Communicating Information to Decision Makers

Markets register information derived from the choices of millions of consumers, producers, and resource suppliers and tabulate it into a summary statistic called the *market price.* This statistic reflects information about preferences, costs, relative scarcity, and matters related to timing, location, and circumstances. Most importantly, prices provide consumers, producers, and resource suppliers with everything they need to know in order to make wise decisions.

For example, suppose a drought in Brazil severely reduces the supply of coffee. Coffee prices will rise. Even if consumers do not know anything about the drought in Brazil, the information transmitted by the higher prices will provide them with the incentive to take the appropriate action—cut back on their consumption of coffee.

Market prices also provide producers with up-to-date information about consumers' valuation of additional units of each commodity. Higher prices signal to producers that the commodity is now more highly valued and encourage producers to expand production. Lower prices signal a reduced desire for the commodity and encourage resources to flow away from the production of such goods into the production of others that are valued more highly relative to their cost. For example, suppose that strong demand pushes the price of soybeans up relative to the price of corn. Many farmers will respond to this change by producing more beans and less corn.

---

[6]Adam Smith, *An Inquiry into the Nature and Causes of the Wealth of Nations* (New York: Modern Library, 1937), p. 423.

Prices also communicate important information about the usage of inputs in the production process. The cost of production, driven by the opportunity cost of resources, tells the business decision maker the relative importance others place on factors of production (for example, skill categories of labor, natural resources, and machinery). A boom in the housing market might cause lumber prices to rise. In turn, furniture makers seeing these higher lumber prices will turn to substitute raw materials such as metal and plastic. Because of market prices, furniture makers will conserve on their usage of lumber, just as if they had known that lumber was now more urgently needed for constructing new housing.

Coordinating Actions of Market Participants

Market prices also coordinate the choices of buyers and sellers, bringing their decisions into line with each other. Excess supply will lead to falling prices, discouraging production and encouraging consumption until the excess supply is eliminated. Alternatively, excess demand will lead to price increases, encouraging consumers to economize on their uses of the good and encouraging suppliers to produce more of it, eliminating the excess demand and bringing the choices of market participants into harmony.

Suppose that farmers produce too few potatoes relative to the desire of consumers. This would lead to higher potato prices. Temporarily, the higher potato prices would discourage consumers from using as many, helping to keep their consumption in balance with the level of production. On the supply side, the higher potato prices would make it more profitable to plant potatoes. In the future, more potatoes will be planted and harvested. Market prices induce responses on both sides of the market in the proper direction to help correct the situation.

The combination of product and resource prices will determine profit (and loss) rates for alternative projects and thereby direct entrepreneurs to undertake the production projects that consumers value most intensely (relative to their cost). If consumers really want more of a good—for example, luxury apartments—the intensity of their demand will lead to a market price that exceeds the opportunity cost of constructing the apartments. The profitable opportunity thus created will soon be discovered by entrepreneurs who will undertake the construction, expanding the availability of the apartments. In contrast, if consumers want less of a good—large cars, for example—the opportunity cost of supplying such cars will exceed the sales revenue from their production, penalizing those who undertake such unprofitable production.

Motivating Economic Players

As many leaders of centrally planned economies discovered, people must be motivated to act before production plans can be realized. Market prices establish a reward-penalty (profit-loss) structure that induces participants to work, cooperate with others, use efficient production methods, supply goods that are intensely desired by others, and invest for the future.

No government agency needs to tell business decision makers to use resources wisely (minimize per-unit cost) or to produce those goods intensely desired by consumers. Self-interest and the pursuit of profit will do these jobs. Self-interested entrepreneurs will seek to produce those goods, and only those goods, that consumers value enough to pay a price that is sufficient to cover their costs. Self-interest will also encourage producers to use efficient production methods and adopt cost-saving technologies because lower costs will mean greater profits. Firms that fail to do so, as even giant firms have learned, will be unable to compete successfully in the marketplace.

Similarly, no one has to tell individuals that they should develop skills that are highly valued by others. Once again the profit motive—in this case higher earnings—will do the job. Why are many young people willing to undertake the necessary work, stress, late hours of study, and financial cost to acquire a medical or law degree, or an advanced degree in economics, physics, or business administration? Why do others seek to master a skill requiring an apprentice program? The expectation of financial reward is not the only factor, but it is an important stimulus, providing motivation to work, create, develop skills, and supply capital assets to those productive activities most desired by others.

Prices and Market Order

At the beginning of this chapter, we asked you to reflect on why the grocery stores in your local community have approximately the right amount of milk, bread, vegetables, and other goods—an amount sufficiently large that the goods are nearly always available but not so large that spoilage and waste are a problem. We might also reflect on other products. How is it that refrigerators, automobiles, and CD players, produced at diverse places around the world, are supplied in the U.S. market in approximately the same amount that they are demanded by consumers? The answer is that the invisible hand of market prices directs self-interested individuals into cooperative action and brings their choices into harmony.

The invisible hand principle is difficult for many people to grasp because there is a natural tendency to associate order with central direction. Surely some central authority must be in charge. But this is not the case. ***The pricing system, reflecting the choices of literally millions of consumers, producers, and resource owners, is providing the direction.*** The market process works so automatically that most give little thought to it. They simply take it for granted that the goods most people value will be produced in approximately the quantities that consumers want to purchase.

Perhaps an illustration will enhance your understanding of both the operation and importance of the invisible hand principle. Visualize a busy limited-access highway with four lanes of traffic moving in each direction. No central planning agency assigns lanes and directs traffic. No one tells drivers when to shift to the right, middle, or left lane. Drivers are left to choose for themselves. Nonetheless, they do not all try to drive in the same lane. Why? Drivers are alert for adjustment opportunities that offer personal gain. When traffic in a lane slows due to congestion, some drivers will shift to other lanes and thereby smooth out the flow of traffic among the lanes. Even though central planning is absent, this process of mutual adjustments by the individual drivers results in order and social cooperation. In fact, the degree of social cooperation is generally well beyond what could be achieved if central coordination were attempted—if, for example, each vehicle were assigned a lane. Drivers acting in their own interests and switching to less congested lanes promote the most orderly and quickest flow of traffic for everyone.

Market participation is a lot like driving on the freeway. Like the amount of traffic in a lane, profits and losses provide market participants with information concerning the advantages and disadvantages of alternative economic activities. Losses indicate that an economic activity is congested, and, as a result, producers are unable to cover their costs. Successful market participants will shift their resources away from such activities toward other, more valuable uses. Conversely, profits are indicative of an open lane, the opportunity to experience gain if one shifts into an activity where price is currently high relative to per-unit cost. As producers and resource suppliers shift away from activities characterized by congestion and into those characterized by the opportunity for gain (profit), they smooth out economic activity and enhance its flow. Remarkably, even though individuals are motivated by self-interest, market prices direct their actions toward activities that also promote both order and economic progress. This is precisely what Adam Smith was referring to when he spoke of the "invisible hand" more than 200 years ago.

Qualifications

As we noted at the beginning, the focus of this chapter was the operation of markets where rival firms are free to enter and compete and where property rights are clearly defined and secure. ***The efficiency of market organization is dependent on (1) competitive markets and (2) well-defined private property rights.*** Competition, the great regulator, can protect both buyer and seller. The presence (or possible entry) of independent alternative suppliers protects the consumer against a seller who seeks to charge prices substantially above the cost of production. The existence of alternative resource suppliers protects the producer against a supplier who might otherwise be tempted to withhold a vital resource unless granted exorbitant compensation. The existence of alternative employment opportunities protects the employee from the power of any single employer. Competition can equalize the bargaining power between buyers and sellers.

Understanding the information, coordination, and motivation results of the market mechanism helps us see all the more clearly the importance of property rights, the things actually traded in markets. Property rights force resource users—including users who own the resources—to bear fully the opportunity cost of their actions, and prohibit persons from engaging in destructive forms of competition. When property rights are well defined, secure, and tradable, suppliers of goods and services will be required to pay resource owners the opportunity cost of each resource employed. They will not be permitted to seize and use scarce resources without compensating the owners—that is, without bidding the resources away from alternative users. Neither will they be permitted to use violence (for example, to attack or invade the property of another) as a means to achieve an economic objective.

Although we incorporated numerous examples designed to enhance your understanding of the supply-and-demand model throughout this chapter, we have only touched the surface. In various modified forms, this model is the central tool of economics. The following chapter will explore several specific applications and extensions of this important model.

LOOKING AHEAD

KEY POINTS

▼ The law of demand states that there will be an inverse relationship between the price of a good and the amount consumers will want to purchase. The height of the demand curve at any quantity shows the maximum price that consumers are willing to pay for that unit.

▼ The degree of responsiveness of consumer purchases to a change in price is shown by the steepness of the demand curve. The more (less) responsive buyers are to a change in price, the flatter (steeper) the demand curve.

▼ A movement along a demand curve is called a change in quantity demanded. A shift of the entire curve is called a change in demand. A change in *quantity demanded* is caused by a change in the price of the good. A change in *demand* can be caused by several factors, such as a change in consumer income or a change in the price of a closely related good.

▼ The opportunity cost of producing a good is equal to the cost of bidding the resources required for the production of the good away from their alternative uses. Profit indicates that the producer has increased the value of the resources used, while a loss indicates that the producer has reduced the value of the resources.

▼ The law of supply states that there is a direct relationship between the price of a product and the amount supplied. An increase in the price of a product will induce established firms to expand their output and new firms to enter the market.

▼ A change in the price of a good will cause a change in *quantity supplied*, a movement along a single supply curve. A change in *supply* is a shift in the curve caused by other factors, such as a change in the price of resources or a technological improvement.

▼ The responsiveness of supply to a change in price is shown by the steepness of the supply curve. The more willing producers are to alter the quantity supplied in response to a change in price, the flatter, or more elastic, the supply curve. The supply curve for most products is more elastic in the long run than in the short run.

▼ Market prices will bring the conflicting forces of supply and demand into balance. There is an automatic tendency for prices to bring about an equilibrium where quantity demanded equals quantity supplied.

▼ Consumer surplus represents the net gain to buyers from market trade, while producer surplus represents the net gain to producers and resource suppliers. In equilibrium, competitive markets maximize these gains, a condition known as economic efficiency.

▼ Changes in the prices of goods are caused by changes in supply and demand. An increase (decrease) in demand will cause prices to rise (fall) and quantity supplied to increase (decline). An increase (decrease) in supply will cause prices to fall (rise) and quantity demanded to expand (decline).

▼ Market prices communicate information, coordinate the actions of buyers and sellers, and provide the incentive structure that motivates decision makers to act. As Adam Smith noted long ago, market prices are generally able to bring the personal self-interest of individuals into harmony with the general welfare (the invisible hand principle). The efficiency of the system is dependent on (1) competitive market conditions and (2) securely defined private property rights.

CRITICAL ANALYSIS QUESTIONS

*1. Which of the following do you think would lead to an increase in the current demand for beef?
   a. higher pork prices
   b. higher consumer income
   c. higher prices of feed grains used to feed cattle
   d. widespread outbreak of mad cow or foot-and-mouth disease
   e. an increase in the price of beef

2. What is being held constant when a demand curve for a specific product (like shoes or apples, for example) is constructed? Explain why the demand curve for a product slopes downward to the right.

3. What is the law of supply? How many of the following "goods" do you think conform to the general law of supply? Explain your answer in each case.
   a. gasoline
   b. cheating on exams
   c. political favors from legislators
   d. the services of heart specialists
   e. children
   f. legal divorces
   g. the services of a minister

4. Are prices an accurate reflection of a good's total value? Are prices an accurate reflection of a good's marginal value? What's the difference? Can you think of a good that has high total value but low marginal value? Use this concept to explain why professional wrestlers earn more than nurses despite the fact that in total nurses probably create more total value to society.

5. What is being held constant when the supply curve for a specific good like pizza or automobiles is constructed? Explain why the supply curve for a good slopes upward to the right.

6. Define consumer and producer surplus. What is meant by economic efficiency, and how does it relate to consumer and producer surplus?

7. Recent tax reforms make college tuition partially tax deductible for certain families. This should lead to more people wishing to attend college (a higher demand for a college education). How will this affect tuition prices? How will this affect the cost of college to families who do not qualify for the tax deduction?

*8. "The future of our industrial strength cannot be left to chance. Somebody has to develop notions about which industries are winners and which are losers." Is this statement by a newspaper columnist true? Who is the "somebody"?

9. What role does time play in the market adjustment process? Explain why the response of both consumers and producers to a change in price will be greater in the long run than in the short run.

*10. "Production should be for people and not for profit." Answer the following questions concerning this statement:
   a. If production is profitable, are people helped or hurt? Explain.
   b. Are people helped more if production results in a loss than if it leads to profit? Is there a conflict between production for people and production for profit?

11. What must an entrepreneur do in order to earn a profit? How do the actions of firms earning profit influence the value of resources? What happens to the value of resources when losses are present? What role do profits and losses play in a market economy?

12. What's Wrong with This Way of Thinking? "Economists claim that when the price of something goes up, producers bring more of it to the market. But the last year in which the price was really high for oranges, there were not nearly as many oranges as usual. The economists are wrong!"

13. What is the *invisible hand principle?* Does it indicate that "good intentions" are necessary if one's actions are going to be beneficial to others? What are the necessary conditions for the invisible hand to work well? Why are these conditions important?

14. What's Wrong with This Way of Thinking? "Economists argue that lower prices will necessarily result in less supply. However, there are exceptions to this rule. For example, in 1970, ten-digit electronic calculators sold for $100. By 1995 the price of the same type of calculator had declined to less than $15. Yet business firms produced and sold five times as many calculators in 1995 as in 1970. Lower prices did not result in less production or in a decline in the number of calculators supplied."

15. What is the difference between substitutes and complements? Indicate two goods that are substitutes for each other. Indicate two goods that are complements.

16. How is the market price of a good determined? When the market for a product is in equilibrium, how will the consumers' evaluation of the marginal unit compare with the opportunity cost of producing the unit? Why is this important?

---

*Asterisk denotes questions for which answers are given in Appendix B.

CHAPTER **4**

Supply and Demand: Applications and Extensions

The division of labour, from which so many advantages are derived, is not originally the effect of any human wisdom, which foresees and intends that general opulence to which it gives occasion. It is the necessary, though very slow and gradual consequence of a certain propensity in human nature . . . ; the propensity to truck, barter, and exchange one thing for another.

—Adam Smith[1]

Nations stumble upon establishments, which are indeed the result of human action, but not the execution of any human design.

—Adam Ferguson[2]

Chapter Focus

- Can wage rates, interest rates, and exchange rates be analyzed within the supply and demand framework?

- What happens when prices are set by law above or below the market equilibrium level?

- How do rent controls affect the maintenance and quality of rental housing? How do minimum wage rates influence the job opportunities of low-skilled workers?

- What are "black markets"? How does the lack of a well-structured legal environment affect their operation?

- How does the imposition of a tax affect a market? What determines the distribution of the tax burden between buyers and sellers?

- What is the Laffer curve? What does it indicate about the relationship between tax rates and tax revenues?

---

[1]Adam Smith, *An Inquiry into the Nature and Causes of the Wealth of Nations* (New York: Modern Library, 1937), p. 13.
[2]Adam Ferguson, *An Essay on the History of Civil Society* (London, 1767), p. 187.

Markets are everywhere. They exist in many different forms and degrees of sophistication. In elementary schools, children trade baseball cards; in households, individuals trade chores ("I'll clean the bathroom if you'll clean the kitchen"); on street corners, people buy and sell illegal drugs or tickets to concerts and sporting events; and in the stock market, individuals who have never met exchange shares of corporate stock and other financial assets worth billions of dollars each business day. Even in the nonmarket-based former Soviet Union, black markets were present where individuals bought and sold goods at market-determined prices.

Markets will exist regardless of whether they are legal or illegal, formal or informal. Why? Trading with other individuals is a natural part of human behavior that exists regardless of legal and societal conditions. As Adam Smith put it more than 200 years ago (see quotation, opening of chapter), human beings have a natural propensity "to truck, barter, and exchange one thing for another." We all want to improve our standard of living, and trade with others often helps us achieve this goal. Whenever and wherever people trade, there is a market. Markets are a result of human action, not of human design, as Adam Ferguson points out.[3]

In the previous chapter we saw how the forces of supply and demand determined market prices and coordinated the actions of buyers and sellers. In this chapter we explore several important applications and extensions of supply and demand. We will begin by analyzing interest rates, wage rates, and foreign exchange rates. We will then see how several types of government interventions alter the operation of markets. As the breadth of topics covered in this chapter shows, the laws of supply and demand are universal. ■

WAGE RATES, INTEREST RATES, AND EXCHANGE RATES

As Juliet says to Romeo in William Shakespeare's *Romeo and Juliet*, "What's in a name? That which we call a rose by any other name would smell as sweet." In different markets, different names are sometimes used for price. The price of labor is generally referred to as a *wage rate*. The term *interest rate* is used when referring to the price paid by a borrower or received by a lender of loanable funds. The price of one currency in terms of another is called the *exchange rate*. Despite their different names, they are still prices. Therefore, when analyzing these markets, these special names will be measured along the vertical (or *price*) axis of a supply and demand diagram. In some instances, special names for the quantity traded in the market are used as well. In the labor market, the number of workers holding jobs, or the number of hours they work in aggregate, is called *employment* rather than *quantity*. Although the names have been changed, the forces of supply and demand and the workings of price within the market remain the same.

Linkage Between Labor and Product Markets

The production process generally involves (a) the purchase of resources—such things as raw materials, labor services, tools, and the services of machines; (b) transformation of these resources into products (goods and services); and (c) the sale of the goods and services in the product market. Business firms are generally utilized to undertake production. Typically, business firms demand resources—labor services and raw materials, for example—while households supply them. Firms demand resources *because* they contribute to the production of goods and services. In turn, households supply them in order to earn income.

---

[3]This theme was a focus of much of the work of Nobel Prize–winning economist Friedrich Hayek.

Resource market
Market for inputs used to produce goods and services.

Just as in product markets, the demand curve in a **resource market** is typically downward-sloping and the supply curve upward-sloping. An inverse relationship will exist between the amount of a resource demanded and its price because businesses will substitute away from a resource as its price rises. In contrast, there will be a direct relationship between the amount of a resource supplied and its price because a higher price will make it more attractive to provide the resource. As in the case of consumer goods, prices will coordinate the choices of buyers and sellers in resource markets, bringing the quantity demanded into balance with the quantity supplied.

The labor market is a large and important component of the broader resource market. It is important to note that there is not just one market for labor, but rather many labor markets, one for each different skill-experience-occupational category.

The markets for resources and products are closely linked. Changes in one will also alter conditions in the other. Using the labor market for low-skill, inexperienced workers, **Exhibit 1** illustrates this point. Reflecting demographic factors, in many areas the supply of youthful, inexperienced workers has declined in recent years. This reduction in supply has pushed the wages of youthful workers upward (increase from $6.25 to $7.50 in Exhibit 1a). The higher price of this resource increases the opportunity cost of goods and services the youthful workers help to produce. In turn, the higher cost reduces the supply (shift from S_1 to S_2) of products like hamburgers at McDonald's and other fast-food restaurants, pushing their price upward (Exhibit 1b). When the price of a resource increases, it will lead to higher cost, a reduction in supply, and higher prices for the goods and services produced with the resource.

Of course, lower resource prices would exert the opposite effect. A reduction in resource prices will reduce costs and expand the supply (a shift to the right) of consumer goods using the lower-priced resources. The increase in supply will lead to a lower price in the product market.

There is also a close relation between the demand for products and the demand for the resources required for their production. An increase in demand for a consumer good, automobiles for example, will lead to higher auto prices, which will increase the profitability of automakers and provide them with an incentive to expand output. But the expansion in output of automobiles will also increase the demand for and prices of the resources (for example, steel, rubber, plastics, and the labor services of autoworkers) required for the production of automobiles. The higher prices of these resources will cause other industries to conserve on their usage, making it possible for automakers to utilize the additional resources required for the expansion in the output of automobiles.

EXHIBIT 1
Resource Prices, Opportunity Cost, and Product Markets

Suppose a reduction in the supply of youthful, inexperienced labor pushes the wage rates of workers hired by fast-food restaurants upward (a). In the product market (b), the higher wage rates will increase the restaurant's opportunity cost, causing a reduction in supply (shift from S_1 to S_2), leading to higher hamburger prices.

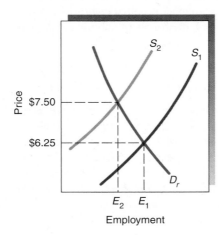

(a) Resource market
(youthful, inexperienced labor)

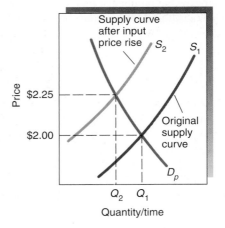

(b) Product market
(fast-food hamburgers)

Of course, the process will work in reverse in the case of a decrease in product demand. A reduction in demand for a product will not only reduce the price of the product but also reduce the demand for and prices of the resources required for its production. As we analyze changes in various markets, we will return to the linkage between product and resource markets again and again.

Loanable Funds Market and the Interest Rate

The **loanable funds market** is highly diverse. Banks, insurance companies, and brokerage firms often act as intermediaries (middlemen) between lenders and borrowers. Bank deposits, bonds, and mutual funds are important financial instruments in this market. In the loanable funds market, borrowers demand the current use of funds in exchange for later repayment, while lenders supply them. As we previously mentioned, the interest rate is the price of loanable funds. To keep things relatively simple, we will assume that there is only a single interest rate. In reality, of course, there is a multitude of interest rates, depending on such factors as risk and length of time the funds are borrowed (or loaned).

The demand and supply curves in this market look like they do in other markets. As part a of **Exhibit 2** illustrates, more funds will be borrowed at lower interest rates. A lower interest rate will make it cheaper for households to purchase consumption goods and for businesses to undertake investment projects *during the current period*. Thus, they will borrow more at lower rates, and, as a result, the demand curve for loanable funds will slope downward to the right. On the other hand, lower interest rates will make it less attractive to save (and loan funds). Thus, the supply curve for loanable funds will slope upward to the right, indicating a direct relationship between the interest rate and the quantity of funds supplied by lenders.

In the loanable funds market, price—the interest rate in this case—will coordinate the actions of borrowers and lenders, just as it coordinates the actions of buyers and sellers in other markets. As Exhibit 2a shows, interest rate r_1 will bring the quantity of funds demanded into balance with the quantity supplied. At interest rates greater than r_1, lenders would want to save more than borrowers will demand. This excess supply of loanable

Loanable funds market
A general term used to describe the broad market that coordinates the borrowing and lending decisions of business firms and households. Commercial banks, savings and loan associations, the stock and bond markets, and insurance companies are important financial institutions in this market.

EXHIBIT 2
Increase in the Demand for Loanable Funds

The interest rate will bring the quantity of loanable funds demanded by borrowers into balance with the quantity supplied by lenders (frame a). An increase in demand for loanable funds will push the interest rate up from r_1 to r_2 (frame b). The higher interest rate will encourage additional savings, making it possible to fund more borrowing.

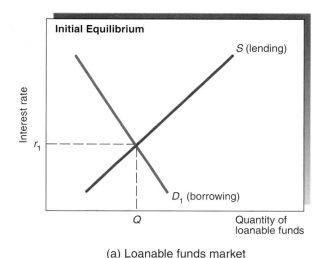

(a) Loanable funds market

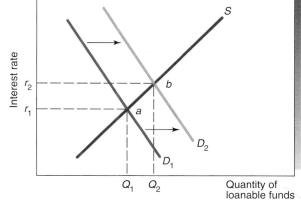

(b) Loanable funds market

funds will place downward pressure on interest rates, pushing them toward equilibrium. If the interest rate was less than r_1, the quantity of funds demanded by borrowers would exceed the quantity supplied by lenders, placing upward pressure on the interest rates. Thus, market forces will direct the interest rate toward r_1, the rate that brings the choices of borrowers and lenders into harmony.[4]

The interest rate is vitally important because it connects the price of things today with their price in the future. In essence, it is the price that must be paid for earlier availability. This relative price—the cost of spending today relative to spending in the future—is central to the decision making of both households and businesses. Should you buy a car this year or wait until next year? Should you reduce your current consumption so you can save more? The interest rate helps you evaluate choices like these. An increase in the interest rate will make it more expensive for households to purchase a car, house, vacation, or any other good during the current period rather than waiting until next year or some other time in the future. The interest rate is a primary determinant of how households allocate their income between current consumption of goods and services and savings for future consumption.

The interest rate is also central to the investment choices of business decision makers. At any point in time, there are literally millions of potential investment projects that might be undertaken. However, profit-seeking business decision makers will only want to undertake projects that are expected to yield a rate of return greater than or equal to the interest rate. If a project's rate of return is less than the interest rate, the potential investor would be better off simply putting the funds into a savings account or using them to purchase a bond. The interest rate confronts business decision makers with the opportunity cost of funds, providing them with a strong incentive to economize on the use of investment funds and allocate them toward the projects that are expected to yield the highest rate of return. This is a vitally important function if an economy is going to grow and get the most out of its resources.

The market interest rate will respond to changing market conditions. Suppose that business decision makers become more optimistic about the future demand for their product, and therefore seek additional funds to expand the scale of their productive capacity. How will this increase in demand for loanable funds influence the interest rate? As part b of Exhibit 2 shows, the stronger demand will push the interest rate up from r_1 to r_2. In turn, the higher interest rate will encourage households to increase their savings (the movement along the supply curve from *a* to *b*). The higher rate will also discourage some investors from undertaking marginal projects that are no longer expected to be profitable at the higher rate of interest. This combination of factors—increased saving and reduction in borrowing for marginal projects—will lead to a new equilibrium at a higher interest rate.

Alternatively, let's consider how the market would respond to a change in supply. Suppose that changes in South America led to a large inflow of savings from that continent. How will that inflow of added savings influence the loanable funds market in the United States? The increase in the supply of loanable funds will reduce interest rates. As interest rates fall, businesses will wish to borrow more funds in order to undertake additional investment projects, and households will borrow additional funds for the purchase of homes, cars, and other items. Equilibrium will be restored at a lower interest rate and higher level of investment.

Market for Foreign Exchange

Foreign exchange market
The market in which the currencies of different countries are bought and sold.

The **foreign exchange market** is the market where the currency of one country is traded for the currency of another. Americans demand various foreign currencies so they can buy goods, services, and assets from sellers in these countries. If you were to go on vacation to Mexico, for example, you would want to conduct many transactions in the Mexican cur-

---

[4]The expectation of inflation will influence the nominal interest rate. This topic will be discussed in a later chapter. For now, when we speak of a change in interest rates, we are referring to a change after adjustment for the effects of inflation.

rency, the peso. One of your first transactions would be to trade some dollars for pesos in the foreign exchange market. However, even if you purchase a Mexican-made product in the United States, it will generally result in a conversion of dollars to pesos so that the Mexican firm can pay its domestic resource suppliers in pesos.

Although purchases from foreigners underlie the demand for a foreign currency, sales to foreigners give rise to the supply. For example, when an American firm sells lumber to a Japanese purchaser, the Japanese buyer will supply yen to the foreign exchange market in order to acquire the dollars used for the lumber purchase. Thus, the sale of goods, services, and assets to foreigners creates a supply of foreign exchange.

Using the currency of Guatemala—the quetzal—part a of **Exhibit 3** shows how "price," the **exchange rate** between the dollar and the quetzal, is determined in the foreign exchange market. (Note: In order to keep the example simple, we assume that the U.S. and Guatemala only trade with each other.) When the dollar price of the quetzal is low, Guatemalan goods will be cheap for Americans. Therefore, Americans will purchase more Guatemalan goods *and therefore more quetzals* at the lower dollar price of the foreign currency. As a result, the dollar demand for quetzals slopes downward to the right. On the other hand, when the dollar price of the quetzal is high, American-produced goods will be cheap for Guatemalans, which will induce them to buy more American goods. Thus, at the higher dollar price of quetzals, American sales to Guatemalans will be greater. As a result, the supply curve for the quetzal will slope upward to the right. The exchange rate will tend to move toward the equilibrium price of $0.10 (10 US cents = 1 quetzal), which will bring the quantity demanded of quetzals into equality with the quantity supplied. This exchange rate could equivalently be quoted as $1 US equals 10 quetzals, however, expressing the exchange rate in terms of one unit of the foreign currency makes the graphical analysis more straightforward.

Suppose that U.S. citizens suddenly increased their desire for Guatemalan coffee. How will this affect the dollar-quetzal exchange rate? Because every purchase of Guatemalan coffee generates a demand for quetzals, the increase in coffee purchases will increase the demand for quetzals. As part b of Exhibit 3 shows, this increase in demand

Exchange rate
The price of one unit of foreign currency in terms of the domestic currency. For example, if it takes $1.50 to purchase an English pound, the dollar-pound exchange rate is 1.50.

EXHIBIT 3
Increase in Demand for Foreign Exchange

Initially, when the dollar price of the Guatemalan quetzal is $0.10 (10 US cents = 1 quetzal), equilibrium is present in this foreign exchange market (frame a). An increase in the demand of Americans for Guatemalan coffee will also increase the demand for the quetzal. As a result, the dollar price of the quetzal will rise (frame b).

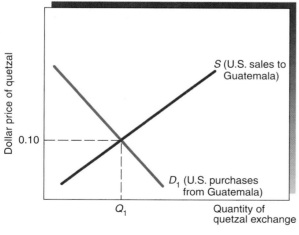

(a) Foreign exchange market

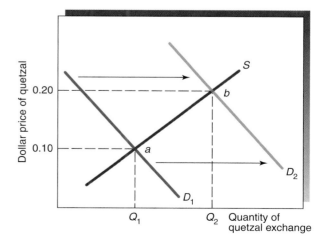

(b) Foreign exchange market

will cause the dollar price of the quetzal to rise to $0.20 (20 cents). How will this affect the cost to a Guatemalan citizen of purchasing a product made in the United States? To answer this, we must first express the exchange rate from the perspective of a Guatemalan citizen. Prior to this change, one quetzal was equal to 10 U.S. cents. Thus, it took 10 quetzals to buy one U.S. dollar. After the dollar price of the quetzal increased to 20 U.S. cents, one U.S. dollar could be purchased for only 5 quetzals. Thus, a U.S.-made product that sells for a price of $100 used to cost the Guatemalan citizen 1,000 quetzals. At the new exchange rate, however, the price of the $100 product has fallen to 500 quetzals. The lower price means that Guatemalan citizens will purchase more American-made products. Thus, the higher U.S. demand for Guatemalan coffee, which results in more imports from Guatemala, will also encourage American exports to Guatemala.

Changes in the exchange rate are vitally important because they alter the prices of all goods, services, and assets that are traded in international markets. They also provide business decision makers with information that will help them compare purchase prices and production costs across countries. Should a business choose to produce output in Mexico, Thailand, the United States, or some other country? Wage rates for most types of labor are likely to be lower in Mexico and Thailand than in the United States. However, there are several disadvantages of locating a plant in another country. If the good is going to be sold in the United States, transportation costs will probably be higher if it is produced in another country. The risks accompanying contract violations and insecurity of property rights are likely to be greater in another country. Exchange rates will help businesses analyze cost advantages and disadvantages like these. As we proceed, we will return to these topics and related issues.

We have shown how market prices, from wage rates to interest rates to exchange rates, coordinate the actions of buyers and sellers. What would happen if prices were fixed either below or above the market equilibrium? We will now turn to this question.

THE ECONOMICS OF PRICE CONTROLS

Price controls
Government-mandated prices; they may be either greater or less than the market equilibrium price.

Buyers often believe that prices are too high, while sellers complain that they are too low. Unhappy with prices established by market forces, various groups may seek to have the government set the prices of certain products. Government-mandated prices are called **price controls**. They may be either price ceilings, which set a maximum price for a product, or price floors, which impose a minimum price. Fixing prices seems like a simple, straightforward solution. However, do not forget the phenomenon of secondary effects.

Price Ceilings

Price ceiling
A legally established maximum price that sellers may charge for a good or resource.

A **price ceiling** is a legal restriction that prohibits exchanges at prices greater than a designated price—the ceiling price. When imposed below the market equilibrium, the price ceiling will alter the operation of the market. **Exhibit 4** illustrates the impact of fixing the price of a product below its equilibrium level. Of course, the price ceiling does result in a lower price than market forces would produce, at least in the short run. At the lower price, however, the quantity that producers are willing to supply decreases, while the quantity that consumers would like to purchase increases. A **shortage** ($Q_D - Q_S$) of the good will result, a situation in which the quantity demanded by consumers exceeds the quantity supplied by producers *at the existing price*. After the imposition of the price ceiling, the quantity of the good exchanged declines and the gains from trade (consumer and producer surplus) fall as well.

Shortage
A condition in which the amount of a good offered for sale by producers is less than the amount demanded by buyers at the existing price. An increase in price would eliminate the shortage.

Normally, the higher price would ration the good to the buyers most willing to pay for it. Because the price ceiling keeps this from happening, other means must be used to allocate the smaller quantity Q_s among consumers seeking to purchase Q_d. Predictably, nonprice factors will become more important in the rationing process. Producers must discriminate on some basis other than willingness to pay as they ration their sales to eager buyers. Sellers will be partial to friends, to buyers who do them favors, and even to buyers who are willing to make illegal "under-the-table" payments. (The accompanying Applica-

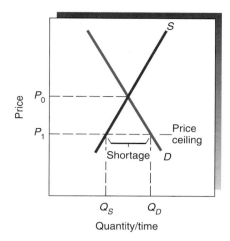

EXHIBIT 4
The Impact of a
Price Ceiling

When a price ceiling like P_1 pushes the price of a product (rental housing, for example) below the market equilibrium, a shortage will develop. Because prices are not allowed to direct the market to equilibrium, nonprice elements will become more important. Given the shortage, the nonprice factors will change in ways favorable to sellers.

tions in Economics box, "The Imposition of Price Ceilings during Hurricane Hugo," highlights this point.) Time may also be used as the rationing device, with those willing to wait in line the longest being the ones able to purchase the good. In addition, the below-equilibrium price reduces the incentive of sellers to expand the future supply of the good. With the passage of time, the shortage conditions will worsen. At the lower price, suppliers will direct resources away from production of this commodity and into other, more profitable areas.

What other secondary effects can we expect? ***In the real world, there are two ways that sellers can raise prices. First, they can raise their money price, holding quality constant. Or, second, they can hold the money price constant while reducing the quality of the good.*** (The latter could include a reduction in the size of the product, such as a decline in the size of a candy bar or loaf of bread.) Confronting a price ceiling, sellers will rely on the latter method of raising prices. Rather than do without the good, some buyers will accept the lower-quality product. It is impossible to repeal the laws of supply and demand.

It is important to note that a shortage is not the same as scarcity. ***Scarcity is inescapable.*** Scarcity exists whenever people want more of a good than nature has provided. This means, of course, that almost everything of value is scarce. ***Shortages, on the other hand, are avoidable if prices are permitted to rise.*** A higher, unfixed price (P_0 rather than P_1 in Exhibit 4) would stimulate additional production, discourage consumption, and increase the incentive of entrepreneurs to search for and develop substitute goods. This combination of forces would eliminate the shortage.

Rent Control: A Closer Look at a Price Ceiling

Rent controls are a price ceiling intended to protect residents from high housing prices. Rent controls are currently in place in many U.S. cities including New York, Washington, D.C., Newark, New Jersey, and San Jose, California. Many were originally enacted either as temporary price controls during World War II or as price controls during the high inflation period during the 1970s. At their peak in the mid 1980s, more than 200 cities, encompassing about 20 percent of the nation's population, imposed rent controls. During this same period, however, more than 30 states adopted laws and constitutional amendments prohibiting the imposition of rent controls.

Because rent controls push the price of rental housing below the equilibrium level, the amount of rental housing demanded by consumers will exceed the amount landlords will make available. Initially, if the mandated price is only slightly below equilibrium, the impact of rent controls may be barely noticeable. With the passage of time, however, their effects will grow. Inevitably, rent controls will lead to the following results.

The Imposition of Price Ceilings During Hurricane Hugo

In the fall of 1989 Hurricane Hugo struck the coast of South Carolina, causing massive property damage and widespread power outages lasting for weeks. While private and government aid from other areas was received, it was often inadequate to deal with immediate problems. The lack of electric power meant that gasoline pumps, refrigerators, cash registers, ATM machines, and many other types of electrical equipment did not work. In the hardest hit coastal areas, such as Charleston, the demand for such items as lumber, gasoline, ice, batteries, chain saws, and electric generators increased dramatically. A bag of ice that sold for $1 before the hurricane went up in price to as much as $10, the price of plywood rose to about $200 per sheet, chain saws soared to the $600 range, and gasoline sold for as much as $10.95 per gallon. At these higher prices, individuals from other states were renting trucks, buying supplies in their home state, driving them to Charleston, and making enough money to pay for the rental truck and the purchase of the goods and to compensate them for taking time off from their regular jobs.

In response to consumer complaints of "price gouging," the mayor of Charleston signed emergency legislation making it a crime, punishable by up to 30 days in jail and a $200 fine, to sell goods at prices higher than their pre-hurricane levels in the city. The price ceilings kept prices down, but also stopped the flow of goods into the area almost immediately. Shippers of items such as ice would stop and sell their goods outside the harder-hit Charleston area in order to avoid the price controls. Shipments that made it into Charleston were often greeted by long lines of consumers, many of whom would end up without goods after waiting in line for up to five hours. Some of the lucky people who got these items would then drive them back out of the city to sell them at the higher, noncontrolled prices. Shortages became so bad that military guards were required to protect shipments of the goods and maintain order when a shipment did arrive.

The price controls resulted in serious misallocations of resources. Grocery stores could not open because of the lack of electric power; inside the stores, food items were spoiling—thousands of dollars' worth, in some stores. Gasoline pumps require electricity to operate, so, although there was fuel in the underground tanks, there was a shortage of gasoline because of the inability to pump it. Consumers were faced with problems of obtaining money, as ATM machines and banks could not operate without electric power. Hard-

ware stores that sold gasoline-powered electric generators before the hurricane typically had only a few in stock, but suddenly hundreds of businesses and residents wanted to buy them. In the absence of price controls, these generators would have risen to thousands of dollars in price. Individual homeowners would have been outbid by businesses who could have put the generators to use in opening stores and gasoline stations and operating ATM machines. It would have been these uses that could have generated enough revenue to cover the high price of the generators. Individuals who had generators at home would have even found it in their interest to sell them to businesses for the high sum of money involved.

However, the price ceilings prevented prices from allocating these generators to those most willing to pay. Instead, individuals kept their generators, and it was commonplace for hardware store owners who had a few generators on hand to take one home for their family, and then sell the others to their close friends, neighbors, and relatives. In the absence of price rationing, these nonprice factors played a larger role in the allocation process. While these families used the generators for household uses (such as running television sets, lighting, electric razors, and hair dryers), gasoline stations, grocery stores, and banks were closed because of their inability to purchase generators. Thousands of consumers could not get goods they urgently wanted because these businesses were closed. In addition, the flow of new generators into the city effectively ceased, and some were being taken from the city to the less-damaged outlying areas to be sold at higher (noncontrolled) prices. Without price controls, the price of generators would have been bid up to the point where they would be (1) purchased by those who had the most urgent uses for them, and (2) imported into the city fairly rapidly because of the high prices they commanded.

The impact of the controls imposed subsequent to Hugo highlights the importance of both price signals and voluntary exchange. Even when major reallocations of goods and resources are needed, such as during a natural disaster, pricing signals will help motivate people to undertake actions that will minimize the damage. The secondary impacts of the price controls imposed in the Charleston area magnified the suffering and retarded the recovery.* In recent years, communities hit by hurricanes and other disasters have been reluctant to impose price controls. Perhaps this reluctance reflects the impact of the controls imposed subsequent to hurricane Hugo.

---

*See David N. Laband, "In Hugo's Path, a Man-Made Disaster," *Wall Street Journal*, September 27, 1989, p. A22; and Tim Smith, "Economists Spurn Price Restrictions," *Greenville News*, September 28, 1989, p. C1.

1. Shortages and black markets will develop.

Since the quantity of housing demanded will exceed the quantity supplied, some persons who value rental housing highly will be unable to find it. Frustrated by the shortage, they will seek methods by which they may induce landlords to rent to them. Some will agree to prepay their rent, including a substantial damage deposit. Others might agree to rent or buy the landlords' furniture at exorbitant prices in order to obtain an apartment. Still others will make under-the-table (black market) payments to secure the cheap housing.

2. The future supply of rental houses will decline.

The below-equilibrium price will discourage entrepreneurs from constructing new rental housing units. Private investment will flow elsewhere, since the controls have depressed the rate of return in the rental housing market. In the city of Berkeley, rental units available to students of the University of California dropped by 31 percent in the first five years after the city adopted rent controls in 1978.[5] In contrast, housing and apartment construction rose dramatically in Boston and some of its suburbs following the repeal of rent controls in the late 1990s. Similar results were observed in Santa Monica, California, following removal of the controls.

3. The quality of rental housing will deteriorate.

When apartment owners are not allowed to raise their nominal prices, they will use reductions in quality to achieve this objective. Normal maintenance and repair service will deteriorate. Tenant parking lots will be eliminated (or rented). Eventually, the quality of the rental housing will reflect the controlled price. Cheap housing will be of cheap quality.

4. Nonprice methods of rationing will increase in importance.

Because price is no longer allowed to play its normal role, other forms of competition will develop. Prohibited from price rationing, landlords will rely more heavily on nonmonetary discriminating devices. They will favor friends, persons of influence, and those with lifestyles similar to their own. In contrast, applicants with many children or unconventional lifestyles, and perhaps racial minorities will find fewer landlords who will rent to them. Since the cost to landlords of discriminating against those with characteristics they do not like has been reduced, such discrimination will become more prevalent in the rationing process. In New York City, which is under rent controls, a magazine article once suggested "joining a church or synagogue" as a useful technique in finding a good connection who could provide leads on an apartment.

5. Inefficient use of housing space will result.

The tenant in a rent-controlled apartment will think twice before moving. Why? Even though the tenant might want a larger or smaller space or might want to move closer to work, he or she will be less likely to move because it is much more difficult to find a vacancy if rent control ordinances are in effect. Turnover will be lower, and many will find themselves in locations and in apartments not well-suited to their needs. In a college town, apartments will end up being rented too heavily to students whose parents live locally (at the cheaper rent they will be less likely to remain living at home and also their parents will have the best connections to local landlords), while students from farther away, to whom the apartments would be better allocated, will find it harder to find a place to rent.

6. Long-term renters will benefit at the expense of newcomers.

People who stay for lengthy periods in the same apartment often pay rents substantially below market value (because the controls restrict rent increases), while newcomers are forced to pay exorbitant prices for units sublet from tenants or for the limited supply of

---

[5]William Tucker, *The Excluded Americans* (Washington, D.C.: Regnery Gateway, 1990), p. 162. For a more detailed exposition on rent controls, see Walter Block, "Rent Controls," in *Fortune Encyclopedia of Economics*, ed. David Henderson (New York: Warner Books, 1993). An excellent discussion of the recent trends in rent control legislation can be found in William Tucker, "Rent Control Drives Out Affordable Housing," in *USA Today Magazine* (July 1998).

Rent controls lead to shortages, poor maintenance, and deterioration in the quality of rental housing.

unrestricted units—typically newly constructed and thus temporarily exempted. Distortions and inequities result. A book on housing and the homeless by William Tucker reports several examples, such as "actress Ann Turkel, who paid $2,350 per month for a seven-room, four-and-a-half bathroom duplex on the East Side (of New York City). . . . Identical apartments in the building were subletting for $6,500."[6] Turkel had been spending only two months each year in New York. "Former mayor Edward Koch . . . pays $441.49 a month for a large, one-bedroom apartment . . . that would probably be worth $1,200 in an unregulated market. Koch kept the apartment the entire twelve years he lived in Gracie Mansion (the official mayor's residence)." Tucker uses these and many other such cases to illustrate the distortions brought on by the control of rental prices.

Imposition of rent controls may look like a simple method of dealing with high housing prices. However, the analysis of price ceilings and the experiences where they have been imposed indicate that they cause other problems, including a decline in the supply of rental housing, poor maintenance, and shortages. Many cities are learning from their poor experience with rent controls and there has been a recent trend toward the repeal of these laws. In the words of Swedish economist Assar Lindbeck: "In many cases rent control appears to be the most efficient technique presently known to destroy a city—except for bombing."[7] Though this may overstate the case somewhat, Lindbeck's point is well taken.

Price Floors

Price floor
A legally established minimum price that buyers must pay for a good or resource.

While price ceilings set a maximum price, **price floors** establish a minimum price that can legally be charged. **Exhibit 5** illustrates the case of a price floor, which fixes the price of a good or resource above the market equilibrium level. At the higher price, sellers will want to bring a larger amount to the market, while buyers will choose to buy less of the good. A

---

[6]Tucker, *The Excluded Americans*, p. 248.
[7]Assar Lindbeck, *The Political Economy of the New Left* (New York: Harper & Row, 1972), p.39.

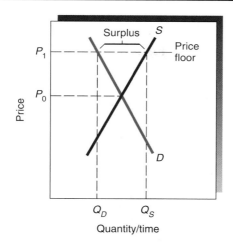

EXHIBIT 5
The Impact of a Price Floor

When a price floor like P_1 keeps the price of a good or service above the market equilibrium, a surplus will result. The surplus will cause the nonprice elements of exchange to change in ways favorable to buyers.

surplus (Q_S-Q_D) will result. As in the case of the price ceiling, nonprice factors will play a larger role in the rationing process because the price control stifles the normal function of prices. But, because there is a surplus rather than a shortage, this time it is buyers who will be in a position to be more selective. Buyers can be expected to seek out sellers willing to offer them favors (better service, discounts on other products, or easier credit, for example). Some sellers may be unable to market their product or service. Unsold merchandise and underutilized resources will result.

Note that a surplus does not mean the good is no longer scarce. People still want more of the good than is freely available from nature, even though they desire less *at the current price* than sellers desire to bring to the market. A decline in price would eliminate the surplus but not the scarcity of the item.

Surplus
A condition in which the amount of a good offered for sale by producers is greater than the amount that buyers will purchase at the existing price. A decline in price would eliminate the surplus.

Minimum Wage: A Closer Look at a Price Floor

In 1938 Congress passed the Fair Labor Standards Act, which provided for a national **minimum wage** of 25 cents per hour. During the past 60 years, the minimum wage has been increased many times. The current minimum wage is $5.15 per hour.

The minimum wage is a price floor. Because most employees in the United States earn wages in excess of the minimum, their employment opportunities are largely unaffected. However, the wages of low-skilled and inexperienced workers will be affected. **Exhibit 6** provides a graphic illustration of the direct effect of a $5.15-per-hour minimum wage on the employment opportunities of a group of low-skilled workers. Without a minimum wage, the supply of and demand for these low-skilled workers would be in balance at a wage rate of $4.00. Because the minimum wage makes low-skilled labor service more expensive, employers will substitute machines and more highly skilled workers (whose wages have not been raised by the minimum) for the now more expensive low-skilled employees. Fewer low-skilled workers will be hired when the minimum wage pushes their wages up. As the wages of low-skilled workers are pushed above equilibrium, there will be more unskilled workers looking for jobs than businesses are willing to employ at the minimum wage. Theory indicates that minimum-wage legislation increases the rate of unemployment among low-skilled workers. The exceedingly high unemployment rate of teenagers (one of the most affected groups) is consistent with this view. In the United States, the unemployment rate for teenagers is more than three times the national average, and the rate for black youth has generally exceeded 30 percent in recent years.

When analyzing the effects of the minimum wage, once again we must remember that the nominal price (wage) is only one dimension of the transaction. As we noted in the previous section, a price ceiling will lead to a deterioration in product quality because sellers

Minimum wage
Legislation requiring that workers be paid at least the stated minimum hourly rate of pay.

EXHIBIT 6
Employment and the
Minimum Wage

If the market wage of a group of employees were $4.00 per hour, a $5.15-per-hour mini-mum wage would increase the earnings of persons who were able to maintain employment, but would reduce the employ-ment of others (E_0 to E_1), pushing them onto the unem-ployment rolls or into less-preferred jobs.

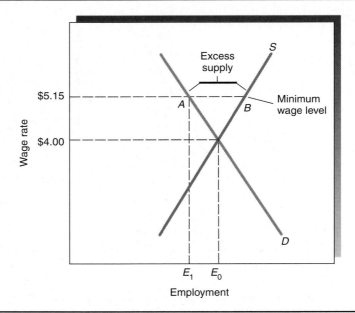

have little incentive to maintain quality in order to attract buyers. Correspondingly, when a price floor pushes price—remember wage rates are a price—above equilibrium, buyers will have little incentive to offer nonprice terms of trade attractive to sellers. At an above-equilibrium wage, employers will have no trouble hiring low-skilled workers. Therefore, they will have little incentive to offer them convenient working hours, training opportuni-ties, continuous employment, and other benefits and nonwage amenities. Predictably, a higher minimum wage will lead to a deterioration of the nonwage attributes of minimum-wage jobs.

The impact of the minimum wage on the opportunity of youthful workers to acquire experience and training is particularly important. Many young, inexperienced workers face a dilemma: They cannot find a job without experience (or skills), but they cannot ob-tain experience without a job. Low-paying, entry-level jobs can provide workers with experience that will help them move up the job ladder to higher-paying positions. Employ-ment experience obtained at an early age, even on menial tasks, can help one acquire self-confidence, work habits, attitudes, skills, and a reputation for these attributes that will enhance one's value to employers in the future. The minimum wage makes this process more difficult. It also reduces the number of jobs providing low-skilled workers with train-ing. Because the minimum wage prohibits the payment of even a temporarily low wage, it is often too costly for employers to offer low-skilled workers jobs with training. Not surprisingly, most minimum-wage jobs are dead-end positions with little opportunity for future advancement.[8]

Of course, workers who are able to maintain employment—most likely the better qualified among those with low skill levels—gain when the minimum wage is increased. Other low-skilled workers, particularly those with the lowest prelegislation wage rates and skill levels, will find it more difficult to find employment. How large are the employment reductions of low-skilled workers? Studies indicate that a 10 percent increase in the mini-mum wage reduces the employment of low-skilled workers by 1 percent to 3 percent. This relatively small decline in employment is not surprising, given the ability of employers to cut training programs and other forms of compensation. Minimum-wage supporters argue

---

[8]For evidence that the minimum wage limits training opportunities, see David Neumark and William Wascher, "Minimum Wages and Training Revisited," National Bureau of Economic Research Working Paper Number 6651, July 1998.

that the higher wages for low-skilled workers are worth these relatively small reductions in employment and job training opportunities.

The proponents of a higher minimum wage nearly always argue that it will help the poor. However, the composition of minimum-wage workers should cause one to question its effectiveness as an antipoverty device. Perhaps surprising to some, most minimum-wage workers belong to families with an income substantially above the poverty line. In fact, about 40 percent of minimum wage workers are members of a family with an income above the median. Only a small proportion of minimum-wage workers—16 percent in 2000—were sole earners responsible for the support of a family. A majority (61 percent) of the minimum-wage workers were working part-time. Approximately one-third (36 percent) were teenagers. The typical minimum-wage worker is a spouse or a teenage member of a household with an income well above the poverty level. Therefore, even if the adverse impacts of a higher minimum wage on employment and nonwage forms of compensation were small, a higher minimum wage would exert little impact on the income of the poor.[9]

BLACK MARKETS AND THE IMPORTANCE OF THE LEGAL STRUCTURE

Not all markets operate within the framework of the law. Some drugs, such as marijuana and cocaine, are illegal. Prostitution is illegal in all states except Nevada. Many states have passed laws making it illegal to sell (and in some cases buy) tickets to concerts and sporting events at prices in excess of the original purchase price. Despite the legal restrictions, when demand is strong and gains from trade are present, markets will develop. Markets that operate outside the legal system, either by selling illegal items or items at illegal prices or terms, are called **black markets**. People may also turn to black markets in order to avoid high taxes and costly regulations. High taxes have created substantial black

Black market
A market that operates outside the legal system, either by selling illegal goods or by selling goods at illegal prices or terms.

Black markets like those for illegal drugs are characterized by less dependable product quality and greater use of violence as a means of settling disputes between buyers and sellers.

---

[9]See William E. Even and David A. Macpherson, "Consequences of Minimum Wage Indexing," *Contemporary Economic Policy*, 14 (October 1996); David Neumark and William Wascher, "Do Minimum Wages Fight Poverty?" National Bureau of Economic Research Working Paper Number 6127, August 1997; and David Neumark and William Wascher, "The Effects of Minimum Wages Throughout the Wage Distribution," National Bureau of Economic Research Working Paper Number 7519, February 2000, for evidence on this point.

markets for cigarettes in such countries as England, Italy, Germany, and Canada. Employees in the United States and other countries are sometimes hired "off the books" and paid in unreported cash in order to avoid payroll and income taxes.

How will black markets work? As in other markets, supply and demand will determine price in black markets. However, because they operate outside the official legal structure, enforcement of contracts and the dependability of quality will be less certain in these markets. Furthermore, participation in black markets involves greater risk, particularly for suppliers. Prices in these markets will have to be high enough to compensate suppliers for the cost of risks they are taking—the threat of arrest, possibility of a fine or jail sentence, and so on. Perhaps most important, there are no legal channels for the peaceful settlement of disputes in black markets. When a buyer or seller fails to deliver, it is the other party who must try to enforce it, usually through the threat of physical force.

Compared to normal markets, black markets are characterized by a higher incidence of defective products, higher profit rates (for those who do not get caught), and greater use of violence. The incidence of phony tickets purchased from street dealers and deaths caused by toxic drugs indicates that the presence of defective goods in these markets is high. Certainly the expensive clothes and automobiles of many drug dealers suggest that monetary profit is relatively high for those who manage to avoid major conflicts with the law. Evidence concerning the use of violence as a means of settling disputes arising from black market transactions is widespread. Illegal drug markets clearly illustrate this point. Crime statistics in urban areas show that a high percentage of the violent crimes, including murder, are associated with bad trades and competition among dealers in the illegal drug market.

The U.S. experience during the Prohibition era also illustrates the elevated role of violence in markets operating outside the rule of law. When the production and sale of alcohol was illegal during the 1920–1933 Prohibition period, gangsters dominated the alcohol trade, and the murder rate soared to record highs. There were also problems with product quality (such as tainted or highly toxic mixtures) similar to the ones present in modern-day illegal drug markets. When Prohibition was repealed and the market for alcoholic beverages once again began operating within the framework of law, these harmful secondary effects disappeared.

The operation of black markets highlights a point that is often taken for granted: A legal system that provides for secure private property rights, enforcement of contracts, and access to an unbiased court system for the settlement of disputes is vitally important for the smooth operation of markets. While markets will exist in any environment, they can be counted on to function efficiently only within the framework of a structured legal environment. Such an environment is largely absent in black markets; therefore, more fraud, deception, and violence are observed here. The analysis of black markets also provides insights into current conditions in Russia and much of the former Soviet Union. A well-structured legal system is often absent in these areas. In fact, markets in Russia are quite similar to black markets in Western Europe and North America. So, too, is their operation. Fraud, deception, and the use of violence are widespread, and, from the viewpoint of economic efficiency, the performance of markets in these areas is relatively poor.

THE IMPACT OF A TAX

Tax incidence
The manner in which the burden of a tax is distributed among economic units (consumers, producers, employees, employers, and so on). The actual tax burden does not always fall on those who are statutorily assigned to pay the tax.

How do taxes affect market exchanges? When a tax is placed on the sale of a good, who bears the burden? Economists use the term **tax incidence** to indicate how the burden of a tax is *actually* shared between buyers (who pay more for what they purchase) and sellers (who receive less for what they sell). When a tax is imposed, the government can make either the buyer or the seller legally responsible for payment of the tax. The legal assignment is called the *statutory incidence* of the tax. However, the person who writes the check to the government—that is, the person statutorily responsible for the tax—is not always the one who bears the tax burden. The *actual incidence* of a tax may lie elsewhere. If, for example, a tax is placed statutorily on a seller, the seller may increase the price of the

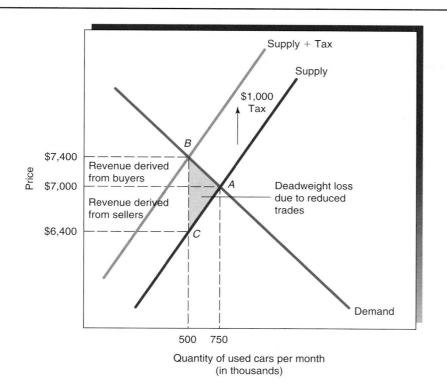

Price
Quantity of used cars per month
(in thousands)

Supply + Tax

Supply

$1,000
Tax

B

$7,400

Revenue derived
from buyers

$7,000

A

Revenue derived
from sellers

Deadweight loss
due to reduced
trades

$6,400

C

Demand

500   750

EXHIBIT 7
The Impact of a Tax
Imposed on Sellers

When a $1,000 tax is imposed statutorily on the sellers of used cars, the supply curve shifts vertically upward by the amount of the tax. The price of used cars to buyers rises from $7,000 to $7,400, resulting in buyers bearing $400 of the burden of this tax. The price received by a seller falls from $7,000 to $6,400 ($7,400 minus the $1,000 tax), resulting in sellers bearing $600 of the burden.

product to consumers, in which case the buyers ends up bearing some, or all, of the tax burden.

To illustrate, **Exhibit 7** shows how a $1,000 tax placed on the sale of used cars would affect the market. (In this hypothetical example, we simplify by assuming that all used cars are identical.) Here, the tax has statutorily been placed on the seller. When a tax is imposed on the seller, it shifts the supply curve upward by exactly the amount of the tax, $1,000 in this example. To understand why, remember that the height of the supply curve at a particular quantity shows the minimum price required to cause enough sellers to offer that quantity of cars for sale. Suppose that you were a potential seller, willing to sell your car for any price over $6,000, but unwilling unless you can pocket at least $6,000 from the sale. Because you will have to pay a tax of $1,000 when you sell your car, the minimum price you will accept *from the buyer* must now rise to $7,000 so that after paying the tax, you will retain $6,000. Other potential sellers will be in an identical position. The tax will push the minimum price at which each seller will be willing to supply the good upward by $1,000. Thus, the after-tax supply curve shifts vertically by this amount.

Before the imposition of the tax, used cars sold for a price of $7,000 (at the intersection of the original supply and demand curves shown by point *A*). After the imposition of this tax, the price of used cars will rise to $7,400 (the intersection of the new supply curve that includes the tax, and the demand curve, shown by point *B*). Thus, despite the tax being statutorily imposed on sellers, the higher price shifts some of the tax burden to buyers. A buyer will now pay $400 more for a used car after the imposition of the tax. A seller now receives $7,400 from the sale of a used car, but, after sending the tax of $1,000 to the government, the seller retains only $6,400. This is exactly $600 less than the seller would have received had the tax not been imposed. Because the distance between the supply curves is exactly $1,000, this net price can be found in Exhibit 7 by following the vertical line down from the new equilibrium to the original supply curve (point *C*) and over to the price axis. In this case, each $1,000 of tax revenue transferred to the government imposes a burden of $400 on the buyer (in the form of higher used-car prices) and a $600 burden on sellers (in the form of lower net receipts from a car sale).

Tax base
The level or quantity of the economic activity that is taxed (e.g., gallons of gasoline sold per week). Because they make the activity less attractive, higher tax rates reduce the level of the tax base.

Tax rate
The per-unit amount of the tax or the percentage rate at which the economic activity is taxed.

Deadweight loss
A loss of gains from trade resulting from the imposition of a tax. It imposes a burden of taxation over and above the burden associated with the transfer of revenues to the government.

Excess burden of taxation
Another term for deadweight loss. It reflects losses that occur when beneficial activities are forgone because they are taxed.

The tax revenue derived from a tax is equal to the **tax base** (in this case, the number of used cars exchanged) multiplied by the **tax rate**. After the imposition of the tax, the quantity exchanged falls to 500,000 cars per month. In this case, the monthly tax revenue derived from the tax would be $500 million (500,000 cars multiplied by $1,000 tax per car).

The Deadweight Loss Accompanying Taxation

Sellers would like to pass the entire tax on to buyers, raising the price by the full amount of the tax, rather than paying any part of it themselves. However, as the price rises, customers respond by purchasing fewer units. Sales decline and sellers must then lower their price toward its pretax level, accepting part of the tax burden themselves in the form of a lower price net of tax. As Exhibit 7 shows, the imposition of the $1,000 tax on used cars causes the number of units exchanged to fall from 750,000 to 500,000. Thus, the imposition of the tax reduces the quantity of units exchanged by 250,000 units. Remember, trade results in mutual gains for both buyers and sellers. The loss of the mutual benefits that would have been derived had the tax not eliminated 250,000 units of exchange also imposes a cost on buyers and sellers. Economists refer to this loss as the **deadweight loss** of taxation. In Exhibit 7, the triangle *ABC* measures the size of the deadweight loss. The deadweight loss generates neither revenue for the government nor gains for any other party. It is a burden imposed on buyers and sellers over and above the cost of the revenue transferred to the government. Thus, it is often referred to as the **excess burden of taxation**. It is composed of losses to both buyers (the lost consumer surplus that is the upper part of the triangle *ABC*), and sellers (the lost producer surplus that is the lower part of the triangle *ABC*).

When a tax is imposed on products currently being produced, the deadweight loss to sellers includes the indirect cost the tax imposes on suppliers of resources to the industry (such as workers). The 1990 luxury boat tax vividly illustrates the potential adverse impact on resource suppliers. Although supporters of the luxury boat tax wanted to shift more of the tax burden toward wealthy yacht purchasers, the actual effects were quite different. As the result of the tax, the sales of luxury boats fell sharply and thousands of workers lost their jobs in the yacht manufacturing industry. Clearly, the boat tax substantially reduced the gains from trade between boat producers and resource suppliers. Thus, the deadweight loss of the tax was quite large. Because of the sharp reduction in luxury boat sales, the tax generated only a meager amount of revenue. This combination—a large deadweight excess burden and meager revenues for the government—eventually led to its repeal. Whenever taxes distort market behavior they create a deadweight loss, regardless of whether the taxes are on income or on goods and services.

The actual burden of a tax is independent of whether it is imposed on buyers or sellers.

By John Trever, *Albuquerque Journal.* Reprinted by permission.

"THIS NEW TAX PLAN SOUNDS PRETTY GOOD... WE GET A 9% CUT AND BUSINESS PICKS UP THE BURDEN...."

Actual Versus Statutory Incidence

Economic analysis indicates that the actual burden of a tax is independent of whether it is statutorily placed on the buyer or seller. To see this, we must first look at how the market responds to a tax statutorily placed on the buyer. Continuing with the above example, suppose that the government places the $1,000 tax on the buyer of the car, rather than the seller. After making a used-car purchase, the buyer must send a check to the government for $1,000. The imposition of a tax on buyers will shift the demand curve downward by the amount of the tax, as is shown in **Exhibit 8**. This is because the height of the demand curve represents the maximum price a buyer is willing to pay for the car. If a particular buyer is willing and able to pay only $5,000 for a car, the imposition of the $1,000 tax would mean that the most the buyer would be willing to pay *to the seller* was now $4,000. This is because the total cost to the buyer is now the purchase price plus the tax.

As Exhibit 8 shows, the price of used cars falls from $7,000 (point *A*) to $6,400 (point *B*) when the tax is statutorily placed on the buyer. Even though the tax is placed on buyers, the resulting reduction in demand causes the price received by sellers to fall by $600. Thus, $600 of the tax is again borne by sellers, just as it was when the tax was placed statutorily on sellers. From the buyer's standpoint, a car now costs $7,400 ($6,400 paid to the seller plus $1,000 in tax to the government). Just as when the tax was imposed on the seller, the buyer now pays $400 more for a used car.

A comparison of Exhibits 7 and 8 makes it clear that the actual burden of the $1,000 tax is independent of its statutory incidence. In both cases, buyers pay a total price of $7,400 for the car (a $400 increase from the pretax level), and sellers receive $6,400 from the sale (a $600 decrease from the pretax level). Correspondingly, the revenues derived by the government, the number of sales eliminated by the tax, and the size of the deadweight loss are identical regardless of whether the law requires payment of the tax by the sellers or by the buyers.

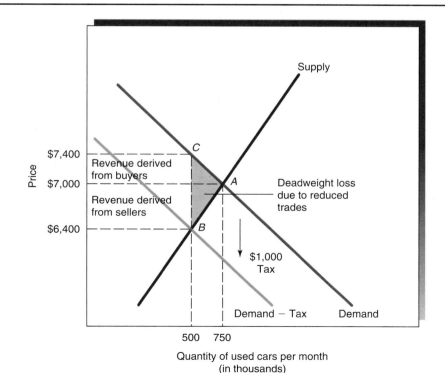

EXHIBIT 8
The Impact of a Tax Imposed on Buyers

When a $1,000 tax is imposed statutorily on the buyers of used cars, the demand curve shifts vertically downward by the amount of the tax. The price of used cars falls from $7,000 to $6,400, resulting in sellers bearing $600 of the burden. The buyer's total cost of purchasing the car rises from $7,000 to $7,400 ($6,400 plus the $1,000 tax), resulting in buyers bearing $400 of the burden of this tax. The incidence of this tax on used cars is the same regardless of whether it is statutorily imposed on buyers or sellers.

The equivalence of the actual burden of a tax regardless of its statutory assignment is true for any tax. The 15.3 percent social security payroll tax, for example, is statutorily levied as 7.65 percent on the employee and 7.65 percent on the employer. The impact is to drive down the net pay received by employees and raise the employers' cost of hiring workers. Economic analysis tells us that the actual burden of this tax will probably differ from its legal assignment. The actual burden imposed on employees and employers, however, will be the same regardless of how the tax is statutorily assigned. Because market prices (here, workers' gross pay) will adjust, the incidence of the tax will be identical regardless of whether the 15.3 percent is levied on employees or on employers or is divided between the two parties.

Elasticity and the Incidence of a Tax

If the actual incidence of a tax is independent of its statutory assignment, what does determine the incidence? The answer: *The incidence of a tax depends on the responsiveness of buyers and of sellers to a change in price*. When buyers respond to even a small rise in price by leaving this market and buying other things, then they will not be willing to accept a price that is much higher. Similarly, if sellers respond to a small reduction in what they receive by shifting to other areas or going out of business, then they will not be willing to accept a much smaller payment, net of tax. The burden of a tax—its incidence—tends to fall more heavily on whichever side of the market has the least attractive options elsewhere, thus is less sensitive to price changes.

In the preceding chapter, we saw that the steepness of the supply and demand curves reflects the degree of responsiveness to a price change. Relatively inelastic demand or supply curves are steeper (more vertical), indicating less responsiveness to a change in price. Relatively elastic demand or supply curves are flatter (more horizontal), indicating a higher degree of responsiveness to a change in price.

Using gasoline as an example, part a of **Exhibit 9** illustrates the impact of a tax when demand is relatively inelastic and supply is relatively elastic. It will not be easy for gasoline consumers to shift—particularly in the short run—to other fuels in response to an increase in the price of gasoline. The inelastic demand reflects this point. When a 20-cent tax is imposed on gasoline, buyers end up paying 15 cents more per gallon ($1.65 instead of $1.50), while the net price of sellers is 5 cents less ($1.45 instead of $1.50). *When, as in the case of gasoline, demand is relatively inelastic and supply elastic, the primary burden of a tax will fall on buyers.*

In contrast, more of the tax burden will fall on sellers and resource suppliers when demand is relatively elastic and supply inelastic. Using a tax on luxury boats as an example, part b of Exhibit 9 illustrates this point. As we mentioned earlier, Congress imposed a tax on the sale of luxury boats in 1990. Later, the tax was repealed because of its adverse impact on sales and employment in the industry. There are many things on which wealthy potential yacht owners can spend their money other than luxury boats *sold in the United States*. For one thing, they can buy a yacht someplace else, perhaps in Mexico, England, or the Bahamas. Or they can spend more time on the golf course, travel to exotic places, or purchase a nicer car or more expensive home. Because there are attractive substitutes, the demand for domestically produced luxury boats is relatively elastic compared to supply. Therefore, when a $25,000 tax is imposed on luxury boats, prices rise by only $5,000 (from $100,000 to $105,000) and output falls substantially (from 10,000 to 5,000). The net price received by sellers falls by $20,000. *When, as in the case of luxury boats, demand is relatively elastic compared to supply, sellers (including resource suppliers) will bear the larger share of the tax burden.*

Elasticity and the Deadweight Loss

We have seen that elasticities of supply and demand determine how the burden of a tax is distributed between buyer and seller. These elasticities also influence the size of the deadweight loss caused by the tax because they determine the total reduction in the quantity of

EXHIBIT 9
How the Burden of a Tax Depends on the Elasticities of Demand and Supply

In part (a) when demand is relatively more inelastic than supply, buyers bear a larger share of the burden of the tax. In part (b) when supply is relatively more inelastic than demand, sellers bear a larger share of the tax burden.

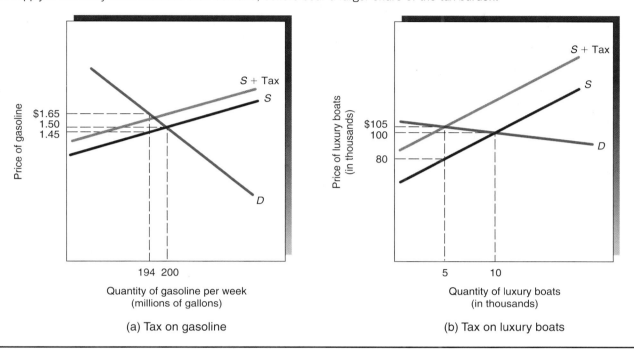

(a) Tax on gasoline

(b) Tax on luxury boats

exchange. When either demand or supply is relatively inelastic, fewer trades will be eliminated by imposition of the tax, so the resulting deadweight loss is smaller. From a policy perspective, the excess burden of a tax system will therefore be lower if taxes are levied on goods and services for which either demand or supply is highly inelastic.

TAX RATES, TAX REVENUES, AND THE LAFFER CURVE

When analyzing the impact of taxation, it is important to distinguish between the average and marginal rates of taxation. The **average tax rate (ATR)** can be expressed as follows:

$$ATR = \text{Tax liability} / \text{Taxable income}$$

For example, if a person's tax liability was $3,000 on an income of $20,000, her average tax rate would be 15 percent ($3,000 divided by $20,000). The average tax rate is simply the percentage of income that is paid in taxes. In the United States, the personal income tax provides the largest single source of government revenue. This tax is particularly important at the federal level. You may have heard reference to the federal income tax being "progressive." A **progressive tax** is defined as a tax in which the average tax rate rises with income. In other words, persons with higher income pay a larger *percentage of their income* in taxes. Alternatively, taxes can be proportional or regressive. A **proportional tax** is one for which the average tax rate is the same across income levels. Here, everyone would pay the same percentage of income in taxes. Finally, a **regressive** tax is one in which the average tax rate falls with income. If someone making $100,000 per year paid $30,000 in taxes (an ATR of 30 percent) while someone making $30,000 per year paid $15,000 in taxes (an ATR of 50 percent), the tax code would be regressive. Note that a

Average tax rate (ATR)
Tax liability divided by taxable income. It is the percentage of income paid in taxes.

Progressive tax
A tax in which the average tax rate rises with income. Persons with higher incomes will pay a higher percentage of their income in taxes.

Proportional tax
A tax in which the average tax rate is the same at all income levels. Everyone pays the same percentage of income in taxes.

Regressive tax
A tax in which the average tax rate falls with income. Persons with higher incomes will pay a lower percentage of their income in taxes.

regressive tax merely means that the *percentage* paid in taxes declines with income; the actual dollar amount of the tax bill might still be higher for those with larger incomes.

The economic way of thinking stresses that what happens at the margin is of crucial importance in personal decision making. The **marginal tax rate (MTR)** can be expressed as follows:

$$MTR = \text{Change in tax liability} / \text{Change in taxable income}$$

The MTR reveals both how much of one's *additional* income must be turned over to the tax collector and how much is retained by the individual. For example, when the MTR is 28 percent, $28 of every $100 of additional earnings must be paid in taxes. The individual is permitted to keep only $72 of his or her additional income. The marginal tax rate is vitally important because it affects the incentive to earn additional income. The higher the marginal tax rate, the less incentive individuals have to earn more income. At high marginal rates, spouses will choose to stay home instead of working, and others will choose not to take on second jobs or extra work. **Exhibit 10** illustrates the calculation of both the average and marginal tax rates within the framework of the 2000 income tax tables provided to taxpayers.

Generally, a person's income is subject to several taxes, and it is the combined marginal tax rate from all applicable taxes that matters to the individuals in their decision making. For example, a married couple with $30,000 in taxable income living in Baltimore, Maryland, would face a 28 percent marginal federal income tax rate, a 7.65 percent marginal social security payroll tax rate, a 5 percent marginal state income tax rate, and a 2.5 percent marginal local income tax rate. If we ignore the relatively small deductions that one tax can generate in calculating certain others, the result is a combined marginal tax rate of 43.15 percent, meaning that an additional $100 of gross income would result in only a $56.85 increase in net take-home income.

Governments generally levy taxes in order to raise revenues. The revenue derived from a tax is equal to the tax base multiplied by the tax rate. As we previously noted, taxes

Marginal tax rate (MTR)
Additional tax liability divided by additional taxable income. It is the percentage of an extra dollar of income that must be paid in taxes. It is the marginal tax rate that is relevant in personal decision making.

EXHIBIT 10
Average and Marginal Tax Rates in the Income Tax Tables

This excerpt from the 2000 federal income tax table shows that in the 28 percent federal marginal income tax bracket, each $100 of additional taxable income (from $32,000 to $32,100) results in tax liability increasing by $28 (from $5,555 to $5,583). Note that the average tax rate for a single taxpayer at $32,000 is about 17.4 percent ($5,555 divided by $32,000).

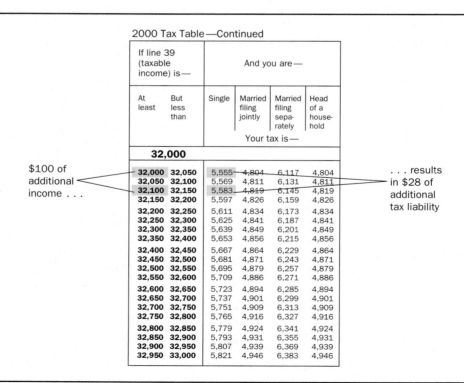

2000 Tax Table—Continued

If line 39 (taxable income) is—		And you are—			
At least	But less than	Single	Married filing jointly	Married filing separately	Head of a household
			Your tax is—		
32,000					
32,000	**32,050**	5,555	4,804	6,117	4,804
32,050	32,100	5,569	4,811	6,131	4,811
32,100	**32,150**	5,583	4,819	6,145	4,819
32,150	32,200	5,597	4,826	6,159	4,826
32,200	32,250	5,611	4,834	6,173	4,834
32,250	32,300	5,625	4,841	6,187	4,841
32,300	32,350	5,639	4,849	6,201	4,849
32,350	32,400	5,653	4,856	6,215	4,856
32,400	32,450	5,667	4,864	6,229	4,864
32,450	32,500	5,681	4,871	6,243	4,871
32,500	32,550	5,695	4,879	6,257	4,879
32,550	32,600	5,709	4,886	6,271	4,886
32,600	32,650	5,723	4,894	6,285	4,894
32,650	32,700	5,737	4,901	6,299	4,901
32,700	32,750	5,751	4,909	6,313	4,909
32,750	32,800	5,765	4,916	6,327	4,916
32,800	32,850	5,779	4,924	6,341	4,924
32,850	32,900	5,793	4,931	6,355	4,931
32,900	32,950	5,807	4,939	6,369	4,939
32,950	33,000	5,821	4,946	6,383	4,946

$100 of additional income . . .

. . . results in $28 of additional tax liability

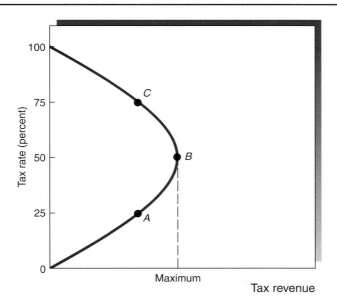

EXHIBIT 11
Laffer Curve

Because taxation affects the amount of the activity being taxed, a change in tax rates will not lead to a proportional change in tax revenues. As the Laffer curve indicates, beyond some point (*B*), an increase in tax rates will cause tax revenues to fall. Because large tax rate increases will lead to only a small expansion in tax revenue as *B* is approached, there is no presumption that point *B* is an ideal rate of taxation.

will lower the level of the activity taxed. The basic postulate of economics indicates that when an activity is taxed more heavily, people will choose less of it. The higher the tax rate, the greater the shift away from the activity. If taxpayers can easily escape the tax by altering their behavior (perhaps by shifting to substitutes), the tax base will shrink significantly as rates are increased. This erosion in the tax base in response to higher rates means that an increase in tax rates will generally lead to a less than proportional increase in tax revenues.

Economist Arthur Laffer has popularized the idea that, beyond some point, higher tax rates will shrink the tax base so much that tax revenues will decline when tax rates are increased. The curve illustrating the relationship between tax rates and tax revenues is called the **Laffer curve**. **Exhibit 11** illustrates the concept of the Laffer curve as it applies to income-generating activities. Obviously, tax revenues would be zero if the income tax rate were zero. What is not so obvious is that tax revenues would also be zero (or at least very close to zero) if the tax rate were 100 percent. Confronting a 100 percent tax rate, most individuals would go fishing—or find something else to do rather than engage in taxable productive activity, since the 100 percent tax rate would eliminate the personal reward derived from additional taxable earnings.

As tax rates are reduced from 100 percent, the incentive to work and earn taxable income increases, income expands, and tax revenues rise. Similarly, as tax rates increase from zero, tax revenues expand. Clearly, at some rate greater than zero but less than 100 percent, tax revenues will be maximized (point *B* in Exhibit 11). This is not to imply that the tax rate that maximizes revenue is ideal. In fact, as rates are increased and the maximum revenue point (*B*) is approached, relatively large tax rate increases will be necessary to expand tax revenue by even a small amount. In this range, the excess burden of taxation in the form of reductions in gains from trade will be exceedingly large relative to the additional tax revenue. Thus, the ideal tax rate will be well below the rate that maximizes revenue.

The Laffer curve illustrates that it is important to distinguish between changes in *tax rates* and changes in *tax revenues*. Higher rates will not always lead to more revenue for the government. Similarly, lower rates will not always lead to less revenue. When higher tax rates lead to a substantial shrinkage in the tax base, the higher rates will raise little additional revenue. In extreme cases, revenue may even decline in response to higher tax rates. Correspondingly, tax rates can sometimes be lower without any significant loss of revenue.

Laffer curve
A curve illustrating the relationship between the tax rate and tax revenue. Tax revenue will be low for both very high and very low tax rates. Thus, when tax rates are quite high, a reduction in the tax rate can increase tax revenue.

APPLICATIONS IN ECONOMICS

The Laffer Curve and Mountain Climbing Deaths

The Laffer curve is a tool that can be used to illustrate many relationships other than the one between tax rates and tax revenues. Economists J. R. Clark and Dwight Lee have used the Laffer curve framework to analyze the relationship between the safety of mountain climbing and the number of mountain climbing deaths on Mt. McKinley. As the probability of death from the climb fell due to increased government involvement in rescue attempts, the number of people seeking to "conquer the mountain" rose significantly. The increase in the number of climbers dominated the reduction in risk, leading to a Laffer curve type relationship: An improvement in safety resulted in a *higher* number of total deaths.

Perhaps a numeric example can best illustrate why this might be the case. Assume that if the probability of death from an attempted climb was 90 percent, only 100 persons would attempt to climb the mountain each year, leading to an annual death rate of 90. Now suppose that increased rescue attempts lower this probability of death to 50 percent. Because incentives matter, the increased safety will result in an increase in the number of people attempting to climb the

mountain. Suppose that the number of climbers increases from 100 to 200. With 200 climbers and a 50 percent probability of death, the annual number of fatalities would increase to 100, 10 more than before the improvement in safety. Viewing this within the Laffer curve framework, the total number of mountain climbing deaths is lowest both when there is a very high and a very low probability of death. The number of deaths is largest in the middle probability ranges. Thus, making a very risky mountain safer can result in more rather than fewer fatalities.

Besides mountain climbing, these same authors have explored a similar relationship between the average prison sentence length and total prison space occupied. Other authors have explored potential Laffer curve relations between the minimum-wage and the earnings of minimum wage workers and the regulatory costs of the Endangered Species Act on the acres of habitat for endangered species.*

---

*See J. R. Clark and Dwight R. Lee, "Too Safe to Be Safe: Some Implications of Short- and Long-Run Rescue Laffer Curves," *Eastern Economic Journal* 23 no. 2 (spring 1997): 127–137; Russell S. Sobel, "Theory and Evidence on the Political Economy of the Minimum Wage," *Journal of Political Economy* 107 no. 4 (August 1999): 761–785; and Richard L. Stroup, "The Endangered Species Act: The Laffer Curve Strikes Again," *The Journal of Private Enterprise*, vol. XIV (special issue 1998): 48–62.

It is interesting to view the 1980s within the framework of the Laffer curve. During the eighties there was a sharp reduction in marginal tax rates imposed on those with high incomes. The top marginal rate was reduced from 70 percent at the beginning of the decade to 33 percent at the end of the decade. Focusing on this sharp reduction in the top marginal rate, critics charged that the 1980s' tax policies were a bonanza for the rich. When analyzing this view, once again it is important to distinguish between tax rates and tax revenue. Even though the top rates were reduced sharply, both the tax revenue (even after adjustment for inflation) and share of the personal income tax paid by high-income taxpayers rose during the 1980s. As **Exhibit 12** illustrates, the real tax revenue (measured in 1982–1984 dollars) collected from the top 1 percent of earners rose from $57.6 billion in 1980 to $87.2 billion in 1990, a whopping increase of 51.4 percent. For the top 10 percent, as a whole, real revenue rose from $149.0 billion in 1980 to $191.9 billion in 1990. Meanwhile, the revenue collected from all other taxpayers was virtually unchanged.

Viewed as percentages of total income tax collections, in 1980 the top 1 percent of earners accounted for just over 19 percent of all income tax revenue collected. By 1990 at the lower tax rates, the top 1 percent accounted for more than 25 percent of income tax revenue. The top 10 percent of earners paid just over 49 percent of total income tax liability in 1980 and 55 percent in 1990. Interestingly, the top 10 percent of earners paid more than half of the total income tax liability.

The data from the 1980s are consistent with the Laffer curve. They indicate that in the case of most taxpayers (those in the range near point *A* of Exhibit 11), lower tax rates lead to a reduction in the revenue collected from the group. When tax rates are higher (in the range near *B* of Exhibit 11), tax rates can be reduced with little or no loss of revenue, and when rates get even higher (in the range near *C* of Exhibit 11), lowering tax rates will produce more tax revenue.

EXHIBIT 12
Changes in Taxes Paid During the 1980s

Measured in 1982–1984 dollars, the personal income taxes paid by the top 1 percent and the top 10 percent of income recipients increased between 1980 and 1990, even though their rates were reduced. In contrast, the tax revenue collected from other taxpayers was virtually unchanged during the decade (left frame). Per return, the revenue collected from the top 1 percent and the top 10 percent rose, while the revenue fell for other taxpayers (right frame).

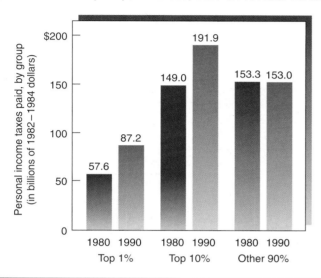

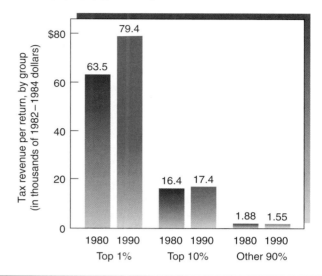

The last two chapters have focused on the operation of markets and the role of market prices. At various points, we have stressed the importance of legal structure and secure property rights for the smooth operation of markets. Governmental policies in these and other areas influence both economic efficiency and progress. The next two chapters will focus on the role and operation of government, a topic that is central to understanding the world in which we live.

LOOKING AHEAD

KEY POINTS

▼ Wage rates, interest rates, and exchange rates are also market prices determined by the forces of supply and demand. In each, these prices play important roles in coordinating the actions of buyers and sellers. Changes in these markets lead to changes in other markets and alter the relative prices of many other goods.

▼ Legally imposed price ceilings result in shortages, while legally imposed price floors will cause surpluses. Both will also cause other harmful secondary effects. Rent controls, for example, will lead to shortages, less investment, poor maintenance, and a deterioration in the quality of rental housing.

▼ The minimum wage is a price floor for unskilled labor. It increases the earnings of some low-skilled workers, but also reduces employment and leads to a reduction in training opportunities and a deterioration in the nonwage job benefits available to minimum-wage workers.

▼ Because black markets operate outside the legal system, they are often characterized by deception, fraud, and the use of violence as a means of enforcing contracts. A legal system that provides secure private property rights and unbiased enforcement of contracts enhances the operation of markets.

▼ The division of the actual tax burden between buyers and sellers is determined by the relative elasticities of demand and supply rather than on whom the tax is legally imposed.

▼ In addition to the cost of the tax revenues transferred to the government, taxes will reduce the level of the activity taxed, eliminate some gains from trade, and thereby impose an excess burden or deadweight loss.

▼ As tax rates increase, the size of the tax base will shrink. Initially, rates and revenues will be directly related—revenues will expand as rates increase. However, as higher and higher rates are imposed, eventually an inverse relation will develop—revenues will decline as rates are increased. The Laffer curve illustrates this pattern.

CRITICAL ANALYSIS QUESTIONS

1. How will a substantial increase in demand for housing affect the wages and employment of carpenters, plumbers, and electricians?

2. What is the interest rate? How does an increase in the interest rate affect the cost of purchasing a good now rather than in the future?

3. What is the exchange rate? If Americans suddenly increased their purchases from foreigners, what would happen to the value of the dollar on the foreign exchange market?

*4. To be meaningful, a price ceiling must be below the market price. Conversely, a meaningful price floor must be above the market price. What impact will a meaningful price ceiling have on the quantity exchanged? What impact will a meaningful price floor have on the quantity exchanged? Explain.

5. a. What is a price ceiling? What will happen if a price ceiling is imposed below the market equilibrium price?
   b. What is a price floor? What will happen if a price floor is imposed above the equilibrium price?
   c. Why are nonprice factors, such as product quality, service, and the characteristics of potential trading partners, more important when price ceilings and price floors are imposed than when prices are freely determined?

*6. Analyze the impact of an increase in the minimum wage from the current level to $10 per hour. How would the following be affected?
   a. Employment in skill categories previously earning less than $10 per hour
   b. The unemployment rate of teenagers
   c. The availability of on-the-job training for low-skilled workers

   d. The demand for high-skilled workers who provide good substitutes for the labor services offered by low-skilled workers, who are paid higher wage rates due to the increase in the minimum wage

7. What is a black market? What are some of the main differences in how black markets operate relative to legal markets?

8. How do you think the markets for organ donation and child adoption would be affected if they were made fully legal with a well-functioning price mechanism? What would be the advantages and disadvantages relative to the current system?

9. What is meant by the incidence of a tax? Explain why the statutory and actual incidence of a tax can be different.

10. What conditions must be met for buyers to bear the full burden of a tax? What conditions would cause sellers to bear the full burden? Explain.

*11. What is the nature of the deadweight loss accompanying taxes? Why is it often referred to as an "excess burden" of the tax?

12. The demand and supply curves for unskilled labor in a market are given in the accompanying table.
   a. Find the equilibrium wage and number of workers hired.
   b. Suppose that a new law is passed requiring employers to pay an unemployment insurance tax of $1.50 per hour for every employee. What happens to the equilibrium wage rate and number of workers hired? How is this tax burden distributed between employers and workers?
   c. Now suppose that, rather than being paid by the employers, the tax must be paid by workers.

How does this affect the equilibrium wage rate and number of workers hired? How is this tax burden distributed between employers and workers?

d. Does it make a difference who is statutorily liable for the tax?

Demand		Supply	
Wage	Quantity Demanded	Wage	Quantity Supplied
$6.50	1,000	$6.50	1,900
$6.00	1,200	$6.00	1,800
$5.50	1,400	$5.50	1,700
$5.00	1,600	$5.00	1,600
$4.50	1,800	$4.50	1,500
$4.00	2,000	$4.00	1,400

13. Currently, the social security payroll tax is statutorily imposed at 7.65 percent on the employee and 7.65 percent on the employer. Show this graphically, being careful to distinguish between the total cost to the employer of hiring a worker, the employee's gross wage, and the employee's net wage. Show how the outcome would differ if all 15.3 percent were imposed on the employee or if all 15.3 percent were imposed on the employer.

*14. Suppose that, recognizing that one cannot support a large family at the current minimum wage, Congress passes legislation requiring that businesses employing workers with three or more children pay these employees at least $10 per hour. How would this legislation affect the employment level of low-skilled workers with three or more children? Do you think some workers with large families might attempt to conceal the fact? Why?

15. "We should impose a 20 percent luxury tax on expensive automobiles (those with a sales price of $50,000 or more) in order to collect more tax revenue from the wealthy." Will the burden of the proposed tax fall primarily on the wealthy? Why or why not?

16. Should policymakers seek to set the tax on an economic activity at a rate that will maximize the revenue derived from the tax? Why or why not? Explain.

17. Suppose that college students in your town convinced the town council to enact a law setting the maximum price for rental housing at $200 per month. Will this help or hurt college students who wish to rent housing? In your answer address how this price ceiling will affect (a) the quality of rental housing, (b) the amount of rental housing available, (c) the incentive of landlords to maintain their property, (d) the amount of racial, gender, and other types of discrimination in the local rental housing market, (e) the ease with which students will be able to find housing, and finally, (f) whether a "black market" for housing would develop.

*Asterisk denotes questions for which answers are given in Appendix B.

CHAPTER 5

The Economic Role of Government

The principal justification for public policy intervention lies in the frequent and numerous shortcomings of market outcomes.

—Charles Wolf[1]

Chapter Focus

- How large is government? What economic activities are undertaken by the government?

- What are the distinguishing characteristics of government?

- How does the nature of decision making in the political and market sectors differ?

- Which functions of government are most likely to promote economic well-being?

- Why might markets fail to achieve ideal economic efficiency?

[1]Charles Wolf, Jr., *Markets or Government* (Cambridge: MIT Press, 1988), p. 17.

As we previously discussed, there are two general methods of organizing economic activity: markets and the political process. The last two chapters focused on how markets work. This chapter and the next will analyze the operation of the political process. As we proceed, we will consider both the potential and limitations of government as a vehicle with which to promote economic progress. ■

GOVERNMENT SPENDING AND TAXATION

As **Exhibit 1** illustrates, total government expenditures were only 9.6 percent of GDP in 1929, and most of that was at the state and local levels. (*Note:* GDP is a measure of the size of the economy. The term will be explained more fully later in macroeconomics.) Federal expenditures accounted for only 2.5 percent of total output in 1929.

During the 1930–1970 period, the size of government grew very rapidly. By 1970 government expenditures had risen to 32.3 percent of the economy, more than three times the level of 1929. Furthermore, almost two-thirds of these expenditures were undertaken at the federal level. Since 1970 the growth of government has slowed. Government expenditures in 2000 were 29.4 percent of GDP, close to the figure for 1970.

Exhibit 2 indicates both the sources of government revenue and the major categories of government spending. These figures cover all levels of government—federal, state, and local. The personal income and payroll taxes provide 31 percent and 18 percent of total government revenue. Thus, governments derive almost half of their revenues from these two taxes. Fourteen percent of the revenues are derived from **user charges**, prices charged for services like electricity, water, and garbage collection. User charges are most likely to be levied at the local level.

User charges
Payments that users (consumers) are required to make if they want to receive certain services provided by the government.

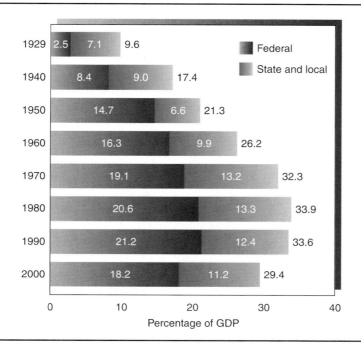

EXHIBIT 1
Growth of Government Expenditures, 1929–2000

Government expenditures as a share of GDP have risen over time.

Source: Bureau of Economic Analysis, www.bea.doc.gov and OECD, *OECD Economic Outlook,* June 2001. Grants to state and local governments are included in federal expenditures.

EXHIBIT 2
Government Revenues and Expenditures by Category, 1997

The major sources of government revenue are personal income taxes, payroll taxes, and user charges. The major categories of government spending are education, health care, Social Security, and other income transfers.

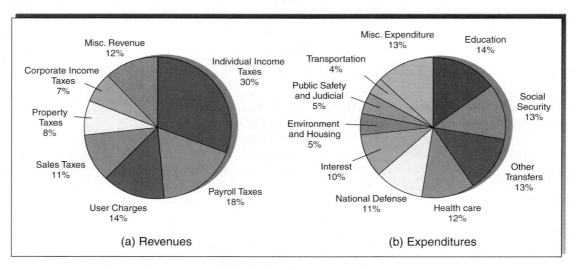

(a) Revenues   (b) Expenditures

Source: U.S. Census Bureau, *Summary of State and Local Government Finances of Government* and Office of Management and Budget, *Budget of the United States Government.*

The largest categories of government spending are education, health care, Social Security, and other transfer payments. These four categories account for 53 percent of all government spending. National defense and interest on the debt account for 11 percent and 10 percent of total spending respectively.

CHARACTERISTICS OF GOVERNMENT

At the most basic level, the distinguishing characteristic of government is its monopoly over the legitimate use of force to modify the actions of adults. Most societies allow parents to use force to influence the actions of their children. But with regard to adults, governments possess the exclusive right to use force. No individual or firm has a right to use violence—or the threat of violence—in order to take your wealth. If a business raises its price or performs unsatisfactorily, you always have the right to exit and take your business elsewhere. But when a government imposes a tax or a new regulation, exit is possible only by moving out of the government's territory—and that is costly, especially when it comes to the national government. Its monopoly on the legitimate use of force to take from its citizens—to tax them and to control their behavior—makes government different from any other form of organization.

Given its unique powers, it is tempting to think of government, particularly democratically elected government, as a tool that can be used to solve all types of problems ranging from the provision of health care to achieving a fair distribution of income. As we will show, governments can perform a number of functions that will enhance the economic well-being of the general populace. But we must not forget that it is merely an alternative form of social organization—an institutional process through which individuals collectively make choices and carry out activities. No matter how lofty the rhetoric of political officials, the people (for example, voters, legislators, lobbyists, and bureau managers) who make the choices that shape political outcomes are ordinary mortals, persons with ethical standards, narrow interests, and personal motivations very much like those present in the market sector. Furthermore, government decision makers often confront a reward structure that encourages them to undertake activities that conflict with a wise use of resources.

Because the incentive structure in the political process generally differs from that of markets, collective outcomes will often differ from market outcomes. For some categories of economic activity, there are reasons to believe that democratic political procedures work quite well. In other instances, there are sound reasons to believe that government allocation will be counterproductive. This chapter and the next will help us understand when—and under what conditions—political decision making is likely to yield positive economic results.

Differences and Similarities between Market and Collective Action

There is at least one important similarity between the market and the public sectors: The choices of individuals will influence outcomes in both. But there are basic structural differences in the way that individuals exercise their influence. Market transactions are characterized by voluntary exchange coordinated by prices. Only transactions that are voluntarily accepted by both buyer and seller will take place in markets. In contrast, when collective action occurs in a democratic setting, majority rule is the key, either directly or through legislative procedures. Let us take a look at both the differences and similarities between the two sectors.

1. Competitive behavior is present in both the market and public sectors.
The nature of the competition and the criteria for success differ between the two sectors, but people compete in both. Politicians compete for elective office. Bureau chiefs and agency heads compete for additional taxpayer dollars. Public-sector employees compete for promotions, higher incomes, and additional power, just as they do in the private sector. Lobbyists compete for program funding, for favorable bureaucratic rulings, and for legislation favorable to the interest groups they represent—including both private and government clients. (See Applications in Economics: Perspectives on the Cost of Political Competition.)

2. Public-sector organization can break the individual consumption-payment link.
In the market, a consumer who wants a commodity must pay the price. In this respect, market and collective action differ in a fundamental way. The government usually does not establish a one-to-one relationship between the individual's payment and receipt of a good. Some individuals receive very large benefits from a government action without any significant impact on their personal tax bill. Others pay substantial taxes while receiving much smaller benefits. In contrast with the market, the amount one pays does not determine the amount one receives in the public sector.

3. Scarcity imposes the aggregate consumption-payment link in both sectors.
Although the government can break the link between an individual's payment for a good and the right to consume the good, the reality of the *aggregate consumption–aggregate payment link* will remain. There are no free lunches. Someone must pay the cost of providing scarce goods, regardless of the sector used to produce (or distribute) them. Free goods provided in the public sector are "free" only to certain individuals. They are certainly not free from the viewpoint of society.

4. Private-sector action is based on mutual agreement, public-sector action on majority rule.
In the private sector, when two parties engage in trade, they do so voluntarily. Corporations, like General Motors and Microsoft, no matter how large or powerful, cannot take

income from you or force you to buy their products. Although mutual gain is the foundation for market transactions, the political process generates losers as well as winners. If a legislative majority decides on a particular policy, the minority must accept the policy and help pay for it, even if that minority strongly disagrees. If $10 billion is allocated by the legislative branch for the development of a super weapon system (or for welfare programs, health care, or foreign aid), the dissenting minority is required to pay taxes that will help finance the project. Similarly, if government regulators mandate that private parties must provide a wildlife habitat, wetlands, housing at below-market prices, or other goods, both the providers of mandated goods and potential buyers who would like to purchase the same resources for their own use must comply with government orders. When issues are decided in the public sector, those who disagree must, at least temporarily, yield to the view of the current majority.

5. When collective decisions are made legislatively, voters must choose among candidates who represent a bundle of positions on issues.

On election day, the voter cannot choose the views of Representative Frank Free Lunch on poverty and business welfare and simultaneously choose the views of challenger Amanda Austerity on national defense and tariffs. ***Inability to support a candidate's views on one issue while rejecting that candidate's views on another greatly reduces the voter's power to make preferences count on specific issues.*** Since the average representative is asked to vote on roughly 2,000 different issues during a two-year term, the enormity of the problem is obvious. The situation in a market is quite different. A buyer can purchase some groceries or items of clothing from one store, while choosing related items from different suppliers. There is seldom a bundle purchase problem in markets.

6. Income and power are distributed differently in the two sectors.

Individuals who supply more highly valued resources in the marketplace have larger incomes. The number of dollar votes available to an individual will reflect his or her abilities, ambitions, skills, perceptiveness, past savings, inheritance, good fortune, and willingness to produce for others, among other things. An unequal distribution of consumer power is the result. In a democratic public sector, ballots call the tune. One citizen, one vote is the rule. But there are other ways of influencing political outcomes. An individual might donate money to help a campaign do its work better and capture more votes. Or an individual might provide more direct assistance to the campaign by visiting friends and neighbors, writing letters, or speaking publicly on behalf of the candidate (or party). The political process gives the greatest rewards to those who are best able and most willing to use their time, persuasive skills, organizational abilities, and financial contributions to help politicians get votes. Persons who have more money and skills of this sort—and are willing to spend them in the political arena—can expect to benefit more handsomely from the political process than can individuals who lack these personal resources. In the public sector as in the market, there is an unequal distribution of influence and "income," although the sources of success and influence differ between the two sectors.

APPLICATIONS IN ECONOMICS

Perspectives on the Cost of Political Competition

Because government is such an extremely important force in our economy and in our lives, individuals and groups try to influence election outcomes by voting and by providing political campaigns with both financial contributions and services of various types.

Competition for elective office is fierce and campaigns are expensive. In preparation for the 2000 elections, for example, candidates for U.S. House and Senate positions raised and spent over $1 billion. This amounts to approximately $2 million per congressional seat. Highly contested seats are often far more expensive.

During and after the election, lobbying groups compete for the attention—the ear—of elected officials. In fact, the greatest portion of campaign funds raised by incumbents is not raised at election time; rather, it accrues over their entire term in office. A large campaign contribution may not be able to "buy" a vote, but it certainly enhances the lobbyist's chance

to sit down with the elected official to explain the power and the beauty of the contributor's position. In the competitive world of politics, the politician who does not at least listen to helpful "friends of the campaign" is less likely to survive.

Campaign contributions are only the tip of the lobbying iceberg. In Washington, D.C., alone, tens of thousands of individuals, many of them extremely talented, hard-working, and well paid, are dedicated to lobbying Congress and the executive branch of the federal government. Furthermore, 65 percent of *Fortune* 200 chief executive officers travel to Washington at least every two weeks, on average. Billions of dollars in budgets, in taxes, and in expenditures required by regulation are at stake. When Congress and the agencies wield such power, competition to obtain the prizes and avoid the penalties naturally results in huge expenditures designed to influence government policy.*

---

*More details on campaign finance can be found in Michael Barone and Grant Ujifusa, *The Almanac of American Politics* (Washington, D.C.: National Journal, annual) or at the Federal Election Commission's Web site (www.fec.gov).

ECONOMIC EFFICIENCY AND THE ROLE OF GOVERNMENT

Government is a powerful force in the economy. It can produce much that is good. But using government is costly. Why do citizens turn to government? How large should the scope of governmental action be? From an economic viewpoint, what are the proper functions of government?

To address these questions, we need a criterion by which to judge alternative institutional arrangements—that is, market- and public-sector policies. Economists often use the standard of **economic efficiency**. The central idea is straightforward. It simply means that, for any given level of effort (cost), we want to obtain the largest possible benefit. A corollary is that we want to obtain any specific level of benefit with the least possible effort. Economic efficiency simply means getting the most value from the available resources—making the largest pie from the available set of ingredients, so to speak.

Why efficiency? Economists acknowledge that individuals generally do not have the efficiency of the economy as a primary goal. Rather, each person wants the largest possible "piece of the pie." However, all might agree that a bigger pie is preferred, particularly if each is allowed a larger slice as a result. Thus, efficiency can be in everyone's interest because it makes a larger pie, and, therefore, larger slices, possible.

What does efficiency mean? When applied to the entire economy, two conditions are necessary for ideal economic efficiency:

> Rule 1. ***Undertaking an economic action will be efficient if it produces more benefits than costs for the individuals of the economy.*** Such actions make it possible to improve the well-being of at least some individuals without creating reductions in the welfare of others. Failure to undertake such activities means that potential gain has been forgone.

Economic efficiency
Economizing behavior. When applied to a community, it implies that (1) an activity should be undertaken if the sum of the benefits to the individuals exceeds the sum of their costs and (2) no activity should be undertaken if the costs borne by the individuals exceed the benefits.

Rule 2. ***Undertaking an economic action will be inefficient if it produces more costs than benefits to the individuals.*** When an action results in greater total costs than benefits, somebody must be harmed. The benefits that accrue to those who gain are insufficient to compensate for the losses imposed on others. Therefore, when all persons are considered, the net impact of such an action is counterproductive.

Both failure to undertake an efficient action (Rule 1) and the undertaking of inefficient activities (Rule 2) will result in economic inefficiency. The concept of economic efficiency applies to each and every possible income distribution, although a change in income distribution may alter the precise combination of goods and services that is most efficient.[2] Positive economics does not tell us how income should be distributed. Of course, we all have ideas on the subject. Most of us would like to see more income distributed our way. Agreement on what is the best distribution of income is unlikely, but for any particular income distribution, there will be an ideal resource allocation that will be most efficient.

Economic efficiency provides us with a criterion for the evaluation of the scope of government. Of course, this does not completely resolve the issue. Philosophers, economists, and other scholars have debated this issue for centuries. While the debate continues, there is substantial agreement that at least two functions of government are legitimate: (1) protection against invasions by others and (2) provision of goods that cannot easily be provided through markets. These two functions correspond to what Nobel laureate James Buchanan conceptualizes as the protective and productive functions of government.

Protective Function of Government

The most fundamental function of government is the protection of individuals and their property against acts of aggression. As John Locke wrote more than three centuries ago, individuals are constantly threatened by "the invasions of others." Therefore, each individual "is willing to join in society with others, who are already united, or have a mind to unite, for the mutual preservation of their lives, liberties, and estates."[3]

The English philosopher John Locke argued that people own themselves and, as a result of this self-ownership, they also own the fruits of their labor. Locke stressed that individuals are not subservient to government. To the contrary, the role of government is to protect the "natural rights" of individuals to their person and property. This view, also reflected in the "unalienable rights" of the American Declaration of Independence, undergirds the protective function of government.

---

[2]Note to students who may pursue advanced study in economics: Using the concept of efficiency to compare alternative policies typically requires that the analyst estimate costs and benefits that are difficult or impossible to measure. Costs and benefits are the values of opportunities forgone or accepted by individuals, *as evaluated by those individuals.* Then these costs and benefits must be added up across all individuals and compared. But does a dollar's gain for one individual really compensate for a dollar's sacrifice by another? Some economists simply reject the validity of making such comparisons. They say that neither the estimates by the economic analyst of subjectively determined costs and benefits nor the adding up of these costs and benefits across individuals is meaningful. Their case may be valid, but most economists today nevertheless use the concept of efficiency as we present it. No other way to use economic analysis to compare policy alternatives has been found.

[3]John Locke, *Treatise of Civil Government*, 1690, ed. Charles Sherman (New York: Appleton-Century-Crofts, 1937), p. 82.

APPLICATIONS IN ECONOMICS

The Importance of the Protective Function

The Case of Russia

Government does not always protect the rights of those who produce value. It sometimes joins with those seeking to restrict trade or plunder the goods of others. The recent experience of Russia vividly illustrates what happens when the protective function of government is poorly performed. Reporter Andrew Higgins, in a front-page article in *The Wall Street Journal* (October 16, 1998) described how regional officials, or "barons," sought to ban the movement of food out of their domains in order to keep food prices low for their regional constituents. "Eager to keep bread cheap, sausages plentiful and their own interests secure," various regional barons restricted the ability of farm producers to trade with buyers outside of their region. As a result, food prices in Moscow and other large northern cities were substantially higher than in the countryside where the food is produced. Sunflower oil, for example, was selling for 2,000 rubles a ton in one region, while the price was 5,000 rubles in another.

The article describes the plight of Mrs. Irina Radinsya, who stored over 250 tons of rye on her farm, along with barley and a sunflower crop. When she and other farmers tried to move their food 375 miles north to Moscow, where hungry people were willing to pay more, regional police stopped them. Some farmers were refused permission to proceed, and others were required to pay bribes of 150 rubles (about $11.50 at the time) per truck moved out of the region. Far from protecting the property of producers and traders, government officials were restricting trade and seizing property. Under these conditions, less food is produced. Furthermore, some of the harvest rots as farmers seek ways around the artificial trade barriers and the lawless demands by government officials for bribes.

The protective function of government involves the maintenance of a framework of security and order—an infrastructure of rules within which people can interact peacefully with one another. Protection of person and property is crucial. The protective function entails the provision of police protection and prosecution of aggressors who take things that do not belong to them. It also involves provision of national defense designed to protect domestic residents against invasion from a foreign power. Legal enforcement of contracts and rules against fraud are also central elements of the protective function. Thus, individuals and businesses that write bad checks, violate contracts, or supply others with false information for example are subject to legal prosecution. As Exhibit 2 shows, in 1997 the U.S. government expenditures on these two items—national defense and public safety (including the operation of a judicial system)—were 11 percent and 5 percent of the total, respectively. These data show that while there is a substantial focus on the protective function, the U.S. government is also heavily involved in other activities.

It is easy to see the economic importance of the protective function. When it is performed well, the property of citizens is secure, freedom of exchange is present, and contracts are legally enforceable. With the freedom of exchange and assurance that if they sow (produce), they will be permitted to reap (enjoy the benefits of their output), individuals will move resources toward their highest valued uses. In contrast, when property rights are insecure and contracts unenforceable, productive behavior is undermined. Plunder, fraud, and economic chaos result. The recent experience of Russia illustrates this point. (See the accompanying Applications in Economics feature on Russia.)

Productive Function of Government

The nature of some goods makes them difficult to provide through markets. Sometimes it is difficult to establish a one-to-one link between payment for a good and receipt of the good. If this link cannot be established, the incentive of market producers to supply such goods is weak. In addition, high transaction costs—particularly, the cost of monitoring use and collecting fees—can sometimes make it difficult to supply a good through the market. When either of these conditions is present, it may be more efficient for the government to supply the good and use its taxing power to cover the cost.

Of all the productive functions that government can provide, a framework of a stable monetary and financial environment is among the most important. If markets are going to work well, individuals have to know the value to others of what they are buying or selling. For market prices to convey this information, a stable monetary exchange system is needed. This is especially true for the many market exchanges that involve a time dimension. Houses, cars, consumer durables, land, buildings, equipment, and many other items are often used and paid for over a period of months or even years. If the purchasing power of the monetary unit, the dollar in the United States, gyrated wildly, previously determined prices would not represent their intended values. Under these circumstances, exchanges involving long-term commitments would be retarded and the smooth operation of markets undermined.

The government's spending and monetary policies exert a powerful influence on economic stability. If properly conducted, these policies contribute to economic stability, full and efficient utilization of resources, and stable prices. However, improper stabilization policies can cause massive unemployment, rapidly rising prices, or both. Economists are not in complete agreement about how public policy can best provide for economic stability and a high level of employment. Those pursuing a course in macroeconomics will find both the potential and the limitations of government action as a stabilizing force discussed further.

THE ROLE OF GOVERNMENT AND POTENTIAL SHORTCOMINGS OF THE MARKET

The protective and productive functions of government can be analyzed within the framework of the invisible hand principle. As we previously discussed, the invisible hand of market forces generally provides resource owners and business firms with a strong incentive to undertake projects that create value. Will this always be true? The answer to this question is no. There are four major factors that may undermine the invisible hand and reduce the efficiency of markets: (1) lack of competition, (2) externalities, (3) public goods, and (4) poorly informed buyers or sellers. We will now consider each of these factors and explain why they may create the potential for productive action through government.

Lack of Competition

Competition is vital to the proper operation of the pricing mechanism. It is competition among sellers that drives the prices of consumer goods down to the level of their cost. Similarly, competition in markets for productive resources prevents (1) sellers from charging exorbitant prices to producers and (2) buyers from taking advantage of the owners of productive resources. The existence of competing buyers and sellers reduces the power of both to rig the market in their own favor.

Because competition is the enemy of prices higher than costs, sellers have a strong incentive to escape from its pressures. When there are only a few firms in a market, rather than competing, sellers may be able to collude effectively. Efforts in this direction should be expected. Competition is something that is good when the other guy faces it. Individually, each of us would prefer to be loosened from its grip. Students do not like stiff competitors at exam time, when seeking entry to graduate school, or in their social or romantic lives. Similarly, sellers prefer few real competitors.

Exhibit 3 illustrates how sellers can gain from collusive action. If a group of sellers could eliminate competition from new entrants to the market, they would be able to raise their prices. The total revenue of sellers is simply the market price multiplied by the quantity sold. The sellers' revenues may well be greater, and their total costs would surely be lower, if the smaller, restricted output Q_2 were sold rather than the competitive output Q_1. The artificially high price P_2 reflects not only resource scarcity, but also a premium due to the reduction in output resulting from collusion among sellers.

It is in the interest of consumers and the community that output be expanded to Q_1. At output Q_1, all units that are valued more than their cost are produced and sold. Thus, Q_1 is

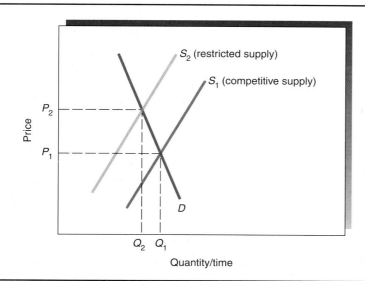

EXHIBIT 3
Rigging the Market

If a group of sellers can restrict the entry of competitors and collude to reduce their own output, they can sometimes obtain more total revenue by selling fewer units. Note that the total sales revenue P_2Q_2 for the restricted supply exceeds the sales revenue P_1Q_1 the competitive supply, in this case. Such behavior reduces the gains from trade, making the market less efficient as a result.

consistent with economic efficiency (Rule 1). It is in the interest of sellers, though, to make the good artificially scarce and raise its price. If sellers could restrict entry into the market and reduce output (to Q_2 for example), they could gain. If this happens, however, inefficiency would result because units valued more than their opportunity cost will not be supplied. There is a potential conflict between the interests of sellers and what is best for the entire community.

What can the government do to ensure that markets are competitive? The first guideline might be borrowed from the medical profession: Do no harm. *A productive government will refrain from using its powers to impose licenses, discriminatory taxes, price controls, tariffs, quotas, and other entry and trade restraints that lessen the intensity of competition.* Competition is ubiquitous. Without the help of government, sellers will generally find it very difficult to limit the entry of rival firms (including rival producers from other countries) into a market. When entry into a market is costly and there are only a few sellers, collusive behavior is more likely. In an effort to deal with such cases, the United States has enacted a series of antitrust laws, most notably the Sherman Antitrust Act (1890) and the Clayton Act (1914), making it illegal for firms to collude or attempt to monopolize a product market.

For the most part, economists favor the principle of government action to ensure and promote competitive markets. There is considerable debate, however, about the effectiveness of past public policy in this area. Many economists believe that, by and large, antitrust policy has been ineffective. Others stress that government regulatory policies have often been counterproductive by restricting entry, protecting existing producers from potential competitors, and limiting price competition. When government takes these actions, it actually *reduces* the competitiveness of markets. As we proceed, we will return to this topic and consider it in more detail.

Externalities—Failure to Register Fully Costs and Benefits

When property rights are not fully enforced, the actions of a producer or consumer might harm the property (or the person) of another, because the law fails to force the party doing the harm to bear the cost or to stop the harm. This failure results in spillover effects called **externalities**, actions of an individual or a group that influence the well-being of others without their consent. When spillover effects are present because, for example, the courts have failed to enforce rights against pollution, markets will fail to register the full costs of the resources used to produce a good or service. As a result, the information conveyed by prices is an inaccurate reflection of relative scarcity.

Externalities
The side effects, or spillover effects, of an action that influence the well-being of nonconsenting parties. The nonconsenting parties may be either helped (by external benefits) or harmed (by external costs).

Externalities resulting from poorly defined and enforced property rights underlie the problems of excessive air and water pollution.

Examples of externalities abound. The steel mill pouring pollution into the air imposes an external cost on surrounding residents. An apartment resident playing loud music may impose a cost on neighbors seeking to study, relax, or sleep. Driving your car during rush hour increases the level of congestion, thereby imposing a cost on other motorists. Similarly, litterbugs, drunk drivers, muggers, and robbers impose unwanted and *unauthorized* costs on others.

The existence of externalities implies the lack of property rights, or a lack of enforcement of those rights. The apartment dweller who is repeatedly bothered by a neighbor's noise either does not have a right to quiet or is unable to enforce the right. In either case, the maker of the noise is not forced to take into account the resulting discomfort of neighbors. Similarly, each motorist adding his or her car to heavy traffic will not be forced to consider the effects on others, unless there is a highway access fee reflecting the costs of congestion. When enforceable property rights are absent, externalities are a natural occurrence.

Not all externalities result in the imposition of a cost. Sometimes human actions generate benefits for nonparticipating parties. The homeowner who keeps a house in good condition and maintains a neat lawn improves the beauty of the entire community, providing benefits for other community members. A flood-control dam project built by upstream residents for their benefit may also generate gains for those who live downstream. Scientific theories benefit their authors, but the knowledge gained also contributes to the welfare of others who do not help to pay for their development. Again, a lack of enforceable property rights to the created benefit prevents the producer of the good or service generating the positive-valued externalities from reaping the full benefit.

Why do externalities create problems for the market mechanism? **Exhibit 4** can help answer this question. With competitive markets in equilibrium, the cost of a good (including the opportunity cost borne by the producer) will be paid by consumers. Unless consumer benefits exceed the opportunity cost of production, the goods will not be produced. What happens, though, when externalities are present?

Suppose that a business firm discharges smoke into the air or sewage into a river. Valuable resources—clean air and pure water—are used essentially for garbage disposal. The polluter may benefit from the garbage removal, but if those downwind or downstream who are harmed cannot successfully sue for damages, neither the firm nor the consumers of its products will pay for these costs. As part a of Exhibit 4 shows, the supply curve will understate the opportunity cost of production when these external costs are present. Since

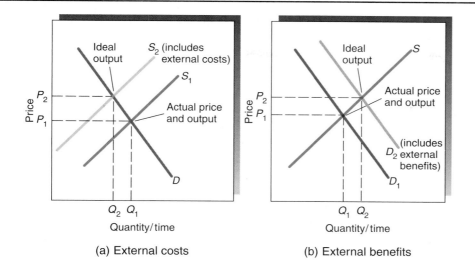

EXHIBIT 4
Externalities and Problems for the Market

When external costs are present (a), the output level of a product will exceed the desired amount. Some units (beyond Q_2) will be produced even though their costs exceed the benefits they generate, causing reduced efficiency. In contrast, market output of goods that generate external benefits (b) will be less than the ideal level. Production that could generate more benefits than costs is not undertaken, and a lack of efficiency results.

the producer has to consider only the cost to the firm and can ignore the costs imposed on secondary parties, supply curve S_1 is present. If the producer had to pay all costs, a smaller supply (S_2) would result.

The actual supply curve S_1 does not register fully the opportunity cost of producing the good. For the producer, the opportunity cost paid is low enough to merit expansion in output beyond Q_2 (to Q_1), *even though the buyer's valuation of the additional units is less than their full opportunity cost.* The second efficiency condition, Rule 2, is violated. Inefficiency results because units are produced even though their value is less than their cost. Excessive air and water pollution are side effects. In the total picture, the harm caused by the added pollution outweighs the net benefits derived by buyers and sellers from the production of units beyond Q_2. The economy would have been better off if the units beyond Q_2 had not been produced. To repeat, this problem is caused by the inability or the failure of courts to protect the property rights of those downwind or downstream who are harmed.

As part b of Exhibit 4 shows, external benefits often result in opportunities forgone. A good, such as a flower garden in the front yard of a home, may be intended for private consumption. But others also benefit without having to shoulder any of the costs. Under these circumstances, the market demand curve D_1 will not register fully the marginal benefits, including those received by persons who do not help pay for their cost. Output Q_1 will result. Could the community gain from a greater output of the product? Yes. The demand curve D_2 reflects both the direct benefits to paying consumers and the benefits bestowed on secondary, nonpaying parties. Expansion of output beyond Q_1 to Q_2 would result in a net gain to the community. But because neither producers nor paying consumers can capture the secondary benefits, consumption level Q_1 will result. The potential net gain from the greater output level Q_2 will be lost. Rule 1 of our ideal efficiency criterion is violated. Units that are valued more highly than their production costs will not be produced because suppliers are unable to collect payment from some of those who benefit from their actions.

Market participants can gain if they can figure out a way to capture the external benefits. Sometimes this can be done by expanding the functions of the firm. For example, developers of golf courses in recent years have typically purchased large tracts of land around the planned course *before it is built.* This places them in a position to resell the land at a higher price after the golf course has been completed, and thereby capture what would otherwise be external benefits.

The development of Walt Disney World in Florida provides an interesting case of entrepreneurial ingenuity designed to capture external benefits more fully. When Walt Disney developed Disneyland in California, the market value of the land in the immediate area soared as a result of the increase in demand for services (food, lodging, gasoline, and so on). Because the land in the area was owned by others, the developers of Disneyland were unable to capture these external benefits. However, when Walt Disney World was developed outside of Orlando, Florida, the owners purchased an enormous plot of land, far more than was needed for the amusement park. The value of this land soared, as the demand for hotels, restaurants, and other businesses increased with the development of Disney World. Through the years, the resale of land near the park has provided a major source of revenue for the Disney Corporation. While efforts of this type are helpful, they are unable to overcome fully the problems created by external benefits. Some unrealized potential gains remain, creating the potential for future improvement.

Summarizing, competitive markets will fail to give consumers and producers the correct signals and incentives when property rights are not fully defined and enforced, creating externalities. The market will tend to overallocate resources to the production of goods that impose external costs on nonconsenting parties and underallocate resources to the production of goods with external benefits. Government might be able to alter this situation. For example, it might be able to define and enforce property rights more clearly. Alternatively, it might levy a tax on goods that generate external costs and provide subsidies to activities that generate external benefits. While there is no assurance that government intervention will improve the situation, externalities do create the potential for productive government action.

Public Goods—a Potential Problem for the Market

Public goods

Jointly consumed goods that are nonexcludable. When consumed by one person, they are also made available to others. National defense, flood control dams, and scientific theories are all public goods.

Public goods are difficult to provide commercially through the marketplace because there is no way to exclude nonpaying customers. For a good to be considered a public good, it must be (1) *joint-in-consumption* and (2) *nonexcludable.* A good is joint-in-consumption when many individuals can share in the consumption of the same unit of output. A radio broadcast signal, for example, can be shared by everyone within the listening range. When a good is joint-in-consumption, additional consumption by one person does not reduce the amount available to others. An additional listener turning on a radio does not reduce the amount of the signal available for other listeners. Thus, the marginal cost of allowing an additional listener to share in the usage of the good is zero. Most goods do not have this shared consumption characteristic, but are instead rival-in-consumption. Two individuals cannot simultaneously consume the same pair of jeans, for example. When one person purchases a pair of jeans, there is one less pair available for someone else.

The second characteristic of a public good is that it is nonexcludable. Nonexcludable means that it is impossible (or at least very costly) to exclude nonpaying customers from receipt of the good. Since those who do not pay cannot be excluded, no one has much incentive to help pay for such goods. This creates a problem with **free riders**, persons who receive the benefits of the good without helping to pay for its cost. When a large number of people become free riders, not very much of the public good is produced. This is precisely the problem with market provision in the case of public goods—they will be undersupplied by the market. This will be true even if the good is quite valuable. Suppose national defense were provided entirely through the market. Would you voluntarily help to pay for it? Your contribution would have little impact on the total supply of defense available to each of us, even if you made a large personal contribution. Many citizens, even though they might value defense highly, would become free riders, and few funds would be available for the finance of national defense.

Free rider

One who receives the benefit of a good without contributing to its costs. Public goods and commodities that generate external benefits offer people the opportunity to become free riders.

It is important to note that it is the characteristics of the good, not the sector in which it is produced, that distinguishes a public good. In reality, government produces both public and nonpublic goods, and so do private markets. Many goods provided in the public sector, ranging from medical services and education to mail delivery and trash collection, do not qualify as public goods. In fact, pure public goods are rare. National defense is probably the closest example. Keeping the air in a city clean also qualifies as a public good. Similarly, the actions of a central banking system and the judicial and legal systems could also be classified as public goods.

Just because a good is a public good does not necessarily mean that markets will fail to supply it. When the benefit of producing these goods is high, entrepreneurs will attempt to find innovative ways to gain by overcoming the free rider problem. For example, radio and television broadcasts, which have both of the public good characteristics, are still produced well by the private sector. The free rider problem is overcome through the use of advertising (which generates indirect revenue from listeners), rather than directly charging listeners. Private entrepreneurs have also used such devices as signal encoders for television broadcasts like HBO and Showtime, copy protection on videotapes, and tie-in purchases (for example, tying the purchase of a software instruction manual with the purchase of the software itself) to overcome the free rider problem. The marketing of computer software provides an interesting illustration. Since the same software program can be copied without reducing the amount available, and it is costly to prevent consumption by nonpayers, software clearly has public good characteristics. Nonetheless, Bill Gates became the richest man in the world by producing and marketing this public good!

In spite of the innovative efforts of entrepreneurs, however, the quantity of a public good supplied strictly through market allocation will often be smaller than the quantity consistent with economic efficiency. This will create the potential for productive public sector action.

Potential Information Problems

Like other goods, information is scarce. Thus, when making purchasing decisions, people are sometimes poorly informed about the price, quality, durability, and side effects of alternative products. The reality of imperfect knowledge is not the fault of the market. In fact, the market provides consumers with a strong incentive to acquire information. If they mistakenly purchase a "lemon" product, they will suffer the consequences. Furthermore, sellers have a strong incentive to inform consumers of the benefits of their products, especially in comparison to competing products. However, circumstances will influence the incentive structure confronted by both buyers and sellers.

The consumer's information problem is minimal if the item is purchased regularly. Consider the purchase of soap. There is little cost associated with trying alternative brands. Since soap is a regularly purchased product, trial and error is an economical means of determining which brand is most suitable to one's needs. Toothpaste, most food products, lawn service, and gasoline also provide examples of **repeat-purchase items**. The consumer can use past experience to good advantage when buying such items.

Repeat-purchase item
An item purchased often by the same buyer.

When dependent on repeat-purchase customers, sellers have a strong incentive to supply consumers with accurate information. Failure to do so would adversely affect future sales. Because future demand is directly related to the satisfaction level of current customers, sellers of repeat-purchase items will want to help their customers make satisfying long-run choices. In this case, there is a harmony of interests between buyers and sellers.

This harmony, however, is not always present. Major problems of conflicting interests, inadequate information, and unhappy customers may arise when goods are either (1) difficult to evaluate on inspection and seldom repeatedly purchased from the same producer or (2) potentially capable of serious and lasting harmful side effects that cannot be predicted by a layperson. Under these conditions, consumers may make decisions that they will later regret.

When customers are unable to distinguish between high-quality and low-quality goods, business entrepreneurs have an incentive to cut costs by reducing quality. Businesses that follow this course may survive and even prosper. Consider the information problem when an automobile is purchased. Are consumers capable of properly evaluating the safety equipment? Most are not. Of course, some consumers will seek the opinion of experts, but this information will be costly and difficult to evaluate. It may be more efficient to have the government regulate automobile safety and require certain safety equipment.

Similar issues arise with regard to product effectiveness. Suppose a new wonder drug promises to reduce the probability that one will be stricken by cancer or heart disease. Even if the product is totally ineffective, many consumers may nonetheless waste their money trying it. When proof of effectiveness is a complicated and lengthy process, it may be better to have "experts" certify its effectiveness. The federal Food and Drug Administration was established to perform this function. However, letting the experts decide is also a less than ideal solution. The certification process is likely to be both costly and lengthy. As a result, the introduction of products that are, in fact, effective may be delayed and once they are introduced they may be more costly than would otherwise be the case.

Information As a Profit Opportunity

Consumers are willing to pay for information that will help them make better decisions. This presents a profit opportunity. ***Entrepreneurial publishers and other providers of information help consumers find what they seek by providing expert evaluations of the special characteristics built into complex products.*** For car buyers and computer buyers, for example, publishers market dozens of specialized magazines containing expert analyses and opinions from almost any point of view. Laboratory test results and detailed product evaluations on a wide variety of goods are provided by *Consumer Reports*, *Consumer Research*, and other publications.

Franchises are another way that entrepreneurs have responded to the need of consumers for more and better information. The tourist traveling through an area for the first time—and very possibly the only time—may find that eating at a franchised food outlet and sleeping at a franchised motel are the cheapest ways to avoid annoying and costly mistakes. The franchiser sets the standards for all firms in the chain and establishes procedures, including continuous inspection, designed to maintain the standards. Franchisers have a strong incentive to maintain their reputation for quality, because if it declines, their ability to sell new franchises is hurt. Even though the tourist may visit a particular establishment only once, the franchise turns that visit into a "repeat purchase," since the reputation of the entire national franchise operation is at stake.

Similarly, the advertising of a brand name nationally develops a reputation that is at stake each time a purchase is made. How much would the Coca-Cola Company pay to avoid the sale of a dangerous bottle of Coke? Surely, it would be a large sum. The company's brand name is worth an estimated $24 billion, and that good name is a hostage to quality control. The firm would suffer enormous damage if it failed to maintain the quality of its product.

Enterprising entrepreneurs have found ways to assure buyers that products meet high standards of quality, even when the producer is small and not so well known. Consider the case of Best Western Motels.[4] Best Western owns no motels; however, building on the franchise idea, it publishes rules and standards with which motel owners must comply if they are to use the Best Western brand name and the reservation service that the company also operates. In order to protect its brand name, Best Western sends out inspectors to see that each Best Western Motel in fact meets the standards. Every disappointed customer harms the reputation and reduces the value of the Best Western name, and reduces the willingness of motel owners to pay for use of the name. The standards are designed to keep customers satisfied. Even though each motel owner has only a relatively small operation, renting the Best Western name provides the small operator with the kind of international reputation formerly available only to large firms. In effect, Best Western acts as a regulator of all motels bearing its name. As it does so, it provides both consumers and producers with a market solution to problems resulting from imperfect information.

Purchase of information from reliable sources, franchising, and brand names can help consumers make more informed decisions. These options are effective, but costly. They will not always provide an ideal solution. Government regulation may sometimes be able to improve the situation, but this too has shortcomings. As in other areas, there is no general solution to the problems that arise because of imperfect information.

---

[4]This section draws from Randall G. Holcombe and Lora P. Holcombe, "The Market for Regulation," *Journal of Institutional and Theoretical Economics* 142, no. 4 (1986): 684–696.

THE OPPORTUNITY COST OF GOVERNMENT

Our analysis indicates that benefits can be derived from government. Governments can make a positive contribution by providing legal and monetary systems that protect individuals and their property from aggression and establish an environment for the smooth operation of competitive markets. Government may also contribute by providing a limited set of public goods and following policies capable of minimizing problems arising from externalities and poor information.

From an efficiency standpoint, however, costs must also be considered. The spending and regulatory activities of government are costly. Taxes provide some information but they do not reflect the full cost of government. Remember, the opportunity cost of an option is what we have to give up in order to enjoy it. Government is no exception. There are three types of cost incurred when taxes are levied and services supplied by the government.

First, there is the opportunity cost of the resources used to produce goods supplied through the public sector. When governments purchase goods and services to provide rockets, education, highways, health care, and other goods, the resources needed must be bid away from private-sector activities. If they were not tied up producing goods provided by government, these resources would be available to produce private-sector goods. This cost is incurred regardless of whether public-sector goods are financed by current taxes, by an increase in government debt, or by money creation. It can be diminished only by reducing the size of government purchases. A similar cost is incurred when government does not purchase goods, but orders the provision of goods without payment, or on terms decreed by regulators rather than terms voluntarily agreed upon by trading parties. The fact that government has not paid a market price does not reduce the cost. The Center for the Study of American Business estimated that the cost of complying with federal regulations, on the part of those regulated, was more than $340 billion (approximately $1,250 per person) in 1998. The first and often largest opportunity cost of an item supplied by government is the best alternative use that could have been made of the resources required to provide the good.

Second, there is the cost of resources expended in the collection of taxes and the enforcement of government mandates. Tax laws and regulatory orders must be enforced. Tax returns and formal notices of compliance with regulations must be prepared and monitored. Resources used to prepare, monitor, and enforce tax and regulatory legislation are unavailable for the production of either private- or public-sector goods. In the United States, studies indicate that it takes businesses and individuals approximately 5.5 billion worker-hours (the equivalent of 2.7 million full-time workers) each year just to complete the taxation paperwork. The total enforcement and compliance costs add approximately 15 percent, over and above the tax revenues, to the cost of government.

Finally, there is the excess burden (or deadweight loss) of taxation that we discussed in Chapter 4. Taxes distort incentives. When buyers pay more and sellers receive less due to the payment of a tax, trade and the production of output become less attractive. Trade and output will decline. Individuals will spend less time on productive (but taxed) market activities and more time on tax-avoidance and untaxed activities, such as leisure. Research indicates that these deadweight losses add between 9 percent and 16 percent to the cost of taxation.[5] These figures along with the costs of enforcement and compliance imply that transferring $1 to the government imposes a cost of approximately $1.25 on the economy. When a government agency can mandate the supply of a resource—for example, a tract of land for use as an endangered species habitat—it will tend to allocate more of the "free" resource and less of other resources that it must purchase from its own budget. Regulatory powers, like taxes, distort prices and incentives. Thus, they also impose a cost over and above the resources transferred to the government.

---

[5]The classic article on this topic is Edgar K. Browning, "The Marginal Cost of Public Funds," *Journal of Political Economy* 84, no. 2 (April 1976): 283–298.

In essence, the cost of government activities is the sum of (1) the opportunity cost of resources used to produce government-supplied goods and services, (2) the cost of tax and regulatory compliance, and (3) the excess-burden cost of taxation and regulation. Thus, government supply of goods and services generally costs the economy a good bit more than either the size of the tax bill or the level of budget expenditures implies.

LOOKING AHEAD

The political process is merely an alternative method of organizing economic activity. There is no assurance that even a democratic government will always "do the right thing." In addition, it is possible in some cases that the benefit from government intervention may not be large enough to offset the cost of government action. Furthermore, people can be expected to turn to government for reasons other than economic efficiency—pursuit of personal gain through subsidies, income transfers, and regulation of rivals, for example. Political decision making is complex, but the tools of economics can enhance our understanding of how it works. The next chapter will focus on this topic—the operation of government, when it is likely to work well, and when there is reason to expect that it will not work so well.

KEY POINTS

▼ In recent years, government spending has accounted for about 30 percent of the U.S. economy.

▼ The distinguishing characteristic of government is its monopoly on the legitimate use of force. In the market sector, economic activity is based on exchange and mutual agreement. In the government sector, it is based on majority rule—either directly or through a legislative body.

▼ There are both similarities and differences between markets and government. Competition is present in both sectors. The government can use its taxing power to break the link between payment and receipt of a good for an individual, but not in aggregate. Scarcity guarantees that someone will pay, regardless of sector. In the public sector, voters face a bundle purchase problem; they are unable to vote for some policies favored by one candidate and other policies favored by the candidate's opponent. Benefits and costs are distributed differently in the public sector, as opposed to the private sector.

▼ Governments can enhance economic well-being by performing both protective and productive functions. The protective function involves (a) the protection of individuals and their property against aggression and (b) the provision of a legal system for the enforcement of contracts and settlement of disputes. The productive function of government can help people obtain goods that would be difficult to supply through markets.

▼ When markets fail to produce the ideal quantity and mix of outputs, the problems can generally be traced to one of four sources: absence of competition, externalities, public goods, and poor information.

▼ Externalities reflect a lack of fully defined, enforced, and tradable property rights. When external costs are present, output is often too large—units are produced even though their cost exceeds their value. In contrast, external benefits sometimes lead to an output that is less than ideal.

▼ The distinguishing characteristics of public goods are (a) jointness in consumption and (b) an inability to exclude nonpaying consumers. Because it is difficult to establish a one-to-one link between payment and receipt of the good, the market supply of public goods will often be less than the ideal quantity.

▼ Entrepreneurs in markets have an incentive to find solutions to each market problem, and new solutions are constantly being discovered. But problems remain, and each creates the potential for improvement through government action.

▼ The cost of government is the sum of the opportunity cost of (a) the resources used to produce goods provided through government; (b) administering, enforcing, and complying with tax and regulatory legislation; and (c) the excess-burden of taxation and regulation. This cost will exceed both the government's tax revenue and level of expenditures.

CRITICAL ANALYSIS QUESTIONS

*1. If producers are to be provided with an incentive to produce a good, why is it important for them to be able to prevent nonpaying customers from receiving the good?

2. What are the similarities between economic allocation through political decision making and economic allocation through markets? What are the differences between the two methods of allocation?

3. What are public goods? Why are they often difficult for markets to allocate efficiently?

*4. Which of the following are public goods? Explain, using the definition of a public good.
   a. an antimissile system surrounding Washington, D.C.
   b. a fire department
   c. tennis courts
   d. Yellowstone National Park
   e. elementary schools

5. Explain in your own words what is meant by external costs and external benefits. Why may market allocations be less than ideal when externalities are present?

6. English philosopher John Locke argued that the protection of each individual's person and property (acquired without the use of violence, theft, or fraud) was the primary function of government. Why is this protection important to the efficient operation of an economy?

7. "The protective function of government is a key to the success of the market sector in the economy." Is this true or false? Explain.

8. "The traveler, in a market economy, has no chance for a fair deal. Local people may be treated well, but the traveler has no way to know, for example, who offers a good night's lodging at a fair price, if the quality and price are not regulated by government." Is this true or false? Explain.

*9. If sellers of toasters were able to organize among themselves, reduce their output, and raise their price, how would economic efficiency be affected? Explain.

10. What are external costs? When are they most likely to be present? When external costs are present, what is likely to be the relationship between the market output of a good and the output consistent with ideal economic efficiency?

*11. "Elementary education is obviously a public good. After all, it is provided by government." Evaluate this statement.

12. What are the necessary conditions for allocative efficiency? What are the major reasons why a market economy might fail to achieve ideal allocative efficiency?

13. Suppose that Abel builds a factory next to Baker's farm, and air pollution from the factory harms Baker's crops. Is Baker's property right to the land being violated? Is an externality present? What if the pollution invades Baker's home and harms her health? Are her property rights violated? Is an externality present? Explain.

*14. Apply the economic efficiency criterion to the role of government. When would a government intervention be considered economically efficient? When would a government intervention be considered economically inefficient?

---

*Asterisk denotes questions for which answers are given in Appendix B.

CHAPTER **6**

The Economics of Collective Decision Making

[Public choice] analyzes the motives and activities of politicians, civil servants and government officials as people with personal interests that may or may not coincide with the interest of the general public they are supposed to serve. It is an analysis of how people behave in the world as it is.

—Arthur Seldon[1]

It does not follow that whenever laissez faire falls short government interference is expedient; since the inevitable drawbacks of the latter may, in any particular case, be worse than the shortcomings of private enterprise.

—Harry Sidgwick, 1887[2]

Chapter Focus

- What are the major forces that determine outcomes under representative democracy?

- Can government action be mutually advantageous to all citizens?

- Does democratic decision making lead to economic efficiency? Is there sometimes a conflict between good economics and good politics? Why?

- Why does representative democracy often tax some people in order to provide benefits to others? What types of income transfers are attractive to politicians?

- Can government action sometimes improve on the efficiency of the market? When is it most likely to do so?

[1]Preface to Gordon Tullock, *The Vote Motive* (London: Institute of Economic Affairs, 1976), p. x.
[2]Quoted in Charles Wolf, Jr., *Markets or Government* (Cambridge: MIT Press, 1988), p. 17.

As we stressed in the previous chapter, the economic role of government is pivotal. The government sets the rules of the game. Its performance with regard to the protection of property rights, enforcement of contracts, and establishment of a stable monetary environment affects the efficiency of market allocation. Governments may also contribute positively through the efficient production of public goods. In addition to these basic functions, modern governments are also often involved in the operation of enterprises, provision of essentially private goods, regulation, and, most significantly, income transfer activities.

Given the size and breadth of government economic activity, it is vitally important to understand how it works. Government decisions are collective, or political, decisions. In most industrialized nations, political control is exercised through a representative democracy. In this chapter, we will use the economic way of thinking to study collective decision making and learn more about how a representative democracy functions and what we can expect from it. In doing so, it will become clear why good economics isn't always good politics, and why sound policies are often not enacted through the political process. ■

AN OVERVIEW OF COLLECTIVE DECISION MAKING

It is important to recognize that government, including one that is controlled democratically, is not a corrective device that will always do the right thing or necessarily undertake policies that promote the general welfare. It is, instead, an alternative method of social organization—an institutional process through which individuals collectively make choices and carry out activities. Just like any other institution, government is imperfect, and will be subject to failure. Economic analysis, however, can give us tools to better understand the conditions when government is likely to work well, and when it is likely to work poorly.

Public-choice analysis is a branch of economics that applies the principles and methodology of economics to the operation of the political process. In analyzing the behavior of people in the marketplace, economists develop a logically consistent theory of behavior that can be tested against reality. Public choice applies this same methodology to collective decision making. It develops a logically consistent theory linking *individual* behavior to political action, analyzes the implications of the theory, and tests them against events in the real world. Since the theory of collective decision making is not as well developed as our theory of market behavior, our conclusions will not always be as well defined. During the past 40 years, however, social scientists have made great strides, enhancing our understanding of public sector resource allocation.[3]

Economists use the self-interest postulate to enhance our understanding of decisions in the market. Likewise, public-choice economists apply the self-interest postulate to political decision making. They assume that, just as people are motivated by narrow interests and the desire for personal wealth, power, and prestige in the market sector, so, too, will these factors influence them when they make decisions in the political arena.

Closely related to self-interest as a motivator for politicians and bureaucrats are the concepts of survival and expansion. In the private sector, even if some managers are not

Public-choice analysis
The study of decision making as it affects the formation and operation of collective organizations, such as governments. In general, the principles and methodology of economics are applied to political science topics.

---

[3]The contributions of Kenneth Arrow, James Buchanan, Duncan Black, Anthony Downs, Mancur Olson, Robert Tollison, and Gordon Tullock have been particularly important. Public choice is something of a cross between economics and political science. Thus, advanced courses are generally offered in both departments.

primarily seeking profits, the profit-making firms are the ones who will be most likely to survive, prosper, and expand because they are the ones better serving their customers; and they are the firms that will be imitated. Similarly, in the public sector, politicians and the bureaucrats they hire must often act in the narrow self-interest of their constituents (and not incidentally in their own career self-interests) if they hope to survive and be reelected. Those who cooperate most closely with powerful constituency groups will obtain more political clout and have the opportunity to lead larger government agencies.

The collective decision process can be thought of as a complex interaction among voters, legislators, and bureaucrats. Citizen-voters elect a legislative body, which levies taxes and allocates budgets to various government agencies and bureaus. Directed by legislators, civil servants utilize the funds to supply government services and income transfers to the voters. In a representative democracy, voter support determines the composition of the legislative body, and a majority vote of the legislature is generally required for the passage of taxes, budget allocations, and regulatory activities. Let us take a closer look at the incentive structure confronting the three primary political players—voters, legislators, and bureaucrats—and consider the implications with regard to the operation of the political process.

The Voter-Consumer

How do voters decide whom to support? No doubt many factors influence their decision. Since voters must choose a candidate to represent them on a great many issues, they cannot know in detail how (and how effectively) the candidate will try to influence each issue in the future. Of necessity, the criteria they use must be very general. Which candidate appears to be the most persuasive, so as to represent best the voters back home? Who appears to be honest, sincere, and competent? Most voters do not know the candidates personally, so several such questions may come down to this: Which one presents the best television image?

The self-interest postulate indicates that voters, like market consumers, will ask, "What can you do for me, and for my goals, and how much will it cost me?" The greater the voter's perceived net personal gain from a particular candidate's election, the more likely it is that the voter will favor that candidate. In contrast, the greater the perceived net economic cost imposed on the voter by the positions of a candidate, the less inclined the voter will be to support the candidate. Other things equal, voters will tend to support those candidates whom they believe will provide them the most government services and transfer benefits, net of personal costs.

Unfortunately, rational voters frequently lack the detailed information needed to cast their ballots in a truly knowledgeable fashion. When decisions are made collectively, the direct link between the individual's choice and the outcome of the issue is broken. ***Most citizens recognize that their vote is unlikely to determine the outcome of an election. So they have little incentive to spend much effort seeking the information needed to cast an informed ballot. Economists refer to this lack of incentive as the*** rational ignorance effect.

Most voters simply rely on information that is supplied to them freely by candidates (via political advertising) and the mass media, as well as conversations with friends and coworkers. The rational ignorance effect explains why the majority of individuals of voting age cannot accurately identify their congressional representatives, much less identify and understand those representatives' positions on such issues as Social Security reform, tariffs, and agricultural policy. The fact that voters acquire scanty information merely indicates that they are responding rationally to economic incentives.

To see in a more personal way why citizens are likely to make better-informed decisions as consumers than as voters, imagine that you are planning to buy a car next week and also to vote for one of two Senate candidates. You have narrowed your choice of a car to either a Ford or a Honda. In the voting booth, you will choose between candidates Smith and Jones. Both the auto purchase and the Senate vote involve complex trade-offs for you. The two cars come with many options, and you must choose among dozens of different combinations; the winning Senate candidate will represent you on hundreds of issues, although you are limited to voting for only one of the two choices.

Which decision will command more of your scarce time for research and thinking about the best choice? Because your choice with regard to the car is decisive, and you must pay for what you choose, an uninformed car purchase could be very costly for you. But if you mistakenly vote for the wrong Senate candidate out of ignorance, the probability is virtually zero that your vote will decide who wins. Because your vote will not swing the election, a mistake or poorly informed choice will have little consequence. It would not be surprising, then, if you spent substantial time considering the car purchase and very little time becoming informed about either the candidates or the political issues at election time. The evidence is consistent with this view. For example, citizens in modern democracies support a great many profitable auto magazines, while even the very best of the magazines focusing on politics and policy cannot operate without donated funds. Citizens simply will not pay enough for even a single political magazine in the United States to earn a profit.

Rational ignorance effect
Voter ignorance resulting from the fact that people perceive their individual votes as unlikely to be decisive. Therefore, they rationally have little incentive to seek the information needed to cast an informed vote.

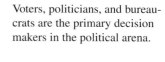

Voters, politicians, and bureaucrats are the primary decision makers in the political arena.

The fact that one's vote is unlikely to be decisive explains more than lack of information on the part of voters. It also helps to explain why many citizens fail to vote. Even in a presidential election, only about half of all voting-age Americans take the time to register and vote. Given the low probability that one's vote will be decisive, this low voter turnout should not be surprising. The rationality of voters is further supported by the fact that, when voters perceive that the election is going to be close, voter turnout is larger. A vote in a close election has a greater chance of actually making a difference.

The Politician-Supplier

Public-choice theory postulates that pursuit of votes is the primary objective shaping the behavior of politicians, or "political suppliers." In varying degrees, such factors as pursuit of the public interest, compassion for the poor, and the achievement of fame, wealth, and power may influence the behavior of politicians. But regardless of ultimate motivation, the ability of politicians to achieve their objectives is sorely dependent upon their ability to get elected and reelected.

Rationally uninformed voters often must be convinced to "want" a candidate. Voter perceptions may be based on realities, but it is always perceptions, not the realities themselves, that influence decisions. This is true regardless of whether the decisions are private or political. As a result, a candidate's positive attributes must be brought to the attention of the rationally ignorant voters, whose attention is likely to be focused on their jobs, various civic activities, and local sports teams (which are probably more entertaining). An expert staff, sophisticated polling to ferret out which issues and which positions will be favored by voters, and high-quality advertising to shape a favorable image for the candidate are vitally important for a successful campaign. Thus, political campaigns are costly. For example, it is not unusual for an incumbent candidate for the U.S. Senate to spend more than $15 million during the two years prior to each election.

Are we implying that politicians are selfish, caring only for their pocketbooks and reelection chances? The answer is no. When people act in the political sphere, they may genuinely want to help their fellow citizens. Factors other than personal political gain, narrowly defined, may influence their actions. On certain issues, political officials may feel strongly that their position is best for the nation, even though it may not be currently popular. The national interest as perceived by the political supplier may conflict with the position that would be most favorable to reelection prospects. Some politicians may opt for the national interest even when it means political defeat in the next election. None of this is inconsistent with an economic view of public choice. It does imply that through time the politicians who are most likely to remain in office are the ones who enact policies that garner votes and support from interest groups.

Just as the general does not want his Camp Swampy Budget cut, most heads of agencies want expanded budgets to help them do more, and to do it more comfortably.

However, the existence of political suicide does not change the fact that most politicians prefer political survival. There is a strong incentive for political suppliers to stake out positions that will increase their vote total in the next election. In fact, competition more or less forces politicians to make decisions in light of political considerations. *Regardless of ultimate motivation, the ability of politicians to achieve their objectives depends on their ability to get elected and reelected. Just as profits are the lifeblood of the market entrepreneur, votes are the lifeblood of the politician.* Many factors undoubtedly influence political suppliers. Political competition, however, limits their options. In the same way that neglect of economic profit is the route to market oblivion, neglect of potential votes is the route to political oblivion.

Government Bureaucrats as Political Participants

Bureaucratic interests can be an additional factor in politics.[4] The interests of bureaucrats are often complementary with those of special interest groups. The bureaucrats who staff an agency usually want to see their agency's goals furthered, whether the goals are to protect more wilderness, increase the number and the pay of public school teachers, or provide additional subsidized irrigation projects. Like other people, bureaucratic decision makers have narrowly focused interests. Many believe strongly in what they are trying to do. To further those interests usually requires larger budgets for the support of favored constituents' interests. Importantly, the larger budgets also provide bureaucrats with expanded career opportunities. Bureaus, therefore, usually work to expand their programs to deliver benefits to their constituencies who, in turn, work with politicians to expand their bureau budgets and programs. Thus, there is a strong tendency for bureaucrats in the Department of Labor, for example, to be favorably disposed toward the interests of organized labor. Those in the Department of Commerce are generally supportive of business, and those in the Department of Agriculture are supportive of farmers, and so on.

    Economic analysis suggests a strong tendency for bureaucrats and public-sector employees to favor expanding their budgets to sizes well beyond what would be considered economically efficient. Legislatures that provide funding for public sector bureaus are generally not very knowledgeable about the cost of production within the agency and the actual resource requirements. This makes it even more likely that political agents in charge of bureaus will be able to obtain funding beyond the level consistent with economic efficiency.

    The political process, which begins with election races and proceeds to legislative decisions and bureaucratic actions, brings about results that please some voters and displease others. In any case, these results help to fuel the next round of activities in the process. The goals of the three major categories of participants—voters, politicians, and bureaucrats—sometimes conflict. Each wants more from the limited supply of resources. But coalitions form among individuals and groups from the three categories, with members of each coalition hoping to enhance their ability to gain from government action.

WHEN VOTING WORKS WELL

Will voting and representative government provide support for productive projects while rejecting unproductive (and counterproductive) ones? People have a tendency to believe that support by a majority makes a political action productive or legitimate. Perhaps

---

[4]The economic analysis of bureaucracy was pioneered by William Niskanen. Reprints of some of his classic articles along with recent updated material can be found in William A. Niskanen, Jr., *Bureaucracy and Public Economics* (Aldershot, U.K.: Edward Elgar Publishing, 1994).

EXHIBIT 1
Benefits Derived by Voters from Hypothetical Road Construction Project

VOTER	BENEFITS RECEIVED (1)	TAX PAYMENT PLAN A (2)	TAX PAYMENT PLAN B (3)
Adams	$20	$5	$12.50
Chan	12	5	7.50
Green	4	5	2.50
Lee	2	5	1.25
Diaz	2	5	1.25
Total	**$40**	**$25**	**$25.00**

surprising to some, if a government project is really productive, it will always be possible to allocate the project's cost so that *all* voters will gain. Thus, all truly productive government projects could pass under a unanimous voting rule. **Exhibit 1** illustrates this point. Column 1 presents hypothetical data on the distribution of benefits from a government road-construction project. These benefits sum to $40, which exceeds the $25 cost of the road. Because voter benefits exceed costs, the project is indeed productive. [*Note:* for the sake of simplicity, the excess burden of taxation and other distortive effects are ignored in this example.] If the project's $25 cost were allocated equally among the voters (Plan A), Adams and Chan gain substantially, but Green, Lee, and Diaz will lose. The value of the project to the latter three voters is less than their $5 cost. If the fate of the project were decided by direct majority vote, the project would be defeated by the "no" votes of Green, Lee, and Diaz.

In contrast, look what happens if the cost of the project is allocated among voters in proportion to the benefits that they receive (Plan B). Under this arrangement, Adams would pay half ($12.50) of the $25 cost, since he receives half ($20) of the total benefits ($40). The other voters would all pay in proportion to their benefits received. Under this finance plan, all voters would gain from the proposal. Even though the proposal could not muster a majority when the costs were allocated equally among voters, it would be favored by all five voters when they are taxed (or charged) in proportion to the benefits that they receive (Plan B).

This simple illustration highlights an extremely important point about voting and productive projects. ***When voters pay in proportion to benefits received, all voters will gain if the government action is productive (and all will lose if it is unproductive).***[5] When the benefits and costs of voters are closely related, productive government actions will be favored by almost all voters. Correspondingly, if a project is counterproductive—if the costs exceed the benefits generated for voters—it will be opposed by almost all voters. ***Therefore, when voters pay taxes in proportion to benefits received, there is a harmony between good politics and sound economics.***

With public-sector action, however, the link between receipt of and payment for a good can be broken in that the beneficiaries of a proposal may not bear its cost. Public-choice theory indicates that the pattern of benefits and costs among voters will influence the workings of the political process. The benefits from a government action may be either

---

[5]The principle that productive projects generate the potential for political unanimity was initially articulated by Swedish economist Knut Wicksell in 1896. See Wicksell, "A New Principle of Just Taxation," in *Public Choice and Constitutional Economics*, James Gwartney and Richard Wagner (Greenwich, Ct.: JAI Press, Inc., 1988). Nobel laureate James Buchanan has stated that Wicksell's work provided him with the insights that led to his large role in the development of modern public-choice theory.

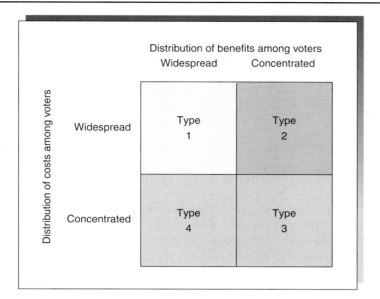

EXHIBIT 2
Distribution of Benefits and Costs Among Voters

It is useful to visualize four possible combinations for the distribution of benefits and costs among voters and to consider how the alternative distributions affect the operation of representative government. When the distribution of benefits and costs are both widespread among voters (1) or both concentrated among voters (3), representative government will tend to undertake projects that are productive and reject those that are unproductive. In contrast, when the benefits are concentrated and the costs are widespread (2), representative government is biased toward adoption of counterproductive activity. Finally, when benefits are widespread but the costs concentrated (4), the political process may reject projects that are productive.

widespread among the general public or concentrated among a small subgroup (for example, farmers, students, business interests, senior citizens, or members of a labor union). Similarly, the costs may be either widespread or highly concentrated among voters. As **Exhibit 2** illustrates, there are four possible patterns of voter benefits and costs: (1) widespread benefits and widespread costs, (2) concentrated benefits and widespread costs, (3) concentrated benefits and concentrated costs, and (4) widespread benefits and concentrated costs.

When both the benefits and costs are widespread among voters (Type 1 issue), essentially everyone benefits and everyone pays. Although the costs of Type 1 measures may not be precisely proportional to benefits, there will be a rough relationship. When Type 1 measures are productive, almost everyone gains more than they pay. There will be little opposition, and political representatives have a strong incentive to support such proposals. In contrast, when Type 1 proposals generate costs in excess of benefits, almost everyone loses, and representatives will confront pressure to oppose such issues. Thus, for Type 1 projects, the political process tends to be consistent with economic efficiency.

Interestingly, the provision of traditional public goods—for example, national defense, a police force and legal system for the protection of persons and property, and stable monetary arrangements to oil the wheels of exchange—best fits Type 1. Nearly everyone pays and nearly everyone benefits from public-sector action of this type.

Similarly, there is reason to believe that the political process will work fairly well for Type 3 measures—those for which both benefits and costs are concentrated on one or more small subgroups. In some cases, the concentrated beneficiaries may pay for the government to provide them a service. This would be the case when user charges finance public services (for example, air safety, electric power, water, sewage) benefiting subgroups of the populace. For these goods, voter-consumers pay roughly in proportion to their consumption of the government-supplied good. Under these circumstances, voter support will provide politicians with an incentive to provide public services that generate value in excess of cost.

Sometimes the subgroup of beneficiaries may differ from the subgroup footing the bill. But even in this case, if the benefits exceed the costs, the concentrated group of beneficiaries will have an incentive to expend more resources supportive of the measure than those harmed by it will expend opposing it. Thus, productive measures will tend to be adopted. Similarly, unproductive measures will tend to be rejected when both the benefits and costs are concentrated.

WHEN VOTING CONFLICTS WITH ECONOMIC EFFICIENCY

While the political process yields reasonable results when there is a close relationship between receipt of benefits and payment of costs, the harmony between good politics and sound economics sometimes breaks down. There are four major reasons why unrestrained majority-rule voting may conflict with economic prosperity.

Special-Interest Effect

Special-interest issue
An issue that generates substantial individual benefits to a small minority while imposing a small individual cost on many other voters. In total, the net cost to the majority might either exceed or fall short of the net benefits to the special-interest group.

Public-choice analysis indicates that problems will arise when issues of a special-interest nature are financed by general taxation. A **special-interest issue** is one that generates substantial personal benefits for a small number of constituents while imposing a small individual cost on a large number of other voters (Type 2 in Exhibit 2). A few gain a great deal individually, while a large number lose a little individually. Examples are not hard to find. The federal government currently spends $75 billion a year on direct subsidies to business. One example is the U.S. Department of Agriculture market promotion program that subsidizes foreign advertising by U.S. corporations selling bakery products, whiskey, and California Chardonnay abroad. Measures of this type are special-interest issues. A number of factors combine to make special-interest groups far more powerful in a representative democracy than their numbers would indicate.

It is easy to see how politicians can improve their election prospects by catering to the views of special interests. Since their personal stake is large, members of the interest group (and lobbyists representing their interests) have an incentive to inform themselves and their allies and to let legislators know how strongly they feel about an issue of special importance. Many of them will vote for or against candidates strictly on the basis of whether they support their specific interests. In addition, such interest groups are generally an attractive source of campaign resources, including financial contributions. In contrast, most other voters will care little about a special-interest issue. For the non-special-interest voter, opportunity cost of the time and energy necessary to examine the issue will generally exceed any possible personal gain from a preferred resolution. Of course, there are many such issues and each would have to be considered separately. Given the costs of information, non-special-interest voters tend to ignore such issues.

If you were a vote-seeking politician, what would you do? Clearly, little gain would be derived from supporting the interest of the largely uninformed and uninterested majority. In contrast, support for the interests of easily identifiable, well-organized groups would generate vocal supporters, campaign workers, and, most important, campaign contributors. *Thus, there is a strong tendency for politicians to support legislation that provides concentrated benefits to interest groups at the expense of disorganized groups (such as taxpayers and consumers). This will often be true even if the total community benefit from the special-interest program is less than its cost. Even if the policy is counterproductive, it may still be a political winner.*

The rational ignorance of voters strengthens the power of special interests. Since the cost imposed on individual voters for each specific issue is small, and since the individual is unable to avoid the cost even by becoming informed, voters bearing the cost of special-interest legislation tend to be uninformed on the issue. This will be particularly true if the complexity of the issue makes it difficult for voters to figure out how the issue affects their personal welfare. Thus, politicians often make special-interest legislation complex in order to hide the cost imposed on the typical voter.

The ability of the voter to punish politicians for supporting special-interest legislation is further hindered by the fact that many issues are bundled together when the voter chooses between one candidate and another. Even if the voter knows and dislikes the politician's stand on several special-interest issues, the bundling of hundreds of issues into one candidate choice severely limits the voter's ability to take a stand at the ballot box for or against any particular issue.

In addition, as we previously discussed, the interests of bureaucrats are often complementary with those of the interest groups they serve. Larger budgets are helpful to both. Thus, bureaucrats will often develop information and provide leadership that will help the interest groups that they serve to achieve their goals.

Yet another force that strengthens the political clout of special-interest groups is **logrolling**, the practice of trading votes by a representative in order to pass intensely desired legislation. Representative A promises to vote for measures favored by other representatives in exchange for their support of a measure that A strongly favors. With logrolling, legislative bodies often pass a bundle of proposals, each of which would be rejected if voted on separately.

Relatedly, **pork-barrel legislation** bundles together a set of projects benefiting regional interests (for example, water projects, dredging of harbors, or expenditures on military bases) at the expense of the general taxpayer. As in the case of logrolling, the bundle of pork-barrel projects can often gain approval even if the items by themselves would be seen as counterproductive and would individually be rejected by the legislative assembly.

Exhibit 3 provides a numeric illustration of the forces underlying logrolling and pork-barrel legislation. Here we consider the operation of a five-member legislative assembly considering three projects: construction of a post office in District A, dredging of a harbor in District B, and expenditures on a military base in District C. In each case, the project is inefficient—the net cost of the project exceeds the net benefit (by a 12-to-10 ratio). If the projects were voted on separately and the representatives reflected the views of their constituents, each project would lose by a 4-to-1 vote. However, when the projects are bundled together through either logrolling or pork-barrel legislation, Representatives A, B, and C will vote yes. The legislative bundle will pass 3 to 2 even though it is counterproductive (on average, the projects as a bundle reduce the wealth of constituents by $6).[6]

Legislation providing subsidies to electricity consumers in California, Nevada, and Arizona illustrates the relevance of logrolling and pork-barrel legislation. Under legislation passed in 1937, electricity generated by Hoover Dam has been sold to residents in the three surrounding states at rates ranging between 10 percent and 25 percent of the market price. The law providing for the subsidized rates was scheduled to expire in 1987. However, before it did, Congress extended the subsidies for another 30 years. The residents of many western states are the recipients of federally subsidized electricity. Every senator west of Missouri voted to continue the subsidized rates for electricity generated by Hoover Dam. In turn, they can expect senators and representatives from California, Arizona, and Nevada to support subsidized electricity rates in their states. In contrast, residents of other states will pay higher taxes so that many residents in western states can enjoy cheap electricity.

Logrolling
The exchange between politicians of political support on one issue for political support on another issue.

Pork-barrel legislation
A package of spending projects benefiting local areas at federal expense. The projects typically have costs that exceed benefits, but are intensely desired by the residents of the district getting the benefits without having to pay much of the costs.

---

[6]Logrolling and pork-barrel policies can lead to the adoption of productive measures. However, if a project is productive, there would always be a pattern of finance that would lead to its adoption even if logrolling and pork-barrel policies were absent. Thus, the tendency for logrolling and pork-barrel policies to result in the adoption of inefficient projects is the more significant point.

EXHIBIT 3
Vote Trading and Passing Counterproductive Legislation

	Net Benefits (+) or Costs (−) to Each Voter in District			
Voters of District[a]	Construction of Post Office in A	Dredging Harbor in B	Construction of Military Base in C	Total
A	+$10	−$ 3	−$ 3	+$4
B	−$ 3	+$10	−$ 3	+$4
C	−$ 3	−$ 3	+$10	+$4
D	−$ 3	−$ 3	−$ 3	−$9
E	−$ 3	−$ 3	−$ 3	−$9
Total	**−$ 2**	**−$ 2**	**−$ 2**	**−$6**

[a]We assume the districts are of equal size.

A unique form of special-interest lobbying is the monopoly held by Crane & Company for supplying the Bureau of Engraving and Printing with the paper on which U.S. currency is printed. The firm has been the sole supplier of paper for U.S. currency since 1879. Legislation was introduced in 1998 to provide for competition in the bidding, but the Massachusetts Congressional delegation fought off the legislation. Crane is located in Dalton, Massachusetts. The four-year contract is expected to total $400 million.

Why don't representatives oppose measures that force their constituents to pay for projects that benefit others? There is some incentive to do so, but the constituents of any one elected representative can capture only a small portion of the benefits of tax savings from improved efficiency, since they would be spread nationwide among all taxpayers. We would not expect the president of a corporation to devote the firm's resources to projects not primarily benefiting stockholders. Neither should we expect an elected representative to devote political resources to projects such as defeating pork-barrel programs, when the benefits of greater efficiency would not go primarily to that representative's constituents. Instead, each representative has a strong incentive to work for programs whose benefits are concentrated among his or her constituents—especially the organized interest groups that can help the representative be reelected. Heeding such incentives is a survival (reelection) characteristic.

The bottom line is clear: Public-choice analysis indicates that majority voting and representative democracy do not work so well when concentrated interests benefit at the expense of widely dispersed interests. This special-interest bias of the political process helps to explain the presence of many programs that reduce the size of the economic pie. As we discuss diverse topics throughout this text, counterproductive political action that has its foundation in the special-interest effect will arise again and again.

The analysis is symmetrical. When the benefits of a government action are widespread and the costs highly concentrated (Type 4 of Exhibit 2), the concentrated interests will strongly oppose the proposal. Most others will be largely uninformed and uninterested. Once again, politicians will have an incentive to respond to the views of the concentrated interests. Projects of this type will tend to be rejected even when they are productive that is, when they would generate larger benefits than costs.

Shortsightedness Effect

The complexity of many issues makes it difficult for voters to identify the future benefits and costs. Will a reduction in tariff rates lead to more rapid economic growth? Does the

Social Security program need reform, and if so, what might best be done about it? What impact will an increase in the national debt have on future prosperity? These questions are hard to answer. The difficulty of predicting the future results of current policies acts to reinforce the rational ignorance effect. Few voters will seriously research and analyze the implications of complex policy alternatives having impacts mainly in the future. Instead, they rely on current conditions when judging the performance of incumbents. To the voter, the most easily seen indicator of performance is, "How are things now?"

Accordingly, politicians seeking reelection have a strong incentive to support policies that generate current benefits in exchange for future costs, particularly if the future costs will be difficult to identify on election day. Public-sector action will therefore be biased in favor of legislation that offers immediate (and easily identifiable) current benefits in exchange for future costs that are complicated and difficult to identify. Simultaneously, there is a bias against legislation that involves immediate and easily identifiable costs (for example, higher taxes) while yielding future benefits that are complex and difficult to identify. Economists refer to this bias inherent in the collective decision-making process as the **shortsightedness effect**.

The shortsightedness effect is compounded by the lack of tradable property rights—the lack of a capital market—in government enterprises. For comparison with the private sector, consider the problem of choosing programs and strategies for a large corporation, such as General Motors. Its stockholders elect a board of directors to set policy and select professional management leadership. The corporation, like a government, faces complex choices of programs that are difficult for the individual stockholder to understand fully and evaluate. However, when evaluating the business programs and strategy of the corporation, the stockholder has an incentive very different from that of a voter. Why? Any stockholder who senses trouble before others do can sell out before the stock price falls. Similarly, the stockholder (or other observer) who recognizes a good program choice by a firm before others do can profit individually by buying stock in the firm.

The choices of informed, quick-to-act stockholders are registered in stock markets and passed on almost instantly. Investor decisions to buy or sell stock cause the stock price to rise or fall, signaling whether trouble or a winning program is forecast by the most attentive buyers and sellers of the stock. A strategy choice or a new program that investors believe will pay off handsomely in the future will quickly lead to a rising share price that rewards management choices well ahead of actual changes in profits and losses. No such advanced market signals, complete with incentives, exist in the collective decision-making processes of government. Thus, the planning horizon of politicians is short because it is difficult for them to capture future benefits. Neither are they held responsible—at least not fully—for future costs.

As a result of the shortsightedness effect, politicians have a strong incentive to promote programs providing easily observable benefits prior to the next election, even when the true cost of these programs outweighs the benefits for citizens as a group. In contrast, their incentive to support programs that generate sizable current costs in order to provide future benefits is reduced.

It is easy to think of instances where positive short-term effects have increased the political attractiveness of policies that exert a long-term detrimental impact. For example, borrowing makes it possible for political officials to increase current spending without raising taxes. Of course, the additional borrowing will mean higher future taxes. It may also lead to higher interest rates and less capital formation. But these costs will be indirect and observable mostly in the future. Thus, it should not be surprising that politicians often find borrowing attractive.

The political attractiveness of price controls is also enhanced because their immediate impact is much more favorable than their longer-term effects. For example, while rent controls may reduce the current cost of rental housing, as we noted in Chapter 4, their long-term effects will be a reduction in the supply of rental units, a deterioration in their quality, and a shortage of rental housing. Similarly, price controls on electricity may keep bills low for a while, but their long-term effects, as policy makers in California recently discovered, will be shortages in the form of blackouts and brownouts.

Shortsightedness effect
Misallocation of resources that results because public-sector action is biased (1) in favor of proposals yielding clearly defined current benefits in exchange for difficult-to-identify future costs and (2) against proposals with clearly identifiable current costs but yielding less concrete and less obvious future benefits.

When buying and selling are controlled by legislation, the first things bought and sold are legislators.

—*P. J. O'Rourke*[7]

Rent seeking
Actions by individuals and interest groups designed to restructure public policy in a manner that will either directly or indirectly redistribute more income to themselves.

Rent Seeking

There are two ways individuals can acquire wealth: production and plunder. When individuals produce goods or services and exchange them for income, they not only enrich themselves but they also enhance the wealth of the society. Sometimes the rules—or lack of rule enforcement—also allow people to get ahead by plundering what others have produced. Such activities enrich some at the expense of others, usually after a strenuous political struggle that consumes additional resources and reduces the wealth of the society.

Rent seeking is the term used by economists when referring to actions taken by individuals and groups seeking to use the political process to plunder the wealth of others.[8] The incentive to engage in rent seeking—perhaps "favor seeking" would be a more descriptive term—is directly proportional to the ease with which the political process can be used for personal (or interest group) gain at the expense of others. When the effective law of the land makes it difficult to take the property of others or force others to pay for projects favored by you and your interest group, rent seeking is unattractive. Under such circumstances, its benefits are relatively low, and few resources flow into rent-seeking activities. In contrast, when government fails to levy user fees or similar forms of financing to allocate goods and services, or when it becomes heavily involved in tax-transfer activities, the payoff for rent seeking expands. Rent seeking will also increase when governments become more heavily involved in erecting trade barriers, mandating employment benefits, providing subsidies, fixing prices, and levying discriminatory taxes (taxes unrelated to the provision of public services to the taxpayer).

When a government, rather than acting as a neutral force protecting property rights and enforcing contracts, attempts to favor some at the expense of others, counterproductive activities will expand while productive activities will shrink. People will spend more time organizing and lobbying politicians and less time producing goods and services. Since fewer resources will be utilized to create wealth (and more utilized in rent-seeking activities), economic progress will be retarded.

Examples of rent seeking abound. Washington D.C. is a beehive of organizations seeking subsidies and other favors from the federal government. More than 3,000 trade associations have offices in Washington and they employ nearly 100,000 people seeking to alter the actions of Congress. Of course, business and labor organizations are well represented, but so too are agricultural interests, health-care providers, trial lawyers, senior citizens, export industries, and many others. Agriculture lobbying organizations argue for additional spending on price supports and other programs designed to benefit farmers. Realtors stress the importance of mortgage interest rate deductibility. Some rent seekers come up with ingenious ways of enhancing their image with policy makers. The dairy farmer's annual Capitol Hill ice cream social that provides free ice cream for congressional staffers illustrates this technique.

The American Association of Retired Persons (AARP) and other senior citizen organizations are perhaps the most effective lobbies in Washington. In 2000, the AARP had 34 million members and spent $56 million on lobbying-related expenses. The endorsement of the AARP is highly coveted by those seeking congressional office. Federal expenditures on Social Security, Medicare, and other programs directed toward the elderly currently account for approximately one-third of the federal budget. By way of comparison, this is about twice the expenditure level on national defense. The AARP and several other senior citizen organizations are vigorously campaigning for inclusion of prescription drugs under Medicare and expansion of other benefits directed toward the elderly. Today, the typical elderly person has an above average income and the poverty rate among the elderly is the lowest of any age group. Thus, targeting additional income transfers toward the elderly is clearly a redistribution from low- to high-income households.

---

[7]Quoted in P. J. O'Rourke, *Insight Magazine*, Jan. 15–25, p. 35.
[8]See the classic work of Charles K. Rowley, Robert D. Tollison, and Gordon Tullock, *The Political Economy of Rent-Seeking* (Boston: Kluwer Academic Publishers, 1988), for additional details on rent seeking.

Inefficiency of Government Operations

Will government goods and services be produced efficiently? Professional pride, and pride in doing a job well, are likely to be present in the public sector as well as the private. However, the incentive to operate efficiently differs in the two sectors. In the private sector, there is a strong incentive to produce efficiently because lower costs mean higher profits, and high costs mean losses and even business failure. This index of performance (profit rate) is unavailable in the public sector. Missing also are signals from the capital market. When a corporation announces a strategy or a plan that closely watching, personally committed investors believe to be faulty, the price of the corporation's stock will drop. There is no mechanism similar to the stock market in the public sector. This makes inefficiency more difficult to detect. In addition, direct competition in the form of other firms trying to take an agency's customers is typically absent in the public sector. As a result, bureaucratic leaders are more free to pursue their narrow goals and interests without a strong regard for the control of costs relative to benefits. (See cartoon below.)

While bankruptcy weeds out inefficiency in the private sector, there is no parallel mechanism to eliminate inefficiency in the public sector. In fact, failure to achieve a targeted objective (for example, a lower crime rate or improvement in student achievement scores) is often used as an argument for *increased* public sector funding. Furthermore, public-sector managers are seldom in a position to gain personally from measures that reduce costs. The opposite is often true. If an agency fails to spend this year's allocation, its case for a larger budget next year is weakened. Agencies typically go on a spending spree near the end of the budget period if they discover that they have failed to spend all the current year's appropriation.

It is important to note that the argument of internal inefficiency is not based on the assumption that employees of a bureaucratic government are lazy or less capable. Rather, the emphasis is on the information and incentives under which managers and other workers toil. Government firms do not have owners that have risked their wealth on the future success of the firm. There is no entity that will be able to reap substantial economic gain if the firm produces more efficiently or incorporates a new product or service that is highly

THE FAMILY CIRCUS   **By Bil Keane**

1-26
© 1998 Bil Keane, Inc.
Dist. by Cowles Synd., Inc.

"Daddy, could you buy a new metal detector? I dropped my quarter in the snow."

Just as the boy considers the quarter more important than the far greater cost of the metal detector, so too does the leader of a bureau often consider the bureau's goals more important than the costs, even if the latter are far greater.

valued relative to its costs. The operation of the firm and appointment of high level management may be influenced by political rather than economic considerations. Because the profitability criteria are absent, performance is difficult to evaluate. There is no test with which to define economic inefficiency or measure it accurately, much less to eliminate it. These perverse incentives are bound to affect efficiency.

The empirical evidence is consistent with this view. Economies dominated by government control, like those of the former Soviet bloc, India, Syria, and Nigeria (and many other African countries) have performed poorly. The level of output per unit of resource input in countries with numerous government enterprises is low. Similarly, when private firms are compared with government agencies providing the same goods or services, the private firms generally have been shown to provide them more economically.

Competition is a key to efficient production and low cost. Units of government can sometimes provide services on a more competitive basis by contracting with private firms or even with other units of government. For example, many cities contract with private firms to provide trash removal services. The city continues to finance the activity through taxes and to specify the level of service. But operational efficiency is greater because competition among potential contractors keeps the cost of the trash removal contracts down. This sort of competitive contracting has increased in recent decades. In the state of Illinois, more than 90 percent of municipalities contracted out their trash removal services. In the United States, 7 state governments were contracting out more than 100 services in 1998, while 14 states contracted out more than 50 services. Even the federal Internal Revenue Service has moved in this direction. The IRS recently awarded a $30.9 million contract to a private partnership to manage its inventory of office equipment and other supplies.

ECONOMIC ORGANIZATION: WHO PRODUCES, WHO PAYS, AND WHY IT MATTERS

The structure of production and consumption will influence economic outcomes. Goods and services may either be produced by private enterprises or supplied through the government. They may be paid for either by the consumer directly or by the taxpayer or some other third party. As **Exhibit 4** shows, this two-by-two matrix means that there are four

EXHIBIT 4
The Private and Government Sector Matrix of Production and Payment

The incentive to economize is influenced by who produces a good and who pays for it. Economizing behavior will be strongest when consumers purchase goods produced by private firms (quadrant 1). The incentive to economize is reduced when payment is made by a third party and when production is handled by the government.

| | Good is paid for by: | |
	Consumer-Purchaser	Taxpayer or other Third party
Private Enterprises	(1) Examples: apples, oranges, television sets, food, housing, most other goods	(2) Examples: health-care, food purchased with food stamps
Government Enterprises or contracting	(3) Examples: Post Office, water and electricity in many cities, toll roads, many hospitals	(4) Examples: public schools, streets and roads, national defense, law enforcement

(Good is produced by:)

possible combinations of production and consumption. Let's take a closer look at each and consider their impact on the allocation of resources and the incentive to economize.

In quadrant 1, goods are produced by private firms and purchased by consumers with their own money. Clearly, consumers will have a strong incentive to economize. They will compare value with cost and purchases will be made only when items are valued more than their purchase price. Correspondingly, the owners of private enterprises have a strong incentive to both cater to the views of consumers and supply goods efficiently. Net revenues can be increased if output can be produced at a lower cost. Producers will continue supplying goods only if consumers are willing to pay an amount sufficient to cover their production costs. Essentially, the supply and demand analysis of Chapter 3 focused on quadrant 1 cases.

Quadrant 2 represents the case where goods are produced privately, but they are paid for by the taxpayer or some other third party. The provision of healthcare financed primarily by government (Medicare and Medicaid) and insurance provides an example of this organizational structure. If someone else is paying, consumers have little incentive to care much about price. Instead of economizing, many consumers will simply purchase from suppliers that they believe offer the highest quality, regardless of price. The behavior of producers will also be affected. If consumers are largely insensitive to price, producers have little reason to control costs and provide services at attractive prices. This can dramatically affect economic efficiency. See the Special Topic at the end of this book, "The Economics of Healthcare," for evidence on this point.

Quadrant 3 represents the situation where consumers pay for the good or service, but production is handled through the government. The provision of first-class mail delivery via the U.S. Postal Service, water and electricity by municipal governments, and the operation of toll roads provide examples of this structure. When consumers pay for a good or service directly, they will economize and seek the most value per dollar of spending. This will be true regardless of whether purchases are from private or government enterprises. As we just discussed, however, there is reason to believe that government-operated firms will generally be less efficient than private enterprises, particularly if the government firms derive some of their revenue from political authorities. Cost consciousness is also likely to be reduced if the government firm is a monopolist—if it is protected from competition with potential private rivals. Competition, however, is difficult to maintain in some markets. When this is the case, government enterprises may offer a reasonable alternative. As we proceed, we will investigate this issue in more detail.

Quadrant 4 represents the case were the government both provides the service and covers its costs through taxation. In this case, the political process determines what will be produced, how it will be produced, and how it will be allocated among the general populace. Consumers acting through markets are in a very weak position to either discipline the suppliers or alter production. Under these circumstances, the incentive for production efficiency is weak and there is likely to be a disconnect between the good produced and

the preferences of consumers. As we discussed in the previous chapter, the nature of public goods—items like national defense and flood control—makes it difficult if not impossible to supply them through markets. In such cases, there is little alternative to provision through government. In other instances, however, there are feasible alternatives. This is true for education. The Special Topic at the end of this book, "School Choice: Can it Improve the Quality of Education in America?" analyzes this issue.

Most goods and services in the United States are allocated under conditions approximating those of quadrant 1. Thus, most of our analysis focuses on this case. However, a sizable portion of economic activity takes place under conditions described by the other three quadrants. Moreover, the incentive structure present in quadrants 2, 3, and 4 often creates problems. As a result, we will often consider modifications that might improve the efficiency of activities currently undertaken in these quadrants.

ECONOMICS OF THE TRANSFER SOCIETY

As **Exhibit 5** illustrates, direct income transfers through the public sector have increased sharply during the past seven decades. In 1929 cash income transfers accounted for less than 1 percent of national income; by 1999 the figure had risen to 13.4 percent. If in-kind benefits, such as food stamps, medical care, and housing, were included, the size of the transfer sector would have constituted over 20 percent of national income.

The ideal distribution of income is largely a matter of personal preference. There is nothing in positive economics that tells us that one distribution of income is better than another. Some people may desire to enhance the living standards of those with low incomes. However, in some respects, income transfers to the poor are a public good. The contributions of any one individual can help specific individuals in need, but can do little to eliminate poverty in the nation. Recognizing this point, even those who would willingly

EXHIBIT 5
The Growth of Government Transfer Payments

The government now taxes approximately 13 percent of national income away from some people and transfers it to others. Means-tested income transfers—those directed toward the poor—account for only about one-sixth of all income transfers.

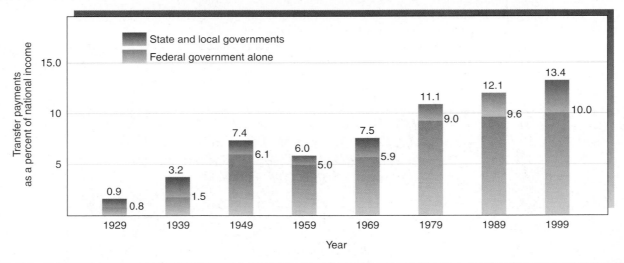

Source: Bureau of Economic Analysis

contribute to reduce the general level of poverty, have an incentive to become *free riders*. If this happens, less than the desired amount of antipoverty effort will be voluntarily supplied. If everyone is required to contribute through the tax system, then the free-rider problem can be overcome. Under these circumstances, transfers directed to the poor may be consistent with economic efficiency.

However, there is also reason to believe that the rent-seeking model underlies a substantial portion of income transfers. In the United States, *means-tested transfers*, those directed toward the poor, constitute only about one-sixth of all transfers. No income test is applied to the other five-sixths, and they are generally directed toward groups that are either well organized (like businesses and labor union interests) or easily identifiable (like the elderly and farmers). The recipients of these transfers often have incomes well above the average.

Within the framework of public-choice analysis, the relatively small portion of income transfers directed toward the poor is not surprising. There is little reason to believe that transfers to the poor will be particularly attractive to vote-seeking politicians. After all, in the United States, the poor are less likely to vote than middle- and upper-income recipients. They are also less likely to be well informed on political issues and candidates. They are not united. Neither are they a significant source of financial resources that exert a powerful influence on the political process.

Whatever the motivation for the income transfers, there are three major reasons why redistribution through the public sector will reduce the size of the economic pie. First, income redistribution weakens the link between productive activity and reward. When taxes take a larger share of one's income, the individual reward derived from hard work and productive service is reduced. The basic economic postulate suggests that when benefits allocated to producers are reduced (and benefits to nonproducers are raised), less productive effort will be supplied.

Second, as public policy redistributes a larger share of income, more resources will flow into wasteful rent-seeking activities. Resources used for lobbying and other means of rent seeking will not be available to increase the size of the economic pie.

Third, higher taxes to finance income redistribution and an expansion in rent seeking will induce taxpayers to focus less on income-producing activities, and more on actions to protect their income. More accountants, lawyers, and tax-shelter experts will be retained as people seek to limit the amount of their income that is redistributed to others. Like the resources allocated to rent seeking, resources allocated to protecting one's wealth from the reach of public policy will also be unavailable for productive activity. Therefore, the incentives generated by large-scale redistribution policies can be expected to reduce the size of the economic pie.

PUBLIC SECTOR VERSUS THE MARKET: A SUMMARY

When considering the usefulness of government and the private sector, it will help to remember two things. The first is the basic characteristic of government: its monopoly on the use of coercive force. It is a powerful tool indeed, for better and for worse. The second thing to remember is that individuals have two fundamental ways to inform and possibly influence an institution such as government or a private firm: exit and voice. Both exit and voice are quite useful in dealing with individuals, firms, and other groups in the private sector. We can speak, and if that doesn't work we can exit from a private arrangement by failing to renew it or by shifting to another alternative. Other buyers and sellers are available even if they do not have identical products in identical locations.

With government, we may be largely limited to voice. In a representative democracy, we can use voice to communicate our displeasure with a new tax or regulation, but exit is usually difficult. We have to move physically from the area of the government's authority.

When government is at the local level, of course, exit is less costly. That is one reason why giving local government more powers is less dangerous than giving the same powers to a national government. Nonetheless, the ability to exit easily and shift to competing entities almost always gives individuals more control in the market than in the public sector.

Economic theory helps explain why both market forces and public-sector action sometimes break down—that is, why they sometimes fail to meet the criteria for ideal efficiency. While there are no *a priori* rules that reveal what the government should and should not do, economics does provide insight with regard to the *strength* of the case for both markets and government. The case for government intervention is obviously stronger for some activities than for others. For example, if property rights cannot be enforced in a manner that will avoid the presence of substantial external effects, market arrangements will often result in economic inefficiency, and public-sector action should be considered; it may allow for greater efficiency. Similarly, when competitive pressures are weak or when there is reason to expect consumers to be poorly informed, market failure may result. And again, government action should be examined. (See the Thumbnail Sketch for a summary of factors that influence the case for market or for public-sector action.)

THUMBNAIL SKETCH

What Weakens the Case for Market-Sector Allocation versus Public-Sector Intervention, and Vice Versa?

These factors weaken the case for market-sector allocation:
1. Lack of competition
2. External costs and benefits
3. Public goods
4. Poor information

These factors weaken the case for public-sector intervention:
1. The power of special interests
2. The shortsightedness effect
3. Rent-seeking costs
4. Lack of signals and incentives to promote operational efficiency

The same analysis holds for the public sector. When there is a good reason to believe that special-interest influence will be strong, the case for government action to correct market failures is weakened. Similarly, the lack of a means to identify and weed out public-sector inefficiency weakens the case for government action. In many cases, the choice of proper institutions may be a choice among evils. For example, we might expect a lack of private-sector competition if a particular activity is left to the market, or perverse regulation due to the special-interest effect if it is turned over to the public sector. Understanding the shortcomings of both the market and the public sectors is important if we are to improve our current economic institutions.

IMPLICATIONS OF PUBLIC CHOICE: GETTING MORE FROM GOVERNMENT

It is important to distinguish between ordinary politics and constitutional rules. Constitutions establish the procedures that will be utilized to make political decisions. They also may reduce the negative results from the problems just discussed, by limiting the reach of the majority. They do so by placing certain matters (for example, the taking of private property without compensation, restrictions on freedom of speech or worship, and various restrictions on voting) beyond the reach of majority rule or normal legislative procedures.

Both bad news and good news flow from public-choice analysis. The bad news is that, for certain classes of economic activity, unconstrained democratic government will predictably be a source of economic waste and inefficiency. Not only does the invisible hand of the market sometimes fail to meet our ideal efficiency criteria; so, too, does political decision making. That makes the growth of government worrisome. But there is also some good news arising from public-choice theory: Properly structured constitutional rules can improve the expected result from government. So the study of how people behave when they make collective choices "in the world as it really is" suggests constructive alternatives for improving the government process. The challenge before us is to develop political economy institutions that are more consistent with economic efficiency and prosperity. Public-choice theory provides us with insight concerning how this objective might be achieved. Needless to say, this topic is one of the most exciting and potentially fruitful areas of study in economics.

Issues involving comparisons between market- and public-sector organization will be discussed repeatedly throughout this book. Public choice—the study of how the public sector works—is an integral and exciting aspect of economic analysis. It helps us to understand the "why" behind many of today's current events. Who said economics is the dismal science?

LOOKING AHEAD

KEY POINTS

▼ In a representative democracy, government is controlled by voters who elect politicians to set policy and hire bureaucrats to run government agencies. All three classes of participants influence political outcomes.

▼ Other things constant, voters have a strong incentive to support the candidate who offers them the greatest gain relative to personal costs. But it is costly to obtain information. Because collective decisions break the link between the choice of the individual and the outcome of the issue, it is rational for voters to remain uninformed on many issues and in many cases to abstain from voting.

▼ Politicians have a strong incentive to follow a strategy that will enhance their chances of getting elected (and reelected). Political competition more or less forces them to focus on how their actions influence their support among voters and special interest groups.

▼ The distribution of the benefits and costs among voters influences how the political process works. When voters pay in proportion to the benefits they receive from a public-sector project, productive projects tend to be approved and counterproductive ones rejected. When the costs of a policy are distributed among voters differently than are the benefits, democratic decision making will tend to be less efficient.

▼ There is a strong incentive for politicians to support special-interest issues. Special-interest groups supply both financial and direct elective support to the politicians, while most other voters tend to be uninformed on special-interest issues.

▼ The shortsightedness effect is another potential source of conflict between good politics and sound economics. Both voters and politicians tend to support projects that promise substantial current benefits at the expense of difficult-to-identify future costs.

▼ Rent seeking moves resources away from productive activities. Widespread use of the taxing, spending, and regulating powers of government will encourage rent seeking. The output of economies with substantial amounts of rent seeking will fall below their potential.

▼ The economic incentive for operational efficiency is weak in the public sector. No individual or relatively small group of individuals can capture the gains derived from improved operational efficiency.

▼ Economic organization influences efficiency. The incentive to economize is strong when consumers use their own money to purchase from private firms. Both payment by a third party and production by the government weaken the incentive to economize.

▼ A large and growing part of government is devoted to transferring income, most of which does not go to poor people. Transfers tend to reduce the size of the overall economic pie.

CRITICAL ANALYSIS QUESTIONS

1. Are voters likely to be well informed on issues and the positions of candidates? Why or why not?

*2. "Government can afford to take a long view when it needs to, while a private firm has a short-term outlook. Corporate officers, for example, typically care about the next three to six months, not the next 50 to 100 years. Government, not private firms, should own things like forests, that take decades to develop." Evaluate this view.

3. "If there are problems with market allocation, democratic decision making will generally be able to intervene and correct the situation." Is this statement true or false? Explain your response.

4. What is rent seeking? When is it likely to be widespread? How does it influence economic efficiency? Explain.

*5. Does the democratic political process incorporate the invisible hand principle? Is the presence or absence of the invisible hand principle important? Why or why not?

*6. "The average person is more likely to make an informed choice when he or she purchases a personal computer than when he or she votes for a congressional candidate." Evaluate this statement.

7. Do you think special-interest groups exert much influence on local government? Why or why not? As a test, check the composition of the local zoning board in your community. How many real-estate agents, contractors, developers, and landlords are on the board? Are there any citizens without real-estate interests on the board?

*8. "Voters should simply ignore political candidates who play ball with special-interest groups, and vote instead for candidates who will represent all the people when they are elected. Government will work far better when this happens." Evaluate this view.

9. If a project is efficient (if total benefits exceed total costs), would it be possible to allocate the cost of the project in a manner that would provide net benefits to each voter? Why or why not? Explain. Will efficient projects necessarily be favored by a majority of voters? Explain.

*10. "When an economic function is turned over to the government, social cooperation replaces personal self-interest." Is this statement true? Why or why not?

*11. What's wrong with this way of thinking? "Public policy is necessary to protect the average citizen from the power of vested interest groups. In the absence of government intervention, regulated industries, such as airlines, railroads, and trucking, would charge excessive prices, products would be unsafe, and the rich would oppress the poor. Government curbs the power of special-interest groups."

12. What is the shortsightedness effect? How does the shortsightedness effect influence the efficiency of public sector action?

13. "Since government-operated firms do not have to make a profit, they can usually produce at a lower cost and charge a lower price than privately owned enterprises." Evaluate this view.

14. Do you think that the political process works to the advantage of the poor? Why or why not?

15. Why does representative democracy often tax some people in order to provide benefits to others? When governments become heavily involved in tax-transfer activities, how will this involvement affect the size of the economic pie? Explain your answer.

16. The United States imposes highly restrictive sugar import quotas that result in a domestic price that is generally about twice the world price. The quotas benefit sugar growers at the expense of consumers. Given that there are far more sugar consumers than growers, why aren't the quotas abolished?

*Asterisk denotes questions for which answers are given in Appendix B.

PART 3

"Growth of output is the key to a

higher living standard"

PART 3

CORE MACROECONOMICS

Macroeconomics is about growth of the economy and fluctuations in output, employment, and the general level of prices. Gross domestic product (GDP) is the broadest and most widely used measure of output. Real GDP, that is, GDP adjusted for inflation has increased at an average annual rate of approximately 3 percent since 1950. Growth of output is highly important because it provides the basis for higher levels of consumption and standards of living.

FLUCTUATIONS IN OUTPUT

Like other countries, the United States has experienced fluctuations in output. What causes economic fluctuations? How can their frequency and intensity be reduced? What can economic policy do to promote more stability? We will analyze these questions in Part 3.

CHAPTER 7

Taking the Nation's Economic Pulse

Chapter Focus

■ What is GDP? What items are included in GDP?

■ How is GDP calculated? What are the major components of GDP?

■ When making comparisons over time, why is it important to adjust nominal GDP for the effects of inflation?

■ What do price indexes measure? How can they be used to adjust for changes in the general level of prices?

■ Is GDP a good measure of output? What are its strengths and weaknesses?

---

[1]As quoted by Milton Friedman in *Economic Freedom: Toward a Theory of Measurement*, edited by Walter Block (Vancouver, B.C.: The Fraser Institute, 1991), p. 11.

Our society likes to keep score. The sports pages supply us with the win-loss records that reveal how well the various teams are doing. We also keep score on the performance of our economy. The scoreboard for economic performance is the *national income accounting system.* Just as a firm's accounting statement provides information on its performance, national income accounts supply performance information for the entire economy.

Simon Kuznets, the winner of the 1971 Nobel Prize in economics, developed the basic concepts of national income accounting during the 1920s and 1930s (see the Outstanding Economist feature). Through the years, these procedures have been modified and improved. In this chapter, we will explain how the flow of an economy's output (and income) is measured. We will also explain how changes in the quantity of goods and services produced are separated from changes that reflect merely inflation (higher prices). Finally, we will analyze the strengths and weaknesses of the measurement tools used to assess the performance of our national economy. ■

GDP—A MEASURE OF OUTPUT

The **gross domestic product (GDP)** *is the market value of final goods and services produced within a country during a specific time period, usually a year.* GDP is the most widely used measure of economic performance. The GDP figures are closely watched both by policymakers and by those in the business and financial communities. In the United States, the numbers are prepared quarterly and released a few weeks following the end of each quarter.

GDP is a "flow" concept. By analogy, a water gauge measures the amount of water that flows through a pipe each hour. Similarly, GDP measures the market value of production that "flows" through the economy's factories and shops each year (or quarter).

Gross domestic product (GDP)
The market value of all final goods and services produced within a country during a specific period.

What Counts Toward GDP?

First and foremost, GDP is a measure of output. Thus, it cannot be arrived at merely by summing the totals on the nation's cash registers during a period. The key phrases in the definition of GDP—"market value" of "final goods and services" "produced" "within a country" "during a specific time period"—reveal a great deal about what should be included in and excluded from the calculation of GDP. Let's take a closer look at this issue.

Only final goods and services count.
If output is to be measured accurately, all goods and services produced during the year must be counted once and only once. Most goods go through several stages of production before they end up in the hands of their ultimate users. To avoid double-counting, care

OUTSTANDING ECONOMIST

Simon Kuznets (1901–1985)

Simon Kuznets provided the methodology for modern national income accounting and developed the first reliable national income measures for the United States. He is often referred to as the "father of national-income accounting." A native Russian, he emigrated to the United States at the age of 21 and spent his academic career teaching at the University of Pennsylvania, Johns Hopkins University, and Harvard University.

Intermediate goods
Goods purchased for resale or for use in producing another good or service.

Final market goods and services
Goods and services purchased by their ultimate user.

must be taken to differentiate between **intermediate goods**—goods in intermediate stages of production—and **final market goods and services**, which are those purchased for final use rather than for resale or further processing.

Sales at intermediate stages of production are not counted by GDP because the value of the intermediate goods is embodied within the final-user good. Adding the sales price of both the intermediate good and the final-user good would exaggerate GDP. For example, when a wholesale distributor sells steak to a restaurant, the final purchase price paid by the patron of the restaurant for the steak dinner will reflect the cost of the meat. Double-counting would result if we included both the sale price of the intermediate good (the steak sold by the wholesaler to the restaurant) and the final purchase price of the steak dinner.

Exhibit 1 will help clarify the accounting method for GDP. Before the final good, bread, is in the hands of the consumer, it will go through several intermediate stages of production. The farmer produces a pound of wheat and sells it to the miller for 30 cents. The miller grinds the wheat into flour and sells it to the baker for 65 cents. The miller's actions have *added* 35 cents to the value of the wheat. The baker combines the flour with other ingredients, makes a loaf of bread, and sells it to the grocer for 90 cents. The baker has *added* 25 cents to the value of the bread. The grocer stocks the bread on the grocery shelves and provides a convenient location for consumers to shop. The grocer sells the loaf of bread for $1, *adding* 10 cents to the value of the final product. Only the final market value of the product—the $1 for the loaf of bread—is included in GDP. This price reflects the value added at each stage of production. The 30 cents *added* by the farmer, the 35 cents by the miller, the 25 cents by the baker, and the 10 cents by the grocer sum to the $1 purchase price.

Financial transactions and income transfers are excluded because they do not involve production.

Remember, GDP is a measure of goods and services "produced." Purely financial transactions and income transfers merely transfer ownership from one party to another. They do not involve current production and therefore they should not be included in GDP. (*Note*: If a financial transaction involves a sales commission, the commission is included in GDP because it involves a service rendered during the current period.)

EXHIBIT 1
GDP and Stages of Production

Most goods go through several stages of production. This chart illustrates both the market value of a loaf of bread as it passes through the various stages of production (column 1) and the amount added to the value by each intermediate producer (column 2). GDP counts only the market value of the final product. Of course, the amount added by each intermediate producer (column 2) sums to the market value of the final product.

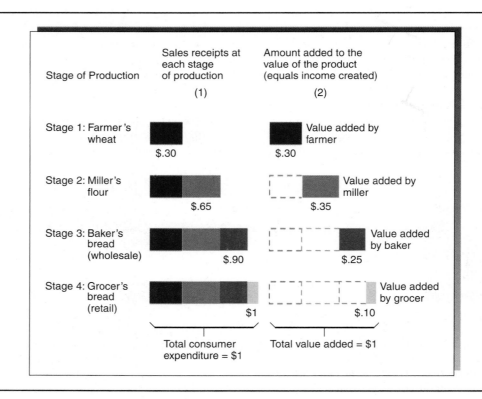

Thus, the purchases and sales of stocks, bonds, and U.S. securities are not included in GDP. Neither are private- and public-sector income transfers. If your aunt sends you $100 to help pay for your college expenses, your aunt has less wealth and you have more, but the transaction adds nothing to current production. Government income transfer payments, such as social security, welfare, and veterans' payments, are also omitted. The recipients of these transfers are not producing goods in return for the transfers. Therefore, it would be inappropriate to add them to GDP.

Only production within the country is counted.

GDP counts only goods and services produced within the geographic borders of the country. When foreigners earn income within U.S. borders, it adds to the GDP of the United States. For example, the incomes of Canadian engineers and Mexican baseball players earned in the United States are included in the U.S. GDP. On the other hand, the earnings of Americans abroad—for example, an American college professor teaching in England—do not count toward the U.S. GDP because this income is not generated within the borders of the United States.

Only goods produced during the current period are counted.

As the definition indicates, GDP is a measure of output "during the current period." Transactions involving the exchange of goods or assets produced during earlier periods are omitted because they do not reflect current production. For example, the purchase of "secondhand" goods, such as a used car or a home built five years ago, are not included in this year's GDP. Production of these goods was counted at the time they were produced and initially purchased. Resale of such items produced during earlier years merely changes the ownership of the goods or assets. It does not add to current production. Thus, it would be inappropriate to include them in current GDP. (*Note*: As in the case of financial transactions, sales commissions earned by those helping to arrange the sale of used cars, homes, or other assets are included in GDP because they reflect services provided during the current period.)

Dollars—The Common Denominator for GDP

In elementary school, each of us was taught the difficulties of adding apples and oranges. Yet, this is precisely the nature of aggregate output. Literally millions of different commodities and services are produced each year. How can the production of apples, oranges, shoes, movies, roast beef sandwiches, automobiles, dresses, legal services, education, heart transplants, astrological services, and many other items be added together? Answer: The "market value" of each is added to GDP.

The vastly different goods and services produced in our modern world have only one thing in common: Someone pays a price for them. Therefore, when measuring output, units of each good are weighted according to their market value—the purchase price of the good or service. If a consumer pays $25,000 for a new automobile and $25 for a nice meal, production of the automobile adds 1,000 times as much to output as production of the meal. Similarly, production of a television set that is purchased for $1,000 will add 1/25 as much to output as the new automobile and 40 times the amount of the meal.

Each good produced increases output by the amount the purchaser pays for the good. The total spending on all goods and services produced during the year is then summed, in dollar terms, to obtain the annual GDP.

TWO WAYS OF MEASURING GDP

There are two ways of looking at and measuring GDP. First, the GDP of an economy can be reached by totaling the expenditures on goods and services produced during the year. National-income accountants refer to this method as the *expenditure approach*. *Alternatively, GDP can be calculated by summing the income payments to the resource suppliers and the other costs of producing those goods and services.* Production of goods

2 approaches

and services is costly because the resources required for their production must be bid away from their alternative uses. These costs generate incomes for resource suppliers. Thus, this method of calculating GDP is referred to as the *resource cost-income approach.*

The prices used to weight the goods and services included in GDP reflect both the market value of the output and the income generated by the resources. From an accounting viewpoint, when a good is produced and sold, the total payments to the factors of production (including the producer's profit or loss) must be equal to the sales price generated by the good.[2] For example, consider a beauty shop operator who leases a building and equipment, purchases various cosmetic products, and combines these items with labor to provide hairdressing services for which customers pay $500 per day. The market value of the output, $500 per day, is added to GDP. Taking the operator's profit or loss into account, the $500 figure is also equal to the income resource owners receive from the provision of the service. Thus, GDP is a measure of both output and income.

The linkage between the market value of a good and the income (including profit and loss) of the resource suppliers is present for each good or service produced, and it is also present for the aggregate economy. This is a fundamental accounting identity.

$$\frac{\text{Dollar flow of expenditures}}{\text{on final goods}} = \frac{\text{Dollar flow of income (and indirect cost)}}{\text{from final goods}}$$

GDP is a measure of the value of the goods and services that were purchased by households, investors, governments, and foreigners. These purchasers valued the goods and services more than the purchase price; otherwise they would not have purchased them. *GDP is also a measure of aggregate income.* Production of the goods involves human toil, wear and tear on machines, use of natural resources, risk, managerial responsibilities, and other of life's unpleasantries. Resource owners have to be compensated with income payments in order to induce them to supply these resources.

Exhibit 2 summarizes the components of GDP for both the expenditure and resource cost-income approaches. Except for a few complicating elements that we will discuss in a moment, the revenues business firms derive from the sale of goods and services are paid directly to resource suppliers in the form of wages, self-employment income, rents, profits, and interest. We now turn to an examination of these components and the two alternative ways of deriving GDP.

EXHIBIT 2
Two Ways of Measuring GDP

There are two methods of calculating GDP. It can be calculated either by summing the expenditures on the "final-user" goods and services purchased by consumers, investors, governments, and foreigners (net exports) or by summing the income payments and direct cost items that accompany the production of goods and services.

EXPENDITURE APPROACH	RESOURCE COST-INCOME APPROACH
PERSONAL CONSUMPTION EXPENDITURES	AGGREGATE INCOME
+	Compensation of employees (wages and salaries)
GROSS PRIVATE DOMESTIC INVESTMENT	Income of self-employed proprietors
+	Rents
GOVERNMENT CONSUMPTION AND GROSS INVESTMENT	Profits
+	Interest
NET EXPORTS OF GOODS AND SERVICES	+
=	NONINCOME COST ITEMS
GDP	Indirect business taxes
	Depreciation
	+
	NET INCOME OF FOREIGNERS
	=
	GDP

---

[2]In the national income accounts, the terms profit and corporate profit are used in the accounting sense. Thus, they reflect both the competitive rate of return on assets (opportunity cost of capital) and the firm's economic profit and loss, which was discussed in Chapter 3.

Deriving GDP by the Expenditure Approach

When derived by the expenditure approach, there are four components of GDP: (1) personal consumption expenditures, (2) gross private domestic investment, (3) government consumption and gross investment, and (4) net exports to foreigners. The left side of **Exhibit 3** presents the values in 2001 for these four components. Later we will discuss the right side, which deals with the resource cost-income approach.

Consumption Purchases

Personal consumption purchases are the largest component of GDP; in 2001 they amounted to $7,065 billion. Most consumption expenditures are for nondurable goods or services. Food, clothing, recreation, medical and legal services, and fuel are included in this category. These items are used up or consumed in a relatively short time. Durable goods, such as appliances and automobiles, comprise approximately one-eighth of all consumer purchases. These products are enjoyed over a longer period of time even though they are fully counted at the time they are purchased.

Personal consumption
Household spending on consumer goods and services during the current period. Consumption is a flow concept.

Gross Private Investment

The next item in the expenditure approach, **private investment**, is the production or construction of capital goods that provide a "flow" of future service. Unlike food or medical services, they are not immediately "used." Business plants and equipment are investment goods because they will help produce goods and services in the future. Similarly, a house is an investment good because it will also provide a stream of services long into the future. Increases in business inventories are also classified as investment because they will provide future consumer benefits.

Gross investment includes expenditures for both (1) the replacement of machinery, equipment, and buildings worn out during the year and (2) net additions to the stock of capital assets. Net investment is simply gross investment minus an allowance for **depreciation** and obsolescence of machinery and other physical assets during the year.

Net investment is an important indicator of the economy's future productive capability. Substantial net investment indicates that the capital stock of the economy is growing, thereby enhancing the economy's future productive potential (shifting the economy's

Private investment
The flow of private sector expenditures on durable assets (fixed investment) plus the addition to inventories (inventory investment) during a period. These expenditures enhance our ability to provide consumer benefits in the future.

Depreciation
The estimated amount of physical capital (for example, machines and buildings) that is worn out or used up producing goods during the period.

EXHIBIT 3
Two Ways of Measuring GDP—2001 Data (Billions of Dollars)

The left side shows the flow of expenditure and the right side the flow of income payments and indirect costs. Both procedures yield GDP.

EXPENDITURE APPROACH			RESOURCE COST-INCOME APPROACH	
PERSONAL CONSUMPTION		$7,065	EMPLOYEE COMPENSATION	$6,010
Durable goods	$ 858		PROPRIETORS' INCOME	744
Nondurable goods	2,055		RENTS	143
Services	4,151		CORPORATE PROFITS	767
GROSS PRIVATE INVESTMENT		1,634	INTEREST INCOME	554
Fixed investment	1,692		INDIRECT BUSINESS TAXES	634
Inventories	−58			
GOV. CONS. & GROSS INV.		1,840	DEPRECIATION	
Federal	616		(CAPITAL CONSUMPTION)[a]	1,351
State and local	1,224		NET INCOME OF FOREIGNERS	5
NET EXPORTS		−330		
GROSS DOMESTIC PRODUCT		$10,208	GROSS DOMESTIC PRODUCT	$10,208

[a]Includes $1,128 billion for the depreciation of privately owned capital and $224 billion for the depreciation of government-owned assets.
Source: U.S. Department of Commerce. These data are also online at www.bea.doc.gov.

production-possibilities frontier outward). In contrast, a low rate of net investment, or even worse, negative net investment, implies a stagnating or even contracting economy. Of course, the impact of investment on future income will also be affected by the productivity of investment—whether the funds invested are channeled into wealth-creating projects. Other things the same, however, countries with a large net investment rate will tend to grow more rapidly than those with a low (or negative) rate of net investment. In 2001, gross private investment expenditures in the United States were $1,634 billion, 16.0 percent of GDP. Of course, a large portion ($1,128 billion) of this figure was for replacement of private assets worn out during the year. Thus, net private investment was $506 billion, only 5.0 percent of GDP.

Because GDP is designed to measure current production, allowance must be made for goods produced but not sold during the year—that is, for **inventory investment**, or changes during the year in the market value of unsold goods on shelves and in warehouses. If business firms have more goods on hand at the end of the year than they had at the beginning of the year, inventory investment will be positive. This inventory investment must be added to GDP. On the other hand, a decline in inventories would indicate that the purchases of goods and services exceeded current production. In this case, inventory *disinvestment* would be a subtraction from GDP. In 2001 the United States disinvested $58 billion in additional inventories.

Government Consumption and Gross Investment

In 2001, federal, state, and local government consumption and investment summed to $1,840 billion, approximately 18 percent of total GDP. The purchases of state and local governments exceeded those of the federal government by a wide margin. The government component includes both (a) expenditures on such items as office supplies, law enforcement, and the operation of veterans' hospitals, which are "consumed" during the current period and (b) the purchase of long-lasting capital goods, such as missiles, highways, and dams for flood control. Remember, transfer payments are excluded from GDP because they do not involve current production. Thus, government purchases of consumption and investment goods are substantially less than total government expenditures. The purchases are valued at their cost to taxpayers rather than their value to those receiving them.

Net Exports

The final item in the expenditure approach is **net exports**, or total exports minus imports. **Exports** are domestically produced goods and services sold to foreigners. **Imports** are foreign-produced goods and services purchased domestically. Remember, GDP is a measure of domestic production—output produced within the borders of a nation. Therefore, when measuring GDP by the expenditure approach, we must (1) add exports (goods produced domestically that were sold to foreigners) and (2) subtract imports (goods produced abroad that were purchased by Americans). For national-income accounting purposes, we can combine these two factors into a single entry:

$$\text{Net exports} = \text{Total exports} - \text{Total imports}$$

Net exports may be either positive or negative. When we sell more to foreigners than we buy from them, net exports are positive. In recent years, net exports have been negative, indicating we were buying more goods and services from foreigners than we were selling to them. In 2001 net exports were *minus* $330 billion.

Deriving GDP by the Resource Cost-Income Approach

The right side of Exhibit 3 illustrates how, rather than summing the flow of expenditures on final goods and services, we could reach GDP by summing the flow of costs incurred and income generated. Labor services play a very important role in the production process. It is therefore not surprising that employee compensation, $6,010 billion in 2001, provides the largest source of income generated by the production of goods and services.

Self-employed proprietors undertake the risks of owning their own businesses and simultaneously provide their own labor services to their firm. Their earnings in 2001 con-

Inventory investment
Changes in the stock of unsold goods and raw materials held during a period.

Net exports
Exports minus imports.

Exports
Goods and services produced domestically but sold to foreigners.

Imports
Goods and services produced by foreigners but purchased by domestic consumers, businesses, and governments.

tributed $744 billion to GDP, 7.3 percent of the total. Together, employees and self-employed proprietors accounted for approximately two-thirds of GDP.

Machines, buildings, land, and other physical assets also contribute to the production process. Rents, corporate profits, and interest are payments to persons who provide either the physical resources or the financial resources required for the purchase of physical assets. Rents are returns to resource owners who permit others to use their assets during a time period. Corporate profits are compensation earned by stockholders, who bear the risk of the business undertaking and who provide financial capital with which the firm purchases resources. Interest is a payment to parties who extend loans to producers.

Not all cost components of GDP result in an income payment to a resource supplier. In order to get to GDP, we need to account also for three other factors: indirect business taxes, the cost of depreciation, and the net income of foreigners.

Indirect Business Taxes

Taxes imposed on the sale of a good that increase the cost of the good to consumers are called **indirect business taxes**. The sales tax is a clear example. When you make a $1.00 purchase in a state with a 5 percent sales tax, the purchase actually costs you $1.05. The $1.00 goes to the seller to pay wages, rent, interest, and managerial costs. The 5 cents goes to the government. Indirect business taxes boost the market price of goods when GDP is calculated by the expenditure approach. Similarly, when looked at from the factor-cost viewpoint, taxes are an indirect cost of supplying the goods to the purchasers.

Indirect business taxes
Taxes that increase the business firm's costs of production and, therefore, the prices charged to consumers. Examples would be sales, excise, and property taxes.

Depreciation

As machines are used to produce goods, they wear out and become less valuable. Even though this decline in the value of capital assets is a cost of producing goods during the current period, it does not involve a direct payment to a resource owner. Thus, it must be estimated. Depreciation is an estimate, based on the expected life of the asset, of the decline in the asset's value during the year. In 2001 depreciation (sometimes called *capital consumption allowance*) of private and public sector capital amounted to $1,351 billion, approximately 13.2 percent of GDP.

Net Income of Foreigners

The sum of employee compensation, proprietors' income, rents, corporate profits, and interest yields **national income**, the income of Americans, regardless of whether that income was earned domestically or abroad. If depreciation and indirect business taxes—the two indirect cost components—are added to national income, the result will be **gross national product (GNP)**, the output of Americans, regardless of whether it is generated in the United States or abroad. Put another way, GNP counts the income that Americans earn abroad, but it omits the income foreigners earn in the United States.

Because GDP is a measure of domestic output, the net income earned by foreigners must be added when GDP is derived by the resource cost-income approach. The **net income of foreigners** is equal to the income foreigners earn in the United States minus the income that Americans earn abroad. If foreigners earn more income in the United States than Americans earn abroad, the net income of foreigners will be positive. In recent years, this has been the case. The net income of foreigners is generally small. In 2001, it was $5 billion, less than one-tenth of 1 percent of GDP. As Exhibit 3 indicates, when this figure is added to the other components, the sum is equal to GDP.

National income
The total income earned by the nationals (citizens) during a period. It is the sum of employee compensation, self-employment income, rents, interest, and corporate profits.

Gross national product (GNP)
The total market value of all final goods and services produced by the citizens of a country. It is equal to GDP minus the net income of foreigners.

Net income of foreigners
The income that foreigners earn by contributing labor and capital resources to the production of goods within the borders of a country minus the income the nationals of the country earn abroad.

Relative Size of GDP Components

Exhibit 4 shows the average proportion of GDP accounted for by each of the components during 1998–2001. When the expenditure approach is used, personal consumption is by far the largest component of GDP. Consumption accounted for 68 percent of GDP during 1998–2001, compared to only 17 and 18 percent for private investment and government purchases respectively. When GDP is measured by the resource cost-income approach,

EXHIBIT 4
Major Components of GDP in the United States, 1998–2001

The relative sizes of the major components of GDP usually fluctuate within a fairly narrow range. The average proportion of each component during 1998–2001 is demonstrated here for both (a) the expenditure and (b) the resource-cost approach.

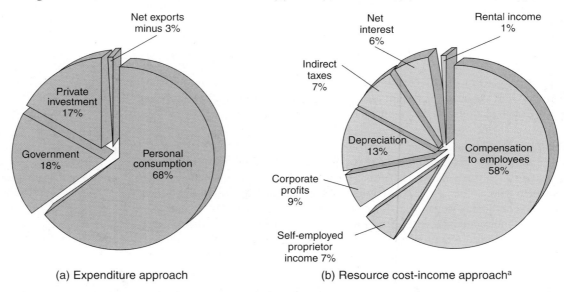

(a) Expenditure approach   (b) Resource cost-income approach[a]

[a]The net income of foreigners was negligible.
Source: Economic Report of the President, 2002.

compensation to employees is the dominant component (58 percent of GDP). During 1998–2001, rents, corporate profits, and interest combined to account for 16 percent of GDP.

ADJUSTING FOR PRICE CHANGES AND DERIVING REAL GDP

GDP was developed in order to help us better assess what is happening to output (and income) over time. This is important because expansion in the production of goods and services that people value is the source of higher incomes and living standards. When comparing GDP across time periods, we confront a problem: The nominal value of GDP may increase as the result of either (1) expansion in the quantities of goods produced or (2) higher prices. Because only the former will improve our living standards, it is very important to distinguish between the two.

When comparing GDP and other income measures across time periods, economists use price indexes to adjust **nominal values** (or *money values*, as they are often called) for the effects of inflation—an increase in the general level of prices over time. When the term **real** accompanies GDP and income data (for example, *real GDP* or *real wages*), this means that the data have been adjusted for changes in the general level of prices through time. When comparing data at different points in time, it is nearly always the real changes that are of most interest.

What precisely is a price index, and how can it be used to adjust GDP and other figures for the effects of inflation? *A price index measures the cost of purchasing a market basket (or "bundle") of goods at a point in time relative to the cost of purchasing the identical market basket during an earlier reference period.* A base year (or period) is chosen and assigned a value of 100. As prices increase and the cost of purchasing the reference bundle of goods rises relative to the base year, the price index increases proportionally. Thus, a price index of 110 indicates that the general level of prices is 10 percent

Nominal values
Values expressed in current dollars.

Real values
Values that have been adjusted for the effects of inflation.

higher than during the base period, an index of 120 implies 20 percent higher prices than the base period, and so on. *Note:* See the Addendum at the end of this chapter for additional details on how price indexes are constructed.

Two Key Price Indexes: The Consumer Price Index and the GDP Deflator

Price indexes indicate what is happening to the general level of prices. The two most widely used price indexes are the consumer price index (CPI) and the GDP deflator. Because the construction of the CPI is simpler, we will begin with it.

The **consumer price index (CPI)** *is designed to measure the impact of price changes on the cost of the typical bundle of goods purchased by households.* A bundle of 364 items that comprised the "typical bundle" purchased by urban consumers during the 1982–1984 base period provides the foundation for the CPI. The quantity of each good reflects the quantity actually purchased by the typical household during the base year. Every month, the Bureau of Labor Statistics surveys approximately 21,000 stores representative of the urban United States in order to derive the average price for each of the food items, consumer goods and services, housing, and property taxes included in the index. The cost of purchasing this 364-item market basket at current prices is then compared with the cost of purchasing the same market basket at base-year prices. The result is a measure of current prices compared to 1982–1984 base-period prices. In 2001 the value of the CPI was 177.1, compared to 100 during the 1982–1984 base period. This indicates the price level in 2001 was 77.1 percent higher than the price level of 1982–1984.

The **GDP deflator** *is a broader price index than the CPI. It is designed to measure the change in the average price of the market basket of goods included in GDP.* In addition to consumer goods, the GDP deflator includes prices for capital goods and other goods and services purchased by businesses and governments. Therefore, in addition to consumer goods, the bundle used to construct the GDP deflator will include such items as large computers, airplanes, welding equipment, and office space. The overall bundle is intended to be representative of those items included in GDP.

The cost of purchasing the typical bundle of goods included in this year's GDP is always compared with the cost of purchasing that same bundle at last year's prices. Each year's inflation rate, based on the updated bundle, is then used to chain together the index. Because of this constant updating of the typical bundle, the impact of price increases is reduced when purchasers substitute away from goods that have risen in price. As a result, the GDP deflator is thought to yield a slightly more accurate measure of changes in the general level of prices than the CPI. As in the case of the CPI, a base year (currently 1996) is chosen for the GDP deflator and assigned a value of 100. As prices rise, the index increases. The year-to-year change in the index provides an estimate of the rate of inflation.

Exhibit 5 presents data for both the CPI and GDP deflator during the past two decades. Even though they are based on different market baskets and procedures, the two measures of the annual rate of inflation are quite similar. Inspection of the annual rate of inflation as measured by each index indicates that the differences between these two alternative measures have been small, usually only a few tenths of a percentage point.

The CPI and GDP deflator were designed for different purposes. Choosing between the two depends on what we are trying to measure. If we want to determine how rising prices affect the money income of consumers, the CPI would be most appropriate because it includes only consumer goods. However, if we want an economy-wide measure of inflation with which to adjust GDP data, clearly the GDP deflator is the appropriate index because it includes a broader set of goods and services.

USING THE GDP DEFLATOR TO DERIVE REAL GDP

We can use the GDP deflator together with **nominal GDP** to measure **real GDP**: GDP in dollars of constant purchasing power. If prices are rising, we simply deflate the nominal GDP during the latter period to account for the effects of inflation.

Consumer price index (CPI)
An indicator of the general level of prices. It attempts to compare the cost of purchasing the market basket bought by a typical consumer during a specific period with the cost of purchasing the same market basket during an earlier period.

GDP deflator
A price index that reveals the cost during the current period of purchasing the items included in GDP relative to the cost during a base year (currently, 1996). Because the base year is assigned a value of 100, as the GDP deflator takes on values greater than 100, it indicates that prices are higher than during the base year.

Nominal GDP
GDP expressed at current prices. It is often called money GDP.

Real GDP
GDP adjusted for changes in the price level.

EXHIBIT 5
Consumer Price Index and
GDP Deflator: 1981–2001

YEAR	CPI (1982–84 = 100)	INFLATION RATE (PERCENT)	GDP DEFLATOR (1996 = 100)	INFLATION RATE (PERCENT)
1981	90.9	10.3	62.4	9.3
1982	96.5	6.2	66.3	6.2
1983	99.6	3.2	68.9	4.0
1984	103.9	4.3	71.4	3.7
1985	107.6	3.6	73.7	3.1
1986	109.6	1.9	75.3	2.2
1987	113.6	3.6	77.6	3.0
1988	118.3	4.1	80.2	3.4
1989	124.0	4.8	83.3	3.8
1990	130.7	5.4	86.5	3.9
1991	136.2	4.2	89.7	3.6
1992	140.3	3.0	91.8	2.4
1993	144.5	3.0	94.1	2.4
1994	148.2	2.6	96.0	2.1
1995	152.4	2.8	98.1	2.2
1996	156.9	3.0	100.0	1.9
1997	160.5	2.3	102.0	2.0
1998	163.0	1.5	103.2	1.2
1999	166.6	2.2	104.7	1.5
2000	172.2	3.4	107.0	2.2
2001	177.1	2.8	109.4	2.2

Source: Economic Report of the President, 2001.

Exhibit 6 illustrates how real GDP is measured and why it is important to adjust for price changes. Between 1996 and 2001, the nominal GDP of the United States increased from $7,813 billion to $10,208 billion, an increase of 30.7 percent. However, a large portion of this increase in nominal GDP reflected inflation rather than an increase in real output. When making GDP comparisons across time periods, we generally do so in terms of the purchasing power of the dollar during the base year of the GDP deflator, currently 1996. The GDP deflator, the price index that measures changes in the cost of all goods included in GDP, increased from 100 in the 1996 base year to 109.4 in 2001. This indicates that prices rose by 9.4 percent between 1996 and 2001. To determine the real GDP for 2001 in terms of 1996 dollars, we deflate the 2001 nominal GDP for the rise in prices:

$$\text{Real GDP}_{2001} = \text{Nominal GDP}_{2001} \times \frac{\text{GDP deflator}_{1996}}{\text{GDP deflator}_{2001}}$$

EXHIBIT 6
Changes in Prices and Real GDP in the United States, 1996–2001

Between 1996 and 2001, nominal GDP increased by 30.7 percent. But when the 2001 GDP is deflated to account for price increases, we see that real GDP increased by only 19.4 percent.

	NOMINAL GDP (BILLIONS OF DOLLARS)	PRICE INDEX (GDP DEFLATOR, 1996 = 100)	REAL GDP (BILLIONS OF 1996 DOLLARS)
1996	$7,813	100.0	$7,813
2001	10,208	109.4	9,331
Percent Increase	30.7	9.4	19.4

Source: Bureau of Economic Analysis (www.bea.doc.gov).

Converting Prior Data to Current Dollars: The Case of Gasoline

We have explained how the GDP deflator can be used to convert nominal GDP data to real GDP (measured in terms of the dollar's purchasing power during the base year of the GDP deflator). Sometimes, however, it makes more sense to convert income or other data during prior years to the purchasing power of the dollar during the current year. A price index can also be used to accomplish this task. In order to convert an earlier observation to current dollars, one merely multiplies the observation by the price index during the current period divided by the price index during the earlier period. If prices have risen in recent years, this will "inflate" the data for the earlier year and thereby bring it into line with the current purchasing power of the dollar.

Let's illustrate this point and at the same time analyze the changes in gasoline prices during the last several decades. As gas prices rose sharply during 2000, the media reported that they had risen to an all-time high in the United States. In nominal terms this was indeed the case, but what about the real price of gasoline?

Chart 1 (column 1) presents data for the nominal price of a gallon of unleaded regular gasoline for various years since 1973. The parallel data for the Consumer Price Index (CPI) are presented in Column 2. The nominal price of gasoline in 1973 was 39 cents. In order to convert this figure to the purchasing power of the dollar in 2000, one merely multiplies the 39 cents by the ratio of the CPI in 2000 divided by the CPI in 1973. This real price measured in terms of the

2000 price level is equal to $1.51 (0.39 × 172.2/44.4). Interestingly, that is precisely what the average price of a gallon of gas was in 2000.

Both crude oil prices and gasoline prices rose sharply throughout the 1970s. By 1980, the nominal price of gasoline had risen to $1.25. This would make the real price of gasoline measured in 2000 dollars equal to $2.61 ($1.25 × 172.2/82.4), substantially higher than the figure for 2000. What was the real price of gasoline in 1976, 1985, and 1990? As an exercise, derive these figures in order to make sure that you understand how to convert data from an earlier time period into the purchasing power of the dollar during the current year.

CHART 1
The Price of a Gallon of Regular Unleaded Gasoline

Year	Nominal Price (1)	CPI (1982–84 = 100) (2)	Real Price (3)
1973	$ 0.39	44.4	$1.51
1976	0.61	56.9	?
1980	1.25	82.4	2.61
1985	1.20	107.6	?
1990	1.16	130.7	?
1995	1.15	152.4	1.30
2000	1.51	172.2	1.51

Source: US Energy Information Administration, *Monthly Energy Review.* The data for regular unleaded were unavailable prior to 1976. Thus, the 1973 observation is for regular leaded, which was slightly cheaper during that period.

Because prices were rising, the latter ratio is less than 1. Measured in terms of 1996 dollars, the real GDP in 2001 was $9,331 billion, only 19.4 percent more than in 1996. So although money GDP (nominal GDP) expanded by 30.7 percent, real GDP increased by only 19.4 percent.

Data on both money GDP and price changes are essential for meaningful output comparisons between two time periods. By itself, a change in money GDP tells us nothing about what is happening to the rate of real production. For example, not even a doubling of money GDP would lead to an increase in real output if prices more than doubled during the time period. On the other hand, money income could remain constant while real GDP increased if there was a reduction in prices. Knowledge of both nominal GDP and the general level of prices is required for real income comparisons over time.

PROBLEMS WITH GDP AS A MEASURING ROD

Even real GDP is an imperfect measure of current output and income. Some productive activities are omitted because their value is difficult to determine. The introduction of new products complicates the use of GDP as a measuring rod. Also, when production involves harmful "side effects" that are not fully registered in the market price of inputs, GDP will fail to accurately measure the level of output. Let us consider some of the major limitations of GDP.

Nonmarket Production

The GDP fails to count household production because such production does not involve a market transaction. Because of this, the household services of millions of people are excluded. If you mow the yard, repair your car, paint your house, pick up relatives from school, or perform similar productive household activities, your labor services add nothing to GDP, because no market transaction is involved. Such nonmarket productive activities are sizable—10 percent to 15 percent of total GDP.

Exclusion of household production results in some oddities in national-income accounting. Suppose, for example, that a woman marries her gardener, and, after the marriage, the spouse-gardener works for love rather than for money. GDP will decline because the services of the spouse-gardener no longer involve a market transaction and therefore will no longer contribute to GDP. On the other hand, if a family member decides to enter the labor force and hire someone to perform services previously provided by household members, there will be a double-barreled impact on GDP. It will rise as a result of (1) the market earnings of the new labor-force entrant plus (2) the amount paid to the person hired to perform the services that were previously supplied within the household.

Most importantly, the omission of household production makes income comparisons across lengthy time periods less meaningful. Compared to the situation today, 50 years ago Americans were far more likely to produce sizable amounts of their own food and clothing. Only a small number of married women worked and child care services were almost exclusively provided within the household. Today, people are also more likely to eat out at a restaurant rather than prepare their own food; hire a lawn service rather than mow their own lawn; and purchase an automatic dishwasher rather than do the dishes by hand. These and many other similar changes involve the substitution of a market transaction, which adds to GDP, for self-provision, which is excluded. Because the share of total production provided within the household has declined relative to production that involves market transactions, current GDP, even in real dollars, is overstated relative to the earlier period. Correspondingly, this factor introduces an upward bias to the growth rate of real GDP.

The Underground Economy

Some people attempt to conceal various economic activities in order to evade taxes or because the activities themselves are illegal. Economists refer to these unreported and therefore difficult to measure activities as the **underground economy**.

Underground economy
Unreported barter and cash transactions that take place outside recorded market channels. Some are otherwise legal activities undertaken to evade taxes. Others involve illegal activities, such as trafficking in drugs and prostitution.

Because cash transactions are difficult for government authorities to trace, they provide the lifeblood of the underground economy. This is why drug trafficking, smuggling, prostitution, and other illegal activities are generally conducted in cash. Not all underground economic activity is illegal. A large portion of the underground economy involves legal goods and services that go unreported in order to evade taxes. The participants in this legal-if-reported portion of the underground economy are quite diverse. Taxicab drivers and waitresses may pocket fees and tips. Small-business proprietors may fail to ring up and report various cash sales. Craft and professional workers may fail to report cash income. Employees ranging from laborers to bartenders may work "off the books" and accept payment in cash in order to qualify for income-transfer benefits or evade taxes (or allow their employers to evade taxes).

Even though they are often productive, these unreported underground activities are not included in GDP. Estimates of the size of the underground economy in the United States range from 10 percent to 15 percent of total output. The available evidence indicates that the size of the underground economy is even larger in Western Europe (where tax rates are higher) and South America (where regulations often make it more costly to operate a business legally).

Leisure and Human Costs

GDP excludes leisure and the human cost associated with the production of goods and services. Only output matters; no allowance is made for how long or how hard people work to generate it. Simon Kuznets, the "inventor" of GDP, believed that these omissions substantially reduced the accuracy of GDP as a measure of economic well-being.

The average number of hours worked per week in the United States has declined steadily over the years. The average nonagricultural production worker spent only 34.2 hours per week on the job in 2001, compared to more than 40 hours in 1947—a 15 percent reduction in weekly hours worked. Clearly, this reduction in the length of the workweek raised the American standard of living, even though it did not enhance GDP.

GDP also fails to take into account human costs. On average, jobs today are less physically strenuous and are generally performed in a safer, more comfortable environment than was true a generation ago.[3] To the extent that working conditions have improved through the years, GDP figures understate the growth of real income.

Quality Variation and Introduction of New Goods

If GDP is going to measure accurately changes in real output, changes in the price level must be measured accurately. This is a difficult task in a dynamic world where new and improved products are constantly replacing old ones. Although statisticians attempt to make some allowance for quality improvements and new products, most believe that they are inadequate. Most economists believe that price indexes, including the GDP deflator, overestimate the rate of inflation by approximately 1 percent *annually*. If so, annual changes in output are underestimated by a similar amount. While 1 percent per year might seem small, errors of this size make a huge difference over lengthy time periods.

Consider the changes in the quality and availability of products during the last 30 years. Today, new automobiles are more fuel-efficient and generally safer than they were in the 1970s. Arthroscopic surgery, MRIs, CAT scans, pharmaceutical products, and various medical breakthroughs have vastly improved the quality of health care. Many commodities that are widely consumed today—compact disc and DVD players, cellular phones, personal computers, video recorders, and electronic mail, to name just a few—were simply unavailable 30 years ago. In a relatively short period of time, scientific breakthroughs and innovative applications have dramatically altered the goods and services available to consumers. The GDP statistics have not been able to keep up.

Harmful Side Effects and Economic "Bads"

GDP makes no adjustment for harmful side effects that sometimes arise from production, consumption, and the destructive acts of man and nature. If they do not involve market transactions, economic "bads" are ignored in the calculation of GDP. Yet, in a modern industrial economy, production and consumption sometimes generate side effects that either

---

[3]For evidence on this point, see *Have a Nice Day*, Federal Reserve Bank of Dallas, 2001 Annual Report (available online at www.dallasfed.org).

detract from current consumption or reduce our future production possibilities. When property rights are defined imperfectly, air and water pollution are sometimes side effects of economic activity. For example, an industrial plant may pollute the air or water while producing goods. Automobiles may put harmful chemicals into the atmosphere while providing us with transportation. GDP makes no allowance for these negative side effects. In fact, expenditures on the cleanup of air and water pollution, should they be undertaken, will add to GDP.

Similarly, GDP makes no allowance for various acts of destruction. Consider the impact of the September 11, 2001 terrorist attacks. In addition to nearly 5,000 fatalities, property losses were estimated at around $20 billion, including the destruction of the World Trade Center, portions of the Pentagon, and four commercial aircraft. But GDP makes no allowance for losses that operate outside of market channels. Therefore, none of this destruction influenced GDP. In fact, the clean-up cost, which continued for months, added to GDP. Of course, GDP was indirectly affected by adjustments and dislocations in response to the attacks. Some of these responses, for example, the reduction in spending on air travel and tourism, reduced GDP. Others, like the increase in expenditures on security, national defense, and reconstruction of the Pentagon, enhanced it. But no allowance was made for the loss of property or life. The same is true for destruction accompanying hurricanes, earthquakes, and other acts of nature. Even if billions of dollars of assets are destroyed, there will be no direct impact on GDP.

DIFFERENCES IN GDP OVER TIME AND ACROSS COUNTRIES

Statistics are merely proxies for the state of the world they attempt to measure. This is particularly true for a statistic like GDP that seeks to provide a single number that accurately represents a remarkably complex phenomenon. It is much easier to point out the shortcomings of GDP than it is to come up with something that is obviously superior.

Production of things that people value provides the foundation for income. When output per person is high, average incomes will also be high. Thus, it should not be surprising that GDP per person is often used to compare income levels across time periods and countries.

Changes in Per Capita GDP Through Time

Exhibit 7 presents the per capita GDP data for the United States for various years since 1930. In 2000, per capita GDP was approximately twice as great as in 1970 and more than five times the figure for 1930. What do these figures reveal?

As we previously discussed, some of the measurement deficiencies of GDP will result in an overstatement of current real GDP relative to earlier periods. For example, current per capita GDP is biased upward because, compared to earlier periods, more output now takes place in the market sector and less in the household sector. Other biases, however, are in the opposite direction. The reduction in time worked and strenuousness of jobs as well as the introduction of improved products and new technologies illustrate this point. On balance, the direction of the overall bias is uncertain.

One thing, however, is for certain: GDP comparisons are less meaningful when there is a dramatic difference in the bundle of goods available. Consider the 1930s compared to today. In the 1930s there were no jet planes, television programs, automatic dishwashers, personal computers, or videocassette players. In 1930 even a millionaire could not have purchased the typical bundle consumed by the average American in 2000.[4] Thus, many

---

[4]The following quotation from the late Mancur Olson, longtime professor of economics at the University of Maryland, illustrates this point:

The price level has risen about eight times since 1932, so a $25,000 income then would be the "equivalent" of an income of $200,000 today—one could readily afford a Rolls-Royce, the best seats in the theater, and the care of the best physicians in the country. But the 1932 Rolls-Royce, for all its many virtues, does not embody some desirable technologies available today in the humblest Ford. Nor would the imposing dollar of 1932 buy a TV set or a home videocassette recorder. And if one got an infection, the best physicians in 1932 would not be able to prescribe an antibiotic.

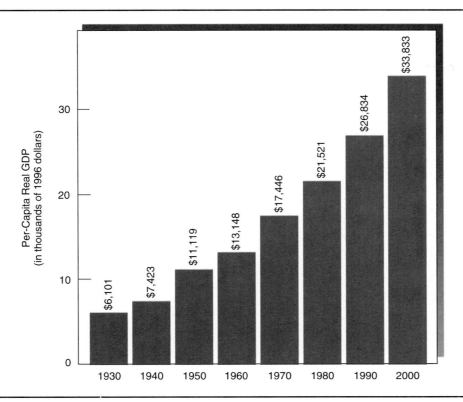

EXHIBIT 7
Per Capita GDP:
1930–2000

In 2000 per capita real GDP was 2.6 times the 1960 level, 4.6 times the 1940 level, and 5.5 times the 1930 value. How meaningful are these numbers?

Source: Derived from U.S. Department of Commerce data.

goods were available in 2001 that were not available in 1930. Under such circumstances, comparative GDP statistics lose some of their precision.

Shortcomings aside, there is evidence that GDP per person is a broad indicator of the living standard available to people. As per capita GDP in the United States has increased over time, the quality of most goods has increased while the amount of work time required for their purchase has declined. In many cases, the changes have been dramatic. (See the boxed feature, "The Time Cost of Goods: Today and Yesterday.") Like GDP, this indicates that our living standards have improved. Broad quality of life variables paint a similar picture. For example, as per capita GDP has risen in the United States, life expectancy and both time and money spent on leisure activities have gone up, while illiteracy and infant mortality rates have gone down.

Cross Country Comparisons

Exhibit 8 presents per capita income data for a number of high, median, and low income countries.[5] (*Note:* these data are for GNP rather than GDP, but for most countries the difference between the two measures is quite small.) The figures indicate that per capita income in the United States is about 20 percent greater than in Japan and Canada, and about 30 percent greater than the parallel figures for Germany, Italy, and the United Kingdom. When considering the significance of data like this, other factors should also be kept in mind. Most believe that the relative size of the underground economy in the high-tax countries of Western Europe is larger than in the United States. If this is true, national income data would understate production in Europe more than in the United States. Euro-

[5]The domestic income data for each country were converted to U.S. dollars through what economists call the "purchasing power parity method." This procedure calculates the quantity of each currency required to purchase a common "typical" bundle of goods and then uses the figure to convert all income data to U.S. dollars. Economists believe that this method provides more accurate cross-country income estimates than those based on exchange rates.

EXHIBIT 8
GNP and Various Other Indicators of Human Welfare: A Cross-Country Comparison

Cross-country comparisons of standard of living on the basis of per capita income are difficult due to differences in the size of the underground economy, production in the household, and time spent working. As a result, relatively modest differences in per capita income should be interpreted with caution. However, the cross-country comparisons show a strong positive relationship between per capita income and various indicators of human welfare such as life expectancy and literacy.

	PER CAPITA GNP MEASURED AT PPP (1999 DOLLARS)	LIFE EXPECTANCY AT BIRTH[1] 1998	ADULT ILLITERACY RATE (% 15 YEARS AND ABOVE) 1998		INFANT MORTALITY RATE PER 1,000 LIVE BIRTHS[1] 1998
			MALE	FEMALE	
HIGH INCOME COUNTRIES					
United States	30,600	77.0	a	a	7
Japan	24,041	80.5	a	a	4
Canada	23,725	79.0	a	a	5
Germany	22,404	77.0	a	a	5
United Kingdom	20,883	77.5	a	a	6
Italy	20,751	78.5	1	2	5
MIDDLE INCOME COUNTRIES					
Malaysia	7,963	72.5	9	18	8
Mexico	7,719	72.0	7	11	30
Russia	6,339	67.0	0	1	17
Brazil	6,317	67.0	16	16	33
Thailand	5,599	72.5	3	7	29
Venezuela	5,268	73.0	7	9	21
Egypt	3,303	66.5	35	58	49
China	3,291	70.0	9	25	31
LOW INCOME COUNTRIES					
Bolivia	2,193	62.0	9	22	60
India	2,149	63.0	33	57	70
Pakistan	1,757	62.0	42	71	91
Bangladesh	1,475	58.5	49	71	73
Kenya	975	51.0	12	27	76
Nigeria	744	53.5	30	48	76

a Source did not provide data for most high income countries. Information from other sources indicates that the illiteracy rate for these countries is close to zero.

[1] Averaged from data reported separately for male and female life expectancy.

Source: World Bank, *World Development Report, 2000–2001: Attacking Poverty* (Tables 1, 2, and 7). Available from the World Bank Web site at http://www.worldbank.org/poverty/wdrpoverty/report/index.htm.

peans generally spend less time working than Americans. For example, only 52.5 percent of Italians aged 15 to 64 were employed in 1999, compared to 74 percent of Americans and 69 percent of Japanese. This too would cause the per capita income figures to overstate the living standard of Americans relative to Western Europeans. As we have stressed throughout, GDP is not a perfect measure and therefore relatively modest differences in per capita GDP should be interpreted with caution.

Exhibit 8 shows that the per capita income of Mexico is only about 25 percent that of the United States. Once again, caution is called for regarding the precision of this figure. A larger share of the total production of Mexico and most other less-developed economies originates in the household sector. For example, Mexican families are more likely than their U.S. counterparts to make their own clothing, raise and prepare their own food, provide their own child-rearing services, and even build their own homes. These productive labor services, originating in the household sector, are excluded from GDP. Because of their larger share of output in the household sector, GDP tends to understate the total output of less developed countries like Mexico relative to that of more developed economies like the United States.

Like the per capita GDP figures over time, the cross-country comparisons also show a

APPLICATIONS IN ECONOMICS

The Time Cost of Goods: Today and Yesterday

Many of you have heard stories from your parents or grandparents about how low prices were when they were young. A bottle of soda cost only a nickel, and a brand new car was less than $2,000. In this chapter you have learned that there is a difference between nominal and real values. When trying to figure out whether a good is now cheaper or more expensive, economists generally use a measure of the overall price level, such as the CPI or GDP deflator, to adjust the nominal prices of earlier periods. There is, however, an alternative way of looking at this issue: One might estimate how long an average person would have to work in order to earn enough to purchase various items. For example, just after telling you that a soda used to cost a nickel, your grandfather might have noted that he used to earn only 25 cents per hour. Thus, for an hour's worth of work, he could earn enough money to purchase five bottles of soda. Today, the price of a soda is approximately 60 cents. To earn the same real wage as your grandfather, you would only need to earn $3 per hour (exactly enough to purchase five sodas with your hour's wage).

Through time, the productivity of the average worker in America has increased substantially. This increased worker productivity is the key to higher real incomes and improved living standards. Using average wage rates, W. Michael Cox and Richard Alm of the Federal Reserve Bank of Dallas have computed the time of work required for the typical worker to purchase many common items. Their analysis shows that Americans today are able to acquire most goods with much less work time than was previously the case. Some examples are shown in the accompanying chart.

To purchase a new automobile in 1908 cost $850, which took the average worker 4,696 hours to earn. In 1955, a new automobile costing $3,030 took 1,638 hours of work to earn, and by 1997, a $17,995 new automobile cost a typical worker only 1,365 hours of work to earn. The time cost of a new car today is less than 30 percent of the time cost in 1908. Furthermore, even today's most economical model is light years advanced from the 1908 version with regard to power, performance, and dependability.

The reductions in price have been particularly dramatic for technologically advanced products, such as computers, microwave ovens, calculators, and cellular phones. Cellular phones and computers now cost only a fraction of the time required for their purchase just 15 years ago. In 1984, it took the average worker over 10 weeks of work to purchase a cellular phone; by 1997 the work time cost had fallen to 9 hours, and the figure is still lower today. In 1901, spending on food, clothing, and shelter consumed 76 percent of the typical worker's paycheck. Because of greater productivity and higher real earnings, today the average worker spends only 38 percent of earnings on these items.

As worker productivity grows, real incomes increase, and the time cost required to purchase products falls. This process generates higher living standards and brings goods that used to be luxuries, costing weeks' or months' worth of a worker's salary, within the reach of most Americans. The next time you call home, remind your parents that in 1915, a 3-minute, coast-to-coast, long-distance telephone call cost more than two-weeks' worth of work at the average wage. Today, it costs only 1.8 minutes of work. Your parents will be happy to hear that, particularly if you are calling collect.

Is an automobile really more expensive than it was in 1955? You might be surprised to learn that in 1955 it took a typical worker 1638 hours of work time to purchase a car. Today, a vastly improved model can be purchased with only 1365 hours.

CHART 1
The Cost of Products to an Average-Wage Worker in Minutes or Hours of Work

Item	Old Cost	Cost in 1997
Eggs (1 dozen)	80 minutes in 1919	5 minutes
Sugar (5 lbs.)	72 minutes in 1919	10 minutes
Coffee (1 lb.)	55 minutes in 1919	17 minutes
Bread (1 lb.)	13 minutes in 1919	4 minutes
Mattress and box spring (twin)	161 hours in 1929	24 hours
Refrigerator	3,162 hours in 1916	68 hours
Clothes washer and dryer	256 hours in 1956	52 hours
Automobile	4,696 hours in 1908	1,365 hours
Coast-to-coast air flight	366 hours in 1930	16 hours
Big Mac	27 minutes in 1940	9 minutes
Long-distance call (3 min.)	90 hours in 1915	1.8 minutes
Calculator	31 hours in 1972	46 minutes
Microwave oven	97 hours in 1975	15 hours
Cellular phone	456 hours in 1984	9 hours
Personal computer	435 hours in 1984	76 hours

Source: W. Michael Cox and Richard Alm, "Time Well Spent: The Declining Real Cost of Living in America," *1997 Annual Report of the Federal Reserve Bank of Dallas,* pp. 2–24. Also see Michael Cox, *Myths of Rich and Poor* (New York: Basic Books, 1999).

strong positive relationship between per capita income and various indicators of human welfare. As Exhibit 8 shows, the residents of countries with higher per capita incomes tend to live longer, have a lower illiteracy rate, and have a lower infant mortality rate than those living in countries with lower incomes. For example, the life expectancy for residents of Japan, which is a high-income country, is 80.5 years. The corresponding figure for residents of Kenya, a low-income country, is only 51.0 years. This suggests that per capita GDP, even with all of its defects, is a broad indicator of economic well-being.

THE GREAT CONTRIBUTION OF GDP

In spite of its shortcomings, per capita GDP provides at least a broad indication of differences in income levels and living standards across time periods and countries. But this is not the major contribution of GDP. When considering the significance of GDP, it is important to keep in mind what it seeks to measure. *GDP was designed to measure the value of the goods and services produced in an economy. In spite of its shortcomings and limitations, real GDP is a reasonably precise measure of the rate of output and it can be used to determine how that output is changing.*

Adjusted for changes in prices, annual and quarterly GDP data provide the information required to track the performance level of the economy. These data allow us to compare the current output of goods and services relative to the rate of output in the recent past. This is a vitally important contribution. Without this information, policymakers would be less likely to adopt productive policies and business decision makers would be less able to determine the future direction of demand for their products.

RELATED INCOME MEASURES

Exhibit 9 illustrates the relationship among five alternative measures of aggregate income. GDP, of course, is the most frequently quoted index of economic performance. The gross national product is a closely related figure that is designed to measure the income of a country's citizenry, regardless of whether earned at home or abroad. Thus, GNP excludes

EXHIBIT 9
Five Alternative Measures of Income

The bars illustrate the relationship among five alternative measures of national income. The alternatives range from the gross domestic product, which is the broadest measure of output, to disposable income, which indicates the funds available to households for either personal consumption or savings.

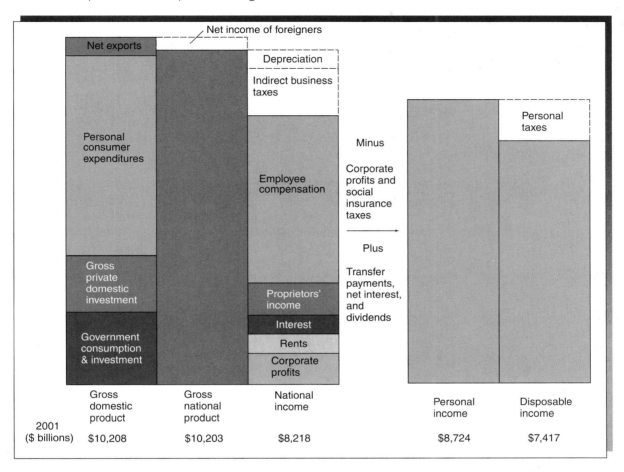

| 2001 ($ billions) | Gross domestic product $10,208 | Gross national product $10,203 | National income $8,218 | Personal income $8,724 | Disposable income $7,417 |

the net income of foreigners, the difference between the earnings of foreigners in the United States and the earnings of Americans abroad. Because this figure (net income of foreigners) is generally small, the difference between GDP and GNP is quite small for the United States and most other countries.

When the net income of foreigners, depreciation, and indirect business taxes are subtracted from GDP, the result is national income, the income earned by the domestic citizens (nationals) at its factor cost. As we previously noted, national income is also equal to the sum of employee compensation, interest, self-employment income, rents, and corporate profits.

Although national income represents the earnings of all resource owners, not all of this income is available for personal use. Exhibit 9 indicates the various adjustments to national income that must be made to derive **personal income**, which is the total of all income received by individuals and noncorporate businesses. As most workers know, the amount shown on your paycheck does not equal your salary. Personal taxes must be deducted. **Disposable income** is the income that is yours to do with as you please. It is simply personal income minus personal taxes.

There are thus five alternative measures of domestic output and income:

Personal income
The total income received by domestic households and noncorporate businesses. It is available for consumption, saving, and payment of personal taxes.

Disposable income
The income available to individuals after personal taxes. It can be either spent on consumption or saved.

1. Gross domestic product

2. Gross national product

3. National income

4. Personal income

5. Disposable income

Each of the five alternatives measures something different, but they are all closely related. Movement of one nearly always parallels movement of the other indicators. Because the five measures move together, economists often use only GDP or the terms *income*, *output*, or *aggregate production* when referring to the general movement of all five indicators of productive activity.

THE LINK BETWEEN OUTPUT AND INCOME

As we have stressed throughout, GDP is a measure of both the market value of output and the income generated by those who produced the output. ***GDP is a measure of both output and income. This highlights a very important point: Increases in output and growth of income are linked. Expansion in output—that is, additional production of goods and services that people value—is the source of higher income levels.***

The linkage between output and income also highlights the importance of improvements in output per worker, what economists call productivity. When the value of the output produced per year increases, average real income levels will rise. Thus, if we want to achieve higher income levels and living standards, we must figure out how to produce more output (things that people value) per worker. We cannot have one without the other. Greater productivity is the source of higher income levels. How can we achieve greater productivity? This is a central question of economics. We have already considered a number of factors that influence productivity, and we will continue to focus on this issue as we proceed.

**LOOKING
AHEAD**

GDP provides us with a measure of economic performance. In the next chapter, we will take a closer look at the path of real GDP in the United States and introduce other indicators of economic performance. Later, we will investigate the factors that underlie both the level of and fluctuations in real GDP.

KEY POINTS

▼ Gross domestic product (GDP) is a measure of the market value of final-user goods and services produced within the borders of a country during a specific time period, usually a year.

▼ Income transfers, purely financial transactions, and exchanges of goods and assets produced during earlier periods are not included in GDP because they do not involve current production.

▼ When derived by the expenditure approach, the four major components of GDP are (1) personal consumption, (2) gross private investment, (3) government consumption and gross investment, and (4) net exports.

▼ When derived by the resource cost-income approach, GDP equals (a) the direct income components (wages and salaries, self-employment income, rents, interest, and corporate profits), plus (b) indirect business taxes, depreciation, and the net income of foreigners.

▼ Price indexes measure changes in the general level of prices over time. They can be used to adjust nominal values for the effects of inflation. The two most widely used price indexes are the GDP deflator and the consumer price index (CPI).

▼ GDP is an imperfect measure of current production. It excludes household production and the underground economy, fails to take leisure and human costs into account, and adjusts imperfectly for quality changes.

▼ Real GDP is vitally important because it is a reasonably accurate measure of short-term fluctuations in business output and market income. Per capita GDP is a broad indicator of income levels and living standards across time periods and countries.

▼ As the alternative ways of measuring GDP highlight, output and income are linked. Increases in output are the source of higher income levels.

CRITICAL ANALYSIS QUESTIONS

*1. Indicate how each of the following activities will affect this year's GDP:
   a. The sale of a used economics textbook to the college bookstore
   b. Smith's $500 doctor bill for setting her son's broken arm
   c. Family lawn services provided by Smith's 16-year-old child
   d. Lawn services purchased by Smith from the neighbor's 16-year-old child who has a lawn-mowing business
   e. A $5,050 purchase of 100 shares of stock at $50 per share plus the sales commission of $50
   f. A multibillion-dollar discovery of natural gas in Oklahoma
   g. A hurricane that causes $10 billion of damage in Florida
   h. $60,000 of income earned by an American college professor teaching in England

2. If a nation's gross investment exceeds its depreciation (capital consumption allowance) during the year, what has happened to the nation's stock of capital during the year? How will this affect future output? Is it possible for the net investment of a nation to be negative? Explain. What would negative net investment during a year imply about the nation's capital stock and future production potential?

*3. A large furniture retailer sells $100,000 of household furnishings from inventories built up last year. How does this sale influence GDP? How are the components of GDP affected?

4. Suppose a group of British investors finances the construction of a plant to manufacture skateboards in St. Louis, Missouri. How will the construction of the plant affect GDP? If the construction project is carried out with American workers, how will it affect GNP? Suppose the plant generates $100,000 in corporate profits this year. Will these profits contribute to GDP? Why or why not?

*5. Why might even real GDP be a misleading index of changes in output between 1950 and 2001 in the United States? Of differences in output between the United States and Mexico?

6. What are price indexes designed to measure? Outline how they are constructed. When GDP and other income figures are compared across time periods, explain why it is important to adjust for changes in the general level of prices.

*7. In 1982 the average hourly earnings of private nonagricultural production workers were $7.68 per hour. By 2000, the average hourly earnings had risen to $13.75. In 2000, the CPI was 172.2, compared to 96.5 in 1982. What were the real earnings of private nonagricultural production workers in 2000 measured in 1982 dollars?

8. The receipts and year of release of the four movies with the largest nominal box office revenues, along with the CPI data of each year are presented on the next page. Assuming that the receipts for each of the movies were derived during their year of release, convert the receipts for each of the movies to real dollars for the year 2000 (2000 CPI = 172.2). Which movie had the largest real box office receipts?

Movies	Box Office Receipts (Millions)	Release Year	CPI in Year Released
Titanic	$600.8	1997	160.5
Star Wars	461.0	1977	60.6
Star Wars: The Phantom Menace	431.1	1999	166.6
E. T.: The Extra Terrestrial	399.9	1982	96.5

*9. How much do each of the following contribute to GDP?

   a. Jones pays a repair shop $1,000 to have the engine of her automobile rebuilt.

   b. Jones spends $200 on parts and pays a mechanic $400 to rebuild the engine of her automobile.

   c. Jones spends $200 on parts and rebuilds the engine of her automobile herself.

   d. Jones sells her four-year-old automobile for $5,000 and buys Smith's two-year-old model for $10,000.

   e. Jones sells her four-year-old automobile for $5,000 and buys a new car for $20,000.

10. What is the difference between the consumer price index (CPI) and the GDP deflator? Which would be better to use if you want to measure whether your hourly earnings this year were higher than they were last year? Why?

*11. Indicate whether the following statements are true or false:

   a. "For the economy as a whole, inventory investment can never be negative."

   b. "The net investment of an economy must always be positive."

   c. "An increase in GDP indicates that the standard of living of people has risen."

*12. How do the receipts and expenditures of a state-operated lottery affect GDP?

13. GDP does not count productive services, such as child care, food preparation, cleaning, and laundry, provided within the household. Why are these things excluded? Is GDP a sexist measure? Does it understate the productive contributions of women relative to men? Discuss.

*14. Indicate how each of the following will affect this year's GDP:

   a. You suffer $10,000 of damage when you wreck your automobile.

   b. You win $10,000 in a state lottery.

   c. You spend $5,100 in January for 100 shares of stock ($5,000 for the stock and $100 for the sales commission) and sell the stock in August for $8,200 ($8,000 for the stock and $200 for the sales commission).

   d. You pay $300 for this month's rental of your apartment.

   e. You are paid $300 for computer services provided to a client.

   f. You receive $300 from your parents.

   g. You get a raise from $8 to $10 per hour and simultaneously decide to reduce your hours worked from 20 to 16 per week.

   h. You earn $2,000 working in Spain as an English instructor.

15. "GDP counts the product of steel but not the disproduct of air pollution. It counts the product of automobiles but not the disproduct of 'blight' due to junkyards. It counts the product of cigarettes but not the disproduct of a shorter life expectancy due to cancer. Until we can come up with a more reliable index, we cannot tell whether economic welfare is progressing or regressing." Is this statement correct? Is this a fair criticism of GDP?

16. The accompanying chart presents 2000 data from the national income accounts of the United States.

Component	(Billions of Dollars)
Personal consumption	$6,757.0
Employee compensation	5,638.2
Rents	140.0
Gov. consumption & investment	1,743.7
Imports	1,468.0
Depreciation	1,257.1
Corporate profits	946.2
Interest income	567.2
Exports	1,097.3
Gross private investment	1,832.7
Indirect business taxes	699.6
Self-employment income	710.4
Net income of foreigners	−4.4

   a. Indicate the various components of GDP when it is derived by the expenditure approach. Calculate GDP using the expenditure approach.

   b. Indicate the various components of GDP when it is derived by the resource cost-income approach. Calculate GDP using the resource cost-income approach.

*17. Fill in the blanks in the following table:

Year	Nominal GDP (In Billions)	GDP Deflator (1996 = 100)	Real GDP (Billions of 1996 Dollars)
1960	$527.4	22.2	a. _____
1970	$1,039.7	29.1	b. _____
1980	$2,795.6	c. _____	$4,900.9
1990	d. _____	93.6	$6,707.9
1992	$6,318.9	e. _____	$6,880.0
1996	$7,813.2	100.0	f. _____
2000	$9,963.1	106.9	g. _____

*Asterisk denotes questions for which answers are given in Appendix B.

ADDENDUM

The Construction of a Price Index

Price indexes are designed to measure the magnitude of changes in the general level of prices through time. The price index during the current year (PI_2) is

$$PI_2 = \frac{\text{Cost of purchasing the typical bundle this year}}{\text{Cost of purchasing the same bundle during the base year}} \times 100$$

The typical (representative) bundle might be the bundle actually chosen during the earlier base year. Alternatively, it could be the bundle chosen this year. *In either case, the quantities of the various goods do not change from year-to-year; only the prices change.*

Let's suppose that the bundle used to calculate the index was the quantities of each good actually chosen during the base year. [This is how the Consumer Price Index is calculated.] In this case, the cost of purchasing the base year bundle this year would be the sum of the price of each good this year (P_2) multiplied by the quantity consumed during the base year (Q_1). The cost of purchasing the **same bundle** during the base year would be the sum of the price of each good during the base year (P_1) multiplied by the quantity of each good chosen during the base year (Q_1). Therefore, the mathematical formula for the price index during the current year (PI_2) could be written;

$$PI_2 = \frac{\Sigma P_2 Q_1}{\Sigma P_1 Q_1} \times 100$$

If prices on average are higher during the current period than was true during the base year, then this expression will be greater than 100. This indicates that it is now more costly to purchase the representative bundle than was true during the base year. Correspondingly, if the general level of prices is currently lower today than during the base period, then PI_2 would be less than 100. Thus, the current price index indicates how the current level of prices compares with the level during the base period.

Let us consider a simple example in order to illustrate more fully how price indexes are constructed. Suppose that your typical daily consumption bundle is 2 hamburgers, 1 order of french fries, and 3 Cokes. Initially, the price of a hamburger was $3, french fries $1 and Coke $1. The price index during this base period is assigned a value of 100. Your expenditures on the bundle during the base period (the denominator in the formula above) were $10 ($6 for the hamburgers + $1 for the french fries + $3 for the 3 Cokes).

Now consider the implications if prices in the current period are $3.50 for hamburgers, $1.75 for french fries, and 75 cents for Cokes. Now the cost of purchasing this bundle (numerator above) is $11 ($7 for the 2 hamburgers, $1.75 for the french fries, and $2.25 for the 3 Cokes). This would yield a price index of 110 ($11 divided by $10 multiplied by 100). The price index of 110 indicates that the general level of prices for the 3-good bundle is now 10 percent higher than during the base period.

Of course, the number of goods and the quantities included in the consumer price index (CPI) and GDP deflator are far greater than the typical bundle considered in this simple illustration. Nonetheless, the general idea is the same. The cost of purchasing the typical bundle in the current period is compared with the cost of purchasing the same bundle during a base year, which is assigned a value of 100. If the cost of purchasing the bundle is now higher than during the base period, the value of this year's price index will be greater than 100. As the price index changes from year to year, it indicates the magnitude of the change in the general level of prices.

CHAPTER **8**

Economic Fluctuations, Unemployment, and Inflation

Chapter Focus

■ What is a business cycle? How much economic instability has the United States experienced?

■ Why do we experience unemployment? Are some types of unemployment worse than others?

■ What do economists mean by full employment? How is full employment related to the natural rate of unemployment?

■ What is the difference between anticipated and unanticipated inflation?

■ What are some of the dangers that accompany inflation?

T he performance of the economy influences our job opportunities, income levels, and quality of life. Thus, key indicators of economic performance, such as growth of real GDP, the rate of unemployment, and the inflation rate, are closely watched by investors, politicians, and the media. This chapter focuses on how several key economic indicators are derived and explains how changes in these measures influence our lives.

The primary objectives of macroeconomic policy are rapid growth of output, a high level of employment, and stability in the general level of prices. There is widespread agreement concerning the desirability of these goals. However, there is considerable controversy with regard to how they can be achieved. As we proceed, the causes of economic instability and the potential of government policy as a stabilizing force will be analyzed in detail. ■

SWINGS IN THE ECONOMIC PENDULUM

During this century, the annual growth rate of real GDP in the United States has averaged approximately 3 percent. The rate of growth, however, has not been steady. During the Great Depression of the 1930s, economic growth plunged. Real GDP declined by 7.5 percent or more each year from 1930 to 1932. In 1933 it was almost 30 percent less than it was in 1929. The 1929 level of real GDP was not reached again until 1939. The Second World War was characterized by a rapid expansion of GDP, which was followed by a decline after the war. Real GDP did not reach its 1944 level again until 1953, although the output of consumer goods did increase significantly in the years immediately following the war.

As **Exhibit 1** illustrates, real GDP has continued to grow at an annual rate of approximately 3 percent from 1960 to 2001. Economic ups and downs have also continued. Real GDP grew rapidly throughout most of the 1960s, 1972–1973, 1976–1977, 1983–1988, and most of the 1990s. Since 1960, however, there have also been seven periods (1960, 1970, 1974–1975, 1980, 1982, 1991, and 2001) of falling real GDP. Compared to the first half of this century, the growth of real GDP has been more stable during the last four decades. During this period, the annual fluctuations in real GDP have fallen within the range of *minus* 2 percent to *plus* 6 percent. This is a definite improvement. Figures on GDP and related data can be obtained from the Bureau of Economic Analysis on the Internet at www.bea.doc.gov.

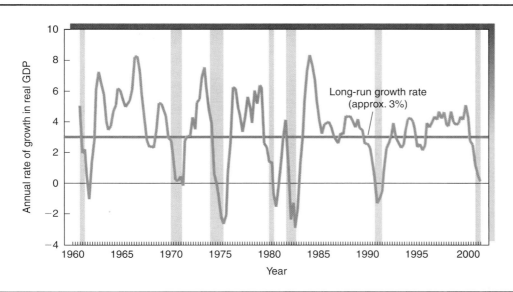

EXHIBIT 1
Instability in the Growth of Real GDP

While real GDP in the United States fluctuates substantially, periods of positive growth outweigh the periods of declining real income. Since 1960, the U.S. growth rate of real GDP has averaged approximately 3.0 percent annually. Economists refer to periods of declining real GDP as recessions. The recessionary periods are shaded.

Source: Economic Report of the President, various issues.

A Hypothetical Business Cycle

The economic record of the United States and other modern economies is characterized by both growth of real GDP and an instability in the pattern of that growth. Periods of economic expansion do not last forever. Inevitably, growth of real GDP has been followed by economic slowdown and contraction. Economists refer to these swings in the rate of output as the **business cycle**. Periods of growth in real output and other aggregate measures of economic activity followed by periods of decline are the distinguishing characteristics of business cycles.

Exhibit 2 illustrates a hypothetical business cycle. When most businesses are operating at capacity level and real GDP is growing rapidly, a *business peak*, or boom, is present. As aggregate business conditions slow, the economy begins the *contraction*, or recessionary, phase of a business cycle. During the contraction, the sales of most businesses fall, real GDP grows at a slow rate or perhaps declines, and unemployment in the aggregate labor market increases.

The bottom of the contraction phase is referred to as the *recessionary trough*. After the downturn reaches bottom, and economic conditions begin to improve, the economy enters the *expansion* phase of the cycle. Here business sales rise, GDP grows rapidly, and the rate of unemployment declines. The expansion eventually blossoms into another business peak. The peak, however, peters out and turns into a contraction, beginning the cycle anew.

The term **recession** is widely used to describe conditions during the contraction and recessionary trough phases of the business cycle—that is, a period during which real GDP declines. Many economists specify that a recession means a decline in real GDP for two or more successive quarters.[1] When a recession is prolonged and characterized by a sharp decline in economic activity, it is called a **depression**.

In one important respect, the term *business cycle* is misleading. *Cycle* generally implies that there is some regularity—like that indicated by the hypothetical business cycle of Exhibit 2—in the timing and duration of the activity. In the real world, as Exhibit 1 illustrates, this is not the case. The expansions and contractions last varying lengths of time, and the swings differ in terms of their magnitude. For example, the recessions of 1961, 1982, and 1990 were followed by eight years or more of uninterrupted growth of output. In contrast, the recession of 1980 was followed by an expansion that lasted only 12 months. The expansionary phase following the recessions of 1970 and 1974–1975 fell

Business cycle
Fluctuations in the general level of economic activity as measured by such variables as the rate of unemployment and changes in real GDP.

Recession
A downturn in economic activity characterized by declining real GDP and rising unemployment. In an effort to be more precise, many economists define a recession as two consecutive quarters in which there is a decline in real GDP.

Depression
A prolonged and very severe recession.

EXHIBIT 2
Business Cycle

In the past, ups and downs have often characterized aggregate business activity. Despite these fluctuations there has been an upward trend in real GDP in the United States and other industrial nations.

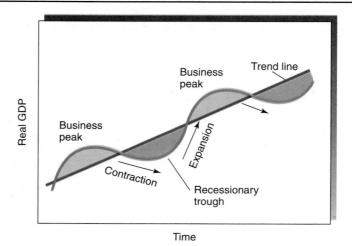

[1]See Geoffrey H. Moore, "Recessions," in *The Fortune Encyclopedia of Economics*, edited by David R. Henderson (New York: Time Warner Inc., 1993), for additional information on recessions in the United States. Also see "Symposium on Business Cycles," *Journal of Economic Perspectives*, Spring 1999, pp. 19–90.

between these two extremes. *In the real world, the observed fluctuations in real output are irregular and unpredictable.*

How can one know where an economy is on the business cycle? Of course, changes in real GDP would provide the answer, but they are only available quarterly and it is usually 4 to 6 weeks after the quarter is over before reliable figures are released. Various indicators that are available monthly or more often can provide clues. For example, auto sales, new housing starts, new factory orders, and even the stock market will generally increase during an expansion and decline when the economy dips into a recession. Thus, these indicators are monitored carefully by those most interested in business cycle conditions.

ECONOMIC FLUCTUATIONS AND THE LABOR MARKET

Fluctuations in real GDP influence the demand for labor and employment. In our modern world, people are busy with jobs, household work, school, and other activities. **Exhibit 3** illustrates how economists classify these activities in relation to the **civilian labor force**, defined as the number of persons age 16 years and over who are either employed or seeking employment. The noninstitutional civilian adult population is grouped into two broad categories: (1) persons not in the labor force and (2) persons in the labor force. There are a variety of reasons why individuals may not currently be in the labor force. Some are retired. Others may be working in their own household or attending school. Still others may not be working as a result of illness or disability. Although many of these people are quite busy, their activities are outside the market labor force.

Civilian labor force
The number of persons 16 years of age and over who are either employed or unemployed. In order to be classified as unemployed, one must be looking for a job.

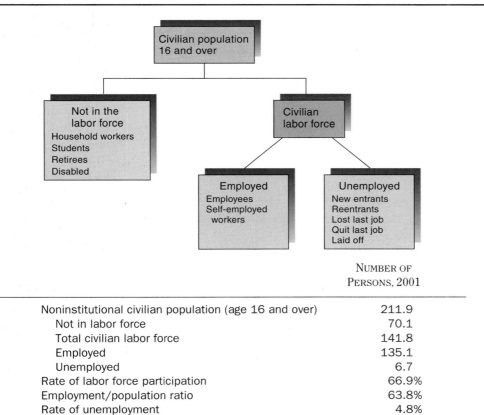

EXHIBIT 3
Population, Employment, and Unemployment, 2001

The accompanying diagram illustrates the alternative participation-status categories for the adult population.

	NUMBER OF PERSONS, 2001
Noninstitutional civilian population (age 16 and over)	211.9
Not in labor force	70.1
Total civilian labor force	141.8
Employed	135.1
Unemployed	6.7
Rate of labor force participation	66.9%
Employment/population ratio	63.8%
Rate of unemployment	4.8%

*Data are measured in millions, except those expressed as percentages.
Source: www.bls.gov.

Unemployed
The term used to describe a person not currently employed who is either (1) actively seeking employment or (2) waiting to begin or return to a job.

Labor force participation rate
The number of persons in the civilian labor force 16 years of age or over who are either employed or actively seeking employment as a percentage of the total civilian population 16 years of age and over.

Rate of unemployment
The percentage of persons in the labor force who are unemployed. Mathematically, it is equal to number of persons unemployed/number of persons in the labor force × 100.

As Exhibit 3 illustrates, **unemployed** workers who are seeking work are included in the labor force along with employed workers. The **labor force participation rate** is the number of persons in the civilian labor force (including both the employed and the unemployed) as a percentage of the civilian population 16 years of age and over. In 2001, the population (16 years of age and over) of the United States was 211.9 million, 141.8 million of whom were in the labor force. Thus, the U.S. labor force participation rate was 66.9 percent (141.8 million divided by 211.9 million).

The labor force participation rate varies substantially across countries. For example, in 2000 the labor force participation rate was 67.2 percent in the United States, 77.4 percent in Canada and 76.2 in Sweden. In contrast, the labor force participation rate was only 56.3 percent in Mexico and 60.0 percent in Italy. The percent of married women in the labor force is generally smaller in countries like Italy and Mexico that have a low labor force participation rate.

In the United States, one of the most interesting labor force developments of the post-World War II era is the dramatic increase in the labor force participation rate of women. **Exhibit 4** illustrates this point. In 2001, 60.1 percent of adult women worked outside the home, up from 32.7 percent in 1948. Married women accounted for most of this increase. More than half of all married women now are in the labor force, compared to only 20 percent immediately following the Second World War. While the labor force participation of women rose, the rate for men fell. In 2001, the labor force participation rate of men was 74.4 percent, down from 83.3 percent in 1960 and 86.6 percent in 1948. Clearly, the composition of workforce participation within the family has changed substantially during the past five decades.

The **rate of unemployment** is a key barometer of conditions in the aggregate labor market. This notwithstanding, the term is often misunderstood. At the most basic level, it is important to note that unemployment is different from not working. As we have already indicated, there are several reasons—including household work, school attendance, retirement, and illness or disability—why a person may be neither employed nor looking for a job. These people, though not employed, are not counted in the unemployment tally.

Moreover, persons must either be employed or unemployed before they are counted as part of the labor force. Part-time as well as full-time workers are counted as employed members of the labor force. The rate of unemployment is the number of persons unemployed expressed as a percentage of the labor force. In 2001 the rate of unemployment in the United States was 4.8 percent (6.7 million out of a labor force of 141.8 million). (See the Applications in Economics box for information on how the Bureau of Labor Statistics derives the unemployment rate.)

EXHIBIT 4
Labor Force Participation of Men and Women, 1948–2001

As the chart illustrates, the labor force participation rate for women has been steadily increasing for several decades, while the rate for men has been declining.

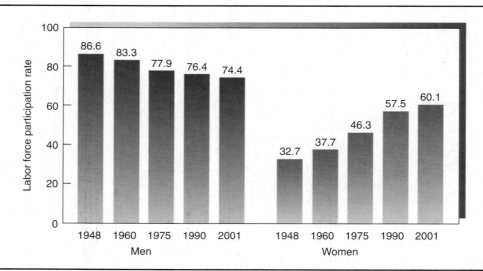

APPLICATIONS IN ECONOMICS

Deriving the Unemployment Rate

Each month, the Bureau of Labor Statistics (BLS) contacts a sample of 50,000 households that reflects the population characteristics of the United States. Specially trained interviewers pose identical questions designed to determine whether each of the approximately 90,000 adults in these households is employed, unemployed, or not in the labor force. Persons aged 16 years and over are considered employed if they (1) worked at all (even as little as one hour) for pay or profit during the survey week, (2) worked 15 hours or more without pay in a family-operated enterprise during the survey week, or (3) have a job at which they did not work during the survey week because of illness, vacation, industrial disputes, bad weather, time off, or personal reasons.

People are considered unemployed if they (1) do not have a job, (2) are available for work, and (3) have actively looked for work during the past four weeks. Looking for work may involve any of the following activities: (1) registration at a public or private employment office, (2) meeting with prospective employers, (3) checking with friends or relatives, (4) placing or answering advertisements, (5) writing letters of application, or (6) being in a union or on a professional register. In addition, those not working are classified as unemployed if they are either waiting to start a new job within 30 days or waiting to be recalled from a layoff.

The BLS uses its survey data to calculate the unemployment rate and other employment-related statistics each month. States use the BLS survey and employment figures from industries covered by unemployment insurance to construct state and area employment statistics. These labor market figures are published by the U.S. Department of Labor in the *Monthly Labor Review* and on the Internet at www.bls.gov.

In addition to the rate of unemployment, many economists also use the **employment/population ratio**—the number of persons employed expressed as a percentage of the population 16 years and over—to monitor labor market conditions. This ratio will tend to rise during an expansion and fall during a recession. Both the number employed and the population age 16 and over are well defined and readily measurable. Their measurement does not require a subjective judgment as to whether a person is actually "available for work" or "actively seeking employment." Thus, some believe that the employment / population ratio is a more objective indicator of job availability than the rate of unemployment. The employment / population ratio was 63.8 percent in 2001. The accompanying Thumbnail Sketch provides the formulas that can be used to calculate the major indicators of conditions in labor markets.

Employment/population ratio
The number of persons 16 years of age and over employed as civilians divided by the total civilian population 16 years of age and over. The ratio is expressed as a percentage.

THUMBNAIL SKETCH

Formulas for Key Labor Market Indicators
1. **Labor force** = Employed + Unemployed
2. **Labor force participation rate** = number in labor force / population (age 16 and over)
3. **Rate of unemployment** = number unemployed / number in labor force
4. **Employment / population ratio** = number employed / population (age 16 and over)

Reasons for Unemployment

Not all people who are unemployed lost their last job. A dynamic economy will be characterized by considerable labor mobility as workers move (1) from contracting to expanding industries and (2) into and out of the labor force. Spells of unemployment often accompany such changes.

EXHIBIT 5
Composition of the Unemployed by Reason

This chart indicates the various reasons why persons were unemployed in 2001. Slightly more than one-third (35.3 percent) of the persons unemployed were dismissed from their last job. More than one-third (36.8 percent) of the unemployed workers were either new entrants or reentrants into the labor force.

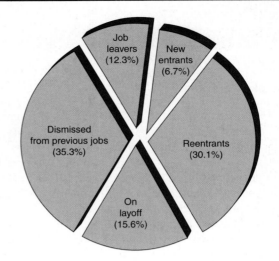

Source: www.bls.gov.

The Department of Labor indicates five reasons why workers may experience unemployment. **Exhibit 5** indicates the share of unemployed workers in each of these five categories in 2001. Interestingly, 6.7 percent of the unemployed workers were first-time entrants into the work force and 30.1 percent were reentering after exiting for additional schooling, household work, or other reasons. Thus, 36.8 percent of the unemployed workers were experiencing unemployment as the result of entry or reentry into the labor force. One out of every eight (12.3 percent) of the unemployed quit their last job. People laid off and waiting to return to their previous positions contributed 15.6 percent to the total. Workers dismissed from their job accounted for slightly more than one-third (35.3 percent) of the unemployed workers.

In a dynamic world where information, like most other things, is scarce and people are free to choose among jobs, some unemployment is inevitable. As new products are introduced and new technologies developed, some firms are expanding while others are contracting. Still other firms may be going out of business. This process results in the creation of new jobs and the disappearance of old ones. Similarly, at any point in time potential workers are switching from school (or nonwork) to the labor force, while others are retiring or taking a leave from the labor force. Workers are mobile as they voluntarily quit and search for better opportunities, or reallocate work responsibilities within the family; some unemployment will always be present.

There is a positive side to job search and unemployment: It generally permits individuals to better match their skills and preferences with the requirements of a job. Such job moves enhance both employee productivity and earnings.

Young workers often switch jobs and move between schooling and the labor force as they search for a career path that best fits their abilities and preferences. As the result of this job switching, the unemployment rate of younger workers is substantially higher than that for more established workers. As **Exhibit 6** shows, in 2001 the unemployment rate of workers 20–24 years of age was more than twice the rate for their counterparts aged 25 years and over. The unemployment rate for teenagers was approximately four times the rate of older workers.

THREE TYPES OF UNEMPLOYMENT

Although some unemployment is perfectly consistent with economic efficiency, this is not always the case. Abnormally high rates of unemployment generally reflect weak demand conditions for labor, counterproductive policies, and/or the inability or lack of incentive on

GROUP	CIVILIAN RATE OF UNEMPLOYMENT, 2001 (PERCENT)
Total, all workers	4.8
Men, Total	4.8
Ages 16–19	15.9
Ages 20–24	8.9
Ages 25 and over	3.6
Women, Total	4.7
Ages 16–19	13.4
Ages 20–24	7.5
Ages 25 and over	3.7

EXHIBIT 6
Unemployment Rate by Age and Gender, 2001

Source: www.bls.gov.

the part of potential workers and potential employers to arrive at mutually advantageous agreements. To clarify matters, economists divide unemployment into three categories: frictional, structural, and cyclical. Let us take a closer look at each of these three classifications.

Frictional Unemployment

Unemployment that is caused by constant changes in the labor market is called **frictional unemployment**. It occurs because (a) employers are not fully aware of all available workers and their job qualifications and (b) available workers are not fully aware of the jobs being offered by employers. In other words, the main cause of frictional unemployment is imperfect information. The number of job vacancies may match the number of persons seeking employment. The qualifications of the job seekers may even meet those required by firms seeking employees. Nonetheless, frictional unemployment will still occur because persons seeking jobs and firms hiring employees with the qualifications of the job seekers do not know about each other. Seeking to improve their options, both employers and employees will search for better alternatives.

Employers looking for a new worker seldom hire the first applicant who walks into their employment office. They want to find the "best available" worker to fill the opening. It is costly to hire workers who perform poorly. It is sometimes even costly to terminate their employment. So, employers search—they expend time and resources screening applicants in an effort to find the best qualified workers willing to accept their wage and employment conditions.

Similarly, job seekers search for their best option among the potential alternatives. They make telephone calls, search newspaper ads and Internet sites, submit to job interviews, use employment services, and so on. Pursuit of personal gain—the landing of a job that is more attractive than the current options of which they are aware—motivates job seekers to engage in job search activities.

As a job searcher finds out about more and more potential job opportunities, it becomes less likely that *additional search* will uncover a more attractive option. Therefore, the *marginal benefit* derived from job search declines with time spent searching for a job, because it becomes less likely that additional search will lead to a better position. The primary cost of job search is generally the opportunity cost of wages forgone as the result of failure to accept one's best current alternative. This cost will increase as better alternatives are found. Thus, the *marginal cost* of job search will rise with the length of one's job search time, primarily because still more search means forgoing wages on more attractive jobs discovered by prior search.

As the marginal benefit from additional search declines and marginal costs rise, eventually the rational job seeker will conclude that potential gain from additional search is not worth the cost. The best alternative resulting from the search process will be accepted. However, this process takes time, and during this time the job seeker is contributing to the frictional unemployment of the economy. It is important to note that, even though frictional

Frictional unemployment
Unemployment due to constant changes in the economy that prevent qualified unemployed workers from being immediately matched up with existing job openings. It results from the scarcity of information and the search activities of both employers and employees for information that will help them make better employment choices.

MYTHS OF ECONOMICS

"Unemployed resources would not exist if the economy were operating efficiently."

Nobody likes unemployment. Certainly, extended unemployment can be a very painful experience. Job search, however, performs an important labor market function: It leads to improvement in the match between worker skills and the requirements of jobs.

In a world of imperfect information, prospective employees will engage in a job search in order to acquire information about employment opportunities and job requirements. In essence, job searchers are "shopping"—they are searching for information about the job opportunity that best fits their skills, earning capabilities, and preferences. Similarly, employers shop when they are seeking labor services. They, too, acquire information about available workers that will help them select employees whose skills and preferences match the demands of the job.

This shopping results in some unemployment, but it also provides both employees and employers with information that will help them make better choices. If the resources of an economy are going to be used effectively, the skills of workers must be matched with the jobs of employers. Waste will result if, for example, a person with high-level computer skills ends up working as a janitor while someone else with minimal computer skills is employed as a computer programmer. Job search improves the match between the skills and preferences of employees and the demands of various jobs.

As workers search to find jobs for which their skills are well suited, they achieve higher wage rates and the economy is able to generate a larger output.

Perhaps thinking about the housing market will help the reader better understand why search time can be both beneficial and productive. As with the employment market, the housing market is characterized by both imperfect information and dynamic change. New housing structures are brought into the market; older structures depreciate and wear out. Families move from one community to another. In this dynamic world, it makes sense for renters from time to time to shop among the available accommodations, seeking the housing quality, price, and location that best fit their preferences and budgets. Similarly, landlords search among renters, seeking to rent their accommodations to those who value them most highly. Housing vacancies, a type of "frictional unemployment," occur. Is this indicative of inefficiency? No. It is the result of imperfect information and the search for a more efficient match on the part of both landlords and renters.

Of course, some types of unemployment, particularly cyclical unemployment, are indicative of inefficiency. However, this is not the case with frictional unemployment. The job searching (as well as the frictional unemployment that accompanies it) helps both job seekers and employers make better choices, and it leads to a more efficient match of applicants with job openings than would otherwise be possible. It is perfectly consistent with economic efficiency.

---

unemployment is a side effect, the job search process typically leads to improved economic efficiency and a higher real income for employees (see the accompanying Myths of Economics box).

Changes that affect the costs and benefits of job search influence the level of unemployment. It is interesting to reflect on the potential impact of the Internet on the job search process. Increasingly, both employers and employees are using Internet sites as a means of communicating with each other. Employers provide information about job openings in various skill and occupational categories, while employees supply information about their education, skills, and experience. This electronic job search process reduces information costs and makes it possible for both employers and employees to consider quickly a wide range of alternatives. As this method of employment search becomes more widespread, it will tend to shorten the job search process and improve the match between employee qualifications and the skills required for high-productivity job performance. Thus, frictional unemployment may well be lower in the future.

On the other hand, a change that makes it cheaper to reject available opportunities and continue searching will encourage employees to lengthen their periods of search. For example, an increase in unemployment benefits would make it less costly to continue looking for a preferred job. As a result, job seekers will expand the length of their search time and the unemployment rate will rise.

Structural Unemployment

In the case of **structural unemployment**, changes in the basic characteristics of the economy prevent the "matching up" of available jobs with available workers. It is not always easy to distinguish between frictional and structural unemployment. In each case, job openings and potential workers searching for jobs are present. The crucial difference between the two is that, with frictional unemployment, workers possess the requisite skills to fill the job openings; with structural unemployment, they do not. Essentially, the primary skills of a structurally unemployed worker have been rendered obsolete by changing market conditions and technology. Realistically, the structurally unemployed worker faces the prospect of either a career change or prolonged unemployment. For older workers in particular, these are bleak alternatives.

There are many causes of structural unemployment. Technological change is of course at the top of the list. The introduction of new products and production technologies can substantially alter the relative demand for workers with various skills. Changes of this type can affect the job opportunities of even highly skilled workers, particularly if their skills are not easily transferable to other industries and occupations. The "computer revolution" has dramatically changed the job opportunities of many workers. The alternatives available to workers with the skills required to operate and maintain high-tech equipment have improved substantially, while the prospects of those without such skills have, in some cases, deteriorated drastically.

Shifts in public sector priorities can also cause structural unemployment. For example, environmental regulations designed to improve air quality led to a reduction in the demand for coal during the 1990s. As a result many coal miners in West Virginia, Kentucky, and other coal mining states lost their jobs. Unfortunately, the skills of many of the job losers were ill-suited for employment in expanding industries. Structural unemployment was the result.

Institutional factors may also make it difficult for some workers to find jobs. For example, minimum wage legislation may push the wages of low-skill workers above their productivity and thereby severely retard the job opportunities that are available to them. Structural unemployment would increase as a result.

> **Structural unemployment**
> Unemployment due to the structural characteristics of the economy that make it difficult for job seekers to find employment and for employers to hire workers. Although job openings are available, they generally require skills that differ from those of the unemployed workers.

Cyclical Unemployment

When there is a general downturn in business activity, **cyclical unemployment** arises. Because fewer goods are being produced, fewer workers are required to produce them. Employers lay off workers and cut back employment.

Unexpected reductions in the general level of demand for goods and services are the major cause of cyclical unemployment. In a world of imperfect information, adjustments to unexpected declines in demand are often painful. When the demand for labor declines generally, workers will at first not know whether they are being laid off because of a specific shift in demand away from their previous employer or because of a general decline in demand. Similarly, they will not be sure whether their current bleak employment prospects are temporary or long-term. Workers will search for employment, hoping to find a job at or near their old wage rate. If their situation was merely the result of shifts among employers in demand, or if the downturn is brief, workers dismissed by employers cutting back output will generally be able to find jobs with employers who are expanding and hiring additional workers. The situation is different, however, when there is a general decline in demand. Many employers will be laying off workers and few will be hiring. Under these circumstances, most workers' search efforts will be fruitless and the duration of their unemployment will be abnormally long.

With time, unemployed workers will lower their expectations and many will be willing to accept employment at a lower wage. This adjustment process, however, will take time. During the adjustment period, an increase in the rate of unemployment is the expected result. As we proceed, we will investigate potential sources of cyclical unemployment and consider policy alternatives to reduce it.

> **Cyclical unemployment**
> Unemployment due to recessionary business conditions and inadequate aggregate demand for labor.

EMPLOYMENT FLUCTUATIONS—
THE HISTORICAL RECORD

Employment and output are closely linked over the business cycle. If we are going to produce more goods and services, we must either increase the number of workers or increase the output per worker. Although productivity, or output per worker, is the primary source of long-term economic growth, it changes slowly from year to year. Thus, rapid increases in output, such as those that occur during a strong business expansion, generally require an increase in employment. As a result, output and employment tend to be positively related. Correspondingly, there is an inverse relationship between growth of output and the rate of unemployment.

The empirical evidence is consistent with this view. As **Exhibit 7** shows, the unemployment rate generally increases during a recession (indicated by shading), and declines during periods of expansion in output. During the recession of 1960–1961, the rate of unemployment rose to approximately 7 percent. In contrast, it declined throughout the economic boom of the 1960s, only to rise again during the recession of 1970. During the recession of 1974–1975, the unemployment rate jumped to more than 9 percent. Similarly, it soared to nearly 11 percent during the severe recession of 1982 and to 7.6 percent during the aftermath of the 1991 recession. Conversely, it declined substantially during the strong expansions of 1983–1989 and 1992–2000.

Full Employment and the Natural Rate of Unemployment

Full employment, a term widely used by economists and public officials alike, does not mean zero unemployment. As we have noted, in a world of imperfect information, both employees and employers will "shop" before they agree to accept a job or hire a new worker. Much of this shopping is efficient, since it leads to a better match between the skills of employees and the skills necessary to carry out productive tasks. Some unemployment is thus entirely consistent with the efficient operation of a dynamic labor market. ***Consequently, economists define full employment as the level of employment that results when the rate of unemployment is normal, considering both frictional and structural factors. In the***

Full employment
The level of employment that results from the efficient use of the labor force after allowance is made for the normal (natural) rate of unemployment due to information cost, dynamic changes, and the structural conditions of the economy. For the United States, full employment is thought to exist when approximately 95 percent of the labor force is employed.

EXHIBIT 7
Unemployment Rate,
1960–2001

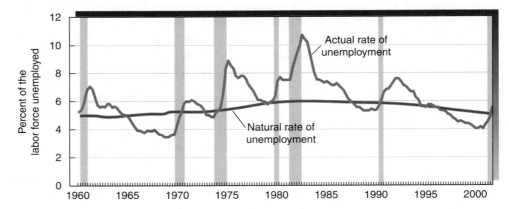

Here we illustrate the rate of unemployment during the 1960–2001 period. As expected, the unemployment rate rose rapidly during each of the seven recessions (the shaded years indicate periods of recession). In contrast, soon after each recession ended, the unemployment rate began to decline as the economy moved to an expansionary phase of the business cycle. Also note that the actual rate of unemployment was substantially greater than the natural rate during and immediately following the recessions.

Source: www.bls.gov and Robert J. Gordon, *Macroeconomics* (Boston: Little Brown, 1990).

United States, full employment is currently believed to be approximately 95 percent of the labor force.

Closely related to the concept of full employment is the **natural rate of unemployment**, the amount of unemployment reflected by job shopping and imperfect information. ***The natural rate of unemployment is not a temporary high or low; it is a rate that is sustainable into the future. Economists sometimes refer to it as the unemployment rate accompanying the economy's "maximum sustainable" rate of output.*** When unemployment is at its natural rate, full employment is present and the economy is achieving the highest rate of output that it can sustain.

The natural rate of unemployment, however, is not immutably fixed. It is influenced both by the structure of the labor force and by changes in public policy. Over time, changes in the demographic composition of the labor force will influence the natural rate. The natural rate of unemployment generally increases when youthful workers expand as a proportion of the workforce. Because youthful workers change jobs and move in and out of the labor force often, they experience high rates of unemployment (refer to Exhibit 6). Therefore the overall rate is pushed upward as they become a larger share of the labor force. This is precisely what happened during the 1960s and 1970s. In 1958 youthful workers (ages 16 to 24) constituted only 15.6 percent of the labor force. As the postwar "baby boom" generation entered the labor market, youthful workers as a share of the labor force rose dramatically. By 1980 one out of every four workers was in the youthful-worker grouping. In contrast, prime-age workers (over age 25) declined from 84.4 percent of the U.S. workforce in 1958 to only 75.3 percent in 1980. As a result of these demographic changes, studies indicate that the natural rate of unemployment rose from approximately 5 percent in the late 1950s to over 6 percent in 1980.

During the last two decades, the situation has reversed. The natural rate of unemployment has receded as the baby boomers moved into their prime working years and youthful workers declined as a share of the labor force. Today, most researchers estimate that the natural rate is once again near the 5 percent level, about the same as during the late 1950s.

Public policy also affects the natural rate of unemployment. When public policy makes it more costly to employ workers and/or less costly for persons to remain unemployed, it increases the natural rate of unemployment. The large European economies illustrate the importance of public policy. The economies of France, Germany, Italy, and Spain are characterized by high unemployment benefits and regulations that both increase the cost of dismissing workers and mandate uniform wages nationwide. Regulations of this type reduce the flexibility of labor markets and make it more costly to hire and employ workers. Thus, they lead to persistently high rates of unemployment.

As **Exhibit 8** shows, the unemployment rates of the major European economies were substantially higher during the last decade than the comparable figures for the United States and Japan, for example. High unemployment rates over such a lengthy time period are indicative of structural rather than cyclical factors. They are also reflective of the adverse impact of public policy on the natural rate of unemployment. See Special Topic "Labor Markets and Unemployment: A Cross-country Analysis," for additional information on this topic.

Exhibit 7 illustrates the relationship between the *actual* unemployment rate and the *natural* unemployment rate for the United States during the past four decades. The actual unemployment rate fluctuates around the natural rate, in response to cyclical economic conditions. The actual rate generally rises above the natural rate during a recession and falls below the natural rate when the economy is in the midst of an economic boom. For example, the actual rate of unemployment was substantially above the natural rate during the recessions of 1974–1975 and 1982, while the reverse was the case during the economic booms of the 1960s and 1990s. As we proceed, we will often compare the actual and natural rates of unemployment. In a very real sense, macroeconomics studies why the actual and natural rates differ and attempts to discern the factors that cause the natural rate to change with the passage of time.

Without detracting from the importance of full employment—in the sense of maximum sustainable employment—we must not overlook another vital point. Employment is

Natural rate of unemployment
The long-run average unemployment rate due to frictional and structural conditions of labor markets. This rate is affected both by dynamic change and by public policy. It is sustainable into the future. The current natural rate of unemployment in the United States is thought to be approximately 5 percent.

EXHIBIT 8
Average Unemployment
Rate for Major Economies,
1990–1999

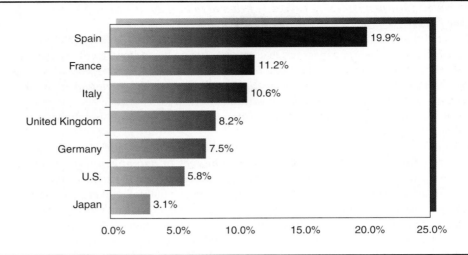

Country	Rate
Spain	19.9%
France	11.2%
Italy	10.6%
United Kingdom	8.2%
Germany	7.5%
U.S.	5.8%
Japan	3.1%

Source: Economic Outlook, OECD (Dec. 2000).

a means to an end. We use employment to produce desired goods and services. Full employment is an empty concept if it means employment at unproductive jobs. It is a meaningful concept only if it refers to productive employment that will generate goods and services desired by consumers at the lowest possible cost.

ACTUAL AND POTENTIAL GDP

If an economy is going to realize its potential, full employment is essential. When the actual rate of unemployment exceeds the natural rate, the actual output of the economy will fall below its potential. Some resources that could be productively employed will be underutilized.

The Council of Economic Advisers defines the **potential output** as: "The amount of output that could be expected at full employment . . . It does not represent the absolute maximum level of production that could be generated by wartime or other abnormal levels of aggregate demand, but rather that which would be expected from high utilization rates obtainable under more normal circumstances."

The concept of potential output encompasses two important ideas: (1) full utilization of resources, including labor, and (2) the potential output is constrained. Potential output might properly be thought of as the maximum *sustainable* output level consistent with the economy's resource base, given its institutional arrangements. Estimates of the potential output level involve three major elements: the size of the labor force, the quality (productivity) of labor, and the natural rate of unemployment. Because these factors cannot be estimated with certainty, some variation exists in the estimated values of the potential rate of output for the U.S. economy. Relying on the projections of potential output developed by the Council of Economic Advisers, **Exhibit 9** illustrates the relationship between the actual and potential output of the United States since 1960.

The relationship between actual and potential GDP reflects the business cycle. Note the similarity in the pattern of the actual real GDP data of Exhibit 9 and the hypothetical data of an idealized business cycle of Exhibit 2. Although the actual data of Exhibit 9 are irregular compared to the hypothetical data, periods of expansion and economic boom followed by contraction and recession are clearly observable. During the boom phase, actual output expands rapidly and may temporarily exceed the economy's long-run potential. In contrast, recessions are characterized by an actual real GDP that is less than its potential. As we proceed, we will focus on how we can achieve the maximum potential output while minimizing economic instability.

Potential output
The level of output that can be achieved and sustained into the future, given the size of the labor force, expected productivity of labor, and natural rate of unemployment consistent with the efficient operation of the labor market. For periods of time, the actual output may differ from the economy's potential.

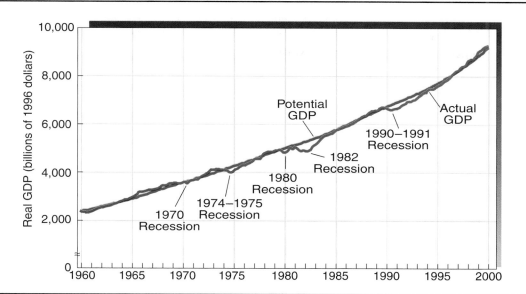

EXHIBIT 9
Actual and Potential GDP

Here we illustrate both the actual and potential GDP. Note the gap (shaded area) between the actual and potential GDP during periods of recession.

Source: U.S. Department of Commerce, Bureau of Economic Analysis.

EFFECTS OF INFLATION: AN OVERVIEW

Inflation is a continuing rise in the general level of prices, such that it costs more to purchase the typical bundle of goods and services that is produced or consumed or both. Of course, even when the general level of prices is stable, some prices will be rising and others will be falling. During a period of inflation, however, the impact of the rising prices will outweigh that of falling prices. Because of the higher prices (on average), a dollar will purchase less than it did previously. Inflation, therefore, might also be defined as a decline in the value (the purchasing power) of the monetary unit.

How do we determine whether prices, in general, are rising or falling? Essentially, we answered that question in the preceding chapter when we indicated how a price index is constructed. When the general level of prices is rising, the price index will also rise. The annual inflation rate is simply the percent change in the price index (PI) from one year to the next. Mathematically, the inflation rate can be written as:

$$\text{inflation rate} = \frac{\text{This year's PI} - \text{Last year's PI}}{\text{Last year's PI}} \times 100$$

If the price index this year was 220, compared to 200 last year, the inflation rate would equal 10 percent:

$$\frac{220 - 200}{200} \times 100 = 10$$

The consumer price index (CPI) and the GDP deflator are the price indexes most widely used to measure the inflation rate in the United States. As we discussed in the preceding chapter, these two measures of the rate of inflation tend to follow a similar path. How rapidly has the general level of prices risen in the United States? Using the annual rate of change in the CPI, **Exhibit 10** presents a picture of the U.S. inflation rate since the early 1950s. During the 1950s and into the mid-1960s, the annual inflation rate was generally low. The average inflation rate during the 1953–1965 period was 1.3 percent. Beginning in

Inflation
A continuing rise in the general level of prices of goods and services. The purchasing power of the monetary unit, such as the dollar, declines when inflation is present.

EXHIBIT 10
The Inflation Rate,
1953–2001

Here we present the annual rate of inflation for the last five decades. Between 1953 and 1965, prices increased at an annual rate of only 1.3 percent. In contrast, the inflation rate averaged 9.2 percent during the 1973–1981 era, reaching double-digit rates during several years. Since 1982, the rate of inflation has been lower (the average annual rate was 3.2 percent during 1983–2001) and more stable.

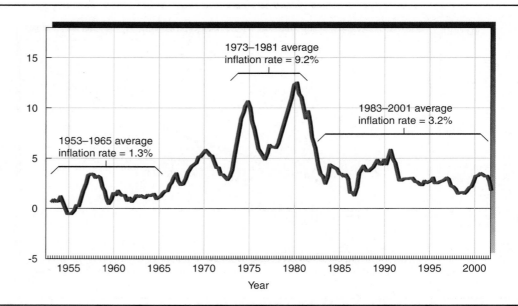

Source: Derived from computerized data supplied by FAME ECONOMICS. Also see *Economic Report of the President* (published annually).

the latter half of the 1960s, inflation began to accelerate upward, jumping to 12 percent or more during 1974, 1979, and 1980. During the 1973–1981 period, the inflation rate averaged 9.2 percent. Price increases moderated again in the mid-1980s, as the inflation rate averaged 3.4 percent during 1983–2001. Additional details on inflation and related measures can be obtained on the Internet at www.bls.gov.

The rate of inflation varies widely among countries. **Exhibit 11** provides data on the annual inflation rates during 1994-2000 for Canada, Germany, Japan, Singapore, and the United States—five countries with low rates of inflation. The annual inflation rate of these countries was generally less than 4 percent during this period; moreover, the year-to-year variation was relatively small. The inflation rate of these countries seldom changed by more than 1 or 2 percent from one year to the next.

Exhibit 11 also presents parallel inflation rate data for six high-inflation countries: Brazil, Bulgaria, Ecuador, Romania, Turkey, and Venezuela. In contrast with the low-inflation countries, the inflation rate of the high-inflation countries was not only higher, it varied substantially more from one year to another. For example, consider the data for Romania. The inflation rate of Romania jumped from 121.6 percent in 1996 to 1,058.4 percent in 1997 and receded to 18.7 percent in 1998 and eventually to 10.4 percent in 2000. (*Note*: An annual inflation rate of 1,000 percent indicates that the general level of prices is 10 times the level of just one year earlier!) The other countries in the high-inflation group also experienced wide fluctuations in the annual rate of inflation. The data of Exhibit 11 reflect a general pattern. ***High rates of inflation are almost always associated with substantial year-to-year swings in the inflation rate.***

Anticipated and Unanticipated Inflation

Unanticipated inflation
An increase in the general level of prices that was not expected by most decision makers.

Before examining the effects of inflation, it is important that we distinguish between unanticipated and anticipated inflation. **Unanticipated inflation** is an increase in the price level that comes as a surprise, at least to most individuals. For example, suppose that, based on the recent past, most people anticipate an inflation rate of 3 percent. If the actual inflation rate turns out to be 10 percent, it will catch people off-guard. When the rate of inflation is high and variable, like the rates for the high-inflation countries of Exhibit 11,

Country	1994	1995	1996	1997	1998	1999	2000
Low Inflation							
Canada	0.2	2.1	1.6	1.6	1.0	1.7	2.7
Germany	2.7	1.7	1.4	1.9	1.0	0.6	2.0
Japan	0.7	−0.1	0.1	1.7	0.7	−0.3	−0.7
Singapore	3.0	1.7	1.4	2.0	−0.3	0.1	1.4
United States	2.6	2.8	2.9	2.3	1.6	2.1	3.4
High Inflation							
Brazil	2050.0	66.1	15.8	6.9	3.2	4.9	7.1
Bulgaria	95.9	62.1	121.6	1058.4	18.7	2.6	10.4
Ecuador	27.4	22.9	24.4	30.6	36.1	52.3	96.1
Romania	137.0	32.3	38.8	154.8	59.1	45.8	45.7
Turkey	106.2	88.0	80.3	85.8	84.6	64.9	54.9
Venezuela	60.7	60.0	99.9	50.0	35.8	23.6	16.2

EXHIBIT 11
Variation in the Annual Inflation Rate of Selected Countries, 1994–2000

Source: International Monetary Fund, *International Financial Statistics* (April 2001, February 2001). The consumer price index was used to measure the inflation rate of each country.

it will be virtually impossible for decision makers to anticipate future rates accurately, and long-range planning will be extremely difficult.

Anticipated inflation is a change in the price level that is widely expected. Decision makers are generally able to anticipate slow steady rates of inflation—such as those present in Canada, Germany, Japan, Singapore, and the United States during 1994–2000—with a high degree of accuracy.

Contrary to the satirical statement presented in the chapter opening quote, inflation will affect the prices of things we sell as well as the prices of goods we buy. Both resource and product prices are influenced by inflation. Before we become too upset about inflation "robbing us of the purchasing power of our paychecks," we should recognize that inflation influences the size of those paychecks. The weekly earnings of employees would not have risen at an annual rate of 7 percent during the 1970s if the rate of inflation had not increased rapidly during that period. Wages are a price, also. Inflation raises both wages and prices.

Anticipated inflation
An increase in the general level of prices that was expected by most decision makers.

Harmful Effects of Inflation

Simply because money income initially tends to rise with prices, it does not follow that there is no need to be concerned about inflation, particularly high rates of inflation. Inflation causes problems! Our modern living standard is the result of gains from specialization, division of labor, and mass-production processes. Realization of gains from these sources is dependent upon trade and a smooth-functioning system of exchange. High and variable rates of inflation will generate uncertainty and weaken the link between income and productive activity. There are three major reasons why inflation will have a harmful impact on the economy.

1. *Because unanticipated inflation alters the outcomes of long-term projects, such as the purchase of a machine or an investment in a business, it will increase the risks and retard the level of such productive activities.* When the price level rises 15 percent one year, 40 percent the next year, and then increases again by 20 or 25 percent the following year, no one knows what to expect. Unanticipated changes of even 5 percent or 10 percent in the rate of inflation can often turn an otherwise profitable project into a personal economic disaster. Given the uncertainty that it creates, many decision makers will simply forgo capital investments and other transactions involving long-term commitments when the rate of inflation is highly variable and therefore unpredictable. As a result, mutually advantageous gains from trade will be lost and the efficiency of markets reduced.

2. *Inflation distorts the information delivered by prices.* Prices communicate important information concerning the relative scarcity of goods and resources. Some prices can be easily and regularly changed. But this will not be true for others—particularly those set by long-term contracts. For example, time delays will occur before the prices accompanying rental lease agreements, items sold in catalogs, mortgage interest rates, and collective bargaining contracts can be changed. Because some prices will respond quickly to inflationary policies while others will change more slowly, an unanticipated change in the rate of inflation will change *relative prices* as well as the *general price level*. The distorted relative prices will be a less reliable indicator of relative scarcity. As a result of these unreliable price signals, producers and resource suppliers will often make choices that they will later regret, and the allocation of resources will be less efficient than would be the case if the general level of prices was more stable.

3. *People will respond to high and variable rates of inflation by spending less time producing and more time trying to protect themselves from inflation.* Since the failure to anticipate accurately the rate of inflation can have a substantial effect on one's wealth, individuals will divert scarce resources from the production of desired goods and services to the acquisition of information on the future rate of inflation and methods to cope with it. The ability of business decision makers to forecast and deal with changes in prices becomes more valuable relative to their ability as managers and organizers of production. Speculative practices are encouraged as people try to out-guess one another with regard to the future direction of prices. Funds flow into speculative investments, such as gold, silver, and art objects, rather than into productive investments (buildings, machines, and technological research) that expand the investor's ability to produce goods and services. Such practices are socially counterproductive. They reduce our production possibilities.

Low and stable rates of inflation will exert a positive impact on real output and the level of prosperity. The U.S. experience illustrates this point. During the 1983–2000 period, inflation in the United States was low and relatively stable. This period was characterized by strong growth and only 8 months of recession. In contrast, when the inflation rate was high and variable during the 1970s, the United States experienced two recessions (1974–1975 and 1979–1980) and sluggish growth of real GDP.

What Causes Inflation?

We must acquire some additional tools before we can answer the question of what causes inflation in detail, but at this point we can outline a couple of theories. First, economists emphasize the link between aggregate demand and supply. If aggregate demand rises more rapidly than supply, prices will rise. Second, nearly all economists believe that a rapid expansion in a nation's stock of money causes inflation. The old saying is that prices will rise because "there is too much money chasing too few goods." The hyperinflation experienced by South American countries and, more recently, the countries of the former Soviet Union has mainly been the result of monetary expansion. Once we develop additional knowledge about the operation of our economy, we will consider this issue in more detail.

LOOKING AHEAD

In this chapter, we have examined the historical record for real income, employment, and prices. Measurement problems and the side effects of economic instability were discussed. In the next chapter, we will begin to develop a macroeconomic model that will help us better understand both the sources of and potential remedies for economic instability.

KEY POINTS

▼ During the past century, real GDP in the United States has grown at an average annual rate of approximately 3 percent.

▼ Real GDP has also been characterized by cyclical movements. The four phases of the business cycle are *expansion, peak (or boom), contraction,* and *recessionary trough*.

▼ A recession is defined as two successive quarters of declining real GDP. If a recession is quite severe, it is called a depression.

▼ There are three types of unemployment: (a) frictional unemployment, (b) structural unemployment, and (c) cyclical unemployment. In a world of imperfect information and dynamic change, some unemployment is inevitable.

▼ Full employment is the employment level consistent with the economy's natural rate of unemployment. Both full employment and the natural rate of unemployment are associated with the economy's maximum sustainable rate of output.

▼ The concept of potential output encompasses two important ideas: (a) full utilization of resources and (b) a supply constraint that limits our ability to produce desired goods and services. Potential output is the maximum *sustainable* output level consistent with the economy's resource base and current institutional arrangements.

▼ Inflation is a general rise in the level of prices. It is important to distinguish between anticipated and unanticipated inflation. Unanticipated changes in the rate of inflation often alter the intended terms of long-term agreements and cause people to make choices that they will later regret.

▼ Inflation, particularly unanticipated inflation, has harmful effects. These include: (a) additional uncertainty accompanying time-dimension contracts, (b) distortion of relative prices, and (c) the shift of resources into activities designed to prevent inflation from eroding one's wealth.

CRITICAL ANALYSIS QUESTIONS

1. List the major phases of the business cycle and indicate how real GDP, employment, and unemployment change during these phases. Are the time periods of business cycles and the duration of the various phases relatively similar and therefore highly predictable?

*2. Explain why even an efficiently functioning economic system will have some unemployed resources.

3. Classify each of the following as employed, unemployed, or not in the labor force:
   a. Brown is not working; she applied for a job at Wal-Mart last week and is awaiting the result of her application.
   b. Martinez is vacationing in Florida during a layoff at a General Motors plant due to a model changeover, but he expects to be recalled in a couple of weeks.
   c. Green was laid off as a carpenter when a construction project was completed. He is looking for work but has been unable to find anything except an $8-per-hour job, which he turned down.
   d. West works 70 hours per week as a homemaker for her family of nine.
   e. Carson, a 17-year-old, works six hours per week as a route person for the local newspaper.
   f. Chang works three hours in the mornings at a clinic and for the last two weeks has spent the afternoons looking for a full-time job.

4. What is full employment? When full employment is present, will the rate of unemployment be zero? Explain.

5. Carefully explain how both the rate of unemployment and the employment/population ratio are derived. Would it be possible for both of these measures to rise during a specific time period? Why or why not?

6. Is the natural rate of unemployment fixed? Why or why not? How are full employment and the natural rate of unemployment related? Is the actual rate of unemployment currently greater or less than the natural rate of unemployment? Why?

*7. How are the following related to each other?
   a. Actual rate of unemployment
   b. Natural rate of unemployment
   c. Cyclical unemployment
   d. Potential GDP

*8. Use the following data to calculate (a) the labor force participation rate, (b) the rate of unemployment, and (c) the employment/population ratio:

Population	10,000
Labor force	6,000
Not currently working	4,500
Employed full-time	4,000
Employed part-time	1,500
Unemployed	500

*9. Persons are classified as unemployed if they are not currently working at a job and if they made an effort to find a job during the past four weeks. Does this mean that there were no jobs available? Does it mean that there were no jobs available for which unemployed workers were qualified? What does it mean?

10. What impact will high and variable rates of inflation have on the economy? How will they influence the risk accompanying long-term contracts and related business decisions?

*11. The nominal salary paid to the President of the United States along with data for the Consumer Price Index (CPI) are given for various years below.

Year	Presidential salary	CPI (2000 = 100)
1920	$ 75,000	11.6
1940	75,000	8.1
1960	100,000	17.2
1980	200,000	47.9
2000	400,000	100.0

a. Calculate the president's salary measured in the purchasing power of the dollar in 2000.
b. Which year was the real presidential salary the highest?
c. The president's nominal salary was constant between 1920 and 1940. What happened to the real salary? Can you explain why?

12. "When employees are dismissed from employment for reasons other than poor performance, unemployment benefits should replace 100 percent of their prior earnings while they are searching for a new job." Evaluate this statement. Do you think the idea expressed is a good one? Would it influence how quickly laid-off workers would find new jobs? What impact would it have on the unemployment rate?

*13. How will each of the following affect a job seeker's decision to reject an available job offer and continue searching for a superior alternative?
a. The rumor that a major firm in the area is going to expand employment next month
b. An increase in unemployment benefits
c. Optimism about the future of the economy

*14. "My money wage rose by 6 percent last year, but inflation completely erased these gains. How can I get ahead when inflation continues to wipe out my increases in earnings?" What's wrong with this way of thinking?

15. Suppose that the consumer price index at year-end 2000 was 150 and by year-end 2001 had risen to 160. What was the inflation rate during 2001?

16. Data for the nominal GDP and the GDP deflator (1995 = 100) in 1999 and 2000 for six major industrial countries are presented in the accompanying **Table A**.
a. Use the data provided to calculate the 1999 and 2000 real GDP of each country measured in 1995 prices. Place in the blanks provided.
b. Use the data for the GDP deflator to calculate the inflation rate of each country. Place in the blanks provided.
c. Which country had the highest growth rate of real GDP? Which had the lowest?

TABLE A

COUNTRY	NOMINAL GDP (BILLIONS OF LOCAL CURRENCY UNITS)		GDP DEFLATOR (1995 = 100)		REAL GDP (IN 1995 CURRENCY UNITS)		INFLATION RATE
	1999	2000	1999	2000	1999	2000	2000
United States	9,268.6	9,872.9	106.7	109.1	_____	_____	_____
Canada	975.3	1,056.0	105.6	109.2	_____	_____	_____
Japan	512.5	511.8	102.6	101.9	_____	_____	_____
Germany	1,982.3	2,032.3	104.1	103.5	_____	_____	_____
France	1,349.8	1,405.4	103.9	104.7	_____	_____	_____
United Kingdom	891.0	934.9	112.0	114.0	_____	_____	_____

Source: International Monetary Fund, *International Financial Statistics,* September 2001.

d. Indicate the countries that had the highest and the lowest inflation rates.

e. Which one of the countries had the most inflation during this period?

17. The following **Table B** presents the 1999 population, employment, and unemployment data for several countries.

a. Calculate the number of people in the labor force for each of the following countries: the United States, Canada, and Japan.

b. Calculate the labor force participation rate for each country and place it in the blanks provided. Which country had the highest rate of labor force participation? Which country had the lowest?

c. Calculate the rate of unemployment for each country, and place it in the blanks provided. Which country had the highest rate of unemployment? Which had the lowest?

*Asterisk denotes questions for which answers are given in Appendix B.

TABLE B

COUNTRY	POPULATION 15 YEARS AND OVER (IN MILLIONS)	NUMBER EMPLOYED (IN MILLIONS)	NUMBER UNEMPLOYED (IN MILLIONS)	RATE OF LABOR FORCE PARTICIPATION (PERCENT)	RATE OF UNEMPLOYMENT (PERCENT)
United States	214.4	133.5	5.9	_____	_____
Canada	24.7	14.5	1.1	_____	_____
Japan	109.9	64.6	3.2	_____	_____
Germany	69.3	36.1	3.5	_____	_____
France	47.9	22.8	2.9	_____	_____
Australia	15.0	8.7	0.7	_____	_____
Italy	48.8	20.5	2.7	_____	_____

Source: OECD, *Labour Force Statistics,* 1979–1999

CHAPTER 9

Macroeconomics is interesting . . . because it is challenging to reduce the complicated details of the economy to manageable essentials. Those essentials lie in the interactions among the goods, labor, and assets [loanable funds] markets of the economy.

—Rudiger Dornbusch and
Stanley Fischer[1]

An Introduction to Basic Macroeconomic Markets

Chapter Focus

■ What is the circular flow of income? What are the major markets that coordinate macroeconomic activities?

■ Why is the aggregate demand for goods and services inversely related to the price level?

■ Why is an increase in the price level likely to expand output in the short run, but not in the long run?

■ What determines the equilibrium level of GDP of an economy? When equilibrium is present, how will the actual rate of unemployment compare with the natural rate?

■ What is the difference between the real interest rate and the money interest rate? Does inflation help borrowers relative to lenders?

■ If equilibrium is present in the loanable funds and foreign exchange markets, how will this influence the leakages from and injections into the circular flow of income?

[1]Rudiger Dornbusch and Stanley Fischer, *Macroeconomics* (New York: McGraw-Hill, 1978).

As we have learned, the U.S. economy has historically grown at an annual rate of about 3 percent. This growth has improved the living standards of Americans. The growth, however, has not been steady. Although growth of real GDP during some years has increased more than the 3 percent average, during others it has fallen well below the average. During recessions, the size of the economy has actually declined. As we noted in Chapter 8, the U.S. economy has also experienced fluctuations in employment and the rate of inflation. The experience of other countries is similar. All countries have experienced short-term fluctuations in output and employment, and varying degrees of inflation.

It is one thing to describe these fluctuations and another to understand their causes. In this chapter, we will develop a simple macroeconomic model. As we proceed, this model will be used to explain why fluctuations in output, employment, and prices occur and to analyze what might be done to reduce them. ■

UNDERSTANDING MACROECONOMICS: OUR GAME PLAN

A model is like a road map; it illustrates relationships between things. The simple model developed in this chapter will help us better understand macroeconomic relationships. It will also help us analyze the impact of policy changes on important economic variables, such as output, employment, and the general level of prices.

Macroeconomic policy is usually divided into two components: fiscal policy and monetary policy. **Fiscal policy** entails the use of the government's taxation and spending policies in order to achieve macroeconomic goals. In the United States, fiscal policy is conducted by Congress and the president. It is thus a reflection of the political process. **Monetary policy** encompasses actions that alter the money supply. The direction of monetary policy is determined by a nation's central bank, the Federal Reserve System in the United States. Ideally, both monetary and fiscal policy are used to promote business stability, high employment, the growth of output, and a stable price level.

Initially, as we develop our basic macroeconomic model, we will assume that monetary and fiscal policies are unchanged. Stated another way, we will proceed as if the government continues to maintain the current tax and spending policies and that the monetary policymakers maintain a constant **money supply**—that they follow policies that keep the amount of cash in our billfolds and deposits in our checking accounts constant. Of course, changes in government expenditures, taxes, and the money supply are potentially important. We will investigate their impact in detail in subsequent chapters. For now, though, things will go more smoothly if we simply assume that policymakers are holding government expenditures, taxes, and the supply of money constant.

Fiscal policy
The use of government taxation and expenditure policies for the purpose of achieving macroeconomic goals.

Monetary policy
The deliberate control of the money supply, and, in some cases, credit conditions, for the purpose of achieving macroeconomic goals.

Money supply
The supply of currency, checking account funds, and traveler's checks. These items are counted as money because they are used as the means of payment for purchases.

FOUR KEY MARKETS: RESOURCES, GOODS AND SERVICES, LOANABLE FUNDS, AND FOREIGN EXCHANGE

Businesses generally purchase resources from households and use them to produce goods and services. In turn, households generally use a substantial portion of the income they earn from the sale of their productive services to purchase goods and services supplied by businesses. ***Thus, there is a circular flow of output and income between these two key sectors, businesses and households. This circular flow of income is coordinated by four key macroeconomic markets: (1) goods and services, (2) resources, (3) loanable funds, and (4) foreign exchange.*** **Exhibit 1** illustrates both the circular flow of income between the household and business sectors and the interrelationships among the key macroeconomic markets. This is a very important exhibit and it is much less complicated than it may first appear. ***In essence, Exhibit 1 provides a visual representation of the macroeconomic model that we will develop and use to analyze the economy.*** It will help students

EXHIBIT 1
Four Key Markets and the Circular Flow of Income

The circular-flow diagram presents a visual model of the economy. The circular flow of income is coordinated by four key markets. First, the resource market (bottom loop) coordinates the actions of businesses demanding resources and households supplying them in exchange for income. Second, the loanable funds market (lower center) brings the net saving of households plus the net inflow of foreign capital into balance with the borrowing of businesses and governments. Third, the foreign exchange market (top right) brings the purchases (imports) from foreigners into balance with sales (exports plus net inflow of capital) to them. Finally, the goods and services market (top loop) coordinates the demand (consumption, investment, government purchases, and net exports) for and supply of domestic production (real GDP).

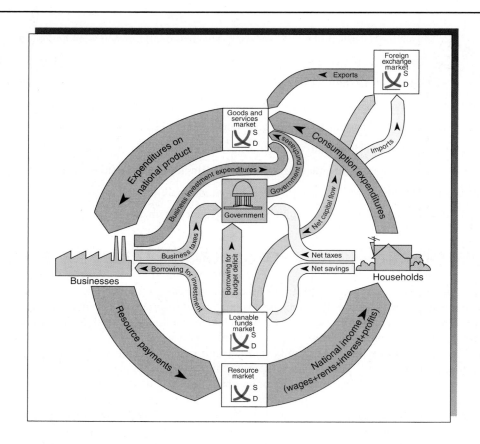

Resource market
A highly aggregated market encompassing all resources (labor, physical capital, land, and entrepreneurship) that contribute to the production of current output. The labor market forms the largest component of this market.

Goods and services market
A highly aggregated market encompassing the flow of all final-user goods and services. The market counts all items that enter into GDP. Thus, real output in this market is equal to real GDP.

visualize more clearly the various spending flows and interrelationships among the key markets.

The bottom loop of this circular-flow diagram depicts the **resource market**, a highly aggregated market that includes the markets for labor services, natural resources, and physical capital. In the resource market, business firms demand resources because of their contribution to the production of goods and services. Households supply labor and other resources in exchange for income. The forces of demand and supply determine prices in the resource market. The payments to the suppliers of resources sum to national income. Some of the income is taxed and used to finance the expenditures of governments. A portion is generally saved, but most of us use the bulk of our income to purchase goods and services.

The **goods and services market** comprises the top loop of the circular-flow diagram. In this market, sometimes referred to as the *product market*, businesses supply goods and services in exchange for sales revenue. As the arrows flowing into the goods and services market (top loop) indicate, there are four major sources of expenditures in this market: (1) household expenditures on consumption (and new housing), (2) business investment, (3) government purchases, and (4) net exports. The expenditures of households, business investors, governments, and foreigners (net exports) compose the aggregate (total) demand for domestic output. As the major demand components indicate, the goods and services market is a highly diverse market. It includes such items as cheeseburgers, pizza, hairstyling, movie tickets, clothing, television sets and DVD players—goods purchased primarily by consumers. It also includes investment goods like tools, manufacturing equipment, and office buildings that are generally purchased by business firms. Finally, such items as highways, fire protection, and national defense, which are usually purchased by governments, are also part of the goods and services market.

There are two other key markets that will help direct the flow of income between the household and business sectors. The **loanable funds market** coordinates the actions of borrowers and lenders. The net **saving** of the household sector supplies funds to the loanable funds market. The demand for funds arises from businesses, to finance investment projects, and from government, to finance budget deficits. In an open economy, such as that of the United States, people also borrow from and lend to foreigners. Note the net inflow of capital from foreign economies into the loanable funds market in Exhibit 1. If the funds borrowed from foreigners exceed the loans to them, there will be a net inflow of funds, increasing supply relative to demand in the loanable funds market. On the other hand, if foreigners are net borrowers, there will be a net outflow of funds. As we discussed in Chapter 4, the interest rate is the price of loanable funds, and it will tend to bring the quantity of funds demanded by businesses and governments into balance with the quantity supplied by households (net saving) and foreigners (net capital inflow). When the borrowed funds are spent on investment goods and government purchases, they return to the circular flow.

Finally, the foreign exchange market coordinates transactions with foreigners. In our world of instant communications and shrinking transportation costs, trade between parties in different countries is common. When Americans purchase goods, services, and assets from foreigners, they will generate a demand for foreign exchange. On the other hand, the sale of items to foreigners will supply foreign exchange. The exchange rate—the price of one currency relative to another—will bring the purchases from foreigners into balance with the sales to them.

Look closely at the right side of Exhibit 1 in order to determine what happens to the flow of income received by households. A major portion of household income is used to purchase consumer goods from domestic producers and therefore these expenditures flow directly into the goods and services market. However, there are three forms of leakage from the circular flow of income: Households will use some of their income to purchase imports; some will be taxed away by the government; and some will be saved. Imports, net taxes, and net saving are leakages from the circular flow of income.

These leakages will tend to be channeled through the loanable funds and foreign exchange markets back into the circular flow. The loanable funds market will tend to direct the net saving of households toward the finance of business investment and government purchases. The foreign exchange market will tend to direct import expenditures toward either spending on exports or net capital inflow. As we proceed, we will investigate in more detail how the loanable funds and foreign exchange markets influence the leakages from and injections into the circular flow of income.

As we noted in Chapter 7, there are two ways of measuring gross domestic product (GDP), the aggregate domestic output of an economy. First, GDP can be measured by adding up the expenditures of consumers, investors, governments, and foreigners (net exports) on goods and services produced during the year. This method is equivalent to measuring the flow of output as it moves through the top loop—the goods and services market—of the circular-flow diagram. Alternatively, GDP can be measured by summing the income payments, both direct and indirect, received by the resource suppliers who produced the goods and services. This method uses the bottom loop—the resource market—to measure the flow of output.

Loanable funds market
A general term used to describe the market arrangements that coordinate the borrowing and lending decisions of business firms and households. Commercial banks, savings and loan associations, the stock and bond markets, and insurance companies are important financial institutions in this market.

Saving
The portion of after-tax income that is not spent on consumption. Saving is a "flow" concept.

AGGREGATE DEMAND FOR GOODS AND SERVICES

What goes on in the aggregate goods and services market is central to the health of an economy. Indeed, if we could keep our eye on just one market in an economy, we would choose the goods and services market. It is important to note that the "quantity" and "price" variables in this highly aggregated market differ from their counterparts in the market for a specific good. In the goods and services market, the "quantity" variable is output as measured by real GDP. The "price" variable is the price level as measured by a general price index (for example, the GDP deflator).

Just as the concepts of demand and supply enhance our understanding of markets for specific goods, they also contribute to our understanding of a highly aggregated market, such as the goods and services market. Because demand in the goods and services market aggregates together the purchases of consumers, investors, governments, and foreigners, it is called "aggregate demand." The **aggregate demand curve** indicates the various quantities of *domestically produced* goods and services that purchasers are willing to buy at different price levels. As **Exhibit 2** illustrates, the aggregate demand curve (*AD*) slopes downward to the right, indicating an inverse relationship between the amount of goods and services demanded and the price level.

Aggregate demand curve
A downward-sloping curve indicating an inverse relationship between the price level and the quantity of domestically produced goods and services that households, business firms, governments, and foreigners (net exports) are willing to purchase during a period.

Why Does the Aggregate Demand Curve Slope Downward?

Both the nature of the aggregate demand curve and the explanation for its downward slope differ substantially from that of the demand for a specific commodity, which we discussed previously in Chapter 3. The inverse relationship between price and the amount demanded of a specific commodity—television sets, for example—reflects the fact that consumers will substitute the good for other commodities when a price reduction makes the good less expensive relative to other goods. A price reduction in the aggregate goods and services market indicates that the level of prices has declined. On average, the prices of all goods are lower. When the prices of all goods produced domestically fall by the same proportion, there will be no incentive for *domestic* purchasers to substitute one good for another.

There are three major reasons why a reduction in the price level will lead to an increase in the aggregate quantity of goods and services demanded by purchasers.

1. *A lower price level will increase the purchasing power of the fixed quantity of money.*
As the level of prices declines, the purchasing power of the fixed quantity of money increases. For example, suppose that you have $2,000 in your bank account. Consider how a

---

EXHIBIT 2
Aggregate Demand Curve

As illustrated here, the quantity of goods and services purchased will increase (to Y_2) as the price level declines (to P_2). Other things constant, the lower price level will increase the wealth of people holding the fixed quantity of money, lead to lower interest rates, and make domestically produced goods cheaper relative to foreign goods. All these factors will tend to increase the quantity of goods and services purchased at the lower price level.

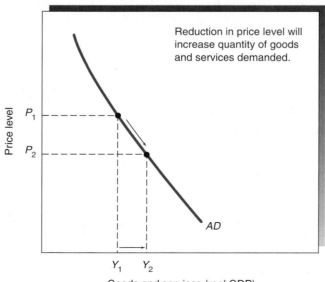

Reduction in price level will increase quantity of goods and services demanded.

20 percent reduction in the level of prices will influence your wealth and spending. At the lower price level, your $2,000 will buy more goods and services. In fact, your $2,000 will buy as much as $2,500 would have purchased at the previous higher level of prices. Other people are in an identical position. As the price level declines, the purchasing power of money and the real wealth of people holding fixed money balances increases. *(Note:* Remember we are assuming that the *nominal* supply of money is fixed.) Because of this increase in wealth, people will purchase more goods and services. Economists refer to this inverse relationship between the price level and the wealth of households and businesses holding a fixed supply of money as the **real balance effect**. It helps explain why a fall in the price level will lead to an increase in the quantity demanded of goods and services.

Real balance effect
The increase in wealth generated by an increase in the purchasing power of a constant money supply as the price level decreases. This wealth effect leads to an inverse relationship between price (level) and quantity demanded in the goods and services market.

2. *The interest rate effect: A lower price level will reduce the demand for money and lower the real interest rate, which will stimulate additional purchases during the current period.*

When the average price of everything is lower, consumers and businesses will need less money to conduct their normal activities. Households will be able to get by just fine with a smaller money balance because, at the lower price level, they will be spending a smaller nominal amount on food, clothing, and other items regularly purchased. Similarly, businesses will need less money to pay employee wages, taxes, and other business expenses. At the lower price level, both consumers and businesses will attempt to reduce their money balances and shift more funds to interest-earning assets like bonds and savings deposits. This will channel more funds into the loanable funds market, placing downward pressure on interest rates.

What impact will a lower interest rate have on the demand for goods and services? A reduction in the interest rate will make it cheaper to purchase goods and services during the current period. Households can be expected to increase their purchases of interest-sensitive consumption goods, such as automobiles and consumer durables. Similarly, firms will expand their current investment expenditures on business expansion and new construction. Thus, the lower price level and accompanying reduction in the interest rate will encourage both households and businesses to demand a larger quantity of goods and services. This interest rate effect also contributes to the downward slope of the aggregate demand curve.

3. *Other things constant, a lower price level will make domestically produced goods less expensive relative to foreign goods.*

At a lower price level, imports will decline as Americans find that many domestically produced goods are now cheaper than products produced abroad. At the lower price level, Americans will tend to purchase fewer Japanese automobiles, Korean textiles, Italian shoes, and other imports because these items are now more expensive relative to domestically produced goods. At the same time, foreigners will increase their purchases of American-made goods that are now relatively cheaper. Therefore, net exports (exports minus imports) will tend to rise.[2] This increase in net exports at the lower U.S. price level will directly increase the quantity demanded of domestically produced goods. This international-substitution effect provides a third reason for the downward slope of the aggregate demand curve.

The Downward-Sloping Aggregate Demand Curve: A Summary

The accompanying Thumbnail Sketch summarizes the reasons why a lower price level will increase the quantity demanded of domestically produced goods and services. A lower price level will (1) increase the purchasing power of the fixed money supply,

---

[2]An increase in exports and a decline in imports will place some upward pressure on the foreign exchange value of the currency. However, the lower interest rates (point 2 above) will result in an outflow of capital, which will place downward pressure on the foreign exchange value of the currency. Most economists believe that this latter effect will dominate. If it does, a depreciation in the nation's currency will stimulate net exports, which will also increase the quantity demanded of goods and services.

Why is the aggregate quantity demanded inversely related to the price level?

A decrease in the price level will raise aggregate quantity demanded because

1. The real wealth of persons holding money balances will increase when prices fall; this will encourage additional consumption.

2. A reduction in the demand for money balances at the lower price level will reduce interest rates, which will encourage current investment and consumption.

3. Net exports will expand (since the prices of domestic goods have fallen relative to foreign goods).

---

(2) lower interest rates, and (3) reduce the price of domestically produced goods relative to goods produced abroad. Each of these factors will tend to increase the quantity demanded in the product market.

The effects would be just the opposite for a higher price level. At a higher price level, (1) the wealth of people holding the fixed supply of money would be less, (2) the demand for money would be greater, which would lead to higher interest rates, and (3) domestic goods would be more expensive relative to those produced abroad. Each of these factors would tend to reduce the quantity demanded of domestically produced goods. Therefore, even though the explanation differs, the quantity demanded in the aggregate goods and services market, like the quantity demanded for a specific product, will be inversely related to price.

AGGREGATE SUPPLY OF GOODS AND SERVICES

In light of our discussion of aggregate demand, it should come as no great surprise that the explanation of the general shape of the **aggregate supply curve** differs from that of the supply curve for a specific good. As we have already noted, an increase in price in the goods and services market indicates that the general level of prices has risen, rather than the price of one good relative to all other goods. Thus, the general shape of the aggregate supply (AS) curve is not a reflection of changes in the relative prices of goods.

When considering aggregate supply, it is particularly important to distinguish between the short run and the long run. In this context, the short run is the time period during which some prices, particularly those in labor markets, are set by prior contracts and agreements. Therefore, in the short run, households and businesses are unable to adjust these prices when unexpected changes occur, including unexpected changes in the price level. In contrast, the long run is a time period of sufficient duration that people have the opportunity to modify their behavior in response to price changes. We now consider both the short-run and long-run aggregate supply curves.

Aggregate Supply in the Short Run

The short-run aggregate supply (SRAS) curve indicates the various quantities of goods and services that domestic firms will supply in response to changing demand conditions that alter the level of prices in the goods and services market. As **Exhibit 3** illustrates, the *SRAS* curve in the goods and services market slopes upward to the right. The upward slope reflects the fact that, in the short run, an unanticipated increase in the price level will, on average, improve the profitability of firms. They will respond with an expansion in output.

The *SRAS* curve is based on a specific expected price level, P_{100} in the case of Exhibit 3, and rate of inflation that generates that price level. When the expected price level is actually achieved, the profitability rate of firms, on average, will be normal and they will supply output Y_0.

Aggregate supply curve
A curve indicating the relationship between the nation's price level and quantity of goods supplied by its producers. In the short run, it is probably an upward-sloping curve, but in the long run most economists believe the aggregate supply curve is vertical (or nearly so).

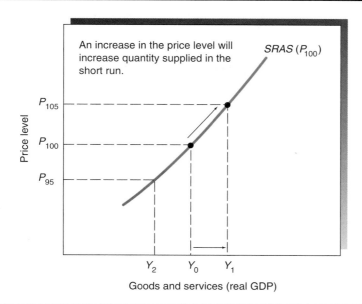

EXHIBIT 3
**Short-run Aggregate
Supply Curve**

The short-run aggregate supply (SRAS) curve shows the relationship between the price level and the quantity supplied of goods and services by domestic producers. In the short run, firms will generally expand output as the price level increases because the higher prices will improve profit margins since many components of costs will be temporarily fixed as the result of prior long-term commitments.

Consider how firms would respond if strong demand led to an unexpected increase in the price level (to P_{105}, for example). In the short run, the higher product prices will enhance profitability. Profit per unit is equal to price minus the producer's per-unit costs. *Important components of producers' costs will be determined by long-term contracts.* Interest rates on loans, collective bargaining agreements with employees, lease agreements on buildings and machines, and other contracts with resource suppliers will influence production costs during the current period. The prices incorporated into these long-term contracts at the time of the agreement are based on the expectation of price level (P_{100}) for the current period. These resource costs tend to be temporarily fixed. *If an increase in demand causes the price level to rise unexpectedly during the current period, prices of goods and services will increase relative to the temporarily fixed components of costs. Profit margins will improve, and business firms will happily respond with an expansion in output (to Y_1).*[3]

An unexpected reduction in the price level to P_{95} would exert just the opposite effect. It would decrease product prices relative to costs and thereby reduce profitability. In response, firms would reduce output to Y_2. Therefore, in the short run, there will be a direct relationship between amount supplied and the price level in the goods and services market.

Aggregate Supply in the Long Run

The long-run aggregate supply (LRAS) curve indicates the relationship between the price level and quantity of output after decision makers have had sufficient time to adjust their prior commitments where possible, or take steps to counterbalance them, in the light of any unexpected changes in market prices. A higher price level in the goods and services market will fail to alter the relationship between product and resource prices in the long run. Once people have time to fully adjust their prior commitments, competitive forces will restore the usual relationship between product prices and costs. Profit rates will return to normal, removing the incentive for firms to supply a larger rate of output. Therefore, as **Exhibit 4** illustrates, the *LRAS* curve is vertical.

---

[3]Other factors may also contribute to the positive relationship between the price level and output in the short run. In response to a general increase in demand, some firms may expand output without much of an increase in price because they believe that their current strong sales are only temporary and that a price increase would drive some of their regular customers to rival suppliers. Other firms may expand output because they mistakenly believe that the demand for their product has increased relative to other products. In the long run, higher costs relative to product prices will make it impossible to sustain such expansions in output.

EXHIBIT 4
Long-run Aggregate
Supply Curve

In the long run, a higher price
level will not expand an economy's rate of output. Once
people have time to adjust
their prior long-term commitments, resource markets (and
costs) will adjust to the higher
level of prices and thereby remove the incentive of firms to
supply a larger output at the
higher price level. An economy's full employment rate of
output—Y_F, the maximum output rate that is sustainable—
is determined by the supply of
resources, level of technology,
and structure of institutions,
factors that are insensitive to
changes in the price level.
The vertical *LRAS* curve illustrates this point.

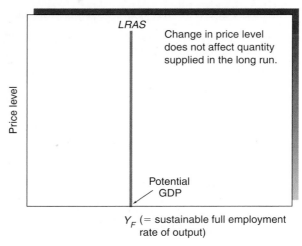

The forces that provide for an upward-sloping SRAS curve are absent in the long run. Costs that are temporarily fixed as the result of contractual agreements will eventually rise. With time, the long-term contracts will expire and be renegotiated. Once the contracts are renegotiated, resource prices will increase in the same proportion as product prices. A proportional increase in costs and product prices will leave the incentive to produce un-changed. Consider how a firm with a selling price of $50 and per-unit costs of $50 will be affected by the doubling of both product and resource prices. After the price increase, the firm's sales price will be $100, but so, too, will its per-unit costs. Thus, neither the firm's profit rate nor the incentive to produce is changed. Therefore, in the long run, an increase in the nominal value of the price level will fail to exert a lasting impact on aggregate output.

As we discussed in Chapter 2, at a point in time, the production possibilities of a nation are constrained by the supply of resources, level of technology, and institutional arrangements that influence the efficiency of resource use. The long-run aggregate supply curve is an alternative way to visualize the economy's production possibilities. Rather than focusing on the output of physical units, as does the production possibilities curve, the long-run aggregate supply curve focuses on the real dollar value of the units produced. The vertical long-run supply curve indicates that a change in the price level does not loosen the constraints that limit our production possibilities. For example, a dou-bling of prices will not improve technology. Neither will it expand the availability of pro-ductive resources, nor improve the efficiency of our economic institutions. Thus, there is no reason for a higher price level to increase our ability to produce goods and services. This is precisely what the vertical *LRAS* curve implies. The accompanying Thumbnail Sketch summarizes the factors that underlie both the short-run and long-run aggregate supply curves.

EQUILIBRIUM IN THE GOODS AND SERVICES MARKET

Equilibrium
A balance of forces permitting the
simultaneous fulfillment of plans
by buyers and sellers.

We are now ready to combine our analysis of aggregate demand and aggregate supply and consider how they act to determine the price level and rate of output. When a mar-ket is in **equilibrium**, there is a balance of forces such that the actions of buyers and

THUMBNAIL SKETCH

Why is the short-run aggregate quantity supplied directly related to the price level?

- As the price level increases, profit margins will improve because initially the product prices of firms will rise relative to cost (important components of which are temporarily fixed by long-term contracts).

Why is the long-run aggregate supply curve vertical?

- Once people have the time to adjust fully to a new price level, the normal relationship between product prices and resource costs is restored.
- The sustainable potential output of an economy is determined by its quantity of resources, technology, and the efficiency of its institutional structures, not by the price level.

sellers are consistent with one another. In equilibrium, buyers are willing to purchase all the units that sellers are willing to supply *at the current price*. Because the equilibrium price clears the market—all units produced are sold—some refer to it as the "market clearing price."

Equilibrium in the Short Run

As **Exhibit 5** illustrates, short-run equilibrium is present in the goods and services market at the price level (*P*) where the aggregate quantity demanded is equal to the aggregate quantity supplied. This occurs at the output rate (*Y*) where the *AD* and *SRAS* curves intersect. At this market clearing price (*P*), the amount that buyers want to purchase is just equal to the quantity that sellers are willing to supply during the current period.

If a price level lower than *P* were present, the aggregate quantity demanded would exceed the aggregate quantity supplied. Purchasers would be seeking to buy more goods and services than producers were willing to produce. This excess demand would place upward pressure on prices, causing the price level to rise toward *P*. On the other hand, at a price level greater than *P*, the aggregate quantity supplied would exceed the aggregate quantity demanded. Producers would be unable to sell all the goods produced. This would result in downward pressure (toward *P*) on prices. Only at the price level *P* would there be a balance of forces between the amount of goods demanded by consumers, investors, governments, and foreigners, and the amount supplied by domestic firms.

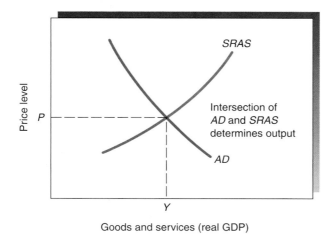

EXHIBIT 5

Short-run Equilibrium in the Goods and Services Market

Short-run equilibrium in the goods and services market occurs at the price level (*P*) where *AD* and *SRAS* intersect. If the price level were lower than *P*, general excess demand in goods and services markets would push prices upward. Conversely, if the price level were higher than *P*, excess supply would result in falling prices.

Equilibrium in the Long Run

In the short run, the goods and services market will gravitate toward a market clearing price—one that brings quantity demanded and quantity supplied into balance. *However, a second condition is required for long-run equilibrium: Decision makers who agreed to long-term contracts influencing current prices and costs must have correctly anticipated the current price level at the time they arrived at the agreements.* If this is not the case, buyers and sellers will want to modify the agreements when the long-term contracts expire. In turn, their modifications will affect costs, profit margins, and output.

Exhibit 6 illustrates a long-run equilibrium in the goods and services market. As in Exhibit 3, the subscripts attached to the *SRAS* and *AD* curves indicate the price level (an index of prices) that was anticipated by decision makers at the time they made decisions affecting the schedules. In this case, when buyers and sellers made their purchasing and production choices, they anticipated that the price level during the current period would be P_{100}, where the subscript 100 refers to an index of prices during an earlier base year. As the intersection of the *AD* and *SRAS* curves reveals, the P_{100} was actually attained. In long-run equilibrium, aggregate demand (*AD*) intersects with *SRAS* along the economy's vertical *LRAS*.

When the price level expectations embedded in the long-term contracts turn out to be correct, then the current resource prices and real interest rates will tend to persist into the future. Profit rates will be normal. The choices of buyers and sellers will harmonize, and neither will have reason to modify their previous contractual agreements when they come up for renegotiation. Thus, current rate of output (Y_F) is sustainable in the future. Long-run equilibrium is present and it will persist into the future until changes in other factors alter *AD* or *SRAS*.

Long-Run Equilibrium, Potential Output, and Full Employment

As we discussed in Chapter 8, potential GDP is equal to the economy's *maximum sustainable output* consistent with its resource base, current technology, and institutional structure. Potential GDP is neither a temporary high nor an abnormal low. When long-

EXHIBIT 6
Long-run Equilibrium in the Goods and Services Market

When the goods and services market is in long-run equilibrium, two conditions must be present. First, the quantity demanded must equal the quantity supplied at the current price level. Second, the price level anticipated by decision makers must equal the actual price level. The subscripts on the *SRAS* and *AD* curves indicate that buyers and sellers alike anticipated the price level P_{100}, where the 100 represents an index of prices during an earlier base year. When the anticipated price level is actually attained, current output (Y_F) will equal the economy's potential GDP and full employment will be present.

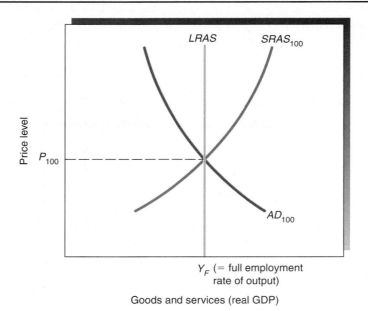

run equilibrium is present, the actual output achieved is equal to the economy's potential GDP.

The long-run equilibrium output rate (Y_F in Exhibit 6) also corresponds with the full employment of resources. When full-employment output is present, the job-search time of unemployed workers will be normal, given the characteristics of the labor force and the institutional structure of the economy. Only frictional and structural unemployment will be present; cyclical unemployment will be absent.

When an economy is in long-run equilibrium, the *actual* rate of unemployment will be equal to the natural rate. Remember, the *natural* rate of unemployment reflects the normal job-search process of employees and employers, given the structure of the economy and the laws and regulations that affect the operation of markets. It is a rate that is neither abnormally high nor abnormally low; it can be sustained into the future. If long-run equilibrium is present, unemployment will be at its natural rate.

Summarizing, in long-run equilibrium, (a) output will be equal to its potential, (b) full employment will be achieved, and (c) the actual rate of unemployment will be equivalent to the natural rate of unemployment. It is this long-run maximum sustainable output that economists are referring to when they speak of "full employment output" or "potential GDP."

Adjustment When Output Differs from Long-Run Potential

Output Greater Than Long-Run Potential

What happens when changes in the price level catch buyers and sellers by surprise? When the actual price level differs from the level forecast by buyers and sellers, some decision makers will enter into agreements that they will later regret—agreements that they will want to change as soon as they have an opportunity to do so.

Consider the situation when the price level *increases* more than was anticipated. Failing to foresee the strong demand and higher product prices, many resource suppliers will have agreed to long-term contracts that are not as attractive as was initially perceived. For example, many union officials and employees will have made commitments to money wages that are now unattractive, given the strong demand and higher general level of prices. Other resource suppliers will find themselves in similar positions. In the short run, the atypically low real wages reduce costs relative to product prices. Profit margins are abnormally high, and firms respond with a larger output. Employment expands and unemployment falls below its natural rate.

But this abnormally large output and high level of employment are not sustainable. The "mistakes," based on a failure to predict the strength of current demand, will be recognized and corrected when contracts expire. Real wages (and other resource prices) will increase and eventually reflect the higher price level and rate of inflation. Profit margins will return to normal. When these adjustments are completed, the temporarily large output rate and high employment level will decline and return to normal.

How can output, even temporarily, be pushed beyond the economy's potential GDP? Remember, potential GDP is a sustainable rate of output; it can be maintained. Motivated by strong demand and high profitability, firms can expand output through intensive supervision, more overtime work, a reduction in down time for maintenance, and similar measures. However, this intense pace cannot be maintained over lengthy periods. The situation is much like that of students who stay up later, watch less television, and spend less time on social and leisure activities in order to increase their study time prior to a major exam. They are able to increase their "productivity" temporarily, but the hectic schedule cannot be maintained. Similarly, business firms can temporarily push output beyond long-run potential, but, given the constraints of the current resource base, the higher output rate cannot be sustained. Markets will adjust and output will recede to its long-run potential.

Output Less Than Long-Run Potential

What will happen if product prices *decline or increase* less rapidly than anticipated? Given the lower than expected price level, many employers will find themselves committed to wages and other resource prices that are extremely high relative to prices in the

The expected rate of inflation influences the prices incorporated into long-term contracts, such as collective bargaining agreements. If the actual price level differs from what was expected, output will differ from long-run equilibrium.

goods and services market. In turn, these commitments will lead to abnormally high costs relative to product prices. Profit margins will be squeezed, causing producers to reduce output and lay off employees. Unemployment will rise above its *natural rate* and current output will fall short of the economy's potential GDP.

Many economists think this is precisely what happened during 1982. After inflation rates of 13 percent in 1979 and 12 percent in 1980, price increases plummeted to 4 percent in 1982. This sharp reduction in the inflation rate caught many decision makers by surprise. Unable to pass along to consumers the large increases in money wages agreed to in 1980 and 1981, employers cut back production and laid off workers. The unemployment rate soared to 10.8 percent in late 1982, up from 7.6 percent in 1981. Eventually, new agreements provided for smaller money wage increases, or even wage reductions, in 1983 and 1984. Unemployment fell. Nevertheless, in 1982 unemployment was well above its natural rate. The necessary adjustments could not be made instantaneously.

In summary, an unexpected change in the price level (rate of inflation) will alter the rate of output in the short run. An unexpected increase in the price level will stimulate output and employment during the next year or two, while an unexpected decline in the price level will cause output and employment to fall in the immediate future.

RESOURCE MARKET

In addition to the aggregate goods and services market, the resource market, loanable funds market, and foreign exchange market help coordinate the circular flow of income between the household and business sectors. All four of these markets are interrelated—changes in one will have repercussions in the others. We will now turn to an analysis of the resource, loanable funds, and foreign exchange markets and their interrelation with the goods and services market

The resource market is the place where labor, raw materials, machines, and other factors of production are bought and sold. Within the framework of our circular flow analysis, households supply resources in exchange for income, and business firms demand resources in order to produce goods and services (see Exhibit 1). By far, the market for labor services is the largest component of the resource market. In the United States, the costs of labor make up approximately 70 percent of production costs. Because of its size and importance, we will focus considerable attention on the labor market.

As in other markets, prices will coordinate the choices of buyers and sellers in the resource market. An increase in the price of labor and other resources will increase the cost of production and make it less profitable for firms to employ resources. As a result, businesses will demand less labor and other resources as their prices increase. Thus, the demand curve in the resource market will have the usual downward slope to the right. Although working and supplying resources generates income, it also requires one to give up something that is valuable: leisure—time for nonwork activities. Higher resource prices will make it more attractive to give up leisure and supply labor and other resources instead. Therefore, the quantity supplied of labor and other resources expands as resource prices increase.

As **Exhibit 7** illustrates, there will be a tendency to move toward a price that will clear the market and bring the amount demanded by business firms into balance with the amount supplied by resource owners. At this price (P_r), the choices of both buyers and sellers in the aggregate resource market harmonize—they are consistent with each other. If the market price were greater than P_r, an excess supply of resources would occur. In turn, this excess supply would push resource prices downward toward equilibrium. In contrast, if resource prices were below equilibrium (less than P_r), excess demand would place upward pressure on the price of resources. Market forces thus tend to move resource prices toward the price that clears the market, the price that brings amount demanded into equality with the amount supplied.

As we discussed in Chapter 4, the markets for resources and products are closely related. The demand for resources is directly linked to the demand for goods and services. In fact, the demand for resources is a *derived demand*—it stems from the demand for goods and services. An increase in demand in the goods and services market will generate additional demand for resources. Similarly, a reduction in aggregate demand in the goods and services market will reduce the demand for resources.

Changes in resource markets will also exert an impact on the goods and services market. The cost of producing goods and services is influenced directly by the price of resources. Other things constant, an increase in resource prices will increase costs and squeeze profit margins in the goods and services market, causing the supply curve (*SRAS*) in the product market to shift to the left. Conversely, a reduction in resource prices will lower costs and improve profit margins in the goods and services market. An increase in

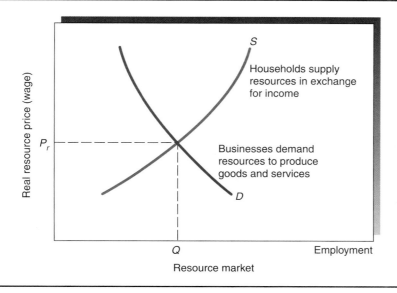

EXHIBIT 7
Equilibrium in the Resource Market

In general, as resource prices increase, the amount demanded by producers declines and the amount supplied by resource owners expands. In equilibrium, resource price brings the amount demanded into equality with the amount supplied in the aggregate-resource market. The labor market is a major component of the resource market.

aggregate supply (a shift to the right in *SRAS*) will result. As we analyze the macroeconomy, the interrelations between these two markets will arise again and again.

When an economy is in long-run equilibrium, the price of resources relative to the price of goods and services will be such that business firms, on average, will be just able to cover their cost of production, including a competitive return on their investment. If this were not the case, producers would seek to either contract or expand output. For example, if the prices of resources were so high (relative to product prices) that firms were unable to cover their costs, many producers would cut back output or perhaps even discontinue production. Aggregate output would thereby be altered. Conversely, if resource prices were so low that firms were able to earn an above-market return, profit-seeking firms would expand output. New firms would begin production. Again, these forces would alter conditions in the goods and services market.

LOANABLE FUNDS MARKET

When we introduced the loanable funds market in Chapter 4, we indicated that borrowers demand loanable funds, while lenders supply them. In essence, borrowers are exchanging future income for purchasing power now. Most of us are impatient; we want things now rather than in the future. *From the borrower's viewpoint, interest is the price paid for earlier availability (purchasing power now rather than in the future). From the lender's viewpoint, interest is a premium received for waiting, for delaying possible expenditures into the future.*

Other things constant, lower interest rates will make it less attractive to save and thereby supply funds to the loanable funds market. On the other hand, the lower rates will make it cheaper for businesses to undertake investment projects and for households to purchase "big ticket" items, such as houses and automobiles. Thus, the supply and demand curves in the loanable funds market have their usual shapes, and the interest rate will tend to bring the quantity of funds demanded by borrowers into equality with the quantity supplied by lenders.[4]

It is important to think of the interest rate in two ways. First, there is the **money interest rate**, the percentage of the amount borrowed that must be paid the lender in addi-

Money interest rate
The percentage of the amount borrowed that must be paid to the lender in addition to the repayment of the principal. It overstates the real cost of borrowing during an inflationary period. When inflation is anticipated, an inflationary premium will be incorporated into this rate. The money interest rate is often referred to as the nominal interest rate.

Banks, savings and loan associations, and brokerage firms help coordinate saving and investment in the loanable funds market.

---

[4]Of course, there are several different interest rates reflecting the time duration of the loan and the creditworthiness of the borrower.

tion to the repayment of the principal. Money interest rates are those typically quoted in newspapers and business publications. Second, there is the **real interest rate**, which reflects the real burden to borrowers and the payoff to lenders in terms of command over goods and services.

The rate of inflation expected by borrowers and lenders will influence the attractiveness of various interest rates. Perhaps an example will illustrate this point and highlight the distinction between the money and real interest rate. Suppose that a borrower and lender—both anticipating that the general level of prices will be stable—agree to a 5 percent interest rate for a one-year loan of $1,000. After a year, the borrower must pay the lender $1,050—the $1,000 principal plus the 5 percent interest. Now, suppose during the year prices rose 5 percent as the result of inflation. Because of this, the $1,050 repayment after a year commands exactly the same purchasing power as the original $1,000 did when it was loaned. The lender receives nothing for making the purchasing power available to the borrower. In this case, the real interest return to the lender (and real cost to the borrower) is zero. Lenders are unlikely to continue making funds available at such bargain rates.

When inflation is present, people will come to anticipate it. Once borrowers and lenders expect a rate of inflation, 5 percent for example, they will build that rate into their loanable funds agreement. Lenders will demand (and borrowers will agree to pay) a higher money interest rate to compensate for the impact of inflation on the purchasing power of the loan proceeds. This premium for the expected decline in purchasing power of the dollar is called the **inflationary premium**. It is equal to the expected rate of inflation. The relationship between the real and money interest rates is:

$$\text{Real interest rate} = \text{Money interest rate} - \text{Inflationary premium}$$

Exhibit 8 illustrates how inflationary expectations influence money interest rates. Here we consider a situation where a 5 percent market rate of interest would emerge when borrowers and lenders anticipate stable prices. Because the expected rate of inflation is zero, there will be no inflationary premium and, under these conditions, the money and real rates are equal. Consider how a persistent inflation rate of 5 percent will influence the choices of both borrowers and lenders. Compared to the zero inflation situation, a 10 percent interest return will be required to provide lenders with the same incentive to loan funds. Similarly, a 10 percent interest rate will provide borrowers with the same incentive to demand funds. Therefore, both the supply and demand curves will shift vertically by 5 percent to compensate for the expected rate of inflation. The money rate of interest will

Real interest rate
The interest rate adjusted for expected inflation; it indicates the real cost to the borrower (and yield to the lender) in terms of goods and services.

Inflationary premium
A component of the money interest rate that reflects compensation to the lender for the expected decrease, due to inflation, in the purchasing power of the principal and interest during the course of the loan. It is determined by the expected rate of future inflation.

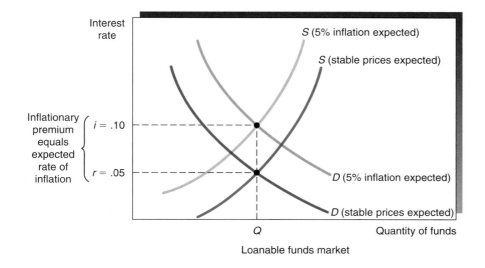

Loanable funds market

EXHIBIT 8
Inflation and Interest Rates

Suppose that when people expect the general level of prices to be stable (zero inflation) in the future, a 5 percent interest rate brings quantity demanded into balance with quantity supplied. Under these conditions, the money and real interest rates will be equal. When people expect prices to rise at a 5 percent rate, the money rate of interest (i) will rise to 10 percent even though the real interest rate (r) remains constant at 5 percent.

increase to 10 percent, 5 percent of which reflects an inflationary premium and 5 percent a real interest return.

Of course, the expected rate of inflation (and therefore the inflationary premium) cannot be directly observed. Therefore, neither can the real interest rate. Nonetheless, it is clear that the money interest rate is often a misleading indicator of the real (remember *real* always means adjusted for inflation) borrowing cost and lending return. The money interest rate will vary directly with the expected rate of inflation. The higher the expected rate of inflation, the greater the inflationary premium and therefore the larger the money rate of interest. However, it is the *real* interest rate that reflects the true cost of borrowing and return to lending.

Does Inflation Help Borrowers?

In a world of uncertainty, decision makers will not always be able to forecast the future rate of inflation accurately. If the actual rate of inflation is higher than was expected, borrowers will tend to gain relative to lenders. For example, suppose borrowers and lenders expect a 3 percent future rate of inflation and therefore agree to an 8 percent interest rate on a loan—5 percent representing the real interest rate and 3 percent the inflationary premium. If the actual rate of inflation turns out to be higher than 3 percent—6 percent, for example—the real amount paid by the borrower and received by the lender will decline. **When the actual rate of inflation is greater than was anticipated, borrowers gain relative to lenders.**

But the converse is true when the actual rate of inflation is less than expected. Suppose that after the borrower and lender agree to the 8 percent loan, the price level is stable while the loan is outstanding. In this case, the borrower ends up paying an 8 percent real interest rate, rather than the 5 percent that was anticipated. **When the actual rate of inflation is less than anticipated, lenders gain at the expense of borrowers.**

Commentators often argue that inflation helps borrowers relative to lenders. This would only be true if borrowers and lenders systematically underestimated the rate of inflation. This is highly unlikely. Of course, forecasting errors will be made. Sometimes the inflation rate will be higher than decision makers anticipated, while in other instances it will be lower. **There is no reason, however, to expect systematic forecasting errors. Thus, there is no reason why inflation will help either borrowers or lenders in a systematic manner.**

Interest Rates and Macroeconomic Markets

The circular-flow diagram (Exhibit 1) illustrates both the inflow and outflow to the loanable funds market. The net saving of households and net capital inflow from foreigners provide the inflow—the supply of funds—into the loanable funds market. The borrowing of businesses for investment projects and of governments for the finance of budget deficits leads to the outflow of funds. This borrowing generates the demand for loanable funds.

Businesses and governments often borrow funds by issuing bonds that yield an interest rate. Issuing bonds is simply a method of demanding loanable funds. In turn, the purchasers of bonds are supplying loanable funds. There is an inverse relationship between bond prices and interest rates. **When interest rates rise, the market value of outstanding bonds will fall. Correspondingly, lower interest rates will push bond prices upward.** (See the Applications in Economics box on bonds and interest rates for a detailed explanation of this point.)

In an open economy like that of the United States, domestic residents are also able to borrow from and lend to foreigners. When foreigners supply more loanable funds than they demand, there will be a net inflow of foreign capital that will supplement domestic saving. On the other hand, if foreigners are net borrowers, there will be a net outflow of capital from the domestic market. The real interest rate in the loanable funds market will

APPLICATIONS IN ECONOMICS

Bonds, Interest Rates, and Bond Prices

Bonds are simply IOUs issued by firms and governments. Issuing bonds is a method of borrowing in the loanable funds market. The entity issuing the bond promises to pay interest at a fixed rate on the amount borrowed (called principal) while the loan is outstanding and to repay the principal on a specified date in the future (for example, five or ten years after the bond is issued). The interest payments are usually made regularly (for example, quarterly or semi-annually) during each year.

Even though interest rates may change with the passage of time, *the bondholder will receive the fixed interest rate as a percentage of the original principal throughout the life of the bond.* Although bonds are issued for lengthy periods of time—the U.S. Treasury issues bonds for up to 30 years—they can be sold to another party prior to their maturity. Each day, sales of previously issued bonds comprise the majority of bonds bought and sold on the bond market.

When overall interest rates rise, the prices of outstanding bonds will fall, and vice versa. Suppose you bought a newly issued $1,000 bond that pays 8 percent per year in perpetuity (forever) on the $1,000 principal.* As long as you own the bond, you are entitled to a fixed return of $80 per year. Let us also assume that after you have held the bond for one year and have collected your $80 interest for that year, the market rate of interest for newly issued bonds like yours increases to 10 percent. How will this increase in the interest rate affect the market price of your bond? Because bond purchasers can now earn 10 percent interest if they buy newly issued bonds, they will be unwilling to pay more than $800 for your bond, which pays only $80 interest per year. After all, why would anyone pay $1,000 for a bond that yields only $80 interest per year when the same $1,000 will now purchase a bond that yields $100 (10 percent) per year? The increase in the interest rate to 10 percent will cause the *market price* of your $1,000 bond (which earns only 8 percent annually) to fall to $800. At that price, the new owners would earn the 10 percent market rate of interest. In this manner, rising market interest rates cause bond prices to decline.

On the other hand, falling interest rates will cause bond prices to rise. If the market interest rate had fallen to 6 percent, what would have happened to the market value of your bond? (*Hint:* $80 is 6 percent of $1,333.) Thus, bond prices and interest rates are inversely linked to each other.

---

*Undated securities of this sort are available in the United Kingdom. They are called *consols*.

---

move toward the rate that will bring the quantity of funds demanded into equality with the quantity supplied, *including the net inflow or outflow of capital.*

In today's global financial markets, the flow of capital to the domestic loanable funds market will be directly related to the real interest rate. As **Exhibit 9** shows, when domestic demand is weak (D_1 for example) and the real interest rate low (r_1), capital will flow outward toward other markets where the rate of return is expected to be higher. In contrast, strong domestic demand (D_2 for example) for loanable funds and high real interest rates will lead to an inflow of capital.

Like the resource market, the loanable funds market is interrelated with the goods and services market. We previously indicated that the reduction in the interest rate that generally accompanies a lower price level when the supply of money is constant helps explain why the *AD* curve slopes downward to the right. In addition, the real interest rate may change for other reasons. When it does, it will affect the aggregate demand schedule. The real interest rate influences how households allocate their income between saving and current consumption. An increase in the interest rate will discourage current consumption by making it more attractive to save and more expensive to borrow. Thus, other things constant, higher interest rates will reduce current consumption and thereby reduce aggregate demand. Lower interest rates will exert the opposite effect. As we proceed, we will analyze in more detail the interrelationship between the loanable funds market and the goods and services market.

When an economy is in long-run equilibrium, the relationship between interest rates in the loanable funds market and prices in product and resource markets will be

EXHIBIT 9
Interest Rates and the Inflow and Outflow of Capital

Demand and supply in the loanable funds market will determine the interest rate. When the demand for loanable funds is strong (like D_2), the real interest rate will be high (r_2) and there will be a net inflow of capital. In contrast, weak demand (like D_1) and low interest rates (like r_1) will lead to net capital outflow.

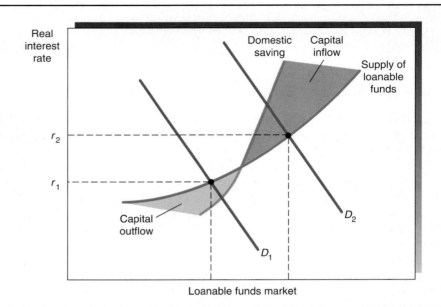

such that the typical firm is just able to earn normal returns on its investments. In other words, the typical producer's return to capital must equal the interest rate, that is, the opportunity cost of capital. Higher returns would induce producers to expand output, while lower returns would cause them to cut back on production.

FOREIGN EXCHANGE MARKET

Look back at Exhibit 1 and note the various transactions with foreigners. Households import some goods and services from foreigners, reducing the flow of spending into the product market. Businesses export some of the domestically produced goods to foreigners, which adds to the flow of spending into the product market. In addition, there is an inflow and outflow of capital in the loanable funds market. As we just discussed, the size and direction of this capital flow are dependent on the real interest rate.

International transactions generally require one of the trading partners to convert their domestic currency to that of the other. For example, an American who purchases pottery from a Mexican supplier typically exchanges dollars for pesos and uses the pesos to pay for the pottery. As we noted in Chapter 4, exchanges like this take place in the foreign exchange market, a market where the currency of one nation is traded for that of another. When Americans buy goods from foreigners and make investments abroad (an outflow of capital), they will require foreign currency for these purchases. Thus, these transactions generate a demand for foreign currency. On the other hand, when Americans sell products and assets (including bonds) to foreigners, the transactions will generate a supply of foreign currency in exchange for dollars. Thus, the dollar demand for foreign currency emanates from the purchases of Americans from foreigners, while the supply of foreign currency in exchange for dollars reflects American sales to foreigners.

Exhibit 10 illustrates how the foreign exchange market will tend to bring the purchases from and sales to foreigners into balance. The dollar price of foreign currency is measured along the vertical axis. A reduction in the dollar price of foreign exchange—a movement down the vertical axis—means that a dollar will buy more units of various foreign currencies. This will make it cheaper for Americans to purchase things from foreign-

EXHIBIT 10
Foreign Exchange Market

Americans demand foreign currencies in order to import goods and services and make investments abroad. Foreigners supply their currency in exchange for dollars in order to purchase American exports and undertake investments in the United States. The exchange rate will bring the quantity demanded into balance with the quantity supplied. This will also bring imports + capital outflow into equality with exports + capital inflow.

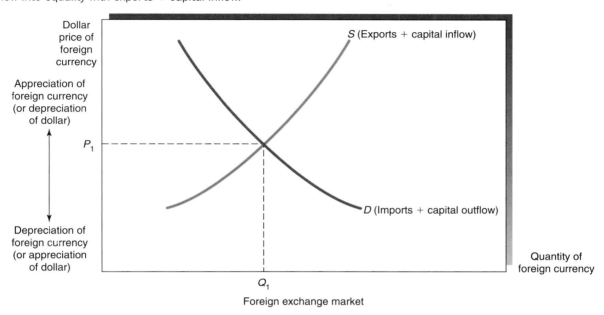

Foreign exchange market

ers. Thus, we say that the dollar has **appreciated**, meaning that it will now buy more foreign goods than was previously true. As the dollar price for foreign exchange falls (movement down the vertical axis), Americans buy more from foreigners and therefore demand a larger quantity of foreign exchange for the purchases. Thus, the dollar demand for foreign currency will slope downward to the right.

In contrast, an increase in the dollar price of foreign exchange—movement up the vertical axis—indicates that more dollars are required to purchase a unit of foreign currency. This makes foreign purchases more expensive for Americans and, therefore, it is referred to as a **depreciation** of the dollar. As the dollar depreciates, a unit of foreign currency will purchase a larger quantity of dollars. This depreciation in the dollar will make American goods less expensive for foreigners. As the dollar depreciates (movement up the vertical axis), foreigners buy more from Americans and therefore supply more foreign currency in exchange for dollars. Thus, the supply curve for foreign exchange will slope upward to the right.

The forces of supply and demand in the foreign exchange market will move the exchange rate toward the equilibrium price (P_1 in Exhibit 10). In equilibrium, the quantity demanded of foreign exchange will just equal the quantity supplied. When this is true, imports plus the outflow of capital for investment abroad will equal exports plus the inflow of capital from the investments of foreigners in the United States. Mathematically, when the exchange market is in equilibrium, the following relationship exists:

$$\text{Imports} + \text{Capital outflow} = \text{Exports} + \text{Capital inflow} \tag{9-1}$$

This relationship can be rewritten in the following manner:

$$\text{Imports} - \text{Exports} = \text{Capital inflow} - \text{Capital outflow} \tag{9-2}$$

Appreciation
An increase in the value of a currency relative to foreign currencies. An appreciation increases the purchasing power of the currency over foreign goods.

Depreciation
A reduction in the value of a currency relative to foreign currencies. A depreciation reduces the purchasing power of the currency over foreign goods.

The right side of Equation 9-2 is also called *net capital inflow*. Because it is a net figure, it can be either positive (indicating an inflow of capital) or negative (indicating an outflow of capital).

The left side of the equation (imports minus exports) indicates the nation's balance of trade. When imports exceed exports, the situation is referred to as a **trade deficit.** On the other hand, if exports exceed imports, a **trade surplus** is present. There is an interesting implication of the relationship between the flow of trade and the flow of capital: When a trade deficit is present, there must be an inflow of capital. The reverse is also true: An inflow of capital implies a trade deficit. Conversely, when a trade surplus (exports are greater than imports) is present, there must also be an outflow of capital.

Trade deficit
The situation when a country's imports of goods and services are greater than its exports.

Trade surplus
The situation when a country's exports of goods and services are greater than its imports.

LEAKAGE AND INJECTIONS FROM THE CIRCULAR FLOW OF INCOME

If you look back at Exhibit 1, you will note that there are three leakages of the income received by households: saving, taxes, and imports. As the three arrows (other than the consumption of households) into the goods and services market indicate, there are also three injections of expenditures into the circular flow of income: investment, government purchases, and exports.

For macroequilibrium to be present, the flow of expenditures on goods and services (top loop of Exhibit 1) must equal the flow of income to resource owners (bottom loop). This will be true if the injections (investment, government purchases, and exports) into the circular flow are equal to the leakages (saving, taxes, and imports) from it. Interestingly, this will be the case when equilibrium is present in the loanable funds and foreign exchange markets. Let's analyze why this is the case.

As Exhibit 1 shows, the net saving of households plus net capital inflow from foreigners provide the supply in the loanable funds market. Business investment and government borrowing to finance budget deficits generate the demand. When the interest rate brings these two forces into balance, it means that the following relationship is present:

(9-3)   Net saving + Net capital inflow = Investment + Budget deficit

The foreign exchange market brings imports plus capital outflow into equality with exports plus capital inflow (Equation 9-1 above). As a result, the net inflow of capital (capital inflow − capital outflow) is equal to imports minus exports (see Equation 9-2 above). Substituting imports minus exports for the net capital inflow in Equation 9-3 yields:

(9-4)   Net saving + Imports − Exports = Investment + Budget deficit

Because the budget deficit is merely government purchases minus net taxes, Equation 9-4 can be rewritten as:

(9-5)   Net saving + Imports − Exports = Investment + Government purchases − Taxes

Finally, moving exports and taxes to the opposite sides of the equation yields:

(9-6)   Net saving + Imports + Taxes = Investment + Government purchases + Exports

Of course, the derivation of Equation 9-6 is based on the presence of equilibrium in both the loanable funds and foreign exchange markets. When interest rates and exchange rates bring these markets into equilibrium, they will also bring the leakage from (left side of Equation 9-6) and injection to (right side of Equation 9-6) the circular flow of income into balance. The accompanying Thumbnail Sketch provides a shorthand summary of the key relationships underlying this proposition.

THUMBNAIL SKETCH

Key Macro Market Relationships

1. Equilibrium in Foreign Exchange Market implies:

   Imports + Capital outflow = Exports + Capital inflow

2. Because net capital inflow is capital inflow minus capital outflow, the equation in 1 can be rewritten as:

   Imports − Exports = Net capital inflow

3. Equilibrium in Loanable Funds Market implies:

   Net saving + Net capital inflow = Investment + Budget deficit

4. Substituting the left side of the equation in 2 for net capital inflow yields:

   Net saving + Imports − Exports = Investment + Budget deficit

5. Because the budget deficit is government purchases minus taxes, the equation in 4 can be rewritten as:

   Net saving + Imports − Exports = Investment + Government purchases − Taxes

6. The equation in 5 can be rewritten as:

   Net savings + Imports + Taxes = Investment + Government purchases + Exports

Therefore, when the loanable funds and foreign exchange markets are in equilibrium, the leakages from the circular flow of income (saving + imports + taxes) and the injections into it (investment + government purchases + exports) will be equal.

Pulling Things Together

We have now discussed all four basic macroeconomic markets: goods and services, resources, loanable funds, and foreign exchange. Like the legs of a chair, these four macroeconomic markets are dependent on each other. When an economy is in long-run equilibrium, the interrelationships among these four markets will be in harmony. The relationship among resource prices, interest rates, and product prices will be such that the firms will earn, on average, only a competitive rate of return. Correspondingly, the interest rates and exchange rates will bring the injections into the circular flow of income into balance with the leakages from it. When people correctly anticipate the current price level (rate of inflation), there are reasons to believe that market adjustments will move an economy toward long-run equilibrium.

This chapter focused on equilibrium. The four basic macroeconomic markets were introduced and the implications of their equilibrium analyzed. However, we live in a world of dynamic change and unexpected events. The following chapter will focus on how changing conditions influence economic performance. Macroeconomics largely concerns tracing the impact of a change in one market through to other markets, particularly the goods and services market. The model developed in this chapter will help us analyze these changes more proficiently.

LOOKING AHEAD

KEY POINTS

▼ The circular flow of income and expenditures highlights the significance of four key markets in the coordination of the macroeconomy: (a) goods and services, (b) resources, (c) loanable funds, and (d) foreign exchange.

▼ The aggregate demand curve indicates the various quantities of domestically produced goods and services purchasers are willing to buy at different price levels. It will slope downward to the right because consumers, investors, governments, and foreigners (net exports) will purchase a larger quantity at a lower price level.

▼ The aggregate supply (AS) curve indicates the various quantities of goods and services domestic suppliers will produce at different price levels. The short-run aggregate supply (SRAS) curve will slope upward to the right because a higher price level will improve profit margins when important cost components are temporarily fixed in the short run.

▼ In the long run, output is constrained by the economy's resource base, current technology, and efficiency of the existing institutions. A higher price level does not loosen these constraints. Thus, the long-run aggregate supply (LRAS) curve is vertical.

▼ Two conditions are necessary for long-run equilibrium in the goods and services market: (a) quantity demanded must equal quantity supplied, and (b) the *actual* price level must equal the price level decision makers *anticipated* when they made buying and selling decisions for the current period. When long-

run equilibrium is present, output will be at its maximum sustainable level.

▼ The aggregate demand/aggregate supply model reveals the determinants of the price level and real output. In the short run, price and output will move toward an intersection of the aggregate demand (AD) and short-run aggregate supply (SRAS) curves. In the long run, price and output will gravitate to the levels represented by the intersection of AD, SRAS, and LRAS.

▼ When the economy is in long-run equilibrium, potential output will be achieved and full employment will be present (the actual rate of unemployment will equal the natural rate).

▼ It is important to distinguish between real and money interest rates. The real interest rate reflects the real burden to borrowers and the payoff to lenders in terms of command over goods and services. The real rate of interest is equal to the money rate of interest minus the inflationary premium. The latter depends on the expected rate of inflation.

▼ When equilibrium is present in the loanable funds and foreign exchange markets, the injections (investment, government purchases, and exports) into the circular flow of income will equal the leakages (saving, taxes, and imports) from it.

▼ Macroeconomic equilibrium requires that equilibrium be achieved in all four key macroeconomic markets and that the interrelationships among these markets must be in harmony.

CRITICAL ANALYSIS QUESTIONS

1. In your own words, explain why aggregate demand is inversely related to the price level. Why does the explanation for the inverse relationship between price and quantity demanded for the aggregate demand curve differ from that of a demand curve for a specific good?

2. What are the major factors that influence our ability to produce goods and services in the long run? Why is the long-run aggregate supply curve vertical?

3. Why does the short-run aggregate supply curve slope upward to the right? If the prices of both (a)

resources and (b) goods and services increased proportionally (by the same percent), would business firms be willing to expand output? Why or why not?

*4. Suppose prices had been rising at a 3 percent annual rate in recent years. A major union signs a three-year contract calling for increases in money wage rates of 6 percent annually. What will happen to the real wages of the union members if the price level is constant (unchanged) during the next three years? If other unions sign similar contracts, what will probably happen to the unemployment rate? Why? Answer the same questions under conditions in which the price level increases at an annual rate of 8 percent during the next three years.

5. What is the current money interest rate on 10-year government bonds? Is this also the real interest rate? Why or why not?

6. If the real interest rate in the loanable funds market increases, what will happen to the net inflow of foreign capital? Explain.

7. Explain why it is possible to temporarily achieve output levels that are beyond the economy's long-run potential. Why can't these high rates of output be sustained?

8. If the price level in the current period is higher than what buyers and sellers anticipated, what will tend to happen to real wages and the level of employment? How will the profit margins of business firms be affected? How will the actual rate of unemployment compare with the natural rate of unemployment? Will the current rate of output be sustainable in the future? Why or why not?

9. Suppose that you purchased a $5,000 bond that pays 7 percent interest annually and matures in five years. If the inflation rate in recent years has been steady at 3 percent annually, what is the estimated real rate of interest? If the inflation rate during the next five years remains steady at 3 percent, what real rate of return will you earn? If the inflation rate during the next five years is 6 percent, what will happen to your real rate of return?

*10. How are the following related to each other?
   a. The long-run equilibrium rate of output
   b. The potential real GDP of the economy
   c. The output rate resulting in the equality of the actual and natural rates of unemployment

11. How will an increase in the inflation rate affect (a) the money rate of interest and (b) the real rate of interest? Explain. Does inflation transfer wealth from lenders to borrowers? Why or why not?

*12. If a bond pays $1,000 per year in perpetuity (each year in the future), what will be the market price of the bond when the long-term interest rate is 10 percent? What would it be if the interest rate were 5 percent?

*13. How are bond prices related to interest rates? Why are they related?

14. When the price of a specific product increases, business firms can generally expand output by a larger amount in the long run than in the short run. For the economy as a whole, however, an unexpected increase in the price level leads to a larger expansion in output in the short run than in the long run. Can you explain this apparent paradox?

15. Show that when equilibrium is present in the loanable funds and foreign exchange markets, the leakages from the circular flow of income will just equal the injections into the circular flow.

16. The following chart indicates the aggregate demand (AD) and short-run aggregate supply (SRAS) schedules of decision makers for the current period. Both buyers and sellers previously anticipated that the price level during the current period would be P_{105}.
   a. Indicate the quantity of GDP that will be produced during this period.
   b. Will it be a long-run equilibrium level of GDP? Why or why not?
   c. What will be the relationship between the actual and natural rates of unemployment during the period? Explain your answer.

AD_{105}	Price Level	$SRAS_{105}$
6,900	90	4,500
6,600	95	4,800
6,300	100	5,100
6,000	105	5,400
5,700	110	5,700
5,400	115	6,000

17. Consider an economy with the following aggregate demand (AD) and short-run aggregate supply (SRAS) schedules. Decision makers have previously made decisions anticipating that the price level during the current period would be P_{105}.
   a. Indicate the quantity of GDP that will be produced during the period.
   b. Is it a long-run equilibrium level of GDP? Why or why not?
   c. How will the unemployment rate during the current period compare with this economy's natural rate of unemployment?
   d. Will the current rate of GDP be sustainable into the future? Why or why not?

AD_{105}	Price Level	$SRAS_{105}$
6,300	90	4,500
6,000	95	4,800
5,700	100	5,100
5,400	105	5,400
5,100	110	5,700
4,800	115	6,000

*Asterisk denotes questions for which answers are given in Appendix B.

CHAPTER 10

Working with Our Basic Aggregate Demand/Aggregate Supply Model

Chapter Focus

- What factors will cause shifts in aggregate demand? What factors will shift aggregate supply?

- How will the goods and services market adjust to changes in aggregate demand?

- How does the economy adjust to changes in aggregate supply?

- What are the causes of recessions and booms?

- Does a market economy have a self-correcting mechanism that will lead it to full employment?

We might as well reasonably dispute whether it is the upper or under blade of a pair of scissors that cuts a piece of paper, as whether value is governed by [demand] or [supply].

—*Alfred Marshall*[1]

[1]Alfred Marshall, *Principles of Economics*, 8th ed. (London: Macmillan, 1920), p. 348.

n Chapter 9, we focused on the equilibrium conditions in the four basic macroeconomic markets. Equilibrium is important, but we live in a dynamic world that continually wars against it. Markets are always being affected by unexpected changes, such as the discovery of a vastly improved computer chip, shifts in consumer confidence, a drought in Midwestern agricultural states, or changes in defense expenditures as the result of national security conditions. Consequently, equilibrium is continually disrupted. Thus, if we want to understand how the real world works, analysis of how macroeconomic markets adjust to dynamic change is of crucial importance.

We are now ready to consider how macroeconomic markets adjust to changes in aggregate demand, aggregate supply, and other macroeconomic factors. As in the preceding chapter, we will continue to assume that the government's tax, spending, and monetary policies are unchanged. For now, we want to help the reader understand how macroeconomic markets work. Once this objective is achieved, we will be better able to understand both the potential and the limitations of macroeconomic policy. ∎

ANTICIPATED AND UNANTICIPATED CHANGES

As we noted in the discussion of inflation in Chapter 8, it is important to distinguish between changes in the general level of prices that are anticipated and those that are unanticipated. This distinction is important in several areas of economics. **Anticipated changes** are foreseen by economic participants. Decision makers have time to adjust to them before they occur. For example, suppose that, under normal weather conditions, a new drought-resistant hybrid seed can be expected to expand the production of feed grain in the Midwest by 10 percent next year. As a result, buyers and sellers will plan for a larger supply and lower prices in the future. They will adjust their decision-making behavior accordingly.

In contrast, **unanticipated changes** catch people by surprise. Our world is characterized by dynamic change: new products are introduced, technological discoveries alter production costs, droughts reduce crop yields, demand expands for some goods and contracts for others. It is impossible for decision makers to foresee many of these changes.

Economics largely concerns how people respond and markets adjust to changing circumstances. As we will explain in a moment, there is good reason to expect that the path of the adjustment process will be influenced by whether or not a change is anticipated.

Anticipated change
A change that is foreseen by decision makers in time for them to adjust.

Unanticipated change
A change that decision makers could not reasonably foresee. Thus, choices made prior to the event did not take the event into account.

FACTORS THAT SHIFT AGGREGATE DEMAND

The aggregate demand curve isolates the impact of the price level on the quantity demanded of goods and services. As we discussed in the previous chapter, a reduction in the price level will (1) increase the wealth of people holding the fixed quantity of money, (2) reduce the real rate of interest, and (3) make domestically produced goods cheaper compared to those produced abroad. All three of these factors will lead to an increase in the quantity of goods and services demanded at the lower price level.

The price level, however, is not the only factor that influences the demand for goods and services. When we constructed the aggregate demand curve, we assumed that several other factors affecting the choices of buyers in the goods and services market were constant. Changes in these "other factors" will shift the entire aggregate demand schedule, altering the amount purchased at each price level. Let us take a closer look at the major factors that will cause shifts in aggregate demand.

1. Changes in Real Wealth
Stock prices in the United States increased by more than 25 percent annually in the period 1995 to 1999. This stock market boom increased the real wealth of stockholders. In contrast, during 2000–2001, stocks listed on the New York Stock Exchange fell by approximately 20

percent. The declines on other exchanges were even greater—50 percent or more. High-tech stocks were particularly hard hit. These sharp declines in stock prices reduced the wealth of many Americans.

How will changes in the wealth of households affect the demand for goods and services? If the real wealth of households increases—perhaps as the result of higher prices in stock, housing, and/or real estate markets—people will demand more goods and services. As **Exhibit 1** illustrates, this increase in wealth will shift the entire aggregate demand (AD) schedule to the right (from AD_0 to AD_1). More goods and services are purchased at each price level. Conversely, a reduction in wealth will reduce the demand for goods and services, shifting the AD curve to the left (to AD_2).

2. Changes in the Real Interest Rate

As we discussed previously, the major macroeconomic markets are closely related. A change in the real interest rate in the loanable funds market will influence the choices of consumers and investors in the goods and services market. A lower real interest rate makes it cheaper for consumers to buy major appliances, automobiles, and houses now rather than in the future. Simultaneously, a lower interest rate will also stimulate business spending on capital goods (investment). The interest rate influences the opportunity cost of all investment projects. If the firm must borrow, the real interest rate will contribute directly to the cost of an investment project. Even if the firm uses its own funds, it sacrifices real interest that could have been earned by loaning the funds to someone else. Therefore, a lower real interest rate reduces the opportunity cost of a project, regardless of whether it is financed with internal funds or by borrowing.

Because a reduction in the real interest rate makes both consumer and investment goods cheaper, both households and investors will increase their current expenditures in response. In turn, their additional expenditures will increase aggregate demand, shifting the entire schedule to the right. In contrast, a higher real interest rate makes current consumption and investment goods more expensive, which leads to a reduction in aggregate demand, shifting the AD curve to the left.

3. Change in the Expectations of Businesses and Households about the Future Direction of the Economy

What people think will happen in the future influences current purchasing decisions. Optimism concerning the future direction of the economy will stimulate current investment. Business decision makers know that an expanding economy will mean strong sales and

EXHIBIT 1
Shifts in Aggregate Demand

An increase in real wealth, such as would result from a stock market boom, for example, will increase aggregate demand, shifting the entire curve to the right (from AD_0 to AD_1). In contrast, a reduction in real wealth decreases the demand for goods and services, causing AD to shift to the left (from AD_0 to AD_2).

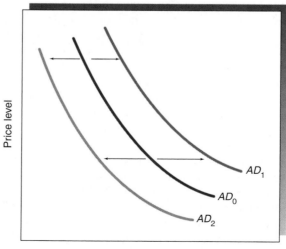

Goods and services (real GDP)

improved profit margins. Investment today may be necessary if business firms are going to benefit fully from these opportunities. Similarly, consumers are more likely to buy big-ticket items, such as automobiles and houses, when they expect an expanding economy to provide them with both job security and rising income in the future. So increased optimism encourages additional current expenditures by both investors and consumers, increasing aggregate demand.

Of course, pessimism about the future state of the economy exerts just the opposite effect. When investors and consumers expect an economic downturn (a recession), they will cut back on their current spending for fear of becoming overextended. This pessimism leads to a decline in aggregate demand, shifting the *AD* schedule to the left.

The University of Michigan publishes a monthly measure of consumer confidence that is based on survey data. Policymakers and others interested in forecasting the future direction of aggregate demand monitor this information closely.

4. Change in the Expected Rate of Inflation

When consumers and investors believe that the inflation rate is going to accelerate in the future, they have an incentive to spend more during the current period. "Buy now before prices go higher" becomes the order of the day. Thus, the expectation of an increase in the inflation rate will stimulate current aggregate demand, shifting the *AD* curve to the right.

In contrast, the expectation of a decline in the inflation rate will tend to discourage current spending. When prices are expected to stabilize (or at least increase less rapidly), the gain obtained by moving expenditures forward in time is reduced. Thus, a reduction in the expected rate of inflation will cause current aggregate demand to fall (a shift to the left in the *AD* curve).

5. Changes in Income Abroad

Changes in the income of a nation's trading partners will influence the demand for the nation's exports. If the income of a nation's trading partners is increasing rapidly, the demand for exports will expand. In turn, the strong demand for exports will stimulate aggregate demand. For example, rapid growth of income in Europe, Canada, and Mexico increases the demand of consumers in these areas for U.S.-produced goods. This will cause U.S. exports to expand, increasing aggregate demand (shifting the *AD* schedule to the right).

Conversely, when a nation's trading partners are experiencing recessionary conditions, they reduce their purchases, including their purchases abroad. Thus, a decline in the income of a nation's trading partners tends to reduce both exports and aggregate demand.

Currently, approximately 12 percent of the goods and services produced in the United States are sold to purchasers abroad. The export sector is still larger for Canada, Mexico, and most Western European countries. The larger the size of the trade sector, the greater the potential importance of fluctuations in income abroad as a source of instability in aggregate demand. If the demand of foreign buyers does not rise and fall at the same time as domestic demand, however, the diversity of markets will reduce the magnitude of fluctuations in domestic demand.

6. Changes in Exchange Rates

As we previously explained, changes in exchange rates will influence the relative price of both imports and exports. An appreciation in the value of the dollar on the foreign exchange market will make it cheaper for Americans to purchase imported goods and more expensive for foreigners to purchase U.S. exports. As a result, U.S. imports will rise and exports will fall. Other things constant, the decline in net exports (exports minus imports) will reduce aggregate demand (shift the *AD* schedule to the left).

Consider the impact of an increase in the foreign exchange value of the dollar relative to the Mexican peso, such as occurred during the mid-1990s. In late 1994 and early 1995, the number of pesos that could be purchased with a dollar approximately doubled in just a few months. The appreciation of the dollar relative to the peso made imports from Mexico cheaper for Americans and U.S. exports more expensive for Mexicans. As U.S. imports rose and exports fell, there was downward pressure on aggregate demand.

A depreciation in the exchange rate value of the dollar will have just the opposite effect. When there is a reduction in the value of the dollar on the foreign exchange market, foreign-produced goods become more expensive for U.S. consumers, while U.S.-produced goods become cheaper for foreigners. As a result, net exports will increase and thereby stimulate aggregate demand (shifting *AD* to the right).[2]

The accompanying Thumbnail Sketch summarizes the major factors causing shifts in aggregate demand. In addition to the factors considered here, the government's spending, taxing, and monetary policies may also shift aggregate demand. In subsequent chapters, we will analyze the impact of fiscal and monetary policy on aggregate demand and economic performance. We now turn to the analysis of the factors that cause shifts in aggregate supply. Then we will be in a position to consider how macroeconomic markets adjust and whether these adjustments will help maintain a high level of output and employment.

THUMBNAIL SKETCH

What Factors Will Influence Aggregate Demand?

These factors will increase (decrease) aggregate demand (*AD*).[1]

1. An increase (decrease) in real wealth.
2. A decrease (increase) in the real rate of interest.
3. An increase in the optimism (pessimism) of businesses and consumers about future economic conditions.
4. An increase (decline) in the expected rate of inflation.
5. Higher (lower) real incomes abroad.
6. A reduction (increase) in the exchange rate value of the nation's currency.

---

[1]The impact of macroeconomic policy will be considered later.

SHIFTS IN AGGREGATE SUPPLY

What factors will cause the aggregate supply curve to shift? The answer to this question will differ depending on whether the change in supply is long-run and sustainable or short-run and only temporary. A long-run change in aggregate supply indicates that it will be possible to achieve and sustain a larger rate of output. For example, the discovery of a lower-cost source of energy would cause a long-run change in aggregate supply. In such a situation, both long-run (*LRAS*) and short-run (*SRAS*) aggregate supply would change.

In contrast, changes that temporarily alter the productive capability of an economy will shift the *SRAS* curve, but not the *LRAS*. A drought in California would be an example of such a short-run change. The drought will hurt in the short run, but it will eventually end, and output will return to the long-run normal rate. Changes that are temporary in nature will shift only *SRAS*. Let us now consider the major factors capable of shifting the *LRAS* and *SRAS* schedules.

Changes in Long-Run Aggregate Supply

Remember, the long-run aggregate supply curve indicates the maximum rate of sustainable output, given the current (1) resource base, (2) level of technology, and (3) institutional arrangements that affect productivity and efficiency of resource use. Changes in any of these three determinants of output would cause the *LRAS* curve to shift.

---

[2]Later, when discussing international finance, we will analyze the determinants of the exchange rate and consider how changes in exchange rates impact both trade and macroeconomic markets in more detail.

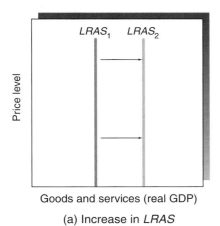

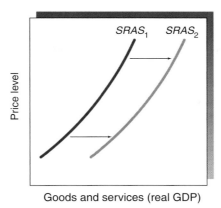

(a) Increase in *LRAS*   (b) Increase in *SRAS*

EXHIBIT 2
Shifts in Aggregate Supply

Such factors as an increase in the stock of capital or an improvement in technology will expand the economy's potential output and shift the *LRAS* to the right (a). Such factors as a reduction in resource prices, favorable weather, or a temporary decrease in the world price of an important imported resource would shift the *SRAS* to the right (b). Of course, changes that resulted in a decrease in either *LRAS* or *SRAS* would shift the respective schedules to the left.

As part a of **Exhibit 2** illustrates, changes that increase the economy's productive capacity will shift the *LRAS* curve to the right. With the passage of time, net investment can expand the supply of physical capital, natural resources, and labor (human resources). Investment in physical capital can expand the supply of buildings, machines, and other physical assets. With the passage of time, changes in population and labor force participation may affect the supply of labor. Similarly, education, training, and skill-enhancing experience can improve the quality of the labor force, and thereby expand the supply of human resources.

Because shifts in long-run aggregate supply will enhance output both now and in the future, they will increase both *LRAS* and *SRAS,* causing both curves to shift to the right. On the other hand, a lasting reduction in the quantity (or quality) of resources will reduce both the current and long-term production capacity of the economy, shifting both *LRAS* and *SRAS* curves to the left.

Improvements in technology—the discovery of economical new products or less costly ways of producing goods and services—also permit us to squeeze a larger output from a specific resource supply. The enormous improvement in our living standards during the last 250 years is, to a large degree, the result of the discovery and adoption of technologically superior ways of transforming resources into goods and services. The development of the internal combustion engine, electricity, and nuclear power, has vastly altered our energy sources. The railroad, automobile, and airplane dramatically changed both the cost and speed of transportation. More recently, numerous high-tech products such as personal computers, electronic mail, fax machines, and the Internet have reduced the cost of doing business and expanded our production capacity. Technological improvements of this type enhance **productivity** and thereby shift both *LRAS* and *SRAS* curves to the right.

Finally, institutional changes may also influence the efficiency of resource use and thereby alter the *LRAS* schedule. Public policy increases aggregate supply when it enhances economic efficiency by providing, for example, public goods at a low cost. In contrast, institutional arrangements sometimes promote waste and increase production costs. For example, studies indicate that minimum-wage legislation reduces employment and restricts the opportunity for training, particularly in the case of youthful workers. Such arrangements reduce aggregate supply.

The long-run growth trend of real GDP in the United States has been approximately 3 percent per year. This indicates that increases in the supply of resources and improvements in productivity have gradually expanded potential real output. Hence, the *LRAS* and *SRAS* curves have gradually drifted to the right at about a 3 percent annual rate, sometimes a little faster and sometimes a little slower.

Productivity
The average output produced per worker during a specific time period. It is usually measured in terms of output per hour worked.

Changes in Short-Run Aggregate Supply

Changes can sometimes influence current output without altering the economy's long-run capacity. When this is the case, the *SRAS* curve will shift even though *LRAS* is unchanged. What types of changes would do this?

1. Changes in Resource Prices

When we derived the *SRAS* schedule in Chapter 9, we noted explicitly that resource prices were being held constant. A change in resource prices will alter *SRAS* but not necessarily *LRAS*. A reduction in resource prices will lower costs and therefore shift the *SRAS* curve to the right, as illustrated in part b of Exhibit 2. However, unless the lower prices of resources reflect a long-term increase in the supply of resources, they will not alter *LRAS*. Conversely, an increase in the price of resources will increase costs, shifting the *SRAS* curve to the left. But unless the higher prices are the result of a long-term reduction in the size of the economy's resource base, they will not reduce *LRAS*.[3]

2. Changes in the Expected Rate of Inflation

As we previously noted, a change in the expected rate of inflation will influence current aggregate demand (*AD*) in the goods and services market. It will also alter *SRAS*. If sellers in the goods and services market expect the future rate of inflation to increase, their incentive to sell at a given price in the current period will be reduced. After all, goods that they do not sell today will be available for sale in the future at what they anticipate will be even higher prices (as the result of the increase in the rate of inflation). Therefore, an increase in the expected rate of inflation will reduce the *current* supply of goods, thereby shifting the *SRAS* curve to the left. Of course, a reduction in the expected rate of inflation will have just the opposite impact. When sellers scale back their expectations concerning future price increases, their incentive to sell in the current period is increased. Why wait, if the price is not going to increase very much in the future? Thus, a reduction in the expected rate of inflation will increase short-run aggregate supply (shift *SRAS* to the right).

Net investment, technological advances, and improvements in institutional arrangements expand the productive capacity of an economy, shifting *LRAS* to the right.

---

[3]The definition of long-run aggregate supply helps clarify why a change in resource prices will affect short-run aggregate supply, but not long-run aggregate supply. When an economy is operating on its *LRAS* curve, the relationship between resource prices (costs) and product prices will reflect normal competitive market conditions. Because both profit and unemployment rates are at their normal levels, there is no tendency for resource prices to change relative to product prices when current output is equal to the economy's long-run potential. Therefore, when an economy is operating on its *LRAS* schedule, any change in resource prices will be matched by a proportional change in product prices, leaving the incentive to supply resources (and output) unchanged.

3. Supply Shocks

Various supply shocks may also alter current output without directly affecting the productive capacity of the economy. <u>Supply shocks</u> are surprise occurrences that temporarily increase or decrease current output. For example, adverse weather conditions, a natural disaster, or a temporary increase in the price of imported resources (for example, oil in the case of the United States) will reduce current supply, even though they do not alter the economy's long-term production capacity. They will thus decrease short-run aggregate supply (shift *SRAS* to the left) without directly affecting *LRAS*. On the other hand, favorable weather conditions or temporary reductions in the world price of imported resources will increase current output, even though the economy's long-run capacity remains unchanged.

The accompanying Thumbnail Sketch summarizes the major factors influencing both long-run and short-run aggregate supply. Of course, macroeconomic policy may also influence aggregate supply. As in the case of aggregate demand, we will consider the impact of macroeconomic policy on supply in subsequent chapters.

Supply shock
An unexpected event that temporarily either increases or decreases aggregate supply.

 THUMBNAIL SKETCH

What Factors Will Influence Long-run and Short-run Aggregate Supply?

These factors will increase (decrease) long-run aggregate supply (*LRAS*).[1]

a. An increase (decrease) in the supply of resources.
b. An improvement (deterioration) in technology and productivity.
c. Institutional changes that increase (reduce) the efficiency of resource use.

These factors will increase (decrease) short-run aggregate supply (*SRAS*).[1]

1. A decrease (increase) in resource prices, that is, production costs.
2. A reduction (increase) in the expected rate of inflation.
3. Favorable (unfavorable) supply shocks, such as good (bad) weather or a reduction (increase) in the world price of an important imported resource.

---

[1]The impact of macroeconomic policy will be considered later.

STEADY ECONOMIC GROWTH AND ANTICIPATED CHANGES IN LONG-RUN AGGREGATE SUPPLY

As we have previously stressed, the impact of changes in market conditions will be influenced by whether the changes are anticipated or unanticipated. When a change takes place slowly and predictably, decision makers will make choices based on the anticipation of the event. Such changes do not generally disrupt equilibrium conditions in markets.

With time, net investment and improvements in technology and institutional efficiency will generally lead to increases in the sustainable rate of output. Such economic growth will shift the economy's *LRAS* curve to the right. When expansions in the productive capacity of an economy are persistent and predictable, they will be anticipated by decision makers. Thus, they need not disrupt macroeconomic equilibrium.

Exhibit 3 illustrates the impact of economic growth on the goods and services market. Initially, the economy is in long-run equilibrium at price level P_1 and output Y_{F_1}. The growth expands the economy's potential output, shifting both the *LRAS* and *SRAS* curves to the right (to $LRAS_2$ and $SRAS_2$). Because these changes are gradual, decision makers have time to anticipate the changing market conditions and adjust their behavior accordingly.

When economic growth expands the economy's production possibilities, a higher rate of real output can be both achieved and sustained. The larger output can be attained even while unemployment remains at its natural rate. If the money supply is held constant, the increase in aggregate supply will lead to a lower price level (P_2).

EXHIBIT 3
Growth of Aggregate Supply

Here we illustrate the impact of economic growth due to capital formation or a technological advancement, for example. The full employment output of the economy expands from Y_{F_1} to Y_{F_2}. Thus, both *LRAS* and *SRAS* increase (to *LRAS$_2$* and *SRAS$_2$*). A sustainable, higher level of real output and real income is the result. If the money supply is held constant, a new long-run equilibrium will emerge at a larger output rate (Y_{F_2}) and lower price level (P_2).

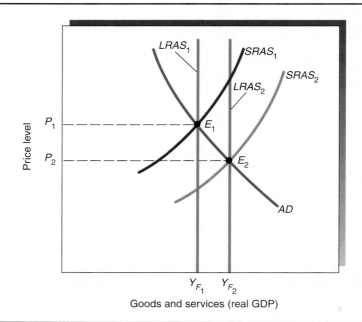

Goods and services (real GDP)

During the past 50 years, real output has expanded significantly in the United States and other countries. However, contrary to the presentation of Exhibit 3, the price level has generally not declined. This is because the monetary authorities have expanded the supply of money. As we will see later, an increase in the money supply stimulates aggregate demand (shifts *AD* to the right) and thereby pushes the price level upward.[4]

UNANTICIPATED CHANGES AND MARKET ADJUSTMENTS

In contrast with anticipated changes, unanticipated changes in aggregate demand and aggregate supply will disrupt long-run equilibrium in the goods and services market. As we have previously discussed, it takes time for decision makers to adjust to unforeseen occurrences. Initially, it may be unclear to decision makers whether a change—an increase in sales, for example—reflects a random occurrence or a real change in demand conditions. It will also take businesses some time to differentiate between temporary fluctuations and more permanent changes. Even after decision makers are convinced that market conditions have changed, time will be required for them to make new decisions and carry them out. In some cases, complete adjustment will also be delayed by the presence of long-term contracts. All these factors will reduce the speed of market adjustments to unexpected changes that disrupt the equilibrium of macroeconomic markets.

Equilibrium may be disrupted by unexpected changes in either aggregate demand or aggregate supply. We will begin by considering the impact of an unanticipated change in aggregate demand.

Unanticipated Increases in Aggregate Demand

Part a of **Exhibit 4** illustrates how an economy that is initially in long-run equilibrium will adjust to an unanticipated increase in aggregate demand. Initially the economy is in long-run equilibrium at output Y_F and price level P_{100} (point E_1). Aggregate demand and aggregate supply are in balance. Decision makers have correctly anticipated the current price level, and the economy is operating at its full-employment level of output.

---

[4]In subsequent chapters, we will explain how stable prices can be achieved as real output increases.

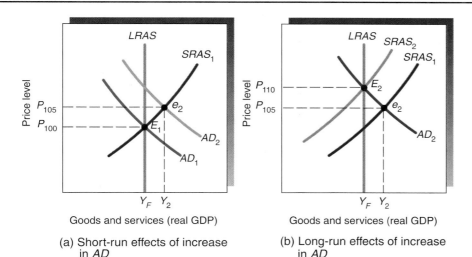

EXHIBIT 4
Unanticipated Increase in Aggregate Demand

(a) Short-run effects of increase in *AD*

(b) Long-run effects of increase in *AD*

In response to an unanticipated increase in aggregate demand for goods and services (shift from AD_1 to AD_2), prices will rise (to P_{105}) in the short run and output will temporarily exceed full-employment capacity (a). However, with the passage of time, prices in resource markets, including the labor market, will rise as the result of the strong demand. The higher resource prices will mean higher costs, which will reduce aggregate supply to $SRAS_2$ (b). In the long run, a new equilibrium at a higher price level (P_{110}) and an output consistent with the economy's sustainable potential will result. Thus, the increase in demand will expand output only temporarily.

Consider what would happen if this equilibrium were disrupted by an unanticipated increase in aggregate demand (shift from AD_1 to AD_2) such as might result from a stock market boom or the rapid growth of income abroad. An excess demand for goods and services would result at the initial price level (P_{100}). Responding to the strong sales and excess demand, businesses would increase their prices. Their profit margins would improve (since product prices increase relative to the cost of resources), and they would expand output along the *SRAS* curve. As part a of Exhibit 4 shows, the economy would move to a short-run equilibrium (e_2), at a larger output (Y_2) and higher price level (P_{105}). (*Note:* A short-run equilibrium is indicated with a lowercase *e*, while a capital *E* is used to designate a long-run equilibrium. This convention will be followed throughout the text.)

In the short run, output will deviate from full employment capacity when prices in the goods and services market deviate from the price level that people anticipated. This will be the case when unexpectedly strong demand pushes prices up more than was expected. For a time, many wage rates, interest payments, rents, and other resource prices will continue to reflect the initial price level (P_{100}) and the previously weaker demand. Because markets do not adjust instantaneously, these resource prices, and therefore costs, will lag behind prices in the goods and services market. Thus, the higher price level will temporarily improve profit margins, which, in turn, will provide the incentive for business firms to expand both output and employment in the short run. As a result, the unemployment rate will drop below its natural rate, and output will temporarily exceed the economy's long-run potential output level.[5]

[5]Thoughtful students may wonder how output (and, by implication, the quantity of resources) can be increased, even temporarily, when real wages and resource prices have fallen. As we noted in the last chapter, firms may temporarily be able to achieve high rates of output through more intense supervision, greater use of overtime, and reduction in downtime for maintenance. In addition, two other factors may contribute to temporary output levels beyond long-run potential. First, in an inflationary environment, workers (and other resource suppliers) may be fooled, at least temporarily, by an increase in money wages (and resource prices) that is less rapid than the inflation rate. Responding to the higher money wages, workers may supply more labor even though their real wages have fallen. Although we have presented the analysis within the framework of a noninflationary environment, the basic linkage between real wages (costs) and *SRAS* still holds. A reduction in the real wage rate, even when it takes the form of a nominal wage increase that is less than the inflation rate, will reduce real costs, and thereby increase *SRAS*. Second, the resource base may temporarily expand in response to strong demand conditions because the cost of entering the labor force will decline during this boom phase of the business cycle. Potential new labor force entrants will be able to find jobs quickly during an economic expansion, causing the size of the labor force to grow rapidly. Conversely, the labor force will tend to shrink (or grow less rapidly) during a business contraction, when the cost of entering the labor force will be high.

This is not the end of the story, however. The strong demand accompanying this high level of output will place upward pressure on prices in resource and loanable funds markets. With time, the strong demand conditions will push wages, other resource prices, and real interest rates upward. As part b of Exhibit 4 illustrates, the rising resource prices and costs will shift the short-run aggregate supply curve to the left (to $SRAS_2$). Eventually, a new long-run equilibrium (E_2) will be established at a higher price level (P_{110}) that is correctly anticipated by decision makers.

Thus, the increase in real GDP above the economy's long-run potential is temporary. It will last only until there is an opportunity to alter the temporarily fixed resource prices (and interest rates) upward in light of the new stronger demand conditions. As this happens, profit margins return to their normal level, output recedes to the economy's long-run potential, and unemployment returns to its natural rate.

Because an increase in aggregate demand does not alter the economy's productive capacity, it cannot permanently expand output (beyond Y_F). The expansion in demand temporarily expands output, but over the long term its major effect will be higher prices (inflation).

Reductions in Aggregate Demand

How would the goods and services market adjust to an unanticipated reduction in aggregate demand? For example, suppose that decision makers become more pessimistic about the future or that an unexpected decline in income abroad reduces the demand for exports. **Exhibit 5** will help us analyze this issue.

Once again, we consider an economy that is in long-run equilibrium (E_1) at output Y_F and price level P_{100} (part a). Long-run equilibrium is disturbed by the reduction in aggregate demand: the shift from AD_1 to AD_2. As the result of the decline in demand, businesses will be unable to sell Y_F units of output at the initial price level of P_{100}. In the short run, business firms will both reduce output (to Y_2) and cut prices (to P_{95}) in response to the weak demand conditions. Because many costs of business firms are temporarily fixed, profit mar-

EXHIBIT 5
Unanticipated Reduction in Aggregate Demand

The short-run impact of an unanticipated reduction in aggregate demand (shift from AD_1 to AD_2) will be a decline in output to Y_2 and a lower price level, P_{95} (a). Temporarily, profit margins will decline, output will fall, and unemployment will rise above its natural rate. In the long run, weak demand and excess supply in the resource market will lead to lower wage rates and resource prices. This will reduce costs, leading to an expansion in short-run aggregate supply (shift to $SRAS_2$) in (b). However, this method of restoring equilibrium (E_2) may be both highly painful and quite lengthy.

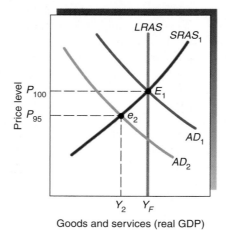

(a) Short-run effects of decline in *AD*

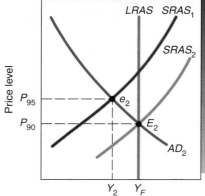

(b) Long-run effects of decline in *AD*

gins will decline. Predictably, firms will cut back on output and lay off workers, causing the unemployment rate to rise. The actual rate of unemployment will rise above the economy's natural rate of unemployment. Weak demand and excess supply will be widespread in resource markets. These forces will place downward pressure on resource prices.

If resource prices quickly adjust downward in response to weak demand and rising unemployment, then the decline in output to Y_2 will be brief. Lower resource prices will reduce costs and thereby increase aggregate supply (shift to $SRAS_2$). As part b of Exhibit 5 illustrates, the result will be a new long-run equilibrium (E_2) at the economy's full employment output rate (Y_F) and a lower price level (P_{90}). Lower interest rates may also play a role. Given the excess production capacity of many firms, weak demand for capital goods (investment) will reduce the demand for loanable funds and thereby place downward pressure on real interest rates. The lower rates will stimulate current spending, which will offset some of the reduction in demand and help direct the economy back to full employment equilibrium.

Resource prices and interest rates, however, may not adjust quickly. Long-term contracts and uncertainty as to whether the weak demand conditions are merely temporary will slow the adjustment process. In addition, individual workers and union officials may be highly reluctant to be the first to accept lower nominal wages. *If resource prices are inflexible in a downward direction, as many economists believe, the adjustment process may be both lengthy and painful. Prolonged periods of economic recession with below-capacity output rates and abnormally high unemployment may occur before the new long-run equilibrium is restored.*

Unanticipated Increases in *SRAS*

By their nature, supply shocks are unpredictable and therefore likely to catch people by surprise. Consider what would happen if a nation's current output expanded as the result of highly favorable weather conditions or a temporary decline in the world market price of oil or some other critical imported resource. **Exhibit 6** addresses this issue. Because the temporarily favorable supply conditions cannot be counted on in the future, they will not directly alter the economy's long-term production capacity. Given that the favorable supply conditions are temporary, short-run aggregate supply will increase (to $SRAS_2$), while *LRAS* will remain constant. Output (and income) will temporarily expand beyond the

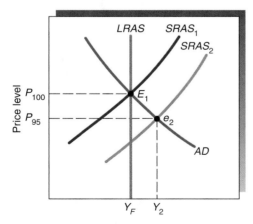

Goods and services (real GDP)

EXHIBIT 6
Unanticipated, Temporary Increase in Aggregate Supply

Here we illustrate the impact of an unanticipated, but temporary, increase in aggregate supply, such as might result from a bumper crop caused by highly favorable weather conditions. The increase in aggregate supply (shift to $SRAS_2$) would lead to a lower price level (P_{95}) and an increase in current GDP to Y_2. Since the favorable supply conditions cannot be counted on in the future, the economy's long-run aggregate supply will not increase.

economy's full-employment constraints. This increase in current supply will place downward pressure on the price level.

With time, however, the temporarily favorable conditions will come to an end. As this happens, the *SRAS* curve will return to its original position and long-run equilibrium will be restored. Thus, the expansion in output will be temporary. Recognizing that they will be unable to maintain their current high level of income, many households will save a substantial portion for use at a future time that is not nearly so prosperous. These savings will make it possible for them to spread some of the benefits of the current high level of income into the future.

What would happen if the favorable conditions increasing supply reflected long-term factors? For example, suppose adoption of a new oil production technology resulted in a decline in the price of oil that was expected to be permanent rather than temporary. In this case, both the *LRAS* and the *SRAS* would increase (shift to the right). This case would parallel the analysis of Exhibit 3. A new long-run equilibrium at a higher output would result.

Unanticipated Reductions in *SRAS*

In recent decades, the U.S. economy has been jolted by several unfavorable supply-side factors. During the summer of 1988, the most severe drought conditions in 50 years resulted in an extremely poor harvest in the U.S. agricultural belt. In 1973, 1979, and again in 1990, the United States and other oil-importing countries were hit with sharply higher oil prices as the result of unstable conditions in the Middle East. Then, after trending downward for almost a decade, the price of crude oil jumped from $18 to almost $35 during 2000. Persistently high crude oil prices along with regulatory factors that limited both the generation and transmission of electric power resulted in sharply higher energy prices and even "blackouts" in some areas during 2001.

How do such unfavorable supply shocks influence macroeconomic markets? **Exhibit 7** illustrates the answer. Both an unfavorable harvest caused by adverse weather conditions and a higher world price of oil will reduce the supply of resources (from S_1 to S_2 in part a)

EXHIBIT 7
Effects of Adverse Supply Shock

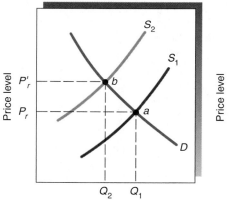

(a) Resource market
(b) Goods and services (real GDP)

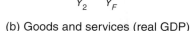

Suppose there is an unanticipated reduction in the supply of resources, perhaps as the result of a crop failure or sharp increase in the world price of a major imported resource, such as oil. Resource prices would rise from P_r to P_r' (a). The higher resource prices would shift the *SRAS* curve to the left. In the short run, the price level would rise to P_{110} (b), and output would decline to Y_2. What happens in the long run depends on whether the reduction in the supply of resources is temporary or permanent. If it is temporary, resource prices will fall in the future, permitting the economy to return to its initial equilibrium (E_1). Conversely, if the reduced supply of resources is permanent, the productive potential of the economy will shrink (*LRAS* will shift to the left) and e_2 will become a long-run equilibrium.

in the domestic market. Resource prices will rise to P_r'. In turn, the higher resource prices will reduce short-run aggregate supply (the shift from $SRAS_1$ to $SRAS_2$ in part b) in the goods and services market. Because supply shocks of this type are generally unanticipated, initially they will reduce output and place upward pressure on prices (the rate of inflation) in the goods and services market.

If an unfavorable supply shock is expected to be temporary, as will generally be the case for a bad harvest, long-run aggregate supply will be unaffected. After all, unfavorable growing conditions for a year or two do not represent a permanent change in climate. Therefore, as normal weather patterns return with the passage of time, both supply and price conditions in the resource market will return to normal, permitting the economy to return to long-run equilibrium at output Y_F.

When an adverse supply-side factor is more permanent, the long-run supply curve would also shift to the left. For example, an increase in the price of oil imports that is expected to prevail for the next several years would reduce long-run as well as short-run aggregate supply. Under these circumstances, the economy would have to adjust to a lower level of real output. Regardless of whether the decline in aggregate supply is temporary or permanent, other things constant, the price level will rise. Similarly, output will decline, at least temporarily.

PRICE LEVEL, INFLATION, AND THE *AD/AS* MODEL

In the basic *AD/AS* model, the general level of prices is measured on the *y*-axis in both the goods and services and resource markets. This approach makes it easier to visualize relative price changes. If prices change in one of the markets, goods and services for example, this indicates that prices in that market have changed *relative* to those in other markets. It is important to note, however, that this structure implicitly incorporates the assumption that the actual and expected rates of inflation are initially zero.

As we have previously discussed, when persistent inflation is present, it will be anticipated and incorporated into long-term contracts affecting important components of production costs in the short run. When the actual and anticipated rates of inflation are equal, persistent price increases will be present in both goods and services and resource markets even though the relative prices between the two markets are unchanged.

However, once decision makers anticipate a given rate of inflation and build it into long-term contracts, an actual rate of inflation that is less than expected is essentially the equivalent of a reduction in the price level when price stability (zero inflation) is anticipated. Both will lead to higher real resource prices and costs, which will squeeze profits and thereby cause firms to cut back on output and employment. For example, consider the situation where 5 percent inflation has been present over a lengthy time period and therefore the 5 percent rate has been built into long-term contracts, including those in resource markets. If weak demand causes the inflation rate to fall to, say, 2 percent, the adjustments will be the same as those for a reduction in product prices when zero inflation is anticipated (see Exhibit 5). In both cases, prices in the goods and services market will fall relative to resource prices. In the short run, profit margins will be squeezed, and firms will cut back on output. Workers will be laid off and the economy may well fall into a recession.

Similarly, the impact of an inflation rate that is greater than was anticipated will be like that of an increase in the price level when price stability is anticipated. Both will increase product prices relative to resource prices, which will enhance profits and thereby induce firms to expand output and employment.

THE BUSINESS CYCLE REVISITED

It is interesting to view the business cycle within the framework of the aggregate demand/aggregate supply (*AD/AS*) model. This model indicates that unanticipated shifts in aggregate demand and aggregate supply underpin economic fluctuations. Such unexpected shifts lead to a misalignment between prices and costs because markets do not adjust instantaneously, and decision makers are not always able to anticipate accurately changes in the price level (and inflation rate).

Recessions occur because prices in the goods and services market are low relative to costs of production (and resource prices). There are two reasons for this: (1) unanticipated reductions in aggregate demand and (2) unfavorable supply shocks. An unanticipated reduction in aggregate demand (illustrated by Exhibit 5a) leads to a lower than expected price level in the goods and services market. Given the weak demand and lower than expected prices, many firms will confront losses, which will force them to reduce output and, in some cases, terminate production. Correspondingly, an adverse supply shock (illustrated by Exhibit 7) leads to higher than expected resource prices and costs. This, too, will cause firms to incur losses and reduce output.

Correspondingly, economic booms—high rates of output that are unsustainable—occur when prices in the goods and services market are high relative to costs (and resource prices). The two causes of booms are: (1) unanticipated increases in aggregate demand and (2) favorable supply shocks. An unanticipated increase in aggregate demand (see Exhibit 4a) leads to a higher than expected price level in the goods and services market. The strong demand, high prices, and attractive profit margins induce firms to expand output to rates that are unsustainable in the long run. Similarly, a favorable supply shock (see Exhibit 6) leads to lower than expected costs and unsustainable rates of output.

Exhibit 8 presents a picture of the economic fluctuations in the United States during the past 40 years. It is interesting to reflect on these figures within the framework of the *AD/AS* model. Real GDP grew substantially. This is what one would expect for an economy characterized by net investment and improvements in technology. Recessions were experienced during 1970, 1974–1975, 1980, 1982, 1990, and 2001. As real output fell during these periods, the rate of unemployment rose above the natural rate (lower frame). (*Note*: Because the natural rate of unemployment is not directly observable, a range of estimates is provided in part b of Exhibit 8.)

The timing of the recessions is particularly interesting. The 1970 recession occurred as the Vietnam War was winding down. The more severe recession of 1974–1975 followed the doubling of crude oil prices (a supply shock) and a sharp reduction in the rate of inflation (suggesting an unanticipated reduction in *AD*). The economic stagnation of 1980 and 1982 reflected these same factors. Oil prices doubled once again in 1978–1979, pushing costs up unexpectedly prior to and during the recession of 1980. The 1982 recession was associated with a reduction in the inflation rate from 12.5 percent in 1980 (and 13.3 percent in 1979) to only 3.8 percent in 1982, suggesting that there was an abrupt, and therefore unexpected, decline in aggregate demand during this period. The 1990 recession was

Plant closings, employee layoffs, and high rates of unemployment are indicative of economic recession. Unanticipated reductions in aggregate demand and/or adverse supply shocks are the primary causes of recession.

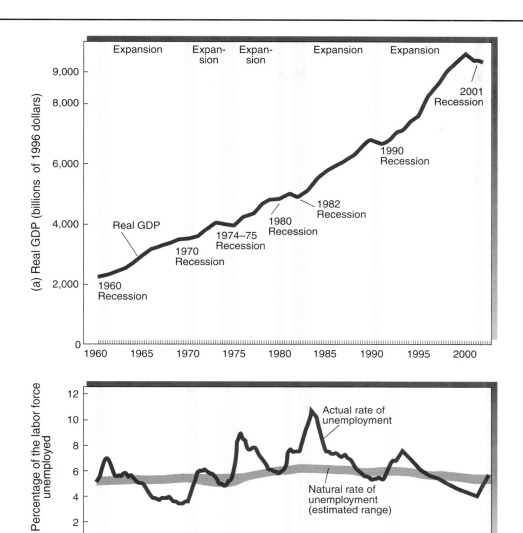

EXHIBIT 8
Expansions, Recessions, and the Rate of Unemployment

Here we illustrate the periods of expansion and contraction (recession) since 1960. Note how the reductions in real GDP (shaded periods) in the top graph are associated with increases in the rate of unemployment well above the natural rate (bottom graph). The *AD/AS* model indicates that recessions are caused by unanticipated reductions in *AD* that are likely to accompany abrupt reductions in the inflation rate and/or adverse supply shocks that might occur, for example, when there is a large increase in the price of a key imported resource, such as crude oil.

Source: Derived from computerized data supplied by *FAME ECONOMICS.*

associated with substantial reductions in defense expenditures following the collapse of communism and economic readjustments accompanying the military buildup and war in Kuwait. Finally, the recession of 2001 was preceded by a surge in the world price of crude oil and a sharp reduction in stock prices. Clearly, supply shocks and unanticipated changes in aggregate demand provided the underpinnings for these recessions.

DOES A MARKET ECONOMY HAVE A SELF-CORRECTING MECHANISM?

In a dynamic world of changing demand conditions and supply shocks, economic ups and downs are inevitable. Are there market forces that will help stabilize an economy and cushion the effects of economic shocks? Does a market economy have a built-in mechanism that will prevent an economic downturn from plunging into a depression? There are three reasons to believe that the answer to both of these questions is yes.

Permanent income hypothesis
The hypothesis that consumption depends on some measure of long-run expected (permanent) income rather than on current income.

1. Consumption demand is relatively stable over the business cycle.

By far, consumption is the largest component of aggregate demand. As incomes fluctuate over the business cycle, there is good reason to expect that consumption spending will be considerably more stable than aggregate income. The **permanent income hypothesis**, developed by Nobel Prize–winning economist Milton Friedman, explains why. According to the permanent income hypothesis, the consumption of households is determined largely by their long-range expected, or permanent, income. Because temporary changes in income, such as those that occur over the business cycle, generally do not exert much impact on long-term expected income, these transitory increases or decreases do not exert a large impact on *current* consumption.[6]

Therefore, when the incomes of many households increase rapidly during an economic expansion, a substantial amount of the above-normal gains in income will be allocated to saving. (Remember "saving"—without an "s" on the end—is income that is not spent on current consumption.) As a result, consumption demand will increase less rapidly than income during the expansion phase of the business cycle. Similarly, when experiencing a temporary decline in income during a recession, many households will reduce their current saving (and draw on their prior savings) in order to maintain a level of current consumption more consistent with their long-term earnings prospects (expected income). Thus, consumer demand will increase less than income during a boom and decline by a smaller amount than income during a recession. This relative stability of the large consumption component will help stabilize aggregate demand over the business cycle.

2. Changes in real interest rates will help to stabilize aggregate demand and redirect economic fluctuations.

Real interest rates will tend to reflect business conditions. During an economic downturn, business demand for new investment projects and therefore loanable funds is generally quite weak. Because of this weak demand, real interest rates will generally fall during the contraction phase of the business cycle. In turn, the lower interest rates will both encourage current consumption and reduce the opportunity cost of investment projects. Both of these factors will help offset the decline in aggregate demand and thereby redirect output toward the full employment level.

During an economic boom, many businesses will borrow in order to undertake capital spending projects needed to meet the strong demand for goods and services. Thus, during business booms, the demand for loanable funds will be strong, placing upward pressure on real interest rates. In turn, the higher real interest rates will make it more expensive to purchase consumer durables and undertake investment projects. This will restrain aggregate demand during a business expansion.

Thus, the movement of interest rates will exert a stabilizing influence on the economy. Lower real interest rates during recessionary periods of weak demand will help to stimulate current spending on goods and services. Correspondingly, higher real interest rates during business booms will help restrain aggregate demand and keep it in line with full employment equilibrium.

Interest-rate adjustments will also help to offset potential disturbances arising from changes in expectations. Suppose that consumers and business operators suddenly became more pessimistic and, as a result, reduced their current level of spending. Other things constant, a reduction in consumer spending implies an increase in saving, while a reduction in investment means weaker demand for loanable funds. Thus, the supply of loanable

---

[6]Perhaps a personal application will help explain why it is important to distinguish between temporary and long-term changes in income. Think for a moment how you would adjust your current spending on goods and services if an aunt left you a gift of $10,000 next month. No doubt you would spend some of the money almost immediately. Perhaps you would buy a new laptop or take a nice vacation. However, you would probably also use a significant portion of this temporary (one-time only) increase in income to pay bills or save for future education. Now, consider how you would alter your current spending if your aunt indicated you were to receive $10,000 per year for the next 30 years. Compared to the one-time gift, the annual gift for 30 years increases your long-term expected income by a much larger amount. In this case, you are likely to spend most of this year's $10,000 almost immediately. You might even borrow money to buy an automobile or make some major expenditures, and thereby expand your spending on goods and services this year by more than $10,000.

funds will increase relative to the demand. This will lead to lower real interest rates, which will help to offset the reduction in spending as the result of the increased pessimism.

Just the opposite would be the case if consumers and businesses suddenly became more optimistic. If they suddenly decide to spend more of their current income, their actions will reduce the supply of loanable funds relative to the demand, causing an increase in real interest rates. But the higher real interest rates will make current spending less attractive and thereby help to stabilize aggregate demand.

3. Changes in real resource prices will help redirect economic fluctuations.

Price adjustments in the resource market will also help keep the economy on an even keel. When the current output of an economy is less than its full employment potential, weak demand and slack employment in resource markets will place downward pressure on real resource prices. Under these conditions, real wages and other resource prices will decline (or increase at a very slow rate). In contrast, when an economy is operating beyond its full employment capacity—that is, when unemployment is less than the natural unemployment rate—strong demand will push the real price of labor and other resources up rapidly.

A Graphic Presentation of the Self-Correcting Mechanism

Exhibits 9 and 10 provide a graphic summary of the economy's self-corrective mechanism. **Exhibit 9** depicts the response of real interest rates and resource prices as market conditions change over the business cycle. When an economy is operating below its full employment potential (Y_F), both real interest rates and real resource prices will tend to decline. Both of these factors will help direct output toward long-run equilibrium (along the vertical *LRAS*). Similarly, when output exceeds the long-run sustainable level, rising real interest rates and resource prices will cause output to recede to the full employment level.

Exhibit 10 depicts the operation of the self-corrective mechanism within the framework of the *AD/AS* model. Part a illustrates the supply and demand conditions in the goods and services market for an economy initially operating beyond full-employment capacity, perhaps as the result of an unanticipated increase in aggregate demand. These are the conditions that one would expect when the expansionary phase of the business cycle results in an unsustainable economic boom. When these conditions are present, the strong demand for goods and services will lead to both a high level of employment and strong demand for investment funds by firms seeking to expand output capacity. As a result, the actual

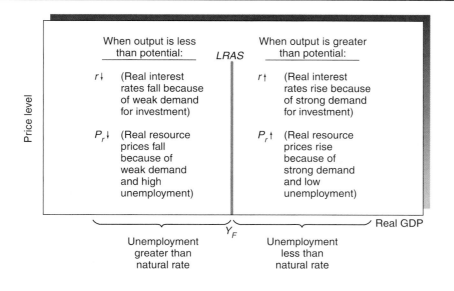

EXHIBIT 9
Changes in Real Interest Rates and Resource Prices Over the Business Cycle

When aggregate output is less than the economy's full employment potential (Y_F), weak demand for investment leads to lower real interest rates, while slack employment in resource markets will place downward pressure on wages and other resource prices (P_r). Conversely, when output exceeds Y_F, strong demand for capital goods and tight labor market conditions will result in rising real interest rates and resource prices.

EXHIBIT 10
The Economy's Self-Corrective Mechanism

In the short run, output may either exceed or fall short of the economy's full-employment capacity (Y_F). If output is temporarily greater than the economy's potential (a), higher real interest rates and resource prices will lead to a lower but sustainable rate of output. The higher interest rates will reduce aggregate demand (shift from AD_1 to AD_2). At the same time, the higher resource prices will increase production costs and therefore reduce short-run aggregate supply (shift to $SRAS_2$ [a]). These forces will direct output toward its full employment potential.

When output is less than capacity (b), lower interest rates (reflecting the weak demand for investment funds) will stimulate aggregate demand (causing the shift to AD_2). In addition, lower resource prices (because of weak demand and abnormally high unemployment) will reduce production costs and thereby stimulate short-run aggregate supply (causing the shift to $SRAS_2$). Thus, output will move toward the economy's full-employment capacity. However, this self-correction process may require considerable time. As we proceed, we will consider policy alternatives that might shorten the adjustment process.

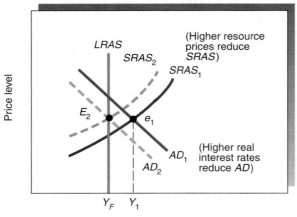

(a) Output is initially greater
than long-run potential

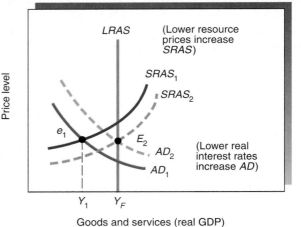

(b) Output is initially less than
long-run capacity

rate of unemployment will be less than the natural rate. However, the strong demand for both loanable funds (to finance investment) and resources will place upward pressure on real interest rates and resource prices, causing both to rise. The higher real interest rates will push up the cost of both investment projects and consumer durables, which will tend to retard the strong demand (shift from AD_1 to AD_2). At the same time, the rising cost of labor and other resources will push production costs upward, causing a reduction in short-run aggregate supply (shift to $SRAS_2$ in part a). As resource prices and costs rise, profit margins will decline to normal competitive rates, and output will recede to its long-run potential. *Eventually, these forces—the higher real interest rates and resource prices— will direct the output of an over-employed economy back to long-run capacity.*

Part b of Exhibit 10 illustrates an economy that is initially in a recession. The initial short-run equilibrium (e_1 of part b) takes place at a rate of output (Y_1) well below the economy's full employment capacity. When current output is less than an economy's long-run potential, the demand for investment funds will be extremely weak. This weak demand for loanable funds will result in lower real interest rates, which lead to an increase in aggregate demand (shift to AD_2 in part b). At the same time, the abnormally high unemployment (initially the actual rate exceeds the natural rate) and weak demand for resources will place downward pressure on real wages and resource prices. Eventually, the excess supply in resource markets will induce suppliers to accept lower wage rates and prices for other resources. This decline in the real price of resources will reduce costs and lead to an increase in short-run aggregate supply (shift to $SRAS_2$ in part b). *With time, this combination of lower interest rates and resource prices will restore the economy's full employment rate of output (equilibrium E_2 of part b).*

The AD/AS model indicates that changes in real interest rates and real resource prices (wages) will redirect both an expansionary boom and a recessionary contraction. A boom will not continue to spiral upward. Neither will a contraction continue to plunge downward.

Exhibit 11 presents data on the estimated real interest rate (Aaa corporate bond rate minus the annual rate of inflation during the last three years) for the peaks and troughs of recent business cycles. Data are also presented for the annual rate of change in the real hourly compensation of nonfarm employees during the periods of expansion and recession. Just as our analysis predicts, real interest rates increased during economic expansions and receded during recessionary periods.

Real wages also followed the expected pattern. The hourly real compensation of nonfarm employees increased less rapidly during each recession than during the preceding (and subsequent) period of economic expansion. In fact, real hourly compensation actually declined during the 1974–1975, 1979–1982, and 1990–1991 recessions.[7] Clearly, the observed pattern of change for both real interest rates and real wages is consistent with the view that they exert a stabilizing influence on the economy.

The Great Debate: How Rapidly Does the Self-Corrective Mechanism Work?

Following the Great Depression of the 1930s, many economists thought that market economies were inherently unstable.[8] They argued that, unless monetary and fiscal policy were used to stimulate and guide the macroeconomy, prolonged recessions would result. Influenced by both a reevaluation of the 1930s and the experience of the last 60 years, most modern economists reject this stagnation view. Today, there is a widespread consensus that market economies possess stabilizing forces.

EXHIBIT 11
Changes in Real Interest Rates and Real Wages Over the Business Cycle

EXPANSIONS AND RECESSIONS	ESTIMATED REAL INTEREST RATE (AT PEAK FOR EXPANSION AND AT TROUGH FOR RECESSION)	ANNUAL PERCENT RATE OF CHANGE IN REAL COMPENSATION PER HOUR (NONFARM BUSINESS SECTOR)
1966–1969 Expansion (Peak, December 1969)	4.2	2.9
1970 Recession (Trough, November 1970)	1.4	1.0
1971–1973 Expansion (Peak, November 1973)	5.9	2.2
1974–1975 Recession (Trough, March 1975)	0.6	−0.4
1976–1979 Expansion (Peak, December 1979)	3.9	1.8
1979–1982 Recession (Trough, November 1982)	1.7	−1.0
1983–1990 Expansion (Peak, July 1990)	4.4	0.5
1990–1991 Recession (Trough, March 1991)	3.3	−1.1
1992–2000 Expansion (Peak, December 2000)	3.4	1.2

Source: The real interest rate data were derived from the *Federal Reserve Bulletin*. The estimated real interest rate is the corporate bond Aaa interest rate minus the expected rate of inflation. The average rate of inflation during the last three years was used to estimate the expected rate of inflation. The real compensation data are from the Department of Labor, Bureau of Labor Statistics. The shaded areas indicate the periods of recession.

---

[7]Officially, there were two recessions during the 1979–1982 stagnation: one of approximately 6 months' duration in 1980 and a second lasting approximately 18 months during 1981–1982. Because the economy recovered only briefly from the initial recession, the entire period was one of economic stagnation.

[8]A detailed analysis of the forces causing and prolonging the Great Depression is presented in Chapter 15.

> *What divides economists is disagreement about how rapidly the self-correcting forces work. This is a key issue. If the self-corrective process works slowly, then market economies will still experience lengthy periods of abnormally high unemployment and below-capacity output.* Many economists believe this is the case. As a result, they have a good deal of confidence that discretionary monetary and fiscal policy can help promote stability and prosperity.

> *Conversely, other economists believe that the self-corrective mechanism of a market economy works reasonably well when monetary and fiscal policy follow a stable course. This latter group argues that macroeconomic policy mistakes are a major source of economic instability.* Thus, they focus on the importance of stable, predictable monetary and fiscal policies, while relying mostly on the self-corrective mechanism of markets to keep the economy on track. When analyzing the impact of monetary and fiscal policy, we will return to this debate.

**LOOKING
AHEAD**

Modern macroeconomics reflects an evolutionary process. The Great Depression and the prolonged unemployment that accompanied it exerted an enormous impact on macroeconomics. John Maynard Keynes, the brilliant English economist, developed a theory that sheds light on the operation of an economy experiencing high rates of unemployment. The next chapter focuses on the Keynesian theory.

KEY POINTS

▼ It is important to distinguish between anticipated and unanticipated changes.

▼ An increase in aggregate demand involves a shift of the entire *AD* schedule to the right. Other than policy, major factors causing an increase in aggregate demand are (a) an increase in real wealth, (b) a lower real interest rate, (c) increased optimism on the part of businesses and consumers, (d) an increase in the expected rate of inflation, (e) higher real income abroad, and (f) a depreciation in the exchange rate. Conversely, if these factors change in the opposite direction, a decrease in aggregate demand will result.

▼ It is important to distinguish between long-run and short-run aggregate supply. The following factors will increase *LRAS*: (a) increases in the supply of labor and capital resources, (b) improvements in technology and productivity, and (c) institutional changes improving the efficiency of resource use. Changes in resource prices, the expected rate of inflation, and supply shocks will cause shifts in short-run aggregate supply (*SRAS*).

▼ An increase in output due to economic growth (an increase in the economy's production capacity) will increase both short-run and long-run aggregate supply, permitting the economy to achieve and sustain a larger output level.

▼ Unanticipated changes in either aggregate demand or aggregate supply will disrupt long-run equilibrium and cause current output to differ from the economy's long-run potential.

▼ Unanticipated increases in aggregate demand and favorable supply shocks can cause economic booms that push output beyond the economy's long-run potential and unemployment below its natural rate. However, as decision makers adjust to the strong demand, resource prices and interest rates will rise and output will recede to long-run capacity.

▼ Unanticipated reductions in aggregate demand and adverse supply shocks can lead to below-capacity output, and abnormally high rates of unemployment. Eventually, lower resource prices (and lower real interest rates) will direct the economy back to long-run equilibrium. However, the process may be both lengthy and painful, particularly if wages and prices are inflexible downward.

▼ Changes in real interest rates and resource prices provide a market economy with a self-corrective mechanism. During a recession, lower interest rates will stimulate aggregate demand, and lower resource prices (including wages) will increase short-run aggregate supply. Both of these forces will help

direct output toward its full employment potential. Similarly, when current output exceeds potential GDP, higher real interest rates and rising real resource prices cause output to recede to the economy's potential capacity.

▼ There is considerable debate among economists concerning how rapidly the economy's self-corrective mechanism works.

CRITICAL ANALYSIS QUESTIONS

*1. Explain how and why each of the following factors would influence current aggregate demand in the United States:
   a. Increased fear of recession
   b. Increased fear of inflation
   c. Rapid growth of real income in Canada and Western Europe
   d. A reduction in the real interest rate
   e. A higher price level (be careful)

*2. Indicate how each of the following would influence U.S. aggregate supply in the short run:
   a. An increase in real wage rates
   b. A severe freeze that destroys half the orange trees in Florida
   c. An increase in the expected rate of inflation in the future
   d. An increase in the world price of oil, a major import
   e. Abundant rainfall during the growing season of agricultural states

3. What is the difference between the production possibilities constraint and the long run aggregate supply curve? How would changes in conditions that move the Production Possibilities Curve affect the *SRAS* and *LRAS?* What impact has the increased use of computer technology had on the cost of doing business during the last 15 years? How has this affected production possibilities and the long-run aggregate supply curve?

*4. When current output is less than full employment capacity, explain how the self-correcting mechanism will direct output toward the economy's long-run potential. Can you think of any reason why this mechanism might not work? Discuss.

5. What is the difference between an anticipated and an unanticipated increase in aggregate demand? Provide an example of each. Which is most likely to result in a temporary spurt in the growth of real output?

*6. Assume that both union and management representatives agree to wage increases because of their expectation that prices will rise 10 percent during the next year. Explain why the unemployment rate will probably increase if the actual rate of inflation next year is only 3 percent.

7. During 2000 there was a sharp reduction in stock prices and a sharp increase in the world price of crude oil. Using the *AD/AS* model, indicate the expected impact of these two factors on output.

*8. When the actual output exceeds the long-run potential of the economy, how will the self-correcting mechanism direct the economy to long-run equilibrium? Why can't the above-normal output be maintained?

*9. Are the real wages of workers likely to increase more rapidly when the unemployment rate is high or when it is low? Why?

10. Suppose consumers and investors suddenly become more pessimistic about the future and therefore decide to reduce their consumption and investment spending. How will a market economy adjust to this increase in pessimism? What will happen to the real rate of interest?

11. How will (a) a 3 percent price reduction in the goods and services market when price stability was expected differ from (b) 1 percent inflation when 4 percent inflation had been expected? What impact would (a) and (b) have on the real price of resources, profit margins, output, and employment? Explain.

*12. Suppose that an unexpectedly rapid growth in real income abroad leads to a sharp increase in the demand for U.S. exports. What impact will this change have on the price level, output, and employment in the short run? In the long run?

13. If the real interest rate increases, how will this affect the incentive of consumers and investors to purchase goods and services? How will it affect the *AD* curve?

14. Construct the *AD*, *SRAS*, and *LRAS* curves for an economy experiencing (a) full employment, (b) an economic boom, and (c) a recession.

15. As the result of changing international conditions, there was a decline in real national defense expenditures of approximately 15 percent between 1989 and 1991. What is the expected impact of a decline in defense expenditures on aggregate demand and output in the short run? If the United States is able to spend less on national defense in the future, how will this factor influence the standard of living of Americans? Discuss.

16. Consider an economy with the following aggregate demand (*AD*) and aggregate supply (*AS*) schedules. These schedules reflect the fact that, prior to the period in question, decision makers entered into contracts and made choices anticipating that the price level would be P_{105}.

AD_{105} (in trillions)	Price Level	$SRAS_{105}$ (in trillions)
$5.1	95	$3.5
4.9	100	3.8
4.7	105	4.2
4.5	110	4.5
4.3	115	4.8

a. Indicate the quantity of GDP that will be produced and the price level that will emerge during this period.

b. Is the economy in long-run equilibrium? Why or why not?

c. How will the unemployment rate during the current period compare with this economy's natural rate of unemployment?

d. What will tend to happen to resource prices in the future? How will this affect the equilibrium rate of output?

e. Will the rate of GDP produced during this period be sustainable into the future? Why or why not?

17. Suppose that the price level that emerges from aggregate demand and aggregate supply conditions during the current period is lower than decision makers had anticipated.

a. Construct *AD*, *SRAS*, and *LRAS* schedules that reflect these conditions.

b. During the current period, how will the actual rate of unemployment compare with the natural rate? How will actual output compare with the economy's potential?

c. As the result of the current conditions, what will tend to happen to resource prices and interest rates? Why?

*18. What impact did the events of September 11, 2001 have on aggregate demand, aggregate supply, and the long-run potential real output of the United States?

---

*Asterisk denotes questions for which answers are given in Appendix B.

CHAPTER 11

Keynesian Foundations of Modern Macroeconomics

Chapter Focus

- What are the major components of the Keynesian model? What is the major factor that causes the level of output and employment to change?

- What was Keynes's explanation for the high rates of unemployment that persisted during the Great Depression?

- What determines the equilibrium level of output in the Keynesian model?

- What is the multiplier principle? Why is it important?

- Why do Keynesians believe market economies experience business instability?

I believe myself to be writing a book on economic theory which will largely revolutionize not, I suppose, at once but in the course of the next ten years the way the world thinks about economic problems.

—*John Maynard Keynes*[1]

[1]Letter from John Maynard Keynes to George Bernard Shaw, New Year's Day, 1935.

M odern macroeconomics is the product of an evolutionary process. Prior to the Great Depression of the 1930s, most economists thought market adjustments would automatically guide an economy to full employment within a relatively brief time. The presence of double-digit unemployment rates throughout the 1930s undermined the credibility of this view. The experience of the Great Depression also led to the development of a new theory, one designed to explain the persistently high unemployment levels of the period.

The new theory, developed by the English economist John Maynard Keynes (pronounced "canes"), provided a reasonable explanation for the widespread and prolonged unemployment of the 1930s.[2] It also exerted an enormous influence on the development of macroeconomics. Several basic concepts and much of the terminology we use today can be traced to Keynes. Modern macroeconomics is built on the foundation of Keynesian analysis. This chapter presents the Keynesian view and illuminates its influence on modern macroeconomic theory. ■

OUTSTANDING ECONOMIST

John Maynard Keynes (1883–1946)

Keynes might properly be referred to as the "father of macroeconomics." The son of a prominent nineteenth-century economist (John Neville Keynes), he earned a degree in mathematics from King's College, Cambridge, where he would later return and spend most of his career as an economist. His *General Theory of Employment, Interest, and Money*, published in 1936, revolutionized the way that economists think about macroeconomics. This work, written in the midst of the Great Depression, provided both a plausible explanation for the massive unemployment and a strategy for ending it. Keynes married an idea with a moment in time.

His work was both path-breaking and controversial. His view that governments should run budget deficits during a recession in order to stimulate demand and direct the economy back to full employment challenged the entrenched views of both policymakers and classical economists. He correctly anticipated that his ideas would be influential (see the chapter's opening quote). This was certainly the case during the three decades following his untimely death in 1946. While the influence of his ideas has waned since the inflation, high unemployment, and instability of the 1970s, the terminology and issue focus of macroeconomics continue to reflect the Keynesian perspective.

Classical economists
Economists from Adam Smith to the time of Keynes who focused their analyses on economic efficiency and production. With regard to business instability, they thought market prices and wages would decline during a recession quickly enough to bring the economy back to full employment within a short period of time.

Say's Law
The view that production creates its own demand. Demand will always be sufficient to purchase the goods produced because the income payments to the resource suppliers will equal the value of the goods produced.

THE GREAT DEPRESSION AND MACROECONOMICS

Mainstream economists before the time of Keynes (often called **classical economists**) emphasized the importance of total production (aggregate supply) and paid little heed to aggregate demand. Classical economists adhered to **Say's Law**, named for nineteenth-century French economist J. B. Say. According to Say's Law, a general overproduction of goods relative to total demand is impossible, since supply (production) creates its own demand. The reasoning here is that the purchasing power necessary to buy (demand) desired

---

[2]See the classic book by Keynes, *The General Theory of Employment, Interest, and Money* (London: Macmillan, 1936), for the presentation of this theory.

The Keynesian model was an outgrowth of the Great Depression. It provided an explanation for the widespread, prolonged unemployment of the 1930s.

products is generated by production. A farmer's supply of wheat generates income to meet the farmer's demand for shoes, clothes, automobiles, and other desired goods. Similarly, the supply of shoes generates the purchasing power with which shoemakers (and their employees) demand the farmer's wheat and other desired goods.

Of course, producers might produce too much of some goods and not enough of others. But the pricing system would correct such imbalances. The prices of goods in excess supply would fall, and the prices of products in excess demand would rise. According to the classical view, deficient total demand could never be a problem because the production of the goods would always generate a demand that was sufficient to purchase the goods produced.

According to the classical view, markets would always adjust and quickly direct the economy toward full employment, conditions parallel to those of long-run equilibrium of the aggregate demand/aggregate supply model developed in the preceding two chapters. If unemployment was temporarily high, wages would fall, which would reduce costs and lower prices until the excess supply of labor was eliminated. Similarly, market-determined interest rates would assure balance between saving and investment.

Before the Great Depression, the classical view seemed reasonable. But the depth and the prolonged duration of the decline during the 1930s challenged its validity and provided the foundation for what we now refer to as Keynesian economics. For those who are familiar only with the relative stability of recent decades, the depth of the economic decline during the 1930s is difficult to comprehend. Real GDP in the United States fell by more than 30 percent between 1930 and 1933. In 1933, 25 percent of the U.S. labor force was unemployed. The depressed conditions continued throughout the decade. In 1939, a decade after the plunge began, per capita income was still nearly 10 percent less than in 1929. Other industrial countries experienced similar conditions.

Keynesian View of the Great Depression

Keynes developed a theory that provided an explanation for prolonged depressed conditions like those of the 1930s. Rejecting the classical view, Keynes offered a completely new concept of output determination. ***Keynes believed that spending induced business firms to supply goods and services. From this, he argued that, if total spending fell (as it might, for example, if consumers and investors became pessimistic about the future or*** *tried to save more of their current income), then business firms would respond by cutting back production. Less spending would thus lead to less output.*

Keynes and his followers rejected the classical view that wage and price reductions would eliminate unemployment. They argued that wages and prices were highly inflexible, particularly in a downward direction. Even when demand was weak, Keynesians believed that large business firms and powerful trade unions would resist price and wage reductions, and thereby retard movement toward full employment.

Keynes also introduced a different concept of equilibrium and a different mechanism for its achievement. *In the Keynesian view, equilibrium takes place when the level of total spending is equal to current output. When this is the case, producers will have no reason to either expand or contract output.* Keynesians believe that changes in output rather than changes in prices direct the economy to equilibrium. If total spending is less than full employment output, output will be cut back to the level of spending, and, most significantly, it will remain there until the level of spending changes. Therefore, if total spending is deficient, equilibrium output will be less than full employment output, and high rates of unemployment will continue. This is precisely what Keynes believed was happening during the 1930s.

The central message of Keynes can be summarized as follows: Businesses will produce only the quantity of goods and services they believe consumers, investors, governments, and foreigners will plan to buy. If these planned aggregate expenditures are less than the economy's full employment output, output will fall short of its potential. When aggregate expenditures are deficient, there are no automatic forces capable of assuring full employment. Prolonged unemployment will persist. Against the background of the Great Depression, this was a compelling argument.

Keynesian Model of Spending and Output

The key to the basic Keynesian model is the concept of *planned* aggregate expenditures. As with aggregate demand, the four components of *planned* aggregate expenditures are consumption, investment, government purchases, and net exports. Before we develop the Keynesian model, however, it's useful to make a few assumptions in order to simplify the analysis. First, as with the *AD/AS* model developed in Chapters 9 and 10, we will assume there is a specific full employment level of output. Only the natural rate of unemployment is present when full employment capacity is attained. Second, following in the Keynesian tradition, we will assume that wages and prices are completely inflexible until full employment is reached. Once full employment is achieved, though, additional demand will lead only to higher prices. Strictly speaking, these polar assumptions will not hold in the real world. They may, however, approximate conditions in the short run. Finally, we will continue to assume that the government's taxing, spending, and monetary policies are constant.

Planned Consumption Expenditures

The most important component of planned aggregate expenditures is *planned* consumption (C). Keynes believed that current income is the primary determinant of consumption expenditures. As he stated:

> Men are disposed, as a rule and on the average, to increase their consumption as their income increases, but not by as much as the increase in their income.[3]

---

[3]Keynes, *The General Theory of Employment, Interest, and Money*, p. 96.

According to Keynes, disposable income is by far the major determinant of current consumption. If disposable income increases, consumers will increase their planned expenditures.

This positive relationship between consumption spending and disposable income is called the **consumption function**. **Exhibit 1** illustrates this relationship for an economy. At low levels of aggregate income (less than $7 trillion), the consumption expenditures of households will exceed their disposable income. When income is low, households dissave—they either borrow or draw from their past savings to purchase consumption goods. Because consumption does not increase as rapidly as income, the slope of the consumption function will be less than 1. So the consumption schedule is flatter than the 45-degree line of Exhibit 1. As income increases, household aggregate income eventually equals and exceeds current consumption. For aggregate incomes above $7 trillion, saving increases as income rises.

Consumption function
A fundamental relationship between disposable income and consumption, in which, as disposable income increases, current consumption expenditures rise, but by a smaller amount than the increase in income.

Planned Investment Expenditures

Investment (I) encompasses (1) expenditures on fixed assets, such as buildings and machines, and (2) changes in the inventories of raw materials and final products not yet sold. Keynes argued that, in the short run, investment was best viewed as an **autonomous expenditure**, one independent of income. In the Keynesian model, planned investment does not change with the level of income. Instead, investment is primarily a function of current sales relative to plant capacity, expected future sales, and the interest rate. Changes in these latter factors would alter investment—they would cause the entire schedule to shift either upward or downward. But when focusing on the forces pushing an economy toward an equilibrium level of output, the basic Keynesian model postulates a constant level of planned investment expenditures.

Autonomous expenditures
Expenditures that do not vary with the level of income. They are determined by factors (such as business expectations and economic policy) that are outside the basic income-expenditure model.

Planned Government Expenditures

As with investment, planned government (G) expenditures in the basic Keynesian model are assumed to be independent of income. These expenditures need not change with the level of income. In the Keynesian model, government expenditures are a policy variable

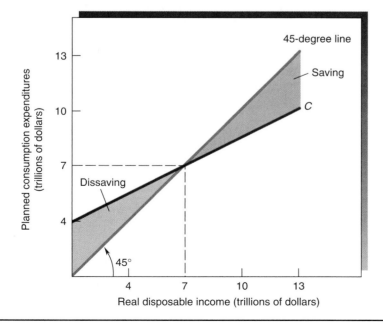

EXHIBIT 1
Aggregate Consumption Function

The Keynesian model assumes that there is a positive relationship between consumption and income. However, as income increases, consumption expands by a smaller amount. Thus, the slope of the consumption function (line C) is less than 1 (less than the slope of the 45-degree line).

determined by the political process. Governments can, and often do, spend more than they receive in taxes. Perceiving government expenditures as autonomous of income allows us to focus more clearly on the stability characteristics of a private economy. Later, we will analyze how changes in government expenditures influence output and employment within the framework of the Keynesian aggregate expenditure model.

Planned Net Exports

Exports are dependent on spending choices and income levels abroad. These decisions are, by and large, unaffected by changes in a nation's domestic income level. Therefore, as **Exhibit 2** illustrates, exports remain constant (at $1.2 trillion) when income changes. In contrast, increases in domestic income will induce consumers to purchase more foreign as well as domestic goods. So the level of imports increases as income rises.

Because exports remain constant and imports increase as aggregate income expands, net exports (*NX*) will decline as income expands (see Exhibit 2). Accordingly, the Keynesian model postulates a negative relationship between income and net exports.

Planned Versus Actual Expenditures

It is important to distinguish between planned and actual expenditures. Planned expenditures reflect the choices of consumers, investors, governments, and foreigners, *given their expectations as to the choices of other decision makers*. Planned expenditures, though, need not equal actual expenditures. If purchasers spend a different amount on goods and services than business firms anticipate, the firms will experience unplanned changes in inventories. When this is the case, actual investment will differ from planned investment because inventories are a component of investment in our national income accounts.

Consider what would happen if the planned expenditures of consumers, investors, governments, and foreigners on goods and services were less than what business firms thought they would be. If this were the case, business firms would be unable to sell as much of their current output as they had anticipated. Their *actual* inventories would increase as they unintentionally made larger inventory investments than they *planned*. On the other hand, consider what would happen if purchasers bought more goods and services than businesses expected. The unexpected brisk sales would draw down inventories and result in less inventory investment than business firms planned. In this case, actual inventory investment would be less than they *planned*.

Actual and *planned* expenditures are equal only when purchasers buy the quantity of goods and services that business decision makers anticipated they would purchase. Only then will the plans of buyers and sellers in the goods and services market harmonize.

EXHIBIT 2
Income and Net Exports

Because exports are determined by income abroad, they are constant at $1.2 trillion. Imports increase as domestic income expands. Thus, planned net exports fall as domestic income increases.

Total Output (Real GDP in Trillions)	Planned Exports (Trillions)	Planned Imports (Trillions)	Planned Net Exports (Trillions)
$ 9.4	$1.2	$1.00	$0.20
9.7	1.2	1.05	0.15
10.0	1.2	1.10	0.10
10.3	1.2	1.15	0.05
10.6	1.2	1.20	0.0

KEYNESIAN EQUILIBRIUM

Equilibrium is present in the Keynesian model when planned aggregate expenditures equal the value of current output. When this is the case, businesses are able to sell the total amount of goods and services that they produce. There are no unexpected changes in inventories. Thus, producers have no incentive to either expand or contract their output during the next period. In equation form, Keynesian macroequilibrium is attained when:

$$\underbrace{\text{Total output}}_{\text{Real GDP}} \quad = \quad \underbrace{\text{Planned } C + G + NX}_{\text{Planned aggregate expenditures}}$$

As an example of Keynesian macroeconomic equilibrium, let's take a look at the hypothetical economy described by **Exhibit 3**. To begin, let's focus on columns 1 and 2. At what level of total output is this economy in Keynesian macroeconomic equilibrium? Stop now and attempt to figure out the answer.

The answer is $10 trillion, because only there is total output exactly equal to planned aggregate expenditures. When real GDP is equal to $10 trillion, the planned expenditures of consumers, investors, governments, and foreigners (net exports) are precisely equal to the value of the output produced by business firms. To see this, note that only at $10 trillion do columns 3 + 4 + 5 equal column 1. Because of this equality, the spending plans of purchasers mesh with the production plans of business decision makers. Given this balance, there is no reason for producers to change their plans.

What happens at other output levels? At any output other than equilibrium, the plans of producers and purchasers will conflict. If output is $9.7 trillion, for example, planned aggregate expenditures will be $9.85 trillion, $150 billion more than the current level of output. When expenditures (purchases) exceed output, inventories will decline. Under these circumstances, firms will expand their output in order to rebuild their inventories to normal levels. Therefore, when aggregate expenditures exceed current output, there will be a tendency for output to expand and move toward equilibrium.

On the other hand, if aggregate expenditures are less than current output, firms will cut back on production. For example, at $10.3 trillion, output will be greater than planned aggregate expenditures, and unwanted inventories will accumulate. Of course, business firms will not continue to produce goods they cannot sell, so they will reduce production and output will recede toward the $10 trillion equilibrium.

Equilibrium at Less Than Full Employment

Because Keynesian equilibrium is dependent on equality between planned aggregate expenditures and output, it need not take place at full employment. If an economy is in

TOTAL OUTPUT (REAL GDP) (1)	PLANNED AGGREGATE EXPENDITURES (2)	PLANNED CONSUMPTION (3)	PLANNED INVESTMENT + GOVERNMENT EXPENDITURES (4)	PLANNED NET EXPORTS (5)	TENDENCY OF OUTPUT (6)
$ 9.4	$ 9.70	$ 7.1	$ 2.4	$ 0.20	Expand
9.7	9.85	7.3	2.4	0.15	Expand
10.0	10.00	7.5	2.4	0.10	Equilibrium
10.3	10.15	7.7	2.4	0.05	Contract
10.6	10.30	7.9	2.4	0.00	Contract

EXHIBIT 3
Example of Keynesian Macroeconomic Equilibrium

Note: All figures are in trillions of dollars. Column 2 equals the sum of columns 3 + 4 + 5.

Keynesian equilibrium, there will be no tendency for output to change even if output is well below full employment capacity.

To see this in our example, assume that full employment is at an output of $10.3 trillion, in Exhibit 3. Given the current planned spending, the economy will fail to achieve full employment. The rate of unemployment will be high. In the Keynesian model, neither wages nor other resource prices will decline in the face of abnormally high unemployment and excess capacity. Therefore, output will remain at less than the full employment rate as long as insufficient spending prevents the economy from reaching its full potential.

This is precisely what Keynes thought was happening during the Great Depression. He believed that Western economies were in equilibrium at an employment rate substantially below capacity. Unless aggregate expenditures increased, therefore, the prolonged unemployment had to continue—as it did throughout that period.

Keynesian Equilibrium—a Graphic Presentation

The Keynesian analysis is presented graphically in **Exhibit 4**, where planned aggregate consumption, investment, government, and net export expenditures are measured on the *y*-axis and total output is measured on the *x*-axis. The 45-degree line that extends from the origin maps out all the points where aggregate expenditures (*AE*) are equal to total output (GDP).

Because aggregate expenditures equal total output for all points along the 45-degree line, the line maps out all possible equilibrium income levels. As long as the economy is operating at less than its full employment capacity, producers will produce any output along the 45-degree line they believe purchasers will buy. Producers, though, will supply a level of output only if they believe planned expenditures will be large enough to purchase it. Depending on the level of aggregate expenditures, each point along the 45-degree line is a potential equilibrium.

Using the data of Exhibit 3, **Exhibit 5** graphically depicts the Keynesian equilibrium. The *C* + *I* + *G* + *NX* line indicates the total planned expenditures of consumers, investors, governments, and foreigners (net exports) at each income level. *Reflecting the consumption function*, the aggregate expenditure (*AE*) line is flatter than the 45-degree line. Remember, as income rises, consumption also increases, but by less than the increase in income. Therefore, as income expands, total expenditures increase by less than the expansion in income.

EXHIBIT 4
Aggregate Expenditures (*AE*)

Aggregate expenditures will be equal to total output for all points along a 45-degree line from the origin. The 45-degree line thus maps out potential equilibrium levels of output for the Keynesian model.

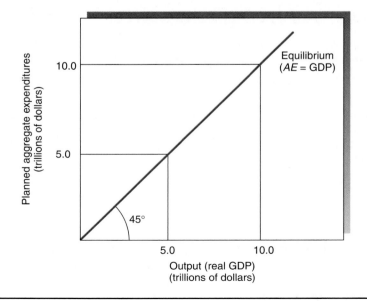

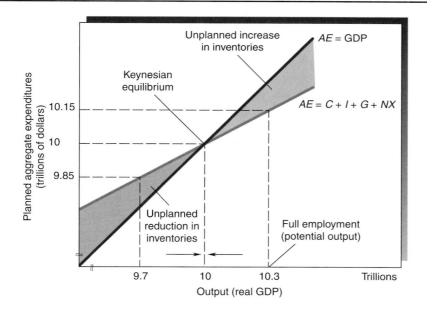

EXHIBIT 5
Aggregate Expenditures and Keynesian Equilibrium

Here the data of Exhibit 3 are presented within the Keynesian graphic framework. The equilibrium level of output is $10.0 trillion because planned expenditures ($C + I + G + NX$) are just equal to output at that level of income. At a lower level of income, $9.7 trillion, for example, unplanned inventory reduction would cause business firms to expand output (right-pointing arrow). Conversely, at a higher income level, such as $10.3 trillion, accumulation of inventories would lead to a reduction in future output (left-pointing arrow). Given current aggregate expenditures, only the $10.0 trillion output could be sustained. Note the $10.0 trillion equilibrium income level is less than the economy's potential of $10.3 trillion.

The equilibrium level of output will be $10.0 trillion, the point at which the total expenditures (measured vertically) are just equal to total output (measured horizontally). Of course, the aggregate expenditures function $C + I + G + NX$ will cross the 45-degree line at the $10.0 trillion equilibrium level of output.

As long as the aggregate expenditures function remains unchanged, no other level of output can be sustained. When total output exceeds $10.0 trillion (for example, $10.3 trillion), the aggregate expenditure line lies below the 45-degree line. Remember that, when the $C + I + G + NX$ line is less than the 45-degree line, total spending is less than total output. Unwanted inventories will then accumulate, leading businesses to reduce their future production. Employment will decline. Output will fall back from $10.3 trillion to the equilibrium level of $10.0 trillion. Note that it is changes in output and employment, not price changes, that restore equilibrium in the Keynesian model.

In contrast, if total output is temporarily below equilibrium, there is a tendency for income to rise. Suppose output is temporarily at $9.7 trillion. At that output level, the $C + I + G + NX$ function lies above the 45-degree line. Aggregate expenditures exceed aggregate output. Businesses are selling more than they currently produce. Their inventories are falling. Excess demand is present. They will react to this state of affairs by hiring more workers and expanding production. Income will rise to the $10.0 trillion equilibrium level. Only at the equilibrium level, the point at which the $C + I + G + NX$ function crosses the 45-degree line, will the spending plans of consumers, investors, governments, and foreigners sustain the existing output level into the future.

As Exhibit 5 illustrates, the economy's full employment potential income level is $10.3 trillion. At this income level, though, aggregate expenditures are insufficient to purchase the output produced. Given the aggregate expenditures function, output will remain below its potential. Unemployment will persist. Within the Keynesian model, equilibrium need not coincide with full employment.

Aggregate Expenditures, Output, and Employment

How could the economy reach its full employment capacity? According to the Keynesian model, it will not do so unless there is a change in the aggregate expenditures schedule. Because the Keynesian model assumes that prices are fixed until potential capacity is reached, wage and price reductions are ruled out as a feasible mechanism for directing the economy to full employment. Neither is the interest rate capable of stimulating demand and directing the economy to full employment.

If consumers, investors, governments, and foreigners could be induced to expand their expenditures, output would expand to full employment capacity. **Exhibit 6** illustrates this point. If additional spending shifted the aggregate expenditures schedule (AE) upward to AE_2, equilibrium output would expand to its potential capacity. At the higher level of expenditures, AE_2, total spending would equal output at $10.3 trillion.

What would happen if aggregate expenditures exceeded the economy's production capacity? For example, suppose aggregate expenditures rose to AE_3. Within the basic Keynesian model, aggregate expenditures in excess of output lead to a higher price level once the economy reaches full employment. Nominal output will increase, but it merely reflects higher prices, rather than additional real output. Total spending in excess of full employment capacity is inflationary within the Keynesian model.

Aggregate expenditures are the catalyst of the Keynesian model. Changes in expenditures make things happen. Until full employment is attained, supply is always accommodative. An increase in aggregate expenditures, caused, for example, by an increase in government expenditures, will thus lead to an increase in real output and employment. Once full employment is reached, however, additional aggregate expenditures lead merely to higher prices.

The Keynesian model implies that regulation of aggregate expenditures is the crux of sound macroeconomic policy. If we could assure aggregate expenditures large enough to achieve capacity output, but not so large as to result in inflation, the Keynesian view implies that maximum output, full employment, and price stability could be attained.

EXHIBIT 6
Shifts in Aggregate Expenditures and Changes in Equilibrium Output

When equilibrium output is less than the economy's capacity, only an increase in expenditures (a shift in *AE*) will lead to full employment. If consumers, investors, governments, or foreigners would spend more and thereby shift the aggregate-expenditures schedule to AE_2, output would reach its full employment potential ($10.3 trillion). Once full employment is reached, further increases in aggregate expenditures, such as indicated by the shift to AE_3, would lead only to higher prices. Nominal output will expand (the dotted segment of the *AE* = GDP schedule), but real output will not.

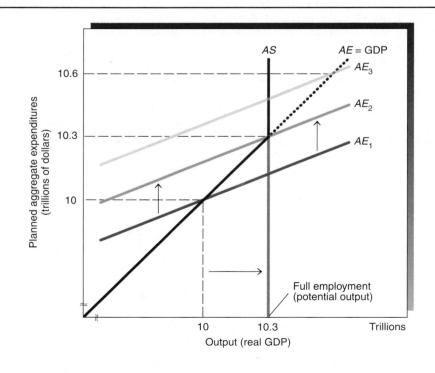

THE KEYNESIAN MODEL WITHIN THE *AD/AS* FRAMEWORK

The Keynesian model can also be presented within the now familiar aggregate demand/aggregate supply (*AD/AS*) framework of the previous two chapters. The only difference in the graphic analysis is that the short-run aggregate supply curve (*SRAS*) has a different shape than in previous chapters because of the assumptions of the Keynesian model. Take a look at **Exhibit 7.** Note that the *SRAS* is completely flat at the existing price level until full employment capacity is reached. This is because the Keynesian model assumes that, at less than full employment output levels, prices (and wages) are fixed because they are inflexible in a downward direction. In essence, firms have a horizontal supply curve when operating below normal capacity, so any change in aggregate demand will lead to a corresponding change in output. Economists sometimes refer to this horizontal segment as the *Keynesian range* of the aggregate supply curve.

What happens to the SRAS in Exhibit 7 when capacity is reached? In this situation, firms raise their prices to allocate the capacity output to those willing to pay the highest prices. Thus, the economy's *SRAS* is vertical at full employment capacity. So both *SRAS* and *LRAS* are vertical at the full employment rate of output (Y_F in Exhibit 7).

Part a of **Exhibit 8** illustrates the impact of a change in aggregate demand within the polar assumptions of the Keynesian model. When aggregate demand is less than AD_2 (for example, AD_1), the economy will languish below potential capacity. Because prices and wages are inflexible downward, below-capacity output rates (Y_1, for example) and abnormally high unemployment will persist unless there is an increase in aggregate demand. When output is below its potential, any increase in aggregate demand (for example, the shift from AD_1 to AD_2) brings previously idle resources into the productive process at an unchanged price level. In this range, the Keynesian analysis essentially turns Say's Law (supply creates an equivalent amount of demand) on its head. In the Keynesian range, an increase in demand creates its own supply. Of course, once the economy's potential output constraint (Y_F) is reached, additional demand would merely lead to higher prices rather than to more output. Because both the *SRAS* and *LRAS* curves are vertical at capacity output, an increase in aggregate demand to AD_3 fails to expand real output.

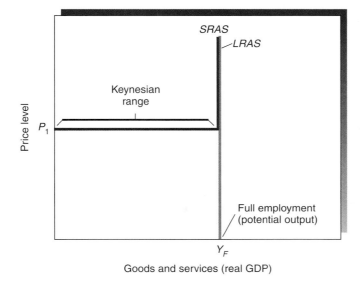

Goods and services (real GDP)

EXHIBIT 7
Keynesian Aggregate Supply Curves

The Keynesian model implies a 90-degree, angle-shaped aggregate supply curve. Because the model postulates downward wage and price inflexibility, the *SRAS* curve is flat for outputs less than potential GDP (Y_F). In this range, often referred to as the Keynesian range, output is entirely dependent on the level of aggregate demand. The Keynesian model implies that real output rates beyond full employment are unattainable. Thus, both *SRAS* and *LRAS* are vertical at the economy's full employment potential output.

EXHIBIT 8
***AD/AS* Presentation of Keynesian Model**

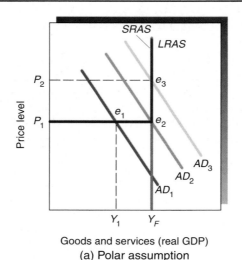

(a) Polar assumption

Goods and services (real GDP)

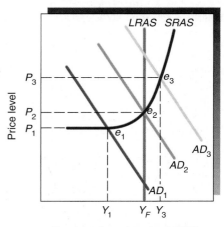

(b) Central implication

Goods and services (real GDP)

Part a illustrates the polar implications of the Keynesian model. When output is less than capacity (for example, Y_1), an increase in aggregate demand such as illustrated by the shift from AD_1 to AD_2 will expand output without increasing prices. But, increases in demand beyond AD_2, such as a shift to AD_3, lead only to a higher price level (P_2). Part b relaxes the assumption of complete price inflexibility and short-run output inflexibility beyond Y_F. The *SRAS* curve therefore turns from horizontal to vertical more gradually. This would imply that unanticipated increases in aggregate demand would lead (1) primarily to increases in output when output is below capacity (for example, Y_1), and (2) primarily to increases in the price level when output is greater than capacity (for example, Y_3).

When constructing models, we often make polar assumptions to illustrate various points. The Keynesian model is no exception. In the real world, prices will not be completely inflexible. Similarly, in the short run, unanticipated increases in demand will not lead solely to higher prices. Nevertheless, the Keynesian model implies an important point that is illustrated more realistically by part b of Exhibit 8. The horizontal segment of the *SRAS* curve is an oversimplification intended to reinforce the idea that changes in aggregate demand exert little impact on prices and substantial impact on output when an economy is operating well below capacity. *Therefore, under conditions like those of the 1930s—when idle factories and widespread unemployment are present—an increase in aggregate demand will generally exert its primary impact on output.*

On the other hand, the vertical segment of the aggregate supply curve is a simplifying assumption meant to illustrate the concept that there is an attainable output rate beyond which increases in demand will lead almost exclusively to price increases (and only small increases in real output). *When aggregate demand is already quite strong (for example, AD_3), increases in aggregate demand will predictably exert their primary impact on prices rather than on output.*

THE MULTIPLIER

Expenditure multiplier
The ratio of the change in equilibrium output to the independent change in investment, consumption, or government spending that brings about the change. Numerically, the multiplier is equal to 1 *divided by* (1 - MPC) when the price level is constant.

The multiplier occupies a central position in the Keynesian model. It focuses on the impact of changes in autonomous expenditures—spending unrelated to income that is determined by factors external to the basic income-expenditure model. Changes in autonomous expenditures—for example, an increase in the level of investment due to improved business expectations or an increase in net exports as the result of higher incomes abroad—will shift the entire aggregate expenditure schedule and generally lead to an expansion in income greater than the initial shift in expenditures. The **expenditure multiplier** is defined as the change in total income (equilibrium output) divided by the autonomous expenditure change that brought about the enlarged income.

 The multiplier principle builds on the point that one individual's expenditure becomes the income of another. As we previously discussed, consumption expenditures are directly related to income—an increase in income (or wealth) will lead to an increase in consumption. Predictably, income recipients will spend a portion of their additional earnings on consumption. In turn, their consumption expenditures will generate additional income for others who will also spend a portion of it.

 Perhaps an example will illuminate the multiplier concept. Suppose that there were idle unemployed resources and that an entrepreneur decided to undertake a $1 million investment project. Because investment is a component of aggregate demand, the project will increase demand directly by $1 million. This is not the entire story, however. The investment project will require plumbers, carpenters, masons, lumber, cement, and many other resources. The incomes of the suppliers of these resources will increase by $1 million. What will they do with this additional income? Given the link between one's income and consumption, the resource suppliers will predictably spend a fraction of the additional income. They will buy more food, clothing, recreation, medical care, and thousands of other items. How will this spending influence the incomes of those who supply these additional consumption products and services? Their incomes will increase, also. After setting aside (saving) a portion of this additional income, these persons will also spend some of their additional income on current consumption. Their consumption spending will result in still more additional income for other product and service suppliers.

 The term *multiplier* is also used to indicate the number by which the initial investment would be multiplied to obtain the total summation of the increases in income. If the $1 million investment resulted in $4 million of additional income, the multiplier would be 4. The total increase in income would be four times the amount of the initial increase in spending. Similarly, if total income increased by $3 million, the multiplier would be 3.

The Size of the Multiplier

The size of the multiplier depends on the proportion of the additional income that households choose to spend on consumption.[4] Keynes referred to this fraction as the **marginal propensity to consume (MPC)**. Mathematically:

$$\text{MPC} = \frac{\text{Additional consumption}}{\text{Additional income}}$$

Marginal propensity to consume (MPC)
Additional current consumption divided by additional current disposable income.

 For example, if your income increases by $100 and you therefore increase your current consumption expenditures by $75, your marginal propensity to consume is 3/4, or 0.75.

 Exhibit 9 illustrates why the size of the multiplier is dependent on the MPC. Suppose the MPC is equal to 3/4, indicating that consumers spend 75 cents of each additional dollar earned. Continuing with our previous example, we know that a $1 million investment would initially result in $1 million of additional income in round 1. Because the MPC is 3/4, consumption would increase by $750,000 (the other $250,000 would flow into saving), contributing that amount to income in round 2. The recipients of the round 2 income of $750,000 would spend three-fourths of it on current consumption. Hence, their spending would increase income by $562,500 in round 3. Exhibit 9 illustrates the additions to income through other rounds. In total, income would increase by $4 million, given an MPC of 3/4. The multiplier is 4.

 If the MPC had been greater, income recipients would have spent a larger share of their additional income on current consumption during each round. Thus, the additional

---

[4]For the purposes of simplicity when calculating the size of the multiplier, we will assume that all additions to income are either (1) spent on domestically produced goods or (2) saved. This assumption means that we are ignoring the impact of taxes and spending on imports as income expands via the multiplier process. At the conclusion of our analysis, we will indicate the significance of this assumption.

EXHIBIT 9
The Multiplier Principle

EXPENDITURE STAGE	ADDITIONAL INCOME (DOLLARS)	ADDITIONAL CONSUMPTION (DOLLARS)	MARGINAL PROPENSITY TO CONSUME
Round 1	1,000,000 →	750,000	3/4
Round 2	750,000	562,500	3/4
Round 3	562,500	421,875	3/4
Round 4	421,875	316,406	3/4
Round 5	316,406	237,305	3/4
Round 6	237,305	177,979	3/4
Round 7	177,979	133,484	3/4
Round 8	133,484	100,113	3/4
Round 9	100,113	75,085	3/4
Round 10	75,085	56,314	3/4
All Others	225,253	168,939	3/4
Total	4,000,000	3,000,000	3/4

EXHIBIT 10
A Higher MPC Means a Larger Multiplier

MPC	SIZE OF MULTIPLIER
9/10	10
4/5	5
3/4	4
2/3	3
1/2	2
1/3	1.5

income generated in each round would have been greater, increasing the size of the multiplier. There is a precise relationship between the expenditure multiplier and the MPC. The expenditure multiplier, *M*, is:

$$M = \frac{1}{1 - \text{MPC}}$$

Exhibit 10 indicates the size of the multiplier for several different values of MPC.

Real-World Significance of the Multiplier

Within the framework of the Keynesian model, the multiplier is important because it explains why even small changes in investment, government, or consumption spending can trigger much larger changes in output. The multiplier magnifies the fluctuations in output and employment that emanate from autonomous changes in spending.

There are both positive and negative sides to the amplified effects. On the negative side, the multiplier principle indicates that a small reduction in investment expenditures, perhaps due to a decline in business optimism, can be an important source of economic instability. As a result, many Keynesian economists believe that the stability of a market economy is quite fragile and constantly susceptible to even modest disruptions. On the positive side, the multiplier principle illustrates the potential of macroeconomic policy to stimulate output even if it is able to exert only a small impact on autonomous expenditures.

APPLICATIONS IN ECONOMICS

Sports Stadiums, Development Subsidies, and the Multiplier

Arguing that they will promote economic development and employment, many local governments have constructed or heavily subsidized sports stadiums, civic and art centers, and even hotels. The multiplier concept is often used in support of such projects. Proponents buttress their case by claiming, for example, that a $100 million project will promote additional spending of three or four times this amount, and thereby generate additional income and tax revenue for the financing of the project.

The construction of BOB (Bank One Ballpark) is typical of such projects. This nearly 50,000-seat stadium is used by the Arizona Diamondbacks major league baseball team. Opening in 1998, the facility cost $360 million, three-fourths of which was financed with taxpayer funds generated by a 1/4 cent increase in the local sales tax.

Does the multiplier enhance the attractiveness of projects like BOB? When thinking about this question, it is important to keep two points in mind. First, the multiplier applies only for shifts in expenditures, that is, spending that otherwise would not have taken place. Economists refer to spending of this type as "exogenous expenditures." Clearly, the $360 million spent on the stadium substantially overstates the net increase in expenditures. The tax increase (and government borrowing) drained approximately $270 million from local taxpayers. If these funds had not been used to finance BOB, taxpayers would have purchased more food, housing, recreation, health care, and numerous other items in the local economy. This reduction in spending is a partial offset against the increased spending resulting from the stadium construction.

Second, if the multiplier is going to work its magic and expand real income, resources that would have otherwise been unemployed must be brought into the production process. Unless this is the case, the expansion in demand will merely lead to higher prices. At the time of BOB's construction, the rate of unemployment in Phoenix and other areas of the country was very low. Given these conditions, a large portion of any increased demand derived from the stadium construction would merely push prices upward, rather than expanding employment and real income.

What about the spending of people attending the games? Again, a substantial portion of this spending will be replacement in nature. If people did not spend their income on major league baseball, most would spend it on other things—basketball and football games, movies, other forms

Do government expenditures on projects like the construction of the Bank One Ballpark in Phoenix, Arizona, exert a multiplier effect?

of entertainment, and eating out, for example. The composition of spending is affected, but there is little, if any, impact on the level of expenditures. Of course, there will be some increase in local spending generated by those attending games from out of town. This spending will generate a multiplier effect for the local economy. However, Diamondback fans in the Phoenix area may follow the team to other cities, and, as a result, spend less in the local economy. This would, at least partially, offset the additional spending in the Phoenix area by those from out of town.

Several economists have examined the impact of sports teams and the construction of sports stadiums on economic activity. A recent survey of eight such studies concludes that there is no evidence that sports teams and facilities generate any additional economic growth.[1] This indicates that the multiplier for sports teams is zero.

Rhetoric aside, local government spending projects for sports, entertainment, and the arts are generally more about rent-seeking—trying to extract favors from the government—than economic development. All of us would like to have others help pay for things we enjoy, or things that will increase the value of assets we own. As the public choice model highlights, rent-seeking is an important motivation for public sector action. Viewed from this perspective, exaggerated claims of multiplier effects by proponents seeking to gain through public sector action are an expected occurrence.

[1]See John Siegfried and Andrew Zimbalist, "The Economics of Sports Facilities and Their Communities," *Journal of Economic Perspectives*, Summer 2000, pp. 95–114.

In evaluating the significance of the multiplier, it is important to keep three points in mind. *First, in addition to saving, leakages in the form of taxes and spending on imports will also reduce the size of the multiplier.* In order to keep things simple, we assumed that all income was either saved or spent on domestically produced goods throughout our analysis. Like saving, taxes and imports will siphon some of the additional income away from spending on domestic goods and services. These leakages from the flow of spending will dampen the effects of the multiplier. Therefore, the actual multiplier will be somewhat smaller than the simple expenditure multiplier of our analysis.

Second, it takes time for the multiplier to work. In the real world, several weeks or perhaps even months will be required for each successive round of spending. Only a fraction of the multiplier effect will be observed quickly. Most researchers believe that only about one-half the total multiplier effect will be felt during the first six months following a change in expenditures.

Third, the multiplier implies that the additional spending brings idle resources into production, leading to additional real output rather than to increased prices. When unemployment is widespread, this is a realistic assumption. However, when there is an absence of abundant idle resources, the multiplier effect will be dampened by an increase in the price level.

KEYNESIAN VIEW OF THE BUSINESS CYCLE

Keynesian economists believe that a market economy, if left to its own devices, is unstable and likely to experience prolonged periods of recession. The Keynesian view emphasizes the destabilizing potential of autonomous changes in expenditures powered by the multiplier and changes in optimism. Suppose there is an increase in aggregate demand triggered by what appears to be a relatively minor disruption—for example, higher incomes abroad, an increase in consumer optimism, or a burst of business optimism generated by a new innovation. Keynesians believe that such changes will often lead to an expansion in output that will have a tendency to feed on itself. The initial increase in demand, *magnified by the multiplier*, will lead to an expansion in employment and a rapid growth of income. In turn, the higher incomes will lead to additional consumption and strong business sales. Inventories will decline, and businesses will expand output (to rebuild inventories) and move investment projects forward as they become more optimistic about the future. Unemployment will decline to a low level as the economy experiences a boom.

Can this expansionary phase continue indefinitely? The answer is no. Eventually, full employment capacity will be reached. Constrained by the availability of both labor and machines, the growth rate of the economy will slow. The slower growth will dampen the optimism of business decision makers and cause them to cut back on fixed investments. Again, the multiplier will magnify the impact of the change in demand. Thus, the reduction in investment and increased pessimism about the future will often lead to a sharp reduction in output. As the economy plunges into a recession, inventories will rise as businesses are unable to sell their goods because of the low level of demand. Workers will be laid off. The ranks of unemployed workers will grow. Bankruptcies will become more common.

This is what Keynes perceived was happening in the 1930s. Consumers were not spending because their incomes had fallen and they were extremely pessimistic about the future. Similarly, businesses were not producing because there was little demand for their products. Investment had come to a complete standstill because underutilized resources and capacity were abundantly available.

Wide fluctuation in private investment is the villain of Keynesian business cycle theory. An economic expansion accelerates into a boom because investment, amplified by the multiplier, stimulates other sectors of the economy. At the first sign of a slowdown, though, investment plans are sharply curtailed. Eventually, machines will wear out and the capital stock will decline to a level consistent with the current level of income. At that point, *additional* investment will be necessary for replacement purposes. The new investment will stimulate additional output and employment, and start the cycle anew.

Thus, Keynesian economists believe that market economies will tend to sway back and forth between recession and boom. They have little confidence that changes in wages and interest rates will keep the economy on a path of steady growth.

EVOLUTION OF MODERN MACROECONOMICS

Major Insights of Keynesian Economics

Keynesian economics and the aggregate expenditure (*AE*) model dominated the thinking of macroeconomists for three decades following the Second World War. Three major insights of the Keynesian model stand out.

1. *Changes in output, as well as changes in prices, play a role in the macroeconomic adjustment process, particularly in the short run.* The classical model emphasized the role of prices in directing an economy to macroeconomic equilibrium. Keynesian analysis highlights the importance of changes in output.

2. *The responsiveness of aggregate supply to changes in demand will be directly related to the availability of unemployed resources.* Keynesian analysis emphasizes that, when idle resources are present, output will be highly responsive to changes in aggregate demand. Conversely, when an economy is operating at or near its capacity, output will be much less sensitive to changes in demand. So the *SRAS* curve is relatively flat when an economy is well below capacity and relatively steep when the economy is operating near and beyond capacity (see Exhibit 8).

3. *Fluctuations in aggregate demand are an important potential source of business instability.* Abrupt changes in demand are a potential source of both recession and inflation. Policies that effectively stabilize aggregate demand—that minimize abrupt changes in demand—will substantially reduce economic instability.

Diminished Popularity of the *AE* Model

As we have stressed, both Keynesian economics and the *AE* model were an outgrowth of the Great Depression. Keynesian analysis provides an explanation for what happened during the 1930s. However, other explanations are also possible. Many economists believe misguided economic policies, particularly monetary policy, contributed to the depth and duration of the Great Depression. According to this view, markets were unable to restore full employment within a reasonable length of time during the 1930s because policies were adopted that not only inadvertently hampered recovery, but actually depressed economic conditions. This monetary view of the business cycle will be presented in Chapters 14 and 15.

In recent years, the popularity of the Keynesian aggregate expenditure model has diminished. There are two major reasons for this. First, the *AE* model is unable to explain the simultaneous occurrence of inflation and high unemployment. In the *AE* model, aggregate expenditures are either too low (resulting in recession) or too high (leading to inflation). Because the model fails to incorporate expectations, it is unable to explain the simultaneous presence of both high unemployment and inflation, such as occurred during the 1970s.

The second factor contributing to the decline of the aggregate expenditure model is the stability of recent years. The *AE* model was designed to explain lengthy recessions— equilibrium at less than full employment—and the fragile nature of business stability. This played well in the aftermath of the Great Depression. But it is less relevant today. During the past 50 years, there have been fewer recessions and those that have occurred have been relatively short. Just as the classical model appeared to have little relevance to the 1930s, a model stressing the recession-prone nature of a market economy seems out of place today. Of course, this may change—it is way too early to pronounce the death of the business cycle. As long as the current stability continues, however, there is likely to be more emphasis on long-run growth and less on economic fluctuations.

The Hybrid Nature of Modern Macroeconomics

Modern macroeconomics is a hybrid, reflecting elements of both classical and Keynesian analysis as well as some unique insights drawn from other areas of economics. As we discussed in the previous chapter, various shocks (unanticipated changes in *AD* or *AS*) can disrupt full employment equilibrium and lead either to recessionary unemployment or to an inflationary boom in the short run. Furthermore, macroeconomic markets do not adjust instantaneously. In the short run, incorrect perceptions of the current price level and "sticky" wages and prices may lead to output levels that differ from long-run equilibrium. This is reflective of the Keynesian view.

However, modern analysis also indicates that changes in real wages and interest rates will act as a stabilizing force, directing a market economy toward full employment. When an economy is operating below its potential during a recession, falling real wages and interest rates will help restore full employment. Similarly, rising real wages and interest rates will tend to retard an economic boom. These long-run implications of modern analysis are reflective of the classical view.

Economic conditions during the past several decades are consistent with the modern view. We continue to experience economic ups and downs that are short-run disequilibrium conditions resulting from various shocks. But economic downturns do not spiral downward and result in prolonged periods of stagnation. The self-corrective characteristics of a market economy are more potent than was previously thought.

In addition, modern macroeconomics indicates that the impact of economic change is more complex than either the earlier classical or Keynesian economists realized. When analyzing the impact of a change, it makes a difference whether the change is anticipated or unanticipated. It is also important whether people expect the change to be temporary or permanent. Today, both Keynesians and non-Keynesians integrate these factors into their analysis.

Several key elements of modern macroeconomics are more easily visualized within the framework of the multimarket *AD/AS* model we developed in Chapters 9 and 10. The *AD/AS* model also makes it easier to understand and distinguish between long-run and short-run conditions. In essence, the classical model is a long-run equilibrium model, while the Keynesian aggregate expenditure model is a short-run excess-capacity model. The *AD/AS* model incorporates and highlights the importance of both the short and long runs. The *AD/AS* model is more flexible, and it can be used to address a broader range of topics than either the classical or Keynesian models. As a result, it will be our primary tool as we seek to develop more depth in our understanding of macroeconomic issues.

LOOKING AHEAD

In the Keynesian model, full employment is dependent upon the maintenance of aggregate demand at the proper level. While Keynesian analysis provided an explanation for the prolonged unemployment of the Great Depression, it also highlighted the potential of fiscal (tax and expenditure) policy as a means to achieve full employment. The following chapter will analyze the workings of fiscal policy and consider its potential as a stabilization tool.

KEY POINTS

▼ Classical economists believed production created an equivalent amount of current demand (Say's Law) and that flexible wages, prices, and interest rates would assure full employment. The Great Depression undermined the credibility of the classical view.

▼ The concept of planned aggregate expenditures is central to the Keynesian analysis. In the Keynesian model, as income expands, consumption increases, but by a lesser amount than the expansion in income. Both planned investment and government expenditures are independent of income in the Keynesian model. Planned net exports decline as income increases.

▼ The Keynesian model postulates that business firms will produce the amount of goods and services they believe consumers, investors, governments, and foreigners (net exports) plan to buy. Thus, equilibrium is present when planned total expenditures are equal to output.

▼ When total expenditures are less than current output, business firms will accumulate unplanned additions to inventories that will cause them to cut back on future output and employment. On the other hand, when total expenditures are greater than output, inventories will fall and businesses will respond with an expansion in output in an effort to restore inventories to their normal levels. Aggregate expenditures must equal current output (AE = GDP) for equilibrium to occur.

▼ Keynesian equilibrium need not occur at the full employment level of output.

▼ Changes in aggregate expenditures are the catalyst of the Keynesian model. When an economy is operating below full employment capacity, increases in aggregate expenditures lead to an expansion in both output and employment. Once capacity is reached, further expansions in expenditures lead only to

higher prices. The Keynesian model highlights the importance of maintaining demand at a level consistent with full employment equilibrium.

▼ The expenditure multiplier indicates that independent changes in planned investment, government expenditures, and consumption will cause income (and output) to increase by some multiple of the initial increase in spending. The multiplier is the number by which the initial change in spending is multiplied to obtain the total amplified increase in income. The size of the multiplier increases with the marginal propensity to consume.

▼ In evaluating the importance of the multiplier, one should remember that (a) taxes and spending on imports will dampen the size of the multiplier; (b) it takes time for the multiplier to work; and (c) the amplified effect on real output will be valid only when the additional spending brings idle resources into production without price changes.

▼ According to the Keynesian view of the business cycle, upswings and downswings tend to feed on themselves. During a downturn, business pessimism, declining investment, and the multiplier principle combine to plunge the economy deeper into recession. During an economic upswing, business and consumer optimism and expanding investment interact with the multiplier principle to propel the economy to an inflationary boom. The theory suggests that a market-directed economy, left to its own devices, will tend to fluctuate between economic recession and inflationary boom.

▼ While modern macro analysis incorporates elements of both Keynesian and classical economics, it also highlights the role of expectations and the importance of distinguishing between market adjustments in the long and short runs.

CRITICAL ANALYSIS QUESTIONS

1. What determines the equilibrium rate of output in the Keynesian model? Explain why an equilibrium level of output will continue to persist. What did Keynes think had happened during the prolonged, high level of unemployment of the Great Depression?

*2. How will each of the following factors influence the consumption schedule?
   a. The expectation that consumer prices will rise more rapidly in the future
   b. Pessimism about future employment conditions

c. A reduction in income taxes

d. An increase in the interest rate

e. A decline in stock prices

f. A redistribution of income from older workers (age 45 and over) to younger workers (under 35)

g. A redistribution of income from the wealthy to the poor

3. What is the major reason for fluctuations in output within the framework of the Keynesian model? What is necessary for maintenance of full employment?

*4. What is the multiplier principle? What determines the size of the multiplier? Does the multiplier principle make it more or less difficult to stabilize the economy? Explain.

5. In the Keynesian *AE* model, why does an increase in aggregate spending lead to an equal increase in real GDP as long as output is at less than full employment capacity? What does this imply about the shape of the aggregate supply curve?

6. The Great Depression undermined the credibility of the classical view. Correspondingly, the high rates of inflation and unemployment during the 1970s undermined the Keynesian view. Can you explain why both of these phenomena were true?

*7. What role do declining real wages and resource prices play in the restoration of full employment in the Keynesian model? If output is currently below the full employment rate, what will direct the economy to full employment in the Keynesian model?

8. Suppose that individuals suddenly decided to spend less on consumption and save more of their current income. Compare and contrast this change within the framework of the Keynesian *AE* and the *AD/AS* models.

9. Would an increase in federal spending on the space program generate a multiplier effect on the U.S. economy? What impact would the additional spending have in Houston, Huntsville, Florida's Space Coast, and similar areas with a heavy concentration of space facilities? What impact would higher taxes to finance the additional spending have in other areas of the country?

10. How would an increase in income abroad influence the equilibrium level of output at home within the framework of the Keynesian *AE* model? Would the results differ within the framework of the *AD/AS* model? Explain.

11. Economists often state that the Keynesian *AE* model has its greatest relevance in the short run, while the classical model is most relevant to the long run. In what sense is this true?

*12. In recent years, approximately 35 percent of the income of Canadians has been spent on imports. In the United States, spending on imports constitutes about 12 percent of income. Would you expect the size of the multiplier to be larger or smaller in Canada than in the United States? Explain.

13. Who is helped and who is hurt when local and regional governments raise taxes in order to finance stadiums for major league sports teams? How do these subsidies influence the income of team owners and professional athletes? What impact do they have on income inequality? Indicate why you either support or oppose the subsidies.

14. The recently constructed stadium of the San Francisco Giants was financed privately. Will the multiplier effects of privately funded projects differ from those financed through taxes and government subsidies? Why or why not?

15. The rate of output and planned expenditures for an economy are indicated in the accompanying table.

Total Output (Real GDP in Billions)	Planned Aggregate Expenditures (in Billions)
$5,000	$5,250
5,500	5,500
6,000	5,750
6,500	6,000
7,000	6,250

a. If the current output rate is $5.0 trillion, what will tend to happen to business inventories, future output, and employment?

b. If the current output rate is $6.5 trillion, what will tend to happen to inventories, future output, and employment?

c. What is the equilibrium rate of income of this economy?

d. If the economy's full employment rate of output is $6.0 trillion, will the rate of unemployment be high, low, or normal, assuming the current planned demand persisted into the future?

e. What would happen if there was an autonomous increase in investment of $250 billion?

---

*Asterisk denotes questions for which answers are given in Appendix B.

CHAPTER 12

Fiscal Policy

Chapter Focus

■ How does fiscal policy affect aggregate demand? How does it affect aggregate supply?

■ What is the Keynesian view of fiscal policy? How do the crowding-out and new classical models modify the basic Keynesian analysis?

■ How difficult is it to time fiscal policy properly? Why is proper timing important?

■ Is there a synthesis view of fiscal policy? What are its major elements?

■ Are there supply-side effects of fiscal policy?

In the early stages of the Keynesian revolution, macroeconomists emphasized fiscal policy as the most powerful and balanced remedy for demand management. Gradually, shortcomings of fiscal policy became apparent. The shortcomings stem from timing, politics, macroeconomic theory, and the deficit itself.[1]

—Paul Samuelson, Nobel Laureate

[1]Paul A. Samuelson and William D. Nordhaus, *Economics*, 15th ed. (New York: McGraw-Hill, 1995), p. 644.

As we indicated in Chapter 9, fiscal policy involves the use of the government's spending and taxing authority. Until now, we have assumed that the government's fiscal policy remained unchanged. We are now ready to relax this assumption and investigate the impact of fiscal policy on output, prices, and employment.

There is some disagreement among economists with regard to both how fiscal policy works and its potential to improve the performance of a market economy. In fact, views on this topic have changed in recent decades. This chapter will cover four alternative fiscal policy models—the Keynesian, crowding-out, new classical, and supply-side. We will consider how and why views toward these models have changed in recent decades. The basic *AD/AS* macroeconomic model will be used to illustrate each of the fiscal policy perspectives.

Because we want to isolate the impact of changes in fiscal policy from changes in monetary policy, we will continue to assume that the monetary authorities maintain a constant supply of money. We will begin our analysis of monetary policy in the following chapter. ■

BUDGET DEFICITS AND SURPLUSES

Balanced budget
A situation in which current government revenue from taxes, fees, and other sources is just equal to current government expenditures.

Budget deficit
A situation in which total government spending exceeds total government revenue during a specific time period, usually one year.

Budget surplus
A situation in which total government spending is less than total government revenue during a time period, usually a year.

Fiscal policy is reflected through the government's spending, taxing, and borrowing policies. It is one of the major tools that might be used to help promote the goals of full employment, price stability, and rapid economic growth. When the supply of money is constant, government expenditures must be financed with either: (1) taxes and other revenues derived from the sale of services or assets or (2) borrowing. When government revenues from taxes and sales are equal to government expenditures (including both purchases of goods and services and transfer payments), the government has a **balanced budget**. The budget need not be in balance, however. A **budget deficit** is present when total government spending exceeds total government revenue from all sources. When a budget deficit is present, the government must borrow funds to finance the excess of its spending relative to revenue. It borrows by issuing interest-bearing bonds that become part of what we call the national debt, the total amount of outstanding government bonds. Conversely, a **budget surplus** is present when the government's revenues exceed its total expenditures. The surplus allows the government to reduce its outstanding debt.

The federal budget is much more than a mere revenue and expenditure statement of a large organization. Of course, its sheer size means that it exerts a substantial influence on the economy. Its importance, though, stems from its position as a policy variable. The federal budget is the primary tool of fiscal policy. In contrast with private organizations that are directed by the pursuit of income and profit, the federal government can alter its budget with an eye toward influencing the future direction of the economy.

Changes in the size of the federal deficit or surplus are often used to gauge whether fiscal policy is adding additional demand stimulus or imposing additional demand restraint. It is important to note, however, that changes in the size of the deficit or surplus may arise from two different sources. *First, changes in the size of the deficit or surplus may merely reflect the state of the economy.* During a recession, tax revenues generally fall and expenditures on transfer programs increase as the result of the weak economic conditions. This will shift the budget toward a deficit even if there is no change in fiscal policy. Just the opposite will happen during the expansion phase of the business cycle. Tax revenue will increase and transfer payments decline as the result of the rapid growth of income. This will shift the budget toward a surplus (or smaller deficit) during a strong economic expansion. *Second, changes in the deficit or surplus may reflect* **discretionary fiscal policy.** Policymakers may institute deliberate changes in tax laws or spending on government programs in order to alter the size of the budget deficit (or surplus). When we speak of "changes in fiscal policy," we are referring to changes of this type—deliberate

Discretionary fiscal policy
A change in laws or appropriation levels that alters government revenues and/or expenditures.

changes in government expenditures or tax policy or both that are designed to affect the size of the budget deficit or surplus.

KEYNESIAN VIEW OF FISCAL POLICY

Prior to the 1960s, the desirability of a balanced federal budget was widely accepted among business and political leaders. Keynesian economists, though, were highly critical of this view. Keynesians argued that the federal budget should be used to promote a level of aggregate demand consistent with the full employment rate of output.

How might policy makers use the budget to stimulate aggregate demand? First, an increase in government purchases of goods and services will directly increase aggregate demand. As the government spends more on highways, flood control projects, education, and national defense, for example, these expenditures will increase demand in the goods and services market. Second, changes in tax policy will also influence aggregate demand. For example, a reduction in personal taxes will increase the current disposable income of households. As their after-tax income rises, individuals will spend more on consumption. In turn, this increase in consumption will stimulate aggregate demand. Similarly, a reduction in business taxes increases after-tax profitability, which will stimulate both business investment and aggregate demand.

When an economy is operating below its potential capacity, the Keynesian model suggests that government should institute **expansionary fiscal policy**. In other words, the government should either increase its purchases of goods and services or cut taxes or both. Of course, this policy will increase the government's budget deficit. In order to finance the enlarged budget deficit, the government will have to borrow from either private domestic sources or foreigners.[2]

Exhibit 1 illustrates the case for expansionary fiscal policy when an economy is experiencing abnormally high unemployment caused by deficient aggregate demand. Initially, the economy is operating at e_1. Output is below potential capacity, Y_F, and unemployment exceeds its natural rate. As we discussed in Chapter 10, if there is no change in policy, abnormally high unemployment and excess supply in the resource market would eventually reduce real wages and other resource prices. The accompanying lower costs would increase aggregate supply (shift to $SRAS_3$) and guide the economy to a full employment equilibrium (E_3) at a lower price level (P_3). In addition, lower real interest rates resulting from weak business demand for investment funds may help stimulate aggregate demand and restore full employment.

As we noted in the previous chapter, Keynesians believe that wages and prices are inflexible—particularly in a downward direction. Thus, they have little confidence in the ability of lower wages and falling interest rates to restore full employment in the midst of a recession. Keynesians recommend government action—a shift to a more expansionary fiscal policy in order to speed up the movement toward full employment equilibrium. Keynesians advocate more government spending or a reduction in taxes or both—that is, a deliberate increase in the budget deficit—as a means of stimulating aggregate demand. Furthermore, they argue that the multiplier process will magnify the initial increase in spending. Suppose that the government holds taxes constant and increases its spending on highways and school construction by $20 billion. The additional spending will enhance the incomes of those undertaking the construction by $20 billion. As these individuals use a portion of this income to buy consumer goods, this will provide additional demand stimulus. Thus, Keynesians expect that the total

Expansionary fiscal policy
An increase in government expenditures and/or a reduction in tax rates such that the expected size of the budget deficit expands.

---

[2]Alternatively, the government could borrow from its central bank—the Federal Reserve Bank in the United States. However, as we will see in the following chapter, this method of financing a budget deficit would expand the money supply. Since we want to differentiate between fiscal and monetary effects, we must hold the supply of money constant. So for now, we assume that the government deficit must be financed by borrowing from private sources.

EXHIBIT 1
Expansionary Fiscal Policy to Promote Full Employment

Here we illustrate an economy operating in the short run at Y_1, below its potential capacity of Y_F. There are two routes to a long-run full employment equilibrium. First, policy makers could wait for lower wages and resource prices to reduce costs, increase supply to $SRAS_3$, and restore equilibrium at E_3. Keynesians believe this market-adjustment method will be slow and uncertain. Alternatively, expansionary fiscal policy could stimulate aggregate demand (shift to AD_2) and guide the economy to E_2.

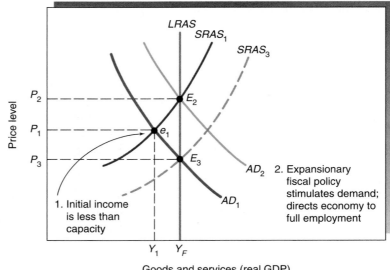

1. Initial income is less than capacity

2. Expansionary fiscal policy stimulates demand; directs economy to full employment

Goods and services (real GDP)

Restrictive fiscal policy
A reduction in government expenditures and/or an increase in tax rates such that the expected size of the budget deficit declines (or the budget surplus increases).

Countercyclical policy
A policy that tends to move the economy in an opposite direction from the forces of the business cycle. Such a policy would stimulate demand during the contraction phase of the business cycle and restrain demand during the expansion phase.

increase in aggregate demand will be substantially greater than the initial $20 billion increase in government purchases.

When an economy is operating below its potential capacity, the Keynesian prescription calls for expansionary fiscal policy—a deliberate change in expenditures and/or taxes that will increase the size of the government's budget deficit. An appropriate dose of expansionary fiscal policy, if timed properly, would stimulate aggregate demand (shift the curve to AD_2 in Exhibit 1) and guide the economy to full employment equilibrium (E_2).

The Keynesian view also provides a fiscal policy remedy for inflation. Suppose that an economy is experiencing an inflationary economic boom as the result of excessive aggregate demand. As **Exhibit 2** illustrates, in the absence of a change in policy, the strong demand (AD_1) would push up wages and other resource prices. In time, the higher resource prices would increase costs, reduce aggregate supply (from $SRAS_1$ to $SRAS_3$), and lead to a higher price level (P_3). The basic Keynesian model, however, indicates that **restrictive fiscal policy** could be used to reduce aggregate demand (shift to AD_2) and guide the economy to a noninflationary equilibrium (E_2). A reduced level of government purchases would diminish aggregate demand directly. Alternatively, higher taxes on households and businesses could be used to dampen consumption and private investment. The restrictive fiscal policy—a spending reduction and/or an increase in taxes—would shift the government budget toward a surplus (or smaller deficit). *The Keynesian analysis suggests that a shift toward a more restrictive fiscal policy is the proper prescription with which to combat inflation generated by excessive aggregate demand.*

The Keynesian revolution challenged the view that a responsible government should constrain spending within the bounds of its revenues. Rather than balancing the budget annually, the Keynesian view stressed the importance of countercyclical policy, *that is, policy designed to "counter" or offset fluctuations in aggregate demand.* When an economy is threatened by a recession, the government should shift to a more expansionary fiscal policy, increasing spending or reducing taxes in a manner that will increase the size of the budget deficit. On the other hand, fiscal policy should become more restrictive—the budget should be shifted toward a smaller deficit or larger surplus—in response to a threat of inflation. According to the Keynesian view, fluctuations in aggregate demand are the major source of economic disturbances. Moreover, wise use

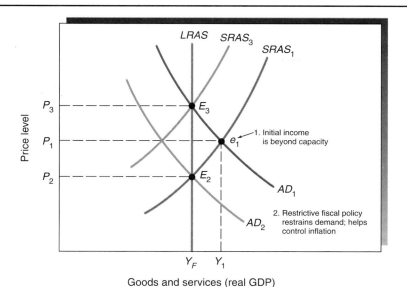

EXHIBIT 2
Restrictive Fiscal Policy to Combat Inflation

Strong demand such as AD_1 will temporarily lead to an output rate beyond the economy's long-run potential (Y_F). If maintained, the high level of demand will lead to long-run equilibrium (E_3) at a higher price level. However, restrictive fiscal policy could restrain demand to AD_2 (or better still, prevent demand from expanding to AD_1 in the first place) and thereby guide the economy to a noninflationary equilibrium (E_2).

OUTSTANDING ECONOMIST

Paul Samuelson (1915–)

The first American to win the Nobel Prize in Economics, Paul Samuelson played a central role in the development and acceptance of Keynesian economics in the 1950s and 1960s. Through the years, his views regarding the effectiveness of fiscal policy have gradually changed (see chapter opening quote). A professor of economics at MIT for more than four decades, Samuelson's *Collected Scientific Papers* encompass five lengthy volumes.[1]

[1]Paul Samuelson, *Collected Papers of Paul Samuelson* (Cambridge: MIT Press, 1966).

of fiscal policy can help stabilize and maintain demand at or near the full employment rate of output.

FISCAL POLICY AND THE CROWDING-OUT EFFECT

By the early 1960s, the Keynesian view was widely accepted both by economists and by policy makers. At that time, it was generally believed that changes in the size of the budget deficit exerted a powerful impact on aggregate demand and output. More recently, however, economists have noted that there are secondary effects that tend to weaken the potency of fiscal policy.

When the government borrows funds to finance an enlarged deficit, typically it will do so by issuing additional bonds. As we previously discussed, issuing bonds is simply a means of demanding loanable funds. The total demand for loanable funds will increase as government borrowing competes with private borrowing for the available supply of funds. Thus, the additional government borrowing to finance a larger deficit will increase the demand for loanable funds and thereby place upward pressure on the real interest rate.

What impact will a higher real interest rate have on private spending? Consumers will reduce their purchases of interest-sensitive goods, such as automobiles and consumer durables. More important, a higher interest rate will increase the opportunity cost of investment projects. Businesses will postpone spending on plant expansions, heavy equipment, and capital improvements. Residential housing construction and sales will also be hurt. Thus, the higher real interest rates caused by the larger deficit will retard private spending. Economists refer to this squeezing out of private spending by a deficit-induced increase in the real interest rate as the **crowding-out effect**.

Crowding-out effect
A reduction in private spending as a result of higher interest rates generated by budget deficits that are financed by borrowing in the private loanable funds market.

The crowding-out effect suggests that budget deficits will exert less impact on aggregate demand than the basic Keynesian model implies. Because financing the deficit pushes up interest rates, budget deficits will tend to retard private spending, particularly spending on investment. This reduction in private spending as the result of higher interest rates will at least partially offset additional spending emanating from the deficit. Thus, the crowding-out effect implies that expansionary fiscal policy will exert little, if any, impact on demand, output, and employment.

Furthermore, the crowding-out effect indicates that the budget deficit will change the composition of aggregate demand. As the higher interest rates accompanying the deficits crowd out private investment, the output of capital goods will decline. As a result, the future stock of capital (for example, heavy equipment, other machines, and buildings) will be smaller than would otherwise have been the case. To the extent that budget deficits crowd out private investment, they will reduce the supply of capital available to future workers and thereby reduce their productivity and income.

Many Keynesians argue that, while crowding-out may occur when an economy is at or near full employment, it is unlikely to be very important during a recession, particularly a serious one. When widespread unemployment is present during a serious recession, an increase in government purchases may well exert a substantial multiplier effect on output, employment, and real income. If the incomes of households increase, they will save more, which will permit the government to finance its enlarged deficit without much upward pressure on interest rates. In addition, when applied during a recession, the demand stimulus may improve business profit expectations and thereby stimulate additional private investment.

The implications of the crowding-out analysis are symmetrical. Restrictive fiscal policy will "crowd in" private spending. If the government increases taxes and/or reduces its spending, the budget will shift toward a surplus (or smaller deficit). As a result, the government's demand for loanable funds will decrease, placing downward pressure on the real interest rate. The lower real interest rate will stimulate additional private investment and consumption. So the fiscal policy restraint will be at least partially offset by an expansion in private spending. *As the result of this crowding in, restrictive fiscal policy may not be very effective as a weapon against inflation.*

The Crowding-Out Effect in a World of Global Financial Markets

Today, financial capital can rapidly move into and out of countries. How does the global nature of financial markets influence the crowding-out effect? Suppose that the budget deficit of the United States increased and that the additional borrowing of the Treasury pushed real interest rates upward just as the crowding-out theory implies. Think how investors will respond to this situation. The higher real interest yields on bonds and other financial assets will attract funds from abroad. In turn, this inflow of financial capital will increase the supply of loanable funds and thereby moderate the rise in real interest rates in the United States.[3]

---

[3]For students who are unsure about the demand for and supply of loanable funds, this would be a good time to review the topic within the framework of our basic macro model outlined by Exhibit 1 in Chapter 9. As this exhibit indicates, household saving and the inflow of financial capital from abroad supply loanable funds. In turn, private investment and borrowing by the government to finance budget deficits generate the demand for these funds.

At first glance, the crowding-out effect would appear to be weakened because the inflow of funds will moderate the upward pressure on domestic interest rates. Closer inspection, though, reveals this will not be the case. Foreigners cannot buy more U.S. bonds and financial assets without "buying" more dollars. Thus, additional bond purchases will increase the demand for U.S. dollars (and supply of foreign currencies) in the foreign exchange market—the market that coordinates exchanges of the various national currencies. As foreigners demand more dollars in order to increase their financial investments in the United States, their actions will cause an appreciation in the foreign exchange value of the dollar. The appreciation of the dollar will make imports cheaper for Americans. Simultaneously, it will make U.S. exports more expensive for foreigners. Predictably, the United States will import more and export less. Thus, net exports will decline (or net imports increase), causing a reduction in aggregate demand. Therefore, while the inflow of capital from abroad will moderate the increase in the interest rate and the crowding out of private domestic investment, it will also reduce net exports and thereby retard aggregate demand.

Exhibit 3 summarizes the crowding-out view of budget deficits in an open economy. The additional government borrowing triggered by the budget deficits will cause interest rates to rise and this will lead to two secondary effects that will dampen the stimulus impact of the deficits. First, the higher interest rates will reduce private investment, which will directly restrain aggregate demand. Second, the higher interest returns will also attract an inflow of foreign capital. While the capital inflow will moderate both the rise in real interest rates and the reduction in domestic private investment, it will also cause the dollar to appreciate in the foreign exchange market. In turn, the appreciation of the dollar will reduce both net exports and aggregate demand. *According to the crowding-out theory, these two factors will largely, if not entirely, offset the stimulus effects of a larger budget deficit.*

NEW CLASSICAL VIEW OF FISCAL POLICY

Some economists stress still another possible offsetting secondary effect that may weaken the impact of budget deficits on aggregate demand. Rather than spending more, households may save more so they will be better able to pay the higher future taxes implied by

EXHIBIT 3
Visual Presentation of the Crowding-Out Effect in an Open Economy

An increase in government borrowing to finance an enlarged budget deficit will place upward pressure on real interest rates. This will retard private investment and thereby aggregate demand. In an open economy, the higher interest rates will also increase the inflow of capital from abroad, which will cause the dollar to appreciate and net exports to decline. Thus, the higher interest rates will trigger reductions in both private investment and net exports, which will weaken the expansionary impact of a budget deficit.

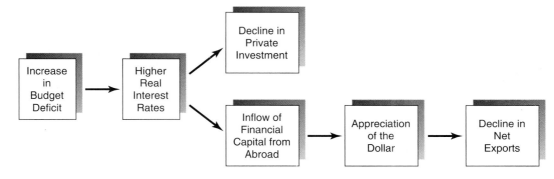

New classical economists
Economists who believe there are strong forces pushing a market economy toward full employment equilibrium and that macroeconomic policy is an ineffective tool with which to reduce economic instability.

Ricardian equivalence
The view that a tax reduction financed with government debt will exert no impact on current consumption and aggregate demand because people will fully recognize the higher future taxes implied by the additional debt.

the larger outstanding debt. Until now, we have implicitly assumed that the current saving decisions of taxpayers are unaffected by the higher future taxes implied by budget deficits. Some economists argue that this is an unrealistic view. Robert Lucas (University of Chicago), the 1995 Nobel laureate, Thomas Sargent (University of Minnesota), and Robert Barro (Harvard University) have been leaders among a group of economists arguing that taxpayers will reduce their current consumption and increase their saving in anticipation of the higher future taxes implied by the debt financing. Because this position has its foundation in classical economics, these economists and their followers are referred to as **new classical economists**.

In the basic Keynesian model, a reduction in current taxes financed by borrowing increases the current disposable income of households. Given their additional disposable income, households increase their current consumption. New classical economists argue that this analysis is incorrect because it ignores the impact of the higher future tax liability implied by the budget deficit and the interest payments required to service the additional debt. *New classical economists stress that debt financing simply substitutes higher future taxes for lower current taxes. Thus, budget deficits affect the timing of the taxes, but not their magnitude.*

A mere change in the timing of taxes will not alter the wealth of households. Therefore, there is no reason to believe that current consumption will change when current taxes are cut and government debt and future taxes are increased by an equivalent amount. According to the new classical view, households will reduce their current consumption in response to additional government debt (and the higher taxes that the debt implies) just as surely as if the equivalent amount of current taxes had been levied. In essence, households will simply save the reduction in their current taxes so they will have the funds with which to pay the higher future taxes implied by the additional government debt. In turn, the increase in saving will allow the government to finance its deficit without an increase in the interest rate. Thus, the substitution of debt for taxes will leave private consumption, aggregate demand, and real interest rates unchanged. This view that taxes and debt financing are essentially equivalent is known as **Ricardian equivalence**, after the nineteenth-century economist, David Ricardo, who initially developed the idea.

Perhaps an illustration will help explain the underlying logic of the new classical view. Consider the following alternative methods of paying a $2,000 tax liability: (1) a one-time payment of $2,000 or (2) payments of $200 each year in the future. When the interest rate is 10 percent, the opportunity cost of a $200 liability each year is $2,000. Therefore, just as the first option reduces current wealth by $2,000, so, too, does the second.

Now let us consider the impact of the two options on future income. If you dip into your savings to make a one-time $2,000 payment, your future interest income will be reduced by $200 each year in the future (assuming a 10 percent interest rate). Just as the second option reduces your future net income by $200 each year, so, too, does the first. In both cases, current wealth is reduced by $2,000. Similarly, in both cases the flow of future net income is reduced by $200 each year. Because of this, the new classical economists believe the two options are essentially the same.

Exhibit 4 illustrates the implications of the new classical view as to the potency of fiscal policy. Suppose the fiscal authorities issue $50 billion of additional debt in order to cut taxes by an equal amount. The government borrowing increases the demand for loanable funds (D_1 shifts to D_2 in part b of Exhibit 4) by $50 billion. If the taxpayers did not recognize the higher future taxes implied by the debt, they would expand consumption in response to the lower taxes and the increase in their current disposable income. Under such circumstances, aggregate demand in the goods and services market would expand to AD_2 (part a). In the new classical model, though, this will not be the case. Recognizing the higher future taxes, taxpayers will maintain their initial level of consumption spending and use the tax cut to increase their savings in order to generate the additional income required to pay the future taxes implied by the $50 billion of addi-

EXHIBIT 4
New Classical View—Higher Expected Future Taxes Crowd Out Private Spending

New classical economists emphasize that budget deficits merely substitute future taxes for current taxes. If households did not anticipate the higher future taxes, aggregate demand would increase to AD_2. However, demand remains unchanged at AD_1 when households fully anticipate the future increase in taxes (a). Simultaneously, the additional saving to meet the higher future taxes will increase the supply of loanable funds to S_2 and permit the government to borrow the funds to finance its deficit without pushing up the real interest rate (b). In this model, fiscal policy exerts no effect. The real interest rate, real GDP, and level of employment all remain unchanged.

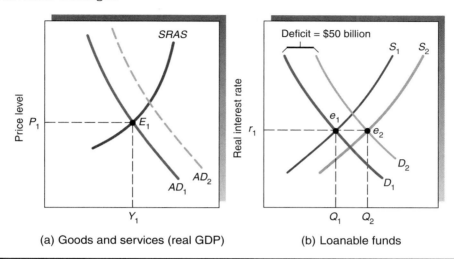

(a) Goods and services (real GDP)   (b) Loanable funds

tional debt. Because consumption is unchanged, aggregate demand also remains constant (at AD_1). At the same time, the additional saving (to pay the implied increase in future taxes) allows the government to finance its deficit without an increase in the real interest rate. In this polar case, fiscal policy exerts no demand stimulus. In fact, it does not change much of anything. Output, employment, the price level, and even the real interest rate all remain constant.

The new classical view might be summarized as follows: The substitution of government debt for current taxes will fail to alter either the wealth or permanent income of the taxpaying households. Households will continue to maintain the same level of consumption even if the government cuts taxes and increases its outstanding debt. Thus, budget deficits will not stimulate aggregate demand. Neither will they affect output and employment. Similarly, the real interest rate is unaffected by deficits since people will save more in order to pay the higher future taxes. According to the new classical view, fiscal policy is completely impotent.

This new classical theory of fiscal policy is controversial.[4] Critics argue that it is unrealistic to expect that taxpayers will anticipate all or even most of the future taxes implied by additional government debt. In addition, even if people did anticipate the higher future taxes, in our world of limited life spans, many would recognize that they will not be around to pay, at least not in full, the future tax liability implied by debt financing. Many economists reject the new classical view of fiscal policy, at least in its pure form. Nonetheless, the significance of the new classical theory and its implications

---

[4]See Robert J. Barro, "The Ricardian Approach to Budget Deficits," *Journal of Economic Perspectives* (spring 1989): pp. 37–44; and John J. Seater, "Ricardian Equivalence," *Journal of Economic Literature* (March 1993): pp. 142–190.

with regard to fiscal policy continue to provide one of the lively topics of debate in modern macroeconomics.

FISCAL POLICY: PROBLEMS OF PROPER TIMING

If fiscal policy is going to reduce economic instability, changes in policy must inject stimulus during a recession and restraint during an inflationary boom. But proper timing of fiscal policy is not an easy task. Because forecasting a forthcoming recession or boom is a highly imperfect science, there is usually a time lag between when a change in policy is needed and when its need is widely recognized by policymakers.

In addition, there is generally a lag between the time when the need for a fiscal policy change is recognized and the time when it is actually instituted. Discretionary fiscal policy requires changes in tax laws and government expenditure programs. The time required for such changes is likely to be quite lengthy. This will be particularly true for a political structure like that of the United States, with a number of checks and balances built into the system.[5] Congressional committees must meet, hear testimony, and draft legislation. Key legislators may choose to delay action if they can use their positions to obtain special favors for their constituencies. A majority of the lawmakers must be convinced that a proposed action is in the interest of the country, and the details of the policy must be arranged such that they will also believe that their own districts and supporters will not be disadvantaged. All these things take time.

An excellent example of the delays involved in conducting discretionary fiscal policy is the 2001 tax cut. The legislation to implement the tax decrease moved slowly through Congress in 2001 due to a debate about who would get their taxes cut. In particular, the argument centered on how much of the tax cut would be directed to high-income families relative to low-income families. While policymakers debated, conditions deteriorated and the economy fell into a recession.

Finally, still another factor adds to the complexity of fiscal policy making: Even after a policy is adopted, it may be six to twelve months before its major impact is felt. If government expenditures are going to be increased, time will be required for competitive bids to be submitted and new contracts granted. Contractors may be unable to begin work right away. Although a tax reduction will generally exert demand stimulus more quickly, it will take time for these effects to work their way through the economy.

Macroeconomic policymaking is a little bit like lobbing a ball at a moving target that sometimes changes directions unpredictably. In order to institute fiscal policy in a manner that will help stabilize the economy, policymakers need to know what economic conditions are going to be six, twelve, or eighteen months in the future. Unfortunately, our ability to forecast future economic conditions is limited. Therefore, in a world characterized by dynamic change and unpredictable events, some policy errors are inevitable.

Exhibit 5 illustrates the implications of the difficulties involved in the proper timing of fiscal policy. Suppose that policymakers attempt to use expansionary fiscal policy to stimulate aggregate demand during an economic downturn. If inability to forecast a recession and delays accompanying the adoption of a policy change take a substantial period, the economy's self-corrective mechanism may already have restored full employment by the time the fiscal stimulus begins to exert its primary impact. If so, the fiscal stimulus may well create excessive demand that will soon lead to inflation. Similarly, restrictive fiscal policy to cool an overheated economy may cause a recession if aggregate demand declines prior to the fiscal restraint.

In the real world, a discretionary change in fiscal policy is like a two-edged sword— it has the potential to do harm as well as good. If timed correctly, it will reduce economic instability. If timed incorrectly, however, the fiscal change will increase rather than reduce economic instability.

---

[5]The time required for the institution of a change in fiscal policy may be shorter under a parliamentary political system, such as that of Canada or the United Kingdom. This is highly likely to be the case if a single party has a parliamentary majority.

EXHIBIT 5
Why Proper Timing of Fiscal Policy Is Difficult

Here we consider an economy that experiences shifts in AD that are not easy to forecast. Initially, the economy is in long-run equilibrium (E_0) at price level P_0 and at output Y_0. At this output, only the natural rate of unemployment is present. However, an investment slump and business pessimism result in an unanticipated decline in aggregate demand (to AD_1). Output falls and unemployment increases. After a time, policymakers institute expansionary fiscal policy seeking to shift aggregate demand back to AD_0. By the time fiscal policy begins to exert its primary effect, though, private investment has recovered and decision makers have become increasingly optimistic about the future. So aggregate demand is already, on its own accord, shifting back to AD_0. Thus, the expansionary fiscal policy overshifts aggregate demand to AD_2 rather than AD_0. Prices rise as the economy is now overheated. Unless the expansionary fiscal policy is reversed, wages and other resource prices will eventually increase, shifting *SRAS* to the left, thus pushing the price level still higher to (P_3). Alternatively, suppose an investment boom disrupts the equilibrium. The increase in investment shifts aggregate demand to AD_2, placing upward pressure on prices. Policymakers respond by increasing taxes and cutting government expenditures. By the time the restrictive fiscal policy exerts its primary impact, though, investment returns to its normal rate. As a result, the restrictive fiscal policy overshifts aggregate demand to AD_1 and throws the economy into a recession. Since fiscal policy does not work instantaneously, and since dynamic factors are constantly influencing private demand, proper timing of fiscal policy is not an easy task.

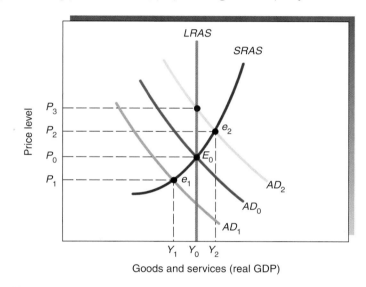

Goods and services (real GDP)

Automatic Stabilizers

Fortunately, there are a few fiscal programs that tend automatically to apply demand stimulus during a recession and demand restraint during an economic boom. Programs of this type are called **automatic stabilizers**. They are automatic in that, without any new legislative action, they tend to increase the budget deficit (or reduce the surplus) during a recession and increase the surplus (or reduce the deficit) during an economic boom.

The major advantage of automatic stabilizers is that they institute countercyclical fiscal policy without the delays associated with policy changes that require legislative action. Thus, they minimize the problem of proper timing. When unemployment is rising and business conditions are slow, these stabilizers automatically reduce taxes and increase government expenditures, giving the economy a shot in the arm. On the other hand, automatic stabilizers help to apply the brakes to an economic boom, increasing tax revenues and decreasing government spending. Three of these built-in stabilizers deserve specific mention: unemployment compensation, corporate profit tax, and progressive income tax.

Automatic stabilizers
Built-in features that tend automatically to promote a budget deficit during a recession and a budget surplus during an inflationary boom, even without a change in policy.

Unemployment Compensation
When an economy begins to dip into a recession, government payments for unemployment benefits will increase as the number of laid-off and unemployed workers expands. Simultaneously, the receipts from the employment tax that finances the system will decline because

employment falls during a recession. Therefore, this program will automatically run a deficit during a business slowdown. In contrast, during an economic boom, the tax receipts from the program will increase because more people are now working, and the amount paid out in benefits will decline since fewer people are unemployed. Thus, the program will automatically tend to run a surplus during good times. So without any change in policy, the unemployment compensation program has the desired countercyclical effect on aggregate demand.[6]

Corporate Profit Tax

Tax studies show that the corporate profit tax is the most countercyclical of all the automatic stabilizers. This results because corporate profits are highly sensitive to cyclical conditions. During a recession, corporate profits decline sharply, and so too do corporate tax payments. In turn, the decline in tax revenues will enlarge the size of the budget deficit. In contrast, when the economy is expanding, corporate profits typically increase much more rapidly than wages, income, or consumption. This increase in corporate profits will result in a rapid increase in the "tax take" from the business sector during the expansion phase of the business cycle. Thus, corporate tax payments will go up during an expansion and fall rapidly during a contraction, even though no new legislative action has been instituted.

Progressive Income Tax

When income grows rapidly, the average personal income tax liability of individuals and families increases. With rising incomes, more people will find their income above the "no tax due" cutoff. Others will be pushed into a higher tax bracket. Therefore, during an economic expansion, revenue from the personal income tax increases more rapidly than income. Other things constant, the budget moves toward a surplus (or smaller deficit), even though the economy's tax rate structure is unchanged. On the other hand, when income declines, many individuals will be taxed at a lower rate or not at all. Income tax revenues will fall more rapidly than income, automatically enlarging the size of the budget deficit during a recession.

FISCAL POLICY AS A STABILIZATION TOOL: A MODERN SYNTHESIS

During the 1960s the basic Keynesian view was widely accepted. Fiscal policy was thought to be highly potent. Furthermore, it was widely believed that political decision makers, with the assistance of their economic advisors, were fully capable of instituting discretionary fiscal policy changes in a manner that would help stabilize the economy. During the 1970s and 1980s, both the operation of fiscal policy and its efficacy as a stabilization tool were analyzed and hotly debated among professional economists. A synthesis view has emerged from that debate. Most macroeconomists—both Keynesian and non-Keynesian—now accept the following three elements of the modern synthesis view.

1. *Proper timing of discretionary fiscal policy is both difficult to achieve and of crucial importance.* Given our limited ability to forecast turns in the business cycle and the political delays that inevitably accompany a change in fiscal policy, the effectiveness of discretionary fiscal policy as a stabilization tool is highly questionable. Therefore, most macroeconomists now place less emphasis on fiscal policy. (*Note:*

---

[6]Although unemployment compensation has the desired countercyclical effect on demand, it also reduces the incentive to accept available employment opportunities. Research in this area indicates that the existing unemployment compensation system increases the length of job search by unemployed workers and thereby increases the long-run natural (normal) unemployment rate.

The chapter opening quotation from Paul Samuelson, a long-time Keynesian, highlights this point.)

2. ***Automatic stabilizers reduce the fluctuation of aggregate demand and help to direct the economy toward full employment.*** Since they are not dependent on legislative action, automatic stabilizers are able consistently to shift the budget toward a deficit during a recession and toward a surplus during an economic boom. Thus, they add needed stimulus during the recession and act as a restraining force during an inflationary boom. Although some question their potency, most all would agree that they exert a stabilizing influence.

3. ***Fiscal policy is much less potent than the early Keynesian view implied.*** The current debate among macroeconomists concerning the impact of fiscal policy during normal times is not whether crowding out takes place, but rather how it takes place. The crowding-out and new classical models highlight this point. Both models indicate that there are side effects of budget deficits that will substantially, if not entirely, offset their impact on aggregate demand. In the crowding-out model, higher real interest rates and a decline in net exports as the result of currency appreciation reduce private demand and offset the expansionary effects of budget deficits. In the new classical model, higher anticipated future taxes lead to the same result. Both models indicate that fiscal policy will exert little, if any, impact on current aggregate demand, employment, and real output during normal economic times.

SUPPLY-SIDE EFFECTS OF FISCAL POLICY

Thus far, we have focused on the potential demand-side effects of fiscal policy. However, when fiscal changes alter tax rates, they influence the incentive of people to work, invest, and use resources efficiently. Thus, tax changes may also influence aggregate supply. Prior to 1980, macroeconomists generally ignored the supply-side effects of changes in tax rates, thinking they were of little importance. **Supply-side economists** challenged this view. The supply-side argument was central to the tax rate reductions of the 1980s and it also played a role in the structure of the tax legislation passed in 2001.

Supply-side economists
Modern economists who believe that changes in marginal tax rates exert important effects on aggregate supply.

From a supply-side viewpoint, the marginal tax rate is of crucial importance. As we discussed in Chapter 4, the marginal tax rate determines the breakdown of one's additional income between tax payments on the one hand and personal income on the other. A reduction in marginal tax rates increases the reward derived from added work, investment, saving, and other activities that become less heavily taxed. People shift into these activities away from leisure (and leisure-intensive activities), tax shelters, consumption of tax-deductible goods, and other forms of tax avoidance. Supply-side economists believe that these substitutions both enlarge the effective resource base and improve the efficiency with which the resources are applied.

The source of the supply-side effects accompanying a change in tax rates is fundamentally different from the source of the demand-side effects. A change in tax policy affects aggregate demand through its impact on disposable income and the flow of expenditures. ***In contrast, changes in tax rates, particularly marginal tax rates, will affect aggregate supply through their impact on the relative attractiveness of productive activity in comparison to leisure and tax avoidance.***

Exhibit 6 graphically depicts the impact of a supply-side tax cut, one that reduces marginal tax rates. The lower marginal tax rates increase aggregate supply as the new incentive structure encourages taxpayers to earn additional income and use resources more efficiently. If the tax change is perceived as long-term, both long- and short-run aggregate supply (*LRAS* and *SRAS*) will increase. Real output and income expand. As real income expands, aggregate demand will also increase (shift to AD_2). If the lower marginal rates are financed by a budget deficit, aggregate demand may increase by a larger amount than aggregate supply, placing upward pressure on the price level.

EXHIBIT 6
Tax Rate Effects and Supply-Side Economics

Here we illustrate the supply-side effects of a reduction in marginal tax rates. The lower marginal tax rates increase the incentive to earn and use resources efficiently. Since these effects are long-run as well as short-run, both *LRAS* and *SRAS* increase (shift to the right). Real output expands. In turn, the higher income levels accompanying the expansion in real output will stimulate aggregate demand (shift to *AD₂*).

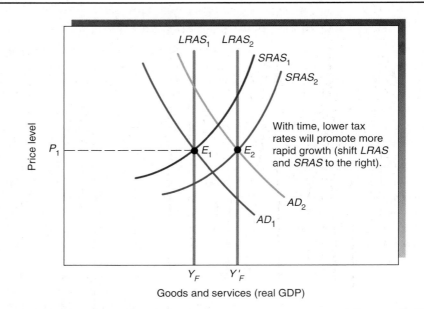

Supply-side economics should not be viewed as a short-run countercyclical tool. It will take time for changing market incentives to move resources out of tax-motivated investments and into higher-yield activities. The full positive effects of lower marginal tax rates will not be observed until labor and capital markets have time to adjust fully to the new incentive structure. ***Clearly, supply-side economics is a long-run, growth-oriented strategy.***

Why High Tax Rates Tend to Retard Output

There are three major reasons why high tax rates are likely to retard the growth of output. First, high marginal tax rates discourage work effort and reduce the productive efficiency of labor. When marginal tax rates soar to 55 percent or 60 percent, individuals get to keep less than half of what they earn—and when the payoff from working declines, people tend to work less. Some (for example, those with a working spouse) will drop out of the labor force. Others will simply work fewer hours. Still others will decide to take more lengthy vacations, forgo overtime opportunities, retire earlier, or forget about pursuing that promising but risky business venture. In some cases, high tax rates will even drive highly productive citizens to other countries where taxes are lower. High tax rates will also result in inefficient utilization of labor. Some individuals will substitute less-productive activities that are not taxed (for example, do-it-yourself projects) for work opportunities yielding taxable income.

Second, high tax rates will adversely affect the rate of capital formation and the efficiency of its use. When tax rates are high, foreign investment will be repelled and domestic investors will search for investment projects abroad where taxes are lower. In addition, domestic investors will direct more of their time and effort into hobby businesses (for example, collecting antiques, raising horses, or giving golf lessons) that provide both enjoyable activities and tax-shelter benefits. This process will divert investment resources away from projects with a higher rate of return but fewer tax-avoidance benefits. As the result of the tax-shelter benefits, individuals will often be able to gain even though the "investments" reduce the value of resources. Scarce capital is wasted and resources are channeled away from their most productive uses.

Third, high marginal tax rates encourage individuals to substitute less-desired tax-deductible goods for more-desired nondeductible goods. Here the inefficiency stems from the fact that individuals do not bear the full cost of tax-deductible purchases. High marginal tax rates make tax-deductible expenditures cheap for persons in high tax brackets. Since the personal cost, but not the cost to society, is cheap, taxpayers confronting high marginal tax rates will spend more money on pleasurable, tax-deductible items, such as plush offices, professional conferences held in favorite vacation spots, and various fringe benefits (for example, a company luxury automobile, business entertainment, and a company retirement plan). Because such tax-deductible purchases reduce their taxes, people will often buy such goods even though they do not value them as much as the cost of producing them.

How Important Are Supply-Side Effects?

There is division among economists with regard to the strength of the supply-side incentive effects. Critics of supply-side economics stress that the rate reductions of the 1980s were associated with a modest growth rate of output, a significant reduction in the real tax revenue of the federal government, and large budget deficits. These outcomes do not indicate that the supply-side effects are highly potent. Defenders of the supply-side position respond by noting that the rate reductions of both the 1960s and the 1980s resulted in impressive growth and lengthy economic expansions. They also stress that the supply-side response in the top brackets—where lower rates have the largest incentive effects—is particularly strong.[7]

It is interesting to view the supply-side perspective within the framework of the Laffer Curve analysis of Chapter 4. The Laffer Curve indicates that the revenues collected from a tax will expand as tax rates are increased. Eventually, however, higher and higher rates will lead to a revenue maximum point and rate increases beyond this level will actually reduce the revenue collected. It is also important to note that tax rates at or near the revenue maximum point are highly inefficient because in that range the high rates are eliminating a substantial amount of beneficial economic activity without raising much additional revenue (see Exhibit 11 in Chapter 4). Tax rates on the backward bending portion of the Laffer Curve involve a double barrel negative impact: productive economic activity is eliminated and the government loses revenue by imposing such high rates.

During the last four decades, there has been a substantial reduction in the personal income tax rates applicable to those with high incomes. As the top marginal rates have fallen, the share of income tax revenue derived from those in the upper brackets has increased. **Exhibit 7** on the next page presents data on the share of the personal income tax derived from the top one-half percent of income recipients since 1960. When the top marginal tax rate was sliced from 91 percent to 70 percent by the Kennedy-Johnson tax cut of 1964, the share of the personal income tax paid by the top half percent rose from 16 percent to 18 percent. In contrast, as inflation pushed more and more taxpayers into higher brackets during the 1970s, the share paid by the top half percent declined. When the tax cuts of the 1980s once again reduced the top rates, the share paid by the top half percent climbed to more than 20 percent of the total. As the top marginal rate was increased in 1991 and again in 1993, there was little change in the share of taxes paid by the top group. Beginning in 1997, the tax rate on income from capital gains was cut from 28 percent to 20 percent. This rate reduction was accompanied by a substantial increase in revenues

---

[7]The incentive effects are greater in the upper brackets because a similar percentage rate reduction will have a greater impact on take-home pay in this area. For example, if a 70 percent marginal tax rate is cut to 50 percent, take-home pay per additional dollar of earnings will increase from 30 cents to 50 cents, a 67 percent increase in the incentive to earn. On the other hand, if a 14 percent marginal rate is reduced to 10 percent, take-home pay per dollar of additional earnings will increase from 86 cents to 90 cents, only a 5 percent increase in the incentive to earn.

EXHIBIT 7
How Have Changes in Marginal Tax Rates Affected the Share of Taxes Paid by the Rich?

The accompanying graph indicates the share of the personal income tax paid by the top one-half percent of earners during 1960–1998. There were four major reductions in marginal tax rates during this period. First, the Kennedy-Johnson tax cut reduced the top rate from 91 percent in 1963 to 70 percent in 1965. During the Reagan years, the top rate was reduced from 70 percent in 1980 to 50 percent in 1982 and in 1986 it was sliced again to approximately 30 percent. Most recently, the capital gains tax rate was sliced from 28 to 20 percent in 1997. Interestingly, the share of the tax bill paid by these "super-rich" earners increased following each of these tax cuts. These findings suggest that, at least for this group of high-income recipients, strong supply-side effects accompanied the rate cuts. Perhaps surprising to some, these high-income taxpayers paid a larger portion of the tax bill when the top marginal rate was less than 40 percent (1986–1998) than was true during the 1960s and 1970s when the top marginal rate was 70 percent or more.

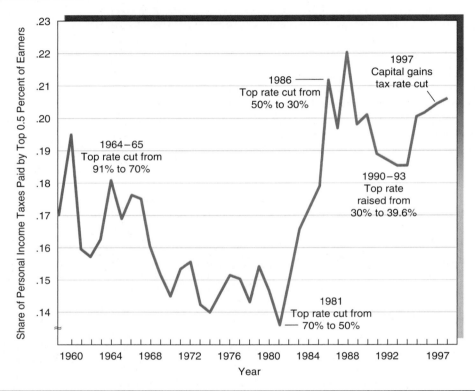

derived from the taxation of capital gains and an increase in the share of the personal income tax collected from high-income taxpayers.[8]

Supply-side economists argue that findings like these illustrate that economic activity is quite sensitive to changes in tax rates, particularly the highest marginal rates. They also indicate that high marginal tax rates, like those of the 1960s and 1970s are counterproductive; they reduce productive activity without raising any appreciable revenue. Since 1986 the top marginal personal income tax rate has been less than 40 percent compared to 70 percent or more prior to 1981. Nonetheless, those with high incomes are now paying more. For example, 25.7 percent of the personal income tax was collected from the top half percent of earners in 1998, up from the 16 to 18 percent range of the early 1960s. Perhaps the supply-siders have found a way to "soak the rich"—keep their marginal tax rates relatively low.

Gradual rate reductions are an integral part of the tax legislation passed in 2001. This bill will reduce the top marginal rate to 35 percent in 2006, down from 39.6 percent in

---

[8]In 1996, capital gains income was $261 billion, which yielded tax revenues of $66 billion. By 2000, income due to capital gains had risen to $652 billion, with corresponding tax revenues of $129 billion.

2000. The 28%, 31% and 36% rates of 2000 will be phased downward to 25%, 28% and 33% by 2006. The proponents of this legislation believe that it will improve supply-side incentives and thereby enhance long-run economic growth. In the years immediately ahead, it will be interesting to track both the level of economic activity and the revenues collected from those with high incomes.

In today's global economy, tax policy is not conducted in a vacuum. Taxes can influence the choices of both business and labor. Ireland provides a vivid illustration of this point. During the last 15 years, Ireland has significantly reduced both personal and corporate income taxes. The lower tax rates help it attract foreign business, expand employment, and promote economic growth. During the 1990s, Ireland had the highest growth rate in Europe and many Irish immigrants who had moved abroad to find work returned to their homeland.

On the other hand, high taxes can drive both business and labor elsewhere.[9] Taxes are generally higher in Europe than the United States, and many believe that this has contributed to Europe's sluggish growth. Several high-tax European countries—including Belgium, Denmark, France, Germany, Netherlands, and Sweden—confront a "brain drain" problem, an exodus of high-skill (and therefore high-income) business and professional workers. While supply-side effects of this type do not dramatically alter year-to-year growth rates, they can exert a significant impact on income levels with the passage of time.

THE FISCAL POLICY OF THE UNITED STATES

The accompanying Thumbnail Sketch summarizes the major implications of the alternative theories with regard to the impact of expansionary fiscal policy. In general, the effects of restrictive fiscal policy would be just the opposite. As we previously mentioned, economists use changes in the size of the deficit or surplus, rather than the absolute amount, to determine whether fiscal policy is shifting toward expansion or restriction. Movement toward a larger deficit (or a smaller surplus) relative to GDP indicates that fiscal policy is becoming more expansionary. Conversely, a reduction in the deficit as a share of GDP (or increase in the surplus) would imply a more restrictive fiscal policy.

 THUMBNAIL SKETCH

Impact of Expansionary Fiscal Policy—A Summary of Four Models

1. **Basic Keynesian model:** An increase in government spending and/or a reduction in taxes will be magnified by the multiplier process and lead to a substantial increase in aggregate demand. When an economy is operating below capacity, real output and employment will also increase substantially.

2. **Crowding-out model:** Expansionary fiscal policy will exert little or no impact on aggregate demand and employment because borrowing to finance the budget deficit will push up interest rates and crowd out private spending, particularly investment. In an open economy, the higher interest rates will lead to an inflow of capital, a currency appreciation, and a decline in net exports.

3. **New classical model:** Expansionary fiscal policy will exert little or no impact on aggregate demand and employment because households will anticipate the higher future taxes implied by the debt and reduce their spending (and increase their saving) in order to pay them. Like current taxes, debt (future taxes) will crowd out private spending.

4. **Supply-side model:** A reduction in marginal tax rates will increase the incentive to earn (produce) and improve the efficiency of resource use, leading to an increase in aggregate supply (real output) in the long run.

[9]See Fabio Padovano and Emma Galli, "Tax Rates and Economic Growth in the OECD Countries," *Economic Inquiry* (January 2001): pp. 44–57, for evidence on the relationship between taxes and growth.

Exhibit 8 presents data on federal expenditures and revenues as a share of GDP during the last four decades. While deficits were present throughout most of the 1960s and 1970s, they were small relative to the size of the economy except during the recessions of 1970 and 1974–1975. Budget deficits have generally increased during recessions (indicated by the shaded bars) and shrunk during expansions. However, the changes in the size of the deficit over the business cycle have been primarily the result of automatic stabilizers rather than discretionary use of fiscal policy. Major discretionary changes motivated by business conditions have generally been too late to have much countercyclical impact. For example, this was the case with the 1968 tax increase to combat inflation during the Vietnam War and the anti-recession tax rebate of 1975.

Business cycle conditions are not the only factor underlying fiscal policy. Sometimes changes in external conditions (the threat of war) or demographic factors (like a change in the number of retirees or prime-age workers) exert a strong impact on expenditure and revenue levels. This was true during the last two decades. Fiscal policy during the first half of the 1980s was driven by a supply-side tax cut and expansion in defense expenditures. These two factors along with the severe recession of 1982 pushed the federal deficit to peacetime highs in the mid-1980s. The deficit declined as the economy grew rapidly during the latter half of the 1980s, but increased once again during the recession and sluggish growth of the early 1990s.

How Were the Deficits Transformed into Surpluses?

Several factors played a role in the transformation of the federal budget from deficit to surplus during the 1990s. While modest tax increases were passed in both 1990 and 1993, strong growth of the economy propelled revenues in the latter half of the decade. The growth of real income within the framework of a progressive tax structure increases effective tax rates. As real income expands, more and more income is pushed into higher tax

---

EXHIBIT 8
Federal Government Expenditures and Revenues as a Percentage of GDP, 1960–2000

Except during recessions (indicated by shaded bars), budget deficits were small as a share of the economy prior to 1980. After a period of persistently large deficits during the 1980s, the federal deficit shrank and by the late 1990s a surplus was present. Revenue increases propelled by a strong economy and spending reductions on defense (see the following exhibit) were the primary factors underlying the shift from deficits to surpluses.

Source: Economic Report of the President, 2001, tables B-1 and B-79.

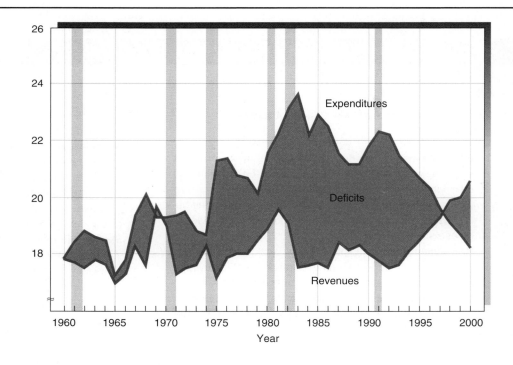

brackets, which automatically increases both average tax rates and tax revenues as a share of income. As Exhibit 8 shows, federal tax revenues rose from 17.5 percent of GDP in 1992 to a post–World War II high of 20.6 percent in 2000.

While increases in defense spending expanded the deficit during the 1980s, defense cuts helped shrink it in the 1990s. **Exhibit 9** illustrates this point. During the mid-1980s, real defense expenditures (4-year moving average) grew at an annual rate of almost 8 percent. This rapid growth pushed up federal expenditures as a share of the economy and contributed to the large deficits of the decade. In the aftermath of the Cold War, however, defense expenditures plunged. By the mid-1990s, real defense expenditures were declining at an annual rate of 4 percent. Real defense spending continued to decline throughout the 1990s, slowing the growth of total federal expenditures. During 1996–2000, real federal spending grew at an annual rate of only 1 percent, the slowest rate of any 5-year period since the end of World War II. This combination of factors—rapid expansion in revenues propelled by both economic growth and higher average tax rates and slow growth of spending due to defense cuts—eliminated the federal deficit in the late 1990s.

Demographic factors smoothed the path for deficit reduction. The huge baby boom generation (persons born between 1946 and 1960) moved into their prime earning years during the 1990s. By 1999, persons age 35–54 comprised 48.3 percent of the labor force, up from 41.6 percent at the beginning of the decade. This increase in prime-age earners contributed to the strong growth of both personal income and federal tax revenues in the 1990s. On the other hand, most of those retiring during the 1990s were born during the 1930s. Because the birthrate was low during these Great Depression years, the growth of retirees during the 1990s was low. This made it easier to control expenditures on Social Security and Medicare, two of the largest federal programs.

While fiscal policy was highly expansionary during the 1980s, the inflation rate fell from the double-digit levels of 1979–1980 to 4 percent in 1983. The economy grew rapidly throughout the remainder of the decade and inflation remained in check. In contrast with the 1980s, fiscal policy was highly restrictive in the 1990s. Nonetheless, the

As a share of GDP government expenditures fell and tax revenues increased in the 1990s. This combination substantially reduced the budget deficit (see Exhibit 8). Reduction in national defense spending from 5.2 percent to 3.0 percent of GDP between 1990 and 2000 was the primary reason for the lower expenditures, while the higher average tax rates accompanying the growth of income was primarily responsible for the increase in revenues.

EXHIBIT 9
Growth Rate of Real Federal Government and Defense Expenditures, 1980–2000

The growth rates of both total and defense spending adjusted for inflation are shown here. During the 1980s, rapid growth of defense spending pushed total federal expenditures upward and contributed substantially to the large deficits of the decade. During the 1990s, defense cuts in the aftermath of the Cold War retarded the growth of federal spending and thereby contributed substantially to the recent surpluses.

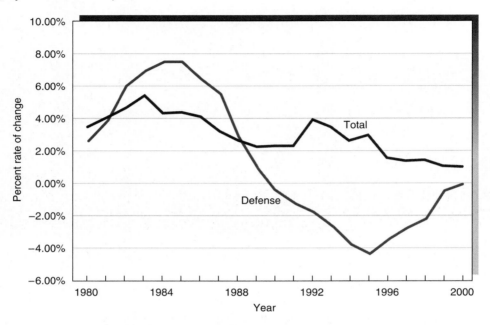

Source: Bureau of Economic Analysis, Web site http://www.bea.doc.gov. The growth rates are calculated as a four-year moving average of the annual rates in order to reduce the impact of the business cycle on changes in expenditures.

economy grew rapidly and inflation remained at a low level. Even though fiscal policy was quite expansionary during the 1980s and quite restrictive during the 1990s, both decades were characterized by strong growth and low rates of inflation. These results do not indicate that fiscal policy—either expansionary or restrictive—exerts a strong impact on aggregate demand. Thus, they are more consistent with the crowding out and new classical theories than the Keynesian view.

The Future

As the budget surplus soared to more than 2 percent of GDP during 2000, large surpluses were projected for several years into the future. This was true even after the effects of the 2001 tax cut were taken into account. However, all of this changed with the September 11 attacks and the War on Terrorism. Federal expenditures increased in several areas including national defense, intelligence gathering, domestic security (a new cabinet level office was established), airport security, and subsidies to the airline industry. The spending increases along with the adverse impact of the recession quickly dissipated the budget surplus.

What is likely to happen to the budget when the economy recovers and growth returns? The answer to this question is dependent on factors that are very difficult to forecast, things like the cost of the War on Terrorism and the perceived likelihood of future terrorist attacks. If the War on Terrorism is relatively short and the related long-term spending increases on national defense and domestic security are small, budget surpluses might well reemerge. Even if this is the case, however, there is reason to question their political viability. Public choice analysis indicates that vote-maximizing politicians have an incentive to increase spending on their constituents, particularly if they can do so without having to raise taxes. The presence of surpluses would make it tempting for political decision makers to undertake new spending projects. Thus, the occurrence of persistent budget surpluses over a lengthy period of time seems unlikely.

The demographics will continue to exert a favorable budgetary impact through the first decade of the twenty-first century. A large share of the labor force will remain in the prime-earning age categories, while the number of new retirees will grow slowly. However, all of this will change dramatically once the baby boomers begin to retire around 2010. Approximately one-third of the federal budget is devoted to spending on the elderly through Medicare and Social Security. The retirement of the baby boomers will push spending on these programs up substantially. As this happens, an era of large deficits is likely to return.

During the last four decades, we have pretty much come full circle with regard to fiscal policy. In the 1960s, most economists thought that fiscal policy was highly potent and that it could be used successfully to smooth the business cycle. Few now adhere to that view. Confidence in the ability of Congress and the president to institute fiscal policy in a counter-cyclical manner has waned. There is also greater awareness of offsetting secondary effects—the factors highlighted by both the crowding out and new classical models. Thus, most economists now believe that fiscal policy exerts only a modest impact on aggregate demand, at least during normal times.

All of this elevates the importance of monetary policy—the other major stabilization weapon. We are now ready to integrate the monetary system into our analysis. Chapter 13 will focus on the operation of the banking system and the factors that determine the supply of money. In Chapter 14, we will analyze the impact of monetary policy on real output, interest rates, and the price level.

LOOKING AHEAD

KEY POINTS

▼ The federal budget is the primary tool of fiscal policy. Discretionary fiscal policy encompasses deliberate changes in the government's spending and tax policies designed to alter the size of the budget deficit and thereby influence the overall level of economic activity.

▼ According to the Keynesian view, fluctuations in aggregate demand are the major source of economic instability. Policies that help to maintain aggregate demand at a level consistent with the economy's full employment capacity will reduce economic instability.

▼ Rather than balancing the budget annually, Keynesian analysis indicates that fiscal policy should reflect business cycle conditions. During a recession, fiscal policy should become more expansionary (a

larger deficit should be planned). During an inflationary boom, fiscal policy should become more restrictive (shift toward a budget surplus).

▼ The crowding-out model indicates that expansionary fiscal policy will lead to higher real interest rates and less private spending, particularly for investment. In an open economy, the higher interest rates will also lead to an inflow of capital, appreciation of the dollar, and a reduction in net exports. The crowding-out theory implies that these secondary effects will largely offset the demand stimulus effects of expansionary fiscal policy. The secondary effects of restrictive fiscal policy will also render it impotent.

▼ The new classical model stresses that substitution of debt for tax financing changes the timing, but not the level, of taxes. According to this view, the higher expected future taxes implied by the bond financing of the deficit will lead to more saving and less private spending, which will offset the expansionary effects of the deficit.

▼ Changes in fiscal policy must be timed properly if they are going to exert a stabilizing influence on an economy. The ability of policymakers to time fiscal policy changes in a countercyclical manner is reduced by (a) our limited ability to forecast future macroeconomic conditions, (b) predictable delays in the institution of policy changes, and (c) a time lag between when a policy change is instituted and when it will exert its primary impact.

▼ The problem of proper timing is reduced in the case of automatic stabilizers—programs that apply stimulus during a recession and restraint during a boom even though no legislative action has been taken.

▼ A modern synthesis concerning the impact of fiscal policy as a stabilization tool has emerged. The major points of the synthesis view are: (1) Proper timing of discretionary fiscal policy is both difficult to achieve and crucially important; (2) automatic stabilizers reduce the fluctuation of aggregate demand and thereby help to promote economic stability; and (3) fiscal policy is much less potent than the early Keynesian view implied.

▼ When fiscal policy changes marginal tax rates, it influences aggregate supply by altering the relative attractiveness of productive activity compared to leisure and tax avoidance. Other things constant, lower marginal tax rates will increase aggregate supply. Supply-side economics should be viewed as a long-run strategy, not a countercyclical tool.

▼ The United States ran large budget deficits throughout the 1980s, but the deficits were eliminated and transformed into surpluses in the late 1990s. Rapid growth of tax revenues during the expansion of the 1990s and slow growth of expenditures resulting from a plunge in defense spending were the primary factors underlying the shift from deficits to surpluses.

▼ Demographic factors—rapid growth of prime-age earners and slow growth of retirees—enhanced revenues and made it easier to control spending growth during the 1990s. These factors will exert the opposite impact once the baby boomers begin retiring during the years following 2010.

CRITICAL ANALYSIS QUESTIONS

1. Suppose that you are a member of the Council of Economic Advisers. The president has asked you to prepare a statement on the question "What is the proper fiscal policy for the next 12 months?" Prepare such a statement, indicating (a) the current state of the economy (that is, unemployment rate, growth in real income, and rate of inflation) and (b) your fiscal policy suggestions. Should the budget be in balance? Explain the reasoning behind your suggestions.

*2. What is the crowding-out effect? How does it modify the implications of the basic Keynesian model with regard to fiscal policy? How does the new classical theory of fiscal policy differ from the crowding-out model?

3. From a stabilization standpoint, why is proper timing of a change in fiscal policy important? Is it easy to time fiscal policy changes properly? Why or why not?

*4. What are automatic stabilizers? Explain their major advantage.

5. Outline the supply-side view of fiscal policy. How does this view differ from the various demand-side theories? Would a supply-side economist be more likely to favor a $500 tax credit or an equivalent reduction in marginal tax rates? Why?

6. According to the Keynesian view, what fiscal policy actions should be taken if the unemployment rate is high and current GDP is well below the economy's potential output rate?

7. How do persistently large budget deficits affect capital formation and the long-run rate of economic growth? Do the proponents of the Keynesian, crowding-out, and new classical theories agree on the answer to this question? Discuss.

*8. "If we set aside our reluctance to use fiscal policy as a stabilization force, it is quite easy to achieve full employment and price stability. When output is at less than full employment, we run a budget deficit. If inflation is a problem, we run a budget surplus. Quick implementation of proper fiscal policy will stabilize the economy." Evaluate this view.

9. Suppose that the government provides each taxpayer with a $600 tax rebate that is financed by issuing additional Treasury bonds. Outline alternative views with regard to how this fiscal action will influence interest rates, aggregate demand, output, and employment.

*10. Some people argue that the growth of output and employment in the 1980s was the result of the large budget deficits. As one politician put it, "Anyone could create prosperity if he wrote $200 billion of hot checks every year." Evaluate this view. If demand stimulus created the prosperity, what would you expect to happen to the rate of inflation? Did this happen during the 1980s?

11. During the 1990s, the federal budget moved from a deficit to a surplus. What factors accounted for this change? Were the budget surpluses of the late 1990s good for the economy? Would it have been better to have reduced taxes and balanced the budget during 1999–2000? Why or why not?

12. Marginal tax rates were cut substantially during the 1980s and while rates were increased in the early 1990s, the marginal rates applicable in the highest income brackets were still well below the top rates of the 1960s and 1970s. How did the lower rates of the 1980s and 1990s affect the share of taxes paid by high-income taxpayers? Were the lower rates of the 1980s and 1990s good or bad for the economy? Discuss.

*13. If the impact on tax revenues is the same, does it make any difference whether the government cuts taxes by (a) reducing marginal tax rates or (b) increasing the personal exemption allowance? Explain.

14. Are discretionary changes in fiscal policy likely to be instituted in a manner that will help smooth the ups and downs of the business cycle? Why or why not?

15. Does fiscal policy exert a strong impact on aggregate demand? Did the large budget deficits of the 1980s lead to excessive demand? Did the budget surpluses of the late 1990s restrain aggregate demand? Discuss.

16. If budget surpluses are present, should Congress cut taxes, increase spending, or use the surpluses to pay down outstanding debt? Explain your answer. If taxes are not reduced, do you think the level of spending will be affected? Why or why not?

17. The personal income tax is indexed for inflation, but not for the growth of real income. Therefore, taxpayers confront higher effective tax rates and the federal government receives a larger share of taxable income as the result of real growth. Do you think this automatic tax increase reflects sound policy or would you like to see the tax structure indexed for the growth of real income?

---

*Asterisk denotes questions for which answers are given in Appendix B.

CHAPTER **13**

Money and the Banking System

Chapter Focus

- What is money? How is the money supply defined?

- What is a fractional reserve banking system? How does it influence the ability of banks to create money?

- What are the major functions of the Federal Reserve System?

- What are the major tools with which the Federal Reserve controls the supply of money?

- How are financial innovations and other changes affecting the nature of money? What will money be like in the future?

Money is whatever is generally accepted in exchange for goods and services—accepted not as an object to be consumed but as an object that represents a temporary abode of purchasing power to be used for buying still other goods and services.

—Milton Friedman[1]

[1]Milton Friedman, *Money Mischief: Episodes in Monetary History* (New York: Harcourt Brace Jovanovich, 1992), p. 16.

The simple macroeconomic model we have developed thus far has four major markets: (1) goods and services, (2) resources, (3) loanable funds, and (4) foreign exchange. When people make exchanges in any of these markets, they generally use money. Money is used to purchase all types of goods, services, physical assets such as houses, and financial assets such as stocks and bonds.

This chapter focuses on the nature of money, how the banking system works, and how the **central bank**—the Federal Reserve System in the United States—controls the supply of money. Money and monetary policy play an important role in the operation of an economy. Reflecting this importance, the next two chapters will focus primarily on how monetary policy works and the impact that it has on the level of prices, output, employment, and the business cycle. ■

WHAT IS MONEY?

Money is the item that is commonly used as a means of payment for goods, services, assets, and outstanding debt. (See the chapter opening quotation of Professor Friedman.) Paradoxically, most modern money has no intrinsic worth. Nonetheless, most of us would like to have more of it. Why? Because money is an asset that performs three basic functions: It serves as a medium of exchange, it provides a means of storing value for future use, and it is used as an accounting unit.

Central bank
An institution that regulates the banking system and controls the supply of money of a country.

Medium of Exchange

Money is one of the most important inventions in human history because of its role as a **medium of exchange**. Money simplifies and reduces the costs of transactions. This reduction in transaction cost permits us to realize the enormous gains from specialization, division of labor, and mass-production processes that underlie our modern standard of living. Without money, exchange would be complicated, time-consuming, and enormously costly. Think what it would be like to live in a barter economy—one without money, where goods were traded for goods. If you wanted to buy a pair of jeans, for example, you would have to first find someone willing to sell you the jeans who was also willing to purchase your labor services or something else you were willing to supply. Such an economy would be highly inefficient.

Money oils the wheels of trade and makes it possible for each of us to specialize in the supply of those things that we do best while purchasing (and consuming) a broad cross-section of goods and services consistent with our individual preferences. People simply sell their productive services or assets for money and, in turn, use the money to buy the goods and services they want. For example, if a farmer wants to exchange a cow for electricity and medical services, the cow is sold for money, which is then used to buy the electricity and the medical services. Money permits a society to escape cumbersome barter procedures.

Medium of exchange
An asset that is used to buy and sell goods or services.

Store of Value

Money is a financial asset—a method of storing value and moving purchasing power from one time period to another. There are some disadvantages of money as a **store of value**. Many methods of holding money do not yield an interest return. During a time of inflation, the purchasing power of money will decline, imposing a cost on those who are holding wealth in the form of money.

Money is not the only way of storing value. Other assets, such as food products, land, houses, stocks, or bonds, might be used to store value for the future. *Money, however, has*

Store of value
An asset that will allow people to transfer purchasing power from one period to the next.

Liquid asset
An asset that can be easily and quickly converted to purchasing power without loss of value.

one big advantage—because of its use as a medium of exchange, money is the most **liquid** *of all assets.* It can be easily and quickly transformed into other goods at a low transaction cost and without an appreciable loss in its nominal value. In contrast, it will take time to locate an acceptable buyer for a house, a plot of land, or an office building. Thus, these assets are illiquid. While stocks and bonds are quite liquid—they can usually be sold quickly for only a small commission—they are not readily acceptable as a direct means of payment. Money provides readily available purchasing power for dealing with an uncertain future. Thus, most people hold some of their wealth in the form of money.

Unit of Account

Unit of account
The units of measurement used by people to post prices and keep track of revenues and costs.

Money also serves as a **unit of account**. Just as we use yards or meters to measure distance, units of money are used to measure the exchange value and costs of goods, services, assets, and resources. The value (and cost) of movie tickets, personal computers, labor services, automobiles, houses, and numerous other items is measured in units of money. Money serves as a common denominator for the expression of both costs and value. If consumers are going to spend their income wisely, they must be able to compare the costs of a vast array of goods and services. Prices measured in units of money help them make such comparisons. Similarly, sound business decisions require cost and revenue comparisons among vastly different productive services. Resource prices and accounting procedures measured in money units facilitate this task.

WHY IS MONEY VALUABLE?

At various times in the past, societies have used gold, silver, beads, seashells, cigarettes, precious stones, and other commodities as money. When commodities are used as money, people will employ scarce resources—resources that could be used to produce valuable goods and services—trying to produce more of the thing that is used as money. Because of this, the opportunity cost of commodity-based money is high.

Money is the item commonly used to buy and sell things. During the Second World War, prisoners of war used cigarettes as money in POW camps.

If a society uses something as money that costs little or nothing to produce, more scarce resources are available for the production of desired goods and services. Thus, most modern nations use **fiat money**, money that has little or no intrinsic value. A dollar bill is just a piece of paper. Checking account deposits are nothing more than accounting numbers. Coins have some intrinsic value as metal, but in most cases this value is considerably less than their value as money.

Why is fiat money valuable? To a degree, its value is based on the confidence of the people who use it. People are willing to accept fiat money because they know it can be used to purchase real goods and services. Governments issuing fiat money often designate it as "legal tender," meaning it is acceptable for payment of debts.

The main thing that makes money valuable, however, is the same thing that generates value for other commodities: Demand relative to supply. People demand money because it reduces the cost of exchange. When the supply of money is limited relative to the demand, money will be valuable.

The value of a unit of money—a dollar, for example—is measured in terms of what it will buy. Its value, therefore, is inversely related to the level of prices. An increase in the level of prices and a decline in the purchasing power of a unit of money are the same thing. If the purchasing power of money is to remain stable over time, the supply of money must be controlled. Assuming a constant rate of use, if the supply of money grows more rapidly than the real output of goods and services, prices will rise. In layman's terms, there is "too much money chasing too few goods."

When government authorities rapidly expand the supply of money, it becomes less valuable in exchange and is virtually useless as a store of value. The rapid growth in the supply of money in Germany following the First World War provides a dramatic illustration of this point. During the period 1922–1923, the supply of German marks increased by 250 percent *per month* for a time. The German government was printing money almost as fast as the printing presses would run. Since money became substantially more plentiful in relation to goods and services, it quickly lost its value. As a result, an egg cost 80 billion marks and a loaf of bread 200 billion. Workers picked up their wages in suitcases. Shops closed at the lunch hour to change price tags. The value of money had eroded. More recently (in the 1980s and 1990s), Argentina, Bolivia, Brazil, Israel, Yugoslavia, Russia, and Ukraine (and several other countries of the former Soviet Union) have experienced this same cycle of rapid growth in the money supply (to pay for government expenditures) and hyperinflation.

THE SUPPLY OF MONEY

How is the supply of money defined? There is no straightforward, single answer to this question. Economists and policy makers have developed several alternative measures. We will briefly describe the two most widely used of these money supply measures.

The M1 Money Supply

Above all else, money is a medium of exchange. The narrowest definition of the money supply, **M1**, focuses on this function. Based on its role as a medium of exchange, it is clear that currency (including both coins and paper bills) and checkable deposits should be included in the supply of money. Deposits that can be drawn from by writing a check are called **transaction accounts**. There are two general categories of transaction accounts. First, there are **demand deposits**, non-interest-earning deposits with banking institutions that are available for withdrawal ("on demand") at any time without restrictions. Demand deposits are usually withdrawn by writing a check. Second, there are **other checkable deposits** that earn interest but carry some restrictions on their transferability. Interest-earning checkable deposits generally either limit the number of checks written each month

Fiat money
Money that has neither intrinsic value nor the backing of a commodity with intrinsic value; paper currency is an example.

M1 (money supply)
The sum of (1) currency in circulation (including coins), (2) checkable deposits maintained in depository institutions, and (3) traveler's checks.

Transaction accounts
Accounts, including demand deposits and interest-earning checkable deposits, against which the account holder is permitted to transfer funds for the purpose of making payment to a third party.

Demand deposits
Non-interest-earning checking deposits that can be either withdrawn or made payable on demand to a third party. Like currency, these deposits are widely used as a means of payment.

Other checkable deposits
Interest-earning deposits that are also available for checking.

or require the depositor to maintain a substantial minimum balance ($1,000, for example). Like currency and demand deposits, interest-earning checkable deposits are available for use as a medium of exchange. Traveler's checks are also a means of payment. They can be freely converted to cash at parity (equal value). ***Thus, the M1 money supply comprises (1) currency in circulation, (2) checkable deposits (both demand deposits and interest-earning checkable deposits), and (3) traveler's checks.***

As **Exhibit 1** shows, the total M1 money supply in the United States was $1,203 billion at year-end 2001. Demand and other checkable deposits accounted for approximately two-thirds of the M1 money supply. This large share reflects the fact that most of the nation's business is conducted by check.

The Broader M2 Money Supply

In modern economies, several financial assets can easily be converted into checking deposits or currency; therefore, the line between money and "near monies" is often blurred. Broader definitions of the money supply include various assets that can be easily converted to checking account funds and cash. The most common broad definition of the money supply is **M2**. It includes all the items included in M1 plus (1) savings deposits (including money market deposit accounts), (2) time deposits of less than $100,000 at all **depository institutions**, and (3) money market mutual funds.

Although the non-M1 components of the M2 money supply are not generally used as a means of making payment, they can be easily and quickly converted to currency or checking deposits for such use. For example, if you maintain funds in a savings account, you can easily transfer them to your checking account for use as a means of payment. **Money market mutual funds** are interest-earning accounts offered by brokerage firms that pool depositors' funds and invest them in highly liquid short-term securities. Because these securities can be quickly converted to cash, depositors are permitted to write checks (which reduce their share holdings) against these accounts.

M2 (money supply)
Equal to M1 plus (1) savings deposits, (2) time deposits (accounts of less than $100,000) held in depository institutions, and (3) money market mutual fund shares.

Depository institutions
Businesses that accept checking and savings deposits and use a portion of them to extend loans and make investments. Banks, savings and loan associations, and credit unions are examples.

Money market mutual funds
Interest-earning accounts offered by brokerage firms that pool depositors' funds and invest them in highly liquid short-term securities. Since these securities can be quickly converted to cash, depositors are permitted to write checks (which reduce their share holdings) against their accounts.

EXHIBIT 1
Composition of Money Supply in the United States

The size and composition (as of December 2001) of the two most widely used measures of the money supply are shown. M1, the narrowest definition of the money supply, is comprised of currency, checking deposits, and traveler's checks. M2, which contains M1 plus the various savings components indicated, is approximately four times the size of M1.

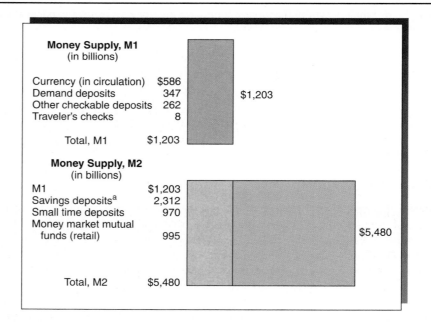

Money Supply, M1 (in billions)	
Currency (in circulation)	$586
Demand deposits	347
Other checkable deposits	262
Traveler's checks	8
Total, M1	$1,203

$1,203

Money Supply, M2 (in billions)	
M1	$1,203
Savings deposits[a]	2,312
Small time deposits	970
Money market mutual funds (retail)	995
Total, M2	$5,480

$5,480

[a]Including money market deposit accounts.
Source: www.federalreserve.gov

Money is an asset; it is part of the wealth of the people who hold it. In contrast, credit card purchases create a liability. They are merely a convenient method of arranging a short-term loan.

Many economists—particularly those who stress the store-of-value function of money—prefer the broader M2 definition of the money supply to the narrower M1 concept. As Exhibit 1 shows, at year-end 2001 the M2 money supply was $5,480 billion, approximately four times the M1 money supply. Other definitions of the money supply have been developed for specialized purposes, but the M1 and M2 definitions are the most important and most widely used.

Credit Cards Versus Money

It is important to distinguish between money and credit. Money is a financial asset that provides the holder with future purchasing power. **Credit** is a liability acquired when one borrows funds. This distinction sheds light on a question students frequently ask: "Because credit cards are often used to make purchases, why aren't credit card expenditures part of the money supply?" In contrast with money, credit cards are not purchasing power. They are merely a convenient means of arranging a loan. When you use your Visa or MasterCard to buy a DVD player, for example, you are not really paying for the player. Instead, you are taking out a loan from the institution issuing your card, and that institution is paying for the player. Payment is not made by you until you write a check to settle your credit card bill and thereby reduce your money balances. Thus, credit card purchases are not money; they are not an asset representing future purchasing power.

Although credit cards are not money, their use will influence the amount of money people will want to hold. Credit cards make it possible for people to buy things throughout the month and then pay for them with a single transaction at the end of the month. This makes it possible for people to conduct their regular business affairs with less money than would otherwise be needed. Thus, widespread use of credit cards will tend to reduce the average quantity of money people hold.

Credit
Funds acquired by borrowing.

THE BUSINESS OF BANKING

We must understand a few things about the business of banking before we can explain the factors that influence the supply of money. The banking industry in the United States operates under the jurisdiction of the **Federal Reserve System**, the nation's central bank.

Federal Reserve System
The central bank of the United States; it carries out banking regulatory policies and is responsible for the conduct of monetary policy.

Not all banks belong to the Federal Reserve, but under legislation enacted in 1980, only a nominal difference exists between member and nonmember banks. We will discuss the Federal Reserve System in detail later in this chapter.

The banking system is an important component of the capital market. Like other private businesses, banks are profit-seeking operations. Banks provide services (for example, safekeeping of funds and checking-account services) and pay interest in order to attract both checking and savings depositors. *They help to bring together people who want to save for the future with those who want to borrow in order to undertake investment projects.* Income derived from loans in support of investment projects is the primary source of revenue for banks.

When deciding whether to fund a project, bankers have a strong incentive to judge both the project's expected profitability and the borrower's creditworthiness. Borrowers may be unable to repay their loans if the funds are channeled into unprofitable investments. In turn, lenders who finance business failures may lose all or part of their funds. Efficient allocation of investment funds is an important source of economic growth. Profitable business projects increase the value of resources and promote economic growth; unprofitable projects have the opposite effect. An efficiently operating capital market, of which the banking system is an integral part, will extend loans and provide financial support for projects that are more likely to be winners—that is, profitable rather than unprofitable.

In the United States, the banking system consists of savings and loan institutions, credit unions, and commercial banks. **Savings and loan associations** accept deposits in exchange for shares that pay dividends. **Credit unions** are cooperative financial organizations of individuals with a common affiliation (such as an employer) that accept deposits, pay interest (or dividends) on them, and generate earnings primarily through the extension of loans to members. **Commercial banks** offer a wide range of services—including checking and savings accounts and extension of loans—and are owned by stockholders. Under legislation passed in 1980, all these depository institutions are authorized to offer both checking and savings accounts and to extend a wide variety of loans to customers.

All these depository institutions are now under the jurisdiction of the Federal Reserve System, which applies similar regulations and offers similar services (for example, check clearing and access to borrowing from the Fed) to each. *Therefore, when we speak of the banking industry, we are referring to not only commercial banks, but savings and loan associations and credit unions as well.*

The consolidated balance sheet of commercial banking institutions (**Exhibit 2**) illustrates the major banking functions. It shows that the major liabilities of banks are transac-

Savings and loan associations
Financial institutions that accept deposits in exchange for shares that pay dividends. Historically, these funds have been channeled into residential mortgage loans. Under banking legislation adopted in 1980, S&Ls are permitted to offer a broad range of services similar to those of commercial banks.

Credit unions
Financial cooperative organizations of individuals with a common affiliation (such as an employer or a labor union). They accept deposits, including checkable deposits, pay interest (or dividends) on them out of earnings, and channel funds primarily into loans to members.

Commercial banks
Financial institutions that offer a wide range of services (for example, checking accounts, savings accounts, and extension of loans) to their customers. Commercial banks are owned by stockholders and seek to operate at a profit.

EXHIBIT 2
Functions of Commercial Banking Institutions

Banks provide services and pay interest to attract transaction (checking), savings, and time deposits (liabilities). Most of the deposits are invested and loaned out, providing interest income for the bank. Banks hold a portion of their assets as reserves (either cash or deposits with the Fed) to meet their daily obligations toward their depositors.

CONSOLIDATED BALANCE SHEET OF COMMERCIAL BANKING INSTITUTIONS, YEAR-END 2001 (BILLIONS OF DOLLARS)

ASSETS		LIABILITIES	
Vault cash	$ 32	Transaction deposits	$ 665
Reserves at the Fed	9	Savings and time deposits	3,596
Loans outstanding	3,964	Borrowings	1,241
U.S. government securities	832	Other liabilities	515
Other securities	648	Net worth	453
Other assets	985		
Total	$6,470		$6,470

Source: www.federalreserve.gov

tion (checking), savings, and time deposits. *From the viewpoint of a bank*, these are liabilities because they represent an obligation of the bank to its depositors. Outstanding interest-earning loans comprise the major class of banking assets. In addition, most banks own sizable amounts of interest-earning securities—bonds issued by either governments or private corporations.

Banking differs from most businesses in that a large portion of the liabilities are payable on demand. However, even though it would be possible for all depositors to demand the money in their checking accounts on the same day, the probability of this occurring is generally quite remote. Typically, while some individuals are making withdrawals, others are making deposits. These transactions tend to balance out, eliminating sudden changes in demand deposits.

Thus, banks maintain only a fraction of their assets in reserves to meet the requirements of depositors. As Exhibit 2 illustrates, bank reserves—vault cash plus reserve deposits with the Federal Reserve—were only $41 billion at year-end 2001, compared to transaction (checking) deposits of $665 billion. Thus, on average, banks were maintaining less than 10 percent of their assets in reserve against the checking deposits of their customers.

Bank reserves
Vault cash plus deposits of the bank with Federal Reserve banks.

Fractional Reserve Goldsmithing

Economists often like to draw an analogy between our current banking system and the goldsmiths of the past. In the past, gold was used as the means of making payments. It was money. People would store their money with a goldsmith for safekeeping, just as many of us open a checking account for safety reasons. Gold owners received a certificate granting them the right to withdraw their gold anytime they wished. If they wanted to buy something, they would go to the goldsmith, withdraw gold, and use it as a means of making a payment. Thus, the money supply was equal to the amount of gold in circulation plus the gold deposited with goldsmiths.

The day-to-day deposits of and requests for gold were always only a fraction of the total amount of gold deposited. A major portion of the gold simply "lay idle in the goldsmiths' vaults." Taking notice of this fact, goldsmiths soon began loaning gold to local merchants. After a time, the merchants would pay back the gold, plus pay interest for its use. What happened to the money supply when a goldsmith extended loans to local merchants? The deposits of persons who initially brought their gold to the goldsmith were not reduced. Depositors could still withdraw their gold anytime they wished (as long as they did not all try to do so at once). In addition, the merchants were now able to use the gold they borrowed from the goldsmith as a means of payment. *As goldsmiths lent gold, they increased the amount of gold in circulation, thereby increasing the money supply.*

It was inconvenient to make a trip to the goldsmith every time one wanted to buy something. Because the certificates were redeemable in gold, they began to circulate as a means of payment. The depositors were pleased with this arrangement because it eliminated the need for a trip to the goldsmith every time something was exchanged for gold. As long as they had confidence in the goldsmith, sellers were glad to accept the certificates as payment.

As gold certificates began to circulate, the daily withdrawals and deposits with goldsmiths declined even more. Local goldsmiths would keep about 20 percent of the total gold deposited with them so they could meet the current requests to redeem the gold certificates in circulation. The remaining 80 percent of their gold deposits would be loaned out to merchants, traders, and other citizens. Therefore, 100 percent of the gold certificates was circulating as money. That portion of gold that had been loaned out, 80 percent of the total deposits, was also circulating as money. The total money supply, gold certificates plus gold, was now 1.8 times the amount of gold that had been originally deposited with the goldsmith. Because the goldsmiths issued loans and kept only a fraction of the total gold deposited with them, they were able to increase the money supply.

As long as the goldsmiths held enough reserves to meet the current requests of the depositors, everything went along smoothly. Most gold depositors probably did not even realize that the goldsmiths did not have their actual gold and that of other depositors, precisely designated as such, sitting in the "vaults."

Goldsmiths derived income from loaning gold. The more gold they loaned, the greater their total income. Some goldsmiths, trying to increase their income by extending more and more interest-earning loans, depleted the gold in their vaults to imprudently low levels. If an unexpectedly large number of depositors wanted their gold, these imprudent goldsmiths would be unable to meet their requests. As this happened, the system of fractional reserve goldsmithing would tend to break down.

Fractional Reserve Banking

Fractional reserve banking
A system that permits banks to hold reserves of less than 100 percent against their deposits.

In principle, our modern banking system is very similar to goldsmithing. The United States has a **fractional reserve banking** system. Banks are required to maintain only a fraction of their deposits in the form of cash and other reserves. Just as the early goldsmiths did not have enough gold to pay all their depositors simultaneously, neither do our banks have enough reserves (vault cash and deposits with Federal Reserve banks) to pay all their depositors simultaneously. (*Note:* As Exhibit 2 illustrates, the vault cash plus the reserves held with the Federal Reserve are less than 10 percent of the transaction—that is, checking—deposits of commercial banks.) The early goldsmiths expanded the money supply by issuing loans. So do present-day bankers. The amount of gold held in reserve to meet the requirements of depositors limited the ability of the goldsmiths to expand the money supply. The amount of cash and other **required reserves** limits the ability of present-day banks to expand the money supply.

Required reserves
The minimum amount of reserves that a bank is required by law to keep on hand to back up its deposits. Thus, if reserve requirements were 15 percent, banks would be required to keep $150,000 in reserves against each $1 million of deposits.

However, there are also important differences between modern banking and early goldsmithing. Today, the actions of individual banks are regulated by a central bank. The central bank is supposed to follow policies designed to promote a healthy economy. It also acts as a lender of last resort. If all depositors in a specific bank suddenly attempted to withdraw their funds simultaneously, the central bank would intervene and supply the bank with enough funds to meet the demand.

BANK RUNS, BANK FAILURES, AND DEPOSIT INSURANCE

Compared to other businesses, banks are more vulnerable to failure (and abuse), and the consequences of failure exert a larger impact on the economy. The vulnerability of banks reflects the fact that their liabilities to depositors are current, while many of their assets are illiquid. This means that if a significant share of depositors lose confidence and withdraw their funds, it will quickly lead to problems. In turn, when a bank fails, it affects not only the owners and employees, but the depositors as well. These secondary effects can undermine the operation of an economy.

The U.S. economy has had its share of banking problems. Between 1922 and 1933, more than 10,000 banks (one-third of the total) failed. Most of these failures were the result of "bank runs," panic withdrawals as people lost confidence in the banking system. Remember, under a fractional reserve system, banks do not have a sufficient amount of reserves to redeem the funds of all (or even most) depositors seeking to withdraw their funds at the same time.

Federal Deposit Insurance Corporation (FDIC)
A federally chartered corporation that insures the deposits held by commercial banks and thrift institutions.

The bank failures of the 1920s and 1930s led to the establishment of the **Federal Deposit Insurance Corporation (FDIC)** in 1934. The FDIC guarantees the deposits of banking customers up to some limit—currently $100,000 per account. Even if the bank should fail, the depositors will be able to get their money (up to the $100,000 limit). Member banks pay an insurance premium to the FDIC for each dollar on deposit, and the FDIC uses these premiums to reimburse depositors with funds in a bank that fails. The FDIC restored confidence in the banking system and brought bank runs to a halt. As a result, bank failures are extremely rare now.

HOW BANKS CREATE MONEY BY EXTENDING LOANS

Under a fractional reserve system, an increase in reserves will permit banks to extend additional loans and thereby create additional transaction (checking) deposits. Since transaction deposits are money, the extension of the additional loans expands the supply of money. To enhance our understanding of this process, let us consider a banking system without a central bank, one in which only currency acts as a reserve against deposits. Initially, we will assume that all banks are required by law to maintain vault cash equal to at least 20 percent of the checking accounts of their depositors. This proportion of the percent of reserves that must be maintained against checkable transaction deposits is called the **required reserve ratio**. The required reserve ratio in our example is 20 percent.

Suppose you found $1,000 that your long-deceased uncle had apparently hidden in the basement of his house. How much would this newly found $1,000 of currency expand the money supply? You take the bills to the First National Bank, open a checking account of $1,000, and deposit the cash with the banker. First National is now required to keep an additional $200 in vault cash, 20 percent of your deposit. However, it received $1,000 of additional cash, so after placing $200 in the bank vault, First National has $800 of **excess reserves**, reserves over and above the amount it is required by law to maintain. Given its current excess reserves, First National can now extend an $800 loan. Suppose it loans $800 to a local citizen to help pay for a car. At the time the loan is extended, the money supply will increase by $800 as the bank adds the funds to the checking account of the borrower. No one else has less money. You still have your $1,000 checking account, and the borrower has $800 for a new car.

When the borrower buys a new car, the seller accepts a check and deposits the $800 in a bank, Citizen's State Bank. What happens when the check clears? The temporary excess reserves of the First National Bank will be eliminated when it pays $800 to the Citizen's State Bank. But when Citizen's State Bank receives $800 in currency, it will now have excess reserves. It must keep 20 percent, an additional $160, as required reserves against the $800 checking account deposit of the automobile seller.

The remaining $640 could be loaned out. Because Citizen's State, like other banks, is in business to make money, it will be quite happy to "extend a helping hand" to a borrower. When the second bank loans out its excess reserves, the deposits of the person borrowing the money will increase by $640. Another $640 has now been added to the money supply. You still have your $1,000, the automobile seller has an additional $800, and the new borrower has just received an additional $640. Because you found the $1,000 and deposited it in the bank, the money supply has increased by $1,440 ($800+$640).

Of course, the process can continue. **Exhibit 3** follows the potential creation of money resulting from the initial $1,000 through several additional stages. When the reserve requirement is 20 percent, the money supply can expand to a maximum of $5,000, the initial $1,000 plus an additional $4,000 in demand deposits that can be created by extending new loans.

The multiple by which new reserves increase the stock of money is referred to as the **deposit expansion multiplier**. The amount by which additional reserves can increase the supply of money is determined by the ratio of required reserves to deposits. In fact, the **potential deposit expansion multiplier** is merely the reciprocal of the required reserve ratio (*r*). Mathematically, the potential deposit expansion multiplier is

Required reserve ratio
A percentage of a specified liability category (for example, transaction accounts) that banking institutions are required to hold as reserves against that type of liability.

Excess reserves
Actual reserves that exceed the legal requirement.

Deposit expansion multiplier
The multiple by which an increase (decrease) in reserves will increase (decrease) the money supply. It is inversely related to the required reserve ratio.

Potential deposit expansion multiplier
The maximum potential increase in the money supply as a ratio of the new reserves injected into the banking system. It is equal to the inverse of the required reserve ratio.

EXHIBIT 3
Creating Money from New Reserves

When banks are required to maintain 20 percent reserves against demand deposits, the creation of $1000 of new reserves will potentially increase the supply of money by $5000.

BANK	NEW CASH DEPOSITS: ACTUAL RESERVES	NEW REQUIRED RESERVES	POTENTIAL DEMAND DEPOSITS CREATED BY EXTENDING NEW LOANS
Initial deposit (Bank A)	$1,000.00	$ 200.00	$ 800.00
Second stage (Bank B)	800.00	160.00	640.00
Third stage (Bank C)	640.00	128.00	512.00
Fourth stage (Bank D)	512.00	102.40	409.60
Fifth stage (Bank E)	409.60	81.92	327.68
Sixth stage (Bank F)	327.68	65.54	262.14
Seventh stage (Bank G)	262.14	52.43	209.71
All others (other banks)	1,048.58	209.71	838.87
Total	$5,000.00	$1,000.00	$4,000.00

equal to $1/r$. In our example, the required reserves are 20 percent, or one-fifth of the total deposits. So the potential deposit expansion multiplier is 5. If only 10 percent reserves were required, the potential deposit expansion multiplier would be 10, the reciprocal of one-tenth. ***The lower the percentage of the reserve requirement, the greater is the potential expansion in the money supply resulting from the creation of new reserves. The fractional reserve requirement places a ceiling on potential money creation from new reserves.***

The Actual Deposit Multiplier

Will the introduction of new currency reserves necessarily have a full deposit expansion multiplier effect? The answer is no. The actual deposit multiplier will generally be less than the potential for two reasons.

First, the deposit expansion multiplier will be reduced if some persons decide to hold the currency rather than deposit it in a bank. For example, suppose the person who borrowed the $800 in the preceding example spends only $700 and stashes the remaining $100 away for a possible emergency. Only $700 can then end up as a deposit in the second stage and contribute to the excess reserves necessary for expansion. The potential of new loans in the second stage and in all subsequent stages will be reduced proportionally. When currency remains in circulation, outside the banks, it reduces the size of the deposit expansion multiplier.

Second, the actual deposit multiplier will be less than its maximum potential when banks fail to use all the new excess reserves to extend loans. Banks, though, have a strong incentive to loan out or invest most of their new excess reserves. Idle excess reserves do not earn interest. Because banks are in business to earn income, they will maintain only a very small portion of their assets—mostly currency needed for daily transactions—in the form of excess reserves. In recent years, excess reserves have accounted for less than 1 percent of the total reserves of banks.

Currency leakages and idle excess bank reserves will result in a deposit expansion multiplier that is less than its potential maximum. However, because people generally keep most of their money in bank deposits (rather than currency) and the excess reserves of banks are typically small, the injection of new reserves into the system can be counted on to expand the supply of money by a multiple of the additional reserves.

THE FEDERAL RESERVE SYSTEM

Most countries have a central banking authority that controls the money supply and conducts monetary policy. As we previously noted, the central bank of the United States is the Federal Reserve System. In the United Kingdom, the central bank is the Bank of England; in Canada, it is the Bank of Canada; in Japan, it is the Bank of Japan. Central banks are responsible for the conduct of their nation's monetary policy.

Structure of the Fed

The major purpose of the Federal Reserve System (and other central banks) is to regulate the money supply and provide a monetary climate that is in the best interest of the entire economy. Congress has instructed the Federal Reserve, or the Fed, as it is often called, to conduct monetary policy in a manner that promotes both full employment and price stability. Unlike commercial banks, the Federal Reserve is not a profit-making institution. The earnings of the Fed, over and above its expenses, belong to the Treasury.

    Exhibit 4 illustrates the structure of the Fed. There are three major centers of decision making within the Federal Reserve: (1) the Board of Governors, (2) the district and regional banks, and (3) the Federal Open Market Operations Committee.

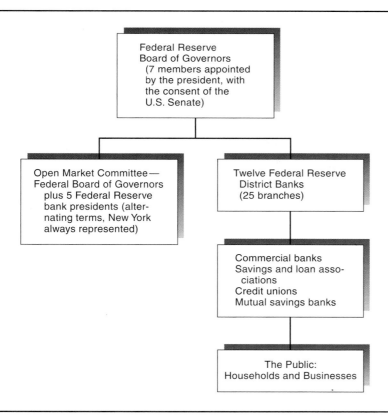

EXHIBIT 4
Structure of Federal Reserve System

The Board of Governors of the Federal Reserve System is at the center of the banking system in the United States. The board sets the rules and regulations for all depository institutions. The seven members of the Board of Governors also serve on the Federal Open Market Committee, a 12-member board that establishes Fed policy with regard to the buying and selling of government securities, the primary mechanism used to control the money supply in the United States.

Board of Governors

The Board of Governors is the decision-making center of the Fed. This powerful board consists of seven members, each appointed to a staggered 14-year term by the president with the advice and consent of the Senate. The president designates one of the seven members as chair for a four-year term. (See the Outstanding Economist box on Alan Greenspan.) The Board of Governors establishes the rules and regulations applicable to all depository institutions. It sets the reserve requirements and regulates the composition of the asset holdings of depository institutions. The board is the rule maker, and often the umpire, of the banking industry.

Federal Reserve District Banks

There are 12 Federal Reserve District banks with 25 regional branches spread throughout the nation. **Exhibit 5** shows the regions covered by each of the 12 district banks. These district and regional banks operate under the supervision of the Board of Governors. Federal Reserve banks are bankers' banks; they provide banking services for commercial banks. Private citizens and corporations do not bank with the Fed.

The district banks are primarily responsible for the monitoring of the commercial banks in their region. They audit the books of depository institutions regularly in order to assure their compliance with reserve requirements and other regulations of the Fed. The district banks also play an important role in the clearing of checks through the banking system. Most depository institutions, regardless of their Fed membership status, maintain deposits with Federal Reserve Banks. As a result, the clearing of checks through the Federal Reserve System becomes merely an accounting transaction. The district and regional banks handle approximately 85 percent of all check-clearing services of the banking system.

Federal Open Market Committee (FOMC)

The **Federal Open Market Committee** is a powerful committee that determines the Fed's policy with respect to the purchase and sale of government bonds. As we shall soon see, this is the Fed's most frequently used method of controlling the money supply in the United States. This important policy-making arm of the Fed is made up of (1) the

Federal Open Market Committee (FOMC)
A 12-member board that establishes Fed policy with regard to the buying and selling of government securities, the primary mechanism used to control the money supply in the United States.

OUTSTANDING ECONOMIST

Alan Greenspan

From 1954 to 1974, Greenspan ran a very successful economic consulting firm in New York City. After serving as the chair of the Council of Economic Advisers (1974–1977) during the Ford administration, he returned to his consulting firm for the following ten years. During this period, he also served as Chairman of the National Commission on Social Security Reform and as a board member of many corporations. In 1987, President Reagan appointed him to a four-year term as chairman of the Fed's Board of Governors. Later, he was reappointed to that position by both Presidents Bush and Clinton. The Fed chairman directs the staff, presides over Board meetings, and testifies frequently before Congress. Because of the importance of monetary policy and the power of the position, the Fed chairman is often said to be the second most influential person—next to the president—in the United States. As the result of the low rate of inflation and the lengthy economic expansion of the 1990s Greenspan is given high marks for his tenure as chairman.

EXHIBIT 5
The Twelve Federal Reserve Districts

The map indicates the 12 Federal Reserve districts and the city in which the district bank is located. These district banks monitor the commercial banks in their region and assist them with the clearing of checks. If you look at any dollar bill, it will identify the Federal Reserve district bank that initially issued the currency. The Board of Governors of the Fed is located in Washington, D.C.

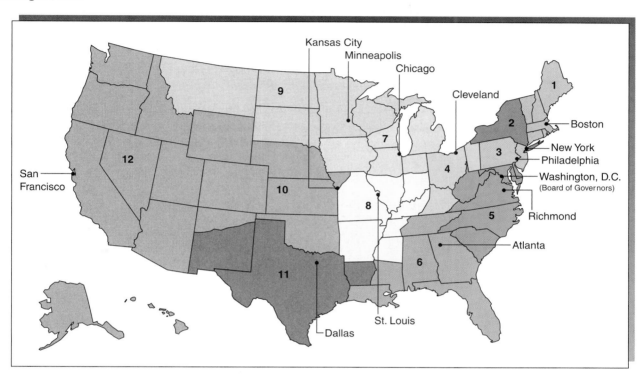

seven members of the Board of Governors, (2) the president of the New York District Bank, and (3) four (of the remaining eleven) additional presidents of the Fed's District Banks, who rotate on the committee. Although they do not always have a vote, all 12 Federal Reserve district bank presidents participate in the FOMC meetings, held every five to eight weeks.

The Independence of the Fed

Like the Supreme Court, the Federal Reserve operates with considerable independence from both Congress and the executive branch of government. Several factors contribute to this independence. The lengthy terms—14 years—protect the seven members of the Fed's Board of Governors from political pressures. Because their terms are staggered—a new governor is appointed only every two years—even two-term presidents are well into their second term before they are able to appoint a majority of the Fed's governing board. The Fed's earnings on its financial assets, mostly government bonds, provide it with substantially more funding than is needed to cover its operating costs. Thus, it is not dependent on Congress for funding allocations. The Fed does not even have to undergo audits from the General Accounting Office, a government agency that audits the books of most government operations. This independence of the Fed is designed to reduce the likelihood that political pressures will adversely affect its ability to follow a stable, noninflationary monetary policy.

Does the independence of a central bank affect policy? There is considerable variation in the independence of central banks. Like the Fed, the German Bundesbank was largely insulated from the political authorities. (*Note:* With the development of a European currency, the Bundesbank has been replaced by the European central bank.) In other instances, central banks are directly beholden to political officials. The central banks of many Latin American countries fit into this category. Studies of this topic indicate that when a country's central bank is strongly influenced by political considerations, the bank is more likely to follow inflationary policies.

How the Fed Controls the Money Supply

The Fed has three major means of controlling the money stock: (1) establishing reserve requirements for depository institutions, (2) buying and selling U.S. government securities in the open market, and (3) setting the interest rate at which it will loan funds to commercial banks and other depository institutions. We will analyze in detail how each of these tools can be used to regulate the amount of money in circulation.

Reserve Requirements

The Federal Reserve System requires banking institutions (including credit unions and savings and loan associations) to maintain reserves against the demand deposits of their customers. The reserves of banking institutions are composed of (1) currency held by the bank (vault cash) and (2) deposits of the bank with the Federal Reserve System. A bank can always obtain additional currency by drawing on its deposits with the Federal Reserve. So both cash-on-hand and the bank's deposits with the Fed can be used to meet the demands of depositors. Both therefore count as reserves.

Exhibit 6 indicates the required reserve ratio—the percentage of each deposit category that banks are required to keep in reserve (that is, in the form of either vault cash or deposits with the Fed). As of December 2001, the reserve requirement for transaction accounts was set at 3 percent for amounts above $5.7 million and up to $41.3 million and 10 percent for amounts in excess of $41.3 million. Currently, banks are not required to keep reserves against their savings and time deposits or on the first $5.7 million of transactions deposits.

Why are commercial banks required to maintain assets in the form of reserves? One reason is to prevent imprudent bankers from overextending loans and thereby placing themselves in a poor position to deal with any sudden increase in withdrawals by deposi-

---

EXHIBIT 6
Required Reserve Ratio of Banking Institutions

Banking institutions are required to maintain 3 percent reserves against transaction-account deposits of over $5.7 million and up to $41.3 million and 10 percent reserves for transaction deposits over $41.3 million (in effect December 2001).

	TRANSACTION ACCOUNTS[a]		
	$0–$5.7 MILLION	$5.7–$41.3 MILLION	OVER $41.3 MILLION
Required reserves as a percent of deposits	0%	3%	10%

[a]The dividing points are adjusted each year to reflect changes in total transaction-account deposits in all banking institutions.
Source: www.federalreserve.gov

tors. The quantity of reserves needed to meet such emergencies is not left totally to the judgment of individual bankers. The Fed sets the rules.

The Fed's control over reserve requirements, however, is important for another reason. By altering reserve requirements, the Fed can alter the money supply. The law does not prevent commercial banks from holding reserves over and above those required by the Fed, but, as we previously noted, banking institutions will want to hold interest-earning assets (like loans to customers and bonds) rather than excess reserves. Because reserves draw no interest, profit-seeking banks will shave their excess reserves to a low level. As a result, an increase in reserve requirements will typically force banks to reduce their outstanding loans and investments. As the volume of loans (and other forms of credit) extended by banks declines, so, too, will the money supply. ***Thus, an increase in the reserve requirements will reduce the supply of money.***

A reduction in reserve requirements will have the opposite impact. When the Fed reduces the reserve requirements, it creates additional excess reserves for banks. Predictably, profit-seeking banks will use a large portion of these newly created excess reserves to extend additional loans and undertake other investments. As they do so, their actions will expand the supply of money. ***Thus, lower reserve requirements increase the capacity of banks to lend and, as they extend additional loans, the money supply increases.***

In recent years, the Fed has seldom used its regulatory power over reserve requirements to alter the supply of money. Why? For one thing, changes in reserve requirements can be disruptive of banking operations. An increase in the required reserve ratio may force many banks to sell securities quickly or call in loans even if there has been no change in the level of their deposits. Furthermore, reserve requirement changes are a blunt instrument—small changes in reserve requirements can sometimes lead to large changes in the money supply. The magnitude and timing of a change in the money stock resulting from a change in reserve requirements are difficult to predict with precision. For these reasons, the Fed has usually preferred to use other monetary tools.

Open Market Operations

The most common tool used by the Fed to alter the money supply is **open market operations**—the buying and selling of U.S. securities on the open market. As we indicated earlier, Fed policy in this area is conducted by the Federal Open Market Committee (FOMC). This committee meets every few weeks to map out the Fed's policy. Open market operations can be undertaken easily and quietly. Because they influence the money supply either directly or through their impact on bank deposits, open market operations are less disruptive than changes in reserve requirements.

Unlike individuals, businesses, and even other government agencies, the Fed can write a check without funds in its account. When the Fed buys things, it creates money. The primary thing that the Fed buys is the national debt bonds that were originally issued by the U.S. Treasury and sold to private parties in order to finance budget deficits.

If the Fed wanted to expand the money supply, it would merely instruct its bond traders at the New York Federal Reserve Bank to buy bonds. (*Note:* Because of its location near major financial markets, the New York bank handles the Fed's bond trading.) ***When the Fed purchases U.S. securities, it injects "new money" into the economy in the form of additional currency in circulation and deposits with commercial banks.***

Let us consider a hypothetical case. Suppose the Fed purchases $10,000 of U.S. securities from Maria Valdez. The Fed receives the securities and Valdez receives a check for $10,000. If she merely cashes the check drawn on the Federal Reserve, the amount of currency in circulation would expand by $10,000, increasing the money supply by that amount. If, as is more likely to be the case, she deposits the funds in her checking account at City Bank, the supply of checking-account money will increase by $10,000 and new bank reserves are created. City Bank is required to maintain additional reserves of only a fraction of Valdez's $10,000 deposit. Assuming a 10 percent required reserve ratio, City

Open market operations
The buying and selling of U.S. government securities in the open market by the Federal Reserve.

Bank can now extend new loans of up to $9,000 while maintaining its initial reserve position. As the new loans are extended, they too will contribute to a further expansion in the money supply. Part of the new loans will eventually be deposited in other banks, and they also will be able to extend additional loans. As the process continues, the money supply expands by a multiple of the securities purchased by the Fed.

Open market operations can also be used to reduce the money stock. *If the Fed wants to reduce the money stock, it sells some of its current holdings of government securities.* When the Fed sells securities, the buyer pays for them with a check drawn on a commercial bank. As the check clears, both the buyer's checking deposits and the reserves of the bank on which the check was written will decline. Thus, the action will reduce the money supply both directly (by reducing checking deposits) and indirectly (by reducing the quantity of reserves available to the banking system).

Monetary base
The sum of currency in circulation plus bank reserves (vault cash and reserves with the Fed). It reflects the stock of U.S. securities held by the Fed.

The Fed's purchase and sale of U.S. securities influence the size of the **monetary base**. The monetary base is equal to the reserves of commercial banks (vault cash and reserve deposits with the Fed) plus the currency in circulation. As **Exhibit 7** illustrates, the monetary base provides the foundation for the money supply of the United States. Of course, the currency in circulation ($594 billion in December 2001) contributes directly to the money supply. In turn, the bank reserves ($41 billion in December 2001) underpin the checking deposits ($609 billion). Fed purchases of U.S. securities increase the monetary base. Some of the proceeds (received by those selling bonds to the Fed) will circulate as currency. Each new dollar of currency in circulation will increase the money supply by exactly $1. In addition, many of those receiving proceeds from bond sales to the Fed will deposit the funds in a bank. When this happens, bank reserves increase and most of the additional reserves will be used to extend loans, causing additional expansion in the money supply.

By how much will the money supply change as the Fed injects and withdraws reserves through open market operations? Given the reserve requirements present in the early 2000s (see Exhibit 6), an increase in the monetary base could potentially expand the money supply (M1) by a multiple of 10 or more. However, leakages in the form of additional currency in circulation and increases in excess bank reserves will result in an actual deposit expansion multiplier that is substantially less than the potential. Exhibit 7 shows that the M1 money supply was approximately twice the size of the monetary base in 2001. This suggests that changes in the monetary base as the result of the Fed's open market op-

EXHIBIT 7
Monetary Base and Money Supply (Year-end 2001)

The monetary base (currency plus bank reserves) provides the foundation for the money supply. The currency in circulation contributes directly to the money supply, while the bank reserves provide the underpinnings for checking deposits. Fed actions that alter the monetary base will affect the money supply (all figures are in billions).

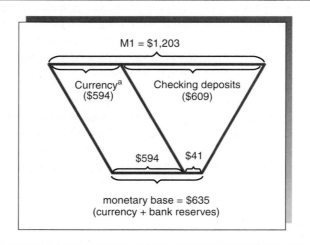

M1 = $1,203

Currency^a ($594)   Checking deposits ($609)

$594 $41

monetary base = $635 (currency + bank reserves)

^aTraveler's checks are included in this category.

erations will change the M1 money supply by about $2 for every $1 change in the monetary base.

Discount Rate—The Cost of Borrowing from the Fed

When banking institutions borrow from the Federal Reserve, they must pay interest on the loan. The interest rate that banks pay on loans from the Federal Reserve is called the **discount rate**. Borrowing from the Fed is a privilege, not a right. The Fed does not have to loan funds to banking institutions. Banks borrow from the Fed primarily to meet temporary shortages of reserves. They are most likely to borrow from the Fed for a brief period of time while they are making other adjustments in their loan and investment portfolios that will permit them to meet their reserve requirement.

An increase in the discount rate makes it more expensive for banking institutions to borrow from the Fed. Borrowing is discouraged, and banks are more likely to build up their reserves to ensure that they will not have to borrow from the Fed. *An increase in the discount rate is thus restrictive. It tends to discourage banks from shaving their excess reserves to a low level.*

In contrast, a reduction in the discount rate is expansionary. At the lower interest rate, it costs banks less if they have to turn to the Fed to meet a temporary emergency. Therefore, as the cost of borrowing from the Fed declines, banks are more likely to reduce their excess reserves to a minimum, extending more loans and increasing the money supply.

The general public has a tendency to overestimate the importance of a change in the discount rate. Many people think an increase in the discount rate means their local banker will (or must) charge them a higher interest rate for a loan.[2] This is not necessarily so. Reserves acquired through transaction and time deposits are the major source of loanable funds for commercial banks. Borrowing from the Fed amounts to less than one-tenth of 1 percent of the available loanable funds of commercial banks. Since borrowing from the Fed is such a negligible source of funds, a 0.5 percent change in the discount rate has something less a profound impact on the availability of credit and the supply of money. Certainly, it does not necessarily mean that your local bank will alter the rate at which it will lend to you.

Discount rate
The interest rate the Federal Reserve charges banking institutions for borrowing funds.

The Federal Funds Interest Rate

If a bank has to borrow to meet its reserve requirements, it need not turn to the Fed. Instead, it can go to the **federal funds market**. In this market, banks with excess reserves extend short-term (sometimes for as little as a day) loans to other banks seeking additional reserves. If the interest rate in the federal funds market is lower or approximately the same as the discount rate, banks seeking additional reserves will generally borrow from the federal funds market rather than the Fed. The federal funds rate and the discount rate tend to move together. If the federal funds rate is significantly higher than the discount rate, banks will attempt to borrow heavily from the Fed. Typically, when this happens, the Fed will raise its discount rate, removing the incentive for banks to borrow from it rather than from the federal funds market.

In recent years, the announcements of the Fed regarding monetary policy have focused on its target for the federal funds rate. This does not conflict with the earlier statement that open market operations are the primary tool used by the Federal Reserve to control the supply of money. The Fed uses open market operations to control the federal funds rate. If the Fed wants to lower the federal funds interest rate, it will purchase government securities and thereby inject additional reserves into the banking system. This will both reduce the federal funds rate and expand the supply of money.

Federal funds market
A loanable funds market in which banks seeking additional reserves borrow short-term (generally for seven days or less) funds from banks with excess reserves. The interest rate in this market is called the federal funds rate.

---

[2]The discount rate is also sometimes confused with the prime interest rate, the rate at which banks loan money to low-risk customers. The two rates are different. A change in the discount rate will not necessarily affect the prime interest rate.

Conversely, if the Fed wants to increase the federal funds rate, it will sell some of its bond holdings and thereby drain reserves from the system. In turn, the reduction in the supply of reserves will both push the federal funds rate upward and reduce the supply of money. The relationship between the money supply and interest rate will be discussed in more detail in Chapter 14.

Controlling the Money Supply—A Summary

Exhibit 8 summarizes the monetary tools of the Federal Reserve. *If the Fed wants to follow an expansionary policy, it can decrease reserve requirements, purchase additional U.S. securities, and/or lower the discount rate.* If it wants to reduce the money stock, it can increase the reserve requirements, sell U.S. securities, and/or raise the discount rate. Because the Fed typically seeks only small changes in the money stock (or its rate of increase), it typically uses only one or two of these tools at a time to accomplish a desired objective.

The Fed and the Treasury

Many students have a tendency to confuse the Federal Reserve with the U.S. Treasury, probably because both sound like monetary agencies. The Treasury is a budgetary agency. If there is a budgetary deficit, the Treasury will issue U.S. securities as a method of financing the deficit. Newly issued U.S. securities are almost always sold to private investors (or government trust funds). Bonds issued by the Treasury to finance a budget deficit are seldom purchased directly by the Fed. In any case, the Treasury is primarily interested in obtaining funds so it can pay Uncle Sam's bills. Except for nominal amounts, mostly coins,

---

EXHIBIT 8
Summary of Monetary Tools of the Federal Reserve

FEDERAL RESERVE POLICY	EXPANSIONARY MONETARY POLICY	RESTRICTIVE MONETARY POLICY
1. Reserve requirements	*Reduce reserve requirements,* because this will create additional excess reserves and induce banks to extend additional loans, which will expand the money supply.	*Raise reserve requirements,* because this will reduce the excess reserves of banks, causing them to make fewer loans; as the outstanding loans of banks decline, the money stock will be reduced.
2. Open market operations	*Purchase additional U.S. securities,* which will expand the money stock directly, and increase the reserves of banks, inducing bankers in turn to extend more loans; this will expand the money stock indirectly.	*Sell previously purchased U.S. securities,* which will reduce both the money stock and excess reserves; the decline in excess reserves will indirectly lead to an additional reduction in the money supply.
3. Discount rate	*Lower the discount rate,* which will encourage more borrowing from the Fed; banks will tend to reduce their reserves and extend more loans because of the lower cost of borrowing from the Fed if they temporarily run short on reserves.	*Raise the discount rate,* thereby discouraging borrowing from the Fed; banks will tend to extend fewer loans and build up their reserves so they will not have to borrow from the Fed.

FRANK AND ERNEST® by Bob Thaves

Source: Frank and Ernest reprinted by permission of Newspaper Enterprise Association, Inc.

the Treasury does not issue money. Borrowing—the public sale of new U.S. securities—is the primary method used by the Treasury to cover any excess of expenditures in relation to revenues from taxes and other sources.

Whereas the Treasury is concerned with the revenues and expenditures of the government, the Fed is concerned primarily with the availability of money and credit for the entire economy. The Fed does not issue U.S. securities. It merely purchases and sells government securities issued by the Treasury as a means of controlling the economy's money supply. Unlike the Treasury, the Fed can purchase government bonds by writing a check on itself without having deposits, gold, or anything else to back it up. In doing so, the Fed creates money out of thin air. The Treasury does not have this power. The Fed does not have an obligation to meet the financial responsibilities of the U.S. government. That is the domain of the Treasury. Although the two agencies cooperate with each other, they are distinctly different institutions established for different purposes (see accompanying Thumbnail Sketch).

It is important to recognize that the buying and selling of bonds by the Treasury and by the Fed have different effects on the supply of money. The key point here is that the Treasury and the Fed handle revenues collected from the selling of bonds in a different manner. When the Treasury issues and sells bonds, it does so to pay for federal government expenditures. After all, the Treasury issues the bonds in order to generate the required revenue for its spending. The people who buy the bonds from the Treasury have less money, but when the Treasury spends, the recipients of its spending will have more money. Thus, Treasury borrowing and spending does not change the supply of money.

In contrast, when the Fed sells bonds, it, in effect, takes the revenues and holds them, keeping them out of circulation. Because this money is out of circulation and can no longer be used for the purchase of goods and services, the money supply shrinks. On the other hand, if the Fed later wishes to increase the money supply, it can buy bonds, which will increase the availability of bank reserves and the money supply.

AMBIGUITIES IN THE MEANING AND MEASUREMENT OF THE MONEY SUPPLY

In the past, economists have generally used the *growth rate* of the money supply (either M1 or M2) to gauge the direction of monetary policy. A rapid growth rate of the money supply was indicative of expansionary monetary policy—a policy that was adding stimulus to the economy. Conversely, slow growth, or a decline, in the money stock implied a more restrictive monetary policy.

Both the history of money and recent developments in financial markets are causing many economists to reconsider the significance of growth rate figures. Historically, major shifts in the nature of money (for example, the shift from precious metals to a fiat

What are the Differences between the U.S. Treasury and the Federal Reserve Banking System?

U.S. Treasury
1. Concerned with the finances of the federal government
2. Issues bonds to the general public to finance the budget deficits of the federal government
3. Does not determine the money supply

Federal Reserve
1. Concerned with the monetary climate for the economy
2. Does not issue bonds
3. Determines the money supply—primarily through its buying and selling of bonds issued by the U.S. Treasury

currency) have substantially influenced the lives of people. Financial innovations continue to affect our methods of payment and the meaning of the various money supply measures.

Throughout most of the 1970s, M1 was comprised almost entirely of currency and demand deposits. At the time, regulations virtually prohibited banks from offering their customers interest-earning checking accounts. Increased competition from mutual funds led to the repeal of the regulatory restraints in 1980, and, as **Exhibit 9** illustrates, this repeal was followed by rapid growth of interest-earning checking deposits. In turn, growth of these deposits pushed up the growth rate of the M1 money supply. The growth of M1 during the 1980s, however, was deceptive. To a degree, it reflected a change in the nature of the M1 money supply. Interest-earning checking accounts are less costly to hold than currency and demand deposits. In essence, interest-earning checking accounts are partly medium-of-exchange money and partly savings. As a result, the M1 money supply of the 1980s is not precisely comparable with the figures for earlier years.

Another innovation influenced the M1 money supply in the 1990s. Beginning in 1994, a number of banks began to encourage customers to move deposits from interest-earning checking accounts into money market deposit accounts. Each of these accounts provides customers with similar services. However, because interest-earning checking deposits are included in M1 but money market deposits are not, this shift reduced the size of

EXHIBIT 9
The Changing Nature of the M1 Money Supply

As a result of deregulation during the 1980s, interest-earning checkable deposits grew rapidly and they now account for approximately one-quarter of the M1 money supply. Since the opportunity cost of holding these other checkable deposits is less than for other forms of money, strictly speaking, the money supply today is not exactly comparable to the money supply prior to 1980.

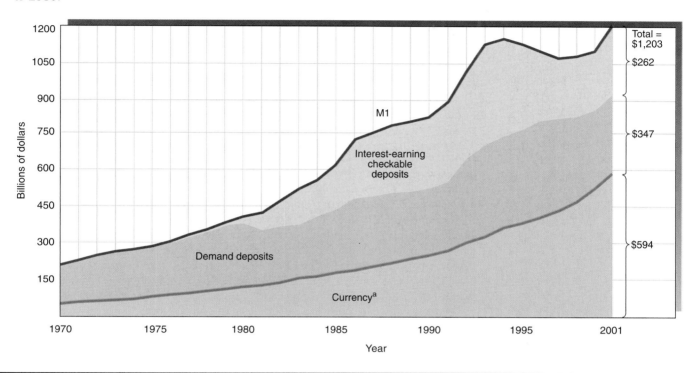

^{a}Traveler's checks are included in this category.
Source: http://www.federalreserve.gov.

the M1 money supply figures. It was largely responsible for the decline in the M1 money supply during the period 1995–1997 (see Exhibit 9). As with the introduction of interest-earning checking during the 1980s, these shifts distorted the M1 money supply statistics and reduced their comparability across time periods.

Other structural changes and financial innovations—some of which are already present and others of which are likely to develop in the near future—are altering the nature of money, and therefore the usefulness of money growth figures (both M1 and M2), as an indicator of monetary policy. Let's consider three of these factors.

1. *Widespread use of the U.S. dollar outside the United States.* The U.S. dollar is widely used in other countries. To a degree, this has been true for a long time. However, a number of countries have recently relaxed legal restraints limiting the domestic use of foreign currencies (and the maintenance of foreign currency bank accounts).[3] As noted earlier, the currency component of the M1 money supply was approximately $586 billion at year-end 2001. According to a recent study by the

---

[3]The number of countries where it is legal for citizens to maintain a foreign currency bank account rose from 38 in 1985 to 62 in 1995. See James Gwartney, Robert Lawson, and Walter Block, *Economic Freedom of the World: 1975–1995* (Washington, D.C.: Cato Institute, 1996), p. 81.

Federal Reserve, more than one-half and perhaps as much as two-thirds of this currency is held overseas. The movement of these funds abroad (and our inability to measure it with any degree of precision) substantially reduces the reliability of the M1 money supply figures. (*Note:* There is also some impact on M2. However, since the currency component is a much smaller proportion of M2 than M1, the distortion of M2 is less severe.)

2. ***The increasing availability of low-fee stock and bond mutual funds.*** Until recently, financial investors were generally required to pay a substantial start-up, or load, fee when purchasing stock and bond mutual funds. This reduced their attractiveness relative to the various savings instruments included in the M2 money supply. No-load stock and bond mutual funds—that is, funds without an initial fee—are now increasingly available. Because stock and bond mutual fund investments are not counted in any of the monetary aggregates, movement of funds from various M2 components (money market mutual funds, for example) will distort the M2 money supply figures.[4]

3. ***Debit cards and electronic money.*** Financial innovators are currently developing a more convenient and versatile debit card. A card of this type would transfer funds from the cardholder's bank account to that of the seller. If more and more businesses accept payment via debit cards in the future, Americans will have less reason to hold currency. As less money is held in the form of currency (and more as bank deposits), the money supply will grow rapidly unless the Fed takes offsetting actions. Like other changes in the nature of money, innovations in this area will reduce the future reliability of the money supply data, particularly the M1 figures, as indicators of monetary policy.

Finally, there is the expected development of electronic money. It is difficult to forecast the nature of changes in this area. However, if individuals and businesses can economically and safely use electronic cash, instead of checking deposits and currency, it will clearly change the nature of money and the meaning of the monetary aggregates. If, as is anticipated, these electronic deposits can safely be maintained outside the banking system, they may also change the major functions of the banking system.

Exhibit 10 presents data on the annual growth rates of both M1 and M2. Reflecting the factors we have just discussed, the M1 money supply has recently shown more variability than the M2 figures. When using money supply growth rates as an indicator of monetary policy, most analysts now rely on M2 (rather than M1). We will follow this convention. However, we should keep in mind that future innovative changes are likely to alter the nature of money and therefore the reliability of the money supply figures (including those for M2) as an indicator of monetary policy.

THE FUTURE OF MONEY

Technological Changes

Will electronic money alter your future? Consider a world where your "paycheck" is deposited in an electronic cash account accessible through your personal computer, but protected with a personal code. With the touch of a few computer keys, you can transfer

[4]For additional information on this topic, see Sean Collins and Cheryl L. Edwards, "Redefining M2 to Include Bond and Equity Mutual Funds," *Federal Reserve Bank of St. Louis Review*, November/December 1994, pp. 7–30; Kenneth N. Daniels and Neil B. Murphy, "The Impact of Technological Change on the Currency Behavior of Households: An Empirical Cross-Section Study," *Journal of Money, Credit, and Banking* 26 (November 1994): 867–874; and John V. Duca, "Should Bond Funds Be Included in M2?" *Journal of Banking and Finance* 19 (April 1995): 131–152.

EXHIBIT 10
The Growth Rate of the M1 and M2 Money Supply: 1970–2001

Here we present the annual growth rates for both the M1 and M2 money supply figures. Since the mid-1980s, the variability of the M1 supply has been much greater than that for M2. To a large degree, the greater variability of M1 reflects regulatory changes and innovations in financial markets that have changed the nature of M1.

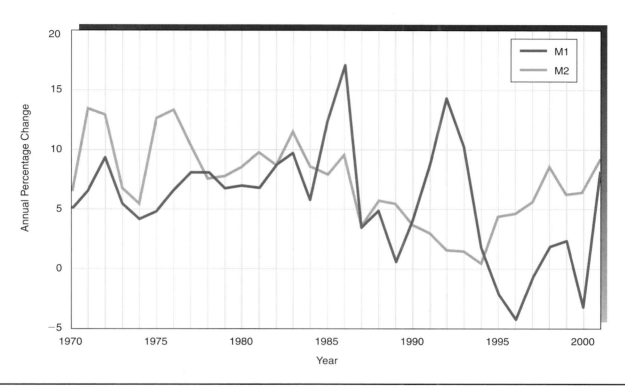

Source: http://www.federalreserve.gov.

funds to pay your monthly utility bill, mortgage and auto loan payments, and other regular expenditures. You can also shop on the Internet and use your deposits to pay for magazines, financial advice, and numerous consumer goods. Your funds can also be used to purchase stocks, bonds, mutual funds, and other financial investments. Like your paycheck, earnings from (or future sales of) these investments can be automatically deposited into your electronic cash account. If you want to withdraw some electronic cash, you merely insert a card and load it with transferable purchasing power, which is widely accepted by restaurants, recreation facilities, retail stores, and other business establishments. If you want to give or receive funds from family or friends, you simply merge their "cash cards" with yours and funds can be added to one card and subtracted from another. In effect, your electronic money allows you to do anything you can currently do with currency or checking deposits—and you can do it faster, safer, and more conveniently.

Many think that this world, or something very much like it, is only a few years away. Already at over 40 colleges and universities such as Colby College, Florida State University, and Pennsylvania State University, student identification cards have become so-called Smart Cards. Students can store money on these Smart Cards, which can be used to make purchases at retail stores as well as pay university fees such as parking tickets and tuition. Technological innovations such as these will certainly alter the nature of money and reduce the importance of the banking system. They may even limit the ability of central banks to conduct monetary policy.

Institutional Changes

Introduction of a New Currency—The Euro

If you have ever traveled in Europe in the past, you know that as you went from country to country, you had to exchange currencies in order to do business. Starting in January 2002, this was no longer necessary. Twelve European nations (Austria, Belgium, Finland, France, Germany, Greece, Ireland, Italy, Luxembourg, Netherlands, Portugal, and Spain) now use a single European currency, the euro. This new currency is managed by a new central bank, the European Central Bank (ECB).

The relationship between the ECB and the former central banks of the 12 countries is much like that between the Board of Governors of the Fed and the District Federal Reserve banks. The ECB sets policy; the national central banks are expected to carry it out. The ECB, located in the Eurotower in Frankfurt, is directed by a 6-member executive committee and a 18-member council comprised of the six executive committee members plus the central bank governor from each of the 12 euro countries. On paper, the ECB is largely independent of political forces—some have called it the world's most independent central bank. Its prime objective laid out in the Maastricht Treaty is price stability. The current target rate of inflation is 2 percent or less. The euro is expected not only to reduce transactions costs within the monetary union, but also to challenge the dollar and the yen for use in international markets. It will be interesting to follow the development of this new currency. One thing is certain—credibility is an important element influencing the choice of currency. Thus, it will be vitally important for the euro to get off to a good start to begin establishing a record of price stability along with sound economic growth.

Movement Toward Fewer Currencies

The number of independent currencies in the world is shrinking. Smaller countries have been linking their currencies to those of larger countries. For example, Hong Kong ties its domestic currency—the Hong Kong dollar—to the U.S. dollar at a 7.7-to-one rate. Other countries adopting a similar strategy include Lithuania, Bosnia, Bulgaria, and Estonia. When a country ties its currency to a strong foreign currency and backs each unit with assets denominated in the foreign currency, people are more likely to be persuaded that the currency will maintain its future value. This increased credibility is an important benefit, particularly for countries with a long history of hyperinflation and monetary instability.

Another factor reducing the number of currencies has been the informal use or outright adoption of a strong foreign currency as a means of payment. The U.S. dollar has been formally adopted as the official currency in Panama, El Salvador, and Ecuador. Currently, dollars are also widely held and, in some cases, used as a means of exchange in Russia (and several other countries of the former Soviet Union), Argentina, Bolivia, Mexico, and other Latin American countries. As we previously noted, an estimated $300 billion of U.S. currency—more than half of the total—is held abroad.

There are three distinct advantages for foreign countries to use U.S. dollars or another strong currency as the means of payment. First, it increases trade as their citizens can buy and sell with more people without converting into another currency. Second, the U.S. dollar and several other currencies have a history of relatively stable value and thus are a more reliable store of value. Third, increased foreign investment is likely since investors won't have to worry as much about exchange rate risk.

How do these holdings of dollars by foreigners affect the U.S. economy? Foreigners acquired the dollars by providing goods and services to Americans. In effect, Americans got valuable goods and services by simply issuing pieces of paper—dollar bills. The dollars held abroad are very much like an interest-free loan to the U.S. government and, indirectly, the taxpayers of the United States. If foreigners were not willing to hold these dollars at a zero interest rate, the U.S. Treasury would have to issue more bonds (perhaps as much as $300 billion more) and pay interest to the bondholders. As a result, the annual interest costs of the federal government would be about $15 billion higher.

What does the future hold? The U.S. dollar is likely to become the dominant currency in the Americas. If the euro gains credibility, then European countries which do not belong to the European Union are likely to adopt the euro or link their currency to it. Likewise, the Japanese yen may emerge as the primary currency in Asia. Therefore, in the relatively near future, most of the world's trade—both domestic and foreign—may well be conducted with only three or four currencies.

In this chapter, we focused on the banking industry and the mechanics of monetary policy. We are now ready to analyze the impact of monetary policy on output, growth, and prices. How do Fed policies influence the economy? Have they exerted a stabilizing influence? These topics and related issues will be considered in the next two chapters.

LOOKING AHEAD

KEY POINTS

▼ Money is a financial asset that is widely accepted as a medium of exchange. It also provides a means of storing purchasing power into the future and is used as a unit of account. Without money, exchange would be both costly and tedious. Money derives its value from its scarcity (supply) relative to its usefulness (demand).

▼ Economists use alternative measures of the money supply to judge the conduct of monetary policy. The narrowest definition of the money supply (M1) includes only (a) currency in the hands of the public, (b) checkable deposits (both demand and interest-earning) held in depository institutions, and (c) traveler's checks.

▼ The broader M2 money supply includes M1 plus (a) savings deposits, (b) time deposits (of less than $100,000), and (c) money market mutual fund shares.

▼ Banking is a business. Banks provide their depositors with safekeeping of money, check-clearing services on demand deposits, and interest payments on time deposits. Banks derive most of their income from the extension of loans and investments in interest-earning securities.

▼ Under legislation adopted in 1980, savings and loan associations and credit unions are permitted to provide essentially the same services as commercial banks. The Federal Reserve System imposes similar regulation on all these depository institutions. In essence, they are all part of an integrated banking system.

▼ Under a fractional reserve banking system, banks are required to maintain only a fraction of their deposits in the form of reserves (vault cash or deposits with the Fed). Excess reserves may be invested or loaned to customers. When banks extend additional loans, they create additional deposits and thereby expand the money supply.

▼ The Federal Reserve System is a central banking authority designed to provide a stable monetary framework for the entire economy. The Fed is a banker's bank. The structure of the Fed is designed to insulate it from political pressures so that it will have greater freedom to follow policies more consistent with economic stability.

The Fed has three major tools with which to control the money supply.

a. ***Establishment of the required reserve ratio.*** When the Fed lowers the required reserve ratio, it creates excess reserves and allows banks to extend additional loans, expanding the money supply. Raising the reserve requirements has the opposite effect.

b. ***Open market operations.*** When the Fed buys U.S. securities, the money supply will expand because bond buyers will acquire money and bank reserves will increase, placing banks in a position to expand the money supply through the extension of additional loans. When the Fed sells securities, the money supply will contract because bond buyers are giving up money in ex-

change for securities and the reserves available to banks will decline (causing them to extend fewer loans).

c. ***The discount rate.*** An increase in the discount rate is restrictive because it discourages banks from borrowing from the Fed to extend new loans. A reduction in the discount rate is expansionary because it makes borrowing from the Fed less costly.

▼ The Federal Reserve and the U.S. Treasury are distinct agencies. The Fed is concerned primarily with the money supply and the establishment of a stable monetary climate, while the Treasury focuses on budgetary matters—tax revenues, government expenditures, and the financing of government debt.

▼ Historically, the rate of change of the money supply has been used to judge the direction and intensity of monetary policy. However, recent financial innovations and other structural changes (for example, the widespread use of U.S. currency in other countries) have blurred the meaning of money and reduced the reliability of the various money supply measures. In the computer age, continued change in this area is likely.

CRITICAL ANALYSIS QUESTIONS

*1. What is meant by the statement, "This asset is illiquid"? List some things that you own, ranking them from most liquid to most illiquid.

2. What determines whether or not a financial asset is included in the M1 money supply? Why are interest-earning checkable deposits included in M1, while interest-earning savings accounts and Treasury bills are not?

*3. What makes money valuable? Does money perform an economic service? Explain. Could money perform its function better if there were twice as much of it? Why or why not?

4. "People are poor because they don't have very much money. Yet, central bankers keep money scarce. If people had more money, poverty could be eliminated." Evaluate this view. Do you think it reflects sound economics?

5. Why can banks continue to hold reserves that are only a fraction of the demand deposits of their customers? Is your money safe in a bank? Why or why not?

*6. Suppose you withdraw $100 from your checking account. How does this transaction affect (a) the supply of money, (b) the reserves of your bank, and (c) the excess reserves of your bank?

7. Explain how the creation of new bank reserves would cause the money supply to increase by some multiple of the newly created reserves.

*8. How will the following actions affect the money supply?
   a. A reduction in the discount rate
   b. An increase in the reserve requirements
   c. Purchase by the Fed of $100 million of U.S. securities from a commercial bank
   d. Sale by the U.S. Treasury of $100 million of newly issued bonds to a commercial bank
   e. An increase in the discount rate
   f. Sale by the Fed of $200 million of U.S. securities to a private investor

9. What's wrong with this way of thinking? "When the government runs a budget deficit, it simply pays its bills by printing more money. As the newly printed money works its way through the economy, it waters down the value of paper money already in circulation. Thus, it takes more money to buy things. Budget deficits are the major cause of inflation."

*10. If the Federal Reserve does not take any offsetting action, what would happen to the supply of money if the general public decided to increase its holdings of currency and decrease its checking deposits by an equal amount?

11. What is the federal funds interest rate? If the Fed wants to use open market operations to lower the federal funds rate, what action should it take? Explain.

*12. If the Fed wants to expand the money supply, why is it more likely to do so by purchasing bonds rather than by lowering reserve requirements?

*13. Are the following statements true or false?
   a. "You can never have too much money."
   b. "When you deposit currency in a commercial bank, cash goes out of circulation and the money supply declines."
   c. "If the Fed would create more money, Americans would achieve a higher standard of living."

14. How has the nature of the M1 money supply changed in recent years? How have these changes influenced the usefulness of M1 as an indicator of monetary policy? Why do many analysts prefer to use M2 rather than M1 when comparing the monetary policy of the 1990s with that of earlier periods?

15. Why do foreigners often hold U.S. dollars? How does the holding of dollars by foreigners affect the welfare of Americans?

*16. Suppose that the Federal Reserve purchases a bond for $100,000 from Donald Truck, who deposits the proceeds in the Manufacturer's National Bank.
   a. What will be the impact of this transaction on the supply of money?
   b. If the reserve requirement ratio is 20 percent, what is the maximum amount of additional loans that the Manufacturer's Bank will be able to extend as the result of Truck's deposit?
   c. Given the 20 percent reserve requirement, what is the maximum increase in the quantity of checkable deposits that could result throughout the entire banking system because of the Fed's action?

d. Would you expect this to happen? Why or why not? Explain.

17. Suppose that the reserve requirement is 10 percent and the balance sheet of the People's National Bank looks like the accompanying example.
   a. What are the required reserves of People's National Bank? Does the bank have any excess reserves?
   b. What is the maximum loan that the bank could extend?
   c. Indicate how the bank's balance sheet would be altered if it extended this loan.
   d. Suppose that the required reserves were 20 percent. If this were the case, would the bank be in a position to extend any additional loans? Explain.

Assets		Liabilities	
Vault Cash	$ 20,000	Checking deposits	$200,000
Deposits at Fed	30,000	Net worth	15,000
Securities	45,000		
Loans	120,000		

*18. Suppose that the reserve requirements are 10 percent and that the Federal Reserve purchases $2 billion of additional securities on a given day.
   a. How will this transaction affect the M1 money supply?
   b. If the brokerage firm that sold the bonds to the Fed deposits the proceeds of the sale into its account with City Bank, what is the maximum amount of additional loans that City Bank will be able to extend as the result of this deposit?
   c. If additional loans are extended throughout the banking system and the proceeds are always redeposited back into a checking account, by how much will the M1 money supply increase if banks use all their additional reserves to extend new loans?
   d. Suppose that banks use all their additional reserves to extend new loans but that 10 percent of the loan proceeds (and the additional funds of the brokerage firm) are held as currency rather than being redeposited into a checking account. When this is the case, by how much will the Fed's action increase the money supply?
   e. Suppose that banks use 5 percent of their additional reserves to build up their excess reserves and that 10 percent of the proceeds of new loans (and the initial bond sale) end up circulating as currency rather than being redeposited into a checking account. By how much will the Fed's action increase the money supply? Indicate the size of both the potential and actual money deposit multiplier in this case.

f. Why is the actual money deposit multiplier generally less than the potential multiplier?

19. How would the following influence the growth rates of the M1 and M2 money supply figures over time?

   a. An increase in the quantity of U.S. currency held overseas

   b. A shift of funds from interest-earning checking deposits to money market mutual funds

   c. A reduction in the holdings of currency by the general public because debit cards have become more popular and widely accepted

   d. The shift of funds from money market mutual funds into stock and bond mutual funds because the fees to invest in the latter have declined

*Asterisk denotes questions for which answers are given in Appendix B.

CHAPTER **14**

Modern Macroeconomics: Monetary Policy

The conventional wisdom once held that money doesn't matter. Now there is wide agreement that monetary policy can significantly affect real economic activity in the short run, though only price level in the long run.

—Daniel L. Thornton and David C. Wheelock[1]

Chapter Focus

- What are the determinants of the demand for money? How is the supply of money determined?

- How does monetary policy affect interest rates, output, and employment?

- Can monetary policy stimulate real GDP in the short run? Can it do so in the long run?

- Does it make any difference whether people quickly anticipate the effects of a change in monetary policy? Why?

- Does an increase in the supply of money cause inflation?

[1]Daniel L. Thornton and David C. Wheelock, "Editor's Introduction," *Federal Reserve Bank of St. Louis: Review* (May/June 1995): vii.

n the preceding chapter we noted that many consider the chairman of the Federal Reserve System to be the second most important person—next to the president—in the United States. Why is this so? Along with other members of the Fed's Board of Governors and Federal Open Market Committee, the Fed chairman is in charge of monetary policy. Monetary policy exerts a powerful impact on the economy. The central objective of monetary policy is the establishment of a stable environment so the economy can achieve high levels of both output and employment. Price stability—a persistently low rate of inflation—is crucial for the achievement of this objective. When conducted appropriately, monetary policy provides the foundation for economic prosperity. In contrast, the consequences of inappropriate monetary policy are often disastrous.

As we have used the aggregate demand/aggregate supply model up to this point, we have assumed that the supply of money was constant. We will now relax this assumption. The previous chapter outlined the tools the Fed has to alter the supply of money. This chapter will focus on how monetary policy works—how changes in the supply of money affect interest rates, output, and prices. ■

IMPACT OF MONETARY POLICY

Like the modern view of fiscal policy, the modern view of monetary policy is the product of an evolutionary process. In the aftermath of the Great Depression and Keynesian Revolution, there was a great debate concerning the importance of monetary policy. During the 1950s and 1960s, most Keynesians argued that monetary policy could be used to control inflation, but that it was often ineffective as a means of stimulating aggregate demand. It was popular to draw an analogy between monetary policy and the workings of a string. Like a string, monetary policy could be used to pull (hold back) price increases and thereby control inflation. However, just as one cannot push with a string, according to this popular view, monetary policy could not be used to push (stimulate) aggregate demand.

Beginning in the late 1950s, this position was hotly contested by Milton Friedman, later a Nobel laureate, and a group of economists, subsequently called **monetarists**. In contrast with the Keynesians of that era, the monetarists argued that changes in the stock of money exerted a powerful influence on output (in the short run), as well as prices (in the long run). Indeed, the monetarists charged that erratic monetary policy was the primary source of both business instability and inflation. Milton Friedman summarized the monetarist position in his 1967 presidential address to the American Economic Association when he stated,

> Every major contraction in this country has been either produced by monetary disorder or greatly exacerbated by monetary disorder. Every major inflation has been produced by monetary expansion.[2]

A modern view of monetary policy emerged from this debate. While minor disagreements remain, both modern Keynesians and monetarists now agree that monetary policy produces an important impact on our economy.[3] The following sections present the modern consensus view with regard to how monetary policy affects the economy.

Monetarists
A group of economists who believe that (1) monetary instability is the major cause of fluctuations in real GDP and (2) rapid growth of the money supply is the major cause of inflation.

---

[2]Milton Friedman, "The Role of Monetary Policy," *American Economic Review* (March 1968): 12.

[3]The evolution of the views of Paul Samuelson, who might properly be regarded as the father of American Keynesian economics, best illustrates the change in the Keynesian view with regard to the relative importance of monetary and fiscal policy. Commenting on the 12th edition of his classic text in 1985, Samuelson stated: "In the early editions of the book, fiscal policy was top banana. In later editions that emphasis changed to equality. In this edition we've taken a stand that monetary policy is most important."

OUTSTANDING ECONOMIST

Milton Friedman (1912–)

The 1976 recipient of the Nobel Prize, Friedman is widely regarded as the most influential spokesman for a free market economy in the twentieth century. With the assistance of other monetarists, he eventually convinced even his critics that monetary policy exerts a strong impact on the economy. Friedman maintains that business fluctuations are the result of monetary instability. His popular books *Capitalism and Freedom* (1962) and *Free to Choose* (1980), coauthored with his wife, Rose, are classical treatises in support of economic freedom. After spending years at the University of Chicago, he is currently on the faculty at Stanford University. Now in his nineties, he continues to be an active scholar and writer.

Demand and Supply of Money

Why do individuals and businesses want to hold cash and checking-account money rather than bonds, stocks, automobiles, buildings, and consumer durables? When considering this question, one must not confuse (1) the desire to hold money balances with (2) the desire for more wealth (or income). Of course, all of us would like to have more wealth, but we may be perfectly satisfied with our holdings of money in relation to our holdings of other goods, *given our current level of wealth*. When we say people want to hold more (or less) money, we mean that they want to restructure their wealth toward larger (smaller) money balances.

People hold money for a variety of reasons. As we discussed in the previous chapter, money provides us with instant purchasing power. At the most basic level, we hold money so we can conduct transactions. Households hold money balances so they can pay for the weekly groceries, the monthly house payment, gasoline for the car, lunch for the kids, and other items purchased regularly. Businesses demand money so they can meet the weekly payroll, pay the utility bills, purchase supplies, and conduct other transactions. Most individuals also hold money so they will be in a better position to deal with the uncertainties of the real world—an unexpected repair bill, an accident, or a medical emergency, for example. Economists refer to this as the *precautionary motive* for holding money. In addition, money is an asset—a means of storing value. Some may hold money as a method of storing purchasing power for future use.

Higher interest rates make it more costly to hold money. Consider the cost of holding $1,000 in the form of currency and demand deposits (which do not earn interest) rather than in interest-earning bonds, for example. If the interest rate is 10 percent, it will cost you $100 per year to hold an additional $1,000 of noninterest-earning money. In contrast, if the interest rate is 1 percent, the annual cost of holding the $1,000 money balance will be only $10. Even if you maintain money balances in an interest-earning checking account, higher interest returns are generally available if you are willing to tie up the funds in a bond or some other less liquid form of savings. Thus, the opportunity cost of holding money is directly related to the nominal interest rate.

A curve that outlines the relationship between the interest rate (measured on the y-axis) and the quantity of money (measured on the x-axis) is called the **demand for money.** *As part a of* **Exhibit 1** *illustrates, there is an inverse relationship between the interest rate and the quantity of money demanded.* This inverse relationship reflects the fact that higher interest rates make it more costly to hold money instead of interest-earning assets like bonds. Therefore, as interest rates rise, individuals and businesses will try to manage their affairs with smaller money balances.

Demand for money
A curve that indicates the relationship between the interest rate and the quantity of money people want to hold. Because higher interest rates increase the opportunity cost of holding money, the quantity demanded of money will be inversely related to the interest rate.

EXHIBIT 1
Demand and Supply of Money

The demand for money is inversely related to the money interest rate (a). The supply of money is determined by the monetary authorities (the Fed) through their open market operations, discount-rate policy, and reserve requirements (b).

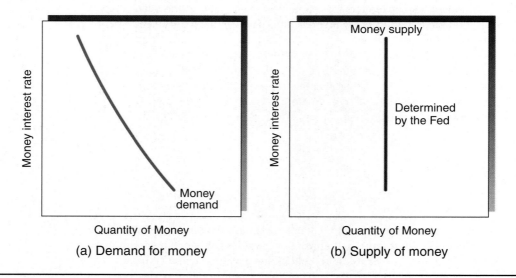

(a) Demand for money

(b) Supply of money

Like other demand curves, the demand curve for money is constructed holding other things constant. The demand for money balances will generally increase with the nominal value of transactions. If wages and prices increase, more money will be required by households to purchase the costlier weekly market basket, and more money will be required by businesses to pay the larger wage bill. Similarly, if prices remain constant, while the quantity of goods bought and sold increases, larger money balances will be required to conduct the larger volume of business. In essence, as nominal GDP increases as the result of either higher prices or the growth of real output, the demand for money balances will also increase—that is, the entire demand for money schedule will shift to the right. Conversely, a decline in nominal GDP will decrease the demand for money, shifting the schedule to the left.

With the passage of time, changes in institutional factors will also influence the demand schedule for money. Both evidence and logic indicate that changes in institutional arrangements have reduced the demand for money in recent years. The widespread use of general purpose credit cards makes it easier for households to reconcile their bills with their receipt of income. Readily available short-term loans have reduced the need to maintain substantial cash balances for emergencies. These changes have gradually reduced the demand for money (shifting the entire schedule to the left).

As we discussed in the previous chapter, the quantity of money available to the economy is determined by the monetary authorities, the Fed in the case of the United States. The Fed can use its control over reserve requirements, the discount rate, and especially open market operations to set the supply of money at whatever level it wants. Changes in the interest rate do not alter the Fed's ability to determine the supply of money. Therefore, as Exhibit 1 (part b) illustrates, the money supply schedule is vertical. The vertical supply curve reflects that the quantity of money is determined by Fed policy and it is not affected by changes in the interest rate.

EXHIBIT 2
Money Supply, Money Demand, and Equilibrium

The money interest rate will tend to gravitate toward equilibrium, i_e, where the quantity of money demanded by households and businesses will equal the quantity of money supplied by the Fed.

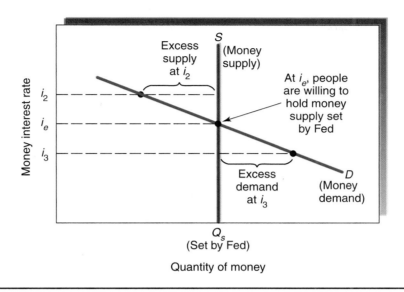

Equilibrium Between Money Demand and Money Supply

Exhibit 2 brings the money demand and money supply together and illustrates how they determine the equilibrium rate of interest. The money interest rate will move toward i_e, where the quantity of money demanded by households and businesses is just equal to the quantity supplied by the Fed. At the equilibrium interest rate, people are willing to hold the stock of money the Fed has supplied to the economy.

At an above equilibrium interest rate, i_2 for example, people would not want to hold as much money as the Fed has supplied. Accordingly, they would try to reduce their money balances. They might do so by using some of their money balances to buy bonds. This increase in demand for bonds would drive bond prices up and interest rates down. (*Remember*: Higher bond prices imply lower interest rates.) As a result, the money interest rate would move toward the i_e equilibrium. On the other hand, at a below equilibrium money interest rate, i_3 for example, an excess demand for money would be present. Excess money demand indicates that people would like to hold a larger quantity of money than the Fed has supplied. Under these circumstances, they might sell bonds in an effort to get their hands on more money. In turn, their sale of bonds would reduce bond prices and place upward pressure on interest rates, causing them to move toward i_e. Therefore, only the equilibrium interest rate i_e would tend to persist into the future.

Transmission of Monetary Policy

How will a change in the money supply affect the economy? As we previously noted, the Fed typically uses open market operations to control the supply of money. If the Fed wants to shift to a more **expansionary monetary policy**, it will buy bonds. **Exhibit 3** illustrates the impact on the economy. Initially, we consider the situation where the money interest rate (i_1 in the money balances market) is equal to the real interest rate

Expansionary monetary policy
A shift in monetary policy designed to stimulate aggregate demand. Bond purchases, creation of additional bank reserves, and an increase in the growth rate of the money supply are generally indicative of a shift to a more expansionary monetary policy.

EXHIBIT 3
Transmission of Monetary Policy

When the Fed shifts to a more expansionary monetary policy, it will generally buy additional bonds. This will supply the banking system with additional reserves. Both the Fed's bond purchases and the banks' use of the additional reserves to extend new loans will increase the supply of loanable funds (shift from S_1 to S_2, part b) and place downward pressure on the real rate of interest. As the real interest rate falls (to r_2), aggregate demand increases (to AD_2 in part c). Since the effects of the monetary expansion were unanticipated, the expansion in AD leads to both an increase in current output (to Y_2) and higher prices (inflation) in the short run.

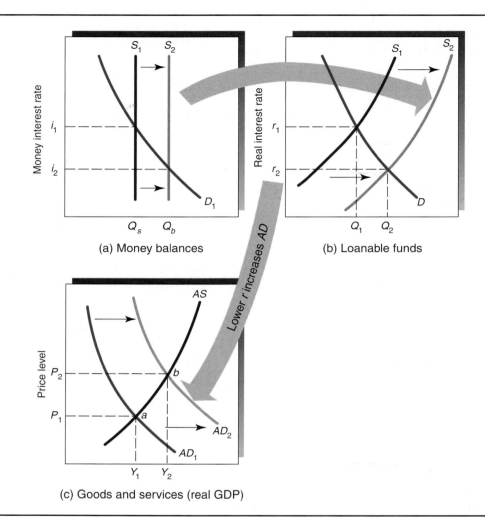

(a) Money balances

(b) Loanable funds

(c) Goods and services (real GDP)

(r_1 in the loanable funds market). This indicates that the expected rate of inflation is zero. When the Fed purchases bonds in order to increase the money supply (shift from S_1 to S_2 in part a), it bids up bond prices and injects additional reserves into the banking system. Profit-seeking banks will not let the additional reserves lie idle; they will seek to attract additional loan customers so that the available reserves can be fully invested in interest-earning assets. This combination of factors—higher bond prices and additional reserves that the banks will use to extend loans—will increase the supply of loanable funds (shift to S_2 as shown in part b of Exhibit 3). In the short run, the real interest rate will fall to r_2.

How will the Fed's bond purchases, creation of additional bank reserves, and lower real interest rate influence the demand for goods and services? As part c of Exhibit 3 illustrates, aggregate demand will increase (shift from AD_1 to AD_2). Economists stress the importance of three factors that contribute to this increase in aggregate demand.[4]

1. ***The lower real interest rate will make current investment and consumption cheaper relative to future spending.*** At the lower interest rate, entrepreneurs will undertake

---

[4]See the *Federal Reserve Bank of St. Louis: Review* (May/June 1995) and the *Journal of Economic Perspectives* (Fall 1995) for additional details on how changes in monetary policy affect aggregate demand.

some investment projects they otherwise would have forgone. Spending by firms on structures and equipment will increase. Similarly, consumers will decide to expand their purchases of automobiles and consumer durables, which can now be enjoyed with smaller monthly payments.

2. ***The lower interest rate may also lead to an outflow of capital, which will cause the dollar to depreciate and thereby stimulate the net export component of aggregate demand.*** As domestic interest rates fall, both domestic and foreign investors will shift some of their financial investments to other countries where rates of return are more attractive. As investors shift funds abroad, they will supply dollars and demand foreign currencies in the foreign exchange market. This will cause the dollar to depreciate. In turn, the depreciation in the exchange-rate value of the dollar will make imports more expensive for Americans and U.S. exports cheaper for foreigners. As a result, U.S. imports will decline and exports will expand. This increase in net exports will also stimulate aggregate demand.

3. ***The lower interest rates will tend to increase asset prices—for example, the prices of stocks, houses, and other structures—which will also stimulate current demand.*** As the prices of real and financial assets rise, household wealth increases, which will stimulate additional consumption. Perhaps more important, the higher prices of houses and other physical assets will make new construction of these assets more profitable. The increased profitability will induce entrepreneurs to undertake additional construction in these areas, which will expand both investment and aggregate demand.

The Thumbnail Sketch on page 326 outlines the complex sequence of events through which Fed bond purchases expand the money supply and stimulate aggregate demand. This sequence is sometimes referred to as the interest rate transmission mechanism of monetary policy.[5]

Unanticipated Expansionary Monetary Policy

As we have previously discussed, modern macroeconomic analysis stresses the importance of whether a change is anticipated or unanticipated. If people do not anticipate the increase in aggregate demand accompanying an expansionary monetary policy, costs will rise less than prices in the short run. Profit margins will improve. Businesses will respond with an expansion in the output of goods and services (as illustrated by the increase in real output from Y_1 to Y_2 in part c of Exhibit 3).

Modern analysis indicates that an unexpected increase in the supply of money will reduce the real rate of interest, thereby triggering an increase in the demand for goods and services. In turn, the increase in aggregate demand will expand real output and employment in the short run.

Part a of **Exhibit 4** illustrates the potential of expansionary monetary policy to direct a recessionary economy to full employment. Consider an economy initially at output Y_1, below full employment capacity (Y_F). Expansionary monetary policy will increase aggregate demand (to AD_2). Real output will expand (to Y_F). In essence, the expansionary monetary policy provides an alternative to the economy's self-corrective mechanism. In the absence

---

[5]There is also a more direct route through which expansionary monetary policy may stimulate aggregate demand. When the Fed expands the supply of money, it will create an "excess supply of money" *at the initial money interest rate*. People may respond by directly increasing their purchases of goods and services in an effort to reduce their money balances to desired levels. Obviously, this will increase aggregate demand. This direct path is most relevant when the government expands the supply of money by paying its bills with newly created currency. Because the money supply of the United States is generally expanded via open market operations, we have focused on the transmission of monetary policy through the interest rate. The implications of both the direct and indirect paths are identical—both indicate that expansionary monetary policy will stimulate aggregate demand.

THUMBNAIL SKETCH

Transmission of Monetary Policy—A Summary

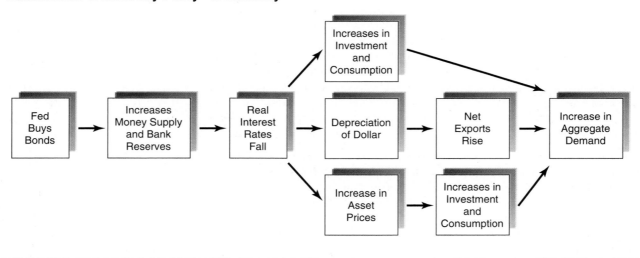

EXHIBIT 4
Effects of Expansionary Monetary Policy

If the impact of an increase in aggregate demand accompanying expansionary monetary policy is felt when the economy is operating below capacity, the policy will help direct the economy to a long-run full-employment equilibrium (a). In this case, the increase in output from Y_1 to Y_F will be long term. In contrast, if the demand-stimulus effects are imposed on an economy already at full employment (b), they will lead to excess demand and higher product prices. Output will temporarily increase (to Y_2). However, in the long run, the strong demand will push up resource prices, shifting short-run aggregate supply to $SRAS_2$. The price level will rise to P_3 and output will recede (to Y_F) from its temporary high.

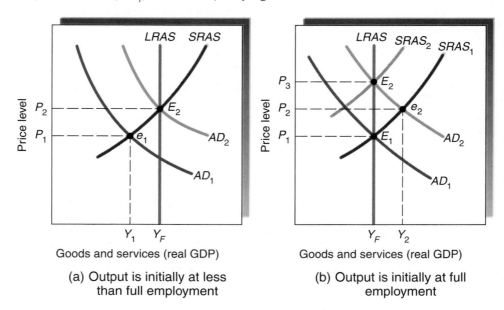

(a) Output is initially at less than full employment

(b) Output is initially at full employment

of demand stimulus, declining resource prices and real interest rates will eventually restore full employment. But many economists believe that expansionary monetary policy can hasten the return to full-employment equilibrium.

How would a shift to expansionary monetary policy influence output and the price level if the economy were already at full employment? Although this is generally not a desirable strategy, nonetheless it is interesting to analyze the outcome. As part b of Exhibit 4 illustrates, the monetary expansion will increase aggregate demand, causing product prices to rise relative to costs, important components of which are temporarily fixed by long-term contracts. The shift in demand will *temporarily* push real output to Y_2, beyond the economy's long-run capacity of Y_F. Output and employment will expand. However, the high rates of output (Y_2) and employment will not be sustainable. Eventually, long-term contracts based on the previously weaker demand (AD_1) will expire. New agreements will reflect the stronger demand. Resource prices will rise, shifting *SRAS* upward to the left. Eventually, long-run equilibrium (E_2) will result at a higher price level (P_3). Output will recede to Y_F. Thus, when an economy is already at full employment, an unexpected shift to a more expansionary monetary policy will temporarily increase output, but in the long run it merely leads to higher prices. Hence, the wisdom of such a shift is highly questionable.

Unanticipated Restrictive Monetary Policy

Suppose the Fed moves toward a more **restrictive monetary policy**. It would generally do so by selling bonds to the general public, which will reduce both the supply of money and the reserves of banks. **Exhibit 5** illustrates the impact of the more restrictive monetary policy on the loanable funds and goods and services markets. The Fed's sale of bonds reduces bond prices and drains reserves from the banking system (reducing the ability of banks to extend loans). As a result, the supply of loanable funds will decline, causing the

Restrictive monetary policy
A shift in monetary policy designed to reduce aggregate demand and place downward pressure on the general level of prices (or the rate of inflation). Bond sales by the Fed, a decline in bank reserves, and a reduction in the growth rate of the money supply are generally indicative of a restrictive monetary policy.

EXHIBIT 5
Short-run Effects of a More Restrictive Monetary Policy

When the Fed shifts to a more restrictive policy, it sells bonds, which reduces the reserves available to banks, decreases the supply of loanable funds, and places upward pressure on interest rates (a). The higher interest rates will decrease aggregate demand (shift to AD_2 in b). When the reduction in aggregate demand is unanticipated, real output will decline (to Y_2) and downward pressure on prices will result.

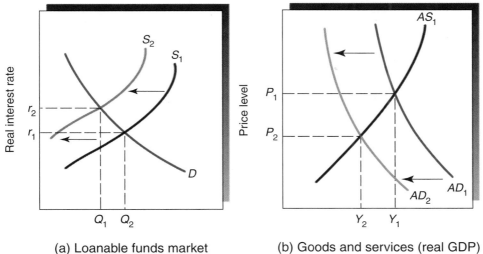

(a) Loanable funds market   (b) Goods and services (real GDP)

real interest rate to rise (from r_1 to r_2 in frame a of Exhibit 5). The higher real interest rates will tend to reduce current spending on both investment and consumer durables. They are also likely to cause an inflow of capital and appreciation in the exchange-rate value of the dollar. In turn, this appreciation of the dollar will encourage imports and discourage exports, leading to a reduction in net exports (and aggregate demand). The higher interest rates may also reduce the prices of housing and other assets, thereby discouraging new construction. All these factors will tend to reduce aggregate demand in the goods and services market (shift from AD_1 to AD_2 in part b of Exhibit 5).

The unexpected decline in the demand for goods and services will place downward pressures on prices, squeeze profit margins, and reduce output in the goods and services market. As part b of Exhibit 5 illustrates, the price level will decline (to P_2) and output will fall (to Y_2) as the result of the restrictive monetary policy.

The appropriateness of a restrictive policy depends on the initial state of the economy. **Exhibit 6** illustrates this point. When an economy is experiencing upward pressure on prices as the result of strong demand, restrictive policy is an effective weapon against inflation. Suppose that, as illustrated by part a of Exhibit 6, an economy is temporarily operating at e_1 and Y_1, beyond its full employment real GDP of Y_F. Strong aggregate demand is placing upward pressure on prices. The problem is inflation, not recession. Under these circumstances, restrictive policy makes good sense. It would help control the inflation. If the proper dosage is timed correctly, restrictive policy would retard aggregate demand (to AD_2) and direct the economy to a noninflationary, long-run equilibrium at P_2 and Y_F (that is, E_2).

As part b of Exhibit 6 illustrates, however, an unanticipated shift to restrictive policy would be damaging if applied to an economy in full-employment equilibrium. If the out-

EXHIBIT 6
Effects of Restrictive Monetary Policy

The stabilization effects of restrictive monetary policy depend on the state of the economy when the policy exerts its primary impact. Restrictive monetary policy will reduce aggregate demand. If the demand restraint comes during a period of strong demand and an overheated economy, then it will limit or even prevent the occurrence of an inflationary boom (a). In contrast, if the reduction in aggregate demand takes place when the economy is at full employment, then it will disrupt long-run equilibrium, reduce output, and result in a recession (b).

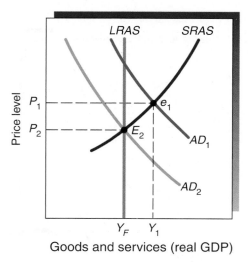

(a) Restrictive policy to control inflation

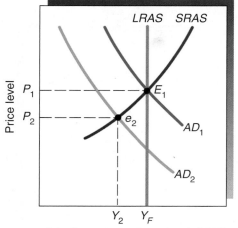

(b) Restrictive policy that causes a recession

put of an economy is at full employment (or worse still, at less than full employment), a shift to restrictive policy would reduce aggregate demand (shift to AD_2) and throw the economy into a recession. Real GDP would decline from Y_F to Y_2. Output would fall below the economy's full employment capacity, and unemployment would rise above the natural rate of unemployment.

Proper Timing

As with fiscal policy, monetary policy must be properly timed if it is to help stabilize an economy. Exhibits 4 and 6 highlight this point. When an economy is operating below its long-run capacity, expansionary monetary policy can stimulate demand and push the output of the economy to its sustainable potential (part a of Exhibit 4). Similarly, if properly timed, restrictive monetary policy can help control (or prevent) inflation (part a of Exhibit 6).

If it is timed improperly, however, monetary policy can be destabilizing. Expansionary monetary policy is a source of inflation if the effects of the policy are felt when the economy is already at or beyond its capacity (part b of Exhibit 4). Similarly, if the effects of a restrictive policy come when an economy is operating at its potential GDP, recession is the likely outcome (part b of Exhibit 6). Worse still, the impact of restrictive policy may be disastrous if imposed on an economy already in the midst of a recession.

Proper timing of monetary policy is not an easy task. While the Fed can institute policy changes rapidly, there may be a substantial time lag before the change in policy will exert a significant impact on aggregate demand. Economists who have studied this issue estimate that this impact lag will be five or six months at a minimum. Some economists, particularly monetarists, estimate that the primary impact of a change in monetary policy on output and employment is often as much as 12 to 18 months after the change is instituted. In terms of its impact on the price level and rate of inflation, the estimated impact lag is even longer, perhaps as much as 36 months. Given our limited ability to forecast the future, such lengthy time lags clearly reduce the potential effectiveness of discretionary monetary policy as a stabilization tool.

MONETARY POLICY IN THE LONG RUN

Since the middle of the eighteenth century, economists have argued that excessive money growth leads to inflation. Nearly a hundred years ago, Englishman Alfred Marshall and American Irving Fisher formalized the **quantity theory of money** in support of this view. *The quantity theory indicates that an increase in the supply of money will cause a proportional increase in the price level.*

Quantity theory of money
A theory that hypothesizes that a change in the money supply will cause a proportional change in the price level because velocity and real output are unaffected by the quantity of money.

The quantity theory of money can be more easily understood once we recognize that there are two ways of viewing GDP. As the *AD/AS* model shows, nominal GDP is the sum of the price, P, times the output, Y, of each final-product good purchased during the period. In aggregate, *P* represents the economy's price level, while Y indicates real income or real GDP. There is also a second way of visualizing GDP. When the existing money stock, *M*, is multiplied by the number of times, *V*, that money is used to buy final products, this, too, yields the economy's nominal GDP. Therefore,

$$PY = \text{GDP} = MV$$

The **velocity of money** (V) is simply the average number of times a dollar is used to purchase a final product or service during a year. Velocity is equal to nominal GDP divided by the size of the money stock. For example, in 2000 GDP was equal to $9,963 billion, while the M1 money supply was $1,088 billion. On average, each dollar in the M1 money supply was used 7.8 times to purchase final-product goods and services

Velocity of money
The average number of times a dollar is used to purchase final goods and services during a year. It is equal to GDP divided by the stock of money.

included in GDP. The velocity of the M1 money stock therefore was 9.2. The velocity of the M2 money stock can be derived in a similar manner. In 2000, the M2 money stock was $4,945 billion. Thus, the velocity of M2 was 2.0 ($9,963 billion divided by $4,945 billion).

The concept of velocity is closely related to the demand for money. When decision makers conduct a specific amount of business with a smaller amount of money, their demand for money balances is reduced. Each dollar, though, is being used more often—the velocity of money has increased. Thus, for a given income level, when the demand for money declines, the velocity of money increases. Correspondingly, an increase in the demand for money is a reflection of a reduction in velocity.

When considering the behavior of prices, output, money, and velocity over time, we can write the quantity theory equation in terms of growth rates:

$$\text{Rate of inflation} + \text{Growth rate of real output} =$$
$$\text{Growth rate of the money supply} + \text{Growth rate of velocity}$$

Equation of exchange
$MV = PY$, where M is the money supply, V is the velocity of money, P is the price level, and Y is the output of goods and services produced.

The $MV = PY$ relationship is simply an identity, or a tautology. Economists refer to it as the **equation of exchange**, because it reflects both the monetary and real sides of each final-product exchange. The quantity theory of money, though, postulates that Y and V are determined by factors other than the amount of money in circulation. Classical economists believed that real output Y was determined by such factors as technology, the size of the economy's resource base, and the skill of the labor force. These factors were thought to be insensitive to changes in the money supply. Similarly, the velocity of money was thought to be determined primarily by institutional factors, such as the organization of banking and credit, the frequency of income payments, the rapidity of transportation, and the communication system. These factors would change quite slowly. Thus, classical economists thought that, for all practical purposes, both Y and V were constant (or changed only by small amounts) over periods of two, three, or four years. If both Y and V are constant, then the $MV = PY$ relationship indicates that an increase in the money supply will lead to a proportional increase in the price level. Correspondingly, an increase in the growth rate of the money supply can be expected to cause a similar increase in the rate of inflation.

Long-Run Implications of Modern Analysis

What does modern analysis indicate with regard to the validity of the quantity theory of money? In addressing this question, it will be helpful to focus on the dynamic long-run implications of the *AD/AS* model. Thus far, we have used comparative statics to analyze monetary policy. Within this framework, an increase in the supply of money is reflective of more expansionary policy. In the real world, however, shifts in monetary policy generally involve changes in the *growth rate* of the money supply. An increase in money growth suggests a move toward a more expansionary monetary policy, while a reduction in the growth rate of the money supply implies a shift to a more restrictive policy. Similarly, in a comparative static framework, an increase in the price level implies inflation. However, inflation is a dynamic concept—a rate of increase in prices, not a once-and-for-all movement to a higher price level.

In order to both add realism and analyze the long-run implications more fully, this section will recast the prior static analysis into a dynamic framework. We will begin with a simple dynamic case. Suppose that the real GDP of an economy is growing at a 3 percent annual rate and that the monetary authorities are expanding the money supply by 3 percent each year. In addition, let's assume that the velocity of money is constant. This would imply that the 3 percent annual increase in output would lead to a 3 percent annual increase in the demand for money. Under these circumstances, the 3 percent monetary growth would be consistent with stable prices (zero inflation). Initially, we will assume

EXHIBIT 7
Long-run Effects of More Rapid Expansion in the Money Supply—Goods and Services Market

Here we illustrate the long-term impact of an increase in the annual growth rate of the money supply from 3 to 8 percent. Initially, prices are stable (P_{100}) when the money supply is expanding by 3 percent annually. The acceleration in the growth rate of the money supply increases aggregate demand (shift to AD_2). At first, real output may expand beyond the economy's potential (Y_F). However, abnormally low unemployment and strong demand conditions will create upward pressure on wages and other resource prices, shifting aggregate supply to AS_2. Output will return to its long-run potential and the price level will increase to P_{105} (E_2). If the more rapid monetary growth continues in subsequent periods, *AD* and *AS* will continue to shift upward, leading to still higher prices (E_3 and periods beyond). The net result of the process is sustained inflation.

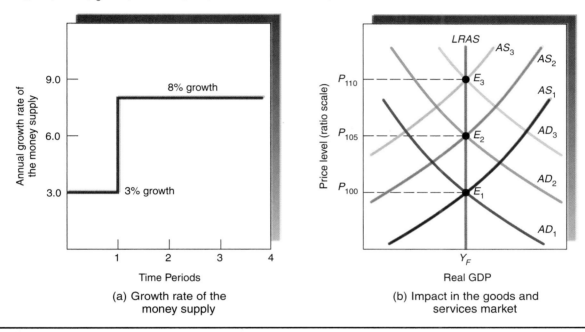

(a) Growth rate of the money supply

(b) Impact in the goods and services market

that the economy's real interest rate is 4 percent. Because the inflation rate is zero, the nominal rate of interest is also equal to 4 percent. **Exhibits 7** and **8** illustrate an economy initially (Period 1) characterized by these conditions.

What will happen if the monetary authorities permanently increase the growth rate of the money supply from 3 percent to 8 percent annually (see part a of Exhibit 7, beginning in Period 2)?[6] In the short run, the expansionary monetary policy will reduce the real interest rate and stimulate aggregate demand (shift to AD_2 in part b of Exhibit 7), just as we previously explained (Exhibits 3 and 4). For a time, real output may exceed the economy's potential. However, as they confront strong demand conditions, many resource suppliers (who previously committed to long-term agreements) will want to modify these agreements in light of the strong demand conditions. With the passage of time, more and more resource suppliers (including labor represented by union officials) will have the opportunity to alter their prior contracts. As this happens, wages and other resource prices will increase. As they do, costs will rise and profit margins will recede to normal levels. The higher costs will reduce aggregate supply (shift to AS_2). As the rapid monetary growth

---

[6]In the preceding chapter, we noted the difficulties involved in the measurement of the money supply (both M1 and M2). Changes in the growth rate of the money supply may not always be indicative of a shift in monetary policy. More generally, the example presented here assumes that the Fed has shifted to a more expansionary monetary policy—one that will lead to an increase in the rate of inflation—regardless of whether the monetary aggregates as currently measured reflect this shift.

EXHIBIT 8
Long-run Effects of More Rapid Expansion in the Money Supply—Loanable Funds Market

When prices are stable, supply and demand in the loanable funds market are in balance at a real and nominal interest rate of 4 percent. If more rapid monetary expansion leads to a long-term 5 percent inflation rate (see Exhibit 7), borrowers and lenders will build the higher inflation rate into their decision making. As a result, the nominal interest rate (i) will rise to 9 percent—the 4 percent real rate plus a 5 percent inflationary premium.

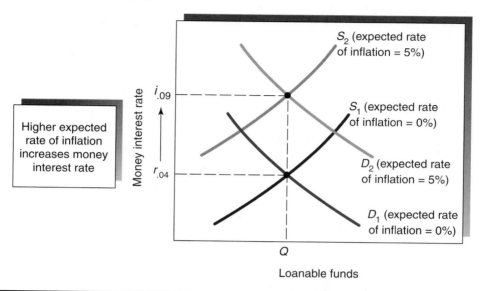

continues in subsequent periods (periods 3, 4, and so on), both *AD* and *AS* will shift upward. The price level will rise to P_{105}, P_{110}, and on to still higher levels as the money supply continues to grow more rapidly than the monetary growth rate consistent with stable prices. The continuation of the expansionary monetary policy leads to a higher and higher price level—that is, a sustained inflation.

Suppose an inflation rate of 5 percent eventually emerges from the more rapid growth rate (8 percent rather than 3 percent) of the money supply. With the passage of time, more and more people will adjust their decision making in light of the persistent 5 percent inflation. In the resource market, both buyers and sellers will eventually incorporate the expectation of the 5 percent inflation rate into long-term contracts, such as collective bargaining agreements. Once this happens, resource prices and costs will rise as rapidly as prices in the goods and services market. ***When the inflation rate is anticipated fully, it will fail to either reduce real wages or improve profit margins. Unemployment will return to its natural rate.***

Exhibit 8 illustrates the adjustments in the loanable funds market once borrowers and lenders expect the 5 percent inflation rate. When lenders anticipate a 5 percent annual increase in the price level, a 9 percent interest rate will be necessary to provide them with as much incentive to supply loanable funds as 4 percent interest provided *when stable prices were expected*. Thus, the supply of loanable funds will shift vertically by the 5 percent expected rate of inflation. Simultaneously, borrowers who were willing to pay 4 percent interest on loans when they expected stable prices will be willing to pay 9 percent when they expect prices to increase by 5 percent annually. The demand for loanable funds will therefore also increase (shift vertically) by the expected rate of inflation. Once borrowers and lenders anticipate the higher (5 percent) inflation rate, the equilibrium money interest rate will rise to 9 percent. Of course, the real interest rate is equal to the money interest rate (9 percent) minus the expected rate of inflation (5 percent). In the long run, a 4 percent real interest rate will emerge with inflation, just as it did with stable prices.[7] Inflation, then, will fail to reduce the real interest rate in the long run.

The long-run implications of modern analysis are consistent with those of the earlier quantity theory of money. ***In the long run, the major consequence of rapid money growth is inflation. While an unanticipated shift to a more expansionary policy may exert a positive impact on output and employment in the short run, this will not be the case in the long run. Rapid monetary growth will neither reduce unemployment nor stimulate real output in the long run.***

MONETARY POLICY WHEN EFFECTS ARE ANTICIPATED

Thus far, we have assumed that decision makers come to anticipate the effects of monetary policy only after they begin to occur. For example, we assumed that borrowers and lenders began to anticipate a higher inflation rate only after prices began to rise more rapidly. Similarly, resource suppliers anticipated the inflation only after it had begun.

What if enough decision makers in the market catch on to the link between expansionary monetary policy and an increase in the inflation rate? Suppose borrowers and lenders start paying attention to the money supply figures and other monetary policy indicators. Observing a shift toward a more expansionary monetary policy, they revise upward their expectation of the future inflation rate. Lenders become more reluctant to supply loanable funds. Simultaneously, borrowers increase their demand for loanable funds at existing rates of interest because they also anticipate a higher rate of future inflation and they want to buy now before prices rise. Under these circumstances, a reduction in supply and an increase in demand for loanable funds will quickly push up the money interest rate. If borrowers and lenders quickly and accurately forecast the future rate of inflation accompanying the monetary expansion, the real interest rate will decline for only a short period of time, if at all.

If buyers and sellers in the goods and services market also anticipate a shift to a more expansionary monetary policy, they too may anticipate its inflationary consequences. As buyers anticipate future price increases, many will buy now rather than later. Current aggregate demand will rise. Similarly, expecting an acceleration in the inflation rate, sellers will be reluctant to sell except at premium prices. Current aggregate supply will fall. This combination of factors will quickly push prices of goods and services upward.

Simultaneously, if buyers and sellers in the resource market believe that more rapid monetary growth will lead to a higher rate of inflation, they too will build this view into long-run contracts. Union officials will demand and employers will pay an inflationary premium for future money wages, based on their expectation of inflation. Alternatively, they may write an **escalator clause** (sometimes called cost-of-living adjustments) into their collective bargaining agreements. Such provisions will automatically raise money wages when the inflation transpires. If decision makers in the resource market correctly anticipate the inflation, real resource prices will not decline once prices accelerate upward.

Escalator clause
A contractual agreement that periodically and automatically adjusts money wage rates upward as the price level rises. They are sometimes referred to as cost-of-living adjustments or COLAs.

As **Exhibit 9** illustrates, when individuals correctly anticipate the effects of expansionary monetary policy *prior to their occurrence*, the short-run impact of monetary policy is much like its impact in the long run. The price level will increase, pushing up money income (P_2Y_1), but real income (Y_1) will be unchanged. Nominal interest rates will rise, but real interest rates will be unchanged. Thus, when the effects of expansionary monetary policy are fully anticipated, they exert little impact on real economic activity.

Are people likely to anticipate the effects of monetary policy? This is a topic of hot debate among economists, and we will consider it in more detail in the next chapter. Because

---

[7]Higher rates of inflation are generally associated with an increase in the variability of the inflation rate. Thus, greater risk (the possibility of either a substantial gain or loss associated with a sharp change in the inflation rate) accompanies exchange in the loanable funds market when inflation rates are high. This additional risk may result in higher real interest rates than would prevail at lower rates of inflation. The text discussion does not introduce this consideration.

EXHIBIT 9
Short-run Effects of Anticipated Monetary Expansion

When decision makers fully anticipate the effects of monetary expansion, the expansion does not alter real output even in the short run. Suppliers, including resource suppliers, build the expected price rise into their decisions. The anticipated inflation leads to a rise in nominal costs (including wages), causing aggregate supply to decline (shift to $SRAS_2$). While nominal wages, prices, and interest rates rise, their real counterparts are unchanged. The result: inflation without any change in real output (Y_1).

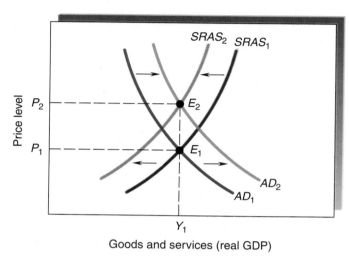

Goods and services (real GDP)

the effects of monetary policy differ substantially depending on whether they are anticipated, the question is clearly a very important one.

INTEREST RATES AND MONETARY POLICY

Can the Fed control interest rates? How quickly will a shift in monetary policy exert a significant impact on output and prices in the goods and services market? These two questions are linked. Let us begin with the interest rate question. In order to simplify matters, we have proceeded as if there were only a single interest rate in the loanable funds market. In the real world loanable funds market, of course, there are numerous interest rates reflecting loans of differing risk and time length. For example, there are short-term interest rates, such as those for federal funds, Treasury bills, and savings deposits. In addition, there are longer-term rates, such as those for home mortgages and long-term bonds.

When the Fed moves toward a more expansionary policy for example, when it purchases bonds and injects additional reserves into the system, there is an immediate impact on short-term interest rates, like the rate in the federal funds market—the market where banks with excess reserves extend short-term loans to banks with insufficient reserves. As the federal funds rate declines, so too will other short-term interest rates—for example, the rates on savings deposits, three-month Treasury bills, and bank certificates of deposit (CDs).

However, the impact of the expansionary monetary policy on long-term interest rates, such as home mortgages and ten-year bonds, will be more modest and less predictable. There are two reasons for this: First, the long-term rates are influenced more by real factors, such as the demand for investment funds, than by monetary factors. Second, to the extent that monetary factors influence long-term interest rates, they op-

erate primarily through their impact on the expected rate of inflation. The expected long-term future rate of inflation is an important component of long-term nominal interest rates. If people expect a higher future rate of inflation as the result of the shift to a more expansionary policy, long-term rates may rise rather than fall. Thus, although a shift in Fed policy is able to exert a substantial impact on short-term interest rates rather quickly, its impact on longer-term rates is both less certain and likely to occur with a substantially longer time lag. Because long- and medium-term rates are most relevant for the investment decisions of businesses and households, the ambiguity concerning the impact of monetary policy on these rates is particularly important.

Short-Term Interest Rates, Velocity of Money, and Time Lag of Monetary Policy

Furthermore, the impact of the change in short-term nominal interest rates on the velocity of money adds an additional complication. A reduction in the short-term rates will reduce the opportunity cost of holding money balances. Predictably, the velocity of money will decline, which will tend to dampen the initial stimulus effects of the monetary expansion. Of course, if the more expansionary monetary policy persists, a combination of lower real interest rates—particularly short-term rates—and more readily available credit will eventually stimulate aggregate demand (see Exhibit 3). With time, the additional demand will place upward pressure on prices, which will also serve to increase both the expected rate of inflation and nominal interest rates, including short-term nominal rates. When this happens—and several quarters may pass before it does—the higher short-term nominal interest rates will increase the velocity of money and amplify the demand-stimulus effects of the policy. It is at this point in time that the primary effects of the expansionary monetary policy will be most potent.

The same forces are also present in the case of a shift to a more restrictive monetary policy. When the Fed shifts to a more restrictive policy, it typically drains reserves from the banking system, which will quickly place upward pressure on the federal funds rate and other short-term interest rates. The restrictive policy, however, will generally exert less impact on longer-term interest rates. If people perceive that inflation is a smaller threat as the result of the more restrictive monetary policy, this factor will place downward pressure on long-term interest rates, which will at least partially offset the restraining effects emanating from the increase in the short-term rates.

At the same time, the higher short-term rates will increase the opportunity cost of holding money and, as a result, its velocity. This increase in the velocity of money will promote additional spending, which will, *for a time*, tend to dampen the restrictive effects of the policy. Of course, the restrictive policy, if continued, will eventually begin to retard inflation and lower nominal interest rates (including short-term rates), which will reduce the velocity of money. Once this happens, and many months may pass before it does, the restrictive policy will be highly potent—it will substantially reduce aggregate demand, output, and prices.

All these factors suggest that the linkage between a change in monetary policy and a change in output and prices is likely to be both lengthy and variable. When there is a shift in monetary policy, the potency of the short-run effects may differ substantially from the potency of the policy shift over a longer period of time. Obviously, these factors will complicate the job of monetary policy makers and make it more difficult for them to institute changes in a manner that will exert a stabilizing influence on the economy.

Money Supply and the Federal Funds Rate

Throughout, we have used shifts in the money supply to indicate the direction of changes in monetary policy. In recent years, however, the Fed has often used interest rates—particularly the federal funds rate—as a means of instituting changes in monetary policy. If the

Fed wants to shift toward a more expansionary policy, it may announce that it is reducing its target for the federal funds interest rate. The Fed controls this rate through its open market operations. In order to achieve the lower rate, it will buy more bonds and thereby inject additional reserves into the system, which will place downward pressure on the federal funds rate. Of course, the Fed's buying of bonds will also increase the money supply. Therefore, even though the news media and others may highlight the change in the federal funds rate, the impact on the economy will be the same as for an increase in the money supply. On the other hand, when the Fed shifts to a more restrictive policy, it may seek to increase the federal funds rate. However, the Fed achieves this objective through its sale of bonds, which will reduce the reserves available to the banking system. Again, the result will be the same as for a reduction in the money supply.

Dangers of Using Interest Rates as an Indicator of Monetary Policy

Are interest rates indicative of Fed policy? For example, do low interest rates indicate that the Fed is following an expansionary policy? Here, it is vitally important to distinguish between the short run and the long run. When the Fed shifts to a more expansionary policy, it generally injects additional reserves into the banking system. In the short run, this will place downward pressure on interest rates—particularly for short-term rates. However, think what would happen if the Fed continued on a highly expansionary course, seeking to push interest rates down over a long period of time. In the long run, the monetary expansion will lead to inflation. As people come to expect the inflation, nominal interest rates will rise instead of fall. Once the inflation is anticipated fully, even real interest rates will return to their normal level.

Paradoxically, while expansionary monetary policy can reduce interest rates in the short run, in the long run the result will be just the opposite. A persistent expansionary monetary policy will lead to inflation and higher nominal interest rates. Similarly, a shift to a more restrictive policy will increase interest rates in the short run. But when pursued over a lengthy time period, restrictive policy will lead to deflation (falling prices) and low interest rates.

Thus, interest rates are often a misleading gauge of monetary policy. In the United States, interest rates were high during the 1970s, a period of expansionary monetary policy and inflation. On the other hand, interest rates were relatively low during the 1960s and 1990s, periods of more restrictive monetary policy. During the Great Depression, interest rates fell to less than 1 percent. But this was not indicative of expansionary monetary policy. To the contrary, it was reflective of a highly restrictive monetary policy that was causing deflation and the expectation of a falling price level. Internationally, the picture is the same. The highest interest rates in the world are found in countries experiencing hyperinflation—Argentina and Brazil in the 1980s and Russia in the 1990s, for example. In the late 1990s, several interest rates in Japan fell below 1 percent. Like the United States during the Great Depression, the low Japanese interest rates are reflective of a highly restrictive monetary policy, one that has led to a falling price level and the expectation of deflation.

EFFECTS OF MONETARY POLICY—A SUMMARY

The accompanying Thumbnail Sketch summarizes the theoretical implications of our analysis. The impact of monetary policy on major economic variables is indicated for three alternatives: (1) the short run when the effects are unanticipated, (2) the short run when the effects are anticipated, and (3) the long run. Note that the impact of monetary policy in the latter two cases is the same. When decision makers quickly anticipate the effects of monetary policy, the adjustment process speeds up, and therefore the short-run effects are identical to the long-run effects. Under these circumstances, only nominal vari-

THUMBNAIL SKETCH

What Is the Impact of Monetary Policy?

	Short-Run Effects When Policy Is Unanticipated (1)	Short-Run Effects When Policy Is Anticipated[a] (2)	Long-Run Effects (3)
Impact of Expansionary Monetary Policy on			
Inflation rate	Only a small increase, particularly if excess capacity is present	Increase	
Real output and employment	Increase, particularly if excess capacity is present	No change	
Money interest rate	Short-term rates will probably decline	Increase	
Real interest rate	Decrease	No change	
Impact of Restrictive Monetary Policy on			
Inflation rate	Only a small decrease	Decrease	
Real output and employment	Decrease, particularly if economy at less than capacity	No change	
Money interest rate	Short-term rates will probably increase	Decrease	
Real interest rate	Increase	No change	

[a]Beginning from long-run equilibrium

ables (money interest rates and the inflation rate) are affected. Real variables (real GDP, employment, and the real interest rate) are unaffected.

Five major predictions flow from our analysis:

1. *An unanticipated shift to a more expansionary (restrictive) monetary policy will temporarily stimulate (retard) output and employment.* As Exhibits 3 and 4 illustrate, an increase in aggregate demand emanating from an unanticipated increase in the money supply will lead to a short-run expansion in real output and employment. Conversely, as Exhibit 5 shows, an unanticipated move toward a more restrictive monetary policy reduces aggregate demand and retards real output.

2. *The stabilizing effects of a change in monetary policy are dependent upon the state of the economy when the effects of the policy change are observed.* If the effects of an expansionary policy come when the economy is operating at less than capacity, then the demand stimulus will push the economy toward full employment. However, if the demand stimulus comes when the economy is operating at or beyond capacity, it will contribute to an acceleration in the inflation rate. Correspondingly, restrictive policy will help to control inflation if the demand-restraining effects are felt when output is beyond the economy's long-run capacity. On the other hand, restrictive policy will result in recession if the reduction in demand comes when the economy is at or below long-run capacity.

3. *Persistent growth of the money supply at a rapid rate will cause inflation.* Although the short-run effects of expansionary monetary policy may be primarily on output, particularly if excess capacity is present, a persistent expansion in the money supply at a rate greater than the growth of real output will cause inflation. The more rapid the

sustained growth rate of the money supply (relative to real output), the higher the accompanying rate of inflation.

4. ***Money interest rates and the inflation rate will be directly related.*** As the inflation rate rises, money interest rates will eventually increase because both borrowers and lenders will begin to expect the higher rate of inflation and build it into their decision making. Conversely, as the inflation rate declines, a reduction in the expected rate of inflation will eventually lead to lower money interest rates. Therefore, when monetary expansion leads to an acceleration in the inflation rate, it will also result in an increase in nominal interest rates.

5. ***There will be only a loose year-to-year relationship between shifts in monetary policy and changes in output and prices.*** It takes time for markets to adjust to changing demand conditions. Some prices in both product and resource markets are set by long-term contracts. Obviously price responses in these markets will take time. In some cases, people may anticipate the effects of a policy change and adjust quickly; in others, the reaction to a policy change may take more time. Differences in this area will weaken the year-to-year relationship between monetary indicators and important economic variables.

In addition, a monetary policy shift will initially exert a far greater impact on short-term interest rates than on longer-term rates. Movements in the short-term nominal rates are likely to cause changes in the velocity of money that will tend to dampen the initial effects of a monetary policy shift. This, too, will tend to weaken the year-to-year link between changes in monetary policy and changes in output and prices. Therefore, even though our analysis indicates that monetary policy does influence output and prices, the year-to-year relationships are likely to be weak.

TESTING THE MAJOR IMPLICATIONS OF MONETARY THEORY

Is the real world consistent with our analysis? The next four exhibits provide evidence on this topic. Our analysis indicates that a shift to a more expansionary monetary policy will initially stimulate output, while a shift to monetary restriction will retard it. **Exhibit 10** shows the relationship between changes in the growth rate of the money supply and real output since 1960 for the United States. In order to smooth the temporary quarterly fluctuations, the annual rates for both figures are for a 4-quarter moving average. Because the introduction of interest-earning checking accounts dramatically changed the nature of M1 (and affected its growth rate) during the 1980s, the M2 money-supply measure is used here. Of course, changes in the growth rate of M2 may not always accurately reflect the direction of monetary policy and other factors such as supply shocks and fiscal policy changes will also influence the growth of output. Thus, the relationship between changes in the money supply and the growth of real GDP will probably be fairly loose. However, close inspection of the data reveals that periods of sharp acceleration in the growth rate of the money supply were generally associated with an acceleration in the growth rate of real GDP. For example, an acceleration in the growth rate of the money supply during 1961–1964, 1971–1972, 1976, and 1983 was associated with an increase in the growth rate of real GDP.

The converse was also true: Periods of sharp deceleration in the growth rate of the money supply were generally associated with (or followed by) economic recession. A decline in the growth rate of the money supply preceded the recessions of 1960, 1970, and 1974–1975. Similarly, a sharp decline in the growth rate of the money stock from 13 percent in 1976–1977 to less than 8 percent in 1978–1979 preceded the back-to-back recessions and sluggish growth of 1979–1982. Prior to the 1990 recession, the growth rate (4-quarter moving average) of the money supply fell from 9.3 percent in 1987 (first quarter)

EXHIBIT 10
Monetary Policy and Real GDP

Sharp declines in the growth rate of the money supply, such as those of 1968–1969, 1973–1974, 1977–1978, 1988–1991, and 1999–2000 have generally preceded reductions in real GDP and periods of recession (indicated by shading). Conversely, periods of sharp acceleration in the growth rate of the money supply, such as 1971–1972 and 1976, have often been followed by a rapid growth in GDP. The monetary authorities have generally increased the growth rate of the money supply during recessions. Note that the growth rate of the money supply has been slower and more stable in the last decade.

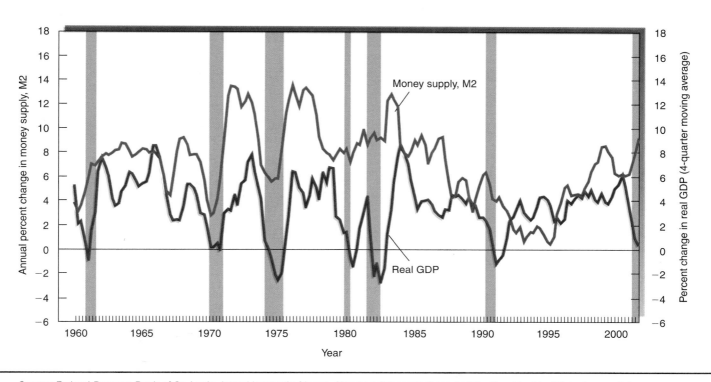

Source: Federal Reserve Bank of St. Louis, http://www.stls.frb.org. Also see *Economic Report of the President* (published annually).

to only 2.6 percent in 1989 (fourth quarter). After increasing at an annual rate of less than 5 percent throughout the 1990s, the money growth rate jumped to more than 8 percent during 1998–1999 before receding to 6 percent at year-end 2000. Between October 1999 and July 2000, the Fed increased its discount rate and target federal funds rate five times. The more restrictive monetary policy of 2000 contributed to the recession of 2001. Just as our theory predicts, there does appear to be a relationship between shifts in monetary policy and changes in real GDP.

Exhibit 11 presents a graphic picture of the relationship between monetary policy and the inflation rate for the United States. Although our theory indicates that persistent, long-term growth of the money supply will be closely associated with inflation, it also indicates that time is required for a monetary expansion (or contraction) to alter demand relationships and impact prices. Most economists believe that the time lag between shifts in monetary policy and observable changes in the level of prices is often two or three years. Reflecting these views, Exhibit 11 compares the current money supply (M2) data with the inflation rate three years in the future. Once again, though the linkage is far from tight, it definitely exists. Most noticeably, the rapid monetary acceleration during 1971–1972 was followed by a similar acceleration in the inflation rate during 1973–1974. Similarly, the sharp monetary contraction of 1973–1974 was accompanied by not only the recession of 1974–1975, but also a substantial reduction in the inflation rate during 1975–1976.

EXHIBIT 11
Effect of Changes in Money Supply on Inflation

Here we illustrate the relationship between the rate of growth of the money supply (M2) and the annual inflation rate three years later. While the two are not perfectly correlated, the data do indicate that periods of monetary acceleration (for example: 1971–1972 and 1975–1976) tend to be associated with an increase in the inflation rate about three years later. Similarly, a slower growth rate of the money supply, like that of the 1990s, is generally associated with a reduction in the rate of inflation.

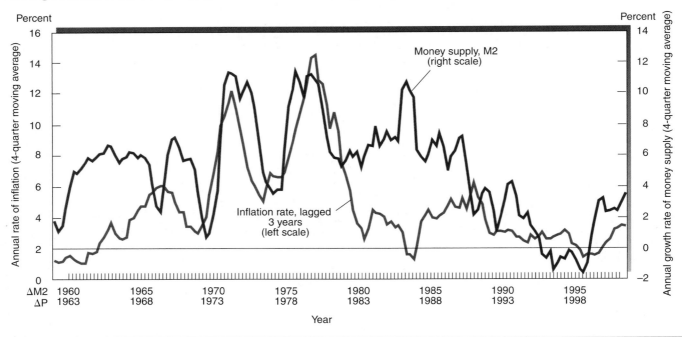

Source: Federal Reserve Bank of St. Louis, http://www.stls.frb.org. Also see *Economic Report of the President* (published annually). The consumer price index was used to measure the rate of inflation.

However, as monetary policy again shifted toward expansion in 1976–1977, the double-digit inflation rates of 1979–1980 were soon to follow.

During the 1980–1986 period, the linkage between monetary growth and the inflation rate a few years later appeared to weaken. To some degree this may reflect the financial innovations and changing nature of money during this period. There is some evidence that the relationship is once again becoming more predictable now that the transition period to interest-earning checking accounts has been completed. During the 1987–1993 period, the annual growth rate of the money supply (M2) decelerated from more than 8 percent to less than 2 percent. With a lag, the inflation rate followed a similar path. Furthermore, the low rate of money growth during the 1990s—the money growth rate averaged approximately 3 percent during this period—has been associated with low rates of inflation.

Exhibit 12 shows the relationship between the inflation rate (change in CPI) and the nominal interest rate. Because our measure of inflation is the rate of change in the price level during the last year, we will compare it with a short-term nominal interest rate—the three-month Treasury bill rate. Our theory implies that nominal interest rates will tend to rise with the rate of inflation. The empirical evidence indicates that is indeed the case. As the inflation rate rose significantly during the late 1960s, so also did the nominal rate of interest. During the 1970s, sharp increases in the inflation rate, particularly during 1977–1980, were accompanied by substantial increases in the nominal interest rate. Similarly, as the inflation rate decelerated from the double-digit levels of the late 1970s, the money interest rate also plunged during 1981–1987. Later, a modest increase in the inflation rate during 1988–1990 resulted in a similar modest increase in short-term interest

EXHIBIT 12
Inflation Rate and the Money Interest Rate

The expectation of inflation (a) reduces the supply and (b) increases the demand for loanable funds, causing money interest rates to rise (see Exhibit 8). Note how the short-term money rate of interest has tended to increase when the inflation rate accelerates (and decline as the inflation rate falls).

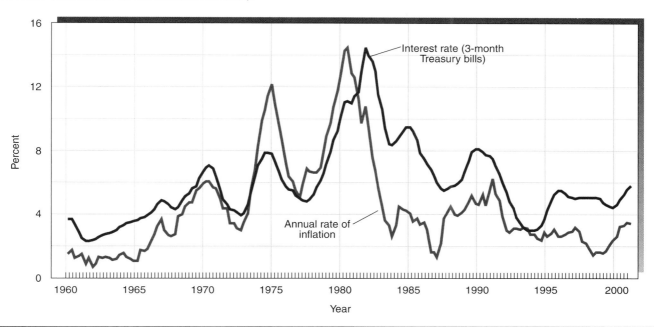

Source: Federal Reserve Bank of St. Louis, http://www.stls.frb.org. Also see *Economic Report of the President* (published annually). The consumer price index was used to measure the rate of inflation.

rates. Finally, as the inflation rate hovered around 3 percent during 1994–2000, the short-term nominal interest rate fluctuated near the 5 percent range. These data provide strong evidence that, just as our theory predicts, the choices of borrowers and lenders are strongly influenced by the inflation rate and expectations concerning its path in the future.

A major implication of our analysis is that rapid growth rates in the money supply over long periods of time will be associated with high rates of inflation. **Exhibit 13** presents data on the annual growth rate of the money supply (adjusted for the growth rate of the nation's output) and the rate of inflation for a diverse set of countries during the 1980–1999 period. The results clearly illustrate the linkage between monetary policy and inflation. Countries with single-digit rates of money growth—for example, Belgium, Japan, Malaysia, Switzerland, and the United States—experienced single-digit rates of inflation. Similarly, countries with rates of money growth in the 10 percent to 20 percent range experienced rates of inflation in this same range. The data for the Philippines, South Africa, Kenya, Hungary, and Chile illustrate this point. Countries like Mexico, Ghana, and Poland with money growth rates in the 30 percent to 50 percent range had inflation rates within this same range. Finally, look at the data for Argentina and Brazil. The average annual rate of money growth of these two countries exceeded 100 percent during this period. So too did their average inflation rate. Most of the money growth of Argentina and Brazil occurred during the 1980s. Predictably, the substantially lower rates of money growth during the 1990s resulted in substantially lower rates of inflation.

When considered over a lengthy time period, the linkage between money growth and inflation is one of the most consistent relationships in all of economics. Inflation is a monetary phenomenon. Persistently low rates of money growth lead to low rates of inflation. Similarly, high rates of money growth lead to high rates of inflation.

EXHIBIT 13
Money and Inflation—An International Comparison, 1980–1999

The relationship between the average annual growth rate of the money supply and the rate of inflation is shown here for the 1980–1999 period. Clearly, there is a close relationship between the two. Higher rates of money growth lead to higher rates of inflation.

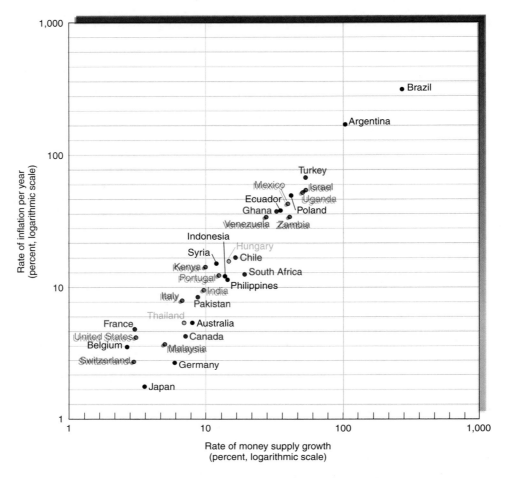

Note: The money supply data are the actual growth rate of the money supply minus the growth rate of real GDP. Data for members of the European Monetary Union are for 1980–1998.

Source: International Monetary Fund, *International Financial Statistics Yearbook*; 1993, 1997, 2001. *Penn World Tables;* and The World Bank, *World Development Indicators,* 2001.

**LOOKING
AHEAD**

As we discussed in this chapter, theory indicates that the impact of monetary policy will be influenced by whether economic agents anticipate its effects. Thus far, we have said little about how decision makers form expectations about the future. The next chapter will consider this important issue.

KEY POINTS

▼ The quantity of money people want to hold is inversely related to the money rate of interest, because higher interest rates make it more costly to hold money instead of interest-earning assets like bonds. The supply of money is vertical because it is determined by the Fed. The money interest rate will gravitate toward the rate where the quantity of money people want to hold is just equal to the stock of money the Fed has supplied.

▼ The impact of a shift in monetary policy is generally transmitted through interest rates, exchange rates, and asset prices.

▼ When instituting a more expansionary monetary policy, the Fed generally buys bonds, which will both increase bond prices and create additional bank reserves, placing downward pressure on real interest rates. In the short run, an *unanticipated* shift to a more expansionary policy will stimulate aggregate demand and thereby increase output and employment.

▼ When instituting a more restrictive monetary policy, the Fed sells bonds, which will depress bond prices and drain reserves from the banking system. An unanticipated shift to a more restrictive monetary policy will increase real interest rates and reduce aggregate demand, output, and employment in the short run.

▼ The quantity theory of money postulates that the velocity of money is constant (or approximately so) and that real output is independent of monetary factors. When these assumptions hold, an increase in the stock of money will lead to a proportional increase in the price level.

▼ In the long run, the primary impact of monetary policy will be on prices rather than on real output. When expansionary monetary policy leads to rising prices, decision makers eventually anticipate the higher inflation rate and build it into their choices. As this happens, money interest rates, wages, and incomes will reflect the expectation of inflation, so real interest rates, wages, and output will return to their long-run normal levels.

▼ When the effects of expansionary monetary policy are anticipated prior to their occurrence, the short-run impact of an increase in the money supply is similar to its impact in the long run. Nominal prices and interest rates rise, but real output remains unchanged.

▼ While the Fed can strongly influence short-term interest rates, its impact on long-term rates is much more limited. Interest rates can be a misleading indicator of monetary policy. In the long run, expansionary monetary policy leads to inflation and high interest rates, rather than low interest rates. Similarly, restrictive monetary policy when pursued over a lengthy time period leads to low inflation and low interest rates.

▼ The empirical evidence indicates that changes in monetary policy influence real GDP in the short run.

▼ Both the U.S. experience and international comparisons strongly indicate that persistent, rapid growth in the money supply is closely linked with inflation. Countries with low (high) rates of growth in the money supply tend to experience low (high) rates of inflation.

CRITICAL ANALYSIS QUESTIONS

1. Why do people hold money? How will an increase in the interest rate influence the amount of money that people will want to hold?

*2. How would each of the following influence the quantity of money that you would like to hold?
  a. An increase in the interest rate on checking deposits
  b. An increase in the expected rate of inflation
  c. An increase in income
  d. An increase in the differential interest rate between money market mutual funds and checking deposits

*3. What is the opportunity cost of the following: (a) obtaining a $100,000 house, (b) holding the house during the next year, (c) obtaining $1,000, and (d) holding the $1,000 in your checking account during the next year?

4. Historically, shifts toward more expansionary monetary policy have often been associated with increases in real output. Why? Would a more expansionary policy increase the long-term growth rate of real GDP? Why or why not?

5. What impact will an unanticipated increase in the money supply have on the real interest rate, real out-

put, and employment in the short run? How will expansionary monetary policy affect the economy when the effects are widely anticipated? Why does it make a difference whether the effects of monetary policy are anticipated?

6. How rapidly has the money supply (M1) grown during the past 12 months? How rapidly has M2 grown? Do you think the monetary authorities should increase or decrease the growth rate of the money supply during the next year? Why? (The data necessary to answer this question for the United States are available in the *Federal Reserve Bulletin*. They may also be found at the Web site of the Federal Reserve Bank of St. Louis, http://www.stls.frb.org.)

*7. If the Fed shifts to a more restrictive monetary policy, it will generally sell bonds in the open market. How will this action influence each of the following? Briefly explain each of your answers.
   a. The reserves available to banks
   b. Real interest rates
   c. Household spending on consumer durables
   d. The exchange rate value of the dollar
   e. Net exports
   f. The prices of stocks and real assets like apartment or office buildings
   g. Real GDP

8. Will a budget deficit be more expansionary if it is financed by borrowing from the Federal Reserve or from the general public? Explain.

9. Political officials often call on the monetary authorities to expand the money supply more rapidly so that interest rates can be reduced. Will expansionary monetary policy reduce interest rates in the short run? Will it do so in the long run? Explain. The highest interest rates in the world are found in countries that expand the supply of money rapidly. Can you explain why?

*10. Many economists believe that there is a "long and variable time lag" between when a change in monetary policy is instituted and when the change exerts its primary impact on output, employment, and prices. If true, how does this long and variable time lag affect the ability of policy makers to use monetary policy as a stabilization tool?

*11. "Historically, when interest rates are high, the inflation rate is high. High interest rates are a major cause of inflation." Evaluate this statement.

*12. If the supply of money is constant, how will an increase in the demand for money influence aggregate demand?

13. a. What is the quantity theory of money?
    b. Is the quantity theory of money valid?
    c. Is it a complete theory with regard to the impact of shifts in monetary policy on the economy? Why or why not?

*14. The accompanying chart presents data on the money supply, price level, and real GDP for three countries during the 1993–1996 period.
   a. Fill in the missing data.

	MONEY SUPPLY (IN BILLIONS OF LOCAL CURRENCY)	GDP DEFLATOR (1990=100)	NOMINAL GDP (IN CURRENT CURRENCY UNITS)	REAL GDP (IN 1990 CURRENCY UNITS)	PERCENT RATE OF CHANGE	
					MONEY SUPPLY	PRICE LEVEL
UNITED STATES						
1993	1,231	109.7	6,553	_____	X	X
1994	1,232	112.2	6,936	_____	_____	_____
1995	1,221	115.0	7,254	_____	_____	_____
1996	1,238	117.2	7,576	_____	_____	_____
CHILE						
1993	1,629	157.3	18,454	_____	X	X
1994	1,892	179.2	21,918	_____	_____	_____
1995	2,313	201.1	26,702	_____	_____	_____
1996	2,687	208.2	29,645	_____	_____	_____
VENEZUELA						
1993	409	205.0	5,454	_____	X	X
1994	981	334.1	8,632	_____	_____	_____
1995	1,367	505.5	13,504	_____	_____	_____
1996	1,349	1,068.8	28,091	_____	_____	_____

Source: International Monetary Fund, *International Financial Yearbook,* 1997.

b. Which country followed the most expansionary monetary policy (highest average rate of growth in the money supply) between 1993 and 1996?

c. Which country experienced the highest average annual rate of inflation during the 1993–1996 period?

d. Which country experienced the most rapid increase in real output during the 1993–1996 period?

15. As signs of economic weakness appeared during the first half of 2001, the Fed reduced its discount rate and the federal funds interest rate several times. What was the Fed trying to do? What is the expected impact of the Fed's actions on aggregate demand, output, employment, and the general level of prices? Might such actions cause future inflation? With the benefit of hindsight, how would you evaluate the Fed's actions during this period?

---

*Asterisk denotes questions for which answers are given in Appendix B.

CHAPTER 15

Stabilization Policy, Output, and Employment

Chapter Focus

■ Historically, how much has real output fluctuated? Are economic fluctuations becoming more or less severe?

■ Can active use of discretionary macroeconomic policy moderate the business cycle?

■ Why is proper timing of changes in macroeconomic policy both crucially important and difficult to achieve?

■ How are expectations formed? Do expectations influence how macroeconomic policy works?

■ What is the modern view of stabilization policy?

■ Did perverse macroeconomic policy cause the Great Depression?

[1]Robert J. Gordon, *Macroeconomics* (Boston: Little, Brown, 1978), p. 334.

n previous chapters we have analyzed the impact of both fiscal and monetary policy on output, employment, and prices. We have also noted that the initial impact of policy changes often differs from the impact over a more lengthy time period. We now want to consider the potential of macro policy as a stabilization tool. Can active management of fiscal and/or monetary policy reduce economic instability? What types of fiscal and monetary policy are best for the economy? This chapter will focus on the tools that enhance and the factors that limit the achievement of a stable economic environment. We will also consider alternative theories about how expectations are formed and investigate their implications with regard to how macroeconomic policy works. We will begin by taking a look at the magnitude of economic fluctuations during this century. ■

ECONOMIC FLUCTUATIONS—THE HISTORICAL RECORD

Wide fluctuations in the general level of business activity—in income, employment, and the price level—make personal economic planning extremely difficult. Such changes can cause even well-devised investment plans to go awry. The tragic stories of unemployed workers begging for food and newly impoverished investors jumping out of windows during the Great Depression vividly portray the enormous personal and social costs of economic instability and the uncertainty that it generates.

Historically, substantial fluctuations in real output have occurred. **Exhibit 1** illustrates the growth record of real GDP in the United States during the past 90 years. Prior to the

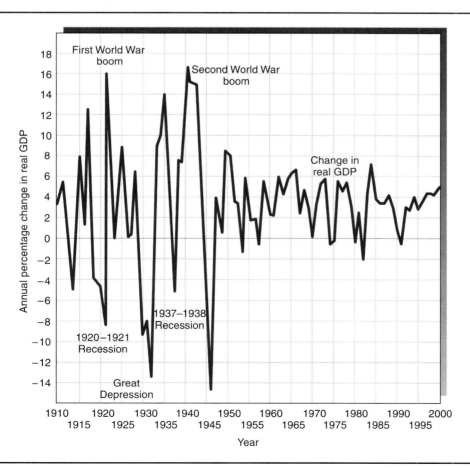

EXHIBIT 1
Post-Second World War Decline in Economic Instability

Prior to the conclusion of the Second World War, the United States experienced double-digit increases in real GDP in 1918, 1922, 1935–1936, and 1941–1943. In contrast, real output fell by 5 percent or more in 1920–1921, 1930–1932, 1938, and 1946. As illustrated here, fluctuations in real GDP have moderated during the last five decades. Most economists believe that more appropriate macro policy—particularly monetary policy—deserves much of the credit (see Exhibit 2).

Sources: Historical Statistics of the United States, p. 224; and Bureau of Economic Analysis, www.bea.doc.gov.

Second World War, double-digit swings in real GDP during a single year were not uncommon. Real GDP rose by more than 10 percent annually during the First World War, during an economic boom in 1922, during a mid-1930s recovery, and again during the Second World War. In contrast, output fell at an annual rate of 5 percent or more during the 1920–1921 recession, in the depression years of 1930–1932 and 1938, and again following the Second World War. Since 1950, economic ups and downs have been more moderate. Nevertheless, substantial fluctuations are still observable.

PROMOTING ECONOMIC STABILITY— ACTIVIST AND NONACTIVIST VIEWS

There is widespread agreement concerning the goals of macroeconomic policy. Economists of almost all persuasions believe that the performance of a market economy would be improved if economic fluctuations were minimal, the general level of prices stable, and employment maintained at a high level (unemployment at the natural rate).

How to achieve these goals is, however, a hot topic of debate among macroeconomists. Many economists argue that the major macroeconomic goals can best be achieved through the active use of discretionary monetary and fiscal policy. The proponents of an **activist strategy** believe that macro policy can be used successfully to speed the adjustment process and reduce the swings of the business cycle. Activists often argue that the economy's self-corrective mechanism works slowly. Therefore, when economic shocks disrupt equilibrium, activists believe that policymakers will be able to manage demand in a manner that will keep the economy on track and minimize the adverse consequences of disruptions.

In contrast, **nonactivists** argue that discretionary use of monetary and fiscal policy in response to changing economic conditions is likely to do more harm than good. According to the nonactivist view, the economy's self-corrective mechanism, if not stifled by perverse macro policy, will prevent prolonged periods of economic decline and high unemployment. Nonactivists charge that erratic policy, particularly the instability of monetary policy, is a major source of economic fluctuations. They note that the really serious cases of economic instability, such as the Great Depression of the 1930s and the inflation of the 1970s, were primarily the result of policy errors. Rather than altering macro policy in a discretionary manner, nonactivists believe that economic stability can best be achieved by following rules and guidelines that will provide for stable monetary and fiscal policy.

There are points of agreement between activists and nonactivists. Both recognize that policy errors have contributed to economic instability. Prior to the Keynesian revolution, governments often raised taxes to balance the budget when revenue declined during a recession. Of course, modern analysis implies that such a policy may add to the severity of a recession. Both activists and nonactivists recognize the potential dangers of monetary instability. As **Exhibit 2** illustrates, extreme gyrations in the money supply characterized monetary policy prior to the Second World War. Sharp contractions in the money supply often accompanied major recessions, while double-digit money growth was observed during the inflationary periods of the First and Second World Wars. Activists and nonactivists agree that erratic policy changes, particularly those in the monetary area, have contributed to economic instability. (See Applications in Economics, "Perverse Macroeconomic Policy and the Great Depression," on page 350 for evidence on the tragic role of policy during the 1930s.)

As Exhibit 2 shows, swings in monetary policy have moderated considerably since the end of the Second World War. So too have business cycle fluctuations. Activists and nonactivists agree that the link between the more stable monetary policy and moderation of the business cycle is no coincidence. We now turn to an analysis of how macroeconomic policy might be actively used to smooth the ups and downs of the business cycle.

Activist strategy
Deliberate changes in monetary and fiscal policy in order to inject demand stimulus during a recession and apply restraint during an inflationary boom and thereby, it is hoped, minimize economic instability.

Nonactivist strategy
The maintenance of a steady monetary and fiscal policy during all phases of the business cycle. According to this view, adjusting macro policy in response to current cyclical conditions is likely to increase, rather than reduce, instability.

EXHIBIT 2
Post-Second World War Decline in Monetary Instability

Prior to 1950, monetary policy was characterized by wide swings. Huge increases (15 percent or more) in the supply of money (M2) were often followed by sharp monetary contractions. Since the end of the Second World War, the fluctuations in the supply of money have declined, as the monetary authorities followed a more stable course. As the prior exhibit illustrates, the more stable monetary policy has been associated with a more stable economy.

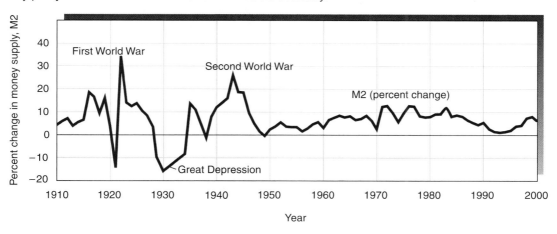

Sources: Federal Reserve, www.federalreserve.gov; and Robert J. Gordon, *Macroeconomics* (Glenview, Ill: Scott Foresman, 1990).

As we proceed, we will consider some of the limitations of this strategy. Later, we will also present the nonactivist view of macroeconomic policy.

THE CONDUCT OF DISCRETIONARY STABILIZATION POLICY

Macroeconomic policy reduces instability only if it injects stimulus and applies restraint at the proper phase of the business cycle. Proper timing is the key to effective stabilization policy. But how can policymakers know whether they should be stimulating aggregate demand or applying the economic brake?

Of course, economic indicators, such as the growth of real GDP and the rate of unemployment, provide policymakers with information on the current state of the economy. However, this is not exactly what policymakers need. Because it takes time for macroeconomic policy to work, policymakers really need to know about the future—where the economy is going to be six to twelve months from now. They need to know whether a business recession or an inflationary boom is around the corner. If they do not know where the economy is going, a policy change may fail to exert its primary impact quickly enough to offset a downturn or restrain future inflation.

How can policymakers find out where the economy is going in the future and when a turn in the macroeconomic road is about to occur? The two most widely used sources of information on the future direction of the economy are the index of leading economic indicators and economic forecasting models.

Index of Leading Indicators

The **index of leading indicators** is a composite statistic based on 10 key variables that generally turn down prior to a recession and turn up before the beginning of a business

Index of leading indicators
An index of economic variables that historically has tended to turn down prior to the beginning of a recession and turn up prior to the beginning of a business expansion.

APPLICATIONS IN ECONOMICS

Perverse Macroeconomic Policy and the Great Depression

As we previously discussed, the Great Depression exerted an enormous impact both on economic thought and on economic institutions. **Table 1** presents data that illustrate both the severity and length of the economic contraction. For four successive years (1930–1933), real output fell. Unemployment soared to nearly one-quarter of the workforce in 1932 and 1933. Although recovery did take place during 1934–1937, the economy again fell into the depth of depression in 1938. Ten years after the catastrophe began, real GDP was virtually the same as it had been in 1929.[1]

Armed with knowledge of how monetary and fiscal policies work, one can clearly see that at least the severity of the calamity was the result of perverse macroeconomic policy. Three important factors contributed to the economic collapse of the 1930s.

1. ***A sharp reduction in the supply of money during 1930–1933 reduced aggregate demand and real output.***
The supply of money expanded slowly but steadily throughout the 1920s.[2] As Table 1 shows, monetary policy suddenly shifted in 1930. The money supply fell by 6.9 percent during 1930, by 10.9 percent in 1931, and by 4.7 percent in 1932. As banks failed and the money supply collapsed, the Fed failed to inject new reserves into the system. Neither did it act as a lender of last resort. The quantity of money in 1933 was 27 percent less than in 1929! A sudden shift to a restrictive monetary policy will reduce both aggregate demand and real output. Our analysis indicates that a drastic reduction in the money supply, such as that of the early 1930s, will almost surely result in a drastic reduction in output. This is precisely what happened. Real output plunged. By 1933, real GDP was 29 percent lower than the 1929 level.

2. ***A large tax increase in the midst of a severe recession made a bad situation worse.*** Prior to the Keynesian revolution, the dominant view was that the federal budget should be balanced. Reflecting the ongoing economic downturn, the federal budget ran a deficit in 1931, and an even larger deficit was shaping up for 1932. Assisted by the newly elected Democratic majority in the House of Representatives, the Republican Hoover administration passed the largest peacetime tax rate increase in the history of the United States. At the bottom of the income scale, marginal tax rates were raised from 1.5 percent to 4 percent in 1932. At the top of the scale, tax rates were raised from 25 percent to 63 percent. As our prior analysis of fiscal policy suggests, a huge tax increase in the midst of a severe recession will further reduce aggregate demand and the incentive to earn. Table 1 shows the degree to which this happened. As tax rates were increased in 1932, real GDP fell by 13.3 percent. Unemployment rose from 15.9 percent in 1931 to 23.6 percent in 1932.

3. ***Tariff increases retarded international exchange.*** Concerned about low agricultural prices, an influx of imports, rising unemployment, and declining tax revenues, Congress adopted various trade restraints. Tariffs (taxes on imported goods) on a wide range of products were increased substantially in early 1930.[3] Other countries promptly responded by increasing their tariffs, further reducing the volume of trade between nations. As the flow of trade diminished, so too did the mutual gains trading partners derive from specialization and exchange.

When discussing the Great Depression, historians often stress the role of the 1929 stock market crash. Since the stock market crash diminished the wealth of many, it was a contributing factor to the reduction in aggregate demand and output. However, the severity of the Great Depression was the result of disastrous macroeconomic policy, not an inevitable consequence of a stock market crash. The experience following the October 1987 crash illustrates this point. In just a few days, the stock market lost a third of its value in 1987, just as it did in 1929. But that is where the parallel ends. In contrast with the response to the 1929 crash, in 1987 the Fed moved quickly to supply

Perhaps the most catastrophic example of inappropriate stabilization policy was that of the Great Depression. A sharp reduction in the supply of money, a huge tax increase, and protectionist trade policies turned a recession into the worst depression in U.S. history.

TABLE 1
The Economic Record of the Great Depression

Year	Real GDP in 1989 Dollars (billions)	Implicit GDP Deflator (1929 = 100)	Unemployment Rate	Percent Change in the Money Supply (M1)
1929	821.8	100.0	3.2	+1.0
1930	748.9	96.8	8.7	−6.9
1931	691.3	88.0	15.9	−10.9
1932	599.7	77.6	23.6	−4.7
1933	587.1	76.0	24.9	−2.9
1934	632.6	82.4	21.7	+10.0
1935	681.3	84.8	20.1	+18.2
1936	777.9	84.8	16.9	+13.9
1937	811.4	89.6	14.3	+4.7
1938	778.9	87.2	19.0	−1.3
1939	840.7	86.4	17.2	+12.1

Source: Economic Report of the President: 1993 (Washington, D.C.: U.S. Government Printing Office, 1993); and Bureau of the Census, *The Statistical History of the United States from Colonial Times to the Present* (New York, Basic Books, 1976).

reserves to the banking system. The money supply did not fall. Tax rates were not increased. And even though there was a lot of political rhetoric about "the need to protect American businesses," trade barriers were not raised. In short, sensible policies were followed subsequent to the crash of 1987. Continued growth and stability were the result. Inadvertently, perverse macroeconomic policies were followed subsequent to the crash of 1929. Economic disaster was the result.

[1] See Robert J. Samuelson, "Great Depression," in *The Fortune Encyclopedia of Economics,* ed. David R. Henderson (New York: Warner Books, 1993), for an interesting and informative commentary on this time period.

[2] From 1921 through 1929, the money stock expanded at an annual rate of 2.7 percent, slightly less rapidly than the growth in the output of goods and services. Thus, the 1920s were a decade of price stability, even of slight deflation.

[3] The high-tariff policy was ineffective as a revenue measure. Even though the taxes on imported goods were increased by approximately 50 percent, imports declined so sharply that tariff revenues fell from $602 million in 1929 to $328 million in 1932.

expansion (see Measures of Economic Activity, "Index of Leading Indicators"). **Exhibit 3** illustrates the path of the index during the 1959–2000 period. Three consecutive monthly declines in the index are considered a warning that the economy is about to dip into a recession. This index has forecast each of the seven recessions since 1959. On four occasions, the downturn occurred eight to eleven months prior to a recession, providing policymakers with sufficient lead time to modify policy, particularly monetary policy. In other instances it has been quite lengthy, as when it turned down 18 months prior to the 1990–1991 recession.

A downturn in the index is not always an accurate indicator of the future. On five occasions (1962, 1966, 1984, 1987, and 1995), a decline in the index of leading indicators forecast a future recession that did not materialize. This has given rise to the quip that the index has accurately forecast twelve of the last seven recessions.

Forecasting Models

Economists have developed highly complex econometric (statistical) models to improve the accuracy of macroeconomic forecasts. In essence, these models use past data on economic interrelationships to project how currently observed changes will influence the future path of key economic variables, such as real GDP, employment, and the price level. The most elaborate of these models use hundreds of variables and equations to simulate the various sectors and macroeconomic markets. Powerful, high-speed computers are

EXHIBIT 3
Index of Leading Indicators

The shaded periods represent recessions. The index of leading indicators forecast each of the seven recessions during the 1959–2001 period. As the arrows show, however, the time lag between when the index turned down and when the economy fell into a recession varied. In addition, on five occasions (1962, 1966, 1984, 1987, and 1995), the index forecast a recession that did not occur.

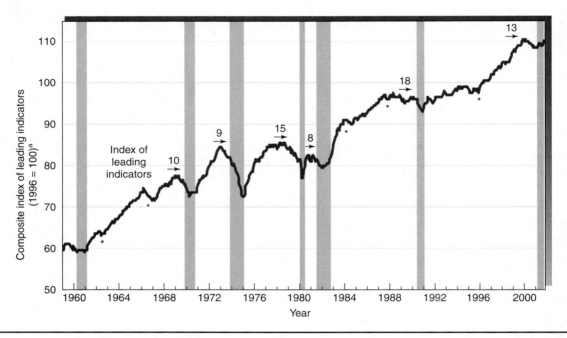

[a]The arrows indicate the number of months that the downturn in the index preceded a recession. An asterisk (*) indicates a false signal of a recession.
Source: Conference Board, www.globalindicators.org.

employed to analyze the effects of various policy alternatives and attempt to predict the future.

To date, the record of computer forecasting models is mixed. When economic conditions are relatively stable (for example, when the growth of real GDP and the rate of inflation follow a steady trend), the models have generally provided accurate forecasts for both aggregate economic variables and important subcomponents of the economy. Unfortunately, however, they have generally missed the major turns in the economic road. For example, none of the major computer models forecast the recessions of 1990 and 2001.

Many economists maintain that accurate forecasts are beyond the reach of economics. Two major factors underlie this view. First, business cycle conditions often reflect economic shocks and unforeseen events—for example, an unexpected policy change, discovery of a new resource or technology, abnormal weather, or political upheaval in an important oil-exporting nation. There is no reason to believe that economists or anyone else will be able to predict such changes accurately and consistently. Thus, while economic theory helps to predict the implications of unforeseen events, it cannot foretell what those events will be and when they might occur. Second, the critics of forecasting models argue that the future will differ from the past because people will often make different choices as the result of what they learned from previous events. Therefore, forecasting models based on past relationships—including elaborate computer models—will never be able to generate consistently accurate predictions.

MEASURES OF ECONOMIC ACTIVITY

Index of Leading Indicators

History indicates that no single indicator is able to forecast accurately the future direction of the economy. However, several economic variables do tend to reach a high or low prior to the peak of a business expansion or the trough of an economic recession. Such variables are called leading economic indicators.

To provide more reliable information on the future direction of the economy, economists have devised an index of 10 such indicators:

1. Length of the average workweek in hours
2. Initial weekly claims for unemployment compensation
3. New orders placed with manufacturers
4. Percentage of companies receiving slower deliveries from suppliers
5. Contracts and orders for new plants and equipment
6. Permits for new housing starts

7. Interest rate spread, 10-year Treasury bonds less fed funds rate
8. Index of consumer expectations
9. Change in the index of stock prices (500 common stocks)
10. Change in the money supply (M2)

The variables included in the index were chosen both because of their tendency to lead (or predict) turns in the business cycle and because they are available frequently and promptly. In some cases, it is easy to see why a change in an economic indicator precedes a change in general economic activity. Consider the indicator of "new orders placed with manufacturers" (measured in constant dollars). An expansion in the volume of orders is generally followed by an expansion in manufacturing output. Similarly, manufacturers will tend to scale back their future production when a decline in new orders signals the probability of weak future demand for their products. The index of leading indicators is published by the Conference Board in *Business Cycle Indicators*.

Market Signals and Discretionary Monetary Policy

Some economists believe that information supplied by certain markets can also provide policymakers with an early warning of the need to institute a change in policy. For example, since they fluctuate daily and are determined in auction markets, changes in commodity prices often foretell future changes in the general price level. An increase in a broad index of commodity prices implies that money is plentiful (relative to demand). This suggests the Fed should shift toward a more restrictive policy in order to offset future inflation. In contrast, falling commodity prices indicate that deflation is a potential future danger, in which case the Fed might want to shift toward a more expansionary policy.

Exchange rates also provide policymakers with information about the relative scarcity of money and fear of inflation. Because exchange rates, to a degree, reflect the willingness of foreigners to hold U.S. dollars, a decline in the exchange rate value of the dollar (the value of the dollar relative to other currencies) often implies a fear of higher inflation and a reluctance to hold dollars. This would signal the need to shift to a more restrictive policy. Conversely, an increase in the exchange rate value of the dollar is a strong vote of confidence in the future purchasing power of the dollar. This provides the Fed with some leeway to move toward a more expansionary policy.

Commodity prices, exchange rates, and other market signals can help us judge the early effects and likely future impact of current policies. They are best used as a supplement to, rather than as a substitute for, other economic indicators and forecasting devices.

Discretionary Policy—The Activist View

Activists recognize that it is difficult to institute countercyclical macroeconomic policy. However, they believe that the index of leading indicators, forecasting models, sensitive market variables, and other economic indicators provide policymakers with an early warning system. Thus, they are able to alter policy in a manner that will smooth business ups and downs. Responding to the early signals, policymakers can initially undertake moderate changes. With the passage of time, more substantial changes can be instituted if more comprehensive information indicates they are needed.

The following scenario outlines the essentials of the activist view. Suppose the economy were about to dip into a recession. Prior to the recession, the index of leading indicators would almost surely alert policymakers to the possibility of a downturn. This would permit them to shift toward macroeconomic stimulus, expanding the money supply more rapidly. Initially, the shift toward macroeconomic stimulus could be applied in moderate doses, which could easily be reversed in the future if necessary. On the other hand, if the signs of a downturn became more pronounced and current business conditions actually weakened, additional stimulus could be injected. Perhaps a tax reduction or a speedup in government expenditures might be used to supplement the more expansionary monetary policy.

Policymakers can constantly monitor the situation, adjusting their actions as additional information becomes available. If the weakness persists, the expansionary policy can be continued. Conversely, when the signs point to a strong recovery, policymakers can move toward restraint and thereby head off potential inflationary pressure. According to the activist view, policymakers are more likely to keep the economy on track when they are free to apply stimulus or restraint based on forecasting devices and current economic indicators.

Lags and the Problem of Timing

Discretionary changes in both monetary and fiscal policy must be timed appropriately if they are going to exert a stabilizing influence on the economy. There are three time lags that make proper timing difficult. First, there is the **recognition lag**, the time period between a change in economic conditions and recognition of the change by policymakers. It generally takes a few months to gather and tabulate reliable information on the recent performance of the economy in order to determine whether it has dipped into a recession or whether the inflation rate has accelerated, and so forth.

Second, even after the need for a policy change is recognized, there is generally an additional time period before the policy change is instituted. Economists refer to this delay as administrative lag. In the case of monetary policy, the **administrative lag** is generally quite short. The Federal Open Market Committee meets every few weeks and is in a position to institute a change in monetary policy quickly. This is a major advantage of monetary policy. For discretionary fiscal policy, the administrative lag is likely to be much longer. Congressional committees must meet. Legislation must be proposed and debated. Congress must act, and the president must consent. Each of these steps takes time.

Finally, there is the **impact lag**, the time period between the implementation of a macro policy change and when the change exerts its primary impact on the economy. Although the impact of a change in tax rates is generally felt quickly, the expansionary effects of an increase in government expenditures are usually much less rapid. It will take time for the submission of competitive bids and the letting of new contracts. Several months may pass before work on a new project actually begins. The impact lag in the case of monetary policy is likely to be even longer. The time period between a shift in monetary policy, a change in interest rates, and, in turn, a change in the level of spending may be quite lengthy.

Economists who have studied this topic, including Milton Friedman and Robert Gordon, conclude that the combined duration of these time lags is generally 12 to 18 months in the case of monetary policy, and even longer in the case of fiscal policy. This means that, if a policy is going to exert the desired effect at the proper time, policymakers cannot wait until a problem develops before they act. Rather, they must correctly forecast the future direction of the economy and act before there is a contraction in real GDP or an observable increase in the rate of inflation. Given our ability to forecast the future, nonac-

Recognition lag
The time period after a policy change is needed from a stabilization standpoint but before the need is recognized by policymakers.

Administrative lag
The time period after the need for a policy change is recognized but before the policy is actually implemented.

Impact lag
The time period after a policy change is implemented but before the change begins to exert its primary effects.

EXHIBIT 4
Time Lags and Effects of Discretionary Policy

Beginning with *A*, we illustrate the path of a hypothetical business cycle. If a forthcoming recession can be recognized quickly and a more expansionary policy instituted at point *B*, the policy may add stimulus at point *C* and help to minimize the magnitude of the downturn. Activists believe that discretionary policy is likely to achieve this outcome. However, if delays result in the adoption of the expansionary policy at *C* and if it does not exert its major impact until *D*, the demand stimulus will exacerbate the inflationary boom. In turn, an anti-inflationary strategy instituted at *E* may exert its primary effects at *F*, just in time to increase the severity of a recession beyond *F*. Nonactivists fear that improper timing of discretionary macro policy will exert such destabilizing effects.

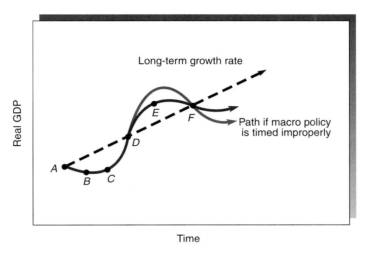

tivists argue that proper timing of discretionary policy changes is unrealistic. Furthermore, even if forecasting were a more precise science, the time lags accompanying changes in monetary and fiscal policies are long and variable. This also reduces the viability of discretionary policy as a stabilization tool.

Exhibit 4 presents a graphic illustration of the difference between the views of the activists and nonactivists. When the economy begins to dip into a recession, activists argue that policymakers can reasonably be expected to recognize the danger and shift to a more expansionary policy at point *B*. If the demand-stimulus effects are felt quickly (before the economy gets to point *C*), the shift to the more expansionary macro policy will help to minimize the decline in output accompanying the business downturn.

In contrast, nonactivists believe that policymakers are unlikely to act so quickly, and, even if they did, the time lags accompanying changes in monetary and fiscal policies are likely to make their actions ineffective. The shift to the more expansionary policy will not come until point *C*, according to this reasoning, and its effects will not be significant until point D. In this case, the expansionary policy will contribute to the severity of the inflationary boom (beyond point *D*). Similarly, a subsequent shift to an anti-inflationary policy may begin to exert its major impact at point *F*, just in time to make an oncoming recession worse (beyond point *F*). Therefore, nonactivists believe that discretionary policy shifts are likely to be destabilizing rather than stabilizing.

HOW ARE EXPECTATIONS FORMED?

Throughout this text, we have carefully differentiated between anticipated and unanticipated changes. A change may exert a very different impact, depending on whether it is widely expected or catches people by surprise. Given the importance of expectations, we need to analyze how they are formed. There are two general theories in this area. Let us outline the essentials of each.

Adaptive Expectations

Adaptive-expectations hypothesis
The hypothesis that economic decision makers base their future expectations on actual outcomes observed during recent periods. For example, according to this view, the rate of inflation actually experienced during the past two or three years would be the major determinant of the rate of inflation expected for the next year.

The simplest theory concerning the formation of expectations is that people rely on the past to predict future trends. According to this theory, which economists call the **adaptive-expectations hypothesis**, decision makers believe that the best indicator of the future is what has happened in the recent past. For example, individuals would expect the price level to be stable next year if stable prices had been present during the past two or three years. Similarly, if prices had risen at an annual rate of 4 or 5 percent during the past several years, people would expect similar increases next year.

Exhibit 5 presents a graphic illustration of the adaptive-expectations hypothesis. In period 1, prices were stable (part a). Therefore, on the basis of the experience of period 1, decision makers assume that prices will be stable in period 2 (part b). However, the actual rate of inflation in period 2 jumps to 4 percent. Continuation of the 4 percent inflation rate throughout period 2 (the periods may range from six months to two or three years in length) causes decision makers to change their expectations. Relying on the experience of period 2, they anticipate 4 percent inflation in period 3. When their expectations turn out to be incorrect (the actual rate of inflation during period 3 is 8 percent), they again alter their expectations accordingly. Then, during period 4, the actual rate of inflation declines to 4 percent, less than the expected rate. Again, decision makers adjust their expectations as to the rate of inflation in period 5.

Of course, one would not expect the precise mechanical link between past occurrences and future expectations outlined in Exhibit 5. Rather than simply using the inflation rate of the immediate past period, people may use a weighted average of recent inflation rates when forming their expectations. It is the structure, however, that is important. With adaptive expectations, decision makers will always expect the next period to be pretty much like the recent past.

Rational Expectations

Rational-expectations hypothesis
The hypothesis that economic decision makers weigh all available evidence, including information concerning the probable effects of current and future economic policy, when they form their expectations about future economic events (such as the probable future inflation rate).

The idea that people form their expectations about the future on the basis of all available information, including knowledge about policy changes and how they affect the economy, is called the **rational-expectations hypothesis**. According to this view, rather than merely

---

EXHIBIT 5
Adaptive-Expectations Hypothesis

According to the adaptive-expectations hypothesis, the actual occurrence during the most recent period (or set of periods) determines people's future expectations. Thus, the expected future rate of inflation (b) lags behind the actual rate of inflation (a) by one period as expectations are altered over time.

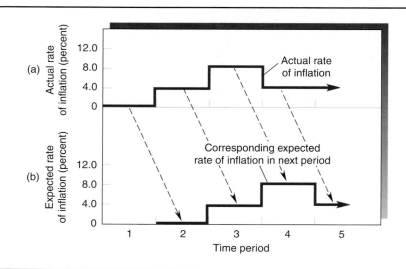

OUTSTANDING ECONOMIST

Robert Lucas (1937–)

The 1995 Nobel laureate, Robert Lucas is generally given credit for the introduction of the rational-expectations theory into macroeconomics. His technical work in this area has substantially altered the way economists think about macroeconomic policy. He is a longtime professor of economics at the University of Chicago.

assuming the future will be pretty much like the immediate past, people also consider the expected effects of changes in policy. Based on their understanding of economic policy, people alter their expectations with regard to the future when the government, for example, runs a larger deficit or expands the supply of money more rapidly.

Perhaps an example will help clarify the rational-expectations hypothesis. Suppose prices had increased at an annual rate of 3 percent during each of the past three years. In addition, assume that decision makers believe there is a relationship between the growth rate of the money supply and rising prices. They note that the money stock has expanded at a 12 percent annual rate during the last nine months, up from the 4 percent rate of the past several years. According to the rational-expectations hypothesis, they will integrate the recent monetary acceleration into their forecast of the future inflation rate. Thus, they may project an increase in the inflation rate, perhaps to the 6 to 10 percent range. In other words, they will expect the future inflation rate to respond to the more rapid growth of the money supply. In contrast, the adaptive-expectations hypothesis implies that people would expect the inflation rate for the next period to be the same as that for the last period (or the last several periods).

The rational-expectations hypothesis does not assume that forecasts will always be correct. We live in a world of uncertainty. Even rational decision makers will err. But they will learn from their past mistakes; they will not continue to make the same types of errors. Thus, the rational-expectations hypothesis assumes that the errors of decision makers will tend to be random. For example, sometimes decision makers may overestimate the increase in the inflation rate caused by monetary expansion, and at other times they may underestimate it. But because they learn from prior experience, people will not continue to make systematic errors year after year.

Recent technological innovations have increased the availability of low-cost information. For example, information on economic matters is now readily available through both the Internet and a proliferation of finance-related networks and programs. As a result, ordinary Americans may now be better prepared to develop well informed forecasts about the future direction of the economy. If so, this will tend to enhance both the relevance and validity of the rational expectations hypothesis.

Major Differences Between Adaptive and Rational Expectations

The adaptive- and rational-expectations theories differ in two major respects: (1) how quickly people adjust to a change and (2) the likelihood of systematic forecasting errors. If the adaptive-expectations theory is correct, people will adjust more slowly. When a more expansionary policy leads to inflation, for example, there will be a significant time lag before people come to expect the inflation and incorporate it into their decision making. In contrast, the rational-expectations theory implies that people will begin to anticipate more inflation as soon as they observe a move toward a more expansionary policy, perhaps even before there is an actual increase in the rate of inflation. Therefore, with rational expectations, the time lag between a shift in policy and a change in expectations is likely to be brief.

Systematic errors will occur with adaptive expectations. For example, when the inflation rate is rising, decision makers will systematically tend to underestimate the future rate of inflation. In contrast, when the rate of inflation is falling, individuals will tend systematically to overestimate its future rate. With rational expectations, the errors will be random. People will be as likely to overestimate as to underestimate the future rate of inflation.

HOW MACRO POLICY WORKS: THE IMPLICATIONS OF ADAPTIVE AND RATIONAL EXPECTATIONS

From the viewpoint of macro policy, does it make any difference how quickly people alter their expectations and whether errors are random or systematic? The *AD/AS* model can be used to address this question. Suppose that there is a shift to a more expansionary macro policy—an increase in the money growth rate, for example. As part a of **Exhibit 6** illustrates, the policy shift will stimulate aggregate demand and place upward pressure on the price level (or the inflation rate in the dynamic case). Under adaptive expectations, people will initially fail to anticipate the higher prices. Therefore, as we have previously discussed, output will temporarily increase to Y_2, beyond the economy's long-run potential. Correspondingly, employment will expand and un-

EXHIBIT 6
Expectations and the Short-run Effects of Demand Stimulus

Under adaptive expectations, anticipation of inflation will lag behind its actual occurrence. As a result, a shift to a more expansionary policy will increase aggregate demand and lead to a temporary increase in real GDP from Y_F to Y_2, (a). In contrast, under rational expectations, decision makers will quickly anticipate the inflationary impact of a demand-stimulus policy. Thus, resource prices and production costs will rise as rapidly as prices. While aggregate demand shifts upward, so too will short-run aggregate supply (shift to $SRAS_2$) (b). With rational expectations, the demand-stimulus policy will increase prices without altering real output even in the short run.

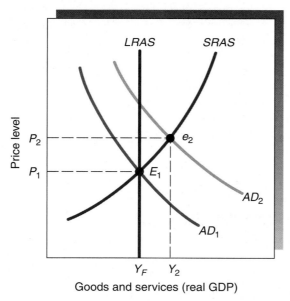

(a) Expansionary policy under
adaptive expectations

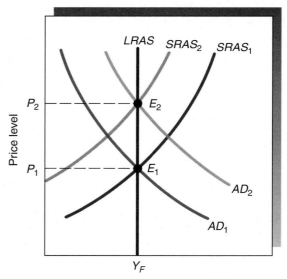

(b) Expansionary policy under
rational expectations

employment will recede below the economy's natural rate. When the effects of expansionary policy are unanticipated, both output and employment increase in the short run. Of course, the output rate beyond the economy's capacity will be unsustainable. Eventually, strong demand for resources and the expectation of a higher price level (or rate of inflation) will push resource prices up also. Thus, the high level of output and employment will only be temporary. When decision makers adjust slowly, however, it may be possible to maintain the higher rate of output for a year or two, perhaps even a little longer.

Part b of Exhibit 6 illustrates the impact of expansionary macroeconomic policy under rational expectations. Remember with rational expectations, decision makers will quickly begin to anticipate the probable effects of the more expansionary policy—stronger demand and a rising rate of inflation, for example—and alter their choices accordingly. Agreements specifying future wage rates and resource prices will quickly make allowance for an expected increase in the price level. These agreements may even incorporate escalator clauses providing for automatic increases in nominal wages as the general price level rises. When buyers and sellers in the resource market anticipate fully and adjust quickly to the effects of the demand-stimulus policies, wage rates and resource prices will rise as rapidly as product prices. Hence, the short-run aggregate supply curve will shift upward (to $SRAS_2$) as rapidly as the aggregate demand curve. When people quickly and accurately anticipate the inflationary effects of the more expansionary policy, the result will merely be an increase in the general level of prices (move from E_1 to E_2 in part b of Exhibit 6). Neither real output nor employment will expand.

The implications are symmetrical for restrictive policy. Under adaptive expectations a shift to a more restrictive policy will reduce both aggregate demand and real output. Under rational expectations, however, the weaker demand and lower prices will be anticipated quickly. Thus, there will also be downward pressure on resource prices and costs, which will make it possible to maintain the initial level of output, even though the general price level has fallen.

The proponents of rational expectations believe that the effects of a change in policy will be widely and quickly anticipated by decision makers. Once this occurs, the policy will fail to exert a systematic impact on real output and employment. Economists refer to this phenomenon as the **policy-ineffectiveness theorem**.

As we noted, rational-expectations theory does not imply that forecasts will always be correct. But the errors will be random. This means that, for example, when there is a shift to a more expansionary macro policy, people will be as likely to overestimate the inflationary side effects as to underestimate them. If people underestimate the future rate of inflation, product prices will rise relative to costs (resource prices) leading to a temporary increase in output. However, if decision makers overestimate the inflationary side effects, costs will increase relative to product prices and output will fall. As we noted, when the increase in inflation accompanying a more expansionary policy is accurately forecast, real output will remain unchanged. Thus, the theory of rational expectations implies that the impact of a shift in monetary and/or fiscal policy on output is unpredictable. A shift in macro policy is as likely to cause a reduction in output as an increase. This unpredictability explains why proponents of rational expectations argue that macro policy should follow a steady course and focus on long-range objectives.

Policy-ineffectiveness theorem
The proposition that any systematic policy will be rendered ineffective once decision makers figure out the policy pattern and adjust their decision making in light of its expected effects. The theorem is a corollary of the theory of rational expectations.

Policy Implications: A Summary

Thus, the adaptive- and rational-expectations theories have quite different implications with regard to the likely short-run effects of changes in macroeconomic policy. *With adaptive expectations, there will be a time lag before people anticipate the eventual effects of a shift to a more expansionary policy. Therefore, policies that stimulate demand and place upward pressure on the general level of prices will temporarily increase output and employment. In contrast, when the inflationary side effects of expansionary policies are anticipated quickly, as the rational-expectations theory*

Expectations and the Impact of Shifts in Macro Policy

	Under Adaptive Expectations (1)	Under Rational Expectations (2)		Under Adaptive Expectations (1)	Under Rational Expectations (2)
Impact in the Short Run			**Impact in the Long Run**		
Shift to a More Expansionary Policy	Higher prices (inflation); increase in output	Higher prices (inflation); no change in output	Shift to a More Expansionary Policy	Higher prices (inflation); no change in output	Higher prices (inflation); no change in output
Shift to a More Restrictive Policy	Lower prices (deflation); reduction in output	Lower prices (deflation) no change in output	Shift to a More Restrictive Policy	Lower prices (deflation); no change in output	Lower prices (deflation) no change in output

Note: Price stability was initially assumed to be present. If inflation was initially present, the shift to a more restrictive policy would reduce the rate of inflation rather than lead to deflation.

implies, the primary impact of the demand stimulus will be an increase in the price level.

While the implications of the two expectations theories differ with regard to the short-run effects of policy changes, their long-run implications are identical. Like rational expectations, the adaptive-expectations theory indicates that decision makers will eventually anticipate the long-run effects of more expansionary policy. As this happens, output will recede to the economy's long-run potential. Therefore, both theories imply that the long-run effects of a more expansionary macro policy will be inflation, rather than sustainable increases in output. The accompanying Thumbnail Sketch summarizes the implications of both adaptive and rational expectations regarding how a change in macro policy will impact the price level (inflation) and real output in both the long and short runs.

NONACTIVIST STABILIZATION POLICY

Timing problems, the public choice perspective, and the theory of rational expectations provide the foundation for the nonactivist view of macro policy. While nonactivists often arrive at their position from different paths, they have two major points in common. They believe that (1) discretionary policy changes will increase rather than reduce economic instability and (2) greater stability would result if stable, predictable policies based on predetermined rules or guidelines were followed.

Nonactivists recommend that policymakers choose a long-run policy path (for example, a low, stable rate of inflation and no change in tax rates or real government expenditures) and inform the public of this choice. This course should then be pursued regardless of cyclical ups and downs. As policymakers stay on course, they will gain credibility. The public will develop confidence in the future stability of the policy. Uncertainty will be reduced, thereby increasing the efficiency of private decision making. Nonactivists are confident this strategy would result both in less instability and in more rapid growth than Western economies have experienced in the past.

Nonactivist Monetary Policy

Suppose we are going to adopt a nonactivist strategy. What rules or guidelines would we choose? Nonactivists believe that monetary policy should focus on achieving either (1) a stable growth rate of the money supply or (2) a stable price level.

Monetary Growth Rule

Many nonactivists favor the constant money growth rule long championed by Milton Friedman. Under this plan, the money supply would be expanded continuously at an annual rate (3 percent, for example) that approximates the long-run growth of the U.S. economy. When real output is growing rapidly (for example, 5 percent annually), the supply of money would decline relative to real GDP. Thus, monetary policy would automatically exert a restraining influence during a period of rapid growth. In contrast, during a recession, the constant money growth rate would exceed the growth of real output, offsetting any tendency toward a downward spiral.

Nonactivists note that monetary policy has often followed a stop-and-go pattern. Many times, after expanding the money supply and causing inflation, policymakers have slammed on the monetary brakes and thrown the economy into a recession (see Exhibit 1). The nonactivists believe that monetary instability is the major source of economic instability. Rather than responding to forecasts and current economic indicators, the Fed, they say, would be a more stabilizing force if it simply increased the supply of money, month after month, at a low (noninflationary) constant rate.

The experience of the 1980s highlighted a potential drawback of the monetary rule approach. The introduction of interest-earning checking deposits drastically changed the nature of the M1 money supply during the 1980s. As the interest-earning checking accounts were legalized and more people began using them, the M1 money supply grew rapidly and fluctuated substantially. But this growth was not indicative of a highly expansionary monetary policy. The inflation rate declined sharply during the early 1980s and was relatively constant during the remainder of the decade. When the nature of money is changing, steady money growth may fail to yield monetary and price stability.

Furthermore, as people shift their savings among financial instruments, the shifts influence the growth of the various money supply measures. This can result in conflicting signals. For example, the M1 money supply contracted at a –0.4 percent annual rate during 1999–2000, suggesting that monetary policy was quite restrictive. During the same period, the annual growth of the M2 money supply was 6.2 percent, indicating that monetary policy was moderately expansionary. Technological developments in the financial sector have substantially reduced the usefulness of the money supply figures as an indicator of monetary policy. In a dynamic world, changes in this area are almost sure to continue. (Some of these changes were discussed in Chapter 13 in the sections on measurement problems and the future of money.)[2]

Price Level Rule

The shortcomings of money supply figures as an indicator of monetary policy have enhanced the attractiveness of price level targeting. Under this approach, the monetary authorities would directly target a broad price index, such as the GDP deflator or consumer price index. The advocates of a price level rule argue that, in the long run, monetary policy cannot determine real output, employment, interest rates, or other real variables. What it can and does determine is the level of prices. Therefore, why not require that the monetary authorities maintain a persistently low rate of inflation and hold them accountable for their

---

[2]In recent years, economists have generally placed more confidence in the M2 money supply figures. But there are no assurances that future financial innovations will not also alter the nature of M2 and undermine its use as a gauge of monetary policy. In fact, evidence of such changes is already present. In response to recent reductions in the start-up cost of stock and bond mutual funds, many individuals shifted funds from various savings instruments that are part of the M2 money supply to the mutual funds, which are not. These shifts reduced both the growth rate of the M2 money supply during 1994–1995 and the reliability of these figures as an indicator of monetary policy.

actions? Under this plan, if the general price index were rising, the monetary authorities would have an incentive to institute more restraint. Conversely, if the price level were falling, a move toward expansion would be in order. The proponents of this rule argue that it would reduce both instability arising from monetary sources and the uncertainty of time-dimension transactions (for example, loan agreements and other long-term contracts).

New Zealand adopted a price level rule in 1990. Although the Central Bank of New Zealand is fully responsible for monetary policy, it is legally required to maintain the inflation rate within a narrow range, currently between zero and 2 percent. If the central bank fails to meet this target, the bank's governor is subject to dismissal. This structure requires the central bank to focus on a well-defined target (a low rate of inflation) that is achievable with monetary policy and holds it accountable for failure to meet the objective. To date, the policy has been highly successful. Prior to 1990, New Zealand had the highest and most variable inflation rate among the high-income industrial nations. In contrast, its rate of inflation has been low (between 0.1 percent and 2.7 percent) since the legislation took effect. Other countries appear to be moving in this direction. The new European Central Bank has committed itself to the achievement of price stability. Several other central banks have also set targets and designated price stability as their primary objective.

Nonactivist Fiscal Policy

In the area of fiscal policy, the simplest rule would require that the budget be balanced annually. Because revenues and expenditures fluctuate over the business cycle, however, a balanced budget rule would require tax increases and/or expenditure reductions during a recession. The opposite changes would be required during a period of rapid growth. Such changes are inconsistent with the nonactivist pursuit of stable (unchanged) policies.

In theory, the proper nonactivist fiscal strategy is a balanced budget *over the business cycle*. Under this plan, the same tax rates and expenditure policies would remain in effect during both booms and recessions. Surpluses would result during periods of prosperity, while deficits would accrue during recessions. Unfortunately, this rule is an elastic band constraint. At any point in time, it is difficult to assess if current tax and expenditure policy will balance the budget over the cycle. Thus, nonactivists, particularly those of a public choice persuasion, recognize that a "balance the budget over the business cycle" rule is unlikely to impose a steady course on policymakers.

Some nonactivists believe that a constitutional amendment limiting both government spending and budget deficits is a necessary ingredient for stable fiscal policy. Pressure from special interest groups and the short time horizon of political officials elected for limited terms biases the political process toward expansionary fiscal policy (increased spending and debt). Because of this, some nonactivists argue that a supramajority (for example, 60 percent) should be required for congressional approval for either (1) deficit-financed government spending or (2) rapid increases (more rapid than the growth of national income) in federal spending.

It is one thing to favor a general strategy and another to develop a workable program for implementation. Clearly, the nonactivists have not yet arrived at a detailed fiscal policy program that would command wide acceptance among even the proponents of nonactivism.

ROLE OF MONETARY POLICY: A CONSENSUS VIEW

Price Stability

 When monetary policymakers consistently achieve price stability, they are providing the foundation for both economic stability and the efficient operation of markets.

A modern consensus view has developed with regard to the proper role of monetary policy. *Economists of almost all persuasions now believe that monetary policy should focus on price stability—the attainment of persistently low rates of inflation.* Achievement of this objective will promote economic stability and provide the framework for healthy long-term economic growth.

The high standard of living that Americans enjoy is the result of gains from specialization, division of labor, and mass production processes. Price stability and the smooth operation of the pricing system will help individuals more fully realize the potential gains from these sources. In contrast, high and variable rates of inflation create uncertainty, distort relative prices, and reduce the efficiency of a market economy.

There is no conflict between price stability and full employment. When the general level of prices is approximately stable, the uncertainties of time dimension activities like investment will be reduced. This will help promote both full employment (low unemployment) and strong economic growth. When price stability is achieved and maintained, monetary policymakers have done their job well.

EMERGING CONSENSUS ON OTHER MATTERS

Monetary policy is not the only area where a consensus is emerging. There is also substantial agreement in three other areas of stabilization policy.

1. *Demand stimulus policies cannot reduce the rate of unemployment below the natural level—at least not for long.*

In the 1960s and 1970s, many economists thought that there was a trade-off between inflation and unemployment. While recognizing demand stimulus policies would lead to some inflation, many believed that they would also reduce the unemployment rate. Expectations theories highlight the error of this view. Once people come to expect inflation, the inflation–unemployment trade-off dissipates. While the adaptive-expectations theory implies that an unanticipated shift to a more expansionary policy can temporarily reduce the unemployment rate, the rational-expectations theory indicates that even the temporary reduction is questionable. Given the uncertainty of the short-run trade-off and clear absence of a long-lasting trade-off, most economists now believe that stimulating inflation in an effort to reduce unemployment is both destabilizing and shortsighted. (See the Special Topic, "The Phillips Curve: Is There a Trade-off Between Inflation and Unemployment?" for an in-depth view of this issue.)

2. *Wide swings in both monetary and fiscal policy should be avoided.*

Given our limited forecasting ability and knowledge about how quickly changes in monetary and fiscal policy impact the economy, policymakers should not attempt to respond to every turn in the economic road. Major changes in tax policy, budget deficits, and the money supply *in response to business cycle conditions* are likely to increase rather than reduce instability. More stability will result if the policymakers adopt a long-range strategy and stick with it.

3. *Use of discretionary fiscal policy as an effective stabilization tool is impractical, particularly in countries like the United States.*

Proper timing is essential for the effective use of stabilization policy. Given the checks and balances built into the U.S. political structure, it is unrealistic to expect speedy changes in fiscal policy. The crowding-out effect creates additional uncertainty with regard to the potency of fiscal policy. These shortcomings have caused even longtime Keynesians like Paul Samuelson to conclude that fiscal policy is an impractical stabilization tool.

STABILIZATION POLICY AND THE U.S. ECONOMY

The focus of stabilization policy has changed dramatically during the last four decades. In the 1960s, it was widely believed that macro policy—particularly fiscal policy—could be effectively used both to smooth the ups and downs of the business cycle and to promote a high level of employment. Both the integration of expectations into macro models and the instability of the 1970s dampened the earlier enthusiasm for fine-tuning policies.

Rather than trying to control output and employment, the focus shifted to the achievement of price stability during the 1980s and 1990s. Paradoxically, this shift and the accompanying low and more stable rates of inflation were associated with a reduction in economic fluctuations. **Exhibit 7** illustrates this point. From 1910 to 1959, the U.S. economy was in recession 32.8 percent of the time. Between 1960 and 1982, recession was present 22.8 percent of the time. By way of comparison, 1983–2000 was an unprecedented period of economic stability. Over this 216-month period, the economy was in recession only eight months—3.7 percent of the time.

What accounts for the recent stability? The public tends to credit as well as blame the president for the state of the economy. Though the president has the power of the veto and can initiate legislative proposals, he is only one player in the formulation of policy. Members of Congress, particularly party leaders and chairmen of key committees, also play an important role in the development of fiscal and regulatory policy.

Furthermore, economists—particularly proponents of the crowding-out and new classical theories—are increasingly skeptical about the potency of fiscal policy. During the 1980s, taxes were cut and increases in defense expenditures pushed the overall level of federal spending upward. The federal government ran large budget deficits, indicating that fiscal policy was highly expansionary. Nonetheless, the inflation receded from the double-digit levels of the 1970s. This suggests that the demand-side effects of the expansionary fiscal policy were relatively weak. During the 1990s, fiscal policy was far more restrictive. Defense expenditures were cut, federal spending declined as a share of the economy, and the federal budget shifted to a surplus. Once again, there was little evidence that the fiscal policy changes exerted much impact. Growth continued at a brisk pace, while the inflation rate remained under control.

The experience of Japan during the 1990s also raises doubts about the potency of fiscal policy. Between 1991 and 2000, the Japanese economy grew at an annual rate of only

EXHIBIT 7
Reduction in the Incidence of Recession

The U.S. economy was in recession 32.8 percent of the time during the 1910–1959 period and 22.8 percent of the time between 1960 and 1982, but only 3.7 percent of the time during 1983–2000.

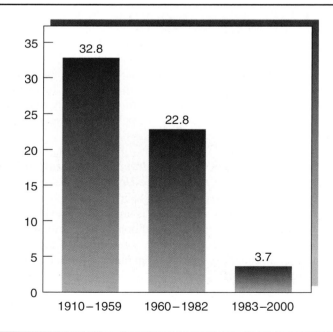

Sources: R.E. Lipsey and D. Preston, *Source Book of Statistics Relating to Construction* (1966); and National Bureau of Economic Research, www.nber.org.

1.2 percent, far below its growth of more than 4 percent during the prior decade. The Japanese shunned expansionary monetary policy. The broad money supply (comparable to M2) grew at an annual rate of only 2.6 percent during 1991–2000 compared to 9.9 percent during 1975–1990. Instead, the Japanese shifted to a highly expansionary fiscal policy in an effort to stimulate the economy. Measured as a share of the economy, government expenditures rose from 30.9 percent in 1991 to 38.1 percent in 1999. During the same period, government revenues declined from 33.8 percent of GDP to 31.1 percent.[3] The budget of the Japanese government went from a surplus of 2.9 percent of GDP in 1991 to a deficit of 7 percent of GDP in 1999. (By way of comparison, the largest general government deficit in the United States during the last 50 years was the 1986 deficit of 5.3 percent of GDP.) In spite of this highly expansionary fiscal policy, demand stagnated and the Japanese economy continued to struggle.

Economists now believe that fiscal policy is far less potent than was thought to be the case during the 1960s. Thus, most would give the more stable policies of the Federal Reserve the primary credit for the economic stability in the United States during the last two decades. Under the leadership of first Paul Volcker and later Alan Greenspan, the Fed avoided wide swings in the rate of inflation. During the entire 1983–2000 period, the inflation rate (as measured by the GDP deflator) remained in a narrow range between 1.1 percent and 4.3 percent. Even more impressive, the year-to-year change in the inflation rate never exceeded 1.2 percent. In essence, the Fed followed policies consistent with a low and stable rate of inflation, and these policies resulted in both economic stability and strong growth.

The Future

Even though the economic record of the 1980s and 1990s was highly impressive, clouds began to appear on the horizon during 2000. The price of crude oil rose from $12 to $32 per barrel during 1999–2000, pushing gasoline and other petroleum-based products sharply higher. The growth of the late 1990s moved more and more income into higher tax brackets and, as a result, federal taxes as a share of national income rose to the highest levels since World War II. Fed policy was also restrictive during the first half of 2000, and stock prices collapsed during the second half of the year. This combination of shocks—sharply higher oil prices, high taxes, restrictive monetary policy, and sharp reduction in stock values—slowed the economy and eventually led to recession beginning in March of 2001. As real GDP declined, the unemployment rate rose from 4.0 percent in December 2000 to nearly 6 percent a year later.

The Federal Reserve reversed its earlier policy and moved aggressively to combat the recession. The Fed supplied additional reserves and lowered key short-term interest rates just about every month during 2001. Congress and the Bush Administration cut taxes and sent $600 tax rebate checks to millions of taxpayers. But it takes time for monetary policy to work and the potency of fiscal policy is questionable. (See prior discussion of the Japanese experience during the 1990s.)

In September of 2001, a U.S. economy that was already in recession was hit with another shock: A terrorist attack on the World Trade Center and the Pentagon that killed nearly 4,000. This led to a military build up and a War on Terrorism. These events, along with anthrax attacks through the postal system, created uncertainty and shook the confidence of many Americans. Airlines, hotels, and other transportation sectors of the economy were hit particularly hard.

Will the actions of the Fed stimulate recovery? Will fiscal policy actions be helpful or harmful? Will the War on Terrorism be lengthy and expensive? Policymakers are now dealing with these questions, and the future stability of the U.S. economy is dependent upon the answers that emerge.

---

[3]See Robert H. Rasche and Daniel L. Thornton, "The Monetary/Fiscal Policy Debate: A Controlled Experiment," *Monetary Trends*, Federal Reserve Bank of St. Louis, page 1. Oct. 2001 for additional details on this topic.

Following up on the topic of economic stability, the next chapter will analyze the determinants of economic growth. Why do some economies grow more rapidly than others? What can policy do to promote high and sustainable rates of economic growth? These questions and related issues will be addressed in the following chapter.

**LOOKING
AHEAD**

KEY POINTS

▼ Historically, the United States has experienced substantial swings in real output. Prior to the Second World War, year-to-year changes in real GDP of 5 to 10 percent were experienced on several occasions. During the last five decades, the fluctuations of real output have been more moderate.

▼ While stable growth, price level stability, and full employment are widely recognized as desirable, there is considerable disagreement concerning how these objectives can be achieved. Activists believe that discretionary use of macro policy can contribute to the achievement of these goals, while nonactivists argue that steady, more passive policies are better.

▼ After a change in policy has been undertaken, there will be a time lag before it exerts a major impact on economic activity. This means the policymakers need to forecast economic conditions several months in the future in order to institute policy changes effectively.

▼ The index of leading indicators and other forecasting tools provide policymakers with information about the likely future economic conditions. Activists argue that policymakers can initially respond with caution to signals indicating the need for a policy change and then act more aggressively if the situation merits it. Activists are confident that discretionary monetary and fiscal policy can be used effectively to promote economic stability.

▼ Nonactivists believe that a market economy's self-corrective mechanism works quite well if it is not short-circuited by perverse macroeconomic policy. Furthermore, they argue that the problems of proper timing and political considerations under-

mine the effectiveness of discretionary macro policy as a stabilization tool. Rather than reacting to cyclical conditions, nonactivists favor steady, predictable policies.

▼ There are two major theories as to how expectations are formed. According to the adaptive-expectations hypothesis, individuals form their expectations about the future on the basis of data from the recent past. The rational-expectations hypothesis assumes that people use all pertinent information, including data on the conduct of current policy, in forming their expectations about the future.

▼ With adaptive expectations, an unanticipated shift to a more expansionary policy will temporarily stimulate output and employment. In contrast, with rational expectations, expansionary policy will fail, even temporarily, to systematically increase output. Both expectations theories indicate that sustained expansionary policies will lead to inflation without permanently increasing output and employment.

▼ Analysis of the Great Depression indicates that the severity and length of the economic plunge, if not its onset, were the result of perverse macroeconomic policy—a sharp contraction in the money supply, a huge tax increase, and a sharp rise in tariff rates.

▼ While debate about macro policy continues, most economists now believe that monetary policy consistent with approximate price stability is the key ingredient of effective stabilization policy. In contrast with the 1960s, use of fiscal policy as an effective stabilization tool is now thought to be impractical.

CRITICAL ANALYSIS QUESTIONS

1. The chair of the Council of Economic Advisers has requested that you write a short paper indicating how economic policy can be used to stabilize the economy and achieve a high level of economic growth during the next five years. Be sure to make specific proposals. Indicate why your recommendations will work. You may submit your paper to your instructor.

*2. How does economic instability during the past four decades compare with instability prior to the Second World War? Is there any evidence that stabilization policy has either increased or decreased economic stability during recent decades?

3. Evaluate the effectiveness of monetary and fiscal policy during the past three years. Has it helped to promote stable prices, rapid growth, and high employment? Do you think policymakers have made mistakes during this period? If so, indicate why.

4. State in your own words the adaptive-expectations hypothesis. How does the theory of rational expectations differ from that of adaptive expectations?

*5. Why do many nonactivists favor a monetary rule such as expansion of the money supply at a constant annual rate? What are some of the practical problems with a monetary rule? Do you think a monetary rule could be devised that would reduce economic instability? Why or why not?

6. Compare and contrast the impact of an unexpected shift to a more expansionary monetary policy under both rational and adaptive theories of expectations. Are the implications of the two theories different in the short run? Are the long-run implications different? Explain.

7. What is the index of leading indicators? Why is it useful to macro policymakers?

*8. What are some of the practical problems that limit the effectiveness of discretionary monetary and fiscal policy as stabilization tools?

9. Many central banks now indicate that their primary objective is to keep inflation at a persistently low rate. If the rate of inflation is persistently low, will this help reduce the instability of the business cycle? Why or why not?

*10. "The Great Depression indicates that the self-correcting mechanism of a market economy is weak and unreliable." Evaluate this statement.

*11. (a) What is the most important thing the Fed can do to promote economic stability? (b) Can expansionary monetary policy reduce interest rates and stimulate a higher growth rate of real output in the long run? (c) If monetary policy is too expansionary, how will nominal interest rates and the general level of prices be affected?

12. What were the major causes of the Great Depression? Did the stock market crash of October 1929 make the Great Depression inevitable? Have advances in macroeconomic understanding made the prospects of another Great Depression unlikely? Why or why not?

13. Who do you think deserves the major credit for the economic stability and strong growth of the 1983–2000 period: (a) Presidents Reagan, Bush, and/or Clinton, (b) Congress, or (c) Federal Reserve policymakers? Explain the reason for your answer.

*Asterisk denotes questions for which answers are given in Appendix B.

CHAPTER 16

Economic Growth

Certain fundamental principles—formulating sound monetary and fiscal policies, removing domestic price controls, opening the economy to international market forces, ensuring property rights and private property, creating competition, and reforming and limiting the role of government—are essential for a healthy market economy.

—Economic Report of the President, 1991

Chapter Focus

- Why is economic growth important?

- How does per-capita income vary among nations?

- How does sustained economic growth change income levels and the lives of people?

- What are the major sources of economic growth?

- What impact do the role and size of government have on economic growth?

- Does economic freedom enhance growth?

Throughout history, most of the world's population has struggled 50, 60, and 70 hours per week just to obtain the basic necessities of life—food, clothing, and shelter. During the last two centuries, sustained economic growth has changed that situation for most people in North America, Europe, Oceania, and Japan. Rising incomes and improvements in the standard of living have not always been present in Western countries. According to Phelps Brown, the real income of English building-trade workers was virtually unchanged between 1215 and 1798, a period of nearly six centuries.[1] In other parts of Europe, workers experienced a similar stagnation of real earnings throughout much of this period.

Low incomes and widespread poverty are still the norm in most countries—particularly those of South and Central America, Africa, and South-Central Asia. Why have income levels in some countries grown rapidly, while they have continued to stagnate in others? What are the key ingredients of economic growth? What can governments do to enhance growth? We have already considered several aspects of these questions. We are now prepared to pull together the lessons of basic economics and address the topic of economic growth and sources of prosperity in a more comprehensive manner. ■

THE IMPORTANCE OF ECONOMIC GROWTH

Economic growth is important because it is a necessary ingredient for higher incomes and living standards. Remember, there are two ways of measuring GDP. It can be measured by summing either (1) the expenditures on all the output produced during a period or (2) the incomes received by those who supplied the resources required to produce the output. Thus, GDP is a measure of both output and income. This fact highlights a very important point: Growth of output is necessary for the growth of income. Without more output, it will be impossible to achieve more income.

Economic growth expands the productive capacity of an economy. The impact of growth can be shown within the framework of the production possibilities concept discussed in Chapter 2. Suppose that a country experienced economic growth during the last decade. As a result, it will be possible to produce a larger quantity of both consumer and capital goods in 2002 than was true in 1992. As **Exhibit 1** (frame a) shows, the growth during the decade will shift the economy's production possibilities curve outward (from *AA* to *BB*).

Exhibit 1 (frame b) illustrates the impact of economic growth within the framework of the *AD/AS* model. The long-run aggregate supply indicates the economy's maximum sustainable rate of output. As the economy grows, the *LRAS* curve will move to the right. Therefore, the growth of the last decade will shift the long-run aggregate supply curve from $LRAS_{92}$ to $LRAS_{2002}$ and the equilibrium level of output will expand from Y_{92} to Y_{2002}.

When a nation's GDP is increasing more rapidly than its population, **per capita GDP**—*that is, GDP per person—will also expand. Growth of per capita GDP means more goods and services per person.* Typically, this leads to a higher standard of living for most people, as well as improvement in life expectancy, literacy, and health.

per capita GDP
Income per person. Increases in income per person are vitally important for the achievement of higher living standards.

Impact of Sustained Economic Growth

There is a tendency to think that a 1 percent or 2 percent difference in growth is of little consequence. However, when sustained over a lengthy period, seemingly small differences in growth can exert a huge impact. If the income per person in Country A grows at an annual rate of 3.5 percent, per capita income will double every 20 years. In contrast, if the growth rate of Country B is 1.75 percent, it will take 40 years for per capita income to double. If the two countries start with the same income level, after 40 years the income of Country A will be twice that of Country B. The principle of compound return is at work here.

---

[1]Phelps Brown, *A Century of Pay: The Course of Pay and Production in France, Germany, Sweden, the United Kingdom, and the United States* (London: Macmillan, 1968).

EXHIBIT 1
Economic Growth, Production Possibilities, and Aggregate Supply

Economic growth expands the sustainable output level of an economy. This can be illustrated by either an outward shift in the production possibilities curve (frame a) or an increase in long-run aggregate supply (shift from $LRAS_{92}$ to $LRAS_{2002}$ in frame b). If monetary policy maintains the initial price level (P_1), equilibrium real GDP will increase from Y_{92} to Y_{2002}.

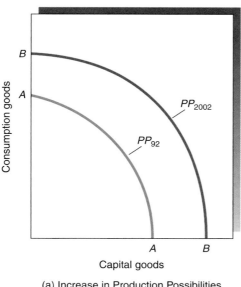

(a) Increase in Production Possibilities

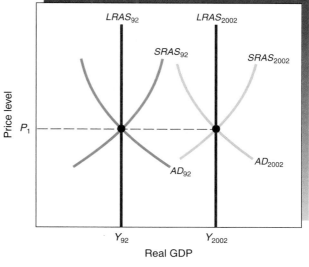

(b) Increase in Real GDP

The **rule of 70** makes it easy to figure how many years it will take for income to double at various rates of growth. If you divide 70 by a country's average growth rate, it will approximate the number of years required for an income level to double.[2] For example, at an average annual growth rate of 5 percent, it will take 14 years (70 divided by 5) for the income level to double. As we just noted, when the growth rate is 3.5 percent, income will double in 20 years (70 divided by 3.5). At a 1 percent growth rate, it will take 70 years for income to double. (*Note:* The rule of 70 also applies to the rate of return on savings and investments. Thus, when maintained over a long period, small differences in rates of return can make a big difference in the accumulated value of your savings or investment.)

Differences in sustained growth rates over a few decades will substantially alter the relative incomes of countries. Nations that experience sustained periods of rapid economic growth will move up the income ladder and eventually achieve high-income status. On the other hand, nations that grow slowly or experience declines in real GDP per capita will slide down the economic ladder.

Using the actual per capita real income figures (measured in 1985 dollars) for Venezuela, Argentina, Mexico, Japan, Hong Kong, and Singapore, **Exhibit 2** vividly illustrates how sustained growth over a lengthy period influences relative incomes. Look at the figures for 1960. The per capita incomes of Hong Kong and Singapore were substantially less than those of the three Latin American countries. In 1960, Japan's per capita income was about the same as that of Mexico and well below the comparable figures for Argentina and Venezuela. During the next four decades, Venezuela's real income per capita stagnated, Argentina's grew slowly (1 percent annual rate), and Mexico's increased at a modest rate (2.3 percent). During the same period, the annual growth of per capita income averaged 4.4 percent in Japan, 5.4 percent in Hong Kong, and 6.2 percent in Singapore.

Rule of 70
If a variable grows at a rate of x percent per year, $70/x$ will approximate the number of years required for the variable to double.

---

[2]Sometimes this rule is called the rule of 72, rather than 70. While 70 yields more accurate estimates for growth rates of less than 5 percent, 72 yields slightly more accurate estimates when the annual rate of growth exceeds 5 percent.

EXHIBIT 2
Differences in Long-term Growth Rates and Changes in Per Capita Income

The impact of long-term growth on income levels is illustrated here. During the 1960–1999 period, the per capita growth rates of Japan, Hong Kong, and Singapore were 4.4 percent, 5.4 percent, and 6.2 percent, respectively. Conversely, the growth rates of Mexico, Argentina, and Venezuela were 2.3 percent, 1.0 percent and −0.1 percent during the same period. Note how the more rapid growth rates of the three Asian countries dramatically increased their income levels relative to the three Latin American nations.

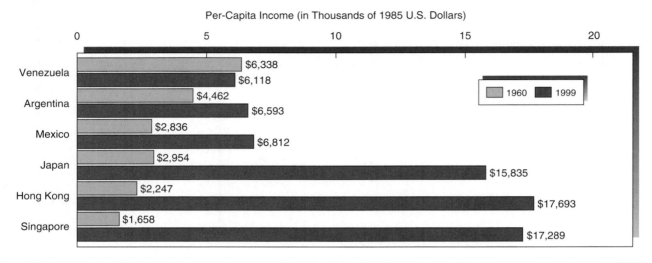

Source: Robert Summers and Alan Heston, *Penn World Tables, Mark 5.6* (Cambridge, MA: National Bureau of Economic Research, 1994) and World Bank, *World Development Indicators, 2001*, CD-ROM.

Now look at the figures for 1999. The rapid growth rates of Hong Kong and Singapore paid off in a big way. The per capita incomes of these two countries, which were the lowest in 1960, were the highest among the six in 1999. In fact, the 1999 per capita incomes of Hong Kong and Singapore were about two and a half times those of the Latin American countries. Japan's income level, which was about the same as that of Mexico in 1960 ($2,954 versus $2,836) was now $15,835 compared to $6,812 for Mexico. Even though Japan's growth rate was only about two percentage points higher than Mexico's, this differential made a dramatic impact over the four decade period. The income level of Venezuela, the country with the highest per capita income in 1960, was now the lowest. Clearly, the differences in growth rates among these countries dramatically altered their relative incomes.

THE BEST AND WORST GROWTH RECORDS

Less-developed countries (LDCs)
Low-income countries generally characterized by rapid population growth and an agriculture-household sector that dominates the economy. Sometimes these countries are referred to as developing countries.

Observing the income differences between the wealthy industrial nations and **less developed countries (LDCs)**, some have argued that the rich are consistently getting richer while the poor are getting poorer. Is this true? Which countries are growing most rapidly? Which are falling behind? **Exhibit 3** presents data on the growth of per capita GDP for (a) high-growth economies, (b) high-income industrial nations, and (c) the economies with the worst growth records.

Only ten countries (left side of Exhibit 3) with a population of at least 2 million were able to achieve an average growth rate of 3.5 percent or more during 1980–1999. China, South Korea, Taiwan, Singapore, Thailand, and Ireland head the list. Except for Ireland, all of the high-growth countries were classified as LDCs at the beginning of the period. Remember, a 3.5 percent annual growth rate means that per capita GDP doubles every 20 years. Thus, the income per person of the high-growth economies has at least doubled during the two decades. Several of the high-growth countries, particularly those in Asia, have experienced recent slowdowns. However, even after taking this into account, their long-

EXHIBIT 3
The Growth of Per Capita GDP for High-Income Industrial Countries, High-Growth LDCs, and Low-Growth LDCs (1980–1999)

HIGH-GROWTH LDCs[*]	GROWTH OF PER CAPITA GDP 1980–1999	HIGH-INCOME INDUSTRIAL COUNTRIES	GROWTH OF PER CAPITA GDP 1980–1999	LOW-GROWTH LDCs[**]	GROWTH OF PER CAPITA GDP 1980–1999
China	8.2%	Japan	2.2%	Congo (Zaire)	−4.7%
South Korea	5.8%	Australia	2.1%	Sierra Leone	−3.5%
Taiwan	5.3%	United States	1.9%	Niger	−2.5%
Singapore	4.8%	United Kingdom	1.9%	Haiti	−2.2%
Thailand	4.7%	Italy	1.8%	Côte d'Ivoire	−2.2%
Ireland	4.4%	Netherlands	1.8%	Zambia	−2.0%
Hong Kong	3.9%	France	1.6%	Madagascar	−1.8%
India	3.7%	Germany	1.5%	Nicaragua	−1.8%
Malaysia	3.7%	Canada	1.4%	Central African Republic	−1.3%
Chile	3.6%	Switzerland	0.9%	Nigeria	−1.1%

* Countries classified as LDC in 1980 with 1980–1999 growth rates of more than 3.5%.
**Countries classified as LDC in 1980 with 1980–1999 negative growth rates less than −1%.

Source: Data are from World Bank, *World Development Indicators CD-ROM, 2001;* and Republic of China, *Statistical Yearbook of the Republic of China, 2000.* Only countries with a population of 2 million or more in 1999 were included in this table. In a few cases, the 1999 data were unavailable. When this was true, the growth rate for the period 1980–1998 was used as a proxy.

term growth is highly impressive. In these high-growth economies, per capita income has increased sharply and living standards improved dramatically in recent decades.

Among the high-income industrial economies, Japan—a country with current economic difficulties—and Australia had the highest annual growth rates during the 1980–1999 period, 2.2 percent and 2.1 percent, respectively. The growth rates of the United States, United Kingdom, Italy, Netherlands, France, Germany, and Canada were bunched within a narrow range between 1.4 percent and 1.9 percent. Switzerland's growth of per capita income lagged behind. Most of the other smaller high-income economies (not included in the exhibit) also had growth rates between 1 percent and 2 percent during the period. Thus, per capita incomes of the high-growth economies—mostly LDCs at the beginning of the period—were expanding at two or three times the rate of the typical high-income industrial countries.

Unfortunately, LDCs dominate not only the high-growth list, but also the list with the worst economic record (right side of Exhibit 3). The income levels of this latter group have not only failed to grow, they have regressed. The per capita incomes of the ten nations with the worst growth record have fallen at an average annual rate of more than 1 percent during the last two decades. In the case of Congo (formerly Zaire), Sierra Leone, Niger, Haiti, Côte d'Ivoire, and Zambia the income reductions averaged 2 percent or more. This implies that the per-person income level of these countries in 1999 was only about half the level of 1980.

The growth picture of LDCs is clearly one of diversity. The fastest-growing countries in the world are LDCs. These rapidly growing countries have closed the income gap relative to their wealthier counterparts.[3] *At the same time, other LDCs are doing very poorly and falling farther and farther behind.*[4]

---

[3]In fact, the income levels of two of the high-growth countries, Hong Kong and Singapore, have risen so much that they are no longer classified as less developed.

[4]For additional analysis of the diversity of growth rates among LDCs, see Stephen L. Parente and Edward C. Prescott, "Changes in the Wealth of Nations," *Quarterly Review: Federal Reserve Bank of Minneapolis* (Spring 1993): 3–16.

APPLICATIONS IN ECONOMICS

China: Is It a Special Case?

Some may be surprised to find China among the high-growth countries of Exhibit 3. After all, isn't China a centrally planned socialist economy that has generally followed policies inconsistent with growth and prosperity?

Even though the Communist Party is in charge of the government, the Chinese economy has experienced remarkable change in recent years. Following the 1978 Communist Party Congress, China began to introduce reforms that have dramatically changed the structure of the economy. ***Today, there are essentially two Chinese economies: (1) agriculture, small businesses, and "special economic zones," and (2) the state enterprises. The first is now a relatively free economy, while the second continues to be centrally planned.***

Initially, China took several important steps toward economic liberalization of the agricultural sector. The collective farms were dismantled and replaced with what the Chinese refer to as a contract responsibility system. Under this organizational form, individual families are permitted to lease land for 15 years or more in exchange for supplying the state with a fixed amount of production at a designated price (which is generally below the market price). Amounts produced above the required quota belong to the individual farmers and may be either directly consumed or sold at a free market price.

Even though the legal ownership remains with the state, this system of long-term land leases provides farmers with something akin to a private property right. This is particularly true since renewal of the lengthy leases is now virtually automatic. Because the state quota is relatively low—approximately 15 percent—and the farmers are permitted to keep all production above the fixed quota, the effective marginal tax rate is zero. Clearly, this provides a strong incentive for farmers to expand output. Markets play a key role in the allocation of agricultural products. Currently, more than 85 percent of the grain (rice, wheat, and barley) output is produced privately and sold at market-determined prices. Restrictions on individual stock breeding, household sideline occupations, transport of agricultural goods, and trade fairs (marketplaces) have been removed. Farmers are now permitted to own tractors and trucks, and even hire laborers to work in their leased fields.

Success in agriculture encouraged reforms in other sectors. Restrictions on the operation of small-scale service and retail businesses were relaxed in the 1980s. Private restaurants, stores, and repair shops sprang up and began to compete with state-operated enterprises. By the mid-1980s, Chinese cities were teeming with sidewalk vendors, restaurants, small retail businesses, and hundreds of thousands of individuals providing personal services.

At the same time, China has established so-called special economic zones. Approximately 20 percent of the Chinese labor force now works in these zones. In these areas, people are permitted to establish businesses, engage in trade with foreigners, maintain bank accounts in foreign currencies, and undertake investment without having to obtain government approval. Taxes in the special zones are generally quite low. During the past decade these zones attracted substantial investment from abroad, which has contributed to the growth of the Chinese investment rate. Economic activity in these regions has also made a sizable contribution to the growth of the trade sector, which has tripled as a share of the economy since 1980. With China's entry into the World Trade Organization, it will almost surely become more fully integrated into the world economy in the future.

Although the moves toward liberalization have contributed substantially to growth, there may also be a second factor at work: China's growth may well be exaggerated. Clearly, this was the case for the former Soviet Union and the countries of Eastern Europe during the 1970s and 1980s. Since centrally planned economies do not rely on product prices to allocate goods and services, output is measured by the physical quantities of goods produced and inputs used. These factors may be a highly unreliable indicator of the value of what is actually being produced. As China has moved away from a command/barter economy in recent years toward greater reliance on markets, some productive activities that were not counted (or were counted only at a depressed level) are now being counted as part of GDP. This will tend to exaggerate the growth of GDP. Thus, the growth estimates of China should be interpreted with caution.

SOURCES OF ECONOMIC GROWTH

Why do some countries grow rapidly, while others stagnate and even experience income reductions? *The process of economic growth is complex. Several factors contribute to growth and they are often interrelated. Much as the performance of an athletic team reflects the joint output of the team members, economic growth is jointly determined by several factors.* And just as one or two weak players can substantially reduce overall team performance, a counterproductive policy in one or two key areas can substantially harm the overall performance of an economy. Although economics cannot provide us with a precise recipe for economic growth, it does reveal important sources of such growth: (1) investment in physical and human capital, (2) technological advances, and (3) institutions and policies consistent with efficient economic organization.

Investment in Physical and Human Capital

Machines can have a substantial impact on a person's ability to produce. Even Robinson Crusoe on an uninhabited island can catch more fish with a net than he can with his hands. Farmers working with modern tractors and plows can cultivate many more acres than could their great-grandparents, who probably worked with hoes. Similarly, education and training that improve the knowledge and skills of workers can vastly improve their productivity. For example, a cabinetmaker, skilled after years of training and experience, can build cabinets far more rapidly and efficiently than a neophyte.

Investment in both physical capital (machines) and human capital (knowledge and skills) can expand the productive capacity of a worker. In turn, people who produce more goods and services valued by others will tend to have higher incomes. Economics suggests that, other things constant, countries using a larger share of their resources to produce tools, machines, and factories will tend to grow more rapidly. Correspondingly, allocation of more resources to education and training will also enhance economic growth.

Of course, investment is not a free lunch; an opportunity cost is involved. When more resources are used to produce machines and factories and develop skills, fewer resources are available for production of current-consumption goods. Economics is about trade-offs. It does, however, indicate that people who save and invest more will be able to produce more in the future.

Technological Progress

Technological advancement—the adoption of new, improved techniques or methods of production—enables workers to produce more output with the same amount of resources. Clearly, improved technology—the result of using brainpower to discover economical new products and/or less costly methods of production—has substantially enhanced our production possibilities. During the last 250 years, the substitution of power-driven machines for human labor; the development of miracle grains, fertilizer, and new sources of energy; and improvements in transportation and communication have vastly improved living standards around the world.

Today, technological progress and entrepreneurial ingenuity are perhaps more important than ever before. As we discussed in Chapter 2, the role of innovators is vitally important for the effective adoption and dissemination of technological improvements. Innovators know how to apply scientific knowledge in a practical manner. For example, Henry Ford played a minor role in the invention and development of the automobile. Nonetheless, he literally "put America on wheels" with his innovative assembly line production techniques that made low-cost production of automobiles possible. More recently Fred Smith, the president and founder of Federal Express, realized that the computer age would generate a strong demand for a rapid delivery system. He figured out how to combine both ground and air transportation into a network delivery system capable of transporting a package overnight between any two locations in the United States. Propelled by this innovative idea, today Federal Express is an $11 billion business. Without innovators like Ford, Smith, and millions of others operating on a smaller scale, scientific breakthroughs are merely ideas waiting to be exploited.

Modern technology is available to all nations—rich and poor alike. Poor nations do not have to invest in research and development—they can emulate (or import at a low cost) the proven technologies of the developed countries. Other things constant, the opportunity for innovative behavior promoting economic growth is greater in low-income countries than for those with higher levels of income. This factor helps explain why countries like South Korea, Taiwan, Hong Kong, Singapore, and even Ireland that were relatively poor

Technological advancement
The introduction of new techniques or methods that enable production of a greater output per unit of input.

Henry Ford was the central figure in the development of the automobile in the United States. He started not only Ford, but also the company that eventually became General Motors. His major contribution was an innovation (the assembly line shown here). As a source of economic progress, innovations are often even more important than inventions.

just a few years ago dominate the list of the world's fastest-growing economies (see Exhibit 3 for evidence on this point).

However, it is important to keep the contribution of technology in perspective. If technology were the primary factor limiting the creation of wealth, most low-income countries would be growing more rapidly than developed nations. This is not the case. Many low-income countries continue to perform poorly even though the proven technologies of high-income industrial countries are readily available to them (see Exhibit 3). Clearly, access to modern technology does not guarantee growth. In fact, it is of little value when the institutional and policy environment undermine the potential attractiveness of entrepreneurial and innovative business activity.

Institutional Environment and Growth

Following the approach outlined in a classic article by Nobel laureate Robert Solow, traditional models of economic growth have stressed the importance of inputs.[5] In fact, the growth of output has often been attributed to the growth of the human capital and physical capital inputs, plus an unexplained residual that was credited to improvements in technology. Clearly, investment in capital goods, education, and technology are important. By themselves, however, they do not necessarily produce economic growth. The experience of the former centrally planned economies illustrates this point. These economies had both very high rates of capital formation and rapid improvements in schooling levels. Despite this growth of inputs, their economic performance was unimpressive. Slow growth and poor living standards eventually led to their collapse.

The last decade has seen a renewal of interest in the effects of institutions and policies on economic growth. Building on the work of Peter Bauer and Douglass C. North, this "new growth theory" stresses the importance of an economic environment that is consistent with the development and efficient use of resources.[6] Proponents of the new growth theory, such as Robert Barro of Harvard and Gerald Scully of the University of Texas, argue that inappropriate institutions and policies can cause growth to fall well below its potential.[7] Further-

---

[5]Robert Solow, "A Contribution to the Theory of Economic Growth," *Quarterly Journal of Economics* 70, no. 1 (February 1956): 65–94.

[6]See Peter T. Bauer, *Dissent on Development: Studies and Debates in Development Economics* (Cambridge: Harvard University Press, 1972); and Douglass C. North, *Institutions, Institutional Change, and Economic Performance* (Cambridge: Cambridge University Press, 1990).

[7]See Robert Barro and Xavier Sala-I-Martin, *Economic Growth* (New York: McGraw-Hill, 1995); and Gerald Scully, *Constitutional Environments and Economic Growth* (Princeton: Princeton University Press, 1992).

more, the more recent approach stresses that when nations establish a sound environment, people will develop their skills (human capital), and investors—both foreign and domestic—will supply the necessary physical capital. In many ways, this recent view is a return to the approach of Adam Smith, who also stressed the importance of policies and institutions.

INSTITUTIONS AND POLICIES CONDUCIVE TO ECONOMIC GROWTH

What types of institutions and policies will promote economic growth? Of course, numerous factors are of some significance, but economic theory suggests a few that are vitally important. We have already discussed several of them; others will be considered in more detail as we proceed. The accompanying Thumbnail Sketch lists six primary ingredients for the creation of an environment that promotes economic efficiency and growth. Let us consider each of them.

THUMBNAIL SKETCH

Sources of Economic Growth

1. Investment in physical and human capital
2. Advancements in technology
3. Institutions and policies that improve economic efficiency

Key Institutions and Policies that Enhance Efficiency and Growth

1. Secure property rights and political stability
2. Competitive markets
3. Stable money and prices
4. Free trade
5. Open capital markets
6. Avoidance of high marginal tax rates

Security of Property Rights and Political Stability

As we have previously discussed, private ownership provides legal protection against those who would use violence, theft, and fraud to take things that do not belong to them. Most important is the incentive structure that emanates from private ownership. ***When the property rights of all citizens—including the vitally important property right to their labor—are clearly defined and securely enforced, production and trade replace plunder as the means of acquiring wealth. When property ownership rights are well defined and enforced, people get ahead by helping and cooperating with others.*** Employers, for example, have to provide prospective employees and other resource suppliers with at least as good a deal as they can get elsewhere. To succeed, business owners will have to develop and provide potential customers with goods and services that they value highly (relative to cost). Moreover, private owners have an incentive to practice wise maintenance and conservation. An owner who fails to maintain the owned assets properly will see the value of those assets, and thus the owner's wealth, decline.

Throughout history, people have searched for and established other forms of ownership that they thought would be more humanitarian or more productive. These experiences have ranged from unsuccessful to disastrous. To date, we do not know of any institutional arrangement that provides individuals with as much freedom and incentive to use resources productively and efficiently as does private ownership.[8]

A volatile political climate undermines the security of property rights. Historically, some governments have confiscated physical and financial assets, imposed punitive taxes, and used regulations to punish those out of favor with the current political regime. Countries with a history like this will find it difficult to restore confidence and reestablish the security of property rights.

Unfortunately, the political climate of many poor, less-developed countries is highly unstable. In some cases, prejudice, injustice, and highly unequal wealth status create a fertile environment for political upheaval. In other instances, political corruption and a history of favoritism to a ruling class provide the seeds for unrest. Regardless of its source, one thing is clear: Potential political upheaval that reduces the security of property rights will repel capital investment and retard economic growth. In recent years, this factor has contributed to the dismal economic performance of several nations, including the Democratic Republic of Congo, Haiti, Nicaragua, Russia, and several other countries of the former Soviet Union (see Exhibit 3).

Competitive Markets

As Adam Smith stressed long ago, when competition is present, even self-interested individuals will tend to promote the general welfare. Conversely, when competition is weakened, business firms have more leeway to raise prices and pursue their own objectives and less incentive to innovate and develop better ways of doing things. Such policies as free entry into businesses and occupations, and freedom of exchange with foreigners, will enhance competition and thereby help to promote economic progress. In contrast, such policies as business subsidies, price controls, entry restraints, and trade restrictions stifle competition and conflict with economic progress.

Competition is a disciplining force for both buyers and sellers. In a competitive environment, producers must provide goods at a low cost and serve the interests of consumers since they will have to woo them away from other suppliers. Firms that develop improved products and figure out how to produce them at a low cost will succeed. Sellers that are unwilling or unable to provide consumers with quality goods at competitive prices will be driven from the market. This process leads to improvement in both products and production methods, while directing resources toward projects where they are able to produce more value. It is a powerful stimulus for economic progress.

Stable Money and Prices

A stable monetary environment provides the foundation for the efficient operation of a market economy. In contrast, monetary and price instability make both the price level and relative prices unpredictable, generate uncertainty, and undermine the security of contractual exchanges. When prices increase 20 percent one year, 50 percent the next year, 15 percent the year after that, and so on, individuals and businesses are unable to develop sensible long-term plans. The uncertainty will reduce the attractiveness of time-dimension ex-

---

[8]For evidence that a legal system that protects property rights, enforces contracts, and relies on rule-of-law principles for the settlement of disputes among parties promotes economic growth, see Stephen Knack and Philip Keefer, "Institutions and Economic Performance: Cross-Country Tests Using Alternative Institutional Measures," *Economics and Politics* 7 (1995): 207–227.

changes, particularly investment decisions. Rather than deal with the uncertainties that accompany double- and triple-digit inflation rates, citizens will save less, while many investors and business decision makers will move their activities to countries with a more stable environment. Foreigners will invest elsewhere, and citizens will often go to great lengths to get their savings (potential funds for investment) out of the country. As a result, potential gains from capital formation and business activities will be lost.

International Trade and an Open Economy

In the absence of trade barriers, producers in various countries will be directed toward those areas where they have a comparative advantage, and the competition from abroad will help keep domestic producers on their toes. International trade allows the residents of each country to use more of their resources to supply goods they can produce at a low cost, while using the proceeds from these sales to purchase goods that could be produced domestically only at a high cost. As a result, the trading partners are each able to produce a larger output and purchase a wider variety of products at more economical prices than would otherwise be possible.

Policies that retard international trade stifle this process and thereby retard economic progress. Obviously, tariffs (taxes on imported goods) and quotas fall into this category because they limit the ability of domestic citizens to trade with people in other countries. So, too, do exchange rate controls. When a nation fixes the exchange rate value of its currency above the market level, the country's export products will be unattractive to foreigners. But if domestic citizens sell less to foreigners, they will have less foreign currency with which to buy from foreigners. Thus, exchange rate controls will reduce the volume of international trade and thereby retard economic progress.

Open Capital Market

If investment is going to increase the wealth of a nation, capital must be channeled into productive projects. When the value of the additional output derived from an investment exceeds the cost of the investment, the project will increase the value of the resources, and thereby create wealth. In contrast, if the value of the additional output is less than the cost of the investment, undertaking the project will reduce the wealth of the nation. If a nation is going to realize its potential, it must have a mechanism capable of attracting savings and channeling them into wealth-creating projects. A competitive capital market performs this function.

When a nation's capital market is integrated with the world capital market, it will be able to attract savings (financial capital) from throughout the world at the cheapest possible price (interest rate). Similarly, its citizens will have access to the most attractive investment opportunities regardless of where those opportunities are located.

In a competitive capital market, private investors have a strong incentive to evaluate projects carefully and allocate their funds toward those projects expected to yield the highest rates of return. In turn, profitable projects will tend to increase the wealth not only of the investor but also of the nation.

When governments fix interest rates and tax some activities heavily while subsidizing others, they undermine the ability of the capital market to bring savers and investors together and channel funds into wealth-creating projects. If investment funds are allocated by governments rather than capital markets, political clout rather than the expected rate of return will determine which projects are undertaken. When politics replaces economic considerations, predictably more funds will be channeled into unprofitable and unproductive projects.

The experience of Eastern Europe and the former Soviet Union highlights this point. For four decades (1950–1990), the investment rates (as a share of GDP) of these countries were among the highest in the world. These countries channeled approximately one-third of GDP into investment. But even these high rates of investment did little to improve living standards. Without the direction of a capital market, the investment funds were often channeled toward political and military projects favored by the planners rather than toward projects that would increase the future availability of consumer goods.

Avoidance of High Marginal Tax Rates

When high marginal tax rates take a large share of the fruits generated by productive activities, the incentive of individuals to work and undertake business projects is reduced. High tax rates may also drive a nation's most productive citizens to other countries (where taxes are lower) and discourage foreigners from financing domestic investment projects. In short, economic theory indicates that high marginal tax rates will retard productive activity, capital formation, and economic growth.

The most detailed study of the impact of high marginal tax rates on the economic growth of LDCs has been conducted by Alvin Rabushka of Stanford University.[9] Rabushka found that the countries that kept marginal tax rates low (or applied high marginal rates only at exceedingly high income thresholds) generally experienced more rapid economic growth. He summarized his findings as follows:

> Good economic policy, including tax policy, fosters economic growth and rising prosperity. In particular, low marginal income tax rates, or high thresholds for medium- and high-rate tax schedules, appear consistent with higher growth rates. The key in any system of direct taxation is to maintain low tax rates or high (income) thresholds.[10]

High taxes on employment can also reduce economic efficiency. A large gap between the employer's cost of hiring a worker and the employee's take-home pay will reduce employment in the formal economy. Such policies tend to drive workers into the "informal," or underground, economy, where the legal structure is less certain and property rights less secure. This reduces the gains from investment and trade, and thereby retards economic growth.

THE ROLE OF GOVERNMENT AND ECONOMIC PROGRESS

Government and the Environment for Prosperity

 Governments can promote economic progress by establishing an environment that encourages entrepreneurship, investment, skill development, and technological improvements. Key elements of this are the protection of individuals and their property, enforcement of contracts, open competition, price stability, free trade, low taxes, and provision of a limited set of "public goods."

Throughout this text, we have analyzed how governments influence the efficiency of resource use and the growth of income. Both the preceding section and the accompanying Key to Prosperity statement highlight functions of government that are vitally important for the smooth operation of markets and the efficient allocation of resources. These activities might be called the core functions of government. Although there is room for debate concerning the precise activities that comprise these core functions, two general categories emerge: (1) activities that protect persons and their property from plunder and (2) provision of a limited set of public goods that, for various reasons, markets may find it difficult to provide.

When governments create a legal, monetary, and regulatory environment for the efficient operation of markets, they enhance economic growth. In addition, government provision of public goods like roads and national defense is also likely to promote growth. Public sector expenditures that expand educational opportunity and the development of

[9]See Alvin Rabushka, "Taxation, Economic Growth, and Liberty," *Cato Journal* (Spring–Summer 1987): 121–148.

[10]Alvin Rabushka, "Taxation and Liberty in the Third World" (paper presented at conference on Taxation and Liberty, Santa Fe, New Mexico, September 26–27, 1985).

human capital may also be beneficial. As governments move beyond the core functions, however, the beneficial effects will eventually wane and become negative. There are four major reasons why expansion in the size of government will eventually retard growth.

1. *As the size of government expands, the marginal cost of taxation becomes higher and higher.* The adverse disincentive effects and excess burden (deadweight losses) of taxation will increase as tax rates rise. (For more detail on this topic, review the material on excess burden of taxation and the Laffer curve analysis of Chapter 4.) Therefore, even if the productivity of government expenditures did not decline, the net gains derived from government would diminish as government grows and the cost of taxation increases.

2. *As government expands relative to the market sector, diminishing returns will reduce the rate of return derived from government activity.* A government that concentrates on those functions for which it is best suited (for example, the core functions discussed above) and performs these functions well will clearly enhance the smooth operation of markets and stimulate economic growth. As it grows, however, government will become more and more involved in activities for which it is ill-suited. Such expansion will adversely affect economic growth. For example, this is likely to result when governments become involved in the provision of private goods—goods for which the consumption benefits accrue to individual consumers. Goods like food, housing, medical service, and child care fall into this category. There is no reason to expect governments to produce or allocate such goods more efficiently than markets.

3. *Government is less innovative and slower to respond to change than the market sector.* To a large degree, growth is a discovery process. Profits provide entrepreneurs with a strong incentive to develop better products, adopt improved technologies quickly, and figure out better ways of doing things.[11] On the other hand, losses impose swift and sure punishment on those that have high cost or use resources unproductively. In markets, entrepreneurs gain by constantly channeling resources toward uses that are more highly valued. There is no similar mechanism that performs this function effectively in the public sector. Thus, the freedom and incentive to innovate is weaker and the adjustment to change slower in the public sector. By way of comparison with markets, the required time for the weeding out of errors (for example, bad investments) and adjusting to changing circumstances, new information, and improved technologies is more lengthy for governments. This is a major shortcoming for economic growth.

4. *As government grows, it invariably becomes more heavily involved in the redistribution of income and regulatory activism. In turn, these activities will encourage wasteful rent-seeking.* As we discussed in Chapter 6, government income transfers and discriminatory regulations will induce individuals to shift resources away from wealth-creating activities toward the pursuit of government favors. This shift will retard economic growth and lead to income levels well below the economy's potential.

In summary, while government activities that focus on the areas where it has a comparative advantage will enhance growth, continued expansion will eventually exert a negative impact on the economy. **Exhibit 4** illustrates the implications with regard to the expected relationship between the size of government and economic growth, *assuming that governments undertake activities based on their rate of return.* As the size of government, measured on the horizontal axis, expands from zero (complete anarchy), initially the growth rate of the economy—measured on the vertical axis—increases. The *A* to *B* range of the curve illustrates this situation. As government continues to grow as a share of the economy, expenditures are channeled into less-productive (and later counterproductive) activities, causing the rate of economic growth to diminish and eventually decline. The

---

[11]Israel Kirzner and Joseph Schumpeter have contributed the classic literature on this topic. See Kirzner, *Competition and Entrepreneurship* (Chicago, IL: University of Chicago Press, 1973); and Schumpeter, *The Theory of Economic Development* (1912). Translated by R. Opie, 1934. Reprinted 1961. Transaction Publishers

EXHIBIT 4
The Size of Government-Growth Curve

If governments undertake activities in the order of their productivity, government expenditures will promote economic growth (moves from *A* to *B* above), but additional expenditures will eventually retard growth (moves along the curve to the right of *B*).

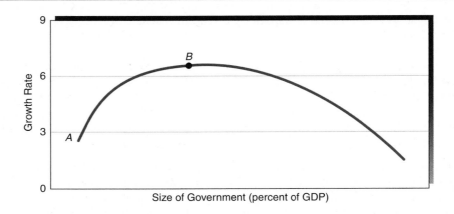

range of the curve beyond *B* illustrates this point.[12] Thus, our analysis indicates that there is a set of activities and size of government that will maximize economic growth. Expansion of government beyond (and outside of) these functions will retard growth.

Size of Government and Economic Growth—Empirical Evidence

How large is the growth-maximizing size of government? Do large governments actually retard economic growth? These are complex questions, but they have been addressed by several researchers.

Exhibit 5 sheds light on these issues. This exhibit presents data on the relationship between size of government (*x*-axis) and economic growth (*y*-axis) for the 23 long-standing members of the Organization for Economic Cooperation and Development (OECD). The exhibit contains four dots (observations) for each of the 23 countries—one for each of the four decades during 1960–1999. Thus, there are 92 dots in total. Each dot represents a country's total government spending as a share of GDP *at the beginning of the decade* and its accompanying growth of real GDP *during that decade*. As the plot illustrates, there is a clearly observable negative relationship between size of government and long-term growth of real GDP. Countries with higher levels of government spending grew less rapidly.

The "best fit" line drawn through the points of Exhibit 5 indicates that a 10 percentage point increase in government expenditures as a share of GDP leads to approximately a 1 percentage point reduction in economic growth. During this period, government expenditures of the countries ranged from a low of around 15 percent of GDP to a high of more than 60 percent. Interestingly, most of the dots for the countries with government expenditures of less than 20 percent were above the line. Thus, there was little evidence that the size of the government was too small in these countries. Put another way, the evidence indicates that these countries were to the right of point *B* on the size of government growth curve of Exhibit 4.[13]

Exhibit 6 presents data on growth during the 1990s for the OECD countries with the largest and smallest governments. As the upper part of the exhibit shows, seven OECD members—Sweden, Denmark, France, Finland, Austria, Italy, and Belgium—had total

---

[12]In the real world, governments may not undertake activities based on their rate of return and comparative advantage. Many governments that are small relative to the size of the economy fail to focus on the core activities that are likely to enhance economic growth. Thus, one would expect that the relationship between size of government and economic growth will be a loose one. The empirical evidence is consistent with this view.

[13]The findings presented here are from James Gwartney, Robert Lawson, and Randall Holcombe, *The Size and Functions of Government and Economic Growth* (Washington, DC: Joint Economic Committee of the U.S. Congress, 1998). These authors also found that the OECD countries with largest increases in size of government between 1960 and 1996 had the largest reductions in economic growth during this period.

EXHIBIT 5
Government Spending and Economic Growth Among the 23 OECD Countries: 1960–1999

Here we show the relationship between size of government and growth of real GDP for the 23 long-time OECD members over each of the past four decades. These data indicate that a 10 percent increase in government expenditures as a share of GDP reduces the annual rate of growth by approximately 1 percent. They also imply that the size of government in these countries is beyond the range that would maximize economic growth.

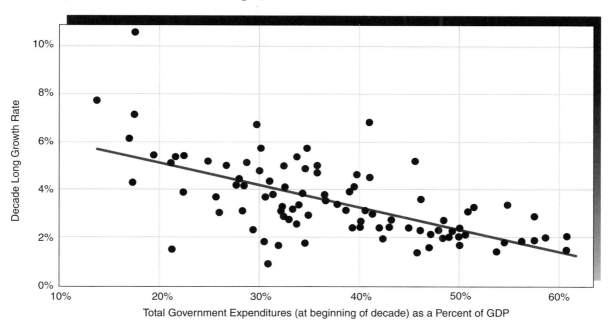

Total Government Expenditures (at beginning of decade) as a Percent of GDP

Source: OECD, *OECD Economic Outlook* (various issues) and World Bank, *World Development Indicators, 2001,* CD-ROM.

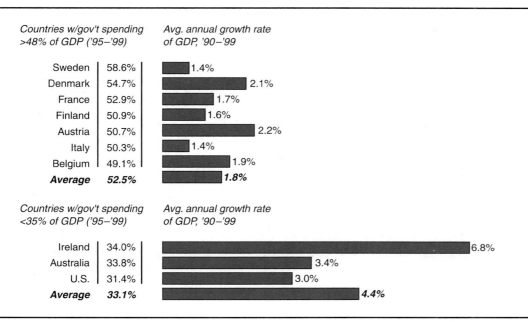

Countries w/gov't spending >48% of GDP ('95–'99)		Avg. annual growth rate of GDP, '90–'99
Sweden	58.6%	1.4%
Denmark	54.7%	2.1%
France	52.9%	1.7%
Finland	50.9%	1.6%
Austria	50.7%	2.2%
Italy	50.3%	1.4%
Belgium	49.1%	1.9%
Average	*52.5%*	*1.8%*

Countries w/gov't spending <35% of GDP ('95–'99)		Avg. annual growth rate of GDP, '90–'99
Ireland	34.0%	6.8%
Australia	33.8%	3.4%
U.S.	31.4%	3.0%
Average	*33.1%*	*4.4%*

EXHIBIT 6
Growth During the 1990s: Big versus Small Government Countries

The average annual growth rate during the 1990s of OECD countries with the largest governments (spending greater than 48 percent of GDP) was 1.8 percent, substantially less than the 4.4 percent average for those with small governments (spending less than 35 percent of GDP).

Source: OECD, *OECD Economic Outlook* (various issues) and World Bank, *World Development Indicators, 2001,* CD-ROM.

government expenditures of 48 percent or more of GDP in 1999. Within this group, growth rates during the decade ranged from the 1.4 percent of Italy and Sweden to Austria's 2.2 percent. The average growth rate for the seven "big government" nations was 1.8 percent. As the bottom frame of Exhibit 6 shows, government spending in three OECD countries—Australia, Ireland, and the United States—was less than 35 percent of GDP. The growth rates within the "small government" group ranged from the 3.0 percent of the United States to Ireland's 6.8 percent. The growth rate average of the small government group was 4.4 percent, more than twice the average of the group with high levels of government spending. The highest growth rate among the big government group, Austria's 2.2 percent, was still lower than any of the small government countries.

While Exhibits 5 and 6 utilize cross-country data, time series data for specific countries have also been used to investigate the link between size of government and growth. Edgar Peden estimates that for the United States, the "maximum productivity growth occurs when government expenditures represent about 20% of GDP." Gerald Scully estimates that the growth-maximizing size of government (combined federal, state, and local) is "between 21.5 percent and 22.9 percent of gross national product (GNP)." Although the methodology of these studies differs, they do have one thing in common: They all indicate that size of government in high-income industrial countries is greater than the growth-maximizing level.[14]

ECONOMIC FREEDOM AND GROWTH

Since the time of Adam Smith, economists have generally argued that freer economies are likely to be more productive. Is this really true? Economic freedom is complex and multi-dimensional. Therefore, it is difficult to measure. In the mid-1980s, the Fraser Institute began work on a special project designed to develop a cross-country measure of economic freedom. Several leading scholars, including Nobel laureates Milton Friedman, Gary Becker, and Douglass North, participated in the endeavor. This eventually led to the devel-

Hong Kong is a modern economic miracle. Its real income per person in 2000 was approximately 8 times the figure for 1960 (see Exhibit 2). The economy of Hong Kong is one of the most free if not the freest in the world. Will it remain that way now that it is once again united with China?

[14]See Edgar Peden, "Productivity in the United States and Its Relationship to Government Activity: An Analysis of 57 Years, 1929–1986," *Public Choice* 69 (1991): 153–173; and Gerald Scully, *What Is the Optimal Size of Government in the United States?* (Dallas, TX: National Center for Policy Analysis, 1994).

opment of the Economic Freedom of the World (EFW) index that is now published annually by a worldwide network of more than 50 institutes.[15]

The EFW index is designed to measure the consistency of a nation's institutions and policies with personal choice, freedom of exchange, and protection of private property. The following are included among the 21 different components of the index: government consumption as a share of GDP, government enterprises as a share of the economy, the standard deviation of the inflation rate, freedom to use alternative currencies, rule of law, the average tariff rate, and the restrictiveness of exchange rate and capital market controls. In order to achieve a high economic freedom rating, countries have to do some things but refrain from doing others. They have to follow rule of law principles and create a stable monetary environment. But they also have to keep taxes low, refrain from creating barriers to both domestic and international trade, and rely more fully on markets (rather than government expenditures and regulations) to allocate goods and resources. It is important to note that the EFW index is designed to measure economic freedom, rather than political freedom or the degree of democracy.

Currently, 123 countries are included in the EFW index. **Exhibit 7** indicates the 10 most free and 10 least free economies in 1999. Hong Kong, Singapore, United Kingdom, New Zealand, and the United States head the list of the world's freest economies. At the other end of the spectrum, the economies of Myanmar, Algeria, the Democratic Republic of Congo, Romania, Russia, and Syria were among the least free in the world.

1999 ECONOMIC FREEDOM RANKING	COUNTRY	1999 ECONOMIC FREEDOM RATING	PPP GDP PER CAP 1999	PER CAPITA GDP GROWTH RATE* 1990–1999
1	Hong Kong	9.4	$22,090	2.0%
2	Singapore	9.1	$20,767	4.6%
3	United Kingdom	8.8	$22,093	1.6%
4	New Zealand	8.7	$19,104	1.2%
4	United States	8.7	$31,872	1.7%
6	Australia	8.5	$24,574	2.2%
6	Ireland	8.5	$25,918	6.1%
8	Luxembourg	8.3	$42,769	3.8%
8	Netherlands	8.3	$24,215	2.2%
8	Switzerland	8.3	$27,171	0.2%
		Average:	**$26,057**	**2.6%**
114	Central African Republic	4.3	$1,166	–0.9%
114	Gabon	4.3	$6,024	0.0%
116	Syria	4.2	$4,454	3.0%
117	Russia	3.9	$7,473	–5.3%
118	Romania	3.8	$6,041	–2.5%
119	Sierra Leone	3.5	$448	–6.6%
120	Guinea-Bissau	3.3	$678	–1.6%
121	Congo (Zaire)	3.0	$801	–8.2%
122	Algeria	2.6	$5,063	–0.8%
123	Myanmar	1.9	$1,200	4.2%
		Average:	**$3,335**	**–1.8%**

EXHIBIT 7
Income and Growth of the Most and Least Free Economies of the World

* GDP per capita growth rates are calculated using real GDP figures in local currency units.
Source: Data are from World Bank, *World Development Indicators CD-ROM, 2001;* Central Intelligence Agency, *The World Factbook, 2000;* and James Gwartney and Robert Lawson, *Economic Freedom of the World, 2001 Annual Report* (Vancouver: Fraser Institute, 2001). The economic freedom rating is on a 0–10 scale.

[15]For additional details, see James Gwartney and Robert Lawson, *Economic Freedom of the World: 2001 Report* (Vancouver: Fraser Institute, 2001) and the Web site www.freetheworld.com.

In many respects, the EFW index reflects the institutional factors listed in the Thumbnail Sketch that are most likely to enhance economic efficiency and growth. If secure property rights, monetary stability, free trade, and reliance on markets really matter, this index should be closely correlated with prosperity and growth. Exhibits 7 and 8 indicate that this is indeed the case.

Exhibit 7 presents the 1999 per capita income and the annual growth rate of real GDP per capita during the 1990s for the 10 most free and 10 least free economies. The average per capita income of the 10 freest economies was $26,057, approximately eight times the figure for the 10 least free economies. Correspondingly, the per capita GDP of the 10 freest economies increased at an average rate of 2.6 percent during the 1990s. Income per person increased in all of the free economies. In contrast, per capita income *declined* at an annual rate of 1.8 percent in the 10 least free economies and only two—Syria and Myanmar—experienced an increase in income per person.

Exhibit 8 takes a closer look at the relationship between economic freedom and performance. The 123 countries of the EFW index were arrayed from the most free to the least free and divided into quintiles. The average per capita income and growth rate for each of the quintiles was then derived. Once again, the data clearly indicate that countries with more economic freedom in 1999 also had both a higher average per-capita GDP and more rapid growth during the 1990s.

Although the data of Exhibit 8 are not adjusted for other factors, such as initial income level, demographic factors, investment, and years of schooling, more comprehensive analysis indicates that even after these factors are taken into consideration, countries with more economic freedom tend to grow more rapidly.[16] This indicates that, like additional capital equipment and improved technology, sound institutions and policies also enhance economic growth.

EXHIBIT 8
Economic Freedom, Income, and Growth

The economic freedom ratings of the 123 countries rated by the Fraser Institute were arrayed from lowest to highest and divided into quintiles. Per capita income in 1999 and the growth rate during the 1990s for each of the quintiles is shown here. Countries with more economic freedom generally had higher income levels and more rapid growth rates than those that were less free.

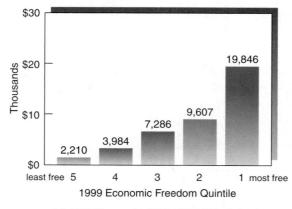

(a) 1998 Per-capita GDP (1998 U.S. dollars)

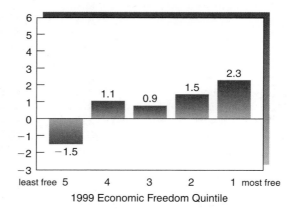

(b) Annual Growth Rate of Real GDP Per Capita, 1990–1999

Source: James Gwartney and Robert Lawson, *Economic Freedom of the World: 2001 Annual Report* (Vancouver: Fraser Institute, 2001), p. 11. The *Economic Freedom of the World:* annual reports can also be found on the Web at www.freetheworld.com.

---

[16]For a comprehensive analysis indicating that economic freedom enhances growth, see John W. Dawson, "Institutions, Investment, and Growth: New Cross-Countries and Panel Data Evidence," *Economic Inquiry* 36 (October 1998): 603–619; Stephen T. Easton and Michael Walker, "Income, Growth, and Economic Freedom," *American Economic Review* 87, no. 2 (May, 1997): 328–332; and James Gwartney, Randall Holcombe, and Robert Lawson, "Economic Freedom and the Environment for Economic Growth," *Journal of Institutional and Theoretical Economics* (December 1999): 643–663.

SOUND POLICY AND THE IRISH MIRACLE: A CASE STUDY

The experience of Ireland in the last four decades illustrates the importance of sound economic policy. From the early 1960s to the mid 1980s, the Irish government followed policies that hampered economic growth. Government spending rose from 28 percent of GDP in 1960 to 43 percent in 1974 and 52 percent in 1986. As the next four exhibits illustrate, the Irish economy in the mid-1980s was characterized by a large and growing government, high taxes, price level instability, and substantial restrictions on international trade. By 1987, Ireland was on the verge of collapse. Real growth had fallen sharply. Unemployment soared to more than 17 percent during 1985–1987. People were leaving the country in search of opportunity.

Ireland's U-turn

As Ireland faced a financial crisis in the mid-1980s, it began to shift toward policies consistent with growth and prosperity. Government spending was slashed, tax rates were lowered, monetary policy became more stable, and trade became more open. Let us take a closer look at each of these four factors.

1. Smaller government
Propelled by spending increases and budget deficits, the outstanding debt of the Irish government soared to 120 percent of GDP in 1986. An attempt in 1983 to balance the budget by raising taxes had failed, throwing the economy into recession and leading to even higher levels of government debt. The government's credit rating was plunging in international markets. Mostly out of desperation, the Irish government cut its expenditures sharply in 1987. Government employment was reduced by about 10 percent between 1986 and 1989. As **Exhibit 9** shows, total government outlays fell from 50 percent of GDP in 1986 to less than 40 percent in 1989. They continued to recede in the 1990s, reaching 28 percent of GDP in 2000.

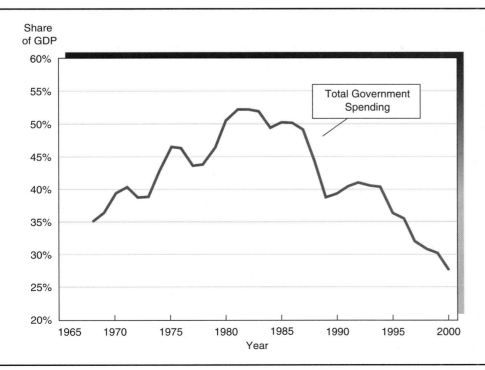

EXHIBIT 9
The Rise and Fall of Ireland's Government Expenditures

Measured as a share of GDP, Ireland's government spending rose rapidly during 1968–1986. Confronting a financial crisis in 1987, the government cut expenditures sharply and spending continued to decline throughout the 1990s. By 2000, government spending had fallen to less than 30 percent of GDP, down from more than 50 percent in the mid-1980s.

Source: OECD, *OECD Economic Outlook* (various issues) and OECD, *OECD Historical Statistics, 1960–1982.*

2. Lower tax rates

As the size of government shrank, the tax burden on both individuals and businesses was systematically reduced. As **Exhibit 10** shows, the top marginal rate imposed on personal income was cut from 65 percent in 1984 to 58 percent in 1986 and 48 percent in 1992. The Irish government continued to reduce taxes and by 2002 the top marginal personal income tax rate had fallen to 42 percent.

Corporate taxes were also reduced. The top corporate rate was reduced from 50 percent in 1986 to 40 percent in the early 1990s and 32 percent in the latter part of the decade. The Irish government has continued to cut the corporate rate. Under current law, it is scheduled to fall to 12.5 percent by 2003. The lower tax rates have attracted foreign investment and increased the incentive to work and innovate.

3. Sound monetary policy and price stability

Monetary policy has improved substantially since the early 1980s. As **Exhibit 11** shows, Ireland's annual rate of inflation fell sharply during the 1980s, and it has become more stable. Since 1987, inflation has averaged 3 percent a year, down from 12.7 percent during 1970–1986. Obviously, the lower and more stable rate of inflation makes it easier for both investors and business decision makers to plan and make contracts for the future.

4. Openness to international trade

When Ireland joined the European Union (EU) in 1973, it was required to harmonize its trade policy with that of the EU over the next decade. By the mid-1980s, Irish tariffs were phased out and replaced by those of the EU. Ireland benefited from both free trade within the EU and from EU tariff rates, which were lower than those previously imposed by the Irish government. **Exhibit 12** illustrates the response to the increased openness of the Irish economy. Ireland's international trade (imports + exports) rose from 101 percent of GDP in 1986 to 121 percent in 1993 and 172 percent in 2000. Once heavily dependent upon neighboring Britain as a trading partner, Ireland's trade is now more diversified. Britain now accounts for only 25 percent of Irish exports, down from 47 percent in 1979.

EXHIBIT 10
Ireland's Top Marginal Tax Rates, 1980–2002

In the midst of the 1987 financial crisis, Ireland not only reduced government spending, but also cut taxes. Personal and corporate tax rates were also reduced several times during the 1990s. The Irish tax rates are now the lowest in Europe.

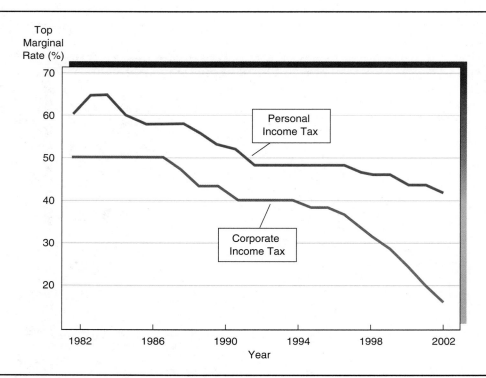

Source: Price Waterhouse, *Individual Taxes: A Worldwide Summary* (various issues).

Annual change
in CPI (%)

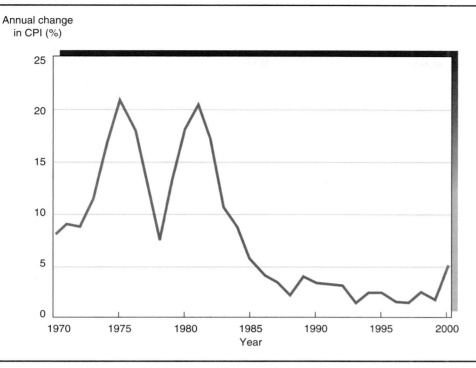

EXHIBIT 11
Ireland's Inflation Rate

After fluctuating substantially during the 1970s and the first half of the 1980s, Ireland's inflation rate was both lower and more stable during the 1990s.

Source: OECD, *OECD Historical Statistics, 1960–1980* (Table 8.11) and OECD, *OECD Economic Outlook*, December 2000.

Imports plus Exports
as a % of GDP

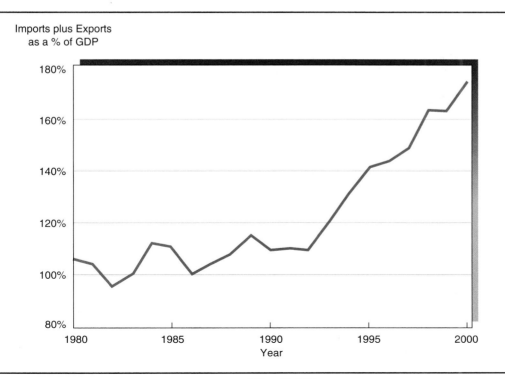

EXHIBIT 12
Ireland's Trade Sector, 1980–2000

The size of the international trade sector (exports + imports) increased substantially as a share of the Irish economy during the 1990s.

Source: World Bank, *World Development Indicators* 2001, CD-ROM.

EXHIBIT 13
Ireland's Rate of Economic Growth

Ireland's economy has responded to the sounder policies of the last 15 years. Its growth rate increased from 2.3 percent in 1982–1987 to 4.8 percent in 1988–1993 and 9.3 percent in 1994–2000. The Irish economy is now one of the fastest-growing in the world.

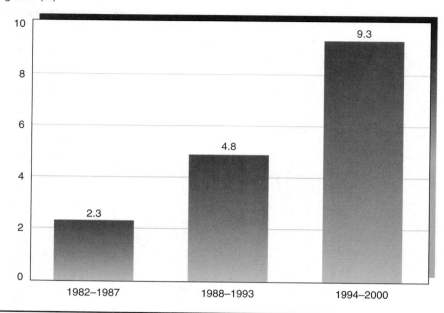

Annual real GDP growth (%)

Source: OECD, *OECD Economic Outlook* (various issues).

The Impact of the Policy Changes

What impact have these policies had on the Irish economy? The turnaround since the late 1980s has been remarkable. As **Exhibit 13** shows, the annual growth rate of real GDP rose from 2.3 percent in 1982–1987 to 4.8 percent in 1988–1993. From 1994 to 2000 the Irish economy grew at a remarkable rate of 9.3 percent. Since 1990 Ireland has been one of the fastest-growing economies in the world. Its growth rate stands in stark contrast with that of other Western European economies, which have generally been growing at an annual rate of around 1.5 percent.

The Irish economy has a number of attractive features. Its legal system is guided by rule of law principles and the judiciary is relatively free of political favoritism. Location between the large and relatively open economies of North America and Europe makes it attractive to many businesses. But these factors were present when the economy was stagnating in the 1970s and 1980s. Thus, the Irish policy U-turn during the mid-1980s indicates that open and competitive markets, government spending restraint, low tax rates, and stable monetary policy matter—indeed, they matter a great deal.

IMPORTANCE OF INSTITUTIONS AND POLICIES— CONCLUDING THOUGHTS

It is vitally important to incorporate the institutional and policy structure into the analysis of growth. While investment and improvements in technology are central elements of the growth process, they do not take place in a vacuum. They are influenced by a country's institutional structure and policy environment. Both investment capital and entrepreneurial talent will flow toward economies with low taxes, secure property rights, sound money, and sensible regulatory policies. In contrast, when these factors are absent, people will find more attractive environments elsewhere.

Modern transport and communications increase the mobility of both labor and capital. They also do something else that is often overlooked: they limit the exploitative power of governments. In today's fast-moving global economy, nations that follow sound policies will often be able to grow very rapidly. The experience of economies like Hong Kong, Singapore, Taiwan, and Ireland illustrate this point. On the other hand, countries that are unable or unwilling to adopt sound policies will continue to stagnate and many will regress. Perhaps more than ever before, prosperity is dependent on getting the institutional and policy environment right.

International trade and global financial markets exert an increasingly important impact on our lives. As was noted in this chapter, both international trade and financial markets capable of directing capital toward productive projects are key ingredients of prosperity. The next two chapters will focus on these topics.

**LOOKING
AHEAD**

KEY POINTS

▼ Economic growth increases the production possibilities of an economy. The growth of per capita real GDP means more goods and services per person, which typically leads to higher living standards and improvements in life expectancy, literacy, and health.

▼ Even seemingly small differences in growth rates sustained over two or three decades will substantially alter relative incomes. For example, if Country A and Country B have the same initial income but the growth rate of A is 2 percentage points greater than that of B, after 35 years the income level of Country A will be twice that of B.

▼ The growth picture of LDCs is clearly one of diversity. Over the last several decades, the fastest-growing countries in the world have been LDCs. These rapidly growing countries have closed the income gap relative to their wealthier counterparts. At the same time, other LDCs are doing very poorly and falling farther and farther behind.

▼ Economic growth is a complex process. Economists stress the importance of three major sources of economic progress: (1) investment in physical and human capital, (2) technological advances, and (3) in-

stitutional and policy changes that improve the efficiency of economic organization.

▼ The following are important for the efficiency of economic organization: (a) secure property rights and political stability, (b) competitive markets, (c) monetary stability, (d) freedom to trade with foreigners, (e) a capital market that directs investment toward productive projects, and (f) avoidance of high tax rates.

▼ When governments focus on the provision of (a) a legal and enforcement structure that protects people and their property from aggression by others and (b) a limited set of public goods, they promote economic growth. However, when governments expand into activities for which they are ill-suited, they deter growth.

▼ More economic freedom is present when people are permitted to choose for themselves, trade freely with others in both domestic and international markets, and live in an environment where property rights are secure and money has a stable value. Countries with more economic freedom tend to grow more rapidly.

CRITICAL ANALYSIS QUESTIONS

1. How does economic growth influence the living standards of people? Does it really make much difference whether an economy grows at 2 percent or 4 percent annually? Discuss.

2. How does the role of government influence economic growth? As the size of government increases as a share of the economy, how is the growth rate of real GDP likely to be affected? Explain.

*3. "Without aid from the industrial nations, poor countries are caught in the poverty trap. Because they are poor, they are unable to save and invest; and, lacking investment, they remain poor." Evaluate this view.

4. More than 200 years ago, Adam Smith argued that the wealth of nations was dependent upon gains from (a) specialization and trade, (b) expansion in the size of the market, and (c) the discovery of better (more productive) ways of doing things. Explain why you either agree or disagree with Smith's view.

5. Evaluate each of the following with regard to their impact on the growth and prosperity of a nation.
   a. Adoption of a regulation that would limit foreign ownership of domestic businesses
   b. Imposition of a surtax on the corporate profits of foreign firms operating in the country
   c. Legislation limiting the number of hours any employee can work during a week to 32
   d. Adoption of a minimum wage equal to 75 percent of the country's average hourly wage
   e. Legislation requiring employers to provide health care for all of their employees
   f. Legislation requiring employers to provide one year of severance pay to any employee who is dismissed from employment

6. How do changes in productivity, that is, output per worker, influence economic growth? During the 1990s, the share of the workforce between the ages of 40 and 55 years increased substantially. How did this influence the growth of productivity during the decade?

*7. Do you think that the absence of international trade barriers would be more important for a small country like Costa Rica than for a larger country like Mexico? Explain.

*8. "Since government-operated firms do not have to make a profit, they can usually produce at a lower cost and charge a lower price than privately owned enterprises." Evaluate this view.

9. "Governments can promote economic growth by using taxes and subsidies to direct investment funds toward high-tech, heavy manufacturing, and other growth industries that will enhance the future income of the nation." Evaluate this view.

*10. What impact do natural resources have on economic growth? Will it be possible for a country with few natural resources to grow rapidly? Why or why not?

11. "The institutional environment is the key to economic growth. If a nation creates an environment conducive to economic growth, people will supply and develop the resources and technology." Evaluate this view. Is the proper economic environment more important than the supply of resources? Why or why not?

*12. The diversity of goods available to consumers today is much greater than in the past. How does this influence consumer welfare? Do the GDP growth figures capture the impact of the increased diversity? Why or why not?

13. Why has Ireland grown more rapidly than other European economies during the last decade? If Mexico followed policies like those of Ireland during the 1990s, could it achieve a similar rate of economic growth? Why or why not? Discuss.

14. Suppose that you have just been appointed to a high-level position in the economic analysis unit of the State Department. The secretary of state has asked you to prepare a memo describing the key policies and economic arrangements that less-developed countries should follow in order to achieve rapid growth and high income levels. Briefly describe your response. Be sure to indicate why each factor that you mention is important if a nation is going to attain a high level of economic progress.

15. Are the rich countries getting richer while the poor are getting poorer? Discuss.

---

*Asterisk denotes questions for which answers are given in Appendix B.

PART 4

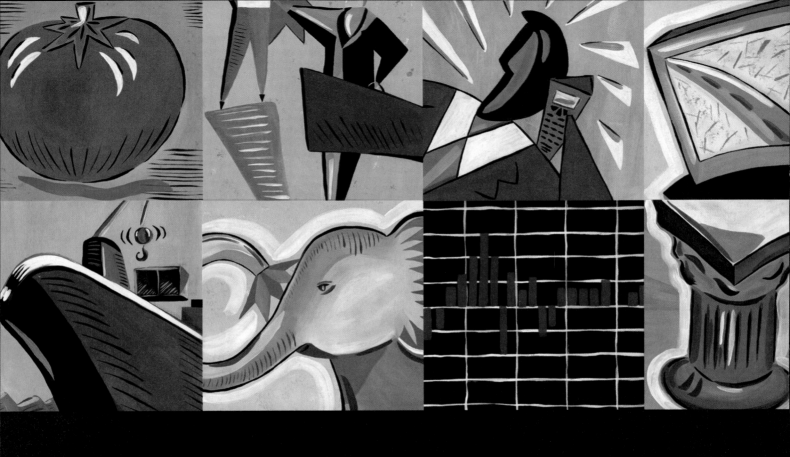

"The world is becoming

INTERNATIONAL ECONOMICS

The volume of international trade has grown dramatically in recent decades. Lower costs of both transportation and communications along with more liberal trade policies have helped propel the growth of trade. The size of the trade sector as a share of the economy varies substantially across countries. Smaller, less populous countries (like Singapore, Hong Kong, and Ireland) generally have larger trade sectors as a share of total output.

MAJOR TRADING PARTNERS OF THE UNITED STATES

Canada, Mexico, and Japan are the major trading partners of the United States. Nearly half of the international trade of the United States is with these three countries. During the last decade, trade with Mexico has expanded rapidly. Although the same general principles apply to trade among individuals, business firms, and nations, the latter generally involves the exchange of one currency for another. Thus, this section will analyze the impact of both international trade and the operation of the foreign exchange market.

PART **4**

CHAPTER 17

Gaining from International Trade

Chapter Focus

- How has the magnitude of international trade changed in recent decades?

- Under what conditions can a nation gain from international trade?

- What impact do trade restrictions have on an economy?

- Do trade restrictions create jobs? Does trade with low-wage countries depress wage rates in high-wage countries like the United States?

- How have open economies performed relative to those that are more closed?

- What accounts for the political popularity of trade restraints?

The evidence is overwhelmingly persuasive that the massive increase in world competition—a consequence of broadening trade flows—has fostered markedly higher standards of living for almost all countries who have participated in cross-border trade. I include most especially the United States.

—*Alan Greenspan*[1]

[1]Speech before the Alliance for the Commonwealth Conference on International Business, Boston, Massachusetts, on June 2, 1999.

We live in a shrinking world. The breakfast of many Americans includes bananas from Honduras, coffee from Brazil, or hot chocolate made from Nigerian cocoa beans. Americans often drive a car produced by a Japanese or European manufacturer that consumes gasoline refined from petroleum extracted in Saudi Arabia or Venezuela. Similarly, many Americans work for companies that sell a substantial amount of their products to foreigners. Spurred by cost reductions in transportation and communications, the volume of international trade has grown rapidly in recent decades. Approximately 21 percent of the world's total output is now sold in a country other than that in which it was produced—double the figure of four decades ago.

Perhaps surprising to some, most international trade is not between the governments of the nations involved but rather between individuals and business firms that happen to be located in different countries. Why do people engage in international trade? The expectation of gain provides the answer. Domestic producers are often able to sell their products to foreigners at attractive prices, while domestic consumers sometimes find that the best deals are available from foreign suppliers. Like other voluntary exchange, international trade results because both the buyer and the seller expect to gain and generally do. If both parties did not expect to gain, they would not agree to the exchange. ∎

CROSS COUNTRY DIFFERENCES IN THE SIZE OF THE TRADE SECTOR

The size of the trade sector varies substantially among nations. Some of the difference is due to size of country. For industries in which economies of scale are important, the domestic market of a less-populated country may not be large enough to support cost-efficient firms. Therefore, in small countries, firms in such industries will tend to export a larger share of their output, and consumers will be more likely to purchase goods produced abroad. As a result, the size of the trade sector as a share of the economy tends to be inversely related to the population of the country.

Even among countries of similar size, there is considerable variation in the size of the trade sector. Among the countries with a large population (120 million or more), the trade sector is largest in Indonesia. In 1999, exports accounted for 35 percent of GDP in Indonesia, about three times the figure for Japan, Brazil, and the United States. Among the mid-size countries (population between 40 million and 65 million), the trade sectors of Thailand, Philippines, and South Korea are quite large, while those of Egypt and Turkey are small. As a share of domestic output, Singapore and Hong Kong have the largest international trade sectors in the world. Both import large quantities of raw materials and unfinished goods and manufacture them into products that are often exported abroad. Therefore, the gross exports of these two vibrant trade centers actually exceed their gross domestic product.

THE TRADE SECTOR OF THE UNITED STATES

As **Exhibit 1** illustrates, the size of the trade sector of the United States has grown rapidly during the last several decades. In 1960, total exports of goods and services accounted for 4.8 percent of the U.S. economy, while imports summed to 4.3 percent. By 1975, both exports and imports were approximately 7.5 percent of the economy. Since 1975 the size of the trade sector as a *share of the economy* has nearly doubled. In 2000, exports accounted for 11.2 percent of total output, while imports summed to 14.9 percent.

EXHIBIT 1
The Growth of the Trade Sector in the United States: 1960–2000

During the past several decades, international trade has persistently risen as a share of GDP. Imports rose from 7.5 percent of GDP in 1975 to 14.9 percent in 2000. During the same period, exports rose from 8.3 percent to 11.2 percent of GDP.

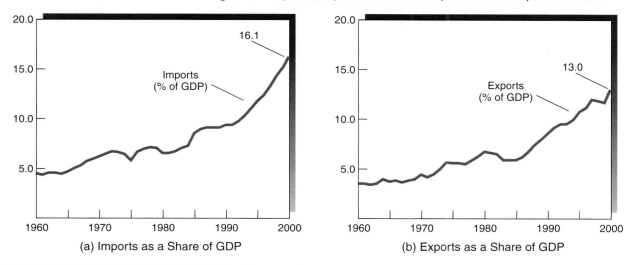

(a) Imports as a Share of GDP   (b) Exports as a Share of GDP

Source: Economic Report of the President, 2001, Table B-2. The figures are based on data for real imports, exports, and GDP.

Who are the major trading partners of Americans? Canada, Japan, and Mexico head the list. In 1999, approximately 45 percent of U.S. exports were sold to purchasers in these three countries. Canadians purchased 24 percent of U.S. exports, while Mexicans purchased 13 percent, and the Japanese 8 percent. These three countries also supplied approximately 43 percent of the U.S. imports—19 percent by Canadians, 13 percent by Japanese, and 11 percent by Mexicans. The nations of the European Union (particularly Germany, the United Kingdom, France, and Italy), China (including Hong Kong), and several other smaller Asian countries (Taiwan, South Korea, Singapore, and Malaysia) are also major trading partners of the United States.

What are the leading imports and exports of the United States? The United States both imports and exports a substantial quantity of capital goods, such as automobiles, computers, semiconductors, telecommunications equipment, and industrial machines. The markets for these items are worldwide. Producers in the United States sell substantial quantities abroad, while, at the same time, many U.S. consumers purchase these goods from foreign manufacturers. Civilian aircraft, electrical equipment, chemicals, and plastics are also among the leading export products of the United States, while crude oil, textiles, toys, sporting goods, and pharmaceutical products are major imports. (See the exhibits in the part opener preceding this chapter for additional details.)

Clearly, the impact of international trade differs across industries. In some industries, domestic producers find it very difficult to compete with their rivals abroad. For example, approximately 90 percent of the shoes purchased by Americans and nearly two-thirds of the radio and television sets, watches, and motorcycles are produced abroad. Imports also supply a high percentage of the clothing and textile products, paper, cut diamonds, and VCRs consumed in the United States. On the other hand, a large proportion of the aircraft, power-generating equipment, scientific instruments, construction equipment, and fertilizers produced in the United States is exported to purchasers abroad.

Comparative advantage
The ability to produce a good at a lower opportunity cost than others can produce it. Relative costs determine comparative advantage.

Absolute advantage
A situation in which a nation, as the result of its previous experience and/or natural endowments, can produce more of a good (with the same amount of resources) than another nation.

GAINS FROM SPECIALIZATION AND TRADE

As we discussed in Chapter 2, the law of **comparative advantage** explains why a group of individuals, regions, or nations can gain from specialization and exchange. *International trade leads to mutual gain because it allows the residents of each country to: (1) specialize more fully in the production of those things that they do best, and (2) import goods when foreigners are willing to supply them at a lower cost than domestic producers.* Labor-force skills and resource endowments differ substantially across countries. These differences influence costs. Therefore, a good that is quite costly to produce in one country may be economically produced in another. For example, the warm, moist climate of Brazil, Colombia, and Guatemala enhances the economical production of coffee. Countries like Saudi Arabia and Venezuela with rich oil fields can produce petroleum cheaply. Countries with an abundance of fertile land, like Canada and Australia, are able to produce products like wheat, feed grains, and beef at a low cost. In contrast, land is scarce in Japan, a nation with a highly skilled labor force. The Japanese, therefore, specialize in manufacturing, using their comparative advantage to produce cameras, automobiles, and electronic products for export. With international trade, the residents of each country can gain by specializing in the production of goods that they can produce economically and using the proceeds to import goods that would be expensive to produce domestically.

Because failure to comprehend the principle of mutual gains from trade is often a source of "fuzzy thinking," we will take the time to illustrate the principle in detail. To keep things simple, we will consider a case involving only two countries, the United States and Japan, and two products, food and clothing. Furthermore, we will assume that labor is the only resource used to produce these products. In addition, since we want to illustrate that gains from trade are nearly always possible, we are going to assume that Japan has an **absolute advantage**—that the Japanese workers are more efficient than the Americans— in the production of both commodities. **Exhibit 2** illustrates this situation. Perhaps due to their prior experience or higher skill level, Japanese workers can produce three units of food per day, compared with only two units per day for U.S. workers. Similarly, Japanese workers are able to produce nine units of clothing per day, compared to one unit of clothing per day for U.S. workers.

Let us consider the following question: Can two countries gain from trade if one of them can produce both goods with fewer resources? Perhaps surprising to some, the answer is yes. As long as *relative* production costs of the two goods differ between Japan and the United States, gains from trade will be possible. Consider what would happen if the United States shifted three workers from the clothing industry to the food industry. This reallocation of labor would allow the United States to expand its food output by six units (two units per worker), while clothing output would decline by three units (one unit per worker). Suppose Japan reallocates labor in the opposite direction. When Japan moves one worker from the food industry to the clothing industry, Japanese clothing production expands by nine units while food output declines by three units. The exhibit shows that this reallocation of labor *within* the two countries has increased their joint output by three units of food and six units of clothing.

The source of this increase in output is straightforward: Aggregate output expands because the reallocation of labor permits each country to specialize more fully in the production of those goods that it can produce at a *relatively* low cost. Our old friend, the opportunity-cost concept, reveals the low-cost producer of each good. If Japanese workers produce one additional unit of food, they sacrifice the production of three units of clothing. Therefore, in Japan the opportunity cost of one unit of food is three units of clothing. On the other hand, one unit of food in the United States can be produced at an opportunity cost of only one-half unit of clothing. American workers are therefore the low-

[2]Adam Smith, *An Inquiry into the Nature and Causes of the Wealth of Nations* (1776; Cannan's ed., Chicago: University of Chicago Press, 1976), pp. 478–479.

EXHIBIT 2
Gains from Specialization and Trade

Columns 1 and 2 indicate the daily output of either food or clothing of each worker in the United States and Japan. If the United States moves 3 workers from the clothing industry to the food industry, it can produce 6 more units of food and 3 fewer units of clothing. Similarly, if Japan moves 1 worker from food to clothing, clothing output will increase by 9 units while food output will decline by 3 units. With this reallocation of labor, the United States and Japan are able to increase their aggregate output of both food (3 additional units) and clothing (6 additional units).

	OUTPUT PER WORKER DAY		POTENTIAL CHANGE IN OUTPUT[a]	
COUNTRY	FOOD (1)	CLOTHING (2)	FOOD (3)	CLOTHING (4)
United States	2	1	+6	−3
Japan	3	9	−3	+9
Change in Total Output			+3	+6

[a]Change in output if the United States shifts three workers from the clothing to the food industry and if Japan shifts one worker from the food to the clothing industry.

opportunity-cost producers of food, even though they cannot produce as much food per day as the Japanese workers. Simultaneously, Japan is the low-opportunity-cost producer of clothing. The opportunity cost of producing a unit of clothing in Japan is only one-third unit of food, compared to two units of food in the United States. The reallocation of labor illustrated in Exhibit 2 expanded joint output because it moved resources in both countries toward areas where they had a comparative advantage.

As long as the relative costs of producing the two goods differ in the two countries, gains from specialization and trade will be possible. When this is the case, each country will find it cheaper to trade for goods that can be produced only at a high opportunity cost. For example, both countries can gain if the United States trades food to Japan for clothing at a trading ratio greater than one unit of food equals one-half unit of clothing (the U.S. opportunity cost of food) but less than one unit of food equals three units of clothing (the Japanese opportunity cost of food). Any trading ratio between these two extremes will permit the United States to acquire clothing more cheaply than it could be produced within the country and simultaneously permit Japan to acquire food more cheaply than it could be produced domestically.

How Trade Expands Consumption Possibilities

Because trade permits nations to expand their joint output, it also allows each nation to expand its consumption possibilities. The production-possibilities concept can be used to illustrate this point. Suppose that there were 200 million workers in the United States and 50 million in Japan. Given these figures and the productivity of workers indicated in Exhibit 2, the production-possibilities curves for the two countries are presented in **Exhibit 3.** If the United States used all of its 200 million workers in the food industry, it could produce 400 million units of food per day—two units per worker—and zero units of clothing (point *N*). Alternatively, if the United States used all its workers to produce clothing, daily output would be 200 million units of clothing and no food (point *M*). Intermediate output combinations along the production-possibilities line (*MN*) intersecting these two extreme points also could be achievable. For example, the United States could produce 150 million units of clothing and 100 million units of food (point US_1).

Part b of Exhibit 3 illustrates the production possibilities of the 50 million Japanese workers. Japan could produce 450 million units of clothing and no food (*R*), 150 million

EXHIBIT 3
Production Possibilities of the United States and Japan Before Specialization and Trade

Here we illustrate the daily production possibilities of a U.S. labor force of 200 million workers and a Japanese labor force of 50 million workers, given the cost of producing food and clothing presented in Exhibit 2. In the absence of trade, consumption possibilities will be restricted to points such as US_1 in the United States and J_1 in Japan along the production possibilities curve of each country.

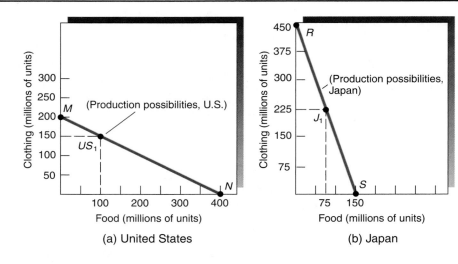

(a) United States

(b) Japan

units of food and no clothing (*S*), or various intermediate combinations, like 225 million units of clothing and 75 million units of food (J_1). The slope of the production-possibilities constraint reflects the opportunity cost of food relative to clothing. Because Japan is the high-opportunity-cost producer of food, its production-possibilities constraint is steeper than the constraint for the United States.

In the absence of trade, the consumption of each country is constrained by the country's production possibilities. Trade, however, expands the consumption possibilities of both. As we previously indicated, both countries can gain from specialization if the United States trades food to Japan at a price greater than one unit of food equals one-half unit of clothing but less than one unit of food equals three units of clothing. Suppose that they agree on an intermediate price of one unit of food equals one unit of clothing. As part a of **Exhibit 4** illustrates, when the United States specializes in the production of food (where it has a comparative advantage) and trades food for clothing (at the price ratio where one unit of food equals one unit of clothing), it can consume along the line *ON*. If the United States insisted on self-sufficiency, it would be restricted to consumption possibilities like US_1 (100 million units of food and 150 million units of clothing) along its production-possibilities constraint of *MN*. With trade, however, the United States can achieve such combinations as US_2 (200 million units of food and 200 million units of clothing) along the line ON. Trade permits the United States to expand its consumption of both goods.

Simultaneously, Japan is able to expand its consumption of both goods when it is able to trade clothing for food at the one-to-one price ratio. As part b of Exhibit 4 illustrates, Japan can specialize in the production of clothing and consume along the constraint *RT* when it can trade one unit of clothing for one unit of food. Without trade, consumption in Japan would be limited to points like J_1 (75 million units of food and 225 million units of clothing) along the line RS. With trade, however, it is able to consume combinations like J_2 (200 million units of food and 250 million units of clothing) along the constraint *RT*.

Look what happens when Japan specializes in clothing and the United States specializes in food. Japan can produce 450 million units of clothing, export 200 million to the United States (for 200 million units of food), and still have 250 million units of clothing remaining for domestic consumption. Simultaneously, the United States can produce 400 million units of food, export 200 million to Japan (for 200 million units of clothing), and still have 200 million units of food left for domestic consumption. After specialization and trade, the United States is able to consume at the point of US_2 and Japan at point J_2, con-

EXHIBIT 4
Consumption Possibilities with Trade

With specialization and trade, the consumption possibilities of a country can be expanded. If the United States can trade one unit of clothing for one unit of food, it can specialize in the production of food and consume along the *ON* line (rather than its original production-possibilities constraint, *MN*). Similarly, when Japan is able to trade one unit of clothing for one unit of food, it can specialize in the production of clothing and consume any combination along the line *RT*. For example, with specialization and trade, the United States could increase its consumption from US_1 to US_2, gaining 50 million units of clothing and 100 million units of food. Simultaneously, Japan could increase consumption from J_1 to J_2, a gain of 125 million units of food and 25 million units of clothing.

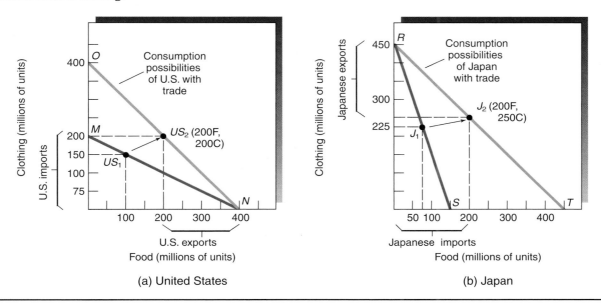

(a) United States   (b) Japan

sumption levels that would be unattainable without trade. Specialization and exchange permit the two countries to expand their joint output, and, as a result, both countries can increase their consumption of both commodities.

The implications of the law of comparative advantage are clear: Trade between nations will lead to an expansion in total output and mutual gain for each trading partner when each country specializes in the production of goods it can produce at a relatively low cost and uses the proceeds to buy goods that it could produce only at a high cost. It is comparative advantage that matters. As long as there is some variation in the relative opportunity cost of goods across countries, each country will always have a comparative advantage in the production of some goods.

Some Real-World Considerations

In order to keep things simple, we ignored the potential importance of transportation costs, which, of course, reduce the potential gains from trade. Sometimes transportation and other transaction costs, both real and artificially imposed, exceed the potential for mutual gain. In this case, exchange does not occur.

We also assumed that the cost of producing each good was constant in each country. This is seldom the case. Beyond some level of production, the opportunity cost of producing a good will often increase as a country produces more and more of it. Rising marginal costs as the output of a good expands will limit the degree to which a country will specialize in the production of a good. This situation would be depicted by a production-possibilities curve that was convex, or bowed out from the origin. In cases of increasing cost there will still be gains from trade but there need not be complete specialization.

International Trade

Trade Openness, Income, and Living Standards

 When people are permitted to engage freely in international trade, they are able to achieve higher income levels and living standards than would otherwise be possible.

Most of us specialize in a relatively few productive activities and use the income from these activities to purchase most of the goods and services that we consume. Of course, the domestic market of our country provides opportunity for gains from specialization and trade. This is particularly true for those who live in a country such as the United States with a large domestic market. International trade makes it possible for individuals to buy from and sell to an even larger market. Thus, it expands the opportunity for gains from trade.

Specialization and comparative advantage provide the foundation for gains from international trade. As we have just explained, trade makes it possible for the residents of each nation to trade for those things for which they are a high opportunity cost producer and, at the same time, focus more of their resources on things they do well. When trading partners use more of their time and resources producing things they do best, they are able to produce a larger output and consume a larger, more diverse bundle of goods than would otherwise be attainable. In addition to these benefits, other gains are also derived from trade openness. We will briefly discuss three of them.

Greater Realization of Gains from Large-scale Production

International trade allows both domestic producers and consumers to gain from reductions in per-unit costs that often accompany large-scale production, marketing, and distribution. Trade expands the potential size of the market available to both domestic and foreign firms. When economies of scale are important in an industry, successful domestic firms will be able to produce larger outputs and achieve lower costs than would be possible if they were unable to sell abroad.

This point is particularly important for small countries. For example, textile manufacturers in Malaysia, Taiwan, and South Korea would have much higher costs if they could not sell abroad. The domestic textile markets of these countries are too small to support large, low-cost firms in this industry. With international trade, however, textile firms in these countries operate at a large scale and compete quite effectively in the world market.

International trade also benefits domestic consumers by permitting them to purchase from large-scale producers abroad. The aircraft industry provides a vivid illustration of this point. Given the huge design and engineering costs, the domestic market of almost all countries would be substantially less than the quantity required for the efficient production of jet planes. With international trade, however, consumers around the world are able to purchase planes economically from large-scale producers like Boeing.

Gains from More Competitive Markets

Openness to international trade promotes competition and thereby encourages both innovative and efficient production. At the same time, it provides consumers with a much broader array of goods than would be available in the absence of trade. The competition from abroad helps keep domestic producers on their toes and provides them with a strong incentive to improve the quality of their products. The experience of the U.S. auto industry illustrates this point. Faced with stiff competition from Japanese firms during the 1980s, U.S. auto makers worked hard to improve the quality of their vehicles. As a result, the reliability of the automobiles and light trucks available to American consumers—including those produced by domestic manufacturers—is almost certainly higher than would have been the case in the absence of international competition.

Brain power and innovation are important sources of economic growth. Trade across national boundaries will lead to greater awareness of technologies and innovative ideas employed elsewhere. In many cases, local entrepreneurs will emulate procedures and products that have been successful in other countries. They may also introduce modifications that make products more suitable for the local market. Dynamic competition of this type is an important source of growth and prosperity, particularly for less developed countries.

Gains from the Adoption of Better Institutions and Policies

Not only do firms of an open economy face more intense competition, so too does government. Openness provides political officials with a strong incentive to establish sound institutions and follow constructive policies. If they do not, both labor and capital will move toward a more favorable environment. For example, neither domestic nor foreign investors will want to place their funds in countries characterized by hostility toward business, monetary instability, legal uncertainty, high taxes and low-quality public services. When labor and capital are free to move elsewhere, policies that penalize success and undermine productive activities become more costly. Even though this indirect effect is generally overlooked, it may well be one of the most beneficial attributes of an open economy.

EXPORT-IMPORT LINK

Doubts about the merits of international trade often result from a failure to consider all the consequences. Why are other nations willing to export their goods to the United States? So they can obtain dollars. Yes, but why do they want dollars? Would foreigners be willing to continue exporting oil, televisions, watches, cameras, automobiles, and thousands of other valuable products to Americans in exchange for pieces of paper? If so, Americans could all be semi-retired, spending only an occasional workday at the dollar printing-press office! Of course, foreigners are not so naive. They trade goods for dollars so they can use the dollars to buy U.S. goods and purchase ownership rights to U.S. assets.

Exports, broadly perceived to include goods, services, and assets, provide the buying power that makes it possible for a nation to import.[3] If a nation did not export, it would not have the foreign currency that is required for the purchase of imports. Similarly, if a nation did not import, foreigners would not have the purchasing power to buy that nation's export items. Therefore, if imports decline, so will the demand for the nation's exports. Exports and imports are closely linked.

SUPPLY, DEMAND, AND INTERNATIONAL TRADE

International trade can also be analyzed within the framework of supply and demand. This approach highlights how trade influences price and output in domestic markets. Given our modern transportation and communication networks, the market for many commodities is worldwide. When a product can be transported long distances at a low cost (relative to its value), the domestic price of the product is in effect determined by the forces of supply and demand in the world market.

Consider the market for a good that U.S. producers are able to supply at a low cost. Using soybeans as an example, **Exhibit 5** illustrates the relationship between the domestic and world markets. The price of soybeans is determined by the forces of supply and demand in the world market. In an open economy, domestic producers are free to sell and domestic consumers are free to buy the product at the world market price (P_w). At this price, U.S. producers will supply Q_p, while U.S. consumers will purchase Q_c. Reflecting their low cost (comparative advantage), U.S. soybean producers will export $Q_p - Q_c$ units at the world market price.

Let us compare the open-economy outcome with the situation in the absence of trade. If U.S. producers were not allowed to export soybeans, the domestic price would be determined by the domestic supply (S_d) and demand (D_d) only. A lower "no-trade"

---

[3]The data of Exhibit 1 indicate that imports have exceeded exports in recent years. These data are for goods and services only; they omit the purchase and sale of assets. In the following chapter, we will illustrate that once the asset transactions with foreigners are also included, the equality between imports and exports is indeed present.

EXHIBIT 5
Producer Benefits from Exports

The price of soybeans and other internationally traded commodities is determined by the forces of supply and demand in the world market (b). If U.S. soybean producers were prohibited from selling to foreigners, the domestic price would be P_n (a). Free trade permits the U.S. soybean producers to sell Q_p units at the higher world price (P_w). The quantity $Q_p - Q_c$ is exported abroad. Compared to the no-trade situation, the producers' gain from the higher price ($P_w bcP_n$) exceeds the cost imposed on domestic consumers ($P_w acP_n$) by the triangle abc.

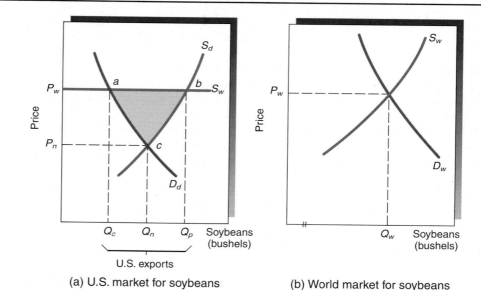

(a) U.S. market for soybeans

(b) World market for soybeans

price (P_n) would emerge. Who are the winners and losers as the result of free trade in soybeans? Clearly, soybean producers gain. Free trade allows domestic producers to sell a larger quantity (Q_p rather than Q_n). As a result, the net revenues of soybean producers will rise by $P_w bcP_n$. On the other hand, domestic consumers of soybeans will have to pay a higher price under free trade. Soybean consumers will lose (1) because they have to pay P_w rather than P_n for the Q_c units they purchase, and (2) because they lose the consumer surplus on the $Q_n - Q_c$ units now purchased at the higher price. Thus, free trade imposes a net cost of $P_w acP_n$ on consumers. As can be seen in Exhibit 5, however, the gains of soybean producers outweigh the losses to the consumers by the triangle abc. Free trade leads to a net welfare gain.

When one focuses only on an export product, it appears that free trade benefits producers relative to consumers—but this ignores the secondary effects. How will foreigners generate the dollars they need to purchase the export products of the United States? If foreigners do not sell goods to Americans, they will not have the purchasing power necessary to purchase goods from Americans. U.S. imports—that is, the purchase of goods from low-cost foreign producers—provide foreigners with the dollar purchasing power necessary to buy U.S. exports. In turn, the lower prices in the import-competitive markets will benefit the U.S. consumers who appeared at first glance to be harmed by the higher prices (compared to the no-trade situation) in export markets.

Using shoes as an example, **Exhibit 6** illustrates the situation when the United States is a net importer. In the absence of trade, the price of shoes in the domestic market would be P_n, the intersection of the domestic supply and demand curves. However, the world price of shoes is P_w. In an open economy, many U.S. consumers would take advantage of the low shoe prices available from foreign producers. At the lower world price, U.S. consumers would purchase Q_c units of shoes, importing $Q_c - Q_p$ from foreign producers.

Compared to the no-trade situation, free trade in shoes results in lower prices and an expansion in domestic consumption. The lower prices lead to a net consumer gain of $P_n abP_w$. Domestic producers lose $P_n acP_w$ in the form of lower sales prices and reductions in output. However, the net gain of the shoe consumers exceeds the net loss of producers by abc.

International competition will direct resources toward their area of comparative advantage. If domestic producers have a comparative advantage in the production of a good,

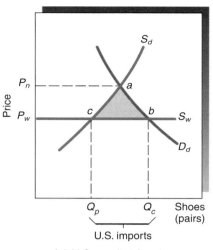
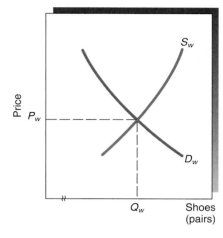

(a) U.S. market for shoes   (b) World market for shoes

EXHIBIT 6
Consumer Benefits from Imports

In the absence of trade, the domestic price of shoes would be P_n. Since many foreign producers have a comparative advantage in the production of shoes, international trade leads to lower prices. At the world price P_w, U.S. consumers will demand Q_c units, of which $Q_c - Q_p$ are imported. Compared to the no-trade situation, consumers gain $P_n abP_w$, while domestic producers lose $P_n acP_w$. A net gain of abc results.

they will be able to compete effectively in the world market and profit from the export of goods to foreigners. In turn, the exports will generate the purchasing power necessary to buy goods that foreigners can supply more economically.

As supply and demand analysis shows, trade makes it possible for the people of a nation to (a) sell goods they can produce cheaply at higher prices and (b) buy items that would be costly to produce at lower prices. Gain is derived from both the high prices received for exports and the lower prices paid for imports. Furthermore, trade permits the residents of each nation to concentrate on the things they do best (produce at a low cost), while trading for those they do least well. The result is an expansion in both output and consumption compared to what could be achieved in the absence of trade.

The pattern of U.S. exports and imports is consistent with this view. The United States is a nation with a technically skilled labor force, fertile farmland, and substantial capital formation. Thus, we export computers, aircraft, power-generating equipment, scientific instruments, and land-intensive agricultural products—items we are able to produce at a comparatively low cost. Simultaneously, we import substantial amounts of petroleum, textile (clothing) products, shoes, coffee, and diamonds—goods costly for us to produce. Clearly, trade permits us to gain by specializing in those areas in which our comparative advantage is greatest.

ECONOMICS OF TRADE RESTRICTIONS

Despite the potential benefits from free trade, almost all nations have erected trade barriers. Tariffs, quotas, and exchange-rate controls are the most commonly used trade-restricting devices. Let us consider how various types of trade restrictions influence the economy.

Economics of Tariffs

A **tariff** is nothing more than a tax on imports from foreign countries. As **Exhibit 7** shows, average tariff rates of between 30 percent and 50 percent of product value were often levied prior to 1945. The notorious Smoot-Hawley trade bill of 1930 pushed the average tariff rate upward to 60 percent. Many economists believe that this legislation was a major contributing factor to the length and severity of the Great Depression. During the past 50 years, the tariff rates of the United States have declined substantially. In 1999, the average tariff rate on imported goods was only 4 percent.

Tariff
A tax levied on goods imported into a country.

EXHIBIT 7
How High Are U.S. Tariffs?

Tariff rates in the United States fell sharply during the period from 1935 to 1950. Subsequently, after rising slightly during the 1950s, they have trended downward since 1960. In 1999, the average tariff rate on merchandise imports was 4.0 percent.

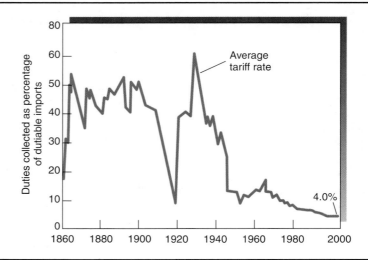

EXHIBIT 8
Impact of a Tariff

Here we illustrate the impact of a tariff on automobiles. In the absence of the tariff, the world price of automobiles is P_w: U.S. consumers purchase Q_1 units (Q_{d_1} from domestic producers plus $Q_1 - Q_{d_1}$ from foreign producers). The tariff makes it more costly for Americans to purchase automobiles from foreigners. Imports decline and the domestic price increases. Consumers lose the sum of the areas $S + U + T + V$ in the form of higher prices and a reduction in consumer surplus. Producers gain the area S and the tariff generates T tax revenues for the government. The areas U and V are deadweight losses due to a reduction in allocative efficiency.

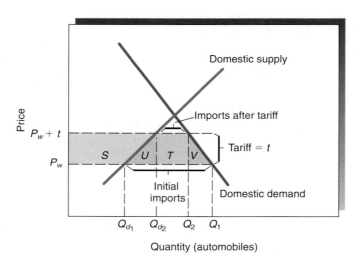

Exhibit 8 illustrates the impact of a tariff on automobiles. In the absence of a tariff, the world market price of P_w would prevail in the domestic market. At that price, U.S. consumers purchase Q_1 units. Domestic producers supply Q_{d1}, while foreigners supply $Q_1 - Q_{d1}$ units to the U.S. market. When the United States levies a tariff, t, on automobiles, Americans can no longer buy cars at the world price. U.S. consumers now have to pay $P_w + t$ to purchase an automobile from foreigners. At that price, domestic consumers demand Q_2 units (Q_{d2} supplied by domestic producers and $Q_2 - Q_{d2}$ supplied by foreigners). The tariff results in a higher price and lower level of domestic consumption.

The tariff benefits domestic producers and the government at the expense of consumers. Since they do not pay the tariff, domestic producers will expand their output in response to the higher (protected) market price. In effect, the tariff acts as a subsidy to domestic producers. Domestic producers gain the area S (Exhibit 8) in the form of additional net revenues. The tariff raises revenues equal to the area T for the government. The areas U and V represent costs imposed on consumers that do not benefit either producers or the government. Simply put, U and V represent *deadweight losses* in the form of reductions in the consumer surplus that buyers would have derived if the tariff had not been imposed.

As a result of the tariff, resources that could have been used to produce goods that U.S. firms produce efficiently (compared to producers abroad) are diverted into the production of automobiles. Thus, we end up producing less in areas where we have a comparative advantage and more in areas where we are a high-cost producer. Potential gains from specialization and trade go unrealized.

Economics of Quotas

An **import quota**, like a tariff, is designed to restrict foreign goods and protect domestic industries. A quota places a ceiling on the amount of a product that can be imported during a given period (typically a year). The United States imposes quotas on several products, including brooms, steel, shoes, sugar, dairy products, and peanuts. As in the case of tariffs, the primary purpose of quotas is to protect domestic industries from foreign competition.

Since 1953 the United States has imposed a quota to limit the importation of peanuts to 1.7 million pounds per year, approximately two peanuts per American. Using peanuts as an example, **Exhibit 9** illustrates the impact of a quota. If there were no trade restraints, the domestic price of peanuts would be equal to the world market price (P_w). Under those circumstances, Americans would purchase Q_1 units. At the price P_w, domestic producers would supply Q_{d_1}, and the amount $Q_1 - Q_{d_1}$ would be imported from foreign producers.

Import quota
A specific limit or maximum quantity (or value) of a good permitted to be imported into a country during a given period.

EXHIBIT 9
Impact of a Quota

Here we illustrate the impact of a quota, such as the one the United States imposes on peanuts. The world market price of peanuts is P_w. If there were no trade restraints, the domestic price would also be P_w, and the domestic consumption would be Q_1. Domestic producers would supply Q_{d_1} units, while $Q_1 - Q_{d_1}$ would be imported. A quota limiting imports to $Q_2 - Q_{d_2}$ would push up the domestic price to P_2. At the higher price, the amount supplied by domestic producers increases to Q_{d_2}. Consumers lose the sum of the area $S + U + T + V$, while domestic producers gain the area S. In contrast with tariffs, quotas generate no revenue for the government. The area T goes to foreign producers who are granted permission to sell in the U.S. market.

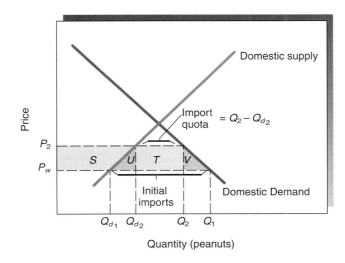

Now consider what happens when a quota limits imports to $Q_2 - Q_{d_2}$, a quantity well below the free-trade level of imports. Since the quota reduces the foreign supply of peanuts to the domestic market, the price of the quota-protected product increases (to P_2). At the higher price, U.S. consumers will reduce their purchases to Q_2, and domestic producers will happily expand their production to Q_{d_2}. With regard to the welfare of consumers, the impact of a quota is similar to that of a tariff. Consumers lose the area $S + U + T + V$ in the form of higher prices and the loss of consumer surplus. Similarly, domestic producers gain the area S, while the areas U and V represent deadweight losses in the form of reductions in consumer surplus, gains that buyers would have derived in the absence of the quota.

While the adverse impact of a quota on consumer welfare is similar to that of a tariff, there is a big difference with regard to the area T. Under a tariff, the U.S. government would collect revenues equal to T, representing the tariff rate multiplied by the number of units imported. With a quota, however, these revenues will go to foreign producers, who are granted licenses (quotas) to sell various amounts in the U.S. market. Clearly, this right to sell at a premium price (since the domestic price exceeds the world market price) is extremely valuable. Thus, foreign producers will compete for the permits. They will hire lobbyists, make political contributions, and engage in other rent-seeking activities in an effort to secure the right to sell at a premium price in the U.S. market.

In many ways, quotas are more harmful than tariffs. With a quota, foreign producers are prohibited from selling additional units regardless of how much lower their costs are relative to those of domestic producers. In contrast to a tariff, a quota brings in no revenue for the government. While a tariff transfers revenue from U.S. consumers to the Treasury, quotas transfer these revenues to foreign producers. Obviously, this politically granted privilege creates a strong incentive for foreign producers to engage in wasteful rent-seeking activities. Thus, by rewarding both domestic producers with higher prices and foreign producers with valuable import permits, quotas generate two strong interest groups supportive of their continuation. As a result, removal of a quota is often even more difficult to achieve than a tariff reduction.

In addition to tariffs and quotas, governments sometimes use regulations and political pressure to restrain competition. For example, the United States prohibits foreign airlines from competing in the domestic air travel market. Japanese regulations make it illegal for domestic dealers to handle both foreign and domestically produced autos. This makes it more difficult for foreign manufacturers to establish the network of dealerships needed for effective penetration of the Japanese market. In the 1980s, the United States used political pressure, including the threat of quota restrictions, in order to induce Japanese auto manufacturers to "voluntarily" restrict their imports to the U.S. market. Like tariffs and quotas, regulatory barriers such as these reduce the supply to the domestic market and thereby push prices upward. Overall output is reduced, while producers benefit at the expense of domestic consumers.

Exchange-Rate Controls as a Trade Restriction

Some countries fix the exchange-rate value of their currency above the market rate and impose restrictions on exchange-rate transactions. At the official (artificially high) exchange rate, the country's export goods will be extremely expensive to foreigners. As a result, foreigners will purchase goods elsewhere, and the country's exports will be small. In turn, the low level of exports will make it extremely difficult for domestic residents to obtain the foreign currency required for the purchase of imports. Such exchange-rate controls both reduce the volume of trade and lead to black-market currency exchanges. Indeed, a large black-market premium indicates that the country's exchange-rate policy is substantially limiting the ability of its citizens to trade with foreigners. While exchange rate controls have declined in popularity, they are still an important trade barrier in many less-developed countries.

WHY DO NATIONS ADOPT TRADE RESTRICTIONS?

As Henry George notes (see quote), trade restraints are an effort to keep people from trading with foreigners. Why would political officials erect blockades against their own people? Several factors play a role. Trade restrictions reflect the political power of concentrated interests: Even though the populace as a whole is harmed, some people are able to gain. Economic illiteracy may also play a role. We will now take a look at each of these factors.

Partially Valid Arguments for Restrictions

There are three major, at least partially valid, arguments for protecting certain domestic industries from foreign competitors: the national-defense, infant-industry, and anti-dumping arguments.

National-Defense Argument

According to the national-defense argument, certain industries—aircraft, petroleum, and weapons, for example—are vital to national defense and therefore should be protected from foreign competitors so that a domestic supply of necessary materials would be available in case of an international conflict. Would we want to be entirely dependent on Arabian or Russian petroleum? Would complete dependence on French aircraft be wise? Many Americans would answer no, even if trade restrictions were required to prevent such dependence by preserving domestic industries.

Although the national-defense argument has some validity, it is often abused. Relatively few industries are truly vital to our national defense. If a resource is important for national defense, often it would make more sense to stockpile the resource during peacetime rather than follow protectionist policies to preserve a domestic industry. Furthermore, it is important to recognize that a strong economy capable of producing large volumes of the goods necessary to sustain a large war effort is itself part of a strong defense. Because the national-defense argument is often used by special interests to justify protection for their industry at the expense of the economy in general, the merits of each specific case must be carefully evaluated.

Infant-Industry Argument

Advocates of the infant-industry argument hold that new domestic industries should be protected from older, established foreign competitors. As the new industry matures, it will be able to stand on its own feet and compete effectively with foreign producers, at which time protection can be removed.

The infant-industry argument has a long and often notorious history. Alexander Hamilton used it to argue for the protection of early U.S. manufacturing. Although it is an argument for only temporary protection, the protection, once granted, is generally difficult to remove. For example, a century ago, this argument was used to gain tariff protection for the newly emerging steel industry in the United States. With time, the steel industry developed and became very powerful, both politically and economically. Despite this maturity, the tariffs remained. To this day, legislation continues to provide the steel industry with various protections that limit competition from abroad.

Anti-Dumping Argument

Dumping involves the sale of goods by a foreign firm at a price below cost or below the price charged in the firm's home-base market. Dumping is illegal and if a domestic industry is harmed, current law provides relief in the form of anti-dumping duties (tariffs

Protective tariffs are as much applications of force as are blockading squadrons, and their objective is the same—to prevent trade. The difference between the two is that blockading squadrons are a means whereby nations seek to prevent their enemies from trading; protective tariffs are a means whereby nations attempt to prevent their own people from trading.

—Henry George[4]

Dumping
The sale of a good by a foreign supplier in another country at a price below that charged by the supplier in its home market.

---

[4]Henry George, *Protection or Free Trade*, 1886, p. 37.

imposed against violators). The number of anti-dumping cases has been increasing. In recent years, the United States has levied charges against, for example, Argentine textile producers, Canadian manufacturers of radial tires, and steel producers in Korea and Brazil.

Dumping raises the concern that foreign producers will temporarily cut prices until the domestic firms are driven from the market and then use their monopoly position to gouge consumers. However, there is reason to question the effectiveness of this strategy. After all, the high prices would soon attract competitors, including other foreign suppliers.

Anti-dumping cases nearly always involve considerable ambiguity. The prices charged in the home market generally vary and the production cost of the firms charged with dumping are not directly observable. This makes it difficult to tell whether a dumping violation has occurred. Furthermore, there is a fine line between dumping and aggressive competitive behavior. Domestic firms facing the latter may well levy charges of the former.

When analyzing the merits of anti-dumping restrictions, it is important to keep two points in mind. First, price cutting is an integral part of the competitive process. When demand is weak and inventories are large, firms will often find it in their interest to offer goods at prices below the average total cost of production. Domestic firms are permitted to engage in this practice. Why should foreign firms be prohibited from doing so? Second, the use of anti-dumping laws to reduce the competitiveness of domestic markets is sure to be contagious. As a few industries are protected from the competition of foreign rivals, others will seek similar treatment. Unless restricted to extreme cases, anti-dumping cases may soon become simply another rather thinly veiled mechanism to stifle competition.

Special Interests and the Politics of Trade Restrictions

> *Protectionism is a politician's delight because it delivers visible benefits to the protected parties while imposing the costs as a hidden tax on the public.*
>
> —Murray L. Weidenbaum[5]

While trade restrictions arise from multiple sources, as Professor Weidenbaum points out, there is no question as to the primary reason for their adoption. *Trade restrictions provide highly visible, concentrated benefits for a small group of people, while imposing widely dispersed costs that are often difficult to identify on the general citizenry. As we discussed in Chapter 6, politicians have a strong incentive to favor issues of this type, even if they conflict with economic efficiency.*

Trade restrictions nearly always provide sizable benefits to well-organized industrial and labor interests at the expense of consumers and taxpayers. The latter two groups are poorly organized and the costs of the restrictive policies are almost always spread thinly and in ways that are often difficult to identify. As a result, consumers generally ignore protectionist policies, even though, in aggregate, their cost is substantial. In contrast, the beneficiaries of trade restraints often derive sizable personal gain. These gains will motivate them to supply politicians with not only votes, but also campaign funds and other political perks. Thus, politicians can often gain by catering to their views even when the restrictive policies are harmful to the economy.

The sugar program provides a vivid illustration of how the process works. Americans pay about twice the world price for sugar because domestic sugar growers and makers of corn syrup, a sugar substitute, have lobbied the government to impose import quotas that keep low-cost foreign sugar out of the United States. The cost to consumers is estimated at about $3 billion a year. For the fewer than three dozen firms that are the big beneficiaries of the sugar program, the benefits from restricting trade are in the tens or even hundreds of millions of dollars per firm. It is worthwhile for the sugar lobby to spend millions of dollars defending its privileges. For a family of four, though, the average savings from lower-cost sugar would be perhaps $60 a year. It is not worthwhile for consumers to spend time or effort to lobby Congress over such a small amount per family. Hence the U.S. government prevents free trade in sugar even though it is in the best interest of American consumers.

[5]Personal correspondence with the authors. Professor Weidenbaum is a former chairman of the President's Council of Economic Advisers and long-time director of the Center for the Study of American Business of Washington University.

With regard to protectionist policies, this story is repeated over and over again. It explains why trade restrictions are imposed and why it so difficult to remove them. The U.S. tariff code itself is a reflection of these political forces. It is highly complex, lengthy (the schedule fills 3,825 pages), and costly to administer. High tariffs are imposed on some products (for example, apparel, tobacco, and footwear), while low tariffs are imposed on others. Highly restrictive quotas limit the import of a few commodities. Even though this system of targeted trade restrictions squanders resources, it is no accident. It reflects the rent seeking of interest groups and the political side payments, particularly campaign contributions, politicians derive from it. Here, as in the case of other special interest issues, there is often a conflict between sound economics and winning politics. The Applications in Economics box "Tomatoes, Regulations, and Trade Restrictions" provides additional evidence on this point.

Trade Barriers and Popular Trade Fallacies

Despite the gains derived from trade, fallacies abound. Why is there so much misunderstanding surrounding trade issues? The primary source of confusion is a point we discussed in Chapter 1: the failure to consider the secondary effects. Key elements of international trade are closely linked—you cannot change one element without changing the other. Failure to recognize the secondary effects is undoubtedly the most common source of error in international trade. Two of the most popular trade fallacies involve the effects of imports on employment and the impact of trade with low-wage countries. Let us take a closer look at both.

Trade Fallacy 1: "Trade restrictions that limit imports save jobs for Americans."
Like most other fallacies, this one has just enough truth to give it some credibility. When tariffs, quotas, and other trade barriers limit imports, they may well promote employment in the industries shielded from competition, but this is only half of the story. They will simultaneously destroy jobs in other sectors.

If import restraints reduce the sales of foreigners to us, there will be an automatic secondary effect—foreigners will have fewer dollars with which to buy goods, services, and assets from Americans. As a result, the demand for American exports declines, causing output and employment in export industries to shrink. This will act as an offset to any jobs saved in sectors shielded by the trade barriers.

As Exhibit 1 shows, U.S. imports grew rapidly—far more rapidly than GDP—during the 1980s and 1990s. But this did not retard employment. Civilian employment in the United States rose from 99 million in 1980 to 119 million in 1990 and 135 million in 2000. Thus, the unprecedented growth of imports during the last two decades has been accompanied by an unprecedented growth in employment.

Once the link between imports and exports is recognized, this growth of employment is not surprising. As imports grew, so too did exports. There was also an inflow of capital that lowered interest rates, further increasing output and employment. As the trade sector grew, jobs were reshuffled, not destroyed. More Americans were employed producing things we do well (where we had a comparative advantage) and fewer were tied up producing things we do poorly. As a result, we were able to produce a larger output than would otherwise have been possible.

When trade restraints are lowered (or there is discussion about lowering them), predictably many workers and business officials in import-competitive industries will charge that jobs will be lost to foreign competitors. In contrast, the additional jobs in the export industries do not yet exist. No one will be saying, "I will not be employed next year if the trade restraints are not lowered." Because the jobs (and employees) in the import-competitive industries are highly visible, while the future jobs in the exporting industries are invisible, it is difficult to maintain open markets.

Even though trade does not reduce the availability of jobs, it is nonetheless a mistake to focus on the employment issue. After all, income and high productivity, not jobs, are the sources of prosperity. Consider the following: If import restrictions are a good idea, why don't we use them to restrict trade among the 50 states? After all, think of all the jobs

Tomatoes, Regulations, and Trade Restrictions

In 1995–1996, Florida tomato growers complained to the Clinton administration and Congress that the import of cheap tomatoes from Mexico was driving them out of business. Blaming the North American Free Trade Agreement (NAFTA) for their plight, they sought to have Congress declare "winter vegetables" a separate industry so they would qualify for greater protection. They also filed an anti-dumping suit with the Commerce Department seeking the imposition of higher tariffs on Mexican tomatoes.

When these strategies failed, the growers asked Congress to pass special package and labeling legislation. While the hard, unripe Florida tomatoes are shipped in solid-tray boxes, the Mexican tomatoes are ripened on the vine, hand-packaged, and shipped in cushioned cartons. At least some consumers believe that this procedure makes the tomatoes tastier. This issue aside, the Florida growers wanted legislation that would require all growers to use the hard-tray cartons. Of course, this would make it difficult for the riper Mexican tomatoes to be shipped without being battered or bruised. Interestingly, the problems of the Florida growers had little to do with NAFTA. The major factor contributing to the increased competitiveness of the Mexican-grown tomatoes was the sharp reduction in the exchange rate of the peso relative to the dollar during 1994–1995.

This case illustrates why it is so difficult to maintain freedom of exchange in international markets. Rather than simply argue for trade restraints, organized interest groups

often support regulations that they say will be "safer," or "more convenient," or "facilitate inspection." Of course, such regulations also just happen to give the special-interest groups a competitive edge over their rivals. This is true in all countries. Japan, in particular, has been charged with the use of such diversionary tactics.

Neither is Mexico blameless. For example, the Mexican government attempted to impose cumbersome labeling and inspection procedures in an effort to reduce the competitiveness of American tires in the Mexican market. Mexico continues to prohibit American express delivery firms, such as United Parcel Service, from using large trucks south of the border. Consumers are the losers when restrictions of this type are imposed. Unfortunately, since consumers are disorganized and generally unaware they are being harmed, support of well-organized interest groups is often politically attractive.

that are lost when, for example, Michigan "imports" oranges from Florida, apples from Washington, wheat from Kansas, and cotton from Georgia. All of these products could be produced in Michigan. However, the residents of Michigan generally find it cheaper to "import" these commodities. Michigan gains by using its resources to produce and "export" automobiles (and other goods it can produce economically) and then using the sales revenue to "import" goods that would be expensive to produce in Michigan.

Most people recognize that free trade among the 50 states is a major source of prosperity for each of the states. Similarly, most recognize that "imports" from other states do not destroy jobs—at least not for long. The implications are identical for trade among nations.

Of course, sudden removal of trade barriers might harm producers and workers in protected industries. It may be costly to transfer quickly the protected resources to other, more productive activities. Gradual removal of the barriers would minimize this shock effect and the accompanying cost of relocation.

Trade Fallacy 2: "Free trade with low-wage countries, such as Mexico and China, will reduce the wages of Americans."

Many Americans believe that if it were not for trade restrictions, American wages would fall to the level of workers in poor countries. How can Americans compete with workers in countries such as Mexico and China who are willing to work for $1 per hour or less? This fallacy stems from a misunderstanding of both the source of high wages and the law of comparative advantage. Workers in the United States are well-educated, possess a high skill level, and work with large amounts of capital equipment. These factors contribute to their high productivity, which is the source of their high wages. Similarly, in countries like Mexico and China, wages are low precisely because productivity is low.

When analyzing the significance of wage and productivity differentials across countries, one must remember that gains from trade emanate from comparative advantage, not absolute advantage (see Exhibits 2, 3, and 4). The United States cannot produce everything cheaper than Mexico or China merely because U.S. workers are more productive and work with more capital than workers in Mexico and China. Neither can the Mexicans and Chinese produce everything cheaper merely because their wage rates are low compared to those of U.S. workers.

Comparative advantage will determine which goods are imported and which are exported. Both high- and low-wage countries will gain when they are able to focus more of their resources on those productive activities that they do well. The comparative advantage of low-wage countries is likely to be in the production of labor-intensive goods, such as toys, textiles, and assembled manufactured products. On the other hand, the comparative advantage of the United States lies in the production of high-tech manufacturing products and other goods produced economically by a well-educated labor force.

Trade reflects relative advantage, not wage levels. We recognize this point with regard to domestic trade. No one argues that trade between doctors and lawn service workers, for example, will cause the wages of doctors to fall. Because of their different skills and costs of providing alternative goods, both high-wage doctors and low-wage lawn care workers can gain from trade. The same is also true for trade between rich and poor nations.

If foreigners, including low-wage foreigners, are willing to sell us a product cheaper than we ourselves can produce it, we can gain by using our scarce resources to produce other things. Perhaps an extreme example will illustrate this point. Suppose a foreign producer (perhaps because workers were willing to work for nothing) was willing to supply us quality automobiles free of charge. Would it make sense to impose tariffs or quotas to keep out the autos? Of course not. Resources that were previously used to produce automobiles could now be freed to produce other goods. The real income and availability of goods would expand. It makes no more sense to erect trade barriers to keep out cheap foreign goods than to keep out free autos.

IMPACT OF TRADE OPENNESS—EMPIRICAL EVIDENCE

Economic theory indicates that more open economies should perform better than those that are more closed. Is this really true? In order to address this issue, a measure of openness—the freedom of individuals to engage in voluntary exchange across national boundaries—is needed. One of the authors was recently involved in a study that derived a Trade Openness Index (TOI) for the 1980–98 period.[6] In order to score high on the zero to ten scale of the index, a country must have low tariffs, a freely convertible currency, a large trade sector given its size and location, and avoid capital market controls.

Exhibit 10 (column 1) shows the 1980–98 TOI ratings for the 12 highest and 12 lowest rated countries among the 91 for which the required data could be obtained. The TOI ratings reflect the average degree of openness for the entire 1980–98 period. This is important because the gains from increased openness will be realized over a lengthy period. Expanding the openness of trade is a long-term growth strategy, not a short-term quick fix. Credibility is also important. Countries that lower trade barriers and then re-impose them a few years later will derive only limited benefits. In order to isolate the full impact of openness, the key relations must be considered over a lengthy period.

---

[6]See James Gwartney, Robert Lawson, and Charles Skipton, "Trade Openness, Income Levels, and Economic Growth," in *Economic Freedom of the World: 2001 Annual Report* (Fraser Institute: Vancouver, B.C., 2001). The analysis of this section borrows freely from that publication.

EXHIBIT 10
Trade Openness, Growth, and Income

Country	TOI (80–98)	Effective Average Tariff Rate 1980	Effective Average Tariff Rate 1999	Actual vs. Expected Size of Trade Sector 1998	PPP GDP per Capita 1999	Avg. Annual Growth Rate of Real GDP per Capita 1980–1999
Hong Kong	9.9	1%	1%	106%	$22,090	3.9%
Singapore	9.8	1%	0%	115%	$20,767	4.9%
Belgium	9.1	1%	1%	49%	$25,443	1.7%
Germany	8.5	1%	1%	13%	$23,742	1.4%
UK	8.5	1%	1%	−3%	$22,093	1.9%
Netherlands	8.4	1%	1%	18%	$24,215	1.8%
Luxembourg	8.3	0%	0%	−3%	$42,769	3.9%
Switzerland	8.0	5%	1%	−20%	$27,171	0.9%
USA	7.8	2%	2%	0%	$31,872	1.9%
Malaysia	7.8	15%	3%	286%	$8,209	3.7%
Sweden	7.8	1%	1%	19%	$22,636	1.4%
Ireland	7.7	7%	1%	64%	$25,918	4.4%
Top 12:	**8.5**	**3%**	**1%**	**54%**	**$24,744**	**2.7%**
India	3.5	31%	22%	8%	$2,110	3.7%
Brazil	3.4	20%	17%	−33%	$6,908	0.6%
Argentina	3.3	19%	9%	−37%	$12,554	0.3%
Tanzania	3.2	15%	24%	−1%	$482	3.3%
Madagascar	3.1	17%	20%	−2%	$776	−1.8%
Algeria	2.9		18%	1%	$4,869	−0.5%
Syria	2.5	14%	7%	9%	$3,749	1.1%
Sierra Leone	1.9	27%	32%	−68%	$487	−3.5%
Iran	1.9	34%	18%	−30%	$5,389	−0.2%
Burundi	1.5	36%	18%	−73%	$581	−1.1%
Bangladesh	1.5	27%	19%	−27%	$1,412	2.4%
Myanmar	0.1	28%	72%	−97%	$1,200	−0.1%
Bottom 12:	**2.4**	**24%**	**23%**	**−29%**	**$3,250**	**0.4%**

Exhibit 10 also presents data for the mean tariff rate and the actual size of the trade sector relative to the expected, given the country's size and location in relationship to the concentration of world demand. When the latter variable is positive, this indicates that the country has a larger trade sector than countries of similar size and location. For example, the 106 percent and 115 percent figures for Hong Kong and Singapore, respectively, indicate that their trade sectors are more than twice as large as what would be expected, given their size and location. On the other hand, the −33 percent figure for Brazil indicates that its trade sector is one-third smaller than expected. Clearly, the more open economies have substantially lower tariff rates and larger trade sectors than those that are more closed. The trade openness ratings reflect these factors, as well as the restrictiveness of exchange rate and capital market controls.

Hong Kong, Singapore, Belgium, Germany, and the United Kingdom head the list of the most open among the 91 economies. The United States ranks ninth tied with Malaysia and Sweden. At the other end of the spectrum, the TOI indicates that Myanmar, Bangladesh, Burundi, Iran, and Sierra Leone were the least open economies during the period.

If trade makes a difference, the countries with persistently high openness ratings should have higher per capita incomes and grow more rapidly than those with persistently low ratings. As Exhibit 10 shows, this was indeed the case. The $24,744 GDP per person of the 12 most open economies is almost eight times the comparable figure for the 12 least open economies. The per capita GDP of the 12 most open economies grew at an annual rate of 2.7 percent during 1980–1999, compared to 0.4 percent a year for the 12 least open economies. All 12 of the open economies had positive growth rates and all but one grew at an annual rate of 1.4 percent or more. In contrast, six of the least open economies experienced reductions in per capita GDP and only four of the twelve achieved a growth rate in excess of 1 percent. These striking differences suggest that openness exerts a major impact on growth and prosperity.

A more detailed statistical analysis of the 91 countries showed that there was a strong positive relationship between openness and both per capita GDP and economic growth. Openness continued to exert a positive and statistically significant impact on both growth and income even after the effects of cross-country differences in the variability of the inflation rate and quality of the legal system were taken into account. Furthermore, the positive impact of openness on economic performance was even stronger when the analysis was undertaken for less developed and small countries separately. These findings provide strong evidence for the economic view that open markets and international trade enhance economic performance.[7]

THE CHANGING NATURE OF GLOBAL TRADE

As we previously mentioned, international trade has approximately doubled as a share of the world economy since 1970. The growth of the trade sector has been propelled by technological advancements, lower transport cost, and more liberal trade policies. The growth of trade—some might say the globalization of the economy—has also triggered a reaction. This section will consider the changing nature of the world economy and its implications for the future.

GATT and the WTO

Following World War II, the major industrial nations established the **General Agreement on Tariffs and Trade** (GATT). For five decades, GATT played a central role in the multilateral tariff reductions and the relaxation (or elimination) of quotas. The average tariff rates of GATT members fell from approximately 40 percent in 1947 to less than 5 percent in 1998.

When the most recent round of trade negotiations—the Uruguay Round—was completed at year-end 1993, GATT was given a new name: the **World Trade Organization (WTO)**. This organization of 141 countries is now responsible for the monitoring and enforcement of the trade agreements developed through GATT. The WTO also provides a forum for consideration of trade rules and settlement of trade disputes among members.

General Agreement on Tariffs and Trade (GATT)
An organization formed following the Second World War to set the rules for the conduct of international trade and reduce barriers to trade among nations.

World Trade Organization (WTO)
The new name given to GATT in 1994; it is currently responsible for monitoring and enforcing the multilateral trade agreements among the 133 member countries.

NAFTA and Other Regional Trade Agreements

In 1988, the United States and Canada negotiated a trade agreement designed to reduce barriers limiting both trade and the flow of capital between the two countries. A few years later, the United States, Canada, and Mexico finalized the **North American Free Trade Agreement (NAFTA)**, which took effect in 1994. As the result of NAFTA, tariffs on the shipment of most products among the three countries will be eliminated by 2004. The agreement will also remove limits on financial investments, liberalize trade in services such as banking, and establish uniform legal requirements for the protection of intellectual property.

Reflecting its proximity, Canada has been a major trading partner of the United States for many decades. On the other hand, U.S. trade with Mexico was small prior to the 1990s. Historically, Mexico has been a relatively closed economy. This began to change in the mid-1980s, prior to its NAFTA membership, when Mexico began cutting its tariff rates and unilaterally removing other trade barriers. In addition to its participation in NAFTA, Mexico has

North American Free Trade Agreement (NAFTA)
A comprehensive trade agreement between the United States, Mexico, and Canada that went into effect in 1994. Tariff barriers will continue to be phased out under the agreement until 2004.

---

[7]For additional information on the relationship between international trade and economic growth, see Jeffrey A. Frankel and David Romer, "Does Trade Cause Growth?" *American Economic Review,* June, 1999, pp. 379-399; and Jeffrey D. Sachs and Andrew Warner, "Economic Reform and the Process of Global Integration." *Brookings Papers on Economic Activity,* 1995 (1), pp. 1–95.

also adopted a free trade agreement with the European Union. During the last 15 years Mexico has moved from one of the world's more protectionist to one of its more open economies.

As **Exhibit 11** shows, U.S. trade with both Mexico and Canada grew rapidly during the 1990s. Measured as a share of GDP, trade with Mexico jumped from 1.1 percent in 1991 to 2.0 percent in 1998. During the same period, trade with Canada rose from 2.9 percent of GDP to 3.8 percent.

This growth of trade, particularly with Mexico, has not been without controversy. Residents along major transportation routes often complain of increased congestion and road damage resulting from the transport of goods by large trucks. Business and labor groups often blame employment contractions and plant closings on competition with Mexican firms. The news media generally gives such stories ample exposure. However, there is no evidence that increased trade with Mexico has adversely affected either output or total employment. While trade with both Mexico and Canada expanded rapidly during the latter half of the 1990s, the U.S. economy experienced strong growth and unemployment fell to a 30-year low. Clearly the dire predictions about the "jobs going to Mexico" have not been realized.

Historically, Europe has been characterized by trade barriers. During the last several decades, this situation has gradually changed. Most barriers limiting the movement of goods among the 15 members of the European Union have now been removed. With the exception of agricultural and a few other commodities, the external tariff rates of the EU are relatively low. In some cases, the combination of a common market among EU members and low external tariffs has exerted a dramatic impact. As a result, several economies—Ireland, Spain, and Greece, for example—that were relatively closed to trade in the 1970s now rank among the world's more open economies. The 12 members of the European Monetary Union have now taken another dramatic step, the adoption of a common currency. This, too, will reduce the cost of exchange within the union and thereby increase the volume of trade.

The Future

Observing the success of open economies like Hong Kong and Singapore, many less-developed countries have unilaterally reduced their trade restrictions. On average, the tar-

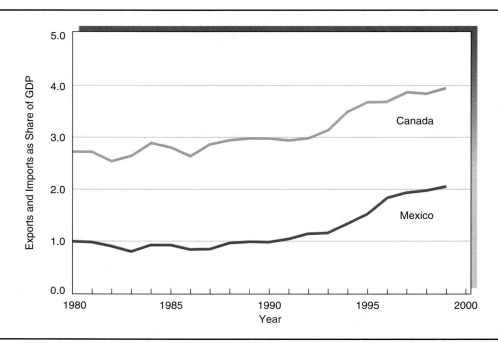

EXHIBIT 11
U.S. Trade with Canada and Mexico, 1980–1999

Trade between the United States and Mexico as well as Canada increased with the passage of NAFTA.

Sources: Statistical Abstract of the United States (various years) and *Economic Report of the President* (2000).

iff rates of less-developed countries are now only about half the level of the early 1980s. Exchange rate controls are becoming increasingly rare and capital market controls are much less restrictive than was true a decade ago. These factors, coupled with the rate reductions of the earlier GATT agreements and increased trade liberalization within regions, have contributed substantially to the worldwide growth of trade.

As demonstrations at recent WTO meetings illustrate, the growth of trade has also generated controversy. Some critics argue that globalization of economic activity is undermining cultural and national identities. Labor and environmental regulations have also been injected into the debate. At the same time, the Internet and other technological changes continue to reduce the costs of transportation and communications, thereby encouraging additional movement of goods, ideas, and people across national boundaries. All of this promises to enliven trade issues in the future.

There are many similarities between trade within national borders and trade across national boundaries. However, there is also a major difference. In addition to the exchange of goods for money, trade across national borders generally involves the exchange of national currencies. The next chapter deals with the foreign exchange market and other dimensions of international finance.

LOOKING AHEAD

KEY POINTS

▼ The volume of international trade has grown rapidly in recent decades. Over 20 percent of the world's output is sold outside the country in which it was produced. The size of the trade sector is generally larger in countries with a smaller population.

▼ Comparative advantage rather than absolute advantage is the source of gains from trade. As long as the relative production costs of goods differ among nations, all nations will be able to gain from trade. Specialization and trade allow trading partners to maximize their joint output and expand their consumption possibilities.

▼ Exports and imports are closely linked. The exports of a nation are the primary source of purchasing power used to import goods. When a nation restricts imports, it simultaneously limits the ability of foreigners to acquire the purchasing power necessary to buy the nation's exports.

▼ Relative to the no-trade alternative, international exchange and specialization result in lower prices for products that are imported and higher domestic prices for products that are exported. However, the net effect is an expansion in the aggregate output and consumption possibilities available to a nation.

▼ Import restrictions, such as tariffs and quotas, reduce foreign supply to the domestic market thereby causing the domestic price to rise. Thus, such restrictions are subsidies to producers (and workers) in protected industries at the expense of (a) consumers and (b) producers (and workers) in export industries. Jobs protected by import restrictions are offset by jobs destroyed in export industries.

▼ National-defense, infant-industry, and anti-dumping arguments can be used to justify trade restrictions for specific industries under certain conditions. It is clear, though, that the power of special-interest groups and voter ignorance about the harmful effects of trade restrictions are the major explanations for real-world policies.

▼ Persistently open economies have grown more rapidly and achieved higher per capita income levels than those that are more closed to international trade.

CRITICAL ANALYSIS QUESTIONS

*1. "Trade restrictions limiting the sale of cheap foreign goods in the United States are necessary to protect the prosperity of Americans." Evaluate this statement made by an American politician.

2. Suppose as the result of the Civil War that the United States had been divided into two countries and that through the years high trade barriers had grown up between the two. How might the standard of living in the "divided" United States have been affected? Explain.

*3. Can both of the following statements be true? Why or why not?
   a. "Tariffs and import quotas promote economic inefficiency and reduce the real income of a nation. Economic analysis suggests that nations can gain by eliminating trade restrictions."
   b. "Economic analysis suggests that there is good reason to expect that trade restrictions will exist in the real world."

4. "The average American is hurt by imports and helped by exports." Do you agree or disagree with this statement?

*5. "An increased scarcity of a product benefits producers and harms consumers. In effect, tariffs and other trade restrictions increase the domestic scarcity of products by reducing the supply from abroad. Such policies benefit domestic producers of the restricted product at the expense of domestic consumers." Evaluate this statement.

*6. The United States uses an import quota to maintain the domestic price of sugar well above the world price. Analyze the impact of the quota. Use supply-and-demand analysis to illustrate your answer. To whom do the gains and losses of this policy accrue? How does the quota affect the efficiency of resource allocation in the United States? Why do you think Congress is supportive of this policy?

7. Suppose that a very high tariff were placed on steel imported into the United States. How would that affect employment in the U.S. auto industry? (*Hint:* Think about how higher steel prices will impact the cost of producing automobiles.)

*8. "Getting more Americans to realize that it pays to make things in the United States is the heart of the competitiveness issue." (This is a quote from an American business magazine.)
   a. Would Americans be better off if more of them paid higher prices in order to "buy American" rather than purchase from foreigners? Would U.S. employment be higher? Explain.
   b. Would Californians be better off if they bought only goods produced in California? Would the employment in California be higher? Explain.

*9. It is often alleged that Japanese producers receive subsidies from their government that permit them to sell their products at a low price in the U.S. market. Do you think we should erect trade barriers to keep out cheap Japanese goods if the source of their low price is governmental subsidies? Why or why not?

10. How do tariffs and quotas differ? Can you think of any reason why foreign producers might prefer a quota rather than a tariff? Explain your answer.

11. In recent years, the European Union has reduced trade barriers among its members. Twelve EU members have formed a monetary union and they will soon have a common currency. What impact are these changes likely to have on European economies?

*12. Does international trade cost American jobs? Does interstate trade cost your state jobs? What is the major effect of international and interstate trade?

13. "The U.S. is suffering from an excess of imports. Cheap foreign products are driving American firms out of business and leaving the U.S. economy in shambles." Evaluate this view.

14. As U.S. trade with low-wage countries like Mexico increases, will wages in the United States be pushed down? Why or why not? Are low-wage workers in the United States hurt when there is more trade with Mexico? Discuss.

*15. "Tariffs not only reduce the volume of imports, they also reduce the volume of exports." Is this statement true or false? Explain your answer.

16. "Physical obstacles like bad roads and stormy weather increase transaction costs and thereby reduce the volume of trade. Tariffs, quotas, exchange-rate controls, and other human-made trade restrictions have similar effects." Evaluate this statement. Is it true? Why or why not?

---

*Asterisk denotes questions for which answers are given in Appendix B.

CHAPTER **18**

International Finance and the Foreign Exchange Market

Currencies, like tomatoes and football tickets, have a price at which they are bought and sold. An exchange rate is the price of one currency in terms of another, such as the price of a French franc in U.S. dollars or German marks.

—*Gary Smith*[1]

Chapter Focus

■ What determines the exchange-rate value of the dollar relative to other currencies?

■ What information is included in the balance-of-payments accounts of a nation? Will the balance-of-payments accounts of a country always be in balance?

■ Will a healthy economy run a balance-of-trade surplus? Does a balance-of-trade deficit indicate that a nation is in financial trouble?

■ How do monetary and fiscal policies influence the exchange-rate value of a nation's currency?

■ How have international financial arrangements changed in recent years? How are they likely to change in the future?

[1]Gary Smith, *Macro Economics* (New York: W. H. Freeman, 1985), p. 514.

Trade across national boundaries is complicated by the fact that nations generally use different currencies to buy and sell goods in their respective domestic markets. The British use pounds, the Japanese yen, the Mexicans pesos, and so on. Therefore, when a good or service is purchased from a seller in another country, it is generally necessary for someone to convert one currency to another. This adds to the complexity of international exchange. This complication could be avoided if the trading partners were to use a common currency. This is precisely what 12 European nations have decided to do. These countries have adopted a common currency—the euro—that is now used to conduct trade throughout the entire region.

Most exchanges across national boundaries, however, still involve currency conversions. If you travel in Europe, Asia, or South America, you will generally have to convert your dollars to another currency in order to purchase items. As we previously discussed, the forces of supply and demand will determine the exchange-rate value of currencies in the absence of government intervention. This chapter will focus more directly on the foreign exchange market. We will consider how exchange rates both exert an impact on and are influenced by the flow of trade and the flow of capital across national boundaries. We will also analyze alternative exchange rate regimes and consider some of the recent changes in the structure of currency markets around the world. ■

FOREIGN EXCHANGE MARKET

Foreign exchange market
The market in which the currencies of different countries are bought and sold.

When trading parties live in different countries, an exchange will often involve a currency transaction. Currency transactions take place in the **foreign exchange market**, the market where currencies of different countries are bought and sold. Suppose you own a sporting goods shop in the United States and are preparing to place an order for athletic shoes. You can purchase them from either a domestic or foreign manufacturer. If you decide to purchase the shoes from a British firm, either you will have to change dollars into pounds at a bank and send them to the British producer, or the British manufacturer will have to go to a bank and change your dollar check into pounds. In either case, purchasing the British shoes will involve an exchange of dollars for pounds.

The British producer has offered to supply the shoes for 30 pounds per pair. How can you determine whether this price is high or low? To compare the price of the British-supplied shoes with the price of those produced domestically, you must know the **exchange rate** between the dollar and the pound. *The exchange rate is one of the most important prices because it enables consumers in one country to translate the prices of foreign goods into units of their own currency. Specifically, the dollar price of a foreign good is determined by multiplying the foreign product price by the exchange rate (the dollar price per unit of the foreign currency).* For example, if it takes $1.50 to obtain 1 pound, then the British shoes priced at 30 pounds would cost $45 (30 times the $1.50 price of the pound).

Exchange rate
The domestic price of one unit of foreign currency. For example, if it takes $1.50 to purchase one English pound, the dollar-pound exchange rate is 1.50.

Suppose the exchange rate is $1.50 = 1 pound and that you decide to buy 200 pairs of athletic shoes from the British manufacturer at 30 pounds ($45) per pair. You will need 6,000 pounds in order to pay the British manufacturer. If you contact an American bank that handles foreign exchange transactions and write the bank a check for $9,000 (the $1.50 exchange rate multiplied by 6,000), it will supply the 6,000 pounds. The bank will typically charge a small fee for handling the transaction.

Where does the American bank get the pounds? The bank obtains the pounds from British importers who want dollars to buy things from Americans. *Note that the U.S. demand for foreign currencies (such as the pound) is generated by the demand of Americans for things purchased from foreigners. On the other hand, the U.S. supply of foreign exchange reflects the demand of foreigners for things bought from Americans.*

Exhibit 1 presents data on the exchange rate—the cents required to purchase a European euro, Japanese yen, British pound, and Canadian dollar—during 1990–2000. An index of the exchange-rate value of the dollar against 26 major currencies is also shown. Under the flexible rate system present in most industrial countries, the exchange rate between currencies changes from day to day and even from hour to hour. Thus, the annual exchange-rate data given in Exhibit 1 are really averages for each year.

An **appreciation** in the value of a nation's currency means that fewer units of the currency are now required to purchase one unit of a foreign currency. For example, in 2000, only 92.3 cents were required to purchase a European euro, down from 106.5 in 1999.[2] *As the result of this appreciation in the value of the dollar relative to the euro, goods purchased from countries in the euro zone became less expensive to Americans.* The direction of change in the prices that those in the euro zone paid for American goods was just the opposite. An appreciation of the U.S. dollar relative to the euro is the same thing as a depreciation in the euro relative to the dollar.

When a **depreciation** occurs, it will take more units of the domestic currency to purchase a unit of foreign currency. Between 1993 and 1998, the dollar depreciated against the British pound (see Exhibit 1). In 1993, it took 150.16 cents to purchase a British pound; by 1998, the figure had risen to 165.73. As the number of cents required to purchase a British pound rose, British goods became more expensive for Americans.

The 26-currency index of the dollar's exchange-rate value presented in Exhibit 1 provides evidence on what is happening to the dollar's general exchange-rate value.[3] An increase in the index implies an appreciation in the dollar, while a decline is indicative of a depreciation. Between 1996 and 2000, the dollar appreciated by approximately 25 percent.

Appreciation
An increase in the value of the domestic currency relative to foreign currencies. An appreciation increases the purchasing power of the domestic currency for foreign goods.

Depreciation
A reduction in the value of the domestic currency relative to foreign currencies. A depreciation reduces the purchasing power of the domestic currency for foreign goods.

EXHIBIT 1
Foreign Exchange Rates, 1990–2000

		U.S. Cents per Unit of Foreign Currency			Index of Exchange-Rate Value of the Dollar (26 Currencies)[a]
Year	Euro	Japanese Yen	British Pound	Canadian Dollar	
1990	—	0.690	178.41	85.7	70.0
1991	—	0.743	176.74	87.3	73.2
1992	—	0.789	176.63	82.7	76.0
1993	—	0.900	150.16	77.5	82.9
1994	—	0.979	153.19	73.2	90.5
1995	—	1.064	157.85	72.9	92.5
1996	—	0.919	156.07	73.3	97.4
1997	—	0.826	163.76	72.2	104.4
1998	—	0.763	165.73	67.4	116.5
1999	106.5	0.879	161.72	67.3	116.9
2000	92.3	0.928	151.56	67.3	120.3

[a]January 1997 = 100. In addition to the currencies listed above, the index also includes 22 other currencies.
Source: www.stls.frb.org

[2]Because an appreciation means a lower price of foreign currencies, some may think it looks like a depreciation. Just remember that a lower price of the foreign currency means that one's domestic currency will buy more units of the foreign currency and thus more goods and services from foreigners.

[3]In the construction of this index, the exchange rate of each currency relative to the dollar is weighted according to the proportion of U.S. trade with the country. For example, the index weights the U.S. dollar–Japanese yen exchange rate more heavily than the U.S. dollar–Swiss franc exchange rate because the volume of U.S. trade with Japan exceeds the volume of trade with Switzerland.

Flexible exchange rates
Exchange rates that are determined by the market forces of supply and demand. They are sometimes called floating exchange rates.

Frequently, people will use the terms "strong" and "weak" when referring to the exchange-rate value of a currency. A strong currency is one that has appreciated substantially in value, while a weak currency is one that has declined in value on the foreign exchange market.

A pure **flexible exchange rate** system is one where market forces alone determine the foreign exchange value of the currency. The exchange-rate system in effect since 1973 might best be described as a managed flexible rate regime. It is flexible because all the major industrial countries allow the exchange-rate value of their currencies to float. But the system is also "managed" because the major industrial nations have from time to time attempted to alter supply and demand in the foreign exchange market by buying and selling various currencies. Compared to the total size of this market, however, these transactions have been relatively small. Thus, the exchange-rate value of major currencies like the U.S. dollar, British pound, Japanese yen, and the new European euro is determined primarily by market forces. Several countries link their currency to major currencies, such as the U.S. dollar, English pound, or Japanese yen. As we proceed, we will investigate alternative methods of linking currencies and analyze the operation of different regimes.

DETERMINANTS OF THE EXCHANGE RATE

To simplify our explanation of how the exchange rate is determined, let us assume that the United States and Great Britain are the only two countries in the world. When Americans buy and sell with each other, they use dollars. Therefore, American sellers will want to be paid in dollars. Similarly, when the British buy and sell with each other, they use pounds. As a result, British sellers will want to be paid in pounds.

If Americans want to buy from British sellers, they will need to acquire pounds. *In our two-country world, the demand for pounds in the exchange-rate market originates from the purchases by Americans of British goods, services, and assets (both real and financial).* For example, when U.S. residents purchase men's suits from a British manufacturer, travel in the United Kingdom, or purchase the stocks, bonds, or physical assets of British business firms, they demand pounds from (and supply dollars to) the foreign exchange-rate market to pay for these items.

The supply of foreign exchange (pounds in our two-country case) originates from sales by Americans to foreigners. When Americans sell goods, services, or assets to the British, for example, the British buyers will supply pounds (and demand dollars) in the exchange-rate market in order to acquire the dollars required to pay for the items purchased from Americans.[4]

Exhibit 2 illustrates the demand and supply curves of Americans for foreign exchange—British pounds in our two-country case. The demand for pounds is downward sloping because a lower dollar price of the pound—meaning a dollar will buy more pounds—makes British goods cheaper for American importers. The goods produced by one country are generally good substitutes for the goods of another country. This means that when foreign (British) goods become cheaper, Americans will increase their expenditures on imports (and therefore the quantity of pounds demanded will increase). Thus, as the dollar price of the pound declines, Americans will both buy more of the lower-priced (in dollars) British goods and demand more pounds, which are required for the purchases.

Similarly, the supply curve for pounds is dependent on the sales by Americans to the British (that is, the purchase of American goods by the British). An increase in the dollar price of the pound means that a pound will purchase more dollars and more goods priced in dollars. Thus, the price (in pounds) of American goods, services, and assets to British purchasers declines. The British will purchase more from Americans and therefore supply

---

[4]We analyze the foreign exchange market in terms of the demand for and supply of foreign currencies. Alternatively, this analysis could be done in terms of the supply of and demand for dollars. Since one currency is traded for another, the same actions that generate a demand for foreign exchange simultaneously generate a supply of dollars. Correspondingly, the same exchanges that create a supply of foreign currencies simultaneously generate a demand for dollars in the foreign exchange market.

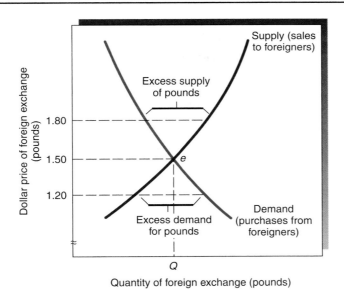

EXHIBIT 2
Equilibrium in Foreign
Exchange Market

The dollar price of the pound
is measured on the vertical
axis. The horizontal axis indicates the flow of pounds to
the foreign exchange market.
The equilibrium exchange rate
is $1.50 = 1 pound. At the
equilibrium price, the quantity
demanded of pounds just
equals the quantity supplied.
A higher price of pounds, such
as $1.80 = 1 pound, would
lead to an excess supply of
pounds, causing the dollar
price of the pound to fall. On
the other hand, a lower price,
for example, $1.20 = 1 pound,
would result in an excess demand for pounds, causing the
pound to appreciate.

more pounds to the foreign exchange market as the dollar price of the pound rises. Because of this, the supply curve for pounds tends to slope upward to the right.

As Exhibit 2 shows, equilibrium is present at the dollar price of the pound that brings
the quantity demanded and quantity supplied of pounds into balance, $1.50 = 1 pound in
this case. *The market-clearing price of $1.50 per pound not only equates demand and sup-
ply in the foreign exchange market, it also equates (1) the value of U.S. purchases of items
supplied by the British with (2) the value of items sold by U.S. residents to the British.* Demand and supply in the currency market are merely the mirror images of these two factors.

What would happen if the price of the pound were above equilibrium—$1.80 =
1 pound, for example? At the higher dollar price of the pound, British goods would be
more expensive for Americans. Americans would cut back on their purchases of shoes,
glassware, textile products, financial assets, and other items supplied by the British. Reflecting this reduction, the quantity of pounds demanded by Americans would decline. Simultaneously, the higher dollar price of the pound would make U.S. exports cheaper for
the British. For example, an $18,000 American automobile would cost British consumers
12,000 pounds when 1 pound trades for $1.50, but it would cost only 10,000 pounds when
1 pound exchanges for $1.80. If the dollar price of the pound were $1.80, the British
would supply more pounds to the foreign exchange market than Americans demand. As
can be seen in Exhibit 2, this excess supply of pounds would cause the dollar price of the
pound to decline until equilibrium is restored at the $1.50 = 1 pound price.

At a below-equilibrium price, such as $1.20 = 1 pound, an opposite set of forces
would be present. The lower dollar price of the pound would make English goods cheaper
for Americans and American goods more expensive for the British. At the $1.20 price for
a pound, the purchases of Americans from the British would exceed their sales to them,
leading to an excess demand for pounds. In turn, the excess demand would cause the dollar price of the pound to rise until equilibrium was restored at $1.50 = 1 pound.

*The implications of the analysis are general. In our multi-country and multi-
currency world, the demand for foreign currencies in exchange for dollars reflects the
purchases by Americans of goods, services, and assets from foreigners. The supply of
foreign currencies in exchange for dollars reflects the sales by Americans of goods, services, and assets to foreigners. The equilibrium exchange rate will bring the quantity of
foreign exchange demanded by Americans into equality with the quantity supplied by*

foreigners. It will also bring the purchases by Americans from foreigners into equality with the sales by Americans to foreigners.

Changes in Exchange Rates

When exchange rates are free to fluctuate, the market value of a nation's currency will appreciate and depreciate in response to changing market conditions. Any change that alters the quantity of goods, services, or assets bought from foreigners relative to the quantity sold to foreigners will also alter the exchange rate. What types of change will alter the exchange-rate value of a currency?

Changes in Income

An increase in domestic income will encourage the nation's residents to spend a portion of their additional income on imports. When the income of a nation grows rapidly, the nation's imports tend to rise rapidly as well. As **Exhibit 3** illustrates, an increase in imports also increases the demand for foreign exchange (the pound in our two-country case). As the demand for pounds increases, the dollar price of the pound rises (from $1.50 to $1.80). This depreciation of the dollar reduces the incentive of Americans to import British goods and services, while increasing the incentive of the British to purchase U.S. exports. These two forces will restore equilibrium in the foreign exchange market at a new, higher dollar price of the pound.

American consumer purchases an auto from a Japanese manufacturer.

American vacationer buys a ticket on British Airways.

Foreign student pays tuition to Harvard.

Foreign investor purchases a bond from a U.S. corporation.

How will each of these transactions influence the demand for and supply of foreign currencies in exchange for the dollar?

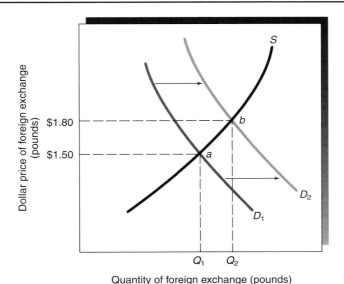

EXHIBIT 3
Growth of Income and Growth of Imports

Other things constant, if incomes grow in the United States, U.S. imports will grow. The increase in the imports will increase the demand for pounds, causing the dollar price of the pound to rise (from $1.50 to $1.80).

Just the opposite takes place when the income of a trading partner (Great Britain in our example) increases. Rapid growth of income abroad will lead to an increase in U.S. exports, causing the supply of foreign exchange (and demand for dollars) to increase. This will cause the dollar to appreciate—the dollar price of the pound will fall.

What will happen if both countries are growing? Other things constant, it is the relative growth rate that matters. A country that grows more rapidly than its trading partners will increase its imports relative to exports, which will cause the exchange-rate value of its currency to fall. Correspondingly, sluggish growth of income relative to one's trading partners will lead to a decline in imports relative to exports. ***Paradoxical as it may seem, sluggish growth relative to one's trading partners will tend to cause a nation's currency to appreciate.***

Differences in Rates of Inflation

Other things constant, domestic inflation will cause the value of a nation's currency to depreciate in the foreign exchange market, whereas deflation will result in appreciation. Suppose prices in the United States rise by 50 percent while our trading partners are experiencing stable prices. The domestic inflation will cause U.S. consumers to increase their demand for imported goods (and foreign currency). In turn, the inflated domestic prices will cause foreigners to reduce their purchases of U.S. goods, thereby reducing the supply of foreign currency to the exchange market. As **Exhibit 4** illustrates, the exchange rate will adjust to this set of circumstances. The dollar will depreciate relative to the pound.

Exchange-rate adjustments permit nations with even high rates of inflation to engage in trade with countries experiencing relatively stable prices.[5] A depreciation in a nation's currency in the foreign exchange market compensates for the nation's inflation rate. For example, if inflation increases the price level in the United States by 50 percent, and the value of the dollar in exchange for the pound depreciates (such that the value of the foreign currency increases 50 percent), then the prices of American goods measured in pounds are unchanged to British consumers. Thus, when the exchange-rate value of the dollar changes from $1.50 = 1 pound to $2.25 = 1 pound, the depreciation in the dollar restores the original prices of U.S. goods to British consumers even though the price level in the United States has increased by 50 percent.

---

[5]However, high rates of inflation are likely to cause greater variability in the foreign exchange value of a currency across time periods. In turn, this increased variability of the exchange rate will generate uncertainty and reduce the volume of international trade—particularly transactions involving a time dimension. Thus, exchange-rate instability is generally harmful to the health of an economy.

EXHIBIT 4
Inflation with Flexible Exchange Rates

If prices were stable in Britain while the price level increased 50 percent in the United States, the U.S. demand for British products (and pounds) would increase, whereas U.S. exports to Britain would decline, causing the supply of pounds to fall. These forces would cause the dollar to depreciate relative to the pound.

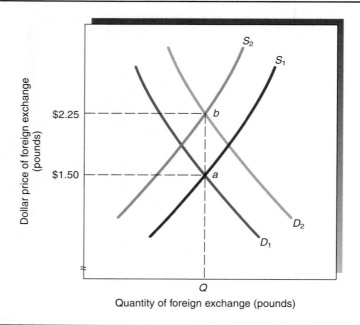

When domestic prices are increasing more rapidly than those of one's trading partners, the value of the domestic currency will tend to depreciate in the foreign exchange market. On the other hand, if a nation's inflation rate is lower than that of its trading partners, then its currency will tend to appreciate.

Changes in Interest Rates

Financial investments will be quite sensitive to changes in real interest rates—that is, interest rates adjusted for the expected rate of inflation. International loanable funds will tend to move toward areas where the expected real rate of return (after compensation for differences in risk) is highest. ***Thus, increases in real interest rates relative to a nation's trading partners will tend to cause that nation's currency to appreciate.*** For example, if real interest rates rise in the United States relative to Britain, British citizens will demand dollars (and supply their currency, pounds) in the foreign exchange market to purchase the high-yield American assets. The increase in demand for the dollar and supply of pounds will cause the dollar to appreciate relative to the British pound.

In contrast, when real interest rates in other countries increase relative to rates in the United States, short-term financial investors will move to take advantage of the higher yields abroad. As investment funds move from the United States to other countries, there will be an increase in the demand for foreign currencies and an increase in the supply of dollars in the foreign exchange market. A depreciation in the dollar relative to the currencies of the countries with the higher real interest rates will be the result.

Changes in the Investment Climate

The inflow and outflow of capital will be influenced by the quality of the investment environment. The monetary and legal climate are particularly important here. Countries that follow a monetary policy consistent with price stability and establish a legal system that provides for the protection of property rights and evenhanded enforcement of contracts will tend to attract capital. In turn, the inflow of capital will strengthen the demand for the domestic currency and thereby cause it to appreciate. In contrast, when investors are concerned about the stability of the monetary climate and fairness of the legal system, they will move their financial capital elsewhere. This outflow of capital will cause the domestic currency to depreciate in the foreign exchange market.

What Factors Cause a Nation's Currency to Appreciate or Depreciate?

These Factors Will Cause a Nation's Currency to Appreciate:

1. Slow growth of income (relative to trading partners) that causes imports to lag behind exports
2. A rate of inflation that is lower than that of one's trading partners
3. Domestic real interest rates that are higher than real interest rates abroad
4. A shift toward sound policies that attract an inflow of capital

These Factors Will Cause a Nation's Currency to Depreciate:

1. Rapid growth of income (relative to trading partners) that stimulates imports relative to exports
2. A rate of inflation that is higher than that of one's trading partners
3. Domestic real interest rates that are lower than real interest rates abroad
4. Movement toward unsound policies that cause an outflow of capital

Other things constant, the currency of a country will tend to appreciate when its policy environment is improving. On the other hand, it will tend to depreciate if investors believe that the nation's policy environment is deteriorating. The accompanying Thumbnail Sketch summarizes the major forces that cause a nation's currency to appreciate or depreciate when exchange rates are determined by market forces.

BALANCE OF PAYMENTS

Just as countries calculate their gross domestic product (GDP) so that they have a general idea of their domestic level of production, most countries also calculate their balance of international payments in order to keep track of transactions across national boundaries. The **balance of payments** summarizes the transactions of the country's citizens, businesses, and governments with foreigners. Balance-of-payments accounts are kept according to the principles of basic bookkeeping. Any transaction that creates a demand for foreign currency (and a supply of the domestic currency) in the foreign exchange market is recorded as a debit, or minus, item. Imports are an example of a debit item. Transactions that create a supply of foreign currency (and demand for the domestic currency) on the foreign exchange market are recorded as a credit, or plus, item. Exports are an example of a credit item. ***Because the foreign exchange market will bring quantity demanded and quantity supplied into balance, it will also bring the total debits and total credits into balance.***

Exhibit 5 summarizes the balance of payments accounts of the United States for 2000. As the exhibit shows, the transactions can be grouped into three basic categories: current account, capital account, and official reserve account. Let us take a look at each of these major categories.

Balance of payments
A summary of all economic transactions between a country and all other countries for a specific time period, usually a year. The balance-of-payments account reflects all payments and liabilities to foreigners (debits) and all payments and obligations received from foreigners (credits).

Current-Account Transactions

Trade of goods and services dominates **current account** transactions. The export and import of merchandise goods are the largest components. When U.S. producers export their products, foreigners will supply their currency in exchange for dollars in order to pay for the U.S.-produced goods. Because U.S. exports generate a supply of foreign exchange and demand for dollars in the foreign exchange market, they are a credit (plus) item. In contrast, when Americans import goods, they will demand foreign currencies and supply dollars in the foreign exchange market. Thus, imports are a debit (minus) item.

Current account
The record of all transactions with foreign nations that involve the exchange of merchandise goods and services, current income derived from investments, and unilateral gifts.

EXHIBIT 5
U.S. Balance of Payments, 2000 (in Billions of Dollars)

	DEBITS	CREDITS	BALANCE: DEFICIT (−) OR SURPLUS (+)
CURRENT ACCOUNT			
1. U.S. merchandise exports		+772.2	
2. U.S. merchandise imports	−1224.4		
3. Balance of merchandise trade (1 + 2)			−452.2
4. U.S. service exports			
5. U.S. service imports		+293.5	
6. Balance on service trade (4 + 5)	−217.0		+76.5
7. Balance on goods and services (3 + 6)			−375.7
8. U.S. investment income on United States assets abroad			
9. Foreign income on foreign assets in the United States		+352.9	
10. Net investment income (8 + 9)	−367.7		−14.8
11. Net unilateral transfers			−54.1
12. Balance on current account (7 + 10 + 11)	−54.1		−444.7
CAPITAL ACCOUNT			
13. Foreign investment in the United States (capital inflow)		+986.6	
14. U.S. investment abroad (capital outflow)	−579.3[a]		
15. Balance on capital account (13 + 14)			+407.3
OFFICIAL RESERVE TRANSACTIONS			
16. Official Reserve Account Balance			+37.3
17. Total (12 + 15 + 16)			0.0

[a]Statistical discrepancy is included in this figure.
Source: www.bea.doc.gov.

Balance of merchandise trade
The difference between the value of merchandise exports and the value of merchandise imports for a nation. The balance of merchandise trade is only one component of a nation's total balance of payments. Also called simply balance of trade or net exports.

In 2000, the United States exported $772.2 billion of merchandise goods compared to imports of $1,224.4 billion. The difference between the value of a country's merchandise exports and the value of its merchandise imports is known as the **balance of merchandise trade** (or *balance of trade*). If the value of a country's merchandise exports falls short of the value of its merchandise imports, it is said to have a balance-of-trade deficit. In contrast, the situation where a nation exports more than it imports is referred to as a trade surplus. In 2000, the United States ran a merchandise-trade deficit of $452.2 billion (line 3 of Exhibit 5).

The export and import of services are also sizable. Service trade involves the exchange of items like insurance, transportation, banking services, and items supplied to foreign tourists. Like the export of merchandise goods, service exports generate a supply of foreign exchange and demand for dollars. For example, a Mexican business that is insured with an American company will supply pesos and demand dollars with which to pay its premiums. Thus, service exports are recorded as credits in the balance of payment accounts. On the other hand, the import of services from foreigners generates a demand for foreign currency and a supply of dollars in the exchange market. Therefore, service imports are a debit item.

As Exhibit 5 illustrates, in 2000, U.S. service exports were $293.5 billion, compared with service imports of $217.0 billion. Thus, the United States ran a $76.5 billion surplus on its service trade transactions (line 6 of Exhibit 5). When we add the balance of service exports and imports to the balance of merchandise trade, we obtain the **balance on goods and services**. In 2000, the United States ran a $375.7 billion deficit (the sum of the $452.2 billion merchandise-trade deficit and the $76.5 billion service surplus) in the goods and services account.

Balance on goods and services
The exports of goods (merchandise) and services of a nation minus its imports of goods and services.

Two other relatively small items are also included in current account transactions: (1) net income from investments and (2) unilateral transfers. In the past, Americans have made substantial investments in stocks, bonds, and real assets in other countries. As these investments abroad generate income, dollars will flow from foreigners to Americans. This flow of income to Americans will supply foreign currency (and create a demand for dollars) in the foreign exchange market. Thus, it enters as a credit on the current account. Correspondingly, foreigners earn income from their investments in the United States. This income of foreigners is recorded as a debit because it creates a demand for foreign exchange (and supply of dollars).

As Exhibit 5 shows, in 2000, Americans earned $352.9 billion from investments abroad, while foreigners earned $367.7 billion from their investments in the United States. On balance, Americans earned $14.8 billion less on their investments abroad than foreigners earned on their investments in the United States. This $14.8 billion net outflow of investment income added to the deficit on current-account transactions.

Gifts to foreigners, such as U.S. aid to a foreign government or private gifts from U.S. residents to their relatives abroad, generate a demand for foreign currencies and supply of dollars in the foreign exchange market. Thus, they are a debit item. Correspondingly, gifts to Americans from foreigners are a credit item. Because the U.S. government and private U.S. citizens gave $54.1 billion more to foreigners than we received from them, this net unilateral transfer was entered as a debit item on the current account in 2000.

Balance on Current Account

The difference between (1) the value of a country's current exports and earnings from investments abroad and (2) the value of its current imports and the earnings of foreigners on their domestic assets (plus net unilateral transfers to foreigners) is known as the **balance on current account**. Current-account transactions involve only current exchanges of goods and services and current income flows (and gifts). They do not involve changes in the ownership of either real or financial assets. The current-account balance provides a summary of all current-account transactions. As with the balance of trade, when the value of the current-account debit items (import-type transactions) exceeds the value of the credit items (export-type transactions), we say that the country is running a current-account deficit. Alternatively, if the credit items are greater than the debit items, the country is running a current-account surplus. In 2000, the United States ran a current-account deficit of $444.7 billion.

Balance on current account
The import-export balance of goods and services, plus net investment income earned abroad, plus net private and government transfers. If the value of the nation's export-type items exceeds (is less than) the value of the nation's import-type items plus net unilateral transfers to foreigners, a current-account surplus (deficit) is present.

Because trade in goods and services dominates current-account transactions, the trade and current account balances are closely related. Countries with large trade deficits (surpluses) almost always run substantial current-account deficits (surpluses).

Capital-Account Transactions

In contrast with current-account transactions, **capital-account** transactions focus on changes in the ownership of real and financial assets. These transactions are composed of (1) direct investments by Americans in real assets abroad (or by foreigners in the United States) and (2) loans to and from foreigners. When foreigners make investments in the United States—for example, by purchasing stocks, bonds, or real assets from Americans—their actions will supply foreign currency and generate a demand for dollars in the foreign exchange market. Thus, these capital inflow transactions are a credit.

Capital account
The record of transactions with foreigners that involve either (1) the exchange of ownership rights to real or financial assets or (2) the extension of loans.

On the other hand, capital outflow transactions are recorded as debits. For example, if a U.S. investor purchases a shoe factory in Mexico, the Mexican seller will want to be paid in pesos. The U.S. investor will supply dollars (and demand pesos) on the foreign exchange market. Since U.S. citizens will demand foreign currency (and supply dollars) when they invest in stocks, bonds, and real assets abroad, these transactions enter into the balance-of-payments accounts as a debit. In 2000, foreign investments in the United States (capital inflow) summed to $986.6 billion, while U.S. investments abroad (capital outflow) totaled $579.3 billion.[6] Since the capital inflow exceeded the outflow, the United States ran a $407.3 billion capital-account surplus in 2000.

Official Reserve Account

As we noted earlier, the current exchange rate regime is not a pure flexible rate system. Governments sometimes seek to modify the foreign exchange value of their currency by engaging in official reserve transactions. A substantial appreciation of a currency will make it more difficult for a nation's export industries to compete in world markets. In an effort to improve the competitiveness of export industries, governments will sometimes respond to an appreciation by purchasing foreign currency reserves (and selling the domestic currency) in the foreign exchange market. Conversely, if a nation's currency is depreciating rapidly, the government may seek to halt the depreciation by using some of its foreign currency reserves to purchase the domestic currency in the foreign exchange market.

Under the current (primarily) flexible rate system, these official reserve transactions are modest relative to the total of international transactions. The United States ran a surplus of $37.3 billion in its official reserve transactions in 2000.

The Balance of Payments Must Balance

The sum of the debit and credit items of the balance-of-payments accounts must balance. Thus, the following identity must hold:

$$\frac{\text{Current-Account}}{\text{Balance}} + \frac{\text{Capital Account}}{\text{Balance}} + \frac{\text{Official Reserve Account}}{\text{Balance}} = 0$$

However, the specific components of the accounts need not balance. For example, the debit and credit items of the current account need not be equal. Specific components may run either a surplus or a deficit. Nevertheless, since the balance of payments as a whole must balance, a deficit in one area implies a surplus in another.

If a nation is experiencing a current-account deficit, it must experience an offsetting surplus on the sum of its capital-account and official reserve account balances. This has been the case for the United States in recent years. In 2000, the United States ran a $444.7 billion current-account deficit and a $407.3 billion capital-account surplus. The difference between these two figures—a $37.3 billion deficit—was exactly offset by a $37.3 billion surplus in the official reserve account. Thus, the deficits and surpluses of the current-, capital-, and official reserve accounts summed to zero as is shown in Exhibit 5 (line 17).

Under a pure flexible rate system, official reserve transactions are zero. When this is the case, a capital-account surplus (inflow of capital) implies a current-account deficit. Similarly, a capital-account deficit (outflow of capital) implies a current-account surplus. ***With flexible exchange rates, changes in the net inflow of capital will influence the current-account balance. If a nation is experiencing an increase in net foreign invest-***

---

[6]The statistical discrepancy is also included in the investments abroad category. This item was approximately $30 billion in 2000. International transactions—particularly those conducted in cash—can be difficult to monitor. As we noted when discussing the money supply, 60 percent or more of the U.S. currency supply circulates abroad. Because this "outflow" of currency is not included in balance-of-payments accounts, such movements would contribute to the statistical discrepancy. Illegal drug trade may also increase the size of this item.

ment, perhaps as the result of higher real interest rates, this increase in the capital-account surplus will enlarge the current-account deficit. In contrast, capital flight (outflow of capital) will move the current account toward a surplus.

MORE POPULAR TRADE FALLACIES

As we noted in the previous chapter, fallacies abound in the area of international trade. Confusion about the significance of current account (predominantly trade) balances provide still another illustration of this point. Let us consider two popular fallacies in this area.

Trade Balance Fallacy 1: "A trade deficit is bad. It is indicative of a weak economy."

There is a natural tendency to believe that a trade deficit is bad for an economy. This is understandable: the word "deficit" suggests things like excessive spending relative to income, bank overdrafts, indebtedness, and a future day of reckoning. A trade deficit, however, is not like this. A trade deficit occurs when a nation's imports exceed its exports. Many times, this occurs because a nation is growing more rapidly than its trading partners. Rapid domestic growth stimulates imports, while slow growth abroad weakens demand for a nation's exports. This combination often causes a trade deficit.

In addition, trade balances are influenced by capital flows. In a global economy where capital moves rather freely across borders, countries that offer attractive investment opportunities relative to those available elsewhere will experience an inflow of capital. With flexible exchange rates, the capital inflow will push the foreign exchange value of the nation's currency upward. This currency appreciation will stimulate imports relative to exports and thereby shift the trade balance toward a deficit. In essence, trade (and current account) deficits are the flip side of capital inflows. Economies that offer attractive investment opportunities relative to the supply of domestic saving will tend to experience both inflows of capital and trade deficits.

Thus, trade deficits are primarily the result of rapid economic growth and investment opportunities that attract an inflow of capital. **Exhibit 6** illustrates this point. This exhibit provides data on the foreign exchange value of the dollar, current account balance, and inflow of capital for the United States during the last three decades. During 1973–1982 both the trade deficits and inflow of capital (net foreign investment) were relatively small. However, as the U.S. economy grew briskly following the 1982 recession, net foreign investment (bottom panel) in the United States increased sharply. Simultaneously, the U.S. dollar appreciated and the trade deficit widened. As the U.S. economy slowed during the late 1980s and the recession of the early 1990s, the capital inflow fell to a trickle and the current account actually registered a small surplus in 1991. As the economy recovered from the recession and experienced strong growth during 1993–2000, once again net foreign investment increased substantially, the U.S. dollar appreciated, and the current account moved toward a large deficit.

As the middle and lower panels illustrate, net foreign investment (net inflow of capital) and the trade deficit are almost mirror images. When net foreign investment increases, the current account (trade) balance shifts toward a deficit. Correspondingly, when net foreign investment shrinks, so too does the current account deficit. This is the expected outcome under a flexible rate system. With flexible rates, the overall payments to and receipts from foreigners must balance. Thus, a deficit in one area is not an isolated event. If a nation runs a current-account (trade) deficit, it must also run a capital-account surplus of equal magnitude. The reverse is also true—a capital-account surplus implies a current account deficit.

The U.S. economy has grown rapidly and provided an attractive environment for investment during the last two decades. These two factors are primarily responsible for the trade deficits of the period. Would the United States have been better off if growth had been slower or the investment environment less attractive? This question answers itself. Recent trade deficits reflect the strength of the U.S. economy, not its weakness.

EXHIBIT 6
The Exchange Rate, Current-Account Balance, and Net Foreign Investment

Here we illustrate the relationship between the exchange rate, the current-account deficit, and net foreign investment (capital inflow). The shaded areas represent recessions.

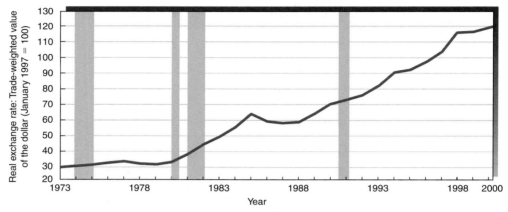

(a) Exchange-rate value of the dollar (compared with 26 currencies)

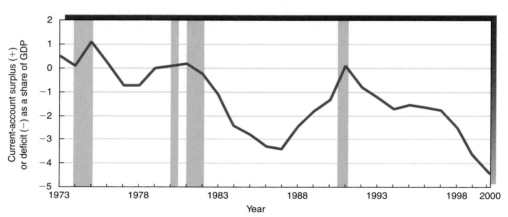

(b) Current-account balance as a share of GDP

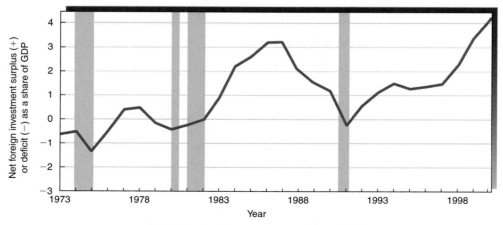

(c) Net foreign investment as a share of GDP

Note: Data are given in billions of dollars.
Source: www.bea.doc.gov and www.stls.frb.org.

Doesn't a trade deficit mean greater indebtedness to foreigners? Not necessarily. Much of the foreign investment involves the purchase of stocks and physical assets like buildings and business assets. Americans benefit because they are able to sell these assets to foreigners at more attractive prices than would otherwise be possible. Foreign investments of this type do not increase American indebtedness to foreigners. Some foreign investments are in the form of loans or the purchase of bonds, which mean lower interest rates for Americans. If the investments are sound, they will generate a future income stream that is more than sufficient to repay the loans. In such cases, the loans are helpful to the U.S. economy.

Can a country continue to run trade deficits? Perhaps surprisingly, the answer is "yes." Trade deficits are primarily a reflection of the inflow of capital. The inflow can and will continue as long as investors find the U.S. economy more attractive than other economies. Put another way, foreigners will be happy to supply investment capital to the U.S. economy as long as they can earn competitive returns. In the case of debt financing, as long as the net income generated by the investment is large enough to cover the borrowing costs, there is no reason why the process cannot continue indefinitely. The historical evidence is consistent with this view. The United States experienced trade deficits and capital inflows year after year from 1820 to 1870. During that period, investment opportunities in the New World were more attractive than those in Europe, so Europeans were quite willing to continue financing undertakings in the New World.

When considering the significance of the U.S. trade deficit, one should remember that the United States has a system of secure property rights, a stable monetary and political environment, and a rapidly growing labor force (compared with Europe and Japan, for example). This makes the United States an attractive country in which to invest. On the other hand, the saving rate of the United States is low compared to our major trading partners. To a large degree, the U.S. current-account deficit reflects this combination of factors—an attractive domestic investment environment and a low saving rate.

A trade deficit is quite different from a business loss or even the budget deficit of a government. No legal entity is responsible for the trade deficit. It reflects an aggregation of the voluntary choices of businesses and individuals. As the late Herbert Stein, a former chairman of the President's Council of Economic Advisers, once put it: "The trade deficit does not belong to any individual or institution. It is a pure-statistical aggregate, like the number of eggs laid in the U.S. or the number of bald-headed men living here."[7]

Trade Balance Fallacy 2: "Bilateral trade between countries should be balanced. If other countries are treating us fairly, our exports to them should be approximately equal to our imports from them."

In recent years, U.S. imports from Japan and China have been substantially greater than U.S. exports to them. As a result, several high-ranking U.S. political officials have charged that the trading policies of these countries are unfair and, in some cases, they have called for trade restraints limiting imports from them. This view is based on a misconception about bilateral trade balances. While flexible exchange rates will bring the total purchases of goods, services, and assets from foreigners into balance with the sales to them, there is no reason to expect the imports and exports to any specific country to be in balance. Instead the predictable result is (a) trade deficits (purchases that exceed sales) with trading partners that are low-cost suppliers of goods and services that we import intensely and (b) trade surpluses (sales that exceed purchases) with trading partners that buy a lot of the things we supply at a low cost.

There is no more reason to expect bilateral trade to balance between nations than between individuals. Consider the trade "deficits" and "surpluses" of a doctor who likes to golf. The doctor can be expected to run a trade deficit with sporting goods stores, golf

---

[7]Herbert Stein, "Leave the Trade Deficit Alone," *The Wall Street Journal*, March 11, 1987.

courses, and favorite suppliers of items like lawn care, plumbing, and auto repairs. Why? The doctor is highly likely to purchase these items from others. On the other hand, the doctor can be expected to run trade surpluses with medical insurers, elderly patients, and those with chronic illnesses. These trading partners are major purchasers of the services provided by the doctor. The same principles are at work across nations. A country can expect to run sizeable surpluses with trading partners who buy a lot of the things the country exports, while trade deficits will be present with trading partners that are low-cost suppliers of the items imported. This is the major factor underlying the U.S. trade deficits with Japan and China. Japan is a major importer of resources like oil and a major exporter of high-tech manufacturing goods. Americans import a lot of the latter, but they export very little of the former. If the United States were a low-cost supplier of energy, its trade balance with Japan would look much different. Major energy exporters—including Indonesia, Oman, Saudi Arabia, and the United Arab Emirates—all run sizeable trade surpluses with Japan.

The situation is much the same with China. China is a low-cost producer of labor-intensive items like toys and textile products, items that are costly for a high-wage country like the United States to produce domestically. Thus, the United States imports substantial quantities of these goods from China. On the other hand, the United States is a low-cost producer of high-tech products and other commodities that can be supplied efficiently by well-educated, technically proficient workers. Because China is a low-income country, its purchases of such commodities are relatively small.

In recent years, the United States has run trade surpluses with the Netherlands, Australia, Belgium, Luxembourg, Brazil, and the United Kingdom. Do these bilateral trade surpluses indicate that the United States treats these countries unfairly? Of course not. The surpluses merely reflect that these countries import goods that American producers supply cheaply.

MACROECONOMIC POLICY, EXCHANGE RATES, AND CAPITAL FLOWS

During the post–Second World War period, there has been a dramatic increase in both international trade and the flow of investment capital across national boundaries. This increasing mobility of both goods and capital influences the effects of macroeconomic policy, even in a country such as the United States with a relatively small trade sector. Throughout this text, we have focused on the impact of macroeconomic policy within the framework of an open economy. However, we have paid little attention to the impact of macro policy on exchange rates and the flow of capital. We now turn to these issues.

Because monetary and fiscal policies exert an impact on income growth, inflation, and real interest rates, they will also influence exchange rates. These two major macro-policy tools differ with regard to their impact on the foreign exchange market. Thus, we will consider them separately.

Monetary Policy and the Foreign Exchange Market

Suppose the United States began to follow a more expansionary monetary policy. How would this policy influence the foreign exchange market? *As we discussed in Chapter 14, an unanticipated shift to a more expansionary monetary policy will lead to a lower real interest rate, upward pressure on the general level of prices, and more rapid economic growth.*[8] Each of these factors will increase the demand for foreign exchange, causing the dollar to depreciate (see prior Thumbnail Sketch). The rapid growth of income will stimu-

---

[8]As we previously noted when considering monetary policy, the impact of a policy change is dependent on whether the effects of the change are anticipated or unanticipated. Neither growth nor the real interest rate will change if people fully anticipate the effects of the change in monetary policy on the price level. In this chapter, we assume for simplicity that the price-level effects accompanying a shift in monetary policy are not fully anticipated. Clearly, this is more likely to be true in the short run than in the long run.

late imports. Similarly, the increase in the U.S. inflation rate (relative to our trading partners) will make U.S. goods less competitive abroad, causing a decline in exports. Simultaneously, the lower real interest rate will encourage investors, both domestic and foreign, to shift funds from the United States to other countries where they can earn a higher rate of return. This outflow of capital will place additional downward pressure on the foreign exchange value of the dollar. ***Thus, an unanticipated shift to a more expansionary monetary policy will cause the dollar to depreciate.***

How will expansionary monetary policy influence the current-account balance? When answering this question, one must consider the mobility of capital relative to trade flows. ***Financial capital is highly mobile. Investors can and do quickly shift their funds from one country to another in response to changes in interest rates. In contrast, importers and exporters often enter into long-term contracts when buying and selling goods. Thus, they are likely to respond more slowly to changing market conditions. Consequently, the impact of the lower interest rates is likely to dominate in the short run.*** For a time, therefore, the shift to a more expansionary monetary policy will tend to cause an outflow of capital that will shift the capital account toward a deficit (or smaller surplus) and the current account toward a surplus (or smaller deficit).

The expected outcome of an unanticipated switch to a more restrictive monetary policy will be just the opposite. The restrictive monetary policy will push real interest rates upward, and thereby retard both inflation and the growth of output. Investment funds from abroad will be drawn by the high real interest rates. At the same time, slow growth will reduce imports. This combination of factors—an inflow of capital and a reduction in imports—will cause the dollar to appreciate. If the inflow of capital dominates in the short run, the current account will move toward a deficit.

Fiscal Policy and the Foreign Exchange Market

Fiscal policy tends to generate conflicting influences on the foreign exchange market. Suppose the United States increases taxes, cuts government expenditures, and thereby shifts to a more restrictive fiscal policy. Just as with restrictive monetary policy, the restrictive fiscal policy will tend to cause a reduction in aggregate demand, an economic slowdown, and a decline in the rate of inflation. These factors will discourage imports and stimulate exports, placing upward pressure on the exchange-rate value of the dollar. However, restrictive fiscal policy will also mean less government borrowing, which will reduce real interest rates in the United States. The lower real interest rates will cause financial capital to flow from the United States. This will increase the supply of dollars in the foreign exchange market, and thereby place downward pressure on the exchange-rate value of the U.S. dollar. In the short run, the outflow of capital is likely to dominate. If so, the foreign exchange value of the currency will depreciate, at least temporarily. Simultaneously, if the outflow of capital dominates, the current account will shift toward a surplus (or smaller deficit).

The analysis of expansionary fiscal policy is symmetrical. To the extent that larger budget deficits stimulate aggregate demand and domestic inflation, they will encourage imports, which will place downward pressure on the exchange-rate value of a nation's currency. However, the increased borrowing to finance larger budget deficits will push real interest rates up and draw foreign investment to the United States, causing the dollar to appreciate. In the short run, the latter effect is likely to dominate. If so, the expansionary fiscal policy will cause the dollar to appreciate, at least temporarily. Correspondingly, the inflow of capital will shift the current account toward a deficit. The accompanying Thumbnail Sketch summarizes the expected impacts of unanticipated shifts in monetary and fiscal policy.

Empirical Evidence

The dramatic change in both monetary and fiscal policy in the early 1980s illustrates how macro policy influences the foreign exchange market. Monetary policy became much more restrictive while fiscal policy was more expansionary. Responding to the

THUMBNAIL SKETCH

How Will Monetary and Fiscal Policy Affect the Exchange-Rate and Balance-of-Payments Components?

A. The Impact of Unanticipated Shift in Monetary Policy:

	Expansionary Monetary Policy	Restrictive Monetary Policy
Exchange rate[a]	Depreciates	Appreciates
Real interest rates	Decline	Increase
Flow of capital	Capital outflow	Capital inflow
Current account	Shifts toward a surplus	Shifts toward a deficit

B. The Impact of Unanticipated Shift in Fiscal Policy:

	Expansionary Fiscal Policy	Restrictive Fiscal Policy
Exchange rate[a]	Uncertain, but the interest rate effect is likely to cause appreciation	Uncertain, but the interest rate effect is likely to cause depreciation
Real interest rates	Increase	Decline
Flow of capital	Capital inflow	Capital outflow
Current account	Shifts toward a deficit	Shifts toward a surplus

[a]Value of domestic currency.

double-digit inflation rates of 1979–1980, the Federal Reserve reduced the rate of money growth and pushed real interest rates upward in the early 1980s. At the same time, fiscal policy was expansionary. Increases in defense expenditures coupled with a reduction in tax rates led to a substantial increase in the federal budget deficit.

Our analysis indicates that this policy combination—a more restrictive monetary policy coupled with expansionary fiscal policy—will cause higher real interest rates, an inflow of capital, currency appreciation, and a current-account deficit (see the prior Thumbnail Sketch). As Exhibit 6 shows, this is precisely what happened. In the early 1980s, real interest rates rose to historic highs. In turn, the higher interest rates led to a sharp increase in net foreign investment in the United States (frame c of Exhibit 6). This inflow of capital increased the demand for the dollar, causing it to appreciate sharply during 1981–1985 (frame a). The inflow of capital and appreciation of the dollar led to a dramatic increase in the current-account deficit (frame b). The annual current account of the United States shifted from a small surplus in 1981 to a deficit of more than 3 percent of GDP in the mid-1980s. These outcomes—an inflow of capital, appreciation of the dollar, and expansion in the size of the current-account deficit—are precisely what our model predicts.

The 1990s were characterized by both low inflation and strong growth. This combination of factors attracted investment from abroad and helped keep the dollar strong in the foreign exchange market. Furthermore, financial instability in both Latin America and Asia during 1997–1998 caused many investors to look for a safe haven. Dollar investments in U.S. stocks and bonds fit this bill. Thus, net foreign investment in the United States increased, pushing the exchange-rate value of the dollar upward. In turn, the capital inflow and appreciation of the dollar led to sizable current-account deficits in the late 1990s (see Exhibit 6).

INTERNATIONAL FINANCE AND EXCHANGE-RATE REGIMES

There are three major types of exchange-rate regimes: (1) flexible rates, (2) fixed rate, unified currency, and (3) pegged exchange rates. We have already explained how a flexible rate system works. We will now consider the operation of the other two.

Fixed Rate, Unified Currency System

Obviously, the 50 states of the United States have a unified currency, the dollar. In addition, the U.S. dollar has been the official currency of Panama for almost a century. Ecuador adopted the U.S. dollar as its official currency in 2000 and El Salvador did so in 2001. The currency of Hong Kong is also closely linked to the U.S. dollar. Hong Kong has a **currency board** that has the power to create currency only in exchange for a specific quantity of U.S. dollars (7.7 HK dollars = $1 in the United States). Thus, the United States, Panama, Ecuador, El Salvador, and Hong Kong have a unified currency regime.

Twelve countries of the European Union—Austria, Belgium, Finland, France, Germany, Greece, Ireland, Italy, Luxembourg, Netherlands, Portugal, and Spain—recently established a unified currency regime. The official currency in each of these countries is the euro. In turn, the foreign exchange value of the euro relative to other currencies, such as the dollar and yen, is determined by market forces (flexible exchange rates).

The distinguishing characteristic of a fixed rate, unified currency regime is the presence of only one central bank with the power to expand and contract the supply of money. For the dollar, that central bank is the Federal Reserve System; for the euro, it is the European Central Bank. Those linking their currency at a fixed rate to the dollar or the euro are no longer in a position to conduct monetary policy. For example, the former central banks of the countries now using the euro no longer have the power to create money. In essence, they are now branches of the European Central Bank, much like the regional and district Federal Reserve banks are branches of the Fed.

The adoption of a currency board provides a method of unifying one currency with another that has greater credibility in international financial markets. This attribute is particularly attractive for countries with a long history of monetary expansion and hyperinflation. *A currency board does two things. First, it issues domestic currency at a fixed rate in exchange for a designated foreign currency. Second, the foreign currency is then invested in bonds denominated in that currency. This means that the money issued by the currency board is backed 100 percent by the foreign currency.* Therefore, the holders of the money issued by the currency board know that it will always have sufficient funds to exchange the domestic currency for the foreign one at the fixed rate.

Under a currency board regime, if domestic citizens buy more (imports) from foreigners than they sell to them (exports), the amount of the domestic currency exchanged for the foreign one will increase. This will cause the domestic money supply to fall, which will place downward pressure on the price level (rate of inflation). In turn, the lower level of prices will encourage exports relative to imports, and thereby automatically keep the value of the two currencies in line. Countries that adopt the currency board approach are no longer in a position to conduct monetary policy. Instead, they essentially accept the monetary policy of the nation to which their currency is tied. They also accept the exchange-rate fluctuations of that currency relative to other currencies outside of the unified zone.

A pure gold standard system, where each country sets the value of its currency in terms of gold and fully backs its domestic money supply with gold, is also a fixed rate, unified system. In this case, the world supply of gold (rather than a central bank) determines the total supply of money. If a country were importing more than it was exporting, its supply of gold would fall, which would reduce the domestic supply of money. This would place downward pressure on the domestic price level and bring the payments to and receipts from foreigners back into balance. Things would change in the opposite direction if a country were exporting more than it was importing. International financial arrangements approximated those of a gold standard during the period between the American Civil War and the establishment of the Federal Reserve System in 1913.

Between 1944 and 1971, most of the world operated under a system of **fixed exchange rates**, where each nation fixed the price of its currency relative to others. In essence, this was a quasi-unified system. It was unified in the sense that the value of one currency was fixed relative to others over lengthy time periods. But it was not a fully

Currency board
An entity that (a) issues a currency with a fixed designated value relative to a widely accepted currency (for example, the U.S. dollar), (b) promises to continue to redeem the issued currency at the fixed rate, and (c) maintains bonds and other liquid assets denominated in the other currency that provide 100 percent backing for all currency issued.

Fixed exchange rate
An exchange rate that is set at a determined amount by government policy.

International Monetary Fund (IMF)
An international banking organization, with more than 180 member nations, designed to oversee the operation of the international monetary system. Although it does not control the world supply of money, it does hold currency reserves for member nations and makes currency loans to national central banks.

unified system because the countries continued to exercise control over monetary policy. Nations maintained reserves with the **International Monetary Fund**, which could be drawn on when payments to foreigners exceeded receipts from them. This provided each with some leeway in its conduct of monetary policy. However, countries running persistent payment deficits would eventually deplete their reserves. This constrained the country's monetary independence and provided its policy makers with an incentive to keep monetary policy approximately in line with that of its trading partners. Under this fixed exchange-rate regime, nations confronting balance-of-payments problems often imposed tariffs, quotas, and other trade barriers in an effort to keep their payments and receipts in balance. Various restrictions on the convertibility of currencies were also common. These problems eventually led to the demise of the system.

Pegged Exchange Rates

Pegged exchange-rate system
A commitment to use monetary and fiscal policy to maintain the exchange-rate value of the domestic currency at a fixed rate or within a narrow band relative to another currency (or bundle of currencies).

A **pegged exchange-rate system** is one in which a country commits itself to the maintenance of a specific exchange rate (or exchange-rate range) relative to another, stronger currency (such as the U.S. dollar) or a bundle of currencies. In contrast with the currency board approach, however, countries adopting the pegged exchange rate continue to conduct monetary policy. Thus, an excess of payments (imports) relative to receipts (exports) does not force the country to reduce its domestic money supply.

In order for a pegged rate system to be effective, a country must follow a monetary policy consistent with the fixed rate. Maintenance of the pegged rate requires the country to give up monetary independence. A nation can either (1) follow an independent monetary policy and allow its exchange rate to fluctuate or (2) tie its monetary policy to the maintenance of the fixed exchange rate. It cannot, however, maintain the convertibility of its currency at the fixed exchange rate while following a monetary policy more expansionary than that of the country to which the domestic currency is tied. Attempts to do so will lead to a financial crisis—a situation where falling foreign currency reserves eventually force the country to forgo the pegged exchange rate.

This is precisely what happened in Mexico. During 1989–1994, Mexico sought to peg the value of the peso to the U.S. dollar. At the same time, Mexico expanded its domestic money supply much more rapidly than the United States. This led to a higher rate of inflation in Mexico than in the United States. Responding to the different inflation rates, more and more people shifted away from the Mexican peso and toward the dollar. By December 1994, Mexico's foreign exchange reserves were virtually depleted. As a result, it could no longer maintain the fixed exchange rate with the dollar. Mexico devalued its currency, triggering a crisis that affected several other countries following similar policies.

More recently, much the same thing happened in Brazil and several Asian countries (Thailand, South Korea, Indonesia, and Malaysia). As in Mexico, these countries sought to maintain fixed exchange rates (or rates within a narrow band), while following monetary and fiscal policies that were inconsistent with the fixed rate. As their reserves declined, they were forced to abandon their exchange-rate pegs. This was extremely disruptive to these economies. Imports suddenly became much more expensive and therefore less affordable. Businesses (including banks) that had borrowed money in dollars (or some other foreign currency) were unable to repay their loans as the result of the sharp decline in the exchange-rate value of the domestic currency. These economies experienced sharp economic declines during 1997–1998.

The Future

Currently, international financial arrangements are in a state of flux. The recent failures of pegged rate systems have created a vacuum. Many countries are reluctant either to (a) give up their monetary policy independence and rigidly tie their currency to another (such as the U.S. dollar) or (b) adopt a purely flexible exchange rate. Both economic theory and real-world experience indicate that either of these two approaches will work reasonably well. On the other hand, the pegged exchange approach is something like a time bomb. Pushed by political considerations, monetary policy makers in most countries are unable to follow a course consistent with the maintenance of pegged rates.

As the relative size of international exchange continues to grow, so too will the demand for a currency of stable value. During the past decade, there has been a dramatic increase in the number of countries where citizens are free to use and maintain bank accounts in any currency they choose, including those issued by other governments. In most areas of the world, the U.S. dollar is the preferred foreign currency. As a result, more than half the currency issued by the Federal Reserve circulates in other countries.[9] The legalization of foreign currencies is an important structural change. The availability of competitive currencies reduces the incentive of the domestic monetary authorities to inflate. If they do, more and more people will shift to the dollar and other, more stable currencies. In essence, the use of a foreign currency provides citizens with an alternative to the uncertainties accompanying an unstable domestic monetary regime.

The shape of financial and exchange-rate regimes is likely to change substantially in the years immediately ahead. Much of Europe has already moved toward a unified currency. As the euro gains credibility, the three EU members (Denmark, Sweden, and the United Kingdom) that have not yet adopted the euro are likely to do so. So too are several Eastern European countries, either through a currency board arrangement or by directly joining the monetary union. It would not be surprising to see a similar trend in North and South America. Brazil, Mexico, and several other countries in the Americas may well seek currency stability through some form of linkage with the dollar. A substantial share of international trade is also conducted in Japanese yen. In the future, the dollar, euro, and yen perhaps along with two or three other currencies may well emerge as the dominant currencies used throughout the world for domestic as well as international trade. These developments make this an exciting time to follow international finance.

KEY POINTS

▼ Because countries generally use different currencies, international trade usually involves the conversion of one currency to another. The currencies of different countries are bought and sold in the foreign exchange market. The exchange rate is the price of one national currency in terms of another.

▼ The dollar demand for foreign exchange arises from the purchase (import) of goods, services, and assets by Americans from foreigners. The supply of foreign currency in exchange for dollars arises from the sale (export) of goods, services, and assets by Americans to foreigners. The equilibrium exchange rate will bring these two forces into balance.

▼ With flexible exchange rates, the following will cause a nation's currency to appreciate: (1) rapid growth of income abroad (and/or slow domestic growth), (2) low inflation (relative to trading partners), (3) rising domestic real interest rates (and/or falling rates abroad), and (4) improvement in the environment for investment. The reverse of these conditions will cause a nation's currency to depreciate.

▼ The balance-of-payments accounts provide a summary of transactions with foreigners. There are three major balance-of-payments components: (1) current account, (2) capital account, and (3) official reserve account. The balances of these three components must sum to zero, but the individual components of the accounts need not be in balance.

▼ Under a pure flexible rate system, there will not be any official reserve account transactions. Under these circumstances, the current and capital accounts must balance. Therefore, an inflow of capital will shift the current account toward a deficit, while

---

[9]If this currency did not circulate outside of the United States, it would be necessary for the U.S. government to have a larger quantity of interest-bearing debt outstanding. When foreigners hold dollars, in essence they are extending an interest-free loan to the U.S. government. Thus, the circulation of dollars abroad is advantageous to the United States.

an outflow of capital will move the current account toward a surplus.

▼ There is no reason to believe that trade deficits are bad and surpluses good. Countries that grow rapidly and follow policies that investors find attractive will tend to experience an inflow of capital and a trade deficit. On the other hand, those that grow slowly and follow policies that are unattractive to investors will tend to experience an outflow of capital and a trade surplus.

▼ There is no reason to expect that bilateral trade between countries will balance.

▼ An unanticipated shift to a more restrictive monetary policy will raise the real interest rate, reduce the rate of inflation, and, at least temporarily, reduce aggregate demand and the growth of income. These factors will all cause the nation's currency to appreciate. The effects of a more expansionary monetary

policy will be just the opposite: lower interest rates, an outflow of capital, and a currency depreciation.

▼ An unanticipated shift to a more expansionary fiscal policy will tend to increase real interest rates, lead to an inflow of capital, and an exchange rate appreciation. The effects of a shift to a more restrictive fiscal policy will be just the opposite: lower interest rates, an outflow of capital, and exchange rate depreciation.

▼ There are three major types of exchange-rate regimes: (1) flexible rates; (2) fixed rate, unified currency; and (3) pegged exchange rates. Both flexible rate and fixed rate, unified currency systems work quite well. Pegged rate systems, however, often lead to problems because they require that the nation follow a monetary policy consistent with the maintenance of the pegged rate. Political pressure often makes this difficult to do.

CRITICAL ANALYSIS QUESTIONS

*1. If the dollar depreciates relative to the Japanese yen, how will this affect your ability to purchase a Honda Accord? How will this change influence the quantity of Hondas purchased by Americans? How will it affect the dollar expenditures of Americans on Hondas?

2. How will the purchases of items from foreigners compare with the sales of items to foreigners when the foreign exchange market is in equilibrium? Explain.

3. Will a flexible exchange rate bring the imports of goods and services into balance with the exports of goods and services? Why or why not?

*4. The accompanying chart indicates an actual newspaper quotation of the exchange rate of various currencies. On February 2, did the dollar appreciate or depreciate against the British pound? How did it fare against the Canadian dollar?

	U.S. Dollar Equivalent	
	February 1	**February 2**
British pound	1.755	1.746
Canadian dollar	0.6765	0.6775

*5. Suppose the exchange rate between the United States and Mexico freely fluctuates in the open market. Indicate whether each of the following would

cause the dollar to appreciate or depreciate relative to the peso.

a. An increase in the quantity of drilling equipment purchased in the United States by Pemex, the Mexican oil company, as a result of a Mexican oil discovery

b. An increase in the U.S. purchase of crude oil from Mexico as a result of the development of Mexican oil fields

c. Higher real interest rates in Mexico, inducing U.S. citizens to move their financial investments from U.S. to Mexican banks

d. Lower real interest rates in the United States, inducing Mexican investors to borrow dollars and then exchange them for pesos

e. Inflation in the United States and stable prices in Mexico

f. An increase in the inflation rate from 2 percent to 10 percent in both the United States and Mexico

g. An economic boom in Mexico, inducing Mexicans to buy more U.S.-made automobiles, trucks, electric appliances, and television sets

h. Attractive investment opportunities, inducing U.S. investors to buy stock in Mexican firms

6. Explain why the current-account balance and capital-account balance must sum to zero under a pure flexible rate system.

7. "A nation cannot continue to run a deficit on its current account. A healthy, growing economy will not persistently expand its indebtedness to foreigners. Eventually, the trade deficits will lead to national bankruptcy." Evaluate this view.

*8. In recent years, a substantial share of the domestic capital formation in the United States has been financed by foreign investors. Is this dependence on foreign capital dangerous? What would happen if the inflow of foreign capital came to a halt?

*9. Suppose that the United States was running a current-account deficit. How would each of the following changes influence the size of the current-account deficit?
   a. A recession in the United States
   b. A decline in the attractiveness of investment opportunities in the United States
   c. An improvement in investment opportunities abroad

10. Several politicians have suggested that the federal government should run a sizable budget surplus during the next decade in order to "save social security." If the federal government does run a large surplus, what is the expected impact on interest rates, the inflow of capital, the current-account deficit, and the foreign exchange value of the dollar? Explain the reasoning underlying your answer.

*11. If foreigners have confidence in the U.S. economy and therefore move to expand their investments in the United States, how will the U.S. current-account balance be affected? How will the exchange-rate value of the dollar be affected?

12. Is a trade surplus indicative of a strong, healthy economy? Why or why not?

13. Rapidly growing strong economies often experience trade deficits, while economies with sluggish growth often have trade surpluses. Can you explain this puzzle?

*14. "Changes in exchange rates will automatically direct a country to a current-account balance under a flexible exchange-rate system." Is this statement true or false?

*15. In recent years, many American political figures have been highly critical of the fact that U.S. imports from Japan have consistently exceeded U.S. exports to Japan.
   a. Under a flexible exchange-rate system, is there any reason to expect that the imports from a given country will tend to equal the exports to that country?
   b. Can you think of any reason why the United States might persistently run a trade deficit with a country such as Japan?
   c. If Japan purchased substantially more American goods, would this significantly reduce the current-account deficit the United States has been running? Why or why not?

*Asterisk denotes questions for which answers are given in Appendix B.

PART 5

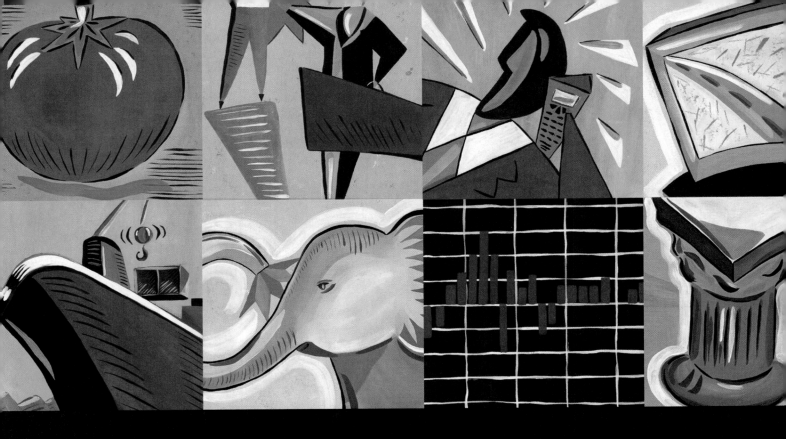

"Microeconomics focuses on the

choices of consumers, the operation

of firms, and the earnings of

resource suppliers"

CORE MICROECONOMICS

Consumers are the ultimate judge of both products and business firms. Their choices will determine which will survive and which will fail. The competitive process is highly dynamic. Numerous businesses come and go. Each year, newly incorporated businesses account for approximately 10 percent of the total. Approximately 1 percent of businesses file for bankruptcy during a typical year. In addition, many others close their doors or sell their assets to other, more successful (or more optimistic) operators.

HOW LARGE ARE BUSINESS PROFITS?

Public opinion surveys indicate that people believe that the profits of business firms average approximately 25 cents out of every dollar of sales. The actual figure is much less. During recent decades, the accounting profit of manufacturing firms has averaged approximately 5 cents per dollar of sales and 14 cents per dollar of stockholder equity invested. The profit rates of nonmanufacturing firms are generally lower than the rates shown here. The Core Microeconomics section takes a closer look at the decision making of consumers, competition among business firms, and the choices of resource suppliers and employers.

CHAPTER 19

Demand and Consumer Choice

Chapter Focus

■ What are the fundamental postulates underlying consumer choice?

■ How does the law of diminishing marginal utility help explain the law of demand?

■ How do the demand curves of individuals translate into a market demand curve?

■ What determines consumer preferences for a specific item? How important are product quality, advertising, time, and risk?

■ What is demand elasticity? What factors determine it and how is it used to analyze consumer spending and a firm's revenue?

[1]David R. Henderson, "Demand," in *The Concise Encyclopedia of Economics*, ed. David R. Henderson www.econlib.org/library/CEE.html.

[2]Quoted in Michael Jackman, ed., *Macmillan Book of Business and Economic Quotations* (New York: Macmillan, 1984), p. 150.

he statement of David Henderson highlights the central position of the law of demand in economics. As Publilius Syrus noted more than 2,000 years ago, demand reflects the willingness of individuals to pay for what is offered in the market. In this section, we begin our examination of microeconomic markets for specific products with an analysis of the demand side of markets. In essence we will be going "behind" the market demand curve to see how it is made up of individual consumer demands, and what factors determine the choices of individual consumers.[3] ■

THE FUNDAMENTALS OF CONSUMER CHOICE

Each of us must decide how to allocate our limited income among the many possible things we could purchase. The prices of goods, *relative to each other*, are very important determining factors. If your favorite cereal doubled in price, would you switch to a different brand? Would your decision be different if all cereals, not just yours, doubled in price? Your choice *between* brands of cereal will be affected only by the change in relative prices. If all cereal prices rose, you might quit purchasing cereal, but this would not give you a strong reason to switch to a different brand. Relative prices measure opportunity cost. If cereal is $5.00 per box when movie tickets are $10, you must give up two boxes of cereal to purchase a movie ticket.

There have been some substantial changes during the past few decades in the way American consumers allocate their income. For example, as a share of total consumption, spending on food (including beverages and tobacco) fell from 26 percent in 1963 to 15 percent in 1999. Out of each food dollar, spending on food away from home and snacks rose from 34 cents in 1970 to 42 cents in 1999. Between 1950 and 1999, spending on housing, excluding utilities and similar items, slightly more than doubled as a share of total consumption. During the last 15 years, spending on clothing has been relatively stable.

Several fundamental principles of consumer behavior account for these changes, as well as for consumer choice more generally.

1. *Limited income necessitates choice.*
Because of scarcity we all have limited incomes. The limited nature of our income requires us to make choices about which goods we will and will not purchase. When more of one good or service is purchased, we must purchase less of some other goods if we are to stay within our budget. This is the meaning of the "cost" of purchasing something.

2. *Consumers make decisions purposefully.*
The goals that underpin consumer choice can usually be met in alternative ways. If two products have an equal cost, a consumer would choose to purchase the one expected to have the higher benefit. On the other hand, if two products yield equal benefits, the consumer would choose to purchase the cheaper one. Fundamentally, we assume that consumers are rational—they are able to weigh the costs and benefits of alternative choices.

3. *One good can be substituted for another.*
Consumers can achieve *utility*—that is, satisfaction—from many different alternatives. Either a hamburger or a taco might satisfy your hunger, while going either to a movie or to a football game might satisfy your desire for entertainment. With $600, you might either buy a new TV set or take a short vacation. No single good is so precious that some of it will not be given up in exchange for a large enough quantity of other goods. There are many competing wants, and each can be satisfied in alternative ways.

---

[3]You may want to review the section on demand in Chapter 3 before proceeding with this chapter.

We have been discussing "wants," but how about our "need" for basic commodities such as water or energy? The need of a person for an item is closely related to its cost—what must be given up to obtain the item. Do southern California residents need water from the north? More expensive water leads individual residents to plant cactus instead of grass, pay a plumber to fix leaking faucets, and use flow constrictors on shower heads. Each of these reduces the need for water, illustrating that need depends on cost to the user. People living in Montana, where household electricity in recent years cost nearly twice as much as in nearby Washington, used about half as much electricity per household. Other factors besides the price of electricity enter their decisions, but Montanans clearly were able to reduce their "need" for electricity by substituting gas, fuel oil, insulation, and wool sweaters for the relatively more expensive electricity. Each of the things we purchase has substitutes.

4. Consumers must make decisions without perfect information, but knowledge and past experience will help.

In Chapter 1 we noted that information is costly to acquire. Asking family and friends, searching through magazines such as *Consumer Reports*, and contacting the local Better Business Bureau are all ways of gathering information about products and potential sellers. The likelihood that a consumer will spend the necessary time, effort, and money to gather this information is directly related to its value to the consumer. Many people will collect this information when deciding on the purchase of a new automobile, but very few would do the same for a purchase of a pencil or a roll of paper towels. When even a bad decision will not be very costly, consumers will rationally remain less informed.

No human being has perfect foresight. Consumers will not always correctly anticipate the consequences of their choices. They will, however, have a good chance of doing so in areas of common knowledge and experience. You have a pretty good idea of what to expect when you buy a cup of coffee, five gallons of gasoline, or a box of your favorite cereal. Why? Because you have learned from experience—your own and that of others. Your expectations may not always be fulfilled precisely (for example, the coffee may be stronger than expected or the gasoline may make your car's engine knock), but even then, you will gain valuable information that will help you project the outcome of future choices more accurately. Being a good consumer includes learning through previous choices.

5. The law of diminishing marginal utility applies: As the rate of consumption increases, the marginal utility derived from consuming additional units of a good will decline.

Law of diminishing marginal utility
The basic economic principle that, as the consumption of a commodity increases, the marginal utility derived from consuming more of the commodity (per unit of time) will eventually decline.

Marginal utility
The additional utility received from the consumption of an additional unit of a good.

Utility is a term economists use to describe the subjective personal benefits that result from an action. The **law of diminishing marginal utility** states that the **marginal** (or additional) **utility** derived from consuming successive units of a product will eventually decline as the rate of consumption increases. For example, the law says that even though you might like ice cream, your marginal satisfaction from additional ice cream will eventually decline. Ice cream at lunchtime might be great. An additional helping for dinner might also be good. However, after you have had it for lunch and dinner, another serving as a midnight snack will be less attractive. When the law of diminishing marginal utility sets in, the additional utility derived from still more units of ice cream declines.

The law of diminishing marginal utility explains why, even if you really like a certain product, you will not spend your entire budget on it. Consumers would be unlikely to stop purchasing a good if an additional unit yielded more satisfaction than the previous one. Failure to purchase an additional unit indicates that the buyer has reached the point where additional units provide less and less marginal utility. Utility-seeking buyers will not operate in the range of increasing marginal utility, but in the range where their marginal utility is declining.

Marginal Utility, Marginal Benefit, and the Demand Curve

The law of diminishing marginal utility helps us to understand the law of demand and the shape of the demand curve. The height of an individual's demand curve at any specific unit is equal to the maximum price the consumer would be willing to pay for that unit—

its **marginal benefit** to the consumer—given the number of units already purchased. Although marginal benefit is measured in dollars, it reflects the opportunity cost of the unit, in terms of other goods forgone. If a consumer is willing to pay, at most, $5 for an additional unit of the product, this indicates a willingness to give up, at most, $5 worth of other goods. *Because a consumer's willingness to pay for a unit of a good is directly related to the utility derived from consuming the unit, the law of diminishing marginal utility implies that a consumer's marginal benefit, and thus the height of the demand curve, falls with the rate of consumption.*

Exhibit 1 shows this relationship for a hypothetical consumer Jones, relative to her weekly consumption of frozen pizza. The law of diminishing marginal utility applies—each additional pizza consumed per week will generate less marginal utility for Jones than the previous pizza. For this reason, Jones's maximum willingness to pay—her marginal benefit—will fall as the quantity consumed increases. In addition, the steepness of Jones's demand curve, or its responsiveness to a change in price—its elasticity—is a reflection of how rapidly marginal utility diminishes with additional consumption. An individual's demand curve for a good whose marginal value declines more rapidly will be steeper.

Given knowledge about a consumer's maximum willingness to pay for additional units of a good, we are now in a position to discuss the choice of how many units a consumer will choose to purchase. *At any given price, consumers will purchase all units of a good for which their maximum willingness to pay—their marginal benefit—is greater than the price.* They will stop at the point where the next unit's marginal benefit would be less than the price. Although there are some problems with divisibility (it is hard to purchase half a car), we can generally say that a consumer will purchase all units of a good up to the point where the marginal benefit equals the price of the good ($MB = P$).

Returning to Exhibit 1, if the price of frozen pizza were $2.50, Jones would purchase three frozen pizzas per week.[4] Remember from Chapter 3 that consumer surplus is defined as the difference between the maximum price the consumer would be willing to pay and

Marginal benefit
The maximum price a consumer would be willing to pay for an additional unit. It is the dollar value of the consumer's marginal utility from the additional unit, and thus falls as consumption increases.

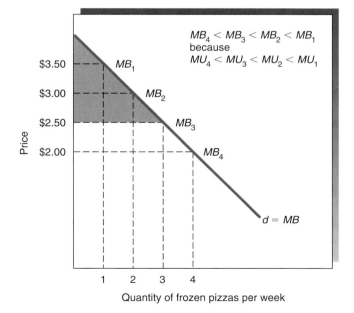

EXHIBIT 1
Diminishing Marginal Utility and the Individual's Demand Curve

An individual's demand curve, Jones's demand for frozen personal pizzas in this case, reflects the law of diminishing marginal utility. Because marginal utility (*MU*) falls with increased consumption, so does the consumer's maximum willingness to pay—marginal benefit (*MB*). A consumer will purchase until *MB* = *Price*, so at $2.50 Jones would purchase 3 pizzas and receive a consumer surplus shown by the shaded triangle.

---

[4]Jones would certainly purchase the second unit because $MB > P$. For the third unit, $MB = P$, so Jones would be indifferent between buying the unit and not purchasing it. For a good that is easily divisible, say, pounds of roast beef, the consumer would continue purchasing up to 2.9999 pounds. Thus, economists are comfortable with simply concluding that the consumer will purchase this final unit, implying that Jones will purchase three frozen pizzas.

the price actually paid. Jones's maximum willingness to pay for the first unit is $3.50, which, at a price of $2.50, generates $1.00 of consumer surplus for Jones. When a consumer has purchased all units to the point where $MB = P$, total consumer surplus is the total triangular area under the demand curve, but above the price. Total consumer surplus for Jones is shown as the shaded area in Exhibit 1.

Within this framework, how would a consumer respond to a decline in the price of a good? Answer: Purchases will be increased to the point where marginal benefit diminishes to the level of the new lower price. If marginal utility declines rapidly with consumption, the consumer will expand purchases only slightly. If marginal utility declines less rapidly, it will take a larger expansion in purchases to reach this point. If the price were to rise, the consumer would cut back purchases, eliminating those for which marginal benefit was now less than the price. It is through this linkage of marginal benefit with maximum willingness to pay that the law of diminishing marginal utility underlies an individual demand curve.

Consumer Equilibrium with Many Goods

The last time you were at the mall, you probably saw something, perhaps a nice billfold, that you liked. After all, there are many things we would like—many different alternatives that would give us utility. Next, you looked at the price tag: "$50, wow! That's too much." What you were really saying was "I like the billfold, but not as much as the $50 worth of other goods that I would have to give up." Consumer choice is a constant comparison of value relative to price. Consider another example—you may prefer steak to less costly hamburger. Nonetheless, your happiness may be better served by buying the hamburger, and saving the extra money to spend on something else.

The idea that choices across goods are based upon a relative comparison of marginal utility (MU) to price (P) can be expressed more precisely. If a consumer is spending a limited income across products so as to maximize total utility, the following relationship will be present:

$$\frac{MU_A}{P_A} = \frac{MU_B}{P_B} = \ldots = \frac{MU_n}{P_n}$$

Using experimental methods, researchers have found that the economic fundamentals of consumer choice theory can even explain the consumption choices of rats and other animals. Other economists have found that these theories can also be used to explain such things as a family's choice concerning how many children to have and a criminal's decision regarding the commission of crimes.

Here *MU* represents the marginal utility derived from the last unit of a product, and *P* represents the price of the good. The subscripts $_{A}$, $_{B}$, . . . , $_{n}$ indicate the different products available to the consumer. ***In the continuous case, this expression implies that the consumer will maximize his or her satisfaction (or total utility) by ensuring that the last dollar spent on each commodity yields an equal degree of marginal utility. Alternatively stated, the last unit of each commodity purchased should provide the same marginal utility per dollar spent on it.*** Thus, if the price of a gallon of ice cream is twice as high as the price of a liter of Coke, a consumer will purchase these items to the point where the marginal utility of the last gallon of ice cream is twice as high as the marginal utility of the last liter of Coke.

Perhaps the best way to grasp this point is to think about what happens when your ratios of marginal utility to price are not equal for two goods. Suppose that you are at a local restaurant eating buffalo chicken wings and drinking Coke. For simplicity, assume that a large Coke and an order of wings each costs $2. With your $10 budget, you decide to purchase four orders of wings, and one large Coke. When you finish your Coke, there are still lots of wings left. You have already eaten so many wings that those remaining do not look as attractive. You could get more utility with fewer wings and another Coke, but it is too late. You have not spent your $10 in a way that gets the most for your money. Instead of satisfying the above condition, you find that the marginal utility of wings is lower than the marginal utility of a Coke, and because they both have the same price ($2), this implies

$$\frac{MU_{wings}}{P_{wings}} < \frac{MU_{Coke}}{P_{Coke}}$$

If you had purchased fewer wings and more Coke, your total utility would be higher. Spending more on Coke would decrease its marginal utility, lowering the value of the right side of the equation. Simultaneously, spending less on wings would raise the marginal utility of wings, increasing the value of the left side of the equation. You will maximize your utility—and get the most "bang for the buck" from your budget—when you make these values (the ratios) equal.

The equation can also be used to derive the law of demand. Beginning from a situation where the two sides were equal, suppose the price of wings increased. It would lower the value of *MU/P* for wings below the *MU/P* for Coke. In response you would reallocate your budget, purchasing fewer of the more costly wings and more Coke. Thus we have the law of demand—as the price of wings rises you will purchase less. When people try to spend their money in a way that gives them the greatest amount of satisfaction, the consumer decision-making theory outlined here is difficult to question. In the next section, we take the theory a little farther.

Price Changes and Consumer Choice

The demand curve or schedule shows the amount of a product that consumers would be willing to purchase at alternative prices during a specific time period. The law of demand states that the amount of a product purchased is inversely related to its price. We have seen how the law of demand can be derived from fundamental principles of consumer behavior. Now, we go farther and distinguish two different phenomena underlying a consumer's response to a price change. First, as the price of a product declines, the lower opportunity cost will induce consumers to buy more of it—even if they have to give up other products. Economists refer to this tendency to substitute a product that has become cheaper for goods that are now relatively more expensive as the **substitution effect** of a price change.

Second, with a fixed money income, a reduction in the price of a product will increase a consumer's real income—the amount of goods and services consumers are able to purchase with their fixed amount of money income. A rent or mortgage payment decline by $100 per month would allow you to buy more of numerous other goods. This increase in

Substitution effect
That part of an increase (decrease) in amount consumed that is the result of a good being cheaper (more expensive) in relation to other goods because of a reduction (increase) in price.

Income effect
That part of an increase (decrease) in amount consumed that is the result of the consumer's real income (the consumption possibilities available to the consumer) being expanded (contracted) by a reduction (rise) in the price of a good.

your real income has the same effect as if the rent had remained the same, but your income had risen by $100 per month. Because of this equivalence, this second way in which a price change affects consumption is referred to as the **income effect**. Typically, consumers will respond by purchasing more of the cheaper product and other products as well, because they can now better afford to do so. (Both the income and substitution effects are derived graphically in the addendum to this chapter, titled "Consumer Choice and Indifference Curves.") The substitution and income effects will generally work in the same direction, causing consumers to purchase more as the price falls and less as the price rises.[5]

Time Cost and Consumer Choice

You may have heard the saying that "time is money." It is certainly true that time has value, and this value can sometimes be measured in dollars. For example we might ask how much a person would be willing to pay to save an hour (perhaps for a nonstop airline flight that takes one hour less travel time, or for a house with a shorter commute to work). Another measure of the value people place on their time is their wage rate, the price at which they are selling an hour of their time.

The monetary price of a good is not always a complete measure of its cost to the consumer. Consumption of most goods requires time as well as money; and time, like money, is scarce to the consumer. So a lower time cost, like a lower money price, will make a product more attractive. For example, patients in a dentist's office would prefer a shorter wait before receiving care. One study showed that dental patients are willing to pay more than $5 per minute saved, to shorten their times in the waiting room.[6] The rise in expenditures on fast foods, mentioned above, is another illustration. Indeed, commodities such as automatic dishwashers, prepared foods, air travel, and taxi service are demanded mainly for the time savings they offer. People are often willing to pay relatively high money prices for such goods.

Time costs, unlike money prices for goods, differ among individuals. They are higher for persons with higher wage rates, for example. Other things being equal, high-wage consumers choose fewer time-intensive (and more time-saving) commodities than persons with a lower time cost. High-wage consumers are overrepresented among air and taxi-cab passengers but underrepresented among television watchers, chess players, and long-distance bus travelers. Can you explain why? You can, if you understand how both money and time costs influence the choices of consumers.

Failure to account for time costs can lead to bad decisions. For example, which is cheaper for consumers: (a) waiting in line three hours to purchase a $25 concert ticket or (b) buying the same ticket for $40 without standing in line? A consumer whose time is worth more than $5 per hour will find that $40 without the wait in line is less costly. Time costs matter. For example, when government-imposed price ceilings (discussed in Chapter 4) create shortages, rationing by waiting in line is frequently used. In many cases, the benefit of the lower price to consumers will be largely, if not entirely, offset by their increased time cost.

MARKET DEMAND REFLECTS THE DEMAND OF INDIVIDUAL CONSUMERS

The market demand schedule is the relationship between the market price of a good and the amount demanded by all the individuals in the market area. Because individual consumers purchase less at higher prices, the amount demanded in a market area as a total is also inversely related to price.

---

[5]The substitution effect will always work in this direction. The income effect, however, may work in the reverse direction for some types of goods known as inferior goods. These will be addressed later in this chapter.

[6]Rexford E. Santerre and Stephen P. Neun, *Health Economics: Theories, Insights and Industry Studies* (Orlando: Harcourt, 2000), p. 113.

EXHIBIT 2
Individual and Market Demand Curves

The market demand curve is merely the horizontal sum of the individual demand curves. It will slope downward to the right just as the individual demand curves do.

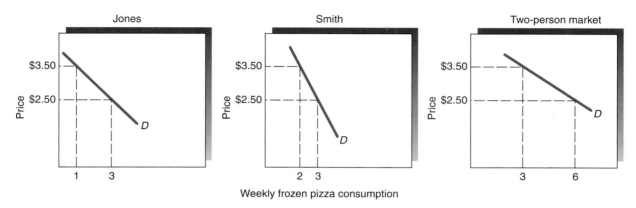

Weekly frozen pizza consumption

Exhibit 2 illustrates the relationship between individual demand and market demand for a hypothetical two-person market. The individual demand curves for both Jones and Smith are shown. Jones and Smith each consume three frozen pizzas per week at a price of $2.50. The amount demanded in the two-person market is six pizzas. If the price rises to $3.50 per pizza, the amount demanded in the market will fall to three pizzas, one demanded by Jones and two by Smith. ***The market demand is simply the horizontal sum of the individual demand curves.***

Market demand reflects individual demand. Individuals buy less as price increases. Therefore, the total amount demanded in the market declines as price increases. That is not difficult to understand, when we think about it. Comparing market prices of different goods, however, can introduce a puzzle.

Total Versus Marginal Value

The classical economists, including Adam Smith, were puzzled that water, which is necessary for life, sells so cheaply, while diamonds have a far greater price. Does this mean that people value diamonds more than water? This same confusion can be found in everyday life. For example, a spouse or good friend might inquire, "You are going out to play golf? Is golf more important to you than I am?"

A century after Smith's time, economists solved this puzzle when they discovered the importance of the marginal analysis we have been discussing. The total value of a good includes consumer surplus for all units consumed; thus, total value can be quite large even though the price (which reflects the marginal value) is quite low. These factors provide the explanation for why market price has so little to do with the total contribution that a good makes to the welfare of users.

It is possible for something to have a large total value, but a very small marginal value, and also for something with high marginal value to have a low total value. Spending time with a spouse or friend can be more valuable in total than playing golf, but it can simultaneously be true that one *additional* hour spent with that person is less valuable than an *additional* hour of golf.

The willingness to pay for additional units depends on one's valuation of the marginal unit, not on the value of all units taken together. While, in total, water is far more valuable to

Nothing is more useful than water; but it will purchase scarce anything. . . . A diamond, on the contrary, has scarce any value in use; but a very great quantity of other goods may frequently be had in exchange for it.

—Adam Smith[7]

[7]Adam Smith, *An Inquiry into the Nature and Causes of the Wealth of Nations*, 1776, ed. Edwin Cannan (Chicago: University of Chicago Press, 1976), p. 33.

you than diamonds, you may well value an additional cup of diamonds more than an additional cup of water. If you had no diamonds and no water, you would certainly value the first cup of water more than the first cup of diamonds. But this is not where you are. You consume hundreds of gallons of water per year, but you may only have one or two diamonds.

Items available at a low cost will be consumed until their marginal value is low enough to match the low cost. Because the supply of water is large, water has a low price. At this low price people use water for frequent showers, fish tanks and many other low-valued uses. If diamonds were as plentiful as water, and sold for only pennies per pound, we might use them for gravel in the bottom of our fish tanks. On the other hand, if water became significantly less abundant, its price would be very high and we might quit taking showers because each costs $1,000 worth of water.

DETERMINANTS OF SPECIFIC PREFERENCES: WHY CONSUMERS BUY WHAT THEY BUY

Did you ever wonder why a friend spent hard-earned money on something that you would not want even if it were free? People have different tastes and preferences, but what determines these preferences? Economists have not been able to say very much on this topic. Without a theory of preferences, the best strategy has generally been to take preferences as given, using price and other demand-related factors to explain and predict human behavior. Still, several observations about what influences consumer preferences have been made:

1. *The determining factors in consumer preferences are frequently complex.*
People looking for a house want far more than just a shelter: They want an attractive setting, a convenient location, higher-quality public services, and a great many other things. Moreover, each person may evaluate the same housing attribute differently. For example, living near a school may be a high priority for a family with children but a nuisance to a retired couple.

2. *Consumer preferences are shaped by attitudes toward time and risk.*
A consumer would nearly always prefer to receive a good now rather than later. The degree of this difference, however, differs across consumers. Those with a higher rate of time preference will be willing to pay extra (perhaps by taking out a loan and paying interest) to make goods available earlier, while others will save and let their money grow in the bank with interest until they can make their desired purchase. This interest is the reward earned for delaying current consumption.

In addition to time preference, consumers also differ in the degree of risk they are willing to take (or more precisely how much they are willing to pay to reduce risk). Would you prefer to pay $20 more for a brand name product, or take a gamble on an unknown product that costs less? A risk taker may choose the cheaper product. Buying insurance is another way to reduce risk. Some consumers will decide to purchase flood insurance for their homes, or dental insurance, while others will not. They will prefer to save the money from the premiums and pay out-of-pocket for any expenses incurred.

With regard to risk preference, a person may be either *risk loving*, *risk neutral*, or *risk averse*. Suppose you could have either $50 cash or a chance to flip a fair coin where heads wins $100 and tails wins nothing. Which would you choose—the certain $50 or the 50 percent chance at winning $100? A risk-loving person would prefer to take the gamble at winning $100, a risk-averse person would take the cash, and a risk-neutral person would be indifferent between the two alternatives.

3. *Advertising influences consumer choice and preferences.*
Advertisers would not spend more than $100 billion in the United States each year if they did not get results. But exactly how does advertising affect consumers? Does it simply

provide valuable information about product quality, price, and availability? Or does it use repetition and misleading information to manipulate consumers? Economists are not of one opinion. Let us take a closer look at this important issue.

Advertising—Is It Useful to Consumers?

Advertising revenues reduce the purchase price of newspapers and magazines, and make broadcast television free to viewers. But since the consumers of the advertised products indirectly pay for these benefits, advertising cannot be defended solely on the basis of its sponsorship role.

Advertising does convey information about product price, quality, and availability. New firms or those with new products, new hours, new locations, or new services can use advertising to keep consumers informed, thus facilitating more efficient trading. After all, people who do not know the advantages of the newly available product or service, and how and where to get it, are not likely to become customers.

Is advertising wasteful?

Some repetitious commercials offer little or no new information, but rather seek to take customers from competitors or promote their brand name. A multimillion-dollar media campaign by a soft drink or automobile manufacturer designed to capture a larger market share may be offset by a similar campaign waged by a competitor. The consumers of these products end up paying the costs of these battles for their attention and their dollars. Consumers, though, are under no obligation to purchase advertised products. If advertising results in higher prices with no compensating benefits, consumers can turn to cheaper, unadvertised products. Many, however, buy the advertised brand names. How can brand names, especially those created by competing advertising campaigns, possibly benefit consumers?

A brand name in which people have confidence, even one established by advertising, has a function beyond gaining the attention of consumers. It is an asset at risk for the seller. People value buying from sellers in whom they have confidence, and will pay a premium to do so. That premium makes a brand name valuable. If something happens to damage the reputation of a brand name, the willingness of consumers to purchase the product falls. In a very real sense, the brand name is hostage to consumer satisfaction.

When brand names are not allowed, as in the case of alcoholic beverages during Prohibition, consumers often suffer. For example, with no brand name reputations to protect, anonymous moonshiners sometimes were careless and allowed dangerous impurities into the brew. Some consumers were blinded, and others died. Today the situation is different. Those who buy Johnnie Walker scotch know that the distiller has an enormous sum of money tied up in the brand—about $3 billion by one estimate.[8] The Guinness Corporation, owner of the brand, would spend a large amount of money to avoid even one death from an impure batch. And this brand's value is dwarfed by many others. The estimated value of the brand name for Microsoft is more than $56 billion, and for Coca-Cola, more than $83 billion. Alternative brands of software and soft drinks compete with these two giants, and do far less advertising. Is a brand name, promoted by costly advertising, worthwhile to the customer? In a market, each buyer decides.

Is advertising misleading and manipulative?

Unfair and deceptive advertising—including false promises, whether spoken privately by a seller or packaged by an advertising agency—is illegal; and a publicly advertised false claim is easier to prosecute than the same words spoken in private.

What about ads that are not fraudulent, but simply attempt to manipulate, or shape the preferences of people? In evaluating the manipulative effect of advertising, two things

---

[8]*Financial World* magazine estimated the Johnnie Walker Red brand name to be worth $3.2 billion (expressed in year 2000 dollars).

should be kept in mind. First, business decision makers are likely to choose the simplest route to economic gain. Generally, it is easier for business firms to cater to the actual desires of consumers than to attempt to reshape their preferences or persuade them to purchase an undesired product. Second, when advertising influences preferences, does it follow that this is bad? College classes in music and art appreciation, for example, may also change preferences for various forms of art and music. Does this make them bad? Economic theory is neutral. It neither condemns nor defends advertising—or college classes—as they try to change the tastes of target audiences.

From market demand and the preferences that lie behind it, we turn now to the measurement of buyer and seller responsiveness to market changes. Intelligent pricing decisions for businesses, universities, and individuals depend on the ability of decision makers to understand this responsiveness and even in some cases to look for measures of buyer responses. The same is true for government decision makers considering tax changes.

ELASTICITY OF DEMAND

Buyers will predictably demand fewer units when the price rises. If a university raises tuition, fewer students will enroll. How many fewer? That depends on a number of factors, including the available substitutes, the cost of change, and the time available to make the change. Entering freshmen may be more responsive to the price change than seniors who would have trouble transferring credits to another school. Students wanting a specific program that is unavailable other places may also be less responsive to the tuition change.

Similarly, when electricity prices rise, as they recently did in California, consumers will buy less. Per-person consumption of electricity there is already the lowest in the nation, but much more conservation is possible. How responsive will consumers be to a specific change in the price of electricity? Again, many factors will enter, from the options available to consumers to the period of time we want to consider. Consumer response to a specific price increase will be greater over a five-year period than a five-week period. Over time, users can gradually replace appliances, lighting fixtures, and water heaters with energy-saving models, learn the habit of switching off unused lights and computers, or switch from electric to gas heat, all in response to the higher electricity price. Estimating short- and long-run responses to a change in price is crucial for government regulators and for electric utility managers.

To learn about and describe buyer responsiveness to price change, economists have developed a concept called *elasticity*. The responsiveness of buyers to a change in price is measured by the **price elasticity of demand**, defined as:

Price elasticity of demand
The percent change in the quantity of a product demanded divided by the percent change in the price causing the change in quantity. Price elasticity of demand indicates the degree of consumer response to variation in price.

$$\text{Price elasticity of demand } = \frac{\text{Percentage change in quantity demanded}}{\text{Percentage change in price}} = \frac{\%\Delta Q}{\%\Delta P}$$

This ratio is often called the *elasticity coefficient*. To express it more briefly, we use the notation $\%\Delta Q$ to represent percent change in quantity and $\%\Delta P$ to represent percent change in price. (The Greek letter delta (Δ) means "change in.") The law of demand states that an increase in price lowers quantity purchased, while a decrease in price raises it. Because a change in price causes the quantity demanded to change in the opposite direction, the price elasticity coefficient is always negative, although economists often ignore the sign and simply use the absolute value of the coefficient.

To see how the concept of elasticity works, suppose that the price of the Ford Taurus rose 10 percent, while other prices remained the same. Ford could expect Taurus sales to fall substantially—perhaps 30 percent—as car buyers responded by switching to the many competing cars whose price had not changed. The strong responsiveness of buyers means that the demand for the Taurus is elastic.

Now consider a different situation. Suppose that because of a new tax, the price of not only the Taurus *but all new cars* rises 10 percent. Consumer options in responding to *this* price increase are much more limited. They can't simply switch to a cheaper close substitute, as they could if the price of the Taurus alone rose. They might either simply pay the extra money for a new car or settle for a used car instead. The 10 percent rise in the price of all new cars will lead to a smaller response, perhaps a 5 percent decline in sales of new cars.

To calculate the elasticity coefficient for the Taurus in our example above, we begin with the 30 percent decline in quantity demanded, and divide by the 10 percent rise in the price that caused the decline. Thus, the elasticity of demand for the Taurus would be:

$$\frac{\%\Delta \text{Quantity}}{\%\Delta \text{Price}} = \frac{-30\%}{+10\%} = -3$$

(or 3.0 if we ignore the minus sign), implying that the percentage change in quantity demanded is three times the percentage change in price.

To calculate the demand elasticity for *all* cars (our second example), we see that the percentage change in quantity, 5 percent, divided by the percentage change in price, 10 percent, gives us $-\frac{1}{2}$, or -0.5. The price elasticity of demand for all cars implies that the percentage change in quantity is half the percentage change in price, using our hypothetical numbers.

To calculate elasticity, we usually begin with the quantities purchased at different prices and first compute the percentage changes. Suppose we begin with a price change from P_0 to P_1, which causes a change in quantity demanded, from Q_0 to Q_1. The change in quantity demanded is $Q_0 - Q_1$. To calculate the percentage change in quantity we divide the actual change by the midpoint (or average) of the two quantities.[9] Although it is often easy to find the midpoint without a formula (halfway between \$4 and \$6 is \$5), it can also be found as $(Q_0 + Q_1)/2$. Finally, because 0.05 is simply 5 percent, we multiply by 100. Thus, we may express the percentage change in quantity demanded as:

$$\frac{Q_0 - Q_1}{(Q_0 + Q_1)/2} \times 100$$

Similarly, when the change in price is $P_0 - P_1$, the *percentage* change in price is

$$\frac{P_0 - P_1}{(P_0 + P_1)/2} \times 100$$

Dividing the resulting percentage change in quantity by the percentage change in price gives the elasticity.

Using these expressions for the percentage changes suggests a more direct method of computing elasticity from the numbers. Dividing the percentage change in quantity by the percentage change in price and simplifying gives

$$\frac{(Q_0 - Q_1)/(Q_0 + Q_1)}{(P_0 - P_1)/(P_0 + P_1)}$$

(Because each term is multiplied by 100 and the denominator of each term contains a 2, these factors cancel out of the final expression.)

A numerical example may help to illustrate. Suppose that Trina's Cakes can sell 50 specialty cakes per week at \$7 each, or 70 of the cakes at \$6 each. The percentage difference in quantity is the difference in the quantity ($50 - 70 = -20$), divided by the midpoint (60), times 100. The result is a -33.33 percent change in quantity ($-20 \div 60 \times 100 = -33.33$). The percentage change in price is the difference in price (\$7 $-$ \$6 $=$ \$1) divided by the midpoint price (\$6.50) times 100, or a 15.38 percent change in price ($1 \div 6.5 \times 100 = 15.38$).

---

[9]This formula uses the average of the starting point and the ending point of the change so that it will give the same result whether we start from the lower or the higher price. This arc elasticity formula is not the only way to calculate elasticity, but it is the most frequently used.

Dividing the percentage change in quantity by the percentage change in price ($-33.33 \div 15.38$) gives an elasticity coefficient of -2.17. Alternatively, we could have expressed this directly as:

$$\frac{[(50 - 70)/(50 + 70)]}{[(7 - 6)/(7 + 6)]} = \frac{-20/120}{1/13} = \frac{-1/6}{1/13} = \frac{-13}{6} = -2.17$$

The same result is obtained either way. The elasticity of -2.17 indicates that the percentage change in quantity is just over twice the percentage change in price.

The elasticity coefficient lets us make a precise distinction between elastic and inelastic. When the elasticity coefficient is greater than 1 (ignoring the sign), as it was for the demand for Trina's Cakes, demand is elastic. When it is less than 1, demand is inelastic. Demand is said to be of *unitary elasticity* if the price elasticity is exactly 1.

Graphic Representation of Price Elasticity of Demand

Exhibit 3 presents demand curves of varying elasticity. A demand curve that is completely vertical is termed *perfectly inelastic*. In the real world, such a demand is nonexistent. The substitutes for a good become more attractive as the price of that good rises, and since the income effect is also present, we should expect that a higher price will always reduce

EXHIBIT 3
Elasticity of Demand

a) Perfectly inelastic: Despite an increase in price, consumers still purchase the same amount. In fact, the substitution and income effects prevent this from happening in the real world.
b) Relatively inelastic: A percent increase in price results in a smaller percent reduction in sales. The demand for cigarettes has been estimated to be highly inelastic.
c) Unitary elastic: The percent change in quantity demanded is equal to the percent change in price. A curve of decreasing slope results. Sales revenue (price times quantity sold) is constant.
d) Relatively elastic: A percentage increase in price leads to a larger percent reduction in purchases. When good substitutes are available for a product (as in the case of apples), the amount purchased will be highly sensitive to a change in price.
e) Perfectly elastic: Consumers will buy all of Farmer Jones's wheat at the market price, but none will be sold above the market price.

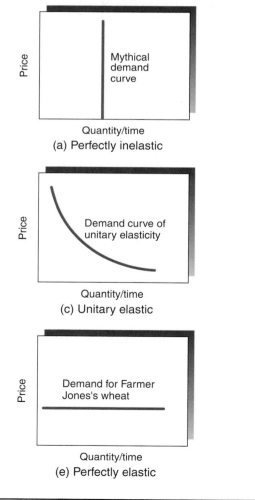

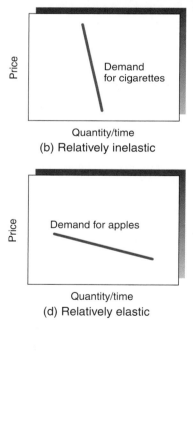

quantity demanded, other things remaining the same. Still, the (mythical) perfectly inelastic demand curve is shown in part a of Exhibit 3.

The more inelastic the demand, the steeper the demand curve *over any specific price range*. Inspection of the demand for cigarettes (part b of Exhibit 3), which is highly inelastic, and the demand for apples (part d), which is relatively elastic, indicates this. When demand elasticity is unitary, as part c illustrates, a demand curve that is convex to the origin will result. When a demand curve is completely horizontal, an economist would say that it is *perfectly elastic*. Demand for the wheat marketed by a single wheat farmer, for example, would approximate perfect elasticity (part e).

Because elasticity is a relative concept, the elasticity of a straight line demand curve will differ at each point along the demand curve. As **Exhibit 4** illustrates, the elasticity of a straight line demand curve (one with a constant slope) will range from highly elastic to highly inelastic. Here, when the price rises from $10 to $11, sales decline from 20 to 10. According to the formula, the price elasticity of demand is −7.0. Demand is very elastic in this region. In contrast, demand is quite inelastic in the $1 to $2 price range. As the price increases from $1 to $2, the amount demanded declines from 110 to 100. The 10-unit change in quantity is the same, but it is a smaller *percentage* change. And the $1 change in price is the same, but it is now a larger *percentage* change. The elasticity of demand in this range is only −0.14; demand here is highly inelastic.

It is clear now that elasticity is more than just the slope of the demand curve. This is important because unlike the slope, elasticities are independent of the units of measure. The elasticity is the same whether we talk about dollars per gallon or cents per liter, even though the slope changes. Elasticity is the appropriate measure, because people do not care what units of measurement are used; their response depends on the actual terms of exchange.

How large is the price elasticity of demand for various goods? What determines those elasticities? The next section reports some estimates and steps back to explain them.

Price Elasticities and Their Determinants

Economists have estimated the price elasticity of demand for many products. As **Exhibit 5** illustrates, the elasticity of demand varies substantially among products. The demand is highly inelastic for several products—salt, toothpicks, matches, light bulbs, and newspapers,

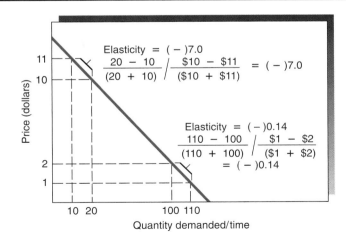

EXHIBIT 4
Slope of Demand Curve Versus Price Elasticity

With this straight line (constant slope) demand curve, demand is more elastic in the high price range. The formula for arc elasticity shows that, when price rises from $1 to $2 and quantity falls from 110 to 100, demand is inelastic. A price rise of the same magnitude (but of a smaller percentage), from $10 to $11, leads to a decline in quantity of the same size (but of a larger percentage), so that elasticity is much greater. (Price elasticities are negative, but economists often ignore the sign and look only at the absolute value.)

EXHIBIT 5
Estimated Price Elasticity of Demand for Selected Products

INELASTIC		APPROXIMATELY UNITARY ELASTICITY	
Salt	– 0.1	Movies	– 0.9
Matches	– 0.1	Housing, owner occupied, long run	– 1.2
Toothpicks	– 0.1		
Airline travel, short run	– 0.1	Shellfish, consumed at home	– 0.9
Gasoline, short run	– 0.2		
Gasoline, long run	– 0.7	Oysters, consumed at home	– 1.1
Residential natural gas, short run	– 0.1	Private education	– 1.1
Residential natural gas, long run	– 0.5	Tires, short run	– 0.9
		Tires, long run	– 1.2
Coffee	– 0.25	Radio and television receivers	– 1.2
Fish (cod), consumed at home	– 0.5		
Tobacco products, short run	– 0.45	**ELASTIC**	
Legal services, short run	– 0.4	Restaurant meals	– 2.3
Physician services	– 0.6	Foreign travel, long run	– 4.0
Dental services	– 0.7	Airline travel, long run	– 2.4
Taxi, short run	– 0.6	Fresh green peas	– 2.8
Automobiles, long run	– 0.2	Automobiles, short run	– 1.2–1.5
		Chevrolet automobiles	– 4.0
		Fresh tomatoes	– 4.6

Sources: Hendrick S. Houthakker and Lester D. Taylor, *Consumer Demand in the United States, 1929–1970* (Cambridge: Harvard University Press, 1966, 1970); Douglas R. Bohi, *Analyzing Demand Behavior* (Baltimore: Johns Hopkins University Press, 1981); Hsaing-tai Cheng and Oral Capps Jr., "Demand for Fish," *American Journal of Agricultural Economics,* August 1988; U.S. Department of Agriculture; and Rexford E. Santerre and Stephen P. Neun, *Health Economics: Theories, Insights and Industry Studies* (Orlando: Harcourt, 2000).

for example—in their normal price range. On the other hand, the demand curves for fresh tomatoes, Chevrolet automobiles, and fresh green peas are highly elastic. The primary factors explaining this variation are the availability of good substitutes and to some extent the share of the typical consumer's total budget expended on a product.

Availability of Substitutes
The most important determinant of the price elasticity of demand is the availability of substitutes. When good substitutes for a product are available, a price rise induces many consumers to switch to other products. Demand is elastic. For example, if the price of felt tip pens increased, many consumers would simply switch to pencils, ballpoint pens, or (for children) crayons. If the price of apples increased, consumers might substitute oranges, bananas, peaches, or pears.

When good substitutes are unavailable, the demand for a product tends to be inelastic. Medical services are an example. When we are sick, most of us find witch doctors, faith healers, palm readers, and aspirin to be highly imperfect substitutes for the services of a physician. Not surprisingly, the demand for physician services is inelastic.

The availability of substitutes increases as the product class becomes more specific, thus increasing price elasticity. For example, as Exhibit 5 shows, the price elasticity of Chevrolets, a narrow product class, exceeds that of the broad class of automobiles in general. If the price of Chevrolets alone rises, many substitute cars are available. But if the prices of all automobiles rise together, consumers have fewer good substitutes.

Share of Total Budget Expended on Product
If the expenditures on a product are quite small relative to the consumer's budget, the income effect will be small even if there is a substantial increase in the price of the product. This will make demand less elastic. Compared to one's total budget, expenditures on some

commodities are almost inconsequential. Matches, toothpicks, and salt are good examples. Most consumers spend only $1 or $2 per year on each of these items. A doubling of their price would exert little influence on the family budget. Therefore, even if the price of such a product were to rise sharply, consumers would still not find it in their interest to spend much time and effort looking for substitutes.

Exhibit 6 provides a graphic illustration of both elastic and inelastic demand curves. In part a, the demand curve for ballpoint pens is elastic, because there are good substitutes—for example, pencils and felt tip pens. Therefore, when the price of the pens increases from $1.00 to $1.50, the quantity purchased declines sharply from 100,000 to only 25,000. The calculated price elasticity equals −3.0. The fact that the absolute value of the coefficient is greater than 1 confirms that the demand for ballpoint pens is elastic over the price range illustrated.

Part b of Exhibit 6 illustrates the demand curve for cigarettes. Because most smokers do not find other products to be a good substitute, the demand for cigarettes is highly inelastic. If a unit of six cigarettes is worth a dollar, a substantial (from $1.00 to $1.50) increase in price leads to only a small reduction in quantity demanded. The price elasticity coefficient is −0.26, substantially less in absolute value than 1, confirming that the demand for cigarettes is inelastic. (*Exercise:* Use the price elasticity formula to verify the values of these elasticity coefficients.)

Time and Demand Elasticity

As changing market conditions raise or lower the price of a product, both consumers and producers will respond. However, their response will not be instantaneous, and it is likely to become larger over time. *In general, when the price of a product increases, consumers will reduce their consumption by a larger amount in the long run than in the short run. Thus, the demand for most products will be more elastic in the long run than in the short run. This relationship between the elasticity coefficient and the length of the adjustment period is sometimes referred to as the second law of demand.*

EXHIBIT 6
Inelastic and Elastic Demand

As the price of ballpoint pens (a) rose from $1.00 to $1.50, the quantity purchased plunged from 100,000 to 25,000. The percent reduction in quantity is larger than the percent increase in price. Thus, the demand for the pens is elastic. In contrast, an increase in the price of cigarettes from $1.00 to $1.50 results in only a small reduction in the number purchased (b). Reflecting the inelasticity of demand for cigarettes, the percent reduction in quantity is smaller than the percent increase in price.

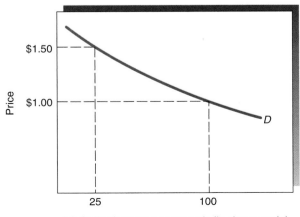

(a) Ballpoint pens per week (in thousands)

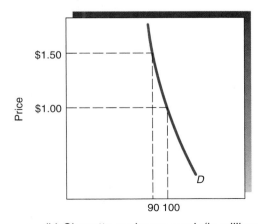

(b) Cigarette packs per week (in millions)

The first law of demand says that buyers will respond predictably to a price change, purchasing more when the price is lower than when the price is higher, if other things remain the same. The second law of demand says that the buyers' response will be greater after they have had time to adjust more fully to a price change.

TOTAL EXPENDITURE, TOTAL REVENUE, AND THE PRICE ELASTICITY OF DEMAND

In this section we examine the relationship between the price elasticity of demand and the total expenditure on an item (or revenue derived from its sale). Demand elasticity can be used to determine changes in total consumer expenditures at three levels: (1) for an individual's total spending on a product using the demand elasticity from an individual's demand curve for the product, (2) for the total combined expenditures of all consumers on a product using the elasticity from the total market demand curve for a product, or (3) for total consumer expenditures on the product of an individual business firm using the demand curve facing that firm.

If the price of a product rises, total consumer expenditures on it can either rise, fall, or stay the same, depending on the elasticity of demand. According to the law of demand, as the price rises the quantity purchased will fall, and as price falls the quantity purchased will rise:

$$\text{Total Expenditures} = \text{Price} \times \text{Quantity}$$
$$? = \uparrow \times \downarrow$$
$$? = \downarrow \times \uparrow$$

Because total expenditures are equal to price times quantity, and because price and quantity move in opposite directions, the net effect on total expenditures depends upon whether the (percent) price change or the (percent) quantity change is greater. When demand is inelastic, the price elasticity coefficient is less than one. This means that the percentage change in price is greater. ***Therefore, when demand is inelastic, a change in price will cause total expenditures to change in the same direction.***

When demand is elastic, the effect of the change in quantity will be greater than the effect of the change in price. ***Therefore, a change in price will cause total expenditures to move in the opposite direction when demand is elastic.***

When demand elasticity is unitary, the change in quantity will be equal in magnitude to the change in price. With regard to their impact on total expenditures, these two effects will exactly offset each other. ***Thus, when price elasticity of demand is equal to one, total expenditures will remain unchanged as price changes.***

The demand curves shown in Exhibit 6 can be used to illustrate the linkage between elasticity of demand and changes in total revenue. In the case of cigarettes (part b), the price elasticity of demand for the price increase from $1.00 to $1.50 is 0.26, indicating that demand is inelastic. This increase in cigarette prices leads to an increase in expenditures on the product from $100 million ($1.00 × 100 million units) to $135 million ($1.50 × 90 million units). If the change had occurred in the opposite direction, with the price falling from $1.50 to $1.00, total expenditures would have declined.

The price elasticity of demand for ballpoint pens for a price increase from $1.00 to $1.50 (part a of Exhibit 6) is 3.0, indicating that demand is elastic. This increase in the price of ballpoint pens leads to a reduction in total consumer expenditures from $100,000 ($1.00 × 100,000 pens) to $37,500 ($1.50 × 25,000 pens). If the change had occurred in the opposite direction, with the price falling from $1.50 to $1.00, total expenditures would have risen.

Exhibit 7 summarizes the relationship between changes in price and total expenditures for products with demands of varying elasticity. The (inelastic) demand for cigarettes

EXHIBIT 7
Demand Elasticity and How Changes in Price Affect Total Consumer Expenditures or a Firm's Total Revenue

PRICE ELASTICITY OF DEMAND	NUMERICAL ELASTICITY COEFFICIENT (IN ABSOLUTE VALUE)	IMPACT OF RAISING PRICE ON TOTAL CONSUMER EXPENDITURES OR A FIRM'S TOTAL REVENUE	IMPACT OF LOWERING PRICE ON TOTAL CONSUMER EXPENDITURES OR A FIRM'S TOTAL REVENUE
Elastic	1 to ∞	decrease	increase
Unitary Elastic	1	unchanged	unchanged
Inelastic	0 to 1	increase	decrease

implies that a price increase will result in higher total consumer expenditures on them. But a price increase for ballpoint pens, with their elastic demand, would lead to lower total expenditures on that item.

This same analysis can be performed using a particular firm's demand curve, rather than the total market demand curve for the product. Here, total consumer expenditures are, from the firm's perspective, the firm's total revenues—the price per unit times the quantity sold. As we discussed earlier in this chapter, the demand curve facing one specific firm in an industry will be substantially more elastic than the demand curve for the entire market. (Remember the demand elasticity comparison between the Ford Taurus and all automobiles.)

Depending on the relationship between price and quantity sold, a firm's total revenue can rise, fall, or stay the same in response to a change in price. Again, the outcome is determined by price elasticity of demand. When demand for the firm's product is inelastic, its total revenues will rise if it increases its price, or fall if it lowers its price. When demand is elastic, however, revenue will fall if price is increased, and will rise if price is reduced. When demand elasticity is unitary, a change in price will leave total revenue unaffected. **Exhibit 8** gives a numerical example to illustrate this point.

Part a of the exhibit shows how a firm's total revenue is calculated from data on price and quantity sold. In addition, the price elasticity has been computed using the formula. These same data are shown graphically along with the firm's demand curve in part b of the exhibit. As the firm lowers its price from $9 to $8 to $7, the firm's revenues expand from $0 to $8 to $14. In this range, the firm's demand curve is elastic, so total revenue is rising as price falls. Intuitively, as the firm lowers its price, it is losing revenue from customers who would have paid more for some units but it is gaining revenue from customers, including new ones, who are buying more at the lower price. When demand is elastic, the expansion in revenue from additional sales is more than enough to offset the reductions in revenue on some units due to the lower price. An example of this is shown by the shaded areas in part b of the exhibit. At a price of $7, the firm sells 2 units. Total revenue is $14, which is shown by the red shaded area. When price is lowered to $6, sales increase to 3 units, and total revenue is $18, shown by the shorter rectangle that includes the blue shaded area. The small part of the red shaded area above the blue area is lost revenue on existing sales, while the small part of the blue area to the right of the red area is the gain in revenue on new sales. Because the gain is greater than the loss, revenue increases.

This process continues until demand reaches unitary elasticity between a price of $4 and $5. In this range total revenue is unchanged at $20 regardless of whether price is $4 or $5. Here, as price is lowered, the revenue from new sales exactly offsets the loss in revenue from existing sales.

As price falls further from $4 to $3 to $2, the firm's total revenues begin to fall. Here, price reductions result in lower revenue because the lower part of the demand curve is inelastic. The revenue from the new sales is not enough to offset the losses in revenue due to the lowered price.

EXHIBIT 8
Demand Elasticity and a Firm's Total Revenue

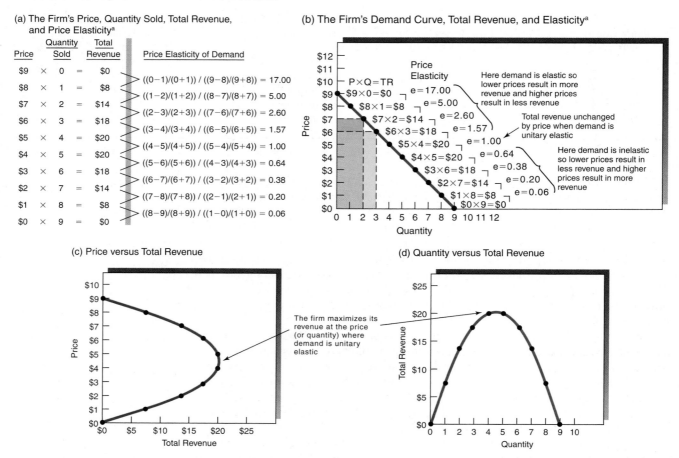

(a) The Firm's Price, Quantity Sold, Total Revenue, and Price Elasticity[a]

(b) The Firm's Demand Curve, Total Revenue, and Elasticity[a]

(c) Price versus Total Revenue

(d) Quantity versus Total Revenue

The firm maximizes its revenue at the price (or quantity) where demand is unitary elastic

[a]The sign of all elasticity coefficients is negative.

Of course, this example could be viewed in reverse. As the firm raises its price up from $1, revenues expand until demand is unit elastic, and, above this, revenues fall with further price increases as demand becomes elastic. The issue is whether the higher revenue from the sales that remain is sufficient to offset the lower revenue from the lost sales.

This relationship between the firm's total revenue and its price is shown in part c of the exhibit. Alternatively, we may view this as a relationship between the quantity and the total revenue, as shown in part d. The firm maximizes its revenue at the price (or quantity) where demand is unit elastic.[10] We might notice a similarity between the graph shown in part c of the exhibit and the Laffer curve between tax rates and total tax revenue from Chapter 4. It is indeed the elasticity of the tax base to a tax rate change that underlies the Laffer curve in a similar manner.

Firms attempt to maximize profit, not revenue. Profit is total revenue *minus total cost.* The price or output where demand is unit elastic and revenue is maximized is not the same as the one where total profit is maximized—unless output can be increased at zero cost. They will be close, however, for some types of firms whose costs are mostly upfront (or

---

[10]An astute student might note that total revenue is really maximized at a price of $4.50 and a quantity of 4.5 (if possible, say, 4.5 pounds of roast beef). Here total revenue is $20.25. Because the elasticity formula uses the midpoint as a basis, the elasticity shown for the price change from $4 to $5 is really the elasticity at the midpoint between these two prices, or $4.50.

"fixed") with little marginal cost of producing additional units. For a concert or sporting event, most of the cost is of this type, and there is very little additional cost of allowing more people into the event.

Suppose that the exhibit shown is for the price, quantity (in thousands), and total revenue (also in thousands) for a firm selling tickets to a concert. Can you explain why even if the capacity of the stadium was 10 thousand, the firm might decide to set the ticket price at a level that does not sell out the stadium? Alternatively, suppose the exhibit was the relationship between a university's tuition (in thousands) and its enrollment (also in thousands). If current tuition was $6 thousand, can you explain why the university could get more tuition revenue by lowering its tuition? If you can, you understand the importance of price elasticity of demand for decision makers in the business firm.

Beyond the price elasticity of demand, two other elasticity relationships are important in any given market. We end this chapter with a brief discussion of income elasticity of demand and of price elasticity of supply.

INCOME ELASTICITY

Increases in consumer income will increase the demand (the quantity demanded at each price) for most goods. Income elasticity indicates the responsiveness of the demand for a product to a change in income. **Income elasticity** is defined as:

$$\text{Income Elasticity} = \frac{\text{Percentage change in quantity demanded}}{\text{Percentage change in income}}$$

As **Exhibit 9** shows, although the income elasticity coefficients for products vary from one good to another, they are normally positive. In fact, the term **normal good** refers to any good with a positive income elasticity of demand. Some normal goods have lower income elasticities than others, however. In general, goods that people regard as "necessities" will have low income elasticities (between 0 and 1). Significant quantities are purchased even at low incomes, and, as income increases, spending on these items will increase by less than a proportional amount. It is understandable that such items as fuel, electricity, bread, tobacco, economy clothing, and potatoes have a low income elasticity.

Goods that consumers regard as "luxuries" generally have a high (greater than 1) income elasticity. For example, private education, new automobiles, recreational activities, donations to environmental groups, swimming pools, and vacation air travel are all highly income elastic. As income increases, the demand for these goods expands even more rapidly, and therefore spending on these items increases as a proportion of income.

Income elasticity
The percentage change in the quantity of a product demanded divided by the percentage change in consumer income causing the change in quantity demanded. It measures the responsiveness of the demand for a good to a change in income.

Normal good
A good that has a positive income elasticity, so that, as consumer income rises, demand for that good rises also.

EXHIBIT 9
Estimated Income Elasticity of Demand for Selected Products

LOW INCOME ELASTICITY		HIGH INCOME ELASTICITY	
Margarine	−0.20	Private education	2.46
Fuel	0.38	New cars	2.45
Electricity	0.20	Recreation and amusements	1.57
Fish (haddock)	0.46	Alcohol	1.54
Food	0.51		
Tobacco	0.64		
Hospital care	0.69		

Sources: Hendrick S. Houthakker and Lester D. Taylor, *Consumer Demand in the United States, 1929–1970* (Cambridge: Harvard University Press, 1966); L. Taylor, "The Demand for Electricity: A Survey," *Bell Journal of Economics* (Spring 1975); F. W. Bell, "The Pope and the Price of Fish," *American Economic Review 58* (December 1968); and Rexford E. Santerre and Stephen P. Neun, *Health Economics: Theories, Insights and Industry Studies* (Orlando: Harcourt, 2000).

A few commodities, such as margarine, low-quality meat cuts, and bus travel, actually have a negative income elasticity. Economists refer to goods with a negative income elasticity as **inferior goods**. As income expands, the demand for inferior goods will decline. Conversely, as income declines, the demand for inferior goods will increase.

PRICE ELASTICITY OF SUPPLY

We may also define the **price elasticity of supply**, which is the percentage change in quantity supplied, divided by the percentage change in the price causing the supply response. Because this measures the responsiveness of sellers to a change in price, it is analogous to the price elasticity of demand. However, the price elasticity of supply will be positive because the quantity producers are willing to supply is directly related to price. As in the case of demand elasticity, time plays a role. Supply elasticities will be greater when suppliers have a longer time to respond to a price change. In the next two chapters we will discuss more fully the factors that determine supply elasticity. For now, it is important simply to recognize the concept of supply elasticity and the fact that suppliers (like buyers) will be more responsive to a price change when they have had more time to adjust to it.

Demand, Choice, and Price-Responsive Consumers

In today's market economies, consumers face complex choices. Substitutes are everywhere, so the demand curve for any one product slopes downward to the right. Movies, sports, camping, TV, swimming, and bowling are all substitutes for one another, for many people. Time is the individual's unique constraint; not the supplier's action or price. Further, the demand for the product of any one firm is generally elastic, reflecting the large range of choices among goods competing for the dollars of consumers. Is there only one movie theater in town? Substitutes for a movie at the theater nonetheless abound, from competing activities like those above, to rental movies on tape or DVD. The price elasticity of demand at the theater is thus likely to be large, even when other local theaters are unavailable. This fact is important for policymakers as well as consumers, as we will see in later chapters.

LOOKING AHEAD

The market demand indicates how strongly consumers desire each good or service. In the following chapter, we turn to a firm's costs of production—costs that arise because resources are demanded in alternative uses. In fact, the cost of producing a good is precisely the value that consumers place on the alternative goods that could be produced with those same resources. An understanding of these two topics—consumer demand and cost of production—is essential if we are to understand how market prices result in resources being allocated toward the production of goods most highly valued by consumers.

KEY POINTS

▼ Consumer choice is a process of allocating limited income among a multitude of goods and services in a way that maximizes utility. The role of relative prices, information, preferences for risk and time,

and the law of diminishing marginal utility help explain these choices. These ideas underlie the position and shape of an individual's demand curve for a product.

▼ The market demand curve reflects the demand of individuals. It is simply the horizontal sum of the demand curves of individuals for the product.

▼ A good with high total value can have low marginal value, and vice versa. Because market price reflects marginal valuations, it has little relationship to the total value of the good.

▼ The advertising budgets of profit-seeking business firms indicate that advertising influences the choices of consumers. Advertising can reduce the search time of consumers, help them make more informed choices and, through brand names, provide assurances with regard to quality.

▼ Price elasticity reveals the responsiveness of the amount purchased to a change in price. When there are good substitutes available and the item forms a sizable component of the consumer's budget, its demand will tend to be more elastic. Typically, the price elasticity of a product will increase as more

time is allowed for consumers to adjust to a change in price. This direct relationship between size of the elasticity coefficient and the length of the adjustment period is often referred to as the *second law of demand.*

▼ The concept of elasticity is useful in determining how a change in price will affect total consumer expenditures on an item or a firm's total revenue. An increase in price will lower total revenue (or expenditure) when demand is elastic, but increase it when demand is inelastic. A decrease in price will raise total revenue (or expenditure) when demand is elastic, but decrease it when demand is inelastic. When demand is of unitary elasticity, total revenue (or expenditure) is unaffected by a change in price.

▼ The concept of elasticity can also be applied to consumer income (income elasticity of demand) and supply (the price elasticity of supply).

CRITICAL ANALYSIS QUESTIONS

*1. Suppose that in an attempt to raise more revenue, Nowhere State University (NSU) increases its tuition. Will this necessarily result in more revenue? Under what conditions will revenue (a) rise, (b) fall, or (c) remain the same? Explain this in words, focusing on the relationship between the increased revenue from the students who enroll despite the higher tuition and the lost revenue from lower enrollment. If the true price elasticity were -1.2, what would you suggest the university do to expand revenue?

2. A bus ticket between two cities costs $50 and the trip will take 28 hours while an airplane ticket costs $300 and takes 3 hours. Mary values her time at $12 per hour, and Michele values her time at $8 per hour. Will Mary take the bus or the plane? Which will Michele take? Explain.

*3. Recent research confirms that the demand for cigarettes is inelastic, but also indicates that smokers with incomes in the lower half of all incomes respond to a given price increase by reductions in their purchases that are more than four times as large as purchase reductions made by smokers in the upper half of all incomes. How can consideration of the income and substitution effects of a price change help to explain this finding?

4. A consumer is currently purchasing 3 pairs of jeans and 5 T-shirts per year. The price of jeans is $30,

and T-shirts cost $10. At the current rate of consumption, the marginal utility of jeans is 60 and the marginal utility of T-shirts is 30. Is this consumer maximizing his utility? Would you suggest he buy more jeans and fewer T-shirts, or more T-shirts and fewer jeans?

5. A few years ago, when residential electricity in the state of Washington cost about half as much as in nearby Montana, the average household in Washington used about 1,200 kilowatt-hours per month, whereas Montanans used about half that much per household. Do these data provide us with two points on the average household's demand curve for residential electricity in this region? Why or why not?

*6. What's wrong with this way of thinking? "Economics is unable to explain the value of goods in a sensible manner. A quart of water is much cheaper than a quart of oil. Yet water is essential to both animal and plant life. Without it, we could not survive. How can oil be more valuable than water? Yet economics says that it is."

*7. The wealthy are widely believed to have more leisure time than the poor. However, even though we are a good deal wealthier today than our great-grandparents were 100 years ago, we appear to live more hectic lives and have less free time. Can you explain why?

8. What are the major determinants of a product's price elasticity of demand? Studies indicate that the demand for Florida oranges, Bayer aspirin, watermelons, and airfares to Europe are elastic. Why?

9. Most systems of medical insurance substantially reduce the costs to the consumer of using additional units of physician services and hospitalization. Some reduce these costs to zero. How does this method of payment affect the consumption levels of medical services? Might this method of organization result in "too much" consumption of medical services? Discuss.

*10. Are the following statements true or false? Explain your answers.
  a. A 10 percent reduction in price that leads to a 15 percent increase in amount purchased indicates a price elasticity of more than 1.
  b. A 10 percent reduction in price that leads to a 2 percent increase in total expenditures indicates a price elasticity of more than 1.
  c. If the percentage change in price is less than the resultant percentage change in quantity demanded, demand is elastic.

*11. Respond to the following questions: If you really like pizza, should you try to consume as much pizza as possible? If you want to succeed, should you try to make the highest possible grade in your economics class?

*12. Sue loves ice cream but cannot stand frozen yogurt desserts. In contrast, Carole likes both and can hardly tell the difference between the two. Who will have the more elastic demand for yogurt?

*13. "If all the farmers reduced their output to one-half the current rate, farm incomes would increase, the total utility derived from farm output would rise, and the nation would be better off." Is this statement true or false? Explain your answer.

*14. "Market competition encourages deceitful advertising and dishonesty." Is this statement true or false? Explain your answer.

15. Patsy's Specialty Bakery projects the following demand for Patsy's pies:

Price	Quantity Purchased
$ 9	130
$10	110
$11	95

  a. Calculate the price elasticity of demand between $9 and $10. Is demand in this range elastic or inelastic?
  b. Calculate the price elasticity of demand between $10 and $11. Is demand in this range elastic or inelastic?

*Asterisk denotes questions for which answers are given in Appendix B.

ADDENDUM: CONSUMER CHOICE AND INDIFFERENCE CURVES

Advanced Material

In the text of this chapter, we used marginal utility analysis to develop the demand curve of an individual. In developing the theory of consumer choice, economists usually rely on a more formal technique—*indifference curve analysis*. Because this technique is widely used at a more advanced level, many instructors like to include it in their introductory course. In this addendum, we use indifference curve analysis to develop the theory of demand in a more formal—some would say more elegant—manner.

What are indifference curves?

There are two elements in every choice: (1) preferences (the desirability of various goods) and (2) opportunities (the attainability of various goods). The **indifference curve** relates to the former: the preferences of an individual. It separates better (more preferred by this individual) bundles of goods from inferior (less preferred) bundles, providing a diagrammatic picture of how an individual ranks alternative consumption bundles.

To illustrate indifference curves, we begin with the title character from the classic *Robinson Crusoe*, by Daniel Defoe, published in 1719 and thought to be the first English novel. Crusoe was shipwrecked on a desert island. In **Exhibit A1**, we assume that he is initially consuming 8 fish and 8 breadfruit per week (point *A*). This initial bundle provides him with a certain level of satisfaction (utility). He would, however, be willing to trade this initial bundle for certain other consumption alternatives if the opportunity presented itself. Since he likes both fish and breadfruit, he would especially like to obtain bundles to the northeast of point *A* in the diagram, since they represent more of both goods. However, he would also be willing to give up some breadfruit if in return he received a compensatory amount of fish. Similarly, if the terms of trade were right, he would be willing to exchange fish for breadfruit. The trade-offs he is just willing to make—those that would make him no better and no worse off—lie *along* the indifference curve. Of course, he is happy to move to any bundle on a higher indifference curve.

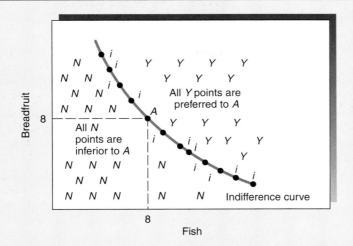

EXHIBIT A1
The Indifference Curve of Robinson Crusoe

The curve generated by connecting Crusoe's "I do not care" answers separates the combinations of fish and breadfruit that he prefers to the bundle *A* from those that he judges to be inferior to *A*. The *i* points map out an indifference curve.

Starting from point *A* (8 fish and 8 breadfruit), we ask Crusoe if he is willing to trade that bundle for various other bundles. He answers "Yes" (*Y*), "No" (*N*), or "I do not care" (*i*). Exhibit A1 illustrates the pattern of his responses. Crusoe's "I do not care" answers indicate that the original bundle (point *A*) and each alternative indicated by an *i* are valued equally by Crusoe. These *i* points, when connected, form the indifference curve. This line separates the preferred bundles of fish and breadfruit from the less-valued combinations. Note that such a curve is likely to be entirely different for any two people. The preferences of individuals vary widely.

We can establish a new indifference curve for the individual by starting from any point not on the original curve and following the same procedure. If we start with a point (a consumption bundle) to the northeast of the original indifference curve, all points on the new curve will have a higher level of satisfaction for Crusoe than any on the old curve. The new curve will probably have about the same shape as the original.

Characteristics of Indifference Curves

In developing consumer theory, economists assume that the preferences of consumers exhibit certain properties. These properties enable us to make statements about the general pattern of indifference curves. What are these properties, and what do they imply about the characteristics of indifference curves?

1. ***More goods are preferable to fewer goods—thus, bundles on indifference curves lying farthest to the northeast of a diagram are always preferred.*** Assuming the consumption of only two commodities that are both desired, the individual will always prefer a bundle with more of one good (without loss of the other) to the original bundle. This means that combinations to the northeast of a point on the diagram will always be preferred to points lying to the southwest.

2. ***Goods are substitutable—therefore, indifference curves slope downward to the right.*** As we indicated in the text of this chapter, individuals are willing to substitute one good for another. Crusoe will be willing to give up some breadfruit if he is compensated with enough fish. Stated another way, there will be some amount of additional fish such that Crusoe will stay on the same indifference curve, even though his consumption of breadfruit has declined. However, in order to remain on the same indifference curve, Crusoe must always acquire more of one good to compensate for the loss of the other. The indifference curve for goods thus will always slope downward to the right (run northwest to southeast).

3. ***The valuation of a good declines as it is consumed more intensively—therefore, indifference curves are always convex when viewed from below.*** The slope of the indifference curve represents the willingness of the individual to substitute one good for the other. Economists refer to the amount of one good that is just sufficient to compensate the consumer for the loss of a unit of the other good as the **marginal rate of substitution**. It is equal to the slope of the indifference curve. Reflecting the principle of diminishing marginal utility, the marginal rate of substitution of a good will decline as the good is consumed more intensively relative to other goods. Suppose Crusoe remains on the same indifference curve while continuing to expand his consumption of fish relative to breadfruit. As his consumption of fish increases (and his consumption of breadfruit declines), his valuation of fish relative to breadfruit will decline. It will take more and more units of fish to compensate for the loss of still another unit of breadfruit. The indifference curve will become flatter, reflecting the decline in the marginal rate of substitution of fish for breadfruit as Crusoe consumes more fish relative to breadfruit.

Of course, just the opposite will happen if Crusoe's consumption of breadfruit increases relative to that of fish—if he moves northwest along the same indifference curve. In this case, as breadfruit is consumed more intensively, Crusoe's valuation of it will decline relative to that of fish, and the marginal rate of substitution of fish for breadfruit will rise (the indifference curve will become steeper and steeper). Therefore, since the valuation of each good declines as it is consumed more intensively, indifference curves must be convex when viewed from the origin.

4. *Indifference curves are everywhere dense.* We can construct an indifference curve starting from any point on the diagram. This simply means that any two bundles of goods can be compared by the individual.

5. *Indifference curves cannot cross—if they did, rational ordering would be violated.* If indifference curves crossed, our postulate that more goods are better than fewer goods would be violated. **Exhibit A2** illustrates this point. The crossing of the indifference curves implies that points *Y* and *Z* are equally preferred, since they both are on the same indifference curve as *X*. Consumption bundle *Y*, though, represents more of both fish and breadfruit than bundle *Z*, so *Y* must be preferred to *Z*. Whenever indifference curves cross, this type of internal inconsistency (irrational ranking) will arise. So, the indifference curves of an individual must not cross.

The Consumer's Preferred Bundle

Used together with the opportunity constraint of the individual, indifference curves can be used to indicate the most preferred consumption alternatives available to an individual. The **consumption opportunity constraint** separates consumption bundles that are attainable from those that are unattainable.

Assuming that Crusoe could produce only for himself, his consumption opportunity constraint would look like the production possibilities curves discussed in Chapter 2. What would happen if natives from another island visited Crusoe and offered to make exchanges with him? If a barter market existed that permitted Crusoe to exchange fish for breadfruit at a specified exchange rate, his options would resemble those of the market constraint illustrated by **Exhibit A3**. First, let us consider the case where Crusoe inhabits a barter economy in which the current market exchange rate is 2 fish to 1 breadfruit. Suppose as a result of his expertise as a fisherman, Crusoe specializes in this activity and is able to bring 16 fish to the market per week. What consumption alternatives will be open to him? Since 2 fish can be bartered in the market for 1 breadfruit, Crusoe will be able to consume 16 fish, or 8 breadfruit, or any combination on the market constraint indicated by the line between these two points. For example, if he trades 2 of his 16 fish for 1 breadfruit, he will be able to consume a bundle consisting of 14 fish and 1 breadfruit. Assuming that the set of indifference curves of Exhibit A3 outlines Crusoe's preferences, he will choose to consume 8 fish and 4 breadfruit. Of course, it will be possible for Crusoe to choose many other combinations of breadfruit and fish,

EXHIBIT A2
Indifference Curves Cannot Cross

If the indifference curves of an individual crossed, it would lead to the inconsistency pictured here. Points *X* and *Y* must be equally valued, since they are both on the same indifference curve (i_1). Similarly, points *X* and *Z* must be equally preferred, since they are both on the indifference curve (i_2). If this is true, *Y* and *Z* must also be equally preferred, since they are both equally preferred to *X*. However, point *Y* represents more of both goods than *Z*, so *Y* has to be preferred to *Z*. When indifference curves cross, this type of internal inconsistency always arises.

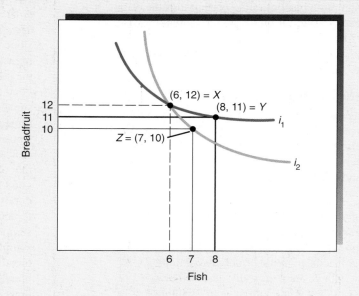

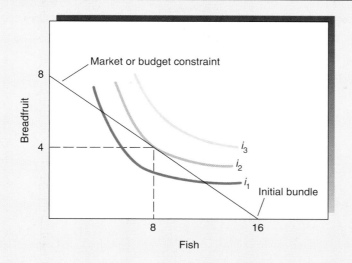

EXHIBIT A3
Consumer Maximization—Barter Economy

Suppose that the set of indifference curves shown here outlines Crusoe's preferences. The slope of the market (or budget) constraint indicates that 2 fish trade for 1 breadfruit in this barter economy. If Crusoe produces 16 fish per week, he will trade 8 fish for 4 breadfruit in order to move to the consumption bundle (8 fish and 4 breadfruit) that maximizes his level of satisfaction.

but none of the other attainable combinations would enable him to reach as high a level of satisfaction. Because he is able to bring only 16 fish to the market, it would be impossible for him to attain an indifference curve higher than i_2.

Crusoe's indifference curve and the market constraint curve will coincide (they will be tangent) at the point at which his attainable level of satisfaction is maximized. At that point (8 fish and 4 breadfruit), the rate at which Crusoe is willing to exchange fish for breadfruit (as indicated by the slope of the indifference curve) will be just equal to the rate at which the market will *permit* him to exchange the two (the slope of the market constraint). If the two slopes differ at a point, Crusoe will always be able to find an attainable combination that will permit him to reach a *higher* indifference curve. He will always move down the market constraint when it is flatter than his indifference curve, and up if the market constraint is steeper.

Crusoe in a Money Economy

As far as the condition for maximization of consumer satisfaction is concerned, moving from a barter economy to a money income economy changes little. **Exhibit A4** illustrates this point. Initially, the price of fish is $1, and the price of breadfruit is $2. The market therefore permits an exchange of 2 fish for 1 breadfruit, just as was the case in Exhibit A3. In Exhibit A4, we assume that Crusoe has a fixed money income of $16. At this level of income, he confronts the same market constraint (usually called a **budget constraint** in an economy with money) as in Exhibit A3. Given the product prices and his income, Crusoe can choose to consume 16 fish, or 8 breadfruit, or any combination indicated by a line (the budget constraint) connecting these two points. Given his preferences, Crusoe will again choose the combination of 8 fish and 4

breadfruit if he wishes to maximize his level of satisfaction. As was true for the barter economy, when Crusoe maximizes his satisfaction (moves to the highest attainable indifference curve), the rate at which he is willing to exchange fish for breadfruit will just equal the rate at which the market will permit him to exchange the two goods. Stated in more technical terms, when his level of satisfaction is at a maximum, Crusoe's marginal rate of substitution of fish for breadfruit, as indicated by the slope of the indifference curve at E_1, will just equal the price ratio (P_F/P_b, which is also the slope of the budget constraint).

What will happen if the price of fish increases? Exhibit A4 also answers this question. Since the price of breadfruit and Crusoe's *money* income are constant, a higher fish price will have two effects. First, it will make Crusoe poorer, even though his money income will be unchanged. His budget constraint will turn clockwise around point A, illustrating that his consumption options are now more limited—that is, his real income has declined. Second, the budget line will be steeper, indicating that a larger number of breadfruit must now be sacrificed to obtain an additional unit of fish. It will no longer be possible for Crusoe to attain indifference curve i_2. The best he can do is indifference curve i_1, which he can attain by choosing the bundle of 5 fish and 3 breadfruit.

Using the information supplied by Exhibit A4, we can now locate two points on Crusoe's demand curve for fish. When the price of fish was $1, Crusoe chose 8 fish; when the price rose to $2, Crusoe reduced his consumption to 5 (see **Exhibit A5**). Of course, other points on Crusoe's demand curve could also be located if we considered other prices for fish.

The demand curve of Exhibit A5 is constructed on the assumption that the price of breadfruit remains $2 and that Crusoe's money income remains constant at $16. If either

EXHIBIT A4
Consumer Maximization—
Money = Income
Economy

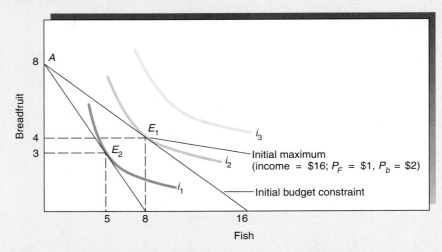

Suppose that Crusoe's income is $16 per day, the price of fish (P_F) is $1, and the price of breadfruit (P_b) is $2. Thus, Crusoe confronts exactly the same price ratio and budget constraint as in Exhibit A3. Assuming that his preferences are unchanged, he will again maximize his satisfaction by choosing to consume 8 fish and 4 breadfruit. What will happen if the price of fish rises to $2? Crusoe's consumption opportunities will be reduced. His budget constraint will turn clockwise around point A, reflecting the higher price of fish. His fish consumption will decline to 5 units. (*Note:* Because Crusoe's real income has been reduced, his consumption of breadfruit will also decline.)

EXHIBIT A5
Crusoe's Demand for Fish

As Exhibit A4 illustrates, when the price of fish is $1, Crusoe chooses 8 units. When the price of fish increases to $2, he reduces his consumption to 5 units. This gives us two points on Crusoe's demand curve for fish. Other points on the demand curve could be derived by confronting Crusoe with still other prices of fish. (*Note:* Crusoe's money income [$16] and the price of breadfruit [$2] are unchanged in this analysis.)

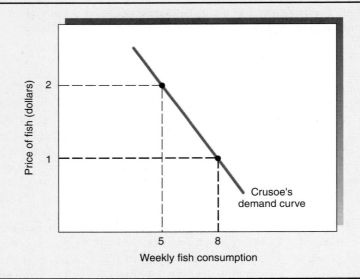

of these factors were to change, the entire demand curve for fish, illustrated by Exhibit A5, would shift.

The indifference curve is a useful way to illustrate how a person with a fixed budget chooses between two goods. In the real world, of course, people have hundreds, or even thousands, of goods to choose from, and the doubling of only one price usually has a small impact on a person's overall consumption and satisfaction possibilities. In our simple example, the twofold increase in the price of

fish makes Crusoe much worse off, because he spends a large portion of his budget on the item.

The Income and Substitution Effects

In the text, we indicated that, when the price of a product rises, the amount consumed will change as a result of both an *income effect* and a *substitution effect*. Indifference curve analysis can be used to separate these two effects. **Exhibit A6** is similar to Exhibit A4. Both exhibits illus-

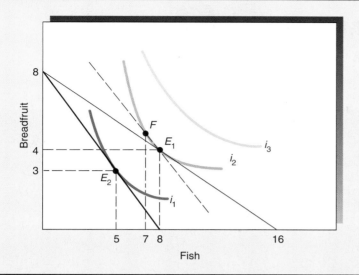

EXHIBIT A6
The Income and
Substitution Effects

Here we break down Crusoe's response to the rise in the price of fish from $1 to $2 (see Exhibit A4) into the substitution and income effects. The move from E_1 to F illustrates the substitution effect, whereas the move from F to E_2 reflects the income effect.

trate Crusoe's response to an increase in the price of fish from $1 to $2 when money income ($16) and the price of breadfruit ($2) are held constant. Exhibit A6, however, breaks down his total response into the substitution effect and the income effect. The reduction in the consumption of fish solely because of the substitution (price) effect, holding Crusoe's real income (level of utility) constant, can be found by constructing a line tangent to Crusoe's original indifference curve (i_2), and having a slope indicating the higher price of fish. This line (the broken line in Exhibit A6), which is parallel to Crusoe's actual budget constraint (the line containing point E_2), reflects the higher price of fish. It is tangent to the original indifference curve i_2, so Crusoe's real income is held constant. As this line indicates, Crusoe's consumption of fish would fall from 8 to 7, due strictly to the fact that fish are now more expensive. This move from E_1 to F is a pure substitution effect.

Real income, though, has actually been reduced. As a result, Crusoe will be unable to attain point F on indifference curve i_2. The best he can attain is point E_2, which de-

creases his consumption of fish by another 2 units to 5. Since the broken line containing F and the budget constraint containing E_2 are parallel, the relative price of fish and breadfruit is held constant as Crusoe moves from F to E_2. This move from F to E_2 is thus a pure income effect. (*Note:* Because the consumption of both goods drops in this move, when income falls but the prices do not change, both goods must be normal goods.) This reduction in the consumption of fish (and breadfruit) in the move from F to E_2 is due entirely to the decline in Crusoe's real income.

Indifference curve analysis highlights the assumptions and considerations that enter into consumer decisions. The logic of the proof that there is an inverse relationship between the price and the amount demanded is both elegant and reassuring. It is elegant because of the internal consistency of the logic and the precision of the analysis. It is reassuring because it conforms with our expectations, which are based on the central postulate of economics—that incentives matter in a predictable way.

CHAPTER 20

Costs and the Supply of Goods

From the stand-point of society as a whole, the "cost" of any-thing is the value that it has in al-ternative uses.

—*Thomas Sowell*[1]

Chapter Focus

- Why are business firms used by societies everywhere to organize production?

- How are firms organized in market economies?

- What are explicit and implicit costs, and how do they guide the behavior of the firm?

- How does economic profit differ from accounting profit, and what role does it play?

- How do short-run costs differ from long-run costs, and what factors shift the firm's cost curves?

[1]Thomas Sowell, *Basic Economics* (New York: Basic Books, 2000), p. 10.

Demand and supply interact to determine the market price of a product. In the preceding chapter, we illustrated that the demand for a product reflects the strength of consumer desire for that product. In this chapter, we focus on the cost of production. The resources needed to produce one good could be used to produce other goods instead. As Thomas Sowell points out in the quotation that begins this chapter, the cost to society of anything is the value that it has in alternative uses. The market for resources makes that cost clear to producers: The maker of soccer balls, for example, must compete against producers of other goods in purchasing the machines, materials, and labor needed to produce the balls. The producer passes that cost message along to consumers. The firm must gain sufficient revenue from selling the product to cover the cost of the resources, and thus the cost of the balls. The cost of a good in the product market reflects the value in alternate uses of the resources needed to produce it.

Costs carry an important message to producers from the rest of society. If the cost of producing a good exceeds its price, the market is signaling that, although the good may be desired, there is an even greater desire for other goods that could be produced with the same resources. The message comes with an important incentive attached. Producers suffer losses when the per-unit cost of a good exceeds the price they can get for it. In a market economy, they are unlikely to continue supplying the good under such conditions. Thus, supply and cost of production are closely linked. For example, a producer who faces a cost of $1,500 to produce a high quality TV set is unlikely to continue supplying the sets for very long if their market price is $1,000. In the long run, sets that cost $1,500 will be supplied only if their market price is at least that amount.

In this chapter, we lay the foundation for a detailed investigation of the links between costs, business output, and market supply. What do economists mean by costs? How do costs guide the owners and managers of firms in a market economy? Why are costs important to managers, even when they personally do not pay them? We discuss these and related questions in this chapter. ■

ORGANIZATION OF THE BUSINESS FIRM

The business firm is an entity designed to organize raw materials, labor, and machines with the goal of producing goods and/or services. Firms (1) purchase productive resources from households and other firms, (2) transform them into a different commodity, and (3) sell the transformed product or service to consumers.

Economies differ in the amount of freedom they allow business decision makers and also in the incentive structure used to stimulate and guide business activity. Yet every society relies on business firms to organize resources and transform them into products. In market economies, most business firms choose their own price, output level, and methods of production. They reap the benefits of sales revenues, but they also pay the costs necessary to earn those revenues. In socialist countries, government policy often sets the selling price and constrains the actions of business firms in various other ways. Firms typically do not pay all their bills from their revenues, and they are often not allowed to keep revenues that exceed costs. In any case, the business firm is the entity used to organize production in capitalist and socialist economies alike. In this chapter we focus on the organization and behavior of firms in a market economy.

Incentives, Cooperation, and the Nature of the Firm

In capitalist countries, most firms are privately owned. Owners risk their wealth on the success of the business. If the firm is successful and earns profits, these financial gains go to the owners. Conversely, if the firm suffers losses, the owners must bear the consequences.

Residual claimants
Individuals who personally receive the excess, if any, of revenues over costs. Residual claimants gain if the firm's costs are reduced or revenues increased.

Team production
A process of production wherein employees work together under the supervision of the owner or the owner's representative.

Shirking
Working at less than a normal rate of productivity, thus reducing output. Shirking is more likely when workers are not monitored, so that the cost of lower output falls on others.

Principal-agent problem
The incentive problem arising when the purchaser of services (the principal) lacks full information about the circumstances faced by the seller (the agent) and thus cannot know how well the agent performs the purchased services. The agent may to some extent work toward objectives other than those sought by the principal paying for the service.

Because the owners receive what remains after the revenue of the firm is used to pay the contractual costs, they are called **residual claimants**.

In a market economy, the property right of owners to the residual income of the firm plays a very important role: It provides owners with a strong incentive to organize and structure their business in a manner that will keep their cost of producing output low (relative to the value of the output). The wealth of these residual claimants is directly influenced by the success or failure of the firm. Thus, they have both the authority and a strong incentive to see that resources under their direction are used efficiently and directed toward production of goods that are valued more highly than their costs.

There are two ways of organizing productive activity: contracting and **team production**, in which workers are hired by a firm to work together under the supervision of the owner, or the owner's representative—a manager. Most business firms use both contracting and team production.

In principle, all production could be accomplished solely through contracting. For example, a builder might have a house built by contracting with one person to pour the concrete, another to construct the wooden part of the house, a third to install the roofing, a fourth to do the electrical wiring, and so on. No employees would have to be involved in such a project. More commonly though, goods and services are produced with some combination of contracting and the use of team production by employees of a firm.

Why do firms use team production? If contracting alone is used to produce something, the producer must, for each project (1) determine what is required to produce the desired result in the best way, given the circumstances and the current technology and prices, (2) search out reliable suppliers, and (3) negotiate and enforce the contracts. The entrepreneur who wants to produce by this method must have specialized knowledge in a variety of areas and must devote a great deal of time and effort to the planning and contracting processes. Not many people have the expertise or the time to perform all these tasks by themselves except on a small scale. Team production for certain tasks may be more practical and less costly.

Accordingly, a builder is likely to hire knowledgeable, experienced workers to plan the construction process, to purchase materials, and to build such structures as houses and office buildings. The firm itself will then contract with others to obtain materials and specialized labor services.

A firm, then, is a business organization that may use team production to reduce many of the transaction costs associated with contracting. Team production, however, raises another set of problems. Team members—that is, the employees working for the firm—must be monitored and given incentives to avoid shirking, or working at less than a normal rate of productivity. Taking long work breaks, paying more attention to their own convenience than to work results, and wasting time when diligence is called for are examples of **shirking**. A worker will shirk more when the costs of doing so are shifted to other team members, including the owners of the firm. Hired managers, even including those at the top, must be monitored and provided with the incentive to avoid shirking.

When team production is utilized, the problem of imperfect monitoring and imperfect incentives is always present. It is part of a larger class of what economists call **principal-agent problems**. Any person taking a car to an auto mechanic experiences such a problem. The mechanic wants to get the job done quickly and to make as much money on it as possible. The car owner wants to get the job done quickly also, but in a way that permanently fixes the problem, at the lowest possible cost. Because the mechanic typically knows far more about the job than the customer, it is hard for the customer to monitor the mechanic's work. There is a possibility, therefore, that the mechanic may charge a large amount for a "quick fix" that will not last.

The owner of a firm is in a similar situation. It is often difficult to monitor the performance of individual employees and provide them with an incentive structure that will encourage high productivity. Nonetheless, the ability of the firm to use resources effectively, and to succeed in a competitive market, depends crucially upon resolving these problems. To keep costs low and the value of output high, a firm must discover and use an incentive structure that motivates managers and workers, and discourages shirking. The problem extends all the way to the top.

Even top-level executives hired to manage a firm do not have the same objectives as owners—primarily profit maximization—unless, of course, the managers are the owners. So the judgments of executives, too, are influenced by what is in their personal best interests. They want perks, personal job security, and other benefits that may not be consistent with profit maximization for the firm. The problem becomes more serious as firms grow larger and acquire more managers and employees. Ultimately it is the job of the owners, as residual claimants, to develop an incentive structure that minimizes the principal-agent problem. For the owner, the saying "the buck stops here" always applies.

Three Types of Business Firms

Business firms can be organized in one of three ways: as a proprietorship, a partnership, or a corporation. The structure chosen determines how the owners share the risks and liabilities of the firm and how they participate in the making of decisions.

A **proprietorship** is a business firm that is owned by a single individual who is fully liable for the debts of the firm. In addition to assuming the responsibilities of ownership, the proprietor often works directly for the firm, providing managerial and other labor services. Many small businesses, including neighborhood grocery stores, barbershops, and farms, are business proprietorships. As **Exhibit 1** shows, proprietorships account for 73 percent of the business firms in the United States. Because most proprietorships are small, however, they account for only 7 percent of all business revenues.

A **partnership** consists of two or more persons acting as co-owners of a business firm. The partners share risks and responsibilities in some prearranged manner. There is no difference between a proprietorship and a partnership in terms of owner liability. In both cases, the owners are fully liable for all business debts incurred by the firm. Many law, medical, and accounting firms are organized along partnership lines. This form of business structure accounts for only 7 percent of the total number of firms and 5 percent of all business revenues.

The business firms that are **corporations** account for 88 percent of total business revenue, even though they comprise only 20 percent of all firms. What accounts for the attractiveness of the corporate structure? First, although the stockholders of the corporation are the legal owners, their liability is limited to the extent of their explicit investment. If a corporation owes you money, you cannot directly sue the stockholders. Of course, you can sue the corporation. However, if a corporation goes bankrupt, you and others to whom the firm owes money may simply be out of luck. This limited liability makes it possible for

Proprietorship
A business firm owned by an individual who possesses the ownership right to the firm's profits and is personally liable for the firm's debts.

Partnership
A business firm owned by two or more individuals who possess ownership rights to the firm's profits and are personally liable for the debts of the firm.

Corporation
A business firm owned by shareholders who possess ownership rights to the firm's profits, but whose liability is limited to the amount of their investment in the firm.

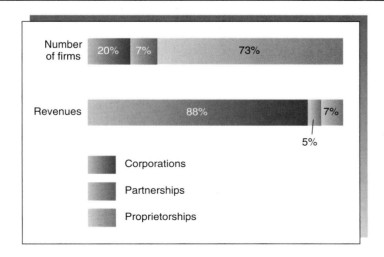

EXHIBIT 1
How Business Firms Are Organized

Nearly three out of every four firms are proprietorships, but only 6 percent of all business revenue is generated by proprietorships. Corporations account for only one out of every five firms, but generate 88 percent of all revenues.

Source: Statistical Abstract of the United States, 2000, Table 855. (Data are for 1997.)

corporations to attract investment funds from a large number of "owners" who do not participate in the day-to-day management of the firm.

Second, ownership can easily be transferred under the corporate structure. The shares, or ownership rights, of an owner who dies can be sold by the heirs to another owner without disrupting the business firm. Because of this, the corporation is an ongoing concern. Similarly, stockholders who become unhappy with the way a corporation is run can bail out merely by selling their stock.

The stockholders of large corporations, through their elected board of directors, usually hire managers—trained experts—to operate the firm. Will the managers operate the firm efficiently and satisfy customers? Offering consumers value at a low cost is the ticket to profitability. In an owner-managed firm, the owner's property right to the residual income provides a strong incentive both to reduce costs and to please consumers.

For a large corporation with many stockholders—millions in some cases—the situation is more complex. Although the stockholders own the residual income, professional managers operate the firm. The objectives of managers may conflict with those of stockholders. For example, managers may prefer high salaries, large offices, first-class travel and other cost-raising benefits for themselves. They may also prefer the power and prestige of business expansion, even if it reduces profitability. Can the stockholders control the actions of managers and direct them toward the pursuit of profitability? Direct control is unlikely. Stockholders elect a board of directors, which in turn appoints high-level managers, but few individual stockholders own enough shares to give them either the incentive or the information to exercise direct control. Most find it too expensive even to attend the annual shareholder's meeting. As the following section describes, however, all is not lost. Internal corporate policies and market activities originating outside the firm both reduce this important form of the principal-agent problem.

COSTS, CONSUMERS, AND CORPORATIONS

Three major factors promote cost efficiency and customer service within the corporation, thus limiting the power of corporate managers. Let us consider each.

1. Competition for Investment Funds and Customers
Even without the ability to exercise direct control of the corporation, stockholders (and the investment advisors, pension fund managers, and others hired to help them) have an incentive to monitor the corporation's management in order to anticipate problems and direct constructive changes. Investors who are the first to spot a good, new management strategy can buy stock early, before others realize the opportunity and bid the price up. A rising stock price is both a signal of approval to good managers and an incentive to manage well. In the case of decisions that are interpreted to be against the interest of stockholders, the opposite occurs. Stockholders who are the first to spot a problem can bail out by selling their stock before others see the problem and dump their stock, thus depressing the price. So managers get constant feedback via stock price changes, which can be just as important as current profits to stockholders and boards of directors.

Similarly, consumers have an incentive to monitor the quality and price of the firm's output. No one forces them to buy the corporation's product; so, if other firms supply superior products or offer a lower price, consumers can take their business to rival firms. Thus, the corporation's need to meet the competition limits the ability of managers to pursue their personal objectives at the expense of either stockholders or customers.

2. Compensation and Management Incentives
The compensation of managers can be structured in a manner that will bring the interests of managers into harmony with those of shareholders. Corporations usually tie the compensation of managers to the market success of the business. Salary increases and bonuses of most high level managers are directly related to the firm's profitability and the price of its shares. How important are these incentives? In 2001, a survey of 200 large U.S. corporations showed that nearly 60 percent of the chief executives' compensation was in the form

of stock options-to-buy.[2] These options are extremely valuable if the market value of the firm's shares rises over time, but may become worthless if it falls. Only 9 percent of these executives' pay was in salary. Such policies encourage corporate managers to maximize the flow of the firm's profits (and the value of the shares), reducing the conflict between the interests of managers and shareholders. Further encouragement comes from the fact that managers often change jobs. More than 21 percent of the chief executives of the top 200 corporations left those firms in 2000. Managers with a record of adding value to the firms they serve earn greater job security and an obvious advantage in finding better positions.

3. Threat of Corporate Takeover

Managers who do not serve the interests of their shareholders are vulnerable to a takeover, a move by an outside person or group to gain control of the firm. As we previously noted, shareholders who lose confidence in management can exit the arrangement by selling their shares. When a significant number of shareholders follow this course of action, the market value of the firm's stock will decline. This will increase the attractiveness of the firm to takeover specialists shopping for a poorly run business, the value of which could be substantially increased by a new management team.

Consider a firm currently earning $1.50 per share. Reflecting current earnings that are expected to continue, the market value of the firm's stock might be $15 per share (assuming a 10 percent interest rate). If the earnings of the firm are low because the current

Competition for investment funds and for consumers, management compensation in the form of stock options, and the threat of a takeover increase the incentive of corporate managers to serve the interests of customers and stockholders.

---

[2]Study of top 200 U.S. industrial and service companies, online at http://www.execpay.com/trends2001.htm#Intro.

management team is pursuing its own objectives at the expense of profitability, then a corporate takeover could lead to substantial gain. Suppose some outside persons believe that they could restructure the firm, improve the management, and thereby increase the firm's earnings to $3 per share. Therefore, they tender a takeover bid—an offer to buy the firm's stock from shareholders (or they make the offer directly to the board, in a "bear hug" that tries to use stockholder pressure to force the board to sell) at $20 per share. If the takeover team gains control, improves the firm's performance, and it increases its earnings to $3 per share, then the stock value of the firm will rise accordingly (to $30 per share).

Of course, the current management has an incentive to resist the takeover. After all, they are likely to lose their jobs if the potential new owners are successful. Managers seldom give such outsiders a warm welcome. Shareholders or their board of directors, however, will decide whether to accept the outsiders' offer. In any case, the presence of large inefficiencies is a powerful attraction for an effective takeover. The mere potential of the takeover reduces the likelihood that managers will stray too far from the profit maximization strategy.

Corporations: Controlling Costs and Serving Customers

How well does the corporate business structure serve consumers and investors? Perhaps history provides the best answer. If the corporate structure were not an effective form of business organization, it would not have continued to survive, nor would it be so prevalent. Rival forms of business organization, including proprietorships, partnerships, consumer cooperatives, employee ownership, and mutually owned companies can and do compete in the marketplace for investment funds and in the product market for customers. In certain industries, some of these alternative forms of business organization are dominant. Nonetheless, in most industries, the corporate structure is the dominant form of business organization (see Exhibit 1). This is strong evidence that, despite its defects, it is generally a cost-efficient, consumer-sensitive form of organization.

ECONOMIC ROLE OF COSTS

Consumers would like to have more economic goods, but resources to produce them are scarce. How much of each desired good should be produced? Every economic system must balance consumers' competing desires. When decisions are made in the political arena, the budget process performs this balancing function. Congress (or the central committee, or the king) decides which goods will be purchased or produced and which will be forgone. Taxes and budgets are set accordingly.

In a market economy, consumer demand and cost of production are central to the performance of this balancing function. ***The demand for a product represents the voice of consumers instructing firms to produce a good, while costs of production represent the desire of consumers for other items that could be produced instead, with the same resources.*** A profit-seeking firm will try to produce only those units of output for which buyers are willing to pay the full cost. Proper measurement and interpretation of costs by the firm are critical both to the firm's profitability and the efficient use of resources.

Calculating Economic Costs and Profits

Business firms, regardless of their size, are primarily concerned with profit. Profit, of course, is the firm's total revenue minus its total costs. But to state profit correctly, costs must be measured properly. Most people, including some who are in business, think of costs as amounts paid for raw materials, labor, machines, and similar inputs. However this concept of cost, which stems from accounting procedures, may exclude some important components of the firm's costs. When cost is miscalculated, so, too, is profit because it is merely revenue minus cost. Bad economic decisions may result from a miscalculation of cost and profit.

The key to understanding the economist's concept of profit is remembering the idea of *opportunity cost*—the highest valued alternative foregone by the resource owner when the resource is used. These costs may either be explicit or implicit. **Explicit costs** result when the firm makes a monetary payment to resource owners. Money wages, interest, and rental payments are a measure of what the firm gives up to employ the services of labor and capital resources. Firms may also incur **implicit costs**—those associated with the use of resources owned by the firm. Since implicit costs do not involve a direct money or contractual payment, they are sometimes excluded from accounting statements. For example, the owners of small proprietorships often work for their own business. There is an opportunity cost associated with the use of this resource (the owner's labor services); other opportunities for the owner's time have to be given up because of the time spent in the operation of the business. The highest valued alternative forgone is the opportunity cost of the labor service provided by the owner. The **total cost** of production is the sum of the explicit and implicit costs incurred by the employment of all resources involved in the production process.

Accounting statements generally omit the implicit cost of equity capital—the cost of funds supplied by owners. If a firm borrows financial capital from a bank or other private source, it will have to pay interest. Accountants properly record this interest expense as a cost. In contrast, when the firm acquires financial capital through the issuance of stock, accountants make no allowance for the cost of this financial capital. Regardless of whether it is acquired by borrowing or stock (equity capital), the use of financial capital involves an opportunity cost. Persons who supply equity capital to a firm expect to earn at least a normal rate of return—a return comparable to what they could earn if they chose other investment opportunities (including bonds). If they do not earn this normal rate of return, investors will not continue to supply financial capital to the business.

When calculating costs, economists use the normal return on financial capital as a basis for determining the implicit **opportunity cost of equity capital**. If the normal rate of return on financial capital is 10 percent, equity investors will refuse funds to firms that persistently fail to earn a 10 percent rate of return on capital assets.

Accounting Profit and Economic Profit

Because economists seek to measure the opportunities lost due to the production of a good or service—the cost to society of that production—they include both explicit and implicit costs in total cost. **Economic profit** is equal to total revenues minus total costs, including both the explicit and implicit cost components. Economic profits will be positive only if the earnings of the business exceed the opportunity cost of all resources used by the firm, including *the opportunity cost of the assets owned by the firm.* Zero economic profit, then, includes just the market wage for the unpaid work of owners, and the normal or competitive rate of return (in investments of similar risk) for their capital. In contrast, economic losses result when the earnings of the firm are insufficient to cover explicit and implicit costs. That is why the **normal profit rate** is zero economic profit, providing just the competitive rate of return on the capital (and labor) of owners. A higher rate will draw more entry into the market, while a lower rate will cause an exit of investors and capital.

Remember that zero economic profits do not imply that the firm is about to go out of business. On the contrary, they indicate that the owners are receiving exactly the normal profit rate, or the competitive market rate of return on their investment (the value of the assets owned by the firm).

Because accounting procedures often omit implicit costs, such as those associated with owner-provided labor services or capital assets, the accounting costs of the firm generally understate the opportunity costs of production. This understatement of cost leads to an overstatement of profits. Therefore, the **accounting profits** of a firm are generally greater than the firm's economic profits (see the Applications in Economics box on accounting costs). When the omission of the costs of owner-provided services is unimportant, as is the case for most large corporations, accounting profits approximate the returns to the firm's equity capital. High accounting profits (measured as a rate of return on a firm's assets), relative to the average for other firms, suggest that a firm is earning an

Explicit costs
Payments by a firm to purchase the services of productive resources.

Implicit costs
The opportunity costs associated with a firm's use of resources that it owns. These costs do not involve a direct money payment. Examples include wage income and interest forgone by the owner of a firm who also provides labor services and equity capital to the firm.

Total cost
The costs, both explicit and implicit, of all the resources used by the firm. Total cost includes an imputed normal rate of return for the firm's equity capital.

Opportunity cost of equity capital
The implicit rate of return that must be earned by investors to induce them to continue to supply financial capital to the firm.

Economic profit
The difference between the firm's total revenues and its total costs, including both the explicit and implicit cost components.

Normal profit rate
Zero economic profit, providing just the competitive rate of return on the capital (and labor) of owners. An above-normal profit rate will draw more entry into the market, while a below-normal rate will cause an exit of investors and capital.

Accounting profits
The sales revenues minus the expenses of a firm over a designated time period, usually one year. Accounting profits typically make allowances for changes in the firm's inventories and depreciation of its assets. No allowance is made, however, for the opportunity cost of the equity capital of the firm's owners, or other implicit costs.

APPLICATIONS IN ECONOMICS

Economic and Accounting Costs: A Hypothetical Example

The revenue-cost statement for a corner grocery store owned and operated by Terry Smith is presented here.

Terry works full-time as the manager, chief cashier, and janitor. Terry has $140,000 worth of refrigeration and other equipment invested in the store. Last year, Terry's total sales were $170,000; suppliers and employees were paid $100,000. Terry's revenues exceeded explicit costs by $70,000.

Did Terry make a profit last year? The accounting statement for the store will probably show a net profit of $70,000. However, if Terry did not have a $140,000 personal investment in equipment, these funds could be earning 5 percent interest. Thus, Terry is forgoing $7,000 of interest each year. Similarly, if the building that Terry owns was not being used as a grocery store, it could be rented to someone else for $1,500 per month. Rental income thus forgone is $18,000 per year. In addition, since Terry is tied up working in the grocery store, a $50,000 managerial position with the local Safeway is forgone. Considering the interest, rental, and salary income that Terry had to forgo in order to operate the

TOTAL REVENUE	
Sales (groceries)	$170,000
Costs (explicit)	
Groceries, wholesale	$76,000
Utilities	4,000
Taxes	6,000
Advertising	2,000
Labor services (employees)	12,000
Total (explicit) costs	$100,000
Net (accounting) profit	$70,000
Additional (implicit) costs	
Interest (personal investment)	$ 7,000
Rent (Terry's building)	18,000
Salary (Terry's labor)	50,000
Total (implicit) costs	$75,000
TOTAL EXPLICIT AND IMPLICIT COSTS	$175,000
ECONOMIC PROFIT (TOTAL REVENUE MINUS EXPLICIT AND IMPLICIT COSTS)	−$5,000

grocery store last year, Terry's implicit costs were $75,000. The total costs were $175,000. The total revenue of Terry's grocery store was less than the opportunity cost of the resources utilized. As a result, Terry incurred an economic loss of $5,000, despite the accounting profit of $70,000.

economic profit. Correspondingly, a low rate of accounting profit implies economic losses. Either positive or negative economic profits, of course, call for a change in output. Such a change will take time.

SHORT RUN AND LONG RUN

A firm cannot instantaneously adjust its output. Time plays an important role in the production process. All of a firm's resources can be expanded (or contracted) over time, but for specialized or heavy equipment, expanding (and contracting) availability quickly may be very expensive or even impossible. Economists often speak of the **short run** as a time period so short that the firm is unable to alter its present plant size. In the short run, the firm is "stuck" with its existing plant and heavy equipment. They are "fixed" for a given time period. The firm can alter output, however, by applying larger or smaller amounts of "variable" resources, such as labor and raw materials. Existing plant capacity can thus be used more or less intensively in the short run.

In sum, we can say that the short run is that period of time during which at least one factor of production, usually the size of the firm's plant, cannot be varied. How long is the short run? The length varies from industry to industry. A trucking firm might be able to hire more drivers and buy or rent more trucks, and double its hauling capacity in a few months. In other industries, particularly those that use assembly lines and mass production techniques (for example, the automotive factory supplying trucks), increasing production capacity might take a year or even several years.

The **long run** is a time period of sufficient length to allow a firm the opportunity to alter its plant size and capacity and all other factors of production. All resources of the

Short run (in production)
A time period so short that a firm is unable to vary some of its factors of production. The firm's plant size typically cannot be altered in the short run.

Long run (in production)
A time period long enough to allow the firm to vary all factors of production.

firm are variable in the long run. In the long run, from the viewpoint of an entire industry, new firms may be established and enter the industry; other firms may dissolve and leave the industry. Thus, the short run may be alternatively viewed as a time period during which the number of firms in the industry is fixed.

Perhaps an example will help to clarify the distinction between the short- and long-run time periods. If a battery manufacturer hired 200 additional workers and ordered more raw materials to squeeze a larger output from the existing plant, it would be making a short-run adjustment. In contrast, if the manufacturer built an additional plant (or expanded the size of its current facility) and installed additional heavy equipment, it would be undertaking a long-run adjustment.

CATEGORIES OF COSTS

To describe various aspects of the firm's costs and the relationship of those costs to the level of output, even without detailed knowledge of the production process, we need some definitions. We have emphasized that in the short run some of a firm's factors of production, such as the size of the plant, will be fixed. Other productive resources will be variable. In the short run, then, we can break the firm's costs into these two categories—fixed and variable. Examining how each category of costs behaves, and seeing that behavior graphically, will illustrate characteristics of the profit-maximizing level of output for a firm. It will be important to distinguish between a firm's total costs and its per-unit costs, which will be called "average" costs.

Each of the firm's fixed costs, and their sum, **total fixed cost** *(TFC)*, will remain unchanged when output is altered in the short run. For example, a firm's insurance premiums, its property taxes, and, most significantly, the opportunity cost of using its fixed assets will be present whether the firm produces a large or small rate of output. These costs will not vary with output. They are "fixed" as long as the firm remains in business. Fixed costs will be present at all levels of output, including zero. They can be avoided only if the firm goes out of business.

What will happen to **average fixed cost** *(AFC)*, fixed costs per unit, as output expands? Remember that the firm's fixed cost will be the same whether output is 1, 100, or 1,000. The *AFC* is simply fixed cost divided by output. As output increases, AFC declines because the fixed cost will be spread over more and more units (see part a of **Exhibit 2**).

Some costs vary with output. For example, additional output can usually be produced by hiring more workers and buying more raw materials. The sum of those and other costs that rise as output increases comprise the firm's **total variable cost** *(TVC)*. At any given

Total fixed cost
The sum of the costs that do not vary with output. They will be incurred as long as a firm continues in business and the assets have alternative uses.

Average fixed cost
Total fixed cost divided by the number of units produced. It always declines as output increases.

Total variable cost
The sum of those costs that rise as output increases. Examples of variable costs are wages paid to workers and payments for raw materials.

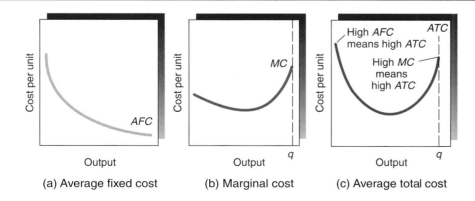

(a) Average fixed cost   (b) Marginal cost   (c) Average total cost

EXHIBIT 2
General Characteristics of Short-Run Cost Curves

Average fixed costs (a) will be high for small rates of output, but they will always decline as output expands. Marginal cost (b) will rise sharply as the plant's production capacity q is approached. As graph (c) illustrates, *ATC* will be a U-shaped curve, since *AFC* will be high for small rates of output and *MC* will be high as the plant's production capacity is approached.

Average variable cost
The total variable cost divided by the number of units produced.

Average total cost
Total cost divided by the number of units produced. It is sometimes called per-unit cost.

Marginal cost
The change in total cost required to produce an additional unit of output.

level of output, the firm's **average variable cost (AVC)** is the total variable cost divided by output.

We have noted that total cost *(TC)* includes explicit and implicit costs. The total cost of producing a good is also the sum of the fixed and variable costs at each output level. At zero output, total cost will equal total fixed cost. As output expands from zero, variable cost and fixed cost must be added to obtain total cost. **Average total cost (ATC)**, sometimes referred to as unit cost, can be found by dividing total cost by the total number of units produced. *ATC* is also equal to the sum of the average fixed and average variable costs. It indicates the amount per unit of output that must be gained in revenue if total cost is to be covered.

The economic way of thinking emphasizes the importance of what happens "at the margin." How much does it cost to produce an additional unit? **Marginal cost (MC)** is the change in total cost that results from the production of one additional unit. The profit-conscious decision maker recognizes *MC* as the addition to cost that must be covered by additional revenue if producing the marginal unit is to be profitable. In the short run, as illustrated by Exhibit 2b, *MC* will generally decline if output is increased, reach a minimum, and then increase. The rising *MC* simply reflects the fact that it becomes increasingly difficult to squeeze additional output from a plant as the facility's maximum capacity (the dotted line of part b of Exhibit 2) is approached. The accompanying Thumbnail Sketch summarizes the interrelationships among a firm's various costs.

THUMBNAIL SKETCH

Compact Glossary on Cost

Term	Symbol	Equation	Definition
Fixed cost			Cost that is independent of the output level
Variable cost			Cost that varies with the output level
Total fixed cost	TFC		Cost of the fixed inputs (equals sum of quantity times unit price for each fixed input)
Total variable cost	TVC		Cost of the variable inputs (equals sum of quantity times unit price for each variable input)
Total cost	TC	$TC = TFC + TVC$	Cost of all inputs (equals fixed costs plus variable costs)
Marginal cost	MC	$MC = \Delta TC \div \Delta q$	Change in total cost resulting from a one-unit rise in output (*q*) [equals the *change* in total cost divided by the *change* in output]
Average fixed cost	AFC	$AFC = TFC \div q$	Total fixed cost per unit of output (equals total fixed cost divided by total output)
Average variable cost	AVC	$AVC = TVC \div q$	Total variable cost per unit of output (equals total variable cost divided by total output)
Average total cost	ATC	$ATC = AFC + AVC$	Total cost per unit of output (equals average fixed cost plus average variable cost)

OUTPUT AND COSTS IN THE SHORT RUN

As a firm alters its rate of output in the short run, how will unit cost be affected? First, let us look at this question intuitively. In the short run, the firm can vary output by using its fixed plant size more (or less) intensively. As Exhibit 2 illustrates, there are two extreme situations that will result in a high unit cost of output. First, when the output rate of a plant is small relative to its capacity, it is obviously being underutilized. Under these circumstances, *AFC* will be high, and therefore *ATC* will also be high. It will be costly and inefficient to operate a large plant substantially below its production capacity. At the other extreme, overutilization can also result in high unit cost. An overutilized plant will mean congestion, time spent by workers waiting for machines, and similar costly delays. As output approaches the maximum capacity of a plant, overutilization will lead to high *MC* and therefore to high *ATC*.

Thus, the ATC curve will be U-shaped, as pictured in part c of Exhibit 2. ATC will be high for both an underutilized plant (because AFC is high) and an overutilized plant (because MC is high).

Diminishing Returns and Production in the Short Run

Our analysis of the changes in unit cost as the output rate rises reflects a long-established economic law. This **law of diminishing returns** states that, as more and more units of a variable factor are applied to a fixed amount of other resources, output will eventually increase by smaller and smaller amounts. Therefore, in terms of their impact on output, the returns to the variable factor will diminish. The impact on costs is clear: When the returns to the variable factor are rising, marginal costs (the additions to total variable cost from adding a unit of output) are falling. Similarly, when the returns to the variable factor are falling, marginal cost is increasing.

The law of diminishing returns is as famous in economics as the law of gravity is in physics. It is based on common sense and real-life observation. Have you ever noticed that, as you apply a single resource more intensively, the resource eventually tends to accomplish less and less? Consider a wheat farmer who applies fertilizer (a resource) more and more intensively to an acre of land (a fixed factor). At some point, the application of additional 100-pound units of fertilizer will expand the wheat yield by successively smaller amounts.

Essentially, the law of diminishing returns is a constraint imposed by nature. If it were not valid, it would be possible to raise all the world's food on an acre of the best land, or even in a flowerpot. Logically, then, there would be no point in cultivating any of the less-fertile land. We would be able to increase output simply by applying another unit of labor and fertilizer to the world's most fertile flowerpot! In the real world, of course, this is not the case; the law of diminishing returns is valid and it restricts our options.

Exhibit 3 illustrates the law of diminishing returns numerically. Column 1 indicates the quantity of the variable resource, labor in this example, that is combined with a specified amount of the fixed resource. Column 2 shows the **total product** that will result as the utilization rate of labor increases. Column 3 provides data on the **marginal product**,

Law of diminishing returns
The postulate that, as more and more units of a variable resource are combined with a fixed amount of other resources, employment of additional units of the variable resource will eventually increase output only at a decreasing rate. Once diminishing returns are reached, it will take successively larger amounts of the variable factor to expand output by one unit.

Total product
The total output of a good that is associated with alternative utilization rates of a variable input.

Marginal product
The increase in the total product resulting from a unit increase in the employment of a variable input. Mathematically, it is the ratio of the change in total product to the change in the quantity of the variable input.

(1) UNITS OF THE VARIABLE RESOURCE, LABOR (PER DAY)	(2) TOTAL PRODUCT (OUTPUT)	(3) MARGINAL PRODUCT	(4) AVERAGE PRODUCT
0	0		—
		8	
1	8		8.0
		12	
2	20		10.0
		14	
3	34		11.3
		12	
4	46		11.5
		10	
5	56		11.2
		8	
6	64		10.7
		6	
7	70		10.0
		4	
8	74		9.3
		1	
9	75		8.3
		−2	
10	73		7.3

EXHIBIT 3
Law of Diminishing Returns (Hypothetical Data)

the change in total output associated with each additional unit of labor. Without the application of labor, output would be zero. As additional units of labor are applied, total product (output) expands. As the first three units of labor are applied, total product increases by successively larger amounts (8, then 12, then 14). Beginning with the fourth unit, however, diminishing returns are confronted. When the fourth unit is added, marginal product—the change in the total product—declines to 12 (down from 14, when the third unit was applied). As additional units of labor are applied, marginal product continues to decline. It is increasingly difficult to squeeze a larger total product from the fixed resources (for example, plant size and equipment). Eventually, marginal product becomes negative (beginning with the tenth unit).

Average product
The total product (output) divided by the number of units of the variable input required to produce that output level.

Column 4 of Exhibit 3 provides data for the **average product** of labor, which is simply the total product divided by the units of labor applied. Note the average product increases as long as the marginal product is greater than the average product. Whenever the marginal unit's contribution is greater than the average, it must cause the average to rise. Here, this is true through the first four units. The marginal product of the fifth unit of labor, though, is 10, less than the average product for the first four units of labor (11.5). Therefore, beginning with the fifth unit, the average product declines as additional labor is applied. When marginal productivity is below the average, it brings down the average product.

Using the data from Exhibit 3, **Exhibit 4** illustrates the law of diminishing returns graphically. Initially, the total product curve (part a) increases quite rapidly. As diminishing marginal returns are confronted (beginning with the fourth unit of labor), total product increases more slowly. Eventually, a maximum output (75) is reached with the application

EXHIBIT 4
Law of Diminishing Returns

As units of variable input (labor) are added to a fixed input, total product will increase, first at an increasing rate and then at a declining rate (a). This will cause both marginal and average product curves (b) to rise at first and then decline. Note that the marginal product curve intersects the average product curve at its maximum (when 4 units of labor are used). The smooth curves indicate that labor can be increased by amounts of less than a single unit.

(a) Total product curve

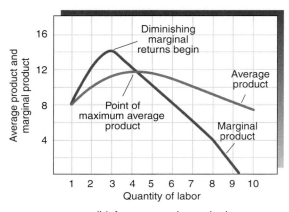

(b) Average and marginal product curve

of the ninth unit of labor. The marginal product curve (part b) reflects the total product curve. Geometrically, marginal product is the slope—the rate of increase—of the total product curve. That slope, the marginal product, reaches its maximum with the application of three units of labor. Beyond three units, diminishing returns are present. Eventually, at ten units of labor, the marginal product becomes negative. When marginal product becomes negative, total product is necessarily declining. The average product curve rises as long as the marginal product curve is above it, since each added unit of labor is raising the average. The average product reaches its maximum at four units of labor. Beyond that, each additional unit of labor brings down the average product, and the curve declines.

Diminishing Returns and Cost Curves

What impact will diminishing returns have on a firm's costs? Once a firm confronts diminishing returns, larger and larger additions of the variable factor are required to expand output by one unit. This will cause marginal costs (MC) to rise. As MC continues to increase, eventually it will exceed average total cost. Until that point, MC is below ATC, bringing ATC down. When MC is greater than ATC, the additional units cost more than the average, and ATC must increase. To make the point clear, consider a similar case in another setting. What happens when you make an additional exam grade above your current class average? Your class average goes up. What happens if a unit of above-average cost is added to output? Average total cost rises. The firm's MC curve therefore crosses the ATC curve at the ATC's lowest point. For output rates beyond the minimum ATC, the rising MC causes ATC to increase.

Exhibit 5 numerically illustrates the implications of the law of diminishing returns for a firm's short-run cost curve. Here, we assume that Royal Roller Blades, Inc., combines units of a variable input with a fixed factor to produce units of output (pairs of inline skates). Columns 2, 3, and 4 indicate how the total cost schedules vary as output is expanded. Total fixed costs *(TFC)*, representing the opportunity cost of the fixed factors of production, are $50 per day at all levels of output. For the first four units of output, total variable costs *(TVC)* increase at a decreasing rate. Why? In this range, there are increasing returns to the variable input. Beginning with the fifth unit of output, however, diminishing marginal returns are present. From this point on, *TVC* and *TC* increase by successively larger amounts as output is expanded.

EXHIBIT 5
Numerical Short-Run Cost Schedules of Royal Roller Blades, Inc.

	TOTAL COST DATA (PER DAY)			AVERAGE/MARGINAL COST DATA (PER DAY)			
(1) OUTPUT PER DAY	(2) TFC	(3) TVC	(4) TC (2) + (3)	(5) AFC (2) ÷ (1)	(6) AVC (3) ÷ (1)	(7) ATC (4) ÷ (1)	(8) MC $\Delta(4) \div \Delta(1)$
0	$50	$ 0	$ 50	—	—	—	—
1	50	15	65	$50.00	$15.00	$65.00	$15
2	50	25	75	25.00	12.50	37.50	10
3	50	34	84	16.67	11.33	28.00	9
4	50	42	92	12.50	10.50	23.00	8
5	50	52	102	10.00	10.40	20.40	10
6	50	64	114	8.33	10.67	19.00	12
7	50	79	129	7.14	11.29	18.43	15
8	50	98	148	6.25	12.25	18.50	19
9	50	122	172	5.56	13.56	19.11	24
10	50	152	202	5.00	15.20	20.20	30
11	50	202	252	4.55	18.36	22.91	50

EXHIBIT 6
Costs in the Short Run

Using data from Exhibit 5, this exhibit illustrates the general shape of the firm's short-run total cost curves (a), and average and marginal cost curves (b). Note that when output is small (for example, 2 units), *ATC* will be high because the *AFC* is so high. Similarly, when output is large (for example, 11 units), per-unit cost *(ATC)* will be high because it is extremely costly to produce the marginal units. Thus, the short-run *ATC* curve will be U-shaped.

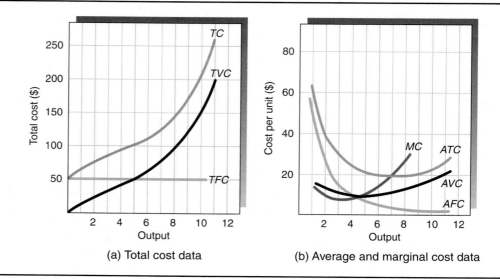

(a) Total cost data

(b) Average and marginal cost data

Columns 5 through 8 of Exhibit 5 reveal the average and marginal cost schedules. For small output rates, the *ATC* of producing roller blades is high, primarily because of the high *AFC*. Initially, *MC* is less than *ATC*, so *ATC* is falling. When diminishing returns set in for output rates beginning with five units, however, *MC* rises. Beginning with the sixth unit of output, *MC* exceeds *AVC*, causing *AVC* to rise. Beginning with the eighth unit of output, *MC* exceeds *ATC*, causing it also to rise. *ATC* thus reaches its minimum at seven units of output. Look carefully at the data of Exhibit 5 to be sure that you fully understand the relationships among the various cost curves. Do you understand how columns 4 to 8 are derived from columns 1 to 3?

Using the numeric data of Exhibit 5, **Exhibit 6** graphically illustrates the total, the average, and the marginal cost curves. Note that the *MC* curve intersects both the *AVC* and *ATC* curves at their minimum points (part b). As *MC,* driven up by diminishing returns, continues to rise above *ATC*, unit costs rise higher and higher as output increases beyond seven units.

In sum, the firm's short-run cost curves reflect the law of diminishing marginal returns. Assuming that the price of the variable resource is constant, *MC* declines so long as the marginal product of the variable input is rising. This results because, in this range, smaller and smaller additions of the variable input are required to produce each extra unit of output. The situation is reversed, however, when diminishing returns are confronted. Once diminishing returns set in, more and more units of the variable factor are required to generate each additional unit of output. *MC* will rise, because the marginal product of the variable resource is declining. Eventually, *MC* exceeds *AVC* and *ATC*, causing these costs also to rise. A U-shaped short-run average total cost curve results.

OUTPUT AND COSTS IN THE LONG RUN

The short-run analysis relates costs to output *for a specific size of plant*. Firms, though, are not committed forever to their existing plant. In the long run, a firm can alter its plant size and all other factors of production. All resources used by the firm are variable in the long run. Thus, there are no fixed and variable cost categories in the long run.

How will the firm's choice of plant size affect per unit production costs? **Exhibit 7** illustrates the short-run *ATC* curves for three different plant sizes, ranging from small to large. If these three plant sizes were the only possible choices, which one should be chosen, as the firm plans for the future? The answer depends on the rate of output the firm expects to produce from the plant to be built. The smallest plant would have the lowest cost

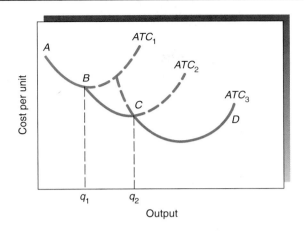

EXHIBIT 7
Long-run Average Total Cost

The short-run average total cost curves are shown for three alternative plant sizes. If these three were the only possible plant sizes, the long-run average total cost curve would be *ABCD*.

if an output rate of less than q_1 were produced. The medium-sized plant would provide the least-cost method of producing output rates between q_1 and q_2. For any output level greater than q_2, the largest plant would be the most cost-efficient.

The long-run ATC curve shows the minimum average cost of producing each output level when the firm is free to choose among all possible plant sizes. It can best be thought of as a planning curve, because it reflects the expected per-unit cost of producing alternative rates of output while plants are still in the blueprint stage.

Exhibit 7 illustrates the long-run *ATC* curve when only three plant sizes are possible, and the planning curve *ABCD* is thus mapped out. Of course, given sufficient time, firms can usually choose among many plants of various sizes. **Exhibit 8** presents the long-run planning curve under these circumstances. It is a smooth curve, with each short-run *ATC* curve tangent to it.

It is important to keep in mind that no single plant size could produce the alternative output rates at the costs indicated by the planning curve **LRATC** *in Exhibit 8.* Any of the planning curve options are available before a plant size is chosen and the plant is built; however, although the firm can plan for the long run, choosing among many options, it can *operate* only in the short run. The *LRATC* curve outlines the possibilities available in the planning stage, indicating the expected average total costs of production for each of a large number of plants, which differ in size.

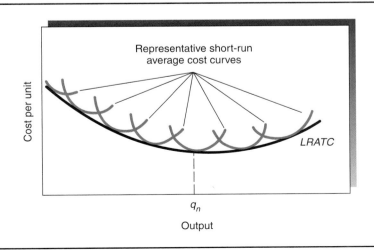

EXHIBIT 8
Planning Curve (*LRATC*)

When many alternative plant sizes are possible, the long-run average total cost curve (*LRATC*) is mapped out.

When firms are able to plan large volumes of output, the use of mass-production methods will generally lead to lower per-unit costs. This helps explain why the *LRATC* has a downward-sloping portion.

Economies and Diseconomies of Scale

Do larger firms have lower minimum unit costs than smaller ones? The answer to this question depends on which industries are being considered. There is a sound basis, though, for expecting some initial reductions in per-unit cost from large-scale production methods. Why? Large firms typically produce a large total volume of output.[3] Volume of output denotes the total number of units of a product that the firm expects to produce.[4] There are three major reasons why planning a larger volume generally reduces, at least initially, unit costs: (1) economies accompanying the use of mass-production methods, (2) higher productivity as a result of specialization and "learning by doing," and (3) economies in promotion and purchasing. Let us consider each of these factors.

Mass-production techniques usually are economical only when large volumes of output are planned, since they tend to involve large development and setup costs. Once the production methods are established, though, marginal costs are low. For example, the use of molds, dies, and assembly line production methods reduce the per-unit cost of automobiles only when the planned volume is in the millions. High-volume methods, although cheaper to use for high rates of output and high volumes, will typically require

---

[3]Throughout this section, we assume that firms with larger plants necessarily plan a larger volume of output than do their smaller counterparts. Reality approximates these conditions. Firms choose large plants because they are planning to produce a large volume.

[4]Note the distinction between rate and volume of output. Rate of output is the number of units produced during a specific period (for example, the next six months). Volume is the total number of units produced during all time periods. For example, Boeing might produce two 777 airplanes per month (rate of output) while planning to produce a volume of two hundred 777s during the expected life of the model. Increasing the rate (reducing the time period during which a given output is produced) tends to raise costs, whereas increasing the volume (total amount produced) tends to lower costs.

high fixed costs, and therefore will cause unit costs to be far higher for low volumes of production.

Large-scale operation also permits specialized use of labor and machines. In a giant auto plant, hundreds of different jobs must be done, and many of them require a training period for each worker. In a small plant, the same worker might do 10 or 20 of these jobs, so each worker would have a much longer, more costly training period. Even then, the worker doing so many tasks might never fully develop the same level of proficiency of the more specialized worker. Baseball players improve by playing baseball, and pianists by playing the piano. Similarly, the employees of a firm improve their skills as they experience "learning by doing" in their jobs. Even better, concentration on a narrower range of tasks may help workers discover or develop cost-reducing techniques. The result of greater size and specialization is often more output per unit of labor.

Large firms may also be able to achieve lower costs by spreading fixed costs (such as the costs of advertising, developing specialized equipment, and searching out or negotiating better input prices) over many more units. For example, both McDonald's and General Motors are able to spread these costs over a large number of stores and volume of sales. The cost advantages of scale come in many forms.

Economic theory explains why, at least initially, larger firms have lower unit costs than comparable smaller firms. Declining unit costs mean that **economies of scale** are present over the initial range of outputs. The long-run *ATC* curve is falling.

Economies of scale
Reductions in the firm's per-unit costs that are associated with the use of large plants to produce a large volume of output.

What about *dis*economies of scale? As output continues to expand, is there reason to believe that larger firms will eventually have higher average total costs than smaller ones? The underlying causes of diseconomies of scale are less obvious, but they do occur. As a firm gets bigger and bigger, beyond some point, bureaucratic inefficiencies *may* result. Code-book procedures tend to replace managerial genius and innovation is more difficult. Motivating the workforce and carrying out managerial directives are also more complex when the firm is larger, and principal-agent problems grow as the number of employees increases and more levels of monitoring need to be done.

Circumstances vary, so diseconomies of scale set in earlier for some kinds of firms than for others. For example, the firms in the fast food industry can be very large and remain efficient; economies of scale apparently outweigh the diseconomies even for giants like McDonalds. Yet in the fine dining portion of the restaurant industry, the best restaurants seem to be small. In those firms, customers demand individual attention, and a constantly changing and innovative menu is important. Diseconomies seem to set in at a much smaller size for that portion of the industry.

The bottom line for diseconomies of scale is this: For some firms, bureaucratic inefficiencies, principal-agent problems, difficulties with innovation, and similar problems cause long-run average total costs to rise beyond some output level in the firm. However, there is considerable variation among industries and even among firms in the same industry concerning the precise output level at which diseconomies of scale begin to occur.

It is important to note that scale economies and diseconomies stem from sources different from those of increasing and diminishing returns. ***Economies and diseconomies of scale are long-run concepts. They relate to conditions of production when all factors are variable. In contrast, increasing and diminishing returns are short-run concepts, applicable only when the firm has a fixed factor of production.***

Alternative Shapes of the LRATC

Exhibit 9 outlines three different long-run average total cost *(LRATC)* curves, each describing real-world conditions in differing industries. For a firm described by the cost curve in part a, both economies and diseconomies of scale are present. Higher per-unit costs will result if the firm chooses a plant size other than the one that minimizes the cost of producing output q. If each firm in an industry faces the same cost conditions, we can generalize and say that all plants larger or smaller than this ideal size will experience higher unit costs. A very narrow range of plant sizes would be expected in industries with

EXHIBIT 9
Three Different Types of Long-run Average Total Cost Curves

For one type of *LRATC* curve, economies of scale are present for output levels less than *q*, but immediately beyond *q*, diseconomies of scale dominate (a). In another instance, economies of scale are important until some minimum output level (q_1) is attained. Once the minimum has been attained, there is a wide range of output levels (q_1 to q_2) that are consistent with the minimum ATC for the industry (b). In a third situation, economies of scale exist for all relevant output levels (c). As we will see later, this type of LRATC curve has important implications for the structure of the industry.

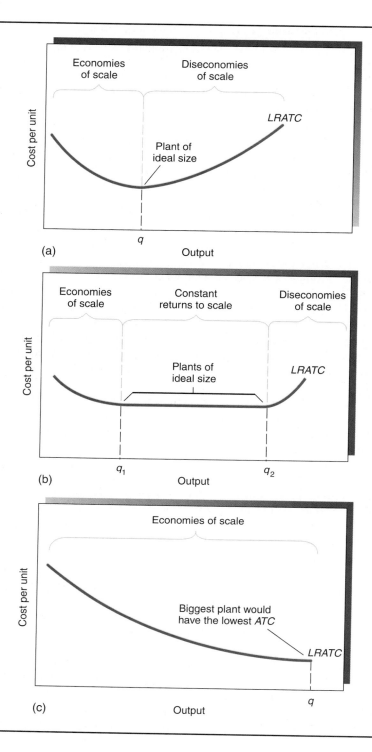

Constant returns to scale
Unit costs that are constant as the scale of the firm is altered. Neither economies nor diseconomies of scale are present.

the *LRATC* depicted by part a. Some lines of retail sales and agriculture might approximate these conditions.

Part b demonstrates the general shape of the *LRATC* that economists believe is present in most industries. Initially, economies of scale exist, but once a minimum efficient scale is reached, wide variation in firm size is possible. Firms smaller than the minimum efficient size would have higher per-unit costs, but firms larger than that would not gain a cost advantage. **Constant returns to scale** are present for a broad range of output rates (between q_1 and q_2). This situation is consistent with real-world conditions in many industries. For example, small firms can be as efficient as larger ones in such industries as apparel, lumber, publishing, and several lines of retailing.

In part c of Exhibit 9, economies of scale exist for all relevant output levels. The larger the firm size, the lower the per-unit cost. The *LRATC* in the local telephone service industry may approximate the curve shown here.

WHAT FACTORS CAUSE COST CURVES TO SHIFT?

In outlining the general shapes of a firm's cost curves in both the long run and short run, we assumed that certain other factors—resource prices, taxes, regulations, and technology—remained constant as the firm altered its rate of output. Let us now consider how these other factors would affect production costs if they did not remain constant.

Prices of Resources

If the price of resources used should rise, the firm's cost curves will shift upward, as **Exhibit 10** illustrates. Higher resource prices will increase the cost of producing each alternative output level. For example, what happens to the cost of producing automobiles when the price of steel rises? The cost of producing automobiles also rises. Conversely, lower resource prices will result in cost reductions. Thus, the cost curves for any specific plant size will shift downward.

Taxes

Taxes are a component of a firm's cost. Suppose that an excise tax of 20 cents were levied on the seller, for each gallon of gasoline sold. What would happen to the seller's costs? They would increase, just as they did in Exhibit 10. The firm's average total and marginal cost curves would shift upward by the amount of the tax. If the tax were an annual business license fee instead, it would raise the average cost, but not the variable cost.

Regulations

The government often imposes health, safety, environmental, and production regulations on business firms. Regulations may require businesses to provide a certain number of water fountains and rest rooms for customers and workers. The Americans With

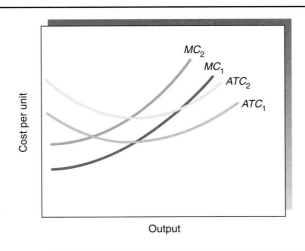

EXHIBIT 10
Higher Resource Prices and Cost

An increase in resource prices will cause the firm's cost curves to shift upward.

"OF COURSE YOU MAY REGISTER A COMPLAINT ABOUT ALL THE GOVERNMENT PAPERWORK, SIR... BUT IT HAS TO BE IN WRITING."

Disabilities Act forces many firms to make their facilities accessible for persons in wheelchairs. Regulations may force firms to include certain features in a product (for example, strong bumpers and air bags for automobiles). Although regulations yield benefits, they are also costly. Merely processing the required paperwork for submission to regulators is costly, and so are the other requirements. Like tax increases, increases in regulatory compliance costs will shift cost curves upward. In some cases, only fixed costs will be affected, while in other instances variable costs will be altered as well. In both cases, the firm's *ATC* will be higher.

Technology

Technological improvements often make it possible to produce a specific output with fewer resources. For example, computers and robots have reduced costs in many industries. The rapid expansion through the Internet of business-to-business or "B2B" services has made it easier to locate and contract for shared services, ranging from building maintenance, computer, and bookkeeping services to important components for manufacturing processes. Small firms can gain from specialization without being large themselves, and even large firms are participating. Federated Department stores, owners of Bloomingdales, Macy's, Burdines and the Bon Marché among others, recently contracted with a specialty firm to manage all of its building facilities worldwide. Federated expects to save $150 million per year from the change.[5] The *Wall Street Journal* reported that Micropub Systems of Rochester, N.Y., can install an entire brewery in 96 square feet, allowing the premium local brews to be made and delivered at lower cost than those currently available from the largest national brewers.[6] As **Exhibit 11** shows, a technological improvement will shift the firm's cost curves downward, reflecting the reduction in the amount of resources used to produce alternative levels of output.

[5]"Economies of Scale: Spend to Save," *Chain Store Age*, Vol. 76, Issue 2, Feb. 2000, p. 2B.
[6]Thomas Petzinger, Jr., "The Rise of the Small and Other Trends to Watch This Year," *Wall Street Journal*, Jan. 9, 1998, p. B1.

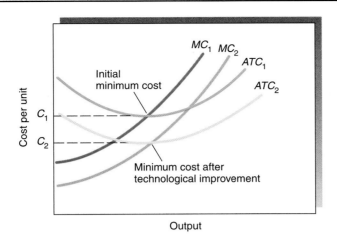

EXHIBIT 11
Egg-Production Costs and Technological Change

Suppose that an egg producer discovers (or develops) a "super" mineral water that makes it possible to get more eggs from the same number of chickens. Because of this technological improvement, various output levels of eggs can now be produced with less feed, space, water, and labor. Costs will be reduced. The egg producer's *ATC* and *MC* curves will shift downward.

ECONOMIC WAY OF THINKING ABOUT COSTS

When analyzing the firm's costs, economists often present a highly mechanical—some would say unrealistic—view. The role of personal choice in a world of uncertainty is often glossed over.

It is important to keep in mind that costs are incurred when choices are made. When business decision makers choose to purchase raw materials, hire new employees, or renew the lease on a plant, they incur costs. All these decisions, like other choices, must be made under conditions of uncertainty. Of course, past experience can help business decision makers to anticipate the likely costs of various decisions. But the world is constantly changing; the future may differ substantially from the past.

Opportunity costs are expected costs—they represent the highest valued option that the decision maker expects to give up as the result of a choice. Think for a moment of what the cost curves developed in this chapter really mean. The firm's short-run *MC* curve represents the opportunity cost of expanding output, *given the firm's current plant size*. The firm's long-run *ATC* curve represents the opportunity cost per-unit of output associated with varying plant sizes and rates of output, *given that the alternative plants are still on the drawing boards*. Opportunity costs look forward, reflecting expectations as to what will be forgone as a result of current decisions. At the time decisions must be made, neither the short-run MC nor the long-run *ATC* can be determined from accounting records, since accounting costs look backward. Accounting figures yield valuable information about historical costs, but, as the following section illustrates, they must be interpreted carefully when forecasting future costs.

Sunk Costs

Sunk costs are historical costs associated with past decisions that cannot be reversed. While sunk costs provide knowledge relevant to current decisions, the specific costs themselves are no longer relevant. When past choices cannot be reversed, money that has been spent is gone for good. Current choices must be based on the costs and benefits expected in relation to *current and future* market conditions, if mistakes are to be avoided (see the Myths of Economics box).

If they are to minimize costs, business decision makers must recognize the irrelevance of sunk costs. Let us consider a simple example that emphasizes this point. Suppose that the firm of Exhibit 5 pays $100,000 to purchase and install a roller blade producing machine.

Sunk costs
Costs that have already been incurred as a result of past decisions. They are sometimes referred to as historical costs.

MYTHS OF ECONOMICS

"A good business decision maker will never sell a product for less than its production costs."

This statement contains a grain of truth. A profit-seeking entrepreneur would not undertake a project knowing that the costs could not be covered. However, this view fails to emphasize (1) the time dimension of the production process and (2) the uncertainty associated with business decisions. The production process takes time. Raw materials must be purchased, employees hired, and plants equipped. Retailers must contract with suppliers. As these decisions are made, costs result. Many of the firm's costs of production are incurred long before the product is ready for marketing.

Even a good business decision maker is not always able to predict the future. Market conditions may change in an unexpected manner. At the time the product is ready for sale, buyers may be unwilling to pay a price that will cover the seller's past costs of production. These past costs, however, are now sunk costs and no longer relevant. Current decisions must be made on the basis of current cost and revenue considerations.

Should a grocer refuse to sell oranges that are about to spoil because their wholesale cost cannot be covered? The grocer's current opportunity cost of selling the oranges may be nearly zero. The alternative may be to throw them in the garbage next week. Almost any price, even one far below past costs, would be better than letting the oranges spoil.

Consider another example. Suppose a couple who own a house plan to relocate temporarily. Should they refuse to rent their house for $500 (if this is the best offer available) because their monthly house payment is $800? Of course not. The house payment will go on, regardless of whether they rent the house. If the homeowners can cover their opportunity costs (perhaps wear and tear plus a $60 monthly fee for a property management service), they will gain by renting rather than leaving the house vacant.

Past mistakes provide useful lessons for the future, but they cannot be reversed. Bygones are bygones, even if they resulted in business loss. There is no need to fret over spilt milk, burnt toast, or yesterday's business losses.

The machine is expected to last ten years. The company's books record the cost of the machine as $10,000 each year under the heading of depreciation. The machine can be used only to make roller blades. Since dismantling and reinstallation costs are high, it cannot be leased or sold to another firm. Also, it has no scrap value. In other words, there are no alternative uses for the machine. The machine's annual production of roller blades will generate $50,000 of revenues for the firm when it is employed with raw materials and other factors of production that cost $46,000. Thus, the net revenue generated by the machine is $4,000.

Should the firm continue to use the machine? Its annual depreciation cost suggests that the machine cost the firm $10,000, compared to the $4,000 of net revenue it generates. Thus, the accounting records indicate that the machine reduces the firm's profit by $6,000 annually. The machine's depreciation cost, however, is a sunk cost. It was incurred when the machine was installed. The current opportunity cost of the machine is precisely zero. The firm is not giving up anything by continuing to use it. Since use of the machine generates $4,000 of additional net revenue, the firm can gain from its continued operation. Of course, if current market conditions are not expected to improve, the firm will not purchase a similar machine or replace the machine when it wears out, but this should not influence the decision of whether to continue operating the current one. The irrelevance of sunk costs helps explain why it often makes sense to continue using older equipment (it has a low opportunity cost), even though it may not be wise to purchase similar equipment again.

Cost and Supply

Economists are interested in cost because they seek to explain the supply decisions of firms. A strictly profit-maximizing firm will compare the expected revenues derived from a decision or a course of action with the expected costs. If the expected revenues exceed costs, the course of action will be chosen because it will expand profits (or reduce losses).

In the short run, when making supply decisions, the marginal cost of producing additional units is the relevant cost consideration. A profit-maximizing decision maker will compare the expected marginal costs with the expected additional revenue from larger sales. If the latter exceeds the former, output (the quantity supplied) will be expanded.

Whereas marginal costs are central to the choice of short-run output, the expected average total cost is vital to a firm's long-run supply decision. *Before entering an industry* (or purchasing capital assets for expansion or replacement), a profit-maximizing decision maker will compare the expected market price with the expected long-run average total cost. Profit-seeking potential entrants will supply the product if, and only if, they expect the market price to exceed their long-run average total cost. Similarly, existing firms will continue to supply a product only if they expect that the market price will enable them at least to cover their long-run average total cost.

In this chapter, we outlined several basic principles that affect costs for business firms. We will use these basic principles when we analyze the price and output decisions of firms under alternative market structures in the chapters that follow.

LOOKING AHEAD

KEY POINTS

▼ The business firm is used to organize productive resources and transform them into goods and services. There are three major types of business structure—proprietorships, partnerships, and corporations.

▼ To solve the principal-agent problem, which tends to reduce worker efficiency in team production, every firm must provide work incentives and monitoring.

▼ The demand for a product indicates the intensity of consumers' desires for the item. The (opportunity) cost of producing the item indicates the intensity of consumer desires for other goods that could have been produced instead, with the same resources.

▼ In economics, total cost includes not only explicit payments for resources employed by the firm, but also the implicit costs associated with the use of productive resources owned by the firm (such as the opportunity cost of the firm's equity capital or owner-provided services).

▼ Because accounting methods omit the cost of equity capital (and sometimes other implicit costs),

they generally understate the opportunity cost of producing a good and overstate the firm's economic profit.

▼ Economic profit (loss) results when a firm's sales revenues exceed (are less than) its total costs, both explicit and implicit. Firms that are making the market (or "normal") rate of return on their assets will therefore make zero economic profit.

▼ The firm's short-run average total cost *(ATC)* curve will tend to be U-shaped.

▼ The law of diminishing returns explains why a firm's short-run marginal and average total costs will eventually rise. When diminishing marginal returns are present, successively larger amounts of the variable input will be required to increase output by one more unit.

▼ The long-run *ATC (LRATC)* reflects the costs of production for plants of various sizes. When economies of scale are present, *LRATC* will decline. When constant returns to scale are experienced,

LRATC will be constant. When diseconomies of scale are present, *LRATC* will rise.

▼ Changes in: (a) resource prices, (b) taxes, (c) regulations, and (d) technology will cause the cost curves of a firm to shift.

▼ Sunk costs are costs that have already been incurred and cannot be recovered. While they may provide information helpful for future decisions, sunk costs are no longer directly relevant for decision making.

CRITICAL ANALYSIS QUESTIONS

*1. What is economic profit? How might it differ from accounting profit? Explain why firms that are making zero economic profit are likely to continue in business.

*2. Which of the following statements do you think reflect sound economic thinking? Explain your answer.
   a. "I paid $400 for this economics course. Therefore, I'm going to attend the lectures even if they are useless and boring."
   b. "Because we own rather than rent, and the house is paid for, housing doesn't cost us anything."
   c. "I own 100 shares of stock that I can't afford to sell until the price goes up enough for me to get back at least my original investment."
   d. "Private education is costly to produce, whereas public schooling is free."

3. Suppose a firm produces bicycles. Will the firm's accounting statement reflect the opportunity cost of the bicycles? Why or why not? What costs would an accounting statement reveal? Should current decisions be based on accounting costs? Explain.

4. What is the principal-agent problem? When will the principal-agent problem be most severe? Why might there be a principal-agent problem between the stockholder-owners and the managers of a large corporation?

5. Suppose that Ajax, Inc., is the target of a takeover attempt by the management of Beta Corporation, which is offering to buy stock from any Ajax stockholder who wants to sell at 20 percent above the current price. Explain how the resistance of Ajax management to the takeover attempt might illustrate the principal-agent problem. Is it possible that Beta Corporation management's action is itself an illustration of the principal-agent problem? Explain.

6. What are some of the advantages of the corporate business structure of ownership for large business firms? What are some of the disadvantages? Is the corporate form of business ownership cost-efficient? In a market economy, how would you tell whether the corporate structural form was efficient?

*7. Explain the factors that cause a firm's short-run average total costs to decline initially, but eventually to increase as the rate of output rises.

8. Which of the following are relevant to a firm's decision to increase output: (a) short-run average total cost, (b) short-run marginal cost, (c) long-run average total cost? Justify your answer.

9. Economics students often confuse (a) diminishing returns to the variable factor and (b) diseconomies of scale. Explain the difference between the two, and give one example of each.

10. "Firms that make a profit have increased the value of the resources they used; their actions created wealth. In contrast, the actions of firms that make losses reduce wealth. The discovery and undertaking of profit-making opportunities are key ingredients of economic progress." Evaluate the statement.

*11. Is profit maximization consistent with the self-interest of corporate owners? Is it consistent with the self-interest of corporate managers? Is there a conflict between the self-interest of owners and that of managers?

*12. What is the opportunity cost of (a) borrowed funds and (b) equity capital? Under current tax law, firms can take the opportunity cost of borrowed funds, but not equity capital, as an expense. How does this tax feature affect the debt/equity ratio of business firms?

*13. "If a firm maximizes profit, it must minimize the cost of producing the profit maximizing output." Is this statement true or false? Explain your answer.

14. Why do economists consider normal returns to capital as a cost? How does economic profit differ from normal profit?

*15. Draw a U-shaped short-run *ATC* curve for a firm. Construct the accompanying *MC* and *AVC* curves.

16. What is shirking? If the managers of a firm are attempting to maximize the profits of the firm, will they have an incentive to limit shirking? How might they go about doing so?

17. What are implicit costs? Do implicit costs contribute to the opportunity cost of production? Should an implicit cost be counted as cost? Give three examples of implicit costs. Does the firm's accounting statement take implicit costs into account? Why or why not?

*18. Consider a machine purchased one year ago for $12,000. The machine is being depreciated $4,000 per year over a three-year period. Its current market value is $5,000, and the expected market value of the machine one year from now is $3,000. If the interest rate is 10 percent, what is the expected cost of holding the machine during the next year?

*19. Investors seeking to take over a firm often bid a positive price for the business even though it is currently experiencing losses. Why would anyone ever bid a positive price for a firm operating at a loss?

20. Fill in the blanks in the following table:
   a. What happens to total product when marginal product is negative?
   b. What happens to average product when marginal product is greater than average product?
   c. What happens to average product when marginal product is less than average product?
   d. At what point does marginal product begin to decrease?
   e. At what point does marginal cost begin to increase?
   f. Summarize the relationship between marginal product and marginal cost.
   g. What happens to marginal costs when total product begins to fall?
   h. What is happening to average variable costs when they equal marginal costs?
   i. Marginal costs equal average variable costs between what output levels?
   j. What is happening to average total costs when they equal marginal costs?
   k. Marginal costs equal average total costs between what output levels?

---

*Asterisk denotes questions for which answers are given in Appendix B.

Units of Variable Input	Total Product	Marginal Product	Average Product	Price of Input	Total Variable Cost	Average Variable Cost	Total Fixed Cost	Total Cost	Average Total Cost	Marginal Cost
0	0	____	____	$1	____	____	$2	____	____	____
1	6	____	____	$1	____	____	$2	____	____	____
2	15	____	____	$1	____	____	$2	____	____	____
3	27	____	____	$1	____	____	$2	____	____	____
4	37	____	____	$1	____	____	$2	____	____	____
5	45	____	____	$1	____	____	$2	____	____	____
6	50	____	____	$1	____	____	$2	____	____	____
7	52	____	____	$1	____	____	$2	____	____	____
8	50	____	____	$1	____	____	$2	____	____	____

CHAPTER 21

Price Takers and the Competitive Process

Chapter Focus

- How do firms that are price takers differ from those that are price searchers?

- What determines the output of a price taker?

- How do price takers respond when price changes in the short run? In the long run?

- How does time influence the elasticity of supply?

- What must firms do in order to make profits? How do profits and losses influence the supply and market price of a product?

- How does competition provide an incentive for producers to supply goods that consumers want at a low cost?

Competition means decentralized planning by many separate persons.

—Friedrich A. von Hayek[1]

[I]t is competition that drives down costs and prices, induces firms to produce the goods consumers want, and spurs innovation and the expansion of new markets . . .

—President's Council of Economic Advisers[2]

[1] F. A. Hayek, "The Use of Knowledge in Society," *American Economic Review* 35 (September 1945): 521.

[2] President's Council of Economic Advisers, *Economic Report of the President, 1996* (Washington, D.C.: U.S. Government Printing Office, 1996), p. 155.

n the previous chapters we saw how firms make production decisions and how costs affect those decisions. In this and the next two chapters, we take a closer look at how the product prices and profit levels that emerge from market trading will influence production. How much will be produced in a given market? What determines the profitability of firms, and how does the level of profit influence market supply over time? When goods and services are allocated by markets, will resources be allocated efficiently? Is there any reason to believe that there will be a linkage between market allocation and economic prosperity? These are the major questions that we will address in the next several chapters. ■

PRICE TAKERS AND PRICE SEARCHERS

This chapter will focus on markets where the firms are **price takers**: They simply take the price that is determined in the market. *In a price-taker market, the firms all produce identical products (for example, wheat, eggs, or regular unleaded gasoline) and each seller is small relative to the total market. Thus, the output supplied by any single firm exerts little or no effect on the market price. Each firm can sell all its output at the market price, but it is unable to sell any of its output at a price higher than the market price.* When a firm is a price taker, there is no price decision to be made. Price takers will merely attempt to choose the output level that will maximize profit, given their costs and the price determined by the market.

Price takers are assumed to seek profits, like all other firms. They need to be sensitive to cost, in order to thrive, or even to survive in a competitive environment. However, price-taker markets and price-searcher markets have differing degrees of competition, ease of entry, and perhaps differing scale economies as well. Competition for consumer business requires each firm to provide a high level of delivered benefits per dollar, compared to what consumers can find elsewhere. No firm can force consumers to purchase its product, and all products have many substitutes. Successful firms are those that stay ahead of competitors and potential competitors.

In the real world, most firms are not price takers. If the firm lowers its price, it will generally attract additional customers. Correspondingly, firms are usually able to increase their price, at least a little, without losing all their customers. For example, if Nike increased the price of its athletic shoes by 10 percent, the number of shoes sold would decline, but it would not fall to zero. Firms like Nike are **price searchers**: They choose the price they will charge for their product, but the quantity that they are able to sell is very much related to that price. As price searchers seek maximum profit, they must not only decide how much to produce, but also what price to charge. We will examine markets where the firms are price searchers in the following two chapters.

If most real-world firms are price searchers rather than price takers, why take the time to analyze the latter? There are several reasons to do so. First, although most firms are not price takers, there are a number of important markets, particularly in agriculture, where the firms do essentially take the price determined in the market. Second, the price-taker model helps clarify the relationship between the decision making of individual firms and market supply in both price-taker and price-searcher markets. Finally, and perhaps most important, the study of markets where firms are price takers enhances our knowledge of **competition as a dynamic process**. Understanding how the competitive process works when firms are price takers will also contribute to our understanding of the process as it applies to many price searchers.

Historically, the term **pure competition** has been used when referring to markets where firms are price takers. However, these markets are increasingly referred to as "price-taker markets" because this expression is more descriptive. Furthermore, this label avoids the implication that competitive forces are necessarily less pure or less intense in price-searcher markets. Often this is not the case. Many price searchers use a broad array of competitive weapons—for example, quality of product, style, convenient location, advertising,

Price takers
Sellers who must take the market price in order to sell their product. Because each price taker's output is small relative to the total market, price takers can sell all their output at the market price, but they are unable to sell any of their output at a price higher than the market price.

Price searchers
Firms that face a downward sloping demand curve for their product. The amount that the firm is able to sell is inversely related to the price that it charges.

Competition as a dynamic process
A term that denotes rivalry or competitiveness between or among parties (for example, producers or input suppliers), each of which seeks to deliver a better deal to buyers when quality, price, and product information are all considered. Competition implies a lack of collusion among sellers.

Pure competition
A market structure characterized by a large number of small firms producing an identical product in an industry (market area) that permits complete freedom of entry and exit. Also called price-taker markets.

APPLICATIONS IN ECONOMICS

The Aalsmeer Flower Auction: An Illustration of a Competitive Market

The Aalsmeer Flower Auction, located near Amsterdam, illustrates a highly competitive market with a large number of both buyers and sellers. Approximately 5,000 growers from the Netherlands and other countries such as Israel, Kenya, and Zambia supply their products to this market. On a typical day, several thousand buyers representing wholesale florists from around the world participate in the auction. More than 18 million flowers and 2 million plants are sold each day from a building equal in size to 125 football fields.

The 50,000 daily transactions are made possible by the Dutch auction system. Under this system, a clock runs backward from the highest to the lowest price per unit. The buyer pushes a button indicating a willingness to purchase when

the clock reaches an acceptable per unit-price. The purchaser is the first buyer to push the button. Flowers and plants auctioned in the morning at Aalsmeer will be available in shops around the world within 24 hours.

Barriers to entry
Obstacles that limit the freedom of potential rivals to enter and compete in an industry or market.

and price—all in an effort to attract consumers. When **barriers to entry** are low, the competitive process is just as important in price-searcher markets as it is when the firms are price takers.

Nonetheless, it should be noted that price-taker markets and purely competitive markets are merely alternative names for the same thing. Thus, if you hear someone speak of pure competition or a purely competitive market, the person is referring to markets that have characteristics like those analyzed in this chapter.

MARKETS WHEN FIRMS ARE PRICE TAKERS

Consider the situation of Les Parrot, a Texas cattle rancher. As Parrot consults the financial pages of the local newspaper, he finds that the current market price of quality steers is 88 cents per pound. Even if his ranch is quite large, there is little that Parrot can do to change the market price of beef cattle. After all, there are tens of thousands of farmers who raise cattle. Thus, Parrot supplies only a small portion of the total cattle market. The amount that he sells will exert little or no impact on the market price of cattle. Parrot is a price taker.

The firms in a market will be price takers when the following four conditions are met:

1. All the firms in the market are producing an identical product (for example, beef cattle of a given grade).

2. A large number of firms exist in the market.

3. Each firm supplies only a very small portion of the total amount supplied to the market.

4. No barriers limit the entry or exit of firms in the market.

When these conditions are met, the firms in the market must accept the market price. This is why they are called price takers. **Exhibit 1** illustrates the relationship between the

Producers in the wheat farming and beef cattle markets are price takers. If they are going to sell their output, they must do so at the price determined by the market. Because individual producers are small relative to the total market, they can sell as many units as they like at the market price.

market forces (frame *b*) and the demand curve facing the price-taking firm (frame *a*). If the firm sets a price above the market level, consumers will simply buy from other sellers. Why pay the higher price when the identical good is available elsewhere at a lower price? For example, if the price of wheat were $5.00 per bushel, a farmer would be unable to find buyers for wheat at $5.50 per bushel. A firm could set its price below the market level. However, since one firm is small relative to the total market, the firm can already sell as much as it wants at the market price. A price reduction would merely reduce revenues. A firm that is a price taker thus confronts a perfectly elastic demand for its product. (Note in the exhibit, that a lower case *d* is used to denote the demand curve faced by the *firm* while a capital *D* indicates the *market* demand curve.)

OUTPUT IN THE SHORT RUN

The firm's output decision is based on comparison of benefits with costs. If a firm produces at all, it will expand output as long as the benefits (additional revenues) from the production and sales of the additional units exceed their marginal costs. How will changes in output influence the firm's costs? In the preceding chapter, we discovered that the firm's short-run marginal costs will eventually increase as the firm expands its output by working its fixed plant facilities more intensively. The law of diminishing marginal returns assures us that this will be the case. Eventually, both the firm's short-run marginal and average total cost curves will turn upward.

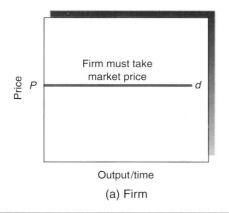

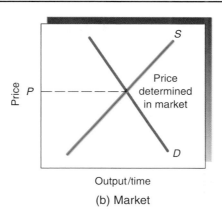

EXHIBIT 1
Price Taker's Demand Curve

The market forces of supply and demand determine price (b). Price takers have no control over price. Thus, the demand for the product of the firm is perfectly elastic (a).

Marginal revenue *(MR)*
The incremental change in total revenue derived from the sale of one additional unit of a product.

What about the benefits or additional revenues from output expansion? **Marginal revenue (*MR*)** is the change in the firm's total revenue per unit of output. It is the additional revenue derived from the sale of an additional unit of output. Mathematically,

$$MR = \text{Change in total revenue/Change in output}$$

The price taker sells all units at the same price; therefore, its marginal revenue will be equal to the market price.

In the short run, the price taker will expand output until marginal revenue (its price) is just equal to marginal cost. This decision-making rule will maximize the firm's profits (or minimize its losses).

Exhibit 2 helps explain why. Since the firm can sell as many units as it would like at the market price, the sale of one additional unit will increase revenue by the price of the product. Does the firm gain by producing an extra unit? The answer is yes, as long as the marginal revenue (price, for the price taker) is greater than or equal to the marginal cost of that unit. Profit is simply the difference between total revenue and total cost. Profit will increase as long as production and sale of a unit add more to revenue than to cost. Thus, the firm will gain from an increase in output as long as marginal revenue exceeds marginal cost. Eventually, however, as the firm produces a larger and larger quantity from its fixed size of plant, marginal costs will rise and exceed price and marginal revenue. When production of an additional unit adds more to cost than it adds to revenue, profit will be reduced if the unit is produced. Thus, the profit of the price taker is maximized at the output rate where $P = MR = MC$. In Exhibit 2, this occurs at output level q.

A profit-maximizing firm with the cost curves indicated by Exhibit 2 would produce exactly q. The total revenue of the firm would be the sales price P multiplied by output sold q. Geometrically, the firm's total revenues would be $P0qB$. The firm's total cost would be found by multiplying the average total cost (*ATC*) by the output level. Geometrically, total costs are represented by $C0qA$. The firm's total revenues exceed total costs, and the firm is making short-run economic profit (the shaded area).

In the real world, of course, decisions are not made by entrepreneurs who spend time drawing demand and marginal cost curves. Many have not even heard of these concepts. A business decision maker who has never heard of the $P = MR = MC$ rule for profit maximization, however, probably has another rule that yields approximately the same outcome. For example, the rule might be to produce those units, and only those units, that add more to revenue than to cost. This ensures maximum profit (or minimum loss). It also takes the firm to the point at which $P = MR = MC$. Why? To stop short of that point would mean not producing some profitable units that would add more to revenue than to cost. Similarly, the decision maker would not go beyond that point because production of such units would add

EXHIBIT 2
Profit Maximization When the Firm Is a Price Taker

The price taker would maximize profits by producing the output level q, where $P = MC$.

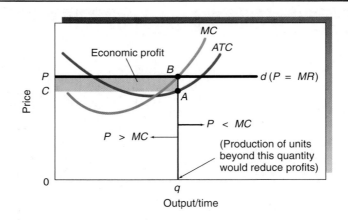

APPLICATIONS IN ECONOMICS

Experimental Economics: The Significance of Competition

Do individual decision makers, without any economics training, behave as if they understand marginal costs? Do they act as price takers, even though not all the assumptions of that model are satisfied? Or, when there are only a few sellers, do they collude successfully so as to raise price above marginal cost?

A normal economic event that we can observe may be the result of more than one cause; therefore, the economist seeking to isolate the impact of one causal factor must try to be sure that other factors influencing the outcome do not vary, or else try to take them into account in the analysis. This is not an easy task. In other disciplines, scientists use carefully designed laboratory experiments to test and verify the basic principles on which their science is built.

Beginning about the middle of the twentieth century, economists also began to conduct laboratory experiments. A good many experiments have been conducted to investigate the predictive power of the price-taker model. In one of the earliest, conducted in 1956 by leading experimental economist Vernon Smith of the University of Arizona, individuals were brought into a laboratory setting and arbitrarily assigned roles as buyers and sellers, in a game-like setting. Each buyer was given a different "limit price" (that is, a maximum price he or she was allowed to pay) for a paper asset. Any buyer who could purchase the paper commodity for less than the limit price received a cash payment equal to the difference between the limit price and the amount actually paid. Therefore, as in other markets, each buyer gained financially by purchasing at lower prices. The sellers were treated in a parallel fashion. Each had a "limit price" (a minimum selling price) and received in cash any extra revenue above that price.

Buyers and sellers were free to make verbal offers to buy or sell. How did markets develop? Did the outcomes resemble a market where sellers compete, or did sellers collude, controlling the market price for their own benefit and controlling entry into the market?

The price-taker model predicts that all mutually advantageous trades among buyers and sellers will occur and that the price of the good will converge toward a single price—the market price. Prior to the work in experimental economics, many economists thought this model was relevant only under highly restrictive conditions. By changing the number of sellers, the type of trading rules, and so on, experimental researchers have generated similar results under a wide variety of conditions. Their findings suggest that outcomes approximating those of the price-taker model often emerge even when the strict assumptions of the model are absent. For example, even if the number of sellers is relatively small, say ten to fifteen, outcomes similar to those predicted by the price-taker model generally occur.

Participants in these experiments are often startled to discover that their competitive trading generated the largest possible joint income gain and, furthermore, that the competitive model presented in this chapter predicted this occurrence. Vernon Smith cites cases where, after the experiment, participants describe the experimental market as "unorganized, unstable, chaotic, and confused." Generally, they are amazed when shown that their actions (trades) achieved the maximum income for the group, and that a sealed envelope, given to them prior to the experiment, predicted the approximate amount of their (maximum) joint gain.

Smith himself was at first surprised at the efficient outcomes resulting from economic experiments. He had not been prepared to believe Adam Smith's principle that markets cause individual traders to reach efficient outcomes, even though this is not their intention. These results are achieved even when the individual participants are far from proficient traders. After numerous experiments, the modern Smith stated:

> In many experimental markets, poorly informed, error-prone, and uncomprehending human agents interact through the trading rules to produce social algorithms which demonstrably approximate the wealth maximizing outcomes traditionally thought to require complete information and cognitively rational actors.[1]

Experimental economics has confirmed that Adam Smith was right in 1776 when he described the invisible hand of the market at work. It has also established that the invisible hand does not require very much beyond the desire of each individual to better his or her own situation. Perfect information, perfect traders, and perfect markets are not necessary for traders to reach efficient solutions, when they can trade freely.

Experimental economics has researched many additional economic questions. Vernon Smith and his colleague Arlington Williams, another leading researcher in this area, summarize the findings of their work in the following manner:

> Experimental market research has provided an empirical foundation for tenets of economic theory that were already well established, and it has also yielded insight into the details of how particular rules affect the outcome of the trading process. Thirty years of experiments

have also brought good news: under most circumstances, markets are extremely efficient in facilitating the movement of goods from the lowest-cost producers to the consumers who place the highest value on them. Organized exchange thus effectively advances human welfare.[2]

[1] Vernon L. Smith, "Economics in the Laboratory," *Journal of Economic Perspectives* 8, no. 1 (winter, 1994): 118.

[2] Vernon L. Smith and Arlington W. Williams, "Experimental Market Economics," *Scientific American* 267 (December 1992): 121. See also Smith, "Economics in the Laboratory," 113–32.

more to cost than to revenue. This commonsense rule thus leads to the same outcome as our model, even when the decision maker knows none of the technical jargon of economics. No wonder economics is sometimes thought of as "organized common sense."

Just how accurate is the price taker's competitive model in predicting behavior in real markets? Do other models, which assume that sellers collude to eliminate competition, yield better predictions? Direct scientific evidence bearing on such questions is highly desirable. As the Applications in Economics box on the significance of competition indicates, such evidence has been produced repeatedly in recent decades by the relatively new subdiscipline of experimental economics. The evidence indicates that the general implications of the price-taker model are valid under a variety of circumstances.

Profit Maximizing—A Numeric Example

Exhibit 3 uses numeric data to illustrate profit-maximizing decision making for a firm that is a price taker. Put yourself in the place of the owner of this firm. Your short-run total and marginal cost schedules have the general characteristics we discussed in the previous

EXHIBIT 3
Profit Maximization for a Price Taker: A Numeric Illustration

(1) OUTPUT (PER DAY)	(2) TOTAL REVENUE (TR)	(3) TOTAL COST (TC)	(4) MARGINAL REVENUE (MR)	(5) MARGINAL COST (MC)	(6) PROFIT (TR − TC)
0	$ 0.00	$ 25.00	$0.00	$ 0.00	$−25.00
1	5.00	29.80	5.00	4.80	−24.80
2	10.00	33.75	5.00	3.95	−23.75
3	15.00	37.25	5.00	3.50	−22.25
4	20.00	40.25	5.00	3.00	−20.25
5	25.00	42.75	5.00	2.50	−17.75
6	30.00	44.75	5.00	2.00	−14.75
7	35.00	46.50	5.00	1.75	−11.50
8	40.00	48.00	5.00	1.50	− 8.00
9	45.00	49.25	5.00	1.25	− 4.25
10	50.00	50.25	5.00	1.00	− 0.25
11	55.00	51.50	5.00	1.25	3.50
12	60.00	53.25	5.00	1.75	6.75
13	65.00	55.75	5.00	2.50	9.25
14	70.00	59.25	5.00	3.50	10.75
15	75.00	64.00	5.00	4.75	11.00
16	80.00	70.00	5.00	6.00	10.00
17	85.00	77.25	5.00	7.25	7.75
18	90.00	85.50	5.00	8.25	4.50
19	95.00	95.00	5.00	9.50	0.00
20	100.00	108.00	5.00	13.00	− 8.00
21	105.00	125.00	5.00	17.00	−20.00

chapter. Since the firm confronts a market price of $5 per unit, its marginal revenue is $5. Total revenue thus increases by $5 per additional unit of output produced and sold. You will maximize your profit when you supply an output of 15 units.

There are two ways of viewing this profit-maximizing output rate. First, profit is equal to the difference between total revenue and total cost. Thus, profit will be maximized at the output rate at which this difference (*TR* minus *TC*) is greatest. Column 6 of Exhibit 3 provides this information. For small output rates (less than 11), you and your firm would actually experience losses. But at 15 units of output, an $11 profit is earned ($75 total revenue minus $64 total cost). A look at the profit figures of column 6 indicates that it would be impossible to earn a profit larger than $11 at any other rate of output.

Exhibit 4 presents in part a the total revenue and total cost approach in graph form. (However, the curves are drawn smoothly, as though output could be increased by tiny amounts, not just in whole-unit increments as shown in Exhibit 3.) Profits will be greatest when the total revenue line exceeds the total cost curve by the largest vertical amount. That takes place, of course, at 15 units of output.

You can also use the marginal approach to determine the profit-maximizing rate of output for this competitive firm. Remember, as long as price (marginal revenue) exceeds marginal cost, production and sale of additional units will add to the firm's profit (or reduce its losses). A look at columns 4 and 5 of Exhibit 3 reveals that *MR* is greater than *MC* for the first 15 units of output. Producing these units will expand the firm's profit. In contrast, producing any unit beyond 15 adds more to cost than to revenue. Profit will

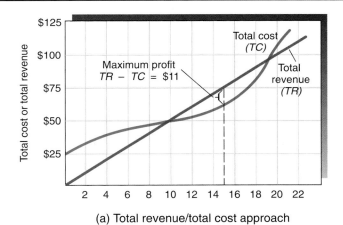

(a) Total revenue/total cost approach

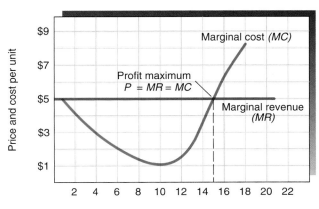

(b) Marginal revenue/marginal cost approach

EXHIBIT 4
Profit Maximization—
The Total and Marginal
Approaches

Using the data of Exhibit 3, here we provide two ways of viewing profit maximization. In the first, the profits of the price taker are maximized at the output level at which total revenue exceeds total cost by the maximum amount (a). In the second, the maximum-profit output is identified by comparing marginal revenue and marginal cost (b).

EXHIBIT 5
Operating with Short-run Losses

A firm making losses will operate in the short run if it (1) can cover its variable costs now and (2) expects price to be high enough in the future to cover all its costs.

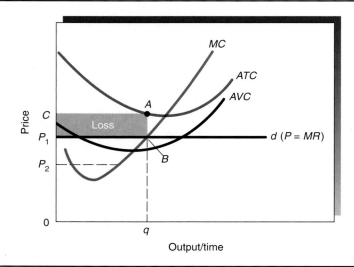

therefore decline if you expand output beyond 15 units. Given the firm's cost and revenue schedule, you will maximize profit by producing 15, and only 15, units per day.

Part b of Exhibit 4 graphically illustrates the marginal approach. Note here that the output rate (15 units) at which the marginal cost and marginal revenue curves intersect coincides with the output rate in part a at which the total revenue curve exceeds the total cost curve by the largest amount. Beyond that output rate, MR is less than MC, so profit must decline.

Losses and Going Out of Business

Suppose changes take place in the market that depress the price below a firm's average total cost. How will a profit maximizer (or loss minimizer) respond to this situation? The answer to this question depends both on the firm's current sales revenues relative to its variable cost and on its expectations about the future. The firm's owner has three options: (1) continue to operate in the short run, (2) shut down temporarily, or (3) go out of business.

If the firm anticipates that the lower market price is temporary, it may want to continue operating in the short run as long as it can cover its variable cost.[3] **Exhibit 5** illustrates why. The firm shown in this exhibit would minimize its loss at output level q, where $P = MR = MC$. But at q, total revenues ($OqBP_1$) are less than total costs ($OqAC$). The firm faces short-run economic losses. Even if it shuts down completely, it will still incur fixed costs, *unless the firm goes out of business*. If it anticipates that the market price will increase enough that the firm will be able to cover its average total costs in the future, it may not want to terminate operations and sell its assets. It may choose to produce q units in the short run, even though losses are incurred. At price P_1, production of output q is clearly more advantageous than shutting down, because the firm is able to cover its variable costs and pay some of its fixed costs. If it were to shut down, *but not sell out*, the firm would lose the entire amount of its fixed cost.

---

[3] Keep in mind the opportunity-cost concept. The firm's fixed costs are opportunity costs that do not vary with the level of output. They can be avoided if, and only if, the firm goes out of business. To specify fixed costs, we need to know (1) how much the firm's fixed assets would bring if they were sold or rented to others and (2) any other costs, such as operating license fees and debts, that could be avoided if the firm declared bankruptcy and/or went out of business. Since fixed costs can be avoided if the firm goes out of business, the firm will foresee greater losses from operating even in the short run if it does not expect conditions to improve.

This ice cream store in Morgantown, West Virginia, closes for several months each winter and reopens during the summer. During these short-run shutdowns, the store still pays fixed costs, such as rent, taxes, and insurance. Only variable costs are avoided during the winter months.

What if the market price declines below the firm's average variable cost (for example, P_2)? Under these circumstances, a temporary **shutdown** is preferable to short-run operation. Continuing to operate in the short run would add more to cost than to revenue, so operating losses merely add to losses resulting from the firm's fixed costs. Therefore, even if the firm's owner expects the market price to increase later, enabling it to survive and prosper in the future, shutting down in the short run will reduce losses when the market price falls below the firm's average variable cost (AVC). Temporary shutdowns are actually planned on a regular basis in some markets. For example, many ski resorts, golf courses, hotels, and restaurants in vacation areas plan to shut down in slow seasons, operating only when tourists or other seasonal purchasers provide enough demand. The price-taker model predicts that these firms will operate only when they expect to cover at least their variable costs.

The firm's third option is **going out of business** immediately. Since a cost that cannot be avoided by closing the business is not a cost of operating the business, even the losses resulting from the firm's fixed costs can be avoided if the firm sells out. When market conditions are not expected to change for the better, going out of business is the preferred option.

Shutdown
A temporary halt in the operation of a business firm. Because the firm anticipates returning to the market in the future, it does not sell its assets and go out of business. The firm's variable cost is eliminated by the shutdown, but its fixed costs continue.

Going out of business
The sale of a firm's assets and its permanent exit from the market. By going out of business, a firm is able to avoid fixed costs, which would continue during a shutdown.

Firm's Short-run Supply Curve

The price taker that intends to stay in business will maximize profits (or minimize losses) when it produces the output level at which $\mathbf{P} = \mathbf{MR} = \mathbf{MC}$ *and variable costs are covered. Therefore, the portion of the firm's short-run marginal cost curve that lies above its average variable cost is the short-run supply curve of the firm.*

EXHIBIT 6
Short-run Supply Curve for the Firm and the Market

As price increases, firms will expand output along their MC curve. Thus, the firm's MC curve is also its supply curve (a). When resource prices are constant, the short-run market supply is merely the sum of the supply produced by all the firms in the market area (b).

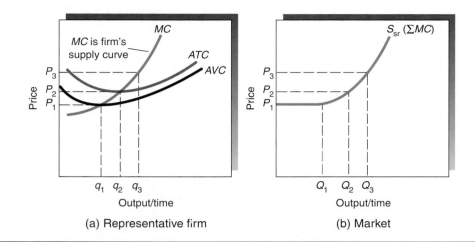

(a) Representative firm

(b) Market

Part a of **Exhibit 6** illustrates that, as the market price increases, the firm will expand output along its *MC* curve. If the market price were less than P_1, the firm would shut down immediately because it would be unable to cover even its variable costs. If the market price is P_1, however, a price equal to the firm's average variable cost, the firm may supply output q_1 in the short run. Economic losses will result, but the firm would incur similar losses if it shut down completely. As the market price increases to P_2, the firm will happily expand output along its *MC* curve to q_2. At P_2, price is also equal to average total costs. The firm is making a "normal rate of return," or zero economic profits. Higher prices will result in a still larger short-run output. The firm will supply q_3 units at market price P_3. At this price, economic profits will result. At still higher prices, output will be expanded even more. As long as price exceeds average variable cost, higher prices will cause the firm to expand output along its *MC* curve, which therefore becomes the firm's short-run supply curve.

Short-run Market Supply Curve

The short-run market supply curve corresponds to the total amount supplied by all the firms in the market. *When the firms are price takers, the short-run market supply curve is the horizontal summation of the marginal cost curves (above the level of average variable cost) for all firms in the market. Since individual firms will supply a larger amount at a higher price, the short-run market supply curve will slope upward to the right.*

Part b of Exhibit 6 illustrates this relationship. As the price of the product rises from P_1 to P_2 to P_3, the individual firms expand their output along their marginal cost curves. Since the individual firms supply a larger output as the market price increases, the total amount supplied to the market also expands.

Our construction of the short-run market supply curve assumes that the prices of the resources used by the industry are constant. When the entire industry (rather than just a single firm) expands output, resource prices may rise. If so, the short-run market supply curve (reflecting the higher prices of purchased inputs) will be slightly more inelastic (steeper) than the sum of the supply curves of the individual firms. The reason, of course, is that when just one firm expands, it has a minuscule effect on the market for resources, but when the entire industry expands output, the rise in resource demand is larger, so resource prices are more likely to rise.

The short-run market supply curve, together with the demand curve for the industry's product, will determine the market price. At the short-run equilibrium market price, each firm will have expanded output until marginal costs have risen to the market price. Firms will have no desire to change output, *given their current size of plant*.

OUTPUT ADJUSTMENTS IN THE LONG RUN

In the long run, firms have the opportunity to alter their plant size and enter or exit an industry. As long-run adjustments are made, output in the whole industry may either expand or contract.

Long-run Equilibrium

In addition to the balance between quantity supplied and quantity demanded necessary for short-run equilibrium, firms that are price takers must earn the normal rate of return, and only the normal rate, before long-run equilibrium can be attained. *If economic profit is present, new firms will enter the industry, and the current producers will have an incentive to expand the scale of their operations. This increase in supply will place downward pressure on prices. In contrast, if firms in the industry are suffering economic losses, they will leave the market. This decrease in supply will place upward pressure on prices.*

Therefore, as **Exhibit 7** illustrates, when a price-taker market is in long-run equilibrium (1) the quantity supplied and the quantity demanded will be equal at the market price, and (2) each firm in the industry will be earning normal (zero) economic profit (that is, its minimum *ATC* will just equal the market price).

Adjusting to an Expansion in Demand

Suppose a price-taker market is in equilibrium. What will happen if there is an increase in demand? **Exhibit 8** presents an example. An entrepreneur introduces a fantastic new candy product. Consumers go wild over it. However, since it sticks to one's teeth, the market demand for toothpicks increases from D_1 to D_2. The price of toothpicks rises from P_1 to P_2. What impact will the higher market price have on the output level of toothpick-producing firms? It will increase (from q_1 to q_2 in part a of the exhibit) as the firms expand output along their *MC* curves. In the short run, the toothpick producers will make economic profits. The profits will attract new toothpick producers to the industry and cause the existing firms to expand the scale of their plants. Hence, the market supply will increase (shift from S_1 to S_2) and eventually eliminate the short-run profits. If the prices

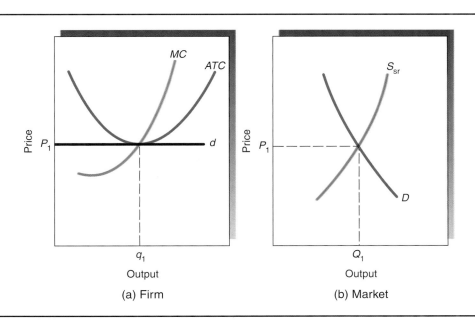

(a) Firm

(b) Market

EXHIBIT 7
Long-run Equilibrium in a Price-Taker Market

The two conditions necessary for equilibrium in a price-taker market are depicted here. First, quantity supplied and quantity demanded must be equal in the market (b). Second, the firms in the industry must earn zero economic profit (that is, the "normal rate of return") at the established market price (a).

EXHIBIT 8
Market Response to Increased Demand

The introduction of a new candy product that sticks to one's teeth causes the demand for toothpicks to increase to D_2(b). Toothpick prices rise to P_2, inducing firms to expand output. Toothpick firms make short-run profits (a), which draw new competitors into the industry. Thus, the toothpick supply expands (shifts from S_1 to S_2). If cost conditions are unchanged, the expansion in supply will continue until the market price of toothpicks has declined to its initial level of P_1.

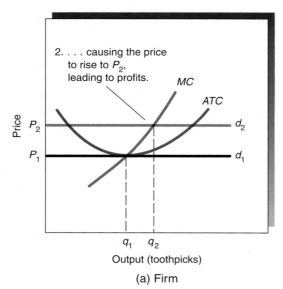

2. . . . causing the price to rise to P_2, leading to profits.

Output (toothpicks)

(a) Firm

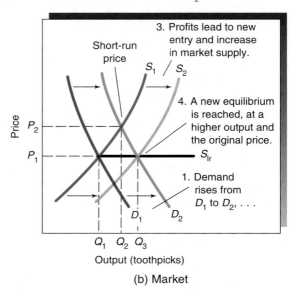

3. Profits lead to new entry and increase in market supply.

Short-run price

4. A new equilibrium is reached, at a higher output and the original price.

1. Demand rises from D_1 to D_2, . . .

Output (toothpicks)

(b) Market

of resources supplied to the industry are unchanged, the market price for toothpicks will return to its initial level, even though output has expanded to Q_3.

Adjusting to a Decline in Demand

Economic profits attract new firms to an industry. In contrast, economic losses (when they are expected to continue) encourage capital and entrepreneurship to move out of the industry and into other areas where the profitability potential is more favorable. Economic losses mean that the owners of capital in the industry (or firms that purchase the services of the capital) are earning less than the market rate of return. The opportunity cost of continuing in the industry exceeds the gain.

Exhibit 9 illustrates how market forces react to economic losses. Initially, assume that an equilibrium price exists in the industry. The firms are able to cover their average costs of production. Now suppose there is a reduction in consumer income, causing the market demand for the product to decrease and the market price to decline. At the new, lower price, firms in the industry will not be able to cover their costs of production. In the short run, they will reduce output along their *MC* curve. This reduction in output by the individual firms results in a reduction in the quantity supplied in the market. For an example of how firms react to changes in market price, see the Applications in Economics boxed feature on coffee production in a price-taker market.

In the face of short-run losses, the inflow of capital will decline and the industry's capital assets will shrink as firms fail to replace equipment when it wears out. Some firms will leave the industry as their fixed costs become variable and they are no longer able to cover their variable costs at the prevailing price. Others will reduce the scale of their operations, producing only those units for which the new, lower revenues can still justify the production costs. These factors will cause the industry supply to decline, indicated by the shift from S_1 to S_2. What impact will this have on price? It will rise. Over time, given no other shifts in demand, the short-run market supply curve will decline—will continue shifting to

EXHIBIT 9
Impact of Decline in Demand

A reduction in market demand will cause price to fall and short-run losses to occur. The losses will cause some firms to go out of business and others to reduce their scale. In the long run, the market supply will fall, causing the market price to rise. The supply will continue to decline and price will continue to rise until the short-run losses have been eliminated.

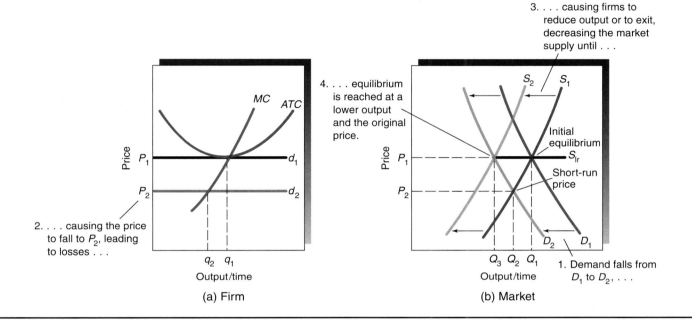

3. . . . causing firms to reduce output or to exit, decreasing the market supply until . . .

4. . . . equilibrium is reached at a lower output and the original price.

2. . . . causing the price to fall to P_2, leading to losses . . .

1. Demand falls from D_1 to D_2, . . .

(a) Firm

(b) Market

Coffee Production in a Price-Taker Market

Sellers to the world's coffee market are price takers. Hundreds of thousands of farmers produce coffee beans, and no grower has a significant impact on the world price. Each grower takes the price as given, and is free to respond to any price change. Changes can be dramatic in the coffee market. The market price rose from less than $1 per pound on average to more than $2 during the 1990s.

As growing coffee became more profitable, coffee production around the world expanded. For example, Vietnam growers more than quadrupled their coffee production, from 92,000 tons in 1990 to 487,000 tons in 1999. By 2000, Vietnam had became the world's second largest coffee-producing nation after Brazil.

But the expanded production proved to be more than consumers were willing to pay for. The market price fell. The price decline began in 1998; by August of 2001, coffee bean prices were averaging below $.60 per pound. Many coffee plantations could not cover their costs at such low prices,

and growers began to shift some of these crop lands to other uses. Some landowners in Indonesia, for example, planted rice. Others, especially in Central and Latin America, moved toward planting shade-grown coffee (in the shade of larger trees), organic, and other specialty coffee requiring special expertise and supervision, with lower yields but offering higher prices. Still other producers, including some in Vietnam, simply abandoned the least profitable plantations, at least temporarily. In Mexico, more than 300,000 farmers are estimated to have left their coffee farms to seek other opportunities, unable to cover even their variable costs.

The world coffee market illustrates very clearly how producers in price-taker markets can quickly expand production when rising prices are seen or expected, but can also contract production in response to falling prices and profits.

Source: The information presented is from Howard LaFranchi, "Economic Upheaval over Coffee," *Christian Science Monitor,* Aug. 15, 2001, p. 1, and from London's BBC Website at http://www.bbc.co.uk/worldservice/business/story_fdh200301.shtml, downloaded Sept. 17, 2001.

the left—until the price rises sufficiently to permit the firms remaining in the industry to earn once again "normal profits." At that point, long-run equilibrium is reached.

Long-run Supply

The *long-run market supply curve* indicates the minimum price at which firms will supply various market output levels, given sufficient time both to adjust plant size (or other fixed factors) and to enter or exit from the industry. The shape of the curve depends on what happens to the cost of production as the *industry's* output is altered. Three possibilities emerge, although one is far more likely than the other two.

Constant-Cost Industries

If resource prices remain unchanged, the long-run market supply curve will be perfectly elastic. In terms of economics, this describes a **constant-cost industry**. Exhibits 8 and 9 both picture constant-cost industries. As Exhibit 8 illustrates, an expansion in demand causes prices to increase *temporarily*. With time, however, the higher prices and profits will stimulate expansion and additional production, which will push the market price down to its initial level (and profitability to its normal rate). In the long run, the larger supply will not require a permanent price increase. Similarly, Exhibit 9 illustrates the impact of a decline in demand in a constant-cost industry. The *long-run supply curve* (S_{lr}) is perfectly elastic, reflecting the basically unchanged cost at the lower rate of industry output.

A constant-cost industry is most likely to arise when the industry's demand for resource inputs is quite small relative to the total demand for these resources. For example, the demand of the matches industry for wood, chemicals, and labor is very small relative to the total demand for these resources. Thus, doubling the output of matches would exert very little impact on the price of the resources used by this industry. Matches therefore approximate a constant-cost industry.

Increasing-Cost Industries

In most industries, an increase in market demand and *industry* output will lead to higher per-unit production costs for all the firms in the industry. Economists refer to such industries as **increasing-cost industries**. The rising output and expanded resource demand in

Constant-cost industry
An industry for which factor prices and costs of production remain constant as market output is expanded. Thus, the long-run market supply curve is horizontal.

Increasing-cost industry
An industry for which costs of production rise as output is expanded. Thus, even in the long run, higher market prices will be required to induce the firms to expand the total output in such industries. The long-run market supply curve in such industries will slope upward to the right.

In central areas of large cities, the supply of parking spaces can be expanded only by using higher-cost space and higher-cost techniques, such as taller parking garages that use a large portion of the building for access ramps. As a result, the unit cost of parking spaces increases as the total number is expanded. Thus, provision of parking space is an increasing-cost industry.

EXHIBIT 10
Increasing Costs and Long-run Supply

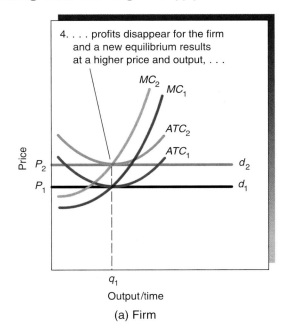

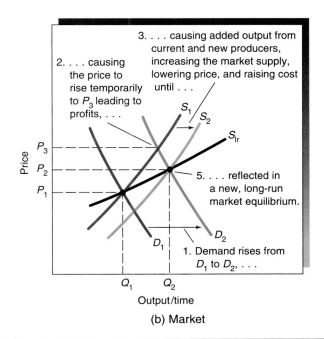

(a) Firm

(b) Market

such industries result in higher prices for at least some resources, causing the firms' cost curves to shift upward. For example, a rising demand for housing places upward pressure on the prices of lumber, window frames, building sites, and construction labor, causing the cost of housing to rise. Similarly, an increase in demand (and market output) for beef may cause the prices of feed grains, hay, and grazing land to rise. Thus, the production costs of beef rise as more of it is produced.

For an increasing-cost industry, an expansion in market demand will bid up resource prices, causing the per-unit cost of the firms to rise. As a result, a larger market output will be forthcoming only at a higher price. The long-run market supply curve for the product will therefore slope upward.

Exhibit 10 depicts an increasing-cost industry. Greater demand causes higher prices and a larger market output. As the industry expands, the price of resources (factors of production) rises so that costs increase. What happens to the firm's cost curves? Both the average and marginal cost curves rise (shift to ATC_2 and MC_2). Greater production cost necessitates a higher long-run price (P_2), so the long-run supply curve slopes upward to the right.

Decreasing-Cost Industries

Sometimes, factor prices will decline when the market output of a product is expanded. The lower resource prices will reduce the unit costs of the firms, placing them in a position to supply a larger market output at a lower price. In such **decreasing-cost industries**, the long-run (but not the short-run) market supply curve will slope downward to the right. For example, as the electronics industry expands, suppliers of certain components may be able to adopt large-scale production techniques that will lead to lower component prices. If rising electronics demand leads to reduced component cost (and if other resource prices do not rise to offset the reductions), then the cost curves of the electronics firms will shift downward. Under these circumstances, the industry supply curve for electronics products—reflecting the lower cost—will slope downward to the right.

Decreasing-cost industry
An industry for which costs of production decline as the industry expands. The market supply is therefore inversely related to price. Such industries are atypical.

In most industries, however, increases in demand and expansion in market output cause higher rather than lower input prices. Thus, increasing-cost industries are the norm, and decreasing-cost industries are quite rare.

Supply Elasticity and the Role of Time

It takes time for firms to adjust to a change in the price of a product. In the short run, firms are stuck with the existing size of their plant. If price increases in the short run, they can expand output only by utilizing their existing plant more intensely. Thus, their output response will be limited. In the long run, however, they will have time to build new plants. This will allow them to expand output by a larger amount in response to an increase in price. Thus, the market supply curve will be more elastic in the long run than in the short run.

The short- and long-run distinction offers a convenient two-stage analysis, but in the real world there are many intermediate production "runs." The delivery rates for some factors that could not be easily increased in a one-week time period can be increased over a two-week period. It might take two weeks, for example to hire reliable workers for jobs requiring no specialized skill. Economical expansion of other factors might require a month, and still others, six months. Ordering a new custom-made machine tool at Boeing, or hiring a competent new manager to expand an eastern Montana ranch operation might take a year. To be more precise, the cost penalty for quicker availability is greater for some productive resources than for others. In any case, a faster expansion usually means that greater cost penalties are necessary to provide for an earlier availability of resources needed for production.

When a firm has a longer time period to plan output and adjust all its productive inputs to the desired utilization levels, it will be able to produce any specific new rate of output at a lower cost. *Because it is less costly to expand output slowly in response to a demand increase, the expansion of output by firms will increase with time, as long as price exceeds cost. Therefore, the elasticity of the market supply curve will be greater when more time is allowed for firms to adjust output.*

Exhibit 11 illustrates the impact of time on the response by producers to an increase in price resulting from an expansion in demand. When the price of a product increases from P_1 to P_2, the immediate supply response of the firms is small, reflecting the high cost of hasty expansion. After one week, firms are willing to expand output only from Q_1 to Q_2. After one month, because of cost reductions made possible by the longer production planning period, firms are willing to offer Q_3 units at the price P_2. After three months, the rate of output expands to Q_4. In the long run, when it is possible to adjust all inputs to the

EXHIBIT 11
Time and Elasticity of Supply

The elasticity of the market supply curve usually increases as more time is allowed for adjustment to a change in price.

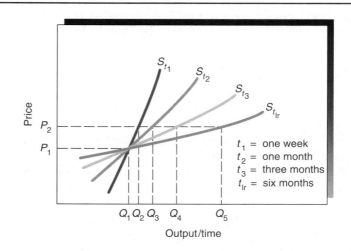

desired utilization levels (after a six-month time period, for example), firms are willing to supply Q_5 units of output at the market price of P_2. The supply curve for products is typically more elastic over a longer time period than over a shorter period.

ROLE OF PROFITS AND LOSSES

The price-taker model highlights the role of profits and losses: They are signals sent to producers by consumers. Economic profits will be largest in those areas where the value of additional units to consumers is highest relative to their production costs. Profit-seeking entrepreneurs will guide additional resources into these areas. Supply will increase, driving prices down and eliminating the profits. ***Free entry and the competitive process will protect the consumer from arbitrarily high prices. In the long run, competitive prices will reflect costs of production.***

Economic profits result because a firm or an entrepreneur acts to increase the value of resources. Business firms purchase resources and use them to produce a product or service that is sold to consumers. Costs are incurred as the business pays workers and other resource owners for their services. If the sales of the business firm exceed the costs of employing all the resources required to produce the firm's output, then the firm will make a profit. ***In essence, profit is a reward that business owners will earn if they produce a good that consumers value more (as measured by their willingness to pay) than the resources required for the good's production (as measured by the cost of bidding the resources away from their alternative employment possibilities).***

For example, suppose that it costs a shirt manufacturer $20,000 per month to lease a building, rent the required machines, and purchase the labor, cloth, buttons, and other materials necessary to produce and market 1,000 shirts per month. Thus, the average cost of the shirts is $20 (the $20,000 monthly cost divided by the 1,000 monthly output). If the manufacturer sells the 1,000 shirts for $22 each, its actions create wealth. Consumers value the shirts more than they value the resources required for their production. The manufacturer's $2 profit per shirt is a reward received for increasing the value of the resources.

In contrast, losses are a penalty imposed on businesses that reduce the value of resources. Losses indicate that the value of the resources used (as measured by their cost) by the firm exceeds the price consumers are willing to pay for the product supplied. Losses, along with bankruptcies, are the market's way of bringing such wasteful activities to a halt.

We live in a world of changing tastes and technology, imperfect knowledge, and uncertainty. Business decision makers cannot be sure of either future market prices or costs of production. Their decisions must be based on expectations. Nonetheless, the reward-penalty structure of a market economy is clear. ***Firms that anticipate correctly the products and services for which future demand will be most urgent (relative to production cost), and produce and market them efficiently will make economic profits. Those that are inefficient and allocate resources incorrectly into areas of weak demand (relative to cost) will be penalized with losses.***

The firms most adept at giving consumers value for money thrive and expand, while those less successful in doing so tend to shrink or even to disappear from the market. When entry barriers are low, small firms are sometimes able to challenge and compete successfully against rivals that are much larger. Michael Dell's success in the personal computer market provides a vivid illustration of this point. In 1984 Dell began producing and marketing personal computers while he was still a student at the University of Texas. At the age of 19, he began operations from his dormitory room with an investment of $1000.[4] Then as now, Dell took orders for PCs, bought component parts from competing sellers, and custom-built the machines almost immediately to fill each order for quick delivery directly to consumers. His firm has very low cost partly because it keeps on hand

[4] These and other facts about Dell are from Michael Dell and Andrew Fisher, "It's Crunch Time for Your Competitors," *Financial Times* (London), Sept. 5, 2001, p. 10.

only 4 days' inventory. This lean operation also allows him to offer and build in the latest technical innovations as soon as they are available. In contrast, IBM, Compaq, and Apple, the dominant firms at the time Dell entered the market, built PCs equipped in one specific way by the thousands and marketed them through retailers.

Dell passes on the firm's low costs, including the constantly falling prices of computer chips and other components. And it contracts with local computer service firms to provide dependable warranty service. Dell's business plan helped the firm build volume year after year until it became the industry leader. By the year 2000, Dell was selling $32 billion worth of computers and related equipment. Michael Dell's stock had made him a billionaire. By 2001, losses had caused IBM to exit the PC market, Compaq was struggling in the PC market and turning its attention to other products, and Apple had a much smaller share of the market than before.

Dell is not truly a price taker, since it does lower price in order to sell more PCs. However, the same low barriers to entry that allowed it to enter and succeed will stop it from raising its price much above the lowest achievable cost, even if its low prices drive other competitors out of business. Many firms, large and small, can quickly enter and expand production of PCs, if Dell raises its prices. A higher price would be an open invitation for others to step in and lure away Dell's customers, just as Dell earlier took customers from the largest firms in the industry. And even if he does not raise his price, there are many college students with $1000, some of them no doubt seeking an even better way to make PCs, or better machines than PCs, standing ready to displace Michael Dell as the top producer in this easy-to-enter business.

COMPETITION AND PROSPERITY

Competition

 Competition provides businesses with a strong incentive to produce efficiently, cater to the views of consumers, and search for innovative improvements.

The price-taker model highlights the importance of the competitive process. Competition places pressure on producers to operate efficiently and use resources wisely. Each business firm will have a strong tendency to produce its output as cheaply as possible. Holding quality constant, pursuit of profit will encourage each firm to minimize the cost of production—to use the least valued set of resources needed to produce the desired output.

Correspondingly, firms in competitive markets will have a strong incentive to discover and produce goods that are valued more highly than the resources required for their production. Thus, resources are drawn to those uses where they are most productive, as judged by the consumers' willingness to pay. The ability of firms freely to expand or contract their businesses, and to enter or exit the market, means that resources that could be more valuable elsewhere will not be trapped unproductively in a particular industry. Resource owners can move them to where they are most highly valued in production.

OUTSTANDING ECONOMIST

Friedrich A. von Hayek (1899–1992)

Remarkably, the writings of this 1974 Nobel Prize recipient spanned seven decades. His work on knowledge and markets both enhanced our understanding of the competitive process and highlighted the fatal defects of central planning. He also made major contributions in areas as diverse as monetary theory, law and economics, business cycles, and capital theory.

Competition weeds out inefficient producers—those who are unable to produce goods and services as economically as their rivals in the marketplace. It also keeps producers on their toes in other areas. The production techniques and product offerings that lead to success today will not necessarily pass the competitive market test tomorrow. Producers who survive in a competitive environment cannot be complacent. As the chapter-opening quotation from the President's Council of Economic Advisers indicates, competition forces firms to be forward-looking and innovative. They must be willing to experiment and quick to adopt improved methods.

In competitive markets, business firms must serve the interests of consumers. As Adam Smith noted more than 200 years ago, competition harnesses personal self-interest and puts it to work, elevating our standard of living and directing our resources toward the production of those goods that we desire most intensely relative to their cost. Smith stated:

> It is not from the benevolence of the butcher, the brewer, or the baker, that we expect our dinner, but from their regard to their own self-interest. We address ourselves, not to their humanity but to their self-love, and never talk to them of our own necessities, but of their advantages.[5]

In a competitive environment, even self-interested individuals and profit-seeking business firms have a strong incentive to recognize and serve the interests of others, and to supply products that are valued more highly than the resources required for their production. This is the path to greater income and larger profits. Paradoxical as it may seem, personal self-interest—a characteristic many view as less than admirable—is a powerful source of economic progress when it is directed by competition.

In the real world, consumers often seek variety in product design, style, durability, service, and location. As a result, the products of one firm are not perfect substitutes for those of another. In such cases, not all consumers switch to other suppliers when the price of one firm's output rises. Most firms are price searchers rather than price takers. In addition, barriers to entry sometimes limit competition. In the next two chapters, we will examine markets where the firms are price searchers and will consider the importance of entry barriers into such markets.

**LOOKING
AHEAD**

KEY POINTS

▼ A firm that confronts a perfectly elastic demand for its product is a price taker. A firm that can raise its price without losing all its customers (and which must lower its price in order to sell more units) is a price searcher.

▼ To maximize profit, a price taker will expand output as long as the sale of additional units adds more to revenues than to costs. Therefore, the profit-maximizing price taker will produce the output level at which marginal revenue (and price) equals marginal cost.

▼ The price taker's short-run marginal cost curve (above its average variable cost) is its supply curve. The short-run market supply curve is the horizontal summation of the marginal cost curves (above *AVC*) of the firms in the industry.

---

[5] Adam Smith, *An Inquiry into the Nature and Causes of the Wealth of Nations* (1776; Cannan's ed., Chicago: University of Chicago Press, 1976), p. 18.

▼ A firm experiencing losses, but anticipating that it will be able to cover its costs in the long run, will operate in the short run if it can cover its average variable costs. Conversely, the firm will shut down if it cannot cover average variable cost. A firm that does not anticipate being able to cover its average total cost even in the long run will minimize losses by immediately going out of business.

▼ When price exceeds average total cost, a firm will make economic profit. When entry barriers are absent, profits will attract new firms into the industry and stimulate the existing firms to expand. This increasing market supply continues and puts downward pressure on price until it reaches the level of average total cost, eliminating the economic profit.

▼ When the market price is less than the firm's average total cost, the resulting losses imply that the resources could be used to produce more value elsewhere. Losses will cause firms to leave the industry or to reduce the scale of their operations. This declining market supply continues and puts upward pressure on price until the firms remaining in the market are able to earn normal returns (zero economic profit).

▼ As the output of an industry expands, marginal costs will increase in the short run, causing the short-run market supply curve to slope upward to the right. Normally, as industry output expands, rising factor prices will push the costs of each firm upward, causing the long-run market supply curve to slope upward to the right.

▼ In the short run, "fixed" resources like the size of the firm's plant will limit the ability of firms to expand output quickly. In the long run, firms can alter the size of their plants and other resources that are fixed in the short run. As a result, the market supply curve will generally be more elastic in the long run.

▼ Firms earn economic profit by producing goods that can be sold for more than the cost of the resources required for their production. Profit is a reward for actions that increase the value of resources. Conversely, losses are a penalty imposed on those who use resources in a way that reduces their value.

▼ The competitive process provides strong pressure for producers to operate efficiently and heed the views of consumers. Competition and the market process harness self-interest and use it to direct producers toward wealth-creating activities.

CRITICAL ANALYSIS QUESTIONS

*1. Farmers are often heard to complain about the high costs of machinery, labor, and fertilizer, suggesting that these costs drive down their profit rate. Does it follow that if, for example, the price of fertilizer fell by 10 percent, farming (a highly competitive industry with low barriers to entry) would be more profitable? Explain.

*2. If the firms in a price-taker market are making short-run profits, what will happen to the market price in the long run? Explain.

3. "In a price-taker market, if a business operator produces efficiently—that is, if the cost of producing the good is minimized—the operator will be able to make at least a normal profit." True or false? Explain.

4. Suppose that the government of a large city levies a 5 percent sales tax on hotel rooms. How will the tax affect (a) prices of hotel rooms, (b) the profits of hotel owners, and (c) gross (including the tax) expenditures on hotel rooms?

*5. Within the framework of the price-taker model, how will an unanticipated increase in demand for a prod-

uct affect each of the following in a market that was initially in long-run equilibrium?
a. The short-run market price of the product
b. Industry output in the short run
c. Profitability in the short run
d. The long-run market price in the industry
e. Industry output in the long run
f. Profitability in the long run

*6. Suppose that the development of a new drought-resistant hybrid seed corn leads to a 50 percent increase in the average yield per acre without increasing the cost to the farmers who use the new technology. If the producers in the corn production industry are price takers, what will happen to the following?
a. The price of corn
b. The profitability of corn farmers who quickly adopt the new technology
c. The profitability of corn farmers who are slow to adopt the new technology
d. The price of soybeans, a substitute product for corn

7. "When the firms in the industry are just able to cover their cost of production, economic profit is zero. Therefore, if there is a reduction in demand causing prices to go down even a little bit, all of the firms in the industry will be driven out of business." True or false? Explain.

8. Why does the short-run market supply curve for a product slope upward to the right? Why does the long-run market supply curve generally slope upward to the right? Why is the long-run market supply curve generally more elastic than the short-run supply curve?

9. How does competition among firms affect the incentive of each firm to (a) operate efficiently (produce at a low per-unit cost) and (b) produce goods that consumers value? What happens to firms that fail to do these two things?

10. Will firms in a price-taker market be able to earn profits in the long run? Why or why not? What are the major determinants of profitability for a firm? Discuss.

*11. During the summer of 1988, drought conditions throughout much of the United States substantially reduced the size of the corn, wheat, and soybean crops, three commodities for which demand is inelastic. Use the price-taker model to determine how the drought affected (a) grain prices, (b) revenue from the three crops, and (c) the profitability of farming.

12. Why is competition in a market important? Is there a positive or negative impact on the economy when strong competitive pressures drive various firms out of business? Discuss.

*13. The accompanying table presents the expected cost and revenue data for the Tucker Tomato Farm. The Tuckers produce tomatoes in a greenhouse and sell them wholesale in a price-taker market.
   a. Fill in the firm's marginal cost, average variable cost, average total cost, and profit schedules.
   b. If the Tuckers are profit maximizers, how many tomatoes should they produce when the market price is $500 per ton? Indicate their profits.
   c. Indicate the firm's output level and maximum profit if the market price of tomatoes increases to $550 per ton.
   d. How many units would the Tucker Tomato Farm produce if the price of tomatoes declined to $450? Indicate the firm's profits. Should the firm continue in business? Explain.

COST AND REVENUE SCHEDULES TUCKER TOMATO FARM, INC.

OUTPUT (TONS PER MONTH)	TOTAL COST	PRICE PER TON	MARGINAL COST	AVERAGE VARIABLE COST	AVERAGE TOTAL COST	PROFITS (MONTHLY)
0	$1,000	$500	___	___	___	___
1	1,200	500	___	___	___	___
2	1,350	500	___	___	___	___
3	1,550	500	___	___	___	___
4	1,900	500	___	___	___	___
5	2,300	500	___	___	___	___
6	2,750	500	___	___	___	___
7	3,250	500	___	___	___	___
8	3,800	500	___	___	___	___
9	4,400	500	___	___	___	___
10	5,150	500	___	___	___	___

14. In the table on the following page, you are given information about two firms that compete in a price-taker market. Assume that fixed costs for each firm are $20.
   a. Complete the table.
   b. What is the lowest price at which firm A will produce?
   c. How many units of output will it produce at that price? (Assume that it cannot produce fractional units.)
   d. What is the lowest price at which firm B will produce?
   e. How many units of output will it produce?
   f. How many units will firm A produce if the market price is $20?
   g. How many units will firm B produce at the $20 price? (Assume it cannot produce fractional units.)
   h. If each firm's total fixed costs are $20 and the price of output is $20, which firm would be receiving a higher net profit or smaller loss?
   i. How much would that net profit or loss be?

	FIRM A				FIRM B		
QUANTITY	TOTAL VARIABLE COST	MARGINAL COST	AVERAGE VARIABLE COST	QUANTITY	TOTAL VARIABLE COST	MARGINAL COST	AVERAGE VARIABLE COST
1	$ 24	_____	_____	1	$ 8	_____	_____
2	30	_____	_____	2	10	_____	_____
3	38	_____	_____	3	16	_____	_____
4	48	_____	_____	4	24	_____	_____
5	62	_____	_____	5	36	_____	_____
6	82	_____	_____	6	56	_____	_____
7	110	_____	_____	7	86	_____	_____

*Asterisk denotes questions for which answers are given in Appendix B.

CHAPTER 22

Price-Searcher Markets with Low Entry Barriers

[T]he price to the price-searcher is not determined for him as if by some impersonal market mechanism. Instead he must search out the optimal (wealth-maximizing) price. And, not knowing the demand schedule exactly, he will have to resort to retrial-and-error search processes.

—Armen A. Alchian and William R. Allen [1]

Chapter Focus

- What are the characteristics of competitive price-searcher markets? How are price and output determined in such markets?

- Why are business failures important for the overall success of an economy?

- What are contestable markets? Can contestable markets be competitive when there is room for only one or two rival firms?

- Why is the role of the entrepreneur left out of economic models? How do the actions of entrepreneurs influence economic progress?

- Why do some economists criticize price-searcher behavior when entry barriers are low, while others like the results?

- Is price discrimination bad?

[1]Armen A. Alchian and William R. Allen, *University Economics*, 2d ed. (Belmont, Calif.: Wadsworth Publishing Co., 1967), p. 113.

I n the previous chapter we learned that price takers must accept the market price. They merely adjust their output to supply more units if they expect the cost of the additional units to be less than the market price. Price searchers have a more complex set of decisions to make in their search for profit. (See the chapter opening quotation from Professors Alchian and Allen.) In this chapter we consider the choices facing price searchers in markets where entry barriers are low. Low entry barriers are the key to competitive markets. When the restraints limiting entry are minimal, any opportunity for profit will attract competitors. Markets with low entry barriers, but where firms can raise their prices without losing all their customers, are described as **competitive price-searcher markets.** ■

Competitive price-searcher market
A market where the firms have a downward-sloping demand curve, and entry into and exit from the market are relatively easy.

Differentiated products
Products distinguished from similar products by such characteristics as quality, design, location, and method of promotion.

Monopolistic competition
Term often used by economists to describe markets characterized by a large number of sellers that supply differentiated products to a market with low barriers to entry. Essentially, it is an alternative term for a competitive price-searcher market.

COMPETITIVE PRICE-SEARCHER MARKETS

Competitive price-searcher markets are characterized by (1) low entry barriers and (2) *firms* that face a downward-sloping demand curve.[2] In contrast with price-taker markets where the firms produce identical products, price searchers produce **differentiated products.** The products supplied by the alternative sellers may differ in their design, dependability, location, ease of purchase, and a multitude of other factors. Sometimes economists use the term **monopolistic competition** to describe markets quite similar to those of the competitive price-searcher model. Since there is nothing "monopolistic" about these markets, we believe that this term is misleading. *Competitive price searcher* is much more descriptive of conditions in these markets. However, students should be aware that the expression "monopolistic competition" is often used to describe markets very much like those analyzed in this chapter.

Product differentiation explains why firms in price-searcher markets confront a downward-sloping demand curve. Ice cream from Häagen-Dazs is not identical to ice cream from Ben and Jerry's, Breyers, or Baskin-Robbins. Since some consumers are willing to pay more in order to get the specific product they like best, the *firm* will not lose all its customers to rivals if it raises its price. Rival firms, however, supply products that are quite similar to those supplied by the price searcher, so as the firm raises its price, some of its consumers will switch to the substitutes. ***Thus, the demand curve faced by the firm in a competitive price-searcher market will be highly elastic, because good substitutes for its output are readily available from other suppliers.***

The price searcher must choose between lower prices with larger quantities sold, and higher prices with smaller sales. ***Although a price searcher can set the price for its products, market forces will determine the quantity sold at alternative prices.*** In trying to find the profit-maximizing price and quantity combination, therefore, price searchers must try to estimate not just one market price, but how buyers will respond to the various prices that might be charged. In effect, price searchers must estimate the relationship between price and quantity demanded for their product. And the complexity does not end there.

Demand is not simply a given, to be discovered by the price searcher. The firm, by changing product quality, location, and service (among many other factors), and by advertising, can alter the demand for its products. It can increase demand by drawing customers from rivals if it can convince consumers that its products provide more value. When an airline adopts a more generous frequent-flier program or a soap manufacturer provides "cents-off" coupons, each is trying to make its product a little more attractive than rival products, for certain potential customers. The precise effects of such decisions cannot easily be predicted, but they can make the difference between profit and loss for the firm. In the real world, most firms occupy this complex and risky territory of the price searcher.

---

[2]It is important to distinguish between the demand curve faced by the firm and the market demand curve. The competitive price-searcher model focuses on the *firm's* demand curve.

In the highly competitive market for custom-fitted golf clubs, firms use style, variable length and flexibility of club shaft, swingweight, advertising, and celebrity endorsements as competitive weapons. Firms in this market are price searchers.

Sellers in competitive price-searcher markets face competition both from firms already producing in the market and from potential new entrants into the market. If profits are present, firms can expect that new rivals will be attracted. Because of the low entry barriers, competitive forces will be strong in price-searcher markets.

Price and Output in Competitive Price-Searcher Markets

How does a price searcher decide what price to charge and what level of output to produce? For the price searcher, reducing price in order to expand output and sales has two conflicting influences on total revenue. As **Exhibit 1** illustrates, the increase in sales (from q_1 to q_2) due to the lower price will, by itself, add to the revenue of the price searcher. The price reduction, however, also applies to units *that would otherwise have been sold at a higher price* (P_1, rather than the lower price, P_2). This factor by itself will cause a reduction in total revenue. As price is reduced in order to sell additional units, these two conflicting forces will result in marginal revenue—that is, change in total revenue—that is less than the sales price of the additional units. Since the price of units that could have been sold at the higher price must also be reduced, the price searcher's marginal revenue will be less than price. As Exhibit 1 shows, the marginal revenue curve of the price searcher will always lie below the firm's demand curve.[3] (Remember, the lowercase d is used when the reference is to the *firm's* demand curve.)

---

[3]For a straight-line demand curve, the marginal revenue curve will bisect any line parallel to the *x*-axis. For example, the *MR* curve will divide the line P_2F into two equal parts, P_2E and EF.

EXHIBIT 1
Marginal Revenue of a Price Searcher

When a firm faces a downward-sloping demand curve, a price reduction that increases sales will exert two conflicting influences on total revenue. First, total revenue will rise because of an increase in the number of units sold (from q_1 to q_2). However, revenue losses from the lower price (P_2) on units that could have been sold at a higher price (P_1) will at least partially offset the additional revenues from increased sales. Therefore, the marginal revenue curve will lie inside the firm's demand curve.

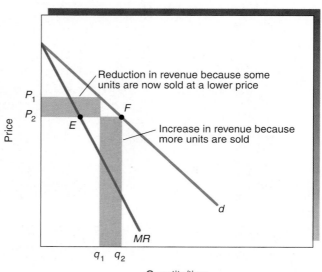

EXHIBIT 2
The Price Searcher's Price and Output

A price searcher maximizes profits by producing output q, for which $MR = MC$, and charging price P. The firm is making economic profits. What impact will they have if this is a typical firm?

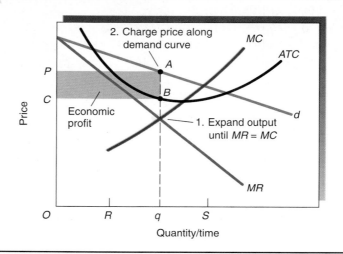

> *Any firm can increase profits by expanding output as long as marginal revenue exceeds marginal cost. Therefore, a price searcher will lower price and expand output until marginal revenue is equal to marginal cost.*

Exhibit 2 illustrates the profit-maximizing price and output. The price searcher will increase profit by expanding output to q, where marginal revenue is equal to marginal cost and price P can be charged. Beyond q, the price reduction required for the sale of additional output would reduce the firm's profit. For any output level less than q (for example, R), a price reduction and sales expansion will add more to total revenues than to total costs. At output R, marginal revenues exceed marginal costs. Thus, profits will be greater if price is reduced so output can be expanded. On the other hand, if output exceeds q (for example, S), sale of additional units beyond q will add more to costs (MC) than to revenues (MR). The firm will therefore gain by raising the price to P, even though the price rise will result in the loss of some customers. Profits will be maximized by charging price P and producing the output level q, where $MC = MR$.

The firm pictured in Exhibit 2 is making an economic profit. Total revenues *PAqO* exceed the firm's total costs *CBqO* at the profit-maximizing output level. Given the low barriers to entry, profits will attract rivals. Other firms will enter the market and attempt to produce a similar product (or service).

What will the entry of new rivals do to the demand for the products of the firms already in the market? These new rivals will draw customers away from existing firms and thereby reduce the demand for their output. As long as new entrants expect to make economic profits, additional competitors will be attracted to the market. This entry of new firms into the market will continue until competition among rivals shifts the demand curve in far enough to eliminate the economic profit. As **Exhibit 3** illustrates, when long-run equilibrium is present in a price-searcher market, price will equal per-unit cost. The firms will produce at the *MR = MC* output level, but they will be unable to earn economic profit because competitive pressures will force the price down to the level of per-unit costs.

If losses are present in a specific market, with time, some of the firms in the market will go out of business. As firms leave, some of their previous customers will buy from other firms. The demand curve facing the remaining firms in the industry will be shifted outward by this process until the economic losses are eliminated and the long-run, zero-profit equilibrium illustrated by Exhibit 3 is restored.

Whenever firms can freely enter and exit a market, profits and losses play an important role in determining the size of the industry. Economic profits will attract new competitors to the market. The increased availability of the product (and similar products) will drive the price down until the profits are eliminated. Conversely, economic losses will cause competitors to exit from the market. The decline in the availability of the product (supply) will allow the price to rise until firms are once again able to cover their average total costs.

Firms in competitive price-searcher markets may make either economic profits or losses in the short run. After long-run adjustments have been made, however, only a normal profit (that is, zero economic profit) will be possible because of the competitive conditions caused by freedom of entry.

Business Failures, the Competitive Process, and Economic Progress

Business failures and cutbacks in output and employment are generally reported under the heading of negative news about the economy. Clearly, they are often painful for the parties directly involved. Owners often lose a substantial amount of their wealth and employees are forced to search for alternative job opportunities. From the standpoint of the entire

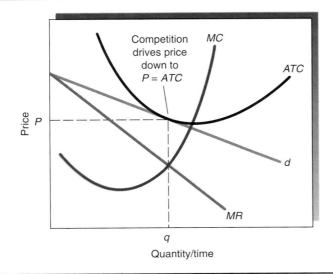

EXHIBIT 3
Competitive Price Searcher and Long-run Normal Profit

Since entry and exit are free, competition will eventually drive prices down to the level of average total cost for the representative price searcher.

economy, however, business failures play an important role that is often overlooked: they release resources so they can be employed more productively elsewhere. The assets and workers of firms that fail become available for use by others supplying goods that consumers value more relative to costs. Without this release of resources, the expansion of both profitable firms and the entire economy would be slowed.

Business failures may occur for a variety of reasons, but the introduction of improved products and adoption of lower-cost production techniques *by rivals* is clearly one of the more important sources. Suppose that an innovative firm figures out how to supply an improved product at a lower cost. The introduction of this product at an attractive price will reduce the demand for the goods supplied by competitors. Facing intense competition from the innovator, some of the existing firms will experience losses and eventually be driven out of business. Viewed from this perspective, business failure is merely the flip side of innovative actions that improved products and reduced costs.

The great Austrian economist Joseph Schumpeter referred to competition arising from the development of new products, new technologies, and superior forms of organization as "creative destruction." This competitive result is both widespread and highly important in price-searcher markets. Such dynamic competition will lead to the expansion of some firms and contraction of others. Examples abound. In early 2001, Lucent, a high-technology firm, announced that its sales had fallen 28 percent, while rival Nortel Networks had experienced a 34 percent increase. Lucent's failure to adopt a new generation of optical technology production quickly forced it to announce the elimination of 16,000 jobs.

Important changes were also taking place in the retail sector. J. C. Penney announced that it would shut 47 stores, 11 months after it had closed 45 others. In 2002, Kmart filed for bankruptcy. Meanwhile, Wal-Mart, Costco, and Target were rapidly expanding across the United States, "the way the Huns blew into Europe," as one news report put it.[4]

In the 1990s, the demand for computer services rose dramatically, as they became more productive and less expensive. Employment in the computer service and data processing industry more than doubled, rising from 736,000 in 1989 to 1,831,000 in 1999. In that same period, however, the demand for guided missiles and space-related equipment fell substantially, as the federal government changed its spending priorities. Employment in that industry fell by more than half, from 194,000 to only 88,000.

Numerous businesses come and go. Each year, newly incorporated businesses account for about 10 percent of the total. Approximately 1 percent of businesses file for bankruptcy during a typical year. In addition, many others close their doors or sell their assets to other, more successful (or more optimistic) operators.

It is important to recognize that business failures do not destroy either the assets owned by the firm or the talents of its workers. Instead, they release these resources for use by other firms that will employ them more productively. The losses underlying the failures indicate that consumers are unwilling to pay enough to cover the cost of the items supplied by these firms. A larger output could be achieved if the resources were released for use by profitable firms supplying goods and services that are more highly valued relative to their cost. It would be a mistake to continue with the operation of the loss-making firms. Thus, even though business failures are painful for the parties involved, they are necessary for the reallocation of resources toward higher-valued uses and the economic progress that this reallocation helps to promote.

CONTESTABLE MARKETS AND THE COMPETITIVE PROCESS

Contestable market
A market in which the costs of entry and exit are low, so a firm risks little by entering. Efficient production and zero economic profits should prevail in a contestable market. A market can be contestable even if capital requirements are high.

If firms can easily enter and exit a market and there is little risk that entry will result in substantial loss of wealth, competitive pressures may be strong even if there are few firms currently operating in the market. Economists refer to such markets as **contestable**

---

[4]Steve Syre and Charles Stein, "Capitalism's Messy Ways Still Come Up Rosy," *Boston Globe,* Jan. 26, 2001, p. C1.

markets.[5] Entry into a contestable market may require substantial amounts of financial capital, but so long as it is largely recoverable, the large capital requirement is not a major deterrent (barrier) to entry. If entry into a contestable market is later judged to be a mistake, exit is relatively easy because large components of the capital costs are recoverable.

When there are no legal barriers restricting entry, an airline route provides a classic example of a contestable market. Consider the case of the airline route between Salt Lake City, Utah, and Albuquerque, New Mexico. Only Delta Airlines provides nonstop service on this route, since it has so little traffic. Further, there would seem to be high barriers to entry, since it takes multimillion-dollar airplanes to compete, as well as facilities for reservations, ticketing, baggage handling, and so on. One might expect Delta, as the only provider of nonstop service, to charge a high price, substantially above its cost. But a deterrent to doing so is the fact that abnormal profits would probably attract direct competitors from the other airlines that are free to enter its nonstop market. Delta is well aware of its rivalry with competitors, some of whom already serve both Salt Lake City and Albuquerque, and in fact provide service between the two, via connecting flights from other cities.

To compete on an airline route may require millions of dollars in equipment, but if there is no problem with renting access to airport facilities, then the barriers to entry are much lower than equipment costs suggest. The nonstop Salt Lake City–Albuquerque market, for example, can be entered simply by shifting aircraft, personnel, and equipment from other routes and locations. Airlines often rent or lease their aircraft in any case. By the same token, if a new entrant (or an established firm) later wants to leave that market, nearly all the invested capital values can be recovered, through shifting the aircraft and other capital equipment to other routes, or leasing them to other firms.

In a contestable market, potential competition, as well as actual entry, can discipline firms selling in the market. When entry and exit are not expensive, even a single seller in a market faces the serious prospect of competition. Contestable markets yield two important results: (1) prices will not for long be higher than the level necessary to achieve zero economic profits, and (2) minimum cost of production will occur. This is true because both prices above costs and inefficiency in production present a profitable opportunity to new

Airliners are extremely expensive and their cost might be a barrier to entry. But airplanes can be leased and are highly mobile among markets, as are pilots, flight attendants, and office workers. These highly mobile resources allow firms to enter into a given air transport market, and to leave it, with relative ease. Such a market is contestable.

---

[5]The classic article on this topic is William J. Baumol's "Contestable Markets: An Uprising in the Theory of Industry Structure," *American Economic Review* 72 (March 1982): 1–15.

entrants. Potential competitors who see an opportunity for economic profit can be expected to enter and drive the price down to the level of per-unit costs.

These results do have a policy implication: If policy makers are concerned that a market is not sufficiently competitive, they should consider what might be done to make the market in question contestable. Much of the enthusiasm of economists for deregulation can be traced to the fact that regulation often is the primary restraint to entry. Many economists believe that deregulation permitting new entry can make many markets contestable, achieving lower prices and more efficiency than can direct regulation of producers.

COMPLEX DECISION MAKING AND THE ENTREPRENEUR

To help us understand facts and make predictions, a scientific model must simplify what it describes, and draw attention to the most important relationships. Economic models are no exception. The price-taker and competitive price-searcher models highlight the choices common to all firms in these markets. But these models leave out some important elements of the business decision-making process. Furthermore, they gloss over the complexity of other decisions that must be made by real-world entrepreneurs.

Would profits increase if prices were raised, or would lower prices lead to larger profits? Real-world decision makers cannot go into the backroom and look at their demand-cost diagram to answer these questions. They must search for clues, experiment with actual price changes, and interpret what they see, often using a great deal of "seat-of-the-pants" judgment. The successful entrepreneur will search and find (or at least approximate) the profit-maximizing price—the $MR = MC$ price-and-output combination that our model shows so simply.

The competitive price-searcher model indicates how entrepreneurs will react to profit and loss in a specific market and explains why their reactions will tend to direct the market toward equilibrium. It does not, however, explain how and when new products will be developed or new production techniques applied. How will consumers react to a potential new product? Can it be produced profitably? Would a new production process or alternative technology reduce cost? Could per-unit costs be reduced if the firm offered a different combination of products and services? Here, as in other areas of profit maximization, the marginal principle applies. If the change adds more to revenue than to cost, it should be made. How much of a change? Up to the point where $MC = MR$! But identifying that point for each potential change is difficult. Such decisions generally involve an important variable that is omitted from our economic models: entrepreneurship.

The Left Out Variable: Entrepreneurship

Entrepreneurial judgment is necessary when there is no decision rule that can be applied using only information that is freely available. For this reason, we are unable to incorporate fully the function of the entrepreneur into economic models. There simply is no way to model these complex decisions that involve uncertainty, discovery, and business judgment. All we can do is note the importance of entrepreneurial judgment and recognize that our models are limited because they are unable to capture this critical element of both business success and economic progress.

If we cannot put entrepreneurship into our models, what can we say about its function? One way to answer this question is to consider a generalized job description for an entrepreneurial position. An investor who lacks the desire, or perhaps the skill, to be an entrepreneur, but nonetheless wants to be in business, may seek someone to act as the business entrepreneur, while the investor provides some of the capital. A newspaper ad to find such a person (though perhaps not the usual way for the investor to search) might read as follows:

> *Wanted: Entrepreneur.* Diverse skills required. Must be (1) alert to new business opportunities and to new problems before they become obvious; (2) willing to back judgments with investments of hard work and creative effort before others

recognize correctness of judgments; (3) able to make correct decisions and to convince others of their validity, so as to attract additional financial backing; and (4) able to recognize own inevitable mistakes and to back away from incorrect decisions without wasting additional resources. Exciting, exhausting, high-risk position. Pay will be very good for success, and very poor for failure.

APPLICATIONS IN ECONOMICS

Entrepreneurs at the Helm of Some Bizarre Occupations

These innovative people see a need and find a niche in the market

BY DAVID YOUNG

(CHICAGO TRIBUNE)

Mike Turk lost a coin toss and wound up with a thousand teak trophy bases he couldn't get rid of. So he bolted Army surplus hand grenades to them and sold them for $15 apiece as desk ornaments. Joseph Tokarski, a postal worker contemplating a post-retirement business, found something of an aftermarket cleaning up Canada goose droppings.

"There are two important dimensions to being an entrepreneur: The first is risk and the second is innovation," said Sumaria Mohan-Neill, professor of entrepreneurship at Roosevelt University's College of Business Administration. "To succeed, a person has to be innovative. Some would call it bizarre," she added.

Turk and Tokarski are among what may be scores of entrepreneurs around Chicago who have found unusual business niches and somehow make their living at bizarre occupations. They manufacture odd products, they provide unusual services and some sell the grotesque. Sometimes these entrepreneurs accidentally find their callings; sometimes out of desperation they gravitate to odd occupations after losing their regular jobs; and in some cases, they are able to turn their hobbies into going business concerns.

"People leverage their knowledge," said Steven C. Michael, business administration professor at the University of Illinois' College of Commerce in Urbana. According to Michael, entrepreneurs have a vision of their mission and are able to sell that to other people, but they also have to be flexible enough to change course.

"Entrepreneurs don't spot markets. They spot needs and assemble the skills to fill them," says Michael, and that's the genesis of Magic Mound Mover, Joseph Tokarski's business. Tokarski said he developed a vacuum system to clean up the backyard scat from his own dogs because no one else in the family would do the chore. The device worked so well that he decided to mount it on a golf cart and go after a problem common in Midwestern open spaces: Canada goose droppings. A

"Complaint Department: Take a number." (Pull the pin of the hand grenade.)

little advertising in local newspapers and by word of mouth has resulted in jobs with apartment complexes, park districts and school systems cleaning up after the ubiquitous geese.

Similarly, coming up with a clever idea to solve a problem played a big role for Turk, who was working in the family-owned surplus business Surplus Trading Corp. in Benton Harbor, Mich. Only for Turk, the problem was what to do with 1,000 teak trophy bases he acquired on the toss of coin that determined their price. "We have all kinds of ways of doing deals in the surplus business," concedes Turk, who over the years has bought and sold 85 dozen women's panties from Victoria's Secret, 60 cases of olive oil and 500 pounds of hard candy. But he couldn't unload the teak at any price, so he decided to turn them into novelty items. He bolted Army surplus hand grenades to the bases and attached plaques that read, "Complaint Department: Take a number." The number is attached to the detonating pin. He has sold hundreds of them.

Turk and Tokarski are lucky ones; the failure rate for entrepreneurs is high, possibly as much as 70 to 80 percent, according to business scholars.

APPLICATIONS IN ECONOMICS

Four Entrepreneurs Who Have Changed Our Lives

Unlike movie stars and athletes, business entrepreneurs seldom command great respect in our society. Often, their contributions are either overlooked or misunderstood. In a competitive economy, entrepreneurs get ahead by discovering better ways of doing things, such as new production techniques that reduce cost or new products that are highly valued (relative to their cost). An interesting aspect of entrepreneurship is that it often comes from unusual sources—people who have an ability to think about and institute unconventional ideas.

Of course, highly successful entrepreneurs make a lot of money. Remember, however, that trade helps both the buyer and the seller. To be successful, entrepreneurs must provide their customers with value—a better deal than they can get elsewhere. Thus, they are an important source of economic progress. Highly successful entrepreneurs often exert enormous impact on our lives, far more than most of us realize. Consider how four key entrepreneurs of our age have affected our lives.

Fred Smith (1944–)

When he was in college in the 1960s, Fred Smith foresaw that computers were going to become a major part of people's lives. And he predicted a logical consequence: If computers were going to replace people for many tasks, the computers would have to be in good working order every day. If something went wrong, they had to be fixed immediately, and parts had to be available right away. As Smith describes it now, computer companies needed a "logistics system that provided the parts and pieces wherever that computer was located whenever it was needed."

Smith developed the idea and described the system in a paper for a business strategy course while studying in the MBA program at Yale. Perhaps because it seemed far-fetched at the time, the professor gave him a "gentleman's C." In the following decade, however, Smith founded Federal Express and created the express delivery system outlined in his paper. Beginning in 1973, FedEx created a giant network of airplane and truck transportation capable of providing overnight delivery around the world. Smith's chief innovation was the development of a transportation system with a "central switch" or "central junction." For FedEx, that was Memphis, Tennessee. When one looks at moving an item from Detroit to Minneapolis via Memphis, it seems inefficient, says Smith. "But when you take all of the transactions on the network together, it's tremendously efficient."

FedEx has revolutionized the express mail and package delivery system. The company has consistently earned a profit and annual revenue now exceeds $20 billion. Furthermore, FedEx has forced competitors, from the U. S. Post Office to United Parcel Service, to become more efficient and make major changes in their operations. Smith has transformed the lives of millions of customers, who use the term FedEx as a verb and know they can get a package anywhere "absolutely positively overnight"—to quote one of the company's past advertising slogans. Smith can take great pride in the fact that the market gave him a much higher grade than his old MBA professor.

For more detail, see "Fred Smith," *Forbes Great Minds of Business*, Gretchen Morgenson ed. (New York: John Wiley & Sons, 1997), 35–71.

Pleasant Rowland

Even though she had never run a business nor studied in an MBA program, Pleasant Rowland used her life savings to start a company. Today, the Pleasant Company is a $250 million-a-year business that sells a popular line of dolls and books known as The American Girl. Rowland was motivated by a mission: the desire for girls age 7 to 12 to experience the love of dolls and the fun of reading that she remembered from her childhood. Rowland's idea began to take shape one Christmas season when she tried to find some dolls for her nieces, then ages 8 and 10. The dolls she found—Cabbage Patch babies and Barbie dolls—seemed of mediocre quality, and they failed to evoke "what it meant to be a girl growing up in America." She had already been thinking about American history. While visiting Colonial Williamsburg, Virginia, she fell in love with the historic buildings and streets. She began to wonder, "Isn't there some way that I can make the magic of this historic place come alive for little girls?"

Her idea was a subtle one, creating a distinctive line of dolls that reflect authentic American history and serve as appealing role models. She had to find designers and craftspeople who could create dolls that captured the imagination and love of young girls, dolls with often poignant stories—a girl who pioneered in the West or one who escaped slavery in the South. Rowland shaped her products as she went along, drawing on all her talents and not being swayed by those who thought she was on the wrong track. She had been a teacher and a writer, so she knew how to communicate with children. She knew that her kind of doll wasn't suited for garish Saturday morning television commercials, where she would be battling against giant companies like Hasbro and Mattel—and she didn't have enough money, anyway. So she marketed her dolls through a catalog, writing her own copy in a "softer" voice.

She was right; there was a void, and her dolls helped fill it. Books and a magazine, *The American Girl*, were natural follow-ons. Rowland says today: "I don't think I'm in the doll business or the book business or the direct mail business. I'm in the little girl business." By following her convictions, Rowland found an audience ready to purchase what she wanted to provide. "The great joy of finding this enormous audience hungry for our values, our quality, our perspective on girlhood has been very, very heartening."

For more detail, see "Pleasant Rowland," in *Forbes Great Minds of Business*, Gretchen Morgenson ed., New York: John Wiley and Sons, 1998. 121–155.

Ted Turner (1938–)

Rejected by Harvard, Ted Turner went to Brown University. Originally enrolled as a humanities major, he eventually shifted his major to economics. His studies in economics, however, did not occupy enough of his time to keep him out of trouble while in college. After being thrown out of his fraternity, Kappa Sigma, he was later expelled from college during his senior year.

After his failed attempt at college, Turner worked in his father's outdoor billboard business and eventually took over the company. In 1970 he risked his assets in the billboard business to acquire an unprofitable TV station, WTCG, in Atlanta. He renamed the station WTBS, the "Superstation," and managed to get it on many of the local cable systems around the country. The station offered mostly movies and major league baseball after Turner purchased the Atlanta Braves.

In 1980, Turner risked all his assets and arranged for additional financing through the "junk bond" market in order to launch a 24-hour news network, a network that is now known to the world as CNN (Cable News Network). Most experts in the TV industry predicted the venture would fail. Prior to his final decision to start CNN, Turner's own employees gave him the following message: "Please, Ted! Don't do this to us! If you commit to a venture of this size you'll sink the whole company!"

Of course, risk taking is an integral part of entrepreneurship. Few, however, have risked so much on an idea so widely viewed as a long shot. Propelled by Turner's determination and confidence concerning what TV viewers wanted, the venture succeeded. The market verified his judgment. By 1991 Turner's cable TV operations (WTBS, CNN, TNT, and Headline News) attracted one-third of the cable TV listening audience. Turner's news stations are now widely viewed around the world. In 1995, he sold his broadcasting businesses to media giant Time Warner, receiving $7.5 billion in the bargain and becoming vice chairman of that firm. In 2001, *Forbes* magazine estimated his net worth at more than $6 billion, despite his prior gifts to the United Nations that had amounted to hundreds of millions of dollars. Who would have thought a college dropout who obtained his business experience in billboard advertising would change the way the world watches television, and become a billionaire in the process?

For more detail, see Gene N. Landrum, *Profiles of Genius* (Buffalo: Prometheus Books, 1993); and Robert F. Hartley, *Management Mistakes and Successes* (New York: John Wiley and Sons, Inc., 1994).

William "Bill" Gates III (1955–)

Even as a child, Bill Gates loved computers. At the early age of 15 he earned $20,000 by writing a computer program to help manage traffic. He entered Harvard at the age of 17, and while still an undergraduate, developed BASIC for the first microcomputer, the MITS Altair. Convinced that eventually most offices and homes would have a microcomputer, Gates, along with his friend Paul Allen, created Microsoft in 1975. The focus of the business was the development of software designed to make microcomputers both more useful and more user friendly.

Gates quickly earned a reputation as a programming genius. When IBM decided to enter the personal computer (PC) market in 1980, they contracted with Gates to provide the basic operating software for their computers, a system now known as MS-DOS. Gates reserved the rights to sell his MS-DOS software to other firms. As IBM (and IBM clones) grew to dominate the PC market during the 1980s, Gates's fortune rose as well. Microsoft developed into the dominant firm in the computer software industry. Gates's programs are now used to run more than 90 percent of the world's computers. Gates's MS-DOS–based software program, Windows 98, along with Windows 2000 and the newer Windows XP, are among the most popular in the world. Doing good for society in this way paid him well. Near the end of 2001, Bill Gates's personal fortune was estimated at more than $50 billion. This was after giving $21 billion to his charitable foundation, and losing more than $9 billion in the falling stock market that year.

Gates attributes his success to his workaholic nature. He continues to work long hours and is still actively involved in the operation and strategic decision making of Microsoft. If you have ever used a computer, you have almost certainly benefitted from programs that Gates created. His remarkable programming genius has changed the way we use personal computers both at home and in the workplace.

For more detail, see Gene N. Landrum, *Profiles of Genius* (Buffalo: Prometheus Books, 1993); and Robert F. Hartley, *Management Mistakes and Successes* (New York: John Wiley and Sons, Inc., 1994).

Entrepreneurship is not for the fainthearted or the lazy. Entrepreneurs are at the center of the action in the real world, even if they do not have a place in most economic models.[6]

ENTREPRENEURSHIP AND ECONOMIC PROGRESS

Entrepreneurship

The entrepreneurial discovery and development of improved products and production processes is a central element of economic progress.

Discovery and development of improved products and production methods propel economic progress. Think of the new products that have been introduced during the last 50 years: microwave ovens, videocassette recorders, color television sets, personal computers, compact disc players, fax machines, cellular telephone service, and coronary artery bypass techniques come to mind. Innovations like these and many others exert an enormous impact on our lives.

But no one knows what the next innovative breakthrough will be or precisely which production techniques will minimize per-unit costs. Better ways of doing things do not just happen; they must be discovered and developed by entrepreneurs. While the potential for financial reward is enormous, entrepreneurial activities are also risky. Is that new visionary idea the greatest thing since the development of the fast-food chain? Or is it simply another dream that will soon turn to vapor?

In a market economy, it is relatively easy to try new business ideas. One only needs to win the support of a few investors willing to finance the innovative new product or production technology. However, competition holds entrepreneurs and the investors who support them accountable: Their ideas must face a "reality check" imposed by production cost and consumer willingness to pay. Consumers are the ultimate judge and jury. If they do not value an innovative new product or service enough to cover its cost, it will not survive in the marketplace.

Furthermore, today's successful product may not pass tomorrow's competitive test. Thus, entrepreneurs must be good at anticipating, identifying, and quickly adopting improved ideas, whether their own or others'. The ongoing reality of dynamic change in a competitive world must constantly be confronted.

Entrepreneurial Decision Making and the Structure, Size, and Scope of Firms

Entrepreneurs must also discover the type of business structure, scale of operation, and scope of activities that best keeps the per-unit cost of their product or service low. Pursuit of profit provides them with a strong incentive to do so.

Unlike other economic systems, a market economy does not mandate or limit the types of firms that are permitted to compete. Any form of business organization is permissible. An owner-operated firm, a partnership, a corporation, an employee-owned firm, a consumer cooperative, a commune, or any other form of business is free to enter the market. In order to be successful, however, a business structure must be cost-effective. A form of business organization that results in high per-unit cost will be driven from a competitive market by lower-cost rivals.

The same is true for the size of a firm. For some products, a business must be quite large to take full advantage of economies of scale. When per-unit costs decline as output increases, small businesses tend to have higher production costs (and therefore higher prices) than their larger counterparts. When this is the case, consumers interested in maximum value for their money will tend to buy from the lower-priced larger firm. In contrast,

---

[6]For a more complete overview of entrepreneurship and references on the topic, see Mark Crosson, "Entrepreneurship," in *The New Palgrave: A Dictionary of Economics,* ed. John Eatwell et al. (New York: Stockton Press, 1987), pp. 151–153.

when personalized service and individualized products are valued highly by consumers, small firms, often organized as individual proprietorships or partnerships, are likely to be more cost-effective. It is up to the entrepreneur to discover the scale of operation that best fits the circumstances of each market.

The scope of a business is another variable requiring entrepreneurial decision making. Should a gasoline station stand alone, or should its scope be expanded to include auto repair services? Or should it instead be combined with a convenience store, or would a different combination create more value relative to cost? Numerous alternative combinations of business activities are possible. Differences in locations and other circumstances will often influence how well each is received. A new and better combination of products and services in the right place can generate a profit, at least temporarily until others catch on and provide close substitutes. In contrast, a business choosing the wrong scope of operation for the situation will earn less and it could be driven from the market by rivals offering a more appropriate scope of activities. Once again, consumer choices and market forces will determine the scope of operation that best fits the circumstances.

Because of the vast array of decisions to be made in price-searcher markets, the role of the entrepreneur is particularly important here. In price-searcher markets, entrepreneurs may use a variety of weapons—quality of product, style, service, convenience of location, advertising, and price to compete with rival firms. But financial success is still dependent on the dollar votes of consumers. *In order to be successful, entrepreneurs must consistently offer consumers at least as much value for their dollar as can be obtained elsewhere. Put another way, they must figure out how to supply consumers with goods and services that are valued highly relative to their costs. As they do so, their actions create wealth and increase the value of resources. Even though many of their activities are omitted from our basic economic models, the vitally important role of entrepreneurs as agents of economic progress is nonetheless abundantly clear.*

AN EVALUATION OF COMPETITIVE PRICE-SEARCHER MARKETS

As we saw earlier, determination of price and output for price searchers is in some ways similar to that for price takers. Because the long-run, equilibrium conditions in price-taker markets are consistent with ideal economic efficiency, it is useful to compare and contrast them with conditions in price-searcher markets when entry barriers are low. There are both similarities and differences.

When barriers to entry are low, businesses must compete for the loyalty of customers. Neither price takers nor price searchers in markets with low entry barriers will be able to earn long-run economic profit. Competing firms drawn by economic profits—that is, returns greater than opportunity costs—will enter until, in the long run, competition has driven the market price down to the level of average total cost. Entrepreneurs in both price-taker and price-searcher markets have a strong incentive to manage and operate their businesses efficiently. Inefficient operation will lead to higher costs, losses, and forced exit from the market. Similarly, price takers and competitive price searchers alike will be motivated to develop and adopt new cost-reducing procedures and techniques because lower costs will mean higher short-run profits (or at least smaller losses).

The response to changing demand conditions in price-taker and price-searcher markets with low entry barriers is also similar. In both cases, an increase in market demand leads to higher prices, short-run profits, expansion of the existing producers, and the entry of new firms. With the entry of new producers, and the concurrent expansion of existing firms, the market supply will increase, placing downward pressure on price. The process will continue until the market price falls to the level of average total cost, squeezing out all economic profit.

Correspondingly, a reduction in demand will lead to lower prices and short-run losses, causing output to fall and some firms to exit. As the market supply declines, prices will

EXHIBIT 4
Comparing Price-Taker and Price-Searcher Markets

Here we illustrate the long-run equilibrium conditions of a price taker and a price searcher when entry barriers are low. In both cases, price is equal to average total cost, and economic profit is zero. However, since the price searcher confronts a downward-sloping demand curve for its product, its profit-maximizing price exceeds marginal cost, and output is not large enough to minimize average total cost when the market is in long-run equilibrium. For identical cost conditions, the price of the product in a price-searcher market will be slightly higher than in a price-taker market. This slightly higher price is considered by some to be indicative of inefficiency, while others perceive it to be the premium a society pays for variety and convenience (price differentiation).

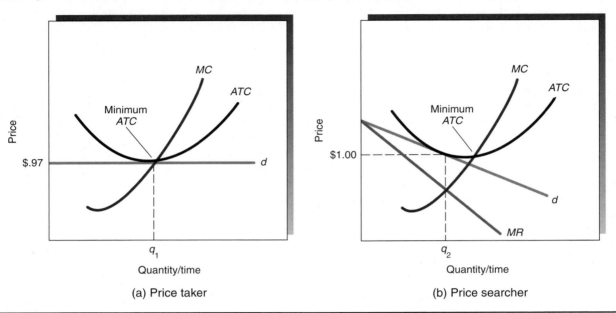

(a) Price taker (b) Price searcher

rise and eventually the short-run losses will be eliminated and the firms remaining in the industry will once again be able to cover their costs. Regardless of whether the firms are price takers or price searchers, profits and losses will direct their output decisions when barriers to entry are low.

As **Exhibit 4** illustrates, while the price taker confronts a horizontal demand curve, the demand curve faced by a price searcher is downward sloping. This is important because it means that the marginal revenue of the price searcher will be less than, rather than equal to, the price charged for the quantity sold. So, when the profit-maximizing price searcher expands output until $MR = MC$, price will still exceed marginal cost (panel b). In contrast, the price charged by a profit-maximizing price taker will equal marginal cost (panel a). In addition, when a price searcher is in long-run equilibrium, the firm's output rate will be less than the rate that would minimize average total cost. The price searcher would have a lower per-unit cost (97 cents rather than $1) if a larger output were produced.

Is the higher cost and price and the greater variety found in the price-searcher market less efficient than the slightly lower price and cost in the price-taker market with less variety? It is impossible to say, since the products in the price-searcher market are substitutes for one another, but they are not quite the same. Thus the output is, for consumers, at least slightly different between the two markets.

Price-searcher firms advertise, but price takers do not. Advertising is costly, and in the long run, consumers cover this cost in the form of higher prices. Do advertised products provide enough information and variety to justify the higher cost from the consumer viewpoint? We cannot know for certain. However, we observe that producers are always free to use low-priced, more uniform and less-advertised products in order to lure buyers away from firms that advertise and provide variety at a higher price. Some firms do, and sometimes the strategy works; yet many consumers choose to buy advertised goods and pay the higher prices. This result suggests that many customers do find that advertised products and greater variety are worth more.

Are resources allocated efficiently in a price-searcher market with low barriers to entry? This question is difficult to answer with certainty. **Allocative efficiency** is achieved when the goods and services most desired by consumers are produced at the lowest possible cost. Clearly, price-taker markets allocate resources efficiently. In a price-searcher market, however, the greater variety of products involves a cost. Therefore, some argue that this is a deviation from ideal allocative efficiency. But a broader range of choices also provides benefits. The greater variety makes it possible for a wider range of consumers to obtain the quality, style, and accompanying service that best fits their preferences. Perhaps most importantly, competitive price-searcher markets provide entrepreneurs with a strong incentive to innovate and discover better ways of doing things. In a dynamic setting, this is vitally important for the efficient use of resources.

Allocative efficiency
The allocation of resources to the production of goods and services most desired by consumers, at the lowest possible cost.

A SPECIAL CASE: PRICE DISCRIMINATION

Thus far, we have assumed that all sellers of a product will charge each customer the same price. Sometimes, though, price searchers can increase their revenues (and profits) by charging different prices to different groups of consumers. Such businesses as hotels, restaurants, and drugstores often charge senior citizens less than other customers. Students and children are often given discounts at movie theaters and athletic events. Grocery stores commonly give discounts to customers who clip "cents off" coupons from newspapers or magazines. Colleges often give financial aid (reduced tuition) to students from less-wealthy families. These practices are called **price discrimination**. *To gain from such a practice, price searchers must be able to do two things: (1) identify and separate at least two groups with differing elasticities of demand, and (2) prevent those who buy at the low price from reselling to the customers charged higher prices.*

Price discrimination
A practice whereby a seller charges different consumers different prices for the same product or service.

Let us take a closer look at why sellers may find price discrimination advantageous. Suppose that a seller has two groups of customers: one with an inelastic demand for its product and the other with an elastic demand. An increase in the price charged the first group will increase the total revenue derived from that group. On the other hand, a reduction in price will increase revenues derived from the latter. Thus, a seller may be able to increase total revenue and profit by charging the first group a higher price than the second.

The pricing of airline tickets illustrates the potential of price discrimination. The airline industry has found that the demand of business fliers is substantially more inelastic than the demand of vacationers, students, and other travelers. Thus, airlines usually charge high fares to persons who are unwilling to stay over a weekend, who spend only a day or two at their destination, and who make reservations a short time before their flight. These high fares fall primarily on business travelers who are less sensitive to price. In contrast, discount fares are offered to fliers willing to make reservations well in advance, travel during off-peak hours, and stay at their destinations over a weekend before returning home. Such travelers are likely to be vacationers and students, who are highly sensitive to price.

Exhibit 5 illustrates the logic of this policy. Panel a shows what would happen if a single price were charged to all customers. Given the demand, the profit-maximizing firm expands output to 100, where *MR* equals *MC*. The profit-maximizing price on coast-to-coast flights is $400, which generates $40,000 of revenue per flight. Since the marginal cost per passenger is $100, this provides the airline with net operating revenue of $30,000 with which to cover other costs.

However, as panel b shows, although the market demand schedule is unchanged, the airline can do even better if it uses price discrimination. When it charges business travelers $500, most of these passengers continue to travel since their demand is highly inelastic. On the other hand, a $100 price cut generates substantial additional ticket sales from vacationers, students, and others whose demands are more elastic. Therefore, with price discrimination, the airline can sell 60 tickets (primarily to business travelers) at $500 and

EXHIBIT 5
Price Discrimination

As panel *a* illustrates, a $400 ticket price will maximize profits on coast-to-coast flights if an airline charges a single price. However, the airline can do still better if it raises the price to $500 for passengers (business travelers) with a highly inelastic demand and reduces the price to $300 for travelers (for example, students and vacationers) with a more elastic demand. When sellers can segment their market, they can gain by (a) charging a higher price to consumers with a less elastic demand and (b) offering discounts to customers whose demand is more elastic.

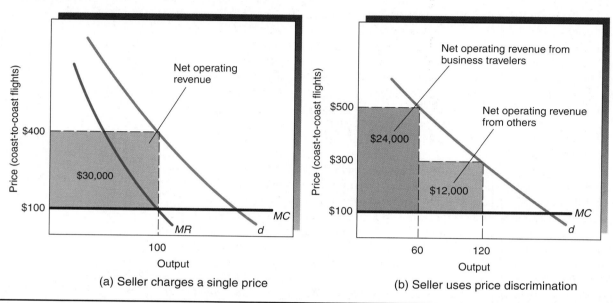

(a) Seller charges a single price

(b) Seller uses price discrimination

60 additional tickets to others at $300. Total revenue jumps to $48,000 and leaves the airline with $36,000 ($48,000 minus 120 times the $100 marginal cost per passenger) of revenue in excess of variable cost. Compared to the single-price outcome (panel a), the price discrimination strategy expands profit by $6,000.

When sellers can segment their market (at a low cost) into groups with differing price elasticities of demand, price discrimination can increase profits. For *each group*, the seller will maximize profit by equating marginal cost and marginal revenue. This rule will lead to higher prices for groups with more inelastic demand and lower prices for groups with more elastic demand. Compared to the single-price situation, price discrimination increases profitability because a higher price increases the net revenue from groups with an inelastic demand, while a lower price increases the net revenue from price-sensitive customers. With price discrimination, the number of units sold also increases (compare panel a with panel b) because the discounts provided to price-sensitive groups increase the quantity sold more than the higher prices charged the less price-sensitive groups reduce sales.

Sometimes price discrimination is subtle. Colleges engage in price discrimination by charging a high standard tuition to get additional revenue from high-income students with a more inelastic demand, while providing low-income students with scholarships based on need (tuition "discounts"). Recently at the University of Maine, for example, tuition at the undergraduate level ran between $12,998 and $20,738, depending on the degree. Financial aid, however, amounted to 54 percent of tuition for students from low-income families, while for high-income students, it was only 17 percent of tuition. Partial-tuition scholarships given to students whose parents are less wealthy enable a school to attract students who have a more elastic demand. Low-income students thus are not so often priced out of the market by the high standard tuition.

How do buyers fare when a seller can price discriminate? Some buyers pay more than they would if a single intermediate price were offered. They purchase fewer units, and

Giving financial aid, in the form of lower tuition charges, to students from families with lower incomes and who thus are likely to be more price-sensitive allows a college to practice price discrimination, charging a higher tuition price to those who are expected to be less price-sensitive.

they are worse off. In contrast, those for whom the price discrimination process lowers the price are better off. Of course, with some products, such as airline transportation, a single buyer might be better off with some purchases and worse off with others.

On balance, however, we can expect that output will be greater with price discrimination than it would be with a single price. The market is not as understocked as it would have been in the absence of the price discrimination. Thus, from an allocative standpoint, price discrimination gets high marks; it allows more trades, reducing the allocative inefficiency due to price being set above marginal cost. Some of the gains that would accrue to consumers with an inelastic demand are transferred to the price searcher as increased revenue, but additional gains from trade are created by the increased output of goods that would be lost if the price searcher did not (or could not) price discriminate.

In some markets, there is an additional gain emanating from price discrimination: Production may occur that would be lost entirely if only a single price could be charged. With price discrimination, some otherwise unprofitable firms may be able to generate enough additional revenue to operate successfully in the marketplace. For example, some small towns in Montana might not provide enough revenue at a single price to enable a local physician to cover her opportunity costs. However, if she is able to discriminate on the basis of income, charging higher-income patients more than normal rates and lower-income patients less, the resulting revenues from practice in the small town may enable the physician to stay in the community. In this case, all residents of the town may be better off as the result of the price discrimination, because it makes it possible for them to access a local physician. After all, even those being charged the highest prices are not disadvantaged if the price discrimination keeps the physician in town. They are just as able to seek physician services elsewhere as they would have been in the absence of the price-discriminating local doctor. With or without price discrimination, access to competing sellers (or buyers) protects market participants from unfair treatment.

> *In summary, if potential customers can be segmented into groups with different elasticities of demand and retrading can be controlled at a low cost, sellers can often gain by charging higher prices to those with the more inelastic demand (and lower prices to those with an elastic demand). Price discrimination can also increase the total gains from trade and thereby reduce allocative inefficiency. Sometimes it even allows production where none would have otherwise occurred.*

LOOKING AHEAD

In this chapter we have analyzed the choices facing price searchers, and their behavior when barriers to entry are low. Next, we will see how barriers to entry might be formed, how price searchers react, and how the results differ when entry barriers are high rather than low.

KEY POINTS

▼ Firms in price-searcher markets with low barriers to entry face a downward-sloping demand curve. They are free to set the prices for the products that they sell, but face strong competitive pressure from existing and potential rivals.

▼ The mark of the price-searcher market with low barriers to entry is product differentiation. Price searchers use product quality, style, convenience of location, advertising, and price as competitive weapons. Because each firm competes with rivals offering similar products, each confronts a highly elastic demand curve for its products.

▼ A profit-maximizing price searcher will expand output as long as marginal revenue exceeds marginal cost, lowering its price in the process, until $MR = MC$. The price charged by the profit-maximizing price searcher will be greater than its marginal cost.

▼ If firms in a price-searcher market with low barriers to entry are making economic profits, rival firms will be attracted to the market. Their entry will expand the supply of the product (and similar products), lowering price and enticing some customers away from established firms. The demand curve faced by each firm will fall (shift inward) until the economic profits have been eliminated.

▼ Economic losses will cause price searchers to exit from the market, raising the demand for each re-

maining firm (shifting it outward) until the losses have been eliminated, ending the incentive to exit.

▼ When barriers to entry are low, firms in a market will make only normal profits in the long run. In the short run, they may make either economic profits or losses, depending on market conditions.

▼ Competition can come from potential as well as actual rivals. If entry and exit can be arranged at low cost, and if there are no legal barriers to entry, the theory of contestable markets indicates that competitive results will be approximated even if there are only a few firms actually in the market.

▼ Although standard economic models do not include the central role of entrepreneurial decision making in a world of uncertainty, economists recognize its importance. Entrepreneurs who discover and introduce lower-cost production methods and new products that are highly valued relative to cost promote economic progress. Entrepreneurs also have a strong incentive to discover the type of business structure, size of firm, and scope of operation that can best keep the per-unit cost of products or services low.

▼ Competitive price-searcher markets provide more variety but may raise costs, relative to price-taker markets because (a) price exceeds marginal cost at the profit-maximizing output level; (b) long-run average cost is not minimized; and (c) advertising is costly. When barriers to entry are low, however, price searchers have an incentive to (a) produce efficiently; (b) undertake production if and only if their actions will increase the value of resources used; and (c) be innovative in offering new product options.

▼ When a price searcher can (a) identify groups of customers that have different price elasticities of de-

mand and (b) prevent customers from retrading the product, price discrimination may emerge. Sellers may be able to gain by charging higher prices to groups with a more inelastic demand and lower prices to those with a more elastic demand. The practice generally leads to a larger output and more gains from trade than would otherwise occur.

CRITICAL ANALYSIS QUESTIONS

1. Street-corner vendors using pushcarts have sometimes engaged in price wars at popular locations within Washington, D.C. Explain why a strategy of cutting price below cost in order to drive out other vendors from a given location would not make sense if there were no legal barriers to entry.

2. Price searchers can set the price of their product. Does this mean that price searchers will charge the highest possible price for their product? What price will maximize the profits of a price searcher? How will the firm's marginal cost compare with price at the profit-maximum output?

*3. What determines the *variety* of styles, designs, and sizes of different products? Why do you think there are only a few different varieties of toothpicks but lots of different types of napkins on the market?

*4. How would the imposition of a per-unit tax of $2,000 on each new U.S. automobile affect a) the higher quality, higher price cars (those selling for more than the media price) compared to b) the lower quality, lower priced cars? What would happen as a result, to the average *quality* of automobiles if the proceeds of the tax are used to subsidize a governmnet operated lottery?

5. What is the primary function of the entrepreneur? Some economists have charged that the major market-structure models of economic theory assume away the function of the entrepreneur. In what sense is this true? Is the function of the entrepreneur important? Discuss.

6. Is quality and style competition as important as price competition? Would you like to live in a country where government regulation restricted the use of quality and style competition? Why or why not? Do you think you would get more or less for your consumer dollar if quality and style competition were restricted? Discuss.

*7. Suppose that a price searcher is currently charging a price that maximizes the firm's total revenue. Will

this price also maximize the firm's profit? Why or why not? Explain.

8. Since price searchers can set their prices, does this mean that their prices are unaffected by market conditions? In price-searcher markets with low barriers to entry, will the firms be able to make economic profit in the long run? Why or why not? What do competitive price searchers have to do in order to make economic profit?

*9. Suppose that a group of investors wants to start a business operated out of a popular Utah ski area, and the group is considering either building a new hotel complex or starting a new local airline serving that market. Each new business would require about the same amount of capital and personnel hiring. The group believes each to have the same profit potential. Which is the safer (less likely to result in a substantial capital loss) investment? Why? Is there an offsetting advantage to the other investment?

10. Would our standard of living be higher if the government "bailed out" troubled businesses? If a firm goes out of business, what happens to the firms assets, workers, and customers? Are business failures bad for the economy? Why or why not?

*11. "When competition is really severe, only the big firms survive. The little guy has no chance." True or false? Explain.

12. Is price discrimination harmful to the economy? How does price discrimination affect the total amount of gains from exchange? Explain. Why do colleges often charge students different prices, based on their family income?

13. What is the primary requirement for a market to be competitive? Is competition necessary for markets to work well? Why or why not? How does competition influence the following: (a) the cost efficiency of producers, (b) the quality of products, and (c) the discovery and development of new products? Explain your answers.

*14. What keeps McDonald's, Wal-Mart, General Motors, or any other business firm from raising prices, selling shoddy products, and providing lousy service?

15. The accompanying graph shows the short-run demand and cost situation for a price searcher in a market with low barriers to entry.
    a. What level of output will maximize the firm's profit level?
    b. What price will the firm charge?
    c. How much revenue will the firm receive in this situation? How much is total cost? Total profit?
    d. How will this situation change with the passage of time?

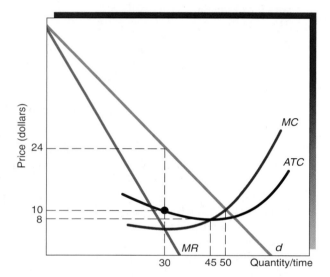

*16. Rod N. Reel owns a dealership that sells fishing boats in an open price-searcher market. In developing his pricing strategy, Rod hired an economist to estimate his demand curve. Columns (1) and (2) of the following chart provide the data for the expected weekly quantity demanded for Rod's fishing boats at alternative prices. Rod's marginal (and av-

erage) cost of supplying each boat is constant at $5,000 per boat no matter how many boats he sells per week in this range. This cost includes all opportunity costs and represents the economic cost per boat.
    a. Find Rod's economic profits at each alternative price by calculating the difference between total revenue and total cost.
    b. Find Rod's marginal revenue and marginal cost from the sale of each additional boat.
    c. If Rod wants to maximize his profits, what price should he charge per boat?
    d. How many boats will Rod sell per week at the profit-maximizing price?
    e. What will Rod's profits be per week at this price and sales volume?
    f. At the price and sales level where profits are maximized, has Rod sold all boats that have higher marginal revenue than marginal cost?
    g. If Rod's profits are typical of all firms in the boat sales business, what might be expected to happen in the future? Will more boat dealers open in the area or will some of the existing ones go out of business? What will happen to the profitability of the boat dealers in the future once the entry/exit has occurred?
    h. Challenge Question: Recall the relationship between elasticity of demand, price changes, and their impact on total revenues. As Rod lowers his price from $9,000 down to $5,000, his total revenues keep increasing. Is demand in this price range elastic, inelastic, or unitary elastic? When Rod lowers his price from $5,000 to $4,000, his total revenues stay the same. Is demand in this price range elastic, inelastic, or unitary elastic? Can you guess what might happen at prices below $4,000? Explain.

*Asterisk denotes questions for which answers are given in Appendix B.

Price of Fishing Boats (1)	Number of Fishing Boats Sold per Week (2)	Total Revenues per Week (3)	Total Cost per Week (4)	Economic Profit per Week (5)	Marginal Revenue (6)	Marginal Cost (7)
$9,000	0	___	___	___	___	___
8,000	1	___	___	___	___	___
7,000	2	___	___	___	___	___
6,000	3	___	___	___	___	___
5,000	4	___	___	___	___	___
4,000	5	___	___	___	___	___

CHAPTER 23

Price-Searcher Markets with High Entry Barriers

If there are economies of scale throughout the region of possible industry outputs, only one or a few firms may be able to exist in the industry.

—George Stigler[1]

Chapter Focus

- What are the barriers to entry that protect some firms against competition from potential rivals?

- What is a monopoly? Does it guarantee the ability to make a profit?

- What is an oligopoly? When are oligopolists likely to collude? Why is it impossible to construct a general theory of output and price for an oligopolist?

- Is competition able to discipline large firms in markets with high barriers to entry? What problems may arise in such markets?

- What policy alternatives might improve the operation of markets with high barriers to entry?

[1]George J. Stigler, *The Theory of Price* (New York: Macmillan, 1987), p. 204.

n the previous two chapters, we analyzed the way firms behave in competitive markets, characterized by low barriers to entry. We now turn to the analysis of firm behavior when entry barriers are high and there are few, if any, rival firms offering the same or similar products. This chapter focuses on factors that increase the difficulty of entry into a market and analyzes how they influence the ability of markets to discipline business firms. The potential of various policy alternatives that might improve the efficiency of resource allocation in these markets will also be considered. ■

WHY ARE ENTRY BARRIERS SOMETIMES HIGH?

What makes it difficult for potential competitors to enter a market? Four factors can be important: economies of scale, government licensing, patents, and control over an essential resource.

Economies of Scale

In some industries, firms experience declining average total costs over the full range of output that consumers are willing to buy. When this is the case, the larger firm will always have lower unit costs. Because the unit costs of smaller firms are higher than those of their larger rivals, it will be difficult for small firms to enter the market, build a reputation, and compete effectively. Under these circumstances, a single firm will tend to emerge in the industry, and the cost advantage resulting from its size will provide the firm with protection from potential rivals.

Government Licensing

Legal barriers are the oldest and most effective method of protecting a business firm from potential competitors. Kings once granted exclusive business rights to favored citizens or groups. Today, governments continue to establish barriers, restricting the right to buy and sell goods. To compete in certain parts of the communications industry in the United States (for example, to operate a radio or television station), one must obtain a government franchise. Similarly, local governments often grant exclusive franchises for the operation of cable television systems.

Licensing limits entry. States and cities often require operators of liquor stores, hair styling shops, taxicabs, funeral homes, drugstores, and many other businesses, to obtain a license. Sometimes these licenses cost little and are designed to ensure certain minimum standards. In other cases, they are expensive and designed primarily to limit competition.

Licensing
A requirement that one obtain permission from the government in order to perform certain business activities or work in various occupations.

Patents

Most countries have patent laws to give inventors a property right to their inventions. A patent grants the owner the exclusive legal right to the commercial use of a newly invented product or process for a limited period of time, 17 years in the United States. Others are not allowed to copy the product or procedure without the permission of the patent holder. For example, when a pharmaceutical company is granted a patent for a newly developed drug, other potential suppliers must obtain permission from the patent holder before producing and selling the product. Others might be able to supply the drug more economically. If they want to do so, however, they will have to purchase the production and marketing rights from the originating firm as long as the patent is in effect.

Costs, as well as benefits, come with a patent system. The entry barrier created by the grant of a patent generally leads to higher consumer prices for products that have already been developed. On the positive side, however, patents increase the potential returns to inventive activity, thus encouraging scientific research and technological improvements. It

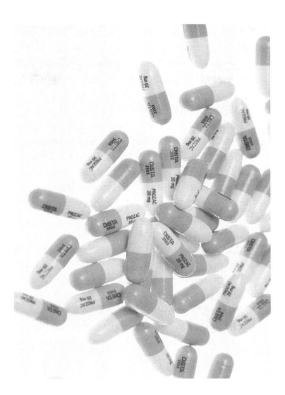

A firm that develops a new drug can use patent protection to restrain production by others for 17 years. Although consumers will pay higher prices than if open competition were permitted, they may benefit from additional investment in research and more rapid development of new products than would be the case in the absence of patent protection.

typically costs $200 million to develop and test a new drug, for example. Without the profit potential from patents on new drugs, less research would be undertaken by drug firms. Eliminating patent protection might well slow the pace of technological innovation.

Control Over an Essential Resource

A single firm with sole control over a resource essential for entry into an industry is free from direct competitors. An example often cited is the Aluminum Company of America, which before World War II controlled the known supply of bauxite conveniently available to American firms. Without this critical raw material, potential competitors could not produce aluminum. With time, however, other supplies of bauxite were found, and this source of monopoly was lost to the company. As this case illustrates, resource monopolies are seldom complete. Profit opportunities provide challengers with an incentive to search for mineral deposits, new technologies, and substitute resources. Over time, they are usually found.

Barriers to entry are often temporary, but they do exist. Let us move on to see what happens when, at least temporarily, there is a barrier to entry high enough to limit the market to only one seller.

THE CASE OF MONOPOLY

The word *monopoly*, derived from two Greek words, means "single seller." We will define **monopoly** as a market characterized by (1) high barriers to entry and (2) a single seller of a well-defined product for which there are no good substitutes. Even this definition is ambiguous, because "high barriers" and "good substitutes" are both relative terms. Are the barriers to entry into the automobile or steel industries high? Many observers would argue that they are. After all, economies of scale are important in these industries and it would take a great deal of financial capital to operate at the least-cost scale of output. However, there are no *physical* or *legal* restraints that prevent an entrepreneur from producing automobiles or steel. If price is well above cost and profit potential is present in these industries, it should

Monopoly
A market structure characterized by (1) a single seller of a well-defined product for which there are no good substitutes and (2) high barriers to the entry of any other firms into the market for that product.

not be too difficult to find the necessary investment capital. Thus, some would argue that entry barriers into these industries are not particularly high.

"Good substitute" is also a subjective term. There is always some substitutability among products, even those produced by a single seller. Is a letter a good substitute for a telephone or e-mail message? For some purposes—correspondence between law firms, for example—a letter delivered by mail is a very good substitute. In other cases, when the speed of communication and immediacy of response are important, telephone and e-mail communication are far superior. Are there any good substitutes for electricity? Most of the known substitutes for electric lighting (candles, oil lamps, and battery lights, for example) are inferior to electric lights in most uses. Natural gas, fuel oil, and wood, though, are often excellent substitutes for electric heating. Also, electric utilities have found that many of their largest industrial customers can generate their own electricity, sometimes at low cost, in conjunction with other fuel-burning operations.

Monopoly, then, is always a matter of degree. Only a small fraction of all markets are served by only one seller. Nevertheless, there are two reasons why it is important to understand how such markets work. First, the monopoly model will help us understand markets in which there are few sellers and little active rivalry. When there are only two or three producers in a market, firms may seek to collude rather than compete, and thus together behave like a monopoly. Second, in a few important industries there is by law often only a single producer in each market. Local telephone and electricity services are examples. The monopoly model will illuminate the operation of such markets.

Price and Output Under Monopoly

Suppose you invent, patent, and produce a microwave device that locks the hammer of any firearm in the immediate area. This fabulous invention can be used to immobilize potential hijackers or armed robbers. Since you own the exclusive patent right to the firearm lock device, you are not concerned about a competitive supplier in the foreseeable future. Although other products are competitive with your invention, they are poor substitutes. In short, you are a monopolist.

What price should you charge for your product? Because you are the only seller of this device, the demand for your product is also the market demand curve. It will be downward sloping because consumers will cut back on their purchases as the price of the firearm lock increases. Like other price searchers, you will have to search to determine the most profitable price to charge. An expansion in output will increase profit as long as the production and sale of additional units add more to revenue than to cost. *Like other price searchers, the monopolist will expand output until marginal revenue equals marginal cost. This profit-maximizing output rate can be sold at a price indicated on the firm's demand curve.*

Exhibit 1 graphically illustrates how a monopolist derives the profit-maximizing output rate.[2] The firm will continue to expand output as long as marginal revenue exceeds marginal cost. Therefore, output will be expanded to Q, where $MR = MC$. The monopolist will be able to sell the profit-maximizing output Q at price P, the height of the demand curve at Q. At any output less than Q, the benefits (marginal revenue) of producing the *additional* units will exceed their costs. In this range, the monopolist will gain by reducing price and expanding output toward Q. For any output greater than Q, the monopolist's costs of producing additional units will be greater than the benefits (marginal revenue). Production of such units would reduce profits. Thus, output rate Q and price P will maximize the firm's profit.

Exhibit 1 also depicts the profits of a monopolist. At output Q and price P the firm's total revenue is equal to $PAQO$, the price times the number of units sold. The firm's total cost would be $CBQO$, the average per-unit cost multiplied by the number of

---

[2]In this chapter we assume that firms are unable to use price discrimination to increase their revenues. If they could, the analysis of price discrimination from the previous chapter would help to describe their decisions.

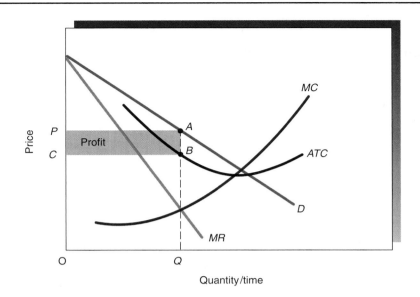

EXHIBIT 1
Short-Run Price and Output of a Monopolist

The monopolist will reduce price and expand output as long as *MR* exceeds *MC*. Output *Q* will result. When price exceeds average total cost at any output level, profit will accrue at that output level.

EXHIBIT 2
Profit Maximization for a Monopolist

Rate of Output (per day) (1)	Price (per unit) (2)	Total Revenue (1) X (2) (3)	Total Cost (per day) (4)	Profit (3) – (4) (5)	Marginal Cost (6)	Marginal Revenue (7)
0	—	—	$50.00	$–50.00	—	—
1	$25.00	$25.00	60.00	–35.00	$10.00	$25.00
2	24.00	48.00	69.00	–21.00	9.00	23.00
3	23.00	69.00	77.00	–8.00	8.00	21.00
4	22.00	88.00	84.00	4.00	7.00	19.00
5	21.00	105.00	90.50	14.50	6.50	17.00
6	19.75	118.50	96.75	21.75	6.25	13.50
7	18.50	129.50	102.75	26.75	6.00	11.00
8	17.25	138.00	108.50	29.50	5.75	8.50
9	16.00	144.00	114.75	29.25	6.25	6.00
10	14.75	147.50	121.25	26.25	6.50	3.50
11	13.50	148.50	128.00	20.50	6.75	1.00
12	12.25	147.00	135.00	12.00	7.00	–1.50
13	11.00	143.00	142.25	.75	7.25	–4.00

units sold. The firm's profits are merely total revenue less total cost, the shaded area of Exhibit 1.

Exhibit 2 provides a numeric illustration of profit-maximizing decision making. At low output rates, marginal revenue exceeds marginal cost. The monopolist will continue expanding output as long as *MR* is greater than *MC*. Thus, an output rate of eight units per day will be chosen. (*Note:* If tiny portions of a unit could be produced and sold, then production would increase to where *MR* = *MC*.) Given the demand for the product, the monopolist can sell eight units at a price of $17.25 each. Total revenue will be $138, compared to a total cost of $108.50. The monopolist will make a profit of $29.50. The profit rate will be smaller at all other output rates. For example, if the monopolist reduces the price to $16 in order to sell nine units per day, revenue will increase by $6. However, the marginal cost of producing the ninth unit is $6.25. Since the cost of producing the ninth unit is greater than the revenue it brings in, profits will decline.

When high barriers to entry are present, they will insulate the monopolist from direct competition with rival firms producing a similar product. In markets with high entry barriers, monopoly profits will not attract—at least not quickly—rivals who will expand supply, cut prices, and spoil the seller's market.

Protected by high entry barriers, a monopolist may be able to continue earning a profit, even in the long run. Does this mean that monopolists can charge as high a price as they want? Monopolists are often accused of price gouging. In evaluating this charge, however, it is important to recognize that, like other sellers, monopolists will seek to maximize *profit*, not *price*. Consumers will buy less as price increases. Thus, a higher price is not always best for monopolists. Exhibit 2 illustrates this point. What would happen to the profit of the monopolist if price were increased from $17.25 to $18.50? At the higher price, only seven units would be sold, and total revenue would equal $129.50. The cost of producing seven units would be $102.75. Thus, when price is $18.50 and output seven units, profit is only $26.75, less than could be attained at the lower price ($17.25) and larger output (eight units). The highest price is not always the best price for the monopolist. Sometimes a price reduction will increase the firm's total revenue more than its total cost.

Will a monopolist always be able to make an economic profit? The profitability of a monopolist is limited by the demand for the product that it produces. In some cases, a monopolist—even one protected by high barriers to entry—may be unable to sell for a profit. For example, there are thousands of clever, patented items that are never produced because demand-cost conditions are not favorable. **Exhibit 3** illustrates this possibility. Here, the monopolist's average total cost curve is above its demand curve at every level of output. Even when operating at the *MR = MC* rate of output, economic losses (shaded area) will occur. While output *Q* could be sold at price *P*, this price is too low to cover the per-unit cost of the monopolist. Under these circumstances, not even a monopolist would want to operate, at least not for long.

EXHIBIT 3
When a Monopolist Incurs Losses

Even a monopolist will incur losses if the average total cost curve lies above the demand curve.

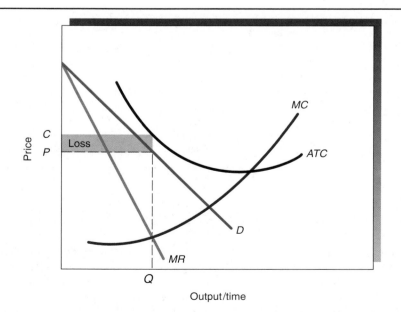

The Monopoly Model and Decision Making in the Real World

Until now, we have proceeded as if monopolists always knew exactly what their revenue and cost curves looked like. Of course, this is not true in the real world. Like other price searchers, a monopolist cannot be sure of the demand conditions for a product. Demand curves frequently shift, and choices must be made without the benefit of perfect knowledge. How many sales will be lost if the price is raised? How many sales will be added if the price is lowered? Like other price searchers, monopolists often experiment with price changes, attempting to find the price at which profit will be maximized. Price will be set on the basis of what the price-searching monopolist expects to happen when price is changed. Thus, the revenue and cost data illustrated in Exhibits 1, 2, and 3 represent *expected* revenues and costs associated with various output levels. To complicate matters further in real life, quality changes of various sorts can be undertaken by the monopolist searching for additional profits. Buyer reactions to potential quality changes, and resulting shifts in demand and cost, must also be considered by the profit-seeking monopolist.

A monopolist, like other business decision makers, seldom calculates what we have called demand, marginal revenue, and cost curves. Given imperfect information, the profit-maximizing price may be only approximated. Like other price searchers, however, the monopolist has a strong incentive to find the profit-maximizing price and output rate and, when it does, the outcome will be as if the $MR = MC$ rule had been used to maximize profit.

It is difficult for a monopolist to predict demand conditions and consumer response to quality and price changes. But life is even more complex for the next class of price searchers we consider: large firms with few rivals in a market protected by high barriers to entry.

CHARACTERISTICS OF OLIGOPOLY

In the United States, the great majority of output in such industries as automobiles, cigarettes, and aircraft is produced by five or fewer dominant firms. These industries are characterized by **oligopoly**. *Oligopoly* means "few sellers." ***The distinguishing characteristics of an oligopolistic market are (1) a small number of rival firms, (2) interdependence among the sellers because each is large relative to the size of the market, (3) substantial economies of scale, and (4) high entry barriers into the market.***

Oligopoly
A market situation in which a small number of sellers compose the entire industry. It is competition among the few.

Interdependence Among Oligopolistic Firms

Since the number of sellers in an oligopolistic industry is small, the decisions of one firm will influence the demand, price, and profit of rivals. This adds to the complexity of the firm's decision making. A firm that is deciding what price to charge, output to produce, or quality of product to offer, must consider the potential reactions of rivals. After all, the demand for its own output depends on the available substitutes offered by rival firms. The business decisions of each firm depend on the policies it expects its major rivals to follow.

Substantial Economies of Scale

In an oligopolistic industry, large-scale production (relative to the total market) is generally required to achieve minimum per-unit cost. Economies of scale are present, so a small number of large-scale firms can produce the entire market demand for the product. Using the automobile industry as an example, **Exhibit 4** illustrates the importance of economies of scale as a source of oligopoly. It has been estimated that each firm must produce approximately 1 million automobiles annually before its per-unit cost of production is minimized. However, when the selling price of automobiles is barely sufficient to cover costs, the total quantity demanded from these producers is only 6 million. To minimize costs, then, each firm must produce at least one-sixth (1 million of the 6 million) of the output

EXHIBIT 4
Economies of Scale and Oligopoly

Oligopoly exists in the automobile industry because firms do not fully realize the cost reductions from large-scale output until they produce approximately one-sixth of the total market.

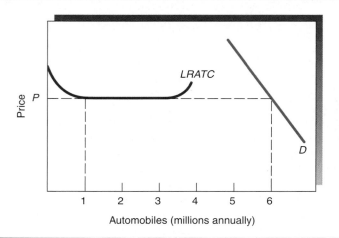

demanded. In other words, the industry can support no more than five or six domestic firms of cost-efficient size.

Significant Barriers to Entry

As with monopoly, barriers to entry limit the ability of new firms to compete effectively in oligopolistic industries. Economies of scale are probably the most significant entry barrier protecting firms in an oligopolistic industry.[3] A potential competitor may be unable to start out small and gradually grow to the optimal size, since it must gain a large share of the market before it can minimize per-unit cost. The manufacture of refrigerators and diesel engines, as well as automobile production, seems to fall into this category. Other factors, including patent rights, control over an essential resource, and government-imposed entry restraints, may also prevent new competitors from entering profitable oligopolistic industries. The presence of high entry barriers is what distinguishes oligopoly from a competitive price-searcher market.

Products May Be Either Identical or Differentiated

The products of sellers in an oligopolistic industry may be either similar or differentiated. When firms produce identical products, such as milk or gasoline, there is less opportunity for nonprice competition. On the other hand, rival firms producing differentiated products are more likely to use style, quality, and advertising as competitive weapons.

PRICE AND OUTPUT IN THE CASE OF OLIGOPOLY

Unlike a monopolist or a price taker, an oligopolist cannot determine the product price that will deliver maximum profit simply by estimating its own costs and the *existing* market demand. The demand facing an oligopolistic firm depends also on the pricing behavior of close rivals. Suppose, for example, that General Motors is considering how to price next year's new Chevrolet model when it comes on the market. The number of Chevrolets it can sell at each price will depend not only on buyer preferences, but also on the prices (and quality) of substitutes available from Ford, Toyota, and other GM rivals. What pric-

---

[3]Economies of scale will not be a barrier to entry in the industry, of course, if resources can be freely moved into and out of the industry at a low cost. Such resource mobility would render the market contestable, a market structure that we discussed in the previous chapter.

ing strategy will each rival use if GM puts a low price on its new model? How would each rival firm react to a higher GM price?

Economics cannot predict these complex interactions among rivals, without making some strong, simplifying assumptions about how each firm reacts when one firm makes a change in price or quality. These simplifying assumptions will not be realistic for the general case, and therefore the precise price and output that will emerge under oligopoly cannot be uniquely determined. Economics does, however, indicate a potential range of prices and the factors that will determine whether prices in the industry will be high or low relative to costs of production.

Consider a typical oligopolistic industry in which seven or eight rival firms produce the entire market output because substantial economies of scale are present. The firms produce nearly identical products and have similar costs of production. **Exhibit 5** depicts the market demand conditions and long-run costs of production of the individual firms for such an industry.

What price will prevail? We can answer this question for two extreme cases. First, suppose that each firm sets its price independently of the other firms. There is no collusion (no agreement among the firms to limit output and keep the price high), so each competitive firm is free to seek additional customers and profits by offering buyers a slightly better deal than its rivals. Under these conditions, the market price would be driven down to P_c. Firms would be just able to cover their per-unit costs of production. If a single firm raised its price, its customers would switch to rival firms, which would now expand to accommodate the new customers. The firm that raised its price would lose out. It would be self-defeating for any one firm to raise its price if the other firms did not raise theirs.

What happens if the current price is greater than P_c, perhaps because the market has not yet adjusted fully to a recent reduction in resource prices that lowered production costs? As a result, price is above per-unit cost and the firms are making economic profit. However, any *individual firm* that reduces its price slightly, by 1 or 2 percent, for example, will gain numerous customers if the other firms maintain the higher price. The price-cutting firm will attract some new buyers to the market, but more important, it will also lure many buyers away from rival firms charging higher prices. Thus, if the rival sellers act independently, each will have a strong incentive to reduce price in order to increase sales and gain a larger share of the total market. But what happens when each firm attempts to undercut its rivals? Price is driven down to P_c, and the economic profit of the firms is eliminated.

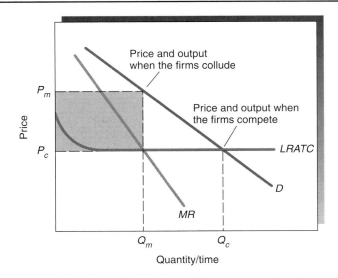

EXHIBIT 5
Range of Price and Output Under Oligopoly

If oligopolists were to act independently and compete with one another, price cutting would drive price down to P_c. In contrast, perfect cooperation among firms would lead to a higher price of P_m and a smaller output (Q_m rather than Q_c). The shaded area shows profit if firms collude. Demand here is the market demand.

When rival oligopolists compete (on the basis of price) with one another, they drive the market price down to the level of costs of production. They do not always compete, however. There is a strong incentive for oligopolists to collude, agreeing to raise price and to restrict output.

Suppose the oligopolists, recognizing their interdependence, acted cooperatively to maximize their joint profit. They might form a **cartel** to accomplish this objective. Probably the world's best-known cartel is the Organization of Petroleum Exporting Countries (OPEC), a group of oil-producing nations formed in 1960 to limit their combined production and thus raise world oil prices. From the beginning, different goals among members caused problems. Members like Saudi Arabia and Kuwait, with few people and large oil reserves, wanted moderately higher prices that would limit the incentives for long-term development of new oil substitutes and new oilfields. Other member nations such as Algeria and Libya, with smaller reserves and more people, wanted much higher prices, to gain more revenue from their limited reserves more quickly. Despite these disagreements, by 1973 OPEC had settled on a production strategy, with quotas for each producer. They succeeded in limiting their output enough to raise oil prices.

Higher oil prices, however, encouraged energy conservation and the greater use of coal, nuclear energy, and other oil substitutes. The higher prices also increased incentives for individual OPEC members to exceed their cartel quotas, and for non-OPEC producers to find and bring to market new oil and to produce more from marginal oilfields. Since the mid-1980s, these factors together have reduced OPEC's ability to keep world oil prices high. OPEC nations control 80 percent of the world's known oil reserves, including those from which oil can be produced most cheaply. Yet in 2001, their production was less than 40 percent of the world's oil output. Cartel agreements are difficult to arrange and to enforce. It is also difficult to protect the cartel market from nonmember producers, who will sell more if the cartel pushes the price up.

Instead of forming a cartel, oligopolists might collude without the aid of a formal organization. Under federal antitrust laws in the United States, collusive action to raise price and expand the joint profit of the firms would be illegal. Nevertheless, let us see what would happen if oligopolists followed this course. Exhibit 5 shows the marginal revenue curve that would accompany the market demand *D* for the product. Under perfect cooperation, the oligopolists would refuse to produce units for which marginal revenue to the group was less than marginal cost. Thus, they would restrict joint output to

Cartel
An organization of sellers designed to coordinate supply decisions so that the joint profits of the members will be maximized. A cartel will seek to create a monopoly in the market.

Collusive agreements among oligopolists and cartels like OPEC are difficult to maintain because any individual cartel member would be better off if it could cheat on the agreement and charge a slightly lower price, if other members do not.

Q_m where $MR = MC$. Market price would rise to P_m. With collusion, substantial joint profits (the shaded area of Exhibit 5) could thus be attained. The case of perfect cooperation would be identical with the outcome under monopoly.

In the real world, the outcome is likely to be between the two polar case extremes of price competition and perfect cooperation. Oligopolists generally recognize their interdependence and try to avoid vigorous price competition, which would drive price down to the level of per-unit costs. But there are also obstacles to collusion, which is why prices in oligopolistic industries are unlikely to rise to the monopoly level. ***Thus, oligopolistic prices are typically above per-unit cost but below those a monopolist would set.***

The Incentive to Collude and to Cheat

Collusion is the opposite of competition. It involves cooperative actions by sellers to turn the terms of trade in their favor and against buyers. Oligopolists as a group can profit by colluding to restrict output and raise price, giving them a strong incentive to do so. To accomplish this, however, the firms must also agree on production shares for each firm, or a division of the market so that production is limited to the level that will be purchased at the chosen cartel price.

Each individual oligopolist also has an incentive to cheat on collusive agreements. **Exhibit 6** explains why. An undetected price cut will enable a firm to attract (1) customers who would not buy from any firm at the higher price and (2) those who would normally buy from other firms. Thus, the demand facing each *individual firm* will be considerably more elastic than the market demand curve. As Exhibit 6 shows, the price P_i that maximizes the industry's profits will be higher than the price P_F that is best for a single oligopolist when the others stay with the higher price. If a firm can use secret rebates or other ways to undercut the price set by the collusive agreement, while other sellers maintain the higher price, the firm's expanded sales (beyond the level agreed upon by the cartel) will more than make up for the reduction in per-unit profit margin.

In oligopolistic industries, there are two conflicting tendencies. An oligopolistic firm has a strong incentive to cooperate with its rivals so that joint profit can be maximized. However, it also has a strong incentive to cheat secretly on any collusive agreement in order to increase its share of the joint profit. Oligopolistic agreements, therefore, tend to

Collusion
Agreement among firms to avoid various competitive practices, particularly price reductions. It may involve either formal agreements or merely tacit recognition that competitive practices will be self-defeating in the long run. Tacit collusion is difficult to detect. In the United States, antitrust laws prohibit collusion and conspiracies to restrain trade.

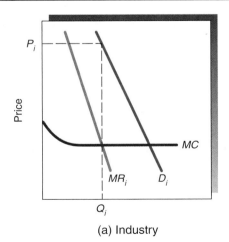

(a) Industry

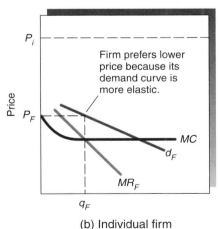

(b) Individual firm

EXHIBIT 6
Gaining from Cheating

The industry demand (D_i) and marginal revenue (MR_i) curves show that the joint profits of oligopolists would be maximized at Q_i where $MR_i = MC$. Price P_i would be best for the industry as a whole (a). However, the demand curve (d_F) facing each firm (under the assumption that no other firms cheat) would be much more elastic than D_i. Given the greater elasticity of its demand curve, an individual firm (b) would maximize its profit by cutting its price to P_F and expanding output to q_F, where $MR_F = MC$. Thus, individual oligopolists could gain by secretly shaving price and cheating on the collusive agreement.

be unstable. This instability exists whether the cooperative behavior is formal, as in the case of a cartel, or informal.

Obstacles to Collusion

There are certain situations in which it is more difficult for oligopolists to collude. Five major obstacles limit collusive behavior.

1. As the number of firms in an oligopolistic market increases, the likelihood of effective collusion declines.

Other things constant, an increase in the number of major firms in an industry will make it more difficult for the oligopolists to communicate, negotiate, and enforce agreements among themselves. In addition, the greater the number of firms, the more likely it is that the objectives of individual firms will conflict with those of the industry. Each firm will want a bigger slice of the pie. Opinions about the best collusive price arrangement will differ because marginal costs, unused plant capacity, and estimates of market demand elasticity are likely to differ among firms. Aggressive, less mature firms may be especially interested in expanding their share of total output. Exactly these problems have reduced the ability of OPEC to maintain high oil prices, as we noted above. Conflicting interests will always make it more difficult to reach a collusive agreement and will contribute to the breakdown of any agreement that is made.

2. When it is difficult to detect and eliminate price cuts, collusion is less attractive.

Unless a firm has a way of policing the pricing activities of rivals, it may be the "sucker" in a collusive agreement. Firms that secretly cut prices may gain a larger share of the market, while those maintaining higher prices are losing customers and profits. OPEC illustrates the explanatory power of the theory. Cheating by members on production and sales quota agreements has been a persistent problem for the cartel.

Price cutting can sometimes be accomplished in ways that are difficult for the other firms to identify. For example, a firm might provide better credit terms, faster delivery, and other related services "free" to improve slightly the package offered to the buyer. In industries where differentiated products are supplied, oligopolists can hold money prices constant and still use improvements in quality and style to provide consumers with more value. "Price cuts" like this are particularly attractive to oligopolists because they cannot be easily and quickly duplicated by rivals. Competitors can quickly match a reduction in money price, but it will take time for them to match an improvement in quality. Collusive agreements on price are of limited value in situations where quality and style are important competitive weapons. The bottom line is this: When cheating (price cutting) is profitable and difficult for rivals to detect and police, collusive agreements—both formal and informal—will be difficult to maintain.

3. Low entry barriers are an obstacle to collusion.

Unless potential new rivals can be excluded, oligopolists will be unable to sustain economic profits. Profitable collusion will merely attract competitors into the industry until the profits drawing the entrants are eliminated. Once again, OPEC illustrates the point. OPEC's member nations produced more than half the world's oil in 1973, when they began to reduce output and raise oil prices. But higher prices led firms in other nations to seek, find, and produce more oil. By 1985, OPEC had cut its production by 12 percent, driving world oil prices up to more than triple their 1973 level. As prices rose, however, the output of non-OPEC members expanded by approximately 30 percent and OPEC's share of the market shrank from 55 percent to only 30 percent. OPEC changed its course, expanding output in order to recapture a larger share of the world oil market. Prices quickly fell by about half, as more and more production came onto the market. Non-OPEC production stopped growing with the lower price, but corrected for inflation, the price of oil in the 1990s was only about one third of its peak in the early 1980s. Even with successful collusion, the benefits to sellers of higher prices must be shared with new entrants, unless entry into the industry can be blocked. Otherwise, entry will continue until falling prices drive economic profits to zero.[4]

Local markets are sometimes dominated by a few firms. For example, many communities have only a small number of ready-mix concrete producers, bowling alleys, accounting firms, and furniture stores. In the absence of government restrictions, however, entry barriers into these markets are generally low. The threat of potential rivals reduces the gains from collusive behavior under these conditions. Even if the number of rival firms is small, the firms will be unable to maintain above-normal profit rates when entry barriers are low. Under these circumstances, the competitive price-searcher model, rather than oligopoly, is more applicable.

4. Unstable demand conditions are an obstacle to collusion.

Demand instability leads to honest differences of opinion among oligopolists about what is best for the industry. One firm may want to expand because it anticipates a sharp increase in future demand, while a more pessimistic rival may want to hold the line on existing industrial capacity. The larger the differences in expectations about future demand, the greater the potential for conflict among oligopolistic firms. Successful collusion is more likely when demand is relatively stable.

5. Vigorous antitrust action increases the cost of collusion.

Under existing antitrust laws, collusive behavior is prohibited. Secret agreements are, of course, possible. Simple informal cooperation might be conducted without discussions or collusive agreements. However, like other illegal behavior, such agreements are not legally enforceable by any firm. Vigorous antitrust action can discourage firms from making such illegal agreements. As the threat of getting caught increases, participants will be less likely to attempt collusive behavior.

Uncertainty and Oligopoly

Uncertainty and imprecision characterize the theory of oligopoly. We know that firms will gain if they successfully restrict output and raise prices. However, collusion is fraught with conflicts and difficulties. In some industries, these difficulties are so great that the **market power** of the oligopolists is relatively small. In other industries, oligopolistic cooperation, although not perfect, may raise prices significantly, indicating a higher degree of market power, which is, in effect, a degree of monopoly power. Analysis of the costs and benefits of collusive behavior, under varying degrees of cooperation and conflict, has become an important part of economics over the last two decades. (See the Applications in Economics feature on **game theory**.) Although this developing field of economics does not yield precise predictions on oligopoly pricing and output, it does suggest the conditions that make it more likely that an oligopolist will face discipline from competitive pressures.

MARKET POWER AND PROFIT—THE EARLY BIRD CATCHES THE WORM

Our analysis of both monopoly and oligopoly indicates that because entry barriers into these markets are often high, firms may be able to earn economic profit over lengthy periods of time. Suppose a well-established firm, such as Disney or IBM, was able to use its market power to persistently earn above-normal returns. Would the current stockholders gain? Surprisingly, the answer is no. The ownership value of a share of corporate stock for

Market power
The ability of a firm that is not a pure monopolist to earn unusually large profits, indicating that it has some monopoly power. Because the firm has few (or weak) competitors, it has a degree of freedom from the discipline of vigorous competition.

Game theory
Analyzes the strategic choices made by competitors in a conflict situation, such as decisions made by members of an oligopoly.

---

[4]We are speaking here of profit from operating the firm. Ownership of a resource, such as an oilfield, does not involve an economic profit or a loss. The market value of the resource (e.g. the oilfield) represents the opportunity cost of using it in production, and the benefit of owning it—the owner could get that value in cash by selling the resource to an oil company, for example. It does not provide profit to the oil producer.

Oligopolistic Decision-making, Game Theory, and the Prisoner's Dilemma

In an oligopoly, a few firms compete by selling into the same market, and the actions of each influence the demand faced by rival sellers. Because they sell similar products and compete for the same customers, the interests of each firm are in conflict with the interests of the others. One firm can gain customers at the expense of the others by reducing its price or increasing its advertising. But if the other firms react competitively by doing the same, then all the firms may lose. Yet if rivals cut price or take other steps to offer consumers a better deal, firms that fail to follow suit will lose customers to their more aggressive competitors. Thus, each firm finds itself on the horns of a dilemma—in this case a variant of the classic "prisoner's dilemma."

Economists have increasingly used game theory, as in the analysis of the prisoner's dilemma, to analyze strategic choices made by competitors in a conflict situation, such as members of an oligopoly. Such choices depend on the anticipated actions of others.

To understand the prisoner's dilemma, consider the hypothetical case of Al and Bob, two touring Americans who just met at a train station in a small foreign country. They are taken prisoner and hauled into the local police station to be questioned separately. They are suspected of being the two men who robbed a local merchant, and each is told that if he makes the job of the police easier by confessing immediately, he will get only a 6-month sentence. But each is also told that if he says nothing while the other confesses, then the one who did not confess immediately will get a 12-month sentence. If neither confesses, both will be held for 3 months while the investigation continues. Al and Bob will not be allowed to communicate with each other. Will they confess?

To analyze such situations, the game theorist begins by laying out the alternative outcomes and showing how they are related to choices made by the players of the game, as we do in **Exhibit 7**. For each man individually, in this version of the dilemma, the box reveals that the best choice depends on what the other does. If Al confesses, then Bob can save 6 months of jail time by also confessing. The same holds for Al, if he thinks Bob will confess. But if neither confesses, both serve only three months in jail.[1] The proper strategy for each prisoner depends heavily on his estimate of the likelihood that the other will confess. The problem becomes more complex if we consider prisoners who face a series of such decisions over time, each prisoner learning the other's previous choice before the next set of choices must be made.

EXHIBIT 7
The Prisoner's Dilemma

		Al's Choice	
		Confess	Not Confess
Bob's Choice	Confess	6 months each	Al: 12 months Bob: 6 months
	Not Confess	Al: 6 months Bob: 12 months	3 months each

Al and Bob must each decide, without communicating with each other, whether to confess. Al knows that if Bob does not confess, then Al can either confess and spend 6 months in jail, or not confess and spend 3 months. But if Bob does confess, then Al's failure to confess would cost him an additional 6 months in jail. Bob is in a similar situation, facing the same options under the same assumptions about whether Al confesses. Each has the incentive to confess if he thinks the other one will, but to not confess if he thinks the other will also remain silent.

Firms in an oligopoly must make decisions somewhat like those of the prisoners: Should a firm cut its price, luring more customers, some from competitors, or should it keep its price high and risk losing customers to competitors who cut prices? If all firms keep the price high, then as a group they will reap more profit. If all cut prices, then as a group they will reap less profit. But the firm that fails to cut price when others do so will lose many customers to the other competing firms. The decision about whether to spend large amounts on advertising has similar characteristics.

For example, consider the pricing policy or advertising strategy of large automakers, such as Ford, General Motors, and Chrysler. Suppose the profit rate of each would be 15 percent if all the major automobile producers raised their prices (or cut their advertising expenditures) by a similar amount. In contrast, each would have a profit rate of only 10 percent if intense competition leads to lower prices and/or larger advertising expenditures. Industry profits are highest when all firms decide to charge high prices. However, if one automaker reduces its price or advertises more heavily, it will be able to win customers away from rivals and increase its profit rate to 20 percent. Thus, if the firm thinks its rivals will continue to charge higher prices (or fail to match its advertising expenditures), it will be able to gain from cutting its prices (and increasing its advertising). If the other firms follow a similar course, however, this strategy will backfire and the profit rate of all the firms in the industry will be less than the level that would have been achieved had they all charged higher prices (or spent less on advertising).

While our simplified analysis highlights the interdependence among the firms and the importance of probability estimates concerning the strategy of rivals, the real world is much more complex. The choices of the rival firms will be repeated over and over again, although often in modified forms. A prior strategy may be modified in light of previous reactions on the part of rivals. The attractiveness of a strategy will be influenced by the likelihood it will be detected by rivals and the speed with which they might be able to react effectively. In addition, the strategies of oligopolistic firms will be influenced by market conditions and the threat of foreign competition, factors that change with the passage of time. Within the framework of game theory models, additional assumptions must be made in order to account for these and other complex factors—factors that often change in the real world. In turn, if the assumptions incorporated into game theory models are not consistent with real-world conditions, the implications of the game theory analysis may well be invalid.

Economists have used game theory extensively to show how results change when the "rules of the game" change for the firms in an oligopolistic market, as well as for auction-bidding markets and other business decision-making situations. When the rules of the game are carefully defined and enforced, as in the case of economic experiments in laboratories, game theory has yielded interesting and important testable conclusions. But in open markets in the real world, empirical work using game theory has been less successful. The use of models is always difficult when the problem to be solved is complex, and human expectations about the changing strategy choices of other human beings must be taken into account. There is no question, however, that game theory can be useful for scholars and business practitioners alike, in helping them to frame the issues involved in strategic decision making.[2]

---

[1]If the numbers were slightly different from those in the accompanying chart, both Al and Bob would have an incentive to confess regardless of what they thought the other would do. For example, if each were told that he would get only a 1-month sentence if he confessed and the other party did not, then confession would become the dominant strategy for both Bob and Al. Under these circumstances, if Bob thought Al would remain silent, then Bob would spend only 1 month in jail if he confessed (compared to 3 months if he also remained silent). Al would be in a similar situation if he believed Bob would remain silent. On the other hand, if Bob thought Al would confess, then Bob's best option would be to also confess since confession would lead to only a 6-month sentence while silence would result in a 12-month jail term. The same would also be true for Al if he thought Bob would confess. Thus, in this classic prisoner's dilemma case, both have an incentive to confess even though confession leads to more jail time for both of them—6 months rather than 3 months. What is best for the individual (or firm) does not always lead to the best outcome from the viewpoint of the group (or industry).

[2]For a further explanation of game theory and the prisoner's dilemma, see Avinash Dixit and Barry Nalebuff, "Game Theory," in David R. Henderson, ed., *The Concise Encyclopedia of Economics*, www.econlib.org/library/CEE.html.

---

such corporations would long ago have begun to reflect their market power and expected future profitability. Many of the present stockholders would have paid high prices for their stock because they expected these firms to be highly profitable. In other words, they paid for any above-normal economic profits that the firm was expected to earn because of its market power.

Do not expect to get rich buying the stock of monopolistic or oligopolistic firms known to be highly profitable. You are already too late. The early bird catches the worm. Those who owned the stock when these firms initially developed their market position have already captured the gain. The value of their stock increased at that time. After a firm's future prospects are widely recognized, subsequent stockholders fail to gain a higher-than-normal rate of return on their financial investment.

DEFECTS OF MARKETS WITH HIGH ENTRY BARRIERS

What types of problems arise when entry barriers limit the number of firms in an industry to a single monopolist or a small group of oligopolists? From Adam Smith's time to the present, economists have generally considered monopoly a necessary evil at best. The attitude toward markets with only a few sellers and high entry barriers is only slightly more tolerant. Open competition, unfettered by high barriers to entry, has been recognized as a key form of market discipline restraining the behavior of producers and encouraging innovation. There are three major reasons for this view.

Monopolists, by keeping the market constantly understocked, by never fully supplying the effectual demand, sell their commodities much above the natural price, and raise their emoluments, whether they consist of wages or profit, greatly above their natural rate.

—Adam Smith[5]

---

[5]Adam Smith, *An Inquiry into the Nature and Causes of the Wealth of Nations* (1776; Cannan's ed., Chicago: University of Chicago Press, 1976), p. 69.

1. When entry barriers are high and there are few, if any, alternative suppliers, the discipline of market forces is weakened.

When entry barriers are low, consumers are well equipped to direct the behavior of suppliers. Producers have little choice but to serve the interest of consumers. The choices of consumers will drive firms from the market if they charge high prices, supply unattractive goods, or otherwise fail to serve the interest of consumers. If you do not like the food at a local restaurant, you eat elsewhere. If you think prices are high and the selection poor at a department store, you patronize rival firms. But consider your alternatives if you do not like the local cable television service. The entry of competitors is typically forbidden in that market. What can you do when the service is bad? You can voice a complaint to the company or your legislative representative, but unlike a competitive situation, you have no exit option other than sacrificing your cable service, perhaps to rely instead on satellite dish service. Cable and satellite service are imperfect substitutes, each with its own disadvantages. When consumers do not have good exit options—when they must either take what the seller offers or do without—their ability to discipline sellers is greatly reduced.

2. Reduced competition results in allocative inefficiency.

Allocative efficiency requires that additional units be produced when they are valued more highly than what it costs to produce them. When barriers to entry are low, production of each good will be expanded until its price is driven down to the level of per-unit costs. With high barriers to entry, however, this will not generally be the case. A monopolist or cartel that does not have to worry about rivals entering the market can often gain by restricting output and raising price. That is, output may not be produced even though consumers value it more than its costs of production. Prices may exceed not only marginal costs, but also average total cost for a long period of time when entry barriers into a market are high. As Adam Smith noted more than 200 years ago, monopolists (and cartels) will understock the market and charge a higher price than would prevail if the producers were disciplined by independent rivals and the threat of new entrants.

3. Government grants of monopoly power will encourage rent seeking; resources will be wasted by firms attempting to secure and maintain grants of market protection.

Grants of special favor by the government will lead to costly activities seeking those favors. As we noted in Chapter 6, economists refer to such activities as rent seeking. When government licenses or the imposition of other entry barriers enhance profitability and provide protection from the rigors of market competition, people will expend scarce resources attempting to secure and maintain these political favors. From an efficiency standpoint, such rent-seeking activities are wasteful; they consume valuable resources without contributing to output. In aggregate, output is reduced as the result of these wasteful activities. These rent-seeking costs from grants of monopoly power add to the welfare losses resulting from the allocative inefficiency mentioned above.

By way of illustration, suppose the government issues a license providing a seller with the exclusive right to sell liquor in a specific market. If this grant of monopoly power permits the licensee to earn monopoly profit, potential suppliers will expend resources trying to convince government officials that they should be granted the license. The potential monopolists will lobby government officials, make political contributions, hire representatives to do consulting studies, and undertake other actions designed to convince politicians and their appointees that they can best "serve the public interest" as a monopoly supplier. Any firm that expects its rent-seeking activities to be successful will be willing to spend up to the present value of the future expected monopoly profits, if necessary, to obtain the monopoly protection. Other suppliers, of course, may also be willing to invest in rent-seeking activities. When several suppliers believe they can win, the total expenditures of all firms on rent-seeking activities may actually consume resources worth more than the economic profit expected from the monopoly enterprise.

POLICY ALTERNATIVES WHEN ENTRY BARRIERS ARE HIGH

What government policies might be used to counteract the problems that result from high barriers to entry? Economists suggest four policy options:

1. Control the structure of the industry in order to assure the presence of rival firms.

2. Reduce artificial barriers that limit competition.

3. Regulate the price and output of firms in the market.

4. Supply the market with goods produced by a government firm.

Each of these policies has been used to either reduce entry barriers or to counteract their negative results. We will briefly consider each of them and analyze both their potential and limitations as tools with which to improve the efficiency of resource use.

Antitrust Policy and Controlling the Structure of an Industry

The major problems raised by high barriers to entry and monopoly power are avoided when rival sellers are present. A firm will be unable to restrict output and raise price when it confronts rivals producing the same product or close substitutes. The United States, to a greater degree than most Western countries, has adopted antitrust laws designed to prevent monopoly and promote competition. Antitrust legislation began in 1890 with the passage of the Sherman Antitrust Act. Additional legislation, including the Clayton Act and the Federal Trade Commission Act of 1914, has buttressed policy in this area.

Antitrust laws provide the U.S. Department of Justice (DOJ) with the power to prosecute firms engaging in collusive behavior or other actions designed to create a monopoly or cartel. They also provide the government with the power to break up an existing monopoly and prevent mergers that significantly reduce competition. The Federal Trade Commission (FTC) is allowed to bring charges under the Sherman Act. Private firms can also bring suits charging antitrust violations by a rival under the Sherman and Clayton acts, and may collect up to three times any actual damages caused by the rival firm. Each year, far more cases are brought by private firms against their competitors than by the two federal agencies. Rival firms can also ask that the two agencies step in to bring antitrust cases against successful competitors who may have, or threaten to gain, monopoly power.

Economists are not in total agreement on the usefulness of strong antitrust laws. Those who support aggressive antitrust policy believe that only by preserving numerous competitors in a market can we be confident that monopoly has been controlled. Opponents point to the danger of protecting high-cost firms at the expense both of consumers and the more aggressive and successful firm(s) in the market. Protection of less efficient firms from successful competitors, they say, is all too common in the actual practice of antitrust policy. Economists on both sides of this lively debate in economics have provided commentary during and after the highly publicized case brought by DOJ against Microsoft Corporation. (See the box feature on "Antitrust, Monopoly and Competition: The Microsoft Case.)

When analyzing the attractiveness of antitrust actions designed to maintain or increase the number of firms in an industry, the potential importance of economies of scale must also be considered. If economies of scale are unimportant, maintaining and/or expanding the number of rivals in an industry can be a good strategy. However, when substantial economies of scale are present, larger firms will have lower per-unit cost than smaller ones. Sometimes economies of scale are so important that per-unit cost of production will be lowest when the entire output of the industry is produced by a few firms (an oligopoly) or even a single firm (a monopoly). In the latter case, the "natural" tendency will be toward a **natural monopoly**—the situation where economies of scale are

Natural monopoly
A market situation in which the average costs of production continually decline with increased output. Therefore, average costs of production will be lowest when a single, large firm produces the entire output demanded.

APPLICATIONS IN ECONOMICS

Antitrust, Monopoly, and Competition: The Microsoft Case

In 1998, the Justice Department filed a highly publicized antitrust case against Microsoft, the software giant. Microsoft's rivals lobbied for this lawsuit. They charged that Microsoft had a monopoly in the market for computer operating systems, and was using its power in that market to give other Microsoft products, and especially its Internet Explorer Web browser, an unfair market advantage. For example, Microsoft had added its Internet Explorer browser to every copy of Windows, its operating system, and thus was giving the browser away free. Critics worried that Microsoft was trying to extend its monopoly on operating systems into the browser market. Several months earlier, IBM had begun to bundle a browser with its OS/2 operating system, but IBM had a much smaller market share. Microsoft's action forced the leading seller of browsers, Netscape, to lower its price to zero also. Like billboard space along a busy road, space on the browser's opening screen is valuable for advertising. Therefore, opportunity for profit was still present, even at a zero price, because a firm with the sizable share of the browser market could promote products and Web sites for itself and for others.

When Microsoft introduced its Internet Explorer in 1995, Netscape's Navigator dominated the browser market. Within a couple of years, Netscape's dominant position in the browser market was eroded and its revenues from browser sales virtually eliminated. Netscape argued that Microsoft's packaging of its browser within its operating system was an unfair competitive tactic. It also retained the services of Robert Bork, one of the nation's leading antitrust lawyers, in an effort to convince the general public and the Department of Justice that antitrust law should be used to protect the future of the Internet. Other rivals of Microsoft joined in the battle. Novell, a Microsoft rival located in Utah, enlisted the help of Utah Senator Orrin Hatch, chairman of the Senate Judiciary Committee. Senator Hatch held hearings to advance the case against Microsoft.

In May 1998, the Justice Department brought a case charging Microsoft with violating antitrust law. There were two primary allegations: (1) Microsoft was compelling computer manufacturers who installed its operating system, Windows, to also license and install Microsoft's Web browser, the Internet Explorer, in an attempt to monopolize the browser market, and (2) Microsoft made contracts that excluded rivals. In addition, Microsoft was charged with various forms of predatory conduct in order to force competitors from the market.

Supporters of the antitrust case against Microsoft argued that a firm with substantial market power cannot be allowed to leverage that power by tying other products to the one that it dominates. Neither can it be allowed to use its market power to bludgeon independent manufacturers not to deal with its competitors, or impose a pricing system that accomplishes the same result. The Justice Department also argued that Microsoft's Windows operating system imposed a serious barrier to entry. A new operating system, such as Linux, faces the problem that far fewer programs are written to be compatible with it, so users are hesitant to adopt it. This enhances Microsoft's market share, and according to the DOJ, justifies judicial intervention.[1]

Opponents of the strong stand taken by the Justice Department argue that antitrust policy is being used to reverse competitive outcomes at the expense of consumers. According to this view, the success of Microsoft's browser had little to do with its Windows operating system. Microsoft defenders buttress their case with evidence from published magazine reviews indicating that Netscape Navigator "was clearly considered the higher quality browser until late 1996, when Explorer became the superior product."[2] After that—and only then—was there a rapid increase in its market share.

More broadly, critics of the antitrust action argue that consumers have benefited from the pricing policies of Microsoft. When Microsoft has entered software markets, prices have consistently fallen, and stayed low. Data for 1988–1995 show that software in markets with direct Microsoft competition fell in price by nearly 60 percent; in markets without a direct Microsoft entrant, prices fell only 15 percent. Critics of the antitrust action stress that, far from restricting output and raising price, as a monopolist would do, Microsoft has substantially lowered the price of software products. In short, the DOJ critics argue that Microsoft's presence has benefited consumers and that most of the restraints that "trust busters" would place on Microsoft would harm consumers, and unfairly harm Microsoft.

The trial judge ruled that Microsoft had maintained its operating system as a monopoly by anticompetitive means and had attempted to establish a monopoly in the browser market by unlawfully bundling Internet Explorer with its Windows operating system. He ordered that Microsoft be split into two firms and established restrictions on the firm's business practices prior to that time.

Microsoft appealed. The appeals court upheld the trial court's ruling on several antitrust violations, but reversed the judge's breakup order and removed him from the case, citing "serious judicial misconduct" regarding his derogatory comments about the company. It ordered that another judge find a remedy that would restore competition and prevent further monopolization of the industry. The new judge encouraged Microsoft and the DOJ to settle the case themselves. The agreement they reached (pending approval from the court as this is written) restrained Microsoft from retaliation against firms that install software from rivals on Microsoft Windows operating systems. It also forced Microsoft to share key parts of its Windows programming codes with its competi-

tors, helping them to design application software to run more smoothly with Windows.

[1]For additional details, see Irwin Stelzer, *Microsoft and the Antitrust Laws: Old-Fashioned Problems and a New Economy*, AEI-Brookings Joint Center for Regulatory Studies, Policy Matters 01-09. March 2001.

[2]For this quote and more evidence on the position of those opposing the antitrust action against Microsoft, see Stan J. Liebowitz and Stephen E. Margolis, *Winners, Losers and Microsoft*, (Independent Institute: Oakland, CA, 1999) and Albert Nichols *Getting the Facts Straight on Microsoft*, AEI-Brookings Joint Center for Regulatory Studies, Policy Matters 01-13, May 2001.

such that unit cost will be minimized only if the entire industry output is produced by a single firm.

In the natural monopoly case, breaking up a large firm in order to increase the number of rivals in the industry is clearly a counter-productive strategy. Expanding the number of firms would lead to higher unit costs of production. Because of their higher costs, the prices charged by the smaller firms might even exceed those of a monopolist. Furthermore, it will be difficult to maintain the larger number of rivals because the firms will have a strong incentive to grow and/or merge in order to achieve the lower unit costs accompanying a larger scale of operation. Thus, use of antitrust laws to expand the number of firms is not an attractive option when an industry is a natural monopoly.

Reduce Artificial Barriers to Trade

Government-imposed restraints such as licensing requirements, tariffs, and quotas often reduce the competitiveness of markets. For example, local governments often require potential entrants into the taxicab business to prove that "additional capacity is needed to serve the market." Hearings must be held to address this issue and existing firms are allowed to explain why the new entrant is not needed. Governments also restrain entry into various occupations through the use of substantial licensing fees, complex examinations, and lengthy training requirements. When government-imposed restrictions are the source of the monopoly power, the appropriate policy action is straightforward: remove the restraints. Of course, this is often easier said than done. The restraints generally reflect the power of special interest groups—the producers currently in the industry—who have a vested interest in restricting competition and keeping prices high.

If a product is traded in international markets, foreign suppliers can enhance the competitiveness of a domestic market. When the domestic market is dominated by a small number of firms, removal of tariffs, quotas, and other obstacles that limit competition from abroad is particularly important. The competition of foreign rivals will help assure that the domestic firms improve quality and keep their costs low.

The U.S. automobile industry illustrates the importance of this approach. Profits for U.S. producers in the highly competitive automobile segment of the industry have been low. The 2.5 percent tariff on imported autos has had only a small impact. In contrast, there is a 25 percent tariff on imported trucks (placed there in 1963 in response to foreign treatment of U.S. frozen chicken exports). The higher tariff protects the same U.S. producers in the truck segment of the industry. There, profits per vehicle are much higher. When General Motors began selling its newly designed line of full-sized pickups in 1998 (the first full updating of those models in 10 years), the profit on a well-equipped $30,000 unit was reported to be $8,000. The tariff keeps the price of foreign imports high, so the level of competition is lower in the U.S. market for new trucks than in the market for cars. Clearly, the competition from abroad has helped keep domestic auto producers on their toes. As a result, most observers believe that the quality of automobiles available to the

American consumer, including those produced by domestic manufacturers, is higher than would have been the case in the absence of the competition from abroad.

As in the case of domestically imposed entry restraints, political considerations often make it difficult to remove obstacles that retard competition from abroad. Trade restraints that limit competition from foreign suppliers are generally a special interest issue. The beneficiaries of the restraints—primarily the owners, managers, and workers in the protected industries—are highly concentrated and generally well organized. In contrast, the costs of the restraints are nearly always thinly spread among poorly organized consumers. The better organized, concentrated interests are likely to prevail. Therefore, even when lower trade barriers are needed to increase the competitiveness of an industry, political factors may reduce the likelihood they will be adopted.

Regulate the Protected Producer

Can government regulation improve the allocative efficiency of a monopoly or an oligopoly? In theory, the answer to this question is clearly yes. **Exhibit 8** illustrates why ideal government price regulation, in the case of a monopolist, would improve resource allocation. Note, the firm illustrated here is a natural monopoly. Its LRATC falls over the entire relevant range of output. Thus, antitrust action that divided the firm into several smaller rivals would be ineffective because the unit cost of the smaller firms would be higher than if the output was produced by a monopolist. Nonetheless, the profit-maximizing monopolist will produce an output that is too small and charge a price that is too high from the viewpoint of allocative efficiency. It will set price at P_0 and produce output Q_0, where $MR = MC$. Consumers, however, would value additional units more than the opportunity cost. Let us consider the potential of two regulatory options and also analyze some of their real-world limitations.

Average Cost Pricing

If a regulatory agency forces the firm in Exhibit 8 to reduce price to P_1, at which the *ATC* curve intersects with the market (and firm) demand curve, the firm will expand output to Q_1. Since it cannot charge a price above P_1, the firm cannot increase revenues by selling a smaller output at a higher price. Once the price ceiling is instituted, the firm can increase revenues by P_1, and by only P_1, for each unit it sells. The regulated firm's *MR* is constant

EXHIBIT 8
Regulation of a Monopolist

If unregulated, a profit-maximizing monopolist with the costs indicated here would produce Q_0 units and charge P_0. If a regulatory agency forced the monopolist to reduce price to P_1, the monopolist would expand output to Q_1. Ideally, we would like output to be expanded to Q_2, where $P = MC$, but regulatory agencies usually do not attempt to keep prices as low as P_2. Can you explain why?

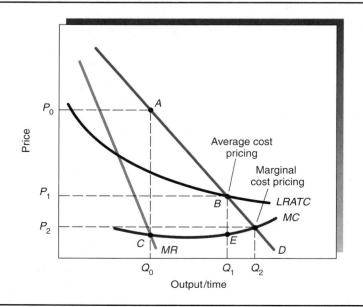

at P_1 for all units sold until output is increased to Q_1. Since the firm's MC is less than P_1 (and therefore less than MR), the profit-maximizing regulated firm shown here will expand output from Q_0 to Q_1. The benefits from the consumption of these units (ABQ_1Q_0) clearly exceed their costs (CEQ_1Q_0). Social welfare has improved as a result of the regulatory action (we will ignore the impact on the distribution of income). At that output level, revenues are sufficient to cover costs. The firm is making zero economic profit (or "normal" accounting profit).

Marginal Cost Pricing
Even at the Q_1 output level, marginal cost is still less than price. Additional welfare gains could be achieved if output were increased to Q_2. However, if a regulatory agency forced the monopolist to reduce price to P_2 (so that price would equal marginal cost at the output level Q_2), economic losses would result. Even a monopolist, unless subsidized, would not undertake production if the regulatory agency set the price at P_2 or any price below P_1. Usually, problems associated with determining and allocating the necessary subsidy would make this option unfeasible.

Problems with Regulation
Even though government regulation of monopoly seems capable of improving market results, as in the preceding average cost pricing example, both economic analysis and history of regulation suggest that regulation will usually not be an ideal solution. Why is regulation an imperfect solution? Four factors tend to reduce both the effectiveness of regulation and the probability that the regulators will act on behalf of all citizens to control monopoly. Let us look at each of these factors.

1. ***Lack of Information.*** In discussing ideal regulation, we assumed that we knew what the firm's ATC, MC, and demand curves looked like. In reality, of course, this would not be the case. The firms themselves have difficulty knowing their costs, and especially their demand curves, with any precision. Furthermore, both supply and demand will vary with time and place. The market for electricity is an excellent example. Because electricity cannot be stored for later use, the highly variable supply and demand conditions in that market cause the opportunity cost of power to change dramatically from one day, or even one hour, to the next. California utilities experienced that problem early in the summer of 2001, as low rainfall reduced hydropower generation, rising natural gas prices increased thermal generation costs, and some hot weather early in the summer added to an already growing demand. These factors combined to sharply raise the marginal cost of delivering electric power. The regulated retail power rates were far too low to cover costs in this situation. Later in the summer, these demand and supply factors had shifted back toward their previous levels, and the marginal cost of power had declined substantially. Meanwhile, however, the resulting power outages and utility revenue shortfalls caused serious problems.

   Because estimates of demand and marginal costs are difficult to obtain, regulatory agencies usually use profits (or rate of return) as a gauge to determine whether the regulated price is too high or too low. The regulatory agency, guarding the public interest, seeks to impose a "fair" or "normal" rate of return on the firm. If the firm is making profits (that is, an abnormally high rate of return), the regulated price must be higher than P_1 of Exhibit 8 and therefore that price should be lowered. Alternatively, if the firm is incurring losses (less than the fair or normal rate of return), this indicates that the regulated price is less than P_1, and therefore the firm should be permitted to charge a higher price.

   The actual existence of profits, though, is not easily identified. Accounting profit is not the same as economic profit, which focuses on opportunity cost. In addition, regulated firms have a strong incentive to adopt reporting techniques and accounting methods that conceal profits. This will make it difficult for a regulatory agency to identify and impose a price consistent with allocative efficiency.

2. *Cost Shifting.* Regulation changes incentives, and therefore it can affect costs. As long as demand is sufficient, the owners of the regulated firm can expect the long-run rate of profit to be essentially fixed, regardless of whether efficient management reduces costs or inefficient management allows costs to increase. If costs decrease, the "fair return" rule imposed by the regulatory agency will force a price reduction; if costs increase, the "fair return" rule will allow a price increase. Compared to the managers of unregulated firms, managers of regulated firms have more freedom to pursue personal objectives and less incentive to seek lower costs. Predictably, they will often fly first-class, entertain lavishly at company expense, grant unwarranted wage increases, and so on. Actions like these will make managerial life more comfortable, but they will also lead to higher unit cost. As the result of the firm's monopoly position, consumers are unable to switch to substitute products (and rival firms) and thereby help to control managerial inefficiency. Normally, wasteful activities would be policed by the owners, but since the firm's rate of return is set by the regulatory agency, the owners have little incentive to be concerned. Prices will be adjusted by regulators to reflect costs as they are. Thus, to a large degree, the incentive structure accompanying price regulation is inconsistent with the minimization of production cost.

3. *Special-Interest Influence.* The difficulties of government regulation discussed thus far are practical limitations that a regulatory agency would confront in seeking to perform its duties efficiently. But, in the political arena, regulatory authorities cannot necessarily be expected to pursue only efficiency. Regulated firms have a strong incentive to see that "friendly," "reasonable" people serve as regulators, and they will invest political and economic resources to this end. Just as rent-seeking activities designed to gain monopoly privileges can be expected, so can activities to influence regulatory decisions.

Each competing segment of a regulated industry will try to use the regulatory mechanism for its own competitive advantage. What services and specialized programming should a regulated cable television firm be allowed to offer, at each price? Alternative providers of TV services, such as satellite companies, will work to see that regulated prices and services of the cable firms are set to minimize the ability of cable firms to compete with the providers of satellite video services.

Consumer interests, in contrast to those of industry, are widely dispersed and disorganized. Ordinarily, consumers cannot be expected to invest the time and resources required to understand regulatory policy and the political contributions that are often necessary to influence its direction. The firms that are regulated can, however, be expected to influence regulators by making such investments. Even though the initial stimulus for regulatory action often comes from consumer interests, economic theory suggests that, with time, regulatory commissions are likely to reflect the views of the business and labor interests they were designed to regulate.

4. *Slow Response to Changing Conditions.* In a time of rapid change, lack of detailed knowledge and understanding of the industry can reduce the rate at which regulators adjust prices. When costs are falling, "regulatory lag" contributes to suppliers' profits. When costs rise, adjustment is also slower.

Tardiness in the adjustment to changing conditions was a major factor underlying the electricity crisis of California during 2000–2001. Sharply higher crude oil and natural gas prices substantially increased the cost of generating electricity during 2000. Because of its heavy dependence on electricity generated from these sources, these price increases were particularly important in California. While the regulatory commission deliberated, various consumer groups lobbied against rate increases and the regulated retail rates remained well below cost for several months. As time passed, one of California's two largest utility companies, Pacific Gas and Electric, was driven into bankruptcy. The other, Southern California Edison, suffered huge losses and was unable to borrow in the credit market. At the low regulated price, consumers had little incentive to reduce their power use or invest in power-saving appliances, computers, and other capital items. These circumstances combined to yield several months of brown-outs and rotating blackouts in areas of California where the regulated rates applied. Eventually, the regulated utilities were permitted to raise their rates and, in order the deal with the shortfall, the state of California entered into long-term contracts for the import of electricity from other regions. As it turned out, the state's long-term contracts for the import of electricity were negotiated at a time when electricity prices were exceedingly high. Electricity and other energy prices fell substantially as the economy weakened in 2001. Thus, the taxpayers of California are now stuck with an estimated bill of $20 billion to cover the cost of these high-priced electricity imports. As the California case illustrates, while regulation has the potential to improve resource allocation, it is not a magic cure.

Supply Market with Government Production

Government-operated firms—socialized firms such as the U.S. Postal Service, the Tennessee Valley Authority, and many local public utilities—present an alternative to both private monopoly and regulation. However, both theory and experience indicate that socialized firms will fail to counteract fully the problems that stem from high barriers to entry. The same perverse managerial incentives—incentives to ignore efficiency and pursue personal or professional objectives at the firm's expense—that regulated firms confront also tend to plague government-operated firms. In addition, the rational ignorance effect comes into play here. Individual voters have little incentive to acquire information about the operation of government firms because their choices will not be decisive. Predictably, the "owners" of a socialized firm (voters) will be uninformed about how well the firm is run, or how it might be run better. This is especially true when there are no direct competitors against which the firm's performance might easily be compared.

Government-operated firms do not provide an environment that rewards efficient management and reductions in cost. Unlike investors in the private sector, no small group of voters normally is in a position to gain substantial wealth by taking over the socialized firm and improving its management. Even more than with monopoly or oligopoly in the private sector, customers of the socialized monopoly (voter-taxpayers) cannot easily switch their business to other sellers. Even those voter-taxpayers who do not consume the product often have to pay taxes to support its provision. When the government operates a business—particularly one with monopoly power—there is typically less investor scrutiny, less reward for efficiency, and less penalty for inefficiency. Higher costs are an expected result.

Government ownership, like unregulated monopoly and government regulation, is a less than ideal solution. Thus, it should not be surprising that those who denounce monopoly in, for instance, the telephone industry seldom point to a government-operated monopoly—such as the postal service—as an example of how an industry should be run.

Pulling It Together

The policy implications that can legitimately be drawn from an analysis of high barriers to entry are less than fully satisfying. We may not like the reduction in competition or its effects, but economic analysis suggests important qualifications to the "solutions" usually put forth.

Most of the policy alternatives are not terribly attractive. Economies of scale often reduce the attractiveness of antitrust actions. When larger firms have lower per-unit costs, restructuring the industry to increase the number of firms will be both costly and difficult to maintain. Antitrust policy can also be used by rivals to increase the cost of successful firms that have simply given consumers a better deal, and taken a large market share from their competitors in the process. Policy actions to stop or to punish such progress is counterproductive, for customers. Government measures, such as tariff reductions and removal of entry barriers into markets, are perhaps the surest recommendation for increasing competition. Such policies, however, will certainly face political opposition, primarily from owners and workers in protected industries.

Regulation is also a less than ideal solution. Regulators do not possess the information necessary to impose an efficient outcome, and they may be susceptible to manipulation by industrial and labor interests. Moreover, since public-sector managers are likely to pursue political objectives at the expense of economic efficiency, public ownership also has shortcomings. Thus, economic theory indicates that there are no ideal solutions when substantial economies of scale are present. Policy choices are made among imperfect alternatives. In this imperfect world, however, consumers have many choices.

THE COMPETITIVE PROCESS IN THE REAL WORLD

How competitive are markets? In a very real sense, every firm competes with every other firm for the consumer's additional dollar of spending. Firms in markets that appear to be unrelated often compete with each other. Sellers of compact discs, for example, compete with the bookstore and the local restaurant for our entertainment budgets. The suppliers of swimming pools compete with airlines, hotels, casinos, and automobile rental companies for the vacation and leisure time expenditures of consumers.

Competition to provide better, lower cost goods and services is everywhere. Innovation and nonprice competition on product quality, design, convenience, and other factors is used constantly by firms seeking greater market share and profitability. Like price reductions, improvements in product quality provide consumers with more value per dollar of expenditure. Competition of this type makes collusion more difficult to agree upon and enforce, and it erodes profits even in industries with few rival firms. Patents and technological innovations may temporarily provide firms a measure of protection from rivals. But there is also a positive side to market power of this type: it encourages innovations that improve products and reduce costs.

The pervasiveness of the competitive process helps explain why profit levels, even in manufacturing industries, are considerably lower than many people think. A national sample poll of adults conducted by Opinion Research of Princeton found that the average person thought profits comprised 29 percent of every dollar of sales in manufacturing. In reality, the after-tax accounting profits of manufacturing corporations are about 4 cents to 5 cents per dollar of sales. Competition among manufacturers is generally strong.

The competitiveness of markets is complex and difficult to measure directly. However, economists generally agree that the U.S. economy has become more competitive over the past several decades. Reductions in transport costs, improvements in communications, the development of the Internet, increased competition from imports, and deregulation of several key markets have all tended to enhance the competitiveness of markets in the United States.

LOOKING AHEAD

The last several chapters have focused on product markets. Of course, resources are required to produce products. The following chapters will focus on resource markets and the employment decisions of both business firms and resource suppliers.

KEY POINTS

- The four major barriers to entry into a market are economies of scale, government licensing, patents, and control of an essential resource.

- Monopoly is present when there is a single seller of a well-defined product for which there are no good substitutes and the entry barriers into the market are high. While there are only a few markets for which the entire output is supplied by a single seller, the monopoly model also helps one better understand the operation of markets dominated by a small number of firms.

- The market demand curve is also the monopolist's demand curve. Like other price searchers, a profit-maximizing monopolist will lower price and expand output as long as marginal revenue exceeds marginal cost. At the maximum-profit output, *MR* will equal *MC*. The monopolist will charge the price on its demand curve consistent with that output.

- If profit is present, high barriers to entry will shield a monopolist from direct competition, and in such cases, monopolists can earn long-run economic profits. Sometimes demand and cost conditions will be such that even a monopolist will be unable to earn economic profit.

- An oligopolistic market is characterized by (1) a small number of rival firms, (2) interdependence among the sellers, (3) substantial economies of scale, and (4) high entry barriers into the market.

- There is no general theory of equilibrium price and output for oligopolistic markets. If rival oligopolists acted totally independent of their competitors, they would drive price down to the per-unit cost of production. Alternatively, if they colluded perfectly, price would rise to the level a monopolist would charge. The actual outcome will generally fall between these two extremes.

- Oligopolists have a strong incentive to collude and raise their prices. However, each firm will be able to gain if it can cut its price (or raise the quality of its product) because the demand curve confronted by the firm is more elastic than the industry demand curve. This introduces a conflict between the interests of individual firms and the industry as a whole. This conflict makes collusive agreements difficult to maintain.

- Oligopolistic firms are less likely to collude successfully against the interests of consumers if (a) the number of rival firms is large; (b) it is costly to prohibit competitors from offering secret price cuts (or quality improvements) to customers; (c) entry barriers are low; (d) market demand conditions tend to be unstable; and/or (e) the threat of antitrust action is present.

- Economists criticize high barriers to market entry because (a) the ability of consumers to discipline producers is weakened, (b) the unregulated monopolist or oligopolist can often gain by restricting output and raising price, and (c) legal barriers to entry will encourage firms to "invest" resources in seeking additional protective barriers and maintaining existing ones.

- A natural monopoly exists when long-run average total costs continue to decline as firm size increases, over the entire range of market demand. Thus, a larger firm always has lower costs.

- When entry barriers are high and competition among rival firms weak, the major policy alternatives are: (a) antitrust action designed to maintain or increase the number of firms in the industry, (b) relaxation of regulations that limit entry and trade, (c) price regulation, and (d) provision of output by government firms. When feasible, option (b) is the most attractive alternative. Under most circumstances, all the other options have shortcomings.

- Competitive forces are present even in markets with high barriers to entry. Quality competition is an important element of the competitive process. Profitability and high prices encourage the development of new technologies and substitute products.

CRITICAL ANALYSIS QUESTIONS

*1. "Barriers to entry are crucial to the existence of long-run profits, but they cannot guarantee the existence of profits." Evaluate.

2. "Monopoly is good for producers but bad for consumers. The gains of the former offset the losses of the latter. On balance, there is no reason to think

that monopoly is bad for the economy." Is this statement true? Why or why not?

*3. Do monopolists charge the highest prices for which they can sell their products? Do they maximize their average profit per sale? Are monopolistic firms always profitable? Why or why not?

4. The retail liquor industry is potentially a competitive industry. However, the liquor retailers of a southern state, with the cooperation of the state legislature, organized a trade association that sets prices for all firms. For all practical purposes, a competitive industry became a monopoly. Compare the price and output policy for a purely competitive industry with the policy that would be established by a profit-maximizing monopolist or trade association. Who benefits and who is hurt by the formation of the monopoly?

5. Does economic theory indicate that an ideal regulatory agency that forces a monopolist to charge a price equal to either marginal or average total cost would improve economic efficiency? Explain. Does economic theory suggest that a regulatory agency will in fact follow a proper regulation policy? What are some of the factors that complicate the regulatory function?

6. Is a monopolist subject to any competitive pressures? Explain. Would an unregulated monopolist have an incentive to operate and produce efficiently? Why or why not?

7. How will high entry barriers into a market influence (a) the long-run profitability of the firms, (b) the cost efficiency of the firms in the industry, (c) the likelihood that some inefficient (high-cost) firms will survive, and (d) the incentive of entrepreneurs to develop substitutes for the product supplied by the firms? Are competitive pressures present in markets with high barriers to entry? Discuss.

*8. Why is oligopolistic collusion more difficult when there is product variation than when the products of all firms are identical?

9. In large cities, taxi fares are often set above the market equilibrium rate. Sometimes the number of licenses is limited in order to maintain the above-market price. Other times licenses are automatically granted to anyone wanting to operate a taxi. When taxi fares are set above market equilibrium, compare and contrast resource allocation under the restricted license system (assume the licenses are tradable) and the free-entry system. In which case will it be easier for customers to get a taxi? In which case will the amount of capital required to enter the taxi business be greater?

10. We have a theory to explain the equilibrium price and output for monopoly, but not for oligopoly. Why? What role can game theory play in helping us to understand decisions made by oligopolists?

*11. Historically, the real cost of transporting both goods and people has declined substantially. What impact does a reduction in transportation cost have on the market power of individual producers? Do you think the U.S. economy is more or less competitive today than it was 100 years ago? Explain.

*12. "My uncle just bought 1,000 shares of Mammoth Manufacturing, one of the largest and most profitable companies in the United States. Given the high profit rate of this company, he will make a bundle from this purchase." Evaluate this statement. Is it necessarily true? Explain.

*13. Gouge-em Cable Company is the only cable television service company licensed to operate in Backwater County. Most of its costs are access fees and maintenance expenses. These fixed costs total $640,000 monthly. The marginal cost of adding another subscriber to its system is constant at $2 per month. Gouge-em's demand curve can be determined from the data in the accompanying table.

Subscription Price (Per Month)	Number of Subscribers
$25	20,000
20	40,000
15	60,000
10	80,000
5	100,000
1	150,000

a. What price will Gouge-em charge for its cable services? What are its profits at this price?
b. Now suppose the Backwater County Public Utility Commission has the data and feels that cable subscription rates in the county are too expensive and that Gouge-em's profits are unfairly high. What regulated price will it set so that Gouge-em makes only a normal rate of return on its investment?

14. Suppose that you produce and sell children's tables in a localized market. Past experience permits you to estimate your demand and marginal cost schedules. This information is presented in the table at the top of the next page.
a. Fill in the missing revenue and cost schedules.
b. Assuming you are currently charging $55 per table set, what should you do if you want to maximize profits?
c. Given your demand and cost estimates, what price should you charge if you want to maximize weekly profit? What output should you produce? What is your maximum weekly profit?

Price	Quantity Demanded (per week)	Marginal Cost	Total Revenue	Marginal Revenue	Fixed Cost	Total Cost
$60	1	$50	_____	_____	$40	_____
55	2	20	_____	_____	_____	_____
50	3	24	_____	_____	_____	_____
45	4	29	_____	_____	_____	_____
40	5	35	_____	_____	_____	_____
35	6	45	_____	_____	_____	_____

15. The diagram shows demand and long-run cost conditions in an industry.
    a. Explain why the industry is likely to be monopolized.
    b. Indicate the price that a profit-maximizing monopolist would charge, and label it P.
    c. Indicate the monopolist's output level, and label it Q.
    d. Indicate the maximum profits of the monopolist.
    e. Will the profits attract competitors to the industry? Why or why not? Explain.

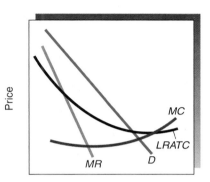

*Asterisk denotes questions for which answers are given in Appendix B.

CHAPTER 24

The Supply of and Demand for Productive Resources

Chapter Focus

■ Why do business firms demand labor, machines, and other resources? Why is the demand for a productive resource inversely related to its price?

■ How do business firms decide which resources to employ and the quantity of each that will be used?

■ How is the quantity supplied of a resource related to its price in the short run? In the long run?

■ What determines the market price of a resource? How do resource prices help to allocate efficiently a society's resources across competing uses?

---

[1]James E. Meade was a longtime professor of economics at Cambridge University.

Recent chapters have focused on product markets, markets where consumers purchase goods and services supplied by business firms. Our analysis now shifts to **resource markets**, markets where firms hire productive resources such as machines and workers and use them to produce goods and services. (*Note*: Because resources are also referred to as *factors or inputs*, these markets are also known as *factor markets* or *input markets*.)

Just as in product markets, the forces of supply and demand combine to determine price in resource markets. The buyers and sellers in resource markets are just the reverse of what they are in product markets. In resource markets, business firms are the purchasers; they demand resources that are used to produce goods and services. Households are the sellers; they (and firms they own) supply resources in exchange for income. The income derived from supplying productive resources, such as the wages received from the sale of labor services, provides the major source of income for most of us. Prices in resource markets coordinate the choices of buyers and sellers and bring the amount of each resource demanded into harmony with the amount supplied. Resource prices also help to allocate factors of production efficiently and channel them into the areas in which they are most productive. This enables us to have higher incomes and a larger supply of consumer goods than would otherwise be the case.

As the circular flow diagram of **Exhibit 1** illustrates, there is a close relationship between product and resource markets. Households earn income by selling factors of production—for example, the services of their labor and capital—to business firms. Their offers to sell form the supply curve in resource markets (bottom loop). The income households derive from the sale of resources provides them with the buying power required to purchase goods and services in product markets. These household expenditures for products generate revenues that provide business firms with the incentive to produce goods and services (top loop). In turn, the business firms demand resources because they contribute to the production of goods and services that can be sold in product markets. ■

HUMAN AND NONHUMAN RESOURCES

Broadly speaking, there are two different types of productive inputs, nonhuman and human. **Nonhuman resources** can be further broken down into the categories of physical capital, land, and natural resources. *Physical capital* consists of human-made resources, such as tools, machines, and buildings, that are used to produce other things.

Net investment can increase the supply of nonhuman resources. Investment, however, involves a cost. Resources that are used to produce machines, upgrade the quality of land, or discover natural resources could be used directly to produce goods and services for current consumption. Why take the roundabout path? The answer is that sometimes indirect methods of producing goods are less costly in the long run. For example, Robinson Crusoe found he could catch more fish by taking some time off from hand-fishing to build a net. Even though his initial investment of time in making the net reduced his current catch, once the net was completed he was able to more than make up for this loss. Benefits and costs will influence investment choices ranging from fishing nets to complex machines. These investments will be undertaken only when decision makers expect the benefits of a larger future output to more than offset the current reduction in the production of consumption goods. Just as the supply of machines can be increased, so, too, can wise land development and soil-conservation practices be used to upgrade both the quantity and quality of land. Similarly, the supply of natural resources can be increased (within limits) by the application of more resources to discovery and development.

Human resources are composed of the skills and knowledge of workers. Investment in such things as education, training, health, and experience can enhance the skill, ability, and ingenuity of individuals, and thereby increase their productivity. Economists refer to

Resource markets
Markets in which business firms demand factors of production (for example, labor, capital, and natural resources) from household suppliers. The resources are then used to produce goods and services. These markets are sometimes called factor markets or input markets.

Nonhuman resources
The durable, nonhuman inputs that can be used to produce both current and future output. Machines, buildings, land, and raw materials are examples. Investment can increase the supply of nonhuman resources. Economists often use the term physical capital when referring to nonhuman resources.

Human resources
The abilities, skills, and health of human beings that can contribute to the production of both current and future output. Investment in training and education can increase the supply of human resources.

573

EXHIBIT 1
The Market for Resources

Until now, we have focused on product markets, where households demand goods and services that are supplied by firms (upper loop). We now turn to resource markets, where firms demand factors of production—human capital (for example, skills and knowledge of workers) and physical capital (for example, machines, buildings, and land)—which are supplied by households in exchange for income (bottom loop). In resource markets, firms are buyers and households are sellers, just the reverse of the case for product markets.

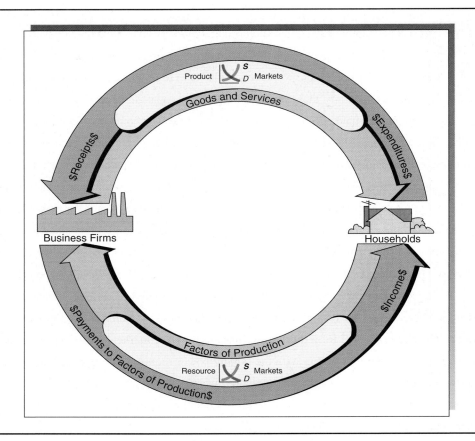

Investment in human capital
Expenditures on training, education, skill development, and health designed to increase human capital and the productivity of an individual.

such activities as **investment in human capital**.[2] Like physical capital, human capital also depreciates (human skills decline with age or lack of use). During any given year, education and training will add to the stock of human capital while depreciation detracts from it.

Decisions to invest in human capital involve all the basic ingredients of other investment decisions. Consider the decision of whether to go to college. As you know, an investment in a college education requires the sacrifice of current earnings as well as payments for direct expenses, such as tuition and books. The investment is expected to lead to a better job (when both monetary and nonmonetary aspects are considered) and other benefits. The rational investor will weigh the current costs against the expected future benefits. College will be chosen only if the benefits outweigh the costs.

Human resources differ from nonhuman resources in two important respects. First, human capital is embodied in the individual. Individuals cannot be separated from their knowledge, skills, and health conditions in the same way that they can be separated from physical capital, such as buildings or machines that they might own. As a result, choices concerning the use of human resources are vitally affected by working conditions, location, job prestige, and similar nonpecuniary factors. Although monetary factors influence human capital decisions, individuals will often choose to trade off some money income for better working conditions.

Second, human resources cannot be bought and sold in nonslave societies. Workers sell only the *services* of their labor, not the ownership to the human resource itself. Individuals have the option of quitting, selling their labor services to another employer, or us-

---

[2]The contributions of T. W. Schultz and Gary Becker to the literature on human capital have been particularly significant. See Ronald G. Ehrenberg and Robert S. Smith, *Modern Labor Economics: Theory and Public Policy*, Seventh Edition (Reading, MA: Addison Wesley, 2000), Chapter 9, for additional detail on human capital theory.

ing them in an alternative manner. Thus, we usually speak of the worker as selling (and the firm as buying) labor services.

In competitive markets, the price of resources, like the price of products, is determined by supply and demand. We will begin our analysis of resource markets by focusing on the demand for resources, both human and nonhuman.

DEMAND FOR RESOURCES

Profit-seeking producers employ laborers, machines, raw materials, and other resources because they help produce goods and services. ***The demand for a resource exists because there is a demand for goods that the resource helps to produce. The demand for each resource is thus a derived demand*; *it is derived from the demand of consumers for products.***

For example, a service station hires mechanics because customers demand repair service, not because the service station owner receives benefits simply from having mechanics

Derived demand
The demand for a resource; it stems from the demand for the final good the resource helps to produce.

The demand for resources is a derived demand. A more complex tax code would increase the demand for (and thus the wages of) accountants, while a simpler tax code would lower the demand for (and wages of) accountants.

EXHIBIT 2
The Demand Curve for a Resource

As the price of a resource increases, producers that use the resource intensely will (1) turn to substitute resources and (2) face higher costs, which will lead to higher prices and a reduction in output. At the lower rate of output, producers will use less of the resource that increased in price. Both of these factors contribute to the inverse relationship between the price and amount demanded of a resource.

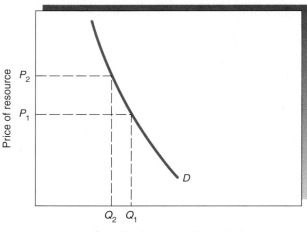

around. If customers did not demand repair service, mechanics would not be employed for long. Similarly, the demand for such inputs as carpenters, plumbers, lumber, and glass windows is derived from the demand of consumers for houses and other consumer products these resources help to make. Most resources contribute to the production of numerous goods. For example, glass is used to produce windows, ornaments, dishes, light bulbs, and mirrors, among other things. The total demand for a resource is the sum of the derived demands for it in each of its uses.

The demand curve for a resource shows the amount of the resource that will be used at different prices. As **Exhibit 2** illustrates, there will be an inverse relationship between the price of a resource and the amount demanded of it. There are two major reasons why less of a resource will be demanded as its price increases: (1) producers will turn to substitute resources and (2) consumers will buy less of goods that become more expensive as the result of higher resource costs. Let us take a closer look at each of these factors.

Substitution in Production
Firms will use the input combination that minimizes their cost. When the price of a resource goes up, firms will turn to lower-cost substitute inputs and cut back on their use of the more expensive resource.

Typically, there are many ways producers can reduce their use of a more expensive resource. For example, if the price of oak lumber increases, furniture manufacturers will use other wood varieties, metals, and plastics more intensely. Similarly, if the price of copper tubing increases, construction firms and plumbers will substitute plastic pipe for the more expensive tubing. Sometimes producers will alter the style and dimensions of a product in order to conserve on the use of a more expensive resource. In other cases, a shift in location may play a role in the substitution process. For example, if prices of office space and land increase in the downtown area of a large city, firms may move to the suburbs in order to cut back on their use of the more expensive resource.

The degree to which firms will be able to reduce their use of a more expensive resource will vary. The easier it is to turn to substitute factors, the more elastic the demand for a resource. *Other things constant, the more (and better) substitute resources that are available, the more elastic the demand for the resource.*

Substitution in Consumption
An increase in the price of a resource will lead to higher costs of production and thus higher prices for the products that the input helps to produce. Faced with these higher prices, *consumers* will turn to substitute products and cut back on their purchases of the

more expensive products. In turn, a smaller quantity of resources (including less of the one that rose in price) will be required to produce the smaller amount demanded by consumers at the now higher price.

The experience of the U.S. auto industry in the early 1980s vividly illustrates the importance of the substitution-in-consumption effect. Substantial wage increases pushed the costs of American automakers upward during this period. As the prices of domestically produced autos rose, many consumers switched to substitutes, particularly automobiles produced abroad. The sales of American producers fell sharply, causing a reduction in the quantity of labor demanded (and employment) in the U.S. automobile industry.

Other things constant, the more elastic the demand for the product, the more elastic the demand for the resource. This relationship stems from the derived nature of resource demand. An increase in the price of a product for which consumer demand is highly elastic will cause a sharp reduction in the sales of the good. There will thus also be a relatively sharp decline in the demand for the resources used to produce the good.

In summary, the demand elasticity of a resource will vary with the ease of substitution in both production and consumption. The demand for a resource will tend to be elastic when it is easy to substitute other resources for it in production and when the resource helps produce goods for which demand is relatively elastic. Conversely, the demand for a resource will tend to be inelastic when it is difficult to find good substitutes in production and when the resource is used to produce products for which demand is more inelastic.

Time and the Demand for Resources

The elasticity of resource demand is also influenced by the length of the time period under consideration. It takes time for producers to adjust fully to a change in the price of a resource. Typically, a producer will be unable to alter a production process or the design of a product immediately in order to conserve on the use of a more expensive input or to make better use of an input whose price has declined. Consumers may also find it difficult to alter their consumption patterns quickly in response to price changes. Thus, the demand for a resource generally becomes more elastic with the passage of time.

Exhibit 3 illustrates the impact of time on the elasticity of resource demand. Because it is generally difficult to substitute quickly away from a more expensive resource, demand is relatively inelastic in the short run. Thus, an increase in price from P_1 to P_2 will lead to only a small reduction in quantity of the resource used (from Q_1 to Q_2). Given more time, however, producers will be able to make a larger substitution away from the

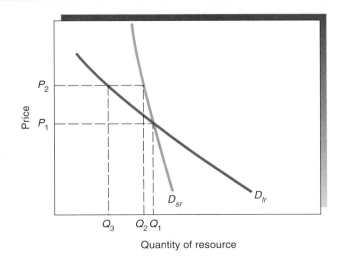

EXHIBIT 3
Time and the Demand Elasticity of Resources

The demand for a resource will be more elastic (1) the easier it is for firms to switch to substitute inputs and (2) the more elastic the consumer demand for the products the resource helps to produce. As we illustrate here, demand for a resource in the long run (D_{lr}) is nearly always more elastic than demand in the short run (D_{sr}).

more expensive resource. Therefore, the P_2 price increase elicits a larger reduction in quantity demanded (to Q_3) with the passage of time. In the long run, the demand for a resource is nearly always more elastic than in the short run.

Shifts in the Demand for Resources

Like the demand schedule for a product, the entire demand curve for a resource may shift. There are three reasons why this may occur.

1. *A change in the demand for a product will cause a similar change in the demand for the resources used to make the product.* Anything that increases the demand for a consumer good simultaneously increases the demand for resources required to make it. Conversely, a decline in product demand will reduce the demand for resources embodied in the product.

   Changes in the music recording industry provide a good example of the linkage between product and resource demand. During the late 1980s and early 1990s, the demand for compact discs increased sharply, driven by the rapidly falling prices of compact disc players. This increase in demand for compact discs led to an increase in demand for workers to produce them. Employment at plants producing the laser optic encoding devices and the types of plastics and metals used to produce the discs expanded rapidly. Similarly, the higher consumer demand for compact discs meant falling demand for vinyl records and tapes. Workers were being laid off at plants producing raw vinyl and related items, such as diamond record player needles. Reflecting the changing demand in product markets, employment in industries related to compact discs expanded, while employment in industries related to records and tapes fell. This reallocation of resources is a natural and integral part of how markets respond to changing consumer demands.

2. *Changes in the productivity of a resource will alter demand—the higher the productivity of a resource, the greater will be the demand for it.* As the productivity of a resource increases so does its value to potential employers. Improvements in the quality or skill level of a resource will increase productivity and therefore the demand for the resource. As workers obtain valuable new knowledge and/or upgrade their skills through investments in human capital, they enhance their productivity. In essence, such workers move into a different skill category, one where demand is greater.

   The productivity of a resource will also depend on the amount of other resources with which it is working. In general, additional capital will tend to increase the productivity of labor. For example, someone with a dump truck can haul more material than the same person with a wheelbarrow. The quantity and quality of the tools with which we work significantly affect our productivity.

   This helps to explain why technological advances, like automation or computer technology, do not have a large negative impact on labor employment. While the substitution that occurs in the production process toward the new capital equipment and away from labor lowers the demand for labor, the technology itself makes labor more productive, which tends to increase the demand for labor. This second effect will partially, and sometimes more than completely, offset the first effect. Improvements in the word-processing equipment have enhanced the productivity of secretaries, journalists, lawyers, and writers. Similarly, computers have substantially increased the productivity of typesetters, telephone operators, scientific researchers, and workers in many other occupations.

   These factors help explain why wage rates in the United States, Canada, Western Europe, and Japan are higher than in most other areas of the world. Given the skill level of workers, the technology, and the capital equipment with which they work, individuals in these countries produce more goods and services per hour of labor than workers in most other countries. In turn, the demand for their labor (relative to supply) is greater because of their high productivity. Essentially, the workers' greater productivity leads to their higher wage rates.

3. *A change in the price of a related resource will affect the demand for the original resource.* A rise in the price of a resource will cause the demand for substitute resources to expand. For example, when the price of lumber increases, the demand for bricks will increase as home builders switch to building more brick homes and fewer wood homes. Conversely, an increase in the price of a resource that is a *complement* to a given resource will decrease the demand for the given resource. Higher prices for lumber would most likely cause the demand for nails, which are used to hold wood in place, to fall.

MARGINAL PRODUCTIVITY AND THE FIRM'S HIRING DECISION

How does a producer decide whether to employ additional units of a resource? Like other decisions, the marginal benefit relative to the marginal cost is the determining factor. Because firms are mostly price takers in resource markets (meaning they can hire as many units of the resource as they wish without affecting the market price of the resource), the marginal cost of hiring one more worker is simply the relevant wage cost, while the marginal cost of purchasing a machine is its price. These represent the increase in the firm's costs that results from employing one more unit of the resource. But what about the marginal benefit of the resource to the firm? It is measured by the increase in the firm's revenue that results from employing one more unit of the resource, the resource's **marginal revenue product *(MRP)*.** A profit-maximizing firm will hire an additional unit of the resource only if the marginal revenue product exceeds the cost of employing the resource.

> **Marginal revenue product *(MRP)***
> The change in the total revenue of a firm that results from the employment of one additional unit of a resource. The marginal revenue product of an input is equal to its marginal product multiplied by the marginal revenue of the good or service produced.

Suppose a retail store was considering hiring a security guard at a wage rate of $25 per hour to help reduce shoplifting. If the security guard could prevent $20 worth of shoplifting per hour, should the profit-maximizing firm hire the guard? Because the marginal cost of employing the security guard (the wage of $25) is higher than the guard's marginal revenue product (the $20 reduction in shoplifting per hour), the wise decision is for the firm not to hire the security guard. Hiring the guard would result in a reduction in the firm's profit of $5 per hour. The guard would be employed only if the reduction in shoplifting would exceed the wage cost. In most situations, the direct impact of hiring an additional resource on a firm's revenue is not as clear, so let's take a closer look at the firm's decision and how marginal revenue product is determined.

Employment of a Variable Resource with a Fixed Resource

When an additional unit of the resource is employed relative to a fixed amount of other resources, the direct result is that the firm's output will increase by an amount equal to the resource's **marginal product *(MP)*.** Because this is measured in units of physical output, it is sometimes referred to as marginal physical product. How much additional revenue can the firm derive from the employment of the resource? Recall that **marginal revenue *(MR)*** is the increase in the firm's revenue that results from the sale of each additional unit of output. Thus, a resource's marginal revenue product is equal to the marginal product of the resource multiplied by the marginal revenue of the good or service produced. *Because of the law of diminishing returns, the marginal product of a resource will fall as employment of the resource expands, and thus the marginal revenue product of a resource will also fall as employment expands.*

> **Marginal product *(MP)***
> The change in total output that results from the employment of one additional unit of a resource, one workday of skilled labor for example.

> **Marginal revenue *(MR)***
> The change in a firm's total revenue that results from the production and sale of one additional unit of output.

The relationship between the marginal revenue a firm derives from selling an additional unit of output and the price for which it is sold is different for *price taker* firms than for *price searcher* firms, however. Because a price taker firm sells all units produced at the same price, the price taker's marginal revenue will be equal to the market price of the product. The price searcher, however, must reduce price (for all units) in order to expand the number of units sold. Thus, the price searcher's marginal revenue will be less than the

EXHIBIT 4
Short-Run Demand Schedule of a Firm

Compute-Accounting, Inc., uses computer technology and data-entry operators to provide accounting services in a competitive market. For each accounting statement processed, the firm receives a $200 fee (column 4). Given the firm's current fixed capital, column 2 shows how total output changes as additional data-entry operators are hired. The marginal revenue product (MRP) schedule (column 6) indicates how hiring an additional operator affects the total revenue of the firm. Since a profit-maximizing firm will hire an additional employee if, and only if, the employee adds more to revenues than to costs, the marginal revenue product curve is the firm's short-run demand curve for the resource (see Exhibit 5).

UNITS OF VARIABLE FACTOR (DATA-ENTRY OPERATORS) (1)	TOTAL OUTPUT (ACCOUNTING STATEMENTS PROCESSED PER WEEK) (2)	MARGINAL PRODUCT (CHANGE IN COLUMN 2 DIVIDED BY CHANGE IN COLUMN 1) (3)	SALES PRICE PER STATEMENT (4)	TOTAL REVENUE (2) × (4) (5)	MRP (3) × (4) (6)
0	0.0	—	$200	$ 0	—
1	5.0	5.0	200	1,000	1,000
2	9.0	4.0	200	1,800	800
3	12.0	3.0	200	2,400	600
4	14.0	2.0	200	2,800	400
5	15.5	1.5	200	3,100	300
6	16.5	1.0	200	3,300	200
7	17.0	0.5	200	3,400	100

Value of marginal product (VMP)
The marginal product of a resource multiplied by the selling price of the product it helps to produce. For a price taker firm, marginal revenue product (MRP) will be equal to the value marginal product (VMP).

sales price of the units. The marginal product of a resource multiplied by the selling price of the product is called the resource's **value marginal product (VMP)**. *For a price taker firm, the* **MRP** *of a resource is equal to its* **VMP** *because price and marginal revenue are equal. For a price searcher firm, however, the* **MRP** *of a resource will be lower than its* **VMP** *because marginal revenue is less than price.*

Using these measures, **Exhibit 4** illustrates how a firm decides how much of a resource to employ. Compute-Accounting, Inc., uses computer equipment and data entry operators to supply clients with monthly accounting statements. The firm is a price taker: It sells its service in a competitive market for $200 per statement. Given the fixed quantity of computer equipment owned by Compute-Accounting, column 2 relates the employment of data entry operators to the expected total output (quantity of accounting statements). One data entry operator can process five statements per week. When two operators are employed, nine statements can be completed. Column 2 indicates how total output is expected to change as additional data entry operators are employed. Column 3 presents the marginal product schedule for data entry operators. Column 6, the *MRP* schedule, shows how the employment of each additional operator affects total revenue. Both fall as additional operators are employed due to the law of diminishing returns.

Because Compute-Accounting is a price taker, the marginal revenue product and the value marginal product of labor are equal. Thus, the marginal revenue product of labor (column 6) can be calculated by multiplying the marginal product (column 3) times the sales price of an accounting statement (column 4).

How does Compute-Accounting decide how many operators to employ? Answer: it analyzes benefits relative to costs. As additional operators are employed, the output of processed statements (column 2) will increase, which will expand total revenue (column 5). Employment of additional operators, though, will also add to production costs because the operators must be paid. Applying the profit-maximization rule, Compute-Accounting will hire additional operators as long as their employment adds more to revenues than to costs. This will be the case as long as the *MRP* (column 6) of the data-entry operators exceeds their wage rate. At a weekly wage of $1,000, Compute-Accounting would hire only one operator. If the weekly wage dropped to $800, two operators would be hired. At still lower wage rates, additional operators would be hired.

Profit-maximizing firms will expand their employment of each variable resource until the **MRP** *of the resource (the firm's additional revenue generated by the resource) is just equal to the price of the resource (the firm's marginal cost of employing the resource). This profit-maximization rule applies to all firms, price takers and price searchers alike.*

MRP and the Firm's Demand Curve for a Resource

Using the data in Exhibit 4, one can construct Compute-Accounting's demand curve for data entry operators. Recall that the height of a demand curve shows the maximum price (here the wage) the buyer (here the firm) would be willing to pay for the unit. Because the marginal revenue product of the first data entry operator is $1,000, the firm would be willing to hire this worker only up to a maximum price of $1,000. Because of this relationship, as **Exhibit 5** illustrates, a firm's short-run demand curve for a resource is precisely the *MRP* curve for the resource.[3] Using this demand curve yields the identical solutions as the table. At a weekly wage of $1,000, Compute-Accounting would hire only one operator. If the weekly wage dropped to $800, two operators would be hired. At still lower wage rates, additional operators would be hired. Underlying the downward-sloping demand curve is the law of diminishing returns causing *MP*, and thus *MRP*, to fall as employment of the resource expands.

The location of the firm's *MRP* curve depends on (1) the price of the product, (2) the productivity of the resource, and (3) the amount of other resources with which the resource is working. Changes in any one of these three factors will cause the *MRP* curve to shift. For example, if Compute-Accounting obtained additional computer equipment that made it possible for the operators to complete more statements each week, the *MRP* curve for labor would increase (shift outward). This increase in the quantity of the other resources working with labor would increase labor's productivity.

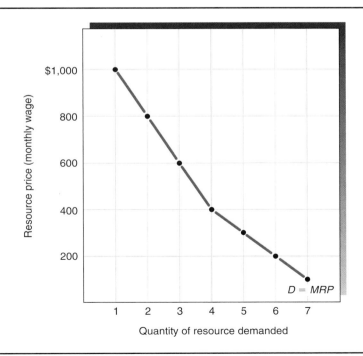

EXHIBIT 5
The Firm's Demand Curve for a Resource

The firm's demand curve for a resource will reflect the marginal revenue product *(MRP)* of the resource. In the short run, it will slope downward because the marginal product of the resource will fall as more of it is used with a fixed amount of other resources. The location of the *MRP* curve will depend on (1) the price of the product, (2) the productivity of the resource, and (3) the quantity of other factors working with the resource.

---

[3]Strictly speaking, this is true only for a variable resource that is employed with a fixed amount of another factor.

Employment Levels When There Are Numerous Factors of Production

Thus far, we have analyzed the firm's hiring decision assuming that it employed one variable resource (labor) and one fixed resource. Production, though, usually involves the use of many resources. How should these resources be combined to produce the product? We can answer this question by considering either the conditions for profit maximization or the conditions for cost minimization.

Profit Maximization When Multiple Resources Are Employed

The same decision-making considerations apply when the firm employs several factors of production. The profit-maximizing firm will expand its employment of a resource as long as the *MRP* of the resource exceeds its employment cost. If we assume that resources are perfectly divisible, the profit-maximizing decision rule implies that, in equilibrium, the *MRP* of each resource will be equal to the price of the resource. Therefore, the following conditions will exist for the profit-maximizing firm:

> *MRP* of skilled labor = Price (wage rate) of skilled labor
>
> *MRP* of unskilled labor = Price (wage rate) of unskilled labor
>
> *MRP* of machine A = Price (explicit or implicit rental price) of machine A and so on, for all other factors.

Cost Minimization When Multiple Resources Are Employed

If the firm is maximizing profits, clearly it must produce the profit-maximizing output at the least possible cost. If the firm is minimizing costs, the marginal dollar expenditure for each resource will have the same impact on output as every other marginal resource expenditure. *Factors of production will be employed such that the marginal product per last dollar spent on each factor is the same for all factors.*

To see why, consider a situation in which a $100 expenditure on labor caused output to rise by ten units, whereas an additional $100 expenditure on machines generated only a five-unit expansion in output. Under these circumstances, five more units of output (at no added cost) would result if the firm spent $100 less on machines and $100 more on labor. The firm's *per-unit* cost would be reduced if it substituted labor for machines.

If the marginal dollar spent on one resource increases output by a larger amount than a dollar expenditure on other resources, costs can always be reduced by substituting resources with a high marginal product per dollar expenditure for those with a low one. Substitution will continue to reduce unit costs (and add to profit) until the marginal product per dollar expenditure on each resource is equalized. This will occur because as additional units of a resource are hired, their marginal product will fall. Thus, the proportional relationship between the price of each resource and its marginal product will eventually be achieved. *Therefore, the following condition exists when per unit costs are minimized:*

$$\frac{\textbf{MP } of\ skilled\ labor}{\textbf{Price } of\ skilled\ labor} = \frac{\textbf{MP } of\ unskilled\ labor}{\textbf{Price } of\ unskilled\ labor} = \frac{\textbf{MP } of\ machine\ A}{\textbf{Price } (rental\ value)\ of\ machine\ A}$$

This relationship, which will be present if a firm is minimizing its per-unit cost of production, indicates why wage differences across skill categories will tend to reflect productivity differences. If skilled workers are twice as productive as unskilled workers, their wage rates will tend toward twice the wage rates of unskilled workers. For example, suppose that a construction firm hiring workers to hang doors is choosing among skilled and unskilled workers. If skilled door hangers can complete four doors per hour, while unskilled workers can hang only two doors per hour, a cost-minimizing firm would hire only skilled workers—as long as their wages are less than twice the wages of unskilled workers. On the other hand, only unskilled workers would be hired if the wages of skilled workers are more than twice that of unskilled workers. With competition, wages across skill categories will tend to mirror productivity differences.

Workers in occupations like nursing that require substantial skill and education will generally earn higher wages than those in occupations requiring little training or experience.

Low wages do not necessarily mean low cost; it is not always cheaper to hire the lowest wage workers. It is not just wages, but rather wages *relative to productivity* that matter. If the wages of skilled workers are twice those of unskilled workers, it will still be cheaper to hire additional skilled workers if their marginal productivity (output per hour) is more than twice that of the unskilled workers.

The importance of wages relative to productivity explains why relatively few firms moved to Mexico following the passage of the North American Free Trade Agreement (NAFTA). Remember the forecast by some of a "giant sucking sound" indicating the movement of both firms and jobs to Mexico? Why didn't the low wages of Mexico cause firms to relocate? *Answer:* While wages are low in Mexico, so, too, is productivity. Given this factor, many firms are able to achieve lower production costs in the high-wage United States than in low-wage Mexico. Suppose that the average wage rate of a U.S. worker is $12 per hour and average hourly productivity is 36 units, while the average wage is $4 per hour in Mexico and average productivity is 8 units. To maximize profits (or minimize costs) a firm should locate wherever *MP/P* is greatest. In the United States the firm would get 3 units of output (36/12) per dollar spent on labor. In Mexico, the firm would get only 2 units of output (8/4) per dollar spent on labor. Thus, a cost-minimizing firm would want to locate in the United States despite the higher wages, because the productivity difference more than makes up for the wage difference. Although U.S. wages are 3 times higher, U.S. productivity is 4.5 times higher. The higher productivity more than compensates for the higher wage cost.

The Central Proposition of the Marginal Productivity Theory of Employment

The central proposition of the marginal productivity theory of resource employment is that firms minimize their per-unit costs of production when they hire additional units of each resource as long as the units' marginal productivity generates revenues in excess of costs. Firms that minimize per-unit costs and maximize profit will never pay more for a unit of input, whether it is skilled labor, a machine, or an acre of land, than the input is worth to them. The worth of a unit of input to the firm is determined by how much additional revenue (marginal revenue product) is expected from its employment.

In the real world, it is sometimes difficult to measure the marginal product of a factor. And, as we have indicated, the marginal product of a resource is influenced by the other factors with which it is employed. Production is a team effort involving interdependent use of resources. We do not mean to imply that business decision makers will necessarily think in terms of equating the marginal product/price ratio *(MP/P)* for each factor of production. Their thought process may well be something like this: "Can we reduce costs by using more of one resource and less of another?" Real-world business decision makers may use experience, trial and error, and intuitive rules as they seek to minimize costs.

Regardless of the methods and procedures used, however, when a firm maximizes profits and minimizes costs, the marginal product/price ratio will be equal for all factors of production. The results will be *as if* the firms had followed the cost-minimization decision-making rules presented earlier. Furthermore, competitive forces will more or less force firms to approximate these minimum cost conditions. Firms that fail to do so will be unable to compete successfully with rivals achieving lower per-unit costs.

The marginal-productivity theory explains the conditions underlying the demand for resources. Of course, resource prices will also be influenced by the supply of resources. We now turn to that topic.

SUPPLY OF RESOURCES

In essence, our analysis of resource demand concludes that employers will hire a resource so long as they can gain by doing so. The same basic postulate also applies to resource suppliers. Resource owners will supply their services to an employer only if they perceive that the benefits of doing so exceed their costs (the value of the other things they could do with their time or resources). Thus, in order to attract factors of production, employers must offer resource owners at least as good a deal as they can get elsewhere. For example, if an employer does not offer a potential employee a package of income payments and working conditions that is as good as or better than the worker can get elsewhere, the employer will be unable to attract that worker.

Resource owners will supply their services to those who offer them the best employment alternative, all factors considered. Other things constant, as the price of a specific resource (for example, engineering services, craft labor, or wheat farmland) increases, the incentive of potential suppliers to provide the resource increases.

An increase in the price of a resource will attract potential resource suppliers into the market. A decrease will cause them to shift into other activities. Therefore, as **Exhibit 6** illustrates, the supply curve for a specific resource will slope upward to the right.[4]

EXHIBIT 6
The Supply of a Resource

As the price of a resource increases, individuals have a greater incentive to supply it. Therefore, a direct relationship will exist between the price of a resource and the quantity supplied.

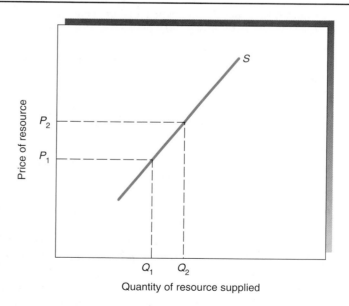

Quantity of resource supplied

[4]Although the supply for nonhuman resources will always slope upward, the supply of labor at very high wage rates can become backward bending. As wages rise, individuals will substitute toward more work, but simultaneously the higher income will cause them to desire more leisure. At very high wage rates the income effect might dominate, causing a negative relationship between wage rates and quantity of labor supplied in this range. For example, at a wage of $10,000 per hour, many individuals would probably supply fewer hours of work than at $500 per hour!

Short-Run Versus Long-Run Resource Supply

As in the case of demand, the supply response in resource markets may vary between the short run and long run. If the wage rate for CPAs rose, for example, we would expect more workers supplying their services as CPAs. But where do these additional CPAs come from? In the short run, the additional supply must come from individuals who possess the necessary skills, but are currently doing other things. The higher wages might induce some college accounting professors and some stay-at-home spouses with accounting credentials to move into employment as CPAs. In the short run, there is insufficient time to alter the availability of a resource through investment in human and physical capital. In contrast, in the long run, resource suppliers have time to adjust their investment choices in response to a change in resource prices. With time, the higher wages for CPAs would cause more students to major in accounting, and others to pursue the necessary additional courses to become CPAs. Higher resource prices will increase the quantity supplied in both the short run and the long run, but the response will be greater in the long run. Therefore, as **Exhibit 7** illustrates, the long-run supply of resources will be more elastic than the short-run supply.

Short-Run Supply

The short-run supply response to a change in price is determined by how easily the resource can be transferred from one use to another—that is, **resource mobility**. The supply of resources with high resource mobility will be relatively elastic even in the short run. Resources that have few alternative uses (or are not easily transferable) are said to be immobile. The short-run supply of immobile resources will be highly inelastic.

Consider the mobility of labor. Within a skill category (for example, plumber, store manager, accountant, or secretary), labor will be highly mobile within the same geographic area. Movements between geographic areas and from one skill category to another are more costly to accomplish. Labor will thus be less mobile for movements of this variety. In addition, because it is easier for a high-skilled person to perform effectively in a lower-skill position than vice versa, short-run mobility will tend to decline as the skill level of the occupation rises. Thus, the short-run supply curve in high-skill occupations like architect, mechanical engineer, and medical surgeon is usually quite inelastic.

Resource mobility
The ease with which factors of production are able to move among alternative uses. Resources that can easily be transferred to a different use or location are said to be highly mobile. Resources with few alternative uses are immobile.

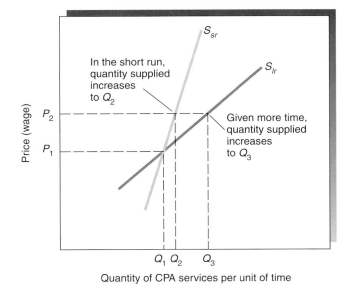

EXHIBIT 7
Time and the Elasticity of Supply for Resources

The supply of certified public accountant (CPA) services and other resources that require a substantial period of time between current investment and expansion in the future quantity supplied will be more elastic in the long run than in the short run.

In the short run, quantity supplied increases to Q_2

Given more time, quantity supplied increases to Q_3

Price (wage)

Quantity of CPA services per unit of time

What about the mobility of land? Land is highly mobile among uses when location does not matter. For example, the same land can often be used to raise corn, wheat, soybeans, or oats. Thus, the supply of land allocated to production of each of these commodities will be highly responsive to changes in their relative prices. Undeveloped land on the outskirts of cities is particularly mobile among uses. In addition to its value in agriculture, such land might be quickly subdivided and used for a housing development or a shopping center. Because land is totally immobile physically, one might think that its supply is unresponsive to changes in price that reflect the desirability of a location. However, the supply of usable space at a specific location can be expanded through the construction of multiple-story buildings. As the demand for a given location increases, higher and higher multilevel construction will be justified. This is why tall buildings are generally located in city centers and major satellite areas, the locations with the strongest demand for space.

Machines are typically not very mobile among uses. A machine developed to produce airplane wings is seldom of much use in the production of automobiles, appliances, or other products. Steel mills cannot easily be converted to produce aluminum. There are, of course, some exceptions. Trucks can typically be used to haul a variety of products. Building space can often be converted from one use to another. In the short run, however, immobility and inelasticity of supply characterize much of our physical capital.

Long-Run Supply

In the long run, the supply of resources can change substantially. Machines wear out, human skills depreciate, and even the fertility of land declines with use and erosion. These factors reduce the supply of resources. On the other hand, investment can expand the supply of productive resources. Additional resources can be used to expand the stock of machines, buildings, and durable assets. Correspondingly, investments in training and education can develop and improve the skills of future labor force participants. Thus, the supply of both physical and human resources in the long run is determined primarily by investment and depreciation.

As the price of a resource increases, more and more people will make the investments necessary to supply the resource. This will be true for human as well as physical resources. Examples abound. As the spread of the computer revolution pushed the salaries of programmers, systems analysts, and computer technicians upward during the early

The supply curve for truck drivers will be considerably more elastic than the supply of doctors. Can you explain why?

1990s, there was a sharp increase in the number of students training for jobs in these areas. In the late 1990s, attractive salaries for physical therapists led to both new programs and expanded enrollments. Higher salaries for lawyers stimulate law school enrollments. According to Harvard University economist Richard Freeman, a 1 percent increase in starting law salaries causes enrollment in the first year of law school to rise by 2 percent.

The long run, of course, is not a specified length of time. Investment can increase the availability of some resources fairly quickly. For example, it does not take very long to train additional over-the-road truck drivers. However, it takes a long time to train physicians, dentists, lawyers, and pharmacists. Higher earnings in these occupations may have only a small impact on their current availability. Additional investment will go into these areas, but it will typically be several years before there is a substantial increase in the quantity supplied in response to higher earnings for these resources.

SUPPLY, DEMAND, AND RESOURCE PRICES

In a market economy, resource prices will be determined by the forces of supply and demand. When factor prices are free to vary, resource prices will bring the choices of buyers and sellers into line with each other. **Exhibit 8** illustrates how the forces of supply and demand push the market wage rates of engineers toward equilibrium, where quantity demanded and quantity supplied are equal. Equilibrium is achieved when the price (wage rate) for engineering services is P_1. Given the market conditions illustrated by Exhibit 8, an excess supply is present if the price of engineering services exceeds P_1. Some engineers will be unable to find jobs at the above-equilibrium wage. This excess supply of engineers will cause the wage rate for engineers to fall, thereby pushing the market toward equilibrium. In contrast, if the resource price is less than P_1, excess demand is present. Employers are unable to obtain the desired amount of engineering services at a below-equilibrium resource price. Rather than doing without the resource, employers will attempt to hire engineers away from other firms by bidding the price up to P_1 and thereby eliminating the excess demand.

How will a resource market adjust to an unexpected change in market conditions? Suppose that there is a sharp increase in the demand for houses, apartments, and office buildings. The increase in demand for these products will also increase the demand for resources required for their construction. Thus, the demand for such resources as steel, lumber, brick, and the labor services of carpenters, architects, and construction engineers will increase. **Exhibit 9** provides a graphic illustration of both the increase in demand for new

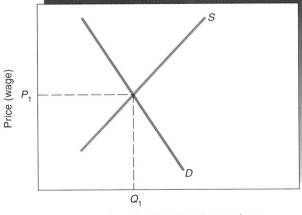

Quantity of engineering services

EXHIBIT 8
Equilibrium in a Resource Market

The market demand for a resource, such as engineering services, is a downward-sloping curve, reflecting the declining *MRP* of the resource. The market supply curve slopes upward because higher resource prices (wage rates) will induce individuals to supply more of the resource. Market price will move toward equilibrium (P_1), where the quantity demanded and quantity supplied are in balance.

EXHIBIT 9
Adjusting to Dynamic Change

An increase in the demand for housing and commercial buildings (frame a) will lead to an increase in demand for the services of construction engineers (frame b) and other resources used in the construction industry. Initially, the increase in the resource price will be substantial (move from a to b), particularly if the supply of the resource is highly inelastic in the short run. The higher resource price will attract additional human capital investment and, with time, the resource supply curve will become more elastic, which will moderate the price (or wage) increase of the resource (move from b to c).

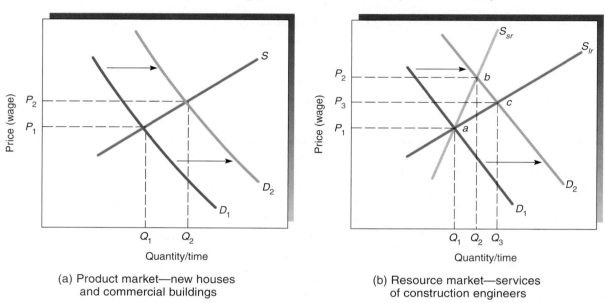

(a) Product market—new houses and commercial buildings

(b) Resource market—services of construction engineers

houses and buildings (frame a) and the accompanying increase in demand for construction engineers. The market demand for the services of construction engineers increases from D_1 to D_2 (frame b) and initially there is a sharp rise in their wages (price increases from P_1 to P_2). The higher wages will induce additional people to undertake the education and training necessary to become a construction engineer. With the passage of time, the entry of the newly trained construction engineers will increase the elasticity of the resource supply curve. As these new construction engineers eventually enter the occupation, the supply curve will become more elastic (S_{lr} rather than S_{sr}), which will place downward pressure on wages in the occupation (the move from b to c). Therefore, as part b of Exhibit 9 illustrates, the long-run price increase (to P_3) will be less than the short-run increase (to P_2).

The supply response and market adjustment for other resources—physical as well as human—will be similar. For example, an unexpected construction boom will generally cause sharp initial increases in the prices of lumber, bricks, and other building materials. With time, however, additional investment will increase the availability of these resources and moderate the increase in their price, just as additional investment in human capital eventually moderated the wage increases of the construction engineers.

The market adjustment to an unexpected reduction in demand for a resource is the same. The price falls farther in the short run than in the long run. At the lower price, some resource suppliers will use their talents in other areas, and the incentive for potential new suppliers to offer the resource will be reduced. Thus, with time, the quantity of the resource supplied will decline, moderating the reduction in price. Those with the poorest alternatives (that is, lowest opportunity cost) will continue to provide the resource at the lower prices. Those with better alternatives will move to other areas.

Pulling things together, our analysis indicates that prices in resource markets play a vitally important role. These prices coordinate the actions of the firms demanding fac-

***tors of production and the households supplying them. Resource prices provide users
with both information on scarcity and the incentive to economize on resource use when
producing output. They also provide suppliers with an incentive to learn skills and provide resources—particularly those that are intensely demanded by users.*** Without the
use of resource markets and the price incentives they provide, efficient use and wise conservation of resources would be extremely difficult to achieve.[5]

The Coordinating Function of Resource Prices

Throughout this text we have stressed that profit is a reward earned by producers who increase the value of resources, while loss is a punishment imposed on producers who reduce the value of resources to society. The key links in this process are the prices of the
products being sold and the prices of the resources used in production. A firm's profits are
its revenues (which are determined by the product price) minus its costs (which are determined by the prices of the resources it uses). The price of the product measures the value
that consumers place on that product. The price of the resources, however, measures the
value that consumers place on *other products* that could be produced with those same resources. Let us explore the importance of this linkage in a little more detail.

As we have shown, the price of a resource will equal the resource's marginal revenue
product when the resource market is in equilibrium. The resource's marginal revenue
product depends upon the price consumers are willing to pay for (and thus their value of)
the output produced by the resource. When a firm wishes to hire a resource, it must offer
that resource a payment at least as attractive as the resource could have earned elsewhere—that is, the resource's MRP in its next best alternative employment. Thus, the
price a firm pays for a resource is equal to the resource's value (as measured by consumer
valuation) in the alternative use. If the output the firm produces with that resource can be
sold at a higher price than the price of the alternative outputs, then and only then will the
firm earn a profit. Thus, profit is a reward to those entrepreneurs who are able to see and
act on opportunities to put resources to higher-valued uses. Because consumer tastes and
preferences continuously change, so do product and resource prices, and thus these opportunities are created and destroyed on a daily basis in a dynamic market economy.

The ability of resource prices to adjust is essential for a properly functioning market
system. They determine the reallocations of resources between industries that allow an
economy to satisfy the changing preferences of consumers. The way in which market
prices provide an incentive for resources to flow continuously to their highest-valued social uses is indeed the essence of Adam Smith's *invisible hand principle*.

In this chapter we presented the theoretical underpinnings of factor markets. This analysis
can be applied to a broad range of economic issues. The next chapter will focus on the labor market and earnings differences among workers. Later, we will focus on the capital market and the allocation of resources over time. The operation of these two markets plays an
important role in determining the distribution of income, a topic that will also be analyzed in
detail in a subsequent chapter.

**LOOKING
AHEAD**

---

[5]Analysis of energy consumption under central planning illustrates this point. The centrally planned economies both used more
energy per unit of output and their energy consumption was less responsive to changes in price than was true for economies that
used markets to allocate energy. For evidence on these points, see Mikhail S. Bernstam, *The Wealth of Nations and the Environment* (London: Institute of Economic Affairs, 1991).

KEY POINTS

▼ Productive assets and services are bought and sold in resource markets. These markets help to determine what is produced, how it is produced, and the distribution of income. There are two broad classes of productive resources: (1) nonhuman capital and (2) human capital.

▼ The demand for resources is derived from the demand for products that the resources help to produce. The quantity of a resource demanded is inversely related to its price because of substitutions made by both producers and consumers.

▼ The demand curve for a resource, like the demand for a product, may shift. The major factors that can increase the demand for a resource are (a) an increase in demand for products that use the resource, (b) an increase in the productivity of the resource, and (c) an increase in the price of substitute resources.

▼ Profit-maximizing firms will hire additional units of a resource up to the point where the marginal revenue product *(MRP)* of the resource equals its price. With multiple inputs, firms will expand their usage of each until marginal product divided by price

(MP/P) is equal across all inputs. When real-world decision makers minimize per-unit costs, the outcome will be as if they had followed these mathematical procedures, even though they may not consciously do so.

▼ The amount of a resource supplied will be directly related to its price. The supply of a resource will be more elastic in the long run than in the short run. In the long run, investment can increase the supply of both physical and human resources.

▼ The prices of resources are determined by supply and demand. Changes in the market prices of resources will influence the decisions of both users and suppliers. Higher resource prices give users a greater incentive to turn to substitutes and suppliers a greater incentive to provide more of the resource.

▼ Changes in resource prices in response to changing market conditions are essential for the efficient allocation of resources in a dynamic world. Profit is a reward to the entrepreneur who is able to see and act on opportunities to put resources to higher-valued uses.

CRITICAL ANALYSIS QUESTIONS

1. "The demand for resources is a derived demand." What is meant by that statement? Why is the employment of a resource inversely related to its price?

2. How does a firm decide whether or not to employ an additional unit of a resource? What determines the combination of skilled and unskilled workers that will be employed by a firm?

*3. Use the information in Exhibit 4 of this chapter to answer the following:
   a. How many employees (operators) would Compute-Accounting hire at a weekly wage of $250 if it were attempting to maximize profits?
   b. What would the firm's maximum profit be if its fixed costs were $1,500 per week?
   c. Suppose there was a decline in demand for accounting services, reducing the market price per monthly statement to $150. At this demand level, how many employees would Compute-Accounting hire at $250 per week in the short run? Would Compute-Accounting be able to stay in business at the lower market price? Explain.

*4. Are productivity gains the major source of higher wages? If so, how does one account for the rising real wages of barbers, who by and large have used the same technique for a half-century? (*Hint:* Do not forget opportunity cost and supply.)

5. Are the following statements both correct? Are they inconsistent with each other? Explain.
   a. "Firms will hire a resource only if they can make money by doing so."
   b. "In a market economy, each resource will tend to be paid according to its marginal product. Highly productive resources will command high prices, whereas less productive resources will command lower prices."

6. Many school districts pay teachers on the basis of their highest degree earned and number of years of service (seniority). They often find it quite easy to fill the slots for English teachers, but very difficult to find the required number of math and science teachers. Can you explain why?

7. Suppose that you were the manager of a large retail store that was currently experiencing a shoplifting problem. Every hour, approximately $15 worth of merchandise was being stolen from your store. Suppose that a security guard would completely eliminate the shoplifting in your store. If you were interested in maximizing your profits, should you hire a security guard if the wage rate of security guards was $20 per hour? Why or why not? What does this imply about the relationship between average shoplifting per hour in the economy and the wage rates of security guards?

*8. A dressmaker uses labor and capital (sewing machines) to produce dresses in a competitive market. Suppose the last unit of labor hired cost $1,000 per month and increased output by 100 dresses. The last unit of capital hired (rented) cost $500 per month and increased output by 80 dresses. Is the dressmaker minimizing cost? If not, what changes need to be made?

9. A firm is considering moving from the United States to Mexico. The firm pays its U.S. workers $12 per hour. Current U.S. workers have a marginal product of 40, while the Mexican workers have a marginal product of 10. How low would the Mexican wage have to be for the firm to reduce its wage cost per unit of output by moving to Mexico?

*10. "The earnings of engineers, doctors, and lawyers are high because lots of education is necessary to practice in these fields." Evaluate this statement.

11. Other things constant, what impact will a highly elastic demand for a product have on the elasticity of demand for the resources used to produce the product? Explain.

*12. The following chart provides information on a firm that hires labor competitively and sells its product in a competitive market:

Units Of Labor	Total Output	Marginal Product	Product Price	Total Revenue	MRP
1	14	___	$5	___	___
2	26	___	$5	___	___
3	37	___	$5	___	___
4	46	___	$5	___	___
5	53	___	$5	___	___
6	58	___	$5	___	___
7	62	___	$5	___	___

a. Fill in the missing columns.
b. How many units of labor would be employed if the market wage rate were $40? Why?
c. What would happen to employment if the wage rate rose to $50? Explain.

13. Leisure Times, Inc., employs skilled workers and capital to install hot tubs. The capital includes the tools and equipment that the workers use to construct and install the tubs. The installation services are sold in a competitive market for $1,200 per hot tub. Leisure Times is able to hire workers for $2,200 per month, including the cost of wages, fringe benefits, and employment taxes. As additional workers are hired, the increase in the number of hot tubs installed is indicated in the table.

Number of Workers Employed	Number of Hot Tubs Installed (per month)
1	5
2	12
3	18
4	23
5	27
6	30
7	32
8	33
9	34

a. Indicate the marginal product and *MRP* schedules of the workers.
b. What quantity of workers should Leisure Times employ if it is maximizing profit?
c. If a construction boom pushes the wages of skilled workers up to $2,500 per month, how many workers would Leisure Times employ if it is maximizing profit?
d. Suppose that strong demand for hot tubs pushes the price of installation services up to $1,500 per month. How would this affect employment of the skilled workers if the wage rate of the workers remained at $2,500 per month?

14. A recent flyer on a university campus stated that consumers should boycott sugar due to the low wages earned by laborers on sugar cane farms in Florida. Using the notion of derived demand, what impact would a boycott on sugar have on the wages of the farm laborers in the short run? In the long run?

---

*Asterisk denotes questions for which answers are given in Appendix B.

CHAPTER 25

Earnings, Productivity, and the Job Market

Chapter Focus

- Why do some people earn more than others?

- Are earnings differences according to race and gender the result of employment discrimination?

- Why are wages higher in the United States than in India or China?

- Why do wages increase? Why has the growth of wages and income per capita increased during the past 5 years?

- Does automation destroy jobs?

[1]The above statement was in response to a question about the amount he was being paid for a popular television show called *The Honeymooners* which ran during the 1950s and 1960s.

The earnings of U.S. workers are among the highest in the world. However, they vary widely. An unskilled laborer may earn $7 per hour, or even less. Lawyers and physicians often earn $100 per hour and more. Dentists and even economists might receive $70 or $80 per hour. How can these variations in earnings be explained? Why are the earnings of Americans so high? How have earnings changed in recent years and what are the factors underlying these changes? This chapter addresses these topics and related issues. ■

WHY DO EARNINGS DIFFER?

The earnings of individuals in the same occupation or with the same amount of education often differ substantially. The earnings of persons with the same family background also vary widely. For example, one researcher found that the average annual earnings differential between brothers was $27,668, compared with $30,642 for men paired randomly.[2] The earnings of persons with the same intelligence quotient, level of training, or amount of experience typically differ.

Several factors combine to determine the earning power of an individual. Some seem to be the result of good or bad fortune. Others are clearly the result of conscious decisions made by individuals. In the previous chapter, we analyzed how the market forces of supply and demand operate to determine resource prices. The subject of earnings differentials can be usefully approached within the framework of the supply and demand model because the wages earned by workers are simply market-determined resource prices.

For simplicity, we have proceeded as if employees earned only money payments. In reality, most workers receive a compensation package that includes **fringe benefits** as well as money wages. The fringe benefit component typically includes items like medical insurance, life insurance, pension benefits, and paid vacation days. When we use the terms wages and earnings in the following discussions, we are referring to the total compensation package that includes both wages and fringe benefits.

The **real earnings** *of all employees in a competitive market economy would be equal if: (1) all individuals were identical in preferences, skills, and background, (2) all jobs were equally attractive, and (3) workers were perfectly mobile among jobs.* If, given these conditions, higher real wages existed in any area of the economy, the supply of workers to that area would expand until the wage differential was eliminated. Similarly, low wages in any area would cause workers to exit until wages in that area returned to normal. However, the conditions necessary for earnings equality do not exist in the real world. Thus, earnings differentials are present. The observed differentials can be explained by the absence of the three conditions that would lead to equality of wages.

Fringe benefits
Benefits other than normal money wages that are supplied to employees in exchange for their labor services. Higher fringe benefits come at the expense of lower money wages.

Real earnings
Earnings adjusted for differences in the general level of prices across time periods or geographic areas. When real earnings are equal, the same bundle of goods and services can be purchased with the earnings.

Earnings Differentials Due to Nonidentical Workers

Workers differ in several important respects that influence both the supply of and demand for their services, and thus create differences in their wage rates.

Worker Productivity and Specialized Skills

The demand for employees who are highly productive is greater than the demand for those who are less productive. Persons who can operate a machine more skillfully, hit a baseball more consistently, or sell life insurance policies with greater regularity will be more valuable to employers. Such employees will contribute more to the firm's revenue—that is, their marginal revenue product *(MRP)* will be higher—than do their

---

[2]Christopher Jencks, *Inequality* (New York: Basic Books, 1972), p. 220. Salary figures are in 2000 dollars.

less-skillful counterparts. In competitive labor markets, workers earn a wage equal to their marginal revenue product. As a result, the labor services of more productive workers will command higher wages in the marketplace.

Worker productivity is the result of a combination of factors, including native ability, parental training, hard work, and investment in human capital. The link between higher productivity and higher earnings provides individuals with the incentive to invest in themselves and thereby upgrade their knowledge and skills. If additional worker productivity did not lead to higher earnings, individuals would have little incentive to incur the direct and indirect costs of productivity-enhancing educational and training programs.

Exhibit 1 illustrates the impact of worker productivity and the cost of investment in human capital on the wages of skilled and unskilled workers. Because the productivity of skilled workers exceeds that of unskilled workers, the demand for skilled workers (D_s) exceeds the demand for unskilled workers (D_u). The vertical distance between the two demand curves reflects the higher marginal product (*MP*) of skilled workers relative to the unskilled workers (part a). Since investments in human capital (for example, education or training) are costly, the supply of skilled workers (S_s) will be smaller than the supply of unskilled workers (S_u). The vertical distance between the two supply curves indicates the wage differential that is necessary to compensate workers for the costs incurred in the acquisition of their skills (part b). Wages are determined by demand relative to supply (part c). Since the demand for skilled workers is large while their supply is small, the equilibrium wage of skilled workers will be high ($20 per hour). In contrast, since the supply of unskilled workers is large relative to the demand, the wages of unskilled workers will be substantially lower ($6 per hour).

Of course, native ability and motivation will influence the rate at which an individual can transform education and training into greater productivity. Individuals differ in the amount of valuable skills they develop from a year of education, vocational school, or on-the-job training. We should not expect, therefore, a rigid relationship to exist between years of education (or training) and skill level. On average, however, there is a strong positive relationship between investment in education and earnings. **Exhibit 2** presents annual earnings data according to educational level for year-round, full-time workers in 2000. The earnings of both men and women increased consistently with additional school-

---

EXHIBIT 1
Demand, Supply, and Wage Rates for Skilled and Unskilled Workers

The productivity—and therefore marginal product (*MP*)—of skilled workers is greater than that of unskilled workers. Therefore, as part a illustrates, the demand for skilled workers (D_s) will exceed the demand for unskilled workers (D_u). Education and training generally enhance skills. Since upgrading skills through investments in human capital is costly, the supply of skilled workers (S_s) is smaller than the supply of unskilled workers at any given wage (part b). As part c illustrates, the wages of skilled workers are high relative to unskilled workers due to the strong demand and small supply of skilled workers relative to unskilled workers. (*Note:* The quantity of skilled labor employed may be far smaller, far larger, or by accident equal to the quantity of unskilled labor hired).

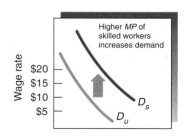
(a) Demand for skilled and unskilled labor

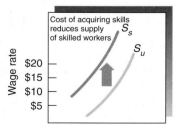
(b) Supply of skilled and unskilled labor

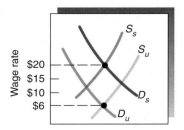
(c) Wages of skilled and unskilled labor

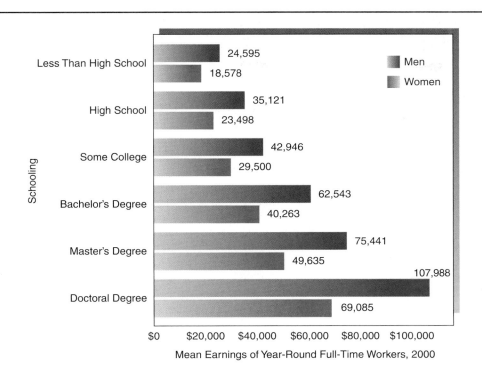

Source: U.S. Department of Commerce, Current Population Reports, P-60 Series. *Money Income in the United States: 2000*, Table 9.

EXHIBIT 2
Education and Earnings

The accompanying graph presents data for mean annual earnings of year-round, full-time workers according to gender and education. Note that the earnings of both men and women increased with additional education. Even though the data are for full-time workers, the earnings of women were only about two-thirds those of men with similar education.

ing. High school graduates earned almost 50 percent more than their counterparts with less than a high school education. Men college graduates working full-time, year-round earned $62,543 compared to $35,121 for men with only a high school education. In the case of women, college graduates earned $40,263 compared to $23,498 for those who only graduated from high school. The earnings of both men and women continued to increase as they earned master's and doctoral degrees.

Some of the additional earnings of those with more education may merely reflect their greater native ability, intelligence, and motivation. (See Applications in Economics box, "A College Degree as a Job Market Signal.") Research, however, indicates that a large proportion of the additional earnings are in fact the result of knowledge and skills acquired from investment in additional education. Economic research has also shown that on-the-job training enhances the earnings of workers.

Investment in human capital and development of specialized skills can protect high-wage workers from the competition of others willing to offer their services at a lower price. Few persons could develop the specialized skills of a Steven Spielberg, Tiger Woods, or Oprah Winfrey. Similarly, the supply of heart surgeons, trial lawyers, engineers, business entrepreneurs, and many other specialized workers is limited in occupations where specific skills, knowledge, and human capital investments contribute to job performance.

The annual earnings of star athletes, entertainers, and television personalities often run into the millions of dollars. What is the marginal revenue product of a superstar entertainer like Julia Roberts? How many more people will go see a movie in which Roberts is the star compared to the number who would attend if the lead actress were less known or less talented? If an additional two million or three million people spend five dollars to attend a movie, this would generate $10 million or $15 million of additional revenue. It is easy to see how a star "box office" attraction would provide the company producing the movie with substantial additional revenues. In turn, competitive labor markets will ensure that big stars get paid their marginal revenue product.

APPLICATIONS IN ECONOMICS

A College Degree as a Job Market Signal: Why You Should Take More Math

"Why should I take *this* difficult course?" "When will I ever use *this*?" Students often complain about taking courses not directly related to their future career. This complaint often reflects an incomplete understanding of exactly why college graduates do better in the job market than those without a college degree. A college degree increases earnings because of both (1) human capital—knowledge that will directly increase job productivity and (2) *signaling*—factors that indicate an individual's attitude and motivational characteristics, as well as his or her general analytical skills.

Suppose an employer is looking for an employee who is a very good analytical problem solver. Without a way to directly observe this ability, the employer may look for indicators that are likely to signal this attribute. For example, even if a job does not directly require calculus, persons with a good calculus grade are likely to possess better problem-solving skills than those with a poor grade (or those who dodged the subject). Thus, employers may favor job applicants with good calculus grades, even if the subject is not directly used on the job.

Persons who attend college and earn a degree are likely to possess greater intellectual ability than those who do not.

Even if college provided no additional direct human capital, a degree could still help employers identify individuals with abilities that are difficult to observe. Similarly, students who are admitted to and graduate from elite universities like Harvard and Yale are likely to have superior abilities relative to those attending lower-level schools. Because of this signaling device, even mediocre graduates from top universities often have better entry-level job market prospects than exceptional students from lesser-known schools. The signaling function also explains why students who choose majors *perceived by others* as "hard" (such as engineering, economics, or finance) generally do better in the job market than those choosing "easy" majors (such as physical education, marketing, or social work).

"When will I ever use this stuff?" "When will a good grade in challenging courses like math and economics matter?" The answer to these questions is, "Soon!" These devices that signal prospective employers about your work habits, motivation, and ability to handle demanding jobs will matter most at the time you enter the job market. It is at the beginning stage of your career when it is difficult for employers to judge your true abilities. As you spend additional years on the job, however, your revealed productivity—and the enhancement of that productivity by your college education—will become more and more important.

Tournament pay
A form of compensation where the top performer (or performers) receives much higher rewards than other competitors, even if the others perform at only a slightly lower level.

What about the large salaries received by CEOs of major corporations? Decisions made by the CEOs of large corporations can and do exert a huge financial impact on the profitability of their companies. A CEO may be particularly valuable when a company is in trouble, faces new competition, or confronts a changing technological or regulatory environment. Like superstar entertainers and athletes, a CEO who transforms business losses into profitability is worth millions to the stockholders of a major corporation.

Economic studies have found that many sports and entertainment superstars have marginal revenue products pretty much in line with their salaries.[3] However, there may be another factor at work here. The earnings in some markets resemble tournaments. Only the top-ranked person receives the big payoff, while those who finish second receive much less. This type of compensation is called **tournament pay**.[4] This name refers to reward systems structured like golf tournaments, in which a slight difference in productivity (perhaps one or two shots) is associated with a difference in pay of several hundred thousand dollars.

In this type of environment, workers basically subject themselves to a lottery where the winner (the person with the highest productivity) receives compensation higher than his or her marginal revenue product, while the losers receive less than their marginal revenue product. There are some constraints against how low the compensation of the losers

[3]Paul M. Sommers and Noel Quinton, "Pay and Performance in Major League Baseball: The Case of the First Family of Free Agents," *Journal of Human Resources* (Summer 1982): 426–435.

[4]Edward Lazear and Sherwin Rosen, "Rank Order Tournaments as an Optimum Labor Contract," *Journal of Political Economy* 89 (October 1981): 841–864; and Robert Frank and Phillip Cook, *The Winner-Take-All Society* (New York: The Free Press, 1995).

What is the marginal revenue product of entertainment stars like Julia Roberts? Do the earnings of star entertainers, athletes, and even business executives reflect the tournament pay nature of markets in these areas?

can be, however, because they could find alternative jobs that would pay a salary equal to their marginal revenue product. Theory suggests that tournament pay environments can work to increase the effort of those in the second tier as they compete to move to the top.

The tournament pay environment creates a strong incentive for potential superstars to expend considerable effort attempting to become a top performer. As a result, many people spend long hours developing skills that will increase their chances of becoming a "star" in athletics, entertainment, professions, and business. The tournament system also encourages those who are unwilling to make such sacrifices to follow another path. Is this good or bad? Economics does not answer that question; it merely explains how these markets work.

Worker Preferences

An important source of earnings differentials that is sometimes overlooked is worker preferences. People have different objectives in life. Some want to make a great deal of money. Many are willing to work two jobs, or very long hours, undergo agonizing training and many years of education, and sacrifice social and family life to make money. Others may be "workaholics" because they enjoy their jobs. Still others may be satisfied with enough money to get by, preferring to spend more time with their family, with the Boy Scouts, in front of the television, on vacation, with a hobby, or at the local tavern.

Economics does not indicate that one set of worker preferences is more desirable than another, any more than it suggests that people should eat more spinach and less pastrami. Economics does indicate, however, that worker preferences toward money, work, and skill development will contribute to differences in earnings. Other things constant, persons who are more highly motivated by monetary objectives will be more likely to do the things necessary to command higher wage rates.

Race and Gender

Discrimination on the basis of race or gender contributes to earnings differences among individuals. **Employment discrimination** may directly limit the earnings opportunities of minorities and women. Employment discrimination exists when minority or women employees are treated in a manner different from similarly productive whites or men. Of

Employment discrimination
Unequal treatment of persons on the basis of their race, sex, or religion, restricting their employment and earnings opportunities compared to others of similar productivity. Employment discrimination may stem from the prejudices of employers, customers, fellow employees, or all three.

course, the earnings of minorities or women may differ from those of whites or men, respectively, for reasons other than employment discrimination. Nonemployment discrimination may limit the opportunity of minority groups and women to acquire human capital (for example, access to high-quality education or specialized training) that would enhance both productivity and earnings. Limited opportunities as the result of growing up in a low-income or a single-parent family may also influence skill development and educational achievement. Thus, factors other than employment discrimination will influence earnings differences among individuals according to race or ethnic status. A later section in this chapter will analyze the impact of employment discrimination in greater detail.

Earnings Differentials Due to Nonidentical Jobs

Nonpecuniary job characteristics
Working conditions, prestige, variety, location, employee freedom and responsibilities, and other nonwage characteristics of a job that influence how employees evaluate the job.

Compensating wage differentials
Wage differences that compensate workers for risk, unpleasant working conditions, and other undesirable nonpecuniary aspects of a job.

When individuals evaluate employment alternatives, they consider working conditions as well as wage rates. Is a job dangerous? Does it offer the opportunity to acquire the experience and training that will enhance future earnings? Is the work strenuous and nerve-racking? Are the working hours, job location, and means of transportation convenient? These factors are what economists call **nonpecuniary job characteristics**. People will accept jobs with undesirable working conditions if the wages are high enough, compared to potential job alternatives with better working conditions. Because the higher wages, in essence, compensate workers for the unpleasant nonpecuniary attributes of a job, economists refer to wage differences stemming from this source as **compensating wage differentials**.

Examples of higher wages that compensate various workers for less-attractive working conditions abound. Because of the dangers involved, aerial window washers (those who hang from windows 20 stories up) earn higher wages than other window washers. Sales jobs involving a great deal of out-of-town travel typically pay more than similar jobs without such inconvenience. Coal miners and sewer workers accept these jobs because they generally pay more than the alternatives available to low-skill workers. Jobs in attractive locations within the United States pay less than similar jobs in less-attractive areas.

Compensating factors even influence the earnings of economists. When economists work for colleges or universities, they generally enjoy a more independent work environment and stimulating intellectual climate than when they are employed in the business sector. Unsurprisingly, the earnings of economists in academia are typically lower than those of economists in business. However, it is important to remember that the academic economist with the lower earnings has chosen this job over business sector employment. The lower earnings do not imply the worker is worse off. As we mentioned previously, differences in worker preferences also play an important role in earnings differences.

Earnings Differentials Due to Immobility of Labor

It is costly to move to a new location or train for a new occupation in order to obtain a job. Such movements do not take place instantaneously. In the real world, labor, like other resources, does not possess perfect mobility. Some wage differentials thus result from an incomplete adjustment to change.

Since the demand for labor resources is a derived demand, it is affected by changes in product markets. An expansion in the demand for a product causes a rise in the demand for specialized labor to produce the product. Since resources are often highly immobile (that is, the supply is inelastic) in the short run, the expansion in demand may cause the wages of the specialized laborers to rise sharply. This happened in the computer industry in the 1980s and 1990s. An expansion in demand for computers triggered a rapid increase in the earnings of computer programmers, system analysts, and other specialized personnel. During the same period, falling demand caused the opposite effect for textile and apparel workers. Increased foreign competition, due to lower trade barriers, reduced the demand for U.S. textiles and apparel. The demand for and employment opportunities of specialized resources in U.S. textile and apparel industries declined substantially as output in these industries fell.[5] Demand shifts in the product market favor those in expanding industries but work against those in contracting industries.

Institutional barriers may also limit the mobility of labor. Licensing requirements, for example, limit the mobility of labor into many occupations—medicine, taxicab driving, architecture, and mortuary science among them. Minimum wage rates may retard the ability of low-skill workers to obtain employment in certain sectors of the economy. These restrictions on labor mobility will influence the size of wage differentials among workers.

Labor unions sometimes create wage differentials by limiting labor mobility and altering the free market forces of supply and demand. As we demonstrated earlier, wages are relatively higher for workers with a greater labor demand or lower labor supply. As a result, unions attempt to raise the demand for union labor and reduce the labor supply in unionized job categories. To the extent they are successful in doing so, unions create higher wages for unionized workers relative to their nonunion counterparts. For more on this topic, see the application titled "Do Labor Unions Increase the Wages of Workers?"

Sources of Wage Differentials: A Summary

As the accompanying Thumbnail Sketch shows, wage differentials stem from many sources, which can be categorized in three main ways: differences in workers, differences in jobs, and immobility of resources. Many of these factors play an important allocative role, compensating people for (1) human capital investments that increase their productivity or (2) unfavorable working conditions. Other wage differentials reflect, at least partially, locational preferences or the desires of individuals for higher money income rather than nonmonetary benefits. Still other differentials, such as those related to discrimination and occupational restrictions, are unrelated to worker productivity or preferences and do not promote efficient production.

THUMBNAIL SKETCH

What Are the Sources of Earnings Differentials?

Differences in Workers

1. Productivity and specialized skills (reflect native ability, parental training, and investment in human capital)
2. Worker preferences (trade-off between money earnings and other factors)
3. Race and gender discrimination

Differences in Jobs

1. Location of job
2. Working conditions (for example, job safety, likelihood of temporary layoffs, and comfort of work environment)
3. Opportunity for training and skill-enhancing work experience

Immobility of Resources

1. Temporary disequilibrium resulting from dynamic change
2. Institutional restrictions (for example, occupational licensing and union-imposed restraints)

The analysis above focuses on factors contributing to differences in real earnings. Nominal earnings will also be influenced by differences in the cost of living. In a large geographically diverse country like the United States, there is substantial variation in the cost of living across cities, regions, and communities. The general level of prices in large cities like New York and San Francisco may well be 50 percent or even 100 percent higher than

---

[5]Between 1980 and 2000, employment in the textile industry fell from 2.1 million to 1.2 million.

America's Millionaires[1]

The number of millionaires has been expanding rapidly. In 1975, there were only 350,000 households with a net worth of $1 million or more. By 1996, the figure had grown to 3.5 million. Only about one-third of the increase was due to inflation, as the number of households worth a million or more in 1975 dollars was about 2.4 million. The growth in the number of millionaires is expected to continue. By 2005 forecasts indicate that there will be 5.6 million millionaire households, 5.2 percent of the total (one out of every 20).

Who are the millionaires?

- In terms of age, millionaires are typically in their late 50s. They tend to be older than the general population because it takes time to accumulate wealth of this magnitude. In addition, older workers have higher earnings enabling them to increase wealth more rapidly.
- Not surprisingly, millionaires tend to be well-educated. About 80 percent have a college degree. In fact, nearly two-fifths have a graduate degree. Those with more education have higher earnings, which is an important source for acquiring wealth.
- Millionaires are disproportionately self-employed entrepreneurs. While less than one-fifth of the workforce is self employed, two-thirds of the millionaires are in this category. To a degree, the income and wealth of millionaires are rewards that compensate them for the greater financial risk accompanying self-employment and business ownership compared to working for a salary.
- The vast majority of millionaires achieved their status through saving and investment. They save on average 20 percent of their income. Most of them are first generation rich. Less than 20 percent received more than 10 percent of their wealth through an inheritance.

---

[1]Based on Thomas J. Stanley and William D. Danko, *The Millionaire Next Door: The Surprising Secrets of America's Wealthy* (New York: Longstreet Press, 1996).

for small communities or rural areas in other parts of the country. Put another way, the quantity of goods and services that can be purchased with $50,000 of earnings is substantially less in New York City than rural Georgia or Kansas, for example. Therefore, in addition to the factors underlying differences in real earnings, cost-of-living differences will also contribute to the variation of nominal earnings among individuals.

THE ECONOMICS OF EMPLOYMENT DISCRIMINATION

How does employment discrimination affect the job opportunities available to women and minorities? Do employers gain from discrimination? Economics sheds light on both these questions. There are two outlets for labor market discrimination: wage rates and employment restrictions. **Exhibit 3** illustrates the impact of wage discrimination. When majority employees are preferred to minority workers (or men to women workers), the demand for the latter groups is reduced. Consequently, the wages of minorities and women decline relative to those of white men.

Essentially, there is a dual labor market—one market for the favored group and another for the group against which the discrimination is directed. The favored group, such as whites, is preferred, but the less expensive labor of minority workers is a substitute productive resource. Both white and minority employees are employed, but the whites are paid a higher wage rate.

Exclusionary practices may also be an outlet for employment discrimination. Either in response to outside pressure or because of their own views, employers may primarily hire whites and males for certain types of jobs. When minority and female workers are excluded from a large number of occupations, they are crowded into a smaller number of remaining jobs and occupations. If entry restraints prevent people from becoming supervisors, plumbers, electricians, and truck drivers, they will be forced to accept alternatives. Thus, the supply of labor in the unrestricted occupations increases, causing wage rates to

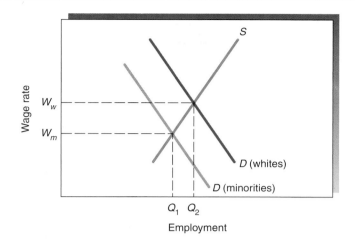

EXHIBIT 3
Impact of Direct Wage
Discrimination

If there is employment discrimination against minorities
or women, the demand for
their services will decline, and
their wage rate will fall from
W_w to W_m.

fall. In turn, the exclusionary practices reduce supply and push wages up in occupations and industries dominated by white males.

Although employment discrimination undoubtedly influences earning opportunities available to minorities and women, economic theory indicates that discrimination is costly to employers when they are merely reflecting their own prejudices. ***If employers can hire equally productive minority employees (or women) at a lower wage than whites (or men), the profit motive gives them a strong incentive to do so. Hiring the higher-wage whites when similar minority employees are available will increase the costs of firms that discriminate.*** Employers who hire employees regardless of their race or gender will have lower costs and higher profits than rival firms who try to fill positions with (mostly) white males. Thus, competitive forces tend to reduce the profitability of firms that discriminate.

Discriminatory hiring practices may stem from factors other than employer prejudice, however. If either the firm's employees or its customers have a preference for or against various groups, this may lead to discriminatory hiring even if the employer is totally unbiased. When we think about discrimination, and possible solutions, it is important to consider the source of the discrimination. If discrimination reflects only employer prejudices, competitive markets will place discriminating firms at a cost disadvantage. However, this is not the case when the employer is simply responding to the biases of customers and employees. When discrimination is customer based, a worker from a favored group will be able to bring in more revenue for the firm. For example, adult nightclubs that hire attractive young women as dancers will generate more revenue than those that hire dancers from all age and gender groups. Similarly, Chinese restaurants that hire all (or almost all) Chinese servers are likely to do better than if the ethnic and racial composition of their employees mirrors that of the labor force.

Historically, customer-based discrimination has often gone unchallenged. This appears to be changing. In a highly publicized case, the Hooters restaurant chain was charged with discrimination against males. Although the Equal Employment Opportunity Commission dropped its four-year investigation, Hooters agreed to pay $3.75 million in damages and begin hiring male servers as the result of privately filed lawsuits in Illinois and Maryland.

Employment Discrimination and the Earnings of Minorities

Earnings may differ among groups for reasons other than employment discrimination. If we want to isolate the impact of employment discrimination, we must (1) adjust for differences between groups in education, experience, and other productivity-related factors and (2) then make comparisons between similarly qualified groups of employees who differ only with regard to race (or gender).

EXHIBIT 4
The Actual and Productivity-Adjusted Wages of Minorities Compared to Whites: 1997–2000.

	MEN		WOMEN	
	ACTUAL	ADJUSTED	ACTUAL	ADJUSTED
White	100	100	100	100
African-American	79	85	90	93
American Indian	83	93	88	96
Asian-American[a]	97	93	104	98
Mexican-American	66	92	75	97
Other Hispanic	80	91	86	96

[a]Primarily Chinese Americans and Japanese Americans.
Source: These data were supplied by David MacPherson. They were derived from the 1997–2000 Current Population Surveys. The data were adjusted for years of schooling, work experience, region, industry, sector of employment, union status, and marital status.

How do the earnings of minorities compare with those of similarly productive whites? **Exhibit 4** presents data on this topic. Both the actual wages of minorities relative to whites and the "productivity-adjusted" minority/white wage ratio are presented. In essence, the adjusted ratio is an estimate of how the wages of minorities would compare with those of whites if the two groups had the same productivity characteristics (schooling, work experience, marital status, regional location, and union and industry status). The actual wages of black men were 79 percent of the wages of white men in 1997–2000. When the workforce characteristics of black men were taken into account, the adjusted hourly earnings of black men rose to 85 percent of the white male earnings. This implies that productivity-related factors accounted for a little more than one-quarter of the wage differential between the two groups. A 15 percent differential, that may well be the result of employment discrimination, remained after adjustment for the productivity characteristics.[6]

Mexican Americans constitute the second-largest minority group in the United States. Even though the actual wages of Mexican-American men were only 66 percent of the wages of white men, their "adjusted" earnings were 92 percent of those for whites. These data were not adjusted for language—inability to speak English. Adjustment for this factor would almost certainly further narrow the differential. This suggests that when Mexican-American men possess the same worker characteristics as white men, their earnings are pretty close to parity with their white counterparts. The actual and corrected earnings for other minority groups are also presented in Exhibit 4. Interestingly, adjustment for productivity factors reduces the wages of Asian Americans relative to whites. This occurs because the productivity characteristics particularly the average level of education—of Asian Americans are higher than those of whites.

Turning to the data for women, the productivity-adjusted wage rates of minority women relative to white women are between 93 percent and 98 percent for each of the groups included in Exhibit 4. This implies that the independent effect of racial discrimination is relatively small. For an analysis of earnings differences according to gender, see the feature "Is Discrimination Responsible for the Earnings Differences Between Men and Women?" in the Special Topics section of this book.

[6]Other researchers using more refined data have found that productivity factors account for a larger share of the earnings differential between whites and blacks. For evidence on this point, see Francine D. Blau and Lawrence M. Kahn, "Race and Gender Pay Differentials," in *Research Frontiers in Industrial Relations and Human Resources,* ed. David Lewin, Olivia S. Mitchell, and Peter D. Scherer (Madison, Wis.: Industrial Relations Research Association, 1992), pp. 381–416; Derek A. Neal and William R. Johnson, "The Role of Premarket Factors in Black-White Wage Differences," *Journal of Political Economy* (October 1996): 869–895; and June O'Neill, "The Role of Human Capital in Earnings Differences between Black and White Men," *Journal of Economic Perspectives* (Fall 1990): 25–45. For a detailed explanation of how the adjusted ratios of Exhibit 4 were derived and information on the significance of productivity differences and employment discrimination on the basis of gender, see David A. Macpherson and Barry T. Hirsch, "Wages and Gender Composition: Why Do Women's Jobs Pay Less?" *Journal of Labor Economics* (July 1995).

THE LINK BETWEEN PRODUCTIVITY AND EARNINGS

 In a market economy, productivity and earnings are closely linked. In order to earn a large income, one must provide large benefits to others.

In a competitive market setting, productivity—that is, output per worker—and earnings are closely linked. When workers are more productive, the demand for their services will be higher and therefore they will be able to command higher wage rates. ***High productivity is the source of high wages. When the output per hour of workers is high, the real wages of the workers will also be high.***

In turn, the linkage between productivity and earnings provides individuals with a strong incentive to develop their talents and utilize their resources in ways that are helpful to others. As the value of the goods and services supplied to others increases, there will also be a tendency for one's earnings to increase. If you want to make a large income, you had better figure out how to provide services that are highly valued. Self-interest is a powerful motivator and, as Adam Smith noted long ago, competitive markets can bring it into harmony with economic progress.

Link between Productivity and Earnings

Improvements in equipment and technology increase worker productivity. In turn, higher productivity is the source of higher earnings.

MYTHS OF ECONOMICS

"Automation Is the Major Cause of Unemployment. If We Keep Allowing Machines to Replace People, We Are Going to Run Out of Jobs."

Machines are substituted for people if, and only if, the machines reduce costs of production. Why did the automatic elevator replace the operator or the power shovel virtually eliminate the job of the ditch digger? Because each is a cheaper method of accomplishing a task.

When automation and technological improvements reduce the cost of producing a good, they allow us to obtain each unit of the product with fewer resources. If the demand for the product is inelastic, consumers will spend less on the good and therefore have more of their income available for spending on other things.

Consider the following example. Suppose that someone develops a new toothpaste that really prevents cavities and sells it for half the price of the current brands. If the demand for toothpaste is inelastic, at the lower price consumers will spend less on this product than was previously the case. Furthermore, the decline in cavities will reduce the demand for and expenditures on dental services. Lower dental care expenditures, however, will increase the income available for consumers to spend on other goods and services. As a result, they will spend more on clothes, recreation, vacations, personal computers, education, and numerous other items. This additional spending, which would not have taken place if dental costs had not been reduced, will generate additional demand and employment in these sectors.

When the demand for a product is elastic, a cost-saving invention can even generate an increase in employment in the industry affected by the invention. This was essentially what happened in the automobile industry when Henry Ford's mass production techniques reduced the cost (and price) of cars. When the price of automobiles fell 50 percent, consumers bought three times as many cars. Even though the worker-hours per car fell by 25 percent between 1920 and 1930, employment in the industry increased by approximately 50 percent during the decade.

Of course, technological advances may diminish the earnings of specific individuals or groups. Home appliances, such as automatic washers and dryers, dishwashers, and microwave ovens, reduced the job opportunities of maids. Computer technology has reduced the demand for telephone operators. In the future, videotaped lectures may even reduce the earnings and job opportunities of college professors. It is understandable why groups directly affected in this manner often fear and oppose automation.

Focusing on the loss of specific jobs, though, conceals the overall impact of technological improvements. Cost-reducing improvements in technology release scarce resources for the expansion of output and employment in other areas. As a result, we are able to produce more and achieve a higher standard of living than would have otherwise been possible.

Furthermore, running out of jobs is not a problem. Jobs represent obstacles, tasks that must be accomplished if we desire to loosen the bonds of scarcity. As long as our ability to produce goods and services falls short of our consumption desires, there will be jobs. A society running out of jobs would be in an enviable position: It would be nearing the impossible goal—victory over scarcity!

Differences in output per worker are the major source of variations in earnings across countries. For example, the earnings per worker are vastly greater in the United States than they are in India or China, because the output of U.S. workers is much greater than the output of their counterparts in those countries. The average worker in the United States is better educated, works with more productive machines, and benefits from more efficient economic organization than the average person in India or China. Thus, the value of the output produced by the average U.S. worker is approximately 15 times that produced by the average worker in India or China. American workers earn more because they produce more. If they did not produce more, they would not be able to earn more.

Productivity differences also underlie changes in earnings across time periods. Today, American workers are substantially more productive than was true 50 years ago.[7] The output of goods and services per hour of U.S. workers in 2000 was approximately twice the

---

[7] For more on productivity growth, see Kevin J. Stiroh, "What Drives Productivity Growth?" Federal Reserve Bank of New York, *Economic Policy Review* (March 2001): 37–59.

Profit-maximizing firms will adopt automated production methods only when they reduce costs. Cost-effective automation releases labor and other resources so they can be used to expand production in other areas. In turn, the expansion in production provides the source for higher earnings.

level of the mid-1950s. Similarly, average real earnings (total compensation) per hour in 2000 were approximately double those of 50 years ago. Earnings rose because productivity increased. If productivity had not increased, the increase in earnings would not have been possible.

Increased availability of physical capital, improvements in the skill level of the labor force, and advances in technology provide the impetus for the growth of both productivity and earnings. For several decades, the educational level (representing investment in human capital) of American workers has steadily increased. Simultaneously, the physical capital per worker has expanded. Technological advances have also enhanced productivity and thereby contributed to the growth of output and income. Some observers argue that technology and automation adversely affect workers (see the accompanying Myth of Economics box). In fact, just the opposite is true. *Once you recognize that expansion in output is the source of higher earnings, the positive impact of improvements in technology is apparent: Better technology makes it possible for workers to produce more and thus to earn more.* For example, accountants can handle more business accounts using microcomputers rather than a pencil and calculator. A secretary can prepare more letters when working with a word processor rather than a typewriter.

Automation
A production technique that reduces the amount of labor required to produce a good or service. It is beneficial to adopt the new labor-saving technology only if it reduces the cost of production.

Productivity and the New Economy

What has happened to productivity in recent decades? **Exhibit 5** presents data on the change in both productivity (output per hour) and real hourly compensation of the United States for 1948–1973, 1974–1995, and 1996–2000. Predictably, productivity growth and increases in real compensation per hour were closely linked. Between 1948 and 1973, both productivity and real compensation per hour grew at an average annual rate of about 3 percent. During the next two decades, the growth of both productivity and real hourly compensation sagged badly. Productivity growth averaged only 1.5 percent

EXHIBIT 5
Productivity and Employee Compensation in the United States, 1948–2000

As illustrated in the graph, worker productivity and employee compensation per hour are closely linked. Between 1973 and 1995, growth of both productivity and real compensation per hour slowed substantially compared to the growth figures achieved during the 1948–1973 period. However, worker productivity and real hourly compensation rebounded during the 1996–2000 period.

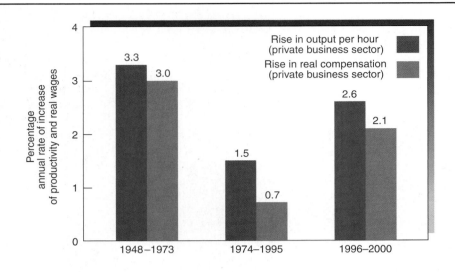

Source: Bureau of Labor Statistics, *www.bls.gov.*

annually and hourly real compensation rose at an annual rate of only 0.7 percent during 1974–1995.

Since 1996, there has been a rebound in the growth of both productivity and real hourly compensation. During 1996–2000, productivity and hourly compensation grew at annual rates of 2.6 percent and 2.1 percent respectively. The acceleration in productivity growth is also reflected in the total output figures. The average annual growth of per capita GDP in the United States rose from 1.8 percent during 1974–1995 to 3.2 percent during 1996–2000.

What accounts for the recent rebound in the growth of productivity? This is currently a topic of hot debate among economists. Some believe that the United States is at the beginning of a "new era economy" characterized by higher productivity growth resulting from the computer revolution and other technological innovations.[8] The proponents of this view believe that the higher productivity since 1996 reflects a new long-term trend. Others argue that the recent resurgence of productivity is merely a temporary phenomena reflecting business cycle conditions. Let us consider these alternative views.

New Era View

As we have previously noted, more and better equipment and tools enhance the productivity of workers. Other things constant, workers are able to produce more when they are working with more physical capital. When the supply of productivity-enhancing capital assets grows more rapidly, the growth of labor productivity also tends to quicken. The proponents of the new era view believe that substantial increases in investment spending on information technology such as computer hardware, software, and communications equipment during the 1990s increased long-term productivity. One study finds that nearly one-half of the acceleration in productivity growth in the second half of the 1990s was due to increased quantities of information technology capital.[9] Spending on other types of capital apparently contributed little to the speedup in productivity growth.

[8]For a discussion of the new economy perspective, see Kevin J. Stiroh, "Is There a New Economy?" *Challenge* (July/August 1999): 82–101.

[9]Stephen D. Oliner and Daniel E. Sichel, "The Resurgence of Growth in the Late 1990s: Is Information Technology the Story?" *Journal of Economic Perspectives* (Fall 2000): 3–22.

Furthermore, new era proponents believe that the pace of technological change has quickened and that new technologies now spread throughout the economy more rapidly. If true, this would enhance the productivity of both labor and capital. As measured by prices, the speed of innovations in computer technology has certainly increased in recent years. For example, the price of computers in the second half of the 1990s fell at nearly twice the rate as in the first half of the 1990s. In fact, one study finds that about one-third of the speedup in productivity growth is due to increased efficiency in the production of computers and semiconductors.[10]

Temporary Factors

Some economists, such as Robert Gordon, are doubtful that the revival in the productivity growth rate is part of a new long-run trend in productivity growth.[11] Gordon argues that the resurgence of productivity growth merely reflects the lengthy boom of the 1990s. Thus, he believes that the recent upturn in productivity growth will fade as the boom comes to an end.

There are two reasons why the rate of productivity growth tends to fall during recessions and rise during booms. First, firms are reluctant to dismiss employees during economic downturns because they don't want to lose their past training investments in workers. As a result, workers are underutilized during recessions and productivity falls. Conversely, firms more fully utilize their employees during an economic boom and therefore productivity rises. Second, consumer demand for durable manufactured goods such as cars and refrigerators rises and falls to a greater extent over the business cycle than the demand for services such as lawn care and hair styling. Because productivity is greater in durable manufacturing than services, the greater fluctuation of the former tends to push productivity up during a boom and pull it down during a recession.

Economists disagree about the role of the economic boom in the productivity revival. Estimates of the portion of the productivity speedup due to cyclical effects range from close to zero to nearly 40 percent.[12] Given the close relationship between the growth of productivity and wages, this debate is important to all Americans. Time will determine the outcome. If productivity growth continues at a high level during the next phase of the business cycle, this would suggest that cyclical factors played only a minor role in the resurgence of productivity. On the other hand, if the growth of productivity recedes in the years immediately ahead, this would indicate that cyclical factors rather than a new era economy were responsible for the higher productivity of the late 1990s.

While this chapter focused on the labor market, the following chapter will analyze the capital market. Real income and output are strongly influenced by the amount of both the physical and human capital with which people work. The next chapter analyzes the factors that underlie the availability of capital and the investment choices of decision makers.

**LOOKING
AHEAD**

---

[10]Ibid.

[11]Robert Gordon, "Does the 'New Economy' Measure up to the Great Inventions of the Past?" *Journal of Economic Perspectives* (Fall 2000): 49–74. Robert Gordon also argues that changes in the measurement of prices accounts for part of the increase in the productivity growth. He points out that in the mid-1990s, the price index was altered so that the measured rate of inflation was lower in future years. This change increased observed measured real output in the second half of the 1990s and thus raised productivity growth. He finds that 11 percent of the productivity speedup was due to this change in the measurement of prices.

[12]The low estimate is from Council of Economic Advisers, *Economic Report of the President, 2001* (Washington, D.C.: Government Printing Office, 2001), Chapter 1, while the high figure is from Robert Gordon. Ibid.

KEY POINTS

▼ The real earnings of individuals would be equal if (1) all individuals were identical in preferences, skills, and background, (2) all jobs were equally attractive, and (3) workers were perfectly mobile among jobs. Earnings differences among individuals result from the absence of these conditions.

▼ Wage differences play an important allocative role. They generally compensate people for (1) investments in education and training that enhance productivity and the development of highly specialized skills and (2) unfavorable working conditions and/or job locations. Wage differences may also result from differences in the preferences of workers (value placed on money income relative to leisure and other factors), employment discrimination, and institutional factors that restrict worker mobility.

▼ Employment discrimination may reduce the wages of a group by either reducing the demand for their services or restricting their entry into various job categories. Productivity differences may also contribute to earnings differentials between groups. Research indicates that the earnings of African-American and Mexican-American males are approximately 85 per-

cent and 93 percent respectively those of white males of similar productivity.

▼ Productivity is the ultimate source of high wages and earnings. Workers in the United States (and other high-income industrial countries) earn high wages because their output per hour is high as the result of (a) greater worker knowledge and skills (human capital) and (b) the use of modern machinery (physical capital).

▼ Automated methods of production will be adopted only if they reduce costs. Although automation might reduce employment in a specific industry, it also releases resources that can be employed in other areas. Improved technology permits us to achieve larger output and income levels than would otherwise be possible.

▼ During the last 5 years, the growth of productivity in the United States has increased well above the growth rate achieved during the prior 20 years. Disagreement exists over whether the acceleration in productivity is the start of a new long-term trend or is only a temporary aberration. If the acceleration in productivity does continue, future improvements in our standard of living will come about more quickly.

CRITICAL ANALYSIS QUESTIONS

1. What are the major reasons for the differences in earnings among individuals? Why are wages in some occupations higher than in others? How do wage differentials influence the allocation of resources? Explain.

*2. Why are real wages in the United States higher than in other countries? Is the labor force itself responsible for the higher wages of American workers? Explain.

3. What are the major factors that would normally explain earnings differences between (a) a lawyer and a minister, (b) an accountant and an elementary school teacher, (c) a business executive and a social worker, (d) a country lawyer and a Wall Street lawyer, (e) an experienced, skilled craftsperson and a 20-year-old high school dropout, and (f) an upper-story and a ground-floor window washer?

4. (a) If minority employees are discriminated against in employment, how will this discrimination influence their earnings? Use supply and demand analy-

sis to explain your answer. (b) If the average earnings differ between two groups of employees (for example, whites and blacks), does this mean that the group with the lower earnings confronts employment discrimination? Why or why not?

5. Is there a relationship between the growth of productivity and changes in wage rates? Can higher earnings be achieved without higher productivity? Why or why not? Discuss.

*6. "Jobs are the key to economic progress. Unless we create more jobs, our standard of living will fall." Is this statement true or false? Explain.

7. "If Jones has a skill that is highly valued, she will be able to achieve high market earnings. In contrast, Smith may work just as hard or even harder, and still earn only a low income."
   a. Does hard work necessarily lead to a high income?
   b. Why are the incomes of some workers high and others low?

c. Do you think the market system of wage determination is fair? Why or why not?

d. Can you think of a more equitable system? If so, explain why it is more equitable.

*8. People who have invested heavily in human capital (for example, lawyers, doctors, and even college professors) generally have higher wages, but they also generally work more hours than other workers. Can you explain why?

*9. "If individuals had identical abilities and opportunities, earnings would be equal." Is this statement true or false?

*10. Other things being constant, how will the following factors influence hourly earnings? Explain your response.

a. The employee must work the midnight to 8:00 A.M. shift.

b. The job involves broken intervals (work 3 hours, off 2 hours, work 3 additional hours, and so on) of employment during the day.

c. The employer provides low-cost child-care services on the premises.

d. The job is widely viewed as prestigious.

e. The job requires employees to move often from city to city.

f. The job requires substantial amounts of out-of-town travel.

*11. Consider two occupations (A and B) that employ persons with the same skill and ability. When employed, workers in the two occupations work the same number of hours per day. In occupation A, employment is stable throughout the year, while employment in B is characterized by seasonal layoffs. In which occupation will the hourly wage rate be highest? Why? In which occupation will the annual wage be highest? Why?

*12. In 2000 the mean weekly earnings of single men were only 64 percent of their married counterparts. Does this indicate that employment discrimination existed against single men and in favor of married men?

13. Productivity growth accelerated in the second half of the 1990s. What do you think caused this resurgence in the growth of productivity?

14. "Technological change eliminates thousands of jobs every year. Unless something is done to slow the growth of technology, ordinary workers will face a bleak future of low wages and high unemployment." Explain why you either agree or disagree with this statement.

---

*Asterisk denotes questions for which answers are given in Appendix B.

CHAPTER 26

To produce capital, people must forgo the opportunity to produce goods for current consumption. People can choose whether to spend their time picking apples or planting apple trees. In the first case there are more apples today; in the second, more apples tomorrow.

—Steven Landsburg[1]

Investment, the Capital Market, and the Wealth of Nations

Chapter Focus

- Why do people invest? Why are capital resources often used to produce consumer goods?

- What is the interest rate? Why are investors willing to pay interest to acquire loanable funds? Why are lenders willing to loan funds?

- Why is the interest rate so important when evaluating costs and revenues across time periods?

- When is an investment profitable? How do profitable and unprofitable investments influence the wealth of nations?

- How does the capital market influence growth and prosperity?

[1]Steven E. Landsburg, *Price Theory and Applications* (Fort Worth: Dryden Press, 1992), p. 581.

n the previous chapter we noted that there was a close relationship between productivity and earnings. In turn, productivity is influenced by investment choices. Consider such choices as whether to construct an office building, purchase a harvesting machine, or go to law school. The returns derived from investments such as these are generally spread over several years (or even decades). Some costs of investments, such as maintenance expenses, may also be incurred over a lengthy time period. Why should we expect profit-seeking individuals and corporate decision makers to pay now to create benefits later—sometimes much later? How can people compare the benefits and costs of an activity when both are spread across lengthy periods of time? Why is the method of allocating investment a vitally important determinant of economic progress? As we explain the investment process and capital markets, this chapter will help you answer these questions. ■

WHY PEOPLE INVEST

Capital is a term used by economists to describe long-lasting resources that are valued because they can help us produce goods and services in the future. As we previously discussed, there are two broad categories of capital: (1) *physical capital*: nonhuman resources, such as buildings, machines, tools, and natural resources, and (2) *human capital*: human resources, that is, the knowledge and skills of people. **Investment** is the purchase, construction, or development of a capital resource. Thus, investment expands the availability of capital resources.

Saving is income not spent on current consumption. *Investment and saving are closely linked. In fact, the two words describe different aspects of the capital formation process. Saving applies to the nonconsumption of income, while investment applies to the use of the unconsumed income to produce a capital resource.* Sometimes saving and investment are conducted by the same person, as when a farmer saves current income (refrains from spending it on consumption goods) in order to purchase a new tractor (an investment good).

It is important to recognize that saving is required for investment. Someone must save—refrain from consumption—in order to provide the resources for investment. When investors finance a project with their own funds, they are also saving (refraining from current consumption). Investors, however, do not always use their own funds to finance investments. Sometimes they will borrow funds from others. When this is the case, it is the lender rather than the investor who is doing the saving.

Considering the alternative use of resources also highlights the linkage between investment and saving. Resources used to produce capital will be unavailable for the direct production of consumption goods. The opportunity cost of investing more and using more of our resources to produce capital resources today is that fewer current resources will be available to produce consumption goods. To invest more, we have to reduce our current consumption.

Why would anyone want to delay consumption in order to undertake an investment? Consumption is the ultimate objective of all production. However, we can sometimes produce more consumption goods by first using resources to produce capital resources and then utilizing these resources to produce the desired consumer goods. Using capital to produce consumption goods makes sense only when it allows us to produce more consumption goods than we otherwise could.

Perhaps a simple illustration can highlight the potential gains from using capital to produce consumption goods. Suppose that Robinson Crusoe can catch fish by either (1) combining his labor with natural resources (direct production) or (2) constructing a net and eventually combining his labor with this capital resource (indirect production). Let us assume that Crusoe could catch 2 fish per day by hand fishing, but could catch 3 fish per day if he constructed and used a net that would last for 310 days. Suppose it would take Crusoe 55 days to build the net. The opportunity cost of constructing the net would be

Capital
Resources that enhance our ability to produce output in the future.

Investment
The purchase, construction, or development of capital resources, including both nonhuman capital and human capital. Investments increase the supply of capital.

Saving
Current income that is not spent on consumption goods.

Savings deposited by some individuals allow resources to be devoted to investments, such as the making of tractors.

110 fish (2 per day not caught, for each of the 55 days Crusoe spent building the net). As the accompanying chart indicates, if Crusoe invested in the capital resource (the net), his output during the next year (including the 55 days required to build the net) would be 930 fish (3 per day for 310 days). Alternatively, hand-fishing during the year would lead to an output of only 730 fish (2 fish per day for 365 days).

NUMBER OF FISH CAUGHT

	WITHOUT NET	WITH NET
Per day	2	3
Annual	730	930

Crusoe's investment in the net will enhance his productivity. With the net, his total output during the year will increase by 200 fish. In the short term, however, investing in the net will impose a sacrifice. During the 55 days it takes to construct the net, Crusoe's production of consumption goods will decline.

How can Crusoe or any other investor know if the value of the larger future output is worth the short-term cost? Most of us have a preference for goods now rather than later. For example, if you are typical, you would prefer a sleek new sports car now rather than the same car 10 years from now. On average, individuals possess a **positive rate of time preference**. By this we mean that, other things being the same, people subjectively value goods obtained sooner more highly than goods obtained later.

When only Crusoe is involved, the attractiveness of the investment in the fishing net is dependent upon his time preference. If he places a high value on a couple of fish per day during the next 55 days, as indeed he may if he is on the verge of starvation, the cost of the investment may well exceed the value of the larger future output. If Crusoe could find someone who would loan him fish while he built the net, however, he could consume the

Positive rate of time preference The desire of consumers for goods now rather than in the future.

borrowed fish now, even while building the net, and pay later from the increase in fish production made possible by the net. If such a loan is available, the attractiveness of the investment (building the net instead of hand fishing now) would be influenced by the price of borrowing fish. Is the payment of additional fish, in order to maintain consumption while investing in the net, worth the extra cost? To answer this question, Crusoe must consider the cost of paying for earlier availability—he must consider, in effect, the interest rate.

INTEREST RATES

The interest rate links the future to the present. It allows individuals to evaluate the value today—the present value—of future income and costs. In essence, it is the market price of earlier availability. From the viewpoint of a potential borrower, the interest rate is the premium that must be paid in order to acquire goods sooner and pay for them later. From the lender's viewpoint, it is a reward for waiting—a payment for supplying others with current purchasing power. The interest rate allows the lender to calculate the future benefit (future payments earned) derived from extending a loan or saving funds today.

In a modern economy, people often borrow funds in order to finance current investments and consumption. Because of this, the interest rate is often defined as the price of loanable funds. This definition is proper. But we should remember that it is the earlier availability of goods and services purchased, not the money itself, that is desired by the borrower.

Determination of Interest Rates

Interest rates are determined by the demand for and supply of loanable funds. Investors demand funds in order to finance capital assets that they believe will increase output and generate profit. Simultaneously, consumers demand loanable funds because they have a positive rate of time preference: They prefer earlier availability.

The demand of investors for loanable funds stems from the productivity of capital. Investors are willing to borrow in order to finance the use of capital in production because they expect that an expansion in future output will provide them with more than enough resources to repay both the amount borrowed—the principal—and interest on the loan. Our prior example of Robinson Crusoe illustrates this point. Remember, Crusoe could increase his output by 200 fish this year if he could take off 55 days from hand fishing in order to build a net. Doing so would reduce Crusoe's fish production by 2 fish per day during the time he was constructing the net. Suppose a fishing crew from a neighboring island visited Crusoe and offered to lend him 110 fish so that he could undertake the capital investment project (building the net). If Crusoe could borrow the 110 fish (the principal) in exchange for, say, 165 fish one year later (110 fish to repay the principal and 55 as interest on the loan), the investment project would be highly profitable. Crusoe could repay the funds borrowed, plus the 50 percent interest rate, and still have 145 additional fish (the 200 additional fish caught minus the 55 fish paid in interest).

Crusoe's demand for loanable fish—and, more generally, the demand of investors for loanable funds—stems directly from the productivity of the capital investment. Crusoe can gain by borrowing to finance the construction of a fishing net only because the net enables him to expand his total output during the year. Similarly, investors can gain by borrowing funds to undertake investment projects only when the capital assets they purchase permit them to expand output (or reduce costs) by enough to make the interest payments and still have more output than they would have without the investment.

As **Exhibit 1** illustrates, the interest rate brings the choices of investors and consumers wanting to borrow funds into harmony with the choices of lenders willing to supply funds. Higher interest rates make it more costly for investors to undertake capital spending projects and for consumers to buy now rather than later. Both investors and consumers will

EXHIBIT 1
Determination of Interest Rate

The demand for loanable funds stems from the consumer's desire for earlier availability and the productivity of capital. As the interest rate rises, current goods become more expensive in comparison with future goods. Therefore, borrowers will demand less loanable funds. On the other hand, higher interest rates will stimulate lenders to supply additional funds to the market.

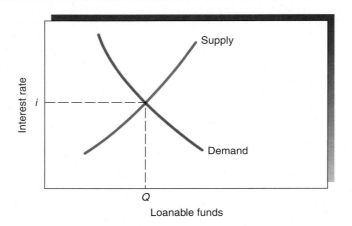

therefore curtail their borrowing as the interest rate rises. Investors will borrow less because some investment projects that would be profitable at a low interest rate will be unprofitable at higher rates. Some consumers will reduce their current consumption rather than pay the high interest premium when the interest rate increases. Therefore, the amount of funds demanded by borrowers is inversely related to the interest rate.

The interest rate also provides a reward to persons (lenders) willing to reduce their current consumption in order to provide loanable funds to others. If some individuals are going to borrow in order to undertake an investment project (or consume more than their current income), others must curtail their current consumption by an equal amount. In essence, the interest rate provides lenders with the incentive to reduce their current consumption so that borrowers can either invest or consume beyond their current income. Higher interest rates provide persons willing to save (willing to supply loanable funds) with the ability to purchase more goods in the future in exchange for the sacrifice of current consumption. Even though people have a positive rate of time preference, they will give up current consumption to supply funds to the loanable funds market if the price is right, that is, if the interest rate is attractive enough. In a market economy, it is often those who are in their peak earning years who are most attracted to saving. By saving now, they can provide for a larger income later, perhaps during their retirement years. But like everyone else, they will tend to save more at higher interest rates. Therefore, as the interest rate rises, the quantity of funds supplied to the loanable funds market expands.

As Exhibit 1 illustrates, the interest rate will bring the quantity of funds demanded into balance with the quantity supplied. *At the equilibrium interest rate, the quantity of funds borrowers demand for investment and consumption now (rather than later) will just equal the quantity of funds lenders save. So the interest rate brings the choices of borrowers and lenders into harmony.*

Money Rate Versus Real Rate of Interest

We have emphasized that the interest rate is a premium paid by borrowers for earlier availability and a reward received by lenders for delaying consumption. However, during a period of inflation—a general increase in prices—the nominal interest rate, or **money rate of interest**, is a misleading indicator of how much borrowers are paying and lenders are receiving. Inflation reduces the purchasing power of a loan's principal. Rising prices mean that when the borrower repays the principal in the future, it will not purchase as much as it would have when the funds were initially loaned.

Money rate of interest
The rate of interest in monetary terms that borrowers pay for borrowed funds. During periods when borrowers and lenders expect inflation, the money rate of interest exceeds the real rate of interest.

Recognizing the declining purchasing power of the dollars to be repaid by borrowers during inflation, lenders are less eager to provide loans at a specified interest rate. They will reduce the amount of loanable funds supplied unless they are compensated for the anticipated rate of inflation by an upward adjustment of the interest rate paid. At the same time, when borrowers anticipate inflation, they will want to purchase goods and services now before they become even more expensive in the future. Thus, they are willing to pay an **inflationary premium**, an additional amount of interest that reflects the expected rate of future price increases. If borrowers and lenders fully anticipate a 5 percent rate of inflation during the life of the loan, for example, they will be just as willing to agree on a 9 percent interest rate as they were earlier to agree on a 4 percent interest rate when both anticipated stability in the general level of prices.

Compared to the situation when the general price level is stable, the supply of loanable funds will decline (the supply curve will shift to the left) and the demand will increase (the demand curve will shift to the right) once decision makers anticipate future inflation. The money interest rate thus rises, overstating the "true" cost of borrowing and the yield from lending. This true cost is the **real rate of interest**, which is equal to the money rate of interest minus the inflationary premium. It reflects the real burden to borrowers and payoff to lenders in terms of command over goods and services.

Our analysis indicates that high rates of inflation will push up the money rate of interest. The real world is consistent with this view. Money interest rates rose to historical highs in the United States as inflation soared to double-digit rates during the 1970s. These same nominal rates fell to the 5 percent range as inflation fell below 2 percent in the 1990s. Cross-country comparisons also illustrate the linkage between inflation and high interest rates. The lowest money interest rates in the 1990s were found in nations such as Germany, Switzerland, and Japan, all with low rates of inflation. In contrast, the highest money interest rates were observed in Russia, Brazil, Turkey, and other countries with high rates of inflation during the period.

Interest Rates and Risk

We have proceeded as though there were only a single interest rate present in the loanable funds market. In the real world, of course, there are many interest rates. There is the mortgage rate, the prime interest rate (the rate charged to business firms with strong credit ratings), the consumer loan rate, and the credit card rate, to name only a few.

Interest rates in the loanable funds market will differ primarily as the result of differences in the risk associated with the loan. It is riskier to loan funds to an unemployed worker than to a well-established business with substantial assets. Similarly, extending an unsecured loan like that accompanying purchases on a credit card is riskier than extending a loan that is secured by an asset, such as a mortgage loan on a house. The risk also increases with the duration of the loan. The longer the time period, the more likely that the ability of the borrower to repay the loan will deteriorate or that market conditions will change unfavorably.

As **Exhibit 2** illustrates, the money rate of interest on a loan has three components. The pure-interest component is the real price one must pay for earlier availability. The inflationary-premium component reflects the expectation that the loan will be repaid with dollars of less purchasing power as the result of inflation. The risk-premium component reflects the probability of default—the risk imposed on the lender by the possibility that the borrower may be unable to repay the loan.

PRESENT VALUE OF FUTURE INCOME AND COSTS

If you deposited $100 today in a savings account earning 6 percent interest, you would have $106 one year from now. To put it another way, the present value of $106 one year from now is equal to the amount ($100) that you would have to invest today in order to have that amount at that time. ***The interest rate allows us to make this calculation. The***

Inflationary premium
A component of the money interest rate that reflects compensation to the lender for the expected decrease, due to inflation, in the purchasing power of the principal and interest during the course of the loan. It is determined by the expected rate of future inflation.

Real rate of interest
The money rate of interest minus the expected rate of inflation. The real rate of interest indicates the interest premium, in terms of real goods and services, that one must pay for earlier availability.

EXHIBIT 2
Three Components of Money Interest

The money interest rate reflects three components: pure interest, inflationary premium, and risk premium. When decision makers expect a high rate of inflation during the period in which the loan is outstanding, the inflationary premium will be substantial. Similarly, the risk premium will be large when the probability of default by the borrower is substantial.

interest rate connects the value of dollars (and capital assets) today with the value of dollars (expected income and receipts) in the future. It is used to discount the value of a dollar received in the future so that its present worth can be determined today.

The **present value (PV)** of a payment received one year from now can be expressed as follows:

$$PV = \frac{\text{Receipts One Year from Now}}{1 + \text{Interest Rate}}$$

Present value (PV)
The current worth of future income after it is discounted to reflect the fact that revenues in the future are valued less highly than revenues now.

If the interest rate is 6 percent, the current value of $100 to be received one year from now is

$$PV = \frac{100}{1.06} = \$94.34$$

If you placed $94.34 in a savings account yielding 6 percent interest, during the year the account would earn $5.66 interest (6 percent of $94.34) and therefore grow to $100 one year from now. Thus, the present value of $100 to be received a year from now is $94.34.

Economists use the term **discounting** to describe this procedure of reducing the value of a dollar to be received in the future to its present worth. Clearly, the value of a dollar in the future is inversely related to the interest rate. For example, if the interest rate is 10 percent, the present value of $100 received one year from now would be only $90.91 ($100 divided by 1.10). At still higher interest rates, the present value of $100 a year from now would be even lower.

Discounting
The procedure used to calculate the present value of future income, which is inversely related to both the interest rate and the amount of time that passes before the funds are received.

The present value of $100 received two years from now is

$$PV = \frac{\$100}{(1 + \text{Interest Rate})^2}$$

If the interest rate is 6 percent, $100 received two years from now would be equal to $89 today ($100 divided by 1.06^2). In other words, $89 invested today would yield $100 two years from now.

The present-value procedure can be used to determine the current value of any future income (or cost) stream. If R represents receipts received at the end of various years in the future (indicated by the subscripts) and i represents the interest rate, the present value of the future income stream is

EXHIBIT 3
Present Value of $100 to be Received in the Future

PRESENT VALUE OF $100 TO BE RECEIVED
A DESIGNATED NUMBER OF YEARS
IN THE FUTURE AT ALTERNATIVE DISCOUNT RATES

YEARS IN THE FUTURE	2 PERCENT	4 PERCENT	6 PERCENT	8 PERCENT	12 PERCENT	20 PERCENT
1	98.04	96.15	94.34	92.59	89.29	83.33
2	96.12	92.46	89.00	85.73	79.72	69.44
3	94.23	88.90	83.96	79.38	71.18	57.87
4	92.39	85.48	79.21	73.50	63.55	48.23
5	90.57	82.19	74.73	68.06	56.74	40.19
6	88.80	79.03	70.50	63.02	50.66	33.49
7	87.06	75.99	66.51	58.35	45.23	27.08
8	85.35	73.07	62.74	54.03	40.39	23.26
9	83.68	70.26	59.19	50.02	36.06	19.38
10	82.03	67.56	55.84	46.32	32.20	16.15
15	74.30	55.53	41.73	31.52	18.27	6.49
20	67.30	45.64	31.18	21.45	10.37	2.61
30	55.21	30.83	17.41	9.94	3.34	0.42
50	37.15	14.07	5.43	2.13	0.35	0.01

The columns indicate the present value of $100 to be received a designated number of years in the future at alternative discount (interest) rates. For example, at a discount rate of 2 percent, the present value of $100 to be received five years from now is $90.57. Note that the present value of the $100 declines as either the interest rate or the number of years in the future increases.

$$PV = \frac{R_1}{(1 + i)} + \frac{R_2}{(1 + i)^2} + \ldots + \frac{R_n}{(1 + i)^n}$$

Exhibit 3 shows the present value of $100 received at various times in the future at several different discount rates. The chart clearly illustrates two points. First, the present value of income received at a date in the future declines with the interest rate. The present value of the $100 received one year from now, when discounted at a 4 percent interest rate, is $96.15, compared to $98.04 when a 2 percent discount rate is applied. Second, the present value of the $100 also declines as the date of its receipt is set farther into the future. If the applicable discount rate is 6 percent, the present value of $100 received one year from now is $94.34, compared to $89 if the $100 is received two years from now. If the $100 is received five years from now, its current worth is only $74.73. *So the present value of a future dollar payment is inversely related both to the interest rate and to how far in the future the payment will be received.*

To see in a more personal way the importance of interest and the value of saving, consider what you could gain by saving just $1,000 per year ($83.33 per month) for 10 years in a tax-free individual retirement account. If you begin at age 25 and continue only until age 35 (putting nothing into the account after that), and the account returns 8 percent annually, the account will be worth $168,627 when you reach age 65. In contrast, if you wait until age 35 and then save $1,000 per year for 30 years (not 10 years of savings as before) with the same 8 percent annual return, by age 65 your account will be worth only $125,228. Ten years of saving, starting with age 25, yields far more than 30 years of saving at the same amount each year but waiting until age 35 to start. Which savings plan is more attractive to you?

PRESENT VALUE, PROFITABILITY, AND INVESTMENT

Investment decisions, like saving decisions, require comparisons of costs and benefits over time. Investment involves an up-front cost of acquiring a machine, skill, or other asset that is expected to generate additional output and revenue in the future. How can an investor know if the expected future revenues will be sufficient to cover the costs? The discounting procedure helps provide the answer. It permits the investor to place both the costs and the

APPLICATIONS IN ECONOMICS

Would You Like to Become a Millionaire?

In the previous chapter, we indicated that approximately one out of every 20 American households has assets worth a million dollars or more. The proportion of millionaires among those 55 to 64 years of age is even higher. Many millionaires earned large incomes in business, professional, and other activities, but others achieved this status even though their incomes were not very much different from those of other Americans. They did so through regular saving and investment throughout their lifetime.

How could a person become a millionaire without making a huge income? Saving and compound interest provide the answer. The real rate of return on a broad portfolio of stock has averaged more than 7 percent during the last 200 years. Moreover, stock investments over 35- to 40-year peri- ods have consistently earned a real return in this range. A real return of 7 percent is highly realistic for even a novice investor. Those with more entrepreneurial talent might well do better. If an individual or family began at age 25 paying funds into a tax-free retirement account, pension fund or similar investment earning a 7 percent real return, how much would they have to save annually in order for the funds to be worth a million dollars (measured in the purchasing power of today's dollar) when they reach age 65? The answer is $5,009. Thus, a household with an income of $50,000 (only slightly above the average) during the working years of life could achieve millionaire status if they were willing to save 10 percent of their earnings. A 5 percent savings rate would do the job for a household with $100,000 of income. The power of compound interest illustrates that millionaire status is well within the reach of many Americans willing to save and invest over lengthy periods of time.

expected future revenues of an investment project into present-value terms. If the present value of the revenue derived from the investment exceeds the present value of the cost, it makes sense to undertake the investment. If revenues and costs of such an investment turn out as expected, the investor will reap economic profit. In turn, profitable investments will increase the value of resources, and thereby create wealth.

On the other hand, if the cost of the project exceeds the discounted value of the future receipts, losses will result. The losses indicate that the resources used to undertake the investment would have more value elsewhere. Investments that result in losses reduce the value of resources and thereby diminish wealth. Such investments are counterproductive.

Let's pencil in the figures for a hypothetical investment option and determine whether it is a good investment. Suppose a truck rental firm is contemplating the purchase of a new $40,000 truck. Past experience indicates that after making allowances for operational and maintenance expenses, the firm can rent out the truck for net revenues of $12,000 per year (received at the end of each year) for the next four years, the expected life of the vehicle.[2] Since the firm can borrow and lend funds at an interest rate of 8 percent, we will discount the future expected income at an 8 percent rate. **Exhibit 4** illustrates the calculation. Column 4 shows how much $12,000, available at year-end for each of the next four years, is worth today. In total, the present value of the expected rental receipts is $39,744—less than the purchase price of the truck. Therefore, the project should not be undertaken.

If the interest rate in our example had been 6 percent, the results would have been different. The present value of the future rental income would have been $41,580.[3] Because it pays to purchase a capital good whenever the present value of the income generated ex-

---

[2]For the sake of simplicity, we assume that the truck has no scrap value at the end of four years.

[3]The derivation of this figure is shown in the following tabulation:

Year	Expected Future Income (dollars)	Discounted Value per Dollar (6% rate)	Present Value of Income (dollars)
1	12,000	0.943	11,316
2	12,000	0.890	10,680
3	12,000	0.840	10,080
4	12,000	0.792	9,504
Total			41,500

YEAR (1)	EXPECTED FUTURE INCOME RECEIVED AT YEAR-END (2)	DISCOUNTED VALUE (8 PERCENT RATE) (3)	PRESENT VALUE OF INCOME (4)
1	$12,000	0.926	$11,112
2	12,000	0.857	10,284
3	12,000	0.794	9,528
4	12,000	0.735	8,820
Total			$39,744

EXHIBIT 4
Discounted Present Value of $12,000 of Truck Rental for Four Years (Interest Rate = 8 Percent)

ceeds the purchase price of the capital good, the project would have been productive (and thus profitable) at the lower interest rate. A lower market interest rate indicates that the alternative projects competing for funds are less profitable.

Expected Future Earnings and Asset Values

The present value of the expected revenue minus the cost of an investment reveals whether the project should be undertaken. However, *once an investment project has been completed*, the present value of the expected future net earnings will determine the market value of the asset. If the present value of the expected net earnings rises (or falls), so too will the value of the asset.

The value of an asset is equal to the present value of the expected net revenues that can be earned by the asset. If the asset is expected to generate a constant annual net income each year in the future, its value would be equal to:

$$\text{Asset Value} = \frac{\text{Annual Net Income from the Asset}}{\text{Interest Rate}}$$

What is the market value of a tract of land if it is expected to generate $1,000 of rental income net of costs each year indefinitely into the future? If the market interest rate is 10 percent, investors would be willing to pay $10,000 for the land. When purchased at this price, the land would provide an investor with the 10 percent market rate of return. Correspondingly, if an asset generates $2,500 of net earnings annually and the market interest rate is 10 percent, the asset would be worth $25,000. There is a direct relationship between the expected future earnings generated by an asset and the asset's market value. *As the present value of the future earnings derived from the ownership of an asset increases, so too does the market value of the asset.*

This linkage between expected future earnings and the price of an asset provides a strong incentive for the owners of business assets to make sure that the assets are being used wisely. Some entrepreneurial investors are particularly good at (1) identifying a business that is poorly operated, (2) purchasing the business at a depressed price, (3) improving the operational efficiency of the firm, and then (4) reselling the business at a handsome profit. Suppose that a poorly run business currently has net earnings of $1 million per year. What is the market value of the business? If the firm is expected to continue earning $1 million per year, the market value of the firm would be $10 million if the interest rate is 10 percent. Suppose that an alert entrepreneur buys the business for $10 million, hires new management, and improves the operational efficiency of the firm. As the result of these changes, the annual net earnings of the firm increase to $2 million per year. Now how much is the firm worth? If the $2 million annual earnings are expected to continue into the future, the net present value of the firm would rise to $20 million. Thus, the entrepreneur who improved the performance of the firm would be able to sell the firm for a very substantial profit.

In a competitive environment, there is a strong incentive for business managers and asset owners to use the resources under their control efficiently. If they do not, the value of

The value of this farmland will be seriously reduced by the erosion. As soon as an appraiser can see the erosion and estimate the loss of future income, the present value of the farmland (and its market price) will decline and thereby reduce the wealth of the farm owner.

the assets will decline, and the business will be vulnerable to a takeover by alert entrepreneurs capable of operating the firm more efficiently (and using the assets more profitably).

Investors and Corporate Investments

In modern market economies, investors typically are not entrepreneurs who personally decide which factories to expand, which machine tools to build, and which research investments to undertake. Instead corporate officers, under the scrutiny of corporate boards of directors, make the entrepreneurial capital investment choices. Nevertheless, individual investors (buyers and sellers of stock) influence that process through the stock market itself. Stock market investors who first believe that a corporation is currently making decisions that are likely to increase future profits will buy more of the corporation's stock, driving up its price. Similarly, stockholders who believe that the corporation's current investment decisions will reduce future profits have an incentive to "bail out" by selling their stock holdings, reducing the market value of the stock. Either way, the price of a corporation's stock shares gives corporate officers very fast feedback on how market investors evaluate their decisions.

Do corporate officers respond to stock price changes? Normally they do. Often they own stock and the value of their pay package depends on the stock price. Also, the members of the corporate board (which hires and fires the officers) are typically large shareholders. Thus, the corporate officers have a strong incentive to act on the feedback provided from the stock market. The choices of individual buyers (and nonbuyers) of the firm's products provide the ultimate judgments on business performance. However, the choices of investors and their fund managers provide early returns on the expected success of business ventures.

INVESTING IN HUMAN CAPITAL

In principle, investments in human capital—an individual's choice to continue in school, for example—involve all the ingredients of other investment decisions. And since the returns and some of the costs normally accrue in the future, the discounting procedure is as helpful here as in decisions about physical capital.

Exhibit 5 is a simplified illustration of the human capital decision confronting Juanita, an 18-year-old high school graduate contemplating the pursuit of a bachelor's de-

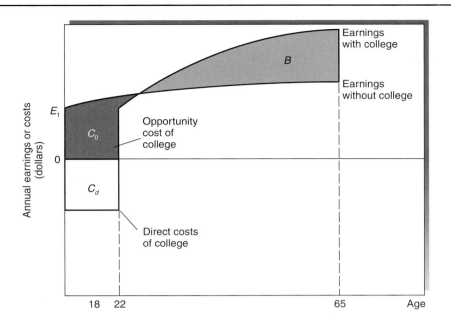

EXHIBIT 5
Investing in Human Capital

Here we provide a simplified illustration of the human capital investment decision confronting Juanita, an 18-year-old who has just finished high school. If Juanita goes to college and majors in business administration, she will incur the direct cost (C_d) of the college education (tuition, books, transportation, and so on) plus the opportunity cost (C_o) of earnings forgone while in college. However, with a business degree, she can expect additions to future earnings (B) during her career. If the discounted present value of the additional future earnings exceeds the discounted value of the direct and indirect costs of a college education, the business degree will be a profitable investment for Juanita.

gree in business administration. Just as an investment in a truck involves a cost in order to generate a future income, so does a degree in business administration. If Juanita does not go to college, she will be able to begin work immediately, starting at annual earnings of E_1. But if she goes to college, she will incur direct costs (C_d) in the form of tuition, books, transportation, and related expenses. She will also bear the opportunity cost (C_o) of lower earnings while in college. However, the study of business will expand Juanita's knowledge and skills, and thereby enable her to earn a higher future stream of income ("Earnings with college" rather than "Earnings without college").

Will the higher future income be worth the cost? To answer this question, Juanita must project her additional income stemming from completion of the business degree, discount each year's additional income, and compare the total with the discounted value of the cost, including the opportunity cost of earnings lost during the period of study. If the discounted present value of the additional future income exceeds the discounted present value of the cost, acquiring the degree is a worthwhile human capital investment.

Of course, nonmonetary considerations may also be important, particularly for human capital investment decisions, since human capital is embodied in the individual. For example, Juanita might prefer working as a college graduate in the business world (rather than in the jobs available to high school graduates) even if she did not make more money. Thus, the nonmonetary attractiveness of business may induce her to pursue the business degree even if the monetary rate of return is low (or even negative).

Although nonmonetary factors are more important in human capital decision making, opportunity cost and the pursuit of profit influence human capital investors just as they do physical capital investors. As with choosing to purchase a new machine, choosing a human capital investment project such as Juanita's degree involves cost, the possibility of profit, and uncertainty. The same principles apply to both types of decisions. Giving due consideration to nonmonetary factors as a potential "benefit," human capital investors, like physical capital investors, seek to undertake only those projects that they anticipate will yield benefits greater than their costs.

UNCERTAINTY, ENTREPRENEURSHIP, AND PROFIT

As we previously discussed, firms and individual investors may be able to earn persistent economic profit—a return in excess of the opportunity cost of funds—if they are able to restrict entry into various industries and occupations. Economic profit, however, may also be present in competitive markets. ***In a competitive market economy, there are two sources of economic profit: uncertainty and entrepreneurship.***

While investment places people in a position to earn a handsome return, it also exposes them to additional uncertainty. We live in a world of uncertainty, imperfect information, and dynamic change. No one knows precisely what will happen in the future. In such a world, investing has elements of a game of chance. Unanticipated changes, changes that no one could have foreseen, create winners and losers. If people did not care whether their income experienced substantial variability or not, the uncertainty accompanying investment projects would not affect the average rate of return. Most people, though, dislike uncertainty. They prefer the certain receipt of $1,000 to a 50-50 chance of receiving either nothing or $2,000. Therefore, people must be paid a premium—an economic profit—if they are going to accept willingly the uncertainty that necessarily accompanies investments. For example, compared to government bonds, the returns to stocks are considerably more uncertain. This uncertainty of return is one reason why stocks have historically yielded a higher average return than bonds.

In a world of imperfect knowledge and foresight, discovery of potential opportunities to combine resources in a manner that increases their value provides a second source of economic profit. Some are better than others at identifying such opportunities. ***At any given time, there is virtually an infinite number of potential investment projects. Some will increase the value of resources and therefore lead to a handsome rate of return on capital. Others will actually reduce the value of resources, generating economic losses. Entrepreneurship involves the ability to recognize and undertake economically beneficial projects that have gone unnoticed by others.*** Originality, quickness to act, and imagination are important aspects of entrepreneurship. Successful entrepreneurship also involves leadership—new buyers must be enticed and financial backers must be convinced to invest. Discovery is vitally important—most profits will be gone by the time the concept is proven and imitators arrive on the scene. Naturally, risk is involved. All too frequently, the entrepreneur's vision turns out to have been a mirage. What appeared to be a profitable opportunity is seen later as an expensive illusion.

The great Harvard economist Joseph Schumpeter believed that entrepreneurship and innovative behavior were the moving forces behind capitalism. According to Schumpeter, this entrepreneurial discovery of new, improved ways of doing things is a central engine of economic progress and improvements in living standards. As Schumpeter put it,

> The fundamental impulse that sets the capitalist engine in motion comes from the new consumer's goods, the new methods of production or transportation, and new markets, and the new forms of industrial organization that capitalist enterprise creates.[4]

Potential entrepreneurs are confined to using their own wealth and that of co-venturers, in addition to whatever can be borrowed. Entrepreneurs with a past record of success will be able to attract funds more readily for investment projects. Therefore, in a market economy, previously successful entrepreneurs will exert a disproportionate influence over decisions as to which projects will be undertaken and which will not.

---

[4]Joseph A. Schumpeter, *Capitalism, Socialism, and Democracy* (New York: Harper Torchbooks, 1950), p. 83.

Joseph Schumpeter (1883–1950)

Born in Austria, Schumpeter was a longtime professor of economics at Harvard University. Generally recognized as one of the top five economists of this century, he is perhaps best known for his views on entrepreneurship and the future of capitalism. He believed that the creative and innovative behavior of business entrepreneurs was the primary fuel of economic progress.

Returns to Physical and Human Capital

Both interest and profit perform important allocative functions. Interest induces people to give up current consumption, a sacrifice that is a necessary ingredient for capital formation. Economic profit provides both human and physical capital decision makers with the incentive to (1) undertake investments yielding an uncertain return and (2) discover and undertake beneficial (wealth-creating) investment opportunities.

Income reflects returns to both human capital and physical capital. As **Exhibit 6** shows, approximately four-fifths of the national income in the United States is earned by employees and self-employed workers. The earnings in these two categories primarily reflect a return to human capital. The other one-fifth—income in the form of interest, corporate profits, and rents—reflects mostly returns to physical capital.[5] These shares to human and physical capital have been relatively constant for several decades.

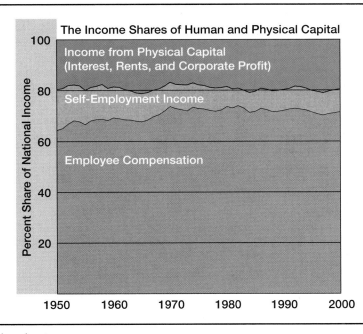

EXHIBIT 6
The Income Shares of Human and Physical Capital

The share of national income earned by employees, self-employed proprietors, and owners of physical capital (interest, corporate profits, and rents) is shown here. Employee compensation and self-employment income represent primarily returns to human capital. These two components have comprised approximately 80 percent of total national income in the United States for several decades.

Source: www.bea.doc.gov.

[5]As used here, rent is income derived by owners who lease (rent) assets like buildings and equipment to another party for a period of time.

THE CAPITAL MARKET AND THE WEALTH OF NATIONS

Innovation and the Capital Market

 If the potential gains from innovative ideas and human ingenuity are going to be fully realized, it must be relatively easy for individuals to try their innovative and potentially ingenious ideas, but difficult to continue if the idea is a bad one.

Knowledge about how to transform resources into desired goods and services is the major reason why we are able to produce a far greater output than our ancestors of a century or two ago. Predictably, improvements in and innovative applications of knowledge will propel future growth and prosperity. The human ingenuity and entrepreneurial talent capable of pushing the frontier of economic progress outward are widely dispersed and often come from unexpected sources. Numerous examples illustrate this point. A college dropout (Ted Turner, founder of CNN), transformed the way people around the world received news during the last two decades of the twentieth century. A relatively unsuccessful marketer of milk shake machines (Ray Kroc) perfected the franchising business and developed McDonalds into the world's largest restaurant chain. A plainspoken owner of a small retail store in one of the poorest states (Sam Walton, founder of Wal-Mart) became America's largest retailer.

It is impossible to determine who will come up with an innovative idea that will promote human progress. This makes it vitally important that individuals from all backgrounds and walks of life are able to try out their ideas at a relatively low cost. Of course, counterproductive projects can waste substantial amounts of resources. Thus, if a nation is going to get the most out of its resources, it must also have a mechanism that will bring unsound projects to a halt.

Competitive capital markets perform these two functions. In a market economy, it is relatively easy to try out a new idea. Entrepreneurs do not have to convince a majority of the populace or key political leaders that their idea is sound. They can undertake the project if they can obtain the required financing. This can be achieved by either putting up one's own money or convincing investors and other potential financiers, including banks and bond purchasers, that the project's profit potential merits the required financial support. Once the project is undertaken, in order to continue, it will have to pass the market test. If the revenues derived from sale of the output are insufficient to cover the cost, it will be difficult to keep the project afloat. Losses will soon drive unprofitable business ventures from the market. Conversely, if a project is profitable, this will encourage operation at a larger scale.

The capital market brings together people who are willing to save with those willing to invest. It is a highly diverse market that includes the markets for stocks, real estate, businesses, and loanable funds. Mutual funds, banks and brokerage firms help organize transactions in this market. The modern capital market accommodates people with widely varying preferences and goals. It allows individuals with widely differing time horizons to gain nonetheless from trading with one another. For example, a person wanting to save for retirement that will begin only 10 years from now may nonetheless be willing to buy a new 20-year bond from General Motors or some other private firm, because the bond market makes it relatively easy to sell the bond to another if the bondholder desires to do so. Varying preferences for risk are also accommodated. Some people want to supply savings in exchange for a fixed rate of return. People who purchase bonds and maintain savings deposits are examples. Others are willing to supply funds in exchange for an uncertain return linked to the success or failure of a business or investment project. Stockholders and partnership investors fall into this category. Still others supply funds to the capital market when they use their own funds to purchase a business or acquire additional schooling.

Private investors, ranging from small business owners to corporate stockholders to venture capitalists, place their own funds at risk in the capital market. This provides them with a strong incentive to search for, discover, and undertake profitable projects. A project will be profitable if the revenues derived from the output are greater than the cost of the investment. Revenues that exceed cost are strong evidence that people value the output produced more than the resources utilized. Thus, profitable investments tend to increase not only the wealth of the investor, but also the wealth of the nation.

In an uncertain world, of course, mistakes will occur. Sometimes projects will be undertaken that prove unprofitable. If investors were unwilling to take chances, many innovative ideas and worthwhile but risky projects would never be tested. In a world of uncertainty, mistaken investments are a necessary price that must be paid for fruitful innovations in new technologies and products. The capital market will at least assure that the mistakes are self-correcting. Unexpected losses will signal investors to terminate unprofitable and unproductive projects, and investors whose own wealth is at stake will be very sensitive to such signals.

Summarizing, the capital market will tend to direct savings toward entrepreneurial activities that are profitable. When property rights are clearly defined and enforced, profitable projects will also be productive—they will create wealth. *Properly guided investment in both physical and human capital is an important source of productivity and income growth.* **Other things constant, countries that invest more and channel more of their investments into productive projects today will tend to have a higher income tomorrow.**

Without a private capital market, it is hard to see how investment funds could be consistently channeled into wealth-creating projects. In today's dynamic world, economic growth is driven by discovery and innovation. Given the pace of dynamic change and the diversity of entrepreneurial talent capable of contributing to economic progress, the knowledge required for sound decision making about the allocation of capital is far beyond the scope of any gifted leader, industrial planning committee, or government agency. Perhaps even more important, when investment funds are allocated by the government rather than by the market, an entirely different set of criteria comes into play. The individual voter, unlike a partner or an owner of stock, has little incentive to be alert for new opportunities or wary of mistaken investments undertaken by government officials. Furthermore, the citizen-voter can neither (1) invest more upon discovery of an attractive project nor (2) opt out (sell) when problems are detected. Thus, voters are in a weak position to monitor and direct government investment effectively. Most simply remain on the sidelines. As they do so, the political clout of special interests replaces market return as the basis for allocating funds. Predictably, investment projects that reduce wealth rather than enhance it become more likely.

The experience of Eastern Europe and the former Soviet Union provides a vivid illustration of what happens when political factors replace economic considerations in the allocation of investment. The investment rates of these countries were among the highest in the world. Their central planners channeled approximately one-third of the national output into capital formation. Even these high rates of investment did little to improve living standards. Government planners and state enterprises were slow to incorporate scientific breakthroughs. Available consumer goods generally reflected outdated technologies. Funds were often wasted on political boondoggles and high-visibility projects favored by important political leaders. Misdirection of investment and failure to keep up with dynamic change eventually led to the collapse of the system.

As the preceding two chapters have stressed, investment in physical and human capital will influence the wealth and income of both individuals and nations. Differences among individuals in these factors will also contribute to income inequality. In the next chapter, we will consider the issue of income inequality in some detail.

LOOKING AHEAD

KEY POINTS

▼ We can often produce more consumption goods by first using our resources to produce physical and human capital resources and then using these capital resources to produce the desired consumption goods. Because resources used to produce capital goods will be unavailable for the direct production of consumption goods, saving is necessary for investment.

▼ People have a positive rate of time preference; they generally value present consumption more highly than future consumption.

▼ The interest rate is the price of earlier availability. It is the premium that borrowers must pay to lenders to acquire goods now rather than later.

▼ Interest rewards lenders who curtail current consumption and supply loanable funds in the market. The demand for loanable funds by investors stems from the productivity of capital resources and the demand by consumers stems from the positive rate of time preference. The market interest rate will bring the quantity of funds demanded by borrowers into balance with the quantity supplied by lenders.

▼ During inflationary times, the money rate of interest incorporates an inflationary premium reflecting the expected future increase in the price level. When inflation is expected, the money rate of interest exceeds the real rate of interest.

▼ The money rate of interest on a specific loan reflects three basic factors—the pure interest rate, an inflationary premium, and a risk premium that is directly related to the probability of default by the borrower.

▼ The interest rate allows individuals to place a current valuation on future revenues and costs. The discounting procedure can be used to calculate the present value of an expected net income stream from a potential investment project. If the present value of the expected revenues exceeds the present value of the expected costs—and if things turn out as expected—the project will be profitable.

▼ The present value of expected future net earnings will determine the market value of existing assets. An increase (decline) in the expected future earnings derived from an asset will increase (reduce) the market value of the asset.

▼ Economic profit plays a central role in the allocation of capital and the determination of which investment projects will be undertaken. In a competitive environment, economic profit reflects uncertainty and entrepreneurship—the ability to recognize and undertake profitable projects that have gone unnoticed by others.

▼ To grow and prosper, a nation must have a mechanism that will attract savings and channel them into investments that create wealth. The capital market performs this function in a market economy. When property rights are clearly defined and enforced, profits and losses will channel investment into projects that promote economic progress.

CRITICAL ANALYSIS QUESTIONS

*1. How would the following changes influence the rate of interest in the United States?
   a. An increase in the positive time preference of lenders
   b. An increase in the positive time preference of borrowers
   c. An increase in domestic inflation
   d. Increased uncertainty about a nuclear war
   e. Improved investment opportunities in Europe

2. "Any return to capital above the pure interest yield is unnecessary. The pure interest yield is sufficient to provide capitalists with the earnings necessary to replace their assets and to compensate for their sacrifice of current consumption. Any return above that is pure gravy; it is excess profit." Do you agree with this view? Why or why not?

3. How are human and physical capital investment decisions similar? How do they differ? What determines the profitability of a physical capital investment? Do human capital investors make profits? If so, what is the source of the profit? Explain.

*4. A lender made the following statement to a borrower: "You are borrowing $1,000, which is to be repaid in 12 monthly installments of $100 each. Your total interest charge is $200, which means your interest rate is 20 percent." Is the effective interest rate on the loan really 20 percent? Explain.

5. In a market economy, investors have a strong incentive to undertake profitable investments. What makes an investment profitable? Do profitable investments create wealth? Why or why not? Do all investments create wealth? Discuss.

*6. Over long periods of time, the rate of return of an average investment in the stock market has exceeded the return on high-quality bonds. Is the higher return on stocks surprising? Why or why not?

7. The interest rates charged on outstanding credit card balances are generally higher than the interest rate that banks charge customers with a good credit rating. Why do you think the credit card rate is so high? Should the government impose an interest rate ceiling of, say, 10 percent? If it did, who would be hurt and who would be helped? Discuss.

*8. If the money rate of interest on a low-risk government bond is 10 percent and the inflation rate for the last several years has been steady at 4 percent, what is the estimated real rate of interest?

9. Suppose you are contemplating the purchase of a commercial lawn mower at a cost of $10,000. The expected lifetime of the machine is three years. You can lease the asset to a local business for $4,000 annually (payable at the end of each year) for three years. The lessee is responsible for the upkeep and maintenance of the machine during the three-year period. If you can borrow (and lend) money at an interest rate of 8 percent, will the investment be a profitable undertaking? Is the project profitable at an interest rate of 12 percent? Provide calculations in support of your answer.

*10. Alicia's philosophy of life is summed up by the proverb, "A penny saved is a penny earned." She plans and saves for the future. In contrast, Mike's view is "Life is uncertain; eat dessert first." Mike wants as much as possible now.
   a. Who has the highest rate of time preference?
   b. Do people like Alicia benefit from the presence of people like Mike?
   c. Do people like Mike benefit from the presence of people like Alicia? Explain.

*11. Some countries with very low incomes per capita are unable to save very much. Are people in these countries helped or hurt by people in high-income countries with much higher rates of saving?

*12. According to a news item, the owner of a lottery ticket paying $3 million over 20 years is offering to sell the ticket for $1.2 million cash now. "Who knows?" the ticket owner explained. "We might not even be here in 20 years, and I do not want to leave it to the dinosaurs."
   a. If the ticket pays $150,000 per year at the end of each year for the next 20 years, what is the present value of the ticket when the appropriate rate for discounting the future income is thought to be 10 percent?
   b. If the discount rate is in the 10 percent range, is the sale price of $1.2 million reasonable?
   c. Can you think of any disadvantages of buying the lottery earnings rather than a bond?

13. Suppose that you are moving into a new apartment that you expect to rent for five years. The owner offers to provide you with a used refrigerator for free and promises to maintain and repair the refrigerator during the next five years. You also have the option of buying a new energy-efficient refrigerator (with a five-year free maintenance agreement) for $700. The new refrigerator will reduce your electric bill by $150 per year and will have a market value of $200 after five years. If necessary, you can borrow money from the bank at an 8 percent rate of interest. Which option should you choose?

*14. Suppose that you are considering whether to enroll in a summer computer training program that costs $2,500. If you take the program, you will have to give up $1,500 of earnings from your summer job. You figure that the program will increase your earnings by $500 per year for each of the next 10 years. Beyond that, it is not expected to affect your earnings. If you take the program, you will have to borrow the funds at an 8 percent rate of interest. From a strictly monetary viewpoint, should you enroll in the program?

15. Are political officials more sensitive to the general welfare of people than business entrepreneurs? Are politicians less greedy than business decision makers? When political officials make investment decisions, what factors will influence their choices? How will this influence economic efficiency?

*16. Will political officials be more likely to channel funds into wealth-creating projects than private investors and entrepreneurs? Why or why not? Discuss.

---

*Asterisk denotes questions for which answers appear in Appendix B.

CHAPTER 27

All animals are equal, but some animals are more equal than others.

—George Orwell[1]

Income Inequality and Poverty

Chapter Focus

- How do resource prices and income differences influence the incentive of people to develop resources and use them productively?

- How much income inequality is there in the United States? Has the degree of inequality changed in recent years?

- How much income mobility exists—do the rich remain rich while the poor remain poor?

- How widespread is poverty? How has the poverty rate changed in recent decades? Did the War on Poverty help reduce the poverty rate?

- Is there too much income inequality? Should the government try to reduce inequality? Why or why not?

---

[1]George Orwell, *Animal Farm* (New York: Harcourt and Brace Company, 1946), p. 112.

Differences in resource prices and the productivity of individuals will cause market incomes to vary. Of course, economic inequality is present in all societies. Substituting politics and central planning for markets does not eliminate inequality. Nonetheless, most of us are troubled by the extremes of inequality—extravagant luxury on the one hand and grinding poverty on the other. How much inequality is there in the United States? Do the same families continually enjoy high incomes, while those in poverty are unable to escape that condition? What impact have income transfer programs had on the welfare of the poor? This chapter focuses on these questions and related issues. ■

PRICES, INCOMES, AND THE AVAILABILITY OF RESOURCES

In a market economy, individuals receive income from selling their resources, such as their labor, at market-determined prices. People differ with regard to their productive abilities, opportunities, preferences, and intestinal fortitude. Some will be able to hit a baseball, perform a rock concert, design a computer, or operate a restaurant so effectively that people will pay millions to consume the product or service that they supply. There will be others with disabilities and/or few skills who may be unable even to support themselves. Thus, incomes vary substantially.

Resource prices reflect both productivity and scarcity. Furthermore, the availability of resources is influenced by their prices—that is, the incomes derived by suppliers. Market participants prosper by supplying resources that are highly valued *by others*. After all, the price at which you can sell a productive resource or service depends on how much others are willing to pay for it. Individuals who supply large amounts of physical and human resources highly valued by others will earn large incomes. The close link between personal prosperity and provision of productive resources provides individuals with a strong incentive to develop those skills, talents, and resources that others value highly relative to their cost.[2]

A market economy does not have a central distributing agency that carves up the economic pie and allocates slices to various individuals. In fact, this fallacious view—the idea that there is a fixed-size economic pie to be divided among individuals—reflects a misunderstanding of the nature of income. Income is created when individuals supply productive resources to others. In turn, the amount of income individuals create is influenced by the incentive structure that they confront. Individuals are motivated to create income precisely because it enhances their personal welfare and that of those about whom they care. When the link between work effort and reward is weakened, individuals have less incentive to create income. Taxes and transfers that alter incomes also alter the incentive to supply scarce resources and thereby expand the size of the economic pie. Therefore, while focusing on the distribution of income and the impact of taxes and transfers, we must not forget the role that differences in resource prices and incomes play in the allocation of resources.

INCOME INEQUALITY IN THE UNITED STATES

Money income is only one component of economic well-being. Such factors as leisure, noncash transfer benefits, the nonpecuniary advantages and disadvantages of a job, and the expected stability of future income are also determinants of economic welfare. Money

---

[2]Adam Smith makes this point in a very famous passage:

> *Every individual is continually exerting himself to find out the most advantageous employment for whatever capital [and other resources] he can command. It is his own advantage, indeed, and not that of the society which he has in view. But the study of his own advantage naturally, or rather necessarily, leads him to prefer that employment which is most advantageous to society. . . . He intends only his own gain, and he is in this, as in many other cases, led by an invisible hand [competitive markets] to promote an end which was not part of his intention.*

See Smith, *An Inquiry into the Nature and Causes of the Wealth of Nations* (New York: Modern Library, 1937), p. 423.

EXHIBIT 1
Share of Money Income by Quintile During Selected Years, 1950–2000

	LOWEST 20 PERCENT OF RECIPIENTS	SECOND QUINTILE	THIRD QUINTILE	FOURTH QUINTILE	TOP 20 PERCENT OF RECIPIENTS
FAMILY INCOME BEFORE TAXES					
1950	4.5	12.0	17.4	23.4	42.7
1960	4.8	12.2	17.8	24.0	41.3
1970	5.4	12.2	17.6	23.8	40.9
1980	5.1	11.6	17.5	24.3	41.6
1990	4.6	10.8	16.6	23.8	44.3
2000	4.3	9.8	15.5	22.8	47.4
IMPACT OF TAXES AND TRANSFERS ON 2000 HOUSEHOLD INCOME					
Before	3.7	9.0	14.8	23.0	49.5
After	4.6	10.3	15.7	22.7	46.7
HOUSEHOLD EXPENDITURES					
1961	7.1	13.2	18.2	24.1	37.4
1972	7.1	12.9	18.0	23.9	38.1
1980	6.8	12.8	18.1	24.1	38.2
1990	7.1	12.4	17.1	23.3	40.1
1995	7.4	12.9	17.5	23.4	38.8

Source: Bureau of the Census, *Current Population Survey,* Series P-60; *Statistical Abstract of the United States, 1995,* Table 733; Congressional Budget Office; 1994, *Green Book;* Bureau of the Census, *Money Income in the United States: 2000;* and Daniel T. Slesnick, *Consumption and Social Welfare: Living Standards and Their Distribution in the United States* (Cambridge: Cambridge University Press, 2001).

income is quite important, however, because it represents command over market goods and services. Moreover, it is readily observable. Consequently, it is the most widely used measure of economic well-being and of the degree of inequality prevailing in society.

Exhibit 1 presents data on money income in the United States. First, consider the data on the share of *before-tax* annual money income by quintile—that is, each fifth of families—ranked from the lowest to the highest. If there were total equality of family annual income, each quintile (20 percent) of families would generate 20 percent of the aggregate income. Given differences in education, skill, ability, work effort, age, family size, and numerous other factors, clearly we would not expect this to be the case. Due to these differences, some families will be able to generate—and thus receive—more income than others. It is, however, informative to observe the shares of income by quintile.

The data indicate that a reduction in before-tax income inequality occurred throughout the 1950s and 1960s. In 1970 the top quintile earned 40.9 percent of the aggregate money income, down from 42.7 percent in 1950. During the same period, the share of income earned by the lowest quintile rose from 4.5 percent in 1950 to 5.4 percent in 1970. Thus, between 1950 and 1970, the income share earned by the top quintile of families declined, while that earned by the bottom quintile rose. Beginning in the 1970s, this trend reversed. During the last two decades, the share of income earned by the top quintile has steadily risen, while that earned by the bottom group has fallen.[3] By 2000, the share of before-tax money income of the top group had risen to 47.4 percent, while that earned by the bottom 20 percent of families had fallen to 4.3 percent of the total. Thus, the top quintile of families earned approximately 11 times as much before-tax money income as the bottom quintile of families in 2000.

[3]A reduction in the share of income earned by the bottom quintile income group does not imply that their income level fell. It merely indicates that their income did not grow as rapidly as that of other groups, particularly the top quintile. In fact, the inflation-adjusted income of the bottom quintile of earners increased during the last two decades.

Low-income families are the primary beneficiaries of noncash transfer programs that provide people with food (food stamps), health care, and housing. Correspondingly, under a system of progressive taxation, taxes take a larger share of income as one's income increases. Therefore, one would expect *after-tax and transfer* income to be less unequal than before-tax income. Exhibit 1 presents data on the distribution of income for households both before and after taxes and transfers. After taxes and transfers, the bottom quintile of households received 4.6 percent of the total income in 2000 (compared to 3.7 percent of the before-tax income). At the same time, the after-tax and transfer share of the top quintile of families was 46.7 percent in 2000 (compared to 49.5 percent before taxes). Taking into account taxes and transfers increases the income share of every quintile except the top two groups. Thus, taxes and transfers do in fact reduce income inequality. [*Note:* Household income is used here because parallel family income data are unavailable. In addition to families, households include individuals living by themselves and unrelated persons living together.]

A Closer Look at Factors Influencing Income Distribution

How meaningful are the data of Exhibit 1? If all families were similar except in the amount of income earned, the use of annual income data as an index of inequality would be quite reasonable. However, the fact is that the aggregate data lump together (1) small and large families, (2) prime-age earners and elderly retirees, (3) multi-earner families and families without any current earners, and (4) husband-wife families and single-parent families.

Consider just one factor: the impact of age and the pattern of lifetime income. Typically, the annual income of young people is low, particularly if they are going to school or are acquiring training. Many persons under 25 years of age studying to be lawyers, doctors, engineers, and economists will have a low annual income during this phase of their life. But this does not mean they are poor, at least not in the usual sense. After completing their formal education and acquiring work experience, such individuals move into their prime working years, when annual income is generally quite high, particularly for families where both husband and wife work. Remember, though, that this is also a time when families are purchasing houses and providing for children. Consequently, all things considered, annual income during the prime working years may overstate the economic well-being of most households. Finally, there is the retirement phase, characterized by less work, more leisure, and smaller family size. Even families who are quite well-off tend to experience income well below the average for the entire population during the retirement phase. *Given the life cycle of income, lumping together families of different ages (phases of their life-cycle earnings) results in substantial inequality in the annual income figures even if incomes over a lifetime were approximately equal.*

Exhibit 2 highlights major differences between high- and low-income families that underlie the distributional data of Exhibit 1. The typical high-income family (top 20 percent) is headed by a well-educated person in the prime working-age phase of life whose income is supplemented with the earnings of other family members, particularly working spouses. In contrast, persons with little education, nonworking retirees, younger workers (under age 35), and single-parent families are substantially overrepresented among low-income families (bottom 20 percent of income recipients). In 2000, 34 percent of the householders in the lowest income quintile failed to complete high school, compared to only 3 percent for the highest income quintile. While only 8 percent of the household heads in the bottom quintile completed college, 58 percent of the householders in the top group did so. Seventy-nine percent of the high-income families had household heads in the prime working-age category (age 35 to 64), compared with only 44 percent of the low-income families. Only one parent was present in 49 percent of the low-income families, whereas 94 percent of the high-income group were husband-wife families. Contrary to the views of some, high-income families are larger than low-income families. In 2000 there were 3.4 persons per family in the top income quintile, compared to only 2.9 family members among the bottom quintile of income recipients.

EXHIBIT 2
Differing Characteristics of High- and Low-income Families, 2001

	BOTTOM 20 PERCENT OF INCOME RECIPIENTS	TOP 20 PERCENT OF INCOME RECIPIENTS
EDUCATION OF HOUSEHOLDER		
Percent with less than high school	34	3
Percent with college degree or more	8	58
AGE OF HOUSEHOLDER (PERCENT DISTRIBUTION)		
Under 35	31	13
35–64	44	79
65 and over	25	8
FAMILY STATUS		
Married-couple family (percent of total)	51	94
Single-parent family (percent of total)	49	6
PERSONS PER FAMILY	2.9	3.4
EARNERS PER FAMILY	0.84	2.2
Percent of married-couple families in which wife works full time	13	63
PERCENT OF TOTAL HOURS WORKED SUPPLIED BY GROUP	9	26

Source: U.S. Department of Commerce, *Money Income in the United States: 2000* (Washington, D.C.: Government Printing Office, 2001).

There was a striking difference in the work time between low- and high-income families. No doubt, much of this difference reflected such factors as family size, age, working spouses, and the incidence of husband-wife families. In high-income families, the average number of workers per family was 2.2, compared with 0.84 for low-income families. Among married couple families, a wife working full time was present only 13 percent of the time in low-income families, compared to 63 percent of the time among the top income group. As we would expect, couples who decide not to have the wife work full-time pay for this choice by falling down the income distribution.

In terms of their work effort supplied to the economy, the top 20 percent of income recipients contributed 26 percent of the total number of hours worked, while the low-income group contributed only 9 percent of the total work time. Thus, high-income families worked 2.9 times as many hours as low-income families and earned approximately 11 times as much before-tax income. This implies that the earnings per hour worked by the top income recipients were only about 3.8 times the earnings per hour worked by the low-income recipients. Clearly, differences in the amount of time worked were a major factor contributing to the income inequality of Exhibit 1.

In summary, Exhibit 2 sheds substantial light on the distributional data of Exhibit 1. *Those with high incomes are far more likely to be well-educated, husband-wife families with dual earners in their prime working years. In contrast, those with low incomes are often single-parent families headed by a poorly educated adult who is either youthful or elderly. The household heads of those families with little income are often either out of the labor force or working only part-time.* Given these factors, it is not surprising that the top 20 percent of recipients have substantially higher incomes, both before and after taxes, than the bottom quintile of family income recipients.[4]

[4]For additional information on income inequality, see: Frank Levy and Richard J. Murnane, "U.S. Earnings Levels and Earnings Inequality: A Review of Recent Trends and Proposed Explanations," *Journal of Economic Literature* (September 1992): 1333–1381; Symposium on "Wage Inequality," *Journal of Economic Perspectives* (spring 1997); and *Economic Report of the President, 1997* (Washington, DC: U.S. Government Printing Office, 1997), Chapter 5.

Why Has Income Inequality Increased?

Exhibit 1 indicates that there has been an increase in income inequality in the United States during the last couple of decades. Why has the gap between the rich and the poor been growing? The answer to this question is a point of controversy among social scientists. Research in this area, however, indicates that at least four factors contributed substantially to the recent shift toward greater inequality.

1. *The increasing proportion of single-parent and dual-earner families has contributed to the increase in the inequality of family income.*

The nature of the family and the allocation of work responsibilities within the family have changed dramatically in recent decades. In 2000 more than one-fourth (27 percent) of all families with children were headed by a single parent, double the figure of the mid-1960s. At the same time, the labor force participation rate of married women increased from 40 percent in 1970 to 61 percent in 2000.

By way of comparison with the late 1960s and early 1970s, we now have both more single-parent families and more dual-earner families. Both of these changes tend to promote income inequality. Perhaps an example will illustrate why. Consider two hypothetical families, the Smiths and the Browns. In 1970 both were middle-income families with two children and one market worker earning $35,000 (in 2002 dollars). Now consider their 2002 counterparts. The Smiths of 2002 are divorced and one of them, probably Mrs. Smith, is trying to work part-time and take care of the two children. The probability is very high that the single-parent Smith family of 2002 will be in the low- rather than the middle-income category. The Smiths may well be in the bottom quintile of the income distribution. In contrast, the Browns of 2002 both work outside the home, and each earns $35,000 annually. Given their dual incomes, the Browns are now a high- rather than a middle-income family. Along with many other dual-income families (see Exhibit 2), the Browns' 2002 family income will probably place them in the top quintile of income recipients.

Even if there were no changes in earnings between skilled and less-skilled workers, the recent changes within the family would enhance income inequality among families and households. More single-parent families like the Smiths increase the number of families with low incomes, while more dual-earner families like the Browns increase the number of high-income families. Both will promote income inequality.

2. *Earnings differentials between skilled and less-skilled workers have increased in recent years, further magnifying income inequality.*

In 1970, workers with little education who were willing to work hard, often in a hot and sweaty environment, were able to command high wages. This is less true today. Throughout the 1950s and 1960s, guidance counselors told high school students that a college education was essential for economic success. For a long time, it appeared that they were wrong. In 1974 the annual earnings of men who graduated from college were only 27 percent higher than the earnings of male high school graduates, hardly a huge payoff for the time and cost of a college degree. Since 1974, however, things have changed dramatically. By the mid-1980s, the earnings premium of male college graduates relative to male high school grads had risen to the 50–60 percent range, approximately twice the premium of 1974. By 1999, the income premium of male college graduates relative to high school graduates had risen to 76 percent. Similarly, the earnings of women college graduates have increased sharply during the last two decades relative to women with only a high school education.

Why have the earnings of persons with more education (and skill) risen relative to those with less education (and skill)? Deregulation of the transport industry and the waning power of unions may have reduced the number of high-wage, blue-collar jobs available to workers with little education. International competition has also played a role. As we mentioned earlier, the international trade sector has grown substantially during the last two decades. Increasingly, American workers compete in a global economy. Furthermore, innovations and cost reductions in both communications and transportation provide firms with greater flexibility with regard to location. Firms producing goods that require substantial amounts of low-skill labor are now better able to move to such places as Korea, Taiwan, and Mexico, where low-skill labor is cheaper. In contrast, the United States is more attractive than most other countries to firms requiring substantial amounts of high-skill, well-educated workers. Thus, globalization tends to reduce the demand for American workers with few skills and little education, while increasing the demand for high-skill workers with college degrees. This widens earnings differentials and increases earnings inequality in high-income countries like the United States. (However, it is worth noting that this process enhances income levels in low-income countries and thereby reduces *worldwide* income inequality.[5])

3. Reductions in communication and transportation costs may have increased the number of markets characterized by a few people at the top with very high earnings.

As we discussed in the chapter on wage differentials, the market compensation of star entertainers and athletes, the most talented professionals, and top business executives is often like that of winner-take-all tournaments. At any point in time, a few people at the top command huge earnings, while most others in these areas have modest or even low incomes. As transport and communication costs have declined, markets have increasingly become national and even global, rather than local. This increases the incomes of a few people at the top, but it also increases the degree of income inequality.

4. The reported incomes of high-income Americans increased sharply because of changes in the tax code.

Prior to 1981, high-income Americans confronted top marginal tax rates of up to 70 percent (50 percent on earnings). Such high marginal tax rates encouraged high-income earners to undertake investments and structure their business affairs in a manner that sheltered much of their income from the Internal Revenue Service. As we indicated in Chapter 4 (see Exhibit 12 of that chapter), the taxable incomes of the top 10 percent of earners expanded sharply when the top marginal tax rates were reduced to the 30 percent range during the 1980s. Some of this increase in income reflected greater work effort due to the increased incentive to earn. Much of it, however, merely reflected a reduction in tax shelter activities in response to the lower marginal tax rates. The flip side of the reduction in tax shelter activities accompanying the lower marginal tax rates of the 1980s was an increase in the visible income of the rich. To the extent this factor contributed to the increase in the measured income of wealthy Americans, the increase in income inequality was more imaginary than real.

INCOME MOBILITY AND INEQUALITY IN ECONOMIC STATUS

Income mobility
Movement of individuals and families either up or down income-distribution rankings when comparisons are made at two different points in time. When substantial income mobility is present, one's current position will not be a very good indicator of what one's position will be a few years in the future.

Statistics on the distribution of annual income fail to reveal **income mobility**—the degree of movement across income groupings—and thus they may be misleading. Consider two countries with identical distributions of annual income. In both cases, the annual income of the top quintile of income recipients is ten times greater than that of the bottom quintile. Now, suppose that in the first country—we will refer to it as Static—the same people are at the top of the income distribution, year after year. Similarly, the poor people of Static remain poor year after year. Static is characterized by an absence of income mobility. In contrast, earners in the second country, which we will call Dynamic, are constantly

---

[5]For additional information on the relationship between international trade and income inequality, see Gary Burtless, "International Trade and the Rise in Earnings Inequality," *Journal of Economic Literature* (June 1995): 800–816; and Symposium on "Income Inequality and Trade," *Journal of Economic Perspectives* (summer 1995).

EXHIBIT 3
Income Mobility—Income Ranking, 1985 and 1995

INCOME STATUS OF INDIVIDUAL, 1985	PERCENTAGE DISTRIBUTION BY INCOME STATUS OF INDIVIDUAL IN 1995				
	TOP-PAID QUINTILE	NEXT-HIGHEST-PAID QUINTILE	MIDDLE QUINTILE	NEXT-LOWEST-PAID QUINTILE	LOWEST-PAID QUINTILE
Top-Paid Quintile	78.4	10.6	6.8	0.1	4.1
Next-Highest-Paid Quintile	42.4	23.9	24.8	4.9	4.0
Middle Quintile	13.4	17.5	45.6	14.4	9.1
Next-Lowest-Paid Quintile	6.2	8.2	37.9	28.6	19.1
Lowest-Paid Quintile	7.8	7.9	12.6	25.4	46.3

Sources: Mary C. Daly and Greg J. Duncan, *Earnings Mobility and Instability, 1969–1995,* Federal Reserve Bank of San Francisco Working Paper 97-06, September 1997.

changing places. Indeed, during every five-year period, each family spends one year in the upper-income quintile, one year in each of the three middle-income quintiles, and one year in the bottom-income quintile. In Dynamic, no one is rich for more than one year (out of each five), and no one is poor for more than a year. Obviously, the nature of economic inequality in Static is vastly different from that in Dynamic. You would not know it, though, by looking at their identical annual income distributions.

The contrast between Static and Dynamic indicates why it is important to consider income mobility when addressing the issue of economic inequality. Until recently, detailed data on income mobility were sparse. This is now beginning to change.[6] **Exhibit 3** presents data on the mobility of individual income between 1985 and 1995. These data compare the relative income positions of the *same individuals* at two different points in time. Based on their 1985 income, each individual was placed into income quintiles ranked from highest to lowest. Later, the 1995 real-income level of the *same individuals* was used to group once again the income of each by quintiles.[7] The first row of Exhibit 3 indicates the relative income position in 1995 of the individuals that were in the top quintile of income recipients in 1985. Approximately four-fifths (78 percent) of those with incomes in the top quintile in 1985 were able to maintain this lofty position 10 years later. Slightly more than one-fifth (22 percent) of the top earners in 1985 had fallen to a lower income quintile by 1995. However, less than one in 20 of the high-income individuals fell to one of the bottom two quintiles of the 1995 income distribution. This suggests that once individuals are able to achieve high-income status, dramatic reductions that push them back to a low level of income are rare.

The bottom row of Exhibit 3 tracks the experience of those in the lowest-income quintile in 1985. Less than half (46.3 percent) of the individuals in the lowest-income quintile remained there in 1995. More than one-quarter (28.3 percent) moved up to one of the top three income quintiles in 1995. Among those in the next-to-lowest income quintile in 1985, more than one-half (52.3 percent) had moved up to a higher-income grouping by 1995.

---

[6]For a review of the literature on income mobility, see Isabel V. Sawhill and Daniel P. McMurrer, *Income Mobility in the United States* (Washington, DC: Urban Institute, 1996). For an early classic work on this topic, see Greg J. Duncan et al., *Years of Poverty, Years of Plenty: The Changing Fortunes of American Workers and Families* (Ann Arbor: Institute for Social Research, University of Michigan, 1984).

[7]The sample includes males aged 25 to 44 with wage and salary earnings in 1985 and who worked more than 250 hours in that year. The 1995 quintile income breakpoints are the 1985 quintile income breakpoints inflated to the 1995 price level using the CPI. As a result, more than 20 percent of the sample may appear in any given 1995 income quintile. Other studies focus on relative income mobility, which defines the 1995 quintile income breakpoints as those which group 20 percent of the sample into each quintile based on the individual's 1995 income. This measure also shows considerable income mobility.

The income mobility data highlight a point that is concealed by the annual figures: There is considerable movement up and down the economic ladder. Relative income positions often change over time. A sizable portion of those with a high relative income during one year subsequently find themselves in a lower income position. At the same time, many of those with low relative incomes during a given year move up to higher-income quintiles in subsequent years.

The data of Exhibit 3 are for the same group of individuals. If new individuals had been included, there would have been even more income mobility, particularly in an upward direction.[8] Often, current income is low because the individual is young and inexperienced or going to school while working part-time. In other cases, the low current income status is the result of a job loss or business setback during the year. In still other cases, it reflects an accident or a temporary health problem. The distribution of income in the United States is dynamic. With time, most of those with low incomes *at a point in time* move up the income ladder only to be replaced by others who are youthful, inexperienced, or victims of current misfortune. Many readers of this book (as college students) currently have a very low annual income and are thus currently poor and in the lower part of the income distribution. After college graduation, however, the earning power of a college degree will place many of these currently poor individuals in the upper-income brackets.

HOUSEHOLD EXPENDITURES AND INEQUALITY

Given the pattern of lifetime income and the mobility up and down the income ladder, many economists argue that differences in household expenditures are a more accurate indicator of economic status than annual income. When the current income of an individual or a household understates either his or her future earning prospects or income level during an earlier period, current expenditures generally exceed current income. On the other hand, if current income is high relative to one's prior or expected future income, more will

Generational Mobility: There is a weak positive correlation between the earnings of fathers and sons. If a father has lifetime earnings 20 percent above the average of his generation, a son can expect to earn about 8 percent more. There is virtually no correlation between the earnings of grandparents and their grandchildren. Apparently, there is some truth in the old saying, "From shirtsleeves to shirtsleeves in three generations."

[8]For evidence on this point, see Michael W. Cox and Richard Alm, "By Our Own Bootstraps: Economic Opportunity and the Dynamic of Income Distribution," *Federal Reserve Bank of Dallas Annual Report, 1995*; and U.S. Department of the Treasury, Office of Tax Analysis, *Household Income Mobility During the 1980s: A Statistical Analysis Based on Tax Return Data* (Washington, DC: U.S. Department of the Treasury, 1992).

be saved, causing expenditures to fall short of current income. To a large degree, current expenditures reflect long-term economic status.

What do expenditures indicate with regard to the degree of inequality in the United States? Daniel Slesnick of the University of Texas has studied this issue extensively. In addition to the income data, Exhibit 1 also presents Slesnick's calculations on share of household expenditures by quintile. In 1995, the 20 percent of households with the smallest consumer expenditure levels undertook 7.4 percent of the aggregate expenditures. On the other hand, the expenditures of the top quintile summed to 38.8 percent of the total. The expenditures of the top group were 5.2 times those of the bottom group. This ratio is significantly lower than the corresponding figure for annual income, both before and after taxes. Thus, the expenditure share of the bottom quintile relative to the top group is significantly greater than the income share.

In contrast with the annual income data, the distribution of household consumption expenditures does not indicate that there has been a major change in economic inequality in the United States during recent decades. Throughout the 1961–1995 period, the expenditures of the bottom quintile were approximately 7 percent of the total, while those of the top quintile were slightly less than 40 percent. This suggests that the increase in inequality as measured by the annual income data is a reflection of dynamic change, temporary fluctuations in annual income, and measurement issues rather than a true increase in economic inequality.

POVERTY IN THE UNITED STATES

In an affluent society, such as that of the United States, income inequality and poverty are related issues. Poverty could be defined in strictly relative terms—the bottom one-fifth of all income recipients, for example. However, this definition would not be very helpful, since it would mean that poverty could never decline.

The official definition of poverty in the United States is based on the perceived minimum income necessary to provide food, clothing, shelter, and basic necessities economically for a family. This **poverty threshold income level** varies with family size and composition, and it is adjusted annually for changes in prices. For purposes of determining whether income is above the poverty threshold, the official poverty rate considers only money income. (See the Measures of Economic Activity feature for additional details on how the poverty rate is measured.)

How many people are poor? According to the official definition of poverty, there were 31.1 million poor people and 6.2 million poor families in 2000. As **Exhibit 4** indicates, 11.3 percent of the population and 8.6 percent of the families were officially classified as poor in 2000. During the 1950s and 1960s, the poverty rate declined substantially. By 1970 the official poverty rate for families had fallen to 10.1 percent, down from 18.1

Poverty threshold income level
The level of money income below which a family is considered to be poor. It differs according to family characteristics (for example, number of family members) and is adjusted when consumer prices change.

	POVERTY RATE (PERCENT)		**EXHIBIT 4**
YEAR	PERSONS	FAMILIES	
1947	n.a.	32.0	
1960	22.2	18.1	
1970	12.6	10.1	
1980	13.0	10.3	
1990	13.5	10.7	
2000	11.3	8.6	

EXHIBIT 4
Poverty Rate of Persons and Families in the United States, 1947–2000

Sources: Bureau of the Census, *Current Population Reports,* Series P60-210; *Poverty in the United States: 2000;* and *Economic Report of the President,* 1964, Table 7.

MEASURES OF ECONOMIC ACTIVITY

Determining the Poverty Rate

Families and individuals are classified as poor or non-poor based on the poverty threshold income level originally developed by the Social Security Administration (SSA) in 1964. Since consumption survey data indicated that low- and median-income families of three or more persons spent approximately one-third of their income on food, the SSA established the poverty threshold income level at three times the cost of an economical, nutritionally adequate food plan. A slightly larger multiple was used for smaller families and individuals living alone. The poverty threshold figure varies according to family size, because the food costs vary by family size and composition. It is adjusted annually to account for rising prices. The following chart illustrates how the poverty threshold for a family of four has increased as prices have risen from 1959 to 2001:

1959	$2,973
1970	3,968
1980	8,414
1990	13,359
2001	18,104

Even though the poverty threshold income level is adjusted for prices, it is actually an absolute measure of economic status. As real income increases, the poverty threshold declines relative to the income of the general populace.

The official poverty rate is the number of persons or families living in households with a money income below the poverty threshold as a percentage of the total. Only money income is considered. Income received in the form of non-cash benefits, such as food stamps, medical care, and housing subsidies, is completely ignored in the calculation of the official poverty rate.

Since noncash benefits targeted for low-income households have grown rapidly since the late 1960s, the failure of the official poverty rate to count this "income" reduces its accuracy as a measurement tool. To remedy this deficiency, the Bureau of the Census has developed several alternative measures of poverty that count the estimated value of non-cash benefits as income. In addition to the official poverty rate, the bureau now publishes annual data for the "adjusted" poverty rates that include a valuation for various non-cash benefits (for example, food stamps, medical care, school lunches, and housing benefits). Of course, inclusion of these benefits reduces the poverty rate. For example, while the official poverty rate for persons was 11.3 percent in 2000, the adjusted poverty rate that included the value of the noncash food, housing, and medical benefits was only 8.6 percent.

The poverty rate is calculated each year based on a survey of about 60,000 households designed to reflect the population of the United States. The two major sources for comprehensive data on this topic are the Bureau of the Census annual publications, *Money Income in the United States* and *Poverty in the United States*.

percent in 1960 and 32.0 percent in 1947. In contrast with the 1950s and 1960s, the official poverty rate has changed by only a small amount since 1970. After rising slightly during the 1970s and 1980s, the official poverty rate fell modestly during the economic expansion of the 1990s. In 2000, the poverty rate of both persons and families was only slightly less than the comparable figure for 1970.

In recent years, the composition of the poverty population has changed substantially. As **Exhibit 5** indicates, elderly persons and the working poor formed the core of the poverty population in 1959. Twenty-two percent of the poor families were headed by an elderly person in 1959. Most poor people (70 percent) worked at least some hours during the year. In 2000, the picture was dramatically different: Only 10 percent of the poor families were headed by an elderly person and only 53 percent of the heads of poor households worked at all during the year.

There has also been a substantial growth in the proportion of female-headed families and an accompanying decline in the proportion of husband-wife families in the general population. Since the poverty rate of female-headed families is several times higher than the rate for husband-wife families (24.7 percent compared with 4.7 percent in 2000), an increase in family instability tends to push the poverty rate upward. In 2000, half of the poor families were headed by a female, compared with only 23 percent in 1959.

	1959	1976	2000
Number of Poor Families (in millions)	8.3	5.3	6.2
Percent of Poor Families Headed by a:			
Female	23	48	50
Black	26	30	27
Elderly person (age 65 and over)	22	14	10
Person who worked at least some during the year	70	55	53
Poverty Rate			
All families	18.5	10.1	8.6
Married couple families	15.8	7.2	4.7
Female-headed families	42.6	32.5	24.7
Whites	18.1	9.1	9.4
Blacks	55.1	31.1	22.0
Children (under age 18)	27.3	16.0	16.1

EXHIBIT 5
Changing Composition of Poor and Poverty Rate of Selected Groups: 1959, 1976, and 2000

Sources: U.S. Department of Commerce, *Characteristics of the Population Below the Poverty Level: 1982,* Table 5; and *Poverty in the United States: 2000,* (P60-214).

The poverty rate of blacks in 2000 was 22.0 percent, compared to 9.4 percent for whites. Nonetheless, 68 percent of the people in poverty were white. Perhaps the most tragic consequence of poverty is its impact on children. Little progress has been made in this area during the last two decades. In 2000, 16.1 percent of the children in the United States lived in poverty, up slightly from 16.0 percent in 1976.

Just as with the income distribution data, there is movement into and out of poverty. A large proportion of poor families remain so for only a brief period of time. For example, even though 14.6 percent of the population was poor during the average month in 1993–1994, only 4.8 percent of the population was poor during the entire period. In fact, the median duration of poverty spells during 1993–1994 was only 4.9 months. Many of these short-term spells of poverty were the result of such factors as medical problems or job changes. Poverty is a long-term problem for only a small number of families. During the typical 10-year period, less than 3 percent of families are poor for 8 or more years.

Transfer Payments and the Poverty Rate

In the mid-1960s, it was widely believed that an increase in income transfers directed toward the poor would substantially reduce, if not eliminate, the incidence of poverty. The 1964 *Economic Report of the President* argued that poverty could be virtually eliminated if the federal government increased its expenditures on transfer programs by approximately 2 percent of aggregate income. Following the declaration of the "War on Poverty" by the Johnson administration, expenditures in this area increased rapidly. Overall transfers, including those directed toward the elderly, approximately doubled as a proportion of personal income between 1965 and 1975. Measured in 1982–1984 dollars, **means-tested income transfers**—those limited to people with incomes below a certain cutoff point—tripled, expanding from $24 billion in 1965 to $70 billion in 1975. *As a proportion of aggregate income*, means-tested transfers jumped from 1.5 percent in 1965 to 3.0 percent in 1975. During the 1975–1990 period, both total transfers and means-tested transfers continued to increase as a percent of income, although at a much slower rate than during the

Means-tested income transfers
Transfers that are limited to persons or families with an income below a certain cutoff point. Eligibility is thus dependent on low-income status.

EXHIBIT 6
Poverty Rate, 1947–2000

The official poverty rate of families declined sharply during the 1950s and 1960s, changed little during the 1970s, and rose during the early 1980s. The rate has fallen by only a small amount since the mid-1980s. The shaded area of the bars indicates the additional reduction in the poverty rate when noncash benefits are counted as income. In 1990, the poverty rate adjusted for noncash benefits was 8.4 percent (compared to 10.7 percent unadjusted) and in 2000 it was 6.4 percent (compared to 8.6 percent unadjusted).

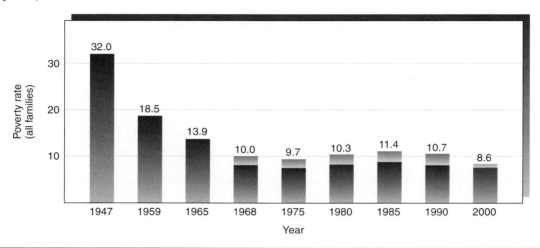

Sources: U.S. Department of Commerce, *Characteristics of the Population Below the Poverty Level: 1982,* Table 5; and *Poverty in the United States: 2000,* (P60-214).

previous decade. By the mid-1990s, means-tested transfers had risen to 5 percent of aggregate income.[9]

Did the expansion in government income transfers reduce the poverty rate as the 1964 *Economic Report of the President* anticipated? Antipoverty programs provide both cash and noncash benefits. **Exhibit 6** shows the poverty rate with and without the benefits of noncash transfer programs counted as income. Continuing the trend of the post-Second World War era, the official poverty rate fell throughout the 1960s. During the 1970s, however, the rate leveled off. By 1980, it was 10.3 percent, virtually unchanged from the 1968 rate. In 2000, the official poverty rate was still 8.6 percent.

Aggregate poverty-rate data as presented in Exhibit 6 conceal an important difference between the experience of the elderly and nonelderly that has often been overlooked. **Exhibit 7** highlights this point. The poverty rate for the elderly has continued to decline throughout the 1970s, 1980s, and 1990s. By 2000, the official poverty rate of the elderly had fallen to 5.4 percent, down from 17.0 percent in 1968 and 30.0 percent in 1959 (see part a of Exhibit 7). The experience of working-age Americans, however, was vastly different. After falling for several decades, the official poverty rate of nonelderly families

[9]The following chart indicates the expenditures on both total income transfers and means-tested transfers as a percentage of aggregate income for 1965, 1975, 1985, and 1995. Both cash and in-kind benefits are included in the figures.

	PERCENT OF AGGREGATE INCOME	
YEAR	TOTAL TRANSFER PAYMENTS	MEANS-TESTED TRANSFER PAYMENTS
1965	8.5	1.5
1975	17.4	3.0
1985	18.4	3.4
1995	20.9	5.0

The means-tested noncash transfers included food (food stamps, school lunch subsidies, and WIC program), housing, and energy assistance benefits, plus Medicaid payments. In addition to these benefits, Medicare payments were also included in the total transfer figures. Expenditures on job training and educational subsidies are not included. See *Statistical Abstract of the United States: 2000,* Tables 600 and 605.

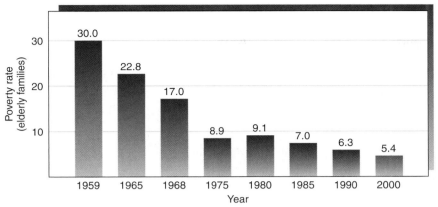

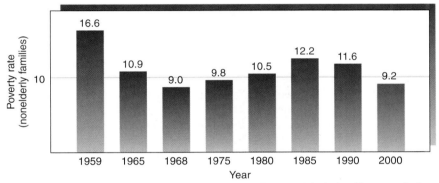

Note: Adjusted for food, medical, and housing benefits.
Sources: Derived from Department of Commerce, *Money Income in the United States: 2000; Poverty in the United States: 1990;* and *Measuring the Effects of Benefits and Taxes on Income and Poverty, 1990 and 1992.* See also James Gwartney and Thomas S. McCaleb, "Have Antipoverty Programs Increased Poverty? *The Cato Journal* (spring/summer, 1985)

EXHIBIT 7
Changing Poverty Rates for Elderly versus Nonelderly, 1959–2000

reached a low in 1968, shortly after the War on Poverty was launched. The nonelderly poverty rate rose during 1970-1985 and it has fallen modestly since. However, the 2000 nonelderly poverty rate of 9.2 percent was still above the 9 percent rate of 1968 (part b of Exhibit 7). If the poverty rates of the elderly and nonelderly were adjusted for the impact of in-kind benefits, the rates would be slightly lower but the general pattern of the changes over time would persist.

Clearly, the income transfer programs of the War on Poverty did not work as anticipated. The 1990s was a period of sustained economic expansion. The unemployment rate fell to a 30-year low. Even more significant, U.S. income per person *adjusted for inflation* was 109 percent higher in 2000 than in 1965. Despite all of these positive factors, the poverty rate in 2000 was virtually unchanged from that of the mid-1960s!

Why wasn't the War on Poverty more effective? Means-tested income transfers generate two major side effects that reduce their effectiveness as an antipoverty weapon. *First, transfer programs that significantly reduce the adversities of poverty will also reduce the opportunity cost of choices that often lead to poverty.* This factor is sometimes called the **Samaritan's dilemma.** To the extent that antipoverty programs reduce the negative side effects of, for example, births by unmarried mothers, abandonment of children by fathers, dependence on drugs or alcohol, or dropping out of school, they inadvertently

Samaritan's dilemma
General assistance to those with low incomes reduces the opportunity cost of choices that lead to poverty. Thus, there is a conflict between providing income transfers to the poor and discouragement of behavior that increases the incidence of poverty.

The poverty rate of the elderly (5.4 percent in 2000) is lower than the poverty rate of those under age 65 (9.2 percent in 2000). Furthermore, during the last three decades, the poverty rate for the elderly has persistently declined, while the rate for the nonelderly has risen slightly.

encourage people to make choices that result in these conditions. Of course, this is not the intent of the transfers, but nonetheless it is one of their side effects. In the short run, these secondary effects are probably not very important. Over the longer term, however, their negative consequences may be substantial.

Second, income-linked transfers reduce the incentive of low-income individuals to help themselves. When the size of transfers is linked to income, larger transfers tend to increase the **implicit marginal tax rate** imposed on the poor. Participants in the food stamp program, for example, have their food stamp benefits reduced by $30 for every $100 of income earned. Thus, every $100 of additional income leads to only a $70 increase in well-being (spendable net income) once the reduction in food stamp benefits is taken into account. When a person qualifies for several programs such as food stamps, Medicaid, and housing benefits, the problem is compounded, and the combined implicit marginal tax rate can frequently exceed 50 or 60 percent. In some cases, the rate may exceed 100 percent—that is, work and additional earnings may actually reduce the family's economic status. Because the high implicit marginal tax rates reduce the incentive of poor families to work and earn, transfers often merely replace income that would have otherwise been earned. When this is the case, they add little or nothing to the *net* income of the poor.

Implicit marginal tax rate
The amount of additional (marginal) earnings that must be paid explicitly in taxes or implicitly in the form of a reduction in income supplements. Since the marginal tax rate establishes the fraction of an additional dollar earned that an individual is permitted to keep, it is an important determinant of the incentive to work.

Estimating the Costs of Redistribution

Economics indicates that the use of income transfers to upgrade the status of those with low incomes is like trying to transfer water with a "leaky bucket." The increases in the marginal tax rates (either explicit or implicit) confronted by both the taxpayer-donor and the transfer recipient adversely affect work incentives and reduce the size of the economic pie. Thus, the cost of the transfers is greater than the amount of income transferred. Furthermore, much of the income received by recipients merely replaces income that they might otherwise have earned.

A study by Sam Allgood and Arthur Snow sought to measure the loss of output due to the reduction in the supply of labor associated with the rise in marginal tax rates accompanying income transfers.[10] Allgood and Snow estimated that it would cost between $1.26 and $3.22 in terms of lost output for every additional dollar taxed from the top 60 percent of income recipients and transferred to the bottom 40 percent.

---

[10]See Sam Allgood and Arthur Snow, "The Marginal Cost of Raising Tax Revenue and Redistributing Income," *Journal of Political Economy* (December 1998). This study builds on earlier work by Edgar K. Browning and William Johnson, "The Trade-off between Equality and Efficiency," *Journal of Political Economy* (April 1984); and Charles L. Ballard, "The Marginal Efficiency Cost of Redistribution," *American Economic Review* (December 1988).

Transferring income from producers to nonproducers is thus an expensive undertaking. Are redistribution programs worth the cost? Economics cannot answer that question. It can only help identify and quantify the cost (in terms of lost output) and expected effectiveness of alternative programs. Hopefully, better information in these areas will help voters and policy makers to make wiser decisions.

INCOME INEQUALITY: SOME CONCLUDING THOUGHTS

Is there too much inequality in the United States? Should public policy attempt to reduce income inequality? These are normative questions and therefore positive economics cannot provide definitive answers. It can, however, provide a sensible way of thinking about them.

Many people, including a good number of economists, would like to see the magnitude of income inequality reduced. Some dimensions of public policy are directed toward this objective. The progressive structure of the income tax, the **Earned Income Tax Credit**, and means-tested programs like food stamps, Medicaid, and housing subsidies provide examples. But the political process is multidimensional and it represents a diverse set of forces, including powerful special interest groups. Therefore, it should not be surprising that the political record in this area, as in others, is mixed. Social Security, the largest income transfer program, redirects income toward the elderly, a group with above-average levels of both income and wealth. Agriculture subsidies constitute another large transfer program and the bulk of these benefits go to large farmers with incomes well above the average. Another sizable share of government transfers is allocated to business interests, including many that are large and highly profitable. Neither public choice analysis nor the real world characteristics of tax-transfer programs indicate that the political process will exert a strong equalizing impact on the allocation of income.

Furthermore, it is important to recognize that income is not like manna from heaven. It is not something that is available to be divided, sliced, and served according to some criteria of fairness. On the contrary, income is something that people produce and earn. It is earned by individuals who provide others with goods and services for which they are willing to pay. The allocation of income reflects the choices of individuals with differing preferences, talents, and abilities. Individuals also differ with regard to their investment in education and training, entrepreneurial skills, willingness to take risk, rate of personal savings, and preference for leisure relative to work and monetary earnings. Wage differentials, profits, losses, and interest rates coordinate the choices of these vastly different individuals and bring them into harmony with each other. Income inequality is an outgrowth of this process. Policies that modify the process may generate perverse incentives and discourage wealth creation.

When considering the issue of fairness, many would argue that the process that generates the outcomes is more important than the resulting pattern. Do individuals have an opportunity to acquire education and training? Are people from all segments of society free to compete in business and labor markets? Are incomes reflective of choices, voluntary exchange, and the productive effort of individuals? These questions are about opportunity, economic freedom, and how income is acquired. Many believe that these ingredients, rather than the distributional pattern, are the key elements of economic fairness.

Perhaps the following example will illustrate the difference between the process and pattern view. Suppose a million people purchase a $10 lottery ticket and the proceeds are used to finance a $10 million jackpot for one person. This activity will clearly increase income inequality. But is it unfair? Those who adhere to the process view would stress that the outcome merely reflects the voluntary choices of participants who were well aware of the rules of the game prior to their purchasing a ticket. According to this view, it is the process rather than the outcome that is the primary determinant of fairness.

In competitive markets, people earn income by supplying others with goods, services, and resources that they value. Individuals who earn a lot must help others a lot. Consider the income of an exceedingly wealthy person—Bill Gates, for example. Gates did not steal from others or force anyone to purchase his software. They did so voluntarily because they

Earned Income Tax Credit
A feature of the personal income tax system that provides supplementary payments to workers with low incomes.

perceived that he provided them with a better deal than was available elsewhere. If individuals earn their income through voluntary exchange and providing services to others, how can the results be unfair?

Economics provides insight on both the allocative role and sources of differences in income. It also indicates that it will be costly, in terms of lost output, to redistribute income through taxes and transfers. Of course, this does not reveal whether there is too much inequality or whether the government should play a larger or smaller role in the allocation of income. It does, however, place one in a position to address these normative issues in a more thoughtful manner.

LOOKING AHEAD

Income transfers are the focal point of many current policy issues, including Social Security and health care. The following Beyond the Basics section contains additional analysis on these and other topics.

KEY POINTS

▼ Market participants create income by supplying resources that are highly valued *by others*. The link between income and provision of productive resources provides individuals with the incentive to develop skills, talents, and resources others value. The view that there is a fixed-size economic pie that can be sliced and divided among the citizenry is fallacious.

▼ In 2000, the bottom 20 percent of families earned 4.3 percent of aggregate income, while the top 20 percent earned approximately 11 times that amount (47.4 percent). After taxes and transfers are taken into account, the top quintile of households earn nearly ten times the income of the bottom quintile. The degree of income inequality declined during the 1950s and 1960s, but it has risen during the last 25 years.

▼ A substantial percentage of the inequality in annual income reflects differences in age, education, family size, marital status, number of earners in the family, and time worked. Young inexperienced workers, students, single-parent families, and retirees are overrepresented among those with low incomes.

▼ While no single factor can explain the recent increase in income inequality, the following four factors probably contributed to it: (a) an increasing proportion of both single-parent *and* dual-earner families, (b) an increase in earnings differentials on the basis of skill and education, (c) more "winner-take-all" markets, and (d) increases in the reported income of those in the top tax bracket due to lower marginal tax rates.

▼ The tracking of household income over time indicates that there is considerable movement both up and down the income spectrum. Annual income data camouflage this movement.

▼ According to the official data, 11.3 percent of the population and 8.6 percent of the families in the United States were officially classified as poor in 2000. Those living in poverty were generally younger, less educated, less likely to be working, and more likely to be living in families headed by a single parent than those who were not poor. There is considerable movement both into and out of poverty. A relatively small proportion of families comprise the long-term poor.

▼ During the last several decades, income transfers—including means-tested transfers—have expanded rapidly both in real dollars and as a share of personal income. As a weapon against poverty, these transfers have been largely ineffective. Even though per capita income increased by more than 100 percent between 1965 and 2000, the poverty rate of working-age Americans was about the same during the two years.

▼ Income supplements large enough to increase the economic status of poor people significantly will (a) encourage behavior that increases the risk of poverty and/or (b) create high implicit marginal tax rates that reduce the recipient's incentive to earn.

▼ Positive economics cannot determine how much inequality should be present. Income inequality reflects differences between individuals and influences their incentive to develop resources and engage in productive activities. The nature of the process as well as the pattern of income distribution is relevant to the issue of fairness.

CRITICAL ANALYSIS QUESTIONS

1. Do you think the current distribution of income in the United States is too unequal? Why or why not? What criteria do you think should be used to judge the fairness of the distribution of income? Is the final outcome more important than the process that generates the income?

*2. Is annual money income a good measure of economic status? Is a family with an $80,000 annual income able to purchase twice the quantity of goods and services as a family with $40,000 of annual income? Is the standard of living of the $80,000 family twice as high as that of the $40,000 family? Discuss.

3. What is income mobility? If there is substantial income mobility in a society, how does this influence the importance of income distribution data?

*4. Consider a table such as Exhibit 3 in which the family income of parents is grouped by quintiles down the rows, and that of their offspring is grouped by quintiles across the columns. If there were no intergenerational mobility in this country, what pattern of numbers would be present in the table? If the nation had attained complete equality of opportunity, what pattern of numbers would emerge? Explain.

5. Do individuals have a property right to income they acquire from market transactions? Is it a proper function of government to tax some people in order to provide benefits to others? Why or why not? Discuss.

*6. Since income transfers to the poor typically increase the marginal tax rate confronted by the poor, does a $1,000 additional transfer payment necessarily cause the income of poor recipients to rise by $1,000? Why or why not?

*7. Sue is a single parent with two children. She is considering a job that pays $800 per month. She is currently drawing monthly cash benefits of $300, plus food stamp benefits of $100, and Medicaid benefits valued at $80. If she accepts the job, she will be liable for employment taxes of $56 per month and

lose all transfer benefits. What is Sue's implicit marginal tax rate for this job?

8. What groups are overrepresented among those with relatively low incomes? Do the poor in the United States generally stay poor? Why or why not?

9. Some argue that taxes exert little effect on people's incentive to earn income. In considering this issue, suppose you were required to pay a tax rate of 50 percent on all money income you earn while in school. Would this affect your employment? How might you minimize the personal effects of this tax?

10. Large income transfers are targeted toward the elderly, farmers, and the unemployed, regardless of their economic condition. Why do you think this is so? Do you think there would be less income inequality if the government levied higher taxes in order to make larger income transfers? Why or why not?

11. The outcome of a state lottery game is certainly a very unequal distribution of the prize income. Some players are made very rich, while others lose their money. Using this example, discuss whether the fairness of the process or the fairness of the outcome is more important, and how they differ.

12. "Means-tested transfer payments reduce the current poverty rate. However, they also create an incentive structure that discourages self-provision and self-improvement. Thus, they tend to increase the future poverty rate. Welfare programs essentially purchase a lower poverty rate today in exchange for a higher poverty rate in the future." Evaluate this statement.

13. Suppose that at birth you do not know if you will be born "poor" or "wealthy" but you can choose how much redistribution will take place in society. However, once you choose the amount of redistribution, it cannot be changed. Would you choose a low or high degree of redistribution in society? Why? What is the impact on efficiency and equity and what are the likely tradeoffs?

14. Suppose that one family has $100,000 while another has only $20,000. Is this outcome fair? What is your initial reaction? Compare and contrast your views under the following processes that might have generated this outcome.

   a. The family with the higher income has both husband and wife working, while the other family has chosen for the wife to remain home with the children rather than work in the labor force.

   b. The family with the higher income is headed by a person who completed a college degree, while the other family is headed by someone who dropped out of high school.

   c. The family with the higher income derived most of its income from the farm subsidy program.

   d. The family with the higher income received it as an inheritance from parents who just died.

---

*Asterisk denotes questions for which answers are given in Appendix B.

PART 6

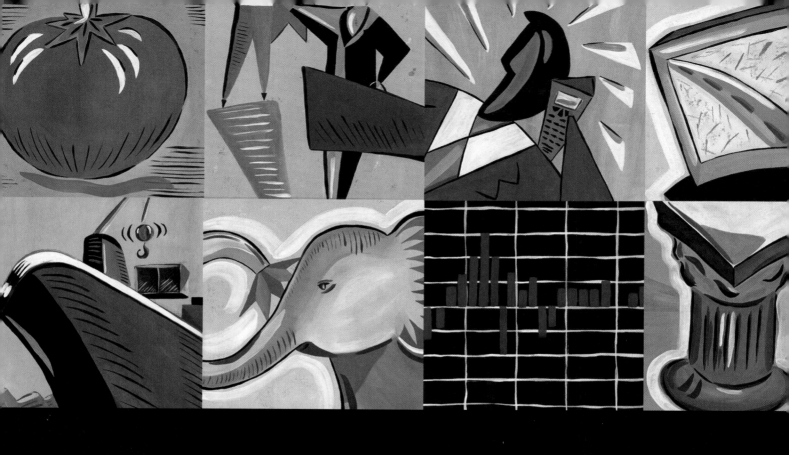

"*Economics is about how the real*

BEYOND THE BASICS: SPECIAL TOPICS IN ECONOMICS

Economics has a lot to say about current issues and real world events. What impact will the Internet have on your life? Why does the current social security system face problems and what might be done to minimize them? Is ownership of stock risky? why is the unemployment rate higher in Europe than the Unites States? What might be done to improve the quality of health care and education? How can we best protect the environment? This section will focus on these topics and several other current issues.

LIST OF SPECIAL TOPICS

1. Government Spending and Taxation

2. The Internet: How Is It Changing the Economy?

3. The Economics of Social Security

4. The Stock Market: What Does It Do And How Has It Performed?

5. The Federal Budget and the National Debt

6. Labor Market Policies and the Natural Rate of Unemployment: A Cross-country Analysis

7. The Phillips Curve: Is There a Tradeoff Between Inflation and Unemployment?

8. The Economics of Health Care

9. School Choice: Can It Improve the Quality of Education in America?

10. Is Discrimination Responsible for the Earnings Differences Between Men and Women?

11. Do Labor Unions Increase the Wages of Workers?

12. How Does Government Regulation Affect Your Life?

13. Natural Resources and the Future

14. Economics and the Environment

SPECIAL TOPIC **1**

If you want to know what people think is important and what has priority, simply follow the money.

—Anonymous

Government Spending and Taxation

Focus

- What are the major categories of government spending and sources of tax revenue?

- How has the size and composition of government changed over time?

- How high are taxes and who pays them?

- How does the size of government in the United States compare with other countries?

n chapters 5 and 6, we analyzed the economic role of government and the operation of the political process. We learned that while the political process and market organization are alternative ways of dealing with scarcity, a sound legal system and stable monetary regime are vitally important for the efficient operation of markets. In this regard, secure property rights, evenhanded enforcement of contracts, and stability in the general level of prices are particularly important. We also noted that, like markets, the political process is imperfect. Even a democratic political system will sometimes go awry.

Building on the earlier analysis, this feature will take a closer look at government in the United States. As the opening quotation indicates, we can learn a great deal about an organization by "following the money." Thus, we will focus on the taxing and spending activities of government. ■

GOVERNMENT SPENDING AND TAXATION

When considering government spending, it is important to distinguish between (1) government purchases of goods and services and (2) transfer payments. Government purchases occur when either consumption or investment goods are supplied through the public sector. Government-supplied consumption goods would include government expenditures on items such as police and fire protection, medical services, and administration. Government investments would include the provision of long-lasting goods such as highways, jet planes, and buildings. Transfer payments are transfers of income from taxpayers to recipients who do not provide current goods and services in exchange for these payments. Simply put, transfer payments take income from some to provide additional income to others.

The political system of the United States is one of federalism. The federal government is primarily responsible for some activities while state and local governments are responsible for others. Approximately three-fifths of the spending by government takes place at the federal level. **Exhibit 1** indicates the major spending categories for the federal and state and local governments. These figures reveal a great deal about the nature of government.

Federal expenditures (part a) on just four things: (1) income transfers (including social security and other income security programs), (2) health care, (3) national defense, and (4) net interest on the national debt accounted for 85.3 percent of federal spending in 2000. This means that expenditures on everything else—the federal courts, national parks, highways, education, job training, agriculture, energy, natural resources, federal law enforcement, and numerous other programs—were less than 15 percent of the federal budget.

Exhibit 1b highlights the functional responsibilities of state and local government. In the United States, public education has traditionally been the responsibility of state and local governments. Spending on education accounts for almost 30 percent of state and local expenditures. Spending on public welfare (income transfers) and health care accounts for just over 20 percent of all state and local spending. Administration, transportation and highways, utilities, insurance trust funds, law enforcement, and fire protection are other major areas of expenditures at the state and local level.

Taxes and Other Sources of Government Revenue

There are no free lunches. Government expenditures must be financed through taxes, user charges, or borrowing.[1] Furthermore, borrowing is simply another name for future taxes that will have to be levied in order to pay the interest on the funds that were borrowed. In the United States, taxes are by far the largest source of government revenue. The power to tax sets governments apart from private businesses. Of course, a private business can put

---

[1]In addition to user charges, taxes, and borrowing, the operations of government might be financed by printing money. But, as we will illustrate later, this is also a type of tax (it is sometimes called an "inflation tax") on those who hold money balances.

EXHIBIT 1
What Governments Buy

About 60 percent of government expenditures take place at the federal level. Income transfers (social security is the largest transfer program), health care, national defense, and interest on the national debt accounted for 85 percent of federal spending in 2000. At the state and local level, the largest categories of spending are education and public welfare.

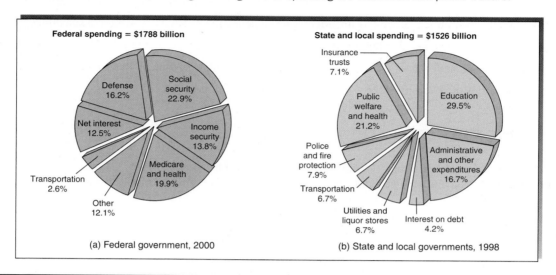

Federal spending = $1788 billion

Defense 16.2%
Social security 22.9%
Net interest 12.5%
Income security 13.8%
Transportation 2.6%
Medicare and health 19.9%
Other 12.1%

(a) Federal government, 2000

State and local spending = $1526 billion

Insurance trusts 7.1%
Public welfare and health 21.2%
Education 29.5%
Police and fire protection 7.9%
Administrative and other expenditures 16.7%
Transportation 6.7%
Utilities and liquor stores 6.7%
Interest on debt 4.2%

(b) State and local governments, 1998

Source: *Economic Report of the President*, 2001 and *Statistical Abstract of the United States*, 2000.

whatever price tag it wishes on its products; but no private business can force you to buy it or to pay for it if you don't consume it. With its power to tax, a government can force citizens to pay, regardless of whether they receive something of equal or greater value in return.

Exhibit 2 indicates the major revenue sources for the federal and state and local levels of government. At the federal level, the personal income tax accounts for almost half of all revenue. Although income from all sources is covered by the income tax, only earnings derived from labor are subject to the payroll tax. Payroll taxes on the earnings of employees and self-employed workers finance social security, Medicare, and unemployment compensation benefits. The payroll tax accounts for almost a third of federal revenue. The remaining sources of revenue, including the corporate income tax, excise taxes, and customs duties, account for less than 20 percent of federal revenue.

Both sales and income taxes are important sources of revenue for state governments. A sales tax is levied by 45 of the 50 states (Alaska, Delaware, Montana, New Hampshire, and Oregon are the exceptions). State and local governments derive 19 percent of their revenue from this source. Personal income taxes are imposed by 42 states (Alaska, Florida, Nevada, New Hampshire, South Dakota, Texas, Washington, and Wyoming are the exceptions) and they provide approximately 12 percent of state and local government revenue.[2] Property taxes (levied mostly at the local level), grants from the federal government, and user charges (prices for services provided by the government) also provide substantial revenues for state and local governments.

GROWTH OF GOVERNMENT

During the first 125 years of the United States, the economic role of the federal government was quite limited and its expenditures were modest. In the nineteenth century, except during times of war, most government expenditures were undertaken at the state and

---

[2]New Hampshire does levy a tax on income derived from dividends and interest.

EXHIBIT 2
Sources of Government Revenue

Almost half of federal revenues are derived from the personal income tax. The payroll tax and corporate income tax are also major sources of federal revenue. The major revenue sources of state and local governments are sales and excise taxes, personal income taxes, user charges, and grants from the federal government.

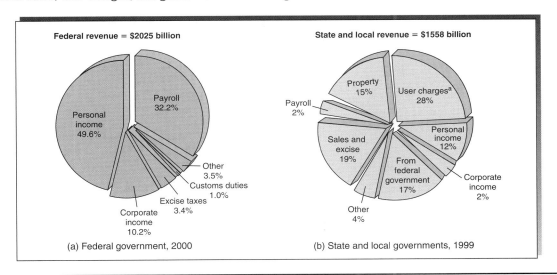

(a) Federal government, 2000

(b) State and local governments, 1999

[a]Revenues from government-operated utilities and liquor stores are included in this category.
Source: Economic Report of the President, 2001 and *Statistical Abstract of the United States,* 2000.

local level. The federal government spent funds on national defense and transportation (roads and canals), but not much else. As recently as 1929, total government spending was less than 10 percent of GDP, and two-thirds of this was at the state and local level.

Exhibit 3 presents data on real federal spending per person (measured in terms of the purchasing power of the dollar in 2000). Just prior to the Civil War, real federal expenditures were $50 per person, not much different than the $40 figure of 1800. Federal spending per person rose sharply during the Civil War, but it soon receded and remained in a range between $90 and $150 throughout the 1870–1916 period. Thus, prior to World War I, federal expenditures per person were low and the growth of government was modest.

Beginning with the World War I spending of 1917, however, the situation changed drastically. Federal spending remained well above the prewar levels during the 1920s and rose rapidly during the 1930s. It soared during World War II and after receding at the end of the war, federal spending continued to grow rapidly throughout the 1950–1990 period. By 1990, per capita real federal spending amounted to $6,640, almost 60 times the $112 figure of 1916. The additional government expenditures came with a cost—the average person in 1990 paid more in federal taxes in *one week* than the average person in 1916 paid in federal taxes for an *entire year,* in real terms.

For the first time in almost a century, this upward trend in federal spending has eased. During the 1990s per capita real federal spending was relatively constant. In fact, it was slightly lower ($6,360) in 2000 than at the beginning of the decade.

THE CHANGING COMPOSITION OF FEDERAL SPENDING

Measured as a share of the economy, total government spending rose from 10 percent in 1929 to approximately 30 percent in the 1960s. Most of this expansion took place at the federal level. Federal spending soared from 3 percent of GDP in 1929 to 17 percent in 1960. After increasing to 23 percent of GDP during the mid-1980s, federal spending has now receded to less than 20 percent of the economy, not much different than in 1960.

EXHIBIT 3
Real Federal Expenditures Per Capita: 1792–2000

Real federal spending per person (measured in 2000 dollars) was generally less than $50 prior to the Civil War and it ranged from $90 to $150 throughout the 1870–1916 period. However, beginning with the spending buildup for World War I in 1917, real federal spending per person soared, reaching $6,645 in 1991. The 1991 figure is nearly 60 times that of 1916.

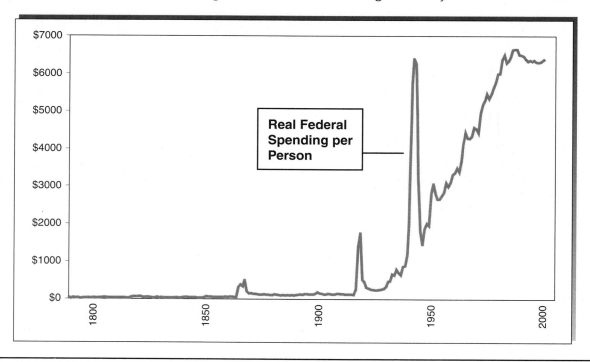

Source: U.S. Census Bureau, *Historical Statistics of the United States*, 1976 and *Economic Report of the President*, 2001.

While federal spending as a share of the economy has changed only modestly since 1960, there has been a dramatic shift in the composition of that spending. Spending on defense has fallen as both a share of the budget and as a share of the economy, while expenditures on transfer payments (income transfers) and health care have soared.

As **Exhibit 4** illustrates, defense expenditures comprised 52.2 percent of federal spending (about 9.1 percent of GDP) in 1960. By 2000, defense spending was only 16.2 percent of the federal budget (about 2.9 percent of GDP). In contrast, government expenditures on income transfers (including social security and other income security programs) and health care (primarily Medicare and Medicaid) rose from 21.5 percent of the federal budget in 1960 to 56.6 percent in 2000.

Thus, there has been a dramatic change in the composition of federal spending during the last four decades. In contrast with earlier times, national defense is no longer the primary focus of the federal government. In essence, the federal government has become an entity that taxes working-age Americans in order to provide income transfers and health care benefits primarily for senior citizens. Furthermore, spending on the elderly is almost certain to increase once the baby boomers begin to retire starting around 2010.

THE PAYMENT AND BURDEN OF TAXATION

As government expenditures have increased, so too have taxes. Beginning with the period immediately following World War II, **Exhibit 5** presents data on revenues as a share of national income for all levels of government and the federal government alone. In 1950,

EXHIBIT 4
The Changing Composition of Federal Spending

In 2000, national defense expenditures accounted for only 16.2 percent of the federal budget, down from 52.2 percent in 1960. In contrast, spending on income transfers and health care rose from 21.5 percent of the federal budget in 1960 to 56.6 percent in 2000.

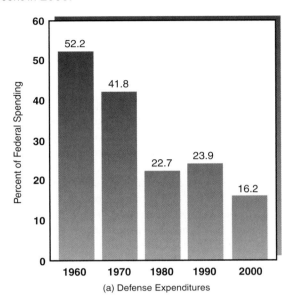

(a) Defense Expenditures

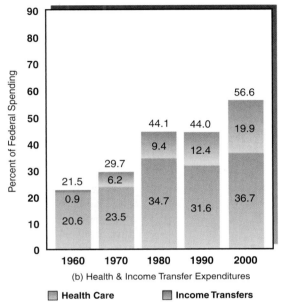

(b) Health & Income Transfer Expenditures

■ Health Care   ■ Income Transfers

Source: Economic Report of the President, 2001.

EXHIBIT 5
Government Revenue As a Share of National Income

In 2000, government revenues consumed 37.9 percent of national income. Federal taxes alone took 25.6 percent of the income generated by Americans. Both of these figures were highs for the post–World War II period.

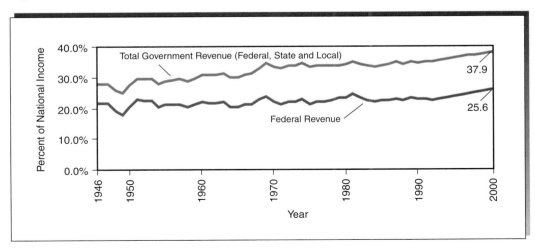

Source: Economic Report of the President, 2001.

total government revenues were approximately one-quarter of national income. By the 1970s, government was taking about a third of national income and by 2000 the figure had risen to 38 percent. The revenues of the federal government followed a similar pattern, increasing from 20 percent of national income in 1950 to 24 percent in 1980 and 26 percent in 2000. Both total and federal taxes took a larger share of national income in 2000 than at any time since World War II.

The Burden of Taxation

A tax dollar extracted from an individual or a business ends up costing the private economy much more than just one dollar. This is the case for two main reasons.

First, the collection of taxes is costly. The administration, enforcement, and compliance of tax legislation requires a sizable volume of resources, including the labor services of many highly skilled experts. The IRS itself employs 100,000 people. In addition, an army of bookkeepers, tax accountants, and lawyers are involved in the collection process. According to the Office of Management and Budget, each year individuals and businesses spend over 5.5 billion hours (the equivalent of 2.7 million full-time year-round workers) keeping records, filling out forms, and learning the tax rules and other elements of the tax compliance process.[3] More than half of U.S. families now retain tax preparation firms like H&R Block and Jackson Hewitt to help file the required forms and comply with the complex rules. Businesses spend roughly $5 billion each year in tax consulting fees to the Big 5 accounting firms, to say nothing of the fees paid to other accounting, law, and consulting firms. In total, the resources involved amount to between 3 percent and 4 percent of national income (or 12 to 15 percent of the revenues collected). If these resources were not tied up with the tax collection process, they could be employed producing goods and services for consumption.

Second, taxes impose an additional burden on the economy because they will eliminate some productive exchanges (and cause people to undertake some counterproductive activities). As the result of the distortions accompanying taxation, particularly high marginal tax rates, the incentive to work, invest, and earn is reduced and more and more economic decisions will be based on tax considerations rather than maximum efficiency. As we discussed in Chapter 4, economists refer to this cost as the excess burden or "deadweight loss" of taxation. It imposes a burden over and above the cost of the revenue transferred to the government.

When considering the burden of taxation, it is important to recognize that all taxes are paid by people. Politicians often speak of imposing taxes on "business" as if part of the tax burden could be transferred from individuals to a nonperson (business). This is not the case. Business taxes, like all other taxes, are paid by individuals. A corporation or business firm may write the check to the government, but it merely collects the money from someone else—from its customers in the form of higher prices, from its suppliers (including employees) in the form of lower wages or prices paid, or from stockholders in the form of lower dividends paid—and transfers the money to the government.

Income Levels and Tax Payments

As we previously noted, the personal income tax accounts for about half of all federal revenues. The payment of this tax is highly skewed towards upper-income individuals. Interestingly, even though the highest marginal tax rates are now much lower than in 1980, the share of taxes collected from high-income taxpayers has increased substantially. As the IRS data of **Exhibit 6** show, the 1 percent of tax filers with the highest incomes (those earning $293,415 and above) paid 36.2 percent of the federal personal income taxes in 1999, up from 19.1 percent in 1980. Two-thirds (66.5 percent) of the personal income tax was collected from the top 10 percent of earners (those earning $87,682 and above) in 1999, compared to 49.3 percent in 1980. The top 50 percent of earners paid 96.0 percent of the personal income

---

[3]Office of Management and Budget, *Information Collection Budget of the United States Government*, fiscal year 1999. Also see Tax Foundation *Special Brief* by Arthur Hall, March 1996.

EXHIBIT 6
Share of Federal Income Taxes Paid by Various Groups

Even though marginal tax rates have been reduced substantially since 1980, upper-income Americans still pay a much larger share of the federal income tax today than during the earlier years.

SHARE OF TOTAL FEDERAL
PERSONAL INCOME TAX PAID

INCOME GROUP	1980	1990	1999
Top 1%	19.1%	25.1%	36.2%
Top 5%	36.8%	43.6%	55.5%
Top 10%	49.3%	55.4%	66.5%
Next 40%	43.7%	38.8%	29.5%
Bottom 50%	7.0%	5.8%	4.0%

Source: Internal Revenue Service.

EXHIBIT 7
Total Federal Taxes As a Share of Income

The federal income tax structure is highly progressive. Federal taxes take 24.6 percent of the income generated by the top quintile (20 percent) of earners, compared to 17.4 percent from the middle-income quintile and 5.9 percent from the lowest quintile of earners.

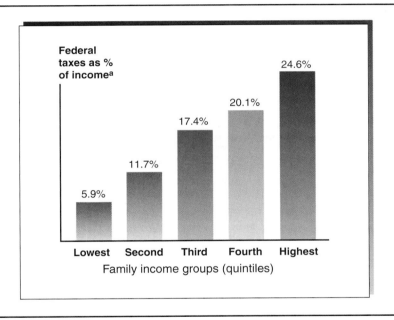

[a] *Total federal taxes include income, excise, payroll, and estate taxes.*
Source: U.S. Department of the Treasury.

tax in 1999, while the bottom half paid only 4.0 percent. The standard deduction and other provisions exempt millions of lower-income families from the personal income tax. More than one-third of the filers either have zero tax liability or actually receive funds from the IRS as the result of the **Earned Income Tax Credit**.

In addition to the personal income tax, the federal government also derives sizable revenues from payroll, corporate income, excise, and estate taxes. How is the overall burden of federal taxes allocated among the various income groups? **Exhibit 7** presents Treasury Department estimates for the average amount of federal taxes paid in 2000 according to income. On average, the top quintile (20 percent) of earners are estimated to pay 24.6 percent of their income in federal taxes. The average federal tax rate for the quintile with the next-highest level of income falls to 20.1 percent and the average tax rate continues to fall as income declines. The average tax rate of the bottom quintile is 5.9 percent, less than one-quarter of the average rate for the top quintile of earners. Clearly, the federal tax system is highly progressive, meaning that it takes a smaller share of the income of those with lower incomes than from those with higher income levels.

Federal income tax brackets are indexed for inflation. Therefore, the tax brackets are widened as inflation increases the nominal incomes of individuals and families. However,

Earned Income Tax Credit
A provision of the tax code that provides a credit or rebate to persons with low earnings (income from work activities). The credit is eventually phased out if the recipient's earnings increase.

no adjustment is made for increases in real incomes. Under a progressive tax system, a larger and larger share of income will be taxed at higher rates as real incomes rise. Therefore, as real incomes grow over time, federal taxes will automatically take a larger share. Put another way, increases in income generate a more than proportional increase in income for the federal government. Some economists, particularly those with a public choice perspective, argue that the automatic tax increases accompanying economic growth adversely affect the efficiency of political decision making. They believe that elected political officials would make better (more efficient) choices if they had to vote for higher taxes in order to adopt new spending programs and expand the relative size of government.

SIZE OF GOVERNMENT IN THE U.S. COMPARED TO OTHER COUNTRIES

There is substantial variation in the size of government across countries. As **Exhibit 8** illustrates, the relative size of government in most other high-income industrial countries is greater than that of the United States. Government spending in 1999 summed to

EXHIBIT 8
Size of Government—An International Comparison, 1999

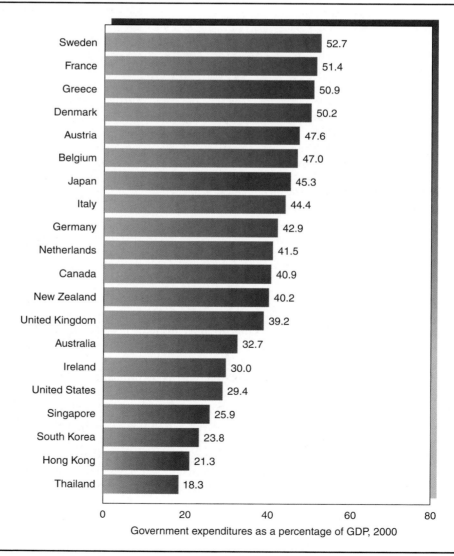

Government expenditures as a percentage of GDP, 2000

Sweden	52.7
France	51.4
Greece	50.9
Denmark	50.2
Austria	47.6
Belgium	47.0
Japan	45.3
Italy	44.4
Germany	42.9
Netherlands	41.5
Canada	40.9
New Zealand	40.2
United Kingdom	39.2
Australia	32.7
Ireland	30.0
United States	29.4
Singapore	25.9
South Korea	23.8
Hong Kong	21.3
Thailand	18.3

Source: OECD Economic Outlook, No 69, June 2001; and Economic Freedom of the World, Annual Report 2001.

more than half of the total output in Sweden, Denmark, France, and Greece. Many other major industrial countries such as Italy, Germany, Canada, the United Kingdom, and Japan had government sectors comprising about 40 to 50 percent of GDP. The government spending/GDP ratios of Australia and Ireland are approximately the same as for the United States. Interestingly, the size of government in South Korea, Singapore, Thailand, and Hong Kong—four Asian nations that have achieved rapid growth and substantial increases in living standards during the last three decades—is smaller than in the United States.

LOOKING AHEAD

As we have shown, the nature of the U.S. government has changed dramatically through time. While real per capita government expenditures declined slightly during the 1990s, that trend is likely to reverse in the near future. Once the baby boomers move into the retirement phase of life beginning around 2010, federal expenditures on both social security and Medicare will increase substantially. Moreover, the recent terrorist attacks illustrate that the world is still a dangerous place. Defense spending, which was sharply curtailed following the collapse of Communism, is likely to increase in response to the terrorist threat. This combination of factors—increased spending on social security, Medicare, and defense—will tend to push both government spending and taxes upward in the near future.

How will the larger government and higher taxes affect the economy? The chapter on economic growth will consider this issue in detail. Even now, however, it is clear that the effects are unlikely to be positive. Higher taxes will mean larger deadweight losses and more significant disincentive effects. Other things constant, this will tend to retard economic growth. Modifications in social security and health care organization might help to alleviate some of the adverse effects. The Special Topic chapters on these subjects will consider alternatives for the improvement of efficiency in these two areas.

KEY POINTS

▼ Government spending includes both purchases of goods and services and income transfers. About three-fifths of government spending takes place at the federal level. Four categories—income transfers (including social security), health care, national defense, and interest on the debt—account for 85 percent of federal spending. Most spending on education takes place at the state and local level.

▼ The federal government derives approximately half of its revenue from the personal income tax and another third from the payroll tax. State and local revenues are derived primarily from sales taxes, income taxes, user charges, and grants from the federal government.

▼ During the first 125 years of U.S. history, federal expenditures per person were small and they grew at a relatively slow rate. In contrast, federal spending

soared throughout most of the twentieth century. In 1990, federal spending per person was nearly 60 times the level of 1916.

▼ During the last four decades, the composition of federal spending has shifted away from national defense and toward spending on income transfers and health care.

▼ In 2000, taxes took a larger share of national income than during any year since World War II. The U.S. tax system is highly progressive—the percentage of income taken from high earners is substantially greater than for those with less income.

▼ The size of government of the United States is smaller than that of Japan and major Western European countries, but larger than for a number of high-growth Asian economies.

CRITICAL ANALYSIS QUESTIONS

*1. How do taxes influence economic efficiency? How much does it cost for the government to raise an additional dollar (or $1 billion) of tax revenue?

2. During the last four decades, a smaller share of the federal budget has been allocated to national defense and a larger share to income transfers and health care. Does economics indicate that this change in expenditure pattern will improve the operation of the economy? Why or why not?

3. A century ago, federal taxes and spending per person were substantially lower than today. How would the U.S. economy be affected if the federal government was, for example, one-third its current size? If this were the case, what programs do you think should be cut? How do you think individuals, families, private organizations, and state and local governments would adjust to the spending cuts?

4. Federal income tax brackets are indexed for inflation, but not for the growth of real income. Because the structure of the personal income tax is progressive, more income is taxed at higher rates as income grows. Therefore, economic growth automatically results in higher taxes unless offsetting legislative action is taken. Do you think this is an attractive feature of the current tax system? Why or why not?

5. Compared to the situation prior to 1980, the marginal tax rates imposed on individuals and families with high incomes are now lower. Are you in favor of or opposed to the lower marginal rates? Do you think it would be a good idea either to raise or lower the current marginal rates? Explain your position.

*Asterisk denotes questions for which answers are given in Appendix B.

SPECIAL TOPIC 2

The Internet: How Is It Changing the Economy?

> *The Internet is kind of like a gold rush where there really is gold.*
>
> —Bill Gates[1]

Focus

- How widely used is the Internet? Who uses the Internet?

- Why is the development of the Internet an important economic phenomenon?

- How is the Internet changing product markets?

- What is the impact of the Internet on the labor market?

---

[1]Bill Gates, *Microsoft Magazine,* January/February 1996.

The Internet is a gigantic library, super shopping mall, and extensive transportation system all wrapped into one. Far more documents can be obtained over the Internet than from even the largest bricks-and-mortar library facility. While a large mall can provide you with access to hundreds of shops in a given locality, the Internet provides access to millions of businesses located around the world. And for only a small fee, you can open your own shop in the world's super mall. Furthermore, many goods including music, movies, software, and financial services can be transported almost instantaneously over the Internet. To top it off, all of this and more is available from your fingertips through the computer in your home or office.

The Internet is changing our lives—how we shop, work, and spend our leisure time. On-line sales of goods and services to consumers such as airline tickets, computers, and books totaled $45 billion in 2000. This figure is expected to rise to $269 billion or 7.8 percent of all projected retail sales by 2005.[2] The Web plays an even more important role in sales between firms. The Internet is expected to account for 40 percent of all business-to-business sales by 2005.[3] The Web is also influencing labor markets by changing how people find new jobs as well as how labor services are provided. This special topic will focus on the Internet and the economic implications of its growth and development. ■

USE OF THE INTERNET

As **Exhibit 1** shows, the number of Web sites on the Internet has exploded in the past decade. In 1992, there were only 16,000 Web sites, but by 2001 there were over 30 million Web sites. This tremendous growth in the number of Web sites has been matched by a dramatic rise in the number of Internet users. By October 2001, over 60 percent of the population or 170 million people were using the Internet in the United States. The typical person uses the Internet quite intensively. The average user spends over 3 hours a week surfing the Web and visits 18 different Web sites per week.[4]

As **Exhibit 2** demonstrates, the use of the Internet has become a worldwide phenomenon. About one-third of Internet users live in the United States. Nearly another one-third of Internet users reside in Europe, and slightly more than one quarter of users live in Asia. Residents of Latin America, the Middle East, and Africa account for a relatively small portion of Internet users.

POTENTIAL GAINS FROM THE INTERNET

Why is the development of the Internet an important economic phenomenon? There are good reasons to believe that the Internet will improve productivity and efficiency—that it will help us generate more value from the available resources. There are three major sources of economic gains from the Internet.

1. **Gains from Lower Transaction Costs.** As we discussed in Chapter 2, trade is vitally important for economic progress. It creates value by moving goods from people who value them less to those who value them more. Trade also creates value by making it possible for the trading partners to produce a larger output as a result of gains from division of labor, specialization, and economies of large-scale production. Transaction

[2]Evie B. Dykema, "On-line Retail's Ripple Effect," September 2000, *Forrester Research Report*, Forrester Research Inc., Cambridge, MA.

[3]Jean G. Henry and John Katsaros, "U.S Business-to-Business Internet Trade Projections," September 2000, *Jupiter Communications Research Report*, Jupiter Communications Inc, Berkeley, CA.

[4]The current number of Internet users as well as usage patterns can be obtained from *www.nielsen-netratings.com*

EXHIBIT 1
Number of Web Sites, 1992–2001

The number of Web sites rose dramatically between 1992 and 2001. By 2001, there were 30 million Web sites.

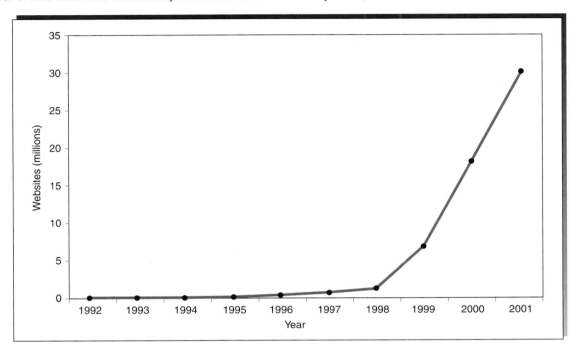

costs are an obstacle to the realization of gains from trade. If these costs could be reduced, the volume of trade would increase and, more importantly, the gains from trade would expand.

The Internet often reduces the cost of transactions, including the cost of information. Through the use of the Internet, many now find it much less costly to search out and identify potential trading partners interested in buying what they have to sell (or selling what they want to buy). In turn, the lower transaction costs increase the gains from trade and thereby make it possible to obtain more value from the available resources. The U.S. economy has already reaped substantial gains from this source, but as use of the Internet expands and people become more aware of its potential, there is reason to believe that the future gains will be even greater.

2. **Gains from Broader and More Competitive Markets.** The cost of establishing an Internet firm are low, often only a few hundred dollars. The costs of identifying potential suppliers through the Internet are also low, and with the development of more efficient search devices, they are declining. As the result of these developments, business firms are now able to compete over a much larger geographic area and buyers are better able to purchase from sellers that are located far away. Thus, markets are becoming more competitive and the location of both buyers and sellers less relevant. This is particularly true for goods that can be transported economically, either through the Internet or via other means of transportation.

3. **Gains from Networking.** Like the telephone of an earlier era, the Internet is a networking system. Telephones were not very valuable when only a few people had one,

EXHIBIT 2
Geographic Distribution of Internet Use, 2001

About one-third of Internet users live in the United States. Nearly another third reside in Europe and slightly more than a quarter are in Asia.

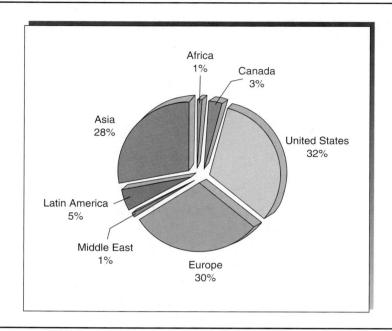

Source: www.nua.ie

but their value increased dramatically as more and more people acquired them. The Internet has this same characteristic. The value of the system to current users increases as more and more people join the network. Growth of the network will make it more likely that Internet sellers will be offering products you want to buy and potential Internet buyers will be searching for goods you are willing to sell. This suggests that the world is just now beginning to tap into the potential economic gains of the Internet.

SOME KEY SECTORS OF INTERNET GROWTH

Exhibit 3 shows that the Internet is now extensively used in several consumer product markets. The percent of sales conducted on-line has now exceeded the 10 percent level in retail markets such as travel, books, and computer hardware and software. The rapid rise in the importance of the Internet in these markets is the result of the relatively low transportation costs for these items as well as the availability of information about these standardized products on-line. A much smaller percentage of the sales of automobiles, food, apparel, and garden and hardware items are conducted on-line. The low market penetration for on-line firms in the food and garden and hardware markets is partly because customers can't observe the condition of these items. The sale of clothing over the Internet is hampered by the fact that one can't examine the fit of clothing on-line. State laws prohibiting the sale of automobiles over the Internet also contribute to their low market share.

The Internet is also quickly transforming how investing is conducted. The number of on-line brokerage accounts has been rapidly increasing. On-line trading accounted for 37 percent of all noninstitutional trading in stocks and options in 1998.[5] By 2000, investors had 12.5 million on-line brokerage accounts.

[5]Brad M. Barber and Terrence Odean, "The Internet and the Investor," *Journal of Economic Perspectives* (Winter 2001): 41–54.

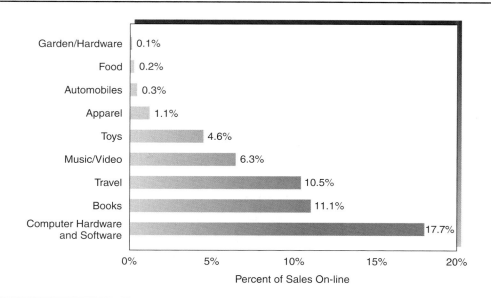

EXHIBIT 3
On-line Market
Penetration 2000

The percent of sales conducted on-line exceeds 10 percent in the travel, books, and computer hardware and software markets. The market share for on-line firms in the automobile, food, apparel, and garden and hardware markets is much smaller.

Source: Shop.org and Boston Consulting Group, *State of Online Retailing 4.0,* May 2001.

The Web has revolutionized the market for used consumer durables. The Web site eBay has made it much easier for people to buy or sell used goods. Buyers search for the items they want with the powerful search engine available on the site. Prior to purchasing an item, buyers can examine earlier customers' ratings of a given seller. Sales are conducted by an on-line auction process. The ease through which trades can be conducted enabled the site to grow to 37.6 million users in 20 countries in 2001. eBay earns revenues by charging a commission for each sale completed and unlike most Internet firms, it has been profitable since its inception.[6]

The Internet is also employed in a variety of ways in sales between firms. The Web is used to automate transactions between buyers and suppliers. Some on-line firms serve as intermediaries between companies. For example, some Web sites are auctioneers of goods such as steel and advertising space. Other on-line companies have set up exchanges for a wide variety of goods. One such exchange is Covisint, which was started by Daimler-Chrysler, Ford, and General Motors to handle their transactions with parts suppliers. Since these three companies purchase almost $250 billion worth of parts each year, this Web site has the potential to become one of the largest firms on the Internet.[7]

PRODUCT MARKETS AND ON-LINE FIRMS

The Internet helps create value in product markets by either reducing costs or improving the match between buyers and sellers.[8] There are several reasons why on-line retail firms may have lower costs. Their handling costs will often be lower because it will not be necessary for the firms to unpack products or put them on display. Losses due to shoplifting, which often are about 3 percent of sales, will be eliminated. Web-based firms are generally

---

[6]Daniel Eisenberg, "Why Are These CEOs Smiling?" *Time,* November 5, 2001, pp. Y2–Y3.

[7]David Lucking-Reiley and Daniel F. Spulber, "Business to Business Electronic Commerce," *Journal of Economic Perspectives* (Winter 2001): 55–68.

[8]For an overview of the impact of the Internet on product markets, see Severin Borenstein and Garth Saloner, "Economics and Electronic Commerce," *Journal of Economic Perspectives* (Winter 2001): 3–12. This section is partly derived from this article.

able to use low-cost warehouses rather than expensive stores in urban or suburban areas. Lastly, on-line retailers will often have lower sales costs than traditional brick-and-mortar firms.

The Internet can also lower costs for sales between companies. For example, switching to an electronic version of the purchasing process from a paper one can substantially reduce the cost of buying goods and services. The cost of completing a paper transaction has been estimated to be roughly $50 per transaction. In addition, improved information from a firm's suppliers about the availability of their products can enable the firm to lower its inventory of inputs and thus its costs.

The Web may also change the production process so that the firm can achieve lower production costs. It can be used to take advantage of differences in time zones. For example, software projects are often transferred over the Internet from programmers in the United States to their counterparts in India at the end of the workday. The Internet can be used in other ways to lower production costs. For instance, a Sun Microsystems Web site allows programmers to bid on contracts to solve clients' software problems.

With regard to matching buyers and sellers, the Internet can often improve information about available goods, increase access to goods, and increase the feasibility of customization. The Internet is an excellent source of information for consumers about available goods and services since an individual can get very specific information about a product or service at a low cost. For example, one can obtain information from on-line versions of product catalogs, product reviews, and price comparison Web sites. In some cases, one can even get product samples of books, music, and software. The powerful search engines available on the Internet, such as Google.com, make it easy to find information about available products. Another important advantage is that consumers can access product information any time of the day or night. Lastly, the Web can customize the process of obtaining information. For instance, Amazon.com provides product recommendations to customers based on their past purchases.

The Web may also make it easier for consumers to obtain access to some goods, particularly specialty products and goods with unique characteristics. For example, it is very expensive for a chain such as The Gap to maintain a large inventory of its products at many different locations. As a consequence, each Gap store branch has only a limited inventory of different styles and sizes of jeans. This results in some consumers having to make compromises on the jeans they purchase. On-line firms can take advantage of economies of scale of centralized inventories and stock a much wider variety of products. This enables Web-based firms to provide a better match to customer's preferences.

A major problem with purchasing goods on-line is that one can't touch, taste, smell, or try on the goods before purchasing them. A potential solution is hybrid stores which act as a showroom for a broad range of products. These stores have for display only a few of each product available for sale. Shoppers can examine the products and then place their order either in the store or later at home on-line. This approach has already been adopted by the Gateway computer company.

The ability of the Internet to provide product customization also increases the quality of matches between sellers and consumers. Dell Computers provides the best example of the impact of product customization. Prior to Dell, the typical personal computer manufacturer forecast demand for various computer models and then produced these computers in batches. The computers were then distributed to wholesalers and retail stores. Changes in inventories and prices were used to create a balance between supply and demand. Dell uses a different business model. On-line Dell customers can customize their computer purchases on several dimensions such as the processor, memory, hard disk size, monitor, and so on. After the order is placed, the computer is made and then shipped directly to the customer. As a result, Dell does not need to manufacture all possible configurations of its computers and therefore is able to achieve lower costs.

The ability of the Internet to improve matches between buyers and sellers also applies to business-to-business transactions. As noted earlier, intermediaries have been set up between firms in a variety of markets. These intermediaries can take the form of exchanges, on-line auctions, and brokers. The intermediaries can often reduce the buyer's search costs and facilitate one-stop shopping and thereby reduce the need for costly contacts with multiple suppliers.

Will Internet firms eventually dominate product markets? It depends on whether they are an efficient method of supplying goods and services. When Internet firms have lower costs or provide consumers with other benefits (for example, broader selection, faster delivery, or greater customization), they will be able to compete effectively. With time, they may even dominate some sectors of the economy. On the other hand, when traditional retailers have lower costs and provide consumers with other benefits (for example, immediate access to the good, inspection of the item, and/or a local service contact), they will survive and prosper. In a market economy, consumers are the ultimate judge. Their choices will determine which firms, be they traditional or on-line, will expand and prosper and which will be driven from the market.

LABOR MARKETS AND THE INTERNET[9]

Job Search

The explosive growth in the Internet is also rapidly changing how people search for jobs. There are now over 3,000 job search sites and 29 million job postings (some of which are duplicates). Monster.com, which is the major job-posting site, indicated in November 2001 that it had over 1 million job-openings and the résumés of over 11 million job seekers.

Job-posting Web sites have several advantages over traditional newspaper help-wanted ads. They contain more job openings and are easier to search. The job openings may be more current since employers can post ads immediately as well as edit them after their initial posting. They also permit individuals to advertise their skills to potential employers as well as the reverse. Lastly, the cost to advertise a job opening is lower. The cost of a 30-day advertisement on Monster.com is less than 5 percent of the cost of a job advertisement in one issue of the Sunday *New York Times*.

Job-posting sites can also help match job seekers with employers. Software can compare the résumés of job seekers with descriptions of open positions. If an appropriate match occurs, then both the employer and the job seeker can be notified. Some programs also learn from job seekers' behavior as they modify their recommendations based on which job openings the individual applied for in the past. Employers can screen candidates by administering personality and skills tests over the Internet.

The Internet is rapidly becoming an important part of the job search process. Currently, the Internet is used in 15 percent of all job searches by unemployed workers. Half of job seekers with Internet access use it in their job search. In fact, the Internet is now more commonly used than traditional job search methods such as contacting friends or relatives and using private employment agencies.

Economic benefits will result from the use of the Internet in the job search process. Job seekers will obtain employment more quickly and thus lower the unemployment rate. This occurs because the Internet permits more initial contacts between potential employers and job seekers. Also, on-line screening of candidates may contribute to a faster and higher quality of match between workers and employers. Productivity should increase since there will be a better match of available positions with job searchers.

The impact on job turnover, however, is uncertain. Better matches between firms and workers should reduce employee turnover. The Internet, however, enables employed workers more easily to search for a new position and so turnover may increase. In fact,

---

[9]This section draws on David H. Autor, "Wiring the Labor Market," *Journal of Economic Perspectives* (Winter 2001): 25–40.

7 percent of the employed indicate that they routinely use the Internet to search for potential new job opportunities.

Delivery of Labor Services

The Internet is also likely to change how workers provide labor services to employers. Remote access to documents and e-mail will permit some workers to provide part or all of their work at home or other locations. In 1997, about 10 percent of workers reported working at home at least sometimes and this figure is rising at 15 percent per year. A potential benefit from telecommuting is that it may reduce the need for unproductive physical commuting time.

The Internet may change how workers obtain their skills. Many employers provide formal and informal training to their workers. This training plays an important role in workers' earnings. On-line delivery of skills training has the potential to reduce the cost and increase the convenience of getting such training.

CONCLUDING THOUGHT

The Internet is an important technological change —perhaps as important as the development of electricity, the railroad, or the automobile. There are reasons to believe that it will improve economic efficiency and help us achieve higher living standards. It will increase the interaction of people around the world. It may also change lifestyles and alter cultural values. It will be exciting to follow these developments in the decades immediately ahead.

KEY POINTS

▼ The use of the Internet has grown dramatically in the past decade and is now a worldwide phenomenon. The Internet is been used extensively in several markets such as investing, airline tickets, books, music, and videos. The volume of business-to-business sales on the Internet is greater than retail sales to consumers.

▼ The Internet tends to improve productivity and the efficiency of resource use because it (a) lowers transaction costs (b) increases the breadth and competitiveness of markets, and (c) becomes more valuable to current users as additional Web sites are added.

▼ The Internet can improve the operation of product markets by reducing costs and improving the matches between buyers and sellers. Costs are reduced due to lower distribution and production costs. Matches are improved through better information about available goods, greater access to goods, and increased customization.

▼ The Internet is rapidly becoming an integral part of the job search process. The reduction in the cost of information through the Internet will tend to lower the rate of unemployment and improve the match between jobs and employee skills. The Internet also makes it possible for many employees to work at home and at other locations.

CRITICAL ANALYSIS QUESTIONS

1. What impact does the Internet have on the efficiency of markets? Explain. How is the Internet likely to influence productivity and the growth of output in the years immediately ahead?

*2. The share of airline tickets bought over the Internet has grown rapidly, while the percent of groceries purchased on-line remains minuscule. What factors likely explain this difference?

3. Instead of being connected to the Internet with slow dial-up modems, many people will soon have fast broadband connections to the Web. How is this change likely to affect product markets?

4. Indicate how the production, marketing, and distribution of each of the following are likely to be influenced by the development of the Internet: (a) popular music, (b) movies, (c) automobiles, (d) commercial employment agencies, (e) beautician services, and (f) health care. Briefly explain your response.

*Asterisk denotes questions for which answers are given in Appendix B.

SPECIAL TOPIC **3**

The Economics of Social Security

Focus

- Why is social security headed for problems?

- Will the Social Security Trust Fund lighten the tax burden of future generations?

- Does social security transfer income from the rich to the poor? How does it impact the economic status of blacks, Hispanics, and those with fewer years of life expectancy?

- Should the social security system be reformed?

---

[1]Mark Weinberger, *Social Security: Facing the Facts* (Washington, D.C.: Cato Institute, 1996), p. 2.

The social security program in the United States is officially known as Old Age and Survivors Insurance (OASI). It offers protection against the loss of income that usually accompanies old age or the death of a breadwinner. In spite of its official title, social security is not based on principles of insurance. Private insurance and pension programs invest the current payments of customers in buildings, farms, or other real assets. Alternatively, they buy stocks and bonds that finance the development of real assets. These real assets generate income that allows the pension fund (or insurance company) to fulfill its future obligations to its customers.

Social security does not follow this saving-and-investment model. Instead, most of the funds flowing into the system are paid out to current retirees and survivors in the program. In essence, the social security system is an intergenerational income-transfer program. Most of the taxes collected from the present generation of workers are paid out to current beneficiaries. Thus, the system is based on "pay-as-you-go" rather than the savings and investment principle.

The social security retirement program is financed by a flat rate payroll tax of 10.6 percent applicable to employee earnings up to a cutoff level. In 2002, the earnings cutoff was $84,900. Thus, employees earning $84,900 or more paid $8,999 in social security taxes to finance the OASI retirement program.[2] The income cutoff is adjusted upward each year by the growth rate of nominal wages. While the payroll tax is divided equally between employee and employer, it is clearly part of the employees' compensation package and most economists believe that the burden of this tax falls primarily on the employee. The formula used to determine retirement benefits favors those with lower earnings during their working years. However, as we will discuss later, the redistributive effects toward those with lower incomes are more apparent than real.

When the program began in 1935, not many people lived past age 65 and the nation had lots of workers and few eligible retirees. As **Exhibit 1** illustrates, there were 16 workers for every social security beneficiary as recently as 1950. That ratio has declined sharply through the years. As a result, higher and higher taxes per worker have been required just to maintain a constant level of benefits. There are currently 3.4 workers per social security retiree. By 2030, however, that figure will decline to only 2.1.

During the early years of social security, there were many workers per beneficiary and therefore it was possible to provide retirees with generous benefits while maintaining a relatively low rate of taxation. Many of those who retired in the 1960s and 1970s received real benefits of three or four times the amount they paid into the system, far better than they could have done had they invested the funds privately. The era of high returns, however, is now over. The program has matured and the number of workers per beneficiary has declined. Payroll taxes have risen greatly over the decades and still higher taxes will be necessary merely to fund currently promised benefits.

Studies indicate that those now age 40 and younger can expect to earn a real rate of return of about 2 percent on their social security tax dollars, substantially less than what they could earn from personal investments. Thus, social security has been a good deal for current and past retirees. It is not, however, a very good deal for today's middle-aged and younger workers. ■

WHY IS SOCIAL SECURITY HEADED FOR PROBLEMS?

The flow of funds into and out of a pay-as-you-go retirement system is sensitive to demographic conditions. The social security system is currently enjoying a period of highly favorable demographics. The U.S. birthrate was low during the Great Depression and World

---

[2]Additional payroll taxes are levied for the finance of disability programs (1.8 percent) and Medicare (2.9 percent). Thus, the total payroll tax sums to 15.3 percent, but only revenues from the 10.6 percent rate are used for the finance of benefits to retirees and surviving dependents. (*Note:* the earnings cutoff does not apply to the Medicare portion of the payroll tax.)

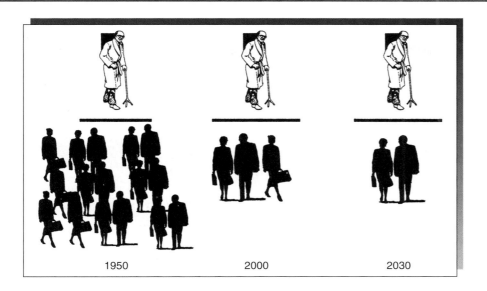

EXHIBIT 1
Workers Per Social Security Beneficiary

In 1950, there were 16 workers per social security beneficiary. By 2000, the figure had fallen to only 3.4. By 2030, there will be only 2.1 workers per retiree. As the worker/beneficiary ratio falls under a pay-as-you-go system, either taxes must be increased or benefits reduced (or both).

Source: 2001 Annual Report of the Board of Trustees of the Federal Old Age and Survivors Insurance and Disability Insurance Trust Funds (Washington, D.C.: Government Printing Office, 2001), p. 122.

War II. The Great Depression/World War II group is now retiring and because it is a relatively small generation, payments to it are also relatively small. The birthrate rose sharply during the two decades following World War II. These baby boomers are now in their prime working years and their large numbers are expanding the flow of revenues into the social security retirement system.

When the baby boomers begin moving into the retirement phase of life around 2011, however, the situation is going to change dramatically. Their retirement, combined with rising life expectancies, will substantially increase the number of retirees relative to the number of workers. As we previously noted, the number of workers per social security retiree will fall from the current 3.4 level to only 2.1 in 2030.

Exhibit 2 illustrates the impact of demographics on the pay-as-you-go social security system. Currently, the funds flowing into the system (pushed up by the large baby boom generation) exceed the expenditures on benefits to retirees (pulled down by the small Great Depression/World War II generation). But the retirement of the baby boomers around 2011 will begin pushing the expenditures of the system upward at a rapid rate. The current surplus of revenues from the payroll tax relative to retirement benefits will end around 2016. After 2016, the deficits will grow larger and larger as the number of beneficiaries relative to workers continues to grow in the decades ahead.

As **Exhibit 3** shows, there are now approximately 25 million persons age 70 and over in the United States. By 2030, the number of septuagenarians will soar to 47.8 million. This increase will be particularly sharp in the years following 2015. The medical expenditures of persons 70 years and over are considerably higher than those of persons a few years younger. These demographic changes will place strong pressure on the Medicare program as well as the social security retirement system. The current pay-as-you-go structure of these two programs will make it exceedingly difficult to control the growth of government and maintain reasonable levels of taxation in the decades ahead.

The revenues derived from the payroll tax have exceeded the benefits paid to current retirees since the mid-1980s (see Exhibit 2). Currently, only about 80 percent of the revenues are required for the payments to current beneficiaries. Thus, the system is currently running a substantial surplus—about $165 billion per year and sizable surpluses are projected in the decade ahead. If other elements of the federal budget were in balance, the

EXHIBIT 2
The Forthcoming Deficit between Payroll Tax Revenues and Benefit Expenditures

Given current payroll taxes and retirement benefit levels, the system will run larger and larger deficits during the 2016–2030 period and beyond.

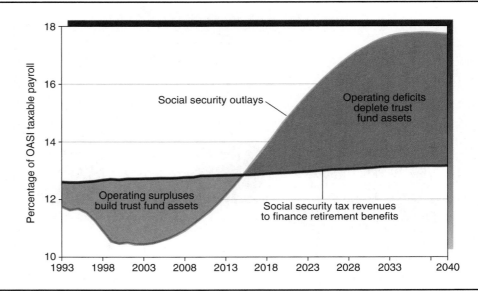

Source: Social Security Administration 2001 OASDI Annual Trustees Report, www.ssa.gov.

EXHIBIT 3
The Increase in the Number of People Age 70 and Over

Between 2000 and 2030, the number of persons age 70 years and over will almost double. The medical expenses of persons in this age group are particularly high. This will place strong pressure on both the social security and Medicare programs.

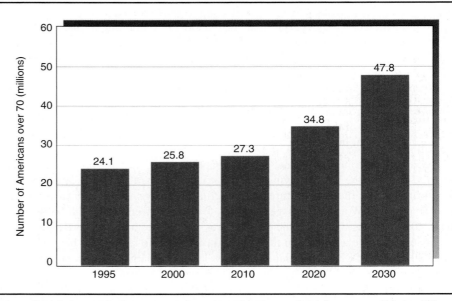

Source: Bipartisan Commission on Entitlement and Tax Reform, Final Report to the President (Washington, D.C.: Government Printing Office, 1995), p. 13; and *1995 Annual Report of the Board of Trustees of the Federal Old Age and Survivors Insurance and Disability Insurance Trust Funds,* p. 21.

social security surpluses could be used to pay off some of the federal government's out-standing debt. In turn, the debt reduction would reduce the government's future interest payments, which would make it easier to deal with rising social security expenditures when the baby boomers retire. Throughout the 1980s and 1990s, however, most of the social security surplus was used to finance current government operations. Only a small portion of the surplus was used to retire outstanding debt.

WILL THE TRUST FUND LIGHTEN THE FUTURE TAX BURDEN?

Under current law, the surpluses are channeled into the Social Security Trust Fund (SSTF). The Trust Fund uses the revenue to buy special nonmarketable bonds from the U.S. Treasury. By 2016, the Social Security Trust Fund is expected to grow to more than $5 trillion. Social security actuaries calculate that this will provide sufficient funds for payment of promised benefits until 2039.

Will a large trust fund make it easier to deal with the retirement of the baby boomers? Some are surprised to learn that there is little reason to believe that it will. Unlike the bonds, stocks, and physical assets held by a private pension fund or insurance company, the SSTF bonds will not generate a stream of future income for the federal government. Neither are they a "pot of money" set aside for the payment of future benefits. Instead the trust fund bonds are an IOU from one government agency—the Treasury—to another—the Social Security Administration. The federal government is both the payee and recipient of the interest and principal represented by the SSTF bonds. ***No matter how many bonds are in the trust fund, their net asset value to the federal government is zero!***

Thus, the number of IOUs in the trust fund is largely irrelevant.[3] The size of the trust fund could be doubled or tripled, but that would not give the government any additional funds for the payment of benefits. Correspondingly, the trust fund could be abolished, and the government would not be relieved of any of its existing obligations or commitments. In order to redeem the bonds and thereby provide the social security system with funds to cover future deficits, the federal government will have to raise taxes, cut other expenditures, or borrow from the public. These options will not change with the depletion of the trust fund.

THE REAL PROBLEM OF THE CURRENT SYSTEM

The real problem faced by the pay-as-you-go social security system will arise around 2016 when the revenues from the payroll tax will begin to fall short of the benefits promised to retirees. The deficits of the system will become larger and larger throughout the 2020s and 2030s. Under current law, revenues will be sufficient to pay only about three-quarters of promised benefits by 2030, and less in later years.

There are only four ways to cover future shortfalls: (1) cut benefits, (2) increase taxes, (3) cut spending in other areas, or (4) borrow. None of these options are attractive and, regardless of how the gap is filled, a slowdown in the rate of economic growth is likely to occur. If benefits are reduced, current beneficiaries and persons near retirement will—quite correctly—feel that a commitment made to them has been broken. It will also be difficult to cover the shortfall with higher taxes. Once the baby boom generation retires, approximately a 50 percent increase in the payroll tax or a 30 percent increase in the personal income tax will be needed to cover social security deficits. Tax increases of this magnitude will exert a negative impact on the economy. Neither will it be easy to cut expenditures in other areas of the federal budget. Defense spending was already cut substantially as a share of the economy during the 1990s and it is likely to be pushed upward in the future by external threats, including those arising from terrorism. Furthermore, the growth of the elderly population is sure to place upward pressure on Medicare spending, another major federal program. Finally, borrowing to cover the shortfall will place upward pressure on interest rates and necessitate higher future taxes merely to cover the interest obligations. Thus, it merely delays the problem.

---

[3]Of course, the SSTF bonds represent funds borrowed by the Treasury from the social security system. This increases the legitimacy of claims on these funds by future social security recipients. It also indicates that the trust fund is similar to what is called budget authority, which provides the legal permission for the government to spend funds on an item.

Not even robust economic growth would eliminate the future shortfall. Retirement benefits are indexed to average growth in nominal wages. If higher productivity enables *real* (inflation-adjusted) wages to rise quickly, so will social security benefits. For example, if inflation is zero and real wages grow 2 percent a year instead of their previous level of 1 percent, the benefits of future recipients will grow by 2 percent rather than 1 percent. Higher economic growth may temporarily improve social security's finances, but under current law the improvement will not last.[4]

WHO IS HELPED AND WHO IS HURT BY SOCIAL SECURITY?

When social security was established in 1935, the population was growing rapidly, only a few Americans lived to age 65, and the labor force participation rate of women was low. Social security was designed for this world. But today's world is dramatically different. Several aspects of the system now seem outdated, arbitrary, and in some cases, unfair.

Does Social Security Help the Poor?

Social Security has gained many supporters because of the belief that it redistributes wealth from rich to poor. The system is financed with a flat tax rate up to the cutoff limit, but the formula used to calculate benefits disproportionately favors workers with low lifetime earnings.[5] However, other aspects of the system tend to favor those with higher incomes. First, workers with more education and high earnings tend to live longer than those with less education and lower earnings. As **Exhibit 4** shows, the age-adjusted mortality rate of persons with less than a high school education is 8 to 10 percent higher than the average for all Americans. As years of schooling increase, mortality rates fall. The age-adjusted mortality rate of college graduates is 21 percent below the average for all Americans, while the rate for persons with advanced degrees is 32 percent below the average. Given the strong correlation between education and earnings, the age-adjusted mortality figures indicate that, on average, Americans with higher earnings live longer than their counterparts with less education and lower earnings. As a result, high-wage workers will, on average, draw social security benefits longer than low-wage workers. Low-wage workers are far more likely to pay thousands of dollars in social security taxes and then die before, or soon after, becoming eligible for retirement benefits.

Second, low-wage workers generally begin full-time work at a younger age. Many work full-time and pay social security taxes for years while future high-wage workers are still in college and graduate school. Low-wage workers generally pay more into the system earlier, and therefore forgo more interest, than high-wage workers.

Third, labor participation tends to fall as spousal earnings increase. As a result, couples with a high-wage worker are more likely to gain from social security's spousal benefit provision, which provides the nonworking spouse with benefits equal to 50 percent of those the working spouse receives.

Two recent studies taking these and other related factors into consideration suggest that social security may actually transfer wealth from low-wage to high-wage workers. A study using data from the Social Security Administration and the Health and Retirement

---

[4]See Garth Davis, "Faster Economic Growth Will Not Solve the Social Security Crisis," *CDA Report 00-01*, Heritage Center for Data Analysis, Feb. 2, 2000.

[5]Retirement benefits are based on the best 35 years of earnings from a worker's career. Benefits are calculated by taking 90 percent of the first $7,104 a year of earnings, 32 percent of earnings between $7,104 and $38,424, and just 15 percent of earnings above $42,804 up to the earnings cutoff of $84,900. Therefore, as base earnings rise, benefits fall as a percentage of average earnings (and payroll taxes paid) during one's lifetime. For example, the retirement benefits of persons with base annual earnings of $10,000 sum to 73 percent of their average working year earnings. In contrast, the retirement benefits of those with base earnings of $60,000 are only 34 percent of their average preretirement earnings. These figures are based on the formula for 2002. The figures are adjusted each year for the growth of nominal wages.

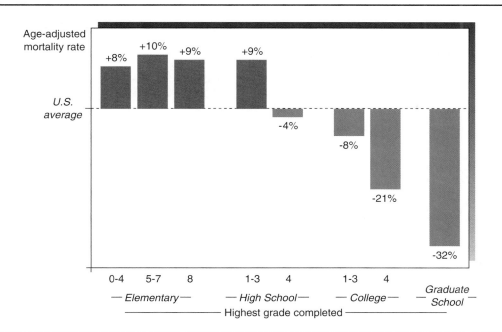

Age-adjusted mortality rate

U.S. average

+8% +10% +9% +9% -4% -8% -21% -32%

0-4 5-7 8 — Elementary —

1-3 4 — High School—

1-3 4 — College—

Graduate School

———— Highest grade completed ————

EXHIBIT 4
Mortality Rates by Level of Education

As shown here the age-adjusted mortality rates are lower for those with more education. Because of the close link between education and income, persons with higher incomes tend to live longer and, therefore, draw social security benefits for a more lengthy time period than those with less education and income.

Source: Center for Data Analysis, Heritage Foundation.

Study found that when social security benefits are assessed for family units, rather than for individuals, the progressivity of the system disappears. Another study adjusted for differences in mortality rates, patterns of lifetime income, and other factors. It found that if a 2 percent real interest rate (discount rate) is used to evaluate the pattern of taxes paid and benefits received, the redistributive effects of social security are essentially neutral. However, at a more realistic 4 percent real interest rate, social security actually favors higher-income households.[6]

Social Security Adversely Affects Blacks and Other Groups with Below-Average Life Expectancy

Currently, the average retiree reaching age 65 can expect to spend 18 years receiving social security benefits, after more than 40 years of paying into the system. But what about those who do not make it into their 80s, or even to the normal retirement age of 65? Unlike private financial assets, social security benefits cannot be passed on to heirs. Thus, those who die before age 65, or soon thereafter, receive little or nothing from their payroll tax payments.

Social security was not set up to transfer income from some ethnic groups to others, but under its current structure, it nonetheless does so. Because of their shorter life expectancy, the social security system adversely affects the economic welfare of blacks. Compared to whites and Hispanics, blacks are far more likely to pay a lifetime of payroll taxes and then die without receiving much in the way of benefits. Thus, the system works to their disadvantage. On the other hand, social security is particularly favorable to Hispanics because of their above-average life expectancy and the progressive nature of the

---

[6]See Alan Gustman and Thomas Steinmeier (2000) "How Effective Is Redistribution under the Social Security Benefit Formula?" National Bureau of Economic Research working paper W7597, March; and Julia Lynn Coronado, Don Fullerton, and Thomas Glass (2000) "The Progressivity of Social Security," National Bureau of Economic Research working paper W7520.

EXHIBIT 5
Rates of Return by Gender, Marital Status, and Ethnicity

The earnings of blacks are lower than whites, but their life expectancy is shorter. The latter effect dominates, so that blacks derive a lower rate of return from social security than whites. On the other hand, Hispanics have both lower earnings and a little longer life expectancy than whites. Thus, their returns from social security are higher than for whites, and substantially higher than blacks.

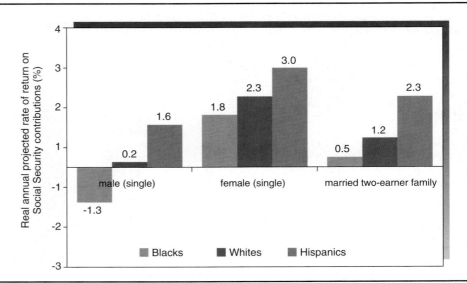

Source: Center for Data Analysis, Heritage Foundation.

benefit formula. As a result, Hispanics derive a higher return than whites and substantially higher than blacks.[7]

Exhibit 5 presents the expected real returns for those born in 1975, according to gender, marital status, and ethnicity.[8] Single black males born in 1975 can expect to derive a real annual return of *negative* 1.8 percent on their social security tax payments, compared to returns of 0.2 percent for single white males and 1.6 percent for single Hispanic males. Similarly, a two-earner black couple born in 1975 can expect a real return of 0.5 percent, compared to returns of 1.2 percent and 2.3 percent for white and Hispanic couples born during the same year. A similar pattern exists when comparisons are made for those born in other years.

The social security retirement system also works to the disadvantage of those with life-shortening diseases. People with diabetes, heart disease, AIDS, and other diseases often spend decades paying 10.6 percent of their earnings into the system, only to die with loved ones unable to receive benefits from the social security taxes they have paid. (People with life-shortening diseases may receive disability insurance, but if they die before retirement they collect nothing from their payments into the retirement system.)

Discrimination Against Working Women

When social security was established, relatively few married women worked outside the home. Therefore, individuals were permitted to receive benefits based on either their own earnings or 50 percent of the benefits earned by their spouse, whichever is greater. This provision imposes a heavy penalty on women in the workforce. In the case of many work-

---

[7]For additional details on the redistributive effects of social security across ethnic groups, see William W. Beach and Gareth Davis (2000), "More for Your Money: Improving Social Security's Rate of Return," in David C. John, editor, *Improving Retirement Security: A Handbook for Reformers*, pp. 25–64, Washington: Heritage Foundation, and Martin Feldstein and Jeffrey Liebman (2000) "The Distributional Effects of an Investment-Based Social Security System," National Bureau of Economic Research working paper W7492.

[8]It is common to calculate a rate of return on financial investments by comparing initial investments with the stream of projected future income (or benefits). Social security is not like a regular financial investment since there is no accumulation of assets and no legal right to benefits. Nonetheless, a rate of return can be calculated by comparing the payroll taxes a worker pays with the future benefits he or she is promised. The rate of return figures of Exhibit 5 were derived in this manner. They assume that the current tax level and promised future benefits will be maintained. However, as we previously noted, projections indicate that current tax rates will cover only about three-fourths of promised benefits by 2030. Thus, higher taxes will be required to maintain the promised benefit levels. In turn, the higher taxes will lower rates of return. Therefore, the figures of Exhibit 5 probably overstate the rates of return for the various groups.

ing married women, the benefits based on the earnings of their spouses are approximately equal to, or in some cases greater than, benefits based on their own earnings. Thus, the payroll tax takes a big chunk of the earnings of many working women without providing them with any significant additional benefits.

PERSONAL RETIREMENT ACCOUNTS AND SOCIAL SECURITY REFORM

When the number of workers is growing rapidly and each successive generation is larger than the one that proceeded it, a pay-as-you-go system can work well and yield a reasonable return. But we are now in an era where the number of retirees is growing more rapidly than the number of workers. In this environment, social security is not a good investment. As we previously mentioned, today's typical worker can expect a return of only 2.0 percent from the taxes paid into the system. Social security uses a worker's highest 35 earning years to calculate benefits. Going back to 1873 (this is as far back as calculations can be made), the average real rate of return derived from a fixed annual payment over a 35-year period into the stock market has been 6.4 percent. The highest return over a 35-year period was 9.5, while the lowest was 2.7 percent.[9] Even this latter figure is higher than can be expected from social security. Social security's low rate of return, along with its structure that sometimes seems outdated, has fostered an environment for change.

When the number of workers is small relative to the number of retirees, a system where individuals finance their own retirement by saving and investing during their working years becomes more attractive. In varying degrees, several countries have already moved toward systems based on personal retirement accounts (PRAs). Beginning in the early 1980s, Chile shifted to a retirement system based on saving and investing through PRAs rather than pay-as-you-go. The Chilean plan was so successful that other Latin American countries, including Mexico, Bolivia, Colombia, and Peru, adopted similar plans in the 1990s. High-income countries have also moved in this direction. In 1986, the United Kingdom began allowing workers to channel 4.6 percentage points of their payroll tax into PRAs in exchange for acceptance of a lower level of benefits from the pay-as-you-go system. The PRA option is highly popular. It is now chosen by nearly three-fourths of British workers. Other countries that now permit at least some substitution of PRAs for payroll taxes and pay-as-you-go benefits include the Netherlands, Australia, Sweden, and Germany.

A shift to a retirement security system based, at least partially, on personal saving accounts raises a number of issues. We will mention four of the most important.

1. **Degree of Investor Choice.** Historical evidence indicates that when held over a lengthy time period, a diverse holding of stocks is a low-risk investment that will generally outperform government bonds. (See the following Special Topic feature.) Furthermore, mutual funds now make it possible for even a small novice investor to hold a diverse stock portfolio while still keeping administrative costs low. If left to their own discretion, however, there is no assurance that investors will choose to hold a diverse portfolio. Some plans would provide individuals with a good deal of discretion concerning how their funds are invested. Others would restrict those choices in order to assure that potential retirement funds are not squandered on risky investments. The issue here is primarily about striking a balance between an attractive rate of return and minimal risk that retirement funds would be wiped out by either unwise financial investments or abrupt changes in the market value of assets.

2. **Share of Payroll Tax Allocated to PRAs and Current System.** How much of the payroll tax should workers be permitted to allocate into PRAs? Several plans would

---

[9]See Liqun Liu, Andrew J. Rettenmaier, and Zijun Wang, "Social Security and Stock Market Risk," NCPA Policy Report No. 244, National Center for Policy Analysis, July 23, 2001.

THE WIZARD OF ID

The projected real rate of return on social security taxes for persons born after 1950 is approximately 2 percent, far below the real rate of return on private sector investments.

permit individuals to channel between 2 and 6 percentage points (out of the current 10.6 percent rate) into a PRA-based system in exchange for acceptance of lower benefits from the current system. With time, other plans would envision full substitution of an investment-based retirement system for the current pay-as-you-go approach. Obviously, this issue is about the relative importance of the two systems in the future.

3. **Protecting the Benefits of Current Retirees and Those Near Retirement.** The benefits promised to current retirees and those near retirement age must be protected. Because most of the payroll tax is needed to finance current benefits, permitting workers to channel more than 1 or 2 percentage points into PRAs would create an immediate shortfall for the current system. Therefore, the transition to a system based more on personal investment may well require an increase in taxes and/or additional borrowing.

4. **Property Rights and PRAs.** Most plans currently under consideration would give individuals a property right to the funds in their account and allow them to be passed along to heirs in case of death prior to retirement. However, funds drawn from a PRA during retirement years would generally have to be converted to a lifetime annuity, an instrument that would pay a regular income for the remainder of one's life.

Policy makers are now searching for ways to provide income security for future retirees without having to increase payroll taxes to levels that will retard work incentives and endanger future growth. Personal retirement accounts may help achieve this objective. The disincentive effects of payments into a PRA, which can be passed along to heirs and used to enhance personal income during retirement, are much less severe than those of higher taxes. Furthermore, PRAs will tend to encourage saving and investment, which will exert a positive impact on future growth of the economy. They will also reduce the dependency of senior citizens on political officials. The ongoing debate about the future structure of social security is particularly important to younger people. It is their lives that will be most affected by how this issue is handled.

KEY POINTS

▼ Social security does not follow the saving-and-investment model. Most of the funds flowing into the system are paid out to current retirees and survivors under the program.

▼ While the current tax revenues exceed the payments to retirees, this will change dramatically as the baby boomers begin to move into the retirement phase of life. Beginning around 2016, the system's current surplus will shift to a deficit, which will persist for several decades.

▼ The current surplus of the social security system is used to purchase U.S. Treasury bonds. Because the federal government is both the payee and recipient of these bonds, their net asset value to the federal government is zero. They will not reduce the level of future taxes needed to cover the social security deficit when the baby boomers begin to retire.

▼ The major problem resulting from the current pay-as-you-go system is that large tax increases, spending cuts, and/or additional borrowing will be required to cover the social security deficits following the retirement of the baby boom generation. Dealing with these deficits is likely to affect the economy adversely.

▼ While the social security benefit formula favors those with lower lifetime earnings, low-wage work-

ers have a lower life expectancy, begin work at a younger age, and gain less from the spousal benefit provisions of the current system. These latter factors largely, if not entirely, offset the egalitarian affects of the benefit formula.

▼ Because of their shorter life expectancy, blacks derive a lower rate of return from social security than whites, and a substantially lower return than Hispanics.

▼ The demographics of the twenty-first century reduce the attractiveness of pay-as-you-go social security. Thus, various plans that would place more interest on investment and personal retirement accounts are now under consideration.

CRITICAL ANALYSIS QUESTIONS

1. Is the social security system based on the same principles as private insurance? Why or why not?

*2. Why does the social security system face a crisis? Are there real assets in the Social Security Trust Fund that can be used to pay future benefits? Will the trust fund help to avert higher future taxes and/or benefit reductions when the baby boomers retire? Why or why not?

3. Do you think workers should be permitted to invest all or part of their social security contribution in private investment funds? What are the advantages and disadvantages of a private option system? If given the opportunity, would you choose the private option or stay with the current system? Why?

4. How does social security affect the economic well-being of blacks relative to whites and Hispanics? Explain.

5. Does the current social security system promote income equality? Why or why not?

6. The social security payroll tax is split equally between the employee and the employer. Would it make any difference if the entire tax was imposed on employees? Would employees be helped if all the tax was imposed on employers? (*Hint:* You may want to consult pages 100–105.)

*Asterisk denotes questions for which answers are given in Appendix B.

SPECIAL TOPIC 4

The Stock Market: What Does It Do and How Has It Performed?

Though the stock market functions as a voting machine in the short run, it acts as a weighing machine in the long run.

—*Ben Graham*[1]
Securities Analyst

Focus

- What is the economic function of the stock market?

- How are stock prices related to the interest rate?

- Why has the stock market risen so much since 1982?

- What is the future outlook for the stock market?

[1]As quoted by Warren Buffett in Carol Loomis, "Warren Buffett on the Stock Market," *Fortune*, December 10, 2001, pp. 80–87.

T he market for corporate shares is called the stock market. The changes in stock prices in recent years have often been front-page news. On the whole, investors in American stocks have done exceedingly well and this has been true over a long period. Since 1802, the returns of stock holdings have averaged 7 percent, corrected for inflation. That means that, on average, stock investments have doubled in value every 10 years.

The Standard and Poor's 500 Index indicates the performance of the broad stock market. This index factors in the value of dividends as if they were reinvested in the market. Thus, it provides a measure of the rate of return received by investors in the form of both dividends and changes in share prices. As **Exhibit 1** illustrates, the S&P 500 stocks generated a 12 percent average annual rate of return during 1950–2000. Even after adjustment for inflation, the returns averaged 8.2 percent during this period. The returns during the 1980s and 1990s were even higher.

The prices of individual stocks can rise and fall spectacularly. Those who buy and sell stocks, especially when they try to outguess market changes, can gain or lose huge sums of money in a very short time. Is the stock market simply a giant casino? Or does it perform functions that are critical for the growth of an economy? Why has the market performed so well during the last 50 years? Will this trend continue or can we expect a downturn or even a stock market crash in the near future? How do changes in factors like the interest rate and the number of people currently in certain age categories affect the demand for stocks? This feature addresses these questions and related issues. ■

THE ECONOMIC FUNCTIONS OF THE STOCK MARKET

The stock market performs several important functions in a modern economy. That is true even though a few active traders in the market treat it much like a casino. Those who constantly buy and sell, trying to predict the movement of each stock price and to outguess others in the market, are gambling. Most will probably lose over time, because buying and selling is itself costly. Traders looking for quick profits face a difficult task. They

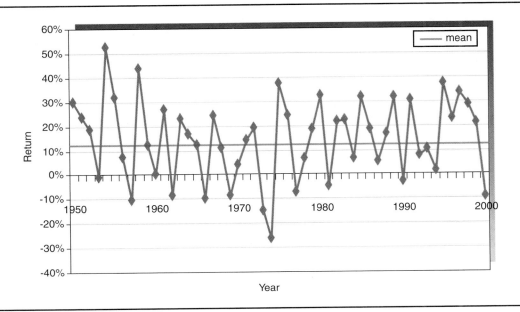

EXHIBIT 1
Annual Return for Stocks, 1950–2000

During the past 50 years, the broad S&P 500 Index indicates that stock investors earned a 12 percent annual rate of return. Double-digit returns were earned in 32 of the 50 years, while returns were negative during only 11 of the years.

Source: Global Financial Data, www.globalfindata.com.

must frequently be right about price changes, just to break even over time. Yet it is very difficult to outguess the others in the market.

Most participants in the stock market have little special expertise. Only a few are willing to take the time to obtain detailed information on a large number of firms. Nonetheless, the stock market provides them with a means through which they can share in the profits (and the risks) of large businesses. Investment fund managers and other advisors offer, for a fee, to manage their investments. Savers have found the stock market to be an excellent place to invest their savings in order to build wealth over time. At the same time, firms seeking funds have found new stock issues to be an excellent method to identify others willing to share the risks and the opportunities that accompany their business activities. Investors and firms seeking investment capital can gain from the exchange of savings for ownership shares. For the economy as a whole, the stock market channels investment funds into profitable activities. It rewards the choice and recognition of successful business strategies. It also disciplines business decision makers who use resources in a wasteful or destructive manner. Let us look at each of these stock market functions more closely.

How the Stock Market Works for Savers and Investors

A large and rapidly growing number of savers invest as a long-term strategy. For them the stock market has been an excellent place to build wealth. Today it is possible for investors to buy shares of ownership in a wide variety of firms and hold them over long periods of time. Such a strategy can substantially reduce risk, although the stock market has no guaranteed returns.

One source of risk for a stock market investor is the fact that individual stocks can rise and fall unpredictably. Investing in any one firm is risky. But investors can reduce their risk of losses by holding a diverse **portfolio**, a collection of stocks characterized by relatively small holdings of a large number of companies. The increases in some stock prices tend to balance out the decreases in others. That way, swings in the value of any one stock do not matter so much. The fees of stockbrokers have fallen over time. For example, trades that might have cost hundreds of dollars 15 years ago can now be made for as little as $5. This makes it cheaper for an investor to purchase shares in a wide array of firms and thereby reduce the variability of his or her earnings and the risk accompanying stock ownership.

Individual investors can also reduce their risk by purchasing a diverse set of firms through an **equity mutual fund**, a corporation that buys and holds shares of stock in many firms. It is also possible to purchase a stock index mutual fund, an equity fund with a portfolio that mirrors one or another of the many stock indexes, such as the S&P 500 Index or the Dow Jones Industrials. These mutual funds do very little trading and as a result have low operating costs. They have had better yields than most of the more actively managed mutual funds—those trading more often in search of greater gains. As **Exhibit 2** shows, the combined holdings of equity mutual funds summed to approximately $4 trillion in 2000. That was about 20 percent of all publicly traded U.S. stocks. Moreover, stock ownership through these mutual funds has been growing rapidly in recent years.

A second source of risk facing investors is the fact that nearly all stocks in the market may rise or fall together, when expectations about the entire economy change. Such change can be sudden. For example, on October 19, 1987, the stocks listed in the Dow Jones Industrial Average lost more than 22 percent of their value in just one trading day. But as **Exhibit 3** shows, investing in stocks for a longer period reduces the risk of large losses.[2] For example, an individual investing in stocks in the S&P Index at the beginning of any year between 1871 and 2000 lost 35.47 percent, after inflation, in the worst case. A gain of 47 percent was the best case. But investing in the index stocks over any 20-year

Portfolio
All the stocks, bonds, or other securities held by an individual or corporation for investment purposes.

Equity mutual fund
A corporation that pools the funds of investors, including small investors, and uses them to purchase a bundle of stocks.

---

[2] The returns are based on the assumption that an individual invests a fixed amount for each year in the investment period.

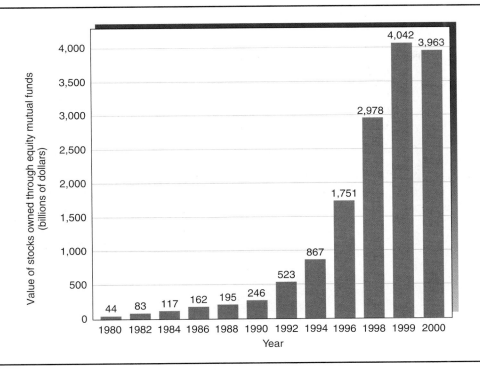

EXHIBIT 2
Value of Equity Mutual Funds

The amount of money that people put into U.S. equity mutual funds, in order to hold shares in the ownership of stocks, rose dramatically in the 1990s. Purchasing shares in a mutual fund is a simple way for an individual to buy and hold an interest in a large variety of stocks with one purchase.

Source: Investor Company Institute, www.ici.org

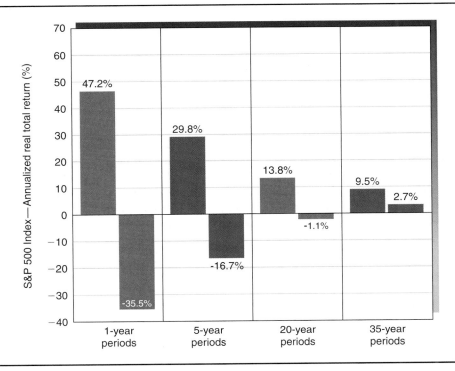

EXHIBIT 3
Stocks Are Less Risky When Invested for a Lengthy Time Period

This graphic highlights the best and the worst annualized real performance for each investment period from 1871 to 2000. It shows that there is less risk of a low or negative return when investment in a portfolio of stocks (S&P 500) is conducted for a longer period of time.

Source: Liqun Liu, Andrew J. Rettenmaier, and Zijun Wang, "Social Security and Market Risk," National Center for Policy Analysis Working Paper Number 244, July 2001. The returns are based on the assumption that an individual invests a fixed amount for each year in the investment period.

Are stocks riskier than bonds? If held for only a short time—1 to 3 years, for example—stocks are more risky. However, when held over lengthy periods like 20 or 30 years, historically, the rate of return on stocks has been both higher and less variable than that of bonds. What does this imply about where persons saving for their retirement while in their twenties and thirties should place their funds?

period brought a small negative real return of −1.05 percent in the worst case. In the best case 20-year period, the real return was 13.79 percent. Over any 35-year period, 2.66 percent was the worst return, while 9.54 percent was the best. Clearly, investing in a portfolio of stocks for a longer period greatly reduces the risk of very low or negative returns to the investor, although it similarly reduces the chance of very large returns.

Two decades ago, the high historical rate of return on stocks was thought to reflect their greater risk relative to bonds and other investments like savings accounts. Indeed, stocks are risky when held for a relatively short time or when only small numbers of stocks are held in one's portfolio. *However, when a diverse set of stocks is held over a lengthy time period, historically, stocks have yielded a high rate of return and the variation of that return has been relatively small. The development of stock mutual funds makes it possible for even small investors to hold a diverse portfolio, add to it regularly, and still keep transaction costs low.*

The development of equity mutual funds both reduced the risk of stock investments and attracted large amounts of funds into the market, helping to push prices upward. During the 1990s, many Americans reached retirement with substantially more wealth than had been expected a few years earlier. In early 2001, U.S. households owned $12 trillion in stocks, up from $7.2 trillion at the end of 1996. About one-half of all households now own stock, either directly or through an equity mutual fund. The wealth of these households has increased substantially as their stock holdings have risen in value.

How the Stock Market Works For Corporations

To raise money to develop new products or expand output, a corporation has several options. It can use retained earnings (profits earned but not paid out to stockholders), it can borrow money, or it can sell stock. In borrowing, it promises to repay to the lender a specific amount, including principal and interest. But when it sells stock, it is selling a share of ownership in the firm. The buyer of the stock is purchasing a fractional share in the firm's future net revenues.

Newly issued stocks are sold through specialized firms to the public. A firm that issues new stock sells it in the **primary market**. When news reports tell us about how stock prices are changing, they are referring to **secondary markets**, where previously issued

Primary market
Market where financial institutions aid in the sale of new securities.

Secondary market
Market where financial institutions aid in the buying and selling of existing securities.

stocks are traded. Secondary markets make it easy to buy and sell listed stock. That is important to the primary market. The initial buyers want to know that their stocks will be easy to sell later. Entry is more attractive when exit will be easy. That helps the corporation that issues new stock to sell it for a higher price.

A stock exchange is a secondary market. It is a place where stockbrokers come to arrange trades for buyers and sellers. The largest and best known stock market is the New York Stock Exchange, where more than 2,500 stocks are traded. There are other such markets in the United States, as well as in London, Tokyo, and other trading centers around the world.

The expectation of future dividends paid from profits and of gains derived from increases in share prices are the major reasons why people buy the stock of a corporation. Periodically, the firm's board of directors determines when the firm will provide dividend payments to its shareholders. A firm that earns greater profits can provide more dividend income to owners of its stock over time.

However, sometimes a firm will not pay out its profits as dividends. Instead it retains those earnings to invest in the firm. If its investments are good, they will increase the firm's future profits. The prospect of greater future profits raises the value of the stock. A good investment is simply one that increases stock value by more than the amount of the forgone dividend. In general, stockholders are happy either with profits now or with a rising stock price. Microsoft, for example, has made many stockholders rich even though it has never paid a dividend. It has used its large profits to invest even more in hiring people and increasing its ability to produce larger profits in the future. In fact, stocks in many new firms, especially those investing in high technology, rise in value before they ever earn a profit. The stock price increase is strictly due to expected future profits.

Either dividend payments or rising stock values will increase the stockholder's wealth. Of course, if the firm does not invest wisely, then future earnings will decline, as will the price of the stock. The value of a firm's stock rises (falls) when investors come to expect future profits to rise (fall). ***Thus when investors believe that a new investment by a corporation is wise—that it will increase future earnings—the stock price will rise. Conversely, when a new management decision seems unwise to investors, many will sell, driving the stock price down.***

It pays for a stockholder, and especially a large stockholder such as a fund manager, to be alert to whether the firm's decisions are good ones. Those who spot a corporation's problems early can sell part or all of their stock in that firm before others notice and lower the price by selling their own stock. Those who first notice decisions that will be profitable can gain by increasing their holdings of the stock. Stockholder alertness benefits the corporation, too. The firm's board of directors can utilize the price changes resulting from investor vigilance to reward good management decisions. They often do so by tying the compensation of the top corporate officers to stock performance. How? Rather than paying these officers entirely in the form of salaries, boards of directors can integrate **stock options** into the compensation package of top executives. When good decisions drive the stock price up, the executives' options will have substantial value. On the other hand, if bad decisions cause the stock price to fall, then the options will have little or no value.

Of course, luck can enter also, as when demand rises or falls in the firm's product market. Some boards of directors make the option price dependent on the firm's performance relative to competing firms. If the firm does well compared to others in the same market, then the reward grows. Because a firm's directors also are normally stockholders, the stock market automatically disciplines them, too. Their own rewards are larger when they choose successful corporate managers and effectively motivate them.

Stock options
The option to buy a specified number of shares of the firm's stock at a designated price. The designated price is generally set so that the options will be quite valuable if the firm's shares increase in price, but of little value if their price falls. Thus, when used to compensate top managers, stock options provide a strong incentive to follow policies that will increase the value of the firm.

How the Stock Market Works for the Economy

We have seen how the stock market benefits stockholders and helps discipline corporate decision makers to be more efficient. As it does so, it is providing both information and the incentives needed to build prosperity. The secondary market in a corporation's shares constantly sends signals to the listed corporation's board of directors and managers. Changing stock prices reward good decisions and penalize bad ones. This provides executives and managers with an incentive to follow policies that increase the firm's value. In order to achieve this objective, the firm must generate an income stream that is worth more than the cost of its assets. Put another way, it must undertake productive projects.

STOCK PRICES AND THE INTEREST RATE

Underlying today's price of a firm's stock is the present value of the firm's expected future net earnings, or profit. What those future profits are worth to an investor today depends on three things: (1) the expected size of future net earnings, (2) when these earnings will be achieved, and (3) how much the investor discounts the future income. The last depends on the interest rate. As we noted in an earlier chapter, the present-value procedure can be used to determine the current value of any future income (or cost) stream. If D represents dividends (and gains from a higher stock price) earned in various years in the future (indicated by the subscripts) and i represents the discount or interest rate, the present value of the future income stream[3] is

$$PV = \frac{D_1}{(1 + i)} + \frac{D_2}{(1 + i)^2} + \ldots + \frac{D_n}{(1 + i)^n}$$

A higher interest rate reduces the present value of future returns from holding shares of a stock. And that is true even if the size of future returns is not affected by changes in the interest rate. Stock analysts often stress that lower interest rates are good for the stock market. This should not be surprising because the lower rates of interest will increase the value of future income (and capital gains). For example, when the interest rate is 12.5 percent, the discounted value of $100 of future income to be received each year in perpetuity is $800 ($100 divided by 0.125). But when the interest rate is 5 percent, the discounted value of this same income stream is $2,000 ($100 divided by 0.05). Other things constant, lower interest rates will increase stock values.

THE STOCK MARKET SINCE 1982: WHAT CAUSED THE DRAMATIC RISE?

On January 1, 1982, the Dow Jones Industrials stood at 875. Eighteen years later on January 1 of 2000, the Dow registered 11,357, almost 13 times the earlier figure. Other stock indexes showed similar increases. During this remarkable 18-year period, the compound annual nominal returns of the S&P 500 were 15.6 percent. The real (adjusted for inflation) returns were 12.7 percent. What factors explain the phenomenal performance of the stock market during 1982–1999? Most observers believe the following four factors played an important role.

▼ **Interest rates and inflation fell.** The interest rate on 10-year Treasury bonds stood at 13.00 percent in 1982. By November 2001, the 10-year bond rate had fallen to 4.75 percent. The lower structure of interest rates in the late 1990s compared to the early 1980s reflected a rather dramatic change in the inflationary environment. In the 2 years prior to 1982, prices had risen 10.7 percent annually; but in the 2 years prior to November 2001, prices rose only 2.8 percent annually.

---

[3]For a specific annual income stream in perpetuity, the present value is equal simply to R/i, where R is the annual revenue stream and i is the interest rate. For example, if the interest rate is 5 percent, the PV of a $100 annual income stream in perpetuity is equal to $100/0.05, or $2,000.

As we just noted, lower interest rates will tend to increase the discounted value of future income derived from stock ownership. In addition, there are two other reasons why lower rates of inflation and interest will tend to boost stock values. First, a lower rate of inflation will reduce the tax burden accompanying capital gains. The United States taxes nominal capital gains. Therefore, if stock prices rise with the general price level, investors will have to pay taxes on the inflationary as well as the real increases in stock values. Stability in the general level of prices, however, will eliminate the tax on the phantom inflationary gains. Second, low and stable rates of inflation reduce the uncertainty of investment and other long-term contracts. This will help both the economy and the stock markets.

▼ **Corporate earnings increased rapidly.** Profits were more than four times larger in the 2 years prior to 2000 than in the 2 years prior to 1982. The 1990s were especially profitable. Per-share operating profits of the S&P 500 Index grew 12 percent per year between 1991 and 2000. There were several reasons for this growth of profits. First, shareholders, especially pension fund and other fund managers with large stock holdings, had begun to insist that firms seek greater earnings. More corporations became willing to sell unprofitable divisions, to merge and grow, or to downsize and lay off managers and workers. Those and other painful measures were taken as shareholders insisted on and got greater productivity and profits.

Second, boards of directors themselves, representing shareholders, more often insisted that their fellow directors hold a significant share of their wealth in the corporation's stock. They also increased the proportion of top managers' compensation paid in the form of stock options rather than salary. Between 1982 and 1994, stock options rose from 15 percent to 29 percent of median CEO compensation.[4] By 1999, nearly two-thirds of average CEO compensation was in the form of stock options.[5] These measures tied the managers' rewards more closely to those of stockholders.

Third, stockholders encouraged firms to take advantage of technological advances that allowed greater productivity. For example, new computerized systems gave managers updated information that helped firms adjust more quickly and operate more efficiently with smaller inventories. This reduced capital requirements and meant that when buyer demands changed, outdated inventories were smaller. Computers also reduced waste by allowing better fuel and industrial process management. Quicker response times and less waste increased productivity and profits.

Fourth, greater productivity increased the firms' ability to compete internationally. The firms represented in the Dow Jones Industrial Average made 35 percent of their sales abroad in 1988. By 1999 they raised that figure to 40 percent. As lower transportation costs and reduced trade barriers expanded world trade, U.S. firms were well positioned to expand their market share.

▼ **The improving U.S. economy drew investment funds from abroad.** Lower tax rates, persistently low rates of inflation, and the general strength of the U.S. economy have attracted substantial investment funds from abroad during the last 19 years. In turn, this inflow of funds into the U.S. stock market has helped push stock prices higher. As **Exhibit 4** shows, foreign holdings of U.S. stocks amounted to $76 billion in 1982. By 2000, the figure had risen to $1.6 trillion. U.S. corporations represented a growing share of the world's stock value. The U.S. stock market rose to 51 percent of world market value in 2000, up from 29 percent in 1988.

---

[4]Brian J. Hall and Jeffrey B. Leibman, "Are CEOs Really Paid Like Bureaucrats?" *Quarterly Journal of Economics*, August 1998.

[5]Nellie Liang and Scott Weisbenner, "Who Benefits from a Bull Market? An Analysis of Employee Stock Option Grants and Stock Prices," Federal Reserve Board of Governors Finance and Economics Discussion Working Paper Number 2001-57, December 2001.

EXHIBIT 4
The Growth of Foreign Investment in the Stock Market

In 1982, foreign holdings of U.S. stocks amounted to $76 billion. By 2000, they had risen to more than $1.5 trillion. This strong demand by foreigners helped to raise U.S. stock prices to record levels.

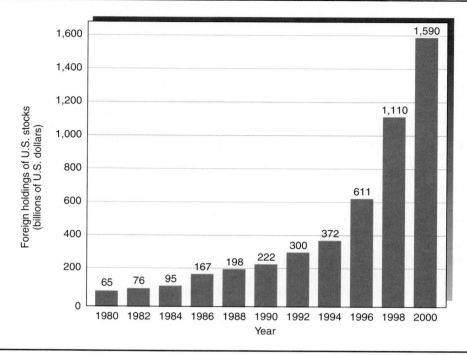

Source: Department of Commerce, Bureau of Economic Analysis.

▼ **Mutual funds expanded their holdings dramatically.** As we previously discussed, equity mutual funds make it possible for even small investors to maintain a diverse portfolio of stocks. These funds have become increasingly attractive, particularly to long-term investors planning for retirement. The recent growth of these funds has also been propelled by the movement of the baby boom generation into the prime-earning and high-saving years of life. As the baby boomers and others have channeled record amounts into retirement plans, the pool of funds invested in stock mutual funds has grown to record levels (see Exhibit 2). In 2000, stock funds gained $25 billion *per month*. This strong demand for stocks purchased through mutual funds has boosted stock prices.

THE OUTLOOK FOR THE STOCK MARKET

The stock market is often a leading indicator. The major stock indexes turned downward early in 2000 and the economy weakened during the latter half of the year. The stock market continued to trend downward as the economy entered a recession in March 2001. Following the terrorist attacks of September 11, the Dow slumped to 8235. By year-end 2001, however, it had rebounded to near 10,000, about 15 percent off its all-time high.

How will the stock market perform in the future? Can long-term investors anticipate attractive returns in the decades ahead? Of course, no one can answer these questions with certainty and, as always, the views of the "experts" differ.

Over the long haul, stock prices are driven by after-tax corporate earnings, changes in interest rates, and the overall performance of the economy. As we previously noted, all of these factors exerted a positive impact on stock prices during 1982–2000. Some are optimistic that productivity improvements, the Internet, and other technological advances will power strong growth of both corporate profits and the economy during the period immediately ahead. They point to the rapid growth of productivity since 1996 as evidence that we are now in a new economic era. These optimists believe that stocks will continue to yield lucrative returns in the years ahead.

However, it is clear that there is reason for caution. In contrast with the 1982–2000 period, stocks are unlikely to get much of an additional boost from lower interest rates. In fact, once the baby boomers begin to retire, the flow of funds into saving and investment is likely to slow. It will also be difficult to pay the promised benefits to baby boom retirees without higher taxes. Both of these factors—a decline in the growth of savings and an increase in taxes—will tend to adversely affect stocks and thus the value of other after-tax future income streams.

The current price/earnings (P/E) ratio also suggests caution. As **Exhibit 5** shows, the P/E ratio of the S&P 500 Stock Index is high by historical standards. The P/E ratio has averaged 16 over the past 50 years. This ratio has risen sharply during the last two decades, moving from the 10-to-14 range during 1982–1985 to the 24-to-32 range during 1997–2001. Stock market pessimists do not believe the current historically high P/E ratio is sustainable. Thus, they are forecasting either a sharp downturn or a lengthy period of little, if any, change in stock prices and a return of the P/E ratio to the "norm" of earlier periods.

Was 1982–2000 a Transition Period?

Prior to the 1980s, small investors faced high transactions costs and difficulties in achieving a diverse stock portfolio. Due to their additional risk, stocks earned a high rate of return, which was reflected in a low price/earnings ratio. As we noted above, sharply lower brokerage fees and the advent of equity mutual funds made it much easier for ordinary investors to build a diverse stock portfolio. This reduced the risk of stock investments relative to those for bonds, for example. Attracted by the lower risk, more and more people began investing in stocks, often through mutual funds. Predictably, this would drive both stock prices and P/E ratios upward. Some believe that this is basically what happened during the 1982–1999 period.

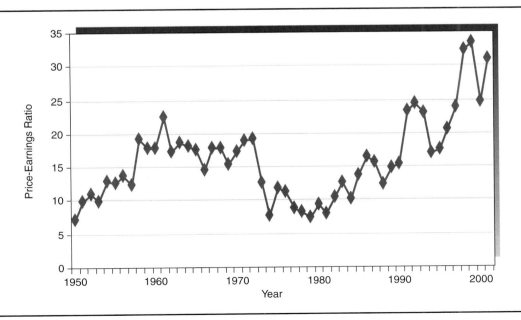

EXHIBIT 5
Price-Earnings Ratio, 1950–2001

The price-earnings ratio for the S&P 500 Index has averaged 16 over the 50 years. The price-earnings ratio has risen over the past two decades and reached 31 in 2001.

Source: www.globalfindata.com and www.economy.com.

Once the transition period is completed, however, the P/E ratio will fluctuate around a new higher plateau and the growth of stock prices will slow. This theory implies that the higher P/E ratio will persist, but the future return derived from stocks will be considerably lower than during the transition period of the last couple of decades. It also suggests that future returns from stocks will be more like those for bonds, which from the standpoint of risk, are now more similar.

CONCLUDING THOUGHT

Random walk theory
The theory that current stock prices already reflect known information about the future. Therefore, the future movement of stock prices will be determined by surprise occurrences. This will cause them to change in a random fashion.

No one knows for sure where the U.S. stock market will go in the future. Most economists adhere to the **random walk theory** of the stock market. According to this theory, current stock prices already reflect the best known information about the future state of corporate earnings, the health of the economy, and other factors that influence stock prices. Therefore, the future direction of stock prices will be driven by surprise occurrences, things that people do not currently anticipate. By their very nature, these factors are unpredictable. If they were predictable, they would already be reflected in current stock prices. Thus, those who hope to get wealthy by predicting the future direction of stock prices are likely to be disappointed.

KEY POINTS

▼ The stock market has allowed many Americans, without special business skills and without the need to make specific business decisions, to participate in the risks and opportunities of corporate America. Many have prospered as a result. Real returns for the past two centuries have averaged 7 percent per year.

▼ Buying and selling individual stocks without specialized knowledge, for a quick profit, is very risky. But holding a diverse portfolio of unrelated stocks, and holding them for long periods of time, greatly reduce the risk of investing in the stock market.

▼ Vigilant investors and investment fund managers, as they buy and sell stocks for their own portfolios, generate price changes that help to allocate capital efficiently and to discipline corporate decision makers in ways that benefit consumers and stockholders in general.

▼ The period 1982–1999 was a remarkable one for the stock market. The real annual rate of return of the S&P 500 was approximately 12 percent over this 18-year period. The following factors enhanced stock market performance during this period:(a) lower inflation and interest rates, (b) rising corporate earnings, (c) increased stock purchases by foreigners, and (d) the growth of equity mutual funds, which made it easier for ordinary investors to hold a diverse portfolio.

▼ Current stock prices already reflect information that is known with a high degree of certainty and our ability to predict future changes is extremely limited. Thus, no one can forecast future stock prices with precision or a high degree of certainty.

CRITICAL ANALYSIS QUESTIONS

*1. A friend just inherited $50,000. She informs you of her investment plans and asks for your advice. "I want to put it into the stock market and use it for my retirement in 30 years. What do you think is the best plan that will provide high returns at a relatively low risk?" What answer would you give? Explain.

2. Suppose that more expansionary monetary policy leads to inflation and higher nominal interest rates.

How is this likely to affect the value of stocks? Explain.

*3. Microsoft stock rose from less than $10 in 1995 to $65 in late 2001. Microsoft has made sizable profits, but never paid a dividend. Why were people willing to pay such a high price knowing that they might not get dividends for many years?

4. In the late 1980s and through the 1990s, as U.S. stocks became more expensive, foreign investors bought more and more of them. Explain why.

*5. The stocks of some corporations that have never made a profit or paid a dividend, especially those in high-technology industries, have risen in price. What causes investors to be willing to buy these stocks?

6. The stock market is generally a leading indicator. Can you explain why stock prices are likely to fall before the economy goes into a recession and rise before it begins to recover? (*Hint:* will stock prices reflect current or future earnings?)

7. If an investment advisor gives you some hot new stock tip, is it likely to be a "sure thing"? Why or why not?

*Asterisk denotes questions for which answers are given in Appendix B.

SPECIAL TOPIC 5

The Federal Budget and the National Debt

Focus

- How large is the national debt? Will the debt have to be paid off?

- Who owns the national debt?

- How are future generations affected by debt financing?

- How does the government debt of the United States compare with other countries?

- How were budget deficits transformed to surpluses during the 1990s? Will the era of budget surpluses end because of the September 11 attacks and the accompanying War on Terrorism?

The attractiveness of financing spending by debt issue to the elected politicians should be obvious. Borrowing allows spending to be made that will yield immediate political payoffs without the incurring of any immediate political cost.

—James Buchanan[1]

[1]James Buchanan, *The Deficit and American Democracy* (Memphis: P. K. Steidman Foundation, 1984).

Historically, attitudes toward government debt have undergone dramatic swings. Prior to the Keynesian revolution, there was a virtual consensus that budget deficits were irresponsible and therefore should be avoided, except perhaps during wartime emergencies. In contrast, during the 1960–1980 Keynesian era, deficits were perceived as an important policy tool that could be used to stimulate growth and help promote stability. But concern about the potential harmful effects of debt financing rose again with the large budget deficits and growth of the national debt during the 1980s. As federal deficits were transformed to surpluses during the 1990s, many argued that it would be prudent to pay off the national debt. This feature will focus on debt financing and its impact on the economy.

DEFICITS, SURPLUSES, AND THE NATIONAL DEBT

When the federal government uses debt rather than taxes and user charges to pay for its expenditures, the U.S. Treasury fills this gap by borrowing in the loanable funds market. When borrowing funds, the Treasury generally issues interest-bearing bonds. These bonds compose the national debt. In effect, the national debt consists of outstanding loans from financial investors to the general fund of the U.S. Treasury.

The federal budget exerts a direct impact on the national debt. The budget deficit or surplus is a "flow" concept (like water running into or out of a bathtub), while the **national debt** is a "stock" figure (like the amount of water in the tub at a point in time). A budget deficit increases the size of the national debt by the amount of the deficit. Conversely, a budget surplus allows the federal government to pay off bondholders and thereby reduce the size of the national debt. In essence, the national debt represents the cumulative effect of all the prior budget deficits and surpluses.

The creditworthiness of an organization is dependent upon the size of its debt relative to its income base. Therefore, when analyzing the significance of budget deficits, surpluses, and the national debt, it makes sense to consider their size relative to the entire economy. **Exhibit 1** presents data for the 1950–2001 period for both the federal budget deficit and the national debt as a percentage of GDP. Because the defense effort of World War II was largely financed with debt rather than taxes, the national debt was quite large during the period immediately following the war. As the top frame of Exhibit 1 shows, budget deficits averaged less than 1 percent of GDP during the 1950–1974 period. Historically, real output in the United States has grown at an annual rate of approximately 3 percent. When the budget deficit as a percent of GDP is less than the growth of real output, the federal debt will decline relative to the size of the economy. This is precisely what happened during the 1950–1974 period. Budget deficits were present, and they pushed up the nominal national debt (from $256.7 billion at year-end 1950 to $492.7 billion at the end of 1974). But GDP grew even more rapidly. By 1974 the national debt had fallen to 33 percent of GDP, down from 87 percent in 1950 (and 127 percent in 1946).

From the mid-1970s to the mid-1990s, federal deficits were both large and continuous. The budget deficits averaged 3 percent of GDP during 1974–1995 (part a of Exhibit 1). Pushed along by the large deficits, the national debt rose from 33 percent of GDP in 1974 to 68 percent in 1995. However, as the economy grew rapidly in the 1990s, the budget deficits were eventually transformed into surpluses. By 2001, the outstanding federal debt had fallen to 56 percent of GDP.

WHO OWNS THE NATIONAL DEBT?

As **Exhibit 2** illustrates, more than two-fifths (41 percent) of the national debt is held by agencies of the federal government. For example, Social Security Trust Funds are often used to purchase U.S. bonds. When the debt is owned by a government agency, it is little

National debt
The sum of the indebtedness of the federal government in the form of outstanding interest-earning bonds. It reflects the cumulative impact of budget deficits and surpluses.

EXHIBIT 1
Budget Deficits and the National Debt as a Percentage of GDP

Throughout most of the 1950s and 1960s, federal budget deficits were small as a percentage of GDP, and occasionally the government ran a budget surplus (a). During this period, the national debt declined as a proportion of GDP (b). During 1974–1995, budget deficits were quite large, causing the national debt to increase as a percentage of GDP. During the last few years, the national debt has fallen as a share of the economy.

(a) Federal budget deficit or surplus as a percentage of GDP

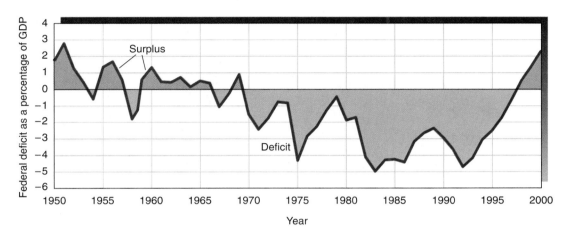

(b) Gross and net federal debt as a percentage of GDP

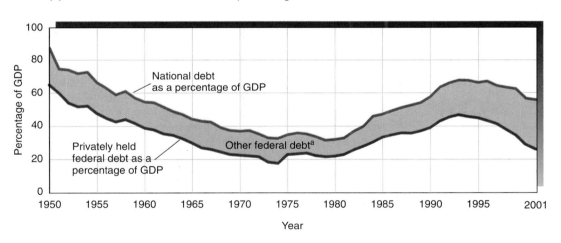

^aFederal debt held by U.S. government agencies and Federal Reserve banks.
Source: www.bea.doc.gov and www.economagic.com.

more than an accounting transaction indicating that one government agency (for example, the Social Security Administration) is making a loan to another (the U.S. Treasury). Even the interest payments in this case represent little more than an internal government transfer.

Another 9 percent of the public debt is held by the Federal Reserve System. When the Fed purchases U.S. securities, it creates money. The bonds held by the Fed, therefore, are indicative of prior government expenditures that have been paid for with "printing-press" money—money created by the central bank. As in the case of the securities held by government agencies, the interest on the bonds held by the Fed is returned to the Treasury after the Fed has covered its costs of operation. The U.S. Treasury both pays and receives

EXHIBIT 2
Who Owns the National Debt?

Of the $5.77 trillion national debt, half is held by government agencies (primarily the Social Security Trust Fund) and Federal Reserve banks. Of the $2.88 trillion federal debt held privately, 58.5% is owned by domestic investors and 41.5% by foreigners.

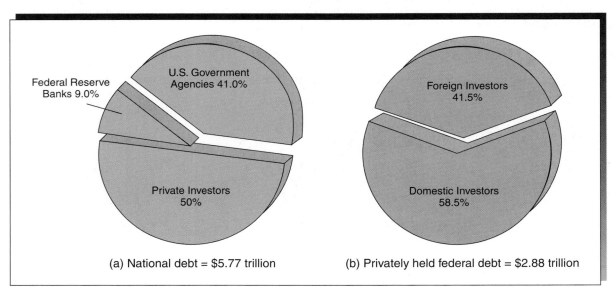

(a) National debt = $5.77 trillion   (b) Privately held federal debt = $2.88 trillion

Source: The Treasury Bulletin, September 2001 and www.federalreserve.gov.

Privately held government debt
The portion of the national debt owed to domestic and foreign investors. It does not include bonds held by agencies of the federal government or the Federal Reserve.

External debt
The portion of the national debt owed to foreign investors.

almost all of the nearly $30 billion of interest on the bonds held by the Federal Reserve. Thus, the bonds held by the Fed, like those held by U.S. government agencies, do not create a net interest liability for the U.S. Treasury.

In contrast, **privately held government debt** imposes a net interest burden on the federal government. In the case of the privately held debt—that is, the bonds held by individuals, insurance companies, mutual funds, and other investors—the federal government will have to impose taxes to meet the future interest payments on these bonds. Therefore, it is important to distinguish between (1) the total national debt and (2) privately held government debt. Only the latter imposes a net interest obligation on the federal government. Currently, the privately held portion of the national debt comprises only half of the total. Thus, the total national debt ($5.8 trillion at mid-year 2001) vastly overstates the net debt obligations of the federal government. Of the $2.9 trillion privately held debt, 58.5 percent is owned by domestic investors and 41.5 percent by foreigners. The portion owned by foreigners is sometimes referred to as **external debt**.

Part b of Exhibit 1 presents data on the size of the privately held federal debt as a percentage of GDP for the 1950–2001 period. Measured as a share of GDP, the general pattern of the privately held debt has been similar to that for the national debt as a whole. However, in recent years the privately held debt has gradually declined as a share of the total. In 2001, the privately held federal debt stood at 27 percent of GDP, up from 18 percent in 1974, but lower than in the 1990s.

How Does Debt Financing Influence Future Generations?

The impact of the national debt on future generations has been a point of controversy for decades.[2] Opponents of debt financing often charge that we are mortgaging the future of

[2]See Richard H. Fink and Jack High, eds., *A Nation in Debt: Economists Debate the Federal Budget Deficit* (Frederick, MD: University Publications of America, 1987), for an excellent set of readings summarizing this debate.

our children and grandchildren—that debt financing permits us to consume today, then send the bill to future generations. In the 1960s and 1970s, the overwhelming bulk of the national debt was held by domestic investors. During this era, Keynesians argued that there was little reason for concern because "We owe it to ourselves." Today, new classical economists take the position that debt affects the timing, but not the magnitude, of taxes. Like Keynesians, the new classicals do not believe that debt financing exerts much impact on the welfare of future generations. Who is right?

When analyzing the issue of debt financing, it is important to keep two points in mind. First, in the case of domestically held debt, our children and grandchildren will indeed pay the taxes to service the debt, but they will also receive the interest payments. Admittedly, those paying the taxes and receiving the interest payments will not always be the same people. Some will gain and others will lose. But both those who gain and those who lose will be members of the future generation.

Second, debt financing of a government activity cannot push the opportunity cost of the resources used by government onto future generations. If current GDP is $10 trillion and the federal government spends $2 trillion on goods and services, then only $8 trillion will be available for consumption and investment by individuals, businesses, and state and local governments. This will be true regardless of whether the federal government finances its expenditures with taxes or debt. When the government builds a highway, constructs an antimissile defense system, or provides police protection, it draws resources with alternative uses away from the private sector. This cost is incurred in the present; it cannot be avoided through debt financing.

If the opportunity cost of resources occurs during the current period, does this mean that the welfare of future generations is unaffected by debt financing? Not necessarily. Debt financing influences future generations primarily through its potential impact on saving and capital formation. If lots of factories, machines, houses, technical knowledge, and other productive assets are available to future generations, then their productive potential will be high. Alternatively, if fewer productive assets are passed along to the next generation, then their productive capability will be less. Thus, the true measure of how government debt influences future generations involves knowledge of its impact on capital formation.

The impact of budget deficits on capital formation is a complex issue. Consider an economy operating at its normal productive capacity. Holding government expenditures constant, how would the substitution of debt financing for current taxation influence capital formation? As our discussion of fiscal policy models implies, economists differ in their responses to this question. We will consider two major theories: the traditional view that budget deficits reduce future capital stock and the opposing new classical view that such deficits exert no significant future impact.

Traditional View: Budget Deficits Reduce Future Capital Stock

Most economists embrace the traditional view that budget deficits will retard private investment and thereby reduce the welfare of future generations. Suppose that the government substitutes borrowing for current taxation. For example, consider what would happen if the government cut the current taxes of each household by $1000 and borrowed the funds to replace the lost revenues. As a result, the after-tax income of each household increases by $1000. Of course, the households may save some of the $1000 addition to their disposable income, but they are also likely to spend some of it on consumption goods, according to the traditional view. If they do not save all the $1000, the additional government borrowing will increase the demand for loanable funds relative to the supply and thereby push real interest rates upward.[3] In turn, the higher real interest rates will retard

---

[3]Alternatively, one could approach this topic from the viewpoint of how households value the government bonds relative to the future tax liability implied by the bonds. If bondholders recognize the asset value of the government bonds while taxpayers fail to recognize fully the accompanying tax liability, then the general populace will have an exaggerated view of its true wealth position. Wealth is an important determinant of consumption. When people think they are wealthier, they will consume more and save less than they would if they had fully recognized their future tax liability. Of course, the increase in consumption and reduction in savings would place upward pressure on the real rate of interest. This is simply an alternative way of viewing the substitution of government debt for current taxation.

private investment, which will reduce the physical capital available to future generations. To the extent future generations work with less capital (fewer productivity-enhancing tools and machines), their productivity and wages will be lower than would have been the case had the budget deficits not crowded out private investment.

In addition, the higher interest rates will attract foreign investors. But investments in the United States will require dollars. As foreigners increase their investments in the United States, they will demand dollars in the foreign exchange market. This strong demand will cause the dollar to appreciate relative to other currencies. In turn, the appreciation in the exchange rate value of the dollar will make U.S. exports more expensive to foreigners and foreign goods cheaper for Americans. These relative price changes will retard exports and stimulate imports. Predictably, net exports will decline.

The inflow of capital from abroad will dampen both the increase in interest rates and the reduction in domestic investment. However, it will also increase the asset holdings of foreigners in the United States. The returns to these assets will generate income for foreigners rather than Americans. Therefore, compared to the situation where government was financed with current taxation, future generations of Americans will inherit both a smaller stock of physical capital and less income from that capital (because the share owned by foreigners has increased). Succeeding generations will be less well-off as a result.

In summary, the traditional view argues that the substitution of debt financing for current taxation will increase current consumption, push up real interest rates, and retard private investment. In addition, the higher real interest rates will lead to an increase in net foreign investment, appreciation in the exchange rate value of the dollar, and a decline in net exports (imports will increase relative to exports). According to the traditional view, budget deficits will retard the growth rate of capital formation, particularly that owned by Americans, and reduce national income and future living standards of Americans.

New Classical View: Budget Deficits Exert Little Impact on Future Capital Stock

Not all economists accept the traditional view of budget deficits. An alternative theory, most closely associated with Robert Barro of Harvard University, encompasses the new classical perspective of fiscal policy.[4] This new classical view stresses that additional debt implies an equivalent amount of future taxes. If, as the new classical model assumes, individuals fully anticipate the added future tax liability accompanying the debt, current consumption will be unaffected when governments substitute debt for taxes. According to this view, when future taxes (debt) are substituted for current taxes, people will save the reduction in current taxes so that they will have the required income to pay the higher future taxes implied by the additional debt. Continuing with our previous example, the new classical theory implies that households receiving a $1000 reduction in current taxes financed by issuing bonds (that imply higher future taxes) will save all the $1000 increase in their current disposable income. This increase in saving, triggered by the anticipation of the higher future taxes, allows the additional government debt to be financed without an increase in the real rate of interest. Since there is no increase in interest rates, private investment is unaffected. Neither is there an influx of foreign capital. Under these circumstances, the substitution of debt for taxes exerts little or no impact on either capital formation or the welfare of future generations.

Empirical Evidence on the Impact of the Deficit

What does the empirical evidence indicate with regard to the validity of the two theories? Empirical studies have found little, if any, relationship between year-to-year changes in the budget deficit and real interest rates. New classical economists argue that these findings are supportive of their theory.

---

[4]See Robert Barro, "Are Government Bonds Net Wealth?" *Journal of Political Economy* 82 (November December 1974): 1095–1117; and "The Ricardian Approach to Budget Deficits," *Journal of Economic Perspectives* 2 (Spring 1989): 35–54.

However, the experience with the large budget deficits subsequent to 1980 would appear to support the traditional theory. As the size of the budget deficit increased substantially during the 1980s, Americans increased their current consumption expenditures and substantially reduced their domestically financed capital formation. Simultaneously, there was an inflow of net foreign investment and a reduction in net exports (imports increased relative to exports). This pattern is precisely what the traditional theory predicts will happen when debt financing is substituted for current taxation. Empirical work on the linkage between (1) the budget deficit on the one hand and (2) interest rates, consumption, and inflow of capital on the other is continuing. At this point, however, the bulk of the evidence appears to be more consistent with the traditional view.

HOW DOES FOREIGN INVESTMENT INFLUENCE THE U.S. ECONOMY?

As Exhibit 2 illustrates, a little more than two-fifths of the privately held federal debt is now owned by foreigners. Furthermore, if debt financing pushes domestic interest rates upward, it will encourage foreign investment. Studies indicate that foreigners currently own about 5 percent of the domestic capital assets of the United States. How does foreign investment affect the U.S. economy? When considering a possible burden emanating from foreign investment, one must keep an eye on both sides of the transaction. The inflow of foreign capital leads to lower interest rates and a higher level of investment than would take place in its absence. An increase in machines, structures, and other capital assets, even if financed by foreign investment, will increase the productivity and wages of American workers. Of course, the inflow of investment funds also enlarges the future profit and interest claims of foreigners. However, if the funds are invested wisely, the projects will generate returns (future income) that provide an offset against the future income claims of foreigners. On the other hand, if the funds are squandered on low-return projects, the wealth of investors will be reduced. But this would be equally true for projects financed solely with domestic funds.

Doesn't this inflow of capital from abroad make the United States more dependent on foreign creditors? In the analysis of this issue, it is important to keep the nature of the foreign investment in mind. Substantial portions of the funds supplied by foreigners are in the form of risk capital—investments in stocks, land, physical structures, and business ventures. Such investments do not involve a contractual repayment commitment. Others are invested in bonds, both corporate and government. These investments are almost entirely fixed interest rate obligations. As long as the investment project is profitable, U.S. citizens as well as foreigners will gain as the result of undertaking the project.

What would happen if foreigners suddenly decided to take their "money" home and quit financing investments in the United States? It is not obvious why literally tens of thousands of foreign investors would be any more likely to "sell out" suddenly than would tens of thousands of domestic investors. But even if they did, market adjustments would exert a stabilizing effect. Remember, the "money" of foreigners is in the form of stocks, bonds, and physical assets. If foreigners suddenly tried to sell these assets, falling prices would create some real bargains for domestic investors. Domestic investors would gain and foreign investors would lose. Similarly, if foreigners cut back their financial investments in the United States, real interest rates would rise. But the higher real interest rates would make U.S. investments more attractive and thereby help deter any outflow of funds.

Finally, the vulnerability accompanying foreign investment almost certainly lies with the foreign investor rather than with the recipient country. It is much easier for a government to expropriate the property of a foreigner than it is for an investor to exercise much control over the policies of a foreign government. History illustrates the vulnerability of the foreign investor. The United States expropriated the property of Germans and Japanese during the Second World War. Several Middle Eastern countries expropriated the property of foreign investors when they nationalized their domestic oil industries in the 1950s and 1960s. Under Fidel Castro, the Cuban government expropriated the assets of foreigners. Foreign investment is a hostage to the domestic policies of the recipient country. A major reason why investment in the United States is attractive to foreigners is the confidence they have that the U.S. government will not abuse its superior position.

GOVERNMENT DEBT: A CROSS-COUNTRY COMPARISON

How does the national debt of the United States compare with that of other countries? **Exhibit 3** provides data on net government debt as a share of GDP for several high-income industrial nations. Among the industrial nations, the net public debt/GDP ratio in 2000 was lowest, 12 percent, for Australia. The parallel figures for the United Kingdom and the United States were 34 percent and 35 percent, respectively. The debt/GDP ratios of France, Germany, and Spain were just over 40 percent. Japan's net public debt was 51 percent of GDP, while the figure for Canada was 66 percent.

Among industrial countries, the debt/GDP ratio was highest for Belgium and Italy. In both countries, the outstanding government debt was approximately 100 percent of GDP. Of course, a large outstanding debt means high interest payments for debt service. As a share of the economy, interest payments on government debt in Italy and Belgium are nearly three times the level of the United States. The governments of Belgium and Italy

EXHIBIT 3
Government Debt of Industrial Countries

The net public debt of the United States is lower than that of most other industrial countries.

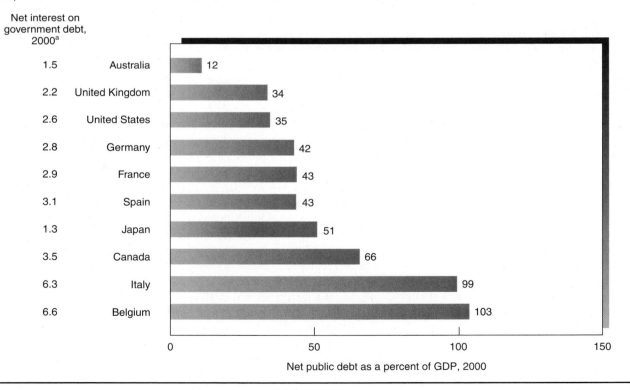

Net interest on government debt, 2000[a]

Net interest	Country	Net public debt (% GDP)
1.5	Australia	12
2.2	United Kingdom	34
2.6	United States	35
2.8	Germany	42
2.9	France	43
3.1	Spain	43
1.3	Japan	51
3.5	Canada	66
6.3	Italy	99
6.6	Belgium	103

Net public debt as a percent of GDP, 2000

[a]As a percent of GDP.
Source: OECD Economic Outlook, June 2001, Annex Tables 33 and 35.

tax away more than 6 percent of the GDP generated by their citizens just to make the interest payments on outstanding debt.

As the size of a nation's debt gets larger and larger, eventually global credit markets will apply some discipline. Countries with large debt/GDP ratios will have to pay higher real interest rates in order to induce investors to purchase their bonds. At some point, credit markets will more or less force governments to bring their spending more closely in line with revenues. This is what happened to Belgium in 1994. Loss of investor confidence led to a sharp decline in the foreign exchange value of the Belgian franc. In order to maintain creditworthiness, the Belgian government was forced to curtail spending—including expenditures on social security, health care, and child care services—and reduce the size of its outstanding debt.

SOCIAL SECURITY, BUDGET DEFICITS, AND THE NATIONAL DEBT

As conventionally measured, the budget deficit includes the revenues and expenditures of government trust funds, including the Social Security Trust Fund. Until recently, the net revenue flowing into this fund was small relative to the size of the budget. Therefore, it really did not make much difference whether it was included or excluded from budget deficit calculations. But this is no longer the case. Under legislation adopted in 1983, social security payroll tax rates were set at levels designed to generate surpluses for the years prior to the retirement of the baby boom generation. The revenues flowing into the social security system are now about $150 billion more than the benefits paid out. As a result, the inclusion of social security in the unified budget calculation makes the deficit appear smaller or the surplus appear larger than would otherwise be the case. For example, if the $150 billion surplus of the social security system had not been included in the 2000 budget calculation, the federal government's budget surplus in 2000 would have been $87 billion rather than $237 billion.

More is at stake here than just a definitional issue. The surplus of the social security system was planned in order to set funds aside for the increase in the share of the population that will draw social security benefits when the baby boom generation begins to retire in the years following 2010. The current social security surpluses are intended to increase the national saving rate and stimulate additional investment, and thereby help to finance

Currently, the social security system is running a surplus, which makes it easier to balance the unified federal budget. But soon after the baby boomers begin to retire around 2010, the social security system will run a deficit, which will make it more difficult to balance the unified budget.

the retirement benefits of the baby boomers. Using these funds to finance current government expenditures completely undermines this strategy.

Given the future demands of the social security system, many economists argue that the federal government should balance its operating budget—that is, its budget exclusive of the social security system. This would imply a surplus at least equal to the annual surplus of the social security system. (For additional discussion of this topic, see Special Topic 3, "The Economics of Social Security.")

POLITICAL ECONOMY, DEMOGRAPHICS, AND DEBT FINANCING

The presence or absence of budget deficits reflects an interesting combination of economics, politics, and demographics. Prior to 1960, almost everyone—including the leading figures of both political parties—thought that the government should balance its budget except perhaps during times of war. In essence, there was widespread implicit agreement—much like a constitutional rule—that the federal budget should be balanced. Against this political background, the budget of the federal government was generally near balanced during times of peace. Therefore, except during times of war, both deficits and surpluses were small relative to the size of the economy prior to 1960.

The Keynesian revolution changed all of this. Rather than balancing the budget, Keynesians argued that the budget should be shifted toward deficit when stimulus was needed and toward surplus when there was concern about inflation. In essence, the Keynesian revolution released political decision makers from the discipline imposed by a balanced budget. Freed from this constraint, politicians consistently spent more than they were willing to tax during the period 1960–1990.[5]

From a public choice viewpoint, the political attractiveness of spending compared to taxation is not surprising. Politicians have a strong incentive to spend money on programs that benefit the voters of their district and special interest groups that will help them win reelection. On the other hand, they do not like to levy taxes because they impose a visible cost on voters. Borrowing provides politicians with an attractive alternative. Because they push the taxes into the future, deficits impose a less visible cost than current taxation. Thus, borrowing allows politicians to supply voters with immediate benefits without having to impose a parallel visible cost in the form of higher taxes or user charges.

By 1990, both the instability of the inflationary 1970s and the integration of expectations into macroeconomic analysis had tempered the views of economists and policymakers alike. The confidence that budget deficits could be planned in a manner that would promote stability and growth had largely dissipated. Therefore, rather than increasing spending and cutting taxes during the 1990 recession, both Congress and the president sought to reduce the size of the deficit which they believed was keeping interest rates high and thereby slowing the recovery.

While loss of confidence in demand stimulus policies contributed to the smaller deficits of the 1990s, three additional factors were also at work. First, the 1990s were a period of strong economic expansion. The revenues of the federal government expanded rapidly with the growth of the economy. Second, sizable reductions in defense expenditures were feasible following the collapse of communism and the end of the Cold War. Defense spending was sliced from approximately 7 percent of GDP in the late 1980s to less than 4 percent by the mid-1990s. Measured as a share of GDP, total federal spending fell by almost precisely the same amount. Third, the demographic changes of the 1990s were highly favorable to both rapid income growth and lower levels of government spending. As the baby boomers moved into the prime earning years of life during the decade, this promoted the rapid growth of both income and government revenue. At the same time, the

[5]See James M. Buchanan and Richard Wagner, *Democracy in Deficit: The Political Legacy of Lord Keynes* (New York: Academic Press, 1977), for a detailed account of the changes wrought by the Keynesian revolution.

number of retirees drawing social security and Medicare expanded slowly during the 1990s because the birthrate was low during the great Depression and World War II (1930–1945). This combination of factors—a larger share of the population in the peak earning years of life and a smaller share in the retirement phase—exerted a highly favorable impact on the federal budget during the 1990s.

Favorable demographic conditions will continue to exert a positive impact on the budget picture during the decade immediately ahead. Given the spending commitments and tax structure in place when the administration of George W. Bush took office in January 2001, sizable budget surpluses were projected through 2010. Some political officials, particularly those favoring smaller government, wanted to cut taxes and return the surpluses to the taxpayer before they were committed to new spending initiatives. Others wanted to use the surpluses to reduce the national debt and expand government spending. Taxes were reduced early in 2001, but the debate about what to do with the remainder of the projected surpluses was drastically altered by two events: recession and the terrorist attacks of September 11, 2001. As the economy slowed and dipped into a recession, the revenues of the federal government fell short of the initial projections. At the same time, the War on Terrorism and demand for additional security measures pushed spending upward. This combination of factors quickly altered the earlier rosy budget picture.

With regard to the future, two points emerge. First, in the aftermath of the September 11 attacks and the accompanying War on Terrorism, federal expenditures on defense and domestic security are almost certain to expand rapidly. As the activities of government claim a larger share of the economy's resources, the earlier projected surpluses are likely to dissipate. Second, an era of large deficits is highly likely, once the baby boomers begin to move into the retirement phase of life beginning around 2010. When this happens, there will be upward pressure on government expenditures for health care and social security, while income growth is likely to slow because of a shrinking share of the workforce in the prime working years of life. Unless major structural changes are undertaken in the near future, both debt financing and debate concerning its impact are sure to continue in the decades ahead.

KEY POINTS

▼ The national debt is the sum of the outstanding bonds of the U.S. Treasury. Budget deficits increase the national debt, while surpluses reduce it. The national debt reflects the cumulative effect of all prior budget deficits and surpluses.

▼ Half of the national debt is owned by U.S. government agencies and Federal Reserve banks. For this portion of the debt, the government both pays and receives the interest (except for the expenses of the Fed). Only the privately held federal debt—the portion of the national debt owned by domestic and foreign investors—generates a net interest obligation for the government.

▼ When considering the impact of the national debt on future generations, one must keep two points in mind. First, the future generations that pay the tax liability accompanying the debt will also receive the interest income implied by the debt. Second, the opportunity cost of resources used by the government

is incurred during the current period regardless of how the government activity is financed.

▼ Budget deficits affect future generations through their impact on capital formation.

▼ According to the traditional view, the substitution of debt financing for taxes will increase real interest rates and reduce the rate of capital formation—particularly capital owned by Americans. Thus, the traditional view indicates that future generations are adversely affected.

▼ In contrast with the traditional view, the new classical theory argues that people will increase their saving in anticipation of the higher future taxes implied by additional debt. In the new classical model, the substitution of debt for taxes leaves interest rates, consumption, and investment unaffected.

▼ A large national debt relative to the size of an economy leads to a large tax burden just to pay the interest on the debt. Several countries have larger government debt to GDP ratios than the United States.

▼ Inclusion of social security in the budget calculations makes the deficit appear smaller or the surplus larger than would be true if these funds were omitted.

▼ Reductions in defense expenditures in the aftermath of the Cold War and favorable demographics

shifted the federal budget from deficit to surplus during the 1990s. In the decade immediately ahead, government spending on both defense and domestic security is likely to increase substantially as the result of terrorism. When the baby boomers begin retiring around 2011, demographic changes will make it more difficult to balance the federal budget. Thus, large budget deficits are likely to reemerge in the future.

CRITICAL ANALYSIS QUESTIONS

*1. Does the national debt have to be paid off at some time in the future? What will happen if it is not?

2. Do we owe the national debt to ourselves? Does this mean the size of the national debt is of little concern? Why or why not?

3. "The national debt is a mortgage against the future of our children and grandchildren. We are forcing them to pay for our current consumption of goods and services." Evaluate this statement.

*4. When government bonds are held by foreigners, the interest income from the bonds goes to foreigners rather than to Americans. Would Americans be better off if we prohibited the sale of bonds to foreigners?

5. How is the social security system currently influencing the size of the budget deficit? If it is not reformed, how will social security influence the budget deficit in the years following 2015? Is this a cause for concern? Why or why not?

*6. Would you predict that government expenditures would be higher or lower if taxes (and user charges)

were required for the finance of all expenditures? Why? Do you think the government would spend funds more or less efficiently if it could not issue debt? Why?

7. Suppose that the federal government ran a sizable budget surplus during the next decade. Compared to balancing the budget, how would this surplus affect interest rates, saving, and investment? Compare and contrast the traditional view and the new classical view.

*8. Does an increase in the national debt increase the supply of money (M1)? Can the money supply increase when the U.S. Treasury is running a budget surplus?

*9. Do you think it would be a good idea for the federal government to raise taxes in order to pay off the national debt? Why or why not?

---

*Asterisk denotes questions for which answers are given in Appendix B.

SPECIAL TOPIC **6**

Labor Market Policies and the Natural Rate of Unemployment: A Cross-Country Analysis

If work does not pay, people will be reluctant to work.

—OECD Jobs Strategy Report[1]

Focus

- Why are unemployment rates substantially higher in Europe than in the United States?

- How do the structure of labor markets and level of unemployment benefits influence the rate of unemployment?

- How have the United Kingdom and New Zealand altered the structure of their labor markets?

[1]OECD, *OECD Jobs Strategy: Making Work Pay* (Paris: OECD, 1997), p. 7.

A s we noted in Chapter 8, the natural rate of unemployment is the minimum unemployment rate that a country will be able to achieve and sustain over an extended period. This rate is influenced by policies and institutional arrangements. The natural rate of unemployment will be higher when the policies of a country (a) push wages above equilibrium, (b) make it more costly for employers to hire and dismiss employees, and (c) make it less costly for job seekers to reject available job offers while continuing to search for a better offer.

Several European countries have followed policies that have made employment of workers more costly and unemployment less costly. As a result, the rate of unemployment throughout much of Europe has been relatively high during the last couple of decades. Of course, the policies were not designed to push the unemployment rate upward. Nonetheless, when perverse incentives were created, higher unemployment was a secondary effect. This feature will focus on this topic and related issues. ■

CROSS-COUNTRY VARIATIONS IN UNEMPLOYMENT RATES

Exhibit 1 presents the standardized unemployment rates during 1991–1995 and 1996–2000 for the five most populous European countries, plus Australia, Canada, Japan, and the United States.[2] These countries are all members of the Organization for Economic Cooperation and Development (OECD). They are perhaps the nine most important market economies in the

EXHIBIT 1
The Standardized Unemployment Rates of Nine Major Industrial Economies 1991–2000

In the 1990s, the unemployment rates of Australia, Canada, and the major European economies have been persistently higher than the rates for the United States and Japan.

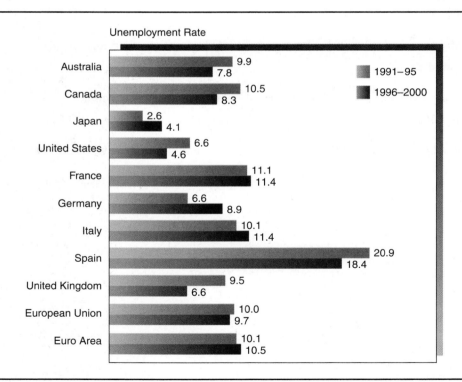

Unemployment Rate

Country	1991–95	1996–2000
Australia	9.9	7.8
Canada	10.5	8.3
Japan	2.6	4.1
United States	6.6	4.6
France	11.1	11.4
Germany	6.6	8.9
Italy	10.1	11.4
Spain	20.9	18.4
United Kingdom	9.5	6.6
European Union	10.0	9.7
Euro Area	10.1	10.5

Source: OECD, *OECD Economic Outlook* (June 2001).

[2]This section borrows freely from Edward Bierhanzl and James Gwartney, "Regulation, Unions, and Labor Markets," *Regulation* (summer 1998): 40–53.

world. The unemployment rate for the European Union as a whole averaged 9.7 percent during 1996–2000. In the Euro area, which excludes the United Kingdom, the rate was even higher, 10.5 percent. The unemployment rates of Italy (11.4 percent), France (11.4 percent) and Spain (18.4 percent) were particularly high. By way of comparison, the unemployment rate of the United States was 4.6 percent during 1996–2000. Similarly, even though the Japanese economy stagnated throughout most of the 1990s, Japan's unemployment rate was still less than half that of the EU during the latter half of the decade.

As Exhibit 1 shows, the situation was similar during the earlier part of the decade. In fact, European unemployment rates have been substantially higher than those of the United States throughout most of the last two decades. This indicates that the higher European unemployment rates reflect long-term factors rather than short-run business conditions. The price stability data are also consistent with this view. The nine economies of Exhibit 1 expanded in the 1990s and the inflation rate of each was low and relatively stable—neither rising nor falling. Under these circumstances, unemployment will move toward the natural rate, the lowest sustainable unemployment rate consistent with the economy's institutional structure.

Employment growth in Europe has also lagged well behind that of the United States and Japan. Total employment for the 15 European Union countries in 2000 was only 11.1 percent higher than the figure for 1980. Employment grew by only 1.9 percent in Italy during the 1980–2000 period. The total growth of employment in Germany, France, the United Kingdom, and Spain was 10 percent or less during this same period. By way of comparison, employment grew by 14.4 percent in Japan and by 35.5 percent in the United States.

THE STRUCTURE OF LABOR MARKETS

Labor market structural characteristics and policies differ substantially among countries. Compared to the United States and Japan, the labor markets of Europe and to some extent those of Australia and Canada, are characterized by (1) higher rates of unionization, (2) greater regulation, and (3) more generous unemployment assistance.[3] Let us look at the cross-country data and consider how each of these factors will influence the rate of unemployment.

Centralized Wage Setting

Exhibit 2 indicates both the percentage of the nonfarm labor force that is unionized and the share of employees whose wages are set by collective bargaining. Among the nine countries, the unionization rate is highest for Italy, Australia, and Canada; it is lowest for France, the United States, and Spain. However, the structure of unions differs substantially across countries. Therefore, membership is often a misleading indicator of the role of unions in the wage-setting process.

Collective bargaining in the United States, Canada, and Japan is decentralized—it takes place at the company or plant level. Unions in Japan are almost exclusively of the "company union" variety. They seldom set wages for an entire industry. Although unions in the United States and Canada may operate across an entire industry, the bargaining process is nearly always between a union and a single employer, or, in some cases, a single plant of the employer. These contracts do not apply to other firms. Under these circumstances, the union density (membership) and the share of workers whose wages are set by collective bargaining are similar (see Exhibit 2).

---

[3]For additional information on this topic, see Charles Bean, "European Unemployment: A Survey," *Journal of Economic Literature*, 1995, no. 2:573–619; Sveinbjorn Blondal and Mark Pearson,"Unemployment and Other Nonemployment Benefits," *Oxford Review of Economic Policy*, 1995, no. 1:136–169; OECD, *Implementing the OECD Jobs Strategy: Member Countries' Experience* (Paris: OECD, 1997); OECD, *Making Work Pay: Taxation, Benefits, Employment and Unemployment* (Paris: OECD, 1997); and Horst Siebert, "Labor Market Rigidities: At the Root of Unemployment in Europe," *Journal of Economic Perspectives*, 1997, no. 3:37–54.

In contrast, the wage-setting process is highly centralized throughout most of Europe as well as in Australia. Negotiations between a union (or federation of unions) and an association of employers set the wages for all or most all workers in various industries, occupations, and/or regions. Statutory legislation extends these agreements to both nonunion employees and nonassociation employers who neither participate in the bargaining process nor agree to the wage contracts. Sometimes political officials are also actively involved in the wage-setting process.

Therefore, as Exhibit 2 shows, the share of employees whose wages are set by collective bargaining in Australia and the populous countries of Europe (except for the United Kingdom in recent years) is far greater than union membership. For example, while union members were only 9 percent of the French labor force in 1995, collective bargaining set the wages for 95 percent of the employees. In Spain, Australia, Italy, and Germany, the pattern was the same. In all of these countries, highly centralized "agreements" set the wages of most workers—both union and nonunion—within various industry and occupational categories. This explains why the proportion of employees whose wages are set by collective bargaining is so much higher than union workers as a share of the workforce.

Does it make any difference whether wages are set at the firm level or for an entire industry, occupation, or region? Economic theory indicates that it does. When union members (and unionized firms) compete with nonunion workers and firms, market forces continue to play an important role. If the unionized workers push wages significantly above the competitive level, it will be more difficult for their employers to compete effectively

EXHIBIT 2

Share of Employees Whose Wages Are Set by Collective Bargaining: 1980 and 1995

Centralized collective bargaining agreements that set wages for all workers in an industry and/or occupation are far more common in Australia and the major European economies than in the United States, Canada, and Japan.

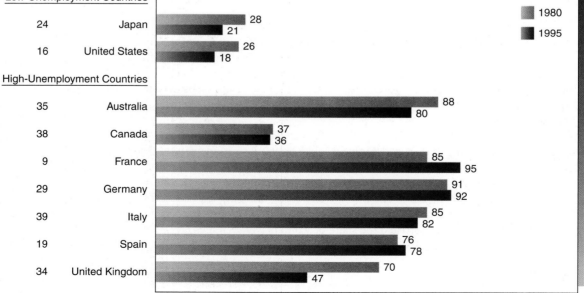

Sources: OECD, *Employment Outlook* (July 1994), Table 5.7; OECD, *Employment Outlook* (July 1997), Table 3.3; and OECD, *Country Surveys* (various issues).

with nonunion rivals. Thus, higher wages for union members would lead to employment reductions in the unionized sector. This will temper the bargaining process.

In contrast, the discipline of market forces is eroded when the wages for all workers and firms in an industry, an occupation, and a region are set centrally. A union that can set the wages of all firms in an industry will have considerable monopoly power. As wages are pushed up, the costs of both union and nonunion employers will rise. There will be less opportunity for nonunion firms to expand and hire workers willing to work at a lower wage. Of course, market forces will not be totally absent. Higher wages will encourage the substitution of capital for labor and make it more difficult for domestic firms to compete in international markets. Some firms will move production operations to other countries, where the services of workers of similar skill are available at a lower cost. The predictable result will be high rates of unemployment (and slow rates of employment growth) like that experienced by European countries during the last two decades.

Centralized wage setting will have fewer adverse effects in small countries with labor forces that are relatively homogeneous in skills and education. In large countries with regional differences in cost of living and greater diversity among labor force participants, centrally determined wage rates will predictably lead to a substantial excess supply of workers in some areas and excess demand in others. In fact, unions and employers in high-wage regions can use the centralized wage-setting process to foist higher costs on rival firms and workers in regions where wages, reflecting educational and skill levels, would normally be lower. By pushing wages up in those regions, lower-wage and lower-skill workers are priced out of the market and rendered less competitive. The incentive for capital to move toward the low-wage regions is thus reduced.

Northern and southern Italy illustrate the significance of this strategy. Workers in southern Italy generally have fewer skills and less education than their counterparts in the North. With centralized labor contracts, however, wages in the various job categories are the same in both regions. As a result, workers in the South are less competitive and the incentive for capital to move toward that region is substantially reduced. Obviously, the northern workers and their union representatives find this arrangement highly attractive. In the South, however, the results are disastrous. In recent years, unemployment rates in southern Italy have ranged between 20 percent and 30 percent—three or four times the rates of the North. Centralized wage setting has also reduced the competitiveness of low-skill

In Europe and Australia, union contracts often set the wages for all workers, both union and nonunion, in industry and occupational categories. The wages of more than three out of four employees are set by unions in Europe, compared to one in five in the United States.

workers in several regions of Spain. As in Italy, the policy has led to both a high overall rate of unemployment and substantial regional disparity.

Regulation of Dismissal and Mandated Severance Pay

Severance pay
Pay by an employer to an employee upon the termination of employment with the firm.

European labor markets are also characterized by laws mandating various periods of prior notification and/or months of **severance pay** for the dismissal of a worker. **Exhibit 3** presents data on the restrictiveness of dismissal regulations in various countries. The graph indicates the number of months of severance pay plus one-half the months of prior notification required for a no-fault dismissal of an employee. Since these mandates generally vary with seniority of the employee, the figures are the average for two workers, one with four years and another with 20 years of seniority.

The sum of the months of severance pay and prior notification required for a dismissal are relatively short in the United States, Japan, and Canada.[4] In contrast, they are quite lengthy in Italy and Spain. For example, Italian employers are required to give a dismissed worker with four years of seniority 1.1 months of notification and 3.5 months of severance pay. If the worker has 20 years of seniority, prior notification of 2.2 months and severance pay of 18 months are required. In addition, several European countries require political approval for mass layoffs. Employers in Italy, Spain, and France must convince various political officials that a business necessity is present before they are permitted to reduce their workforce by a sizable amount.

Proponents argue that regulations mandating notification and severance pay will help protect workers against arbitrary dismissal and provide them with greater job security.

EXHIBIT 3
Restrictiveness of Dismissals: The Average Months of Mandated Severance Pay and Notification for a No-Fault Dismissal, Mid 1990s

In Europe and Australia, government regulations generally require employers to give dismissed employees substantial prior notification and pay them severance pay for lengthy periods of time. These dismissal regulations are particularly restrictive in Italy and Spain.

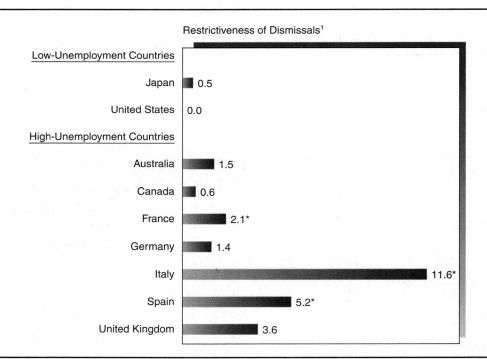

Restrictiveness of Dismissals[1]

Low-Unemployment Countries
Japan 0.5
United States 0.0
High-Unemployment Countries
Australia 1.5
Canada 0.6
France 2.1*
Germany 1.4
Italy 11.6*
Spain 5.2*
United Kingdom 3.6

[1]The average months of mandated severance pay plus one-half of the average months of mandated notification for the no-fault dismissal of a worker (average for workers with 4 years and 20 years of employment).
*Indicates that collective dismissals required approval from political authorities.
Sources: OECD, *OECD Jobs Study: Evidence and Explanations* (1994), Part II, Table 6.5; and OECD, *Country Surveys* (various issues).

[4]Although there is no general notification requirement in the United States, employers with one hundred or more full-time employees are required to give 60-day notice to employees dismissed as the result of a plant closing or mass layoff.

However, regulations that make it more costly to dismiss workers also make it more costly to hire them. When dismissal costs are high, employers will be reluctant to add workers during periods of strong demand because it will be costly to dismiss them if future conditions are less favorable. Thus, firms will often find that it is cheaper to expand output—particularly if the expansion is expected to be temporary—by using more capital, contracting out, or hiring part-time workers not covered by the dismissal regulations.

Furthermore, restrictive dismissal policies reduce the competition between workers with jobs and those seeking employment. They make it more expensive for employers to substitute current job seekers for established workers. In essence, the restrictions make it extremely difficult for new entrants to find jobs and acquire labor force experience. High unemployment among younger workers is an important secondary effect. The data are consistent with this view. The unemployment rate of persons age 15 to 24 years has exceeded 30 percent throughout most of the 1990s in both Spain and Italy, the two major countries with the most restrictive dismissal policies.

Impact of Unemployment Benefits

Unemployment benefits reduce the opportunity cost of job search and thereby encourage more lengthy "spells" of unemployment. When set at a high level, they can become an attractive source of income in comparison to work. The generosity of the benefit levels may also influence unemployment in more subtle ways. Employers in seasonal and other industries offering erratic employment will often be able to pay lower wages because the benefits provide employees with income supplements when they are not working. In essence, the benefits subsidize businesses offering unstable employment and encourage the expansion of such employment.[5] More generous benefits tend to reduce the political repercussions of high unemployment rates. This is particularly important when the government is an active participant in the wage-setting process, as is the case throughout much of Europe. When the benefit levels are high, political officials will have less reason to resist the wage demands of unions even if the higher wages mean fewer jobs and higher rates of unemployment. Therefore, there are good reasons to expect that countries with more generous unemployment benefits will experience higher unemployment.

Unemployment benefit systems are highly complex. Interestingly, the initial **replacement rate** among the major industrial countries is quite similar. However, there is considerable variation with regard to the length of time persons are permitted to draw benefits. The shortest duration periods for the benefits are found in Italy, the United States, the United Kingdom, Canada, and Japan, where the benefits for most unemployed workers expire in a year or less.[6] (*Note*: In the United States, unemployment benefits normally expire after 26 weeks.) In contrast, unemployed workers are permitted to draw benefits for two years or more in Spain, France, Germany, and Australia.

The replacement rate often varies with previous level of earnings, family size and situation, previous length of employment, and duration of unemployment. The OECD has calculated the replacement rate of member countries for recipients at two different income levels, three family situations, and three time periods of unemployment. The average replacement rates for these 18 different categories provide a reasonably good "index of generosity" for the unemployment system of each country.[7]

Replacement rate
The share of previous earnings replaced by unemployment benefits.

---

[5]In several countries, including the United States, employers with more erratic employment patterns are required to pay a higher payroll tax for unemployment insurance. However, the higher tax is generally insufficient to cover the additional benefits paid to the workers laid off or dismissed by these firms, effectively giving them a subsidy.

[6]Italy uses mandated severance pay (see Exhibit 3) as a substitute for unemployment compensation. Until recently, only a token unemployment compensation system was present in Italy.

[7]The OECD figures cover the replacement rate for the first year of unemployment, years two and three, and years four and five. Because the benefits will expire after six months or one year in many countries, this average replacement rate for most countries is substantially lower than the initial replacement rate. For example, unemployment benefits initially replace 60 percent of earnings in the United States. However, since the benefits can only be drawn for six months, the average replacement rate over the five-year time period is much lower than the initial figure.

As **Exhibit 4** shows, the unemployment benefits are generally more attractive (and less restrictive with regard to eligibility) in Europe, Australia, and Canada than in the United States and Japan. The average replacement rates of the United States and Japan generally range from one-half to one-third the replacement rates of the European countries, Australia, and Canada. Predictably, the higher unemployment benefit levels of these latter countries will encourage more lengthy periods of job search and thereby push the unemployment rate up.

Pulling It Together

Compared to the five most populous European countries, as well as Australia and Canada, the labor markets of the United States and Japan are more decentralized, dismissal regula-

EXHIBIT 4
The Average Replacement Rate of Unemployment Benefits in Nine Major Industrial Economies

Compared to Japan and the United States, unemployment benefits in Australia, Canada, and Europe replace a larger proportion of an unemployed worker's lost earnings. How will this influence the natural rate of unemployment?

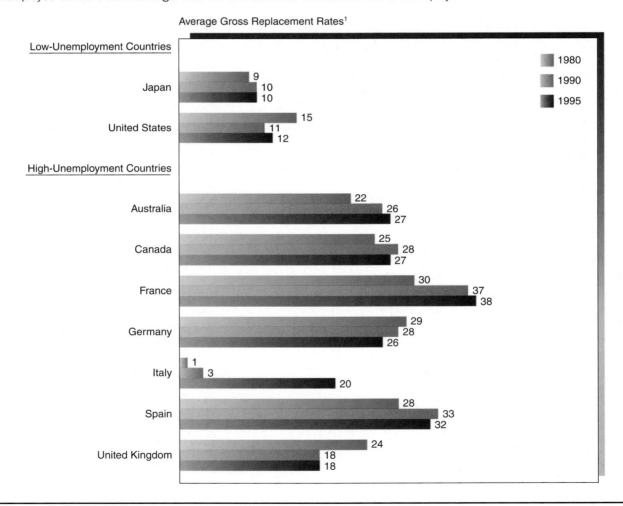

[1]Average for two earnings levels (2/3 average and average earnings), three family situations (single, married with dependent spouse, and married with working spouse), and three duration periods (1 year, 1–3 years, and 3–5 years).
Sources: OECD, *OECD Jobs Strategy: Making Work Pay* (1997), Figure 2; and OECD, *Implementing the OECD Jobs Strategy: Member Countries' Experience*, Table 5.

Business is brisk in this German unemployment office. Compared to the United States and Japan, unemployment benefits are more generous in Europe and Australia. Higher unemployment benefits reduce the opportunity cost of job search and thereby tend to lengthen spells of unemployment. This pushes unemployment rates upward.

tions are less restrictive, and unemployment benefits are less generous. Economic theory indicates that each of these factors will enhance the flexibility of labor markets and help keep unemployment rates low. The evidence is supportive of this view. While the unemployment rates of the United States and Japan were 4.6 percent and 4.1 percent, respectively, during 1996–2000, the average unemployment rate of the seven more interventionist countries was 10.4 percent. For the European Union as a whole, the unemployment rate averaged 9.7 percent during this period. Only one of the more regulated labor markets was able to do better than a 7 percent average rate of unemployment during 1996–2000.

LABOR MARKET REFORMS IN THE UNITED KINGDOM AND NEW ZEALAND

If a country moved toward a more liberal labor market, would it make any difference? The experience of the United Kingdom and New Zealand sheds light on this issue. During the 1980s and 1990s, these two countries adopted major reforms designed to protect the rights of workers and make their labor markets more competitive.

In the United Kingdom, the reforms focused on promotion of democratic decision making and the protection of workers' rights. The Employment Act of 1980 required secret ballot approval prior to the establishment of a closed shop, in which only union members can be hired. Later, legislation was adopted (1) requiring worker approval every five years for the continuation of a closed shop and (2) making strike action to establish a closed shop unlawful. Nonunion workers were also granted legal protection against dismissal and discriminatory actions as the result of their nonunion status. Union members were given the right to join the union of their choice and granted protection against unions seeking to discipline them for failure to support a strike. These changes both weakened the monopoly power of unions and led to a more decentralized wage-setting process. Union membership in the United Kingdom fell from 50 percent of the workforce in 1980 to 34 percent in 1995. More important, centralized bargaining became less commonplace. The share of employees having their wages set by collective bargaining contracts fell from 70 percent in 1980 to 47 percent in 1995. The labor market reforms were supplemented with less generous unemployment benefits. As Exhibit 4 indicates, the average replacement rate in the United Kingdom fell from 24 percent in 1980 to 18 percent in 1990 and 1995.

In New Zealand, the Employment Contracts Act of 1991 restructured the labor market even more rapidly than the English reforms. This act allowed all employees to "choose whether or not to associate with other employees for advancing the employees' collective employment interests." Employees were granted the right to negotiate labor contracts, with or without the assistance of an agent. Most significantly, while rights to strike and lockout were explicitly recognized, these weapons were permitted only at the expiration of labor contracts and then only after employee approval was obtained at the enterprise level. This effectively changed the wage-setting process in New Zealand from a centralized to a decentralized system. As in the United Kingdom, union membership fell and the share of employees having their wages set by union contracts declined from 67 percent in 1990 to 31 percent in 1995.

How have the labor markets of these two countries reacted to economic liberalization? In the United Kingdom, the economy expanded rapidly throughout most of the 1980s and the unemployment rate declined. Following the recession in the early 1990s, the economy rebounded nicely and by 1998, the rate of unemployment in the United Kingdom had receded to less than 6 percent, the lowest rate achieved since the 1970s. In 2000, the unemployment rate of the UK was 5.5 percent. The UK unemployment rate now stands in stark contrast to the double-digit rates of the other populous European countries. Similar results were achieved in New Zealand. The unemployment rate of New Zealand fell from 10.3 percent during 1991–1992 to an average of 6.5 percent during 1995–2000.

LABOR MARKETS IN THE UNITED STATES AND CANADA

Comparisons between the United States and Canadian labor markets are also revealing. Although the Canadian labor market is less regulated and more decentralized than those of the major European economies, it is clearly less liberal than that of the United States. Compared to the United States, the share of employees with wages set by collective bargaining is greater, dismissal regulations are more restrictive, and unemployment benefits are more generous in Canada. Furthermore, the Canadian labor market has been drifting toward the European model. Union membership has been increasing as a share of the labor force in Canada, while it has been declining in the United States. During the last decade, Canada has enacted legislation making it more difficult for employers to dismiss workers and reduce the size of their workforce.

These factors show up in the unemployment statistics. During the 1960s and 1970s, the Canadian average unemployment rate was virtually the same as that of the United States. This is no longer true. During the 1980s, the Canadian average rate of unemployment was about 2 percent greater than the rate of the United States, and in the 1990s the gap widened to approximately 4 percent (see Exhibit 1). Like the high unemployment rates of continental Europe, the differential unemployment rate between the United States and Canada also illustrates the link between labor market policies and the natural rate of unemployment.

KEY POINTS

▼ During the last decade, the major European economies persistently experienced double-digit unemployment rates. In recent years, the unemployment rate of the European Union has been about twice that of the United States.

▼ When used in large and diverse labor markets, a centralized wage-setting process will push wage

rates above market levels in various regions and skill categories. This will tend to cause higher rates of unemployment. Similarly, regulations that make it more costly to dismiss workers will also make employers more reluctant to hire employees. This will lead to sluggish employment growth and high rates of unemployment, particularly for youthful workers seeking to enter the workforce. High unemployment benefits will reduce the opportunity cost of job search, and thereby cause more lengthy spells of unemployment.

▼ Compared to the United States and Japan, the labor markets of Italy, Spain, France, and Germany are characterized by centralized wage-setting processes, more restrictive dismissal regulations, and high unemployment benefit replacement rates. There is reason to believe that these policies have contributed to the high unemployment rates of these economies.

▼ Recent reforms in the United Kingdom and New Zealand have increased the competitiveness of labor markets. The rates of unemployment in both countries have declined and are now significantly lower than the rates of countries that have followed more restrictive labor market practices.

▼ Compared to the United States, the Canadian labor market is characterized by a larger degree of unionization, more restrictive dismissal practices, and more generous unemployment benefits. The data also indicate that the natural rate of unemployment is higher in Canada than in the United States.

CRITICAL ANALYSIS QUESTIONS

*1. Compared to the situation where a union is able to organize only a portion of the firms in an industry, how does the ability to set wages for an entire industry influence the power of a labor union? What does this suggest about the relative strength of unions in Europe versus those in the United States and Japan?

2. Explain why unemployment compensation is an indirect subsidy to employers with a less stable workforce. Is it a good idea to subsidize this type of unemployment? Why or why not?

3. Suppose that legislation was passed requiring all employers in the United States to pay dismissed workers one week of severance pay for every year they were employed by the firm. What impact would this have on (a) the dismissal rate of employees, (b) the productivity of employees, and (c) the unemployment rate of youthful workers? Discuss.

4. Do you think that the United States should move toward the European labor market model characterized by more extensive collective bargaining, greater government regulation, and more generous unemployment benefits? Why or why not?

*Asterisk denotes questions for which answers are given in Appendix B.

SPECIAL TOPIC 7

The Phillips Curve: Is There a Trade-off Between Inflation and Unemployment?

Focus

- What is the Phillips curve?

- Does inflation reduce the unemployment rate?

- Why were the early views about the Phillips curve wrong?

- Have views about the Phillips curve influenced macroeconomic policy?

Inflation does give a stimulus . . . when it starts from a condition that is noninflationary. If the inflation continues, people get adjusted to it. But when people get adjusted to it, when they expect rising prices, the mere occurrence of what has been expected is no longer stimulating.

—*Sir John R. Hicks* [1]

[1]J. R. Hicks, "Monetary Theory and Keynesian Economics," in *Monetary Theory*, ed. R. W. Clower (Harmondsworth: Penguin, 1969), p. 260.

Because it originated with an influential article by British economist A. W. Phillips, a curve indicating the relationship between the rate of inflation and the rate of unemployment is known as the **Phillips curve**.[2] The views of economists and policy makers with regard to the Phillips curve and the potential of demand stimulus to reduce the rate of unemployment have changed twice during the last four decades. Beginning in the early 1960s, several influential economists argued that there was a trade-off between inflation and unemployment—that a lower rate of unemployment could be achieved if we were willing to tolerate a little more inflation.[3] By the end of the 1960s, there was widespread acceptance of this view. However, both the experience of the 1970s and important developments in economic theory led to another shift. By the 1980s, the perceived inflation-unemployment trade-off had lost most of its luster. As views shifted on this topic, so too did macroeconomic policy. This feature focuses on the Phillips curve and analyzes the impact of changing views on the topic. ■

Phillips curve
A curve that illustrates the relationship between the rate of change in prices (or money wages) and the rate of unemployment.

EARLY VIEWS ABOUT THE PHILLIPS CURVE

Exhibit 1, taken from the 1969 *Economic Report of the President*, illustrates that there was an inverse relationship between inflation and unemployment during the 1954–1968 period. At the time, most economists thought the inflation-unemployment relationship was stable. In other words, they believed that expansionary policies would lead to some inflation, but would also lead to a long-lasting lower rate of unemployment.[4]

Influenced by the Phillips curve analysis, both monetary and fiscal policy were more expansionary during the latter half of the 1960s. For a while, it seemed that the demand-stimulus policies were yielding the expected result. As Exhibit 1 shows, the higher inflation rates of the late 1960s were associated with lower rates of unemployment. However, things began to change in the 1970s. As the inflation rate rose from 3 percent in the late 1960s to double-digit levels during 1974–1975, the rate of unemployment rose from less than 4 percent to more than 8 percent. As high rates of inflation continued in the latter half of the 1970s, so too did the high rates of unemployment. In contrast with the predictions of the early Phillips curve proponents, the United States experienced high rates of both inflation and unemployment throughout most of the 1970s.

Error of Early Phillips Curve Proponents: Failure to Consider Expectations

What went wrong? Why did the inflation-unemployment forecasts of the Phillips curve proponents prove so faulty? With the benefit of hindsight, it is easy to see the error: The early Phillips curve proponents failed to integrate expectations into their analysis. Building on the work of an early paper by John Muth, economists began to integrate expectations into their analysis during the 1970s.[5]

---

[2]A. W. Phillips, "The Relationship between Unemployment and the Rate of Change of Money Wages in the United Kingdom, 1861–1957," *Economica* 25 (1958): 238–299.

[3]For example, Nobel prize winners Paul Samuelson and Robert Solow told the 1959 meeting of the American Economic Association,

> In order to achieve the nonperfectionist's goal of high enough output to give us no more than 3 percent unemployment, the price index might have to rise by as much as 4 to 5 percent per year. That much price rise [inflation] would seem to be the necessary cost of high employment and production in the years immediately ahead.

See Paul A. Samuelson and Robert Solow, "Our Menu of Policy Changes," *American Economic Review* (May 1960).

[4]Not all economists accepted the view that there was a trade-off between inflation and unemployment. At the height of its popularity, the theoretical underpinning of the alleged trade-off was independently challenged by both Edmund Phelps and Milton Friedman. See Edmund S. Phelps, "Phillips Curves, Expectations of Inflation and Optimal Employment over Time," *Economica* 3(1967): 254–281; and Milton Friedman, "The Role of Monetary Policy," *American Economic Review* (May 1968): 1–17.

[5]The leading contributors to the integration of expectations in macroeconomics are Robert Barro of Harvard, Robert Lucas of the University of Chicago, and Thomas Sargent of the University of Minnesota.

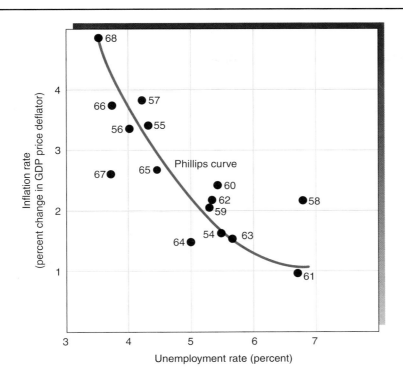

EXHIBIT 1
The Phillips Curve—Before the Inflation of the 1970s

This exhibit is from the 1969 *Economic Report of the President*, prepared by the president's Council of Economic Advisers. Each dot on the diagram indicates, as a coordinate point on the graph, the inflation rate and unemployment rate for the year. The report stated that the chart "reveals a fairly close association of more rapid price increases with lower rates of unemployment." Economists refer to this link as the Phillips curve. In the 1960s it was widely believed that policy makers could pursue expansionary macroeconomic policies and thereby permanently reduce the unemployment rate. More recent experience has caused most economists to reject this view.

Source: *Economic Report of the President*, 1969, p. 95. The Phillips curve is fitted to the points to illustrate the relationship.

How do expectations affect the Phillips curve analysis? Suppose the monetary authorities unexpectedly shift to a more expansionary policy. As our basic macroeconomic model indicates, the more expansionary policy will stimulate aggregate demand. When the increase in demand is unanticipated, the initial effects will be upward pressure on prices and increases in both output and employment. As a result, the unemployment rate will fall.

There are two reasons why an unanticipated increase in the rate of inflation will stimulate employment and reduce the rate of unemployment. First, the unexpected inflation will reduce the real wages of workers employed under long-term contracts and thereby stimulate employment. Union wage contracts and other wage agreements often determine money-wage rates over periods ranging from one to three years. Unanticipated inflation means that the impact of strong demand and upward pressure on prices has not been fully factored into long-term money-wage agreements. As a result, an unexpected increase in the inflation rate will reduce the employee's real-wage rate and the employer's real-wage costs.

Suppose that employees and employers anticipate a 4 percent inflation rate during the next year. From this, they concur on a collective bargaining agreement calling for money wages of $10 during the current year and $10.40 for the year beginning 12 months from now. If the actual inflation rate this year equals the 4 percent expected rate, the $10.40 money-wage rate 12 months from now translates to a $10 real-wage rate *at today's price level*. What happens to the real-wage rate if the inflation rate exceeds the expected rate of 4 percent? If actual inflation during the next 12 months is 8 percent, for example, the real-wage rate one year from now will fall to $9.63 at current prices. The higher the actual inflation rate, the lower the real wages of the employees. Unanticipated inflation tends to reduce the real-wage rates of employees whose money wages are fixed by long-term contracts. At the lower real-wage rate, firms will hire more workers and employment will expand.

There is a second reason why underestimation of the inflation rate will tend to expand employment. Misled by inflation, some job seekers will quickly accept job offers on the basis of a mistaken belief that the offers are particularly good ones in relation to the market for their labor services. When people underestimate the extent to which inflation has increased both prices and money wages, many job seekers will fail to recognize how much nominal wages have increased in their skill category. Unaware of just how much their money-wage opportunities have improved, they will tend to accept offers that are not as good as they think they are (relative to jobs that could be found with additional search). Unemployed workers thus shorten their search time, which lowers the unemployment rate.

Summarizing, unanticipated (or underestimated) inflation reduces the real-wage rate of workers whose money wages are determined by long-term contracts and reduces the search time of job seekers. Both of these factors will expand employment and reduce the unemployment rate below its natural rate.

However, once the importance of expectations is considered, it is clear that the lower rate of unemployment will only be temporary. With time, people will anticipate the higher rate of inflation and adjust their decision making accordingly. The adaptive expectations theory implies that there will be a significant time lag—perhaps one to three years—before people are able to anticipate and adjust to the higher rate of inflation. The rational expectations theory indicates that many will foresee the effects of policy changes and therefore alter their choices more quickly. Both theories of expectations, however, imply that individuals will eventually anticipate the higher rate of inflation and adjust their behavior in light of it.

Once the higher rate of inflation is anticipated, workers and their union representatives will demand and employers will agree to money-wage increases that reflect the higher current and expected future inflation rate. Similarly, job seekers will become fully aware of the extent that inflation has increased (and continues to increase) their money-wage alternatives. As they do so, their search time will return to normal. *Once decision makers fully anticipate the higher rate of inflation and reflect it in their choices, the inflation rate will neither depress real-wage rates nor reduce the search time of job seekers. As this happens, both real output and unemployment will return to their natural (long-run) rates.*

Exhibit 2 uses our aggregate-demand/aggregate-supply (*AD/AS*) model to illustrate the implications of adaptive expectations with regard to the Phillips curve analysis. Beginning from a position of stable prices and long-run equilibrium (point *A*), part a of Exhibit 2 illustrates the impact of an unanticipated increase in aggregate demand. Initially the demand stimulus will increase output (to Y_2) and employment. The unemployment rate will recede below the economy's natural rate. The strong demand and tight resource markets will place upward pressure on resource prices. *For a time*, the economy will experience both rising prices and an output beyond full-employment capacity (point *B*). This high level of output, however, will not be long-lasting. People will eventually anticipate the rising prices (inflation). When this happens, resource prices and costs will rise (from their temporary low levels) relative to product prices, causing the *SRAS* curve to shift to the left. As the previous relationship between resource prices and product prices is restored, output will recede to the economy's full-employment level (point *C*). If the rising prices continue at the same rate, they will be anticipated by decision makers. When this is the case, both the *AD* and *SRAS* curves will continually shift upward (the dotted curves of part a). The price level will steadily increase, but output and employment will remain at the full-employment level.

Part b of Exhibit 2 illustrates the same case within the Phillips curve framework. Because initially stable prices are present and the economy is in long-run equilibrium, unemployment is equal to its natural rate (point *A*). We assume that the economy's natural rate of unemployment is 5 percent. The condition of long-run equilibrium implies that the stable prices are both anticipated and observed. Under adaptive expectations, an unanticipated shift to a more expansionary policy will temporarily increase output and reduce unemployment. It will also place upward pressure on prices. Suppose that demand-stimulus

EXHIBIT 2
AD/AS Model, Adaptive Expectations, and Phillips Curve

When stable prices are observed and anticipated, both full-employment output and the natural rate of unemployment will be present (*A* in both panels). With adaptive expectations, a shift to a more expansionary policy will increase prices, expand output beyond its full-employment potential, and reduce the unemployment rate below its natural level (move from *A* to *B* in both panels). Decision makers though, will eventually anticipate the rising prices and incorporate them into their decision making. When this happens, the *SRAS* curve shifts to the left, output recedes to the economy's full-employment potential, and unemployment returns to the natural rate (moves from *B* to *C* in both panels). As the inflationary policy continues and decision makers anticipate it, both the *AD* and *SRAS* curves will continually shift upward (dotted *AD* and *SRAS* curves in panel a) without leading to an increase in output and employment. Inflation fails to expand output and reduce the unemployment rate when it is anticipated. Thus, the long-run Phillips curve is vertical at the natural rate of unemployment.

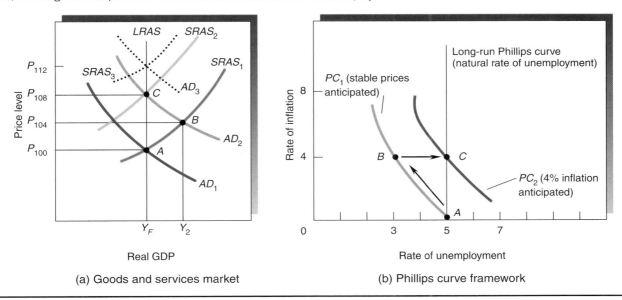

(a) Goods and services market

(b) Phillips curve framework

policies lead to 4 percent inflation and a reduction in the unemployment rate from 5 percent to 3 percent (moving from *A* to *B* along the short-run Phillips curve PC_1). Although point *B* is attainable, it will not be sustainable. After a period of time, decision makers will begin to anticipate the 4 percent rate of inflation. Workers and their union representatives will take the higher expected rate of inflation into account in their job search and collective bargaining decision making. Once the 4 percent rate of inflation is anticipated, the economy will confront a new, higher short-run Phillips curve (PC_2). The rate of unemployment will return to the long-run natural rate of 5 percent, even though prices will continue to rise at an annual rate of 4 percent (point *C*).

The moves from point *A* to point *B* in both panels of Exhibit 2 are simply alternative ways of representing the same phenomenon—a temporary increase in output and reduction in unemployment as the result of an unanticipated increase in aggregate demand. Similarly, the moves from point *B* to point *C* in the two panels both represent the return of output to its long-run potential and unemployment to its natural rate, once decision makers anticipate fully the observed rate of inflation.

What would happen if policy makers tried to keep the unemployment rate low (below its natural rate) by shifting to a still more expansionary policy? As **Exhibit 3** illustrates, this course of action would accelerate the inflation rate to still higher levels. For a time, people may continue to anticipate only the 4 percent rate of inflation. If so, the higher 8 percent rate of inflation will lead to another temporary reduction in unemployment (movement from *C* to *D*). Of course, once the 8 percent rate persists for a while, it too will be fully anticipated. The short-run Phillips curve will again shift to the right (to

EXHIBIT 3
Expectations and Shifts in the Phillips Curve

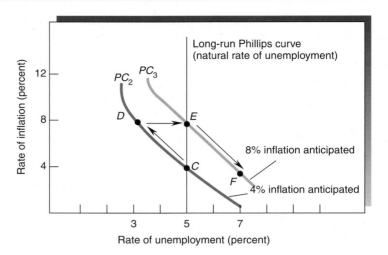

Continuing with the example of Exhibit 2, part b, point *C* illustrates an economy experiencing 4 percent inflation that was antici-pated by decision makers. Because the inflation was anticipated, the natural rate of unemployment is present. With adaptive expectations, demand-stimulus policies that result in a still higher rate of inflation (8 percent, for example) would once again temporarily reduce the unemployment rate below its long-run, normal level (move from *C* to *D* along *PC₂*). After a time, however, decision makers would come to anticipate the higher inflation rate, and the short-run Phillips curve would shift still farther to the right to *PC₃* (move from *D* to *E*). Once the higher rate is anticipated, if macro planners reduce the rate of inflation, unem-ployment will temporarily rise above its long-run natural rate (for example, move from *E* to *F*).

PC₃), unemployment will return to its long-run natural rate, and inflation will continue at a rate of 8 percent (point *E*).

Once decision makers anticipate an inflation rate, how would the economy be affected by a shift to a more restrictive policy? Suppose that wage rates are based on agreements that anticipated a continuation of the 8 percent inflation rate (point *E* of Exhibit 3). If the actual inflation rate falls to 4 percent when 8 percent inflation was expected, the real wages of workers will exceed the real wage present when the actual and expected rates of inflation were equal at 8 percent. The more the actual inflation rate falls short of the ex-pected rate, the higher the real wages of workers will be. Similarly, the search time of job seekers will increase when they overestimate the impact of inflation on money-wage rates. Unaware that the attractive money-wage offers they seek are unavailable, job hunters will lengthen their job search. In the short run, rising unemployment will be a side effect of the higher real wages and more lengthy job searches.

As Exhibit 3 illustrates, an anticipated shift to a more restrictive policy designed to reduce the inflation rate will cause abnormally high unemployment (the move from *E* to *F* along *PC₃*) and economic recession. The abnormally high unemployment rate will con-tinue until a lower rate of inflation convinces decision makers to alter their inflationary expectations downward and revise long-term contracts accordingly.

EXPECTATIONS AND THE MODERN VIEW OF THE PHILLIPS CURVE

Expectations substantially alter the naive Phillips curve view of the 1960s. Three major points follow from the integration of expectations into the Phillips curve analysis.

1. ***Demand stimulus will lead to inflation without permanently reducing unemploy-ment below the natural rate.*** Once people fully anticipate the inflationary side effects

of expansionary policies, resource prices will rise, profit margins will return to normal levels, and unemployment will return to its natural rate. An unanticipated shift to a more expansionary policy may temporarily reduce the unemployment rate, but the lower rate of unemployment will not be sustainable. There is no long-run (permanent) trade-off between inflation and unemployment. Like the *LRAS* curve, the long-run Phillips curve is vertical at the natural rate of unemployment.

2. ***When inflation is greater than anticipated, unemployment falls below the natural rate. Conversely, when inflation is less than expected, unemployment will rise above the natural rate.*** It is the *difference* between the actual and expected rates of inflation that influences unemployment, not the magnitude of inflation, as some economists previously thought. **Exhibit 4** illustrates this point by recasting the Phillips curve within the expectations framework. When people underestimate the actual rate of inflation, abnormally low unemployment will occur. Conversely, when decision makers expect a higher rate of inflation than what actually occurs—when they overestimate the inflation rate—unemployment will rise above its natural rate. Equal changes in the actual and expected inflation rates, though, will fail to reduce the unemployment rate. If actual inflation rates of 5 percent, 10 percent, 20 percent, or even higher are accurately anticipated, they will fail to reduce unemployment below its natural rate.[6]

3. ***When the inflation rate is steady—when it is neither rising nor falling—the actual rate of unemployment will equal the economy's natural rate of unemployment.*** If the inflation rate of an economy is constant (or approximately so), decision makers will come to anticipate the rate. This rate will be reflected in both long-term contracts and the job search of workers. Once this happens, unemployment will return to its natural rate—the minimum rate that can be sustained in the future. In fact, the natural rate of

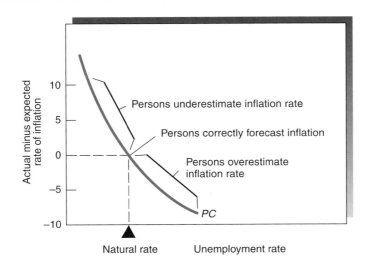

EXHIBIT 4
Modern Expectational Phillips Curve

It is the difference between the actual and expected rates of inflation that influences the unemployment rate, not merely the size of the inflation rate, as the earlier, naive Phillips curve analysis implied. When inflation is greater than anticipated (people underestimate it), unemployment will fall below the natural rate. In contrast, when inflation is less than people anticipate (people overestimate it) unemployment will rise above the natural rate. If the inflation rate is correctly anticipated by decision makers, the natural rate of unemployment will result.

---

[6]Empirically, higher rates of inflation are generally associated with greater variability in the inflation rate. Erratic variability increases economic uncertainty. It is likely to inhibit business activity, reduce the volume of mutually advantageous exchange, and cause the level of employment to fall. Thus, higher, more variable inflation rates may actually increase the rate of unemployment.

unemployment is sometimes defined as the unemployment rate present when the inflation rate is neither rising nor falling.

EXPECTATIONS, INFLATION, AND UNEMPLOYMENT: THE EMPIRICAL EVIDENCE

Integration of expectations into the Phillips curve analysis helps clarify the U.S. data on inflation and unemployment during the last several decades. After nearly 20 years of low inflation (and moderate monetary and fiscal policy) following World War II, decision makers, accustomed to relative price stability, expected low rates of inflation. As a result, the shift toward expansionary policies in the mid-1960s caught people by surprise. Therefore, as Exhibit 1 shows, these policies initially reduced the unemployment rate.

Contrary to the popular view of the 1960s, however, the abnormally low unemployment rate could not be sustained. **Exhibit 5**, which is an updated version of Exhibit 1, makes this point clear. Just as our theory predicts, the inflation-unemployment conditions worsened substantially as the expansionary policy persisted. The Phillips curve consistent with the 1970–1973 data (PC_2) was well to the right of PC_1. During the 1974–1983 period, still higher rates of inflation were observed. As inflation rates in the 6 percent to 10 percent range became commonplace in the latter half of the 1970s, the Phillips curve once again shifted upward, to PC_3.

As monetary policy tightened in 1981–1983 and the Reagan administration promised to bring inflation under control, the inflation rate decelerated sharply. Just as our theory predicts, initially the unemployment rate soared, to 9.7 percent in 1982 and 9.6 percent in 1983, when macroeconomic policy shifted toward restraint. As the restraint continued, the inflation rate declined from the high rates of the late 1970s to the 2.5 to 4.5 percent range during 1984–1993. Soon after the decline in inflation, people scaled their expectations for

EXHIBIT 5
Inflation and Real-world Shifts in the Phillips Curve

While the 1961–1969 unemployment-inflation data mapped Phillips curve PC_1 (see Exhibit 1), as demand-stimulus policies led to higher inflation rates, the Phillips curve shifted outward to PC_2 (for the 1970–1973 period) and PC_3 (for the 1974–1983 period). Just as our theories of expectations indicate, the high rates of inflation failed to reduce permanently the rate of unemployment. Similarly, as lower rates of inflation were achieved and eventually anticipated, the Phillips curve shifted inward. Since 1994, the position of the Phillips curve has been similar to its position during the 1960s.

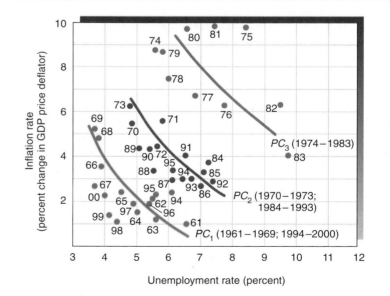

Source: Economic Report of the President, 2001.

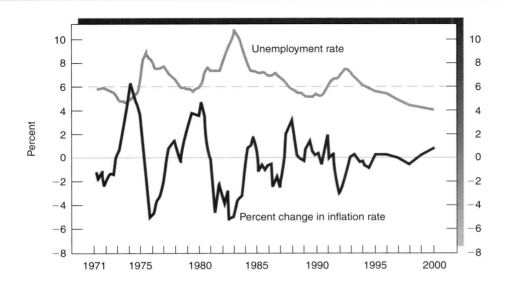

Source: Economic Report of the President, 2001.

EXHIBIT 6
Unemployment Rate and Change in the Rate of Inflation

Here we illustrate the relationship between the rate of unemployment and the change in the rate of inflation (this year's inflation rate minus the rate during the preceding year). Note how the sharp reductions in the rate of inflation during 1975, 1981–1982, and 1991 were associated with recession and substantial increases in the unemployment rate. In contrast, the low and steady inflation rates since 1992 have led to low rates of unemployment.

the inflation rate downward, and the Phillips curve shifted inward (from PC_3 to PC_2). As low rates of inflation were maintained, the 1994–2000 Phillips curve appears to be in a position quite similar to that of the 1960s.

The modern view indicates that it is the difference between the actual and expected rates of inflation that will influence the rate of unemployment. Abrupt changes in the inflation rate are less likely to be correctly anticipated. **Exhibit 6** presents data on changes in the annual rate (12-month moving average) of inflation and the rate of unemployment. As the graph shows, there were sharp reductions in the rate of inflation during 1975, 1981–1982, and 1991. For example, the inflation rate fell from 12.4 percent in 1974 to 6.9 percent in 1975, a drop of more than 5 percentage points. Decision makers are likely to underestimate the magnitude of such sharp reductions in the inflation rate. When this is the case, the actual rate of inflation will be less than the expected rate. Under these circumstances, our analysis indicates that unemployment will rise above its natural rate. As Exhibit 6 shows, the unemployment rate rose substantially in response to the steep declines in the rate of inflation during 1975, 1981–1982, and again in 1991. In contrast, during the period 1993–2000, the year-to-year differences in the inflation rate were quite small. The unemployment rate declined during this period of low (and steady) inflation. Most observers estimated that unemployment in the United States was approximately equal to the natural rate during 1995–2000.

THE PHILLIPS CURVE AND MACRO POLICY

The evolution of views with regard to the Phillips curve illustrates how ideas—even when they are wrong—can influence policy. As we noted, in the 1960s and 1970s, most economists thought that there was a trade-off between inflation and unemployment. If a little inflation would stimulate output and reduce the unemployment rate, why not follow this course? After all, inflation only influences the nominal value of things, whereas changes in real output and employment affect real incomes and living standards. Arguments along these lines provided the foundation for the more expansionary macro policy of the 1970s.

By 1980, however, things were shifting the other way. Both the experience of the 1970s and the integration of expectations into numerous areas of economics, including the

Phillips curve analysis, had convinced many economists that the earlier view of the Phillips curve was fallacious. In the 1980s most believed that even if a trade-off did exist between inflation and unemployment, it would not last long. Thus, attempting to exploit the questionable trade-off would be shortsighted. Once again, there was an impact on policy. During the last two decades, monetary policy has focused on price stability—keeping the inflation rate low.

Interestingly, the pursuit of more expansionary policies during the era when most believed in the inflation-unemployment trade-off led to higher rates of both inflation and unemployment. **Exhibit 7** highlights this point. The average annual rate of inflation rose during the 1970s, but so too did the average rate of unemployment. As the dream of the inflation-unemployment trade-off dissipated, policy makers—particularly those in the monetary area—shifted their emphasis toward the achievement of price stability. Paradoxically, as they did so, the unemployment rate fell.[7]

There are two important lessons to be learned from the Phillips curve era. First, expansionary macro policy will not reduce the rate of unemployment, at least not for long. Efforts to use it in this manner will lead to higher rates of both inflation and unemployment. Second, an environment of price stability will help keep the unemployment rate low. There is no conflict between price stability and a low rate of unemployment.

EXHIBIT 7
Inflation and Unemployment During Various Periods, 1959–2000

When more expansionary policies were pursued during the 1970–1973 and 1974–1982 periods, higher rates of both inflation and unemployment occurred. In contrast, lower rates of unemployment have accompanied the lower inflation rates of the more recent periods. There is no conflict between price stability and low unemployment.

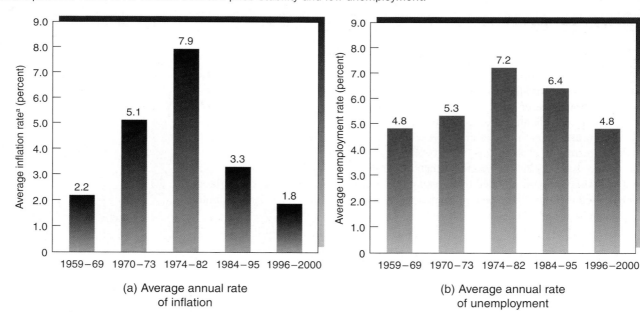

(a) Average annual rate of inflation

(b) Average annual rate of unemployment

Note: [a]The GDP deflator was used to measure the rate of inflation.
Source: Economic Report of the President, 2001.

[7]Youthful workers generally have higher rates of unemployment than their older counterparts. Therefore, as we noted in Chapter 8, the natural rate of unemployment will tend to rise when youthful workers comprise a larger share of the labor force. Youthful workers rose as a share of the labor force during the 1970s and declined during the 1990s. This factor also contributed to the higher unemployment rates during the earlier time period and lower rates of more recent years. For evidence on this topic, see Abbigail J. Chioto and Michael T. Owyang, "Low Unemployment: Old Dogs or New Tricks?" *Regional Economist,* October 2001, Federal Reserve Bank of St. Louis.

KEY POINTS

▼ The Phillips curve indicates the relationship between the unemployment rate and inflation rate. Prior to the late 1970s, it was widely believed that higher inflation would lower the rate of unemployment.

▼ Integration of expectations into the Phillips curve analysis indicates that any trade-off between inflation and unemployment will be short-lived. An unanticipated shift to a more expansionary policy may temporarily reduce the unemployment rate, but as soon as decision makers come to anticipate the higher rate of inflation, unemployment will return to its natural rate. Even high rates of inflation will fail to reduce unemployment once they are anticipated by decision makers.

▼ There is no permanent trade-off between inflation and unemployment.

▼ When the inflation rate is greater than anticipated, unemployment will tend to fall below the natural rate. This often happens when there is an abrupt shift to a more expansionary macro policy and an accompanying jump in the rate of inflation. Conversely, when the inflation rate is less than anticipated, unemployment will rise above its natural rate. This often happens when there is an abrupt shift to a more restrictive policy and a sharp reduction in the rate of inflation.

▼ Unemployment will move toward the natural rate—its minimum sustainable rate—when decision makers are able to forecast accurately the general level of prices and integrate it into their decision making. Because predictably low rates of inflation will be easier for people to forecast accurately, they will lead to low rates of unemployment.

▼ The early inflation-unemployment trade-off view helped promote the more expansionary macro policy of the 1970s. In contrast, the rejection of the inflation-unemployment trade-off during the 1980s created an environment more conducive to price stability. In turn, the increase in price-level stability contributed to the lower unemployment rates of the 1990s.

CRITICAL ANALYSIS QUESTIONS

1. How would you expect the actual unemployment rate to compare with the natural unemployment rate in the following cases?
   a. Prices are stable and have been stable for the last four years.
   b. The current inflation rate is 3 percent, and this rate was widely anticipated more than a year ago.
   c. Expansionary policies lead to an unexpected increase in the inflation rate from 3 percent to 7 percent.
   d. There is an unexpected reduction in the inflation rate from 7 percent to 2 percent.

*2. Prior to the mid-1970s, many economists thought a higher rate of unemployment would reduce the inflation rate. Why? How does the modern view of the Phillips curve differ from the earlier view?

3. If policy makers think that demand stimulus policies will reduce the unemployment rate, how is this likely to influence macro policy? Would you expect acceptance of this view to lead to a more or less expansionary macro policy prior to major elections, such as those for president in the United States? Why or why not?

4. How did integration of expectations into the Phillips curve analysis and rejection of the view that higher inflation will reduce the unemployment rate affect macro policy in the last two decades?

*5. Explain what happens to real wages, the job search time of workers, and the unemployment rate when unanticipated inflation occurs. What happens when the inflation is anticipated?

---

*Asterisk denotes questions for which answers are given in Appendix B.

SPECIAL TOPIC **8**

The Economics of Health Care

Focus

■ How much do Americans spend on health care?

■ Who pays the bill for health care services? Why is this important?

■ Why have the prices of health care services risen so rapidly in recent decades?

■ What is likely to happen to health care prices and expenditures in the future?

■ What can be done to improve the delivery of health care services?

Americans increasingly have been driven to pay for their health care through third party insurers and to purchase that insurance, when possible, from their employers. This, in turn, has led to rising health care costs while making it harder for Americans without employer-provided insurance to obtain coverage.

—Michael Tanner [1]

[1] Michael Tanner, "What's Wrong with the Current System," in *Empowering Health Care Consumers Through Tax Reform*, Edited by Grace-Marie Arnett (Ann Arbor, University of Michigan Press, 1999).

here is considerable dissatisfaction with the operation of the health care industry in the United States. This is not without justification. Both the expenditures on and prices of health care have soared in recent decades. **Exhibit 1** presents the expenditure figures *as a share of GDP*. Health care spending, including both private and government, jumped from 5.1 percent of GDP in 1960 to 8.8 percent in 1980 and 13.2 percent in 2000. What are the factors underlying this growth of health care spending? Is it likely to continue in the future? Is the health care industry in need of fundamental reform? This special topic feature will investigate these questions and related issues.

Some categories of health care spending have substantial public good components. For example, this is true for expenditures on pure research and activities that retard, and in some cases, eliminate the incidence of communicable diseases. In these cases, health care spending can generate spillover benefits for the general populace and it would be difficult, if not impossible, to exclude nonpaying consumers from the receipt of these benefits. As we discussed in Chapter 5, the market may produce less than the ideal quantity of public goods and therefore there is a strong case for government action promoting the supply of such goods. The National Institute of Health and the Center For Disease Control provide examples of government organizations that justify their funding primarily on the basis of the public good nature of their services. However, the vast majority of health care spending, including that of the government, involves private goods, goods for which the benefits accrue primarily to the consumer. This special topic feature focuses on the government's involvement in the financing of health care. ∎

STRUCTURE OF THE HEALTH CARE INDUSTRY

As we discussed in Chapter 6, goods and services may be produced by either private or government-operated firms. Correspondingly, they may be paid for by the consumer directly or by the taxpayer or some other third party. (See Exhibit 4 of Chapter 6.) Because it alters incentives, the structure of production and payment affects the operation of the industry.

Health care in many countries, including Canada and most of the high-income countries of Europe, is a socialized industry.[2] In these countries, hospitals are operated by the government and their services are financed through taxes. Physicians, nurses, and other health care workers are government employees. Of course, socialization does not eliminate the problems of scarcity and rationing. Resources must be attracted to the health care industry and this will involve a cost. No country is able to provide as much health care, free of charge, as its citizens would like. Therefore, when price plays a secondary role, alternative methods must be utilized to allocate health care services. As a result, countries with socialized medicine are characterized by waiting lists for basic medical procedures, an absence (or highly restricted availability) of services such as MRIs that involve expensive equipment, and widespread use of political rules and regulations to determine who will receive and who will be denied various types of health care. When patients in countries with socialized medicine are unable to obtain treatment or lack confidence in that treatment, those who can afford to do so often travel to another country in order to purchase desired health services.

In the United States, there is widespread use of both private and government-operated enterprises in the health care industry. While the services of doctors are generally supplied privately, hospitals are often operated by the government, particularly local

---

[2]For a cross-national comparison of spending on health care, see Uwe E. Reinhardt, "Health Care for the Aging Baby Boom: Lessons from Abroad," *Journal of Economic Perspectives*, Spring 2000, pp. 71–83.

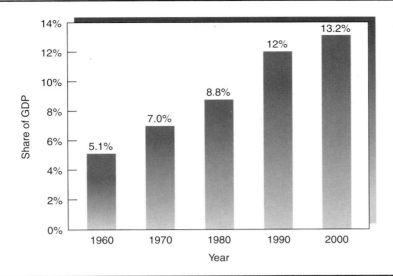

Source: www.hcfa.gov

EXHIBIT 1
Health Care Expenditures As a Share of GDP

Total expenditures (including both private and government-financed) on health care as a share of GDP have persistently increased during the last four decades. In 2000, the United States spent 13.2 percent of its GDP on health care, up from 5.1 percent in 1960.

governments. Many communities, however, also have privately operated hospitals. Some of the privately operated hospitals are for-profit businesses, while others are operated by charitable institutions. In contrast with most other industries, approximately 80 percent of health care spending is paid for by a third party, either the taxpayer or a private insurance company.

The Medicare and Medicaid programs have covered the bulk of the health care cost of the elderly and the poor since their establishment in the mid-1960s. Medicare's hospitalization program (Part A) uses a 2.9 percent tax on the wages and salaries of current workers to finance virtually all of the cost of hospitalization incurred by the elderly (persons age 65 and over). Medicare's Supplementary Medical Insurance (Part B) covers outpatient medical services. It is financed 75 percent by general revenues and 25 percent by beneficiary premiums. The Medicaid program is financed by general revenues and it provides low-income families with access to health care either free or at a nominal cost.

Exhibit 2 presents data for real expenditures (measured in terms of the purchasing power of the dollar in 2000) on the Medicare and Medicaid programs. From the very beginning, spending on the programs rose rapidly. By 1970, combined spending on the two summed to more than $40 billion (measured in 2000 dollars). Real expenditures on the Medicare program doubled between 1970 and 1980 and doubled again between 1980 and 1990. Real Medicare expenditures during the 1990s have increased by about 80 percent. While Medicaid started from a lower base in 1970, real spending on this program has increased even more rapidly than Medicare. In 1999, government spending on Medicaid ($111.6 billion) was ten times the level of 1970.

Health care spending, mostly for Medicare and Medicaid, consumed 19.9 percent of the federal budget in 2000, up from 9.4 percent in 1980 and 0.9 percent in 1960. This makes it the second largest item in the federal budget, greater than the spending on national defense and only slightly less than expenditures on social security. If the present trend continues, health care spending will be the largest item in the federal budget in the near future.[3] (See Exhibits 1 and 4 of Special Topic 1, "Government Spending and Taxation.")

---

[3]For a discussion of the problems facing Medicare, see Mark McClellan, "Medicare Reform: Fundamental Reform, Incremental Steps," *Journal of Economic Perspectives*, Spring 2000, pp. 21–44.

EXHIBIT 2
Real Expenditures on Medicare and Medicaid (Measured in 2000 dollars)

Expenditures on both Medicare and Medicaid have soared during the last three decades. Adjusted for inflation, the 1999 expenditures on Medicare are three times the level of 1980 and seven times the figure for 1970. The real Medicaid expenditures in 1999 were ten times the level of 1970.

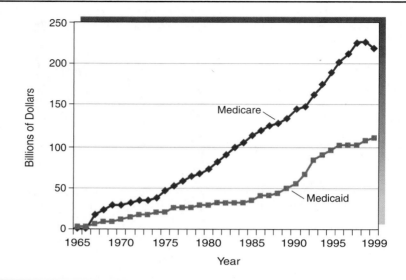

Source: http://w3.access.gpo.gov/usbudget/fy2001/hist.html

Discrimination Against the Direct Purchase of Health Insurance

Health insurance is also an integral part of the health care industry in the United States. About two-thirds of nonelderly adults have health insurance through group plans offered by their employers. Employee compensation in the form of health insurance is not subject to taxation. This makes group health insurance programs provided through one's employer particularly attractive.[4] Interestingly, this favorable tax treatment of employer-provided health insurance is a historical relic dating back to the wage and price controls of World War II. Because health insurance benefits were not counted as wages, employers were able to use them as a means to increase compensation and attract additional workers, while still complying with the wage controls imposed during the war.

In contrast with employer-provided policies, both personal medical bills and the direct purchase of health insurance by an individual or family must be paid for with after-tax dollars. When employees are provided with additional income rather than health insurance benefits, the income is subject to both payroll and personal income taxes. This makes the direct purchase of health insurance far more costly than purchase through an employer. For example, a lower-middle-income family confronting a 15 percent federal income tax and the 15.3 percent payroll tax would have to earn approximately $6,000 of additional income in order to purchase a $4,200 health insurance policy. A family in the 28 percent federal tax bracket would have to earn nearly $7,000 more in order to purchase the policy. If state and local income and payroll taxes were present, these figures would be even higher.

This discriminatory tax treatment encourages employees to demand and employers to provide low-deductible, small copayment health insurance policies. In essence, health care expenses covered in this manner are tax deductible, while those paid for out-of-pocket or through the direct purchase of health insurance are not.[5] As a result of this distortion, more health care bills are paid for by third-party insurers and fewer are covered directly by the health care consumer or through high-deductible insurance plans. As we will see in a moment, this affects the efficiency of health care delivery.

---

[4] In addition to the favorable tax treatment, economies resulting from the group purchase of health insurance may also make employer-provided plans more attractive.

[5] Out-of-pocket health care expenses can only be deducted if the taxpayer files an itemized return. Even in this case, only health care expenses in excess of 7.5 percent of the taxpayer's adjusted gross income are deductible.

The linking of health insurance to employment also reduces employee mobility and increases the number of people without any health insurance coverage. When employees lose their job or change jobs, they often lose their health insurance. Because purchase of a policy with after-tax dollars is so expensive, many unemployed workers remain uncovered until they are able to find a new job. Furthermore, the discriminatory tax treatment of direct purchase policies reduces the competitiveness of the health insurance industry. Unsurprisingly, the industry is dominated by a relatively small number of companies offering primarily "one size fits all" group plans.

THIRD-PARTY PAYMENTS AND HEALTH CARE INFLATION

Following the establishment of the Medicare and Medicaid programs in the mid-1960s, third-party payment of health care expenditures grew rapidly, while the share of medical bills paid directly by the consumer declined. As **Exhibit 3** shows, 55.2 percent of the 1960 medical expenditures were paid directly by consumers. Third parties financed only 44.8 percent of the 1960 total. Through the years, the share paid out-of-pocket has declined while that financed by third parties has risen. By 1999, third-party payments accounted for 82.4 percent of the medical care purchases, 43.3 percent by the government, and 39.1 percent by private insurers. Only 17.6 percent of 1999 medical expenditures were paid for directly by consumers.

Economic theory indicates that the growth of subsidies to health care consumers and accompanying expansion in third-party payments will push prices upward. There are two reasons why this will be the case. First, subsidies like those provided by Medicare and Medicaid will increase the demand for medical care. In turn, the stronger demand will lead to higher prices. Unfortunately, the supply of many health care services is highly inelastic, particularly in the short run. In the health care industry, the short run may be quite lengthy. This is perhaps most evident in the case of the services of doctors. Training for doctors is long and rigorous, and therefore an increase in doctors' fees will not quickly increase the

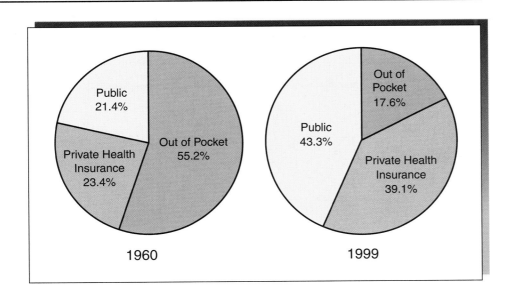

EXHIBIT 3
Out-of-pocket versus Third-Party Payments for Medical Care, 1960 and 1999

In 1960, out-of-pocket medical care expenditures of consumers accounted for 55 percent of the total, while private insurance and government programs paid 45 percent of the medical bills. By 1999, the out-of-pocket payments had declined to only 17.6 percent of expenditures, while those covered by a third party had risen to 82 percent of the total. Economic theory indicates that growth of third-party payments will reduce the incentive to economize and lead to both higher prices and expenditure levels.

Source: www.hcfa.gov

supply of practicing physicians and thereby reverse the upward movement of prices. This is particularly true when medical schools, perhaps unduly influenced by the American Medical Association, are reluctant to expand the size of their classes. Thus, the strong demand generated by Medicare and Medicaid is likely to exert its primary impact on the prices of medical services.

Second, the growth of third-party payments exerts an enormous impact on the incentive of consumers to economize and shop for low-cost services, and for producers to provide the goods at a low price. In a normal market, consumers will shop around and patronize those suppliers that provide the most value per dollar of expenditure. In turn, this shopping by consumers provides suppliers with a strong incentive to control their costs and offer their services at attractive prices. Therefore, high-cost, inefficient producers will find it difficult to compete in a normal market.

Perhaps the following example will help explain why the substitution of third-party payments for out-of-pocket spending will lead to higher prices. Suppose that the government, insurance companies, or some other third party was willing to pay 90 percent of the bill of customers purchasing hair-cutting services. Think how the behavior of both potential consumers and suppliers in the hair-cutting business would be altered. Because someone else is paying most of the bill, many consumers will now get their hair cut more often, search for the very best stylists even if they are quite expensive, and patronize those providing extra services (for example, shoulder massages, pleasant surroundings, and valet parking). The strong demand will make it possible for haircut suppliers to raise their prices and many will begin providing the "extras" designed to convince consumers that their services are the best available. All of these adjustments will drive the price of hair-cutting services upward and cause the third-party expenditures to soar.

Of course, health care is a far more serious matter than getting a haircut and the growth of the third-party health care payment system has taken place gradually over a lengthy time period, rather than abruptly as in our example. Nonetheless, the same general principles apply. *Economic theory indicates that when a third party is paying more and more of the bill, the demand for the service will increase, the incentive to economize will decline, and both the prices and expenditures on the service will rise rapidly.*

The evidence is consistent with this view. As **Exhibit 4** shows, the ratio of the medical care price index to the general consumer price index has doubled since 1960. Thus, during this lengthy time span, on average, the prices of medical services have risen

EXHIBIT 4
Ratio of Health Care Price Indexes Relative to the Consumer Price Index

The ratio of medical care prices to the general level of consumer prices doubled between 1960 and 2000. After increasing less rapidly than the Consumer Price Index during 1960–1980, prescription drug prices have risen more rapidly than the CPI during the last two decades.

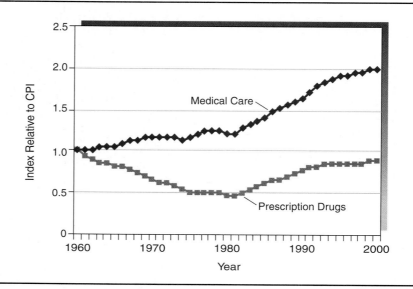

Source: www.bls.gov

twice as rapidly as the index of consumer prices. Furthermore, there is no evidence that the health care inflation is about to subside. In fact, the ratio of health care prices to the general consumer price index grew more rapidly during 1980–1999 than during the 1960s and 1970s. Correspondingly, the prices of prescription drugs, which rose less than the consumer price index during the 1960s and 1970s, have increased more rapidly than the CPI since 1980.

When viewed within the framework of economic theory, the health care inflation (Exhibit 4) and soaring expenditures (Exhibit 1) are not a surprise. Indeed, they are a predictable outcome of the changing incentive structure that has evolved in this industry over the last four decades.

With time, third-party payees, including both insurance companies and the government, will take steps to restrain expenditures. They may limit the amount paid for various services, require consumers to patronize only certain providers, make it more difficult to obtain permission for costly procedures, impose delays, and the like. This is essentially the route taken by the "managed care movement" of the 1990s. Regulatory controls of this type, however, will be difficult to implement successfully because they will generally conflict with the interest of both consumers and health care providers. As the managed care experience already indicates, this path will tend to result in unhappy consumers and decisions that, with the benefit of hindsight, are clearly inappropriate and in some cases life-threatening. Controlling costs through rules and regulations imposed by a third party is an imperfect substitute for competition and the choices of consumers spending their own money.

THE RETIREMENT OF THE BABY BOOMERS AND THE FUTURE OF HEALTH CARE

How are health care prices and expenditures likely to change in the future? **Exhibit 5** provides insight on this question. As the exhibit shows, the elderly population grew by 36 percent during the last two decades (from 25.5 million in 1980 to 34.7 million in 2000). By way of comparison, the number of persons aged 65 and over is projected to grow by 76 percent during the two decades following 2010, more than twice the growth rate of the last 20 years.

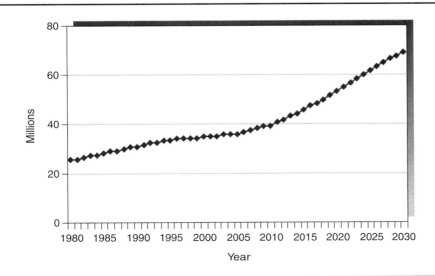

EXHIBIT 5
U.S. Population Age 65 and Over, 1980–2000 and Projections to 2030

As shown here, the growth rate of the elderly population will accelerate as the baby boomers move into the retirement phase of life during the years following 2010. Unless structural changes are undertaken, this increase in the growth rate of the elderly population will cause future health care prices and expenditures to increase even more rapidly than in the past.

Source: www.census.gov

Of course, this acceleration in the growth rate of the elderly population reflects the movement of the baby boom generation into the retirement phase of life. Because medical expenditures tend to be high during the elderly years, the rapid future growth in the number of senior citizens will both increase the demand for medical services and the share of those services financed by third parties. This will push both health care prices and expenditures upward. It will also cause Medicare expenditures to soar and necessitate the need for higher taxes to finance the program. Unless reform is undertaken, the health care inflation and spending growth of recent decades is likely to continue.

AVERTING THE CRISIS: HOW TO MOVE TOWARD A CONSUMER-DRIVEN SYSTEM

Perverse public policy is the primary factor underlying the soaring expenditures and rising prices in the health care industry. By promoting third-party payment of health care expenses and the purchase of medical insurance through employers, health care policy has (a) eroded the incentive of health care consumers and providers to economize, (b) undermined the operation of health care markets, and (c) made it more costly for persons without a job to obtain health insurance. Without fundamental reforms, political officials can be expected to impose more and more regulations, including price controls, on the industry in an effort to control the soaring expenditure levels. The experience of other countries indicates where this will lead. The health care industry is too large, complex, and diverse to plan and regulate centrally. Efforts at central planning will waste resources and produce disappointing results.

Health care costs so much because consumers directly pay for so little of it. When consumers spend their own money, they will choose wisely and their choices will provide suppliers with a strong incentive to control costs and offer quality service. If health care is to become more efficient and cost-effective, greater reliance must be placed on consumer choice and direct payment of medical expenses. How can this be achieved? Several policy changes would be helpful but the following five alternatives are particularly important.

1. **Equalize the tax treatment of out-of-pocket medical expenses and the direct purchase of health insurance with that of health insurance purchased through an employer.** As we discussed above, health insurance purchased through an employer is tax-free, while both medical bills and personal health insurance policies must be paid for with after-tax income. This promotes both third-party payment of medical bills and low copayment insurance plans. The most reasonable and politically feasible method of correcting this distortion is to make out-of-pocket medical expenses and the purchase of personal health insurance tax deductible. This deductibility would not be of much value to taxpayers with low incomes or those filing the short tax forms. These taxpayers could be provided with a 30 percent tax credit, a tax saving similar to that of employer-provided plans, for expenditures on the direct purchase of medical insurance and out-of-pocket payment of medical bills. This would also make it cheaper for persons without access to employer-provided insurance to purchase coverage and pay medical bills directly.

Medical savings accounts
Special savings accounts that individuals could use for the payment of medical bills or the purchase of a catastrophic (high deductibility) health insurance plan. Unfavorable tax treatment compared to employer-provided health insurance and other regulatory restrictions currently reduce their use.

2. **Encourage medical savings accounts (MSAs) and the direct payment of medical bills from the accounts.** To a degree, insurance involves the setting aside of funds on a regular basis for coverage of future medical bills. People should also be permitted to smooth out medical payments through **medical savings accounts**, accounts that individuals would pay into regularly and draw out as needed for the direct payment of medical bills. The tax system should not discriminate against this method of handling medical expenses. Because MSAs will promote economizing behavior and reduce the incidence of third-party payments, the current discriminatory tax treatment is particularly unfortunate.

The tax treatment of payments into MSAs should be identical with that for health insurance purchased through an employer. This means that contributions into these accounts should be fully tax deductible (up to a maximum such as $3,000 for an individual or $6000 for a family, for example). Similarly, contributions by employers into the medical savings accounts of their employees should qualify as a business expense. Current regulations restricting the establishment of medical savings accounts to companies with fewer than 50 employees should be repealed. Individuals should have full ownership of medical savings accounts and be permitted to roll funds not used during one year into the next. With time the funds would grow as the result of both payments into the accounts and interest earnings. Eventually, unused funds could be passed along to heirs. Because of their ownership rights, individuals and families would economize on their use of these funds just as they do for out-of-pocket expenditures. MSAs would be particularly effective when combined with high deductibility medical insurance.

3. **Encourage the purchase of catastrophic health insurance and discourage the purchase of policies with first-dollar coverage and small copayments.** Insurance works well when it compensates people for losses resulting from unpredictable events outside of their control that seldom occur, paying for large losses imposed on the unfortunate parties. Under these circumstances, the premiums of those experiencing little or no damage can be used to compensate those experiencing large losses. Large medical expenses such as those resulting from a severe injury or a catastrophic illness like diabetes or cancer generally fall into this category. It makes sense to promote the purchase of health insurance providing protection against large medical bills resulting from catastrophic illnesses and injuries. Policies with a high deductible, such as one covering most medical expenses in excess of $3,000 per year, are relatively cheap. In 2001, such a policy could be purchased for an annual premium of approximately $1,500. A system of tax credits could be utilized to encourage all (or at least most) citizens to purchase policies of this type.

   In contrast, insurance works poorly when the "losses" are widespread among the insurees and when the actions of those insured influence the size of the benefits they derive. Under these circumstances, many insurees will follow actions that increase the likelihood that events triggering compensation will occur and, as a result, insurance premiums will be costly relative to the benefits. Many health care costs, including those resulting from routine illnesses (for example colds and flu), common childhood diseases, minor injuries, and the like fall into this category. In varying degrees, most everyone can expect to experience such medical problems and there are several alternative ways of dealing with them, some of which are far more costly than others. Predictably insurance will work poorly for medical costs of this type. Furthermore, policies requiring only a small copayment for routine medical expenses promote the third-party payment system that retards economizing behavior. Thus, it makes no sense for public policy to encourage such schemes.

4. **Shift Medicare at least partly from a reimbursement service to a defined-benefit plan.** Under this approach, Medicare recipients would receive a specific amount each year for paying medical bills directly and purchasing private insurance. All Medicare recipients would be required to purchase at least a catastrophic insurance plan. The funds not used in one year could be rolled over for use in subsequent years. This approach would increase the freedom of Medicare recipients to choose the combination of medical services and method of payment that best fits their personal situation.

5. **Place more emphasis on the supply side of the health care market.** Each year the government spends several hundred billion dollars subsidizing demand, helping people purchase medical services. Very little is spent encouraging additional supply. However, without additional supply, demand subsidies merely reallocate health care services among consumers. The subsidy recipients, primarily the elderly and those with

low incomes, obtain more medical care, while others receive less. Furthermore, the primary beneficiaries of the demand-side subsidies are health care suppliers, who receive higher prices for their services. Supply-side programs would focus more on the training of health care providers. For example, they might provide more aid for the growth and development of medical schools—only one new medical school has been established in the United States during the last two decades. Aid to low-income students qualified to attend medical and nursing schools might also be expanded. In contrast with demand subsidies, programs that expand the supply of medical personnel would make it easier to control future costs.

If we want to improve efficiency and avert a future health care crisis, the current system must be reformed. The five proposals outlined above will lead to (a) more direct payment (and less third-party payment) of health care expenses, (b) lower cost of catastrophic insurance protection (but higher cost for low deductibility, high copayment coverage), and (c) greater reliance on expanding supply of medical services rather than stimulation of demand. No doubt, these reforms will not solve all of our health care problems, but economic analysis suggests that they are a step in the right direction.

KEY POINTS

▼ Spending on health care has soared in recent decades. Measured as a share of the economy, total health care spending has risen from 5.1 percent in 1960 to 8.8 percent in 1980, and 13.2 percent in 2000.

▼ Following the enactment of Medicare and Medicaid in the mid-1960s, the direct expenditures of health care consumers gradually declined and those of third-party payees expanded. The out-of-pocket spending of consumers accounted for only 17.6 percent of health care spending in 1999, down from 55 percent in 1960.

▼ The growth of subsidies to health care consumers and greater reliance on third-party payments of recent decades (a) increased the demand for medical services and (b) reduced the incentive of both health care consumers and providers to economize. Both of these factors contributed to the health care infla-

tion and soaring expenditures of recent decades.

▼ Once the baby boomers begin to retire around 2010, the elderly population will grow more rapidly than in recent decades. Under the current Medicare program, this will increase the demand for health care services and the share of medical payments financed by a third party. It can also be expected to result in higher health care prices and increased taxes for the finance of Medicare.

▼ Health care reform that placed (a) more emphasis on direct (rather than third-party) payment of medical bills, (b) encouraged catastrophic insurance protection (but not low deductibility, high copayment plans), and (c) focused more on expansion in supply (rather than demand) of health care would help minimize, if not avert, a crisis that is likely to occur when the baby boomers retire.

CRITICAL ANALYSIS QUESTIONS

1. Currently, health insurance purchased through an employer is tax deductible (it is not counted as taxable income), while the direct purchase of health insurance and payment of medical expenses is not. Do you think this is sound policy? Why or why not?

*2. When an employer provides health insurance benefits as part of the compensation package, does this represent a gift by employers to their employees? Do employees earn these benefits? Why or why not? Justify your response.

3. How does the substitution of third-party payments by insurance companies and the government for the out-of-pocket purchase of health care by consumers influence the demand and price of medical services? Explain.

4. Do individuals have a right to free health care? Do they have a right to force others to provide them with free health care? Discuss.

*5. How did the Medicare and Medicaid programs influence the cost of medical services purchased by Americans who were neither poor nor elderly? Explain.

6. Does it make any difference whether medical services are paid for directly by consumers or by a third party such as the government or an insurance company? Why or why not?

7. Consider the five reform proposals suggested by the authors at the end of this feature. Indicate why you believe each is either a good or a bad idea. Explain your answers.

SPECIAL TOPIC **9**

School Choice: Can It Improve the Quality of Education in America?

Real reform will only come from pressure from outside the system, generated by empowered parents with expanded school choice.

—Howard Fuller [1]

F o c u s

- How has spending on education changed in recent decades? How does the educational spending of the United States compare with other countries?

- How do student achievement scores today compare with those of the past? How does student performance in the United States compare with that of other countries?

- What does economics have to say about the structure of education?

- How can the quality of education be improved?

---

[1]Former School Superintendent, Milwaukee School District, *USA Today*, August 25, 1995.

ncreasingly, brains rather than brawn or resources are the basis of economic development and individual wealth. A good education is more important than ever to economic success. There is, however, widespread concern about the quality of education in the United States. Is a lack of spending the cause of low student achievement in the United States? What are the sources of the deficiencies in the current educational system? How can we reform the educational process? This special topic will investigate these questions and related issues. ■

EDUCATIONAL SPENDING AND STUDENT PERFORMANCE

One source of the dissatisfaction with the education system in the United States is low student performance. As **Exhibit 1** demonstrates, achievement scores fell in the 1970s, changed little during the 1980s, and rose slightly during the 1990s. Clearly, the average achievement scores of high school graduates today are well below those of students 35 years ago.

Cross-country comparisons of achievement scores also illustrate the weak performance of U.S. schools. **Exhibit 2** shows the mathematics achievement scores from the 1999 Third International Mathematics and Science Repeat Study, which compared achievement in 12 countries. U.S. eighth-graders scored 27 points below the country average and 87 points below Korea. The achievement scores for science also show that U.S. students lag well behind those of most developed countries.

Do the performance patterns reflect expenditures? **Exhibit 3** presents data on real spending per pupil on public elementary and secondary education for the 1970–2000 period. As the graph illustrates, educational spending has been steadily increasing. *Measured in 2000 dollars*, expenditures per pupil in public elementary and secondary schools in the United States increased from $3,431 in 1970 to $7,146 in 2000. Thus, real spending per pupil has more than doubled during the last three decades.

How does U.S. spending on education compare with other countries? **Exhibit 4** presents international data for government spending on primary education for 1998, the latest year for which the figures are available. As these figures show, public spending per pupil in the United States is among the highest in the world. The United States spent over $6,000 per primary student, which was 50 percent more than the average across 29 countries.[2] Moreover, this figure omits private spending, which is more extensive in the United

---

EXHIBIT 1
Average Combined SAT Score, 1967–1999

The achievement scores of American students dropped in the 1970s, changed little in the 1980s, and rose modestly during the 1990s.

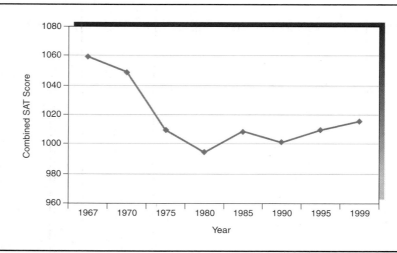

Source: Statistical Abstract of the United States, 2000.

---

[2]The United States spent $7,764 per secondary pupil, which is 38 percent above the OECD average.

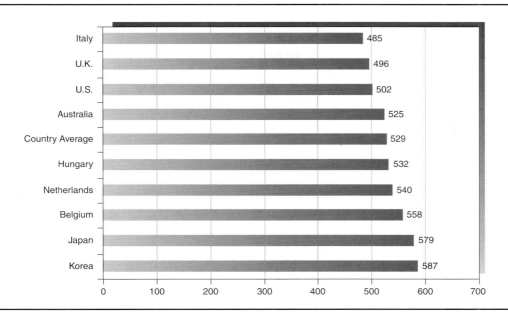

EXHIBIT 2
Average Eighth Grade Mathematics Achievement Scores: A Cross-Country Comparison

The mathematics achievement scores of eighth grade American students lag behind those of other countries.

Source: OECD, *Education at a Glance,* 2001.

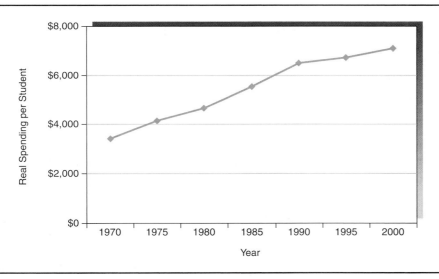

EXHIBIT 3
Real Spending per Elementary and Secondary Pupil, 1970–2000

Real spending per pupil on public elementary and secondary schools more than doubled during the 1970–2000 period.

Source: Statistical Abstract of the United States, 1993 and 2000 and www.nea.org.

States than in many other countries. Thus, lack of spending does not explain the lower performance level of U.S. students compared to other countries.

ECONOMICS AND THE STRUCTURE OF THE EDUCATIONAL SYSTEM

Why are U.S. schools doing so poorly? Many economists believe that part of the answer lies with the structure of the school system. As we discussed in Chapter 6 (see Exhibit 4 in Chapter 6), the operation of a market is influenced by who pays for the good (the consumer or a third party) and who produces it (private or government-operated firms). When consumers

EXHIBIT 4
Spending per Primary Student, 1998: A Cross-country Comparison

Spending per primary student in the United States is among the highest in the world.

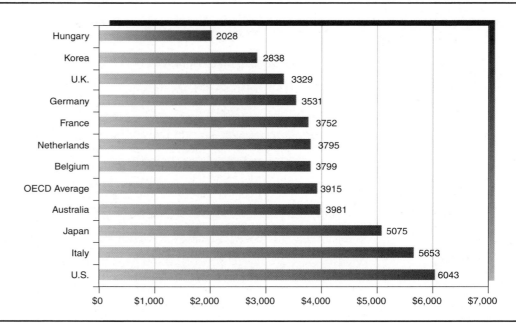

Source: OECD, *Education at a Glance,* 2001.

pay directly for goods and services, they will shop among suppliers and patronize those that provide them with the most value per unit of expenditure. In turn, their choices will provide profit-seeking firms operating in open markets with a strong incentive to operate efficiently, keep their prices down, and cater to the preferences of consumers. As we have stressed throughout, this combination of forces—economizing behavior by consumers and competition among suppliers—is vitally important for the efficient allocation of resources.

The structure of the U.S. schooling market undermines both of these forces. In essence, public schools are government-operated firms with substantial monopoly power. They are protected from the competition of rivals because "free" education is only available to those who attend the local district public school. The impact of economizing behavior on the part of consumers is largely eroded. If students (and their parents) choose a nonpublic school they have to pay for their own education. They lose the government subsidy that would be theirs if they attended public schools. This makes it very costly to switch to rival suppliers. Thus, a public school has to be very bad before it loses many customers.

Furthermore, like the managers of other government-operated firms, school administrators have a strong incentive to build the case for larger government funding. Predictably, they will confront politicians controlling their budgets with the image that marvelous things can be accomplished with additional funds and that any reduction in funding will have drastic consequences. In contrast, the incentive to innovate and figure out how to provide students with a better education at a lower cost is weakened. After all, school revenues come from the politicians, not consumers.

Perhaps a thought experiment will help illuminate some of the problems with the current educational structure. Suppose that the restaurant industry in the United States was set up like our schools. A system of local "restaurant districts" would be established. Taxes would be levied to finance the cost of the government-operated restaurants in each district. Citizens would not be allowed to patronize public restaurants outside their local district. If customers chose to patronize private restaurants, they would have to pay for the food *twice*—once as a taxpayer and again as a consumer. Thus, if a private restaurant were to survive, it would have to figure out how to attract customers from the tax-financed restaurants that were giving food away to district residents.

Clearly, there would be major problems with this organizational structure. Since the managers of the government-operated restaurants would derive their funds from the government, predictably they would spend more time satisfying those with political clout (including worker unions) and less time catering to the needs and preferences of customers. The incentive to keep costs low would be weak. Similarly there would be little reason for restaurant operators to innovate, figure out how to do things better, or search for ways to provide their "customers" with better service. After all, a lower quality of service would merely highlight the need for additional funding of the public-sector restaurants. Since consumers could not take their funding and go elsewhere, they would be in a weak position to discipline the district restaurants that were not doing a good job. The outcome of this organizational structure is predictable. Compared to the current system based on customer choice and competition, restaurant food costs would rise and quality would deteriorate. There would be a disconnect between the preferences of consumers and the product supplied and, as a result, consumers would get less for their food expenditure dollar.

The performance of U.S. education at the college and university level is also instructive. Here, the structure is quite different than at the elementary and secondary level. In higher education, students have a much greater opportunity to choose among a variety of colleges and universities. Financial aid that can be used at either private or government-operated schools is more readily available. Thus, competition between private and government-operated schools (and among public schools) is much stronger at the college level. In contrast with the international standing of elementary and secondary schools, U.S. higher education leads the world in the variety of programs offered, eminence of researchers, quality of facilities, and percentage of high school graduates attending college.

ALTERNATIVE WAYS OF INCREASING COMPETITION AND EXPANDING THE OPTIONS OF CONSUMERS

After years of disappointing results from the growth of educational expenditures, interest in alternative approaches has grown. In recent years, several states have adopted programs providing students and parents with options to the traditional public school system. The following section will briefly consider three of the most common alternatives: school vouchers, charter schools, and choice for children attending failing schools.

School Vouchers

Under a pure voucher plan, rather than financing schools directly, the government would provide parents with a certificate equal to the current educational expenditures per pupil. The parents could then use the voucher to finance their child's education at the public or private school they think is best for their child.

In essence a voucher plan would put competition to work to improve our schools. Since their revenues would be dependent upon their ability to attract students, schools would compete for students and parents would be free to choose among schools. The competition among schools would encourage innovative ideas and the discovery of more effective teaching techniques. It would also mean competition for first-rate educators. The demand for outstanding teachers would increase, which would increase salaries and help attract quality people to the teaching profession. Perhaps just as important, the demand for poor teachers would decline and many would shift to other careers.

A voucher system would also encourage diversity, which would allow a larger number of Americans to choose and receive a type of schooling that is more consistent with their preferences. Some parents would choose a highly structured school; others would prefer the open-school concept. Some would select a school that stresses religious values; others would opt for secularism in education. Some would choose a school with a traditional college prep program, while others would support schools that provide technical and vocational training. Under a system of parental choice, each of these diverse preferences could be satisfied.

Three major objections are typically raised against a voucher system. First, some charge that the primary beneficiaries would be high-income Americans who already send their children to private schools. (*Note:* about 10 percent of the students at the elementary and secondary level currently attend private schools, while approximately 90 percent attend public schools.) Second, others express a fear that a voucher plan would increase the racial imbalance among schools. Third, some argue that vouchers would drain funds away from the public schools, and thereby cause their quality to deteriorate.

A modified voucher targeted toward low- and middle-income families would overcome each of these objections. For example, low-income families with children in a private school might be provided a voucher equal to the full cost per pupil of public spending on education, while the voucher grants to middle-income families might be equal to, say two-thirds of the public school cost, and the grants to high-income families might be even smaller. Above a certain income level, perhaps no aid would be given to high-income families with children in private schools. This type of voucher plan would enhance the educational opportunities available to the children of low- and middle-income families without providing a windfall gain to high-income families sending their children to private schools.

The modified voucher plan would also promote racial and economic balance among schools. Since blacks and other minorities are overrepresented among the low-income families receiving the highest valued vouchers, those groups would also be overrepresented among families shifting to private schools (and high-quality public schools outside the district).

Furthermore, the modified plan should ameliorate fears that public schools would be placed at a financial disadvantage. Except in the case of low-income students, the per pupil aid to public schools would always exceed that provided to students attending private schools. Moreover, if the middle- or high-income students shift from a public to a private school, the per pupil funding remaining with public schools would actually increase. Given the superior aid this plan would provide for public relative to private schools, inability of a public school to compete would speak volumes about the efficiency of its operation and the quality of education it was providing.

Charter Schools

Charter schools provide another mechanism that might be used to expand parental choice and introduce competitive forces into the public school system. Charter schools are publicly funded but run independently from the traditional public school system. They operate under a contract ("charter") with a government agency. The supervising agency usually requires the charter schools to meet a variety of standards including financial, safety, and educational outcomes.

Charter schools differ from voucher programs in some important dimensions. Religious schools are not permitted to be charter schools. Charter schools are not permitted to charge tuition, as all of their students are subsidized by public funds. Since existing private schools charge tuition, they are not allowed to be charter schools (though conversions to a charter school are permitted in some states). In contrast, vouchers are allowed to be used at private schools.

Like vouchers, charter schools would increase the choices available to parents regarding the types of schools their children could attend. Charter schools offering a wide variety of programs have been established. Some schools focus on mathematics and science, others on the arts; some are directed at African-American students; and still others focus on the development of leadership skills among girls.

Choice for Students of Failing Schools

As we noted earlier, in most states, primary and secondary education is a monopoly. Students are assigned to a particular public school, and it is virtually impossible to escape the grasp of a failing school, particularly for children of parents with low incomes. One solution to this dilemma is to provide students in a failing school with a voucher that would cover their cost of attending an alternative private or public school of their choice.

This would increase the incentive of schools to cater to the needs of students and empower those currently trapped in failing schools with a strong weapon: the ability to shift their business elsewhere. It would also provide a strong incentive for weaker public schools to improve. If they did not, like other businesses in a competitive environment, they would lose customers.

Growth of Choice Programs

In 2001 Congress passed an educational bill providing parents with children in failing schools grants of up to $1000 for the purchase of after-school tutoring, summer school programs, or other educational materials. But when it comes to school choice, state and local governments are leading the way. Innovative programs include Florida's A-Plus Education Plan (which allows students in failing schools to switch to private or other public schools); state and locally funded school voucher programs in Milwaukee, Cleveland, and elsewhere; and privately funded efforts to offer scholarships to low-income families in some of the country's worst-performing school districts.

During the 1999–2000 school year, more than 500,000 students participated in public school choice programs including charter schools, magnet schools (drawing pupils from a broad geographic area), and open enrollment policies. Another 60,000 students were involved in school voucher programs. In addition, Arizona, Illinois, Iowa, Minnesota, and Pennsylvania now allow taxpayers a tax deduction (or tax credit) for donations to organizations that provide scholarships to students or for parents who spend personal funds on private school expenses. Choice is also expanding in other countries. Voucher programs that pay some or all of the tuition at private primary and secondary schools already exist in Chile, Colombia, the Netherlands, Sweden, and even post-communist Russia.

IMPACT OF STRUCTURAL CHANGE

It is too early for a full evaluation of voucher programs and charter schools. Structural changes of this type will exert their primary impact in the long run, that is, over a time period of sufficient length for suppliers to innovate and for the competitive process to discover better ways of doing things. Thus, one would not expect dramatic short-term improvements. Moreover, the short-term results will almost certainly understate the potential for longer-term gains. In spite of these limitations, some interesting results are beginning to emerge from early research in this area.[3] First, African-American students tend to earn modestly higher achievement test scores after one to two years in voucher programs. On the other hand, evidence of systematic improvements in the achievement scores of children from other racial groups is limited.

Second, the impact of charter schools on student achievement is inconclusive. In Arizona, charter schools appear to score higher on reading than traditional public schools. In Texas, charter schools that are focused on poorly performing students also do better than conventional public schools. However, other Texas charter schools do slightly worse than traditional public schools. In Michigan, the impact of charter schools on student achievement differs across grade levels. Achievement scores in charter schools do appear to improve after the first year.

Third, most parents of students in charter schools and voucher programs indicate they are highly satisfied with their children's schools. The satisfaction level of parents with children in voucher programs and charter schools exceeds that of parents with children in traditional public schools in the same community.

Lastly, targeted voucher programs do appear to modestly increase racial integration in highly segregated communities. These programs are placing minority children in voucher schools that have a lower percentage of minority students. In contrast, charter schools have

---

[3]The following discussion is based on Brian P. Gill, P. Michael Timpane, Karen E. Ross, and Dominic J. Brewer, *Rhetoric Versus Reality: What We Know and What We Need to Know About Vouchers and Charter Schools* (Santa Monica: RAND, 2001).

racial distributions that are similar to those in local public schools.[4]

CONCLUSION

During the last three decades, educational expenditures have increased substantially but the performance of schools as measured by the achievement level of students has been poor. Given the structure of the schooling system, this is not surprising. There is little incentive for government firms operating in a protected market to provide high quality service at a low cost. On the other hand, competition among rival suppliers works quite well in most markets. Many believe that it would also work well in education and help improve our schools.

KEY POINTS

▼ Real spending per student has risen over the past several decades, but student performance on basic skill exams is now well below the levels of the late 1960s. The United States spends more on primary and secondary education than most countries, but its students have performed below international averages on measures of student achievement.

▼ Economic analysis indicates that the structure of the educational system may well be a contributing factor to the poor performance of recent decades. Education is provided by government-operated firms with substantial monopoly power. Because competition is largely absent and educational consumers have limited choice, the incentive to produce effi-

ciently and cater to the needs of parents and students is weak.

▼ Vouchers, charter schools, and choice for students at failing schools are three possible reforms of the educational system. These changes generally expand the choices of consumers and increase competition among schools.

▼ In the short time they have been operating, charter schools and voucher programs appear to have had modest effects on student achievement. However, parents with children in charter schools and voucher programs indicate a higher level of satisfaction with their children's schools than parents with children in traditional public schools.

CRITICAL ANALYSIS QUESTIONS

1. "The best solution to reverse the decline in student performance in recent decades is to increase spending on education." Evaluate this statement.

*2. How does the lack of competition in the provision of education affect the quality and cost of education? Explain.

3. Should parents have the right to choose which schools their children attend? Why or why not? Discuss.

4. Consider the three reform proposals discussed by the authors at the end of this special topic. Indicate why you believe each is either a good or a bad idea. Explain your answers.

5. Currently, students attending state colleges and universities are heavily subsidized, but those attending private higher educational institutions are not. Do you think this is fair? Would you like to see a voucher system applied to higher education? Why or why not?

---

[4]There is some evidence that greater choice resulting from smaller school districts enhances quality. Most of the students graduating from high school during the 1960s (when SAT scores were much higher) were educated in districts that were much smaller than is now the case. Today, choice is expanded by multiple school districts within cities because this makes it easier for parents to improve the educational opportunities of their children by moving to districts with better schools. In contrast, when school districts cover an entire city, it is costly for parents to express their preferences for schools. Harvard University economist Caroline Hoxby compared results in metropolitan areas that have lots of school districts with those that have only a small number (often only one). Her findings indicate that average achievement levels were higher and expenditure levels lower in cities with more choice. Furthermore, the impact of choice on school productivity was largest in those states where districts have greater financial independence. See Caroline Hoxby, "Does Competition Among Public Schools Benefit Students and Taxpayers?" *American Economic Review*, December 2000, and "Would School Choice Change the Teaching Profession?" NBER Working Paper No. 7866, National Bureau of Economic Research.

SPECIAL TOPIC **10**

Is Discrimination Responsible for the Earnings Differences Between Men and Women?

Over the past 25 years, the gender pay gap has narrowed dramatically and women have increasingly entered traditionally male occupations.

—*Francine D. Blau and Lawrence M. Kahn*[1]

Focus

- Why are the earnings of women substantially lower than those of men? Is employment discrimination responsible?

- How has the economic status of women changed in recent decades?

- How have the educational choices and career goals of women changed? Will this influence their future earnings?

[1] Francine D. Blau and Lawrence M. Kahn, "Gender Difference in Pay," *Journal of Economic Perspectives* (fall 2000).

half-century ago, the typical American woman spent most of her time within the household caring for her children, preparing food, and providing laundry, cleaning, and other services for her family. Fewer than one in four married women worked outside the household in 1950. Today, the situation is dramatically different. Most women, including those who are married, work outside the home. This special topic analyzes earnings differences according to gender and the impact of the changing economic role of women. ■

EMPLOYMENT DISCRIMINATION AND THE EARNINGS OF WOMEN

During the last several decades, there has been a dramatic shift in the household versus market work choices of women. As **Exhibit 1** shows, the labor force participation rate of women rose from 37.6 percent in 1960 to 60.9 percent in 2000. Increased labor force participation by married women accounted for most of this increase.

Exhibit 1 also shows that the female/male (F/M) earnings ratio for full-time workers was approximately 60 percent throughout the 1960–1980 period. Since the early 1980s, the earnings of women have steadily increased relative to men. Nevertheless, women working full-time earned only 73.3 percent as much as their male counterparts in 2000. Women employed full-time, however, still worked approximately 10 percent fewer hours than men. Thus, the hourly earnings of full-time working women were approximately 80 percent of those of their male counterparts in 2000.

Why are the earnings of women so low compared to those of men? Most people blame employment discrimination. There is evidence that appears to support this view. In contrast with minorities relative to whites, the age, education, marital status, language, and

EXHIBIT 1
Labor-Force Experience of Women, 1960–2000

Between 1960 and 2000, the labor force participation of females rose from 37.6 to 60.9 percent. However, the F/M earnings ratio fluctuated around 60 percent during the 1960–1980 period, before climbing throughout the 1980s and 1990s. By 2000, the F/M earnings ratio had risen to 73.3 percent. The hourly earnings ratio of women relative to men was approximately 80 percent in 2000.

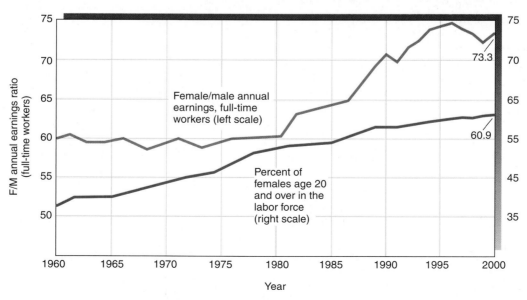

Source: www.census.gov and www.bls.gov.

locational characteristics of men and women are similar. Thus, correcting for these factors does little to reduce the earnings differential between men and women. Occupational data are also consistent with the view that women are crowded into a few low-paying jobs. Until recently, more than half of all women were employed in just four occupations—clerical workers, teachers, nurses, and food service workers.

Despite this evidence, the case that employment discrimination is the sole or even the primary source of the earnings differential between men and women is less than airtight. For one thing, the size of even the adjusted differential should cause one to pause. If an employer could really hire women who are willing and able to do the same work as men for 20 percent less, the profit motive would provide the employer with a strong incentive to do so. If an employer could really cut labor costs 20 percent merely by hiring women (primarily) rather than men, surely many less "sexist" employers (both men and women) would jump at the chance. Of course, as more and more employers substituted women for men workers, the F/M earnings ratio would move toward parity.

When considering earnings differences according to gender, it is important to recognize that married men and women have historically had different areas of specialization within the family. Until quite recently, married men typically pursued paid employment aggressively because they were expected to be the family's primary breadwinner. Given this traditional responsibility for monetary earnings, men were more likely to (1) have continuous labor force participation, (2) move in order to get a higher-paying job, and (3) accept jobs with long hours, uncertain schedules, and out-of-town travel.

In contrast, married women traditionally had the primary responsibility for operating the household and caring for children. Given these areas of specialization, many women sought jobs with more flexible hours and other characteristics complementary with household responsibilities.[2] Because women expected to have temporary spells out of the labor force (for example, when children were small or financial requirements less demanding), jobs requiring skills and credentials that were easily transportable among employers were particularly attractive. Considering these factors, an overrepresentation of women in nursing, teaching, and secretarial positions is not surprising.

How important are gender differences in specialization within the family? Since preferences cannot be directly observed, the family specialization theory is difficult to test. However, **Exhibit 2** sheds some light on its importance. Here we illustrate the median annual earnings of women relative to men, according to marital status. Clearly, married women earn substantially less than married men. Even when working full-time, year-round, married women earn only 70 percent as much as men. However, the earnings gap between men and women is substantially less for singles, the group least influenced by actual and potential differences in specialization within the traditional family. In fact, in 2000 the female/male annual earnings ratio for full-time, full-year workers was 89 percent for singles. Thus, the earnings of single women were only 11 percent less than those of single men. This pattern of earnings differences according to marital status implies that, although employment discrimination may well be a contributing factor, family specialization is also an important determinant of the overall earnings differential between men and women.

THE CHANGING WORKFORCE OBJECTIVES OF WOMEN

Although the career objectives of men and women have differed substantially in the past, the differences have narrowed in recent years. In 1968, a national survey of women 14 to 24 years of age found that only 27 percent expected to be working at age 35. In contrast, a similar survey of young women in 1979 found that 72 percent expected to be working at

---

[2]For an analysis of how family specialization influences the employment and earnings of women, see James P. Smith and Michael P. Ward, "Women in the Labor Market and in the Family," *Journal of Economic Perspectives* (winter 1989): 9–23; and Solomon Polachek, "Discontinuous Labor Force Participation and Its Effect on Women's Market Earnings," in *Sex Discrimination and the Division of Labor*, ed. Cynthia B. Lloyd (New York: Columbia University Press, 1975).

EXHIBIT 2
Female/Male Earnings According to Marital Status, 2000

Although the female/male earnings ratio varies considerably according to marital status and time worked, the earnings of single women relative to the earnings of single men are much higher than the earnings of women in other marital status groupings. This suggests that differences in specialization within the traditional husband-wife family contribute to earnings differentials according to gender.

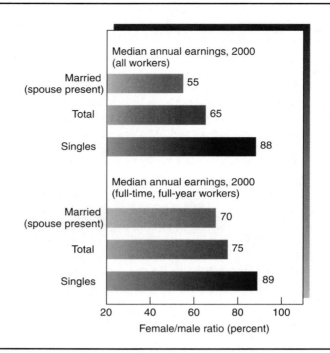

Median annual earnings, 2000 (all workers)

Married (spouse present) 55
Total 65
Singles 88

Median annual earnings, 2000 (full-time, full-year workers)

Married (spouse present) 70
Total 75
Singles 89

Female/male ratio (percent)

Source: Author calculations from March 2001 *Current Population Survey.*

EXHIBIT 3
Women as a Proportion of Persons Earning Selected Professional Degrees, 1970–1971, 1987–1988, and 1997–1998

FIELD OF STUDY	1970–71	1987–88	1997–98
Engineering	0.8	15.3	18.5
Dentistry	1.2	26.1	38.2
Optometry	2.4	34.3	53.4
Law	7.3	40.4	44.4
Veterinary Medicine	7.8	50.0	65.6
Medicine	9.2	33.0	41.6
Accounting	10.1	52.6	57.3
Economics	11.2	32.8	31.7
Architecture	12.0	38.7	35.1
Pharmacy	25.2	59.7	67.3

Source: Commission of Professionals in Science and Technology, *Professional Women and Minorities* (Washington, D.C.: CPST, 1987); and U.S. Department of Education, *Digest of Education Statistics, 1990 and 2000,* (Washington, D.C.: U.S. Government Printing Office).

that age.[3] These figures indicate that there was a dramatic increase during the 1970s in the proportion of young women preparing for a career and planning for a lifetime of labor force participation. As the proportion of women planning for a workforce career rose, their educational choices also changed dramatically. In the early 1970s, women were much less likely than men to study mathematics, engineering, medicine, law, and similar fields leading to high-paying professional jobs. But as **Exhibit 3** shows, the proportion of women earning degrees in accounting, veterinary medicine, dentistry, medicine, law, architecture, pharmacy, and economics increased dramatically in the 1970s and 1980s. By the 1990s,

---

[3]See Chapter 7 of the *Economic Report of the President,* 1987. The numbers presented here are from Table 7-3 of the report.

The female/male earnings ratio hovered around 60 percent throughout the 1950–1980 period. During the 1970s, an increasing proportion of women began to plan for full-time, long-term labor force participation. Reflecting this commitment, the career and educational choices of women shifted toward the professions (see Exhibit 3). As this happened, the earnings of women began to increase steadily relative to men (see Exhibit 1).

parity was achieved in several of these areas. Increasingly, women like men are planning for careers in diverse areas, including high-paying professional and business occupations.

It is interesting to reflect on the importance of employment discrimination, traditional household responsibilities, and educational choices in light of the changes during the last four decades. In 1962, equal pay legislation was passed requiring employers to pay equal wage rates to men and women working on the same job. In 1964 the historic Civil Rights Act, prohibiting employment discrimination on the basis of both race and gender, was passed. Despite these actions, there was little change in the earnings of women relative to men during the 1960s and 1970s. However, as the career objectives of women—perhaps pushed along by earlier legislative actions—began to change during the 1970s, the educational choices of men and women started to become more similar (see Exhibit 3).[4] Soon thereafter, the earnings of women began to rise relative to men (see Exhibit 1). As more and more women who have prepared themselves for professional and business careers acquire experience and move into the prime earning years of life, the upward trend in the F/M earnings ratio will almost surely continue.

KEY POINTS

▼ The annual earnings of women working full time are approximately 75 percent of the figure for males. In the case of singles, the female/male earnings ratio is approximately 90 percent.

▼ In addition to employment discrimination, differences in specialization within the family, educational choices, and career goals contribute to earnings differentials according to gender.

▼ As the educational and career choices of women have become more like those of men during the last two decades, the earnings of women have risen toward those of men. This trend is likely to continue in the future as more and more women prepare and acquire experience in high-paying professional and business areas that have traditionally been dominated by men.

[4]For additional details on recent changes in the male/female earnings gap, see Francine D. Blau, "Trends in the Well-Being of American Women, 1970–95," *Journal of Economic Literature* (March 1998): 112–165; William E. Even and David A. Macpherson, "The Decline of Private Sector Unionism and the Gender Wage Gap," *Journal of Human Resources* (spring 1993): 279–296; June O'Neill and Solomon Polachek, "Why the Gender Gap Narrowed in the 1980s," *Journal of Labor Economics* (January 1993): S205–228; and Claudia Goldin, "Gender Gap," *Fortune Encyclopedia of Economics*, ed. David R. Henderson (New York: Warner Books, 1993).

CRITICAL ANALYSIS QUESTIONS

1. Is employment discrimination the major cause of earnings differences between men and women? Carefully justify your answer.

2. During the last three decades, the labor force participation of married females approximately doubled. What impact did this influx of married workers into the labor force have on (a) the average years of work experience of women relative to men, (b) the mean hours of work time of women relative to men, and (c) the female/male earnings ratio?

3. Physical strength is important on some jobs. Do you think differences in physical strength between men and women contribute to earnings differences according to gender? Why or why not?

*4. In 2000, the median earnings of single men working full-time, year-round were only 70 percent of their married counterparts. Does this indicate that employment discrimination existed against single men and in favor of married men?

* Asterisk denotes questions for which answers are given in Appendix B.

SPECIAL TOPIC **11**

Do Labor Unions Increase the Wages of Workers?

The rise and decline of private sector unionization were among the more important features of the U.S. labor market during the twentieth century.

—*Barry T. Hirsch and Edward J. Schumacher* [1]

Focus

- How much of the U.S. workforce is unionized?

- Can unions increase the wages of their members? What makes a union strong? What factors limit the power of a union?

- Can unions increase the wages of all workers?

[1]Barry T. Hirsch and Edward J. Schumacher, "Private Sector Union Density and the Wage Premium: Past, Present, and Future," *Journal of Labor Research* (summer 2001), p. 487.

A **labor union** is an organization of employees, usually working either in the same occupation or same industry, who have consented to joint bargaining with employers concerning wages, working conditions, grievance procedures, and other elements of employment. The primary objective of a labor union is to improve the welfare of its members. Unions have historically been controversial. Some see them as a necessary shield protecting workers from employer greed. Others charge that unions are monopolies seeking to provide their members with benefits at the expense of other workers, consumers, and economic efficiency. Still others argue that the economic influence of unions—both for good and for bad—is vastly overrated. This feature will consider the impact of unions on the wages of their members and those of other workers. ■

Labor union
A collective organization of employees who bargain as a unit with employers.

UNION MEMBERSHIP AS A SHARE OF THE WORKFORCE

Historically, the proportion of the U.S. labor force belonging to a labor union has fluctuated substantially. In 1910, approximately 10 percent of nonfarm employees belonged to a union. As **Exhibit 1** shows, this figure rose to 18 percent in 1920. In the aftermath of the First World War, union membership declined, falling to 12 percent of nonfarm workers by 1929. Pushed along by favorable legislation adopted during the Great Depression, union membership rose from 13.5 percent of nonfarm employees in 1935 to 30.4 percent in 1945. By 1954, nearly a third of nonfarm workers in the United States were unionized.

Since the mid-1950s, however, union membership has waned. As Exhibit 1 illustrates, it declined slowly as a share of the workforce during 1955–1970, and then more rapidly during the last two decades. By 2000, union members comprised only 13.6 percent of nonfarm employees, down from 24 percent in 1979 (and 32 percent in 1954).

EXHIBIT 1
Union Membership as Share of Nonagricultural Employment

Between 1910 and 1935, union membership fluctuated between 12 percent and 18 percent of nonagricultural employment. During the 1935–1945 period, union membership increased sharply to approximately one-third of the nonfarm workforce. Since the mid-1950s, union membership has declined as a percent of nonfarm employment, and the decline has been particularly sharp since 1979.

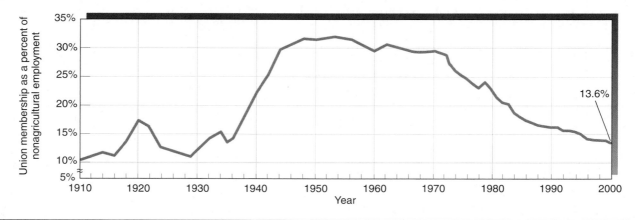

Source: Leo Troy and Neil Sheflin, *Union Source Book: Membership, Structure, Finance, Directory* (West Orange, N.J.: Industrial Relations and Information Services, 1985); and Barry T. Hirsch, David A. Macpherson, and Wayne G. Vroman, "Estimates of Union Density by State," *Monthly Labor Review,* July 2001.

Several factors have contributed to this decline. First, much of the recent employment growth has been in sectors where unions have been traditionally weak. Such sectors include relatively small firms (fewer than 100 employees) in service and high-tech industries. Small firms are costly for unions to organize and thus tend to be nonunion. Also, in recent decades, employment has grown rapidly in the less-organized Sunbelt, while stagnating in the more heavily unionized Northeast and upper Middle West. This regional growth pattern has retarded the growth of union membership. Second, competition has eroded union strength in several important industries. Foreign producers have increased their market share in steel, mining, automobiles, and other heavy-manufacturing industries. Employment has thus been shrinking in these areas of traditional union strength. Deregulation in transportation and communication industries has further reduced the membership of unions. As these industries have become more competitive, unionized firms have faced increased competition from nonunion producers. Finally, union membership has declined in part because workers have reduced their demand for unions over time. Consistent with a falling desire for union representation, opinion surveys reveal that workers believe that unions are less effective in improving their lot now than in the past.[2]

To some extent, several of these trends reflect the impact of unions on the wages of their members. Business investment and employment will tend to move toward geographic areas, industries, and classes of firms where wages are lower *relative to productivity*. Therefore, when unions increase the wages of their members *relative to nonunion workers of similar productivity*, they also retard the growth of employment in unionized sectors.

As **Exhibit 2** shows, there is substantial variation in the incidence of union membership across gender, racial, and occupational groups. Men are more likely than women to belong to a union. In 2000, 15.2 percent of employed men were union members compared to only 11.5 percent of employed women. The incidence of unionization among blacks (17.1 percent) was higher than for whites (13.0 percent) and Hispanics (11.4 percent). There is substantial variation in unionization according to occupation. Less than 10 percent of the workers in technical, sales, clerical, and service occupations were unionized in 2000. In contrast, about 20 percent of the workers in craft, operative, and laborer occupations belonged to a union.

The biggest difference in unionization is found when comparing the private and public sectors. While only 9.0 percent of the private wage and salary workers are unionized, 37.5 percent of the government employees belong to a union. And while the share of the private workforce belonging to a union has been shrinking, unionization has been increasing in the public sector. In fact, the proportion of government employees belonging to a union has more than tripled since 1960.

There is also substantial variation in the rate of unionization among states. **Exhibit 3** indicates the share of wage and salary employees who are unionized for the ten states with the lowest and highest unionization rates. Southern states comprise most of the group of ten with the lowest incidence of union membership. Fewer than 6 percent of employees are unionized in North Carolina, South Carolina, South Dakota, and Virginia. Heading the list of states with the highest rate of unionization are New York, Hawaii, Alaska, Michigan, and New Jersey. The rate of unionization tends to be high in the industrial states of the Northeast and upper Midwest. All the ten states with the lowest incidence of unionization have **right-to-work laws**, legislation that prohibits collective bargaining agreements requiring a worker to join a union as a condition of employment. In contrast, none of the ten states with the highest rate of union membership has right-to-work legislation.[3]

Right-to-work laws
Laws that prohibit the union shop, the requirement that employees must join a union as a condition of employment. Each state has the option to adopt (or reject) right-to-work legislation.

---

[2]Henry S. Farber and Alan B. Krueger, "Union Membership in the United States: The Decline Continues," in *Employee Representation: Alternatives and Future Directions*, ed. Morris Kleiner and Bruce Kaufman (Madison, Wis.: Industrial Relations Research Association, 1993). For several recent studies examining the decline in unionism, see "Symposium on the Future of Private Sector Unions in the United States: Part I," *Journal of Labor Research* (spring 2001); and "Symposium on the Future of Private Sector Unions in the United States: Part II," *Journal of Labor Research* (summer 2001).

[3]In 1947, Congress passed the Taft-Hartley Act; Section 14-B allows states to adopt right-to-work laws. Currently, 22 states, mostly in the Sunbelt, have such legislation.

EXHIBIT 2
Incidence of Union Membership According to Sex, Race, Occupation, and Sector

The incidence of unionism is higher among (a) men than women and (b) blacks than whites and Hispanics. Technical, sales, clerical, and service workers are far less likely to be unionized than are craft, operator, and repair workers. As a share of the workforce, unionization among government employees is four times that of private sector workers.

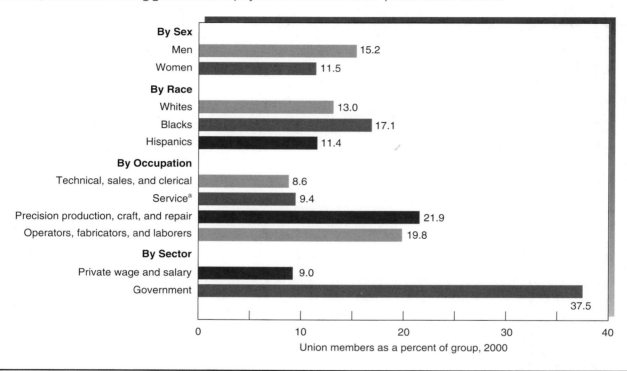

Union members as a percent of group, 2000

ªExcluding protective service workers.
Source: Barry T. Hirsch and David A. Macpherson, *Union Membership and Earnings Data Book: Compilations from the Current Population Survey (2001 edition)* (Washington, D.C.: The Bureau of National Affairs, 2001).

HOW CAN UNIONS INFLUENCE WAGES?

The union-management bargaining process often gives the impression that wages are established primarily by the talents of those sitting at the bargaining table. It might appear that market forces play a relatively minor role. However, as both union and management are well aware, market forces provide the setting in which the bargaining is conducted. They often tip the balance of power one way or the other.

High wages increase the firm's costs. When union employers face stiff competition from nonunion producers or foreign competitors, they will be less able to pass along higher wage costs to their customers. Competition in the product market thus limits the bargaining power of a union. Changing market conditions also influence the balance of power between union and management. When the demand for a product is strong, the demand for labor will be high, and the firm will be much more willing to consent to a significant wage increase. When demand is weak, however, the product inventory level of the firm (or industry) is more likely to be high. Under these circumstances, wage increases will be more difficult to obtain because the firm will be much less vulnerable to a **strike** on the part of the union. (*Note*: When we speak of wage rates, we are referring to the total compensation package, including both fringe benefits and money wages.)

Strike
An action of unionized employees in which they (1) discontinue working for the employer and (2) take steps to prevent other potential workers from offering their services to the employer.

EXHIBIT 3
States with the Lowest and Highest Incidence of Union Members as a Percent of All Wage and Salary Employees

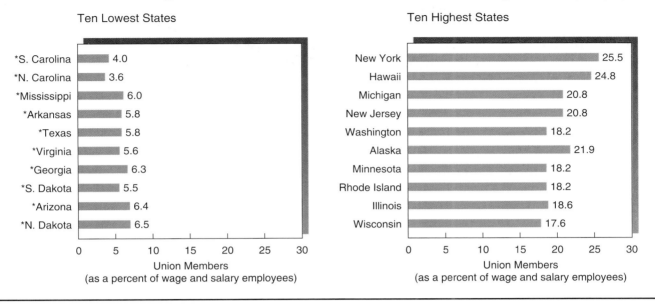

Ten Lowest States

State	Union Members
*S. Carolina	4.0
*N. Carolina	3.6
*Mississippi	6.0
*Arkansas	5.8
*Texas	5.8
*Virginia	5.6
*Georgia	6.3
*S. Dakota	5.5
*Arizona	6.4
*N. Dakota	6.5

Union Members
(as a percent of wage and salary employees)

Ten Highest States

State	Union Members
New York	25.5
Hawaii	24.8
Michigan	20.8
New Jersey	20.8
Washington	18.2
Alaska	21.9
Minnesota	18.2
Rhode Island	18.2
Illinois	18.6
Wisconsin	17.6

Union Members
(as a percent of wage and salary employees)

*Indicates state has a right-to-work law.
Source: Barry T. Hirsch and David A. Macpherson, *Union Membership and Earnings Data Book: Compilations from the Current Population Survey (2001 Edition)* (Washington, D.C.: The Bureau of National Affairs, 2001), Table A.

A union can use three basic strategies to increase the wages of its members: supply restrictions, bargaining power, and increased demand for union labor. We will examine each of these in turn.

Supply Restrictions

If a union can successfully reduce the supply of competitive labor, higher wage rates will automatically result. Licensing requirements, long apprenticeship programs, immigration barriers, high initiation fees, refusal to admit new members to the union, and prohibition of nonunion workers from holding jobs are all practices that unions have used to limit the supply of labor to various occupations and jobs. Craft unions, in particular, have been able to restrict supply into various occupations and boost the wages of union members.

Part a of **Exhibit 4** illustrates the impact of supply restrictions on wage rates. Successful exclusionary tactics will reduce supply, shifting the supply curve from S_0 to S_1. Facing the supply curve S_1, employers will consent to the wage rate W_1. Compared to a free-entry market equilibrium, the wage rate has increased from W_0 to W_1, but employment has declined from E_0 to E_1. At the higher wage rate, W_1, an excess supply of labor, AB, will result. The restrictive practices will prevent this excess supply from undercutting the above-equilibrium wage rate. Because of the exclusionary practices, the union will be able to obtain higher wages for E_1 employees. Other employees who would be willing to accept work even at wage rate W_0 will now be forced into other areas of employment.

Bargaining Power

Must unions restrict entry? Why can they not simply use their bargaining power, enhanced by the strike threat, as a vehicle for raising wages? If they have enough economic power, this will be possible. A strike by even a small percentage of vital employees can sometimes

EXHIBIT 4
Supply Restrictions, Bargaining Power, and Wage Rates

The impact of higher wages obtained by restricting supply is very similar to that obtained through bargaining power. As illustrated in part a, when union policies reduce the supply of one type of labor, higher wages result. Similarly, when bargaining power is used in order to obtain higher wages (part b), employment declines and an excess supply of labor results.

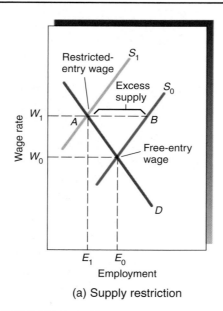

(a) Supply restriction

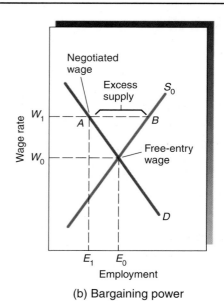

(b) Bargaining power

halt the flow of production. For example, a work stoppage by airline pilots can force major airlines to cancel their flights. Because the pilots perform an essential function, an airline cannot operate without their services, even though they constitute only 10 percent of all airline employees.

If the union is able to obtain an above-free-entry wage rate, the impact on employment will be similar to a reduction in supply. As part b of Exhibit 4 illustrates, employers will hire fewer workers at the higher wage rate obtained through bargaining power. Employment will decline below the free-entry level (from E_0 to E_1) as a result of the rise in wages. An excess supply of labor, AB, will exist, at least temporarily. More employees will seek the high-wage union jobs than employers will choose to hire. Nonwage methods of rationing jobs will become more important.

Increased Demand

Unions may attempt to increase the demand for union labor by appealing to consumers to buy only union-produced goods. Union-sponsored promotional campaigns instructing consumers to "look for the union label" or "buy American" are generally designed to increase the demand for union-made products.

Most people, however, are primarily interested in getting the most for their consumer dollar. Thus, the demand for union labor is usually determined primarily by factors outside the union's direct control, such as the availability of substitute inputs and the demand for the product. Unions, though, can sometimes use their political power to increase the demand for their services. They may be able to induce legislators to pass laws that reduce competition from nonunion and/or foreign workers. In some areas, required inspections on construction projects will only be undertaken if the electrical or plumbing services have been performed by "licensed" (mostly union) craft workers. Unions are often supportive of import restrictions designed to increase the demand for products that they produce. In 2002, the steel workers successfully lobbied for higher tariffs restricting the entry of foreign-produced steel. Garment workers have used their political muscle to raise tariffs and reduce import quotas for clothing produced abroad. Practices that increase the demand for goods and services produced by union labor will increase product prices as well as the wages of unionized workers. Thus, it is not surprising that both management and labor of unionized firms often join together to support various restrictions designed to reduce the competitiveness of goods produced by nonunion employees and foreigners.

WHAT GIVES A UNION STRENGTH?

Not all unions are able to raise the wages of their workers. What are the factors that make a union strong? ***Simply stated, if a union is to be strong, the demand for its labor must be inelastic. This will enable the union to obtain large wage increases while suffering only modest reductions in employment.*** In contrast, when the demand for union labor is elastic, a substantial rise in wages will mean a large loss in jobs.

There are four major determinants of the demand elasticity for a factor of production: (1) the availability of substitutes, (2) the elasticity of product demand, (3) the share of the input as a proportion of total cost, and (4) the supply elasticity of substitute inputs.[4] We now turn to the importance of each of these conditions as a determinant of union strength.

Availability of Good Substitute Inputs

When it is difficult to substitute other inputs for unionized labor in the production of a good, the union is strengthened. The demand for union labor is then more inelastic, and reductions in employment tend to be small if the union is able to use its bargaining power and the threat of a strike to push wages up. In contrast, when there are good substitutes for union labor, employers will turn to the substitutes and cut back on their use of union labor as it becomes more expensive. Under these circumstances, higher union wages will price the union workers out of the market and lead to a sharp reduction in their employment.

Some employers may be able to automate various production operations—in effect, substituting machines for union workers if their wages increase. When machines are a good substitute for union labor, the demand for union labor will be elastic, which will reduce the union's ability to push wages above the market level.

The best substitute for union labor is generally nonunion labor. Thus, the power of unions to gain more for their members will be directly related to their ability to insulate themselves from competition with nonunion labor. When employers are in a position to substitute nonunion labor for unionized workers, the market power of the union will be substantially reduced.

Within a given plant, a union will negotiate the wages and employment conditions for all workers, both union and nonunion. However, as union wages rise, it may be economical for unionized firms to contract with nonunion firms to handle specific operations or to supply various components used in production. Thus, contracting out often permits employers to indirectly substitute nonunion for union workers. In addition, many large firms in automobile, textile, and other manufacturing industries operate both union and nonunion plants. They may be able to substitute nonunion for union labor by shifting more and more of their production to their nonunion plants, including those located overseas or in right-to-work states where unions are generally weaker.

Elasticity of Demand for Products of Unionized Firms

Wages are a component of costs. An increase in the wages of union members will almost surely lead to higher prices for goods produced with union labor. Unless the demand for the good produced by union labor is inelastic, the output and employment of unionized firms will decline if the union pushes up wages (and costs). If a union is going to have a significant impact on wages (without undermining employment opportunities), its workers must produce a good for which the demand is inelastic.

---

[4]Alfred Marshall, *Principles of Economics*, Eighth ed. (New York: Macmillan, 1920).

Deregulation of the trucking industry opened the market to nonunion trucking firms. This led to a sharp reduction in the employment of unionized (Teamsters) truck drivers in the early 1980s. Can you explain why?

Our analysis implies that a union will be unable to significantly increase wages above the free market rate when producing a good that competes with similar (or identical) goods produced by nonunion labor or foreign producers. The demand for the good produced by union labor will almost surely be highly elastic when the same product is available from nonunion and foreign producers. Thus, if higher union wages push up costs, the market share of unionized firms will shrink and their employment will fall substantially.

Both past history and recent events are consistent with this view. In the 1920s, the United Mine Workers obtained big wage gains in unionized coalfields. The union, however, was unable to halt the growth of nonunion mining, particularly in the strip mines of the West. The unionized mines soon lost the major share of their market to nonunionized fields, leading to a sharp reduction in the employment of unionized miners.

More recently, the strength of the Teamsters' union was substantially eroded when deregulation subjected the unionized segment of the trucking industry to much more intense competition from nonunion firms in the early 1980s. With deregulation, nonunion firms with lower labor costs entered the industry. Given their labor-cost advantage, many of the new entrants cut prices and were able to gain a larger market share. In contrast, the output and employment of unionized trucking firms declined. More than 100,000 Teamsters lost their jobs. Given the sharp reduction in the employment of their members, the Teamsters eventually agreed to wage concessions and a reduction in their fringe benefit package.[5]

Union Labor as a Share of Cost of Production

If the unionized labor input comprises only a small share of total production cost, demand for that labor typically will be relatively inelastic. For example, since the wages of plumbers and airline pilots comprise only a small share of the total cost of production in the housing and air travel industries, respectively, a doubling or even tripling of their wages would result in only a 1 percent or 2 percent increase in the cost of housing or air travel. A large increase in the price of such inputs would have little impact on product price, output, and employment. This factor has sometimes been called "the importance of being unimportant," because it is important to the strength of the union.

---

[5]A study on the deregulation of the trucking industry found that the wage premium of unionized truckers fell by approximately 30 percent in the regulated sector of the industry. More drivers were employed, but the percentage of drivers who were union members fell from 60 percent prior to deregulation to 25 percent currently. See Barry T. Hirsch and David A. Macpherson, "Earnings and Employment in Trucking: Deregulating a Naturally Competitive Industry," in *Regulatory Reform and Labor Markets*, ed. James Peoples (Dordrecht, Netherlands: Kluwer Publishers, 1998). For a survey of studies examining the impact of deregulation in a variety of industries, see James Peoples, "Deregulation and the Labor Market," *Journal of Economic Perspectives* (summer 1998).

The airline pilots' union is able to increase the wages of its members substantially relative to nonunion pilots. On the other hand, the wages of union and nonunion grocery clerks are about the same. Why is the pilots' union strong and the clerks' union weak?

Supply Elasticity of Substitute Inputs

We have just explained that if wage rates in the unionized sector are pushed upward, firms will look for substitute inputs, and the demand for these substitutes will increase. If the supply of these substitutes (such as nonunion labor) is inelastic, however, their price will rise sharply in response to an increase in demand. The higher price will reduce the attractiveness of the substitutes. An inelastic supply of substitutes will thus strengthen the union by making the demand for union labor more inelastic.

WAGES OF UNION AND NONUNION EMPLOYEES

The precise impact of unions on the wages of their members is not easy to determine. In order to isolate the union effect, differences in other factors must be eliminated. Comparisons must be made between union and nonunion workers who have similar productivity (skills) and who are working on similar jobs.

Numerous studies have examined the effect of unions on wages. The pioneering work in this area was a 1963 study by H. Gregg Lewis of the University of Chicago.[6] Lewis estimated that, on average, union workers during the 1950s received wages between 10 and 15 percent higher than those of nonunion workers *with similar productivity characteristics*. The findings of other researchers using data from the 1950s and 1960s are generally consistent with the early work of Lewis.[7]

In a 1986 work, Lewis reviewed the evidence from nearly 200 studies on this topic and used more recent data to develop estimates of the union wage premium for the 1960s

---

[6]H. Gregg Lewis, *Unionism and Relative Wages in the United States* (Chicago: University of Chicago Press, 1963).

[7]See Albert Rees, *The Economics of Trade Unions* (Chicago: University of Chicago Press, 1967); and Michael J. Boskin, "Unions and Relative Wages," *American Economic Review* (June 1972).

EXHIBIT 5
The Wage Premium of Union Workers, 1950–2000

Most studies indicate that the wages of union workers have been between 17 and 20 percent higher than those of similar nonunion workers during the last two decades. This union-nonunion wage differential is slightly higher than during the 1950s and 1960s.

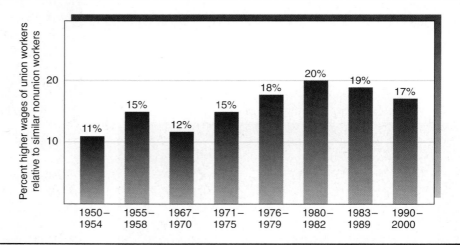

Sources: H. Gregg Lewis, *Unionism and Relative Wages in the United States: An Empirical Inquiry* (Chicago: University of Chicago Press, 1963), p. 222; and H. Gregg Lewis, *Union Relative Wage Effects: A Survey* (Chicago: University of Chicago Press, 1986), p. 9. The 1983–1989 and 1990–2000 figures are from Barry T. Hirsch and David A. Macpherson, *Union Membership and Earnings Data Book: Compilations from the Current Population Survey (2001 edition)* (Washington, D.C.: The Bureau of National Affairs, 2001).

and 1970s.[8] **Exhibit 5** summarizes Lewis's findings and provides similar estimates for more recent periods. Research in this area indicates that the union-nonunion wage differential widened during the 1970s.[9] Lewis estimates that union workers received an 18 percent premium compared with similar nonunion workers during the 1976–1979 period, up from a 12 percent premium during 1967–1970. Labor economists Barry Hirsch and David Macpherson of Florida State University have used data from the annual Current Population Survey to estimate the adjusted union-nonunion wage differential during the 1980s and 1990s.[10] Their work indicates that, on average, union workers earned 17 to 19 percent more than similar nonunion employees during the past decade.[11] *Like other research in this area, this suggests that the average union-nonunion wage differential has been between 15 and 20 percent during the last 25 years.*

Our theory indicates that some unions will be much stronger than others—that is, better able to achieve higher wages for their members. In some occupations, the size of the union-nonunion differential will be well above the average, while in other occupations, unions will exert little impact on wages.

Lewis estimated that strong unions, such as those of the electricians, plumbers, tool and die makers, metal craft workers, truckers (prior to deregulation), and commercial airline pilots, were able to raise the wages of their members substantially more than the aver-

[8]H. Gregg Lewis, *Union Relative Wage Effects: A Survey* (Chicago: University of Chicago Press, 1986).

[9]See Richard B. Freeman and James L. Medoff, *What Do Unions Do?* (New York: Basic Books, 1984); Barry T. Hirsch and John T. Addison, *The Economic Analysis of Unions: New Approaches and Evidence* (Boston: Allen and Unwin, 1986); and Alison L. Booth, *The Economics of the Trade Union* (Cambridge, England: Cambridge University Press, 1995), for evidence on this point.

[10]Barry T. Hirsch and David A. Macpherson, *Union Membership and Earnings Data Book: Compilations from the Current Population Survey (2001 edition)* (Washington, D.C.: The Bureau of National Affairs, 2001). For other studies examining the union wage differential, see Barry T. Hirsch and Edward J. Schumacher, "Unions, Wages, and Skills," *Journal of Human Resources*, (winter 1998); and David G. Blanchflower, "Changes Over Time in Union Relative Wage Effects in Great Britain and the United States," in Sami Daniel and John Grahl (eds.), *The History and Practice of Economics: Essays in Honour of Bernard Corry and Maurice Peston*, (Northampton, Mass.: Edward Elgar), 1999.

[11]The studies referred to in the text compared the wages of similarly productive union and nonunion workers at a point in time. Another approach would be to compare the change in the wages of the same worker in cases where the worker moves from a union to a nonunion job and vice versa. Research using this approach has generally placed the union wage premium at 10 percent or less, somewhat smaller than the estimates derived from cross-section studies. For evidence provided by studies using this methodology, see George Jakubson, "Estimation and Testing of the Union Wage Effect Using Panel Data," *Review of Economic Studies* (October 1991); and Richard B. Freeman, "Longitudinal Analysis and Trade Union Effects," *Journal of Labor Economics* (January 1984). Also see Barry T. Hirsch and Edward J. Schumacher, "Unions, Wages, and Skills," *Journal of Human Resources* (winter 1998); and Christopher J. Bollinger, "Measurement Error and the Union Wage Differential," *Southern Economic Journal* (January 2001).

age for all unions. Other economists have found that the earnings of unionized merchant seamen, postal workers, and rail, auto, and steel workers exceed the wages of similarly skilled nonunion workers by 25 percent or more.

Unionization appears to have had the least impact on the earnings of cotton-textile, footwear, furniture, hosiery, clothing, and retail sales workers. In these areas, the power of the union has been considerably limited by the existence of a substantial number of nonunion firms. The demands of union workers in these industries are moderated by the fear of placing unionized employers at a competitive disadvantage in relation to the nonunion employers of the industry.

Unions, Profitability, and Employment in the Unionized Sector

If unions increase the wages of unionized firms above the competitive market level, the costs of those firms will rise unless (as seems unlikely) there is a corresponding increase in productivity. In the short run, the higher costs will reduce the profitability of the unionized firm. Recent research indicates that this was true during the 1970s. Barry Hirsch found that as the union-nonunion wage premium increased during the 1970s, the profitability of unionized firms lagged behind the profitability of other firms.[12]

If unions are able to transfer profits from unionized firms to union workers, clearly this is a two-edged sword. For a time, workers enjoy higher wages. In the long run, however, investment will move away from areas of low profitability. Like other mobile resources, capital may be exploited in the short run, but this will not be the case in the long run. Therefore, to the extent that the profits of unionized firms are lower, investment expenditures on fixed structures, research, and development will flow into the nonunion sector and away from unionized firms. As a result, the growth of both productivity and employment will tend to lag in the unionized sector. Investment, production, and employment will all shift away from unionized operations and toward nonunion firms. The larger the wage premium of unionized firms, the greater the incentive will be to shift production toward nonunion operations. The findings of Linneman, Wachter, and Carter are highly supportive of this

On average, unions are able to boost the wages of unionized workers by 18 to 20 percent relative to nonunion workers of similar productivity. However, there is no evidence that they are able to increase the wages of all workers or the share of income going to labor relative to capital.

---

[12]Barry T. Hirsch, *Labor Unions and the Economic Performance of Firms* (Kalamazoo, Mich.: Upjohn Institute for Employment Research, 1991). Also see Barry T. Hirsch, "Unionization and Economic Performance: Evidence on Productivity, Profits, Investment, and Growth," in *Unions and Right-to-Work Laws*, ed. Fazil Mihlar (Vancouver, Canada: Fraser Institute, 1997).

view.[13] They found that industries with the largest union wage premiums were precisely the industries with the largest declines in the employment of unionized workers.

IMPACT OF UNIONS ON WAGES OF ALL WORKERS

Although unions have increased the average wages of their members, there is no reason to believe that they have increased the average overall compensation of workers—both union and nonunion. At first glance, this may seem paradoxical. However, the economic way of thinking enhances our understanding of this issue. As unions push wages up in the unionized sector, employers in this sector will hire fewer workers. Unable to find jobs in the high-wage union sector, some workers will shift to the nonunion sector. This increase in labor supply will depress the wages of nonunion workers. Thus, higher wages for union members do not necessarily mean higher wages for all workers.

If labor unions increased the wages of all workers, we would expect labor's share of income to be directly related to union membership. This has not been the case. Even though union membership rose sharply during the 1940s, reached a peak in the 1950s, and has been declining ever since, there was virtually no change in the share of income received by labor (human capital) during this entire period. Similarly, if unions were the primary source of high wages, the real wages of workers would be higher in highly unionized countries, such as Australia, France, and Italy, than they are in the United States. But this is not what we observe.

The real source of high wages is high productivity, not labor unions. Increases in the general level of wages are dependent upon increases in productivity per hour. Income is simply the flip side of output (productivity). Of course, improvements in (1) technology, (2) the machines and tools available to workers (physical capital), (3) worker skills (human capital), and (4) the efficiency of economic organization provide the essential ingredients for higher levels of productivity. ***Higher real wages can be achieved only if the production of goods and services is expanded. Although unions can increase the wages of union workers, they cannot increase the wages of all workers unless their activities increase the total productivity of labor.***

KEY POINTS

▼ Union membership as a share of nonfarm employees has fluctuated substantially during the last 90 years. During the 1910–1935 period, union workers comprised between 12 and 18 percent of nonfarm employees. Unionization increased rapidly during the 1935–1945 period, soaring to one-third of the workforce in the mid-1950s. Since then, union membership has waned, falling to only 13.6 percent of employees in 2000.

▼ A union can use three basic methods to increase the wages of its members: (a) restrict the supply of competitive inputs, including nonunion workers; (b) apply bargaining power enforced by a strike or threat of one; and (c) increase the demand for the labor service of union members.

▼ If a union is going to increase the wages of its members without experiencing a significant reduction in employment, the demand for union labor must be inelastic. The strength of a union is enhanced if (a) there is an absence of good substitutes for the services of union employees, (b) the demand for the product produced by the union labor is highly inelastic, (c) the union labor input is a small share of the total cost of production, and/or (d) the supply of available substitutes is highly inelastic. An absence of these conditions weakens the power of the union.

▼ Studies suggest that the wage premium of union members relative to similar nonunion workers increased during the 1970s. Since the late 1970s, the

---

[13]Peter D. Linneman, Michael L. Wachter, and William Carter, "Evaluating the Evidence on Union Employment and Wages," *Industrial and Labor Relations Review* (October 1990). Linneman, Wachter, and Carter estimate that increases in the union wage premium were responsible for up to 64 percent of the decline in the union share of employment during the last two decades.

union-nonunion wage differential has been in the 17 to 20 percent range.

▼ Even though unions have increased the average wage of their members, there is no indication that they have either increased the average wage of all workers or increased the share of national income going to labor (human capital rather than physical capital).

▼ The real wages of workers are a reflection of their productivity rather than the share of the workforce that is unionized.

CRITICAL ANALYSIS QUESTIONS

1. Assume that the primary objective of a union is to raise the wages of its members.
   a. Discuss the conditions that will help the union achieve this objective.
   b. Why might a union be unable to meet its goal?

*2. Suppose that Florida migrant workers are effectively unionized. What will be the impact of the unionization on (a) the price of Florida oranges, (b) the profits of Florida fruit growers in the short run and in the long run, (c) the mechanization of the fruit-picking industry, and (d) the employment of migrant farmworkers?

3. The Retail Clerks Union has organized approximately one-third of the department stores in a large metropolitan area. Do you think the union will be able to increase the wages of its members significantly? Explain.

4. "Unions cannot repeal the law of demand; they cannot have both high wages and high employment. The more successful they are at raising wages above competitive levels, the smaller the number of unionized employees."
   a. Evaluate this view.
   b. Does the success of unions at enlarging their wage premium tend to undermine their growth? Why or why not?

5. Evaluate the following statements.
   a. "An increase in the price of steel will be passed along to consumers in the form of higher prices for automobiles, homes, appliances, and other products made with steel." Do you agree or disagree?
   b. "An increase in the price of craft union labor will be passed along to consumers in the form of higher prices of homes, repair and installation services, appliances, and other products that require craft union labor." Do you agree or disagree?
   c. Are the interests of labor unions in conflict primarily with the interests of union employers? Explain.

6. What are the major forces that influence the ability of a union to increase the wages of the employees it represents? Why are some unions better able than others to attain higher wages for members? Explain.

*7. "If a union is unable to organize all the major firms in an industry, it is unlikely to exert a major impact on the wages of union members." Indicate why you either agree or disagree.

8. Suppose that the United Automobile Workers (UAW) substantially increases wages in the auto industry. What impact will the higher wages in the auto industry have on the following?
   a. wages of nonunion workers outside the automobile industry
   b. price of automobiles made by the UAW
   c. demand for foreign-produced automobiles
   d. profitability of U.S. automobile manufacturers

9. "Unions provide workers with protection against the greed of employers." Evaluate this statement. Be sure to consider the following questions:
   a. With whom do union workers compete?
   b. When union workers restrict entry into a market, whom are they trying to keep out?

*10. "Unions provide the only protection available to working men and women. Without unions, employers would be able to pay workers whatever they wanted." True or false?

*11. A survey of firms in your local labor market reveals that the average hourly wage rate of unionized production workers is $1.50 higher than the average wage rate of nonunion production workers. Does this indicate that unionization increases the wage rates of workers in your area by $1.50? Why or why not?

*12. Even though the wage scale of union members is substantially greater than the minimum wage, unions have generally been at the forefront of those lobbying for higher minimum rates. Why do you think unions fight so hard for a higher minimum wage?

---

* Asterisk denotes questions for which answers are given in Appendix B.

SPECIAL TOPIC **12**

Sometimes things are not what they seem. And sometimes the illusion is more satisfying than the reality.

—William R. Allen [1]

How Does Government Regulation Affect Your Life?

Focus

- How does regulation influence our lives?

- How does the regulation of health and safety differ from traditional economic regulation?

- What does public choice analysis suggest about the motivation for regulatory activities and differences between their stated objectives and actual effects?

- Who bears the cost of regulation? How do regulatory costs compare to their benefits?

[1]William R. Allen, *The Midnight Economist: Little Essays on Big Truths* (Sun Lakes, Ariz.: Thomas Horton and Daughters, 1997), p. 133.

As we saw in Chapter 5, markets often are not perfectly efficient. When property rights do not hold resource users, polluters, or consumers fully accountable, ideal efficiency will not result. Government regulation might improve efficiency in such cases. Regulation might also improve economic efficiency in a market that is not fully competitive. However, the actual outcomes of regulation often differ from and sometimes conflict with stated objectives. The regulatory process is complex and people may adjust to it in unforeseen ways. Further, efficiency is not the only reason why people seek to influence the regulatory process. Government regulatory restrictions on market activity can also be used by some to gain at the expense of others. For example, producers might find regulations useful to raise the costs of rival firms, or even to keep them out of the market altogether. In those cases, regulatory restrictions may reduce economic efficiency. This special topic feature takes a closer look at how regulation affects our lives. ■

REGULATION OF BUSINESS

Regulatory activity in the United States has a large impact on the economy. Federal regulatory agencies spent $18.9 billion on regulatory activities, and Americans spent far more than that to comply with the regulations. A 2001 study by economists Mark Crain and Thomas Hopkins for the U.S. Department of Commerce[2] estimated the additional cost of complying with federal regulations at $843 billion in 2000. Their estimate excluded taxes paid, but included private sector paperwork required by federal regulations, including record keeping required by tax regulations. Economic regulation accounts for 49 percent of the total, while environmental regulations generated another 23 percent. Regulation can have benefits, but clearly it has substantial costs.

The trend for staffing and spending by federal regulatory agencies has been mostly upward since 1970, except in the early 1980s. From 1970 to 2000, the number of government employees involved in the regulatory process rose 86 percent to nearly 130,000, while regulatory agency budgets grew 203 percent. Economic regulation, however, has sometimes been reversed in recent decades.

Traditional Economic Regulation

Regulation of business activity is not a new development. In 1887, Congress established the Interstate Commerce Commission (ICC), providing it with the authority to regulate both prices and levels of service in the railroad industry. In 1935, the trucking industry was also brought under the ICC's regulatory jurisdiction. State regulatory commissions began to oversee local delivery of electricity, natural gas, and telephone services as early as 1907. Federal commissions were formed during the 1930s to regulate interstate telephone service, broadcasting, airlines, natural gas pipelines, and other industries. These activities focus on **economic regulation** and usually control the product price or the structure of a particular industry rather than specifying the production processes used by business firms.

Sometimes economic regulation was promoted to protect consumers in markets characterized by large-scale production and natural monopoly. In other instances, it was designed to preserve "orderly competition" in industries with high fixed costs and low variable costs. Railroad transport is an example of the latter. Regardless of their original purpose, regulations that fix prices and restrict entry stifle the competitive process. With time, such regulation often ends up protecting inefficient producers and limiting the options of consumers. Later, we will see some examples of this. During the late 1970s, high costs generated widespread dissatisfaction with economic regulations in several industries.

Economic regulation
Regulation of product price or industrial structure, usually imposed on a specific industry. By and large, the production processes used by the regulated firms are unaffected by this type of regulation.

---

[2]W. Mark Crain and Thomas D. Hopkins, *The Impact of Regulatory Costs on Small Firms*, Department of Commerce, found online at: http://www.sba.gov/advo/research/rs207tot.pdf (61 pp.).

Major steps toward deregulation in the ground and air transportation industries resulted. Consumers benefited substantially. Airline deregulation, for example, brought more competition and reduced average airline ticket prices by about 40 percent from their levels in 1978, spurring large increases in airline traffic. Regulatory reform continues in other markets.

Recent Health and Safety Regulation of Business

Health and safety regulation
Legislation designed to improve the health, safety, and environmental conditions available to workers and/or consumers. The legislation usually mandates production procedures, minimum standards, and/or product characteristics to be met by producers and employers.

Along with movement toward less economic regulation, there has been a sharp increase in **health and safety regulation**. In the late 1960s and early 1970s, people had great faith in the ability of government to improve the quality of life. The economy was prospering, and people turned their attention more toward policies to reduce health hazards and preserve environmental quality. As the nation became wealthier, reducing air and water pollution and other externalities became more feasible and more desirable. In addition, activist groups sought regulation to protect individuals against risks from occupational hazards, as well as risks from newly developed drugs and other consumer products.

Reflecting these forces, the new health and safety regulation has expanded rapidly. The expenditures, employment, and powers of such agencies as the Occupational Safety and Health Administration (OSHA), Consumer Product Safety Commission (CPSC), Food and Drug Administration (FDA), and Environmental Protection Agency (EPA) have grown. Their regulatory authority cuts across industries and involves them more in the actual operation of individual firms. In contrast with economic regulation, the health and safety mandates frequently specify in detail the engineering processes to be followed by the regulated firms and industries.

THE POLITICAL ECONOMY OF REGULATION

Regulation involves a complex set of forces, political as well as economic. Public choice analysis provides us with some insight regarding political support of regulation and how we would expect the regulatory process to work. Four factors are particularly important.

1. *The demand for regulation often stems from special interest effects and redistribution considerations rather than from the pursuit of economic efficiency.* The wealth of an individual (or business firm) can be increased if that person or firm becomes more efficient or expands production. Regulation introduces another possibility. Sellers can gain from regulatory policies that either reduce competition in their market or increase the costs of rival firms. Buyers can gain, at least in the short run, if a law forces producers to supply goods below cost. Regulation opens up an additional avenue whereby those most able to influence the political process to their advantage can increase their wealth.

   Public choice analysis (see Chapter 6) indicates that special interest groups, such as well-organized, concentrated groups of buyers or sellers, can be expected to exert a disproportionate influence on the political process. Furthermore, the regulators themselves often comprise a politically powerful interest group. Regulatory bureaucrats are key figures in the process. Their cooperation is important to those who are regulated. These factors suggest that there will be demand for economic regulation even if it contributes to economic inefficiency.

2. *With the passage of time, regulatory agencies will often adopt the views of the business interests they are supposed to regulate.* Once again, the special interest effect indicates why this is an expected result, even if the regulation initially was designed to police the actions of a business group. The personal payoff derived by individual consumers (and taxpayers) from a change in regulatory actions is likely to be small. Often they are lulled into thinking that because a regulatory agency exists, the "public interest" is served. In contrast, firms (and employees) in regulated industries are vitally interested in the structure and composition of regulatory commissions and agencies. Favorable actions by these regulatory bodies could result in larger profits, higher-paying

APPLICATIONS IN ECONOMICS

Limousines and Restraints on Entry*

Occupational and business licensing by state and local governments often restricts entry and reduces competition. John West, an auto mechanic in Las Vegas, felt the brunt of such regulation when he tried to start a limousine business. His experience shows how existing companies, with help from a state agency, often use regulation to keep out competition.

Las Vegas, one of the fastest growing cities in the country and well-known for its entertainment complexes, would be an excellent location for a limousine business, West decided a few years ago. He had worked on limousines and thought he could improve life for himself and his family by starting his own limousine service. But he almost went bankrupt in an effort to obtain permission from the state of Nevada.

To operate a limousine service in Nevada, a person must obtain a "certificate of public convenience and necessity" from the Transportation Services Authority (TSA). It permits existing limousine companies to intervene in the approval process. The TSA commissioners can turn down applicants if the commissioners think that a new entrant will have an "unreasonable and adverse effect" on the present limousine business. In effect, the existing companies can operate as a cartel and pressure the TSA to keep out competition. In John West's case, the TSA delayed action on his application for a year, while the existing limousine companies ("intervenors") demanded extensive information from him, including lists of prospective clients. Then the TSA abruptly and arbitrarily rejected West's application. Of course, the primary effect of such regulations is less competition and higher fare prices.

In 1998, the Institute for Justice, a private nonprofit organization that defends economic freedom, supported West and two other would-be limousine drivers in challenging the practices of the TSA in court. On May 16, 2001, Judge Jon Parraguirre of Nevada's Clark County ruled that the TSA had violated the rights of the applicants. The judge said, "The right to earn a living in one's chosen profession is a liberty interest protected by the due process clauses of both the U.S. and Nevada constitutions."

The cartel didn't give up, however. Very quickly, owners of existing limousine companies went to the Nevada legislature and campaigned for a law limiting entry to the limousine

Rey Vinole, John West, and Ed Wheeler challenged regulations limiting entry into the Las Vegas limousine market. Their legal victory changed the rules to open up entry.

business. The law would have restricted the number of licenses for limousine service and would have divided these licenses among existing operators. However, the proposed law was not passed.

The Institute for Justice assists people in many occupations who face licensing restraints. In 1999, it litigated the case of JoAnne Cornwell, a provider of African hairbraiding services. Regulations of the state of California had prohibited her from opening a salon because she is not a licensed cosmetologist. Obtaining a California cosmetology license would require 1,600 hours of training, none of which actually teaches skills relevant to her specialty. A federal court struck down the California law.

While certain licensing regulations have been successfully challenged in some states, occupational and business licensing appears to be on the increase. Economist Morris M. Kleiner says that more than 800 occupations are licensed in at least one state, ranging from fortune-tellers in Maryland to rainmakers in Arizona, and the percentage of workers covered by licensing is increasing. Regulation of entry is clearly an avenue for cartels to reduce potential competition by excluding competitors.

*This feature is based on www.ij.org/cases/economic and Morris M. Kleiner, "Occupational Licensing," *Journal of Economic Perspectives* (Fall 2000), pp. 189–202.

jobs, and insulation from the uncertainties of competition. Thus, firms and employee groups, recognizing their potential gain, will invest both economic and political resources to influence the actions of regulatory agencies. In return for their organized support, political officials will have a strong incentive to favor their position when setting policy and making appointments to regulatory agencies.

3. *Regulation is inflexible and slow to react to dynamic change.* Changing market conditions often make regulatory procedures obsolete. For example, the advent of trucking vastly changed the competitiveness of the ground transportation industry (previously dominated by railroad interests). Nevertheless, government regulation of price, entry, and routes for both trucking firms and railroads continued for years after competitive forces had eliminated the monopoly power of firms in this industry. Similarly, city building codes that may have been appropriate when adopted have become obsolete and now retard the introduction of new, more efficient materials and procedures. In many cities regulatory procedures have prevented builders from introducing such cost-saving materials as plastic pipes, preconstructed septic tanks, and prefabricated housing units. Other local restraints are also common. Some are used primarily to stifle competition. (See the accompanying boxed feature on regulation of limousine services.)

4. *When approval has to be obtained from regulators, it will be difficult to introduce new products, including those that might potentially save lives.* The activities and management of a regulatory agency, the Food and Drug Administration, for example, will come under severe scrutiny if they inadvertently permit a dangerous product on the market. The victims of such a product are specific persons and the product's harm can often be seen. In contrast, regulators face few problems if they keep a highly beneficial product—including one that would save lives—off the market. Who will know that a specific drug or other product—one that most have never heard about because the tests are still being conducted—*might* have saved an individual's life? Thus, the cost to the regulatory agency of the former error is much greater than that of the latter. As a result, regulatory agencies will predictably apply tests that are too restrictive from the viewpoint of economic efficiency and consumer welfare.

THE COSTS OF REGULATION

Regulators produce benefits by ordering producers to do such things as emit less pollution, make workplaces accessible to handicapped workers, and reduce noise levels in the workplace. Of course, as they do so, costs are incurred. The major cost of health and safety regulation is felt in the form of higher production costs and thus higher prices. And, of course, the process of regulation itself is costly: Employment and operating costs of regulatory agencies must be met, which means higher taxes. When costs are borne by others, and mostly "off-budget," there is little incentive to regulate in the most economical manner. The costs can be surprisingly high. According to EPA estimates, when contractors were hired in 1988 to clean up Superfund hazardous waste sites, the indirect costs—costs of such things as formulating and enforcing the rules—amounted to more than $328 (or $492, measured in 2001 dollars) for every hour spent by a worker involved in the cleanup. These figures—essentially, overhead—were in addition to all payments to the firms and their employees actually planning and undertaking the work at each site.[3] For this and other reasons, the Superfund program is an example of inefficient regulation, open to severe criticism of its effectiveness. (See boxed feature, "Superfund: A Highly Inefficient Cleanup Program.")

The primary cost of health and safety regulation, however, comes in the form of higher operating costs of firms striving to meet the new standards. In effect, these higher costs are like a tax. As **Exhibit 1** illustrates, the higher cost shifts the supply curve to the left for a good affected by the regulation. Higher prices and a decline in the output of the product result. Who pays the cost? As with any tax, the burden is shared by buyers and sellers according to the elasticity of supply and demand. When consumers have more options that they can choose instead of the taxed good, so that their demand is more elastic, they will pay a smaller portion of the tax. In Exhibit 1, the new price ($P_2 + t$) will be closer to P_1 when demand is more elastic. On the other hand, sellers will pay a smaller

---

[3]These figures are from an EPA statement in the *Federal Register* 57, no. 152 (August 6, 1992).

APPLICATIONS IN ECONOMICS

Superfund: A Highly Inefficient Cleanup Program

A classic case of wasteful regulation is EPA's Superfund program, which was enacted in 1980 to clean up hazardous waste sites. Reducing human health risks was the major selling point for the legislation. Yet little in the way of human health benefits could be demonstrated by 1996, when researchers James T. Hamilton and W. Kip Viscusi wrote *Calculating Risks* (Cambridge: MIT Press, 1996). They analyzed the Superfund program in general and 150 Superfund hazardous waste sites in particular. Their conclusions included a number of discouraging findings:

- Most supposed Superfund "risks" do not pose a threat to human health now and they will do so in the future only if people violate commonsense precautions and actually inhabit contaminated sites and disregard known risks there.
- Even if the risks of exposure above did occur, there is less than a 1 percent chance that the risks are as great as EPA estimates, due to extreme assumptions made by EPA about the dangers.
- Cancer risk is the main concern at Superfund sites, but cleanups are expected to avert only 0.1 case of cancer at the majority of sites. Without any cleanup, only 10 of the 150 sites studied were estimated to have one or more expected cases.
- Average cleanup cost per site in the study was $26 million (in 1993 dollars).
- Replacing extreme EPA assumptions with more reasonable averages brought the estimated median cost per cancer case averted to over $7 billion; at 87 of the 96 sites having the necessary data available, the costs per cancer case averted (only some of which would mean a life saved) was above $100 million.
- Other federal programs commonly consider a life saved to be worth about $5 million. Diverting expenditures from most Superfund sites to other sites or other risk-reduction missions could save many more lives or save the same number of lives at far less cost.

Why do we observe such apparent inefficiencies in environmental programs? EPA site managers have little reason to consider that forcing people to spend more money at Superfund sites means spending less on other important goals for society. As Supreme Court Justice Stephen Breyer has put it, each agency decision maker has "tunnel vision."

In Breyer's words, tunnel vision is a "classic administrative disease" that arises "when an agency so organizes or subdivides its tasks that each employee's individual conscientious performance effectively carries single-minded pursuit of a single goal too far, to the point where it brings about more harm than good." Breyer calls this trying to achieve "the last 10 per cent." Thus agency and program officials will try to push beyond the efficient point of cleanup. Indeed, Hamilton and Viscusi estimate that 95 percent of Superfund expenditures are directed at the last 0.5 percent of the risk. The inefficiency of Superfund cleanups clearly demonstrates the importance of encouraging decision makers to consider opportunity cost and to think at the margin as they set the standards at Superfund sites. It also demonstrates the cost we pay when our political process fails to use economic thinking.

*This feature is based on Richard L. Stroup, "Politics or Sound Policy? " *Regulation* Vol. 24, No. 2 (Summer 2001), pp. 50–51 and Stephen Breyer, *Breaking the Vicious Circle: Toward Effective Risk Regulation* (Cambridge: Harvard University Press, 1993), pp. 10–11.

---

portion when the supply curve is more elastic, indicating that resource suppliers in the industry have reasonably attractive options in other industries. The burden imposed on sellers occurs in the form of reduced profits for investors and lower wages (and employment) for workers in the industry. In the short run, resources employed in the industry may have few alternative uses. Therefore, the short-run supply is likely to be inelastic. In the long run, of course, capital and labor are quite mobile among users, resulting in a supply curve that is more elastic.

Sometimes the opportunity cost of health and safety regulation is exceedingly difficult to calculate. For example, former FDA official Henry I. Miller reports that FDA testing requirements and approval delays helped to increase the time from synthesis of a new drug to FDA marketing approval from 14.1 years in the 1980s to an average of 15.2 years in the early 1990s.[4] Partly because of these requirements, it now costs about $400 million

---

[4]Henry I. Miller, "Strong Bush Prescription Needed to Cure an Overactive FDA," published in Findlaw.com, and available online at http://www.cei.org/gencon/019,01957.cfm.

EXHIBIT 1
The Regulation "Tax"

Regulation that requires businesses to adopt more costly production techniques is similar to a tax. If the regulation increases per-unit costs by t, the supply curve shifts upward by that amount. Higher prices and a smaller output result.

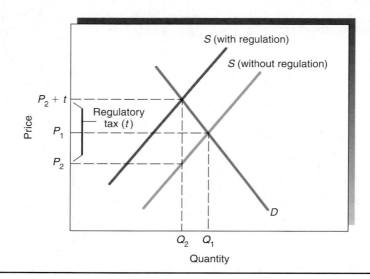

to bring a drug to market in the United States. In addition to these costs, there are two other major opportunity costs of this regulation: (1) some drugs that have a limited profit potential are never developed because of the expensive tests and delays, and (2) people who could have been helped by a drug—had it been approved—have to forgo it for several years. Deaths often result from these delays.

Health and safety regulations often stem from a problem of lack of information. Many people are unaware of the precise effects of drugs, air pollution, or workplace hazards. Even when the information is available to experts, consumers may never receive it because of the cost of communicating information, particularly highly technical information. A case can be made, therefore, that we should let the experts decide which drugs, how much air pollution, and what forms of workplace safety should be sought.

Ironically, however, choosing regulation to protect citizens who do not understand the danger introduces a related problem: When regulators make the decisions, most of the incentive for individuals to learn about comparative risks is removed. Yet these same individuals, now with less incentive to learn about risk, as voters ultimately control the political process and influence the agency's decisions.

The same lack of information that generates much of the demand for health and safety regulation also makes it difficult to evaluate the effectiveness of each regulatory activity. Current health and safety regulations in the United States produce high costs as well as large benefits, but these costs and benefits can only be crudely estimated. When Robert Hahn and John Hird estimated the sum of the costs and benefits from health and safety regulations, they could not state with confidence whether the benefits exceeded the costs. They concluded that the annual costs of these regulations in the late 1980s may have exceeded the benefits by as much as $65 billion, or that, alternatively, benefits may have exceeded costs by as much as $104 billion. They suggest that the benefits of health and safety regulation are probably larger than the costs, but only by a small amount. More recently, Hahn and other respected economists from three Washington, D.C., research organizations jointly published a critique of federal regulations. It stated that a "substantial share" of the regulations are "ineffective."[5]

---

[5] Robert W. Hahn and John A. Hird, "The Costs and Benefits of Regulation: Review and Synthesis," *Yale Journal on Regulation* 8 (Winter 1991): 233–278; and Robert W. Crandall, et al., *An Agenda for Federal Regulatory Reform* (Washington, D.C.: AEI and Brookings, 1997).

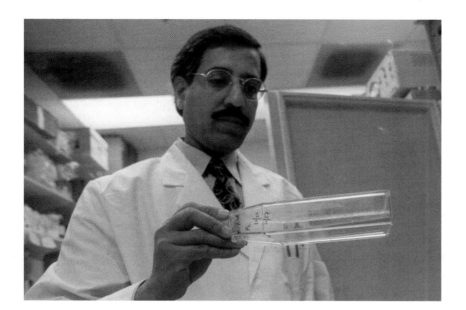

When the FDA announces the approval of a new, life-saving drug after several years of testing, the public can be better assured of its safety and effectiveness. However, this assurance involves costs. This extensive and time-consuming approval process means both higher drug prices and additional pain, suffering, and even loss of life for those who might have been helped by a more rapid approval of the drug.

Case Study: The Costs and Benefits of Fuel Conservation Regulation[6]

Fear of global warming—which some scientists think could be caused by rising levels of carbon dioxide in the air—has led to louder calls for more fuel-efficient cars, since cars that burn less fuel emit less carbon dioxide. Legislation that would require automakers to boost substantially their average mileage per gallon (mpg) of gasoline is once again before Congress. Would such mandatory fuel economy reduce fuel usage significantly? And, if so, at what cost? A look at the history of fuel efficiency regulation is informative. Responding to sharp worldwide increases in petroleum prices, Congress began mandating fuel economy standards in 1975, although the actual effects of the legislation did not occur until the mid 1980s. The experience with this legislation provides insights with regard to both the expected impact of tighter standards and possible unintended consequences that often accompany regulation.

The initial Corporate Average Fuel Economy (CAFE) standards were intended to conserve energy and make the United States less dependent on foreign oil. However, if Congress had simply allowed gasoline prices to rise, the higher prices would have encouraged people to adjust their habits in ways best suited to their personal circumstances. Some consumers would simply have driven less; others would have saved on gasoline by buying smaller cars or having more tune-ups. Some people living far from their workplaces might have bought larger cars and carpooled; others might have moved to places where they would have a shorter commute.

Indeed, well before the CAFE standards had an impact, people began to respond to higher gasoline prices by purchasing fuel-efficient cars. According to the 1986 *Economic Report of the President*, average fuel economy in the United States increased by 43 percent between 1973 and 1979, as consumers responded to higher fuel prices. By the time the fuel efficiency standards influenced the design of cars, which probably occurred with the 1986 model year, much fuel economy had already been achieved and gasoline prices were going down.

By that time, some consumers wanted larger cars, but the CAFE standards forced automakers to offer smaller cars. Although car companies could make some reductions in fuel usage by such steps as redesigning transmissions or fuel injection systems, they had

[6]This case study was written by Jane S. Shaw, Senior Associate at the Political Economy Research Center, Bozeman, Montana.

to reduce vehicle weight to meet the standards. Robert W. Crandall of the Brookings Institution and John Graham of the Harvard School of Public Health estimated that model year 1989 cars were on average 500 pounds lighter than they would have been without the CAFE standards.[7]

A serious problem with lighter cars is that they are less safe than larger cars. Crandall and Graham estimated that 2,200 to 3,900 lives would be lost over a 10-year period as a result of the application of the CAFE standards to the cars of the 1989 model year. A similar number of lives would likely be lost with each succeeding model year. Another study, published in 2000 by the National Academy of Sciences, found that downsizing of cars "probably resulted in an additional 1,300 to 2,600 traffic fatalities in 1993."[8]

There have been other unintended consequences of CAFE standards. To sell enough small cars to raise the fuel economy average, domestic automakers reduced small car prices and raised prices for large cars. Buying decisions were distorted, and consumers paid more on balance for their cars. Because Congress required the car companies to calculate average fuel economy separately for their domestic-manufactured cars and their imports, companies could not use their smaller, more fuel-efficient imports to bring down their domestic fleets' average. This encouraged small car production in the United States, even though it might have been cheaper to produce these cars overseas. At the same time, Ford moved some of its large car production out of the country in order to more easily meet the overall standards. Predictably, the CAFE regulations also led to major lobbying efforts by the auto industry firms, moving additional creative skills and energy away from productive activity.

Did the CAFE standards effectively reduce fuel use? According to the Federal Highway Administration, even though fuel usage per vehicle has fallen since 1969, total fuel consumption has been rising since 1982. With new, large cars more expensive as a result of the standards, some people probably kept their old cars longer, increasing gas consumption (and pollution). At the same time, the lower prices of small cars probably increased the total number of cars purchased. More cars on the road meant greater fuel consumption because the marginal cost of driving in a small car was lower than would otherwise have been the case, and because smaller car sizes led people to share fewer rides. Robert A. Leone of Boston University estimates that a 2 or 3 cent tax on gasoline beginning in 1984 would have saved as much fuel as the CAFE standards, and at a substantially lower cost to society.

The experience with CAFE highlights both the inflexibility of regulation and the unforeseen and unwanted side effects that often accompany it. It is not easy to mandate a specific outcome without triggering adverse consequences. As a result, regulation is generally less effective than it might first appear.

FUTURE DIRECTIONS FOR REGULATORY POLICY

Most people concede that regulation, both economic and social, is like a two-edged sword. Regulations can be beneficial, but they tend to be costly and can also be counterproductive. Some regulations are far more costly than others, even when their major goals are similar. **Exhibit 2** demonstrates this point. A group of well-known risk researchers analyzed several hundred regulations that save lives, issued by several agencies. The researchers estimated the cost per year of life saved of each regulation and averaged the cost for each agency. Some of these cost estimates for various agencies are presented here. The researchers estimated that the median cost of Federal Aviation Administration (FAA) regulations *per life year* saved was $23,000. In contrast, that of the Environmental Protection Agency was $7,600,000, or 330 times that of the FAA. Clearly, if some resources had been

[7]Robert W. Crandall and John D. Graham, "The Effect of Fuel Economy Standards on Automobile Safety," *Journal of Law and Economics* 32, no. 1 (April 1989): 97–118.

[8]Two of the 13 members of the committee dissented with this finding of the report, *Effectiveness and Impact of Corporate Average Fuel Economy (CAFE) Standards*, which can be found online at http://www.nap.edu/books/0309076013/html/.

Agency	Median Cost per Life Year Saved	
Federal Aviation Administration	$23,000	**EXHIBIT 2**
Consumer Product Safety Commission	$68,000	**Regulations and**
National Highway Transportation Safety Administration	$78,000	**Differences in the**
Occupational Safety and Health Administration	$88,000	**Cost of Saving Lives**
Environmental Protection Agency	$7,600,000	

Source: T. O. Tengs et al., "Five Hundred Life-Saving Interventions and Their Cost-Effectiveness," *Risk Analysis* 15 (1995): 369–390.

shifted from EPA regulatory activities to those of the FAA, more lives could have been saved for the same cost.

The cost also varied widely among the rules within each agency. The researchers suggest that if the least costly methods to save lives were chosen, the same expenditures could save tens of thousands of additional lives per year, or alternatively, the same number of lives could be saved while expenditures could be reduced by tens of billions of dollars per year.

Regulation would be significantly improved if the regulations that generate large gains relative to their cost could be adopted while those that generate few, if any, benefits, could be modified or eliminated. However, it is not easy to do this, especially because regulations are the business of many agencies. Without regulations, their existence would be in jeopardy. Predictably, the agency's leadership will lobby for larger budgets and greater authority. While there is strong support for the continuation and expansion of social regulatory activities, the voices favoring regulatory reform, and even deregulation, are growing louder. Improved empirical evidence on the effectiveness of specific regulatory policies will continue to emerge and, in some cases, will alter the direction of regulatory activities.

KEY POINTS

▼ Traditional economic regulation has generally sought to fix prices and/or influence entry into specific industries. During the 1970s, widespread dissatisfaction with economic regulation led to significant deregulation in the trucking and airline industries. This deregulation resulted in new entry, intense competition, and discount prices.

▼ Regulation involves a complex set of economic and political forces. Public choice analysis provides some insight regarding how the regulatory process can be expected to work. The following four points are particularly important:
  a. The demand for regulation often stems from special interest and redistribution considerations.
  b. With the passage of time, regulatory agencies are likely to adopt the views of the interest groups they are supposed to regulate.
  c. Regulation is inflexible; it will be slow to adjust to changing conditions.

  d. Approval of a dangerous product will cause more problems for a regulatory agency than a failure to approve a highly beneficial product. As a result, agencies approving new products (for example, medical drugs) will generally apply tests that are too restrictive from the viewpoint of consumer welfare.

▼ While economic regulation has been relaxed in recent years, health and safety regulation has expanded rapidly. Health and safety regulation seeks to provide a cleaner, safer, healthier environment for workers and consumers. Pursuit of this objective is costly, bringing about higher product prices and higher taxes, as well as unintended safety problems. Since the costs, and particularly the benefits, are often difficult to measure and evaluate, the efficiency of social regulatory programs is both controversial and the subject of much current research.

CRITICAL ANALYSIS QUESTIONS

*1. Legislation mandating stronger side and door panels to protect drivers and passengers against side collisions presumably makes cars both safer and more expensive. The same could be said for air bags. Are laws like these necessary for auto safety? Do they save lives and make auto travel safer? Why or why not?

2. "Without legal safety requirements, products such as lawn mowers would be unsafe." Evaluate this statement.

*3. Will health and safety legislation mandating workplace and product safety standards reduce the profitability of the regulated firms? Who bears the cost and who gains the benefits of such legislation?

4. In large cities, taxi fares are often set above the market equilibrium rate. Sometimes the number of licenses is limited in order to maintain the above-market price. In other cases, licenses are automatically granted to anyone wanting to operate a taxi. When taxi fares are set above market equilibrium, compare and contrast resource allocation under the restricted license system (assume the licenses are tradable) and the free-entry system. In which case will it be easier for customers to get a taxi? In which case will the amount of capital required to enter the taxi business be greater?

5. "Regulations on the introduction of new drugs should be strengthened. Fewer people would die if more research were required prior to the introduction of new drugs. Only an economist could possibly disagree. Sure, it would cost more, but saving even one life would be worth more than whatever it costs." Evaluate this statement.

*6. "People cannot be expected to make good decisions on their own regarding auto safety. Only experts know enough to make such decisions." Evaluate this statement.

7. "Safety regulation is not an economic question. Where lives and health are at stake, economics has no place." Evaluate this statement.

*8. "If we force increased safety measures in the workplace by regulation, business may bear the cost in the short run, but capital will receive the market rate of return in the long run." Evaluate this statement, and explain your reasoning.

9. "EPA has the entire nation's interests at heart when it directs cleanups at Superfund sites. It does not work for a profit. We can expect its cleanups, therefore, to be more cost-effective than a corporation's cleanups would be." Evaluate.

*Asterisk denotes questions for which answers are given in Appendix B.

SPECIAL TOPIC **13**

Natural Resources and the Future

"As we look at oceanic fisheries, rangelands, forests, aquifers, and croplands, we see that these natural support systems are often overtaxed at both the regional and global level. As population increases, so does pressure on these systems."

—Lester R. Brown[1]

Focus

■ What does the economic way of thinking have to say about resource markets?

■ How do private ownership and competitive markets affect the availability and conservation of resources?

■ How do regulations influence conservation when they weaken property rights?

■ Are we in danger of running out of vital natural resources?

---

[1]Lester R. Brown, founder and chair of the board of the Worldwatch Institute, in "Bjorn Again," in *Grist Magazine* 12 Dec. 2001, found at http://www.gristmagazine.com/grist/books/brown121201.asp

For centuries there has been concern that global population growth will place excessive demands on the world's natural resources and that resource depletion might lead to disaster. A well-known report published in 1798 by economist Thomas Malthus, *An Essay on the Principles of Population*, asserted that the human population was likely to grow more rapidly than its ability to feed itself. Since the time of Malthus, resource shortages, energy crises, and famines have occurred periodically. Fisheries are frequently in decline, oil prices sometimes rise quickly, and worries about future timber supply have been common. Lester R. Brown, author of the opening quote, began highlighting these gloomy possibilities in 1984, when he started publishing the annual *State of the World* series of reports. Each volume has focused on the resource depletion problems that seem to loom for our generation. In spite of the gloomy predictions and periodic crises, however, living standards have risen dramatically during the last two centuries. Can progress continue? Will there be enough minerals, water, and other natural resources for future generations? Economics has much to say about using natural resources wisely. This application will focus on these questions and related topics. ■

NATURAL RESOURCE MARKETS

As we have previously stressed, the price of a good or service influences the production, quantity used, and availability of substitutes. A higher price for one good makes others more attractive as substitutes. When there is an increase in the price of movie tickets, a host of substitutes, such as cable television subscriptions, books, and live concerts, become more attractive options for entertainment. The number of people attending movies will decline as the result of the price increase. Similar forces are at work on the supply side, since investors and workers have options as well. For example, when the prices of movie tickets increase, movie exhibitors will be able to bid more land, labor, and capital away from other uses and will supply more theater seats at the higher price.

Are the demand and supply of natural resources shaped by similar influences? Are good substitutes readily available for something so basic as water? Water is used for drinking, cleaning, irrigating crops, and for industrial processes and other purposes as well. In each use, we can substitute reduced activity (using less), more care (spilling or wasting less, for example), different methods of conducting the activity (perhaps drip irrigation rather than sprinklers), or equipment to recycle the water we use. **Exhibit 1** illustrates how several industries adjusted their water use during a lengthy drought in California in the late 1980s. Firms in that area had already seen water costs rise, and many conservation measures had already been taken. During the drought they came to anticipate further cost increases as well as possible supply interruptions. Their response was to install water recycling facilities and to alter production processes in order to conserve more water. Thus, these industrial users cut costs by sharply reducing their use of water per unit of output. Other studies have shown that agricultural users and households respond to increases in the price of water in a similar manner.

When economists examine markets for water, petroleum products, wilderness recreation, and other natural resources, they find that the sensitivity of decision makers to price and cost is similar to that found for other goods and services. Substitutes, it seems, are everywhere. For example, when the price of gasoline rises, users find many ways to use less of it: smaller cars, less distant vacation destinations, fewer shopping trips, and the use of public transportation or carpooling, to name just a few. *Users always seem to find ways to achieve their goals while using less of a resource that has risen in price. Like other goods and services, the amount demanded of a natural resource is negatively related to the price paid by users.*

Market prices influence resource suppliers also, in the usual way. In the case of minerals from the earth, higher prices will induce suppliers to search for and recover more deposits of the resource. For example, when oil prices increase, wildcatters will search new

EXHIBIT 1
Prices and the Industrial Use of Water

As water prices and the uncertainties of future availability increased during the 1986–1989 drought in California, industrial users cut back on their usage. As illustrated here, the amount of water used per unit of output declined by almost 50 percent in several key industries. When the use of water is expensive, people find ways to use less of it. How much water is needed to generate a gallon of paint? That depends very much on how costly water is. The "need" can be reduced if there is a good reason (such as a price increase) to do so.

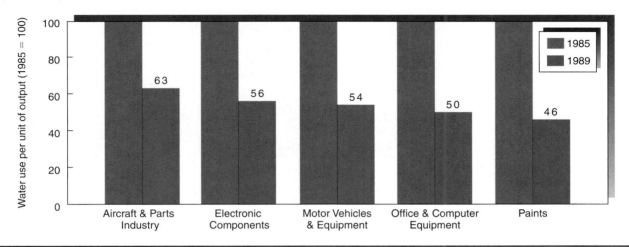

Source: Cost of Industrial Water Shortages, California Urban Water Agencies, 1991; Executive Summary, Table 1-1.

territories, drillers will dig deeper, and water flooding and other techniques will be used to recover more oil from existing wells. ***Thus, the quantity supplied of oil or any other resource is positively related to its price.*** Similarly, as incomes grow and the demand for access to fly fishing, wooded homesites, and hiking trails in relatively undisturbed natural areas increases, owners of land with these attractions will strive to preserve and enhance those characteristics that make the land more valuable. When lands are owned or controlled by government, political pressures will tend to move in the same directions as market pressures, although the decision-making process is different.

As in other markets, the responsiveness of producers and users will vary with time. The longer a sharp rise or fall in price persists, the stronger the response will be to the price change. The adjustment process requires time. Resource users need time to alter their equipment, for example, in order to conserve on the use of a more expensive resource. Similarly, suppliers need time to employ more capital and labor in order to expand output of a resource that has increased in price. And it will take time for product innovation and technological change to have a major impact, both on quantities demanded and on those supplied, when prices change.

Economists have used statistical methods to analyze both the impact of price changes and the role of time in energy markets. **Exhibit 2** summarizes the findings of several studies on the price elasticities of demand for three major energy sources. For residential electricity, the estimated price elasticity of demand is 0.2 in the short run. This implies that a 10 percent rise in price would lead to a 2 percent short-run reduction in quantity demanded. The short run here means one year. When buyers have up to 10 years to respond, the long-run elasticity indicates that the same 10 percent price rise would cause a larger decline—a 7 percent reduction in residential use of electricity, if other factors remain the same.

The price elasticities of demand for natural gas and gasoline follow a similar pattern. In the short run, a change in price will lead to only a small change in amount demanded. With additional time, however, consumers will be able to adjust more fully to a price

When water is scarce and costly, additional capital equipment can be used to provide drip irrigation, which delivers carefully measured amounts of water to exactly the places where plants can best use it. This can greatly reduce the water input needed per acre. Capital equipment and careful planning are being substituted for water.

When people have open access to forests, pasture land, or fishing grounds, they tend to overuse them. Providing land titles to farmers in Thailand has helped reduce damage to forests. The assignment of property titles to slum dwellers in Bandung, Indonesia, has tripled household investment in sanitation facilities. Providing security of tenure to hill farmers in Kenya has reduced soil erosion. Formalizing community rights to land in Burkina Faso is sharply improving land management. And allocating transferable rights to fishery resources has checked the tendency to overfish in New Zealand.

—World Bank [2]

increase and come up with more and better ways to reduce consumption. Thus, the demand for both natural gas and gasoline will also be substantially more elastic in the long run than in the short run.

Both economic theory and statistical studies indicate that resource markets are quite similar to those for other products. Higher resource prices will increase the incentive of consumers to conserve on their use of a resource and to find substitutes for it. The higher price will also bring forth additional production (supply). Lower prices will have the opposite effects, reducing the quantity supplied of the resource and increasing the quantity demanded.

PROPERTY RIGHTS AND RESOURCE CONSERVATION

As the quote from the World Bank indicates, the presence or absence of property rights exerts a powerful influence on the practice of conservation of resources. Energy use in the former Soviet Union and the Eastern European nations also illustrates this point. During the period when these countries were controlled by socialist governments, private property rights were largely absent. The constant adjustments that occur in a market setting as producers reduce costs by economizing on resources did not take place. When Mikhail Bernstam compared the 1986 energy use in the 12 largest industrialized market economies with its use in the Eastern European socialist countries (plus socialist North Korea), he found that the market-based industrial economies used only 37 percent as much energy per $1,000 of output as the socialist nations. Similarly, the socialist economies used more than three times as much steel per unit of output as market economies.[3] Socialist managers may know of new conservation methods, but they normally lack the authority and the incentive to make the stream of changes needed to minimize costs as technologies and resource scarcities change. Failure to minimize costs means that less is produced from the resources used. Costs are higher, resource use is greater per unit of output, waste is not minimized and the environment suffers as a result.

Conservation of land, too, occurs when farmers and private landowners operate in markets, with both the freedom and the profit incentive to adopt technology that makes

[2]The quoted passage is from *World Development Report*, 1992 (New York: World Bank), p. 12.

[3]The facts in this paragraph are from Mikhail Bernstam, *The Wealth of Nations and the Environment* (London: Institute of Economic Affairs, 1991), pp. 1–28.

| | Estimated Elasticity[a] | |
FUEL	SHORT RUN	LONG RUN
Residential electricity	0.2	0.7
Residential natural gas	0.1	0.5
Gasoline	0.2	0.7

EXHIBIT 2
Price Responsiveness of Energy Forms: Estimated Price Elasticities of Demand

[a]When income and other factors such as other fuel prices are held constant, the elasticities indicate the ratio of percent change in quantity to the percent change in price causing the quantity change. Each elasticity is actually a negative number, since price and quantity demanded move in opposite directions.
Source: Douglas R. Bohi, *Analyzing Demand Behavior* (Baltimore: Johns Hopkins University Press, 1981), p. 159.

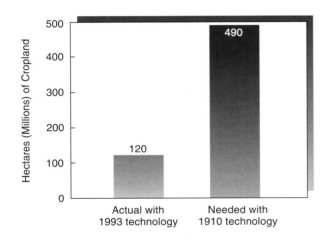

EXHIBIT 3
Croplands Needed for 1993 Level of U.S. Food Production

Without the technological advances that were adopted by U.S. farmers from 1910 to 1993, producing the food needed in 1993 would have required more than four times the cropland actually used, leaving that much less land for other uses, including natural habitat for wildlife and recreation.

Source: Indur Goklany, "Factors Affecting Environmental Impacts: The Effect of Technology on Long-term Trends in Cropland, Air Pollution and Water-related Diseases," *Ambio,* vol. 25, no. 8 (Dec. 1996) p. 498.

their resource more productive. Indur M. Goklany shows that new technologies have enabled farmers to increase the yields per acre of cropland, with the result that much less land is needed to produce any given farm output. **Exhibit 3** illustrates his point. If farmers had, on average, continued with the technology present in 1910, the nation would require nearly five times as much agricultural land now to feed today's population. Far less land would be left for other uses, including the natural habitat that improves environmental quality. In fact when we look at nations today where farmland is not privately owned or where market signals are not the primary guides to farm production, we see that food output per acre is much less. Lower productivity per acre means that more land must be devoted to farming, thereby reducing natural habitat and wildlife populations.

Why Private Ownership Is Important

Private ownership of natural resources, when combined with market organization of production, performs four functions that encourage resource conservation and, in doing so, improve the quality of the environment.

1. *Private property rights provide owners with the incentive to share (sell to others) access to resources, while resource prices provide users with the incentive to conserve.*
   The right to sell forces each owner to confront the opportunity cost of alternative uses of the resource, including uses that improve environmental quality and conserve

resources for future use. Highly valued alternative uses will be reflected in offers to buy the resource or access to it; failure to gain from the sale is the cost to the owner of keeping the resource rather than sharing it. Furthermore, when resources are privately owned, producers have a strong incentive to reduce costs by using less of each resource. The pursuit of profit encourages business firms to implement new technologies that conserve on the use of resources. Thus, it should not be surprising that resource-saving changes tend to occur earlier in a market setting than under socialism. Comparisons of resource conservation among nations and across time support this view.

2. ***A resource owner has a strong incentive to exercise good stewardship.*** Private ownership of property provides owners with an incentive to take good care of things. If the resource is well cared for, it will be more valuable and add more to the personal wealth of its owner. But the owner who allows the resource to deteriorate or be harmed by pollution will personally bear the cost of that negligence as the value of the resource declines. The value of the property right to the resource is, in a very real sense, a hostage to the owner's good care of that resource. That direct personal incentive is generally absent, however, without private ownership.

3. ***A resource owner has legal rights against anyone who would harm the resource.*** A private owner of a farm, a forest, or other resource has more than just the incentive to preserve the value of that resource. Private property rights also provide the owner with legal rights against anyone (including a government agency) who invades—physically or by pollution—and harms the resource. Much environmental damage is prevented this way. The private owner of a forest or a farm will not sit idly by if someone is cutting down the trees or invading the property with hazardous pollutants. Lawsuits can be used to protect those rights. For example, owners of copper and lead smelters in the United States have been forced to compensate owners of agricultural crops and homes for damage from sulfur dioxide emissions. Once such a company has been successfully sued, the decision sets a legal precedent that effectively discourages further pollution.

   When resources are not privately owned, no individual will receive large personal rewards for bringing suit against polluters, even when the source of the pollution is clear. In the United States, fish in a river might be damaged by pollution, but they are not owned by anyone whose personal wealth depends on their safety. Political and bureaucratic authorities must be counted on to protect the resource. In England, by contrast, where fishing rights on a stream are privately owned, the owners jealously guard the quality of the water.

4. ***Changes in the value of a privately owned resource bring the anticipated future benefits and costs of today's resource decisions immediately to bear on the resource owner.*** Property rights provide long-term incentives for maximizing the value of a resource, even for owners whose personal outlook is short term. If erosion on a tract of land reduces its future productivity, the land's value today falls, reducing the owner's wealth immediately. Fewer future services from a privately owned resource mean a fall in the value of that resource now. In fact, as soon as an appraiser or potential buyer can see future problems, the value of the asset declines.

   This is true even if the owner of the resource is a corporation, and the corporate officers, rather than the owner-stockholders, are in control. Corporate officers may be concerned mainly about the short term, not expecting to be present when future problems arise. They are concerned with current profits, but they must be equally concerned about current changes in the value of the corporation's stock. If today's decision reduces future profits, it will reduce the price of the firm's stock today. Why? It is in each stockholder's interest to keep an "ear to the ground" (or to invest in funds managed by those who do) because correctly anticipating market reaction to a corporate decision can allow a discerning investor to buy before good news is fully captured in the stock price or to sell before bad news is fully reflected in a falling stock price. The top corporate managers are hired and fired by the firm's board of directors, which is normally dominated by large shareholders. The top managers cannot afford to let shortsighted policies harm the interests of board members. Such self-interested scrutiny and the resultant decisions of investors, driven by the presence of property rights and the resulting resource ownership and liability for harm, provide a continual assessment of corporate strategies.

In order to properly perform these functions, property rights must be (a) defined (the rights and responsibilities of the owner are known), (b) defendable (at reasonable cost against those who would simply take them from the owner), and (c) tradeable (so that owners can gain from providing them to others, and will feel the cost to themselves of failing to do so). To underscore the positive role of property rights, let us consider what happens to the use of land when well enforced property rights to resources are weakened, as is the case of the Endangered Species Act, or are missing, as with many ocean fisheries.

THE ENDANGERED SPECIES ACT: UNWANTED SECONDARY EFFECTS FROM WEAKER PROPERTY RIGHTS[4]

The intent of the Endangered Species Act (ESA), which the Congress passed in 1973, was to help save endangered species from extinction. To do that, the ESA gave the U.S. Fish and Wildlife Service (FWS) the power to prohibit any land use by private owners (and government land managers) that might disturb the habitat of any animal species listed as endangered under the ESA. The majority of species that are listed are found on private lands. Farming, building, cutting trees, clearing brush, and even walking are activities that have been prohibited on private parcels of land where FWS biologists believe that such activities might harm a listed animal. Under the ESA, when the presence of a listed species is known or suspected, the right to decide on land use is taken from the owner and given (without payment) to the agency to further its mission. The property rights of landowners are severely weakened by the ESA.

On the one hand, colonies of many listed species have benefited from this control. On the other, the control has had a negative impact on land management that may outweigh the benefits to isolated populations of endangered species. Although a public good—habitat provision for endangered species—is produced as a result of these sacrifices, the fact that no compensation is given to owners means that market signals and incentives for conservation are missing.

Landowners affected by the endangered species regulations have often been forced by ESA requirements to sacrifice highly productive activities. Consider the sacrifice—the opportunity cost—required to set aside the habitat favored by the red-cockaded woodpecker, a listed species found in southern pine forests from Virginia to Texas under current FWS regulations. The FWS requires that trees the birds nest in must be left standing for several decades beyond the time they would normally be harvested for wood. Many acres of forage must also be available around the nest. Under the rules set by FWS, most potential uses of land are forbidden within several hundred yards of any tree, once the protected species has built a nest there.

Many landowners dread the possibility that the species will be found on their land, leading to the imposition of restrictions by the FWS. Such landowners can take subtle management steps to make their land unattractive to the listed species, and evidence has appeared that they do just that. Economists Dean Lueck and Jeffrey Michael found that landowners located close to colonies of red-cockaded woodpeckers in North Carolina cut

[4]Sources for this section are: Thomas R. Bourland and Richard L. Stroup, "Rent Payments as Incentives: Making Endangered Species Welcome on Private Land," *Journal of Forestry* 94, no. 4 (April 1996): 18–21; and Richard L. Stroup and Jane S. Shaw, "Technology and the Protection of Endangered Species," in *The Half-Life of Policy Rationales: How New Technology Affects Old Policy Issues,* eds. Fred E. Foldvary and Daniel B. Klein (New York: New York University Press, 2003).

Preservation of endangered species such as the red-cockaded woodpecker can be achieved at a much lower cost if the incentive structure encourages local persons to assist with the protection.

down their trees sooner than did those who were far away from the woodpeckers, where older trees were less likely to draw the listed woodpeckers which could trigger a transfer of control of their land to the FWS. The unwanted secondary effect of the ESA has been a reduction in habitat for listed and candidate species—just the opposite of the goal of the law.

Prior to the ESA's weakening of property rights, landowners often were quite willing to help preserve declining wildlife. When fears arose that bluebirds were in danger of extinction, landowners allowed volunteers to place hundreds of thousands of bluebird nest boxes on their land and to monitor them. Because owners did not fear the loss of their rights, they usually cooperated voluntarily. The bluebird has recovered and as a result never had to be listed. Many similar efforts, large and small, have been successful in gaining landowner cooperation with little or no payment. But finding a landowner willing to help a species now listed under the current ESA is obviously difficult. Few will want to attract species that could bring FWS control of their land. In fact, some will no longer even welcome hikers who might discover and report a listed species on the land.

When regulation weakens property rights and allows regulators to ignore costs their actions impose on others, low-cost solutions to problems—the kind of solutions that helped bluebirds, for example—become less likely. ***Without the signals and incentives of the market mechanism, it is difficult to discover low-cost means of resource conservation. There is also less incentive for decision makers to use low-cost methods, even when they are known.***

OCEAN FISHERIES: A LACK OF PROPERTY RIGHTS CAUSES OVERFISHING[5]

Overfishing in the oceans is a classic example of overexploitation of a resource that is not privately owned. Without ownership of the fish or of fishing rights, each fisher has little to gain from taking fewer fish, since others will get most of what he or she leaves. Since the 1970s, the U.S. government has regulated fishing in marine waters 12 to 200 miles from

[5]This section is based in large part on information found in Donald R. Leal, *Homesteading the Oceans: The Case for Property Rights in U.S. Fisheries,* found at http://www.perc.org/ps19pr.htm and personal communications with Leal.

its shores. To reduce the harvest so that a sufficient breeding stock is left, regulators typically mandate a shorter fishing season. Yet at least a third of U.S. fisheries are known to be overfished. To get more fish as the regulated season becomes shorter, each fisher invests in bigger, better capital equipment. The resulting race to get more fish has led to shorter and shorter seasons and hasty, wasteful harvests.

A strategy increasingly used around the world is to replace limits on season length with property rights strategies for the control of fishing. A prominent example is the adoption of ITQs, or individual transferable quotas, which give fishers ownership of a portion of the annual allowed catch. In New Zealand, these ITQs have become genuine property rights, increasing the value of fisheries and encouraging cooperation among owners in protecting the long-run future of the fishing areas.

In the past, fishers were part of a wasteful and dangerous "race to fish." In order to preserve the stock of fish, governments reduced fishing seasons (often to just a few days) and set limits on the kinds of gear that could be used. This meant that boats went out to sea in dangerous weather, took all the fish they could, even immature fish, and faced accidents and capsizing as their gear became entangled with other fishers' gear. ITQs have changed that frenzied and wasteful competition.

ITQs allow either individual fishers, or groups of fishers acting together, to keep for themselves the gains from slower and more careful fishing. The value of the fish has risen because fishers have the time to handle them more carefully, chilling them or even putting them in tanks for live delivery to market. Because fish can be caught over a longer period of time, the fish is more often fresh, not frozen, and buyers are willing to pay more. Waste is down, production and prices are up, and fishers have become more cooperative. In New Zealand, for example, abalone fishers agreed to limit their catch and invested in research to determine how to increase abalone numbers.

We have seen that markets can, without any central planning, lead to efficient allocation of resources and to innovative resource conservation, as well as resource production. But we have also seen that markets cannot do their work without property rights, and that defendable property rights are not always present. On balance, have conservation and innovation been sufficient to keep us from running out of resources? Will there be enough for our grandchildren and theirs? We turn now to that question.

RESOURCE MARKETS VERSUS RESOURCE DEPLETION

For centuries, various social commentators have argued that the world is about to run out of vital minerals and various sources of energy. In the middle of the nineteenth century, fear arose that the United States was about to run out of whale oil, at that time the primary fuel for artificial lighting.[6] As the demand for whale oil increased, many predicted that all the whales would soon be gone and that Americans would face long nights without light. Whale oil prices rose sharply from 23 cents per gallon in 1820 to $1.42 per gallon in 1850. As with charcoal, higher prices motivated consumers and entrepreneurs to seek alternatives, which included distilled vegetable oils, lard oil, and coal gas. By the early 1850s, coal oil (kerosene) had won out. And soon thereafter, a new substitute for whale oil appeared: Petroleum replaced coal oil as the source of kerosene. As for whale oil, by 1896 its price had fallen to 40 cents per gallon, and even at that price few people used it. The whale oil crisis had passed.

Doomsday predictions about exhaustion emerged almost as soon as large numbers of people began using petroleum. In 1914 the Bureau of Mines reported that the total U.S. supply of oil was 6 million barrels, an amount less than the United States now produces every two years. In 1926 the Federal Oil Conservation Board informed people that the U.S. supply of oil would last only 7 years. A couple of decades later the secretary of the interior forecast that the United States would run out of oil in just a few more years.

---

[6]See Charles Maurice and Charles W. Smithson, *The Doomsday Myth: 10,000 Years of Economic Crises* (Stanford, Calif.: Hoover Institution Press, 1987).

Dire predictions about our natural resource future became commonplace during the 1970s. The U.S. federal government established a Department of Energy. The first energy secretary proclaimed in 1979 that "we must rapidly adjust our economics to a condition of chronic stringency in traditional energy supplies." He appeared to be correct when oil prices rose to $53 per barrel in 1981. But then they fell. By 1986 oil prices were less than $20 per barrel and have stayed in that range for most of the years since. By the end of 2001, the price was hovering near $20 per barrel.

Why Have Doomsday Projections Been Wrong?

There are two major reasons for their inaccuracy. First, "proved reserves" of a mineral resource are the verified quantity of the resource that producers have discovered and that they believe can be produced *at current levels of technology and prices*. But technology can change. In the Gulf of Mexico, for example, oil wells were thought to be fully exploited after about 30 percent of the oil was removed. With improved technology, we are now able to extract 80 percent or more of the oil from these same wells. Furthermore, a better understanding of geophysics and the increasing availability of very large, low-cost computing capabilities are now used to direct the drilling. This, too, has helped to increase proved reserves.

Second, doomsday predictions have generally failed to consider the role of price changes. When a resource becomes more scarce, its price rises. This increase provides additional incentive for (1) resource users to cut back on their consumption, (2) suppliers to develop new methods of discovering and recovering larger quantities of the resource, and (3) both users and producers to search for and develop substitutes. To date, these forces have pushed "doomsday" farther and farther into the future.

In fact, the empirical evidence indicates that the relative scarcity of most resources is declining, and, as a result, the relative price of most resources is falling. A classic study of Harold Barnett and Chandler Morse illustrates this point.[7] Using data from 1870 to 1963, Barnett and Morse found that the real price of resources declined during that long period. Updates and extensions of this work indicate that resource prices are continuing to decline.

In 1980 the late Julian Simon, an economist, drew public attention to the resource price trend by betting doomsday environmentalist Paul Ehrlich that the inflation-adjusted price of a bundle of any five natural resources of Ehrlich's choosing would decline during the 1980s. In fact, the prices fell not only for the bundle, but for each of the five resources chosen by Ehrlich. Simon easily won the highly publicized bet. Resource prices have continued their centuries-long decline, and no end to that trend is in sight.

Continuing technological advances are enhancing our ability to get more value from reduced amounts of material inputs, reinforcing the trend toward cheaper (less scarce) resource inputs. Reduced demands for energy and minerals, together with the ability to produce more food from less land, reduces the pressure on our natural resource base and environment.[8] Population growth has also slowed, and there are indications that the world's population may begin to decline about 2040.[9] Rising wealth, it appears, can—with guidance from properly functioning markets—be achieved without resource destruction or the overtaxing of our supporting natural systems that doomsayers have been concerned about since at least the time of Malthus. While no one can guarantee that markets and technology will continue to triumph over resource depletion, both economic analysis and the historical record provide reason for optimism.

---

[7]Harold Barnett and Chandler Morse, *Scarcity of Growth: The Economics of Natural Resource Availability* (Baltimore: Johns Hopkins University Press for Resources for the Future, 1963). See also Julian L. Simon, *The State of Humanity* (Cambridge, Mass.: Blackwell Publishers, 1995), Part III, Natural Resources.

[8]Lynn Scarlett writes of this in "Doing More with Less: Dematerialization—Unsung Environmental Triumph," in Ronald Bailey, ed., *Earth Report 2000* (New York: McGraw-Hill, 2000), pp. 41–62.

[9]Fertility rates already are well below those needed to sustain the population of most market economies, including those of Europe and North America, as well as China and Japan. See Nicholas Eberstadt, "World Population Prospects for the Twenty-First Century: The Specter of 'Depopulation'?" in Ronald Bailey, ed., *Earth Report 2000* (New York: McGraw-Hill, 2000), pp. 63–84.

KEY POINTS

▼ In resource markets, as in other markets, incentives matter. Both the quantity demanded of a resource and the quantity supplied depend on the resource price. Substitutes abound and they influence the elasticity of both demand and supply. As in other markets, demand and supply in resource markets are generally more elastic in the long run than in the short run.

▼ Private resource ownership is important for resource conservation because it (a) is necessary for the wide, but controlled, access encouraged by the market process, (b) provides an incentive for resource stewardship, (c) gives owners legal standing against those who would overuse or harm the resource, and (d) gives future users a voice in today's markets through the capital value of resource assets.

▼ When property rights are poorly defined and enforced, problems arise. Because of the difficulties of specifying and enforcing ownership of some re-

sources, property rights and market prices are not a panacea. As with other economic issues, government regulation may provide improvements when markets fail. But here, as elsewhere, it is important to recognize that government action is not an automatic corrective device.

▼ Neither economic analysis nor empirical evidence supports the view that the world is about to run out of key natural resources. When private property rights are present, increased scarcity of a natural resource increases the price of the resource and thereby encourages (a) conservation, (b) the use of substitutes, and (c) the development of new technologies capable of both enhancing supply and reducing reliance on a resource. Contrary to the doomsday view of resource scarcity, the real prices of most natural resources have been declining during the last century.

CRITICAL ANALYSIS QUESTIONS

*1. Does a resource that is not owned, and therefore is not priced, have a zero opportunity cost? Might it be treated as if it did? Explain.

2. Why is the price elasticity of demand for resources, such as water and natural gas, greater in the long run than in the short run? What examples of responses to price changes can you think of that are more complete after one year than after one week?

3. "The federal government should do a complete survey of mineral availability in the nation. It is inexcusable that we do not know how much oil, for example, the country can ultimately produce." Evaluate this statement.

*4. Why will more oil in total be produced from an oil well when the price of crude oil is higher?

*5. "Private ownership of a natural resource, such as a lake in the woods, is tantamount to setting aside that resource for the personal, selfish enjoyment of one owner. Society will be better off if it is recognized that such a resource was provided by nature, for all to enjoy." Evaluate this statement.

6. Will the world ever run out of any mineral resource? Why or why not?

*7. "Corporations should not be allowed to own forests. Corporate managers are just too shortsighted. Their philosophy is to make a profit now, regardless of the future consequences. For example, trees may be cut after growing 30 years to get revenue now, even though another 20 years' growth would yield a very high rate of return. The long-run health of our forests is too important to entrust them to this sort of management." Evaluate this statement.

8. "Since our national forests are owned by all the people, their resources will be conserved for the benefit of all, rather than exploited in a shortsighted way, to produce benefits only for the owners." Evaluate this statement.

9. "If more nations become as rich as the United States, the pressures placed on natural systems will quickly become intolerable. Our world cannot sustain such increases in consumption." What evidence can you cite for or against this view?

*10. The movie *The Perfect Storm* is set in a situation where a very short fishing season forces the fishers to go to sea despite the dangerous conditions. Explain how a move to ITQs could solve that problem.

---

*Asterisk denotes questions for which answers are given in Appendix B.

SPECIAL TOPIC **14**

Economics and the Environment

If Fido digs up your flower bed, your recourse is to find Fido's owner and hold him accountable for the damages . . . Where property rights [for the animals] are lacking, problems are inevitable because costs are imposed on unwilling recipients.

—Terry L. Anderson
and Donald R. Leal [1]

In nearly every case, environmental problems stem from insecure, unenforceable, or nonexistent property rights.

—Jane S. Shaw [2]

F o c u s

- **What does the economic way of thinking have to say about environmental decision making?**

- **Is economic growth harmful to the environment?**

- **How do private ownership and competitive markets affect environmental quality?**

- **Can government regulation help protect the environment? Will it always be successful in doing so?**

[1]Terry L. Anderson and Donald R. Leal, *Free Market Environmentalism* (New York: Palgrave, 2001), p. 27.
[2]Jane S. Shaw, "Private Property Rights: Hope for the Environment," *Liberty*, Vol. 2, No. 2 (November 1988), p. 55.

W e have become increasingly sensitive to the environment, especially during the past 30 years. Will the quality of the environment be better in the future? Or will pollution increase as capital formation and technological improvements lead to greater production of goods and services? What does economics have to say about protecting the environment? What role can property rights and market exchange play in environmental matters? This application will focus on these questions and related issues. ■

ECONOMIC PRINCIPLES AND ENVIRONMENTAL DECISIONS

As we previously discussed, markets coordinate the choices of people with regard to natural resource use. Environmental decisions, however, are often made outside the market, and thus without the benefit of fully priced goods and services. There are relatively few markets for clean air, pure water, and endangered species. The absence of clearly defined and securely enforced property rights and the resulting lack of markets and decision maker accountability are at the heart of pollution and other externality problems. Still, in environmental matters as elsewhere, incentives make a difference, values are subjective, and unwanted secondary effects tend to pop up when policies are made. Let us consider how the economic way of thinking enhances our understanding of environmental choices and problems.

1. *Incentives matter.* Nearly a century after they were wiped out, wolves have returned to Yellowstone National Park. The process of reintroducing wolves was not an easy one, and it succeeded largely because one environmentalist understood the importance of incentives. Early in the twentieth century, wolves were eradicated from Yellowstone and the surrounding area. Ranchers didn't want wolves killing their livestock, and park managers wanted to protect animals they considered more desirable, such as elk, deer, and antelope.

   In the mid 1980s, however, attitudes about the wolf were changing in much of the country. Hank Fischer, a Montana employee of the environmental group Defenders of Wildlife, wanted to bring back the wolf, which he felt was important to the park's

Wolves have been reintroduced to Yellowstone Park with the help of a privately financed program to compensate nearby ranchers for the resulting losses to their herds of livestock. The program reduced the incentive for ranchers to oppose reintroduction.

natural ecology.[3] At first, he thought it would be easy. He met with a group of ranchers to learn about their concerns. They were adamantly opposed. At the end of the meeting, one of the ranchers asked, "What's the best caliber to shoot a wolf with, anyway?"

The meeting set Fischer thinking. "I learned that I didn't have a good answer for their most central question: Why should they have to pay the costs of wolf introduction?" he says.

Wolves were already slowly moving into northern Montana from Canada. When a wolf pack killed some livestock, ranchers were outraged, and the kills dominated the local newspapers for months. Then Fischer hit on an idea. Why not pay the ranchers for their losses? He found donors to fund a program that compensates the ranchers for wolf kills. Their anger subsided and the topic dropped out of the newspaper headlines. Since it began in 1987, the fund has paid out about $175,000. Fischer didn't turn ranchers into wolf enthusiasts, but he reduced their incentive to fight introduction. In 1995, the wolf was peaceably introduced into Yellowstone, and the compensation program continues. In the public sector as well as the private, incentives help to determine outcomes.

2. ***The value of a good or service is subjective.*** Environmental values, like all others, are subjective. How valuable is a tract of unroaded wilderness land, relative to the same land with roads and campgrounds added to enhance recreation, or the same land developed for high-quality residential use? Individuals will differ dramatically in their evaluations of those alternatives. Some believe that wilderness is the highest and best use for such a tract of land. Others prefer more intensive recreational use or tastefully planned and easily accessible residential development, where people can be comfortable and also be in close contact with the beauty of nature.

Consider the following question: Will persons living near a river be willing to vote for sewage plant improvements to help clean up a half-mile stretch of the river for better fishing and boating, even though that will add an extra $12 per month to their water bill? Again, we can expect people to differ in how much value they place on making a stretch of river a little cleaner. Some will be quite happy to pay the fee, while others will probably object.

3. ***Remember the secondary effects.*** As in other areas of human action, the secondary effects of environmental actions must be considered. The story of the pesticide DDT shows what happened when first the environmental harms, and later the benefits of DDT were ignored in public policy.[4]

In the 1950s, the U.S. Department of Agriculture sprayed the insecticide DDT on millions of acres of crops and forests to reduce damage by insects and subsidized others to do the same. DDT was cheap and effective, but enormous quantities were being sprayed. Organic farmers were clearly affected and went to court, noting that the spray caused them to lose organic status for their crops in the market. They asked for protection of their right to farm on their land without unwanted pesticides. Their property rights were overruled in court, in favor of the public's general interest in controlling pests. Although individual sprayers of DDT and other pesticides whose sprays drifted and caused similar concerns and damages were being stopped in courts, the federal agency was not held to the same standard. When the Environmental Defense Fund (EDF, now called Environmental Defense) lost one such case in court, they began to take the case against DDT to the public and into the political arena.

Aided by the public fear and outcry raised by Rachel Carson's famous book, *Silent Spring*, EDF helped raise public awareness and outrage against DDT (and dra-

---

[3]The following paragraphs are based on "Who Pays for Wolves?" by Hank Fischer, *PERC Reports* (Bozeman, Mont.: Political Economy Research Center), December 2001.

[4]This discussion is based on overviews of the DDT problem found in Roger E. Meiners and Andrew P. Morriss, *Pesticides and Property Rights* (Bozeman, Mont.: PERC, 2001), available online at http://www.perc.org/issdep.htm; Thomas R. Degregori, *Agriculture and Modern Technology: A Defense* (Ames: Iowa State U. Press, 2001); and Indur M. Goklany, *The Precautionary Principle: A Critical Appraisal of Environmental Risk Assessment* (Washington, D.C.: Cato Institute, 2001).

matically raised its own prominence and funding) to the point where, in 1972, EPA banned DDT, mainly because it was believed to cause damage to wild birds. To this day, there is no verifiable damage to humans. Unfortunately, the ban had unwanted secondary effects. In place of DDT, other pesticides were used that were more costly and more risky to the workers who applied them in the fields.

In other nations, the secondary effects of banning DDT were even more tragic. In Sri Lanka, for example, where the mosquitoes that carry malaria had been controlled by DDT, the incidence of malaria had declined from 2.8 million cases in 1946 to fewer than 20 cases in 1963. After the government of Sri Lanka stopped the use of DDT in 1964, however, the number of malaria cases jumped back up to 2.5 million in 1969. In poor, tropical nations around the world, about 1 million people die each year from malaria. Many of these deaths could be avoided, as they are in some nations, by a light spraying indoors to protect people as they sleep at home. This involves little or no environmental risk, but environmentalists, fearful of damage to wildlife, demand the end to DDT use everywhere. It is important that environmental decision makers, like those in other policy areas, be alert for secondary effects. This basic economic principle is just as important in environmental decision making as in other areas of human action.

Economic principles apply to the choices of people regarding natural resources and the environment just as they do to choices in other areas. But since markets and easily defended property rights are not always present, especially for air and water quality and other environmental services, observers often worry that as an economy grows, more resources will be used and additional waste will be imposed on the environment. Clearly, this is an extremely important concern. What can economists say about the effects of economic growth on environmental quality? We now turn to an examination of this important issue.

IS ECONOMIC GROWTH HARMFUL TO THE ENVIRONMENT?

Is economic growth sustainable? We often hear the claim that growth inevitably means more pollution and ever greater demands on Earth's fixed supply of natural resources. Yet many of the same forces that encourage economic growth, such as market institutions and improvements in technology, also help to *reduce* pressures on the environment. In addition, rising incomes foster the willingness and ability to pay for a cleaner, safer, more pleasant environment. Although environmental protection often imposes some cost on economic activities, growth can still proceed when the controls are intelligently applied. And growth itself, properly controlled to avoid environmental harm, has important beneficial effects on the environment.

Once people have enough income so that they are not struggling to put food on the table, they become more willing and able to take actions to reduce (or avoid) environmental damage and improve the quality of the environment. For example, as incomes have risen in North America, Europe, and other parts of the world, private actions to maintain nature preserves have proliferated. Individuals, firms, and nonprofit groups have established areas for the protection of plant and animal habitats.[5] Profit-seeking firms, such as Big Sky of Montana, find it profitable to buy large tracts of mountainous land, far more than they plan to develop, then sell some of the tracts with environmentally protective restrictions and leave the bulk of what they own permanently for undeveloped wildlife habitat. By providing legal restrictions that protect the pristine surroundings of their development, they increase the total market value of what they own.

---

[5]Chapter 9 of *Environmental Quality* (1984), the annual report of the President's Council on Environmental Quality, describes a representative sample of these private projects, some of which date back to the nineteenth century, to benefit the environment. Contemporary examples are found in Terry L. Anderson and Donald R. Leal, *Free Market Environmentalism: Revised Edition* (New York: Palgrave, 2001).

Economic growth generally leads to environmental improvements because people with higher incomes are willing to pay more for environmental quality. Economist Donald Coursey has studied this topic extensively. He finds that in the United States and in other industrial nations, citizens' support for measures to improve environmental quality is highly sensitive to income changes. In economic terms, willingness to pay for costly environmental measures is highly elastic with respect to income. Coursey estimates that in industrial nations the income elasticity of demand for environmental quality is 2.5. Thus, a 10 percent increase in income leads to a 25 percent increase in citizens' willingness to pay for environmental measures. According to Coursey, the demand for environmental quality has approximately the same income elasticity as the demand for luxury automobiles like the BMW and Mercedes-Benz.

Technological change is another factor that often improves the environment. Economic growth and technological change generally accompany each other. The market processes that reward innovation and produce growth also bring technological advances. In the United States, advancing technology was itself cleaning the environment well before major environmental laws were passed. For example, in 1900, New York City residents used 120,000 horses, each leaving 20 pounds of manure and many gallons of urine—mainly on the streets—each day. Autos today emit pollution, but it is far less noxious. Also, since the late 1960s, about 97 percent of the pollution from each new car has been eliminated. Technology is also reducing our use of many materials, along with the mining, energy production, and other polluting activities necessary for using them. The aluminum beverage cans made in the early 1990s were made with 40 percent less aluminum than in 1963, when the cans were first used. And the percentage of recycled aluminum grew to about half, so that far less mining was needed, and far less energy to make each pound of aluminum. Former Vice President Al Gore summarized our recent history this way: "In the past 50 years, the value of our economy has tripled, while the physical weight of our economy has barely increased at all."[6]

One reason that we have cleaner cars is that a richer United States also strengthened its environmental cleanup laws, especially in the late 1960s and the years following. A recent EPA report on air pollution[7] makes the following points about progress since that agency was established in 1970:

▼ Since 1970, aggregate emissions of six principal pollutants tracked nationally have been cut 29 percent. During that same time period, U.S. Gross Domestic Product increased 158 percent, energy consumption increased 45 percent, and vehicle miles traveled have increased 143 percent.

▼ National air quality levels measured at thousands of monitoring stations across the country have shown improvements over the past 20 years for all six principal pollutants.

Exhibit 1, from the same report, illustrates these advances. New laws and EPA regulations explain some of these gains, while the cost-reducing technological advances mentioned above and long-standing local regulations played a role also. In fact some of the air pollutants were declining even faster prior to the increased federal regulation. Still, as the EPA report also points out, further progress is needed in some areas.

Exhibit 2 illustrates the general relationship between three types of environmental problems and per-capita income. Some environmental problems are ameliorated with higher income, while others may be worsened. Still others are worsened only up to a point and then generally improve with still higher levels of economic development.[8] Such prob-

---

[6]Al Gore, quoted in Lynn Scarlett, "Doing More with Less: Dematerialization—Unsung Environmental Triumph?" in Ronald Bailey, ed., *Earth Report 2000* (New York: McGraw-Hill, 2000), p. 42.

[7]*National Air Quality 2000: Status and Trends* (Washington: EPA, Sept. 2001*)*; the quote and Exhibit 1 are from the Highlights section, found online at http://www.epa.gov/oar/aqtrnd00/.

[8]A concise overview of the connections between growth and environmental quality, with references to leading works, is found in Matthew Brown and Jane S. Shaw, "Does Prosperity Protect the Environment?" in *PERC Reports,* Feb. 1999, pp. 12–14, available at http://www.perc.org/percrept.htm.

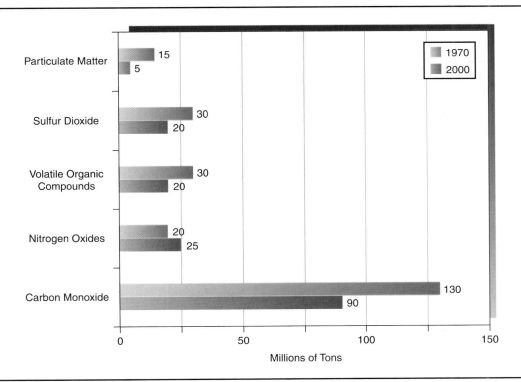

EXHIBIT 1
Comparison of Air Emissions: 1970 and 2000

In the United States, incomes grew 158 percent from 1970 to 2000, with substantial increases in energy use, travel in autos, and other polluting activities. Yet the aggregate of five major types of air pollution declined by 29 percent during that time period. Technological improvements, spurred both by cost reduction measures and by added regulations, help explain the difference.

Source: National Air Quality 2000: Status and Trends (Washington: EPA, Sept. 2001); from the Highlights section, found online at http://www.epa.gov/oar/aqtrnd00/.

lems as a lack of safe drinking water (part a) are steadily reduced as income rises. As people become richer, they can dramatically reduce sickness and death from waterborne diseases by installing sewers to handle human waste and by reducing water contamination by animals. Better stoves and switching from wood to coal, gas, and oil fuels eliminate large health problems from indoor air pollution while also saving forests from devastation. At incomes greater than $3000 per year, economies typically begin to write environmental protections for forests into law. Certain pollutants, however, such as particulates in urban air (part b), tend to become worse with growth until incomes rise above $9000 per year. But as income levels continue to rise, fuel burning and industrial processes become more efficient and emit smaller amounts of waste, and particulates in the air decline. Once minimal income levels are achieved, economic growth generally brings cleaner air and water, along with improvements in habitat preservation and several other aspects of environmental quality.

On balance, per capita income is closely linked with a cleaner and safer environment. Markets and a secure system of property rights help people achieve both higher income levels and better environmental protection from identifiable polluters. Without enforceable rights to resources, both income growth and a clean environment are more difficult to reach. We turn now to a discussion of how property rights have helped the environment in several nations around the world.

PROPERTY RIGHTS AND THE ENVIRONMENT

Income growth helps to increase the demand for environmental quality, while technological advances help to lower the cost of reducing both resource use and pollution. Yet incomes above the poverty level and an understanding of technology are not enough to protect the environment. The opening up of Eastern European nations and the Soviet

EXHIBIT 2
Pollution Problems as
National Income Rises

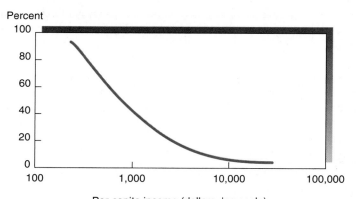

(a) Population without safe water

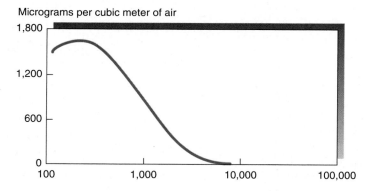

(b) Urban concentration of particulate matter

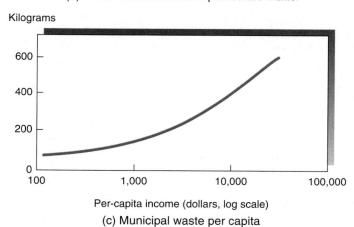

(c) Municipal waste per capita

Note: Estimates are based on cross-country regression analysis of data from the 1980s.
Source: World Bank, *World Development Report,* 1992, p. 11.

Union in the 1990s exposed widespread environmental disasters. These disasters occurred despite the presence of good technical capabilities and above-average per-capita incomes in those nations.

Why did these relatively advanced nations not take better care of their environments? The answer appears to lie in the fact that property rights and market exchange were largely missing. Property rights and markets stimulate resource conservation. The same is true for environmental quality. Reduced use of energy, steel, and other natural resources to produce goods and services usually means less pollution. In addition, property rights give legal standing to those who are threatened by pollution. Owners of land and other resources in a market economy have the right to sue anyone who damages their property with pollution. Citizens have similar rights against polluters who wrongfully bombard the individuals themselves with harmful pollution. Without enforceable property rights, however, citizens must depend on government agencies to protect them. Finally, property rights promote economic prosperity and thereby spur citizen demand for greater emphasis on environmental quality.

Property Rights and the Protection of Water Quality

Could property rights help protect water quality in rivers and streams? The case of fishing rights in England illustrates what happens when private ownership is present. In England the adjacent landowner has title to fishing rights out to the middle of the stream. The fishing right can be rented, leased, or sold. Fishing clubs and owners of country inns are among those who have purchased those rights. Club members and guests of the inns may then have access to fishing in this area.

As trout fishing became more popular during the 1900s and the rights became more valuable, fishing rights owners became more serious about protecting their rights. In 1948, long before the first Earth Day in 1970 and 20 years before the government established authorities to control water pollution, the Anglers' Cooperative Association (ACA, later the Anglers' Conservation Association) was formed to help clubs and anglers obtain damage awards or court orders forcing intruders to cease polluting activities. The ACA won its first major case in 1951 against two chemical companies and the city of Derby for pumping untreated sewage, hot water, and tar products into the River Derwent. Through the years, it won several other cases, including a 1987 case against the Thames Water Authority for fouling the Thames River. The association has established enough court precedents that it seldom has to go to court now. As economist Roger Bate says in his book on the subject, the ACA "is the most efficient and determined pollution prevention body in Britain."[9]

In the United States, fishing rights on most streams are held in trust for the people by state governments, which might in principle sue to protect these rights just as the ACA does in England. However, without their own wealth at stake, bureaucratic decision makers seem less inclined to protect aggressively either the fish or the water quality. Instead, control of water pollution in streams is typically left up to environmental regulators. England, however, has demonstrated what seems to be a more sure and far less expensive way—private ownership of fishing rights—to protect waters that are valuable for fishing.

GOVERNMENT REGULATION AND THE ENVIRONMENT

Substantial contributions to environmental quality are made through the normal operation of property rights and a market system. However, it is sometimes difficult—if not impossible—to define, establish, and protect property rights. When pollution is truly local— when it exerts a significant impact on only a few people—the property rights approach can deal effectively with the problem. Most pollutants capable of doing proven and serious damage are of this sort. But this is not always the case. If the effects of an emitted substance are both serious and widespread over a large population, or if the substance has many sources, then government regulation may be more efficient.

Government regulation is an alternative method of seeking to protect and preserve the quality of the environment. However, as we discussed in the Special Topic on this subject, regulation seldom leads to ideal outcomes, and it can be enormously expensive. Regulation is

---

[9]The quote is from Roger Bate, *Saving Our Streams: The Role of the Anglers' Conservation in Protecting English and Welsh Rivers* (London: Institute of Economic Affairs, 2001), on which this section is based.

seldom based on market signals, and so it is subject to all the problems caused by lack of information and lack of incentives that have plagued the socialist nations. Its benefits can be questionable, since the harms from the actions they regulate might have been dealt with in court, if the uncertainty of their size were not so great. Regulation is often demanded precisely because the harms are uncertain and cannot be demonstrated in court. The issue of global warming provides a good example.

Emissions of carbon dioxide from the efficient burning of all fuels cause no harm where they are emitted. No one's rights are being violated by the invasion of a harmful pollutant. Yet these emissions have been building up in the atmosphere. They may in the future require regulation if the buildup acts as an invisible blanket and causes the earth to warm significantly. Such warming could change weather patterns and might result in rising sea levels around the globe. If the "worst-case scenarios" suggested by scientists were to materialize, some communities would face flooding of their lands, serious ecological disruptions, and related problems.

Some scientists and many environmental groups argue that the threat of global warming is so serious that despite high costs, the nations of the world must impose strong regulations quickly. Government limits of some sort, they point out, are the only way that carbon dioxide emissions can be controlled. Other scientists, and many policy analysts, believe that imposing strong regulation at this time would be a mistake. They point out that the science of global warming is filled with uncertainties. For example:

1. *We do not know whether changes in the earth's cloud cover will do more to enhance the warming effects of carbon dioxide or to offset them.* Water vapor and clouds in the atmosphere account for more than 98 percent of the total warming we now experience. Yet certain kinds of clouds reflect enough of the sun's energy that they reduce warming, while others enhance warming. In fact recent evidence suggest that as oceans warm, the clouds that warm the earth will decline, allowing more heat to escape into space.[10] All scientists agree that the atmospheric models used to predict global warming do not accurately incorporate the effects of atmospheric water vapor, although gradual improvements in the models are being made.

2. *It is true that in the past, over thousands of years, added carbon dioxide has been associated with warming. But does this association mean that the carbon dioxide caused the warming?* Studies of ice cores drilled deep into Antarctica and Greenland allow scientists to measure the levels of carbon dioxide in the atmosphere during earlier years. The evidence indicates that the warming often preceded, rather than followed, the buildup of carbon dioxide. In such cases, how could the buildup cause the warming, when the warming came first?

3. *If warming does occur, will sea levels rise or fall?* A rise in sea level is forecast by many of the scientists who believe that warming will occur. Warming would cause glaciers and ice caps to melt and shrink at the edges. However, warmer air carries more moisture, and the added precipitation would build up snow and ice in the still-frigid centers of the polar ice caps, increasing their thickness. Whether the net effect on the sea level would be positive or negative is unknown. Scientific experts disagree on the question.

These questions and many more are in dispute. We cannot even be sure whether the buildup and a warmer world would, on balance, be better or worse. Some people—particularly those distant from the equator—would gain from a warmer, wetter world. Also, the direct effects of added carbon dioxide are helpful to plants. Owners of greenhouses routinely purchase carbon dioxide to enrich the enclosed atmosphere and enhance plant growth. Certain diseases might also increase in a warmer world, but economist Thomas Gale Moore has shown that warmer climates are generally more healthy on balance.[11]

---

[10]Indur Goklany, *The Precautionary Principle: A Critical Appraisal of Environmental Risk Assessment* (Washington, D.C.: Cato Institute, 2001), citing Richard Lindzen, et al., "Does Earth have an Infrared Iris?" *Bulletin of the American Meteorological Society*, No. 82, pp. 417–432 (2001).

[11]Thomas Gale Moore, *Climate of Fear* (Washington, D.C.: Cato Institute, 1998).

The cost of such policies is another consideration. Economist William Nordhaus recently estimated[12] that signing on to the Kyoto Protocol, while it would have almost no perceptible effect on global temperatures, would cost the United States alone about $125 billion each year for the next century. These estimated costs and the scientific uncertainties combine to make many economists unwilling to endorse strong regulations to force reductions in the emissions of carbon dioxide. As Nordhaus earlier suggested, "The best investment today may be in learning about climatic change, rather than in preventing it."[13] Certainly we know that a world with more wealth is one that can provide more aid to the victims of any disasters that do occur, whatever their source.

In sum, environmental regulation is a powerful tool, capable of providing improvements in environmental quality, but it tends to be very costly, and its unintended consequences can be serious. The results of regulations banning DDT proved that point, as we described earlier, as in the tragic case of Sri Lanka.

Policy makers and analysts considering environmental regulations should recognize that environmental quality is an economic good. Like food, clothing, and shelter, it is something that people are willing to pay for, though not in unlimited amounts. In addition, policy makers should recognize the linkage between environmental quality and economic prosperity. Environmental regulations can exert a powerful influence, for ill as well as for good. Finally, policy makers should not forget that enforceable property rights were for many years our main form of regulating environmental pollution. In addition, they allow farsighted individuals and groups to exercise their visions and preserve natural areas. Overall, property rights continue to play a positive role in the preservation of a quality environment.

KEY POINTS

▼ Even though environmental decisions are often made outside a market context, the basic principles of economics still apply. Purposeful choices, influenced by prices (or their absence) and other incentives, are made without full knowledge. Values are subjective, and the secondary effects of decisions are often important.

▼ Environmental quality and economic growth tend to go together. The demand for environmental quality is positively and strongly linked to income levels.

▼ Market prices provide potential users with an incentive to conserve on their use of resources. The technological improvements spurred by market competition enhance economic growth, reduce resource waste, and enhance our ability to control pollution.

▼ When enforceable property rights cannot be put into place, government regulation is an alternative mechanism that can promote wise use of resources and the environment. However, regulatory choices are not based on information and incentives from market prices. Thus, regulation has the same potential for inefficiency and ineffectiveness faced by the socialist governments whose citizens have suffered many environmental harms.

CRITICAL ANALYSIS QUESTIONS

1. "People want clean air and clean water in their rivers, but they cannot buy them in a market. Government regulation is the only way to provide them." Evaluate this statement.

*2. Is it possible to be "too safe" when it comes to risks from chemicals, such as pesticides that might find their way into food? Why or why not? Explain.

---

[12]William D. Nordhaus, "Global Warming Economics," *Science* Vol. 294 (9 November 2001), pp. 1283–1284.

[13]William Nordhaus, "Global Warming: Slowing the Greenhouse Express," in *Setting National Priorities: Policies for the Nineties*, ed. Henry J. Aaron (Washington, D.C.: The Brookings Institution, 1990), p. 207.

3. Are rich people or poor people more likely to call for tighter environmental laws? Why? What does this imply about the effects of economic growth on environmental quality?

*4. "The buildup of carbon dioxide and other gases in the atmosphere threatens to warm the planet and cause enormous damage worldwide. We must immediately stop this buildup, for the sake of our grandchildren and all future generations." Why do many economists disagree with this statement? Does that indicate that these economists care less for future generations than other commentators who call for an immediate stop to the buildup? Explain.

5. Is environmental quality a good like all others?

*6. "Unlike in a marketplace, where pollution is profitable, government control of resources and pollution can take into account the desires of all the people." What does economic thinking have to say about this statement?

7. "Without tighter regulation, economic growth will inevitably cause us to be buried in our own waste and choked by our own pollution." What does the history of the past century tell us about this concern? How can the economic way of thinking help us avoid this pessimistic possibility?

*Asterisk denotes questions for which answers are given in Appendix B.

APPENDIX A

General Business and Economic Indicators

SECTION 1
Gross Domestic Product and Its Components

Year	Personal Consumption Expenditures (Billions)	Gross Private Domestic Investment (Billions)	Government Consumption and Gross Investment (Billions)	Net Exports (Billions)	Real GDP		
					Gross Domestic Product (Billions)	1996 Prices	Annual Real Rate (Percent)	Real GDP Per Capita
1960	$ 332.3	$ 78.9	$ 113.8	$ 2.4	$ 527.4	$2,376.7	2.5	$13,206
1961	342.7	78.2	121.5	3.4	545.6	2,432.0	2.3	13,291
1962	363.8	88.2	132.2	2.5	586.5	2,578.9	6.0	13,885
1963	383.1	93.8	138.5	3.3	618.7	2,690.4	4.3	14,278
1964	411.7	102.1	145.1	5.5	664.4	2,846.5	5.8	14,896
1965	444.3	118.2	153.7	3.9	720.1	3,028.6	6.4	15,655
1966	481.8	131.3	174.4	1.9	789.3	3,227.4	6.6	16,509
1967	508.7	128.6	195.4	1.4	834.1	3,308.3	2.5	16,762
1968	558.7	141.2	212.8	−1.3	911.5	3,466.1	4.8	17,390
1969	605.5	156.5	224.6	−1.2	985.4	3,571.4	3.0	17,742
1970	649.0	152.4	237.1	1.2	1,039.7	3,578.0	0.2	17,557
1971	702.4	178.2	251.0	−3.0	1,128.6	3,697.7	3.3	17,879
1972	770.7	207.6	270.1	−8.0	1,240.4	3,898.4	5.4	18,628
1973	852.5	244.5	287.9	0.6	1,385.6	4,123.4	5.8	19,510
1974	932.4	249.5	322.4	−3.2	1,501.0	4,099.1	−0.6	19,214
1975	1,030.3	230.2	361.1	13.6	1,635.2	4,084.5	−0.4	18,957
1976	1,149.8	292.0	384.5	−2.3	1,823.9	4,311.7	5.6	19,819
1977	1,278.4	361.4	415.3	−23.7	2,031.4	4,511.8	4.6	20,530
1978	1,430.4	436.0	455.6	−26.1	2,295.9	4,760.6	5.5	21,435
1979	1,596.3	490.7	503.5	−24.0	2,566.4	4,912.1	3.2	21,874
1980	1,762.9	477.9	569.7	−14.9	2,795.6	4,900.9	−0.2	21,569
1981	1,944.2	570.8	631.4	−15.0	3,131.4	5,020.9	2.4	21,881
1982	2,079.3	516.1	684.4	−20.6	3,259.2	4,919.4	−2.0	21,235
1983	2,286.4	564.2	736.0	−51.7	3,535.0	5,132.4	4.3	21,953
1984	2,498.4	735.5	800.8	−102.0	3,932.8	5,505.1	7.3	23,344
1985	2,712.6	736.3	878.3	−114.2	4,213.0	5,717.0	3.8	24,029
1986	2,895.2	747.2	942.3	−131.9	4,452.9	5,912.4	3.4	24,621
1987	3,105.3	781.5	997.9	−142.3	4,742.5	6,113.3	3.4	25,231
1988	3,356.6	821.2	1,036.9	−106.3	5,108.3	6,368.3	4.2	26,046
1989	3,596.7	872.9	1,100.2	−80.7	5,489.1	6,591.8	3.5	26,707
1990	3,831.5	861.7	1,181.4	−71.5	5,803.3	6,707.9	1.8	26,889
1991	3,971.3	800.2	1,235.5	−20.7	5,986.2	6,676.4	−0.5	26,478
1992	4,209.7	866.7	1,270.5	−27.8	6,319.0	6,880.1	3.1	26,978
1993	4,454.7	955.1	1,293.0	−60.5	6,642.3	7,062.7	2.7	27,398
1994	4,716.4	1,097.1	1,327.9	−87.1	7,054.3	7,347.7	4.0	28,225
1995	4,969.0	1,143.8	1,372.1	−84.3	7,400.6	7,543.8	2.7	28,705
1996	5,237.5	1,242.7	1,422.0	−89.0	7,813.2	7,813.2	3.6	29,458
1997	5,529.3	1,390.5	1,487.9	−89.4	8,318.4	8,159.5	4.4	30,470
1998	5,856.0	1,538.8	1,538.5	−151.7	8,781.5	8,508.9	4.3	31,486
1999	6,250.2	1,636.7	1,632.5	−250.9	9,268.6	8,856.5	4.1	32,478
2000	6,728.4	1,767.5	1,741.0	−364.0	9,872.9	9,224.0	4.1	32,776
2001	7,064.5	1,633.9	1,839.5	−329.8	10,208.1	9,333.8	1.2	32,774

Source: www.economagic.com.

	GDP Deflator		Consumer Price Index		SECTION 2
Year	Index (1996 = 100)	Annual Percentage Change	Index (1982–84 = 100)	Percentage Change	**Prices and Inflation**
1960	22.2	1.4	29.6	1.0	
1961	22.4	1.1	29.9	1.1	
1962	22.7	1.4	30.3	1.2	
1963	23.0	1.1	30.6	1.2	
1964	23.3	1.5	31.0	1.3	
1965	23.8	1.9	31.5	1.6	
1966	24.5	2.9	32.5	3.0	
1967	25.2	3.1	33.4	2.8	
1968	26.3	4.3	34.8	4.3	
1969	27.6	4.9	36.7	5.5	
1970	29.1	5.3	38.8	5.8	
1971	30.5	5.0	40.5	4.3	
1972	31.8	4.3	41.8	3.3	
1973	33.6	5.6	44.4	6.2	
1974	36.6	9.0	49.3	11.1	
1975	40.0	9.3	53.8	9.1	
1976	42.3	5.7	56.9	5.7	
1977	45.0	6.4	60.6	6.5	
1978	48.2	7.1	65.2	7.6	
1979	52.2	8.4	72.6	11.3	
1980	57.0	9.2	82.4	13.5	
1981	62.4	9.3	90.9	10.3	
1982	66.3	6.2	96.5	6.1	
1983	68.9	3.9	99.6	3.2	
1984	71.4	3.7	103.9	4.3	
1985	73.7	3.2	107.6	3.5	
1986	75.3	2.2	109.6	1.9	
1987	77.6	3.0	113.6	3.7	
1988	80.2	3.4	118.3	4.1	
1989	83.3	3.8	124.0	4.8	
1990	86.5	3.9	130.7	5.4	
1991	89.7	3.6	136.2	4.2	
1992	91.8	2.4	140.3	3.0	
1993	94.0	2.4	144.5	3.0	
1994	96.0	2.1	148.2	2.6	
1995	98.1	2.2	152.4	2.8	
1996	100.0	1.9	156.9	2.9	
1997	101.9	1.9	160.5	2.3	
1998	103.2	1.2	163.0	1.6	
1999	104.7	1.4	166.6	2.2	
2000	107.0	2.2	172.2	3.4	
2001	109.4	2.2	177.1	2.8	

Source: www.economagic.com.

SECTION 3
Population and
Employment

	POPULATION AND LABOR FORCE			
YEAR	CIVILIAN NONINSTITUTIONAL POPULATION AGE 16+ (MILLIONS)	CIVILIAN LABOR FORCE (MILLIONS)	CIVILIAN LABOR FORCE PARTICIPATION RATE (PERCENT)	CIVILIAN EMPLOYMENT/ POPULATION RATIO (PERCENT)
1959	115.3	68.4	59.3	56.0
1960	117.2	69.6	59.4	56.1
1961	118.8	70.5	59.3	55.4
1962	120.2	70.6	58.8	55.5
1963	122.4	71.8	58.7	55.4
1964	124.5	73.1	58.7	55.7
1965	126.5	74.5	58.9	56.2
1966	128.1	75.8	59.2	56.9
1967	129.9	77.3	59.6	57.3
1968	132.0	78.7	59.6	57.5
1969	134.3	80.7	60.1	58.0
1970	137.1	82.8	60.4	57.4
1971	140.2	84.4	60.2	56.6
1972	144.1	87.0	60.4	57.0
1973	147.1	89.4	60.8	57.8
1974	150.1	91.9	61.3	57.8
1975	153.2	93.8	61.2	56.1
1976	156.2	96.2	61.6	56.8
1977	159.0	99.0	62.3	57.9
1978	161.9	102.3	63.2	59.3
1979	164.9	105.0	63.7	59.9
1980	167.7	106.9	63.8	59.2
1981	170.1	108.7	63.9	59.0
1982	172.3	110.2	64.0	57.8
1983	174.2	111.6	64.0	57.9
1984	176.4	113.5	64.4	59.5
1985	178.2	115.5	64.8	60.1
1986	180.6	117.8	65.3	60.7
1987	182.8	119.9	65.6	61.5
1988	184.6	121.7	65.9	62.3
1989	186.4	123.9	66.5	63.0
1990	189.2	125.8	66.5	62.8
1991	190.9	126.3	66.2	61.7
1992	192.8	128.1	66.4	61.5
1993	194.8	129.2	66.3	61.7
1994	196.8	131.1	66.6	62.5
1995	198.6	132.3	66.6	62.9
1996	200.6	133.9	66.8	63.2
1997	203.1	136.3	67.1	63.8
1998	205.2	137.7	67.1	64.1
1999	207.8	139.4	67.1	64.3
2000	209.7	140.9	67.2	64.5
2001	211.9	141.8	66.9	63.8

Source: www.bls.gov.

	UNEMPLOYMENT RATES			
YEAR	ALL WORKERS	BOTH SEXES, AGE 16 TO 19	MEN AGE 20+	WOMEN AGE 20+
1959	5.5	14.6	4.7	5.2
1960	5.5	14.7	4.7	5.1
1961	6.7	16.8	5.7	6.3
1962	5.5	14.7	4.6	5.4
1963	5.7	17.2	4.5	5.4
1964	5.2	16.2	3.9	5.2
1965	4.5	14.8	3.2	4.5
1966	3.8	12.8	2.5	3.8
1967	3.8	12.9	2.3	4.2
1968	3.6	12.7	2.2	3.8
1969	3.5	12.2	2.1	3.7
1970	4.9	15.3	3.5	4.8
1971	5.9	16.9	4.4	5.7
1972	5.6	16.2	4.0	5.4
1973	4.9	14.5	3.3	4.9
1974	5.6	16.0	3.8	5.5
1975	8.5	19.9	6.8	8.0
1976	7.7	19.0	5.9	7.4
1977	7.1	17.8	5.2	7.0
1978	6.1	16.4	4.3	6.0
1979	5.8	16.1	4.2	5.7
1980	7.1	17.8	5.9	6.4
1981	7.6	19.6	6.3	6.8
1982	9.7	23.2	8.8	8.3
1983	9.6	22.4	8.9	8.1
1984	7.5	18.9	6.6	6.8
1985	7.2	18.6	6.2	6.6
1986	7.0	18.3	6.1	6.2
1987	6.2	16.9	5.4	5.4
1988	5.5	15.3	4.8	4.9
1989	5.3	15.0	4.5	4.7
1990	5.6	15.5	5.0	4.9
1991	6.8	18.7	6.4	5.7
1992	7.5	20.1	7.1	6.3
1993	6.9	19.0	6.4	5.9
1994	6.1	17.6	5.4	5.4
1995	5.6	17.3	4.8	4.9
1996	5.4	16.7	4.6	4.8
1997	4.9	16.0	4.2	4.4
1998	4.5	14.6	3.7	4.1
1999	4.2	13.9	3.5	3.8
2000	4.0	13.1	3.3	3.6
2001	4.8	14.7	4.2	4.1

**SECTION 3 (continued)
Population and
Employment**

Source: www.bls.gov.

SECTION 4
Money Supply, Interest Rates, and Federal Finances

	MONEY SUPPLY					FEDERAL BUDGET			NATIONAL DEBT[1]	
YEAR	M1 (BILLIONS)	ANNUAL CHANGE (PERCENT)	M2 (BILLIONS)	ANNUAL CHANGE (PERCENT)	AAA BONDS (PERCENT)	FISCAL YEAR OUTLAYS (BILLIONS)	FISCAL YEAR RECEIPTS (BILLIONS)	SURPLUS/ DEFICIT (BILLIONS)	BILLIONS OF DOLLARS	PERCENT OF GDP
1960	$ 140.3	0.0	$ 304.3	3.8	4.4	$ 92.2	$ 92.5	$ 0.3	$ 206	39.1%
1961	143.1	2.0	324.8	6.7	4.4	97.7	94.4	(3.3)	212.2	38.9%
1962	146.5	2.4	350.1	7.8	4.3	106.8	99.7	(7.1)	216.3	36.9%
1963	150.9	3.0	379.6	8.4	4.3	111.3	106.6	(4.7)	217.3	35.1%
1964	156.8	3.9	409.4	7.9	4.4	118.5	112.6	(5.9)	218.5	32.9%
1965	163.5	4.3	442.5	8.1	4.5	118.2	116.8	(1.4)	216.3	30.0%
1966	171.0	4.6	471.4	6.5	5.1	134.5	130.8	(3.7)	213.2	27.0%
1967	177.7	3.9	503.6	6.8	5.5	157.5	148.8	(8.7)	221.2	26.5%
1968	190.1	7.0	545.3	8.3	6.2	178.1	153.0	(25.1)	224.7	24.7%
1969	201.4	5.9	578.7	6.1	7.0	183.6	186.9	3.3	221.1	22.4%
1970	209.1	3.8	601.4	3.9	8.0	195.6	192.8	(2.8)	229.1	22.0%
1971	223.2	6.7	674.4	12.1	7.4	210.2	187.1	(23.1)	247	21.9%
1972	239.1	7.1	758.1	12.4	7.2	230.7	207.3	(23.4)	261.7	21.1%
1973	256.3	7.2	831.8	9.7	7.4	245.7	230.8	(14.9)	260.9	18.8%
1974	269.2	5.0	880.7	5.9	8.6	269.4	263.2	(6.2)	271	18.1%
1975	281.4	4.5	963.7	9.4	8.8	332.3	279.1	(53.2)	349.4	21.4%
1976	297.2	5.6	1,086.6	12.8	8.4	371.8	298.1	(73.7)	409.5	22.5%
1977	320.0	7.7	1,221.4	12.4	8.0	409.2	355.6	(53.6)	461.3	22.7%
1978	346.3	8.2	1,322.4	8.3	8.7	458.7	399.6	(59.1)	508.6	22.2%
1979	372.7	7.6	1,425.8	7.8	9.6	504.0	463.3	(40.7)	540.5	21.1%
1980	395.7	6.2	1,540.4	8.0	11.9	590.9	517.1	(73.8)	616.4	22.0%
1981	424.9	7.4	1,679.6	9.0	14.2	678.2	599.3	(78.9)	694.5	22.2%
1982	453.0	6.6	1,833.4	9.2	13.8	745.8	617.8	(128.0)	848.4	26.0%
1983	503.2	11.1	2,057.9	12.2	12.0	808.4	600.6	(207.8)	1,022.6	28.9%
1984	538.6	7.1	2,222.5	8.0	12.7	851.9	666.5	(185.4)	1,212.5	30.8%
1985	586.9	9.0	2,420.1	8.9	11.4	946.4	734.1	(212.3)	1,417.2	33.6%
1986	666.3	13.5	2,616.8	8.1	9.0	990.5	769.2	(221.3)	1,602	36.0%
1987	743.4	11.6	2,786.8	6.5	9.4	1,004.1	854.4	(149.7)	1,731.4	36.5%
1988	774.8	4.2	2,937.0	5.4	9.7	1,064.5	909.3	(155.2)	1,858.5	36.4%
1989	782.2	1.0	3,060.3	4.2	9.3	1,143.7	991.2	(152.5)	2,017.4	36.8%
1990	810.6	3.6	3,228.1	5.5	9.3	1,253.2	1,032.0	(221.2)	2,305.3	39.7%
1991	859.0	6.0	3,348.4	3.7	8.8	1,324.4	1,055.0	(269.4)	2,578.5	43.1%
1992	965.9	12.4	3,411.4	1.9	8.1	1,381.7	1,091.3	(290.4)	2,847.3	45.1%
1993	1,078.5	11.7	3,448.5	1.1	7.2	1,409.5	1,154.4	(255.1)	3,059.6	46.1%
1994	1,145.0	6.2	3,495.0	1.3	8.0	1,461.9	1,258.6	(203.3)	3,177.6	45.0%
1995	1,142.6	−0.2	3,566.1	2.0	7.6	1,515.8	1,351.8	(164.0)	3,307.7	44.7%
1996	1,105.8	−3.2	3,736.7	4.8	7.4	1,560.6	1,453.1	(107.5)	3,431.2	43.9%
1997	1,069.2	−3.3	3,919.8	4.9	7.3	1,601.3	1,579.3	(22.0)	3,414.6	41.0%
1998	1,079.8	1.0	4,206.6	7.3	6.5	1,652.6	1,721.8	69.2	3,334	38.0%
1999	1,101.8	2.0	4,525.6	7.6	7.0	1,702.9	1,827.5	124.6	3,233.9	34.9%
2000	1,104.0	0.2	4,801.0	6.1	7.6	1,788.8	2,025.2	236.4	2,880.4	29.2%
2001	1,137.4	3.0	5,219.4	8.7	7.1	1,856.2	2,136.9	280.7	2,722.6	26.7%

[1]National debt is debt held by private investors at year end. The 2001 figure is based on June 2001 data.
Source: www.economagic.com and www.whitehouse.gov/omb/.

			PURCHASES OF GOODS AND SERVICES (% OF GDP)	NON-DEFENSE PURCHASES OF GOODS AND SERVICES (% OF GDP)	TRANSFER PAYMENTS TO PERSONS (% OF GDP)
YEAR	EXPENDITURES (% OF GDP)	REVENUES (% OF GDP)			
1960	22.7%	24.9%	21.6%	11.1%	4.6%
1961	23.7%	24.9%	22.3%	11.6%	5.2%
1962	23.8%	25.1%	22.5%	11.8%	4.9%
1963	23.8%	25.5%	22.4%	12.3%	4.9%
1964	23.3%	24.4%	21.8%	12.5%	4.7%
1965	23.0%	24.4%	21.3%	12.7%	4.7%
1966	23.7%	25.1%	22.1%	12.7%	4.8%
1967	25.6%	25.4%	23.4%	13.1%	5.4%
1968	26.2%	26.9%	23.3%	13.2%	5.8%
1969	26.3%	28.0%	22.8%	13.4%	6.0%
1970	27.6%	26.9%	22.8%	14.1%	6.9%
1971	28.0%	26.2%	22.2%	14.4%	7.5%
1972	27.8%	27.3%	21.8%	14.2%	7.6%
1973	27.1%	27.4%	20.8%	14.0%	7.8%
1974	28.3%	28.0%	21.5%	14.8%	8.6%
1975	30.4%	26.3%	22.1%	15.5%	10.0%
1976	29.5%	27.0%	21.1%	14.9%	9.7%
1977	28.8%	27.2%	20.4%	14.4%	9.3%
1978	27.6%	27.3%	19.8%	14.1%	8.8%
1979	27.3%	27.4%	19.6%	13.9%	8.8%
1980	29.0%	27.4%	20.4%	14.3%	9.7%
1981	29.5%	28.0%	20.2%	13.8%	9.8%
1982	31.5%	27.3%	21.0%	14.0%	10.5%
1983	31.5%	26.7%	20.8%	13.7%	10.4%
1984	30.3%	26.6%	20.4%	13.2%	9.6%
1985	30.6%	27.0%	20.8%	13.4%	9.6%
1986	30.9%	27.1%	21.2%	13.7%	9.6%
1987	30.7%	27.9%	21.0%	13.6%	9.4%
1988	30.0%	27.6%	20.3%	13.3%	9.3%
1989	29.9%	27.9%	20.0%	13.4%	9.5%
1990	30.6%	27.7%	20.4%	13.9%	9.9%
1991	31.4%	27.7%	20.6%	14.2%	10.8%
1992	32.4%	27.6%	20.1%	14.1%	11.5%
1993	32.1%	28.0%	19.5%	14.0%	11.7%
1994	31.1%	28.3%	18.8%	13.8%	11.5%
1995	31.0%	28.6%	18.5%	13.8%	11.6%
1996	30.5%	29.0%	18.2%	13.6%	11.5%
1997	29.6%	29.3%	17.9%	13.6%	11.2%
1998	28.8%	29.8%	17.5%	13.5%	10.9%
1999	28.3%	30.1%	17.6%	13.7%	10.7%
2000	28.1%	30.6%	17.6%	13.8%	10.5%
2001	28.5%	29.9%	18.0%	14.1%	11.0%

FEDERAL, STATE, AND LOCAL GOVERNMENT[1]

SECTION 5
Size of Government as a Share of GDP, 1960–2001

[1]There are some differences across reporting agencies with regard to accounting procedures and the treatment of government enterprises. This results in some differences in statistical measures of the size of government.

Source: www.bea.doc.gov.

SECTION 6
Share of Federal Income
Taxes Paid by Income
Groupings

FEDERAL INCOME TAX SHARE BY PERCENTILES

YEAR	TOP 1%	TOP 5%	TOP 10%	NEXT 40%	BOTTOM 50%
1980	19.1%	36.8%	49.3%	43.7%	7.0%
1981	17.6%	35.1%	48.0%	44.6%	7.5%
1982	19.0%	36.1%	48.6%	44.1%	7.3%
1983	20.3%	37.3%	49.7%	43.1%	7.2%
1984	21.1%	38.0%	50.6%	42.1%	7.4%
1985	21.8%	38.8%	51.5%	41.4%	7.2%
1986	25.7%	42.6%	54.7%	38.9%	6.5%
1987	24.8%	43.3%	55.6%	38.3%	6.1%
1988	27.6%	45.6%	57.3%	37.0%	5.7%
1989	25.2%	43.9%	55.8%	38.4%	5.8%
1990	25.1%	43.6%	55.4%	38.8%	5.8%
1991	24.8%	43.4%	55.8%	38.7%	5.5%
1992	27.5%	45.9%	58.0%	36.9%	5.1%
1993	29.0%	47.4%	59.2%	36.0%	4.8%
1994	28.9%	47.5%	59.4%	35.8%	4.8%
1995	30.3%	48.9%	60.7%	34.6%	4.6%
1996	32.3%	51.0%	62.5%	33.2%	4.3%
1997	33.2%	51.9%	63.2%	32.5%	4.3%
1998	34.8%	53.8%	65.0%	30.8%	4.2%
1999	36.2%	55.5%	66.5%	29.5%	4.0%

Source: Internal Revenue Service.

SECTION 7
Basic Economic Data for 58 Countries

	POPULATION (MILLIONS) 1999	GDP PER CAPITA (PPP) 1999	AVG ANNUAL GROWTH OF GDP PER CAP (REAL 1996$) 1990–1999	INFLATION—GDP DEFLATOR, AVG ANNUAL COMPOUNDING 1990–1999	INVESTMENT (AS A % OF GDP) 1990–99
HIGH-INCOME COUNTRIES					
Australia	19.0	24,574	2.2%	1.5%	22.6
Austria	8.1	25,089	1.7%	2.4%	24.1
Belgium	10.2	25,443	1.6%	2.3%	21.0
Canada	30.5	26,251	1.2%	1.6%	19.0
Denmark	5.3	25,869	1.7%	2.3%	19.1
Finland	5.2	23,096	1.2%	2.2%	19.4
France	58.6	22,897	1.3%	1.8%	19.7
Germany	82.1	23,742	1.1%[1]	1.7%[1]	22.6
Hong Kong, China	6.7	22,090	2.0%	5.1%	29.8
Italy	57.6	22,172	1.2%	4.4%	19.8
Japan	126.6	24,898	1.4%	0.5%	29.4
Netherlands	15.8	24,215	2.2%	2.0%	21.9
Singapore	4.0	20,767	4.6%	1.8%	35.6
Spain	39.4	18,079	2.3%	4.5%	23.3
Sweden	8.9	22,636	1.0%	3.0%	17.4
Switzerland	7.1	27,171	0.2%	1.9%	22.3
United Kingdom	59.5	22,093	1.6%	3.7%	17.2
United States	278.2	31,872	1.7%	2.3%	18.0
AFRICA					
Botswana	1.6	6,872	2.1%	9.0%	26.0
Cameroon	14.7	1,573	−2.4%	4.1%	16.5
Cote d'Ivoire	15.5	1,654	−0.3%	5.3%	11.9
Ghana	18.8	1,881	1.5%	25.3%	20.3
Kenya	29.4	1,022	−0.4%	13.5%	16.3
Mauritius	1.2	9,107	4.0%	6.8%	28.3
Nigeria	123.9	853	0.2%	26.7%	20.3
South Africa	42.1	8,908	−0.8%	10.9%	14.8
Tanzania	32.9	501	0.3%	22.3%	21.4
Zambia	9.9	756	−2.4%	63.0%	14.1
ASIA AND THE PACIFIC					
Bangladesh	127.7	1,484	3.1%	4.3%	19.1
China	1,253.6	3,618	8.5%	6.7%	38.4
India	997.5	2,248	3.7%	8.8%	23.3
Indonesia	207.0	2,857	2.8%	14.8%	29.7,
Malaysia	22.7	8,209	4.4%	3.7%	36.3
Pakistan	134.8	1,834	1.5%	9.9%	18.6
Philippines	74.3	3,805	0.4%	9.5%	22.4
South Korea	46.9	15,712	5.1%	6.0%	34.4
Taiwan	22.1	14,972	5.5%	2.3%	23.5
Thailand	60.2	6,132	4.0%	4.5%	36.2

(continued)

[1]Germany's GDP growth and inflation calculations are based on data following unification (1991).

SECTION 7 (continued)
Basic Economic Data for 58 Countries

	POPULATION (MILLIONS) 1999	GDP PER CAPITA (PPP) 1999	AVG ANNUAL GROWTH OF GDP PER CAP (REAL 1996$) 1990–1999	INFLATION—GDP DEFLATOR, AVG ANNUAL COMPOUNDING 1990–1999	INVESTMENT (AS A % OF GDP) 1990–99
SOUTH/CENTRAL AMERICA					
Argentina	36.6	12,277	3.0%	49.7%	17.8
Brazil	168.0	7,037	0.3%	320.8%	20.8
Chile	15.0	8,652	4.7%	9.7%	25.0
Colombia	41.5	5,749	0.8%	22.5%	19.9,
Dominican Republic	8.4	5,507	2.6%	15.5%	22.4
Guatemala	11.1	3,674	1.4%	14.4%	15.6
Mexico	96.6	8,297	1.6%	19.8%	22.9
Peru	25.2	4,622	1.4%	108.5%	21.2
Venezuela	23.7	5,495	−0.1%	41.9%	17.8
MIDDLE EAST/MEDITERRANEAN					
Egypt	62.7	3,420	2.4%	9.8%	19.6
Greece	10.5	15,414	1.6%	10.8%	20.9
Iran	63.0	5,531	2.9%	25.2%	26.6
Israel	6.1	18,440	2.1%	11.3%	23.7
Syria	15.7	4,454	3.0%	9.4%	25.4
Turkey	64.4	6,380	2.0%	72.8%	24.3
EASTERN EUROPE					
Bulgaria	8.2	5,071	−2.7%	95.5%	16.2
Hungary	10.1	11,430	0.3%	21.0%	24.1
Poland	38.7	8,450	3.5%	25.4%	21.0
Romania	22.5	6,041	−2.5%	96.6%	25.5
Russia	146.2	7,473	−5.3%	159.3%	25.8

Sources: World Bank, World Development Index, 2001; *International Monetary Fund,* International financial Statistics Yearbook, 2001; and Statistical Yearbook of the Republic of China, 2000.

APPENDIX B

Answers to Selected Critical Analysis Questions

CHAPTER 1: THE ECONOMIC APPROACH

2. Production of scarce goods always involves a cost; there are no free lunches. When the government provides goods without charge to consumers, other citizens (taxpayers) will bear the cost of their provision. Thus, provision by the government affects how the costs will be covered, not whether they are incurred.

4. For most taxpayers, the change will reduce the after-tax cost of raising children. Other things constant, one would predict an increase in the birthrate.

5. False. Intentions do not change the impact of the policy. If the policy runs counter to sound economics, it will lead to a counterproductive outcome, even if that was not the intention of the policy. Bad policies are often advocated by people with good intentions.

7. Raising the price of new cars by requiring safety devices, which customers would not have purchased if given the choice, slows the rate of sales for new cars. Thus the older, less safe cars are driven longer, partially offsetting the safety advantage provided by the newer, safer cars. Also, drivers act a bit differently—they may take more risks—when they believe the safety devices will provide protection should they have an unexpected accident. In fact, economist Gordon Tullock says that the greatest safety device of all might be a dagger built into the center of the steering wheel, pointed directly at the driver's chest!

8. Money has nothing to do with whether an individual is economizing. Any time a person chooses, in an attempt to achieve a goal, he or she is economizing.

9. Positive economics can help one better understand the likely effects of alternative policies. This will help one choose alternatives that are less likely to lead to disappointing results.

10. Association is not causation. It is likely that a large lead, near the end of the game, caused the third team to play more, rather than the third team causing the lead.

CHAPTER 2: SOME TOOLS OF THE ECONOMIST

2. This is an opportunity cost question. Even though the productivity of painters has changed only slightly, rising productivity in other areas has led to higher wages in other occupations, thereby increasing the opportunity cost of being a house painter. Since people would not supply house painting services unless they were able to meet their opportunity costs, higher wages are necessary to attract house painters from competitive (alternative) lines of work.

4. The statement reflects the "exchange is a zero sum game" view. This view is false. No private business can force customers to buy. Neither can a customer force a business to sell. Unless both buyer and seller believe the exchange is in their interest, they will not enter into the exchange. Mutual gain provides the foundation for voluntary exchange.

8. Yes. This question highlights the incentive of individuals to conserve for the future when they have private ownership rights. The market value of the land will increase in anticipation of the future harvest, as the trees grow and the expected day of harvest moves closer. Thus, with transferable private property, the tree farmer will be able to capture the value added by his planting and holding the trees for a few years, even if the actual harvest does not take place until well after his death.

9. In general, it sanctions all forms of competition except for the use of violence (or the threat of violence), theft, or fraud.

11. If the food from land, now and in the future, is worth more than the housing services from the same land, then developers will not be able to bid the land away from farmers. However, comparative advantage determines the efficient use of a resource; thus, even the best farmland, if situated in the right location, may be far more valuable for buildings. Other, poorer land can always be made more productive by the use of different (and more costly) farming techniques, irrigation, fertilizer, and so on. Physical characteristics alone do not determine the value or the most valuable use of a resource, including land.

12. Those who get tickets at the lower price gain, while those who are prevented from offering a higher price to ticket holders may not get a ticket even though both the buyer and some ticket holders would have gained from the exchange at the higher price. Ticket holders may simply break the law, or may sell at the regulated price only to buyers willing to provide them with other favors. Price controls, if they are effective, always reduce the gains from trade.

17. The opportunity cost of those individuals will rise and they will likely consume less leisure.

CHAPTER 3: SUPPLY, DEMAND, AND THE MARKET PROCESS

1. Choices a and b would increase the demand for beef; c and d would affect primarily the supply of beef, rather than the demand; e leads to a change in quantity demanded, not a change in demand.

4. a. Reductions in the supply of feed grains and hay led to sharply higher prices. b. The higher feed grain and hay prices increased the cost of maintaining a cattle herd and thereby caused many producers to sell (an increase in current supply), depressing cattle prices in 1998. c. The reduction in the size of cattle herds led to a smaller future supply and higher cattle prices in 1989.

8. True. "Somebody" must decide who will be the business winners and losers. Neither markets nor the political process leaves the determination of winners and losers to chance. Under market organization, business winners and losers are determined by the decentralized choices of millions of consumers who use their dollar votes to reward firms that provide preferred goods at a low cost and penalize others who fail to do so. Under political decision making, the winners and losers are determined by political officials who use taxes, subsidies, regulations, and mandates to favor some businesses and penalize others.

10. a. Profitable production increases the value of resources owned by people and leads to mutual gain for resource suppliers, consumers, and entrepreneurs. b. Losses reduce the value of resources, which reduces the well-being of at least some people. There is no conflict.

CHAPTER 4: SUPPLY AND DEMAND: APPLICATIONS AND EXTENSIONS

4. Agreement of both buyer and seller is required for an exchange. Price ceilings push prices below equilibrium and thereby reduce the quantity sellers are willing to offer. Price floors push prices above equilibrium and thereby reduce the quantity consumers wish to buy. Both decrease the actual quantity traded in the market.

6. a. Decreases; b. Increases; c. Decreases; d. Increases.

11. The deadweight loss is the loss of the potential gains of buyers and sellers emanating from trades that are squeezed out by the tax. It is an excess burden because even though the exchanges that are squeezed out by the tax impose a cost on buyers and sellers, they do not generate tax revenue (since the trades do not take place).

14. The employment level of low-skill workers with large families would decline. Some would attempt to conceal the presence of their large family in order to get a job.

CHAPTER 5: THE ECONOMIC ROLE OF GOVERNMENT

1. When payment is not demanded for services, potential customers have a strong incentive to attempt a "free ride." However, when the number of nonpaying customers becomes such that the sales revenues of sellers are diminished (and in some cases eliminated), the sellers' incentive to supply the good is thereby reduced (or eliminated).

4. The anti-missile system is a public good for the residents of Washington, D.C. Strictly speaking, none of the other items is a public good since each could be provided to some consumers (paying customers, for example) without being provided to others.

9. By reducing output below the efficient level, there would be some units of the good no longer produced and exchanged, despite the fact that consumers' value of these marginal units exceeded the marginal cost of production. This would violate economic efficiency.

11. A public good reflects the characteristics of the good, not the sector in which it is provided. Elementary education is generally not considered a public good because it is relatively easy to exclude nonpaying customers and establish a one-to-one link between payment for and receipt of the good.

14. A government intervention would be efficient if the benefits from the intervention exceeded the cost of the intervention. All opportunity costs (tax money required, resources utilized, deadweight losses, etc.) would need to be considered in the comparison. A government intervention would be considered inefficient if the costs exceeded the benefits.

CHAPTER 6: THE ECONOMICS OF COLLECTIVE DECISION MAKING

2. Corporate officers, while they surely care about the next few months and the profits during that time, care also about the value of the firm and its stock price. If the stock price rises sufficiently in the next few months—as it will if investors believe that current investments in future-oriented projects (planting new trees, for example) are sound—then the officers will find their jobs secure even if current profits do not look good. Rights to the profits from those (future) trees are salable now in the form of the corporation's stock. There is no such mechanism to make the distant fruits of today's investments available to the political entrepreneurs who might otherwise fight for the future-oriented project. Only if the project appeals to today's voters, and they are willing to pay today for tomorrow's benefits, will the program be a political success. In any case, the wealth of the political entrepreneur is not directly enhanced by his or her successful fight for the project.

5. The invisible hand principle is present only when the self-interest of individuals is consistent with the general welfare. Both the special interest effect and the short-sightedness effect indicate that this will not always be the case, even when political choices are made democratically.

6. True. Since each individual computer customer both decides the issue (what computer, if any, will be purchased) and bears the consequences of a mistaken choice; each has a strong incentive to acquire information needed to make a wise choice. In contrast, each voter recognizes that one vote, even if mistaken, will not decide the congressional election. Thus, each has little incentive to search for information to make a better choice.

8. It is difficult for the voter to know what a candidate will do once elected, and the rationally ignorant voter is usually unwilling to spend the time and effort required to understand issues because the probability that any single vote will decide the issue is exceedingly small. Special interest voters, on the other hand, will know which candidate has promised them the most on their issue. Also, the candidate who is both competent and prepared to ignore special interests will have a hard time getting these facts to voters without financial support from special interest groups. Each voter has an incentive to be a "free rider" on the "good government" issue. Controlling government on behalf of society as a whole is a public good, requiring much private activity. Like other public goods, it tends to be underproduced.

10. No. The government is merely an alternative form of organization. Government organization does not permit us to escape either scarcity or competition. It merely affects the nature of the competition. Political competition (voting, lobbying, political contributions, taxes, and politically determined budgets) replaces market competition. Neither is there any reason to believe that government organization modifies the importance of personal self-interest.

11. When the welfare of a special interest group conflicts with that of a widely dispersed, unorganized majority, the legislative political process can reasonably be expected to work to the benefit of the special interest.

CHAPTER 7: TAKING THE NATION'S ECONOMIC PULSE

1. a, c, f, g, and h will exert no impact on GDP; b and d will increase GDP by the amount of the expenditure; and e will increase GDP by $250 (the commission on the transaction).

3. Since the furniture was produced last year, the sale does not affect GDP this year. It reduces inventory investment by $100,000 and increases consumption by $100,000, leaving GDP unchanged.

5. The reliability of GDP comparisons over long periods of time is reduced because the leisure and human costs may change substantially between the two years, and because the types of goods available for consumption during the two years may be vastly different. Likewise, GDP may not be a good index of output differences between countries (for example, the United States and Mexico) for the same reasons. In addition, there may be substantial differences between countries in the production of (a) economic "bads," (b) goods in the household sector, and (c) the size of the underground economy.

7. $7.71

9. a. $1,000; b. $600; c. $200; d. 0; e. $10,000

11. a. False. Inventory investment indicates whether the holdings of unsold goods are rising or falling. A negative inventory investment (economists refer to this as disinvestment) means that inventories were drawn down during the period. b. False. If gross investment is less than the depreciation of capital goods during the period, net investment would be negative. Net investment in the United States was negative for several years during the Great Depression of the 1930s. c. Not necessarily. Rather, it may be the result of an increase in prices, population, or hours worked.

12. Neither the receipts nor the expenditures on payouts would count toward GDP because they are merely transfers—they do not involve production. However, expenditures on operations, administration, and government-provided goods and services from lottery proceeds would add to GDP.

14. a. 0; b. 0; c. $500; d. $300; e. $300; f. 0; g. 0; h. 0

17. a. $2375.7 billion; b. $3572.9 billion; c. 57.0 d. $5803.2 billion; e. 91.8 f. $7813.2 billion; g. $9320.0 billion.

CHAPTER 8: ECONOMIC FLUCTUATIONS, UNEMPLOYMENT, AND INFLATION

2. Job seekers do not know which employers will offer them the more attractive jobs. They find out by searching. Job search is "profitable" and consistent with economic efficiency as long as the marginal gain from search exceeds the marginal cost of searching.

7. When the actual unemployment rate is equal to the natural rate of unemployment, cyclical unemployment is absent and potential GDP is at its sustainable rate. When the actual unemployment rate is greater (less) than the natural rate of unemployment, cyclical unemployment is positive (negative) and potential GDP is less (greater) than its sustainable rate.

8. a. 60 percent; b. 8.3 percent; c. 55 percent.

9. No. It means that there were now jobs available at wage rates acceptable to the potential workers who were unemployed. Thus, they continued to search for more attractive opportunities.

11. a. $646,552; $925,926; $581,395; $417,537; $400,000 b. 1940; c. The real salary rose because the price level between 1920 and 1940 declined.

13. Each will encourage additional search.

14. The wages people earn are also prices (prices for labor services) and, like other prices, they usually rise as the general level of prices increases. The statement ignores this factor. It implicitly assumes that money wages are unaffected by inflation—that they would have increased by the same amount (6 percent) even if prices would have been stable. Generally, this will not be the case.

CHAPTER 9: AN INTRODUCTION TO BASIC MACROECONOMIC MARKETS

4. If the inflation rate unexpectedly falls from 3 percent to zero, the real wages of union members will rise. If other unions have similar contracts, the unemployment rate will increase because employment costs have risen relative to product prices. Profit margins will be cut and producers will respond by reducing output and laying off workers. In contrast, if the inflation rate rises to 8 percent, profit margins will improve, producers will expand their output, and the unemployment rate will decline.

10. They are all equal.

12. $10,000; $20,000

13. Inversely; an increase in interest rates is the same thing as a reduction in bond prices.

CHAPTER 10: WORKING WITH OUR BASIC AGGREGATE DEMAND/AGGREGATE SUPPLY MODEL

1. Choice a would decrease *AD*; b, c, and d would increase it; and e would leave it unchanged. For the "why" part of the question, see the Factors That Shift Aggregate Demand section at the beginning of the chapter.

2. a, b, c, and d will reduce *SRAS*; e will increase it.

4. When an economy is operating at less than full employment, weak demand in resource markets will tend to reduce (a) the real rate of interest and (b) resource prices relative to product prices and thereby restore normal profit and the incentive of firms to produce the long-run potential output level. If resource prices and the real interest rate were inflexible downward, the self-correcting mechanism would not work.

6. At the lower than expected inflation rate, *real wages* (and costs) will increase relative to product prices. This will squeeze profit margins and lead to reductions in output and employment, causing the unemployment rate to rise.

8. Tightness in resource markets will result in rising resource prices relative to product prices, causing the *SRAS* to shift to the left. Profit margins will decline, output rate will fall, and long-run equilibrium will be restored at a higher price level. The above-normal output cannot be maintained because it reflects input prices that people would not have agreed to and output decisions they would not have chosen if they had anticipated the current price level (and rate of inflation). Once they have a chance to correct these mistakes, they do so; and output returns to the economy's long-run potential.

9. Real wages will tend to increase more rapidly when the unemployment rate is low because a tight labor market (strong demand) will place upward pressure on wages.

12. The increase in demand for exports will increase aggregate demand. In the short run, this unanticipated expansion in demand will tend to increase output and employment, while exerting modest upward pressure on the price level. In the long run, the primary impact will be a higher price level, with no change in output and employment.

18. The assets destroyed (World Trade Center, a portion of the Pentagon, etc.) by the attack reduced the productive assets of the United States and thereby adversely affected potential real output. However, these assets were a relatively small share, less than .01 percent, of U.S. capital assets. Thus, the direct impact on potential output was small. But there were also indirect effects such as increased expenditures on national defense and domestic security. The opportunity cost of these indirect effects reduced the future potential output of *consumer* goods and thereby adversely affected the future living standard of Americans. These indirect effects may well be larger than the impact of the assets destroyed.

CHAPTER 11: KEYNESIAN FOUNDATIONS OF MODERN MACROECONOMICS

2. a. Increase current consumption, as the expectation of rising future prices will induce consumers to buy now. b. Decrease current consumption, as people will attempt to save more for hard times. c. Increase current consumption, as the result of an expansion in disposable income. d. May have little effect. However, the tendency will be toward a reduction in consumption, since households have an incentive to save more at the higher interest rate. e. Decrease consumption, as falling stock prices will reduce the wealth of consumers. f. Increase consumption, as the young typically have a higher marginal propensity to consume than the elderly. g. Increase consumption, as the poor typically have a higher marginal propensity to consume than the wealthy.

4. It is the concept that a change in one of the components of aggregate demand—investment, for example—will lead to a far greater change in the equilibrium level of income. Since the multiplier equals $1/(1 - MPC)$, its size is determined by the marginal propensity to consume. The multiplier makes stabilizing the economy more difficult, since relatively small changes in aggregate demand have a much greater impact on equilibrium income.

7. None. The Keynesian model assumes that wages and prices are inflexible downward. It will take an increase in aggregate expenditures to restore full employment.

12. You would expect the multiplier to be smaller in Canada because Canadians would be expected to spend a larger share of their additions to income on imports, rather than domestic goods. This will reduce the size of the multiplier.

CHAPTER 12: FISCAL POLICY

2. The crowding-out effect is the theory that budget deficits will lead to higher real interest rates, which retard private spending. The crowding-out effect indicates that fiscal policy would not be nearly so potent as the simple Keynesian model implies. The new classical theory indicates that anticipation of higher future taxes (rather than higher interest rates) will crowd out private spending when government expenditures are financed by debt.

4. Automatic stabilizers are built-in features (unemployment compensation, corporate profit tax, progressive income tax) that tend automatically to promote a budget deficit during a recession and a budget surplus (or smaller deficit) during an inflationary boom. Automatic stabilizers have the major advantage of providing needed restraint, or stimuli, without congressional approval—which, in turn, minimizes the problem of proper timing.

8. This statement depicts the views of many economists three decades ago. Today, most economists recognize that it is naive. Given our limited ability to accurately forecast future economic conditions, timing of fiscal policy is more difficult than was previously thought. Political considerations—remember, the government is merely an alternative form of social organization, not a corrective device—reduce the likelihood that fiscal policy will be used as a stabilization tool. Changes in interest rates and private spending may offset fiscal actions and thereby reduce the potency of fiscal policy. All factors considered, it is clear that the use of fiscal policy to stabilize the economy is both difficult and complex.

10. There is a major defect in this view. If the budget deficits stimulated demand and thereby output and employment, we would have expected the inflation rate to accelerate. This was not the case; in fact, the inflation rate declined. The failure of the inflation rate to accelerate during the expansion of the 1980s strongly suggests that factors other than demand stimulus were at work.

13. Yes. Only the lower rates would increase the incentive to earn marginal income and thereby stimulate aggregate supply.

CHAPTER 13: MONEY AND THE BANKING SYSTEM

1. A liquid asset is one that can easily and quickly be transformed into money without experiencing a loss of its market value. Assets such as high-grade bonds and stocks are highly liquid. In contrast, illiquid assets cannot be easily and quickly converted to cash without some loss of their value. Real estate, a family-owned business, business equipment, and artistic works are examples of illiquid assets.

3. Money is valuable because of its scarcity relative to the availability of goods and services. The use of money facilitates (reduces the cost of) exchange transactions. Money also serves as a store of value and a unit of account. Doubling the supply of money, holding output constant, would simply cause its purchasing power to fall without enhancing the services that it performs. In fact, fluctuations in the money supply would create uncertainty as to its future value and reduce the ability of money to serve as a store of value, accurate unit of account, and medium of exchange for time-dimension contracting.

6. a. No change; currency held by the public increases, but checking deposits decrease by an equal amount. b. Bank reserves decrease by $100. c. Excess reserves decrease by $100, minus $100 multiplied by the required reserve ratio.

8. Answers b, e, and f will reduce the money supply; a and c will increase it; if the Treasury's deposits (or the deposits of persons who receive portions of the Treasury's spending) are considered part of the money supply, then d will leave the money supply unchanged.

10. While the transformation of deposits into currency does not directly affect the money supply, it does reduce the excess reserves of banks. The reduction in excess reserves will cause banks to reduce their outstanding loans and thereby shrink the money supply. Therefore, an increase in the holding of currency relative to deposits will tend to reduce the supply of money.

12. There are two major reasons. First, the money supply can be altered quietly via open market operations, while a reserve requirement change focuses attention on Fed policy. Second, open market operations are a fine-tuning method, while a reserve requirement change is a blunt instrument. Generally, the Fed prefers quiet, marginal changes to headline-grabbing, blunt changes that are more likely to disrupt markets.

13. a. False; statements of this type often use money when they are really speaking about wealth (or income). b. False; the checking deposit also counts as money. In addition, the deposit increases the reserves of the receiving bank, and thereby places it in a position to extend additional loans that would increase the money supply. c. False; only an increase in the availability of goods and services valued by people will improve our standard of living. Without an additional supply of goods and services, more money will simply lead to a higher price level.

16. a. Money supply increases by $100,000; b. $80,000; c. $500,000; d. no; there will be some leakage in the form of additional currency holdings by the public and additional excess reserve holdings by banks.

18. a. Money supply will increase by $2 billion; b. $1.8 billion; c. $20 billion; d. approximately $10.5 billion; e. approximately $8.51 billion; the potential money multiplier was 10, but the actual multiplier was only 4.255; f. the leakages in the form of currency held by the public and additions to bank reserves cause the actual money multiplier to be less than the potential multiplier.

CHAPTER 14: MODERN MACROECONOMICS: MONETARY POLICY

2. Choices a and c would increase your incentive to hold money deposits; b and d would reduce your incentive to hold money.

3. a. The cost of obtaining the house is $100,000. b. the cost of holding it is the interest forgone on the $100,000 sales value of the house. c. the cost of obtaining $1,000 is

the amount of goods one must give up in order to acquire the $1,000. For example, if a pound of sugar sells for 50 cents, the cost of obtaining $1,000 in terms of sugar is 2,000 pounds. d. As in the case of the house, the cost of holding $1,000 is the interest forgone.

7. a. bank reserves will decline; b. real interest rates will rise; c. spending on consumer durables will fall; d. the dollar will appreciate because the higher interest rates will attract bond purchases by foreigners; e. exports will decline because the appreciation of the dollar will make U.S. goods more expensive for foreigners; f. the higher real interest rates will tend to reduce real asset prices; and g. real GDP will fall.

10. If the time lag is long and variable (rather than short and highly predictable), it is less likely that policy makers will be able to time changes in monetary policy so that they will exert a *countercyclical* impact on the economy. The policy makers will be more likely to make mistakes and thereby exert a destabilizing influence.

11. Association does not reveal causation. Decision makers—including borrowers and lenders—will eventually anticipate a high rate of inflation and adjust their choices accordingly. As the expected rate of inflation increases, the demand for loanable funds will increase and the supply will decrease. This will lead to higher nominal interest rates. Thus, economic theory indicates that the causation tends to run the opposite direction from that indicated by the statement.

12. Aggregate demand will decline as individuals and businesses reduce spending in an effort to build up their money balances (demand more money).

14. Real GDP: U.S. (7,751, 8,095, 8,448, and 8,752); Chile (28,268, 30,358, 31,380, and 31,037); Turkey (14,772, 15,884, 16,375, and 15,553); Money Supply Growth: U.S. (3.5%, 3.5%, and 10.4%); Chile (20.2%, −13.3%, and 32.9%); Turkey (69.1%, 63.1%, and 77.0%); Price Level Growth: U.S. (1.8%, 1.2%, and 1.6%); Chile (4.0%, 2.7%, and 3.6%); Turkey (81.5%, 75.7%, and 56.2%); b. Turkey; c. Turkey; d. U.S.

CHAPTER 15: STABILIZATION POLICY, OUTPUT, AND EMPLOYMENT

2. Compared with earlier periods, the United States has experienced less economic instability during the last four decades. There is reason to believe that a more stable monetary policy has contributed to the increase in stability.

5. Nonactivists think that a monetary rule would result in less instability from monetary sources. The changing nature of money may reduce the stabilizing effects of a monetary rule.

8. Here are three practical problems that limit the effectiveness of discretionary macro policy as a stabilization tool: (1) inability to forecast the future direction of the economy with a high degree of accuracy, (2) lengthy and uncertain time lags between when a policy change is instituted and when the primary effects are felt, and (3) political factors that make it difficult to alter fiscal policy quickly.

10. The Great Depression certainly indicates that the economy's self-correcting mechanism does not work instantaneously and that it is unable to offset the impact of perverse macro economic policy. Most significantly, it highlights the importance of monetary stability and the damage that occurs when counter-productive policies are undertaken.

11. (a) Keep the inflation rate at a low and highly predictable level, (b) No, (c) Both nominal interest rates and the general level of prices will rise.

CHAPTER 16: ECONOMIC GROWTH

3. A few years ago, many believed that this view was essentially true. However, this is no longer the case. Foreign aid has played an insignificant role in the progress of most of the high-growth LDCs. In some cases, it has adversely affected economies. In the past, aid has disrupted markets and retarded the incentive of producers in less-developed countries. Furthermore, attractive investment alternatives will draw investment from abroad even if domestic saving is inadequate. Thus, the efficacy of aid as a tool to promote economic growth is highly questionable.

7. Yes. Trade barriers limit the ability of both businesses and consumers to benefit from economies associated with an expansion in the size of the market. This limitation will be more restrictive for small countries (like Costa Rica) than for larger countries (like Mexico) because the latter will often have sizable domestic markets.

8. When considering the answer to this question, think about the following: Is there an opportunity cost of the capital used by government firms? Do government firms have a strong incentive to keep costs low? Are government firms innovative?

10. Natural resources are neither a necessary nor sufficient condition for economic growth. Other than their harbors, neither Hong Kong nor Singapore have significant natural resources. Likewise, Japan has few natural resources, and it imports almost all of its industrial energy supply. Nonetheless, the growth rates of all three have been among the most rapid in the world since 1960. In contrast, many resource rich countries such as Nigeria, Venezuela, Ghana, and Bolivia have poor records of economic growth. Without sound institutions and policies, even resource-rich countries tend to stagnate. On the other hand, countries that follow sound policies are able to import the resources required for growth and prosperity.

12. The increase in diversity provides consumers with more options and thereby improves their welfare. For the most part, the GDP figures fail to capture the impact of this factor.

CHAPTER 17: GAINING FROM INTERNATIONAL TRADE

1. Availability of goods and services, not jobs, is the source of economic prosperity. When a good can be purchased cheaper abroad than it can be produced at home, a nation can expand the quantity of goods and services available for consumption by specializing in the production of those goods for which it is a low-cost producer and trading them for the cheap (relative to domestic costs) foreign goods. Trade restrictions limiting the ability of Americans to purchase low-cost goods from foreigners stifle this process and thereby reduce the living standard of Americans.

3. Statements a and b are not in conflict. Since trade restrictions are typically a special interest issue, political entrepreneurs can often gain by supporting them even when they promote economic inefficiency.

5. True. The primary effect of trade restrictions is an increase in domestic scarcity.This has distributional consequences, but it is clear that as a whole, a nation will be harmed by the increased domestic scarcity accompanying the trade restraints.

6. The quota reduces the supply of sugar to the domestic market and drives up the domestic price of sugar. Domestic producers benefit from the higher prices at the expense of domestic consumers. Studies indicate that the quota expanded the gross income of the 11,000 domestic sugar farmers by approximately $130,000 per farm in the mid-1980s, at the expense (in the form of higher prices of sugar and sugar products) of approximately $6 per year to the average domestic consumer. Since the program channels resources away from products for which the United States has a comparative advantage, it reduces the productive capacity of the United States. Both the special interest nature of the issue and rent-seeking theory explain the political attractiveness of the program.

8. a. No. Americans would be poorer if we used more of our resources to produce things for which we are a high opportunity-cost producer and less of our resources to produce things for which we are a low opportunity-cost producer. Employment might either increase or decrease, but the key point is that it is the value of goods produced, not employment, that generates income and provides for the wealth of a nation. The answer to b is the same as a.

9. In thinking about this issue, consider the following points. Suppose the Japanese were willing to give products such as automobiles, electronic goods, and clothing to us free of charge. Would we be worse off if we accepted the gifts? Should we try to keep the free goods out? What is the source of real income—jobs or goods and services? If the gifts make us better off, doesn't it follow that partial gifts would also make us better off?

12. While trade reduces employment in import-competing industries, it expands employment in export industries. On balance, there is no reason to believe that trade either promotes or destroys jobs. The major effect of trade is to permit individuals, states, regions, and nations to generate a larger output by specializing in the things they do well and trading for those things that they would produce only at a high cost. A higher real income is the result.

15. True. If country A imposes a tariff, other countries will sell less to A and therefore acquire less purchasing power in terms of A's currency. Thus, they will have to reduce their purchases of A's export goods.

18. a. Italy b. Chile c. 1 apple/grape to 3 apples/grape d. After specialization and trade, Chile consumes (in millions of bushels) 30 apples and 30 grapes, while Italy consumes 60 apples and 60 grapes. This represents an increase of 10 grapes for Chile and 30 apples for Italy.

CHAPTER 18: INTERNATIONAL FINANCE AND THE FOREIGN EXCHANGE MARKET

1. Hondas will become more expensive; the quantity purchased will decrease; and expenditures on imported Hondas will decline.

4. On February 2, the dollar appreciated against the British pound and depreciated against the Canadian dollar.

5. Answers a and g would cause the dollar to appreciate; b, c, d, e, and h would cause the dollar to depreciate; f would leave the exchange rate unchanged.

8. As trade deficits persist, foreign ownership of real assets, equities, and bonds grows. Some fear that the United States is vulnerable because foreigners might decide to suddenly sell their assets and leave. When considering this argument, it is important to recognize that foreign and domestic investors are influenced by the same considerations. Anything that would cause foreigners to withdraw funds would cause domestic investors to do likewise. In fact, the vulnerability runs the other way. If foreign investors left, the assets financed by their funds would remain. Thus, they are in a weak position to impose harm on the U.S. economy.

9. Each of the changes would reduce the size of the current account deficit.

11. The current account balance will move toward a larger deficit (or smaller surplus) and the dollar will appreciate.

14. False. Flexible exchange rates bring the sum of the current and capital accounts into balance, but they do not necessarily lead to balance for either component.

15. a. No. The exchange rate will bring the sum of the current and capital accounts into balance, but it will not bring about either an overall merchandise trade balance or a trade balance with a specific country. b. Compared to the United States, Japan has a high savings rate. High-income countries with high savings rates tend to invest substantially abroad. In order to pay for these investments, Japan must run a current account surplus. Its trading partners—particularly those with a low saving rate like the United States—will do the opposite. In addition, Japan is a major importer of natural resources and raw materials, two product areas where the United States does not generally have a comparative advantage. Because the United States is generally not a low-cost producer of the primary products imported by the Japanese, the United States tends to export less goods and services to Japan than it imports. c. Americans will not want to hold the additional yen. They can be expected to use them to purchase additional foreign-produced goods, including goods supplied by the Japanese. Clearly, the trade deficit with Japan is only a part of the total current account deficit.

CHAPTER 19: DEMAND AND CONSUMER CHOICE

1. Revenue will rise (fall) if students who enroll pay more (less) extra revenue than is lost due to lower enrollment. Revenue will remain the same if those who enroll pay just enough more to offset the loss from reduced enrollment. A price elasticity of 1.2 implies that raising tuition rates would reduce tuition revenue.

3. a. 0.21; 1.2. b. Substitutes; higher fuel oil prices lead to an increase in demand (and consumption) for insulation.

6. Water is usually cheaper than oil because its marginal utility at current consumption levels is less than that of oil. Since water is so abundant relative to oil, the benefit derived from an additional quart of water is less than the benefit from an additional quart of oil, even though the total utility from all units of water is far greater than the total utility from all units of oil. However, the price of a product will reflect marginal utility, not total utility.

7. Both income and time constrain our ability to consume. Since, in a wealthier society, time becomes more binding and income less binding, time-saving actions will be more common in a wealthier society. As we engage in time-saving actions (fast food, automatic appliances, air travel, and so on) in order to shift the time restraint outward, our lives become more hectic.

10. All three statements are true.

11. a. No. Even for things we like, we will experience diminishing returns. Eventually, the cost of additional units of pizza will exceed their benefits. b. Perfection in any activity is generally not worth the cost. For example, reading every page of this text three, four, or five times may improve your grade, but it may not be worth it. One function of a text is to structure the material (highlighted points, layout of graphs, and so on) so that the reader will be able to learn quickly (at a lower cost).

12. Carole.

13. False. Since the demand for agricultural products is generally inelastic, farm incomes may well increase. But the total utility of farm output reflects not only the sales revenues but also the consumer surplus. For the units produced, the utility is unchanged as the loss of consumer surplus by consumers is exactly offset by higher payments to farmers. However, both the payments to farmers and consumer surplus are lost for those units not produced. Therefore, the decline in production will reduce the total utility of farm output and the nation will be worse off as a result.

14. Deceit and dishonesty will be encouraged by methods of organization that increase the returns to such behavior. The returns to deceitful and dishonest claims will be inversely related to the ease with which they can be countered by rivals. Other things constant, the presence of rivals will tend to reduce deceitful behavior. Is a politician more or less likely to tell the truth when he or she regularly confronts rivals? Is a news medium more or less likely to be balanced and trustworthy when it faces rivals in the news business? Is a court witness more or less likely to tell the truth when there are other witnesses and cross-examination can be expected? Is a firm selling automobiles, cough drops, or hamburgers more or less likely to be honest when it faces competitors? Answers to such questions are obvious.

CHAPTER 20: COSTS AND THE SUPPLY OF GOODS

1. The economic profit of a firm is its total revenues minus the opportunity cost of all resources used in the production process. Accounting profit often excludes the opportunity cost of certain resources—particularly the equity capital of the firm and any labor services provided by an owner-manager. Zero economic profit means that the resources owned by the firm are earning their opportunity cost—that is, the rate of return is as high as the highest valued alternative forgone. Thus, the firm would not gain by pursuing other lines of business.

2. a. Sunk costs are irrelevant. b. There is an opportunity cost of one's house. c. Sunk costs should not affect one's current decision. d. There is an opportunity cost of public education even if it is provided free to the consumer.

7. At low output, the firm's plant (a fixed cost) is underutilized, implying a high average cost. As output rises toward the designed output level, average cost falls, but then rises as the designed or optimal output for that size plant is surpassed and the plant is fully utilized.

11. Because owners receive profits, clearly profit maximization is in their interest. Managers, if they are not owners, have no property right to profit and therefore no direct interest in profit maximization. Since a solid record of profitability tends to increase the market value (salary) of corporate managers, they do have an indirect incentive to pursue profits. However, corporate managers may also be interested in gaining power, having nice offices, hiring friends, expanding sales, and other activities, which may conflict with profitability. Thus, the potential for conflict between the interests of owners and managers is present.

12. a. The interest payments; b. The interest income forgone. The tax structure encourages debt rather than equity financing since the firm's tax liability is inversely related to its debt/equity ratio.

13. True. If it could produce the output at a lower cost, its profit would be greater.

15. Check list: Did your marginal cost curve cross the *ATC* and *AVC* curves at their low points? Does the vertical distance between the *ATC* and *AVC* curves get smaller and smaller as output increases? If not, redraw the three curves correctly.

18. $2,500; the $2,000 decline in market value during the year plus $500 of potential interest on funds that could be obtained if the machine were sold new. Costs associated with the decline in the value of the machine last year are sunk costs.

19. Because they believe they will be able to restructure the firm and provide better management so that the firm will have positive net earnings in the future. If the firm is purchased at a low enough price, this will allow the new owners to cover the opportunity cost of their investment and still earn an economic profit. Alternatively, they may expect to sell off the firm's assets, receiving more net revenue than the cost of purchasing the firm.

CHAPTER 21: PRICE TAKERS AND THE COMPETITIVE PROCESS

1. In a highly competitive industry such as agriculture, lower resource prices might improve the rate of profit in the short run, but in the long run, competition will drive prices down until economic profit is eliminated. Thus, lower resource prices will do little to improve the long-run profitability in such industries.

2. New firms will enter the industry and the existing firms will expand output; market supply will expand, causing the market price to fall until economic profit is eliminated.

5. a. Increase; b. Increase; c. Increase. Firms will earn economic profit; d. Rise (compared with its initial level) for an increasing cost industry, but return to initial price for a constant cost industry; e. Increase even more than it did in the short run; f. Economic profit will return to zero.

6. a. Decline; b. Increase; c. Decline; d. Decline.

11. a. The reduction in supply led to higher prices. b. Since demand is inelastic, the total revenue from sales increased. c. Overall, the profitability of farming increased, although some of the producers that were hardest hit by the drought experienced losses because of their sharp reduction in output.

13. b. Six or seven tons; $250 profit; c. seven or eight tons; $600 profit; d. five or six tons; $50 loss. Since the firm can cover its variable cost, it should stay in business if it believes that the low ($450) price is temporary.

CHAPTER 22: PRICE-SEARCHER MARKETS WITH LOW ENTRY BARRIERS

3. The amount of variety is determined by the willingness of consumers to pay for variety relative to the cost of providing it. If consumers value variety highly and the added costs of producing different styles, designs, and sizes is low, there will be a lot of variety. Alternatively, if consumers desire similar products or if variation can be produced only at a high cost, little variety will be present. Apparently, consumers place a substantial value (relative to cost) on variety in napkins, but not in toothpicks.

4. The tax would increase the price of lower-quality (and lower-priced) automobiles by a larger percentage than higher-quality automobiles. Consumers would substitute away from the lower-quality autos since their relative price has increased. This substitution would increase the average quality of automobiles sold. Since the funds from the tax are rebated back to citizens through the lottery, one would expect this substitution effect to dominate any possible income effect.

7. No. A firm that maximizes *total* revenue would expand output as long as marginal revenue is positive. When marginal costs are positive, the revenue-maximizing price would be lower (and the output greater) than the price that would maximize the firm's profits.

9. Building the new resort is more risky (and less attractive) because if the market analysis is incorrect, and demand is insufficient, it probably will be difficult to find other uses for the newly built resort. If the airline proves unprofitable, however, the capital (airplanes) should be extremely mobile. However, the resort would have one offsetting advantage: If demand were stronger than expected, and profits larger, it would take competitors longer to enter the market (build a new resort), and they would be more reluctant to make the more permanent investment.

11. In a competitive setting, only the big firms will survive if economies of scale are important. When economies of scale are unimportant, small firms will be able to compete effectively.

14. Competition provides the answer. If McDonald's fails to provide an attractively priced, tasty sandwich with a smile, people will turn to Burger King, Wendy's, Dairy Queen, and other rivals. If Wal-Mart does not provide convenience and value, people will turn to Target or other retailers. Similarly, as recent experience has shown, even a firm as large as General Motors will lose customers to Ford, Honda, Toyota, Chrysler, Volkswagen, and other automobile manufacturers if it fails to please the customer as much as rival suppliers.

16. a. Total revenue: $0; $8,000; $14,000; $18,000; $20,000; $20,000; Total cost: $0; $5,000; $10,000; $15,000; $20,000; $25,000; Economic profit: $0; $3,000; $4,000; $3,000; $0; $5,000 (loss). b. Marginal revenue: $8,000; $6,000; $4,000; $2,000; $0; Marginal cost: $5,000; $5,000; $5,000; $5,000; $5,000. c. Profit maximizing price: $7,000 d. Rod will sell 2 boats at the profit-maximizing price of $7,000. e. Rod's economic profits will be $4,000 per week. f. Yes, boats 1 and 2 are the only boats for which marginal revenue is higher than marginal cost. g. Because of the existence of economic profit, more boat dealers will open up in the area. This will result in more competition and lower prices. The entry will continue until boat dealers' economic profits fall to zero. h. When demand is elastic, lowering price increases total revenue; thus Rod's demand is elastic between the prices of $9,000 and $5,000. When demand is unitary elastic, lowering price leaves revenues unchanged; thus Rod's demand is unitary elastic between the prices of $5,000 and $4,000. One could also assume that Rod's demand would eventually become inelastic below a price of $4,000 because the elasticity of demand keeps falling as one moves down along a demand curve. When this happens, Rod's total revenues will begin to fall as he continues to lower price. For example, at a price of $3,000, Rod may sell 6 boats per week, resulting in only $18,000 in revenues, which is less than the revenues Rod receives at a price of $4,000.

CHAPTER 23: PRICE-SEARCHER MARKETS WITH HIGH ENTRY BARRIERS

1. Profits cannot exist in the long run without barriers to entry because without them new entrants seeking the profits would increase supply, drive down price, and eliminate the profits. But as the chapter shows, barriers to entry are no guarantee of profits. Sufficient demand is also a necessary condition.

3. No; No; No.

8. Product variation provides each firm in the oligopoly a chance to "cheat" by raising the quality of its products in order to entice customers away from rivals. This raises cost and helps to defeat the purpose, for the oligopolistic group, of controlling price. But if collusion has raised price much above marginal cost, there will be a powerful incentive for each firm to compete in a hidden way to get more customers.

11. Reductions in the cost of transportation generally increase competition because they force firms to compete with distant rivals and permit consumers to choose among a wider range of suppliers. As a result, the U.S. economy today is generally more competitive, in the rivalry sense, than it was 100 years ago.

12. The stock price, when the uncle bought the stock, no doubt reflected the well-known profits of Mammoth. The previous owners of the stock surely would not have sold it at a low price that failed to reflect the future dividends. In the language of the text, the uncle was not an "early bird." It is unlikely that he will profit, in the economic sense, from the purchase.

13. a. $15, profit = $110,000; b. $10.

CHAPTER 24: THE SUPPLY OF AND DEMAND FOR PRODUCTIVE RESOURCES

3. a. Five; b. $350; c. Four. The firm will operate in the short run but it will go out of business in the long run unless the market prices rise.

4. Yes. General increases in the productivity of the labor force will cause a general increase in wages. The higher general wage rates will increase the opportunity cost of barbering and cause the supply of barbers to decline. The reduction in the supply of barbers will place upward pressure on the wages of barbers, even if technological change and worker productivity have changed little in barbering.

8. No. The dressmaker needs to employ more capital and less labor because the marginal dollar expenditures on the former are currently increasing output by a larger amount than the latter.

10. Other things constant, a lengthy training requirement to perform in an occupation reduces supply and places upward pressure on the earnings level. However, resource prices, including those for labor services, are determined by both demand and supply. When demand is weak, earnings will be low, even though a considerable amount of education may be necessary to perform in the occupation. For example, the earnings of people with degrees in English literature and world history are generally low, even though most people in these fields have a great deal of education.

12. b. 4; c. Employment would decline to 3.

CHAPTER 25: EARNINGS, PRODUCTIVITY, AND THE JOB MARKET

2. U.S. workers are more productive. By investing in human capital, the laborers are somewhat responsible, but the superior tools and physical capital that are available to U.S. workers also contribute to their higher wages.

6. Although this statement, often made by politicians, sounds true, in fact, it is false. Output of goods and services valued by consumers, not jobs, is the key to economic progress and a high standard of living. Real income cannot be high unless real output is high. If job creation was the key to economic progress, it would be easy to create millions of jobs. For example, we could prohibit the use of farm machinery. Such a prohibition would create millions of jobs in agriculture. However, it would also reduce output and our standard of living.

8. The opportunity cost of leisure (nonwork) for higher-wage workers is greater than for lower-wage workers.

9. False. Several additional factors, including differences in preferences (which would influence time worked, the trade-off between money wage and working conditions, and evaluation of alternative jobs), differences in jobs, and imperfect labor mobility, would result in variations in earnings.

10. a, b, e, and f will generally increase hourly earnings; c and d will generally reduce hourly earnings.

11. Hourly wages will be highest in B because the higher wages will be necessary to compensate workers in B for the uncertainty and loss of income during layoffs. Annual earnings will be higher in A in order to compensate workers in A for the additional hours they will work during the year.

12. Not necessarily. Compared with married men, single men tend to be younger, have fewer dependents, be more likely to drop out of the labor force, and be less likely to receive earnings-enhancing assistance from another person. All these factors will reduce their earnings relative to married men.

CHAPTER 26: INVESTMENT, THE CAPITAL MARKET, AND THE WEALTH OF NATIONS

1. All the changes would increase interest rates in the United States.

4. No. The average outstanding balance during the year is only about half of $1,000. Therefore, the $200 interest charge translates to almost a 40 percent annual rate of interest.

6. *Hints:* Which has been considered to be more risky—purchasing a bond or a stock? How does risk influence the expected rate of return?

8. 6 percent.

10. a. Mike; b. Yes, people who save a lot are able to get a higher interest rate on their savings as the result of people with a high rate of time preference; c. Yes, people who want to borrow money will be able to do so at a lower rate when there are more people (like Alicia) who want to save a lot.

11. Helped. This question is a lot like prior questions involving Alicia and Mike. Potential gains from trade are present. If obstacles do not restrain trade, the low-income countries will be able to attract savings (from countries with a high saving rate) at a lower interest rate than would exist in the absence of trade. Similarly, people in the high-income countries will be able to earn a higher return than would otherwise be possible. Each can gain because of the existence of the other.

12. a. Approximately $1.277 million; b. Yes; c. The lottery earnings are less liquid. Since there is not a well-organized market transforming lottery earnings into present income, the transaction costs of finding a "buyer" (at a price equal to the present value of the earnings) for the lottery earnings "rights" may be higher than for the bond, if one wants to sell in the future.

14. No. The present value of the $500 annual additions to earnings during the next ten years is less than the cost of the schooling.

16. Consider the following when answering this question: whose money is being invested by each of the two entities? If a private investment project goes bad, who is hurt? If a private project is successful, who reaps the gain? Answer the same two questions for political officials.

CHAPTER 27: INCOME INEQUALITY AND POVERTY

2. Differences in family size, age of potential workers, nonmoney "income," taxes, and cost-of-living among areas reduce the effectiveness of annual money income as a measure of economic status. In general, high-income families are larger, are more likely to be headed by a prime-age worker, have less nonmoney income (including leisure), pay more taxes, and reside in higher-cost-of-living areas (particularly large cities). Thus, money income comparison between high- and low-income groups often overstates the economic status of the former relative to the latter.

4. If there were no intergenerational mobility, the diagonal numbers would all be 100 percent. If there were complete equality of opportunity and outcomes, the numbers in each column and row would be 20 percent.

6. No. The increase in marginal tax rates will reduce the incentive of the poor to earn income. Therefore, their income will rise by $1,000 minus the reduction in their personal earnings due to the disincentive effects of the higher marginal tax rates.

7. 67 percent.

SPECIAL TOPIC 1: GOVERNMENT SPENDING AND TAXATION

1. Taxes reduce economic efficiency because they eliminate some exchanges and thereby reduce the gains from these transactions. Because of (a) the deadweight losses accompanying the elimination of exchanges and (b) the cost of collecting taxes, the costs of additional tax revenue will be greater than the revenue transferred to the government.

SPECIAL TOPIC 2: THE INTERNET: HOW IS IT CHANGING THE ECONOMY?

2. Airline tickets can be "transported" electronically; groceries cannot. Customers can observe the ticket information Online, but they cannot observe the condition of fruits, vegetables, and other grocery products via the Internet.

SPECIAL TOPIC 3: THE ECONOMICS OF SOCIAL SECURITY

2. The pay-as-you-go social security system will face a crisis sometime around 2016 when the inflow of tax revenue will be insufficient to cover the promised benefits. While the Social Security Trust Fund has bonds, they are merely an IOU from the Treasury to the Social Security Administration. In order to redeem these bonds and provide additional funds to finance social security benefits, the federal government will have to raise taxes (or pay the interest on additional Treasury bonds it sells), or cut other expenditures, or both. Thus, the presence of the SSTF bonds does not do much to alleviate the crisis.

SPECIAL TOPIC 4: THE STOCK MARKET: WHAT DOES IT DO AND HOW HAS IT PERFORMED?

1. History shows that in the U.S. stock market, a relatively low risk with fairly high returns can be gained by holding a diverse portfolio of stocks in unrelated industries, for a period of 20 years or more. Mutual funds are an option that allows a person to purchase a diverse portfolio while keeping commission costs low.

3. High profits now and the expectation of higher profits in the future have driven up the price of the stock, despite the lack of dividend payment in the first years of the firm. Investors are equally happy with high dividends or the equivalent in rising stock value due to the firm's retaining of its profits for further investment.

5. Investors are buying such a stock for its rising value (price), which reflects expected future earnings and dividends.

SPECIAL TOPIC 5: THE FEDERAL BUDGET AND THE NATIONAL DEBT

1. No. Both private corporations and governments can, and often do, have continual debt outstanding. Borrowers can continue to finance and refinance debt as long as lenders have confidence in their ability to pay. This will generally be the case as long as the interest liability is small relative to income (or the potential tax base).

4. No. Remember, trade is a positive-sum game. Bonds are sold to foreigners because they are offering a better deal (acceptance of a lower interest rate) than is available elsewhere. Prohibiting the sale of bonds to foreigners would result in higher real interest rates and less investment, both of which would adversely affect Americans.

6. Lower; voters do not enjoy paying taxes and, therefore, voter dissatisfaction places a restraint on higher taxes, which would also restrain expenditures if the budget had to be balanced. More efficient; the restraint of tax increases would tighten the budget constraint and make the reality of opportunity cost more visible to both voters and politicians.

8. No. Yes.

9. Payment of outstanding debt certainly seems like a sensible policy. However, in the case of the federal debt, there are some additional considerations. First, U.S. Treasury securities play an important role in our financial markets. Treasury securities, particularly those that are indexed for inflation, provide households, businesses, pension funds, and financial institutions with a secure, highly liquid asset that makes it easier for them to deal with an uncertain future. Furthermore, a tax increase would force many private households and businesses to borrow more in order to cover the higher tax liability. In essence, this substitutes riskier, high-interest debt for more secure, low-interest debt. On balance, it is not obvious that this substitution would reduce overall interest costs.

Second, the Federal Reserve manages the money supply through the purchase and sale of U.S. securities in the open market. If Treasury securities were unavailable, the Fed would have to buy and sell a large amount of securities issued by private firms, which would give the Fed an opportunity to play favorites and subject it to political pressure regarding the companies whose securities it purchases.

Third, the U.S. dollar is a "reserve currency." Central banks and other monetary authorities around the globe currently hold more than $600 billion of Treasury securities as reserve assets. If these securities were unavailable to foreigners, the dollar would be a less attractive reserve currency. With time, this could erode its position as the world's leading currency.

Fourth, we must not forget that the national debt is a relatively small portion of the federal government's unfunded liabilities. Currently, the unfunded liabilities of the social security system are estimated to be between $5 trillion and $11 trillion; those of the Medicare program are projected at almost $10 trillion. These liabilities are far greater than the outstanding federal debt. Thus, it would appear to be more important to deal with these liabilities than pay off the national debt.

There is an "optimal amount of debt" for both businesses and governments. Just as the optimal amount is often positive for a strong healthy business, it may also be positive for the federal government.

SPECIAL TOPIC 6: LABOR MARKET POLICIES AND THE NATURAL RATE OF UNEMPLOYMENT: A CROSS-COUNTRY ANALYSIS

1. The ability to organize only a portion of the firms in an industry leaves the organized firms in competition with the unorganized firms. When organized firms pay higher wages, they find it harder to compete with nonunion firms due to higher costs. This restricts the ability of the union to raise wages in the organized firms. Because competition from nonunion firms is less prevalent in Europe than in the United States, European unions are better able to increase the wages of union members than their counterparts in the United States.

SPECIAL TOPIC 7: THE PHILLIPS CURVE: IS THERE A TRADE-OFF BETWEEN INFLATION AND UNEMPLOYMENT?

2. Economists in the mid-1970s thought inflation would reduce unemployment; they failed to recognize that decision makers would eventually come to anticipate the inflation. The modern view of the Phillips curve incorporates expectations into the analysis.

5. With unanticipated inflation, real wages fall because many workers, who did not anticipate the inflation, accepted explicit and implicit contracts at wage rates they would have found unacceptable had they correctly anticipated the magnitude of the price increase. Job search time will decline because many workers will accept jobs at money wage rates they would have rejected if they had been fully aware of how much inflation had increased money wages. Both of these factors will temporarily reduce the unemployment rate. When the inflation is anticipated, it will be fully reflected in long-term wage agreements. Thus, the inflation will fail to reduce real wage rates. Similarly, job search time will be normal because workers will recognize how much inflation has increased the money wages of potential jobs. Thus, anticipated inflation fails to reduce the unemployment rate.

SPECIAL TOPIC 8: THE ECONOMICS OF HEALTH CARE

2. Health insurance benefits are a component of the employee's compensation package. Unless the employer values the services of the employee by an amount greater than or equal to the total cost of the employee's compensation, the worker will not be hired. Thus, like other components of the compensation package, health insurance benefits are earned by employees.

5. Medicare and Medicaid increased both total health-care spending and the share of that spending paid by a third party. Both of these factors increased the demand for and prices of medical services, thereby making them more expensive for persons not qualifying for these programs.

SPECIAL TOPIC 9: SCHOOL CHOICE: CAN IT IMPROVE THE QUALITY OF EDUCATION IN AMERICA?

2. The current educational structure tends to raise costs and lower quality. The incentive to keep costs low is weak since managers in the education system don't face competitive pressures. Since consumers cannot take their funding and go elsewhere, they are in a weak position to discipline the district schools that are not doing a good job. Furthermore, a lower quality of service would merely highlight the need for additional funding of the public-sector schools.

SPECIAL TOPIC 10: IS DISCRIMINATION RESPONSIBLE FOR THE EARNINGS DIFFERENCES BETWEEN MEN AND WOMEN?

4. Not necessarily. Compared with married men, single men tend to be younger, have fewer dependents, be more likely to drop out of the labor force, and be less likely to receive earnings-enhancing assistance from another person. All these factors will reduce their earnings relative to married men.

SPECIAL TOPIC 11: DO LABOR UNIONS INCREASE THE WAGES OF WORKERS?

2. If the union is able to raise the wages of the farmworkers: (a) The cost of Florida oranges will rise, causing supply to decline and price to rise in the long run; (b) profits of the Florida orange growers will decline in the short run, but in the long run they will return to the normal rate; (c) mechanization will be encouraged; and (d) the employment of fruit pickers will decline—particularly in the long run.

7. If only part of an industry is unionized, the costs of nonunion firms in the industry will be lower than the costs of unionized firms, if the unionized firms have higher wage rates. If the union wages are much higher than nonunion wages, then the unionized firms will be unable to compete successfully.

10. False. Competition constrains both employers and employees. Employers must compete with other employers for labor services. In order to gain the labor services of an employee, an employer must offer a compensation package superior to what the employee can get elsewhere. If the employer does not offer a superior package, the employee will work for a rival employer or choose self-employment. Similarly, employees must compete with other employees. Therefore, their ability to demand whatever wage they would like is also restrained. Thus, competition prevents both the payment of low (below-market) wages by employers and the imposition of high (above-market) wages by employees.

11. Not necessarily. Adjustment must be made for differences in (a) the productivity characteristics of the union and nonunion workers, and (b) the types of jobs they occupy (for example, work environment, job security, likelihood of layoff, and so on). Adjustment for these factors may either increase or reduce the $1.50 differential.

12. Remember, union members compete with other workers, including less-skilled workers. An increase in the minimum wage makes unskilled, low-wage workers more expensive. A higher minimum wage increases the demand for high-skill employees who are good substitutes for the low-skill workers. Union members are overrepresented among the high-skill group helped by an increase in the minimum wage. Therefore, while union leaders will generally pitch their support for a higher minimum wage in terms of a desire that all workers be paid a "decent wage," the impact of the legislation on union members suggests that self-interest rather than altruism underlies their support for the legislation.

SPECIAL TOPIC 12: HOW DOES GOVERNMENT REGULATION AFFECT YOUR LIFE?

1. Making cars safer is good, but if the cost has previously kept consumers from demanding the safety measures, it is possible that they are not worth the cost to many consumers. Some very expensive cars, such as Mercedes-Benz, had airbags when there was no requirement, but Volkswagen did not. Should only the more costly cars be sold? If so, then some people, probably the less affluent, will drive older, even less safe cars. This is not a clear-cut issue.

3. Profitability may be adversely affected in the short run, but in the long run, prices will rise enough for the firms to cover their opportunity cost of production. Consumers bear the cost of such legislation and get the associated benefits, large or small.

6. Experts often do know far more about the technical options than do consumers, although consumers can and do read the advice of experts. Suppliers of safer products

also make it a point to advertise data and expert opinion indicating their products are indeed safer. Nevertheless, experts usually do understand the technologies better. On the other hand, experts cannot know about how products will be used. A consumer may prefer to pay for a high degree of safety for the family car, which will carry the whole family at high speeds over long distances, while preferring a much cheaper, less-reliable car for running errands near home. Such choices are hard to allow if all vehicles are strictly regulated for safety. Decision-maker knowledge (and incentives) is, in some cases, better with consumer choice than with thorough and strict regulation.

8. The statement is essentially true. In the short run, capital may be invested in an industry such that it cannot easily be moved elsewhere. If customer demand is elastic, the industry may bear a large part of the cost burden in the short run. In the long run, however, capital is mobile. Factories don't have to be replaced, for example. If costs in the industry are high, relative to the revenues, then capital will migrate over time to other industries, and supply in the regulated industry will fall until the price buyers will pay is again high enough to provide the market rate of return to capital.

SPECIAL TOPIC 13: NATURAL RESOURCES AND THE FUTURE

1. Merely because a resource is unowned and unpriced, it does not follow that its opportunity cost is zero. Use of an unowned, unpriced resource might involve a high opportunity cost. Yet if there is no owner to protect it, or to allocate it to its highest-valued use, then it might indeed be treated as if it had no opportunity cost. This illustrates why private ownership of resources is important for their efficient allocation.

4. Wells are abandoned by producers when the cost of extracting and delivering additional oil exceeds its value. When the value of crude oil rises, additional oil can be produced since water flooding, steam, and chemical measures—all of which are costly—can be paid for by the higher prices gained from the extra oil.

5. Issues for thought: Are resources supplied by nature scarce? If so, what process should be used to ration them among the competing demanders? If a resource is owned by the government rather than privately, how will this affect the incentive to care for, maintain, and conserve it for the future? Do you think that government-owned property like the national forests and parks are better cared for than, for example, Disney World?

7. If an investment, such as leaving the trees to grow another 20 years, yields a higher return than other investments, then the stock price will fall if the trees are cut too soon, or will go higher if a new, more profitable investment path (leaving the trees to grow) is announced. Either way, the stock price immediately rewards good long-term decisions and penalizes bad, shortsighted ones.

10. The ITQ would allow the fishers to go to sea at a time of their own choosing, without losing the opportunity to get the fish catch allowed under the quota.

SPECIAL TOPIC 14: ECONOMICS AND THE ENVIRONMENT

2. Actions taken to reduce one risk can increase others. For example, banning the pesticide DDT raised risks from replacement pesticides in the United States and from malaria in Sri Lanka. It is important to consider the secondary effects of any risk-avoidance activity.

4. The cost of stopping the buildup of carbon dioxide would be very large, if it can be done. When the risk is somewhat speculative, even though it could turn out to be quite real, we must consider the reduction in wealth and prosperity that would be caused by reducing the buildup. Lower wealth and incomes would reduce our ability to reduce other risks. Then too, a warmer world would have many benefits as well as costs. We all want future generations to be better off. Whether reducing the buildup of carbon dioxide would make them better or worse off is the question.

6. Potential polluters must take into account any harm that pollution does to others, if pollution victims can enforce their property rights in court. But if enforcement of those rights is impossible because, for example, the true value of the harm or the source of the harm cannot be found, then regulation might help. However, a government regulator will have the same need for knowledge in seeking to improve the situation. Both markets and government organizations encourage resource owners and potential owners to consider their impacts on others, but neither system is perfect.

GLOSSARY

Absolute advantage A situation in which a nation, as the result of its previous experience and/or natural endowments, can produce more of a good (with the same amount of resources) than another nation.

Accounting profits The sales revenues minus the expenses of a firm over a designated time period, usually one year. Accounting profits typically make allowances for changes in the firm's inventories and depreciation of its assets. No allowance is made, however, for the opportunity cost of the equity capital of the firm's owners, or other implicit costs.

Activist strategy Deliberate changes in monetary and fiscal policy in order to inject demand stimulus during a recession and apply restraint during an inflationary boom and thereby, it is hoped, minimize economic instability.

Adaptive-expectations hypothesis The hypothesis that economic decision makers base their future expectations on actual outcomes observed during recent periods. For example, according to this view, the rate of inflation actually experienced during the past two or three years would be the major determinant of the rate of inflation expected for the next year.

Administrative lag The time period after the need for a policy change is recognized but before the policy is actually implemented.

Aggregate demand curve A downward-sloping curve indicating an inverse relationship between the price level and the quantity of domestically produced goods and services that households, business firms, governments, and foreigners (net exports) are willing to purchase during a period.

Aggregate supply curve A curve indicating the relationship between the nation's price level and quantity of goods supplied by its producers. In the short run, it is probably an upward-sloping curve, but in the long run most economists believe the aggregate supply curve is vertical (or nearly so).

Allocative efficiency The allocation of resources to the production of goods and services most desired by consumers, at the lowest possible cost.

Anticipated change A change that is foreseen by decision makers in time for them to adjust.

Anticipated inflation An increase in the general level of prices that was expected by most decision makers.

Appreciation An increase in the value of the domestic currency relative to foreign currencies. An appreciation increases the purchasing power of the domestic currency for foreign goods.

Automatic stabilizers Built-in features that tend automatically to promote a budget deficit during a recession and a budget surplus during an inflationary boom, even without a change in policy.

Automation A production technique that reduces the amount of labor required to produce a good or service. It is beneficial to adopt the new labor-saving technology only if it reduces the cost of production.

Autonomous expenditures Expenditures that do not vary with the level of income. They are determined by factors (such as business expectations and economic policy) that are outside the basic income-expenditure model.

Average fixed cost Total fixed cost divided by the number of units produced. It always declines as output increases.

Average product The total product (output) divided by the number of units of the variable input required to produce that output level.

Average tax rate (ATR) Tax liability divided by taxable income. It is the percentage of income paid in taxes.

Average total cost Total cost divided by the number of units produced. It is sometimes called per-unit cost.

Average variable cost The total variable cost divided by the number of units produced.

Balance of merchandise trade The difference between the value of merchandise exports and the value of merchandise imports for a nation. The balance of merchandise trade is only one component of a nation's total balance of payments. Also called simply balance of trade or net exports.

Balance of payments A summary of all economic transactions between a country and all other countries for a specific time period, usually a year. The balance-of-payments account reflects all payments and liabilities to foreigners (debits) and all payments and obligations received from foreigners (credits).

Balance on current account The import-export balance of goods and services, plus net investment income earned abroad, plus net private and government transfers. If the value of the nation's export-type items exceeds (is less than) the value of the nation's import-type items plus net unilateral transfers to foreigners, a current-account surplus (deficit) is present.

Balance on goods and services The exports of goods (merchandise) and services of a nation minus its imports of goods and services.

Balanced budget A situation in which current government revenue from taxes, fees, and other sources is just equal to current government expenditures.

Bank reserves Vault cash plus deposits of the bank with Federal Reserve banks.

Barriers to entry Obstacles that limit the freedom of potential rivals to enter and compete in an industry or market.

Black market A market that operates outside the legal system, either by selling illegal goods or by selling goods at illegal prices or terms.

Budget constraint The constraint that separates the bundles of goods that the consumer can purchase from those that cannot be purchased, given a limited income and the prices of the products.

Budget deficit A situation in which total government spending exceeds total government revenue during a specific time period, usually one year.

Budget surplus A situation in which total government spending is less than total government revenue during a time period, usually a year.

Business cycle Fluctuations in the general level of economic activity as measured by such variables as the rate of unemployment and changes in real GDP.

Capital Man-made resources (such as tools, equipment, and structures) that are used to produce other goods and services. Resources that enhance our ability to produce output in the future.

Capital account The record of transactions with foreigners that involve either (1) the exchange of ownership rights to real or financial assets or (2) the extension of loans.

Capitalism An economic system based on private ownership of productive resources and allocation of goods according to the signals provided by market prices.

Cartel An organization of sellers designed to coordinate supply decisions so that the joint profits of the members will be maximized. A cartel will seek to create a monopoly in the market.

Central bank An institution that regulates the banking system and controls the supply of money of a country.

Ceteris paribus A Latin term meaning "other things constant," used when the effect of one change is being described, recognizing that if other things changed, they also could affect the result. Economists often describe the effects of one change, knowing that in the real world, other things might change and also exert an effect.

Choice The act of selecting among alternatives.

Civilian labor force The number of persons 16 years of age and over who are either employed or unemployed. In order to be classified as unemployed, one must be looking for a job.

Classical economists Economists from Adam Smith to the time of Keynes who focused their analyses on economic efficiency and production. With regard to business instability, they thought market prices and wages would decline during a recession quickly enough to bring the economy back to full employment within a short period of time.

Collective decision making The method of organization that relies on public-sector decision making (voting, political bargaining, lobbying, and so on) to resolve basic issues.

Collusion Agreement among firms to avoid various competitive practices, particularly price reductions. It may involve either formal agreements or merely tacit recognition that competitive practices will be self-defeating in the long run. Tacit collusion is difficult to detect. In the United States, antitrust laws prohibit collusion and conspiracies to restrain trade.

Commercial banks Financial institutions that offer a wide range of services (for example, checking accounts, savings accounts, and extension of loans) to their customers. Commercial banks are owned by stockholders and seek to operate at a profit.

Comparative advantage The ability to produce a good at a lower opportunity cost than others can produce it. Relative costs determine comparative advantage.

Compensating wage differentials Wage differences that compensate workers for risk, unpleasant working conditions, and other undesirable nonpecuniary aspects of a job.

Competition as a dynamic process A term that denotes rivalry or competitiveness between or among parties (for example, producers or input suppliers), each of which seeks to deliver a better deal to buyers when quality, price, and product information are all considered. Competition implies a lack of collusion among sellers.

Competitive price-searcher market A market where the firms have a downward-sloping demand curve, and entry into and exit from the market are relatively easy.

Complements Products that are usually consumed jointly (for example, peanut butter and jelly). They are related such that a decrease in the price of one will cause an increase in demand for the other.

Constant returns to scale Unit costs that are constant as the scale of the firm is altered. Neither economies nor diseconomies of scale are present.

Constant-cost industry An industry for which factor prices and costs of production remain constant as market output is expanded. Thus, the long-run market supply curve is horizontal.

Consumer price index (CPI) An indicator of the general level of prices. It attempts to compare the cost of purchasing the market basket bought by a typical consumer during a specific period with the cost of purchasing the same market basket during an earlier period.

Consumer surplus The difference between the maximum price consumers are willing to pay and the price they actually pay. It is the net gain derived by the buyers of the good.

Consumption function A fundamental relationship between disposable income and consumption, in which, as disposable income increases, current consumption expenditures rise, but by a smaller amount than the increase in income.

Consumption opportunity constraint The constraint that separates consumption bundles that are attainable from those that are unattainable. In a money income economy, this is usually a budget constraint.

Contestable market A market in which the costs of entry and exit are low, so a firm risks little by entering. Efficient production and zero economic profits should prevail in a contestable market. A market can be contestable even if capital requirements are high.

Corporation A business firm owned by shareholders who possess ownership rights to the firm's profits, but whose liability is limited to the amount of their investment in the firm.

Countercyclical policy A policy that tends to move the economy in an opposite direction from the forces of the business cycle. Such a policy would stimulate demand during the contraction phase of the business cycle and restrain demand during the expansion phase.

Credit Funds acquired by borrowing.

Credit unions Financial cooperative organizations of individuals with a common affiliation (such as an employer or a labor union). They accept deposits, including checkable deposits, pay interest (or dividends) on them out of earnings, and channel funds primarily into loans to members.

Crowding-out effect A reduction in private spending as a result of higher interest rates generated by budget deficits that are financed by borrowing in the private loanable funds market.

Currency board An entity that (a) issues a currency with a fixed designated value relative to a widely accepted currency (for example, the U.S. dollar), (b) promises to continue to redeem the issued currency at the fixed rate, and (c) maintains bonds and other liquid assets denominated in the other currency that provide 100 percent backing for all currency issued.

Current account The record of all transactions with foreign nations that involve the exchange of merchandise goods and services, current income derived from investments, and unilateral gifts.

Cyclical unemployment Unemployment due to recessionary business conditions and inadequate aggregate demand for labor.

Deadweight loss A loss of gains from trade resulting from the imposition of a tax. It imposes a burden of taxation over and above the burden associated with the transfer of revenues to the government.

Decreasing-cost industry An industry for which costs of production decline as the industry expands. The market supply is therefore inversely related to price. Such industries are atypical.

Demand deposits Non-interest-earning checking deposits that can be either withdrawn or made payable on demand to a third party. Like currency, these deposits are widely used as a means of payment.

Demand for money A curve that indicates the relationship between the interest rate and the quantity of money people want to hold. Because higher interest rates increase the opportunity cost of holding money, the quantity demanded of money will be inversely related to the interest rate.

Depository institutions Businesses that accept checking and savings deposits and use a portion of them to extend loans and make investments. Banks, savings and loan associations, and credit unions are examples.

Depreciation 1) A reduction in the value of the domestic currency relative to foreign currencies. A depreciation reduces the purchasing power of the domestic currency for foreign goods. 2) The estimated amount of physical capital (for example, machines and buildings) that is worn out or used up producing goods during the period.

Depression A prolonged and very severe recession.

Derived demand The demand for a resource; it stems from the demand for the final good the resource helps to produce.

Differentiated products Products distinguished from similar products by such characteristics as quality, design, location, and method of promotion.

Discount rate The interest rate the Federal Reserve charges banking institutions for borrowing funds.

Discounting The procedure used to calculate the present value of future income, which is inversely related to both the interest rate and the amount of time that passes before the funds are received.

Discretionary fiscal policy A change in laws or appropriation levels that alters government revenues and/or expenditures.

Disposable income The income available to individuals after personal taxes. It can be either spent on consumption or saved.

Dumping The sale of a good by a foreign supplier in another country at a price below that charged by the supplier in its home market.

Earned Income Tax Credit A provision of the tax code that provides a credit or rebate to persons with low earnings (income from work activities). The credit is eventually phased out if the recipient's earnings increase.

Economic efficiency 1) A market meets the criterion of economic efficiency if all the gains from trade have been realized. With well-defined property rights and competition, market equilibrium is efficient. 2) Economizing behavior. When applied to a community, it implies that (1) an activity should be undertaken if the sum of the benefits to the individuals exceeds the sum of their costs and (2) no activity should be undertaken if the costs borne by the individuals exceed the benefits.

Economic profit The difference between the firm's total revenues and its total costs, including both the explicit and implicit cost components.

Economic regulation Regulation of product price or industrial structure, usually imposed on a specific industry. By and large, the production processes used by the regulated firms are unaffected by this type of regulation.

Economic theory A set of definitions, postulates, and principles assembled in a manner that makes clear the "cause-and-effect" relationships of economic data.

Economies of scale Reductions in the firm's per-unit costs that are associated with the use of large plants to produce a large volume of output.

Economizing behavior Choosing with the objective of gaining a specific benefit at the least possible cost. A corollary of economizing behavior implies that, when choosing among items of equal cost, individuals will choose the option that yields the greatest benefit.

Employment discrimination Unequal treatment of persons on the basis of their race, sex, or religion, restricting their employment and earnings opportunities compared to others of similar productivity. Employment discrimination may stem from the prejudices of employers, customers, fellow employees, or all three.

Entrepreneur A profit-seeking decision maker who decides which projects to undertake and how they should be undertaken. A successful entrepreneur's actions will increase the value of resources and expand the size of the economic pie.

Equation of exchange $MV = PY$, where M is the money supply, V is the velocity of money, P is the price level, and Y is the output of goods and services produced.

Equilibrium A state of balance between conflicting forces, such as supply and demand, permitting the simultaneous fulfillment of plans by buyers and sellers.

Equity mutual fund A corporation that pools the funds of investors, including small investors, and uses them to purchase a bundle of stocks.

Escalator clause A contractual agreement that periodically and automatically adjusts money wage rates upward as the price level rises. They are sometimes referred to as cost-of-living adjustments or COLAs.

Excess burden of taxation Another term for deadweight loss. It reflects losses that occur when beneficial activities are forgone because they are taxed.

Exchange rate The price of one unit of foreign currency in terms of the domestic currency. For example, if it takes $1.50 to purchase an English pound, the dollar-pound exchange rate is 1.50.

Expansionary fiscal policy An increase in government expenditures and/or a reduction in tax rates such that the expected size of the budget deficit expands.

Expansionary monetary policy A shift in monetary policy designed to stimulate aggregate demand. Bond purchases, creation of additional bank reserves, and an increase in the growth rate of the money supply are generally indicative of a shift to a more expansionary monetary policy.

Expenditure multiplier The ratio of the change in equilibrium output to the independent change in investment, consumption, or government spending that brings about the change. Numerically, the multiplier is equal to 1 *divided by* $(1 - \text{MPC})$ when the price level is constant.

Explicit costs Payments by a firm to purchase the services of productive resources.

Exports Goods and services produced domestically but sold to foreigners.

External debt   The portion of the national debt owed to foreign investors.

Externalities   The side effects, or spillover effects, of an action that influence the well-being of nonconsenting parties. The nonconsenting parties may be either helped (by external benefits) or harmed (by external costs).

Fallacy of composition   Erroneous view that what is true for the individual (or the part) will also be true for the group (or the whole).

Federal funds market   A loanable funds market in which banks seeking additional reserves borrow short-term (generally for seven days or less) funds from banks with excess reserves. The interest rate in this market is called the federal funds rate.

Federal Reserve System   The central bank of the United States; it carries out banking regulatory policies and is responsible for the conduct of monetary policy.

Fiat money   Money that has neither intrinsic value nor the backing of a commodity with intrinsic value; paper currency is an example.

Final market goods and services   Goods and services purchased by their ultimate user.

Fiscal policy   The use of government taxation and expenditure policies for the purpose of achieving macroeconomic goals.

Fixed exchange rate   An exchange rate that is set at a determined amount by government policy.

Flexible exchange rates   Exchange rates that are determined by the market forces of supply and demand. They are sometimes called floating exchange rates.

Foreign exchange market   The market in which the currencies of different countries are bought and sold.

Free rider   One who receives the benefit of a good without contributing to its costs. Public goods and commodities that generate external benefits offer people the opportunity to become free riders.

Frictional unemployment   Unemployment due to constant changes in the economy that prevent qualified unemployed workers from being immediately matched up with existing job openings. It results from the scarcity of information and the search activities of both employers and employees for information that will help them make better employment choices.

Fringe benefits   Benefits other than normal money wages that are supplied to employees in exchange for their labor services. Higher fringe benefits come at the expense of lower money wages.

Full employment   The level of employment that results from the efficient use of the labor force after allowance is made for the normal (natural) rate of unemployment due to information cost, dynamic changes, and the structural conditions of the economy. For the United States, full employment is thought to exist when approximately 95 percent of the labor force is employed.

Game theory   Analyzes the strategic choices made by competitors in a conflict situation, such as decisions made by members of an oligopoly.

GDP deflator   A price index that reveals the cost during the current period of purchasing the items included in GDP relative to the cost during a base year (currently, 1996). Because the base year is assigned a value of 100, as the GDP deflator takes on values greater than 100, it indicates that prices are higher than during the base year.

General Agreement on Tariffs and Trade (GATT)   An organization formed following the Second World War to set the rules for the conduct of international trade and reduce barriers to trade among nations.

Going out of business   The sale of a firm's assets and its permanent exit from the market. By going out of business, a firm is able to avoid fixed costs, which would continue during a shutdown.

Goods and services market   A highly aggregated market encompassing the flow of all final-user goods and services. The market counts all items that enter into GDP. Thus, real output in this market is equal to real GDP.

Gross domestic product (GDP)   The market value of all final goods and services produced within a country during a specific period.

Gross national product (GNP)   The total market value of all final goods and services produced by the citizens of a country. It is equal to GDP minus the net income of foreigners.

Health and safety regulation   Legislation designed to improve the health, safety, and environmental conditions available to workers and/or consumers. The legislation usually mandates production procedures, minimum standards, and/or product characteristics to be met by producers and employers.

Human resources   The abilities, skills, and health of human beings that can contribute to the production of both current and future output. Investment in training and education can increase the supply of human resources.

Impact lag   The time period after a policy change is implemented but before the change begins to exert its primary effects.

Implicit costs   The opportunity costs associated with a firm's use of resources that it owns. These costs do not involve a direct money payment. Examples include wage income and interest forgone by the owner of a firm who also provides labor services and equity capital to the firm.

Implicit marginal tax rate   The amount of additional (marginal) earnings that must be paid explicitly in taxes or implicitly in the form of a reduction in income supplements. Since the marginal tax rate establishes the fraction of an additional dollar earned that an individual is permitted to keep, it is an important determinant of the incentive to work.

Import quota   A specific limit or maximum quantity (or value) of a good permitted to be imported into a country during a given period.

Imports   Goods and services produced by foreigners but purchased by domestic consumers, businesses, and governments.

Income effect   That part of an increase (decrease) in amount consumed that is the result of the consumer's real income (the consumption possibilities available to the consumer) being expanded (contracted) by a reduction (rise) in the price of a good.

Income elasticity   The percentage change in the quantity of a product demanded divided by the percentage change in consumer income causing the change in quantity demanded. It measures the responsiveness of the demand for a good to a change in income.

Income mobility   Movement of individuals and families either up or down income-distribution rankings when comparisons are made at two different points in time. When substantial income mobility is present, one's current position will not be a very good indicator of what one's position will be a few years in the future.

Increasing-cost industry An industry for which costs of production rise as output is expanded. Thus, even in the long run, higher market prices will be required to induce the firms to expand the total output in such industries. The long-run market supply curve in such industries will slope upward to the right.

Index of leading indicators An index of economic variables that historically has tended to turn down prior to the beginning of a recession and turn up prior to the beginning of a business expansion.

Indifference curve A curve, convex from below, that separates the consumption bundles that are more preferred by an individual from those that are less preferred. The points on the curve represent combinations of goods that are equally preferred by the individual.

Indirect business taxes Taxes that increase the business firm's costs of production and, therefore, the prices charged to consumers. Examples would be sales, excise, and property taxes.

Inferior good A good that has a negative income elasticity, so that, as consumer income rises, the demand for that good falls.

Inflation A continuing rise in the general level of prices of goods and services. The purchasing power of the monetary unit, such as the dollar, declines when inflation is present.

Inflationary premium A component of the money interest rate that reflects compensation to the lender for the expected decrease, due to inflation, in the purchasing power of the principal and interest during the course of the loan. It is determined by the expected rate of future inflation.

Innovation The successful introduction and adoption of a new product or process; the economic application of inventions and marketing techniques.

Intermediate goods Goods purchased for resale or for use in producing another good or service.

International Monetary Fund (IMF) An international banking organization, with more than 180 member nations, designed to oversee the operation of the international monetary system. Although it does not control the world supply of money, it does hold currency reserves for member nations and makes currency loans to national central banks.

Invention The creation of a new product or process, often facilitated by the knowledge of engineering and scientific relationships.

Inventory investment Changes in the stock of unsold goods and raw materials held during a period.

Investment The purchase, construction, or development of capital resources, including both nonhuman capital and human capital (such as better education). Investment expands the availability of capital resources in an economy. The process of investment is sometimes referred to as capital formation.

Investment in human capital Expenditures on training, education, skill development, and health designed to increase human capital and the productivity of an individual.

Invisible hand principle The tendency of market prices to direct individuals pursuing their own interests into productive activities that also promote the economic well-being of the society.

Labor force participation rate The number of persons in the civilian labor force 16 years of age or over who are either employed or actively seeking employment as a percentage of the total civilian population 16 years of age and over.

Labor union A collective organization of employees who bargain as a unit with employers.

Laffer curve A curve illustrating the relationship between the tax rate and tax revenue. Tax revenue will be low for both very high and very low tax rates. Thus, when tax rates are quite high, a reduction in the tax rate can increase tax revenue.

Law of comparative advantage A principle that states that individuals, firms, regions, or nations can gain by specializing in the production of goods that they produce cheaply (that is, at a low opportunity cost) and exchanging those goods for other desired goods for which they are high-opportunity-cost producers.

Law of demand A principle that states there is an inverse relationship between the price of a good and the amount of it buyers are willing to purchase. As the price of a product increases, other things constant, consumers will purchase less of the product.

Law of diminishing marginal utility The basic economic principle that, as the consumption of a commodity increases, the marginal utility derived from consuming more of the commodity (per unit of time) will eventually decline.

Law of diminishing returns The postulate that, as more and more units of a variable resource are combined with a fixed amount of other resources, employment of additional units of the variable resource will eventually increase output only at a decreasing rate. Once diminishing returns are reached, it will take successively larger amounts of the variable factor to expand output by one unit.

Law of supply A principle that states there is a direct relationship between the price of a good and the amount of it offered for sale. As the price of a product increases, other things constant, producers will increase the amount of the product supplied to the market.

Less-developed countries (LDCs) Low-income countries generally characterized by rapid population growth and an agriculture-household sector that dominates the economy. Sometimes these countries are referred to as developing countries.

Licensing A requirement that one obtain permission from the government in order to perform certain business activities or work in various occupations.

Liquid asset An asset that can be easily and quickly converted to purchasing power without loss of value.

Loanable funds market A general term used to describe the broad market that coordinates the borrowing and lending decisions of business firms and households. Commercial banks, savings and loan associations, the stock and bond markets, and insurance companies are important financial institutions in this market.

Logrolling The exchange between politicians of political support on one issue for political support on another issue.

Long run A time period of sufficient length to enable decision makers to adjust fully to a market change.

Long run (in production) A time period long enough to allow the firm to vary all factors of production.

Loss Deficit of sales revenue relative to the opportunity cost of production. Losses are a penalty imposed on those who misuse resources in lower-valued uses as judged by buyers in the market.

M1 (money supply)   The sum of (1) currency in circulation (including coins), (2) checkable deposits maintained in depository institutions, and (3) traveler's checks.

M2 (money supply)   Equal to M1 plus (1) savings deposits, (2) time deposits (accounts of less than $100,000) held in depository institutions, and (3) money market mutual fund shares.

Macroeconomics   The branch of economics that focuses on how human behavior affects outcomes in highly aggregated markets, such as the markets for labor or consumer products.

Marginal   Term used to describe the effects of a change in the current situation. For example, the marginal cost is the cost of producing an additional unit of a product, given the producer's current facility and production rate.

Marginal benefit   The maximum price a consumer would be willing to pay for an additional unit. It is the dollar value of the consumer's marginal utility from the additional unit, and thus falls as consumption increases.

Marginal cost   The change in total cost required to produce an additional unit of output.

Marginal product   The increase in the total product resulting from a unit increase in the employment of a variable input. Mathematically, it is the ratio of the change in total product to the change in the quantity of the variable input.

Marginal propensity to consume (MPC)   Additional current consumption divided by additional current disposable income.

Marginal rate of substitution   The change in the consumption level of one good that is just sufficient to offset a unit change in the consumption of another good without causing a shift to another indifference curve. At any point on an indifference curve, it will be equal to the slope of the curve at that point.

Marginal revenue (MR)   The incremental change in total revenue derived from the sale of one additional unit of a product.

Marginal revenue product (MRP)   The change in the total revenue of a firm that results from the employment of one additional unit of a resource. The marginal revenue product of an input is equal to its marginal product multiplied by the marginal revenue of the good or service produced.

Marginal tax rate (MTR)   Additional tax liability divided by additional taxable income. It is the percentage of an extra dollar of income that must be paid in taxes. It is the marginal tax rate that is relevant in personal decision making.

Marginal utility   The additional utility received from the consumption of an additional unit of a good.

Market   An abstract concept that encompasses the trading arrangements of buyers and sellers that underlie the forces of supply and demand.

Market power   The ability of a firm that is not a pure monopolist to earn unusually large profits, indicating that it has some monopoly power. Because the firm has few (or weak) competitors, it has a degree of freedom from the discipline of vigorous competition.

Means-tested income transfers   Transfers that are limited to persons or families with an income below a certain cutoff point. Eligibility is thus dependent on low-income status.

Medical savings accounts   Special savings accounts that individuals could use for the payment of medical bills or the purchase of a catastrophic (high deductibility) health insurance plan. Unfavorable tax treatment compared to employer-pro-

vided health insurance and other regulatory restrictions currently reduce their use.

Medium of exchange   An asset that is used to buy and sell goods or services.

Microeconomics   The branch of economics that focuses on how human behavior affects the conduct of affairs within narrowly defined units, such as individual households or business firms.

Middleman   A person who buys and sells or who arranges trades. A middleman reduces transaction costs.

Minimum wage   Legislation requiring that workers be paid at least the stated minimum hourly rate of pay.

Monetarists   A group of economists who believe that (1) monetary instability is the major cause of fluctuations in real GDP and (2) rapid growth of the money supply is the major cause of inflation.

Monetary base   The sum of currency in circulation plus bank reserves (vault cash and reserves with the Fed). It reflects the stock of U.S. securities held by the Fed.

Monetary policy   The deliberate control of the money supply, and, in some cases, credit conditions, for the purpose of achieving macroeconomic goals.

Money interest rate   The percentage of the amount borrowed that must be paid to the lender in addition to the repayment of the principal. It overstates the real cost of borrowing during an inflationary period. When inflation is anticipated, an inflationary premium will be incorporated into this rate. The money interest rate is often referred to as the nominal interest rate.

Money market mutual funds   Interest-earning accounts offered by brokerage firms that pool depositors' funds and invest them in highly liquid short-term securities. Since these securities can be quickly converted to cash, depositors are permitted to write checks (which reduce their share holdings) against their accounts.

Money rate of interest   The rate of interest in monetary terms that borrowers pay for borrowed funds. During periods when borrowers and lenders expect inflation, the money rate of interest exceeds the real rate of interest.

Money supply   The supply of currency, checking account funds, and traveler's checks. These items are counted as money because they are used as the means of payment for purchases.

Monopolistic competition   Term often used by economists to describe markets characterized by a large number of sellers that supply differentiated products to a market with low barriers to entry. Essentially, it is an alternative term for a competitive price-searcher market.

Monopoly   A market structure characterized by (1) a single seller of a well-defined product for which there are no good substitutes and (2) high barriers to the entry of any other firms into the market for that product.

National debt   The sum of the indebtedness of the federal government in the form of outstanding interest-earning bonds. It reflects the cumulative impact of budget deficits and surpluses.

National income   The total income earned by the nationals (citizens) during a period. It is the sum of employee compensation, self-employment income, rents, interest, and corporate profits.

Natural monopoly A market situation in which the average costs of production continually decline with increased output. Therefore, average costs of production will be lowest when a single, large firm produces the entire output demanded.

Natural rate of unemployment The long-run average unemployment rate due to frictional and structural conditions of labor markets. This rate is affected both by dynamic change and by public policy. It is sustainable into the future. The current natural rate of unemployment in the United States is thought to be approximately 5 percent.

Net exports Exports minus imports.

Net income of foreigners The income that foreigners earn by contributing labor and capital resources to the production of goods within the borders of a country minus the income the nationals of the country earn abroad.

New classical economists Economists who believe there are strong forces pushing a market economy toward full employment equilibrium and that macroeconomic policy is an ineffective tool with which to reduce economic instability.

Nominal GDP GDP expressed at current prices. It is often called money GDP.

Nominal values Values expressed in current dollars.

Nonactivist strategy The maintenance of a steady monetary and fiscal policy during all phases of the business cycle. According to this view, adjusting macro policy in response to current cyclical conditions is likely to increase, rather than reduce, instability.

Nonhuman resources The durable, nonhuman inputs that can be used to produce both current and future output. Machines, buildings, land, and raw materials are examples. Investment can increase the supply of nonhuman resources. Economists often use the term physical capital when referring to nonhuman resources.

Nonpecuniary job characteristics Working conditions, prestige, variety, location, employee freedom and responsibilities, and other nonwage characteristics of a job that influence how employees evaluate the job.

Normal good A good that has a positive income elasticity, so that, as consumer income rises, demand for that good rises also.

Normal profit rate Zero economic profit, providing just the competitive rate of return on the capital (and labor) of owners. An above-normal profit rate will draw more entry into the market, while a below-normal rate will cause an exit of investors and capital.

Normative economics Judgments about "what ought to be" in economic matters. Normative economic views cannot be proved false, because they are based on value judgments.

North American Free Trade Agreement (NAFTA) A comprehensive trade agreement between the United States, Mexico, and Canada that went into effect in 1994. Tariff barriers will continue to be phased out under the agreement until 2004.

Oligopoly A market situation in which a small number of sellers compose the entire industry. It is competition among the few.

Open market operations The buying and selling of U.S. government securities in the open market by the Federal Reserve.

Opportunity cost The highest valued alternative that must be sacrificed as a result of choosing among alternatives.

Opportunity cost of equity capital The implicit rate of return that must be earned by investors to induce them to continue to supply financial capital to the firm.

Opportunity cost of production The total economic cost of producing a good or service. The cost component includes the opportunity cost of all resources, including those owned by the firm. The opportunity cost is equal to the value of the production of other goods sacrificed as the result of producing the good.

Other checkable deposits Interest-earning deposits that are also available for checking.

Partnership A business firm owned by two or more individuals who possess ownership rights to the firm's profits and are personally liable for the debts of the firm.

Pegged exchange-rate system A commitment to use monetary and fiscal policy to maintain the exchange-rate value of the domestic currency at a fixed rate or within a narrow band relative to another currency (or bundle of currencies).

per capita GDP Income per person. Increases in income per person are vitally important for the achievement of higher living standards.

Permanent income hypothesis The hypothesis that consumption depends on some measure of long-run expected (permanent) income rather than on current income.

Personal consumption Household spending on consumer goods and services during the current period. Consumption is a flow concept.

Personal income The total income received by domestic households and noncorporate businesses. It is available for consumption, saving, and payment of personal taxes.

Phillips curve A curve that illustrates the relationship between the rate of change in prices (or money wages) and the rate of unemployment.

Policy-ineffectiveness theorem The proposition that any systematic policy will be rendered ineffective once decision makers figure out the policy pattern and adjust their decision making in light of its expected effects. The theorem is a corollary of the theory of rational expectations.

Pork-barrel legislation A package of spending projects benefiting local areas at federal expense. The projects typically have costs that exceed benefits, but are intensely desired by the residents of the district getting the benefits without having to pay much of the costs.

Portfolio All the stocks, bonds, or other securities held by an individual or corporation for investment purposes.

Positive economics The scientific study of "what is" among economic relationships.

Positive rate of time preference The desire of consumers for goods now rather than in the future.

Potential output The level of output that can be achieved and sustained into the future, given the size of the labor force, expected productivity of labor, and natural rate of unemployment consistent with the efficient operation of the labor market. For periods of time, the actual output may differ from the economy's potential.

Poverty threshold income level The level of money income below which a family is considered to be poor. It differs according to family characteristics (for example, number of family members) and is adjusted when consumer prices change.

Present value (PV)   The current worth of future income after it is discounted to reflect the fact that revenues in the future are valued less highly than revenues now.

Price ceiling   A legally established maximum price that sellers may charge for a good or resource.

Price controls   Government-mandated prices; they may be either greater or less than the market equilibrium price.

Price discrimination   A practice whereby a seller charges different consumers different prices for the same product or service.

Price elasticity of demand   The percent change in the quantity of a product demanded divided by the percent change in the price causing the change in quantity. Price elasticity of demand indicates the degree of consumer response to variation in price.

Price elasticity of supply   The percentage change in quantity supplied, divided by the percentage change in the price causing the change in quantity supplied.

Price floor   A legally established minimum price that buyers must pay for a good or resource.

Price searchers   Firms that face a downward sloping demand curve for their product. The amount that the firm is able to sell is inversely related to the price that it charges.

Price takers   Sellers who must take the market price in order to sell their product. Because each price taker's output is small relative to the total market, price takers can sell all their output at the market price, but they are unable to sell any of their output at a price higher than the market price.

Primary market   Market where financial institutions aid in the sale of new securities.

Principal-agent problem   The incentive problem arising when the purchaser of services (the principal) lacks full information about the circumstances faced by the seller (the agent) and thus cannot know how well the agent performs the purchased services. The agent may to some extent work toward objectives other than those sought by the principal paying for the service.

Private investment   The flow of private sector expenditures on durable assets (fixed investment) plus the addition to inventories (inventory investment) during a period. These expenditures enhance our ability to provide consumer benefits in the future.

Private property rights   Property rights that are exclusively held by an owner, or group of owners, and that can be transferred to others at the owner's discretion.

Privately held government debt   The portion of the national debt owed to domestic and foreign investors. It does not include bonds held by agencies of the federal government or the Federal Reserve.

Producer surplus   The difference between the minimum supply price and the actual sales price. It measures the net gains to producers and resource suppliers from market trade. It is not the same as profit.

Production possibilities curve   A curve that outlines all possible combinations of total output that could be produced, assuming (1) the utilization of a fixed amount of productive resources, (2) full and efficient use of those resources, and (3) a specific state of technical knowledge. The slope of the curve indicates the rate at which one product can be traded off to produce more of the other.

Productivity   The average output produced per worker during a specific time period. It is usually measured in terms of output per hour worked.

Profit   An excess of sales revenue relative to the opportunity cost of production. The cost component includes the opportunity cost of all resources, including those owned by the firm. Therefore, profit accrues only when the value of the good produced is greater than the value of other goods that could have been produced with those same resources.

Progressive tax   A tax in which the average tax rate rises with income. Persons with higher incomes will pay a higher percentage of their income in taxes.

Property rights   The right to use, control, and obtain the benefits from a good or service.

Proportional tax   A tax in which the average tax rate is the same at all income levels. Everyone pays the same percentage of income in taxes.

Proprietorship   A business firm owned by an individual who possesses the ownership right to the firm's profits and is personally liable for the firm's debts.

Public goods   Jointly consumed goods that are nonexcludable. When consumed by one person, they are also made available to others. National defense, flood control dams, and scientific theories are all public goods.

Public-choice analysis   The study of decision making as it affects the formation and operation of collective organizations, such as governments. In general, the principles and methodology of economics are applied to political science topics.

Pure competition   A market structure characterized by a large number of small firms producing an identical product in an industry (market area) that permits complete freedom of entry and exit. Also called price-taker markets.

Quantity theory of money   A theory that hypothesizes that a change in the money supply will cause a proportional change in the price level because velocity and real output are unaffected by the quantity of money.

Random walk theory   The theory that current stock prices already reflect known information about the future. Therefore, the future movement of stock prices will be determined by surprise occurrences. This will cause them to change in a random fashion.

Rate of unemployment   The percentage of persons in the labor force who are unemployed. Mathematically, it is equal to number of persons unemployed/number of persons in the labor force $\times$ 100.

Rational ignorance effect   Voter ignorance resulting from the fact that people perceive their individual votes as unlikely to be decisive. Therefore, they rationally have little incentive to seek the information needed to cast an informed vote.

Rational-expectations hypothesis   The hypothesis that economic decision makers weigh all available evidence, including information concerning the probable effects of current and future economic policy, when they form their expectations about future economic events (such as the probable future inflation rate).

Rationing   An allocation of a limited supply of a good or resource to users who would like to have more of it. Various criteria, including charging a price, can be utilized to allocate the limited supply. When price performs the rationing function, the good or resource is allocated to those willing to give up the most "other things" in order to obtain ownership rights.

Real balance effect   The increase in wealth generated by an increase in the purchasing power of a constant money supply as the price level decreases. This wealth effect leads to an inverse relationship between price (level) and quantity demanded in the goods and services market.

Real earnings Earnings adjusted for differences in the general level of prices across time periods or geographic areas. When real earnings are equal, the same bundle of goods and services can be purchased with the earnings.

Real GDP GDP adjusted for changes in the price level.

Real interest rate The interest rate adjusted for expected inflation; it indicates the real cost to the borrower (and yield to the lender) in terms of goods and services.

Real rate of interest The money rate of interest minus the expected rate of inflation. The real rate of interest indicates the interest premium, in terms of real goods and services, that one must pay for earlier availability.

Real values Values that have been adjusted for the effects of inflation.

Recession A downturn in economic activity characterized by declining real GDP and rising unemployment. In an effort to be more precise, many economists define a recession as two consecutive quarters in which there is a decline in real GDP.

Recognition lag The time period after a policy change is needed from a stabilization standpoint but before the need is recognized by policy-makers.

Regressive tax A tax in which the average tax rate falls with income. Persons with higher incomes will pay a lower percentage of their income in taxes.

Rent seeking Actions by individuals and interest groups designed to restructure public policy in a manner that will either directly or indirectly redistribute more income to themselves.

Repeat-purchase item An item purchased often by the same buyer.

Replacement rate The share of previous earnings replaced by unemployment benefits.

Residual claimants Individuals who personally receive the excess, if any, of revenues over costs. Residual claimants gain if the firm's costs are reduced or revenues increased.

Resource An input used to produce economic goods. Land, labor, skills, natural resources, and capital are examples. Throughout history, people have struggled to transform available, but limited, resources into things they would like to have—economic goods.

Resource market 1) A highly aggregated market encompassing all resources (labor, physical capital, land, and entrepreneurship) that contribute to the production of current out-put. The labor market forms the largest component of this market. 2) Markets in which business firms demand factors of production (for example, labor, capital, and natural resources) from household suppliers. The resources are then used to produce goods and services. This market is sometimes called factor markets or input markets.

Resource mobility The ease with which factors of production are able to move among alternative uses. Resources that can easily be transferred to a different use or location are said to be highly mobile. Resources with few alternative uses are immobile.

Restrictive fiscal policy A reduction in government expenditures and/or an increase in tax rates such that the expected size of the budget deficit declines (or the budget surplus increases).

Restrictive monetary policy A shift in monetary policy designed to reduce aggregate demand and place downward pressure on the general level of prices (or the rate of inflation). Bond sales by the Fed, a decline in bank reserves, and a reduction in the growth rate of the money supply are generally indicative of a restrictive monetary policy.

Ricardian equivalence The view that a tax reduction financed with government debt will exert no impact on current consumption and aggregate demand because people will fully recognize the higher future taxes implied by the additional debt.

Right-to-work laws Laws that prohibit the union shop, the requirement that employees must join a union as a condition of employment. Each state has the option to adopt (or reject) right-to-work legislation.

Rule of 70 If a variable grows at a rate of x percent per year, $70/x$ will approximate the number of years required for the variable to double.

Samaritan's dilemma General assistance to those with low incomes reduces the opportunity cost of choices that lead to poverty. Thus, there is a conflict between providing income transfers to the poor and discouragement of behavior that increases the incidence of poverty.

Saving The portion of after-tax income that is not spent on consumption. Saving is a "flow" concept.

Savings and loan associations Financial institutions that accept deposits in exchange for shares that pay dividends. Historically, these funds have been channeled into residential mortgage loans. Under banking legislation adopted in 1980, S&Ls are permitted to offer a broad range of services similar to those of commercial banks.

Say's Law The view that production creates its own demand. Demand will always be sufficient to purchase the goods produced because the income payments to the resource suppliers will equal the value of the goods produced.

Scarcity Fundamental concept of economics that indicates that there is less of a good freely available from nature than people would like.

Scientific thinking Development of a theory from basic postulates and the testing of the implications of that theory as to their consistency with events in the real world. Good theories are consistent with and help explain real-world events. Theories that are inconsistent with the real world are invalid and must be rejected.

Secondary effects Consequences of an economic change that are not immediately identifiable but are felt only with the passage of time.

Secondary market Market where financial institutions aid in the buying and selling of existing securities.

Severance pay Pay by an employer to an employee upon the termination of employment with the firm.

Shirking Working at less than a normal rate of productivity, thus reducing output. Shirking is more likely when workers are not monitored, so that the cost of lower output falls on others.

Short run A time period of insufficient length to permit decision makers to adjust fully to a change in market conditions. For example, in the short run, producers will have time to increase output by using more labor and raw materials, but they will not have time to expand the size of their plants or to install additional heavy equipment.

Short run (in production) A time period so short that a firm is unable to vary some of its factors of production. The firm's plant size typically cannot be altered in the short run.

Shortage A condition in which the amount of a good offered for sale by producers is less than the amount demanded by buyers at the existing price. An increase in price would eliminate the shortage.

Shortsightedness effect Misallocation of resources that results because public-sector action is biased (1) in favor of proposals yielding clearly defined current benefits in exchange for difficult-to-identify future costs and (2) against proposals with clearly identifiable current costs but yielding less concrete and less obvious future benefits.

Shutdown A temporary halt in the operation of a business firm. Because the firm anticipates returning to the market in the future, it does not sell its assets and go out of business. The firm's variable cost is eliminated by the shutdown, but its fixed costs continue.

Socialism A system of economic organization in which (1) the ownership and control of the basic means of production rest with the state, and (2) resource allocation is determined by centralized planning rather than by market forces.

Special-interest issue An issue that generates substantial individual benefits to a small minority while imposing a small individual cost on many other voters. In total, the net cost to the majority might either exceed or fall short of the net benefits to the special-interest group.

Stock options The option to buy a specified number of shares of the firm's stock at a designated price. The designated price is generally set so that the options will be quite valuable if the firm's shares increase in price, but of little value if their price falls. Thus, when used to compensate top managers, stock options provide a strong incentive to follow policies that will increase the value of the firm.

Store of value An asset that will allow people to transfer purchasing power from one period to the next.

Strike An action of unionized employees in which they (1) discontinue working for the employer and (2) take steps to prevent other potential workers from offering their services to the employer.

Structural unemployment Unemployment due to the structural characteristics of the economy that make it difficult for job seekers to find employment and for employers to hire workers. Although job openings are available, they generally require skills that differ from those of the unemployed workers.

Substitutes Products that serve similar purposes. They are related such that an increase in the price of one will cause an increase in demand for the other (for example, hamburgers and tacos, butter and margarine, Chevrolets and Fords).

Substitution effect That part of an increase (decrease) in amount consumed that is the result of a good being cheaper (more expensive) in relation to other goods because of a reduction (increase) in price.

Sunk costs Costs that have already been incurred as a result of past decisions. They are sometimes referred to as historical costs.

Supply shock An unexpected event that temporarily either increases or decreases aggregate supply.

Supply-side economists Modern economists who believe that changes in marginal tax rates exert important effects on aggregate supply.

Surplus A condition in which the amount of a good offered for sale by producers is greater than the amount that buyers will purchase at the existing price. A decline in price would eliminate the surplus.

Tariff A tax levied on goods imported into a country.

Tax base The level or quantity of the economic activity that is taxed (e.g., gallons of gasoline sold per week). Because they make the activity less attractive, higher tax rates reduce the level of the tax base.

Tax incidence The manner in which the burden of a tax is distributed among economic units (consumers, producers, employees, employers, and so on). The actual tax burden does not always fall on those who are statutorily assigned to pay the tax.

Tax rate The per-unit amount of the tax or the percentage rate at which the economic activity is taxed.

Team production A process of production wherein employees work together under the supervision of the owner or the owner's representative.

Technological advancement The introduction of new techniques or methods that enable production of a greater output per unit of input.

Total cost The costs, both explicit and implicit, of all the resources used by the firm. Total cost includes an imputed normal rate of return for the firm's equity capital.

Total fixed cost The sum of the costs that do not vary with output. They will be incurred as long as a firm continues in business and the assets have alternative uses.

Total product The total output of a good that is associated with alternative utilization rates of a variable input.

Total variable cost The sum of those costs that rise as output increases. Examples of variable costs are wages paid to workers and payments for raw materials.

Tournament pay A form of compensation where the top performer (or performers) receives much higher rewards than other competitors, even if the others perform at only a slightly lower level.

Trade deficit The situation when a country's imports of goods and services are greater than its exports.

Trade surplus The situation when a country's exports of goods and services are greater than its imports.

Transaction accounts Accounts, including demand deposits and interest-earning checkable deposits, against which the account holder is permitted to transfer funds for the purpose of making payment to a third party.

Transaction costs The time, effort, and other resources needed to search out, negotiate, and consummate an exchange.

Unanticipated change A change that decision makers could not reasonably foresee. Thus, choices made prior to the event did not take the event into account.

Unanticipated inflation An increase in the general level of prices that was not expected by most decision makers.

Underground economy Unreported barter and cash transactions that take place outside recorded market channels. Some are otherwise legal activities undertaken to evade taxes. Others involve illegal activities, such as trafficking in drugs and prostitution.

Unemployed The term used to describe a person not currently employed who is either (1) actively seeking employment or (2) waiting to begin or return to a job.

Unit of account   The units of measurement used by people to post prices and keep track of revenues and costs.

User charges   Payments that users (consumers) are required to make if they want to receive certain services provided by the government.

Utility   The subjective benefit or satisfaction a person expects from a choice or course of action.

Value of marginal product (VMP)   The marginal product of a resource multiplied by the selling price of the product it helps to produce. For a price taker firm, marginal revenue product *(MRP)* will be equal to the value marginal product *(VMP)*.

World Trade Organization (WTO)   The new name given to GATT in 1994; it is currently responsible for monitoring and enforcing the multilateral trade agreements among the 133 member countries.

CREDITS

LITERARY CREDITS

Ch. 7, Exhibit 8, p. 172, World Bank, World Development Report, 2000–2001: Attacking Poverty (Tables 1,2 and 7). [On-line.] Available from the World Bank web site at: http://www.worldbank.org/poverty/wdrpoverty/report/index.htm. ©2001 Reprinted with permission from World Bank.

Ch. 8, Exhibit 7, p. 190, Economic Report of the President, 2001 and Robert J. Gordon, Macroeconomics (Boston: Little Brown, 1990). ©1990 Little, Brown & Company. ©AOL Time Warner.

Ch. 8, Exhibit 11, p. 195, International Monetary Fund, International Financial Statistics, (April 2001, February 2001). Reprinted by permission from International Monetary Fund.

Special Topic 13, Exhibit 2, p. 785, "Price Responsiveness of Energy Forms: Estimated Price Elasticity of Demand," from Douglas R. Bohi, Analyzing Demand Behavior (Baltimore: Johns Hopkins University Press, 1981), p.159. Reprinted with permission.

Special Topic 13, Exhibit 3, p. 785, Indur M. Goklany, "Factors Affecting Environmental Impacts: The Effects of Technology on Long-term Trends in Cropland, Air Pollution and Water-related Diseases," Ambio, Vol. 25, No. 8, Dec. 1996. Reprinted with permission from Royal Swedish Academy of Sciences.

PHOTO CREDITS

p. 8	©Photopia
p. 11	©Photopia
p. 29	©Phil Sears
p. 34 (L)	©David Young-Wolff/PhotoEdit
p. 34 (R)	©Leo Snider/The Image Works
p. 35	Courtesy of Berry College, Mount Berry GA
p. 44 (R)	©Jeff Greenberg/PhotoEdit
p. 44 (TR)	©James Nubile/The Image Works
p. 44 (BR)	©Wesley Bocxe/The Image Works
p. 76	©PhotoDisc
p. 99	©Richard Hutchings/PhotoEdit
p. 118	©CORBIS
p. 122	©Charles Kennard/Stock,Boston/PictureQuest
p. 133 (L)	©Tom Prettyman/PhotoEdit
p. 133 (center)	#3970703 ©Newsmakers/Gettyimages
p. 133 (R)	©Bob Daemmrich/The Image Works
p. 173 (L)	©Archive Photos
p. 173 (R)	©AP Photo
p. 212	©Jim West, Detroit MI
p. 214	©Photopia
p. 230	©Mark Richards/PhotoEdit/PictureQuest
p. 230	©Erica Lansner/Black Star Publishing/PictureQuest
p. 238	©Jim West, Detroit MI.
p. 238	©Steve Liss/TimePix
p. 249	©CORBIS
p. 261	©Vance Laforet/Allsport
p. 285	©Kevin Horan/Stock, Boston
p. 292	©CORBIS
p. 295 (L)	©Peter Barrett/Masterfile
p. 295 (R)	©Garry Black/Masterfile
p. 310 (T)	©John Neubauer/PhotoEdit
p. 310 (B)	©Sandra Baker/Liaison International
p. 350	©CORBIS
p. 376	©Walter Edwards/National Geographic Society Image Collection
p. 384	©Jane Tyska/Stock, Boston
p. 414	©Spencer Grant/PhotoEdit
p. 426 (TL)	©Michelle Bridwell/PhotoEdit
p. 426 (TR)	©John Neubauer/PhotoEdit
p. 426 (BL)	©Richard Pasley/Stock, Boston
p. 426 (BR)	©Don Couch Photography, Austin TX
p. 452	©Mark Richards/PhotoEdit
p. 481	©Bill Bachman/The Image Works
p. 492	© M. Greenlar/The Image Works
p. 504	©Dave Bartruff/CORBIS
p. 505 (L)	©A. Ramey/PhotoEdit
p. 505 (R)	©John Eastcott/Stock, Boston
p. 511	©Russell Sobel
p. 516	©John Claude LeJeune/Stock, Boston
p. 527 (TL)	©Photopia
p. 527 (TR)	©Photopia
p. 527 (BL)	©Photopia
p. 527 (BR)	©Photopia
p. 531	©Daniel Sheehan/Liaison Photo
p. 533	©Michael Turk/Surplus Trading
p. 541	©Wojnarowicz/The Image Works
p. 547	©Najlah Feanny/Stock, Boston
p. 554	©UPI/Bettmann
p. 583 (L)	©Digital Vision/PictureQuest
p. 583 (R)	©Mark Anderson/RubberBall Productions/PictureQuest
p. 586 (L)	©Michael Newman/PhotoEdit
p. 586 (R)	©Richard Lord/The Image Works
p. 597	©Russell Einhorn/Gamma Liaison
p. 603 (T)	©Tony Freeman/PhotoEdit
p. 603 (B)	©Myrleen Ferguson/PhotoEdit
p. 605	©Stacy Pick/Stock, Boston
p. 612 (L)	©Bill Aron/PhotoEdit
p. 612 (R)	©Gary Matosa/Contact Press Images/PictureQuest
p. 620	©Townsend P. Dickinson/The Image Works
p. 636	©Paul Conklin/PhotoEdit
p. 642	©Mark Antman/The Image Works
p. 686	©Joseph Giannetti/Stock, Boston/PictureQuest
p. 703	©CORBIS
p. 711	©AP Photo/Hans Edinger
p. 715	©Sean Gallup/Getty Images
p. 755	©Pictor International/Pictor International, Ltd./PictureQuest
p. 764	©Jim West, Detroit MI
p. 765 (L)	©Lien Nibauer/Liaison International
p. 765 (R)	©Frank Siteman/PhotoEdit
p. 767	©Brian Haimer/PhotoEdit
p. 773	©AP Photo

p. 777 Used with permission from Institute of Justice, Washington D.C. http://www.ij.org

p. 784 ©Peter Menzel/Stock, Boston

p. 788 ©AP Photo/Glen Mills

p. 793 ©Jeff Venuga/CORBIS

CARTOON CREDITS

p. 10 BLONDIE reprinted by special permission of King Features Syndicate.

p. 11 THE FAMILY CIRCUS® reprinted by special permission of King Features Syndicate.

p. 14 Reprinted by special permission of King Features Syndicate.

p. 33 From *The Wall Street Journal*—permission, Cartoon Features Syndicate.

p. 102 By John Trever, *Albuquerque Journal.* Reprinted by permission.

p. 116 SHOE reprinted by permission: Tribune Media Services.

p. 134 BEETLE BAILEY by Mort Walker. Reprinted by special permission of King Features Syndicate.

p. 143 FAMILY CIRCUS® reprinted by special permission of King Features Syndicate.

p. 145 FRANK & ERNEST reprinted by permission of Newspaper Enterprise Association, Inc.

p. 167 BEETLE BAILEY by Mort Walker. Reprinted by special permission of King Features Syndicate.

p. 309 FRANK & ERNEST reprinted by permission of Newspaper Enterprise Association, Inc.

p. 496 DUNIGIN reprinted by permission of Tribune Media Services.

p. 575 Dick Wright reprinted by permission of United Feature Syndicate.

INDEX

YEAR	GROSS DOMESTIC PRODUCT			GDP DEFLATOR		CONSUMER PRICE INDEX	
	NOMINAL GDP (BILLIONS OF CURRENT DOLLARS)	REAL GDP (BILLIONS OF CONSTANT 1996 DOLLARS)	ANNUAL REAL GROWTH RATE	INDEX (1996=100)	ANNUAL PERCENTAGE CHANGE	INDEX (1982–84 =100)	ANNUAL PERCENTAGE CHANGE
1960	527.4	2,376.7	2.5	22.2	1.4	29.6	1.0
1961	545.6	2,432.0	2.3	22.4	1.1	29.9	1.1
1962	586.5	2,578.9	6.0	22.7	1.4	30.3	1.2
1963	618.7	2,690.4	4.3	23.0	1.1	30.6	1.2
1964	664.4	2,846.5	5.8	23.3	1.5	31.0	1.3
1965	720.1	3,028.6	6.4	23.8	1.9	31.5	1.6
1966	789.3	3,227.4	6.6	24.5	2.9	32.5	3.0
1967	834.1	3,308.3	2.5	25.2	3.1	33.4	2.8
1968	911.5	3,466.1	4.8	26.3	4.3	34.8	4.3
1969	985.4	3,571.4	3.0	27.6	4.9	36.7	5.5
1970	1,039.7	3,578.0	0.2	29.1	5.3	38.8	5.8
1971	1,128.6	3,697.7	3.3	30.5	5.0	40.5	4.3
1972	1,240.4	3,898.4	5.4	31.8	4.3	41.8	3.3
1973	1,385.6	4,123.4	5.8	33.6	5.6	44.4	6.2
1974	1,501.0	4,099.1	−0.6	36.6	9.0	49.3	11.1
1975	1,635.2	4,084.5	−0.4	40.0	9.3	53.8	9.1
1976	1,823.9	4,311.7	5.6	42.3	5.7	56.9	5.7
1977	2,031.4	4,511.8	4.6	45.0	6.4	60.6	6.5
1978	2,295.9	4,760.6	5.5	48.2	7.1	65.2	7.6
1979	2,566.4	4,912.1	3.2	52.2	8.4	72.6	11.3
1980	2,795.6	4,900.9	−0.2	57.0	9.2	82.4	13.5
1981	3,131.4	5,020.9	2.4	62.4	9.3	90.9	10.3
1982	3,259.2	4,919.4	−2.0	66.3	6.2	96.5	6.1
1983	3,535.0	5,132.4	4.3	68.9	3.9	99.6	3.2
1984	3,932.8	5,505.1	7.3	71.4	3.7	103.9	4.3
1985	4,213.0	5,717.0	3.8	73.7	3.2	107.6	3.5
1986	4,452.9	5,912.4	3.4	75.3	2.2	109.6	1.9
1987	4,742.5	6,113.3	3.4	77.6	3.0	113.6	3.7
1988	5,108.3	6,368.3	4.2	80.2	3.4	118.3	4.1
1989	5,489.1	6,591.8	3.5	83.3	3.8	124.0	4.8
1990	5,803.3	6,707.9	1.8	86.5	3.9	130.7	5.4
1991	5,986.2	6,676.4	−0.5	89.7	3.6	136.2	4.2
1992	6,319.0	6,880.1	3.1	91.8	2.4	140.3	3.0
1993	6,642.3	7,062.7	2.7	94.0	2.4	144.5	3.0
1994	7,054.3	7,347.7	4.0	96.0	2.1	148.2	2.6
1995	7,400.6	7,543.8	2.7	98.1	2.2	152.4	2.8
1996	7,813.2	7,813.2	3.6	100.0	1.9	156.9	2.9
1997	8,318.4	8,159.5	4.4	101.9	1.9	160.5	2.3
1998	8,781.5	8,508.9	4.3	103.2	1.2	163.0	1.6
1999	9,268.6	8,856.5	4.1	104.7	1.4	166.6	2.2
2000	9,872.9	9,224.0	4.1	107.0	2.2	172.2	3.4
2001	10,208.1	9,333.8	1.2	109.4	2.2	177.1	2.8

Sources: www.economagic.com; www.whitehouse.gov/omb/; www.bls.gov; and www.bea.doc.gov